12/15 20X

4/14/15

DATE DUE

JAN 2 4 2009	
FEB 1 7 2009	
APR 2 1 2009	
OCT 1 6 2009	
OCT 3 1 2009	
JAN 2 5 2010	
AUG 1 8 2010	
03- 3- 11	
GAYLORD	PRINTED IN U.S.A.

the all-new ultimate
Southern Living®
COOKBOOK

Compiled and edited by
Julie Fisher Gunter

Foreword by Scott Jones

Oxmoor
House®

©2006 by Oxmoor House, Inc.
Book Division of Southern Progress Corporation
P. O. Box 2262, Birmingham, Alabama 35201-2262

Southern Living® is a federally registered trademark
belonging to Southern Living, Inc.

ISBN-13: 978-0-8487-3114-4
ISBN-10: 0-8487-3114-X
Library of Congress Control Number: 2006924443
Printed in the United States of America
Seventh Printing 2008

Oxmoor House, Inc.
Editor in Chief: Nancy Fitzpatrick Wyatt
Executive Editor: Susan Carlisle Payne
Copy Chief: Allison Long Lowery

Cover: Lemon-Thyme Roasted Chicken (page 374), Roasted
New Potatoes (page 472), Sautéed Green Beans (page 456),
Fan Tans (page 97)
Back Cover: Tomato Salad (page 410), Cream Cheese Pound
Cake (page 151), Stuffed Border Burgers (page 248),
Blackberry Iced Tea (page 65)

To order additional publications, call 1-800-765-6400.
For more books to enrich your life, visit oxmoorhouse.com

***Southern Living*®**
Executive Editor: Scott Jones
Foods Editor: Shannon Sliter Satterwhite
Senior Writers: Donna Florio, Andria Scott Hurst
Associate Foods Editors: Charla Draper, Shirley Harrington,
   Holley Johnson, Kate Nicholson, Mary Allen Perry,
   Vicki A. Poellnitz
Assistant Recipe Editor: John McMillan
Test Kitchens Director: Lyda H. Jones
Assistant Test Kitchens Director: James Schend
Test Kitchens Specialist/Food Styling: Vanessa McNeil Rocchio
Test Kitchens Staff: Marian Cooper Cairns, Rebecca Kracke
   Gordon, Pam Lolley, Alyssa Porubcan, Angela Sellers
Administrative Assistant: Sandra J. Thomas
Production and Color Quality Manager: Katie Terrell Morrow
Copy Chief: Dawn P. Cannon
Copy Editor: Cindy Riegle
Senior Photographers: Ralph Anderson, Van Chaplin,
   Charles Walton IV
Photographers: Tina Cornett, William Dickey, Beth Dreiling
Senior Photo Stylist: Buffy Hargett
Photo Stylists: Lisa Powell Bailey, Rose Nguyen, Cari South,
   Amy Wilson
Photo Librarian: Tracy Duncan
Photo Assistant: Catherine Carr
Photo Services: Lisa Dawn Love
Assistant Production Manager: Jamie Barnhart
Production Coordinators: Christy Coleman, Paula Dennis

The All-New Ultimate Southern Living*® *Cookbook
Editor: Julie Fisher Gunter
Copy Editor: Donna Baldone
Senior Designer: Melissa Jones Clark
Editorial Assistant: Julie Boston
Test Kitchens Director: Elizabeth Tyler Austin
Assistant Test Kitchens Director: Julie Christopher
Food Stylist: Kelley Self Wilton
Test Kitchens Staff: Kristi Carter, Nicole Lee Faber,
   Kathleen Royal Phillips, Elise Weis
Director of Production: Laura Lockhart
Publishing Systems Administrator: Rick Tucker
Senior Production Manager: Greg A. Amason
Production Assistant: Faye Porter Bonner
Photography Director: Jim Bathie
Senior Photo Stylist: Kay E. Clarke
Photo Stylist: Katherine Eckert

Contributors
Editorial: Margaret Agnew, Carol Damsky, Dolores Hydock,
   Jean Wickstrom Liles
Editorial Interns: Meg Kozinsky, Ashley Leath,
   Caroline Markunas, Mary Catherine Shamblin,
   Vanessa Rusch Thomas
Indexer: Mary Ann Laurens
Nutrition: Caroline Grant, M.S., R.D.; Rachel Quinlivan, R.D.
Photographers: Lee Harrelson, Becky Luigart-Stayner
Photo Stylists: Susan Huff, Katie Stoddard

Tomato Salad (page 410)

contents

foreword

For more than 40 years, *Southern Living* has been the guide to our region's fine food and endearing hospitality. Along the way, we've developed a unique connection with generations of devoted readers.

You've invited us into your homes. You've shared your tips and secrets for everything from getting supper on the table during the week to successfully hosting elegant holiday celebrations. Fact is, you've made us part of your extended family. We certainly think of each reader as part of ours.

The foundation of this special bond is that we listen to you each and every month. From letters to phone calls to e-mails, your comments are invaluable. One benefit of these is that we know which cooking basics you'd like to learn more about and which techniques trip you up in the kitchen. We take pleasure in helping you locate special recipes that may have been misplaced, and providing suggestions on how to make a classic family favorite just a little bit healthier.

All of this, and more, is packed into *The All-New Ultimate Southern Living® Cookbook.* There's something for everyone—from the beginner cook to those folks who think of the kitchen as the new living room. We hope this cookbook becomes an indispensable tool in your kitchen, right alongside your favorite cast-iron skillet and wooden spoon.

Scott Jones
Executive Editor, *Southern Living*

introduction

The All-New Ultimate Southern Living® Cookbook is bigger and better than ever. The joy of cooking is set forth in a grand format with fresh, updated recipes, text, and photos. This book was compiled to empower you with basic food knowledge and to boost your interest in food and cooking.

A basic love of food and the desire to try new flavors is still what defines a good home cook today. Flip through the pages of this book to discover or rediscover some timeless principles of cooking. The book begins with Kitchen Basics—a chapter that is, in itself, an invaluable resource. Take pointers for stocking your kitchen and pantry, glance at our cooking glossaries, and see our tips for healthy living as well as entertaining. Our photographed food dictionaries define herbs, spices, sugars, salts, knives, and much more in this chapter and throughout the book.

The heart of the book is the recipe collection. Turn to any of the 19 chapters to find recipes that are *quick, make ahead, vegetarian, for kids, from the grill,* and for *entertaining.* On top of that, the prep and cook times for every recipe are there for you at a glance. And, in keeping with today's trend toward healthy living, you'll find every recipe has a complete nutrient analysis.

There are pages devoted to new chapters on Grilling, Breakfast & Brunch food, Healthy Favorites, and Meatless Main Dishes. And over four dozen menu ideas offer you meal plans from one season to the next.

We hope you'll find lasting inspiration in this culinary resource that's designed to give you the utmost confidence in cooking. Let these recipes and images lure you into the kitchen afresh.

kitchen basics

organizing your kitchen

The secret to becoming a great cook begins with the basics—using the right equipment, ingredients, and techniques. Reduce the time and energy you spend in the kitchen by organizing it to fit your needs. Take stock of your current inventory, and use the suggestions below to help you clean up, toss out, and reorganize.

• **Check dried herbs and spices for freshness.** We recommend storing dried herbs and spices in the freezer, not in racks near the oven or cooktop where heat and light can cause them to deteriorate. Most herbs and spices should stay fresh up to a year if stored properly. To test for freshness, sprinkle a small amount of the seasoning in your hand; if you don't smell an immediate aroma, it's time to replace it.

• **Clean out your pantry.** Check the date on canned goods. Canned foods beyond a year old tend to lose quality as well as nutrient value. Check the date on baking products, too, particularly baking powder and soda. If they're past their expiration dates, they won't do their job of leavening.

• **Plan equipment storage.** Store utensils and small appliances near the area in your kitchen where you'll be using them. Keep pot holders, kitchen towels, and baking pans near the cooktop and oven. Organize drawers by task. Keep flatware and serving utensils close to the dishwasher. Invest in drawer trays to separate small utensils and gadgets.

• **Clean out the freezer.** Bring older packages to the front and use them before using newly purchased items. Do the same with the refrigerator. Remember to stack food away from the back of the freezer and refrigerator so cold air can circulate freely.

• **Maximize efficiency.** Keep a variety of spoons, spatulas, tongs, and other well-used utensils in a canister near your work station or cooktop; then you'll always have them at your fingertips. Invest in a pot rack. Hang your favorite pots and pans overhead and within easy reach. Store knives where they'll be safe and easily accessible in a knife block or on a magnetic strip that hangs on the wall.

Efficient Grocery Shopping

Here are a few tips toward speedy shopping.

• **Write your grocery list** according to categories in the store. For example, list all dairy needs together in one column.

• **Don't shop when you're hungry.** And try to avoid shopping weekdays between 5 and 7 p.m.—the busiest shopping hours.

• **Shop the perimeter of the store first.** This is where the basics are—produce, dairy, meats, deli goods.

• **Stockpile pantry goods and items** you use regularly when they're on sale.

• **Put your groceries through the checkout in categories,** and ask the clerk to bag like items together. Once home, you can put items away quickly, because they'll already be sorted.

our testing procedures

Here's a guide to using the recipes in this book. Follow our lead for foolproof recipes every time. (See page 28 regarding how we analyze recipes.)

• Measure dry ingredients in dry measuring cups (metal or plastic) and liquids in glass or clear plastic liquid measuring cups with a pouring spout. See page 24 for techniques.

• Measure flour by lightly spooning it into a dry measuring cup and leveling it off with a knife.

• Don't sift flour unless a recipe specifies. Cake flour is the one exception that should be sifted before use. Don't sift powdered sugar unless recipe specifies.

• Use Grade A large eggs unless recipe specifies otherwise.

• When a recipe calls for greasing a pan, use vegetable shortening such as Crisco. When a recipe calls for lightly greasing a pan, use vegetable cooking spray. If a recipe calls for a buttered dish, use butter.

• Measure skillets and pans across the top, not the bottom.

• Wash and dry all produce before using.

• When a recipe calls for grated citrus rind, use a grater. When a recipe calls for citrus zest, use a Microplane® grater or citrus zester to get the fine zest and citrus mist.

• Use salted butter unless recipe specifies otherwise. When a recipe calls for softened butter, let butter stand at room temperature about 30 minutes. See photo on page 133 for more baking details.

• If a recipe states to bake covered, use aluminum foil or the lid that comes with the dish. If a recipes doesn't state to cover, then bake it uncovered.

• When a recipe states to mix ingredients, use an electric mixer. When a heavy-duty stand mixer is specified, we tested with a KitchenAid.

• If a recipe states to whisk a mixture, use a wire whisk.

• For baking, preheat oven 10 minutes.

• Use light-colored metal pans for baking. If using dark metal pans and baking sheets, baked goods may brown faster and cook quicker. Keep a close eye on them.

• When a recipe calls for freshly ground pepper, use a pepper mill.

• For freshly grated or shredded Parmesan cheese, use the fine-tooth holes of a box grater. A Microplane® grater produces a lighter, feathery volume of cheese.

• Always salt pasta water and water for cooking rice. See page 328 for amounts.

stock your kitchen

Whether you're planning a kitchen for the first time or adding to your current inventory, investing in good tools makes cooking easier and more fun. Here's a checklist for the well-equipped kitchen.

Equipment Tools

Mixing bowls in graduated sizes
Dry measuring cup set
Liquid measuring cups (1-, 2-, and 4-cup)
Measuring spoons (at least 2 sets)
Set of quality knives; knife block
Mixing spoons (plastic, metal, and wooden)
Kitchen shears
Pastry blender
Thermometers (meat, instant-read, and candy)
Openers (electric, hand, bottle, and corkscrew)
Wire whisk
Vegetable peeler
Timer
Mallet
Colander
Rolling pin
Sifter
Spatulas (rubber and metal)
Wire-mesh strainer
Scales (optional)
Cutting boards (small and large)
Grater (box and Microplane®)
Brushes (pastry and basting)
Spring-loaded tongs
Garlic press
Ladle
Potato masher
Kitchen towels and pot holders
Carving set
Pepper mill

Cookware

Saucepans (1-, 2-, and 3-quart with lids)
Skillets (large and small)
Dutch oven with lid
Stockpot with lid

Bakeware

Pans are metal; dishes are glass.
Two or three 9-inch round cakepans
8- and 9-inch square pans
13- x 9-inch pan
10-inch tube pan
12-cup Bundt pan
13- x 9-inch baking dish
8- or 9-inch square baking dish
1-quart baking dish
Pair of baking sheets
15- x 10-inch jelly-roll pan
Wire cooling racks
9- x 5-inch loafpan
Muffin pan
9-inch glass pieplate
9-inch springform pan

stock your pantry

Canned soups: chicken and beef broth, cream of mushroom, cream of chicken, cream of celery, tomato
Canned tomatoes: diced tomatoes, diced tomatoes and green chiles, Italian-style diced tomatoes, crushed tomatoes, stewed tomatoes, tomato sauce and paste
Canned and jarred vegetables: mushrooms, olives, roasted red pepper, artichoke hearts, green chiles
Canned or packaged beans and peas: great Northern beans, kidney beans, black beans, black-eyed peas, chickpeas
Rice: long-grain rice, quick-cooking rice, long-grain and wild rice mix, Arborio rice, yellow rice
Pasta: spaghetti, fettuccine, macaroni, penne
Sauces: marinara sauce, spaghetti sauce
Milks: sweetened condensed milk, evaporated milk
Baking items: flour, sugar, brown sugar, powdered sugar, salt, baking soda, baking powder
Miscellaneous items: aluminum foil, zip-top freezer bags, parchment paper or wax paper

equipment & ingredients

Cookware

Buy the best pots and pans you can afford—top-quality durable equipment. Consider buying individual pieces you know you'll use rather than a whole set. Choose pots and pans of heavy gauge (thickness) and sturdy construction—those that won't warp, dent, or scorch. Look for thick bottoms, tight-fitting lids, and heat-resistant handles that are securely attached.

Select and collect 1-, 2-, and 3-quart saucepans. Clad metals (several metals fused together) are a good all-purpose choice for heat conductivity, durability, and nonreactive and nonstick properties.

Copper cookware, which is often lined with tin, is an excellent heat conductor; it's expensive, though, and it needs frequent polishing and retinning over the years.

Aluminum cookware heats rapidly, is durable, and is relatively inexpensive, but it can react with acidic foods, altering the taste and color of food. Anodized aluminum has been treated to make it harder and more resistant to corrosion.

Stainless steel and glass pans are poor conductors of heat but are sturdy, nonreactive, and easy to clean. Clad stainless steel, however, boasts rapid and uniform heat conduction, and aluminized steel also heats quickly and evenly, does not corrode, and is durable.

Invest in a Dutch oven as well as a tall, narrow stockpot, both with lids. A 9- or 12-quart stockpot is a smart size for most cooks.

A 12-inch heavy skillet with a lid will prove most useful as well as a 6-inch skillet for omelets and crêpes, and 8- and 10-inch skillets. And a well-seasoned cast-iron skillet is an inexpensive pan every Southern kitchen should stock. For healthy cooking, buy nonstick skillets and try out a grill pan, which has a ridged surface that allows fat to drip away from food. (Read more about Dutch ovens and skillets on the opposite page.)

Bakeware

Shiny aluminum bakeware and stainless steel bakeware produce the best baked goods. They conduct heat evenly and encourage a brown crust. Dark pans can cause overbrowning.

Always use the pan size specified in a recipe. The correct way to measure pans is across the inside top edges.

Baking pans and dishes: Pans are metal; dishes are glass. If a recipe calls for a pan and you have only glass in that size, reduce oven temperature by 25 degrees. You'll often use 8- and 9-inch square pans and/or baking dishes, a 13- x 9-inch pan and baking dish, an 11- x 7-inch baking dish, a small and large roasting pan, and a broiler pan with a rack.

Baking sheets: Purchase at least two large sturdy baking sheets as well as a 15- x 10-inch jelly-roll pan.

Loafpans: Metal pans measuring 9- x 5-inches and 8½- x 4½-inches are most common.

Muffin pans: Purchase a muffin pan that holds 12 muffins, a typical yield for muffin recipes. Most muffin pan cups measure 2½ inches across the top. A mini-muffin pan is handy, too, and gives a petite option.

Pieplates: For pieplates, use glass, ceramic, or dull metal. The standard size is 9 inches. Deep-dish pieplates are 9½ inches.

Cakepans: We suggest owning three each of 8- and 9-inch round cakepans. Also consider a tube pan for angel food cake, a Bundt pan for pound cake, and a 9-inch springform pan for cheesecakes.

Wire racks: Collect two or three large rectangular wire racks for cookie baking. For cake layers, look for small round and oval racks.

Appliances

Ovens: Combination conventional/convection ovens are a popular choice today. They offer the strengths of both oven types.

A *conventional oven* can be gas or electric; this familiar oven has been the mainstay heat source in kitchens for decades. A *convection oven* is equipped with a fan that circulates air flow evenly around food, cooking food about 25% faster than a conventional oven. Convection ovens heat up fast and cook food efficiently. No special equipment is required, but for best results with convection cooking, consider the following factors:

- It's best to use shallow, uncovered casserole dishes and baking pans with sides no higher than an inch or so.
- Deep roasting pans, oven roasting bags, and covered casserole dishes keep heat from circulating around food and block the efficiency of convection cooking.
- Avoid using aluminum foil tents that blow off by the force of circulating air.
- To convert to convection cooking from a conventional recipe, reduce the oven temperature by 25 degrees, and bake for the same time specified. Or keep the oven temperature the same and bake 5 to 10 minutes less.

Grills: Outdoor grills enable you to get great smoky flavor at home. Charcoal grills bestow the best smoke. Choose a grill that has a lid to catch the flavor-infusing smoke. You have to preheat the charcoal and let it burn down to an ashy glow before grilling. A gas grill allows you to control the heat quickly and easily, but the food's smoky flavor is less pronounced. Grilling enthusiasts often have both types of grills. Any grill with a lid can be used for direct grilling (cooking food directly over the fire), including hibachis. For indirect grilling (cooking food over a drip pan that's surrounded by hot coals), you need a covered grill.

Smokers: Smokers are charcoal or electric grills with single or double cooking levels. They come with a cooking grill rack and a water pan. Use charcoal models to smoke, roast, grill, or steam food up to 6 hours using a single pan of charcoal. Smoke food like turkey, chicken, or ribs that cook longer than 6 hours using an electric model that provides constant, even heat.

Microwave: A microwave is a handy oven alternative, noted for cooking vegetables and bacon and for heating foods efficiently. Microwave ovens vary in cooking power from 700 to 1000 watts or more. We tested our microwave recipes for this book with a 1000-watt oven. If your oven has higher or lower wattage, adjust cooking times accordingly.

Bread machine: A bread machine does the mixing, kneading, rising, and baking in its chamber; all you do is add the ingredients and choose the appropriate settings. It's the answer to bread baking for those too busy to bake conventionally. You can set a delayed setting and have fresh baked bread 12 hours later with no attention needed.

Electric blender: A blender is your best bet for smooth soups, sauces, and drinks. Its tall, narrow container holds 5 cups or more. Be careful not to overload it, though, particularly with hot liquid; it could spew out. A blender will also chop small amounts of food for you. An immersion blender is more portable and allows you to blend directly in the pot that you've cooked in.

Electric mixer: There are two kinds: a portable handheld mixer for small mixing jobs and a stand mixer (regular or heavy duty) for substantial baking. Lightweight portable mixers allow you to control the mixer's movement in a freestanding bowl. Heavy-duty stand mixers come with attachments, and the bowl capacity is large, meant to handle thick batter or bread dough. (See more on page 133 in our Cakes chapter.)

Food processor: This appliance will chop, shred, and grate for you. It can also make pastry dough in a jiffy. And you can use a food processor for the same purposes as a blender. Be aware, though, that processor bowls will leak at the base if overloaded with liquid. A mini chopper is a smaller version of this appliance and is made for small chopping jobs.

Griddle and waffle iron: These appliances prepare those well-loved breakfast foods, pancakes and waffles. A thick, flat griddle also works great for sandwiches, fried green tomatoes, and fried eggs.

Panini press: Produce European pressed sandwiches with this quick-to-heat and easy-to-clean trendy appliance.

Pressure cooker: Made of heavy-gauge stainless steel and aluminum, a pressure cooker works by the steam action that builds up in a tightly sealed pot. A valve system controls the pressure, releasing excess steam through the top openings. Pressure cookers cook food up to 10 times faster than other methods, preserving flavor and nutrients and tenderizing tough cuts of meat.

Slow cooker: An electric slow cooker allows you to safely cook a meal while you're away from home. Made of thick stoneware, the slow-cooker bowl or crock is surrounded by an enclosed heating system. The low temperature gently simmers food for hours unattended. Slow cookers come in sizes ranging from 1 to 6 quarts. A 5-quart size is ideal to feed a family of four; a 6-quart cooker is enough for a family of six. Look for programmable slow cookers, which allow you to select timed cooking options, complete with a warm setting that kicks on at the end of cooking.

Toaster/toaster oven: A toaster is still the simplest way to toast all types of bread. A toaster oven will do the same task as well as act as a small oven. Convection toasters are available, too, as an option for cooking small amounts of food. Just be sure to plan for the counter space it will consume.

Wok: Known for stir-frying, a steel wok with a rounded bottom cooks food fast and efficiently with very little fat. With the aid of a wok ring, a steel wok fits easily on your cooktop. Freestanding electric woks are a convenient appliance, too.

about our pots and pans

The Perfect Pot

In our recipes calling for a Dutch oven, we use a pot that holds 5 to 6 quarts of liquid. Sides on this type of pot are shallow enough to be comfortable for average-height cooks to add ingredients and stir mixtures. It should have a tight-fitting lid for simmering things such as spaghetti sauce and chili. For larger amounts, we use a stockpot, which is great for making broth for soups. You can also use it to cook more than a pound of pasta or for seafood boils.

Skillet Smarts

When a large skillet is specified in our recipes, you need a skillet that measures 12 inches across the top. (If you measure the bottom, you may get a variety of sizes due to the sloping sides.) Otherwise, a 10-inch size is fine. Our Test Kitchens use clad stainless steel or anodized aluminum unless the recipe specifies a cast-iron skillet, which is cast iron that has been seasoned for cooking. All three cookware finishes will brown foods well and yield those little browned bits stuck to the bottom that flavor a sauce so well when scraped loose.

If we say to use a nonstick skillet, we're referring to a skillet coated with a high-tech coating that prevents sticking so you can use less fat—or only vegetable cooking spray—when cooking.

Our recipes do not specify flared (often called fry pan, skillet, omelet, or chef's pan) or straight-side skillets (also called sauté pans). Flared skillets work great for foods that you want to slide out of the pan, such as omelets, crêpes, and scrambled eggs. Also, use these shapely skillets for quick-cooking foods such as breakfast pork chops, chicken cutlets, and stir-fry veggies. Straight-sided skillets come with lids and ideally cook thicker meats and skillet suppers. Any time food is partially or fully covered for a portion of the cooking time, a skillet with a lid is essential. If a dish is started on the cooktop and finished in the oven, look for a skillet with an oven-safe handle.

Pastry brush

kitchen equipment dictionary

Bowls: Choose mixing bowls in graduated sizes so they'll be easy to stack and store. Plastic or earthenware bowls work fine for most mixing tasks, but a copper bowl is the ultimate for beating egg whites. Stainless steel bowls and glass bowls are best for cake batter.

Brushes: Both pastry and basting brushes are useful tools for brushing glazes and marinades on breads, meats, and other food. When selecting a brush, be sure the bristles are securely attached to the handle. The best brushes are made of natural boar bristles.

Coffee grinder: An electric coffee grinder not only grinds whole beans, but whole spices as well. Buy two grinders to keep for separate uses.

Colander: A metal or sturdy plastic colander is essential for draining cooked pasta and vegetables, rinsing salad greens, and draining canned beans and vegetables.

Cutting board: A wooden cutting board and a plastic cutting board are standard recommendations. Use a carving board when carving meat to catch the juices. Make it a practice to sanitize boards regularly.

Dough scraper: Also called a bench scraper, use this tool to lift and cut dough on a work surface. The sharp, straight edge can also cut fudge and bar cookies.

Garlic press: Use this tool when a recipe calls for pressed garlic because you'll want the garlic and its juice.

Grater: Invest in a box grater that has four sizes of grating holes. Microplane® graters come in a variety of sizes. Use them for grating feathery light mounds of hard cheese, chocolate, or citrus rind. Other popular graters include a two-piece Mouli grater that makes tableside cheese grating easy, and porcelain graters that have sharp, fine teeth for grating fresh ginger.

Juicer: A hand-juicer simplifies the process of squeezing citrus fruits.

Kitchen shears: These all-purpose scissors cut many foods more easily than a knife does. Use them to snip fresh herbs or to chop canned tomatoes right in the can.

Ladle: This tool helps you transfer soup to serving bowls.

Mallet: Choose a stainless steel mallet for pounding meat and poultry. It will also crack ice and mash garlic.

Measuring cups: Select a nested set of metal or plastic measuring cups for dry ingredients. They come in graduated sizes of 1 cup, ½ cup, ⅓ cup, and ¼ cup. You'll also need glass or clear plastic measuring cups for liquid ingredients; they come in 1-cup, 2-cup, and 4-cup sizes.

Measuring spoons: Select a set of measuring spoons that graduate from ⅛ teaspoon to 1 tablespoon.

Melon baller: This cupped tool makes rounded fruit bites.

Mortar and pestle: These tools, a bowl and tiny bat, work together to crush and blend spices, herbs, and garlic.

Carving board

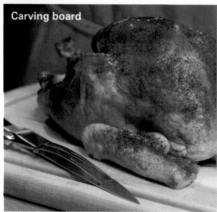
Dough scraper

Kitchen shears

Box grater

Microplane® graters

Porcelain grater

Melon baller

Pastry blender

Potato masher

Citrus reamer

Slicer

Strawberry huller

Thermometers

Tongs

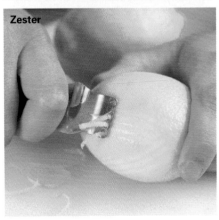
Zester

Mushroom brush: Use these bristles to clean dirt from mushrooms and other vegetables.

Pastry blender: The blades of this tool make it easy to cut fat into pea-size pieces while incorporating it into flour.

Pastry wheel: A pastry wheel cuts smooth or fluted edges of pastry and cookie dough. The fluted wheel seals and crimps edges of turnovers.

Potato masher: Designs vary for this tool that does a fast job of mashing spuds and other soft foods.

Ramekins and custard cups: Use these little dishes for baking custards and soufflés.

Reamer (citrus): This old-fashioned tool does a grand job of squeezing juice from a cut lemon.

Rolling pin: A large wooden rolling pin works well for rolling pastry and bread dough. A marble rolling pin is heavier and helps keep dough cold; a tapered European rolling pin is light and easily maneuvered.

Sifter: Use this to sift cake flour and powdered sugar. Never wash a sifter; just shake out the excess powder.

Slicer: Use this gadget to slice mushrooms, kiwifruit, or hard-cooked eggs.

Spatulas and spoons: Collect several wooden spoons and (heat-resistant) rubber spatulas; they're kitchen workhorses.

Steamer basket: This collapsible metal insert expands to fit snugly in a saucepan for steaming vegetables or other foods.

Strainer: Strainers have a coarse or fine wire mesh. A basic bowl strainer is used to drain or separate liquid from solid. Look for a strainer with stainless steel mesh. A strainer is called a *sieve* when it's used to separate coarse particles from fine ones.

Strawberry huller: This small tool efficiently plucks the caps from strawberries.

Stripper: This single-notched tool will cut a thin strip of peel from citrus fruit.

Thermometer: We recommend three thermometers for cooking: a meat thermometer, a combination candy/deep-fry thermometer that clips onto a pan, and an all-purpose instant-read thermometer. In addition, oven and refrigerator thermometers are inexpensive investments that help you keep a pulse on your appliances.

Tongs: Spring-loaded metal tongs will turn meat and many other foods as they cook without piercing them and releasing their juices.

Vegetable peeler: This tool peels the skin from vegetables and fruits. Buy one with a comfortable grip.

Whisk: Choose small, medium, and large elongated stainless steel wire whisks for blending batters and sauces, and a balloon whisk for whipping egg whites.

Zester: This tool has tiny holes that scrape the outer "zest" of citrus peels plus a fine mist of citrus oil.

knife knowledge

A high-quality set of knives is an investment, but you'll get your money's worth with years of use. Knives come in a variety of sizes, each made for a specific task. With the right knife in your hand, every cooking experience will be better.

Knife prices vary greatly. If a whole knife set isn't in your budget, just buy knives one at a time. And buy only knives that you know you'll use. Select knives based on ease of use, comfort, and value. Keeping your price range in mind, look at the knife's construction.

High-carbon stainless steel is the best-value blade; often called "no stain," this blade remains sharp and is not affected by air or moisture. Carbon steel is also a good-quality blade, but it may stain or rust if not dried immediately after washing.

The *tang* is the part of the knife blade that extends into the handle. Choose a knife with a full tang, which means that the blade extends throughout the length of the handle, adding balance and weight to the knife. Top-quality knives use metal rivets embedded in the handle on both sides to hold the tang in place.

Before you make an investment, be sure the knife fits comfortably in your hand and is well balanced. Test the knife by supporting it with two fingers at the point where the handle joins the blade; it should stay in a horizontal position.

Take the time to care for your knives properly. Always cut on a surface that has some resilience; wood is an excellent choice. Remember to wash your knives immediately after use, and dry them thoroughly. Washing them by hand rather than in the dishwasher is critical to their upkeep. Store knives in a slotted knife block or drawer insert, or on a magnetic bar that hangs on the wall in a safe zone.

To sharpen a knife: Hold the blade at a 20-degree angle against the steel; draw the blade gently across and down the steel's surface in a slight arc, using moderate pressure. Repeat on the other side of the blade. Repeat these steps 5 to 10 times, always alternating the right and left side of the blade. Get into the practice of using the steel every time you use your knife.

The Basics

These include a chef's knife, paring knife, utility knife, and serrated knife. They will take you through most food preparation. The main thing is to select the right knife for the job and for your cooking style.

Chef's knife: A large, tapered blade, about 8 to 10 inches long, used for chopping, slicing, dicing, and mincing.

Paring knife: Similar to a chef's knife with a tapered blade about 3 to 4 inches long, used for peeling and slicing fruits and vegetables.

Utility knife: A larger version of a paring knife, used for slicing meats and large vegetables. Also called a *sandwich knife.*

Bread knife: The long serrated-edged slicing knife slices bread and layer cakes with ease. Its toothed or scalloped edge cuts through anything with a tough skin or crust protecting a soft interior. Use a back-and-forth sawing motion when cutting with a serrated knife.

The shorter serrated knife called a *tomato knife* zips through tomatoes and crusty baguettes easily.

Other Cutlery

Carving/slicing knife: The blade on this knife meant for carving meats is narrower than a chef's knife. The tip can be pointed or rounded, and the blade can have a smooth or serrated edge. The long, smooth-edged blade cuts thin, even slices of meats and large vegetables as well as blocks of cheese. The long, scalloped-edged, rounded-tip knife called a *ham slicer* has a sturdy blade that's excellent for slicing ham and roasts.

Cleaver: This wide-bladed knife is most known for its ability to chop through bone. A cleaver is also good for coarsely chopping meats and vegetables, but its bulky blade makes precision slicing difficult.

Boning knife: This knife's narrow blade is 5 to 7 inches long and is excellent for separating cooked or uncooked meat from the bone, carving a roast, or peeling fruits and vegetables.

Santoku (Japanese cook's knife): This all-purpose Japanese knife makes fast work of large amounts of chopping, and the wide blade is a helpful scoop.

Bird's beak paring knife: This paring knife with a short, curved blade is great for working with round fruits and vegetables. Its small size makes it easy to handle and a good tool for creating garnishes.

Honing steel: This tool is included in many knife sets. It acts like a file on the knife's edge by realigning the edge and keeping the blade sharp. After years of use, the steel may no longer restore the cutting edge; then it's time to have your knives professionally sharpened.

Remember: A properly sharpened knife prevents accidents; cutting with a dull knife is one of the easiest ways to get hurt.

Carving knife

Serrated bread knife

Honing steel

Paring knives

Santoku

Utility knife

Cleaver

Cook's/chef's knives

Boning knife

glossary of staples

Selecting the right ingredients that a recipe specifies is a key factor in successful cooking. This glossary lists many of the basic ingredients in our recipes and describes the ways in which you can buy them.

Breadcrumbs

You can buy packaged or canned breadcrumbs, or you can make your own. Be sure to follow recipe specifics because the textures of different breadcrumbs vary and can influence a recipe's results.

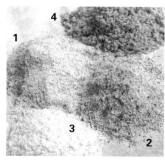

When we call for fine, dry breadcrumbs, we're referring to the store-bought kind. You can purchase them plain (1), Italian seasoned (2), or panko, coarse crumbs that yield an especially crunchy crust when used as a coating (3). If we call for soft breadcrumbs, it refers to home-made crumbs (4) made from sand-wich bread or a loaf. A food processor or mini chopper does a quick job of making crumbs for you (5).

Chocolate See page 205.

Cream

Whipping cream is the richest cream you can buy. It contains 30% to 40% milkfat. Heavy whipping cream has the highest percentage of milkfat (36% to 40%). Some recipes specifically call for heavy whipping cream for its ultimate rich attributes. In our recipes that call for whipped cream, we assume you'll measure the cream and whip it yourself. If a recipe calls for a carton of **frozen whipped topping**, that's the convenience product with its own signature flavor.

Half-and-half, also called light cream, contains about half the amount of fat as whipping cream and is more like the consistency of milk than cream. It will not whip.

Sour cream is a cultured product that's thick and has a slightly sour taste. Although we don't specify using light sour cream in this book, it's a fine substitute in many recipes.

Fats

Fats can be divided into two groups: fats and oils. Fats are solid at room temperature. They include **butter, margarine, shortening, and lard**. Oils are liquid at room temperature. They include canola oil, olive oil, vegetable oil, peanut oil, sesame oil, corn oil, safflower oil, and some nut oils.

Butter and margarine are two fats widely used in cooking and flavoring foods. While butter and margarine are often used interchangeably, they are different products. Butter has milkfat or cream as a base, while most margarines are made from vegetable oil, with some made from a combination of vegetable oil and animal fat. Read labels to know what you're buying.

Both butter and margarine are available in salted, unsalted, and whipped forms. Unsalted butter is the freshest premium butter for baking, but regular salted butter is also acceptable. Don't substitute whipped products for stick butter or margarine in baking. Whipped products have air incorporated to make them more spreadable. **Imitation margarine** (often labeled light, low fat, or low calorie) is a soft margarine used primarily as a spread. It isn't suitable for baking due to its high water content.

Shortening is composed of vegetable or animal fat or a combination of the two. It's solid at room temperature and has a long shelf life. It's tasteless but is commonly used for baking because it adds moisture and tenderness, particularly to piecrusts. Shortening is easy to measure in its stick form. Butter-flavored shortening is processed with a butter flavoring.

Lard is rendered pork fat. In years past, it was used almost exclusively for making pastry and biscuits.

Olive oil is used widely in cooking, particularly in vinaigrettes and recipes where its fresh flavor is noticed. **Extra-virgin olive oil** is from the olive's first pressing. It has the deepest color, richest flavor, and is the least acidic tasting—and the most expensive. Use it where you'll taste it, drizzled over fresh ingredients just before serving. **Vegetable oil** and **corn oil** are all-purpose cooking oils. **Canola oil** is another all-purpose oil, and it offers health benefits, as well. It's low in saturated fat and contains omega-3 fatty acids that are believed to lower cholesterol and triglycerides. **Peanut oil** is excellent for frying because it has a high smoke point. This means it can withstand high-heat cooking without smoking and burning.

Don't substitute oil for shortening in baked products, even when the shortening is to be melted.

Flour

Flour is milled from all kinds of grains—wheat, corn, rye, oats, and barley—each producing one or more kinds of flour. The differences lie in the particular grain used and how it's processed.

Wheat flours are divided into two basic groups: **whole grain** and **white. Whole-grain wheat flours** include whole wheat, graham, and cracked wheat. Among the **white flours** are bread, all-purpose, unbleached all-purpose, and cake flour. These are often enriched with iron and B vitamins to replace nutrients lost when the wheat germ is removed.

Different types of flour are not generally interchangeable in our recipes. That's because wheat flours vary in protein content, and protein affects how a flour performs during baking. When mixed with a liquid, the protein forms gluten, which gives elasticity to batters and doughs and provides the structure or framework for whatever you're baking. In addition, gluten affects the tenderness and volume of baked goods. White flours have more usable protein (gluten) than whole-grain flours.

Bread flour is a hard-wheat flour milled especially for breadmaking. It has a high protein content that produces sturdy yeast breads.

All-purpose flour is a combination of hard- and soft-wheat flour and is commonly used for all types of baked products. All-purpose flours made with more soft wheat (such as White Lily and Martha White) give extra-tender results when used for cakes, quick breads, and sweet rolls, as opposed to all-purpose flours with more hard wheat (such as Pillsbury and Gold Medal), which work better for yeast breads.

Unbleached flour is an all-purpose flour that has no bleaching agents added during processing and can be used interchangeably with all-purpose. Purists like baking with unbleached flour; they claim it lends the freshest taste.

Self-rising flour is an all-purpose flour to which leavening and salt have been added. It's not meant for use in yeast breads. It's best not to substitute self-rising flour for all-purpose flour; however, you can substitute all-purpose flour for self-rising by making these adjustments: For 1 cup self-rising, use 1 cup all-purpose flour plus 1 teaspoon baking powder and ½ teaspoon salt.

Cake flour is a soft-wheat flour and has a much lower protein content than all-purpose flour. Products made with cake flour have a tender, delicate crumb. You can substitute all-purpose flour for cake flour by using 2 tablespoons less all-purpose flour per cup.

Gelatin

You can purchase gelatin either unflavored or sweetened and flavored; the two are not interchangeable. **Unflavored gelatin** is sold in packages containing slightly less than 1 tablespoon. Each package will gel 2 cups of liquid. **Flavored gelatin** is sold in 3- and 6-ounce packages and contains sugar, flavoring, and coloring. Flavored and unflavored gelatins require different softening procedures; always follow the package directions.

Milk

We test recipes using **whole milk** unless otherwise stated. This milk has at least 3.25% fat content. **Fat-free milk** has most of the fat removed and has more calcium than whole milk. It has less than .5% fat. **Low-fat milk** is available from .5% to 2% fat content.

Evaporated milk has had 60% of the water removed. It's available in cans only. You can substitute evaporated milk for fresh milk by blending it with equal parts water.

Sweetened condensed milk has had half its water content removed and 60% sugar added. Buy it in cans. It can't be substituted for fresh milk because it's too thick and sweet.

Nonfat dry milk powder is what remains after the water and fat have been removed from whole milk. It rehydrates easily with water.

Buttermilk is the liquid that remains after butter is made from whole milk. Cultured buttermilk is the product left after skim milk is treated with lactic acid bacteria.

Yogurt is simply fermented milk. It's available plain or flavored. Plain yogurt is often used as a low-calorie substitute for sour cream.

Salt See page 18.

Spices See pages 20-21.

Sugar See page 19.

Syrup

Molasses is the syrup left after making granulated sugar from sugar cane. It's most commonly sold as light or dark molasses. **Unsulphured** and **blackstrap molasses** are less-refined forms that have a stronger flavor. Use them only when specified in a recipe.

Honey is a thick syrup made by bees from the nectar of flowers. It's sweeter than sugar and has a distinctive flavor. Clover honey is widely sold in the marketplace, but there are dozens of flavored honeys available, most of which are named for the flower that produces the honey.

Corn syrup is available in light and dark forms, the lighter being lighter in both flavor and color. Our recipes specify which form to use.

Cane syrup comes from sugar cane that has been boiled down to the consistency of syrup.

Sorghum comes from a coarse grass by the same name. It's processed to obtain a juice, which is then boiled down to a syrup.

Maple syrup comes from the sap of the sugar maple tree. Like sugar cane, it's boiled down to the consistency of syrup.

Thickening Agents

All-purpose flour is the most common thickener. It's used for gravies, sauces, and puddings, and it gives an opaque appearance. Two tablespoons of flour will thicken one cup of liquid.

Use **cornstarch** to thicken puddings and sauces when you want a more translucent look, particularly with fruit sauces. One tablespoon of cornstarch will thicken one cup of liquid.

Arrowroot is not used as often as in the past, but it will thicken fillings and sauces, leaving them sparkling clear. One tablespoon of arrowroot will thicken one cup of liquid. When old recipes call for arrowroot, you can substitute an equal measure of cornstarch.

Use **tapioca** for thickening pie fillings and puddings. It gives a characteristic granular texture to foods. Use about 1½ tablespoons tapioca per cup of liquid.

Vinegar

Vinegar gives a jolt of acidity to foods like salads, dressings, and marinades. **White vinegar** is the most common type. It's colorless, but it has a strong flavor and aroma.

Wine vinegar, either red or white, is mild in flavor and makes a nice addition to marinades and salad dressings.

Cider vinegar, made from the juice of apples, is a strong vinegar commonly used in slaws, fruit salads, and for pickling. Whether you use cider or white vinegar for canning, make sure the label claims 5% acidity.

Balsamic vinegar gets its dark brown color and pungent sweetness from aging in wood barrels. Use this luxurious vinegar sparingly. It enriches a wide range of foods from beef stew to strawberries.

Maine sea salt

Mesquite smoked sea salt

Coconut & kaffir lime sea salt

Coarse sea salt

Fine sea salt

Australian flake salt

salt dictionary

Until recently, salt was just a basic commodity. Now chefs and home cooks across the globe have come to appreciate and distinguish between the distinct qualities of salts and how they enhance the flavors and finish of foods.

The differences between kosher salt and sea salt are mainly their texture and taste. Kosher salt generally comes in flakes rather than granules, and it usually has no additives. Many cooks prefer the texture and flavor of kosher salt in cooking.

Sea salt is unrefined salt harvested from sea water through evaporation. Like kosher salt, sea salt contains no additives. Many people prefer sea salt to table salt because of its bright, pure, clean flavor.

Maine Sea Salt—sun-dried, unrefined, whole sea salt from the Gulf of Maine. A few of these big crystals enhance an ordinary dish.

Mesquite Smoked Sea Salt—Maine sea salt that's been mesquite smoked. Use it to add mesquite flavor to poultry, pork, or fish on the grill, or to add smokehouse flavor to soups.

Australian Flake Salt—delicate peach-colored flakes with a mild flavor. Crystals melt quickly, making it an ideal finishing salt.

Coarse Sea Salt—sea salt for grinding.

Fine Sea Salt—sea salt for shaking out of a shaker.

Coconut & Kaffir Lime Sea Salt—Bali sea salt smoked over coconut shells and Kaffir lime leaves. A nice complement to steamed or grilled vegetables, seafood, and pasta.

Hawaiian (coarse) Sea Salt—sea salt enriched with Alaea baked Hawaiian red clay. Use it for roasting or grilling meats.

French Grey (fine) Sea Salt—fine, moist grey crystals that dissolve quickly and evenly when used in cooking.

French Grey (coarse) Sea Salt—coarse, moist grey crystals produced through natural evaporation of sea water. The grey hue comes from its extremely high level of minerals and nutrients. When used as a finishing salt, it adds a nice crunch to any dish.

Fleur de Sel—a premium salt with a rich history in French cooking. This hand-raked salt harvested from the Guérande region of France is often promoted as a finishing salt—add it at the very end of cooking to preserve its delicate, sweet flavor. It's ideal for grilled meats, cooked fresh vegetables, and salads.

Maldon Sea Salt—sought after by the health conscious and gourmet alike for its texture and flavor. The pyramid-shaped, soft, flaky crystals have a distinctive salty taste, meaning less of it is required in cooking. Use it in cooking, or sprinkle over food before serving.

Kosher Salt—a large flaked salt that's additive-free. The flakes dissolve easily and have a less pungent flavor than table salt.

finishing salts are harvested in special areas around the world and are known for their unique textures that allow them to quickly dissolve when applied to food just before serving. These salts (flake salt, Fleur de Sel, and French sea salt) bring out the depth of natural flavors of any dish.

French grey (fine) sea salt

French grey (coarse) sea salt

Hawaiian sea salt

Fleur de Sel

Kosher salt

Maldon sea salt

Powdered sugar

sugar dictionary

Powdered sugar, also called confectioners' sugar, is granulated sugar that has been crushed and screened until the grains are like powder. You can tell the degree of fineness of powdered sugar by the number of x's indicated on the package. The fine powdered is 4x, the very fine powdered is 6x, and the ultrafine powdered is 10x. The 10x type is what our Test Kitchens use in recipes.

Dark and light brown sugar is granulated sugar combined with molasses, rendering a soft, rich sugar whose color is dependent on the amount of molasses added. While the more delicate flavor of light brown sugar is widely used in baking, the heady flavor of dark brown sugar is savored in gingerbread, baked beans, and other foods with full-bodied flavor. Our recipes specify which one to use when it makes a difference; otherwise, you choose.

Brown sugar will dry out easily after opening because it's moister than granulated sugar. After a package is opened, transfer the unused part to an airtight container; this keeps it soft and moist. You can soften hardened brown sugar by putting it in an airtight container and adding a slice of apple or bread or by brief heating in the microwave.

Muscovado sugar, also known as *Barbados* sugar, is a moist, finely textured raw sugar that's distinctive in its dark brown color and rich molasses flavor. Its heavy characteristics are best suited for barbecue sauces, brown quick breads, and other sweet and savory uses that require sugar with depth and density.

Superfine sugar, also called *castor* sugar, is a granulated sugar with the tiniest and most uniform crystals. Use superfine sugar when you want it to dissolve easily in a recipe, such as meringues. Make your own by pulsing regular granulated sugar in the food processor about 30 seconds.

Sparkling/sanding sugars are coarse or fine white crystals that are prized for adding sparkle to baked goods. Use sanding sugar to add sparkle to the rim of a glass or the top of a cookie because these larger granules offer a satisfying crunch as well as sweetness.

Demerara sugar is from the Demerara area of Guyana in South America. It's a pale golden-yellow sugar with slightly sticky crystals.

Turbinado sugar is an amber-colored sugar with a mild cane flavor. It's prized for its coarse crystals that are often sprinkled on scones and pastries.

Superfine sugar

Dark brown sugar

Coarse sparkling/sanding sugar

Light brown sugar

Fine sparkling/sanding sugar

Muscovado sugar

Turbinado sugar

Demerara sugar

Pink peppercorns

Black peppercorns

Juniper berries

Green peppercorns

White peppercorns

Yellow mustard seeds

Brown mustard seeds

Fennel seeds

Fenugreek

Annato seeds

Poppy seeds

spice dictionary

Storing Your Spices

Dried whole and ground spices are often used as flavor boosts for what's cooking within arm's reach. While the obvious and convenient storage space for spices might appear to be on a rack near your stovetop, spices can lose their potency and color when exposed to light and heat. Spices will last six months to a year when stored in a cool, dark place or in your freezer. Take the sniff test each time you open a spice jar; if there's not an immediate aroma, it's time to pitch and replace.

Savory Spices

Peppercorns—Pepper berries are processed to produce numerous varieties of peppercorns such as black, green, pink, and white. Freshly ground in a pepper mill, dried peppercorns impart maximum flavor to food as compared to store-bought ground pepper, which quickly loses its potency. Dried whole peppercorns can be stored in a cool, dry place up to six months.

Juniper Berries—Most recognizable as the signature flavor in gin, juniper berries also lend their flavor as a dried spice in cooking. Blue-black in color, these berries are usually crushed to release their strong flavor.

Mustard Seeds—There are two main types of mustard seeds, white and brown. White mustard seeds are larger but less pungent than the brown. Brown mustard seeds are the main ingredient in European and Chinese mustards. Both types of seeds are used for pickling and flavoring cooked meats and vegetables. Freshly ground mustard seeds are used in salad dressings and sauces.

Fennel Seeds—A characteristic spice of Italian sausage, fennel seeds are an important ingredient in seasoning blends of the Mediterranean, Italy, China, and Scandinavia. Fennel seeds may be roasted to intensify their flavor. Fennel is used in curry blends, Chinese five spice, and herbes de Provence. Fennel is also used to flavor fish, sausages, baked goods, and liquors.

Fenugreek—Whether whole or ground, fenugreek is a versatile and lesser-recognized spice that is used as a flavor component in curry powders, teas, and spice blends.

Poppy Seeds—Poppy seeds lend crunchy texture and nutty flavor to pastries, coffee cakes, and other baked goods, both as a filling and topping. Because of their high oil content, poppy seeds are prone to rancidity, so store them in an airtight container in the refrigerator or freezer.

Annato/Achiote—A prevalent spice at East Indian, Spanish, and Latin American markets, achiote seed is a musky-flavored spice with a robust rusty-red color. *Annato*, a derivative of the achiote seed, is commercially used as a colorant for butter, margarine, cheese, and smoked fish.

Turmeric, Saffron, and Curry—Turmeric and saffron are boldly colored, pungent spices revered as having a highly exotic fragrance. Turmeric, with its intense yellow-orange color, is an integral component of curry blends. Saffron, sold as threads and powder, is another golden spice known for its strong perfume and high price tag. Saffron is best known for its use in bouillabaisse, paella, and European breads. Widely used in Indian cooking, curry powder is a blend of up to 20 spices, herbs, and seeds. It can lose its potency quickly, so store it airtight up to two months.

Dill Seeds—The characteristic ingredient for the brine in which dill pickles are cured, dill seeds bring an intense flavor to a dish, especially when heated.

Celery Seed—Celery seed is an intensely flavored spice primarily used for pickling, but it's also used in spice blends.

Coriander—The seed from which the cilantro leaf is grown, coriander has a citrusy fragrance and is believed by some to increase the appetite. Once used as a pickling spice, coriander and its aromatic lemony-sage flavor add to a variety of ethnic recipes from Mexican to Southeast Asian fare.

Cumin Seed—With a potent, earthy flavor, cumin is popular in Southwestern, Thai, and Indian cooking and is a key ingredient in curry powder blends and chili powder.

Baking Spices

Anise Seed—Used as a digestive agent for centuries, anise seed, with its familiar licorice flavor, is an intense ingredient used in cookies, cakes, and pickles. Anise contains a fragrant oil, anethol, that's also found in star anise.

Saffron threads · Dill seeds · Celery seeds · Coriander seeds · Cayenne pepper · Paprika · Anise seed · Turmeric · Cumin seed

Cinnamon—The inner bark of a tropical evergreen tree that's harvested and dried to produce cinnamon quills. Ceylon cinnamon is lighter in color and less prominent in flavor than cassia cinnamon, the spicy, reddish-brown variety commonly found in stores. In addition to its presence in baked goods, cinnamon is used in spice blends such as garam masala.

Cloves—With a distinctive floral note, cloves are the dried, unopened flower buds of Indonesia's tropical evergreen clove tree. Cloves are a strong, versatile spice, contributing to familiar foods ranging from ketchup and Worcestershire sauce to Chai tea and mulled cider.

Cinnamon · Cloves · Allspice · Nutmeg

Allspice—Also known as Jamaica pepper, allspice offers a taste that nods to nutmeg, cinnamon, and cloves. Allspice is named for its broad flavor.

Nutmeg and Mace—When the fruit of the nutmeg tree splits, it reveals the nutmeg seed and a lacy membrane that's dried and powdered as nutmeg's sibling spice, mace. Mace is used to flavor savory and sweet foods. Nutmeg is sold whole or ground and is noted for its use in custards as well as spinach dishes.

Cardamom—Encased in small pods about the size of a cranberry, cardamom seeds are a fragrant relative to ginger. Cardamom, sold in both ground and pod form, has a pungent aroma and a spicy, sweet flavor.

Ginger—Powdered ginger is an indispensable ingredient in classic baked goods like gingerbread and spice cakes. The flavor of powdered ginger, with its subtle citrusy impact, differs greatly from its fresh counterpart.

Vanilla Bean—These dried brown beans are so expensive because they're hand harvested from a type of orchid. So rare that they were once reserved for royalty, these fragrant pods have a multitude of uses in baking today. See page 211 for a technique on scraping out the beloved seeds.

Vanilla Bean Paste—A relatively new product available in cook stores, vanilla bean paste can be used like vanilla extract. Use the same amount of paste as you would extract in recipes. It has a syrupy consistency with flecks of vanilla bean. Use it when you want a real punch of vanilla essence.

Vanilla bean paste

herb dictionary

Basil: One of the easiest herbs to grow, basil has a heady fragrance and a faint licorice flavor. Use it in salads, pestos, pasta dishes, pizza, and meat and poultry dishes. Purple ruffles basil has ruffled purple-black leaves and a mild fragrance and flavor. Cinnamon basil, Thai basil, and lemon basil are very flavorful, fragrant basils for cooking.

Bay leaves: Use fresh or dried bay leaves in soups, stews, vegetables, and bouquet garni. Discard bay leaves before serving food.

Chervil: A fragile herb, chervil is commonly known as French parsley. It has a subtle anise flavor and is best fresh or cooked only briefly. Add chervil to egg dishes, soups, and salads, or use it as a substitute for parsley.

Chives: Chives are attractive, rugged herbs that are easy to grow. Snip the leaves and they'll provide a mild onion or garlic flavor to soups, salads, and vegetable dishes. In spring, chives boast globelike lavender-colored blooms that make ideal edible garnishes for salads.

Cilantro: Also known as Chinese parsley, cilantro is grown for its spicy-flavored foliage and for its seeds called coriander. Cilantro is the leaf, and coriander is the seed or powder; the two are not interchangeable in recipes. Slightly bruise a cilantro leaf and it will give off its unmistakable pungent, peppery fragrance. Use the leaves in Southwestern, Mexican, and Asian dishes. Cumin and mint are often paired with cilantro. Coriander seeds are used in Indian dishes as well as in pickles and relishes.

Dill: Finely chop fresh dill for shrimp dishes, eggs, soups, sandwiches, potato salad, and sauces. Dill is a good salt substitute. You can harvest and dry dill seeds and use them in pickles, breads, and salad dressings.

Geranium, scented: Use these scented leaves for flavoring pound cakes, cookies, herb butters, jellies, and iced tea.

Lavender: This edible ornamental herb blooms with fragrant spikes of purple flowers. Harvest the flowers just before they're fully opened, and use them (as well as the leaves) in ice cream or baked goods, marinades, and sauces. Spanish lavender is a gray-leafed plant with needlelike leaves that resemble rosemary.

Lemon balm: This hardy, bushy member of the mint family has a mild lemony flavor. Chop the aromatic leaves to use in tea bread, scones, and salads, or use leaves whole in tea or other cold beverages.

Lemon verbena: The strongest scented lemon herb, lemon verbena has a healthy lemony essence. Use it as you would lemon balm leaves. Pulse a handful of leaves with a cup of sugar in a food processor to make lemon sugar. Store it in a jar. Use the sugar in pound cakes and teas.

Mint: Add this popular herb to lamb, poultry, salads, sauces, teas, and punches. Try cooking with flavorful types of mint such as peppermint, orange mint, apple mint, or chocolate mint.

Nasturtiums: These bright red and orange edible flowers have a peppery

Chives

French tarragon

Flat-leaf parsley

Cilantro

Mexican marigold mint

Lemon balm

Apple mint

Chocolate mint

Lemon verbena

taste. Use them in salads and sandwich spreads or as a versatile garnish.

Oregano: These small green leaves produce a strong flavor. Greek oregano is the most popular oregano for cooking because of its pronounced flavor and aromatic leaves. Add oregano to Italian dishes, meat, fish, eggs, fresh and cooked tomatoes, vegetables, beans, and marinades.

Parsley: Curly parsley's the most common with its ruffly edges and peppery bite. Italian flat-leaf parsley offers a fresh flavor to stews, bean dishes, and salads.

Rosemary: Unlike other herbs, rosemary has a stronger flavor when fresh than when dried. It's a hardy herb with a piney scent and flavor. To harvest rosemary, strip leaves from the stem. Use the strong-flavored leaves sparingly as an accent to soups, meats, stews, breads, and vegetables.

Sage: This fuzzy gray-green herb is best known for use in holiday dressings. Sage is often paired with sausage, too. And its soft texture makes it easy to tuck under the skin of poultry before roasting.

Tarragon: This tender herb plays a classic role in béarnaise sauce. Leaves have a bittersweet, peppery scent with a hint of anise that adds flavor to soups, poultry, seafood, vegetables, and egg dishes.

Thyme: Strip the tiny leaves from stems just before using. Use fresh thyme in marinades for basting seafood, chicken, or pork. Add thyme to meat stews or bean or vegetable dishes.

All about Herbs

Herbs offer simple fresh seasoning to most any type of food. Once you've cooked with herbs, you'll want to grow them, too.

• Some herbs, such as rosemary, lavender, oregano, and thyme, are perennials. Give them a permanent spot in your garden and you can have continual clippings.

• If you grow your own herbs for cooking, snip and use them before they flower. Harvest herbs early in the morning just after the dew has dried. Wash herbs and pat dry.

• If you buy fresh herbs at the grocery store, preserve them up to a week with one of these methods: 1) Wrap stems in a soaking-wet paper towel, taking care to keep herb foliage dry. Place wrapped herbs in a zip-top bag, seal it with air inside, and store in refrigerator, or 2) place stem ends in a glass with two inches of water, cover herb foliage loosely with a zip-top bag, and store in refrigerator.

• If a recipe doesn't specify when to add herbs, it's best to add them at the end of cooking to release their full flavor. Bay leaves are the exception; they typically simmer at length in soups.

• If you want to substitute fresh herbs for dried herbs, which are more concentrated in flavor, use three times the amount of fresh herbs as dried. Rosemary is the exception; use it in equal amounts.

• Don't emphasize more than one strong herb in a dish. Just taste an herb to identify whether it has a pungent, spicy, fruity, or floral taste; then pair it with a compatible food.

• Rosemary, cilantro, thyme, oregano, and sage are strong herbs; go sparingly when adding them to a dish. Medium-flavored herbs are basil, dill, mint, and fennel; use them more generously. Use delicate herbs like parsley and chives in abundance.

terms & techniques

Measuring Ingredients

Successful cooking depends on adding just the right amount of ingredients. Get in the habit of measuring with precision. Liquid and dry ingredients are measured using different techniques and equipment.

Glass measuring cups with a pouring spout are best for liquids. Place them on a flat surface, and read at eye level, filling exactly to the line indicated. If you use a liquid measuring cup for flour, you'll end up with at least an extra tablespoon per cup. It may not sound like much, but it can make a big difference in the moistness of your baked goods.

Nested metal or plastic cups are best for measuring dry ingredients. Flour settles during storage, so stir it before spooning lightly into a dry measuring cup. Fill to overflowing and level it off with the straight edge of a knife or metal spatula.

Measure brown sugar by packing it firmly into a dry measuring cup; then level it off. Always use the measuring cup that holds the exact amount called for in a recipe.

Measure syrup, corn syrup, molasses, and honey by first coating the measuring spoon or cup with cooking spray; then the ingredient can be measured and released with ease.

Cooking Terms

Barbecue: To roast meat slowly over coals on a spit or framework, or to roast in an oven, basting meat occasionally with a sauce or marinade.

Baste: To spoon or brush liquid over meats while they're cooking to keep food moist and flavorful. The liquid can be a sauce, a glaze, butter, or pan drippings.

Beat: To mix vigorously with a brisk motion using a spoon, fork, whisk, or electric mixer.

Blanch: To dip food briefly into boiling water. Blanching loosens tomato and peach skins for easy peeling.

Blend: To combine two or more ingredients until uniformly mixed. You can use an electric mixer, blender, or spoon to blend ingredients.

Boil: To heat liquid until bubbles break vigorously on the surface.

Braise: To cook food slowly with a small amount of liquid in a tightly covered pan. Less tender cuts of meat benefit from this long, slow cooking.

Broil: To cook by direct dry heat under a broiler.

Bruise: To partially crush an ingredient, such as herbs, to release flavor for seasoning food.

Butterfly: To split food like shrimp or boneless leg of lamb horizontally in half, cutting almost, but not all the way, through food. Food is then opened flat to expose more surface area so it can cook evenly and quickly.

Caramelize: To cook sugar in a skillet over medium heat until it forms a golden syrup. Foods like onions that contain natural sugar caramelize and turn golden during oven roasting.

Chop: To cut food roughly into small, irregular pieces.

Core: To remove the tough or seeded center of some fruits and vegetables.

Cream: To beat softened butter, alone or with sugar, until light and fluffy.

Crimp: To pinch dough edges to create a decorative edge on a piecrust or to seal two layers of dough so filling doesn't seep out during baking. Use the tines of a fork or your fingers to crimp.

Cube: To cut food squarely into pieces ½ inch or larger.

Cut in: To incorporate by brief cutting or chopping motions, as in cutting butter or shortening into flour for pastry.

Deglaze: To create a complex, flavorful sauce by pouring liquid into a pan in which meat has been roasted or sautéed in order to absorb the essence and caramelized bits. First sauté meat in a heavy skillet; then remove food from skillet, and add wine or broth. Bring to a boil over high heat, scraping up crusty bits that cling to bottom of skillet. Simmer briefly, season, and pour over food before serving. Add cream, butter, or herbs for richer flavor.

Devein: To remove intestinal vein of shrimp, using a small knife or shrimp deveiner.

Dice: To cut food squarely on all sides into pieces ranging from ⅛ to ½ inch. The smallest (⅛ inch) dice is *brunoise*. The size of a dice can vary; diced is smaller than cubed.

Dissolve: To mix a dry substance with liquid until the dry substance becomes part of the solution.

Dot: To scatter small bits of butter over a casserole, pie, or other food before baking. The butter adds flavor and enhances a golden crust.

Dredge: To coat food lightly with a dry ingredient like flour or breadcrumbs.

Drizzle: To slowly pour liquid such as melted butter in a fine stream, back and forth, over food.

Dust: To sprinkle very lightly with a powdery ingredient such as powdered sugar or flour.

Emulsify: To bind liquids such as oil and water that don't blend together naturally. Add one liquid, usually the oil, to the other liquid in a slow, steady stream while blending.

Flambé: To flame, using alcohol as the burning agent; the flame causes caramelization, enhancing flavor.

Fold: To add a whipped ingredient, such as cream or egg white, to another ingredient or mixture with a spatula by a gentle over-and-under motion.

Fry: To cook food in hot fat, usually oil or melted shortening.

Grate: To obtain very small particles of food such as cheese or chocolate by rubbing on smallest holes of a grater.

Julienne: To cut food into thin, uniform matchsticks that are 2 to 3 inches long and ⅛ to ¼ inch wide.

Knead: To work a food (usually dough) by hand, using a folding-over-and-pressing-forward motion.

Marinate: To flavor (and often tenderize) food by letting it soak in a liquid. The liquid often contains an acid like lemon juice, wine, or vinegar as well as oil and seasonings.

Mince: To chop food into very fine irregular pieces using a chef's knife.

Pan-broil: To cook over direct heat in an uncovered skillet containing little or no fat.

Pan-fry: To cook in an uncovered skillet in a small amount of fat until food is browned and cooked to proper doneness.

Parboil: To partially cook in boiling water before final cooking on a grill or in the oven.

Pipe: To squeeze a smooth mixture through a decorating bag or zip-top freezer bag with a corner snipped to make a shaped dough or design.

Poach: To cook in a small amount of gently simmering liquid. The surface should barely shimmer.

Pound: To flatten meats and poultry to a uniform thickness using a meat mallet or rolling pin. This promotes even thickness and tenderizes tough cuts of meat by breaking up connective tissue.

Preheat: To turn on oven so that desired temperature will be reached before food is inserted for

Dice

Deglaze

Julienne

Mince

Slice diagonally

baking. We recommend preheating an oven 10 minutes before baking.

Prick: To pierce food before cooking.

Proof: To test yeast for potency; the rising stage for yeast breads.

Punch down: To deflate yeast bread dough after it has risen by punching your fist into center of dough and then pulling the edges into the center.

Puree: To form a smooth mixture by blending food in a food processor or blender.

Reduce: To rapidly boil a liquid to concentrate its flavor and to reduce its amount by evaporation.

Render: To melt away fat from surrounding meat. Crispy cracklings will be left.

Roast: To cook, uncovered, in an oven by dry heat.

Sauté: To cook or brown food lightly over fairly high heat in a small amount of fat in a skillet.

Score: To cut shallow gashes on surface of food, as in scoring fat on ham before glazing.

Sear: To brown surface of meat over high heat to deepen flavor and to caramelize the meat's exterior.

Shred: To cut, tear, or grate food into long, narrow pieces or to rub food on the large holes of a grater.

Shuck: To remove the husks of corn with your hands or to remove the shells of oysters, mussels, or clams using a special knife.

Simmer: To cook gently at a temperature just below the boiling point.

Skim: To remove fat from surface of liquid.

Slice: To cut food into a desired thickness, using a chef's knife or slicing knife. Slice **diagonally** by holding knife at a 45-degree angle to the food and slicing to desired thickness. This technique exposes maximum surface area, allowing food to cook quickly (as for stir-frying).

Steam: To cook with steam given off by boiling water either in a pressure cooker, on a platform in a covered pan, or in a special steamer.

Steep: To let food, such as tea, stand in almost boiling water until the flavor is extracted.

Stir-fry: To cook quickly in a small amount of oil over high heat, using light and constant tossing motions to preserve food's texture. A wok is the traditional pan used to stir-fry, but a skillet works, too.

Temper: To heat food gently before adding it to a hot mixture so it doesn't curdle. Temper beaten eggs by adding one-fourth of a hot mixture to eggs to raise the temperature; then stir it back into the hot mixture.

Toss: To mix together gently with light over-and-under motions in order not to bruise delicate food such as salad greens.

Whip: To beat rapidly to incorporate air and increase volume.

working with garlic

Mash garlic by crushing it under the weight of your hand on a chef's knife. The peel should slip right off. ▶

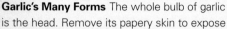

Garlic's Many Forms The whole bulb of garlic is the head. Remove its papery skin to expose individual cloves. Keep garlic in a cool, dry place 2 to 4 months. You can buy minced garlic and roasted garlic in a jar; just be aware that the flavor is more intense than freshly chopped cloves. And garlic salt and garlic powder have their place in sauces, rubs, and quick-and-easy cooking.

jarred garlic · head · cloves · minced fresh · garlic salt · garlic powder

chopping an onion

▲ Halve a peeled onion through root end. Place cut side down on cutting board. Make several horizontal cuts parallel to the board, cutting close to, but not through, root end.

▲ Make lengthwise vertical cuts, to but not through the root.

sectioning citrus

▲ Using a paring knife, slice away peel and white pith from fruit.

▲ Holding fruit over a bowl to catch juice, slice between membrane and one side of fruit segment; then lift segment out with knife.

cleaning mushrooms

▲ Wipe fresh mushrooms clean with a damp paper towel or a mushroom brush.

peeling ginger

▲ Use a small spoon to rub skin from a knob of fresh ginger.

▲ Cut across onion to chop it into small, even pieces.

seeding a tomato

▲ Cut off top of tomato. Using your finger or a small spoon, gently dig out seeds and discard into a bowl.

making a bouquet garni

Tie herbs, such as parsley, bay leaves, and thyme, together with string. Use the bundle to flavor soups and stews; discard before serving. ▶

pitting an olive

◀ Using a cherry/olive pitter, place olive in the tool; press lever to punch out the pit. Otherwise, you can remove an olive pit in the same manner as you mash garlic (top left).

skinning hazelnuts

▲ Toast nuts at 350° for 5 to 10 minutes or until skins begin to split.

▲ Transfer warm hazelnuts to a colander; rub briskly to remove skins.

chiffonade

▲ Tightly roll up leaves of basil, spinach, or similar ingredients. Slice into fine shreds with a chef's knife.

▲ Chiffonade makes a beautiful salad or garnish.

pitting an avocado

▲ Cut avocado in half lengthwise; carefully stab pit with chef's knife. Twist knife to remove pit.

▲ Lay knife blade parallel to cutting board, and pop off pit.

▲ Gently scoop out flesh with a spoon; chop or mash as desired.

roasting peppers

▲ Hold pepper over a gas flame or under broiler in the oven until charred on all sides.

▲ Place pepper in zip-top or paper bag; seal bag, and let pepper sweat 10 minutes.

▲ Gently peel off and discard charred skin. Chop pepper as desired.

seeding jalapeños

◀ Most of the heat in a jalapeño is in the seeds and membranes. Wearing protective gloves, slice pepper in half lengthwise. Using a paring knife, cut out and discard the seeds and membranes. Chop pepper as desired.

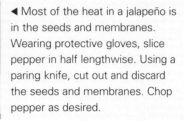

blanching vegetables

▲ Drop vegetables in rapidly boiling water briefly (about 1 minute).

▲ Plunge vegetables into ice water to stop the cooking process. Blanching heightens the color and sets the flavor of food.

steaming vegetables

▲ Place a steamer insert in a large pot of a small amount of boiling water. Add vegetable pieces. Cover and steam until vegetables are crisp-tender when pierced with a knife.

healthy living

Eating right can mean something different to each of us. In general, it's wise to watch portion sizes, be aware of the fat sources in your diet, and be discerning about the foods you eat. And don't forget those two words, balance and moderation. Consider the points on these pages to help you plan wholesome meals for your family.

The New Food Pyramid

To help Americans make more individualized and nutritious food choices, the United States Department of Agriculture (USDA) released an updated version of the Food Guide Pyramid in 2005. This new guide, the *My Pyramid Plan*, incorporates the most current nutrition information from the 2005 Dietary Guidelines for Americans and encourages a personalized approach to healthy eating and exercise based on age, gender, and exercise level. The new pyramid provides general guidelines for Americans over age two that are listed below for a 2,000 calorie-a-day diet, but for personalized recommendations, go to **www.mypyramid.gov** and type in your information; the Web site will provide individualized recommendations for each food group.

And, for the first time, the USDA pyramid includes an exercise component. The aim is to find your own balance between food and exercise with a general goal of staying active for at least 30 minutes on most days of the week. Children and teenagers should be active for 1 hour every day or on most days of the week.

Grains—eat 6 ounces every day.
• These foods are your body's primary energy source, providing complex carbohydrates and fiber. Eat at least 3 ounces of whole-grain cereals, breads, crackers, rice, or pasta every day to help

how we analyze recipes

• If an ingredient has a range in amounts, we analyzed with the first amount.
• Garnishes and optional ingredients are not included in nutrient analyses.
• We consider a recipe *low carb* if it's under 10 grams carbohydrate and doesn't contain a significant amount of refined sugar.
• We consider a recipe *low cholesterol* if it has less than 20 milligrams cholesterol and less than 2 grams saturated fat.
• Entrées (including soups, stews, sandwiches, casseroles, and entrée salads) are considered *low fat* if they contain 12 grams fat or less. Other categories may be considered low fat with 5, 3, and 2 grams fat or less.
• When a recipe says to cook pasta according to package directions, we analyzed adding 1 tablespoon salt to the water per 16 ounces pasta.
• When a recipe calls for hot cooked rice, we analyzed adding ¾ teaspoon salt to the water per cup of uncooked rice.
• A recipe qualifies as *vegetarian* if it has no meat or meat derivatives. And we consider a *meatless main dish* as having 10 or more grams protein.
• For a recipe to qualify as *quick*, it must be prepared in 30 minutes or less.
• *Weekend chef* recipes are more time consuming than the average recipe.

prevent cardiovascular disease and some cancers.
• One ounce = 1 slice of bread, about 1 cup of breakfast cereal, or ½ cup of cooked rice, cereal, oatmeal, or pasta.

Vegetables—eat 2 ½ cups every day.
• Eat more dark green and orange vegetables, but include a variety of colors to get the full range of vitamins and minerals.
• Eat more dried beans such as pinto beans and kidney beans, and peas.

Fruits—eat 2 cups every day.
• Eat a variety of fruits, either fresh, frozen, canned, or dried fruit.
• Limit fruit juices because it's easy to consume lots of calories, and you miss the fiber and vitamins that are often found in the pulp and skin of fresh fruit.

Milk—get 3 cups every day; 2 cups per day for kids age 2 to 8.
• Choose fat-free or low-fat milk, yogurt, and other dairy products.
• If you don't or can't consume milk, choose lactose-free products or other calcium sources such as fortified foods and beverages.

Meat and Beans—eat 5½ ounces every day.
• Choose low-fat or lean meats and poultry, and bake, broil, or grill them for heart health.
• Vary your protein sources—choose more fish, beans, nuts, and seeds.

Fats, Oils, and Sugars—be discerning.
• Know your fats. Limit solid fats such as butter, stick margarine, shortening, and lard, and choose meats and dairy products wisely to decrease your saturated fat consumption.
• For adults who get less than 30 minutes of moderate exercise per day, 5 to 7 teaspoons per day of oils from fish, nuts, cooking oil, or salad dressing should be adequate.
• Choose food and beverages low in added sugars—they add calories, and few, if any, nutrients.

"superfoods" dictionary

Recent studies have heralded a new category of food—the "superfoods." These foods have such high levels of nutrients and health-enhancing properties that they should be included in our diets as often as possible. Many of them contain antioxidants—substances that help

neutralize the damaging effect on cells and tissues by products known as free radicals. Filled with antioxidants, vitamins, minerals, fiber, and other nutritious components, the list of "superfoods" continues to lengthen as scientists make new discoveries about the foods we eat.

However, variety is also the key to nutritional nirvana. These "superfoods" may be packed with disease-fighting properties, but many other fruits, vegetables, and grains contain smaller amounts of these health-enhancing compounds. So be sure to eat an array of foods to get the full range of nutrients needed for good health.

1. Spinach is a great source of folate, an important B vitamin involved in producing and maintaining new cells. It's particularly important during pregnancy to help prevent neural tube defects.

2. Green tea comes from the same plant as black and oolong teas but contains higher amounts of antioxidants because the leaves are steamed rather than fermented. This minimal processing helps retain the antioxidants.

3. Cantaloupe, with its high water content and low calories, is filling and nutritious. It's high in beta-carotene, an antioxidant that is converted to vitamin A in the body and has an essential role in vision, growth, and development.

4. Broccoli is one of the most healthful foods you can eat. In addition to its rich supply of vitamin C, folate, and potassium, it also contains phytochemicals that studies have found to have cancer-fighting effects.

5. Olive oil has the same amount of calories as other oils, but it's a better choice because 86% of the fat is heart-healthy monounsaturated fat that can help decrease total cholesterol levels.

6. Quinoa, although technically not a grain, has been eaten as a substitute for cereal for centuries. It's superior to grains because it's a more complete plant source of protein. (Unlike grains, it includes the amino acid lysine.) And it also contains more iron than most grains.

7. Red wine may have heart-healthy benefits because of the antioxidants present in the skins and seeds of red grapes. Moderate alcohol consumption may help improve cardiovascular health.

8. Oats have earned their heart-healthy label. The high amount of soluble fiber in oats can help lower cholesterol levels because it binds to cholesterol in the digestive tract and prevents it from being absorbed.

9. Black beans are a rich plant source of protein and are also high in fiber, half of which is soluble. And with a slow digestion time, black beans keep you fuller longer.

10. Red kidney beans are not only an excellent plant source of protein, but they are full of complex carbohydrates and insoluble fiber that keeps the digestive tract healthy.

11. Flaxseed contains omega-3 fatty acids, a type of polyunsaturated fat that helps lower cholesterol levels and reduce blood pressure. Research has found that the type of omega-3s found in flaxseed may protect against heart and blood vessel disease.

12. Almonds are high in protein and contain good-for-you unsaturated fats. Almonds are the best nut source of vitamin E (a handful contains about half of the Recommended Dietary Allowance). Vitamin E is a powerful antioxidant that plays a role in immune function and DNA repair.

13. Cranberries contain compounds that prevent the adhesion of certain bacteria that are associated with urinary tract infections. These same bacteria-blocking compounds may also help fight gum disease and stomach ulcers.

14. Walnuts are packed full of omega-3 fatty acids that help lower triglyceride levels and increase HDL ("good" cholesterol) levels, which may help reduce the risk of heart disease, cancer, and diabetes.

15. Blackberries are loaded with antioxidants, such as anthocyanin, vitamins C and E, and ellagic acid. Cooking doesn't seem to destroy the ellagic acid, so even blackberry jam will retain some of this compound's health benefits.

16. Strawberries came in second behind blueberries when the USDA ranked fruits with the most antioxidants. They also have more vitamin C than any other berry.

17. Raspberries are high in ellagic acids and anthocyanins, two substances that have antioxidant properties.

18. Blueberries are ranked by the USDA as the fruit with the highest level of antioxidants, and scientists believe that the pigment anthocyanin, which gives blueberries their color, is responsible. This berry also boasts a high fiber content.

19. Yogurt, in addition to its high protein and calcium content, contains live cultures that contribute good bacteria to the digestive tract and help fight harmful bacteria.

20. Oranges have long been known as a rich source of vitamin C—an antioxidant that's important in wound healing and critical to brain function. It's also known to affect mood.

21. Tomatoes contain vitamins A and C as well as the antioxidant lycopene. Heat-processed tomato products like spaghetti sauce can provide over six times more lycopene than the equivalent amount of fresh tomatoes because the heat used during processing breaks down tomato cell walls, allowing better absorption of lycopene.

22. Edamame is a great source of soy protein, which can be a good substitute for animal products because, unlike some other beans, soy is a complete source of protein—it contains all the amino acids that the body needs.

23. Fresh artichokes are fat- and cholesterol-free, low in sodium and calories, and filled with nutrients, too. They're a good source of folate, magnesium, fiber, and vitamin C.

entertaining

Do some outdoor dining—pull a rustic table outside under a shade tree and add wicker furniture.

When entertaining friends in your home, there are a host of simple things you can do to dress up a table.

Place Setting 101

Arrange the charger and flatware about one inch from the edge of the table; position the flatware pieces beginning at the outside edge according to their order of use. Place the knife, with the blade turned toward the plate, on the right beside the plate, and spoons to the right of the knife. The soup spoon goes to the extreme right. Set the forks on the plate's left, beginning at the far left of the place setting and working in according to their logical order—salad fork, fish fork, and meat or dinner fork. The dessert fork or spoon can be brought in with dessert, or you can use the European placement above the plate parallel to the edge of the table.

Place the water glass above the knife. If you're serving iced tea or wine, set this glass to the right of the water glass above the spoon. If soup or salad is served as a separate course, place the individual dish on the charger. However, salad may be served with the meal; in which case, position the salad plate or bowl on the left side by the fork.

Place bread and butter plates above the forks. When using individual butter spreaders, rest each at the top of a bread plate parallel to the table's edge with the handle to the right. When serving coffee or tea with the meal, the cup and saucer go to the right of the spoons, but if meant to be served with dessert, bring cups and saucers in at that time.

For an informal dinner, salt and pepper containers for every two to three people are correct. On a formal table, place small salt and pepper containers directly above each place setting.

rules to regard

- As soon as you're seated, place your napkin in your lap.
- Wait to begin eating until the hostess takes the first bite. Also follow her lead when in doubt about which utensil to use.
- Once you pick up a piece of flatware, never place it back on the table; rest it on your plate. Leave knife at upper plate edge with blade toward plate. Leave the fork centered on the plate.
- Never butter a whole piece of bread at one time; instead, break off a bite-sized piece, butter, and eat it. Biscuits are an exception.
- Remove olive pits or any seeds from your mouth with the same utensil you used to eat the food.
- Serve dinner plates from the left, and remove plates from the right.
- Pass food around the table to the right at a seated dinner.
- When passing salt and pepper, place the shakers or mills on the table rather than handing them directly to the person requesting them. And always pass both salt and pepper, even if only one is requested.
- Place your knife and fork together at the "3:15" position on your plate to signal that you've finished your meal. And at the end of the meal as you leave the table, place your napkin on the table.

▲ Add color and warmth with linen runners or place mats.
- Use chargers as an added layer of color and interest.
- Let runners or oversized napkins drape off the table at each setting, serving as place mats.
- Use single flower stems at each setting or as napkin rings (far left).

◄ Use garden tags and fresh herbs for garden-themed fun.

▼ Use fruits and vegetables as table decorations and place card holders.

all about beer & wine

Beer Basics
Bolster your love of suds with our easy brew guide.

Stout

Medium-Bodied
Lager

Basic English
Ale

American
Lager

Hefeweizen

Beer Glossary

Beer comes in hundreds of varieties, and it's distinguished by the type of yeast used and the brewing process. Most of our basic American beers are lagers, which are light and probably the most food-friendly type beer. Lagers have more carbonation than ales, so they're considered more refreshing thirst quenchers. Ales are usually robust, complex, and slightly fruity. Here are some other generalities.

Stout: (such as Guinness) Dark, thick, outstanding stuff. Most stouts have a roasted barley addition that infuses a rich flavor such as coffee.

Basic English Ale: (such as Bass) Typically more hearty than lagers, sometimes bitter and strong. A good one melts in your mouth and leaves a pleasant aroma that hovers in the air.

Hefeweizen: (such as Paulaner) These beers have a cloudy appearance due to unfiltered yeast and the addition of malted wheat. Make sure to get every last drop; that's where the flavor is.

Medium-Bodied Lager: (such as Harp Lager) Usually lighter and cleaner tasting than ales. Lagers ferment slow and cold, producing a crystal clear, bubbly beverage that tickles your tongue.

American Lager: (such as Budweiser) Very light in color, high carbonation. This is what we Americans typically drink at football games and cookouts.

The Wonders of Wine

There are several things to ponder when pairing wines with food. First, become familiar with the attributes of wine. Once you've done some reading and experienced a wine tasting or two, then make a friend at your local wine shop. Ask questions each time you purchase wine for a meal. After that, wine selection is a matter of experimenting and personal preference.

Your sense of smell plays a major role in sampling and selecting wines. A wine's fragrance is called its *nose* or *bouquet*. The scents you detect depend on the type of grape used, where it was grown, if it was aged in oak barrels, and how long it's been in the bottle.

To swirl and taste wine, grasp the stem of the glass rather than the bowl so that you don't raise the wine's temperature. Swirl gently with the glass set on the table; then bring the glass quickly to your nose, breathe deeply, and suck in a sip.

The wine you select will reveal its best qualities when served correctly. For example, wine should be served at its optimum temperature, the cork should be extracted neatly, and the wine should be served in an appropriately shaped glass. Here are some pointers:

• **Serve white wines** between 58° and 62°. There's a tendency to serve whites ice cold. Chill no more than one hour. Champagne

Drinking from stubby glasses
and tumblers is a European tradition.
Some stemless glassware is making a hit in this country. It's casual,
dishwasher safe, and sturdier than stemware.

pairing wine and cheese

The general rule is to serve light, acidic wines with young, fresh, creamy cheese and full-bodied wines with aged, more robust cheese. Try these pairing suggestions for a few popular cheeses.

- Soft-ripened, mellow cheese such as Camembert, Brie, and triple-crème call for sparkling wine, Chardonnay, or Pinot Noir.
- Washed-rind cheeses such as Limburger and Taleggio are pungent and thus taste terrific with light, fruity wines such as Riesling, Gewürztraminer, Merlot, Grenache, and Zinfandel.
- Hard cheeses such as Asiago and Parmesan taste great with Riesling, Sangiovese, sherry, and sparkling wines.
- Pungent blue cheeses pair well with Riesling, Gewürztraminer, late-harvest Riesling, and sparkling wines such as brut.

Serve Cheese with Savvy

- A good rule of thumb is to buy 4 or 5 ounces of cheese per person (when cheese is the primary food served).
- Serve each cheese on a cutting board, plate, or piece of marble instead of placing all cheese on one platter. If you're using one serving tray, separate the cheese as much as possible so the mild cheese won't taste like pungent cheese.
- Serve cheeses at room temperature (around 70°) to taste their full flavors. Remove from the refrigerator an hour before the gathering. Cover leftovers in plastic wrap.
- Experts recommend going from the hardest cheese to the softest and saving the blues for last.
- Pair cheeses with nuts (seasoned or plain); dried fruit such as apricots, dates, and figs; and sliced fresh fruit such as Bosc pears or Gala apples.

How to Host an Easy Party

- Offer a few good cheeses along with wine, fruit, olives, and nuts to create an elegant spread with very little preparation.
- Perch white wine and beer bottles in a metal tub of ice for guests to serve themselves.
- A 750-ml bottle of wine will yield about 6 glasses; plan on 1 or 2 glasses of wine per person.
- If you're serving a meal, serve appetizer and dessert courses in different rooms or outside on a porch or deck.
- Let guests get involved in some last-minute food preparation. Friends are often flattered and very willing to lend a hand.

and sparkling wine, on the other hand, are exceptions; they're best served well chilled at around 45°.
- **Most reds are best served** between 62° and 65°, so don't be afraid to stick a bottle in the refrigerator for 20 to 30 minutes before opening.
- **Wine should be opened gently,** using an opener that will enable you to extract the cork cleanly. Be sure to wipe off the rim of the bottle before pouring wine. Twist the bottle as you pour to prevent dripping.
- **A basic glass for white wine** has a tulip shape, while a glass for red wine has a larger balloon shape. But for the vast majority of people, one thin, clear, all-purpose wine glass (whether tulip- or balloon-shaped) with a capacity of about 10 to 12 ounces will do. The one exception is the Champagne flute. The narrow shape concentrates the wine's bubbles and bouquet and helps it stay cold.
- **When serving wine,** don't fill glasses more than halfway. The remaining space allows for swirling and the development of the wine's bouquet.
- **Ideally, the rim of your wine glass** should not be any thicker than the glass itself.

- **If you're serving more than one wine** with a meal, serve dry before sweet, white before red, light before full-bodied, and young before aged.
- **Store leftover wine by** recorking it and refrigerating it up to two days.

the sparkle of champagne

It's important to remember that all Champagne is sparkling wine, but not all sparkling wine is Champagne. In order for a sparkling wine to be called Champagne, it must be made with specific grapes from the Champagne region of northern France. Delicious and affordable sparkling wines are made around the world. However, the most widely available and affordable sparkling wines are made in the U.S., Spain, Italy, and Australia.

The most notable Italian sparklers are Prosecco (pro-SEHK-koh) and Spumante (the Italian word for sparkling or foamy wine). Spain's easy-drinking Cava (KAH-vah) may just be one of the best values around.

cheese dictionary

Soft Cheeses

Boursin: A fresh cheese sold in a cylindrical shape, Boursin has a rich, sweet flavor with a hint of acidity. It's a table cheese for spreading on your favorite bread, or use it for baking. It pairs nicely with white wine.

Brie: Here's one of the great dessert cheeses. In order for it to be enjoyed at its fullest flavor, serve at room temperature. Look for it packaged in a wooden box. The famous **French Camembert** is a similar earthy, creamy cheese that has a delicate salty taste.

Crème fraîche: This rich, thick cream cheese is wonderful served over fruit and rustic fruit desserts. It's not a true cheese because it's made by adding a culture to fresh cream.

Farmer cheese: A very dry cheese, similar to a pressed cottage cheese. This mild, slightly tangy cheese is sold in a loaf, making it firm enough to slice, crumble on your favorite salad, or bake in the oven.

Feta cheese: Often referred to as a pickled cheese, feta is a classic Greek cheese that's stored and cured in its own whey brine. Traditionally, the rich, tangy cheese is produced from sheep's milk or goat's milk, while many manufacturers today use cow's milk.

Goat cheese: The tart goat cheese, or *chèvre*, as you may see it labeled, comes in a variety of shapes and textures and is sometimes covered with edible ash, herbs, pepper, or leaves.

Italian mascarpone: This mild, fresh cheese is supple and spreadable. It's used in some well-known desserts like tiramisù and is a perfect pair for fresh fruit.

Saint André: A French triple crème, Saint André is a decadent, rich, and smooth cheese that's perfect for your party cheese platter.

Semisoft Cheeses

Butterkase: As the name suggests, the German butterkase has a buttery taste and color. It comes in a loaf or wheel, recognizable by its brightly colored rind that ranges from gold to red.

Chaumes: A French cheese noted for its tangerine-orange rind and smooth, rubbery interior, Chaumes has a nutty and almost meaty flavor that's wonderful as both a table cheese or for grilling.

Fontina: One of Italy's famous cheeses, the creamy and versatile fontina is made of cow's milk. It has a mild, nutty flavor and melts easily.

Crème fraîche · Brie · Saint André · Goat cheese · Mascarpone · Farmer cheese · Le Vache de chalais · Camembert · Goat cheese · Boursin · Feta cheese

soft cheeses

Gouda: Gouda is Holland's most well-known cheese with its wax rind and signature yellow interior dotted with tiny holes. Its smooth, nutty flavor can range from very mild to being almost Cheddarlike, depending on its age.

Havarti: The Danish Havarti is pale yellow with small, irregular holes. It has a mild, tangy flavor.

Mozzarella: This cheese is sold in two styles: semisoft and fresh. The semisoft, elastic cheese sold in blocks is popular on pizza due to its excellent melting quality. Fresh mozzarella, of which Buffalo mozzarella is most prized for its moist, delicate texture, is often served simply to highlight its subtle taste, such as with sliced tomatoes and basil in a Caprese salad.

Pepper Jack: A semisoft white melting cheese that contains bits of chile peppers, Pepper Jack was born out of the craze to add flavors to cheese and the chile popularity across America in recent decades. It has a smooth, buttery texture and a fairly mild flavor. There are about a dozen other flavors of Jack cheese available.

Port Salut: First made in the 19th century by monks on France's Brittany coast, Port Salut is a cow's-milk cheese with a distinctive orange rind. Its mild flavor and slightly rubbery texture is well-suited for a fruit-and-cheese plate.

Provolone: This Italian cheese is ideal for the table as well as for cooking and grating. Aged for as little as 2 to 3 months and up to a year or more, provolone has a pale yellow color and a smoky flavor that intensifies with age.

Fresh mozzarella · Braided smoked mozzarella · String cheese

With its many forms, mozzarella is a cheese that accommodates any trend and palate. It can be found anywhere from lunch boxes to haute cuisine.

Reblochon: From the Savoie mountain region of France, Reblochon is a creamy cow's-milk cheese with a velvety rind. Reblochon's subtle nutty flavor is a favorable complement for fruit.

Hard or Firm Cheeses

Asiago: A popular Italian cheese often used like Parmesan, Asiago has a slightly nutty flavor that's well suited to be grated over pasta dishes or used in savory baked recipes.

Comté: Similar to the Swiss Gruyère, Comté is a firm cheese with an assertive yet smooth flavor. Comté lends its unique taste to many regional French recipes, including fondues and gratins.

Gruyère: The inspiration for what Americans know as Swiss cheese, Gruyère is a sweet, nutty cheese with characteristic, small holes. Gruyère is a rich cooking cheese that's often used in fondue or atop French onion soup.

Jarlsberg: The Norwegian Jarlsberg, like Gruyère, is a mild cheese with innumerable uses. Characterized by its irregular holes and yellow color, Jarlsberg is a buttery, rich cheese that works for cooking as well as snacking.

Manchego: Known for its signature crosshatch rind, this cheese has a mild, slightly briny, nutty flavor and is named for the Spanish region of La Mancha.

Parmigiano-Reggiano: Here's the cheese that inspired its industrial American rendition, Parmesan. A true Parmigiano-Reggiano is aged at least two years, providing its complex flavor and distinctive granular texture.

Romano: While Romano exists in many different types, all take their name from the city of Rome. The most popular type of Romano cheese is Pecorino Romano, which is a sharp, tangy sheep's-milk cheese. In general, however, most Romano cheeses in the United States are made of a blend of cow's milk and sheep's milk.

Smoked Cheddar: Smoked Cheddar is a variety of Cheddar cheese that has been cold smoked to give it a deeper flavor.

Vermont white Cheddar: This is a sharp Cheddar cheese from Vermont that has not been dyed by annatto to give the orange color of other Cheddars.

blue cheeses

Stilton Gorgonzola

Maytag

The Blues

Gorgonzola: This Italian cow's-milk cheese is characterized both by its bluish streaks and pungent smell. Its creamy, assertive flavor pairs well with crisp fruits such as apples and pears as well as bold red wines.

Maytag: An American offering of crumbly blue cheese, Maytag blue cheese is handmade in Iowa. The Maytag dairy is owned and operated by the family who founded Maytag appliances. Maytag has a slightly spicy flavor, a moist yet crumbly texture, and a lemony finish.

Stilton: Dubbed as England's "King of Cheeses," Stilton tastes like a blend between the bold Cheddar and blue cheeses. Creamy and rich, Stilton has a crumbly pale yellow interior with bluish-green veins.

hard cheeses

Emmenthaler

Gruyère

Smoked Cheddar

Comté

Vermont white Cheddar

Asiago

Manchego

Jarlsberg

appetizers & beverages

appetizers
snacks

Honey-Nut Snack Mix

prep: 6 min.   cook: 35 min.

4   cups crisp oat cereal squares (we tested
     with Quaker Essentials Oatmeal
     Squares)
1½   cups uncooked regular oats
1½   cups coarsely chopped pecans
1½   teaspoons ground cinnamon
¼   teaspoon salt
½   cup butter or margarine
½   cup firmly packed light brown sugar
½   cup honey
1   (6-ounce) package sweetened dried
     cranberries (about 1⅓ cups)

Combine first 5 ingredients in a large bowl;
set aside.
Combine butter, brown sugar, and honey in
a small saucepan over low heat, stirring until
butter melts and sugar dissolves.
Pour butter mixture over cereal mixture,
stirring to coat. Spread in a single layer on
a lightly greased aluminum foil-lined
15- x 10-inch jelly-roll pan.
Bake at 325° for 20 minutes, stirring once.
Stir in cranberries, and bake 10 more minutes. Spread snack mix immediately on wax
paper; cool. Store in an airtight container.
Yield: 9½ cups.

Per ½ cup: Calories 253 (45% from fat); Fat 12.6g (sat 3.8g, mono 5.4g, poly 2.6g);
Protein 3.3g; Carb 35.3g; Fiber 3g; Chol 13mg; Iron 4.4mg; Sodium 124mg; Calc 44mg

---

snack mixes generally keep up to
5 days in an airtight container. It's important
to bake a snack mix in an even layer so that
all ingredients bake evenly and get crisp. Let
mix cool completely before packaging.

Shown on previous page: Pesto Coins
(page 40), Balsamic Marinated Olives (page 42)

No-Bake Snack Mix

prep: 3 min.

*A big yield makes this mix great for
gift giving.*

2   (8.75-ounce) packages crispy cereal
     squares snack mix (we tested with Bold
     Party Blend Chex Mix)
1   (15-ounce) package raisins
1   (12-ounce) can honey-roasted peanuts
1   (7.2-ounce) package fish-shaped
     Cheddar cheese crackers

Combine all ingredients. Store in an airtight
container. Yield: 15½ cups.

Per ½ cup: Calories 209 (42% from fat); Fat 9.8g (sat 1.3g, mono 2.4g, poly 1.4g);
Protein 5g; Carb 26.1g; Fiber 4.3g; Chol 2mg; Iron 3.5mg; Sodium 269mg; Calc 14mg

Easy Microwave Snack Mix

prep: 3 min.   cook: 4 min.   other: 30 min.

2   (1-ounce) envelopes Ranch dressing mix
½   cup vegetable oil
3   cups crisp oat cereal squares (we tested
     with Quaker Essentials Oatmeal Squares)
3   cups corn-and-rice cereal (we tested
     with Wheat Chex)
3   cups crisp wheat cereal squares (we
     tested with Crispix)
1   (11.5-ounce) can lightly salted mixed
     nuts

Whisk together dressing mix and oil in a
large microwave-safe glass bowl. Add cereals
and nuts, tossing to coat.
Microwave snack mix at HIGH 2 minutes;
stir well. Microwave at HIGH 2 more
minutes, and stir. Spread mixture in a single
layer on wax paper, and let cool 30 minutes.
Store in an airtight container. Yield: 12 cups.

Per ½ cup: Calories 174 (63% from fat); Fat 12.1g (sat 1.5g, mono 6.4g, poly 3.6g);
Protein 3.7g; Carb 18.5g; Fiber 2.2g; Chol 0mg; Iron 4.7mg; Sodium 657mg; Calc 32mg

Popcorn Gorp

prep: 13 min.   other: 30 min.

*This sweet treat is best enjoyed the day it's
made. Use holiday colored candy-coated
pieces to go along with a party theme.*

8   cups popped popcorn
3   cups corn chips, coarsely crushed
2   cups crispy corn puffs cereal (we tested
     with Kix)
1   pound white chocolate, coarsely
     chopped
2   cups candy-coated chocolate pieces

Combine first 3 ingredients in a large bowl.
Microwave white chocolate in a microwave-
safe glass bowl at HIGH 1 to 3 minutes, stirring every 30 seconds, until white chocolate
melts. Drizzle over popcorn mixture, tossing
to coat. Stir in chocolate pieces. Spread on a
wax paper-lined 15- x 10-inch jelly-roll
pan; chill 30 minutes. Break into pieces.
Store in an airtight container. Yield: 16 cups.

Per ½ cup: Calories 173 (45% from fat); Fat 8.7g (sat 4.9g, mono 0.8g, poly 0.8g);
Protein 2g; Carb 20.7g; Fiber 0.7g; Chol 6mg; Iron 0.6mg; Sodium 77mg; Calc 43mg

Popcorn Gorp

Crispy Caramel Corn

prep: 10 min.   cook: 1 hr.

We've found the perfect caramel corn; it's easy, and no candy thermometer's needed.

1	cup sugar
½	cup butter or margarine
½	cup light corn syrup
½	teaspoon salt
1	teaspoon vanilla extract
½	teaspoon baking soda
2	(3-ounce) packages light butter microwave popcorn, popped (16 cups)
1	cup mixed nuts

Stir together first 5 ingredients in a small saucepan; bring to a boil over medium heat, stirring constantly. Remove hot caramel from heat, and stir in baking soda.
Place half of popcorn and nuts in each of 2 lightly greased shallow roasting pans. Pour hot caramel evenly over popcorn mixture; stir well with a lightly greased spatula.
Bake at 250° for 1 hour, stirring every 15 minutes. Spread on wax paper to cool, breaking apart large clumps as popcorn cools. Store in airtight containers. Yield: 16 cups.

Per ½ cup: Calories 102 (51% from fat); Fat 5.8g (sat 2.3g, mono 2.1g, poly 0.7g); Protein 1g; Carb 13.1g; Fiber 0.7g; Chol 8mg; Iron 0.2mg; Sodium 125mg; Calc 6mg

Spicy Pistachios

prep: 5 min.   cook: 30 min.

This snack is a homemade version of the spicy nuts available in pricey food catalogs.

4	cups shelled dry-roasted pistachios (about 8 cups unshelled)
¼	cup Worcestershire sauce
3	tablespoons butter or margarine, melted
2	teaspoons ground chipotle chile pepper (we tested with McCormick Gourmet Collection)
½	teaspoon garlic powder
½	teaspoon ground cinnamon

Combine all ingredients in a large zip-top freezer bag; seal and shake to coat. Arrange pistachios in a single layer on a lightly greased 15- x 10-inch jelly-roll pan.
Bake at 300° for 30 minutes, stirring once. Cool completely on pan. Store in an airtight container up to 3 days. Yield: 4 cups.

Per ¼ cup: Calories 205 (74% from fat); Fat 16.9g (sat 3.1g, mono 8.3g, poly 4.6g); Protein 6.9g; Carb 9.7g; Fiber 3.4g; Chol 6mg; Iron 1.6mg; Sodium 187mg; Calc 42mg

Sugar-and-Spice Peanuts

prep: 3 min.   cook: 40 min.

¾	cup sugar
½	cup water
2	cups shelled raw peanuts
1	teaspoon pumpkin pie spice

Cook sugar and ½ cup water in a heavy 3-quart saucepan over medium-high heat, stirring constantly until sugar dissolves. Stir in peanuts, and cook, stirring often, 7 minutes or until sugar thickens and caramelizes. Remove from heat, and stir in pumpkin pie spice until peanuts are coated. Quickly spread in a single layer on a lightly greased 15- x 10-inch jelly-roll pan.
Bake at 300° for 30 minutes, stirring and breaking apart every 10 minutes. Cool on pan. Store in an airtight container up to 5 days. Yield: 4 cups.

Per ¼ cup: Calories 140 (58% from fat); Fat 9g (sat 1.3g, mono 4.5g, poly 2.8g); Protein 4.7g; Carb 12.4g; Fiber 1.6g; Chol 0mg; Iron 0.9mg; Sodium 4mg; Calc 18mg

Sugared Nuts

prep: 5 min.   cook: 22 min.

These nuts are good sprinkled over a salad, garnishing a dessert, or as a stand-alone snack.

1	large egg white
4	cups pecan halves, walnut halves, or whole almonds
1	cup sugar

Whisk egg white in a large bowl until foamy; stir in pecans, coating well. Stir in sugar, coating well. Spread pecan mixture evenly on a lightly greased 15- x 10-inch aluminum foil-lined jelly-roll pan.
Bake at 350° for 10 minutes. Stir gently with a wooden spoon; bake 10 to 12 more minutes or until sugar is light golden brown. Remove from oven, and cool completely on pan. Store in an airtight container up to 5 days. Yield: 5 cups.

Per ¼ cup: Calories 189 (74% from fat); Fat 15.6g (sat 1.3g, mono 8.8g, poly 4.7g); Protein 2.2g; Carb 13g; Fiber 2.1g; Chol 0mg; Iron 0.6mg; Sodium 3mg; Calc 15mg

Smoky Pecans

prep: 30 min.   cook: 1 hr., 25 min.
other: 30 min.

You don't need a smoker for this recipe. You can get great smoky flavor with indirect heat on your gas grill.

	Hickory wood chips
½	cup butter or margarine, melted
1¾	teaspoons salt
2	pounds pecan halves

Soak wood chips in water 30 minutes; drain well. Shape a 10- x 6- x 2-inch tray from 2 sheets of heavy-duty aluminum foil. Fill foil tray with chips.
Preheat gas grill, using both burners. Set foil tray with wood chips directly on hot lava rocks on left side of grill. Cover grill; continue to heat until wood chips produce a generous amount of smoke (about 15 minutes).
Meanwhile, stir together butter and salt. Place nuts in a large bowl; gradually add butter mixture, stirring until nuts are coated. Spread nuts on a 15¼- x 10½- x 1-inch disposable baking sheet. Turn off right burner of grill. Place nuts on grill rack over right burner. Grill, covered with grill lid, over indirect heat 1 hour and 10 minutes or until nuts are bronze and toasted, stirring after 30 minutes. Store in an airtight container up to 3 weeks. Yield: 9 cups.

Per ¼ cup: Calories 196 (95% from fat); Fat 20.7g (sat 3.2g, mono 10.9g, poly 5.5g); Protein 2.3g; Carb 3.5g; Fiber 2.4g; Chol 7mg; Iron 0.6mg; Sodium 131mg; Calc 19mg

Caribbean Cashews

prep: 5 min.   cook: 23 min.

Orange rind adds a fresh citrus note to these simple spiced nuts.

1½   teaspoons butter or margarine
1   (9¾-ounce) can lightly salted whole cashews (about 2 cups)
2   teaspoons grated orange rind
2   teaspoons Caribbean Jerk Seasoning (we tested with McCormick)

Preheat oven to 350°. Heat butter in an 8-inch cakepan in oven 2 to 3 minutes or until melted; stir in cashews and remaining ingredients, tossing to coat.
Bake at 350° for 20 minutes, stirring occasionally. Arrange cashews in a single layer on wax paper, and let cool. Store in an airtight container up to 5 days. Yield: 2 cups.

Per ¼ cup: Calories 208 (74% from fat); Fat 17.2g (sat 3.4g, mono 9.1g, poly 3g); Protein 5.3g; Carb 10.6g; Fiber 1.2g; Chol 2mg; Iron 2.1mg; Sodium 182mg; Calc 16mg

Roasted Pumpkin Seeds

prep: 4 min.   cook: 7 min.

With a touch of rosemary, these pan-toasted seeds are the perfect snack or salad topper.

2   cups raw green pumpkin seeds*
1   tablespoon olive oil
2   tablespoons chopped fresh rosemary
2   teaspoons kosher salt

Toast pumpkin seeds in a large nonstick skillet over medium heat 5 minutes or until seeds puff and pop, shaking skillet occasionally. Add oil, rosemary, and salt; cook 2 more minutes. Let cool. Store in an airtight container up to 2 weeks. Yield: 2 cups.

Per ¼ cup: Calories 87 (50% from fat); Fat 4.8g (sat 0.8g, mono 2.2g, poly 1.6g); Protein 3g; Carb 8.7g; Fiber 0.7g; Chol 0mg; Iron 0.6mg; Sodium 483mg; Calc 10mg

*Find raw pumpkin seeds (pepitas) at specialty grocery stores or in the organic section of your local supermarket.

Pesto Coins

Pesto Coins

prep: 25 min.   cook: 18 min. per batch
other: 8 hrs.

These savory shortbread bites have all the ingredients you'd find in a traditional pesto. We recommend stirring in the flour by hand instead of using a mixer.

1   cup butter, softened
1   (8-ounce) block Parmesan cheese, shredded
3   garlic cloves, pressed
½   cup pine nuts, finely chopped and toasted
1   tablespoon chopped fresh basil
¼   teaspoon ground red pepper
2   cups all-purpose flour
¼   cup pine nuts

Beat butter and Parmesan cheese at medium speed with an electric mixer until blended. Add garlic and next 3 ingredients, beating just until blended. Gradually stir in flour with a spoon (mixture will be crumbly); stir until mixture is blended and smooth (about 2 to 3 minutes). Or instead of stirring the dough with a spoon after adding flour, you can gently press mixture together with hands, and work until blended and smooth.
Shape dough into 8 (6-inch) logs. Wrap each log in plastic wrap, and chill 8 hours.
Remove plastic wrap. Cut logs into ⅓-inch-thick slices, and place on lightly greased baking sheets. Press 1 pine nut into center of each dough slice.
Bake at 350° for 15 to 18 minutes or until lightly browned. Remove to wire racks, and let cool. Yield: 12 dozen.

Per coin: Calories 29 (68% from fat); Fat 2.2g (sat 1.1g, mono 0.6g, poly 0.3g); Protein 0.9g; Carb 1.5g; Fiber 0.1g; Chol 4mg; Iron 0.1mg; Sodium 34mg; Calc 20mg

Tender, rich, crisp, and crumbly, all in one—that's what shortbread is. Recipes that are "short" have instant melt-in-your-mouth appeal, thanks to a high ratio of fat to flour in the dough.

entertaining • family favorite • freeze it make ahead

Cheese Wafers

prep: 31 min.   cook: 17 min. per batch
other: 10 hrs.

The dough for these crisp wafers can also be fashioned into cheese straws.

1½ cups butter or margarine, softened
1   (1-pound) block sharp or extra-sharp Cheddar cheese, shredded
4   cups all-purpose flour
1½ teaspoons salt
1   teaspoon ground red pepper
½   teaspoon dry mustard
½   teaspoon paprika

Beat butter and cheese at medium speed with an electric mixer until blended; gradually add flour and remaining ingredients, beating until blended. Cover dough, and chill 2 hours.
Shape dough into 4 (8-inch) logs; wrap in plastic wrap, and chill 8 hours. Cut into ¼-inch slices, and place on ungreased baking sheets.
Bake at 350° for 15 to 17 minutes or until lightly browned. Remove to wire racks to cool. Store in an airtight container. Yield: 10 dozen.

Per wafer: Calories 51 (65% from fat); Fat 3.7g (sat 2.4g, mono 0.7g, poly 0.1g); Protein 1.3g; Carb 3.2g; Fiber 0.1g; Chol 10mg; Iron 0.2mg; Sodium 69mg; Calc 28mg

Cheese Straws: Do not chill dough. Use a cookie press fitted with a star-shaped disk to shape dough into straws onto ungreased baking sheets, following manufacturer's instructions. Press dough into parallel lines 1-inch apart on ungreased baking sheets.

Score dough at 2-inch intervals with a sharp knife. (Do not separate straws.) Bake at 350° for 12 minutes or until lightly browned. Immediately after baking, gently break straws apart with the edge of a spatula. Remove straws to wire racks to cool. Yield: about 23 dozen.

entertaining • freeze it • make ahead

Pecan–Cornmeal Shortbreads

prep: 17 min.   cook: 24 min. per batch
other: 1 hr.

Cornmeal puts a nice crunch in these thick, savory cookies. Pair them with Chardonnay or sweet seedless grapes.

1   cup butter, softened
2   cups all-purpose flour
½   cup yellow cornmeal
2   tablespoons sugar
½   teaspoon salt
½   teaspoon ground red pepper
½   cup chopped pecans, toasted

Beat butter at medium speed with an electric mixer until creamy. Combine flour and next 4 ingredients; add to butter, stirring just until blended. Stir in pecans.
Divide dough in half, and shape each portion into a 9-inch log; wrap in plastic wrap, and chill 1 hour. Cut logs into ⅓-inch slices. Place on ungreased baking sheets.
Bake at 350° for 22 to 24 minutes or until bottoms are lightly browned. Remove to wire racks to cool. Yield: 4½ dozen.

Per wafer: Calories 61 (62% from fat); Fat 4.2g (sat 2.2g, mono 1.3g, poly 0.4g); Protein 0.7g; Carb 5.2g; Fiber 0.3g; Chol 9mg; Iron 0.3mg; Sodium 46mg; Calc 3mg

tips for cheese straw prep and storage

• We recommend shredding your own cheese for the Cheese Wafers and Cheese Straws at left, as well as Pesto Coins on the previous page. It's stickier and blends much better than preshredded cheese.
• When cutting a chilled dough log, rotate the log about a quarter turn after every few slices to preserve the rounded shape.
• These recipes call for baking until lightly browned (golden). Baking to a darker golden brown produces a nuttier flavor in shortbread, particularly with those recipes that include Cheddar or Parmesan cheese.
• All three of these savory doughs (unbaked and wrapped in plastic wrap) can be frozen in an airtight container or in zip-top freezer bags up to three months.
• Once baked, these shortbreads and cheese straws can be frozen in an airtight container or in zip-top freezer bags up to one month.

cheese straws have some popular cousins in this savory shortbread recipe (above) and Pesto Coins on the previous page. These doughs can all be frozen and then sliced and baked from the frozen state. You may have to add a minute or so to the baking time.

Balsamic Marinated Olives

prep: 9 min.   other: 8 hrs., 30 min.

*Keep this easy appetizer up to one month in the fridge for a quick
addition to salads or antipasto trays.*

2   (6-ounce) cans ripe olives,
    drained
2   (6-ounce) jars pitted kalamata olives,
    drained
2   (7-ounce) jars pimiento-stuffed olives,
    drained
½   cup olive oil
½   cup balsamic vinegar
1   tablespoon dried Italian seasoning

Place olives in a large nonmetallic bowl.
Stir together oil, vinegar, and Italian season-
ing. Pour over olives, stirring gently to coat.
Cover and chill at least 8 hours.

Let stand at least 30 minutes at room temperature before serving. Yield: 9 cups.

Per ¼ cup (**4 olives**): Calories 67 (83% from fat); Fat 6.2g (sat 0.8g, mono 4.7g, poly 0.6g);
Protein 0.4g; Carb 2.9g; Fiber 0.5g; Chol 0mg; Iron 0.6mg; Sodium 465mg; Calc 19mg

Note: This make–ahead recipe can easily be
halved.

Balsamic Marinated Olives

dips & spreads

Curry Dip

prep: 4 min.

1½ cups mayonnaise
1   teaspoon garlic powder
1   teaspoon dry mustard
¾   teaspoon curry powder
½   teaspoon celery seeds
1½ teaspoons prepared horseradish
1   teaspoon white wine Worcestershire
    sauce
⅛   teaspoon hot sauce

Combine all ingredients in a bowl; stir well. Cover and chill. Serve with assorted fresh vegetables. Yield: 1½ cups.

Per tablespoon: Calories 101 (97% from fat); Fat 10.9g (sat 1.6g, mono 2.7g, poly 5.9g); Protein 0.2g; Carb 0.8g; Fiber 0.1g; Chol 5mg; Iron 0.2mg; Sodium 82mg; Calc 5mg

---

low calorie • low carb • low cholesterol
White Bean Hummus

prep: 10 min. other: 1 hr.

Enjoy this dip as a sandwich spread in a veggie wrap.

2   garlic cloves
1   teaspoon chopped fresh rosemary
2   (15.5-ounce) cans great Northern
    beans, rinsed and drained
3   tablespoons lemon juice
3   tablespoons tahini
¾   teaspoon salt
¼   teaspoon ground red pepper
¼   cup olive oil

Pulse garlic cloves and rosemary in a food processor 3 or 4 times or until minced. **Add** beans and next 4 ingredients; process until smooth, stopping to scrape down sides. **Pour** oil gradually through food chute with processor running; process until smooth. Cover and chill 1 hour. **Serve** with crackers, pita chips, or, for low-carb options, sliced cucumber, pimiento-stuffed olives, and pitted kalamata olives. Yield: 2½ cups.

Per ¼ cup: Calories 106 (66% from fat); Fat 7.8g (sat 1.1g, mono 4.9g, poly 1.6g); Protein 3.3g; Carb 8.6g; Fiber 2.8g; Chol 0mg; Iron 0.9mg; Sodium 381mg; Calc 25mg

---

family favorite • low carb
Vidalia Onion-Cheese Dip

prep: 12 min. cook: 25 min.

3   large Vidalia onions or other sweet
    onions, coarsely chopped
2   tablespoons butter or margarine, melted
2   cups (8 ounces) shredded sharp
    Cheddar cheese
1   cup mayonnaise
½   teaspoon hot sauce
1   garlic clove, minced

Sauté onion in butter in a large skillet over medium-high heat until tender. Combine onion, cheese, and remaining ingredients; stir well. Pour into a greased 1½-quart casserole. Bake, uncovered, at 375° for 20 to 25 minutes or until bubbly and golden. **Serve** with tortilla chips or crackers or, for a low-carb option, celery sticks. Yield: 4 cups.

Per ¼ cup: Calories 181 (84% from fat); Fat 16.9g (sat 5.5g, mono 4.4g, poly 6.1g); Protein 4g; Carb 3.6g; Fiber 0.4g; Chol 24mg; Iron 0.2mg; Sodium 178mg; Calc 112mg

---

entertaining • low carb • quick
Hot Crabmeat Dip

prep: 12 min. cook: 6 min.

Serve this special-occasion appetizer with fancy crackers and a crisp white wine.

3   (8-ounce) packages cream cheese
1   small onion, grated
½   cup mayonnaise
½   teaspoon garlic powder
½   teaspoon salt
¾   teaspoon pepper
¼   cup dry white wine
1   tablespoon prepared mustard
1   to 2 tablespoons prepared horseradish
1   pound fresh lump crabmeat, drained
2   tablespoons chopped fresh chives
2   tablespoons chopped fresh parsley

Combine first 9 ingredients in a saucepan; cook, stirring constantly, over medium heat until cream cheese melts. **Stir** in crabmeat, chives, and parsley; cook, stirring constantly, just until crabmeat is heated. Transfer to a chafing dish, and keep warm. Serve with crackers or, for a low-carb option, red pepper strips. Yield: 6 cups.

Per ¼ cup: Calories 151 (82% from fat); Fat 13.8g (sat 6.8g, mono 3.7g, poly 2.4g); Protein 5.6g; Carb 1.5g; Fiber 0.1g; Chol 49mg; Iron 0.6mg; Sodium 215mg; Calc 43mg

---

entertaining • low carb • test kitchen favorite
Blue Cheese-Bacon Dip

prep: 6 min. cook: 26 min.

This creamy dip goes a long way. Our staff uses it to top baked potatoes and grilled steak, too.

8   bacon slices
2   garlic cloves, minced
2   (8-ounce) packages cream cheese, softened
⅓   cup half-and-half
1   (4-ounce) package crumbled blue cheese
2   tablespoons chopped fresh chives
½   cup chopped walnuts, toasted

Cook bacon, in batches, in a skillet over medium-high heat 6 minutes or until crisp. Drain bacon, reserving 1 tablespoon drippings in skillet. Chop bacon; set aside. Add garlic to skillet, and sauté 30 seconds. **Beat** cream cheese at medium speed with an electric mixer until smooth. Add half-and-half, beating until combined. Stir in half of chopped bacon, garlic, blue cheese, and chives. Spoon mixture evenly into 4 lightly greased (1-cup) individual baking dishes or a lightly greased 1-quart dish. Bake, uncovered, at 350° for 15 minutes or until golden and bubbly. Sprinkle remaining bacon and walnuts over hot dip. Serve with crackers or, for low-carb options, grapes and pear slices. Yield: 3 cups.

Per ¼ cup: Calories 245 (84% from fat); Fat 22.9g (sat 11.8g, mono 6.9g, poly 2.8g); Protein 8.4g; Carb 2.3g; Fiber 0.4g; Chol 58mg; Iron 0.7mg; Sodium 376mg; Calc 92mg

Baked Tortilla Chips

prep: 11 min.   cook: 10 min. per batch

These easy-to-make homemade chips are great for anything from appetizers to salad or soup toppings. Get trendy with some flavored tortillas such as dried tomato or spinach.

8   (8½-inch) flour tortillas
Vegetable cooking spray
¾   teaspoon salt

Cut tortillas into eighths. Working in 3 batches, place triangles in a single layer on a large baking sheet; coat triangles with cooking spray. Sprinkle each batch with ¼ teaspoon salt. Bake at 400° for 8 to 10 minutes or until tortilla chips are crisp and lightly browned. Yield: 64 chips.

Per 4 chips: Calories 54 (25% from fat); Fat 1.5g (sat 0.5g, mono 0g, poly 0g); Protein 2.5g; Carb 8g; Fiber 1g; Chol 0mg; Iron 0mg; Sodium 126mg; Calc 0mg

Fried Tortilla Chips: Pour vegetable oil to a depth of 3 inches into a Dutch oven; heat to 360° to 365°. Fry plain tortilla triangles, a few at a time, in hot oil 1 minute or until golden, turning once. Drain on paper towels; sprinkle with salt. Yield: 64 chips.

Chili-Cheese Tortilla Chips: Add 2 teaspoons chili powder to salt. Sprinkle one-third of spice mixture onto each batch of chips on baking sheets. Sprinkle 2 cups shredded Monterey Jack cheese with peppers evenly over 3 batches of seasoned chips before baking. Bake at 400° for 8 to 10 minutes or until cheese melts. Yield: 64 chips.

Baked Artichoke Dip

prep: 9 min.   cook: 20 min.

1   (14-ounce) can artichoke hearts or hearts of palm, drained and chopped
1   cup grated Parmesan cheese
¾   cup mayonnaise
1   garlic clove, minced
¼   teaspoon Worcestershire sauce
⅛   teaspoon hot sauce

Combine all ingredients, stirring well; spoon into a lightly greased 1-quart casserole. Bake, uncovered, at 350° for 20 minutes or until bubbly. Serve with Melba toast rounds or, for a low-carb option, carrot sticks. Yield: 2 cups.

Per ¼ cup: Calories 204 (84% from fat); Fat 19.1g (sat 4.2g, mono 4.9g, poly 9g); Protein 4.9g; Carb 3.3g; Fiber 0g; Chol 17mg; Iron 0.6mg; Sodium 348mg; Calc 116mg

Benne Seed Pita Triangles

prep: 10 min.   cook: 13 min. per batch

We used a thicker style pita bread here, which makes sturdy chips that are easy to dip.

1   (18-ounce) package large pita bread rounds (we tested with Toufayan Bakeries Pita Bread)
6   tablespoons butter, melted
½   teaspoon freshly ground pepper
2   tablespoons benne or sesame seeds
¼   teaspoon salt

Split each pita round horizontally into 2 rounds; stack rounds, and cut into 6 wedges to make 72 triangles. Arrange triangles on baking sheets.
Stir together butter and pepper. Brush mixture evenly over split sides of pita triangles. Sprinkle evenly with benne seeds and salt.
Bake at 375° for 10 to 13 minutes or until golden. Yield: 12 servings.

Per serving: Calories 176 (35% from fat); Fat 6.9g (sat 3.8g, mono 1.8g, poly 0.8g); Protein 4.2g; Carb 24.1g; Fiber 1.1g; Chol 15mg; Iron 1.4mg; Sodium 317mg; Calc 53mg

Note: Triangles can be made up to a day ahead. Store in zip-top plastic bags until ready to serve.

Red Pepper Hummus

prep: 10 min.   other: 1 hr.

1   (15-ounce) can navy beans or chickpeas, rinsed and drained
2   garlic cloves, chopped
½   cup roasted red bell peppers, drained and chopped
⅓   cup tahini
¼   cup fresh lemon juice
¾   teaspoon salt
¼   teaspoon ground cumin
¼   teaspoon ground coriander
¼   teaspoon ground red pepper
2   tablespoons olive oil
1   tablespoon chopped fresh cilantro
Garnish: fresh flat-leaf parsley

Process first 9 ingredients in a food processor or blender until smooth, stopping to scrape down sides. With processor running, pour oil through food chute in a slow, steady stream; process until smooth. Stir in chopped cilantro; chill 1 hour. Garnish, if desired. Serve with tortilla chips or pita chips or, for low-carb options, fresh vegetables. Yield: 2 cups.

Per ¼ cup: Calories 133 (60% from fat); Fat 8.9g (sat 1.2g, mono 4.5g, poly 2.8g); Protein 4.4g; Carb 10.4g; Fiber 2.3g; Chol 0mg; Iron 1.2mg; Sodium 417mg; Calc 33mg

Red Pepper Hummus,
Benne Seed Pita Triangles

Salsa is simply the Mexican term for sauce. Salsa can be either fresh or cooked. All 5 of these salsa recipes pair perfectly with tortilla chips, but you can also team them with grilled meats or tacos; toss with pasta; or spoon over cream cheese or even ice cream.

Fresh Mango Salsa, Balsamic Strawberry Salsa, Corn Salsa

low calorie • low carb • low cholesterol
low fat • quick

Salsa

prep: 5 min.

4 to 5 plum tomatoes, quartered and seeded
2 garlic cloves, chopped
1 small jalapeño pepper, seeded and sliced
3 tablespoons lime juice
½ teaspoon salt
½ teaspoon pepper
¼ cup chopped fresh cilantro

Process first 6 ingredients in a blender or food processor until smooth, stopping to scrape down sides. Stir in cilantro. Cover and chill until ready to serve. Yield: 1¾ cups.

Per ¼ cup: Calories 10 (9% from fat); Fat 0.1g (sat 0g, mono 0g, poly 0.1g); Protein 0.5g; Carb 2.5g; Fiber 0.6g; Chol 0mg; Iron 0.2mg; Sodium 169mg; Calc 7mg

entertaining • make ahead • quick

Balsamic Strawberry Salsa

prep: 30 min.   other: 1 hr.

The flavors in this unique salsa will surprise you. Who would've thought strawberries and tomatoes taste so good together.

6 tablespoons olive oil
2 tablespoons white balsamic vinegar
½ teaspoon salt
1 pint fresh strawberries, coarsely chopped
8 green onions, chopped
2 pints grape tomatoes or cherry tomatoes, coarsely chopped
½ cup chopped fresh cilantro

Whisk together first 3 ingredients in a large bowl; add strawberries and remaining ingredients, tossing to coat. Cover and chill at least 1 hour. Yield: 4 cups.

Per ¼ cup: Calories 62 (75% from fat); Fat 5.2g (sat 0.7g, mono 3.8g, poly 0.6g); Protein 0.6g; Carb 4g; Fiber 0.9g; Chol 0mg; Iron 0.4mg; Sodium 78mg; Calc 10mg

low calorie • low cholesterol • make ahead

Corn Salsa

prep: 17 min.   other: 2 hrs.

Fresh corn in season makes all the difference in this salsa. Use frozen whole kernel corn as an option.

4 medium ears fresh corn, husks removed
1 (12-ounce) jar roasted red bell peppers, drained and chopped
2 ripe avocados, chopped*
2 green onions, finely chopped
1 large tomato, seeded and minced
1 jalapeño pepper, seeded and minced
3 tablespoons minced fresh cilantro
2 tablespoons fresh lime juice
1 tablespoon white wine vinegar
½ teaspoon salt
¼ teaspoon pepper
¼ teaspoon ground cumin

Cut corn from cobs. Combine corn and remaining ingredients in a large bowl. Cover and chill at least 2 hours. Yield: 4 cups.

Per ¼ cup: Calories 70 (53% from fat); Fat 4.1g (sat 0.6g, mono 2.6g, poly 0.7g); Protein 1.6g; Carb 8.4g; Fiber 2.7g; Chol 0mg; Iron 0.5mg; Sodium 148mg; Calc 8mg

*If you want to make this salsa a day ahead, add avocado just before serving to prevent browning.

Looking for healthy dippers? Whole wheat pita chips, whole grain crackers, or raw vegetables are smart alternatives to potato chips.

low calorie • low cholesterol • low fat
make ahead • quick • test kitchen favorite

Fresh Mango Salsa

prep: 18 min.   other: 3 hrs.

Serve this tropical condiment with grilled pork tenderloin, chicken, or fish.

2 ripe mangoes, cubed*
½ red bell pepper, finely chopped
½ small red onion, finely chopped
3 tablespoons chopped fresh cilantro
2 to 3 tablespoons chopped fresh mint
1 jalapeño pepper, seeded and minced
2 tablespoons fresh lime juice
½ teaspoon salt
¼ teaspoon pepper

Stir together all ingredients. Cover and chill 3 hours. Yield: 2½ cups.

Per ¼ cup: Calories 32 (6% from fat); Fat 0.2g (sat 0g, mono 0.1g, poly 0g); Protein 0.4g; Carb 8.2g; Fiber 1.1g; Chol 0mg; Iron 0.3mg; Sodium 118mg; Calc 9mg

*Substitute 1 (26-ounce) jar mango slices, drained and finely chopped, or papayas, or pineapple, if desired.

Grilled Tomatillo Salsa

prep: 15 min.   cook: 12 min.
other: 2 hrs., 10 min.

This fresh mix is great with tortilla chips as well as grilled meats and poultry.

1½ pounds fresh tomatillos, husks removed (about 12)
2   plum tomatoes
1   to 2 jalapeño peppers
½   medium-size red onion, sliced ¼ inch thick
½   cup chopped fresh cilantro
2   garlic cloves
3   tablespoons fresh lime juice
1   teaspoon salt

Rinse tomatillos under warm water to remove stickiness.
Grill tomatillos and next 3 ingredients, covered with grill lid, over high heat (400° to 500°) 12 minutes or until tomatoes look blistered and onion is tender, turning ingredients twice. Cool 10 minutes. Discard jalapeño seeds, if desired.
Pulse grilled ingredients and remaining ingredients in a blender or food processor 6 times or until salsa is coarsely chopped, stopping to scrape down sides.
Cover and chill salsa at least 2 hours. Yield: 3 cups.

Per ¼ cup: Calories 17 (21% from fat); Fat 0.4g (sat 0.1g, mono 0.1g, poly 0.2g); Protein 0.5g; Carb 3.4g; Fiber 0.9g; Chol 0mg; Iron 0.3mg; Sodium 195mg; Calc 7mg

Guacamole

prep: 12 min.

A splash of lime juice and a sprinkling of cilantro spice up this Mexican favorite. Using a potato masher makes quick work of mashing avocados.

6   ripe avocados, peeled
⅓   cup fresh lime juice
2   tomatoes, finely chopped
3   garlic cloves, minced
1   tablespoon chopped fresh cilantro
¾   teaspoon salt
¼   teaspoon pepper

Place avocados in a bowl; mash, leaving some chunky pieces. Stir in lime juice until blended.
Stir in tomato and remaining ingredients. Cover tightly with plastic wrap; chill 30 minutes, if desired. Serve with tortilla chips or, for a low-carb option, carrot sticks. Yield: 4 cups.

Per ¼ cup: Calories 126 (79% from fat); Fat 11.1g (sat 1.6g, mono 7.4g, poly 1.4g); Protein 1.7g; Carb 7.8g; Fiber 5.3g; Chol 0mg; Iron 0.5mg; Sodium 116mg; Calc 12mg

Tomato Pesto Dip

prep: 20 min.

Serve this thick dip with crusty French bread rounds, breadsticks, and fresh vegetables, or try it as a sandwich spread.

12   dried tomatoes
1   (8-ounce) package cream cheese, softened
1   (7-ounce) jar roasted red bell peppers, drained
½   cup shredded Parmesan cheese
2   garlic cloves, minced
6   fresh basil leaves
2   tablespoons olive oil
1   tablespoon lemon juice
¾   teaspoon salt
¼   teaspoon dried crushed red pepper
Garnishes: green and ripe olives, chopped

Place dried tomatoes in a bowl; cover with boiling water. Let stand 20 minutes; drain.

Process tomatoes, cream cheese, and next 8 ingredients in a food processor or blender until smooth, stopping to scrape down sides. Spoon into a bowl, and sprinkle with olives, if desired. Serve with crostini or, for a low-carb option, Belgian endive. Yield: 1⅓ cups.

Per ¼ cup: Calories 248 (81% from fat); Fat 22.4g (sat 11.6g, mono 8.8g, poly 1.2g); Protein 7.2g; Carb 6.4g; Fiber 0.8g; Chol 52mg; Iron 1.2mg; Sodium 796mg; Calc 140mg

Cranberry Ambrosia–Cream Cheese Spread

prep: 21 min.   cook: 10 min.

This spread is pretty enough for the holiday table. It's also great for breakfast on bagels or English muffins.

2   (8-ounce) packages cream cheese, softened
¼   cup powdered sugar
1   (6-ounce) package sweetened dried cranberries, divided
1   (11-ounce) can mandarin oranges, undrained
2   (8-ounce) cans crushed pineapple
1   (3.5-ounce) can shredded coconut, divided
1   cup chopped pecans, toasted
8   pecan halves, toasted

Stir together cream cheese and sugar until blended. Add dried cranberries, reserving ¼ cup cranberries.
Drain oranges and pineapple; pat dry between layers of paper towels. Set oranges aside. Stir pineapple and coconut into cream cheese mixture, reserving ¼ cup coconut. Stir in chopped pecans. Spoon mixture into a serving bowl. (You will have about 5 cups of spread.)
Sprinkle reserved dried cranberries around edges of bowl; arrange orange sections around inside edge of cranberries. Sprinkle reserved ¼ cup coconut in center, and top with pecan halves. Serve with gingersnaps. Yield: 24 appetizer servings.

Per serving: Calories 162 (67% from fat); Fat 12.1g (sat 5.8g, mono 4.2g, poly 1.5g); Protein 2.2g; Carb 13.3g; Fiber 1.3g; Chol 21mg; Iron 0.5mg; Sodium 68mg; Calc 23mg

Tapenade

prep: 7 min.

Make this classic olive spread ahead and serve it with anything from grilled fish to focaccia. For maximum flavor, let it come to room temperature and stir well before serving.

2 garlic cloves
1 shallot, halved
¼ cup loosely packed fresh parsley leaves
1 (6-ounce) jar pitted kalamata olives, drained
1 anchovy fillet, rinsed
2 teaspoons drained capers
1 tablespoon fresh lemon juice
¼ cup olive oil
Garnishes: olives, lemon slice, fresh parsley

With food processor running, drop garlic through food chute; process until minced. Add shallot and next 5 ingredients. Process 5 seconds or until minced; scrape down sides. With processor running, pour oil through food chute, stopping to scrape down sides. Spoon into a serving dish, and garnish, if desired. Yield: 1 cup.

Per ¼ cup: Calories 251 (89% from fat); Fat 24.9g (sat 3.2g, mono 18.6g, poly 2.7g); Protein 1.5g; Carb 6.4g; Fiber 0.6g; Chol 1mg; Iron 0.8mg; Sodium 775mg; Calc 26mg

low calorie • low carb • make ahead

Chile-Cheese Spread

prep: 11 min.   other: 2 hrs.

Make this spicy appetizer up to three days ahead. Serve leftovers on sandwiches.

2 (8-ounce) packages light cream cheese, softened
1 cup (4 ounces) shredded Cheddar cheese
3 green onions, finely chopped
3 chipotle peppers in adobo sauce
1 teaspoon adobo sauce
½ teaspoon Creole seasoning
½ teaspoon ground cumin
½ teaspoon chili powder
¼ teaspoon Worcestershire sauce
⅛ teaspoon hot sauce
⅓ cup pecan pieces, toasted
Garnishes: sliced green onions, pecan halves

Combine first 10 ingredients in a food processor; pulse 3 times, stopping to scrape down sides. Stir in toasted pecans; cover and chill 2 hours. Garnish, if desired. Serve with assorted crackers or, for a low-carb option, sliced vegetables. Yield: 2¾ cups.

Per tablespoon: Calories 40 (72% from fat); Fat 3.2g (sat 1.7g, mono 1.1g, poly 0.3g); Protein 1.7g; Carb 1g; Fiber 0.2g; Chol 8mg; Iron 0.1mg; Sodium 104mg; Calc 33mg

low carb • make ahead • quick

Herbed Feta Spread

prep: 11 min.

1 (8-ounce) package feta cheese, crumbled
1 (8-ounce) package cream cheese, softened
3 tablespoons chopped fresh basil
3 tablespoons chopped fresh chives
2 tablespoons olive oil
2 tablespoons balsamic vinegar
⅓ cup pine nuts, toasted
Garnish: fresh basil sprigs

Place feta and cream cheese in a small bowl; mash with a fork until combined. Stir in chopped basil and next 3 ingredients. Cover and chill up to 7 days, if desired. Stir in pine nuts just before serving. Garnish, if desired. Serve with crackers or, for a low-carb option, carrot sticks. Yield: 2¼ cups.

Per tablespoon: Calories 55 (85% from fat); Fat 5.2g (sat 2.5g, mono 1.7g, poly 0.6g); Protein 1.6g; Carb 0.9g; Fiber 0.1g; Chol 13mg; Iron 0.2mg; Sodium 89mg; Calc 37mg

entertaining • make ahead • quick

Smoked Salmon Spread With Capers

prep: 10 min.

Rinsing capers helps to remove the brine that capers are packed in so they don't overpower the salmon.

1 (8-ounce) package cream cheese, softened
¼ cup sour cream
⅓ cup minced green onions
1 tablespoon chopped fresh dill
1 tablespoon lemon juice
¼ teaspoon pepper
½ pound smoked salmon, thinly sliced
3 tablespoons capers, rinsed and drained

Pulse first 7 ingredients in a food processor until blended. Stir in capers. Serve with crackers or bagel chips. Yield: 2½ cups.

Per tablespoon: Calories 30 (75% from fat); Fat 2.5g (sat 1.5g, mono 0.8g, poly 0.1g); Protein 1.5g; Carb 0.4g; Fiber 0.1g; Chol 8mg; Iron 0.2mg; Sodium 81mg; Calc 8mg

entertaining • low carb • make ahead

Herb-and-Garlic Goat Cheese Truffles

prep: 30 min.   chill: 3 hrs.

Truffles take a new direction as a surprisingly good appetizer offering. A slightly chilled bottle of Sauvignon Blanc makes a classic pairing with goat cheese.

1 (8-ounce) package cream cheese, softened
1 (6-ounce) log mild, creamy goat cheese
1 teaspoon fresh lemon juice
1 tablespoon minced fresh chives
1 tablespoon minced fresh basil
1 to 2 teaspoons minced roasted garlic
½ teaspoon cracked black pepper
1 cup finely chopped pecans, toasted
Strawberry slices, melon wedges

Beat first 3 ingredients at medium speed with an electric mixer until smooth. Stir in chives and next 3 ingredients. Cover and chill 2 hours or until firm.
Shape cheese mixture into 24 (1½-inch) balls; roll evenly in pecans. Cover and chill at least 1 hour. Serve with fruit. Yield: 2 dozen.

Per truffle: Calories 87 (87% from fat); Fat 8.4g (sat 3.4g, mono 3.3g, poly 1.2g); Protein 2.5g; Carb 1.1g; Fiber 0.5g; Chol 14mg; Iron 0.4mg; Sodium 54mg; Calc 22mg

Prosciutto Bruschetta and Cantaloupe Chutney

prep: 8 min.   cook: 3 min.

True to its Italian roots, this recipe will remind you of the perfect marriage of melon, prosciutto, and crusty bread.

1   French baguette
2   tablespoons olive oil
12   thin prosciutto slices (about 6 ounces)
Cantaloupe Chutney

Cut baguette into 12 (½-inch-thick) diagonal slices; reserve remaining baguette for other uses.
Place baguette slices on a baking sheet, and brush tops with oil. Broil 3 inches from heat 2 to 3 minutes or until toasted, turning once.
Top each toasted baguette slice with 1 slice prosciutto and 1 tablespoon Cantaloupe Chutney. Yield: 12 appetizers.

Per appetizer: Calories 85 (44% from fat); Fat 4.2g (sat 1g, mono 2.5g, poly 0.5g); Protein 4.3g; Carb 8.2g; Fiber 0.3g; Chol 13mg; Iron 0.5mg; Sodium 326mg; Calc 10mg

Cantaloupe Chutney

prep: 18 min.   cook: 50 min.   other: 2 hrs.

Chill any remaining chutney, and serve with pita chips.

½   large cantaloupe, peeled, seeded, and
       diced (about 4 cups)
1   shallot, diced
½   cup firmly packed light brown sugar
¼   cup white wine vinegar
1   tablespoon minced fresh ginger or
       ¼ teaspoon ground ginger
2   garlic cloves, minced
¼   teaspoon salt
¼   teaspoon ground red pepper
2   tablespoons chopped fresh mint

Combine first 8 ingredients in a large non-aluminum saucepan. Bring to a boil. Reduce heat, and cook, uncovered, over medium-low heat 50 minutes or until thickened, stirring often. Cool slightly; stir in mint. Cover and chill at least 2 hours. Yield: 1½ cups.

Per tablespoon: Calories 24 (0% from fat); Fat 0g (sat 0g, mono 0g, poly 0g); Protein 0.2g; Carb 6g; Fiber 0.2g; Chol 0mg; Iron 0.2mg; Sodium 28mg; Calc 7mg

Bruschetta Pomodoro, Prosciutto Bruschetta and Cantaloupe Chutney

Bruschetta Pomodoro

prep: 15 min.   cook: 2 min.   other: 30 min.

Fresh shaved Parmesan makes an excellent garnish for this Italian snack.

1¾   cups seeded and finely chopped plum
       tomatoes (about ¾ pound)
⅓   cup chopped kalamata olives
¼   cup finely chopped red onion
¼   cup chopped fresh basil
2   tablespoons capers, drained
1   tablespoon extra-virgin olive oil
1   tablespoon balsamic vinegar
¼   teaspoon salt
¼   teaspoon pepper
1   French baguette
⅓   cup olive oil

"Pomodoro" is Italian for tomato.

Combine first 9 ingredients in a bowl; cover and let stand 30 minutes.
Cut baguette into 20 (½-inch-thick) diagonal slices. Brush both sides of slices with olive oil. Grill, uncovered, over medium-high heat (350° to 400°) 1 to 2 minutes on each side or until golden. Top evenly with tomato mixture. Yield: 20 appetizers.

Per appetizer: Calories 79 (58% from fat); Fat 5.1g (sat 0.7g, mono 3.6g, poly 0.6g); Protein 1.2g; Carb 7.3g; Fiber 0.6g; Chol 0mg; Iron 0.5mg; Sodium 149mg; Calc 12mg

Cheddar-Pecan Ring With Strawberry Preserves

prep: 18 min.   other: 8 hrs.

1   (1-pound) block sharp Cheddar cheese, shredded
1   cup mayonnaise
½   cup chopped onion
¼   teaspoon salt
¼   teaspoon pepper
¼   to ½ teaspoon ground red pepper
1   cup chopped pecans, toasted
1   (12-ounce) jar strawberry preserves

Beat first 6 ingredients at medium speed with an electric mixer until blended; stir in pecans. Spoon into a lightly greased 4- or 5-cup ring mold or other mold. Cover and chill 8 hours or up to 2 days. Unmold cheese onto a serving platter. Spoon preserves over cheese. Serve with crackers or bread rounds. Yield: 16 appetizer servings.

Per serving: Calories 326 (72% from fat); Fat 26.2g (sat 9.1g, mono 6.5g, poly 7.6g); Protein 6.9g; Carb 15.9g; Fiber 0.8g; Chol 35mg; Iron 0.3mg; Sodium 295mg; Calc 209mg

Marinated Cheese Stack

prep: 29 min.   other: 8 hrs.

Southwestern flavors permeate this impressive layered cheese. Chilling the blocks of cheese makes them easy to slice.

½   cup olive oil
½   cup white wine vinegar
¼   cup fresh lime juice
½   (12-ounce) jar roasted red bell peppers, drained and diced
3   green onions, minced
⅓   cup chopped fresh cilantro
1   teaspoon sugar
½   teaspoon salt
½   teaspoon freshly ground black pepper
1   (8-ounce) block sharp Cheddar cheese, chilled
1   (8-ounce) block Monterey Jack cheese with peppers, chilled
1   (8-ounce) package cream cheese, chilled

Whisk together first 3 ingredients in a bowl until blended; stir in diced bell pepper and

next 5 ingredients. Set marinade aside. **Cut** block of Cheddar cheese in half lengthwise. Cut halves crosswise into ¼-inch-thick slices. Repeat procedure with Monterey Jack cheese and cream cheese. **Arrange** cheese slices alternately in a shallow dish, standing slices on edge. Pour marinade over cheeses; cover and chill at least 8 hours. Using a slotted serving piece, transfer cheese to a serving plate. Spoon remaining marinade over top. Serve with crackers or alone for a low-carb option. Yield: 16 appetizer servings.

Per serving: Calories 233 (82% from fat); Fat 21.3g (sat 10.5g, mono 8.1g, poly 1.1g); Protein 7.3g; Carb 2.7g; Fiber 0.2g; Chol 46mg; Iron 0.3mg; Sodium 310mg; Calc 216mg

Blue Cheese Logs

prep: 15 min.   other: 1 hr.

2   (8-ounce) packages cream cheese, softened
1   (10-ounce) package sharp Cheddar cheese, shredded
2   (4-ounce) packages crumbled blue cheese
½   small onion, diced
1½   tablespoons Worcestershire sauce
½   teaspoon ground red pepper
2   cups finely chopped pecans, toasted and divided
2   cups finely chopped fresh parsley, divided

Process first 6 ingredients in a food processor 1 to 2 minutes until combined, stopping to scrape down sides. **Stir** together cheese mixture, 1 cup pecans, and ½ cup parsley. Cover and chill 1 hour. **Shape** cheese mixture into 4 (7-inch) logs. **Combine** remaining 1 cup pecans and 1½ cups parsley. Roll logs in nut mixture; cover and chill until ready to serve. Serve with crackers. Yield: 24 appetizer servings.

Per serving: Calories 219 (84% from fat); Fat 20.4g (sat 9g, mono 7.8g, poly 2.6g); Protein 7.5g; Carb 2.9g; Fiber 1.2g; Chol 40mg; Iron 1mg; Sodium 274mg; Calc 166mg

Note: Cheese logs can be frozen, if desired. Thaw in refrigerator overnight.

Caponata

prep: 15 min.   cook: 1 hr.   other: 8 hrs.

We recommend this sweet-and-tart eggplant appetizer as part of an antipasto platter. It can be refrigerated up to five days or frozen up to three months.

2   medium eggplants, cut into ½-inch cubes (about 2 pounds)
¼   cup olive oil
2   medium onions, chopped
2   tablespoons olive oil
1   (14½-ounce) can diced tomatoes, undrained
1   cup diced celery (about 3 ribs)
½   cup pimiento-stuffed olives, chopped
1   (2½-ounce) can sliced ripe olives, drained
¼   cup golden raisins
2   tablespoons capers, drained
⅓   cup pine nuts, toasted
½   cup red wine vinegar
1   tablespoon sugar
½   teaspoon salt
¼   teaspoon pepper

Sauté eggplant in ¼ cup hot oil in a Dutch oven over medium-high heat 10 minutes or until tender and slightly brown. Remove eggplant, and set aside. **Sauté** onions in 2 tablespoons olive oil in Dutch oven over medium heat 5 minutes or until golden. Add tomatoes and celery, scraping pan to loosen browned bits. Simmer, stirring occasionally, 15 minutes or until celery is tender. Stir in olives and next 3 ingredients. Return eggplant to Dutch oven. **Stir** vinegar and next 3 ingredients into eggplant mixture. Cover and simmer, stirring occasionally, 30 minutes. Cool. Cover and chill 8 hours. Remove from refrigerator 1 hour before serving. Serve with pita chips or toasted bread rounds or, for a low-carb option, celery sticks. Yield: 7 cups.

Per ¼ cup: Calories 65 (64% from fat); Fat 4.6g (sat 0.6g, mono 2.8g, poly 0.9g); Protein 1g; Carb 5.9g; Fiber 2g; Chol 0mg; Iron 0.5mg; Sodium 159mg; Calc 14mg

Goat Cheese Torta

prep: 12 min.   other: 8 hrs.

Make and freeze Garden Pesto from your summer herb harvest to use in this creamy goat cheese appetizer for parties or anytime.

¾   cup Garden Pesto
4   garlic cloves
1   (10.5-ounce) package goat cheese
1   (8-ounce) package cream cheese, softened
½   teaspoon salt
¼   teaspoon pepper
Garnishes: fresh basil sprigs, pecans, pine nuts
French baguette slices

Prepare Garden Pesto.
With food processor running, drop garlic through food chute; process until minced. Add goat cheese and next 3 ingredients; process until smooth, stopping to scrape down sides.
Line a 3-cup glass bowl with plastic wrap, allowing 3 inches to hang over sides.
Spread half of cheese mixture into bowl; top with pesto. Top with remaining cheese mixture. Cover and chill 8 hours.
Invert chilled torta onto a serving platter; remove plastic wrap. Garnish, if desired. Serve with baguette slices or, for a low-carb option, celery sticks. Yield: 8 appetizer servings.

Per serving: Calories 327 (84% from fat); Fat 30.6g (sat 13.7g, mono 12.7g, poly 2.6g); Protein 11.3g; Carb 2.9g; Fiber 0.7g; Chol 51mg; Iron 1.7mg; Sodium 432mg; Calc 141mg

Garden Pesto

prep: 8 min.   cook: 8 min.

¼   cup chopped pecans
¼   cup pine nuts
2   garlic cloves
2½   cups firmly packed fresh basil leaves
¾   cup loosely packed fresh parsley leaves
¾   cup freshly grated Parmesan cheese
⅔   cup olive oil

Bake pecans and pine nuts in a shallow pan at 350° for 8 minutes or until toasted. Let cool completely.
With processor running, drop garlic through food chute; process until minced.

Add basil and parsley; process until minced. Add nuts and cheese. With processor running, pour oil through food chute; process until smooth, stopping once to scrape down sides. Cover and chill up to 5 days, or freeze up to 1 month, if desired. Yield: 1½ cups.

Per tablespoon: Calories 84 (92% from fat); Fat 8.6g (sat 1.4g, mono 5.4g, poly 1.4g); Protein 1.4g; Carb 0.8g; Fiber 0.4g; Chol 2mg; Iron 0.4mg; Sodium 44mg; Calc 42mg

Pepper-Cheese Terrine

prep: 20 min.   cook: 15 min.
other: 1 hr., 40 min.

2   red bell peppers
2   yellow bell peppers
6   ounces blue cheese or goat cheese, crumbled
2   (8-ounce) packages cream cheese, softened
Tomato-Basil Vinaigrette
Garnish: fresh basil

Cut peppers in half lengthwise; discard seeds and membranes. Place peppers, skin side up, on an aluminum foil-lined baking sheet; flatten with palm of hand. Broil 3 inches from heat 15 minutes or until peppers are charred and blistered.
Place peppers in a zip-top plastic bag; seal and let stand 10 minutes to loosen skins. Peel peppers; pat dry, and chop.
Beat cheeses at medium speed with an electric mixer until smooth. Coat a 7½- x 3-inch loafpan with cooking spray, and line with plastic wrap, allowing plastic to extend over edges. Spoon one-third of cheese mixture into pan; top with half of pepper mixture. Repeat layers, ending with one-third of cheese mixture. Fold plastic wrap over cheese; chill until firm.
Unmold terrine onto a serving platter. Remove plastic wrap. Let stand at room temperature 30 minutes before serving. Spoon Tomato-Basil Vinaigrette over terrine, if desired. Serve with remaining vinaigrette. Garnish, if desired. Serve with crackers or toasted baguette slices or, for a low-carb option, red bell pepper strips. Yield: 12 appetizer servings.

Per serving and 1 tablespoon vinaigrette: Calories 215 (81% from fat); Fat 19.3g (sat 11.2g, mono 6.2g, poly 0.9g); Protein 6.5g; Carb 5.1g; Fiber 1g; Chol 52mg; Iron 0.8mg; Sodium 388mg; Calc 111mg

Tomato-Basil Vinaigrette

prep: 10 min.

¾   cup seeded, diced tomato
¼   cup chopped dried tomatoes in oil
2   tablespoons chopped fresh basil
1   garlic clove, minced
2   tablespoons dried tomato oil
1½   tablespoons balsamic vinegar
½   teaspoon salt
¼   teaspoon freshly ground pepper

Stir together all ingredients in a bowl. Cover and chill until ready to serve. Yield: 1 cup.

Per tablespoon: Calories 24 (75% from fat); Fat 2g (sat 0.3g, mono 0.4g, poly 0.9g); Protein 0.2g; Carb 1.3g; Fiber 0.6g; Chol 0mg; Iron 0.1mg; Sodium 75mg; Calc 2mg

Curried Chicken Pâté

prep: 12 min.   other: 8 hrs.

2   cups chopped cooked chicken breast
1   small Granny Smith apple, peeled and quartered
1   large shallot, quartered
½   cup butter or margarine, softened
½   teaspoon salt
½   teaspoon curry powder
1   teaspoon lemon juice
Garnishes: Italian parsley sprig, chopped pimiento
Hot mango chutney

Process first 3 ingredients in a food processor until smooth, stopping to scrape down sides. Add butter and next 3 ingredients; process until smooth.
Spoon mixture into a lightly greased 6- x 3-inch loafpan. Cover and chill 8 hours. Unmold and garnish, if desired. Serve with hot mango chutney and crackers or Melba rounds or, for a low-carb option, red bell pepper strips. Yield: 3 cups.

Per tablespoon: Calories 28 (68% from fat); Fat 2.1g (sat 1.3g, mono 0.6g, poly 0.1g); Protein 1.9g; Carb 0.4g; Fiber 0g; Chol 10mg; Iron 0.1mg; Sodium 42mg; Calc 2mg

Note: Line your loafpan with plastic wrap, and spray with cooking spray before adding pâté filling. This makes for easy removal and cleanup.

Fiery Cheese-and-Chutney Appetizer

prep: 19 min.   other: 3 hrs.

If you want to add more heat to this cheese ball, use hot mango chutney instead of the milder variety.

1   (8-ounce) package cream cheese, softened
1   (3-ounce) package cream cheese, softened
⅓   cup mango chutney
1   tablespoon habanero pepper hot sauce
½   cup finely chopped honey-roasted peanuts
2   tablespoons chopped fresh cilantro

Stir together first 4 ingredients until blended. Cover and chill 3 hours or until firm enough to be shaped. Shape mixture into a ball; roll in peanuts and cilantro. Serve with crackers. Yield: 8 servings.

Per serving: Calories 206 (73% from fat); Fat 16.6g (sat 8.9g, mono 5.2g, poly 1.3g); Protein 4.3g; Carb 11.6g; Fiber 0.5g; Chol 43mg; Iron 0.9mg; Sodium 254mg; Calc 35mg

Note: If mango chutney has large chunks, chop it before adding to cream cheese.

Shrimp Butter

prep: 11 min.

Many grocery stores now carry toasted baguette slices in the bakery or deli section. They're the ideal accompaniment with this rich seafood spread.

1   pound peeled and cooked shrimp (2 pounds raw in shell)
1   (8-ounce) container cream cheese with chives
½   cup butter, softened
3   tablespoons grated onion
1   tablespoon prepared horseradish
1   tablespoon lemon juice
1   tablespoon chili or cocktail sauce
2   garlic cloves, cut in half
½   teaspoon salt
½   teaspoon hot sauce

Process shrimp in a food processor until coarsely ground. Add cream cheese and

remaining ingredients; process until smooth. Cover and chill until ready to serve. Serve with baguette slices or, for a low-carb option, celery sticks. Yield: 4 cups.

Per tablespoon: Calories 39 (61% from fat); Fat 2.7g (sat 1.7g, mono 0.4g, poly 0.1g); Protein 3.2g; Carb 0.4g; Fiber 0g; Chol 35mg; Iron 0.5mg; Sodium 85mg; Calc 9mg

Phyllo Cups With Smoked Salmon

prep: 25 min.

1   (8-ounce) package cream cheese, softened
¼   cup sour cream
1   tablespoon chopped green onion tops or chopped fresh chives
¼   teaspoon salt
¼   teaspoon freshly ground pepper
2   (2.1-ounce) packages mini phyllo cups
⅓   cup red or black caviar
¼   cup chopped fresh or sliced chives
1   pound smoked salmon, separated and cut into small pieces

Beat cream cheese and sour cream at medium speed with an electric mixer until smooth. Stir in 1 tablespoon chopped green onions, salt, and pepper. Spoon filling into phyllo cups; top each with about ½ teaspoon caviar, and sprinkle with chives.
Arrange salmon on a serving platter. Arrange phyllo cups around salmon for serving. Yield: 15 appetizer servings.

Per serving (2 phyllo cups and 2 salmon pieces): Calories 151 (62% from fat); Fat 10.4g (sat 4.3g, mono 2.6g, poly 0.9g); Protein 9.2g; Carb 4.9g; Fiber 0.1g; Chol 59mg; Iron 1.5mg; Sodium 423mg; Calc 37mg

Cut salmon into small slivers for serving alongside crisp phyllo cups of cheese and caviar.

Phyllo Cups With Smoked Salmon

Miniature Tomato Sandwiches

prep: 10 min.

- ¼ cup mayonnaise
- 1 (3-ounce) package cream cheese, softened
- 1 tablespoon chopped fresh basil
- ¼ teaspoon salt, divided
- ¼ teaspoon pepper, divided
- 1 French baguette
- 4 plum tomatoes, sliced

Stir together mayonnaise, cream cheese, basil, ⅛ teaspoon salt, and ⅛ teaspoon pepper; cover and chill 8 hours, if desired.
Cut baguette into 16 slices.
Spread cheese mixture on baguette slices. Top with tomato, and sprinkle with remaining salt and pepper. Yield: 16 appetizers.

Per appetizer: Calories 167 (41% from fat); Fat 7.6g (sat 2.1g, mono 2.1g, poly 3g); Protein 3.1g; Carb 22.1g; Fiber 1.9g; Chol 7mg; Iron 0.7mg; Sodium 242mg; Calc 10mg

Miniature Tomato Sandwiches

chilled appetizers

Mediterranean Rollups

prep: 27 min.   other: 30 min.

Tahini is a paste made of ground sesame seeds.

- 1 (16-ounce) can chickpeas, drained
- ¼ cup tahini
- 6 garlic cloves
- ⅓ cup olive oil
- ¼ cup lemon juice
- 1 teaspoon salt
- 4 (8-inch) flour tortillas
- 1 medium-size red bell pepper, chopped
- 6 ounces feta cheese, crumbled
- 2 tablespoons thinly sliced fresh mint
- ½ teaspoon pepper
- ¼ teaspoon paprika

Process first 6 ingredients in a food processor until smooth. Spread mixture evenly over tortillas. Sprinkle with red bell pepper, feta, and remaining 3 ingredients; roll up. Chill at least 30 minutes. Cut each roll diagonally into 1-inch slices. Yield: 30 appetizers.

Per appetizer: Calories 77 (61% from fat); Fat 5.2g (sat 1.5g, mono 2.7g, poly 0.9g); Protein 2.4g; Carb 5.7g; Fiber 0.9g; Chol 5mg; Iron 0.5mg; Sodium 176mg; Calc 49mg

The key to neat rollups: Avoid overfilling tortillas, and roll tightly.

Grilled Parsleyed Shrimp and Vegetables

prep: 35 min.   cook: 18 min.   other: 8 hrs.

- 3 pounds unpeeled, jumbo fresh shrimp (16 to 20 count per pound)
- 2 large yellow bell peppers
- 2 large green bell peppers
- 2 large red bell peppers
- 2 large red onions
- 1 cup chopped fresh flat-leaf parsley
- 1 garlic clove, pressed
- 1 (16-ounce) bottle olive oil-and-vinegar dressing (we tested with Newman's Own Olive Oil & Vinegar dressing)
- ¼ cup fresh lemon juice

Garnish: fresh flat-leaf parsley sprigs

Peel shrimp, leaving tails on; devein, if desired.

Grill shrimp, covered with grill lid, over medium-high heat (350° to 400°) 2 to 3 minutes on each side or until shrimp turn pink. Place in a large bowl.
Cut each pepper into 4 large pieces; remove and discard seeds. Cut each onion horizontally into 3 thick slices.
Grill vegetables, covered, over medium-high heat 5 to 7 minutes on each side or until bell peppers look blistered and onions are crisp-tender; cut vegetables into 2-inch pieces. Add grilled vegetables, chopped parsley, and garlic to shrimp in bowl. Pour vinaigrette and lemon juice over mixture, and stir to coat and blend. Divide shrimp mixture in half; place each portion in a large zip-top freezer bag, and seal. Chill 8 hours or overnight. Garnish, if desired. Yield: 14 appetizer servings.

Per serving: Calories 282 (64% from fat); Fat 20.2g (sat 3.3g, mono 0.2g, poly 0.4g); Protein 16.5g; Carb 8g; Fiber 1.7g; Chol 144mg; Iron 2.9mg; Sodium 350mg; Calc 46mg

Sun-Dried Tomato Cheesecake

prep: 14 min.   cook: 41 min.

other: 8 hrs., 35 min.

Find edible flowers to garnish this recipe along with fresh herbs in the produce section of larger grocery stores.

¾   cup minced dried tomatoes in oil
1   (15-ounce) package refrigerated piecrusts
2   (8-ounce) packages cream cheese, softened
3   large eggs
1   (5-ounce) package shredded Swiss cheese
3   green onions, chopped (about ¼ cup)
1   teaspoon salt
½   teaspoon pepper
¼   teaspoon ground red pepper
1¾   cups sour cream
Garnishes: edible pansies, marigolds, and nasturtiums; fresh chives; fresh mint

Drain tomatoes well, pressing between paper towels. Set aside.

Unroll piecrusts; place 1 piecrust on a lightly floured surface, and brush lightly with water. Top with remaining crust. Roll into 1 (12½-inch) circle.

Press piecrust on bottom and 2½ inches up sides of a 9-inch springform pan. Press out folds in piecrust on sides of pan. Crimp with a fork. Freeze piecrust 30 minutes.

Bake at 450° for 9 minutes. Remove piecrust from oven, and reduce oven temperature to 350°.

Beat cream cheese at medium speed with an electric mixer 2 minutes. Add eggs, 1 at a time, beating well after each addition. Stir in tomatoes, Swiss cheese, and next 4 ingredients, mixing well. Pour into baked piecrust.

Bake on lower rack at 350° for 32 minutes or until golden brown and set. Cool 5 minutes. Spread sour cream evenly over top. Cool completely on a wire rack; cover and chill 8 hours.

Release and remove sides of pan. Transfer cheesecake to a serving plate. Garnish and serve with crackers, if desired. Yield: 20 appetizer servings.

Per serving: Calories 263 (72% from fat); Fat 21g (sat 11.4g, mono 7g, poly 2.2g); Protein 6.3g; Carb 13.9g; Fiber 0.3g; Chol 78mg; Iron 0.6mg; Sodium 308mg; Calc 110mg

Note: Use a springform pan without a nonstick coating; otherwise the crust may shrink during the first baking.

hot appetizers

Baked Pimiento Cheese

prep: 10 min.   cook: 30 min.

1   (8-ounce) block extra-sharp Cheddar cheese, shredded
1   (8-ounce) block sharp Cheddar cheese, shredded
1   tablespoon cornstarch
1   cup light mayonnaise
1   (4-ounce) jar diced pimiento, drained
1   teaspoon Worcestershire sauce
1   teaspoon finely grated onion
¼   teaspoon ground red pepper

Combine cheeses in a large bowl; add cornstarch, and toss to coat.

Stir together mayonnaise and next 4 ingredients in a large bowl; stir in cheeses. Spoon mixture into a lightly greased 1-quart baking dish.

Bake at 300° for 30 minutes or until golden and bubbly. Serve with crackers or, for a low-carb option, fresh vegetables. Yield: 3 cups.

Per tablespoon: Calories 58 (78% from fat); Fat 5g (sat 2.6g, mono 1.3g, poly 1g); Protein 2.1g; Carb 0.7g; Fiber 0.1g; Chol 12mg; Iron 0.1mg; Sodium 101mg; Calc 67mg

Beer-and-Cheddar Fondue

prep: 12 min.   cook: 13 min.

A hearty dip—perfect for serving to a crowd of hungry football fans. This dip travels well, too, when put in a slow cooker.

½   pound ground pork sausage
6   tablespoons butter or margarine
1   small onion, chopped
1   garlic clove, chopped
6   tablespoons all-purpose flour
2   cups milk
2   (8-ounce) blocks Cheddar cheese, shredded
1   cup beer (we tested with Dos Equis Amber beer)*
1   (4.5-ounce) can chopped green chiles
½   teaspoon salt
¼   teaspoon ground red pepper
Cubed French bread

Cook sausage in a large saucepan over medium heat, stirring until it crumbles and is no longer pink. Drain and remove sausage from saucepan.

Melt butter in saucepan over medium heat; add onion and garlic, and sauté 5 minutes or until tender.

Add flour, stirring until smooth. Cook, stirring constantly, 1 minute. Gradually add milk, stirring until thickened. Add cheese, stirring until melted. Remove from heat; stir in sausage, beer, and next 3 ingredients. Transfer to a slow cooker or fondue pot; keep warm on LOW. Serve with French bread cubes or, for a low-carb option, celery sticks. Yield: 7 cups.

Per ¼ cup: Calories 127 (68% from fat); Fat 9.6g (sat 5.6g, mono 2.8g, poly 0.4g); Protein 6.2g; Carb 3.3g; Fiber 0.2g; Chol 31mg; Iron 0.3mg; Sodium 204mg; Calc 139mg

*Nonalcoholic beer can be substituted for regular beer.

Spinach–Artichoke Dip

prep: 15 min.   cook: 20 min.

Garlic-and-herb gourmet cheese updates this popular dip.

1   (10-ounce) package frozen chopped spinach, thawed
1   (14-ounce) can quartered artichoke hearts, drained
1   (6.5-ounce) container garlic-and-herb soft spreadable cheese (we tested with Alouette Garlic and Herbes Gourmet Spreadable Cheese)
1   cup shredded Parmesan cheese
1   (8-ounce) container sour cream
½   cup mayonnaise
1   (2-ounce) jar chopped pimiento, drained
6   bacon slices, cooked and crumbled

Drain spinach well, pressing between layers of paper towels. Coarsely chop artichokes.
Stir together spinach, artichoke, and next 5 ingredients. Spoon into a lightly greased 11- x 7-inch baking dish.
Bake at 400° for 20 minutes or until bubbly. Sprinkle with bacon. Serve with crackers or corn chips or, for a low-carb option, carrot sticks. Yield: 4 cups.

Per ¼ cup: Calories 164 (83% from fat); Fat 15.2g (sat 6.4g, mono 3g, poly 0.4g); Protein 5g; Carb 3.1g; Fiber 0.4g; Chol 26mg; Iron 0.7mg; Sodium 306mg; Calc 108mg

Parmesan–Artichoke Crostini

prep: 12 min.   cook: 9 min.

1   French baguette
1   (12-ounce) jar marinated artichoke hearts, drained and chopped
1   (4.5-ounce) can chopped green chiles, drained
1   cup mayonnaise
1   cup freshly shredded Parmesan cheese
¼   cup finely chopped red bell pepper
2   garlic cloves, minced

Cut baguette to make 42 (¼-inch) slices. Reserve any remaining baguette for other uses. Arrange slices on a large baking sheet. Broil slices 1 to 2 minutes or until toasted.
Stir together artichoke hearts and remaining 5 ingredients.

Spread 1 tablespoon artichoke mixture on toasted side of each baguette slice, and place on ungreased baking sheets.
Bake at 450° for 6 to 7 minutes or until lightly browned and bubbly. Serve hot. Yield: 42 appetizers.

Per appetizer: Calories 97 (56% from fat); Fat 6g (sat 1.2g, mono 1.5g, poly 2.8g); Protein 1.9g; Carb 9.1g; Fiber 0.9g; Chol 4mg; Iron 0.3mg; Sodium 156mg; Calc 27mg

Raspberry–Brie Tartlets

prep: 1 hr., 8 min.   cook: 22 min.

You'll want to sneak a few of these gooey appetizers right off the baking sheet. We've called for a whole jar of jam, but you'll have leftovers for hot biscuits or sandwiches.

18   slices white bread (we tested with Sara Lee Classic White)
⅓   cup melted butter or margarine
1   (8-ounce) wedge Brie, cut into 54 pieces
1   (13-ounce) jar seedless raspberry jam

Roll and flatten each bread slice with a rolling pin. Cut 3 circles out of each bread slice with a 2-inch fluted or round cookie cutter.
Brush mini muffin pans with melted butter. Press bread circles on bottom and up sides of muffin cups; brush bread cups with melted butter.
Bake at 350° for 10 to 12 minutes or until lightly toasted.
Remove bread cups from muffin pans; place on ungreased baking sheets. Fill each bread cup with 1 piece of cheese; press lightly with finger to make a slight indentation. Fill each indentation with ¼ teaspoon jam.
Bake at 300° for 10 minutes or until cheese melts. Yield: 4½ dozen.

Per tartlet: Calories 41 (53% from fat); Fat 2.4g (sat 1.5g, mono 0.7g, poly 0.1g); Protein 1.2g; Carb 3.5g; Fiber 0.1g; Chol 7mg; Iron 0.2mg; Sodium 67mg; Calc 15mg

Note: To make ahead, freeze toasted bread shells up to 1 month. Thaw at room temperature about 30 minutes. Assemble tartlets, and bake as directed.

Stuffed Shiitakes Parmigiana

Stuffed Shiitakes Parmigiana

prep: 15 min.   cook: 12 min.

Fresh shiitakes have plump caps and edges that curl under.

12   large shiitake mushrooms
3   tablespoons butter, divided
1   medium onion, diced
½   (4-ounce) package sliced pepperoni, chopped
¼   cup diced green bell pepper
1   garlic clove, minced
⅓   cup chicken broth
12   round buttery crackers, crushed
¼   cup shredded Parmesan cheese
1   tablespoon chopped fresh parsley
½   teaspoon seasoned salt
¼   teaspoon dried oregano
Dash of pepper

Remove and discard stems from mushrooms. Melt 1 tablespoon butter in a large nonstick skillet over medium heat. Add mushrooms in 2 batches, and cook 1 to 2 minutes. Place mushroom caps on a 15- x 10-inch jelly-roll pan; set aside.
Melt remaining 2 tablespoons butter in skillet over medium-high heat. Add onion and next 3 ingredients; sauté until tender.
Add broth and remaining 6 ingredients, stirring until liquid is absorbed.
Spoon mixture onto mushroom caps. Broil 3 inches from heat 2 minutes; serve immediately. Yield: 1 dozen.

Per mushroom: Calories 140 (59% from fat); Fat 9.1g (sat 3.5g, mono 4.7g, poly 0.6g); Protein 3g; Carb 11.9g; Fiber 0.6g; Chol 13mg; Iron 0.9mg; Sodium 334mg; Calc 50mg

Grilled Chicken Quesadillas

prep: 14 min.　cook: 14 min.　other: 2 hrs.

Serve these meaty quesadillas as an appetizer or entrée.

⅓　cup fresh lime juice
2　tablespoons olive oil
1　teaspoon salt
1　teaspoon pepper
1½　pounds skinned and boned chicken breasts
12　(6-inch) flour tortillas
Cilantro-Pecan Pesto
1　cup (4 ounces) shredded Mexican four-cheese blend
Toppings: salsa picante, sour cream, chopped cilantro

Combine first 4 ingredients in a shallow dish or zip-top freezer bag; add chicken. Cover or seal, and chill 2 hours. Remove chicken from marinade, discarding marinade.
Grill chicken, covered with grill lid, over medium-high heat (350° to 400°) 4 minutes on each side or until done. Cut chicken into thin strips. Top 1 side of 6 tortillas evenly with Cilantro-Pecan Pesto, cheese, and chicken. Top with remaining tortillas.
Cook quesadillas in a lightly greased skillet or griddle over medium-high heat 2 to 3 minutes on each side or until browned. Cut each quesadilla into quarters. Serve with desired toppings. Yield: 12 appetizer servings.

Per serving: Calories 298 (50% from fat); Fat 16.5g (sat 4.5g, mono 8g, poly 2.3g); Protein 18.9g; Carb 18.1g; Fiber 1.3g; Chol 46mg; Iron 1.8mg; Sodium 526mg; Calc 141mg

Cilantro-Pecan Pesto

prep: 6 min.

1½　cups fresh cilantro leaves
2　garlic cloves, chopped
⅓　cup olive oil, divided
2　tablespoons chopped pecans
2　tablespoons pine nuts
¼　cup shredded Parmesan cheese
½　teaspoon salt

Process cilantro, garlic, and 2 tablespoons olive oil in a food processor until a rough paste forms. Add pecans and remaining

3 ingredients; process until blended, stopping to scrape down sides. With processor running, pour remaining oil through food chute in a slow, steady stream; process until smooth. Cover and chill up to 5 days, or freeze up to 1 month, if desired. Yield: ⅔ cup.

Per tablespoon: Calories 59 (95% from fat); Fat 6.3g (sat 0.9g, mono 4g, poly 1g); Protein 0.8g; Carb 0.5g; Fiber 0.2g; Chol 0.9mg; Iron 0.2mg; Sodium 95mg; Calc 18mg

Barbecued Pork Quesadillas

prep: 20 min.　cook: 16 min.

For this recipe, pick up some barbecued pork and sauce from your favorite barbecue joint. Be sure to ask for the sauce on the side.

½　pound shredded barbecued pork
½　cup barbecue sauce
¼　cup chopped fresh cilantro
5　green onions, thinly sliced
8　(5½- or 6-inch) flour tortillas
1　cup (4 ounces) shredded Mexican four-cheese blend
2　tablespoons butter or margarine, softened
Toppings: sour cream, sliced green onions, barbecue sauce

Stir together first 4 ingredients.
Spoon pork mixture evenly on tortillas; sprinkle with cheese. Fold tortillas in half, pressing gently to seal. Spread butter on both sides of quesadillas.
Heat a large nonstick or cast-iron skillet over medium heat, and cook quesadillas 3 minutes on each side or until browned. Cut each quesadilla into quarters, if desired. Serve with desired toppings. Yield: 8 appetizer servings.

Per serving: Calories 247 (44% from fat); Fat 12g (sat 6.1g, mono 4.3g, poly 0.9g); Protein 13.3g; Carb 20.8g; Fiber 1.4g; Chol 34mg; Iron 1.6mg; Sodium 752mg; Calc 126mg

Tex-Mex Egg Rolls

prep: 14 min.　cook: 25 min.　other: 15 min.

To help prepare for a party, you can roll the Egg Rolls in advance and fry them just when your guests arrive so the appetizers will stay hot and crunchy.

1　bunch green onions, chopped
½　red bell pepper, finely chopped
3　tablespoons olive oil
6　cups fresh baby spinach
1　(15-ounce) can black beans, rinsed and drained
1　cup frozen whole kernel corn
½　cup chopped fresh cilantro or parsley
1½　teaspoons ground cumin
1　teaspoon salt
1　cup (4 ounces) shredded Monterey Jack cheese with peppers
14　egg roll wrappers
Peanut oil
1　cup salsa
1　cup guacamole (page 46)

Sauté green onions and bell pepper in hot olive oil in a large skillet over medium-high heat 5 minutes or until tender. Stir in spinach, and cook 1 minute or until spinach wilts. Add black beans and next 4 ingredients; cook, stirring occasionally, 4 minutes or until thoroughly heated. Remove from heat; let stand 15 minutes. Stir in cheese.
Spoon ¼ cup mixture in center of each egg roll wrapper. Fold top corner over filling, tucking tip of corner under filling; fold left and right corners over filling. Lightly brush remaining corner with water, tightly roll filled end toward remaining corner, and gently press to seal.
Pour peanut oil to a depth of 1½ inches in a medium saucepan; heat to 350°. Fry egg rolls, in batches, 5 minutes or until golden; drain on paper towels. Serve with salsa and guacamole. Yield: 14 egg rolls.

Per egg roll and 1 tablespoon each salsa and guacamole: Calories 210 (48% from fat); Fat 11.2g (sat 2.9g, mono 6g, poly 1.6g); Protein 6.6g; Carb 25.3g; Fiber 4.6g; Chol 9mg; Iron 1.8mg; Sodium 598mg; Calc 87mg

Pork Picadillo Empanadas

prep: 20 min.   cook: 30 min.   other: 30 min.

These Caribbean-inspired savory pastries can be baked and frozen in advance. Reheat at 350° for 15 minutes before serving.

¾ pound ground pork
½ jalapeño pepper, seeded and minced
1 teaspoon chili powder
1 teaspoon ground cumin
¾ teaspoon ground cinnamon
¼ teaspoon salt
¼ cup golden raisins
1½ cups chipotle salsa, divided
2 tablespoons fresh lime juice
¼ cup chopped almonds, toasted
¼ cup sour cream
1 (16.3-ounce) can refrigerated buttermilk biscuits (we tested with Pillsbury Grands)
1 large egg, lightly beaten

Cook pork in a large nonstick skillet over medium-high heat 8 to 10 minutes or until meat crumbles and is no longer pink; drain. Add jalapeño pepper and next 4 ingredients; cook, stirring occasionally, 2 minutes.
Stir in raisins, ½ cup salsa, and lime juice. Remove from heat, and stir in almonds and sour cream. Cool.
Separate dough into 8 biscuits. Separate each biscuit in half to make 16 rounds. Roll each round on a lightly floured surface to a 4-inch circle.
Spoon 1 heaping tablespoon pork mixture in center of each dough circle. Fold dough over filling, pressing edges with a fork to seal. Cover empanadas with plastic wrap, and chill 30 minutes.
Place empanadas on lightly greased baking sheets. Brush evenly with beaten egg.
Bake at 350° for 18 minutes or until golden. Cool 5 minutes on baking sheets. Serve with remaining 1 cup chipotle salsa. Yield: 16 empanadas.

Per serving (1 empanada and 1 tablespoon salsa): Calories 183 (48% from fat); Fat 9.8g (sat 3.4g, mono 4.9g, poly 0.7g); Protein 7.1g; Carb 16.7g; Fiber 1.4g; Chol 30mg; Iron 1.2mg; Sodium 483mg; Calc 28mg

Blue Cheese Biscuits With Beef Tenderloin and Horseradish Cream

prep: 12 min.   cook: 40 min.   other: 5 min.

Impress guests with these melt-in-your-mouth biscuits filled with tenderloin and a kicky horseradish sauce.

2 cups self-rising flour
1 (8-ounce) container sour cream
½ cup butter, melted
1 (4-ounce) package crumbled blue cheese
2 (6-ounce) beef tenderloin steaks (about 1½ inches thick)
½ teaspoon salt
½ teaspoon freshly ground pepper
1 tablespoon vegetable or olive oil
Horseradish Cream

Stir together first 4 ingredients just until blended. Turn dough out onto a lightly floured surface. Pat dough to a ½-inch thickness; cut with a 2-inch round cutter. Place on lightly greased baking sheets.
Bake at 425° for 13 to 14 minutes or until lightly browned.
Sprinkle steaks with salt and pepper. Heat oil in a skillet over high heat; add steaks, and cook 5 to 6 minutes on each side or to desired degree of doneness. Remove from pan; let stand 5 minutes.
Cut steak into ¼-inch slices. Split biscuits in half, and top each with beef and 1 tablespoon Horseradish Cream. Replace biscuit tops. Yield: 18 appetizers.

Per appetizer: Calories 211 (63% from fat); Fat 14.7g (sat 8.4g, mono 4.3g, poly 0.9g); Protein 7.6g; Carb 12.1g; Fiber 0.4g; Chol 41mg; Iron 1mg; Sodium 410mg; Calc 116mg

Horseradish Cream

prep: 3 min.

1 (8-ounce) container sour cream
1 tablespoon prepared horseradish
1 tablespoon Dijon mustard
1 tablespoon chopped fresh chives

Stir together all ingredients. Cover and chill until ready to serve. Yield: 1 cup.

Per serving: Calories 31 (87% from fat); Fat 3g (sat 1.9g, mono 0.9g, poly 0.1g); Protein 0.5g; Carb 0.7g; Fiber 0g; Chol 6mg; Iron 0mg; Sodium 23mg; Calc 17mg

one wet, one dry——It's a good rule of thumb when battering foods. Use one hand to dip chicken in batter, leaving the other hand clean to work with dry ingredients. That way you don't slow down prep time by constantly washing your hands.

Barbecue-Battered Chicken Nuggets

prep: 10 min.   cook: 6 min. per batch
other: 4 hrs.

2 cups buttermilk
¾ cup honey smoke barbecue sauce
¼ cup barbecue seasoning spice, divided (we tested with McCormick's Grill Mates)
3 pounds skinned and boned chicken breasts, cut into 1-inch pieces
1½ cups all-purpose flour
1 tablespoon salt
1 teaspoon pepper
Peanut or vegetable oil
1½ cups honey smoke barbecue sauce

Combine buttermilk, ¾ cup barbecue sauce, and 1 tablespoon barbecue seasoning in a large zip-top freezer bag; add chicken. Seal and chill 4 hours, turning occasionally.
Remove chicken from marinade, discarding marinade.
Combine flour, salt, pepper, and remaining 3 tablespoons barbecue seasoning in a large shallow dish. Dredge chicken pieces in flour mixture.
Pour oil to a depth of 1½ inches in a deep skillet or Dutch oven; heat to 350°.
Fry chicken, in batches, 5 to 6 minutes or until golden. Drain on wire racks over paper towels. Serve chicken with 1½ cups barbecue sauce. Yield: 12 appetizer servings.

Per serving (3 nuggets and 2 tablespoons sauce): Calories 390 (46% from fat); Fat 20.1g (sat 3.8g, mono 8.7g, poly 6.1g); Protein 27.4g; Carb 22.5g; Fiber 0.2g; Chol 69mg; Iron 1.1mg; Sodium 1214mg; Calc 14mg

Fried Chicken Fingers With Come Back Sauce

prep: 12 min.   cook: 6 min. per batch
other: 4 hrs.

8	skinned and boned chicken breasts
2	cups buttermilk
1	teaspoon salt
½	teaspoon lemon pepper
½	teaspoon black pepper
2	cups all-purpose flour

Vegetable oil
Come Back Sauce

Cut each chicken breast into 4 strips.
Combine chicken strips, buttermilk, and next 3 ingredients in a shallow dish or zip-top freezer bag. Cover or seal, and chill 4 hours.
Remove chicken from marinade, discarding marinade; dredge chicken in flour.
Pour oil to a depth of 2 inches into a large Dutch oven; heat to 350°.
Fry chicken, in batches, 5 to 6 minutes or until golden. Drain on paper towels. Serve with Come Back Sauce. Yield: 16 appetizer servings.

Per serving (2 chicken fingers and 2 tablespoons sauce): Calories 335 (65% from fat); Fat 24.4g (sat 3.4g, mono 10.4g, poly 9.5g); Protein 15.8g; Carb 13.5g; Fiber 0.5g; Chol 39mg; Iron 1.2mg; Sodium 526mg; Calc 39mg

Fried Chicken Fingers With Come Back Sauce

Come Back Sauce

prep: 10 min.   other: 1 hr.

1	cup mayonnaise
⅓	cup chili sauce
¼	cup ketchup
2	tablespoons water
2	teaspoons coarsely ground pepper
4	teaspoons Worcestershire sauce
4	teaspoons prepared mustard
¼	teaspoon hot sauce
⅛	teaspoon paprika
1	medium onion, minced
2	garlic cloves, minced
½	cup olive oil

Whisk together all ingredients except oil in a bowl. Gradually whisk in oil. Cover and chill at least 1 hour. Yield: 3 cups.

Per serving: Calories 58 (92% from fat); Fat 5.9g (sat 0.8g, mono 1.7g, poly 0.2g); Protein 0.1g; Carb 1.3g; Fiber 0.1g; Chol 2mg; Iron 0.1mg; Sodium 102mg; Calc 2mg

family favorite
Sweet-and-Spicy Chipotle Chicken Wings

prep: 9 min.   cook: 8 min. per batch
other: 5 min.

Chipotle-flavored hot sauce gives these wings a smoky-sweet flavor. We loved the finished sauce that's drizzled on the wings. You can serve it with chicken fingers or French fries, too.

1	(15-ounce) can tomato sauce
2	tablespoons butter
½	cup honey
¼	cup chipotle-flavored hot sauce
1	tablespoon grated lime rind (about 3 limes)
3	tablespoons fresh lime juice
¼	teaspoon ground red pepper
4½	pounds chicken wings
1	tablespoon salt
1	teaspoon pepper
1	cup all-purpose flour

Peanut or vegetable oil

Heat tomato sauce and butter in a small saucepan over medium heat, stirring until butter melts. Stir in honey and next 4 ingredients, and bring to a boil. Reduce heat, and simmer, stirring often, 5 minutes. Set tomato sauce mixture aside.
Cut off wing tips, and discard. Cut wings in half at joint, if desired.
Sprinkle wings evenly with salt and pepper; dredge lightly in flour, shaking off excess.
Pour oil to a depth of 1½ inches into a large deep skillet or Dutch oven; heat oil to 375°.
Fry wings, in 3 batches, 8 minutes per batch or until golden and crispy. Remove wings from oil using a slotted spoon; drain on layers of paper towels. (Allow oil to return to 375° before adding next batch of wings.)
Place wings in a large bowl. Drizzle with tomato sauce mixture, tossing well to coat. Let stand 5 minutes before serving. Yield: 6 appetizer servings.

Per serving: Calories 618 (50% from fat); Fat 34.3g (sat 9.9g, mono 13.9g, poly 7.2g); Protein 37.8g; Carb 40.3g; Fiber 1.8g; Chol 120mg; Iron 3.4mg; Sodium 1747mg; Calc 39mg

Buffalo Hot Wings

prep: 13 min. cook: 1 hr.

3   pounds chicken wings
2   (0.7-ounce) envelopes Italian dressing
    mix, divided
½   cup butter, melted
½   to ¾ cup hot sauce
2   tablespoons lemon juice
1   teaspoon garlic powder
Ranch dressing

Cut off wing tips, and discard; cut wings in half at joint, if desired.
Place 1 package Italian dressing mix in a large zip-top plastic bag; add wings, and shake to coat. Place wings, skin side up, in a single layer on a lightly greased aluminum foil-lined 15-x 10-inch jelly-roll pan.
Bake, uncovered, at 425° for 30 minutes or until golden. Remove pan from oven; reduce heat to 350°.
Stir together remaining package of dressing mix, butter, and next 3 ingredients. Pour over wings; bake at 350° for 30 more minutes. Serve with Ranch dressing. Yield: 4 appetizer servings.

Per serving: Calories 519 (71% from fat); Fat 40.8g (sat 15.2g, mono 14.5g, poly 6.4g); Protein 33.9g; Carb 2.3g; Fiber 0.1g; Chol 172mg; Iron 1.8mg; Sodium 1064mg; Calc 27mg

Shrimp Fritters

prep: 15 min. cook: 5 min. per batch
other: 2 hrs.

The batter for these fritters is very wet. Once fried, the results are soft, golden puffs.

1   pound unpeeled, medium-size fresh
    shrimp
6   cups water
1   cup all-purpose flour
1   teaspoon baking powder
1   teaspoon salt
1   teaspoon pepper
2   large eggs
¼   cup light or dark beer
1   medium onion, minced
1   jalapeño pepper, seeded and minced
4   garlic cloves, minced
½   teaspoon dried thyme
Vegetable oil

Peel shrimp, and devein, if desired.
Bring 6 cups water to a boil; add shrimp, and cook 3 to 5 minutes or just until shrimp turn pink. Drain and rinse with cold water. Chill shrimp. Coarsely chop shrimp.
Beat flour and next 5 ingredients at medium speed with an electric mixer until smooth. Stir in shrimp, onion, and next 3 ingredients. Cover and chill 2 hours. (Batter will be very wet.)
Pour oil to a depth of 1½ inches into a Dutch oven; heat to 375°. Drop batter by rounded tablespoonfuls, and fry in batches 4 to 5 minutes or until golden. Drain fritters on paper towels. Serve hot. Yield: 21 fritters.

Per fritter: Calories 67 (31% from fat); Fat 2.3g (sat 0.4g, mono 0.8g, poly 0.8g); Protein 5.7g; Carb 6.8g; Fiber 0.3g; Chol 53mg; Iron 1mg; Sodium 175mg; Calc 31mg

Spicy Jumbo Shrimp Rolls With Soy Dipping Sauce

prep: 40 min. cook: 3 min. per batch

Find red curry paste in the ethnic section of the grocery store. Chill a bottle of Sauvignon Blanc for this appetizer.

28 unpeeled, jumbo fresh shrimp
¼   cup minced fresh cilantro
2   garlic cloves, minced
2   teaspoons red curry paste
28 won ton wrappers
1   egg white, lightly beaten
Vegetable oil
Soy Dipping Sauce

Peel shrimp, leaving tails on; devein, if desired, and set aside.
Combine cilantro, garlic, and curry paste.
Brush 1 side of each won ton wrapper with egg white. Spoon ¼ teaspoon cilantro mixture in the center of each wrapper. Top each with 1 shrimp. Fold wrapper around shrimp; leave tail exposed, and press wrapper to seal.
Pour oil to a depth of 2½ inches in a Dutch oven; heat to 350°. Fry won tons, in small batches, 2 to 3 minutes or until golden, turning once. Drain on wire racks over paper towels. Serve with Soy Dipping Sauce. Yield: 28 shrimp rolls.

Per serving (1 shrimp roll and 1 tablespoon dipping sauce): Calories 58 (45% from fat); Fat 2.9g (sat 0.3g, mono 1.2g, poly 1.2g); Protein 2.1g; Carb 6.3g; Fiber 0.2g; Chol 11mg; Iron 0.5mg; Sodium 967mg; Calc 7mg

Soy Dipping Sauce

prep: 5 min.

This dipping sauce doubles easily.

1   cup lite soy sauce
¼   to ½ teaspoon dried crushed red pepper
4   teaspoons honey

Combine all ingredients, stirring well. Yield: 1 cup.

Per serving: Calories 15 (0% from fat); Fat 0g (sat 0g, mono 0g, poly 0g); Protein 1g; Carb 2.5g; Fiber 0g; Chol 0mg; Iron 0mg; Sodium 605mg; Calc 0.2mg

Garlic-and-Rosemary Shrimp

prep: 28 min. cook: 25 min.

3   pounds unpeeled, large fresh shrimp
1   large garlic bulb
¼   cup butter
¼   cup extra-virgin olive oil
1   cup dry white wine
¼   cup white wine vinegar
¼   cup lemon juice
4   dried red chile peppers
3   bay leaves
¾   teaspoon salt
1   tablespoon chopped fresh rosemary
1   tablespoon fresh oregano or 1 teaspoon
    dried oregano
½   teaspoon dried crushed red pepper

Peel shrimp, leaving tails on; devein, if desired, and set aside.
Separate and peel garlic cloves. Melt butter with oil in a large skillet over medium-high heat. Add garlic cloves to butter mixture, and sauté 2 minutes.
Stir in wine and next 8 ingredients; bring to a boil. Boil, stirring occasionally, 8 to 10 minutes or until reduced by half.
Add half of shrimp. Cook 5 to 6 minutes or just until shrimp turn pink; remove with a slotted spoon. Cook remaining shrimp 5 to 6 minutes or just until shrimp turn pink; remove with slotted spoon. Bring remaining liquid to a boil over medium-high heat, and cook 2 minutes or until slightly thickened. Discard bay leaves. Serve shrimp with warm sauce. Yield: 12 appetizer servings.

Per serving: Calories 168 (50% from fat); Fat 9.3g (sat 3.3g, mono 4.5g, poly 1g); Protein 18.3g; Carb 2.2g; Fiber 0.1g; Chol 178mg; Iron 2.9mg; Sodium 368mg; Calc 44mg

Coconut Shrimp With Mustard Sauce

prep: 30 min.   cook: 3 min. per batch
other: 20 min.

24   unpeeled, jumbo fresh shrimp
     (1½ pounds)
2   cups all-purpose baking mix, divided
¾   cup beer
1   (7-ounce) package sweetened flaked
     coconut
¾   cup Japanese breadcrumbs (panko)
1   teaspoon salt
¼   teaspoon ground red pepper
Peanut or vegetable oil
Mustard Sauce

Peel shrimp, leaving tails on; devein, if desired. Set aside.

Stir together 1 cup baking mix and ¾ cup beer until smooth.
Combine coconut and breadcrumbs in a large shallow dish.
Stir together remaining 1 cup baking mix, salt, and ground red pepper. Dredge shrimp in dry mixture, and dip in beer mixture, allowing excess coating to drip. Roll shrimp in coconut mixture, pressing gently. Arrange shrimp on a baking sheet and freeze 20 minutes.
Pour oil to a depth of 3 inches into a Dutch oven or heavy saucepan, and heat to 350°. Cook shrimp, in batches, 2 to 3 minutes or until golden; remove shrimp, and drain on paper towels. Serve immediately with Mustard Sauce. Yield: 8 appetizer servings.

Per serving (3 shrimp and 2 tablespoons sauce): Calories 463 (48% from fat); Fat 24.5g (sat 9.7g, mono 7.6g, poly 5.1g); Protein 20.1g; Carb 57.4g; Fiber 1.6g; Chol 129mg; Iron 3mg; Sodium 795mg; Calc 79mg

Mustard Sauce

prep: 5 min.

½   cup orange marmalade
¼   cup Creole mustard
2   tablespoons light brown sugar
2   tablespoons beer
¼   teaspoon ground red pepper

Stir together all ingredients. Yield: 1 cup.

Per serving: Calories 35 (0% from fat); Fat 0g (sat 0g, mono 0g, poly 0g); Protein 0.2g; Carb 8.9g; Fiber 0.1g; Chol 0mg; Iron 0.1mg; Sodium 86mg; Calc 5mg

Fried Bacon–Wrapped Oysters

prep: 20 min.   cook: 5 min. per batch

1   cup all-purpose flour
1   teaspoon salt
1   teaspoon pepper
2   pints fresh oysters (about 46), rinsed
     and drained
23   bacon slices, cut in half
Peanut oil

Combine first 3 ingredients in a shallow dish. Dredge oysters in flour mixture. Wrap each oyster with a bacon piece, and secure with a wooden pick.
Pour oil to a depth of 1 inch in a deep cast-iron skillet or Dutch oven; heat to 350°.
Fry oysters, in batches, 3 to 5 minutes or until bacon is cooked. Drain on paper towels. Serve hot. Yield: 23 appetizer servings.

Per serving: Calories 70 (69% from fat); Fat 5.4g (sat 1.8g, mono 2.3g, poly 0.6g); Protein 2.3g; Carb 3g; Fiber 0.1g; Chol 11mg; Iron 1mg; Sodium 170mg; Calc 8mg

Coconut Shrimp With Mustard Sauce

This crunchy shrimp guarantees rave reviews. Freezing the battered shrimp ensures the coconut will adhere during frying.

beverages
hot beverages

On Tea and Coffee

Tea is calming. It's long been associated with meditation and reflection. But tea also is stimulating. It keeps us awake, alert, and aware.

The three most common types of tea are black, green, and oolong. The flavors are determined by where the tea leaf plants are grown (high altitudes are best) and how they're processed.

Black tea leaves are fermented and dried. They produce a full-bodied tea and contain *theophylline,* a cousin to caffeine. In contrast, green tea leaves are steamed and dried without fermenting. The tea has a flowery flavor and slightly bitter taste. Oolong tea leaves are partially fermented. The flavor isn't as bold as black tea or as grassy as green tea. Green tea is prized for its disease-fighting antioxidants. (See more information on green tea on page 63.)

Gaining in popularity is the Indian tea, chai (rhymes with "pie"). This spiced milk tea is made with black tea, whole milk, sugar, and various spices, such as ginger, cloves, pepper, and cardamom. Chai is prized for its taste and soothing effect, and as a digestive aid.

The coffee experience is all about extracting maximum flavor. When buying coffee, freshness matters most. Buying beans and grinding them yourself just before brewing is best. To maintain freshness, store coffee beans in an airtight container in a cool, dry place (not the fridge) and use within two weeks for best flavor. Ground and whole-bean coffee can be frozen, tightly sealed, up to three months.

The type of coffeemaker you choose is a personal preference. Coffee connoisseurs maintain a French press is the best way to achieve rich, robust coffee. It works by pouring boiled water into a French press carafe over coffee grounds and letting it steep 4 to 5 minutes. After steeping, gently press down the attached plunger. (This presses the grounds to the bottom and separates the liquid from the coffee grounds.)

Other coffee fanatics prefer the drip method. Coffee grounds are placed in a paper filter in a basket. Cold water is poured into a chamber, then heated, and allowed to "drip" over the grounds where coffee is extracted into the carafe.

low calorie • low carb • low cholesterol
low fat • quick

Hot Tea

prep: 5 min.

1   regular-size tea bag
¾   cup boiling water

Warm teapot, mug, or cup by rinsing with boiling water. Place tea bag in teapot. Immediately pour ¾ cup boiling water over tea bag. Steep 5 minutes. Remove tea bag; serve with sugar and lemon, if desired. Yield: ¾ cup.

Per ¾ cup: Calories 2 (5% from fat); Fat 0g (sat 0g, mono 0g, poly 0g); Protein 0g; Carb 0.5g; Fiber 0g; Chol 0mg; Iron 0mg; Sodium 5mg; Calc 0mg

family favorite • low calorie • low cholesterol
low fat • make ahead • quick

Spiced Tea Mix

prep: 3 min.

Keep this instant spiced tea on hand to serve when friends drop in to visit. It's an easy recipe to mix up in large quantities— ideal for gift giving.

1¼ cups instant orange-flavored breakfast
     drink (we tested with Tang)
1   cup instant tea
1   (0.23-ounce) package lemonade soft
     drink mix (we tested with Kool-Aid)
¾   cup sugar
1   teaspoon ground cloves
1   teaspoon ground cinnamon

Combine all ingredients; stir well. Store mix in an airtight container. To serve, spoon 1 heaping tablespoon mix into a cup. Add 1 cup boiling water; stir well. Yield: 2⅔ cups mix.

Per 1-tablespoon mix: Calories 19 (0% from fat); Fat 0g (sat 0g, mono 0g, poly 0g); Protein 0g; Carb 5.1g; Fiber 0g; Chol 0mg; Iron 0mg; Sodium 1mg; Calc 15mg

low calorie • low carb • low cholesterol
low fat • quick

Coffee

prep: 1 min.   cook: 5 min.

2   tablespoons ground coffee
¾   cup cold water

Select the particular grind of coffee that your coffeemaker requires.
Drip: Assemble drip coffeemaker according to manufacturer's directions. Place ground coffee in the coffee filter or filter basket. Add water to coffeemaker, and brew.
Percolator: Pour water into percolator; assemble stem and basket in pot. Add coffee. Replace lid. Plug in coffeepot if using an electric percolator. If using a nonelectric model, bring to a boil over high heat; reduce heat, and perk gently 5 to 7 minutes.
Vacuum: Bring water to a boil in lower bowl. Place a filter in the upper bowl, and fill with ground coffee. Reduce heat. Stir water when it rises into upper bowl. Brew 1 to 3 minutes. Remove from heat, and allow coffee to return to lower bowl.
Serve coffee immediately with cream and sugar. Yield: ¾ cup.

Per ¾ cup: Calories 2 (27% from fat); Fat 0g (sat 0g, mono 0g, poly 0g); Protein 0.2g; Carb 0g; Fiber 0g; Chol 0mg; Iron 0mg; Sodium 3.6mg; Calc 4mg

left to right: gold filter baskets, thermal carafe, whole bean grinder, French press pot

to enjoy coffee at its finest, we suggest:

- Start with cold (preferably filtered) water.
- Grind only as much coffee as you plan to brew.
- Use 2 tablespoons coffee for 6 ounces (¾ cup) of water.
- After brewing, serve coffee immediately or transfer to a thermal carafe for up to 15 minutes. Don't leave in coffeemaker where it can develop a scorched taste.
- Don't boil coffee; boiling destroys flavor and makes coffee bitter.

entertaining • quick

Maple Coffee

prep: 2 min.   cook: 5 min.

Maple syrup lends a sweet note to your morning cup of coffee.

2   cups half-and-half
1   cup maple syrup
3   cups strong brewed coffee

Cook half-and-half and maple syrup in a saucepan over medium heat 5 minutes or until thoroughly heated. (Do not boil.) Stir in coffee. Yield: 6 cups.

Per 1 cup: Calories 244 (34% from fat); Fat 9.3g (sat 5.8g, mono 2.7g, poly 0.4g); Protein 2.5g; Carb 39.2g; Fiber 0g; Chol 30mg; Iron 0.7mg; Sodium 40mg; Calc 122mg

Note: To lighten recipe, use fat-free half-and-half, and reduce maple syrup to ⅔ cup.

entertaining • low cholesterol • quick

Almond After-Dinner Coffee

prep: 5 min.   cook: 10 min.

The aroma of this coffee is very inviting.

8   cups brewed dark roast coffee
1   cup sugar
2   teaspoons whole cloves (about 38)
5   (3-inch) cinnamon sticks
⅔   cup amaretto liqueur
½   cup whipped cream
Orange rind strips (optional)

Heat first 4 ingredients in a saucepan over low heat 10 minutes. (Do not boil.) Stir in amaretto. Remove and discard cloves and cinnamon. Pour into mugs; top with whipped cream. Place a strip of orange rind on rim of each mug, if desired. Yield: 8 cups.

Per 1 cup: Calories 192 (18% from fat); Fat 3.9g (sat 1.3g, mono 0.6g, poly 0.1g); Protein 0.5g; Carb 33.5g; Fiber 0g; Chol 8mg; Iron 0mg; Sodium 6mg; Calc 6mg

family favorite • quick

Hot Cocoa

prep: 2 min.   cook: 5 min.

Any type of milk can be used for this familiar hot treat.

⅔   cup sugar
½   cup unsweetened cocoa
⅛   teaspoon salt
4½   cups milk
1   teaspoon vanilla extract
Miniature marshmallows (optional)

Combine first 3 ingredients in a heavy saucepan. Whisk in milk until smooth; heat thoroughly (do not boil). Stir in vanilla; pour into mugs. Top with marshmallows, if desired, and serve immediately. Yield: 5 cups.

Per 1 cup: Calories 257 (29% from fat); Fat 8.3g (sat 4.8g, mono 2.2g, poly 0.5g); Protein 8.8g; Carb 41.4g; Fiber 2.9g; Chol 22mg; Iron 1.3mg; Sodium 148mg; Calc 260mg

coffee primer

Café au lait: French for "coffee with milk," it consists of equal portions of brewed coffee and steamed milk.

Cappuccino: One-third espresso capped with one-third steamed milk and one-third foamed milk.

Demitasse: French for "half-cup." The small cups in which espresso is traditionally served.

Espresso: Strongly brewed coffee made specifically in a steam-pressured espresso machine. When made properly, a shot of espresso will have a golden crema (foam) on top. A close substitute can be made in your own coffeemaker, using 3 to 4 tablespoons ground espresso roast coffee beans to ¾ cup water. Serve espresso in demitasse cups with lemon peel and raw sugar cubes.

Latte: A popular morning coffee drink containing one-third espresso with two-thirds steamed milk and topped with little or no froth.

Macchiato: Espresso "marked" with a dollop of steamed milk foam and served in an espresso cup.

family favorite • low calorie • low cholesterol
low fat • make ahead • quick

Spiced Mocha Mix

prep: 4 min.

1   cup sugar
¾   cup instant nonfat dry milk powder
⅔   cup cocoa
½   cup powdered nondairy coffee creamer
⅓   cup instant coffee granules
½   teaspoon ground allspice
½   teaspoon ground cinnamon
½   teaspoon salt
Marshmallows (optional)

Combine first 8 ingredients. Store in an airtight container. To serve, spoon 3 heaping tablespoons into a mug. Add 1 cup hot milk, stirring until dissolved. Top with marshmallows, if desired. Yield: 2¾ cups mix.

Per 3-tablespoons mix: Calories 97 (13% from fat); Fat 1.4g (sat 0.5g, mono 0.5g, poly 0.3g); Protein 3.2g; Carb 20.1g; Fiber 13.5g; Chol 1mg; Iron 0.6mg; Sodium 117mg; Calc 85mg

Hot Cider Nog

Hot Cider Nog

prep: 5 min.   cook: 20 min.

2   large eggs
2   cups half-and-half
1   cup milk
1   cup apple cider
½   cup sugar
⅛   teaspoon salt
¼   teaspoon ground cinnamon
⅛   teaspoon ground nutmeg
½   cup bourbon (optional)
½   cup whipping cream, whipped
Ground nutmeg (optional)

Whisk eggs in a large heavy saucepan; whisk in half-and-half and next 4 ingredients. Sift cinnamon and nutmeg into egg mixture, and whisk to blend ingredients.
Cook over medium-low heat, stirring constantly, until mixture thickens and coats a spoon (about 20 minutes). Stir in bourbon, if desired.
Serve in individual cups with dollops of whipped cream and, if desired, sprinkle with more ground nutmeg. Serve immediately. Yield: 5 cups.

Per 1 cup: Calories 368 (57% from fat); Fat 23.4g (sat 13.9g, mono 6.9g, poly 1.1g); Protein 7.4g; Carb 33.3g; Fiber 0.1g; Chol 158mg; Iron 0.5mg; Sodium 159mg; Calc 184mg

---

low cholesterol • low fat • quick

Mulled Cranberry Drink

prep: 5 min.   cook: 10 min.

1   (48-ounce) bottle cranberry juice drink
3   cups apple juice
3   cups orange juice
½   cup maple syrup
1½   teaspoons ground cinnamon
¾   teaspoon ground cloves
¾   teaspoon ground nutmeg
1   orange, sliced
Garnish: fresh cranberries

Bring first 7 ingredients to a boil in a Dutch oven. Add orange slices just before serving. Garnish, if desired. Yield: 12 cups.

Per 1 cup: Calories 170 (2% from fat); Fat 0.4g (sat 0.1g, mono 0.1g, poly 0.1g); Protein 0.6g; Carb 42.3g; Fiber 0.7g; Chol 0mg; Iron 0.6mg; Sodium 12mg; Calc 29mg

---

entertaining • low cholesterol • low fat

Spirited Apple Cider

prep: 10 min.   cook: 45 min.

Dark rum adds depth of flavor to this cider.

12   whole cloves
6   whole allspice
3   (3-inch) cinnamon sticks, broken
1   tablespoon grated orange rind
2   quarts apple cider
1   cup orange juice
1   cup cranberry juice cocktail
1   cup pineapple juice
½   cup dark rum
½   cup apple brandy

Tie first 4 ingredients in a cheesecloth bag; combine spice bag and cider in a large saucepan or Dutch oven. Bring mixture to a boil; reduce heat to medium, and cook 35 minutes or until mixture is reduced to 4 cups.
Discard spice bag; stir in orange juice and remaining ingredients. Simmer over medium heat until heated. Yield: 8 cups.

Per 1 cup: Calories 201 (0% from fat); Fat 0.1g (sat 0g, mono 0g, poly 0g); Protein 0.4g; Carb 42g; Fiber 0.2g; Chol 0mg; Iron 0.2mg; Sodium 26mg; Calc 9mg

---

low calorie • low cholesterol • low fat • quick

Hot Spiced Wine

prep: 5 min.   cook: 20 min.

2   (750-milliliter) bottles red wine
2   cups apple juice
1   cup sugar
6   tablespoons mulling spice

Bring all ingredients to a boil in a Dutch oven; reduce heat, and simmer 15 minutes. Pour mixture through a wire-mesh strainer into a pitcher, discarding mulling spices. Serve wine hot. Yield: 9 cups.

Per 1 cup: Calories 121 (0% from fat); Fat 0g (sat 0g, mono 0g, poly 0g); Protein 0.3g; Carb 30.8g; Fiber 0g; Chol 0mg; Iron 0.7mg; Sodium 19mg; Calc 13mg

Note: For best results, use a fruity red wine, such as Beaujolais or Pinot Noir.

---

entertaining • low calorie • low cholesterol
low fat

Wassail

prep: 10 min.   cook: 30 min.

In traditional wassail, small roasted apples float in the brew. We used apple and orange slices.

4   (3-inch) cinnamon sticks, broken
1   teaspoon whole cloves
3   quarts apple cider
1   (11.5-ounce) can apricot nectar
1   (6-ounce) can frozen lemonade concentrate, thawed and undiluted
1   (6-ounce) can frozen orange juice concentrate, thawed and undiluted
⅔   cup firmly packed dark brown sugar
1   teaspoon ground allspice
½   teaspoon ground ginger
½   teaspoon ground cinnamon
1   (12-ounce) bottle dark beer or ale
Garnishes: apple and orange slices

Tie cinnamon sticks and cloves in a cheesecloth bag. Combine spice bag, cider, and next 7 ingredients in a Dutch oven.
Bring to a boil; reduce heat, and simmer, uncovered, 20 minutes. Remove from heat, and stir in beer. Discard spice bag before serving. Garnish, if desired. Yield: 1 gallon.

Per 1 cup: Calories 178 (1% from fat); Fat 0.1g (sat 0g, mono 0g, poly 0g); Protein 0.5g; Carb 44.7g; Fiber 0.4g; Chol 0mg; Iron 0.4mg; Sodium 36mg; Calc 17mg

cold beverages

low calorie • low cholesterol • low fat • quick

Southern Sweet Tea

prep: 15 min.   other: 5 min.

You know you're in the South when you see iced tea on the breakfast menu.

Pour 6 cups boiling water over 4 family-size tea bags; cover and steep 5 minutes. Stir in 1 to 1½ cups sugar. Pour into a 1-gallon pitcher, and add enough water to fill pitcher. Serve over ice in glasses. Add a lemon slice or mint sprig to each serving, if desired. Yield: 1 gallon.

Per 1 cup: Calories 51 (0% from fat); Fat 0g (sat 0g, mono 0g, poly 0g); Protein 0g; Carb 13.2g; Fiber 0g; Chol 0mg; Iron 0.1mg; Sodium 7mg; Calc 0mg

---

entertaining • low calorie • low cholesterol
low fat • make ahead • quick

Peach Iced Tea

prep: 4 min.

For a super-quick beverage, look for already-brewed unsweetened tea in the refrigerated section of your grocery store.

3   (11.5-ounce) cans peach nectar
2   quarts brewed tea
1   cup sugar
¼   cup fresh lemon juice

Stir together all ingredients; cover and chill until ready to serve. Yield: 13½ cups.

Per 1 cup: Calories 103 (0% from fat); Fat 0g (sat 0g, mono 0g, poly 0g); Protein 0.2g; Carb 26.7g; Fiber 0.5g; Chol 0mg; Iron 0.2mg; Sodium 10mg; Calc 4mg

Dress up cold drinks
with frozen lemon and
lime wedges.

---

low calorie • low cholesterol • low fat

Ginger Tea

prep: 15 min.

To make this tea, look for knobs of fresh ginger in the produce section of the store. Peel the brown skin, and grate the fibrous pulp for this surprisingly spicy tea. It's best served over ice, but great hot, too.

2   quarts water
⅓   to ½ cup grated fresh ginger
⅓   cup lemon juice
¼   cup honey
4   regular-size green tea bags
1½   cups sugar

Combine first 4 ingredients in a Dutch oven; bring to a boil. Reduce heat, and simmer 5 minutes, stirring occasionally. Remove from heat.
Add tea bags; cover and steep 5 minutes. Remove tea bags; stir in sugar, and cool.
Pour tea through a wire-mesh strainer into a pitcher; serve over ice. Yield: 8 cups.

Per 1 cup: Calories 183 (0% from fat); Fat 0.1g (sat 0g, mono 0g, poly 0g); Protein 0.2g; Carb 47.6g; Fiber 0.1g; Chol 0mg; Iron 0.1mg; Sodium 3.1mg; Calc 3mg

---

low calorie • low cholesterol • low fat
make ahead • quick

Iced Green Tea

prep: 5 min.   cook: 5 min.   other: 5 min.

If you like your tea on the sweet side, use ¾ cup honey.

6   cups water
1   (1-inch) piece fresh ginger, sliced
6   regular-size green tea bags
¾   cup loosely packed mint leaves
½   cup honey
2   tablespoons lemon juice
Garnish: fresh mint sprigs

Bring water and ginger to a boil in a large saucepan. Pour boiling mixture over tea bags and ¾ cup mint; cover and steep 5 minutes. Remove tea bags. Pour tea through a fine wire-mesh strainer into a pitcher, discarding ginger and mint. Stir in honey and lemon juice. Cover and chill. Serve over ice. Garnish, if desired. Yield: 6 cups.

Per 1 cup: Calories 87 (0% from fat); Fat 0g (sat 0g, mono 0g, poly 0g); Protein 0.1g; Carb 23.6g; Fiber 0.1g; Chol 0mg; Iron 0.1mg; Sodium 2mg; Calc 2mg

green tea power

Green tea has long been praised for its many health benefits. Green tea contains healing antioxidants, which may help prevent various types of cancer, lower cholesterol, and relieve arthritis pain. Studies have shown that green tea can also ease stomach and digestive problems, and possibly accelerate weight loss. There have even been claims that sipping green tea regularly may help fight tooth decay, because it contains fluoride. The recommended daily dosage of green tea is 3 to 4 cups a day.

Compared to other caffeinated beverages, the amount of caffeine in green tea is low. An 8-ounce cup of water with one green tea bag has only 20 milligrams of caffeine, while a 5-ounce cup of coffee has 80 milligrams. Green tea also contains the lowest amount of caffeine among popular teas like black and oolong. Black tea has the most at an average of 40 milligrams per cup, and oolong has 30 milligrams. Herbal teas, such as peppermint or chamomile, however, are naturally caffeine free.

Blackberry Iced Tea

Blackberry Iced Tea

prep: 10 min.   other: 1 hr.

For garnish, thread fresh blackberries onto 6-inch wooden skewers.

3   cups fresh or frozen blackberries, thawed
1   cup sugar
1   tablespoon chopped fresh mint
Pinch of baking soda
4   cups boiling water
3   family-size tea bags
2½ cups sparkling water or cold water
Garnishes: fresh blackberries, fresh mint
    sprigs

Combine 3 cups blackberries and sugar in a large container. Crush blackberries with a wooden spoon. Add chopped mint and baking soda. Set aside.
Pour 4 cups boiling water over tea bags; cover and let stand 3 minutes. Discard tea bags.
Pour tea over blackberry mixture; let stand at room temperature 1 hour. Pour tea through a wire-mesh strainer into a large pitcher, discarding solids. Add 2½ cups sparkling water, stirring until sugar dissolves. Cover and chill until ready to serve. Garnish, if desired. Yield: 7 cups.

Per 1 cup: Calories 118 (1% from fat); Fat 0.1g (sat 0g, mono 0g, poly 0.1g); Protein 0.1g; Carb 30.2g; Fiber 0g; Chol 0mg; Iron 0.1mg; Sodium 17mg; Calc 4mg

Sweet-Tart Lemonade

prep: 25 min.   cook: 5 min.

Enjoy this simple summer sipper anytime. (pictured on page 36)

3   cups cold water
2   cups Sugar Syrup (above right)
1¾ to 2 cups fresh lemon juice
Garnish: lemon wedges

Stir together first 3 ingredients until well blended; serve over ice. Garnish, if desired. Yield: 7 cups.

Per 1 cup: Calories 237 (0% from fat); Fat 0g (sat 0g, mono 0g, poly 0g); Protein 0.2g; Carb 62.4g; Fiber 0.2g; Chol 0mg; Iron 0mg; Sodium 3mg; Calc 8mg

Sugar Syrup

prep: 5 min.   cook: 8 min.

2   cups sugar
1   cup water
¼   teaspoon fresh lemon juice

Stir together all ingredients in a small saucepan. Bring to a boil over medium heat, stirring often. Reduce heat; simmer 1 minute or until sugar dissolves. Remove from heat; cool. Yield: 2 cups.

Per tablespoon: Calories 48 (0% from fat); Fat 0g (sat 0g, mono 0g, poly 0g); Protein 0g; Carb 12.5g; Fiber 0g; Chol 0mg; Iron 0mg; Sodium 0mg; Calc 0mg

Fresh Mint Sugar Syrup: Add 1 cup loosely packed fresh mint leaves to ingredients in saucepan. Bring to a boil and cool as directed above. Pour mixture through a wire-mesh strainer into a pitcher, discarding mint. Yield: 2 cups.

Fresh Mint-Citrus Sipper

prep: 20 min.   cook: 10 min.

This refreshing drink starts out with a mint simple syrup. You can store the syrup in an airtight container in the refrigerator up to two weeks.

1½ cups fresh lemon juice
1   cup fresh lime juice
1   cup fresh orange juice
Fresh Mint Sugar Syrup (above)
1   (25-ounce) bottle lemon-flavored
     sparkling water, chilled (about 3 cups)

Combine first 4 ingredients in a large pitcher, stirring well. Stir in sparkling water just before serving. Serve over ice. Yield: 8 cups.

Per 1 cup: Calories 227 (0% from fat); Fat 0.1g (sat 0g, mono 0g, poly 0g); Protein 0.5g; Carb 59.8g; Fiber 0.4g; Chol 0mg; Iron 0.1mg; Sodium 2mg; Calc 12mg

Fresh Mint-Citrus Sipper by the Glass: Combine 3 tablespoons Fresh Mint Sugar Syrup; 2 tablespoons each fresh lemon, lime, and orange juice; and ¾ cup lemon-flavored sparkling water, chilled. Stir mixture well.

Watermelon-Lemonade Cooler

prep: 25 min.   cook: 10 min.   other: 8 hrs.

This is the perfect pick-me-up for a thirsty crowd.

15 cups seeded and cubed watermelon
2   (12-ounce) cans frozen lemonade
    concentrate, thawed
2   fresh mint sprigs
Ice
Garnishes: watermelon wedges, fresh mint
    sprigs

Process 15 cups watermelon, in batches, in a blender or food processor until smooth. **Combine** lemonade concentrate and 2 mint sprigs, and cook in a saucepan over medium-high heat 10 minutes. Stir together watermelon puree and lemonade mixture; cover and chill 8 hours. Remove and discard mint. Stir and serve over ice. Garnish, if desired. Yield: 14 cups.

Per 1 cup: Calories 137 (2% from fat); Fat 0.3g (sat 0g, mono 0.1g, poly 0.1g); Protein 1.1g; Carb 35.2g; Fiber 0.8g; Chol 0mg; Iron 0.7mg; Sodium 4mg; Calc 15mg

Kiwi-Lemonade Spritzer

prep: 10 min.

4   kiwifruit, peeled
1   (12-ounce) can frozen lemonade
    concentrate, thawed and undiluted
3   cups lemon lime soft drink, chilled

Cut kiwifruit into chunks. Process fruit chunks and lemonade concentrate in a food processor until smooth, stopping to scrape down sides.
Pour mixture through a wire-mesh strainer into a pitcher, discarding solids. Stir in lemon lime soft drink just before serving. Yield: 5 cups.

Per 1 cup: Calories 218 (2% from fat); Fat 0.5g (sat 0g, mono 0g, poly 0.2g); Protein 0.9g; Carb 56.6g; Fiber 2g; Chol 0mg; Iron 0.7mg; Sodium 18mg; Calc 25mg

family favorite • low calorie • low cholesterol
low fat • quick

Homemade Orange Soda

prep: 5 min.

Stir this refreshing beverage occasionally to keep the ingredients blended.

1   (12-ounce) can frozen, pulp-free orange juice concentrate, thawed and undiluted
2   (2-liter) bottles lemon lime soft drink, chilled
1   to 2 oranges, cut into wedges

Stir together orange juice concentrate and lemon lime soft drink when ready to serve. Serve over ice in individual glasses with an orange wedge. Yield: 4½ quarts.

Per 1 cup: Calories 128 (0% from fat); Fat 0.1g (sat 0g, mono 0g, poly 0g); Protein 0.6g; Carb 33.6g; Fiber 0.5g; Chol 0mg; Iron 0.1mg; Sodium 22mg; Calc 13mg

for kids • low calorie • low cholesterol
low fat • make ahead

Cherry Sparkler

prep: 10 min.   other: 8 hrs.

2   (6-ounce) jars red maraschino cherries, drained
2   (6-ounce) jars green maraschino cherries, drained
½   gallon distilled water
1   (2-liter) bottle cherry-flavored, lemon lime soft drink, chilled (we tested with Cherry 7-Up)

Place 1 red or green cherry in each compartment of 4 ice-cube trays. Fill trays with distilled water; freeze 8 hours. Serve soft drink over ice cubes. Yield: 8 cups.

Per 1 cup: Calories 174 (0% from fat); Fat 0.1g (sat 0g, mono 0g, poly 0g); Protein 0.1g; Carb 44.7g; Fiber 1.3g; Chol 0mg; Iron 0.2mg; Sodium 54mg; Calc 22mg

low calorie • low cholesterol • low fat
make ahead

Southern Breeze

prep: 10 min.   other: 8 hrs.

1   cup sugar
1   (0.22-ounce) envelope unsweetened blue raspberry lemonade mix (we tested with Kool-Aid Island Twists Ice Blue Raspberry Lemonade Unsweetened Soft Drink Mix)
7   cups water
1   (6-ounce) can frozen lemonade concentrate, thawed
1   (46-ounce) can unsweetened pineapple juice, chilled
1   (2-liter) bottle ginger ale, chilled

Stir together first 4 ingredients in a 2–quart pitcher; pour evenly into several ice cube trays, and freeze at least 8 hours.
Combine pineapple juice and ginger ale; serve over raspberry ice cubes. Yield: 14 cups.

Per 1 cup: Calories 107 (0% from fat); Fat 0.1g (sat 0g, mono 0g, poly 0g); Protein 0.2g; Carb 27.7g; Fiber 0.1g; Chol 0mg; Iron 0.2mg; Sodium 14mg; Calc 12mg

low calorie

Chocolate Iced Coffee

prep: 10 min.   other: 2 hrs., 10 min.

To keep the drink from being diluted, freeze half-and-half and leftover coffee in ice-cube trays to use in place of ice.

3½ cups water
1   cup ground coffee
2   tablespoons sugar
¾   teaspoon ground cinnamon
2   cups half-and-half
⅓   cup chocolate syrup

Bring 3½ cups water and coffee to a boil in a saucepan; remove from heat, and let stand 10 minutes.
Pour mixture through a fine wire–mesh strainer into a bowl, discarding coffee grounds.
Stir sugar and cinnamon into coffee until sugar dissolves; let cool. Stir in half-and-half and syrup; chill 2 hours. Serve over ice. Yield: 2 quarts.

Per 1 cup: Calories 125 (50% from fat); Fat 6.9g (sat 4.3g, mono 2g, poly 0.3g); Protein 2.2g; Carb 13.9g; Fiber 0.1g; Chol 22mg; Iron 0.3mg; Sodium 35mg; Calc 68mg

Homemade
Orange Soda

punches

entertaining • low cholesterol • low fat • quick

Champagne Punch

prep: 10 min.

*If you prefer a punch that's a little less on
the sweet side, add additional sparkling
water to taste.*

1   (11.5-ounce) can frozen pineapple-
    orange juice concentrate, thawed and
    undiluted
1   (6-ounce) can frozen lemonade
    concentrate, thawed and undiluted
1   (12-ounce) can or 1½ cups ginger ale,
    chilled
1   (750-milliliter) bottle Champagne or
    sparkling white grape juice, chilled
2   cups bottled sparkling water, chilled

Stir together concentrates in punch bowl.
Add ginger ale and remaining ingredients,
stirring gently. Serve immediately. Yield:
2 quarts.

Per 1 cup: Calories 200 (0% from fat); Fat 0g (sat 0g, mono 0g, poly 0g);
Protein 0.7g; Carb 34.5g; Fiber 0g; Chol 0mg; Iron 0.5mg; Sodium 18mg; Calc 24mg

entertaining • low calorie • low cholesterol
low fat • make ahead

Brunch Punch

prep: 5 min.   other: 2 hrs.

*Chill the juices before stirring them together;
this eliminates the need for additional time
in the refrigerator.*

1   (46-ounce) can pineapple juice
3   cups orange juice
2   cups cranberry juice
¾   cup powdered sugar
¼   cup lime juice
Garnishes: fresh mint sprigs, lime slices,
    orange slices, fresh cranberries

Stir together first 5 ingredients. Cover and
chill 2 hours. Stir before serving. Garnish, if
desired. Yield: about 3 quarts.

Per 1 cup: Calories 144 (2% from fat); Fat 0.3g (sat 0g, mono 0.1g, poly 0.1g);
Protein 0.9g; Carb 35.4g; Fiber 0.4g; Chol 0mg; Iron 0.5mg; Sodium 4mg; Calc 29mg

low calorie • low cholesterol • low fat

Cranberry–Pineapple Punch

prep: 10 min.   other: 8 hrs.

1   (48-ounce) bottle cranberry juice drink
1   (48-ounce) can pineapple juice
½   cup sugar
2   teaspoons almond extract
1   (2-liter) bottle ginger ale, chilled

Stir together first 4 ingredients until sugar
dissolves. Cover and chill 8 hours.
Stir in ginger ale just before serving. Yield:
6½ quarts.

Per 1 cup: Calories 107 (1% from fat); Fat 0.1g (sat 0g, mono 0g, poly 0g);
Protein 0.2g; Carb 27.2g; Fiber 0.2g; Chol 0mg; Iron 0.4mg; Sodium 7mg; Calc 14mg

entertaining • quick

Nog Punch

prep: 10 min.

1   gallon vanilla ice cream
½   gallon eggnog
1   teaspoon ground nutmeg
½   teaspoon ground cinnamon
1   (16-ounce) container frozen whipped
    topping, thawed

Scoop ice cream into a punch bowl. Pour
eggnog over ice cream, and sprinkle with
nutmeg and cinnamon; stir in whipped topping. Serve immediately. Stir as needed.
Yield: 1½ gallons.

Per 1 cup: Calories 344 (50% from fat); Fat 19.2g (sat 12.9g, mono 4.5g, poly 0.7g);
Protein 6.3g; Carb 36.5g; Fiber 0.7g; Chol 89mg; Iron 0.3mg; Sodium 116mg; Calc 223mg

entertaining • make ahead • quick

Peppermint Punch

prep: 10 min.

*If you serve this drink in a large punch
bowl, hang peppermint candy canes on the
bowl's rim.*

1   quart eggnog
1   (1-liter) bottle club soda, chilled
½   gallon peppermint ice cream, softened
Hard peppermint candies, crushed

Stir together first 3 ingredients in a punch
bowl or large bowl; sprinkle with peppermint candy, and serve immediately. Yield:
about 1 gallon.

Per 1 cup: Calories 246 (43% from fat); Fat 11.8g (sat 6.9g, mono 3.4g, poly 0.5g);
Protein 4.4g; Carb 30.6g; Fiber 0g; Chol 62mg; Iron 0.1mg; Sodium 99mg; Calc 146mg

Note: Punch can be made ahead, without
crushed peppermint candies, and chilled
2 hours. Stir well, and sprinkle with candies
just before serving.

make ahead • test kitchen favorite

Creamy Eggnog

prep: 12 min.   cook: 30 min.

This is a velvety-thick holiday drink.

2   cups half-and-half
2   cups milk
12 large eggs
¼   teaspoon salt
1½ cups sugar
1   cup bourbon
2   tablespoons vanilla extract
½   teaspoon ground nutmeg, divided
2   cups whipping cream

Heat half-and-half and milk in a large
saucepan over medium heat. (Do not boil.)
Meanwhile, beat eggs and salt at medium
speed with an electric mixer until thick and
pale; gradually add sugar, beating well.
Gradually stir about one-fourth of hot milk
into egg mixture; add to remaining hot
milk, stirring constantly.
Cook over medium-low heat, stirring
constantly, 25 to 30 minutes or until mixture thickens and reaches 160°.
Stir in bourbon, vanilla, and ¼ teaspoon
nutmeg. Remove from heat; cool. Cover
and chill up to 2 days.
Beat whipping cream at medium speed
until soft peaks form. Fold whipped cream
into eggnog. Sprinkle with remaining
¼ teaspoon nutmeg before serving. Yield:
10½ cups.

Per ½ cup: Calories 244 (51% from fat); Fat 13.9g (sat 7.5g, mono 2g, poly 0.5g);
Protein 5g; Carb 18.2g; Fiber 0g; Chol 162mg; Iron 0.6mg; Sodium 87mg; Calc 66mg

shakes, smoothies & slushy drinks

family favorite • for kids • quick

Peanut Butter–Banana–Chocolate Shake

prep: 12 min.

Bite-size peanut butter sandwich cookies make this kids' shake ultra thick.

4	cups vanilla ice cream, slightly softened
¼	cup milk
⅔	cup miniature peanut butter sandwich cookies (we tested with Nutter Butter Bites)
1	(1.5-ounce) package peanut butter cup candies, frozen and chopped
1	ripe banana, sliced
2	tablespoons chocolate syrup

Process first 5 ingredients in a blender just until smooth, stopping to scrape down sides (shake will be thick). Pour into glasses; drizzle each serving with chocolate syrup. Serve immediately. Yield: 4½ cups.

Per ¾ cup: Calories 321 (42% from fat); Fat 15g (sat 7.6g, mono 4.9g, poly 1.3g); Protein 5.4g; Carb 43.9g; Fiber 1.8g; Chol 40mg; Iron 0.6mg; Sodium 155mg; Calc 130mg

family favorite • quick

Rich Vanilla Milk Shake

prep: 3 min.

If you have a blender, you can whip up any one of these six shakes at home.

3	cups premium vanilla ice cream
1	cup milk
½	teaspoon vanilla extract

Process all ingredients in a blender until smooth. Serve immediately. Yield: 2½ cups.

Per 1¼ cups: Calories 629 (57% from fat); Fat 39.9g (sat 25.2g, mono 10.9g, poly 1.8g); Protein 11.7g; Carb 55.1g; Fiber 0g; Chol 216mg; Iron 0.8mg; Sodium 184mg; Calc 398mg

Strawberry Milk Shake: Substitute strawberry ice cream for vanilla ice cream, or add 1 (10-ounce) package frozen strawberries, thawed, or 1 cup fresh strawberries to ingredients in blender.

Chocolate Milk Shake: Substitute chocolate ice cream for vanilla ice cream, or add ¼ cup chocolate syrup to ingredients in blender.

Peach Milk Shake: Add 1 (16-ounce) can sliced peaches, drained, to blender.

Banana Milk Shake: Add 1 large banana, sliced, to ingredients in blender.

Coffee Milk Shake: Substitute coffee ice cream for vanilla ice cream, or add 1 tablespoon instant coffee granules to ingredients in blender.

quick

Pineapple–Buttermilk Shake

prep: 10 min.

The tang of buttermilk balances the sweetness of pineapple in this cooler.

1	(8-ounce) can unsweetened pineapple chunks, drained and frozen
1	quart vanilla ice cream
½	cup firmly packed brown sugar
2	cups buttermilk

Process all ingredients in a blender until smooth, stopping to scrape down sides. Serve immediately. Yield: 6 cups.

Per 1 cup: Calories 287 (33% from fat); Fat 10.4g (sat 6.4g, mono 2.8g, poly 0.4g); Protein 5.9g; Carb 44.6g; Fiber 0.8g; Chol 42mg; Iron 0.6mg; Sodium 164mg; Calc 227mg

Double-Berry Milk Shake

prep: 5 min.

1	pint fresh strawberry halves, frozen
¾	cup milk
¼	cup powdered sugar
1	teaspoon vanilla extract
1	pint strawberry ice cream
Garnishes: sweetened whipped cream, fresh whole strawberries	

Process first 4 ingredients in a blender until smooth. Add ice cream, and process until blended. Garnish, if desired. Yield: 4 cups.

Per 1 cup: Calories 205 (32% from fat); Fat 7.3g (sat 4.3g, mono 2g, poly 0.4g); Protein 4.1g; Carb 32.2g; Fiber 2g; Chol 24mg; Iron 0.5mg; Sodium 59mg; Calc 143mg

family favorite • quick

Chocolate-Yogurt Malt

prep: 5 min.

4	cups low-fat frozen vanilla yogurt
1	cup chocolate 1% low-fat milk or chocolate soy milk
¼	cup chocolate-flavored instant malted milk (we tested with Ovaltine)

Process all ingredients in a blender until smooth, stopping to scrape down sides. Serve immediately. Yield: 4 cups.

Per 1 cup: Calories 321 (11% from fat); Fat 4g (sat 2.5g, mono 1.1g, poly 0.2g); Protein 11.9g; Carb 61.9g; Fiber 1.7g; Chol 12mg; Iron 0.8mg; Sodium 209mg; Calc 391mg

entertaining • for kids • low calorie low cholesterol • low fat • quick

Tropical Smoothie

prep: 6 min.   other: 1 hr., 30 min.

You can make this drink at a moment's notice when you have a supply of banana slices in your freezer. Simply toss fresh slices in lemon juice, and freeze up to six months in a zip-top freezer bag.

1	medium-size ripe banana, cut into 1-inch pieces
2	teaspoons lemon juice
1	medium mango, peeled and cut into 1-inch pieces
1½	cups pineapple-orange juice, chilled
1	(6-ounce) container nonfat vanilla yogurt

Toss banana with lemon juice; drain, reserving lemon juice. Place banana in a small zip-top freezer bag; freeze 1½ hours. **Process** frozen banana, reserved lemon juice, mango, pineapple-orange juice, and yogurt in a blender until smooth. Pour into chilled glasses; serve immediately. Yield: 4 cups.

Per 1 cup: Calories 142 (1% from fat); Fat 0.2g (sat 0.1g, mono 0.1g, poly 0g); Protein 3.1g; Carb 33.8g; Fiber 1.9g; Chol 1mg; Iron 0.2mg; Sodium 36mg; Calc 86mg

Three-Fruit
Yogurt Smoothie

Fruit Parfait Slushy

prep: 10 min.   cook: 5 min.
other: 8 hrs., 30 min.

¾ cup sugar

1¼ cups water

1 (20-ounce) can crushed pineapple in juice

1 (10-ounce) package frozen strawberries

1 (12-ounce) can frozen pink lemonade concentrate, thawed

1 (6-ounce) can frozen orange juice concentrate without pulp, thawed

2 (1-liter) bottles lime-flavored sparkling water

Heat sugar and 1¼ cups water in a saucepan over medium heat 5 minutes or until sugar dissolves and reaches a syrup consistency.

Process crushed pineapple, frozen strawberries, lemonade concentrate, and orange juice concentrate, in batches, in a blender until smooth. Stir in sugar syrup, and freeze at least 8 hours.

Remove from freezer, and let stand 30 minutes or until mixture can be broken into pieces. Stir in sparkling water, and serve immediately. Yield: about 16 cups.

Per 1 cup: Calories 120 (1% from fat); Fat 0.1g (sat 0g, mono 0g, poly 0g); Protein 0.7g; Carb 30.4g; Fiber 0.9g; Chol 0mg; Iron 0.4mg; Sodium 6mg; Calc 26mg

Banana-Peach Buttermilk Smoothie

prep: 8 min.

Cultured dairy products—such as buttermilk and yogurt—are good for maintaining a healthy digestive tract.

2 large ripe bananas, sliced and frozen

2 cups frozen peaches

1 cup whole or fat-free buttermilk

¼ cup fresh orange juice

2 tablespoons honey

Process all ingredients in a blender until smooth, stopping to scrape down sides. Serve immediately. Yield: 4 cups.

Per 1 cup: Calories 170 (13% from fat); Fat 2.5g (sat 1.4g, mono 0.1g, poly 0.1g); Protein 3.7g; Carb 36.9g; Fiber 1.8g; Chol 9mg; Iron 0.5mg; Sodium 74mg; Calc 11mg

Three-Fruit Yogurt Smoothie

prep: 4 min.

If you can't find fresh blueberries and peaches in your area, substitute frozen fruit—no thawing required.

2 cups vanilla or desired fruit-flavored yogurt

1 cup fresh blueberries, frozen

1 cup fresh peach slices, frozen

1 (8-ounce) can unsweetened pineapple chunks, drained and frozen

Process all ingredients in a blender until smooth, stopping to scrape down sides. Serve immediately. Yield: 4½ cups.

Per ¾ cup: Calories 109 (10% from fat); Fat 1.2g (sat 0.7g, mono 0.3g, poly 0.1g); Protein 4.6g; Carb 21.3g; Fiber 1.3g; Chol 4mg; Iron 0.3mg; Sodium 54mg; Calc 147mg

Lemon-Rum Slush

prep: 5 min.   other: 6 hrs.

¼ cup sugar

2 (6-ounce) cans frozen lemonade concentrate

2 cups water

1½ cups pineapple juice

2 cups rum

Combine all ingredients, and freeze 6 hours, stirring occasionally. Remove lemonade mixture from freezer, and stir until slushy. Yield: 7 cups.

Per 1 cup: Calories 292 (0% from fat); Fat 0.1g (sat 0g, mono 0g, poly 0g); Protein 0.3g; Carb 37.4g; Fiber 0.2g; Chol 0mg; Iron 0.6mg; Sodium 5mg; Calc 14mg

Frozen Coffee Cooler

prep: 10 min.

6 cups ice cubes
4 cups brewed coffee, cooled
1 cup coffee liqueur
¾ cup sugar
1 teaspoon ground cinnamon
1 cup half-and-half or milk
Garnishes: whipped cream, ground cinnamon

Process half of first 5 ingredients in a blender until smooth. Pour coffee mixture into a large pitcher. Repeat with remaining half of first 5 ingredients, and pour into pitcher. Stir half-and-half into coffee mixture, and garnish, if desired. Serve immediately. Yield: 8 cups.

Per 1 cup: Calories 230 (14% from fat); Fat 3.6g (sat 2.2g, mono 1g, poly 0.2g); Protein 1.1g; Carb 36.6g; Fiber 0.2g; Chol 11mg; Iron 0.2mg; Sodium 18mg; Calc 38mg

quick • test kitchen favorite

Spiced Mocha Shake

prep: 10 min.   cook: 5 min.

Any style of coffee ice cream will work in this decadent shake.

1 (4-ounce) sweet dark chocolate bar, chopped (we tested with Ghirardelli)
¾ cup milk
1 teaspoon instant espresso granules
1 teaspoon vanilla extract
½ teaspoon almond extract
¼ teaspoon ground cinnamon
4 cups coffee ice cream (we tested with Starbucks Coffee Almond Fudge)

Cook first 6 ingredients in a saucepan over low heat, stirring until chocolate melts. Cool. **Process** coffee ice cream and chocolate mixture in a blender until smooth. Serve immediately. Yield: 4 cups.

Per 1 cup: Calories 715 (62% from fat); Fat 49.6g (sat 28.9g, mono 14g, poly 2g); Protein 13.5g; Carb 58.6g; Fiber 2.1g; Chol 245mg; Iron 0.8mg; Sodium 189mg; Calc 354mg

low calorie • low cholesterol

Café Latte Slush

prep: 15 min.   other: 8 hrs.

½ to ¾ cup sugar
2 cups hot, strong brewed coffee or espresso
2 cups milk or half-and-half, divided*
Garnish: chocolate syrup

Combine sugar and hot coffee in a large bowl, stirring until sugar dissolves; stir in 1 cup milk. Cover and freeze 8 hours. **Let** thaw 2 hours in refrigerator or until it can be cut into chunks; add remaining 1 cup milk. Beat at medium speed with an electric mixer until smooth. Garnish, if desired. Serve immediately. Yield: 6 cups.

Per 1 cup: Calories 114 (21% from fat); Fat 2.7g (sat 1.5g, mono 0.7g, poly 0.2g); Protein 2.7g; Carb 20.3g; Fiber 0g; Chol 8mg; Iron 0mg; Sodium 34mg; Calc 94mg

*Substitute fat-free milk or fat-free half-and-half for regular milk or half-and-half, if desired.

bar drinks

low calorie • low cholesterol • low fat • quick

Spicy Bloody Marys

prep: 7 min.

Hot sauce, horseradish, and pepper give this wake-up drink its kick.

4½ cups tomato juice or spicy vegetable juice, chilled
¼ cup lemon juice, lime juice, or clam juice
3 tablespoons Worcestershire sauce
1 tablespoon prepared horseradish
1 teaspoon celery salt
½ teaspoon freshly ground pepper
¼ to ½ teaspoon hot sauce
1 cup vodka
Garnish: celery stalks

Combine first 7 ingredients; stir well, and chill thoroughly. Stir in vodka, and serve over ice. Garnish, if desired. Yield: 6 cups.

Per 1 cup: Calories 127 (1% from fat); Fat 0.2g (sat 0g, mono 0g, poly 0.1g); Protein 1.5g; Carb 10.5g; Fiber 0.9g; Chol 0mg; Iron 1.4mg; Sodium 833mg; Calc 33mg

Virgin Marys: Omit vodka; add 1 more cup tomato juice or spicy vegetable juice.

entertaining • low cholesterol • low fat

Chocolate Martinis

prep: 3 min.   other: 1 hr.

Dip the rims of the glasses just before serving so cocoa doesn't dissolve.

2 cups vodka, chilled
1¼ cups chocolate liqueur
¼ cup raspberry liqueur
¼ cup half-and-half
¼ cup light corn syrup
¼ cup sweetened ground cocoa

Stir together first 4 ingredients in a pitcher; chill at least 1 hour.
Fill martini glasses with ice. Let stand 5 minutes; discard ice.
Dip rims of chilled glasses in corn syrup; dip in cocoa, coating rims.

Whisk vodka mixture just before serving; pour into glasses. Serve immediately. Yield: 8 servings.

Per ½ cup: Calories 351 (5% from fat); Fat 1.8g (sat 1g, mono 0.3g, poly 0.1g); Protein 0.6g; Carb 33.6g; Fiber 0.5g; Chol 3mg; Iron 0.2mg; Sodium 20mg; Calc 10mg

Note: For testing purposes only, we used Godiva Liqueur for chocolate liqueur, RazzMatazz for raspberry liqueur, and Ghirardelli Sweet Ground Chocolate and Cocoa for sweetened ground cocoa.

Individual Chocolate Martini: Combine ¼ cup vodka, 2 tablespoons chocolate liqueur, 1½ teaspoons raspberry liqueur, 6 ice cubes, and a dash of half-and-half in a martini shaker. Cover with lid, and shake until thoroughly chilled. Remove lid, and strain into a chilled martini glass. Serve immediately. Yield: 1 serving.

Bourbon Sunrise

prep: 15 min.   cook: 10 min.

½   cup water
1   cup sugar
2   large navel oranges, sliced
1½ cups bourbon
1   quart orange juice
1   (10-ounce) jar maraschino cherries with stems, undrained

Combine ½ cup water, sugar, and orange slices in a saucepan, squeezing slices to release juices. Bring to a boil; cook over medium-high heat, stirring often, 5 minutes. Cover; remove from heat. Cool.
Pour syrup through a wire-mesh strainer into a pitcher, discarding orange slices; stir in bourbon and orange juice. Stir in cherry juice and cherries. Serve over ice. Yield: 8½ cups.

Per 1 cup: Calories 301 (1% from fat); Fat 0.5g (sat 0g, mono 0.1g, poly 0.1g); Protein 1.1g; Carb 51.9g; Fiber 0.6g; Chol 0mg; Iron 0.3mg; Sodium 22mg; Calc 35mg

Classic Margaritas

prep: 5 min.   other: 30 min.

2   cups sugar
2   cups water
2   cups orange liqueur
2   cups tequila
2   cups fresh lime juice
Margarita salt
Garnish: lime wedges

Bring sugar and water to a boil over medium heat; cook, stirring constantly, 1 to 2 minutes or until sugar dissolves. Remove from heat; cool.
Stir together sugar mixture, liqueur, tequila, and lime juice; cover and chill at least 30 minutes.
Dip glass rims in water, and dip rims in salt. Serve margaritas over crushed ice. Garnish, if desired. Yield: 8 cups.

Per 1 cup: Calories 538 (0% from fat); Fat 0.2g (sat 0g, mono 0g, poly 0.1g); Protein 0.3g; Carb 80g; Fiber 0.3g; Chol 0mg; Iron 0.1mg; Sodium 967mg; Calc 11mg

Note: For frozen margaritas, freeze 8 hours, and stir before serving.

Mimosas

Rio Grande Limeade

prep: 10 min.   other: 8 hrs.

2   (12-ounce) cans frozen limeade concentrate, thawed
3   cups tequila
3   cups water
2   cups orange liqueur
1   cup fresh lime juice
Garnish: lime slices

Stir together first 5 ingredients. Cover and chill 8 hours. Serve over ice, and garnish, if desired. Yield: 3 quarts.

Per 1 cup: Calories 378 (0% from fat); Fat 0.2g (sat 0g, mono 0g, poly 0.1g); Protein 0.2g; Carb 46.1g; Fiber 0.2g; Chol 0mg; Iron 0.1mg; Sodium 9mg; Calc 11mg

Mimosa

prep: 5 min.

Fresh squeezed juice is what makes a mimosa great.

Pour equal parts of chilled fresh orange juice and Champagne into a Champagne flute. Garnish with an orange slice, if desired. Yield: 1 serving.

Per ⅔ cup: Calories 93 (2% from fat); Fat 0.2g (sat 0g, mono 0g, poly 0.1g); Protein 0.7g; Carb 9.7g; Fiber 0.2g; Chol 0mg; Iron 0.1mg; Sodium 0.8mg; Calc 8mg

mint juleps

The Kentucky Derby is celebrated the first Saturday in May with visitors from around the world gathering at the racetrack and all over Louisville. As "My Old Kentucky Home" plays before the race, julep cups are raised high. To Kentuckians, a mint julep is more than a drink; it's a cup of tradition, full of emotion.

The classic version is served in silver julep cups. These are filled to the rim with a refreshing concoction of the finest bourbon, simple syrup, fresh mint, and crushed ice.

This drink is best made individually "to taste" using only fresh ingredients. While Kentucky Colonel mint is commonly used, other varieties work, too. The ingredients remain constant, but opinions are varied as to the proper way to make them. Many crush the mint and sugar together (referred to as muddling), while others insist that the mint should be smelled not tasted.

Chill cups before filling with crushed ice to prevent the ice from melting quickly.

Before tasting, insert a cocktail straw or coffee stirrer near the mint sprig. Inhale a deep breath, and slowly sip until someone says, "May I fix you another mint julep?"

Classic Mint Julep

low calorie • low carb • low cholesterol
low fat • quick

Classic Mint Julep

prep: 10 min.

Leftover simple syrup keeps in the refrigerator about one week and perfectly sweetens iced tea, in addition to these delectable juleps.

3   fresh mint leaves
1   tablespoon Mint Simple Syrup
Crushed ice
1½ to 2 tablespoons (1 ounce) bourbon
1   (4-inch) cocktail straw or coffee stirrer
1   fresh mint sprig
Powdered sugar (optional)

Place 3 mint leaves and Mint Simple Syrup in a chilled julep cup. Gently press leaves against cup with back of spoon to release flavors. Pack cup tightly with crushed ice; pour bourbon over ice. Insert straw, place 1 mint sprig directly next to straw, and serve immediately. Sprinkle with powdered sugar, if desired. Yield: 1 (8-ounce) julep.

Per serving: Calories 90 (0% from fat); Fat 0g (sat 0g, mono 0g, poly 0g); Protein 0g; Carb 6.3g; Fiber 0g; Chol 0mg; Iron 0mg; Sodium 0mg; Calc 0mg

Mint Simple Syrup

prep: 5 min.   cook: 10 min.   other: 24 hrs.

1   cup sugar
1   cup water
10   to 12 fresh mint sprigs

Bring sugar and water to a boil in a medium saucepan. Boil, stirring often, 5 minutes or until sugar dissolves. Remove from heat; add mint, and let cool completely. Pour into a glass jar; cover and chill 24 hours. Remove and discard mint. Yield: 2 cups.

Per serving: Calories 24 (0% from fat); Fat 0g (sat 0g, mono 0g, poly 0g); Protein 0g; Carb 6.3g; Fiber 0g; Chol 0mg; Iron 0mg; Sodium 0mg; Calc 0mg

To Kentuckians, a mint julep is more than a drink; it's a cup of tradition, full of emotion.

Mint Bellinis

prep: 10 min.   cook: 20 min.

4   (12-ounce) cans peach nectar
2   cups sugar
1   lemon, halved
¼   cup firmly packed fresh mint leaves
1   (750-milliliter) bottle Champagne or
    2½ cups sparkling water
Garnish: lemon slices

Bring first 4 ingredients to a boil, and cook 20 minutes. Cool. Remove and discard lemon and mint; store mixture in an airtight container in refrigerator until ready to serve. Stir in Champagne before serving. Serve over ice; garnish, if desired. Yield: 9½ cups.

Per ½ cup: Calories 152 (0% from fat); Fat 0g (sat 0g, mono 0g, poly 0.1g); Protein 0.2g; Carb 32.7g; Fiber 0.5g; Chol 0mg; Iron 0.2mg; Sodium 6mg; Calc 4mg

Thick 'n' Rich Piña Coladas

prep: 9 min.

Serve this fruity concoction with a straw and a spoon.

1   (8½-ounce) can cream of coconut
1   (8-ounce) can crushed pineapple, drained
⅓   cup flaked sweetened coconut
½   cup light rum
½   teaspoon banana extract
2   cups vanilla ice cream, slightly softened

Process all ingredients in a blender until smooth. Serve immediately. Yield: 4 cups.

Per 1 cup: Calories 364 (49% from fat); Fat 20g (sat 15.7g, mono 2.5g, poly 0.5g); Protein 4.3g; Carb 29.3g; Fiber 2.5g; Chol 29mg; Iron 0.6mg; Sodium 99mg; Calc 92mg

Mock Coladas: Omit rum, and add 1 teaspoon rum extract. Yield: 3½ cups.

Watermelon Daiquiri

prep: 20 min.   other: 8 hrs.

4   cups seeded and cubed watermelon
⅓   cup light rum
¼   to ½ cup orange juice
2   tablespoons orange liqueur
4   teaspoons powdered sugar
2   teaspoons fresh lime juice

Place watermelon in a zip-top freezer bag. Seal bag; freeze 8 hours.
Process watermelon, rum, and remaining ingredients in a blender or food processor until smooth, stopping to scrape down sides. Serve immediately. Yield: 3 cups.

Per 1 cup: Calories 155 (2% from fat); Fat 0.4g (sat 0g, mono 0.1g, poly 0.1g); Protein 1.4g; Carb 22.5g; Fiber 0.9g; Chol 0mg; Iron 0.6mg; Sodium 3mg; Calc 17mg

Mojito

prep: 4 min.

This Cuban cooler has fast become a favorite in the states. If you have access to Key limes, use them for the most authentic flavor.

2   tablespoons sugar
15 fresh mint leaves
¼   cup white rum
2   tablespoons fresh lime juice
¼   cup club soda, chilled
½   cup ice
Garnishes: lime wedge, fresh mint sprig

Place sugar and 15 mint leaves in a 2-cup glass measuring cup; crush mint with a wooden spoon. Add rum and juice; stir until sugar dissolves. Just before serving, stir in club soda. Place ice in an 8-ounce glass; pour mint mixture over ice. Garnish, if desired. Yield: 1 cup.

Per 1 cup: Calories 233 (0% from fat); Fat 0g (sat 0g, mono 0g, poly 0g); Protein 0.2g; Carb 27.7g; Fiber 0.2g; Chol 0mg; Iron 0.1mg; Sodium 14mg; Calc 9mg

Whiskey Sour Slushies

prep: 10 min.   other: 2 hrs., 40 min.

We use brewed tea in this favorite Collins drink, also known as Tennessee Tea when paired with Jack Daniel's whiskey. Instead of freezing, you can chill and serve over ice.

4   regular-size tea bags
2   cups boiling water
2   cups sugar
7   cups water
1   (12-ounce) can frozen orange juice concentrate, thawed
1   (12-ounce) can frozen lemonade concentrate, thawed
2   cups whiskey
Lemon lime soft drink

Combine tea bags and 2 cups boiling water; steep 10 minutes. Discard tea bags.
Bring tea, sugar, 7 cups water, orange juice concentrate, and lemonade concentrate to a boil in a Dutch oven over medium heat, stirring until sugar dissolves. Remove from heat, and stir in whiskey; cool.
Freeze in zip-top freezer bags or plastic containers at least 2 hours. Remove from freezer, and let stand at room temperature 30 minutes. Break up with a fork.
Scoop ½ cup mixture into a cocktail glass. Fill glass with lemon lime soft drink. Serve immediately. Yield: about 15 cups.

Per ½ cup: Calories 297 (0% from fat); Fat 0.1g (sat 0g, mono 0g, poly 0g); Protein 0.6g; Carb 59.1g; Fiber 0.2g; Chol 0mg; Iron 0.3mg; Sodium 17mg; Calc 11mg

Whiskey Sour: Chill instead of freezing. Pour ½ cup mixture into a cocktail glass with ice. Fill glass with lemon lime soft drink.

breads

Bread Basics

Quick bread recipes are speedy to stir together and bake immediately; they're leavened (made to rise) by baking powder or baking soda. Yeast breads are more involved to make but worth any extra effort. Yeast is a living organism which requires mixing with liquid at a certain temperature to activate its growth process. When making yeast breads, the kneading process is crucial to the final product. As you knead dough, its structure develops, and this ultimately leads to a perfectly textured bread.

Equipment

If you love home-baked bread, you can never have too many baking sheets, loafpans, and specialty baking pans. Select good quality, heavy grade baking sheets and pans for long-term use. Choose shiny pans because they reflect heat best and produce baked goods with nicely browned, tender crusts. Nonstick pans tend to brown breads quicker.

The most common size loafpan is 9 x 5 inches, although some bread recipes specify pans 8½ x 4½ inches or smaller. For best results, use the pan size that the recipe calls for; otherwise, expect breads that are shallower or deeper and baking times that vary.

A popover pan, pastry blender, dough scraper, serrated bread knife, and baguette pans are valuable tools for the seasoned bread baker.

Flours for Bread

The type of flour used in a recipe and its protein content play an important role in the texture of the end product. Wheat flour made predominantly from "hard wheat" (such as Pillsbury and Gold Medal) is richer in gluten than flour made predominantly from "soft wheat" (like White Lily and Martha White). Hard wheat flour absorbs liquid more readily and yields heartier textured bread. Soft wheat flour produces more tender bread products.

All-purpose flour is a combination of hard wheat and soft wheat flours and can be used for all types of baking.

Self-rising flour is all-purpose flour that has leavening and salt added. It's best not to substitute self-rising flour for all-purpose; however, you can substitute all-purpose for self-rising with these adjustments: For 1 cup self-rising flour, use 1 cup all-purpose flour plus 1 teaspoon baking powder and ¼ teaspoon salt.

Unbleached flour is all-purpose flour that has no bleaching agents added during processing. Use it interchangeably with all-purpose flour.

Bread flour is produced primarily for yeast bread baking and is a blend of hard wheat flour and a bit of malted barley flour. Its high-protein content makes it absorb liquid differently than all-purpose flour, so use it only in recipes that specify it.

Whole wheat flour is coarse-textured and is ground from the entire wheat kernel, making it higher in fiber, nutrients, and fat content. It's great for hearty breads and some cookies, but not a good choice for delicate baked goods.

Flour is also milled from grains other than wheat, such as **corn, rye, oats,** and **barley**. All absorb water differently so they're not interchangeable in recipes.

Since most flour is sifted during the milling process, there's no need to sift before measuring. To measure flour, stir it lightly; then spoon it into a dry measuring cup (don't pack it). Level the top, using a spatula or other straight edge. Don't shake the cup level, because this packs the flour. Cake flour, however, is the one exception that does need to be sifted before use.

Storing and Freezing Bread

Bread turns stale quickly, so proper storage is important. Contrary to popular belief, bread will get stale faster in the refrigerator than at room temperature (although it will mold faster at room temperature than in the refrigerator). If you want to keep bread for several days, cover it with an airtight wrap, and store it at room temperature.

For longer storage, let bread cool completely after baking, wrap tightly in aluminum foil, place in a freezer bag, and freeze up to three months. To serve, partially unwrap and let stand at room temperature until thawed. Reheat briefly, uncovered, at 350°.

quick breads

Some quick breads start with a batter, some with a dough. The ratio of liquid to flour, the type of fat used, and the number of eggs create many variations in quick breads. And once in the oven, these breads rise quickly, leavened by steam, eggs, and the gases formed by baking powder or soda.

Double-acting baking powder is the most common type of leavening used for quick breads. It contains an acid (typically cream of tartar) and an alkali (baking soda) which, when combined with a liquid, react to give off carbon dioxide. Once in a hot oven, this carbon dioxide forms tiny bubbles that expand quickly, thus giving the bread height and developing its structure. Hence the name double-acting—it reacts initially when added to liquid and again from the heat of the oven.

That means you should bake all quick breads as soon as possible after mixing. Even if they stand at room temperature a few minutes before baking, recipes made with double-acting baking powder will rise better than those made with other types of baking powder. To be sure baking powder maintains its freshness, check the date on the can, and stir before using.

Baking soda starts reacting as soon as it's combined with liquid, so recipes calling for it should be baked immediately. Baking soda is typically used only in recipes that contain an acid, such as buttermilk, lemon juice, sour cream, molasses, or chocolate, to help activate the soda.

A rule of thumb is to bake quick breads until a wooden pick inserted in center comes out clean. Length of time will vary due to bread size and oven temperature.

biscuits

The most tender biscuits start with solid fat, such as (chilled) shortening or cold butter. Cut the fat into the dry ingredients, using a pastry blender until the mixture is crumbly. (Two knives work almost as well if you don't own a pastry blender.) This "cutting" action distributes lumps of fat throughout the dough that melt during baking and give biscuits their trademark flakiness. Add liquid ingredients, and stir just until dry ingredients are moistened. Too much mixing makes biscuits heavy.

Knead the dough on a lightly floured surface only three or four times, just until the dough feels soft and no longer sticky. Quickly roll, "punch" cut, and bake as the recipe directs. If you twist the cutter as you cut biscuits, they won't rise evenly.

A good biscuit has a level and golden top and straight sides. Inside the biscuit should be tender and slightly moist. For the beginner baker, drop biscuits (see recipe, page 79) are a great place to start. They require no kneading, rolling, or cutting.

family favorite • low cholesterol • quick

Baking Powder Biscuits

prep: 6 min.   cook: 15 min.

2   cups all-purpose flour
1   tablespoon baking powder
½   teaspoon salt
⅓   cup shortening
¾   cup milk

Combine first 3 ingredients; cut in shortening with a pastry blender until mixture is crumbly. Add milk, stirring until dry ingredients are moistened.
Turn dough out onto a floured surface, and knead lightly 3 or 4 times. Roll dough to ½-inch thickness; cut with a 2½-inch round cutter, and place on a lightly greased baking sheet.
Bake at 425° for 15 minutes or until golden. Yield: 1 dozen.

Per biscuit: Calories 137 (39% from fat); Fat 6g (sat 1.7g, mono 0.1g, poly 0.1g); Protein 2.7g; Carb 17.4g; Fiber 0.6g; Chol 2mg; Iron 1.1mg; Sodium 225mg; Calc 88mg

◄ Cut shortening into dry ingredients until crumbly.

◄ Knead dough lightly with heel of your hands.

◄ Punch out biscuits with a round cutter.

quick

Whipping Cream Biscuits

prep: 10 min.   cook: 15 min.

1   cup cold butter or margarine, cut into pieces
4   cups self-rising flour
1¾ to 2 cups whipping cream
½   cup butter or margarine, melted

Cut 1 cup butter into flour with a pastry blender or fork until crumbly. Add whipping cream, stirring just until dry ingredients are moistened.
Turn dough out onto a lightly floured surface, and knead lightly 3 or 4 times. Roll or pat dough to ¾-inch thickness; cut with a 2-inch round cutter, and place on a lightly greased baking sheet.
Bake at 400° for 13 to 15 minutes or until golden. Brush warm biscuits with ½ cup melted butter. Yield: 2 dozen.

Per biscuit: Calories 235 (69% from fat); Fat 18g (sat 11.2g, mono 4.8g, poly 0.8g); Protein 2.6g; Carb 16.2g; Fiber 0.6g; Chol 54mg; Iron 1mg; Sodium 352mg; Calc 85mg

Whipping Cream Biscuits

Old-Fashioned Biscuits

prep: 10 min.   cook: 12 min.

¼   cup shortening
2   cups self-rising flour
⅔   cup milk

Cut shortening into flour with a pastry blender or fork until crumbly. Add milk, stirring just until dry ingredients are moistened.
Turn dough out onto a lightly floured surface, and knead lightly 3 or 4 times. (Use all-purpose flour for sprinkling on your work surface rather than self-rising.) Pat or roll dough to ½-inch thickness; cut with a 2-inch round cutter, and place on a lightly greased baking sheet.
Bake at 475° for 10 to 12 minutes or until golden. Yield: 14 biscuits.

Per biscuit: Calories 105 (36% from fat); Fat 4.2g (sat 1g, mono 1.7g, poly 1.2g); Protein 2.2g; Carb 14.2g; Fiber 0.5g; Chol 1.2mg; Iron 0.9mg; Sodium 231mg; Calc 74 mg

Sour Cream Biscuits: Substitute 1 (8-ounce) container sour cream for ⅔ cup milk. Proceed as directed.

quick

Favorite Buttermilk Biscuits

prep: 5 min.   cook: 14 min.

It's the Southern-produced soft wheat flour that gives these biscuits their light-as-a-feather interior. The three ingredients are a snap to stir together and, if you pat the dough instead of rolling it, you can have biscuits ready for the oven in 5 minutes flat.

⅓   cup cold butter or margarine, cut into pieces
2   cups self-rising soft wheat flour (we tested with White Lily)
¾   cup buttermilk
     Butter or margarine, melted

Cut ⅓ cup butter into flour with a pastry blender until mixture is crumbly; add buttermilk, stirring until dry ingredients are moistened.
Turn dough out onto a lightly floured surface; knead 3 or 4 times. Pat or roll dough to ¾-inch thickness; cut with a 2½-inch

round cutter, and place on a lightly greased baking sheet.
Bake at 425° for 12 to 14 minutes or until golden. Brush with melted butter. Yield: 8 biscuits.

Per biscuit: Calories 205 (42% from fat); Fat 9.5g (sat 5.9g, mono 2.5g, poly 0.5g); Protein 4.2g; Carb 25.6g; Fiber 1g; Chol 25mg; Iron 1.4mg; Sodium 507mg; Calc 92mg

low calorie • low cholesterol

Angel Biscuits

prep: 18 min.   cook: 15 min. per batch
other: 35 min.

Angel Biscuits are aptly named because they rise more than traditional biscuits due to the yeast in them. They're lighter and airier—more like a roll.

1   (¼-ounce) envelope active dry yeast
¼   cup warm water (100° to 110°)
5   cups all-purpose flour
1   tablespoon baking powder
1   teaspoon baking soda
1   teaspoon salt
¼   cup sugar
1   cup shortening
2   cups buttermilk

Combine yeast and warm water in a 1-cup liquid measuring cup; let stand 5 minutes.
Combine flour and next 4 ingredients in a large bowl; cut in shortening with a pastry blender until mixture is crumbly. Add yeast mixture and buttermilk; stir just until ingredients are moistened.
Turn dough out onto a lightly floured surface, and knead 6 to 8 times. Roll dough to ½-inch thickness; cut with a 2½-inch cutter, and place on lightly greased baking sheets. Cover and let rise in a warm place (85°), free from drafts, 30 minutes.
Bake at 400° for 15 minutes or until lightly browned. Yield: 32 biscuits.

Per biscuit: Calories 142 (43% from fat); Fat 6.8g (sat 1.4g, mono 2.9g, poly 2.1g); Protein 2.6g; Carb 18g; Fiber 0.6g; Chol 1mg; Iron 1mg; Sodium 174mg; Calc 46mg

Rerolling biscuit dough toughens it a little. For the most tender biscuits, reroll dough with a light touch.

measure flour by lightly spooning it into a dry measuring cup and leveling it off with a straight edge. Accurate measurements prevent dry biscuits.

quick • test kitchen favorite

Sweet Potato Biscuits

prep: 15 min.   cook: 15 min.

4   cups all-purpose flour
2   tablespoons baking powder
2   teaspoons salt
1   cup cold butter or margarine, cut into pieces
1   cup cooked mashed sweet potato
¾   to 1 cup buttermilk

Combine first 3 ingredients. Cut in butter with a pastry blender until crumbly.
Stir together sweet potato and buttermilk; add to dry ingredients, stirring just until moistened.
Turn dough out onto a floured surface; knead 3 or 4 times. Pat or roll dough to ½-inch thickness; cut with a 3-inch round cutter, and place on a lightly greased baking sheet.
Bake at 425° for 10 to 15 minutes or until golden. Yield: 14 biscuits.

Per biscuit: Calories 273 (45% from fat); Fat 13.5g (sat 8.4g, mono 3.4g, poly 0.7g); Protein 4.8g; Carb 33.2g; Fiber 1.6g; Chol 35mg; Iron 2.1mg; Sodium 659mg; Calc 152mg

family favorite

Cheesy Chive Biscuits

prep: 15 min.   cook: 16 min.

These grand biscuits are the perfect accompaniment with a hearty soup, or fill them with sliced smoked turkey or ham.

2   cups all-purpose flour
1   tablespoon baking powder
¾   teaspoon salt
⅓   cup cold butter, cut into pieces
½   cup grated Parmesan cheese
2   tablespoons chopped fresh chives
¾   cup milk

Cutting cold butter into pieces (1 tablespoon amounts) makes it easy to incorporate into flour.

Combine first 3 ingredients in a large bowl. Cut butter into flour mixture with a pastry blender until crumbly; stir in Parmesan cheese and chives. Add milk, stirring until dry ingredients are moistened.

Turn dough out onto a lightly floured surface, and knead lightly 5 or 6 times. Pat or roll dough to ½-inch thickness; cut with a 2¾-inch round cutter, and place on a lightly greased baking sheet.

Bake at 400° for 15 to 16 minutes or until lightly browned. Yield: 7 biscuits.

Per biscuit: Calories 253 (41% from fat); Fat 11.6g (sat 7g, mono 3g, poly 0.6g); Protein 7g; Carb 30.1g; Fiber 1g; Chol 31mg; Iron 2mg; Sodium 618mg; Calc 218mg

family favorite • low calorie
Cornmeal Biscuits

prep: 22 min.   cook: 18 min. per batch

This is an easy recipe, but take care to cut the butter into the flour evenly and finely, until you almost can't see any bits of butter.

4   cups self-rising flour
½   cup yellow cornmeal*
1   cup cold butter, cut into pieces
2   cups buttermilk
Yellow cornmeal
¼   cup milk

Combine flour and ½ cup cornmeal in a large bowl; cut in butter with a pastry blender or fork until mixture is crumbly. Add buttermilk, stirring just until dry ingredients are moistened.

Turn dough out onto a lightly floured surface; knead 2 or 3 times.

Sprinkle cornmeal evenly onto lightly greased baking sheets. Pat or roll dough to ½-inch thickness; cut with a 2-inch round cutter, and place on baking sheets. Brush tops with milk.

Bake at 425° for 15 to 18 minutes or until golden. Yield: 3 dozen.

Per biscuit: Calories 110 (44% from fat); Fat 5.4g (sat 3.3g, mono 1.4g, poly 0.3g); Protein 2.1g; Carb 13g; Fiber 0.5g; Chol 14mg; Iron 0.8mg; Sodium 227mg; Calc 66mg

*White cornmeal can be substituted.

quick
Quick Buttermilk Biscuits

prep: 10 min.   cook: 9 min. per batch

Keep a dozen or two of these tasty gems in the freezer for drop-in company or a last-minute morning treat.

2¼   cups all-purpose baking mix (we tested with Bisquick)
⅓   cup buttermilk
6   tablespoons unsalted butter, melted and divided

Stir together baking mix, buttermilk, and 5 tablespoons melted butter just until blended.

Turn dough out onto a lightly floured surface, and knead 1 or 2 times. Pat to ½-inch thickness; cut with a 1½-inch round cutter, and place on lightly greased baking sheets.

Bake at 450° for 7 to 9 minutes or until lightly browned. Brush tops evenly with remaining 1 tablespoon melted butter. Yield: 2 dozen.

Per biscuit: Calories 74 (56% from fat); Fat 4.6g (sat 2.3g, mono 1.5g, poly 0.3g); Protein 1g; Carb 7.4g; Fiber 0.2g; Chol 8mg; Iron 0.4mg; Sodium 146mg; Calc 22mg

To make ahead: Freeze unbaked biscuits on a lightly greased baking sheet 30 minutes or until frozen. Store in a zip-top freezer bag up to 3 months. Bake frozen biscuits as directed for 8 to 10 minutes or until lightly browned. Proceed with recipe as directed.

family favorite • low calorie • quick
Garlic Cheese Drop Biscuits

prep: 6 min.   cook: 10 min.

These tender little biscuits get a tasty hit from garlic butter.

2   cups all-purpose baking mix (we tested with Bisquick)
⅔   cup milk
½   cup (2 ounces) shredded Cheddar cheese
3   tablespoons butter, melted
¼   teaspoon garlic powder

Stir together first 3 ingredients until soft dough forms. Stir vigorously 30 seconds. Drop dough by tablespoonfuls onto an ungreased baking sheet.

Bake at 450° for 8 to 10 minutes or until lightly browned.

Stir together butter and garlic powder; brush over warm biscuits. Yield: 1 dozen.

Per biscuit: Calories 134 (53% from fat); Fat 7.9g (sat 3.5g, mono 3g, poly 0.4g); Protein 3.1g; Carb 13g; Fiber 0.4g; Chol 13.8mg; Iron 0.7mg; Sodium 307mg; Calc 79mg

family favorite • low calorie
low cholesterol • quick
Fresh Tomato Biscuits

prep: 5 min.   cook: 16 min.

In no time you can dress up ordinary canned biscuits and make them fit for company.

¼   cup mayonnaise
¼   teaspoon salt
¼   teaspoon coarsely ground pepper
¼   cup chopped fresh basil
1   (12-ounce) can refrigerated flaky biscuits (we tested with Pillsbury Buttermilk Biscuits)
2   plum tomatoes, thinly sliced

Combine first 4 ingredients. Set aside.
Place biscuits on a lightly greased baking sheet. Bake at 400° for 6 minutes. Spread each biscuit evenly with a rounded teaspoon of mayonnaise mixture. Top each biscuit with a tomato slice. Bake 10 more minutes or until mayonnaise is bubbly and biscuits are golden. Serve immediately. Yield: 10 biscuits.

Per biscuit: Calories 143 (53% from fat); Fat 8.4g (sat 1.7g, mono 1.1g, poly 2.4g); Protein 2.2g; Carb 14.8g; Fiber 0.2g; Chol 2mg; Iron 0.8mg; Sodium 450mg; Calc 4mg

Classic Cream Scones, Orange-Pecan Scones

Scones are made with cream or milk, butter, and sometimes egg. The dough should be "shaggy" or rough, and as in the biscuit procedure, you should work quickly using cold butter, and keep mixing to a minimum for a flaky product.

quick
Classic Cream Scones

prep: 10 min.   cook: 13 min.

Smear these sugar-crusted scones with crème fraîche or preserves.

2   cups all-purpose flour
2   teaspoons baking powder
⅛   teaspoon salt
¼   cup sugar
⅓   cup cold butter, cut into pieces
½   cup whipping cream
1   large egg
1½   teaspoons vanilla extract
1   egg yolk
1   teaspoon water
1   tablespoon sugar or turbinado sugar

Combine first 4 ingredients. Cut in butter with a pastry blender until crumbly.
Whisk together cream, egg, and vanilla; add to flour mixture, stirring just until dry ingredients are moistened.
Turn dough out onto a lightly floured surface. Pat dough to ¾-inch thickness; cut with a 2½-inch round cutter, and place on a lightly greased baking sheet.
Whisk together egg yolk and 1 teaspoon water; brush over tops of scones. Sprinkle evenly with 1 tablespoon sugar.
Bake at 425° for 13 minutes or until lightly browned. Yield: 8 scones.

Per scone: Calories 283 (45% from fat); Fat 14.1g (sat 8.2g, mono 4.1g, poly 0.8g); Protein 4.5g; Carb 34g; Fiber 0.9g; Chol 92mg; Iron 1.8mg; Sodium 223mg; Calc 81mg

freeze it · quick
Orange-Pecan Scones

prep: 14 min.   cook: 14 min.   other: 5 min.

2   cups self-rising flour
½   cup granulated sugar
2   teaspoons grated orange rind
⅓   cup cold butter, cut into pieces
½   cup chopped pecans, toasted
⅓   cup buttermilk
¼   cup fresh orange juice
1   teaspoon vanilla extract
4   teaspoons turbinado sugar, divided

Combine first 3 ingredients. Cut in butter with a pastry blender until crumbly; add pecans and next 3 ingredients, stirring just until dry ingredients are moistened.

Turn dough out onto a lightly floured surface; knead 3 or 4 times. Divide dough in half; pat each portion into a 6-inch circle, and place on a lightly greased baking sheet. Sprinkle each circle with 2 teaspoons turbinado sugar. Cut each circle into 6 even wedges. (Do not separate wedges.)
Bake at 425° for 13 to 14 minutes or until golden. Let stand 5 minutes before separating wedges. Yield: 1 dozen.

Per scone: Calories 199 (40% from fat); Fat 8.9g (sat 3.6g, mono 3.4g, poly 1.4g); Protein 2.9g; Carb 27.3g; Fiber 1.1g; Chol 14mg; Iron 1.2mg; Sodium 308mg; Calc 85mg

Note: Freeze baked scones up to 1 month. Thaw in refrigerator 8 hours. Reheat at 350° for 10 minutes or until thoroughly heated.

Cut butter into dry ingredients until crumbly. ▶

Sprinkle dough with sugar. ▶

Cut each circle of dough into wedges. ▶

muffins

Muffin tins come in miniature, standard, and jumbo sizes. Standard muffin pans can vary in size (see muffin pans box, page 83). Our recipes were tested using standard 2½-inch muffin pans.

It's important to mix muffin batter using the proper technique. Combine dry ingredients and make a well in the center by using the back of a spoon. Combine liquid ingredients, and pour them into the well; stir just until dry ingredients are moistened. Spoon batter into greased muffins pans, and bake as directed.

Remove muffins from pans as soon as they're baked to keep condensation from forming and making them soggy on the bottom. The well-made muffin has a pebbly top and a rounded even shape. If over-mixed, muffins will be peaked and will have tunnels and a coarse, tough texture.

Muffins that call for beating with an electric mixer contain more sugar than the traditional muffin and have a resulting cakelike texture. This additional mixing works well in this case; however, don't use a mixer unless the recipe specifies using one.

family favorite • freeze it • make ahead
Blueberry-Streusel Muffins

prep: 18 min.   cook: 20 min.

Chock-full of plump berries and topped with a buttery oat crumble, these muffins make for a picture-perfect morning.

¼ cup slivered almonds
¼ cup firmly packed light brown sugar
3 tablespoons all-purpose flour, divided
3 tablespoons butter, cut into pieces
¼ cup uncooked regular oats
2 cups all-purpose flour
½ cup granulated sugar
2 teaspoons baking powder
¼ teaspoon baking soda
½ teaspoon salt
2 teaspoons grated lemon rind
¾ cup buttermilk
⅓ cup vegetable oil
1 large egg, lightly beaten
1½ cups fresh blueberries

Poppy Seed Muffins,
Blueberry-Streusel Muffins,
Gingerbread Muffins

Pulse almonds, brown sugar, 2 tablespoons flour, and butter 4 or 5 times in a food processor or until nuts are chopped and topping is crumbly. Stir in oats; set aside.
Combine 2 cups flour and next 5 ingredients in a large bowl; make a well in center of mixture.
Whisk together buttermilk, oil, and egg; add to flour mixture, stirring just until moistened.
Toss blueberries with remaining 1 tablespoon flour, and gently fold into batter.
Spoon batter into paper-lined, lightly greased muffin pans, filling three-fourths full; sprinkle batter evenly with crumble topping, gently pressing into batter.

Bake at 400° for 20 minutes or until lightly browned and muffins spring back when touched lightly in center. Remove to wire racks to cool. Yield: 14 muffins.

Per muffin: Calories 221 (41% from fat); Fat 10g (sat 2.5g, mono 3.8g, poly 2.8g); Protein 3.7g; Carb 30.3g; Fiber 1.3g; Chol 22mg; Iron 1.3mg; Sodium 161mg; Calc 41mg

Note: Freeze baked muffins up to 1 month.

for well-rounded muffins, a lumpy batter is desirable. Stir gently just until dry ingredients are moistened. A smooth batter is not essential here.

Gingerbread Muffins

prep: 10 min.   cook: 22 min.

1	cup shortening
1	cup sugar
1	cup molasses
3	large eggs
1	cup buttermilk
3	cups all-purpose flour
1	teaspoon baking soda
½	teaspoon salt
1½	tablespoons ground ginger
1	teaspoon ground cinnamon
½	teaspoon ground nutmeg

Beat shortening at medium speed with an electric mixer until fluffy; gradually add sugar, beating well.

Add molasses; beat until blended.

Add eggs, 1 at a time, beating until blended after each addition. Add buttermilk; beat until blended.

Combine flour and next 5 ingredients. Gradually add to buttermilk mixture; beat until blended.

Spoon into greased muffin pans, filling three-fourths full.

Bake at 350° for 20 to 22 minutes. Remove from pans immediately. Yield: 26 muffins.

Per muffin: Calories 204 (39% from fat); Fat 8.9g (sat 1.9g, mono 3.8g, poly 2.6g); Protein 2.6g; Carb 29g; Fiber 0.5g; Chol 25mg; Iron 1.5mg; Sodium 116mg; Calc 44mg

Poppy Seed Muffins

prep: 10 min.   cook: 18 min.

Butter and sour cream lend a luxurious texture to this speckled favorite.

1¾	cups all-purpose flour
1	teaspoon baking soda
½	teaspoon salt
½	cup granulated sugar
3	tablespoons poppy seeds
1	tablespoon grated lemon rind
1	cup sour cream
1	large egg, lightly beaten
⅓	cup butter, melted
2	teaspoons vanilla extract
½	cup powdered sugar
1	tablespoon lemon juice
½	teaspoon vanilla extract

Combine first 6 ingredients in a large bowl, and make a well in center of mixture. Combine sour cream and next 3 ingredients; add to dry ingredients, stirring just until moistened.

Spoon batter into greased muffin pans, filling two-thirds full.

Bake at 400° for 17 to 18 minutes or until lightly browned. Remove from pans immediately, and cool on wire racks.

Combine powdered sugar, lemon juice, and vanilla in a small bowl, stirring until smooth. Drizzle glaze over muffins. Return to wire rack until glaze is set. Yield: 1 dozen.

Per muffin: Calories 224 (43% from fat); Fat 10.6g (sat 6g, mono 2.8g, poly 1.1g); Protein 3.5g; Carb 28.9g; Fiber 0.8g; Chol 39mg; Iron 1.1mg; Sodium 255mg; Calc 60mg

Oat–Bran Muffins

prep: 9 min.   cook: 20 min.   other: 5 min.

These healthy muffins taste similar to an oatmeal cookie. They're full of oats and raisins, and good-for-you bran cereal.

¾	cup shreds of wheat bran cereal (we tested with Bran Buds)
¾	cup uncooked regular oats
1¼	cups milk
1	large egg
¼	cup vegetable oil
½	cup raisins
1¼	cups all-purpose flour
1	tablespoon baking powder
½	teaspoon salt
½	cup sugar

Combine first 3 ingredients in a bowl; let stand 5 minutes. Combine egg, oil, and raisins; stir into bran mixture.

Combine flour and remaining 3 ingredients in a large bowl, and make a well in center of mixture. Add bran mixture to dry ingredients, stirring just until moistened.

Spoon batter into greased muffin pans, filling three-fourths full.

Bake at 400° for 20 minutes or until golden. Remove from pans immediately. Yield: 1½ dozen.

Per muffin: Calories 129 (30% from fat); Fat 4.3g (sat 0.8g, mono 1.7g, poly 1.6g); Protein 2.7g; Carb 21.6g; Fiber 2.5g; Chol 13mg; Iron 1.4mg; Sodium 184mg; Calc 72mg

Peanut Butter Bran Muffins

prep: 18 min.   cook: 30 min.   other: 5 min.

Banana and peanut butter pair well in this high-fiber muffin. Try heating leftovers in the microwave for 15 seconds for a warm snack or dessert.

2	cups shreds of wheat bran cereal (we tested with All-Bran)
1¾	cups milk
1½	cups all-purpose flour
¾	cup sugar
1	tablespoon baking powder
¼	teaspoon salt
1	medium-size ripe banana, mashed
½	cup crunchy peanut butter
¼	cup vegetable oil
1	large egg
	Streusel Topping

Stir together cereal and milk; let stand 5 minutes.

Combine flour and next 3 ingredients in a large bowl; make a well in center of mixture. Stir banana and next 3 ingredients into cereal mixture; add to dry ingredients, stirring just until moistened.

Spoon into greased muffin pans, filling two-thirds full. Sprinkle Streusel Topping evenly over batter.

Bake at 350° for 25 to 30 minutes. Remove from pans immediately, and cool on wire racks. Yield: 1½ dozen.

Per muffin: Calories 253 (43% from fat); Fat 12g (sat 3.3g, mono 4.5g, poly 3g); Protein 5.7g; Carb 34.7g; Fiber 3.3g; Chol 21mg; Iron 2.3mg; Sodium 207mg; Calc 111mg

Streusel Topping

prep: 5 min.

½	cup all-purpose flour
½	cup firmly packed light brown sugar
¼	cup butter or margarine
2	tablespoons peanut butter

Combine flour and brown sugar. Cut butter and peanut butter into flour mixture with a pastry blender or fork until mixture resembles small peas. Yield: 1¼ cups.

Per tablespoon: Calories 62 (45% from fat); Fat 3.1g (sat 1.6g, mono 0.1g, poly 0.3g); Protein 0.8g; Carb 8.1g; Fiber 0.2g; Chol 6mg; Iron 0.3mg; Sodium 26mg; Calc 6mg

standard muffin pans can vary in size. The most common pans measure 2½ inches across the top; they hold ¼ cup batter when a recipe calls for filling cups three-fourths full. There are also standard pans that measure 3 inches across the top. These hold ⅓ cup batter at three-fourths full. Our recipes were tested using the 2½-inch standard pans. If you have the larger pans, your muffin yield may be slightly less, and muffins will be larger.

Muffin top pans produce shallower bread with a more predominant crusty top. If you use them with these recipes, baking times will be shorter and yields will be larger.

---

family favorite

Broccoli Cornbread Muffins

prep: 10 min.   cook: 20 min.   other: 3 min.

1   (8½-ounce) package corn muffin mix
1   (10-ounce) package frozen chopped broccoli, thawed
1   cup (4 ounces) shredded Cheddar cheese
1   small onion, chopped
2   large eggs
½   cup butter or margarine, melted

Combine first 4 ingredients in a large bowl; make a well in center of mixture.
Stir together eggs and butter, blending well; add to broccoli mixture, stirring just until dry ingredients are moistened.
Spoon batter into lightly greased miniature (1¾-inch) muffin pans, filling almost full.
Bake at 325° for 15 to 20 minutes or until golden. Let stand 2 to 3 minutes before removing from pans. Yield: 3 dozen mini muffins.

Per muffin: Calories 70 (60% from fat); Fat 4.7g (sat 2.6g, mono 1.5g, poly 0.3g); Protein 1.9g; Carb 5.3g; Fiber 0.7g; Chol 22mg; Iron 0.3mg; Sodium 118mg; Calc 34mg

---

family favorite

Ham-and-Cheddar Muffins

prep: 15 min.   cook: 23 min.

3   tablespoons butter or margarine
1   medium-size sweet onion, finely chopped
1½   cups all-purpose baking mix
2   cups (8 ounces) shredded Cheddar cheese, divided
½   cup milk
1   large egg
1   cup finely chopped cooked ham
Poppy seeds (optional)

Melt butter in a skillet over medium-high heat; add onion, and sauté 3 to 5 minutes or until tender.
Combine baking mix and half of cheese in a large bowl; make a well in center of mixture.
Stir together milk and egg, blending well; add to cheese mixture, stirring until moistened. Stir in onion and ham.
Spoon batter into lightly greased muffin pans, filling two-thirds full. Sprinkle with remaining 1 cup cheese. Sprinkle with poppy seeds, if desired.
Bake at 425° for 17 to 18 minutes or until golden. Let stand 2 to 3 minutes before removing from pans. Yield: 1 dozen.

Per muffin: Calories 201 (60% from fat); Fat 13.4g (sat 7.1g, mono 4.2g, poly 0.7g); Protein 9.4g; Carb 10.9g; Fiber 0.4g; Chol 53mg; Iron 0.9mg; Sodium 512mg; Calc 176mg

---

family favorite

Buttery Herb-Cheese Mini Muffins

prep: 10 min.   cook: 25 min.

The secret to these delectable bites is a garlic-and-herb cheese spread from the grocery store.

2   cups self-rising flour
1   cup butter, melted
1   (6.5-ounce) package buttery garlic-and-herb spreadable cheese, softened (we tested with Alouette Garlic et Herbes Gourmet Spreadable Cheese)
½   cup sour cream

Stir together all ingredients just until blended.
Spoon batter into lightly greased miniature (1¾-inch) muffin pans, filling full.

Bake at 350° for 25 minutes or until lightly browned. Remove from pans immediately. Yield: 2½ dozen.

Per mini muffin: Calories 112 (72% from fat); Fat 9g (sat 5.6g, mono 1.8g, poly 0.3g); Protein 1.3g; Carb 6.7g; Fiber 0.2g; Chol 26mg; Iron 0.4mg; Sodium 189mg; Calc 40mg

---

low calorie • quick

Parmesan Cheese Muffins

prep: 10 min.   cook: 18 min.

2   cups self-rising flour
¾   cup shredded Parmesan cheese
2   tablespoons sugar
1   cup milk
¼   cup vegetable oil
2   large eggs

Combine first 3 ingredients in a large bowl; make a well in center of mixture.
Whisk together milk, oil, and eggs until well blended. Add to flour mixture, and stir just until dry ingredients are moistened.
Spoon mixture into lightly greased muffin pans, filling two-thirds full.
Bake at 400° for 15 to 18 minutes or until golden. Remove from pans immediately. Yield: 1 dozen.

Per muffin: Calories 169 (42% from fat); Fat 7.9g (sat 2.1g, mono 2.9g, poly 2.3g); Protein 5.7g; Carb 18.7g; Fiber 0.6g; Chol 41mg; Iron 1.2mg; Sodium 369mg; Calc 160mg

---

muffin "musts"

• The less muffin batter is stirred, the better. Overstirring results in muffins that are tough with undesirable tunnels inside.
• Another common cause for tough muffins is too much flour. This is generally caused by "scooping" instead of "spooning." To measure flour accurately, stir it with a fork to aerate; then lightly spoon it into a dry measuring cup, leveling the top with a knife.
• If all the cups aren't used when filling the muffin pan with batter, pour water into the empty cups to keep the pan from buckling.
• Muffins are best when eaten the day they are made, but they freeze well, too. Cover them tightly, and freeze for up to one month.

quick bread loaves

Many of these sweet and savory loaves benefit from the same quick and light-handed mixing procedure as muffins. A small crack down the top center of a quick loaf is characteristic—not to worry.

Be sure to let nut breads cool completely before slicing them so they won't crumble. To cut them, use a sharp serrated-edged knife and a gentle sawing motion.

family favorite • for kids

Banana-Nut Bread

prep: 15 min.   cook: 1 hr., 5 min.
other: 10 min.

Yogurt adds an extra bit of moisture and tang to this banana bread. The recipe still tastes great if you don't have it on hand. Greasing and flouring only the bottom of the loafpan causes the bread to cling to the sides and climb higher.

2	cups self-rising flour
1	cup sugar
½	teaspoon baking soda
1	cup chopped pecans, toasted
½	cup butter or margarine, melted
3	very ripe bananas, mashed (1½ cups)
2	large eggs, lightly beaten
¼	cup plain low-fat yogurt (optional)
1	teaspoon vanilla extract

Grease and flour bottom of a 9- x 5-inch loafpan; set aside.

Combine first 4 ingredients in a large bowl; make a well in center of mixture. Stir together melted butter, mashed banana, eggs, yogurt, if desired, and vanilla; add to dry ingredients, and stir just until moistened. Pour batter into prepared pan.

Bake at 350° for 1 hour to 1 hour and 5 minutes or until a wooden pick inserted in center comes out clean. Cool in pan on a wire rack 10 minutes; remove from pan, and cool completely on wire rack. Yield: 1 loaf.

Per ½-inch slice: Calories 239 (45% from fat); Fat 11.9g (sat 4.3g, mono 4.8g, poly 2g); Protein 3.5g; Carb 31.1g; Fiber 1.9g; Chol 42mg; Iron 1.1mg; Sodium 290mg; Calc 70mg

Banana-Nut Muffins: Spoon batter into lightly greased muffin pans, filling three-fourths full. Bake at 350° for 19 to 21 minutes or until lightly browned. Remove from pans immediately. Let cool on wire racks. Yield: 20 muffins.

Banana-Nut Bread

◀ Make a well in dry ingredients.

◀ Add liquids to the well. Stir just until dry ingredients are moistened.

Overripe bananas lend maximum moisture and sweetness to banana-nut bread.

banana basics

The perfect bananas for this bread don't look so perfect. Let them get ripe, almost black, or very speckled. It takes a week to go from green to ready. To hasten ripening, place in a paper bag with a bruised apple. Once ripe, refrigerate or freeze unpeeled bananas in zip-top freezer bags; thaw before mashing. We tried to freeze mashed bananas, but once thawed, they were watery and not suitable to use.

family favorite

Cream Cheese-Banana-Nut Bread

prep: 15 min.   cook: 1 hr.   other: 40 min.

Warm banana bread is yummy, but to get perfect slices, let bread cool 30 minutes, and cut with a serrated or an electric knife.

¾ cup butter, softened
1 (8-ounce) package cream cheese, softened
2 cups sugar
2 large eggs
3 cups all-purpose flour
½ teaspoon baking powder
½ teaspoon baking soda
½ teaspoon salt
3 very ripe bananas, mashed (1½ cups)
1 cup chopped pecans, toasted
½ teaspoon vanilla extract

Beat butter and cream cheese at medium speed with an electric mixer until creamy. Gradually add sugar, beating until light and fluffy. Add eggs, 1 at a time, beating just until blended after each addition.
Combine flour and next 3 ingredients; gradually add to butter mixture, beating at low speed just until blended. Stir in mashed banana, pecans, and vanilla. Spoon batter into 2 greased and floured 8- x 4-inch loafpans.
Bake at 350° for 1 hour or until a long wooden pick inserted in center comes out clean and sides pull away from pan, shielding with aluminum foil the last 15 minutes to prevent browning, if necessary. Cool bread in pans on wire racks 10 minutes. Remove from pans, and cool 30 minutes on wire racks before slicing. Yield: 2 loaves.

Per ½-inch slice: Calories 221 (46% from fat); Fat 11.3g (sat 5.3g, mono 3.9g, poly 1.3g); Protein 3g; Carb 28.1g; Fiber 1.1g; Chol 37mg; Iron 0.9mg; Sodium 95mg; Calc 20mg

entertaining

Lemon Tea Bread

prep: 15 min.   cook: 1 hr.   other: 10 min.

½ cup butter, softened
1 cup granulated sugar
2 large eggs
1½ cups all-purpose flour
1 teaspoon baking powder
½ teaspoon salt
½ cup milk
2 tablespoons grated lemon rind, divided
1 cup powdered sugar
2 tablespoons fresh lemon juice
1 tablespoon granulated sugar

Beat softened butter at medium speed with an electric mixer until creamy. Gradually add 1 cup granulated sugar, beating until light and fluffy. Add eggs, 1 at a time, beating just until blended after each addition.
Stir together flour, baking powder, and salt; add to butter mixture alternately with milk, beating at low speed just until blended, beginning and ending with flour mixture. Stir in 1 tablespoon grated lemon rind. Spoon batter into a greased and floured 8- x 4-inch loafpan.
Bake at 350° for 1 hour or until a wooden pick inserted in center of bread comes out clean. Let cool in pan 10 minutes. Remove bread from pan, and cool completely on a wire rack.
Stir together powdered sugar and lemon juice until smooth; spoon over top of bread, letting excess drip down sides. Stir together remaining 1 tablespoon lemon rind and 1 tablespoon granulated sugar; sprinkle on top of bread. Yield: 1 (8-inch) loaf.

Per ½-inch slice: Calories 215 (32% from fat); Fat 7.7g (sat 4.5g, mono 2g, poly 0.4g); Protein 2.7g; Carb 34.8g; Fiber 0.5g; Chol 48mg; Iron 0.8mg; Sodium 178mg; Calc 38mg

family favorite • low cholesterol

Cranberry-Walnut Bread

prep: 15 min.   cook: 1 hr., 15 min.   other: 10 min.

Serve this jeweled nut bread for dessert or as a snack.

3 cups all-purpose flour
1¼ cups sugar
4 teaspoons baking powder
2 teaspoons salt
1½ cups milk
1 large egg, lightly beaten
½ cup canola oil
1 teaspoon vanilla extract
1½ cups chopped walnuts or pecans
¾ cup sweetened dried cranberries (we tested with Craisins)

Sift first 4 ingredients into a large bowl, and stir to combine. Add milk and next 3 ingredients, stirring just until moistened. Stir in nuts and cranberries. Pour into a greased and floured 9- x 5-inch loafpan.
Bake at 350° for 1 hour and 10 minutes to 1 hour and 15 minutes or until a long wooden pick inserted in center comes out clean. Cool in pan on a wire rack 10 minutes; remove from pan, and cool completely on wire rack. Yield: 1 loaf.

Per ½-inch slice: Calories 318 (43% from fat); Fat 15.3g (sat 1.5g, mono 6.2g, poly 6.4g); Protein 6.4g; Carb 40.9g; Fiber 1.8g; Chol 16mg; Iron 1.7mg; Sodium 427mg; Calc 107mg

Lemon Tea Bread

Whole Wheat Date–Nut Bread

prep: 15 min.   cook: 1 hr., 15 min.

Don't be surprised by the heavy weight of this hearty bread when you remove it from the pan. Even though the batter has no egg or oil, it still produces a moist and tender loaf.

2   cups whole wheat flour
1   cup all-purpose flour
1   cup chopped pecans, toasted
¾   cup chopped dates or raisins
½   cup sugar
1   teaspoon salt
1   teaspoon baking soda
1½ cups milk
½   cup molasses

Combine first 6 ingredients in a large bowl; make a well in center of mixture.

Dissolve baking soda in milk; stir in molasses. Add to flour mixture, stirring just until dry ingredients are moistened. Spoon into a greased and floured 9- x 5-inch loafpan.

Bake at 325° for 1 hour to 1 hour and 15 minutes or until a wooden pick inserted in center comes out clean. Remove from pan, and cool on a wire rack. Yield: 1 loaf.

Per ½-inch slice: Calories 221 (26% from fat); Fat 6.5g (sat 1g, mono 3.3g, poly 1.8g); Protein 4.5g; Carb 38.8g; Fiber 3.3g; Chol 2mg; Iron 1.7mg; Sodium 238mg; Calc 62mg

cornbread

Cornbread carries a loyal following in the South. Its crisp edge and slightly gritty texture make it a popular staple—all by itself, crumbled over chili, or smeared with butter and honey. And a well-seasoned cast-iron skillet is a must in its preparation.

Cornmeal comes stone-ground, steel-ground, self-rising, or as a mix. It's made from either white or yellow corn, and meal made from the two types of corn can be used interchangeably. Cornbread made with yellow meal tends to be slightly coarser.

Cornbread batter should be fairly thin and pourable. If it seems too thick, add a little more liquid. Pouring the batter into a very hot skillet with a dab of melted fat gives cornbread its crisp crust.

Super-Moist Cornbread

prep: 5 min.   cook: 25 min.

For the crispiest cornbread crust, remove cornbread from skillet to serve.

2   cups self-rising cornmeal
2   cups buttermilk
1   large egg
1   tablespoon sugar
⅓   cup butter

Stir together first 4 ingredients.
Melt butter in a 10-inch cast-iron skillet in a 425° oven 5 minutes. Tilt skillet to coat.

ironclad rules

Cast iron's ability to distribute heat evenly as well as to stand up to high temperatures makes it an admirable addition to any kitchen. Here's how to season it to perfection:

• To season new cast iron, scrub with steel wool soap pads; then wash with dish soap and hot water. Dry thoroughly. Spread a layer of vegetable shortening on the inside of pan, including the underside of the lid. Bake at 250° for 15 minutes. Remove from oven, and wipe out shortening with a paper towel. Bake for 2 more hours. Remove from oven, and cool to room temperature. Repeat coating with shortening and baking two or three times.
• Once your cast-iron cookware is seasoned, never use soap to clean it—and never put it in a dishwasher.
• Clean with a plastic scrubber or stiff brush under hot running water. Dry immediately, and rub with a thin coating of vegetable oil.
• If your skillet loses its seasoning, you can repeat the seasoning procedure—or just fry something in it.

Pour batter into buttered hot skillet.
Bake at 425° for 25 minutes or until golden. Remove cornbread immediately from skillet, and let cool. Yield: 10 servings.

Per serving: Calories 167 (42% from fat); Fat 7.8g (sat 4.4g, mono 2.1g, poly 0.7g); Protein 4.3g; Carb 20.8g; Fiber 1.6g; Chol 39mg; Iron 1.5mg; Sodium 406mg; Calc 149mg

Chile-Cheese Cornbread

prep: 10 min.   cook: 45 min.

This deluxe cornbread boasts corn, chiles, and cheese in the batter.

1   cup self-rising cornmeal
½   teaspoon baking soda
¼   teaspoon salt
1½ cups (6 ounces) shredded Cheddar cheese
½   cup chopped onion
1   (4.5 ounce) can chopped green chiles, drained
1   cup milk
3   tablespoons bacon drippings
1   teaspoon garlic powder
3   large eggs, lightly beaten
1   (7-ounce) can whole kernel corn, drained
1   (2-ounce) jar diced pimiento, drained

Combine first 3 ingredients in a large bowl; add Cheddar cheese and remaining ingredients, stirring just until dry ingredients are moistened. Spoon batter into a greased 10-inch cast-iron skillet.
Bake at 350° for 45 minutes or until golden. Yield: 10 servings.

Per serving: Calories 218 (52% from fat); Fat 12.6g (sat 6g, mono 4.1g, poly 0.9g); Protein 8.4g; Carb 16.4g; Fiber 1.6g; Chol 87mg; Iron 1.3mg; Sodium 552mg; Calc 182mg

a southern tradition

Cornbreads vary in flavor, texture, and the color of cornmeal used (white is traditional). Cornbread can be a sturdy, slightly salty round with a rich buttermilk tang like the traditional version offered, or sweet and crumbly with a cakelike texture (see Soufflé Cornbread, below). The latter gets its dainty, high-rising ways from flour and sugar, two hotly debated ingredients among cornbread purists.

test kitchen favorite
Soufflé Cornbread

prep: 17 min.   cook: 30 min.

The steps involved in preparing this cornbread are well worth it. It's so moist and delicious you won't need extra butter.

1   (14¾-ounce) can cream-style corn
6   tablespoons butter, softened
2   large eggs, separated
½   cup whipping cream
1½   cups yellow cornmeal
1   cup all-purpose flour
1   tablespoon baking powder
1¼   teaspoons salt
⅓   cup sugar
1   tablespoon shortening

Process corn in a blender until smooth, stopping to scrape down sides.
Beat butter and egg yolks in a large mixing bowl at medium speed with an electric mixer until smooth. Add pureed corn and whipping cream, stirring well. (Mixture will be lumpy.)
Combine cornmeal and next 4 ingredients; add to corn mixture, stirring until blended.
Heat shortening in a 9- or 10-inch cast-iron skillet in a 375° oven for 6 minutes.
Beat egg whites at high speed until stiff peaks form; gently fold into cornmeal batter.
Remove skillet from oven. Pour batter into hot skillet.
Bake at 375° for 25 to 30 minutes or until golden. Yield: 8 servings.

Per serving: Calories 380 (41% from fat); Fat 17.2g (sat 9.2g, mono 3.6g, poly 1.3g); Protein 6.4g; Carb 51.4g; Fiber 3g; Chol 95mg; Iron 2.4mg; Sodium 847mg; Calc 116mg

family favorite
Cracklin' Cornbread

prep: 10 min.   cook: 25 min.

Cracklings are crispy brown pieces of rendered pork fat. They lend a light texture and unmistakable Southern flavor to this bread. They're sold in small packages in specialty markets.

1½   cups cornmeal
¼   cup all-purpose flour
1   teaspoon baking soda
1   teaspoon salt
1   large egg, lightly beaten
2   cups buttermilk
1   cup cracklings

Combine first 4 ingredients in a large bowl; add beaten egg and buttermilk, stirring just until dry ingredients are moistened. Stir in cracklings.
Generously grease a 10-inch cast-iron skillet with shortening; place skillet in a 450° oven for 4 minutes or until hot. Remove from oven; pour batter into hot skillet.
Bake at 450° for 25 minutes or until golden. Yield: 10 servings.

Per serving: Calories 231 (56% from fat); Fat 14.3g (sat 4.7g, mono 5.8g, poly 1.6g); Protein 4.3g; Carb 20.9g; Fiber 1.6g; Chol 36mg; Iron 1.1mg; Sodium 421mg; Calc 61mg

Some Southern foods just wouldn't be the same cooked in anything except cast iron. Cornbread's one of them.

Corn Sticks

prep: 10 min.   cook: 20 min.

2   jalapeño peppers, seeded and chopped
2   garlic cloves, minced
⅓   cup vegetable oil
½   cup yellow cornmeal
½   cup all-purpose flour
2   teaspoons baking powder
¾   teaspoon salt
1   tablespoon sugar
1   tablespoon chopped fresh cilantro or
    1 teaspoon dried cilantro
1   large egg, lightly beaten
½   cup milk
Vegetable cooking spray

Cook jalapeño peppers and garlic in oil in a saucepan over medium heat, stirring constantly, until tender; set aside.
Combine cornmeal and next 5 ingredients; add jalapeño pepper mixture, egg, and milk, stirring until smooth.
Coat a cast-iron breadstick or corn stick pan with cooking spray; heat in a 425° oven 3 minutes or until hot. Remove pan from oven; spoon batter into pan.
Bake at 425° for 15 to 20 minutes or until lightly browned. Yield: 6 corn sticks.

Per corn stick: Calories 224 (58% from fat); Fat 14.4g (sat 2g, mono 5.9g, poly 5.6g); Protein 3.9g; Carb 20.7g; Fiber 1.3g; Chol 37mg; Iron 1.4mg; Sodium 629mg; Calc 162mg

Hush Puppies

prep: 10 min.   cook: 6 min. per batch
other: 10 min.

Beer makes this bread light and tangy.

1   cup self-rising white cornmeal mix (we
    tested with White Lily Self-Rising White
    Cornmeal Mix)
½   cup self-rising flour
½   cup diced onion
1   tablespoon sugar
1   large egg, lightly beaten
½   cup milk or beer
Vegetable oil

Combine first 4 ingredients in a large bowl. Add egg and milk to dry ingredients, stirring just until moistened. Let stand 10 minutes.
Pour oil to a depth of 2 inches into a Dutch oven; heat to 375°.

Drop batter by rounded tablespoonfuls into hot oil, and fry in batches 2 to 3 minutes on each side or until golden. Drain on a wire rack over paper towels; serve immediately. Yield: 1½ dozen.

Per hush puppy: Calories 68 (41% from fat); Fat 3.1g (sat 0.5g, mono 1.2g, poly 1.2g); Protein 1.5g; Carb 8.8g; Fiber 0.6g; Chol 12mg; Iron 0.6mg; Sodium 135mg; Calc 46mg

Note: Keep fried hush puppies warm in oven at 225° for up to 15 minutes.

test kitchen favorite
Mexican Hush Puppies

prep: 9 min.   cook: 3 min. per batch

Serve these hush puppies with fried fish. Leftovers freeze well. Reheat in a toaster oven.

2   cups self-rising cornmeal
1   cup self-rising flour
3   tablespoons sugar
3   large eggs, lightly beaten
½   cup milk
1   (14¾-ounce) can cream-style corn
1½ cups (6 ounces) shredded sharp
    Cheddar cheese
2   cups chopped onion
2   jalapeño peppers, seeded and chopped
2   teaspoons chili powder
Vegetable oil

Combine first 3 ingredients in a large bowl; make a well in center of mixture.
Combine eggs and next 6 ingredients in a bowl; add to dry ingredients, stirring just until moistened.
Pour oil to a depth of 2 inches into a Dutch oven; heat to 375°.
Drop batter by rounded tablespoonfuls into hot oil; fry hush puppies, a few at a time,

hush puppy history

So, how did hush puppies get their name? They were perhaps the original treat (aka bribe) for Fido. Legends tell how Southern fishermen and Civil War soldiers first made golden nuggets from scraps just to toss to barking and begging dogs with the command to "Hush, puppy."

3 minutes or until golden, turning once. Drain well on paper towels. Yield: 40 hush puppies.

Per hush puppy: Calories 95 (42% from fat); Fat 4.4g (sat 1.3g, mono 1.6g, poly 1.2g); Protein 2.8g; Carb 11.5g; Fiber 0.9g; Chol 21mg; Iron 0.6mg; Sodium 199mg; Calc 69mg

Creole Hush Puppies

prep: 10 min.   cook: 2 min. per batch

5   cups self-rising cornmeal
1   (14¾-ounce) can cream-style corn
1   (10-ounce) can diced tomatoes and
    green chiles
2   large eggs
2   cups buttermilk
3   medium onions, chopped
1   banana pepper, chopped
½   cup chopped green bell pepper
1   teaspoon Creole seasoning
Vegetable oil

Stir together first 9 ingredients just until moistened.
Pour oil to a depth of 2 inches into a Dutch oven; heat to 375°. Drop batter by teaspoonfuls into oil; fry 2 minutes or until golden, turning once. Yield: 6 dozen.

Per hush puppy: Calories 42 (15% from fat); Fat 0.7g (sat 0.2g, mono 0.1g, poly 0.2g); Protein 1.3g; Carb 8.1g; Fiber 0.8g; Chol 7mg; Iron 0.5mg; Sodium 145mg; Calc 33mg

low carb
Squash Fritters

prep: 10 min.   cook: 10 min.

2   medium-size yellow squash, grated
¼   cup diced onion
2   tablespoons diced green bell pepper
1   teaspoon brown sugar
1   teaspoon salt
1   tablespoon all-purpose flour
1   large egg, lightly beaten
2   teaspoons butter, melted
½   cup olive oil

Stir together first 8 ingredients.
Heat oil in a large heavy skillet. Drop mixture by tablespoonfuls into hot oil; fry in batches until golden, turning once. Drain on paper towels, and serve immediately. Yield: 6 servings.

Per serving: Calories 84 (74% from fat); Fat 6.9g (sat 1.6g, mono 2.7g, poly 2.2g); Protein 2.1g; Carb 4.6g; Fiber 0.9g; Chol 39mg; Iron 0.5mg; Sodium 410mg; Calc 17mg

Griddle Cakes

prep: 10 min.   cook: 5 min. per batch

Serve these little pancakes as appetizers or as an evening meal along with country ham or pork sausage.

1   cup white cornmeal
1   cup all-purpose flour
1   teaspoon baking soda
½   teaspoon salt
½   teaspoon baking powder
1   cup buttermilk
½   cup sour cream
1   large egg, lightly beaten
Honey or maple syrup

Combine first 5 ingredients in a large bowl.
Combine buttermilk, sour cream, and egg; add to dry ingredients, stirring just until moistened.
Pour about 3 tablespoons batter for each cake onto a hot, lightly greased griddle. Cook pancakes 3 minutes or until tops are covered with bubbles and edges look cooked; turn and cook 2 minutes. (Cakes should be golden brown.) Serve with honey or maple syrup. Yield: 1 dozen.

Per pancake: Calories 115 (23% from fat); Fat 3g (sat 1.5g, mono 0.9g, poly 0.3g); Protein 3.4g; Carb 18.4g; Fiber 1.1g; Chol 23mg; Iron 1.1mg; Sodium 255mg; Calc 51mg

taste of the south spoonbread

What could be more comforting and Southern than this freshly baked concoction—made from cornmeal, butter, milk, and eggs—so light, yet so rich and creamy that it requires a spoon? If you've never prepared spoonbread, you'll find that it's surprisingly easy; just be sure to start with plain cornmeal, not a mix which may contain baking soda. One bite and this soufflélike dish could make it become a new favorite. Serve it warm from the oven to keep it from becoming too dense. Spoonbread invites a host of accompaniments—our favorite being any braised meat smothered in gravy, especially when flavored with smoked bacon drippings. It's great for breakfast, lunch, or dinner. Also, try it warmed in the microwave with just a kiss of real butter and a crack of fresh black pepper.

Memmie's Spoonbread

prep: 15 min.   cook: 50 min.   other: 10 min.

3   cups boiling water
2   cups cornmeal (we tested with Quaker yellow cornmeal)
2   teaspoons salt
½   cup butter or margarine, cut into pieces
2   cups milk
4   large eggs, lightly beaten
1   tablespoon baking powder

Pour 3 cups boiling water gradually over cornmeal in a large bowl, stirring until smooth. Add salt and butter, stirring until well blended; let stand 10 minutes.
Gradually stir in milk and eggs. Stir in baking powder. Pour mixture into a lightly greased 13- x 9-inch baking dish.
Bake at 375° for 45 to 50 minutes or until lightly browned. Yield: 12 servings.

Per serving: Calories 201 (49% from fat); Fat 11g (sat 6.1g, mono 3g, poly 0.8g); Protein 5.4g; Carb 20.2g; Fiber 1.7g; Chol 95mg; Iron 1.4mg; Sodium 605mg; Calc 127mg

pancakes and waffles

With a few minutes' preparation and the right equipment, you can make pancakes and waffles from scratch. Before you begin cooking, lightly grease your griddle or waffle iron to prevent sticking. You can tell waffles are done when steam no longer comes from the sides of the waffle iron. Most waffle irons have a signal light to tell you when they're ready.

For pancakes, as soon as the top surface is full of bubbles and the edges begin to look cooked, they're ready to turn. The second side will take only a minute or two to brown. Serve pancakes and waffles immediately after cooking or keep them warm in a single layer in a warm oven. Try not to stack them or they'll get soggy.

Buttermilk Pancakes

prep: 10 min.   cook: 3 min. per batch

Buttermilk makes these pancakes fluffy. Add 1 cup chopped pecans to the batter for some crunch.

2   cups all-purpose flour
2½ teaspoons baking powder
1   teaspoon baking soda
¾   teaspoon salt
2   tablespoons sugar
2   large eggs, lightly beaten
2   cups buttermilk
¼   cup vegetable oil

Combine first 5 ingredients; stir well.
Combine eggs, buttermilk, and oil in a bowl; add to flour mixture, stirring just until dry ingredients are moistened.
Pour about ¼ cup batter for each pancake onto a hot, lightly greased griddle. Cook pancakes until tops are covered with bubbles and edges look cooked; turn and cook other side. (Store unused batter in a tightly covered container in refrigerator up to 1 week. If refrigerated batter is too thick, add milk or water to reach desired consistency.) Yield: 18 (4-inch) pancakes.

Per pancake: Calories 102 (35% from fat); Fat 4g (sat 0.7g, mono 1.6g, poly 1.5g); Protein 3g; Carb 13.5g; Fiber 0.4g; Chol 25mg; Iron 0.8mg; Sodium 271mg; Calc 74mg

Blueberry-Cream Cheese Pancakes

prep: 10 min.   cook: 20 min.

1   (3-ounce) package cream cheese, softened
2   large eggs
1¼ to 1½ cups milk
2   tablespoons butter or margarine, melted
1½ teaspoons vanilla extract
2   cups self-rising flour
2   tablespoons sugar
1½ cups blueberries

Beat cream cheese at medium speed with an electric mixer until creamy; add eggs, 1 at a time, beating after each addition. Add milk, butter, and vanilla, beating at low speed until blended.

Stir together flour and sugar in a large bowl; make a well in center of mixture.

Add milk mixture to dry ingredients, stirring just until dry ingredients are moistened. Stir in blueberries.

Pour about ¼ cup batter for each pancake onto a hot, lightly greased griddle. Cook pancakes until tops are covered with bubbles and edges look cooked; turn and cook other side. Serve with warm maple syrup or sifted powdered sugar. Yield: 21 (4-inch) pancakes.

Per pancake: Calories 94 (34% from fat); Fat 3.6g (sat 2g, mono 1g, poly 0.3g); Protein 2.7g; Carb 12.6g; Fiber 0.6g; Chol 29mg; Iron 0.7mg; Sodium 192mg; Calc 47mg

Banana Pancakes With Peanut Butter and Jelly Syrups

prep: 12 min.   cook: 4 min. per batch

The classic kids' sandwich flavors pair with bananas in these yummy pancakes.

2   cups all-purpose baking mix (we tested with Bisquick)
1   cup buttermilk
1   cup mashed ripe banana (2 bananas)
2   large eggs
½   teaspoon ground cinnamon
¾   cup maple syrup
¼   cup creamy peanut butter
1   cup strawberry syrup (we tested with Smucker's)

Whisk together first 5 ingredients in a large bowl just until dry ingredients are moistened. **Pour** about ¼ cup batter for each pancake onto a hot, lightly greased griddle. Cook pancakes until tops are covered with bubbles and edges look cooked; turn and cook other side.

Whisk together maple syrup and peanut butter in a small saucepan. Heat over low heat until peanut butter melts, whisking constantly. Serve pancakes with peanut butter mixture and strawberry syrup. Yield: 16 (4-inch) pancakes.

Per 2 pancakes and 2 tablespoons of each syrup: Calories 405 (23% from fat); Fat 10.3g (sat 2.6g, mono 4.4g, poly 1.7g); Protein 7g; Carb 74.3g; Fiber 1.8g; Chol 54mg; Iron 1.9mg; Sodium 477mg; Calc 114mg

Gingerbread Pancakes

prep: 6 min.   cook: 8 min.

Gingerbread works well as a pancake flavor, especially with this orange syrup.

1   cup all-purpose flour
2   teaspoons baking powder
½   teaspoon salt
1   tablespoon sugar
1   tablespoon ground cinnamon
½   teaspoon ground ginger
¼   teaspoon ground allspice
⅛   teaspoon ground nutmeg
⅛   teaspoon ground cloves
1   large egg, lightly beaten
1   cup buttermilk
3   tablespoons butter, melted
3   tablespoons vegetable oil
1   tablespoon molasses
    Orange Marmalade Syrup

Combine first 9 ingredients in a large bowl; make a well in center of mixture.

Combine egg and next 4 ingredients; add to dry ingredients, stirring just until moistened.

Spoon about ¼ cup batter for each pancake onto a hot, lightly greased griddle. Cook pancakes until tops are covered with bubbles and edges look cooked; turn and cook other side. Serve with Orange Marmalade Syrup. Yield: 10 pancakes.

Per 2 pancakes and ¼ cup syrup: Calories 485 (32% from fat); Fat 17.1g (sat 5.9g, mono 5.9g, poly 4.2g); Protein 5.7g; Carb 81g; Fiber 1.2g; Chol 62mg; Iron 2.4mg; Sodium 570mg; Calc 231mg

Orange Marmalade Syrup

⅔   cup maple syrup
⅔   cup orange marmalade

Combine ingredients in a small saucepan, and bring to a boil, stirring constantly. Yield: 1⅓ cups.

Per tablespoon: Calories 51 (0% from fat); Fat 0g (sat 0g, mono 0g, poly 0g); Protein 0g; Carb 13.3g; Fiber 0.1g; Chol 0mg; Iron 0.1mg; Sodium 7mg; Calc 11mg

Waffles

prep: 5 min.   cook: 15 min.

Top these crisp and light waffles with ice cream and fresh fruit for dessert.

2   cups all-purpose baking mix (we tested with Bisquick)
½   cup vegetable oil
2   large eggs
1   cup club soda

Stir together first 3 ingredients in a large bowl; add club soda, stirring until batter is blended.

Cook in a preheated, oiled waffle iron until golden. Yield: 10 (4-inch) waffles.

Per waffle: Calories 209 (60% from fat); Fat 13.9g (sat 2.5g, mono 6.7g, poly 5.3g); Protein 3g; Carb 14.9g; Fiber 0.4g; Chol 42mg; Iron 1mg; Sodium 321mg; Calc 43mg

Crispy Waffles

prep: 10 min.   cook: 24 min.   other: 8 hrs.

The beauty of this waffle recipe is that you can make the batter the night before and pop it in the fridge.

1   (¼-ounce) envelope active dry yeast
½   cup warm water (100° to 110°)
2   cups warm milk (100° to 110°)
½   cup butter or margarine, melted
1   teaspoon sugar
1   teaspoon salt
2   cups all-purpose flour
2   large eggs
¼   teaspoon baking soda

Combine yeast and ½ cup warm water in a glass measuring cup; let stand 5 minutes.

Combine yeast mixture, milk, and next 3 ingredients in a large bowl. Add flour, stirring until smooth. Cover and chill 8 hours. **Whisk** eggs and baking soda into batter. **Cook** in a preheated, oiled waffle iron until crisp. Yield: 16 (4-inch) waffles.

Per waffle: Calories 137 (49% from fat); Fat 7.5g (sat 4.4g, mono 2g, poly 0.4g); Protein 3.6g; Carb 13.8g; Fiber 0.5g; Chol 45mg; Iron 0.9mg; Sodium 227mg; Calc 42mg

family favorite • freeze it

Pecan Waffles

prep: 7 min.   cook: 8 min. per batch

These waffles are crisp and light. If the recipe makes more than you need, you can freeze leftovers and reheat in the toaster.

2½ cups all-purpose flour
4   teaspoons baking powder
¾   teaspoon salt
1½ tablespoons sugar
2   large eggs, beaten
2½ cups milk
¾   cup vegetable oil
½   cup finely chopped pecans

Combine first 4 ingredients in a large bowl. **Combine** eggs, milk, and oil; add to flour mixture, stirring with a wire whisk just until dry ingredients are moistened. Stir in pecans. **Cook** in a preheated, oiled waffle iron until golden. Yield: 22 (4-inch) waffles.

Per waffle: Calories 164 (61% from fat); Fat 11.2g (sat 1.7g, mono 4.8g, poly 4g); Protein 3.2g; Carb 13.6g; Fiber 0.6g; Chol 22mg; Iron 0.9mg; Sodium 186mg; Calc 87mg

for kids • low calorie

Belgian Waffles

prep: 18 min.   cook: 4 min. per batch

Belgian waffle irons have deep indentations and produce thick, cakelike waffles.

4   large eggs, separated
2   tablespoons sugar
3   tablespoons butter, melted
1   teaspoon vanilla extract
2   cups all-purpose flour
2   teaspoons baking powder
½   teaspoon salt
2   cups milk
Sweetened whipped cream
Sliced fresh strawberries

Belgian Waffles

Beat egg yolks and sugar at medium speed with an electric mixer until thick and pale. Add butter and vanilla, beating until blended. Combine flour, baking powder, and salt. Add flour mixture and milk to egg mixture, beating until smooth. Beat egg whites until stiff peaks form; fold into batter. **Cook** in a preheated, oiled Belgian waffle iron until golden. Serve with sweetened whipped cream and strawberries. Yield: 1 dozen.

Per waffle: Calories 160 (34% from fat); Fat 6.1g (sat 3.1g, mono 1.7g, poly 0.5g); Protein 5.6g; Carb 20.2g; Fiber 0.6g; Chol 82mg; Iron 1.4mg; Sodium 238mg; Calc 104mg

waffling with leftovers

Make a batch of waffles, and freeze the leftovers in a zip-top freezer bag up to one month. To reheat, toast them straight from the freezer. Top waffles with yogurt for a change.

Popovers bake into crusty, hollow shells that you can smear with butter or fill with anything from chicken salad to ice cream. It's the leavening power of eggs that causes popovers to rise high above their pans once in the oven. Resist the temptation to open the oven door as they bake, so they'll rise promptly. Some popover recipes instruct you to pierce the popovers near the end of baking and then continue baking briefly to further dry them.

Popovers

low calorie
Popovers

prep: 7 min.   cook: 40 min.

1	cup all-purpose flour
¼	teaspoon salt
1	cup milk
2	large eggs, lightly beaten

Combine all ingredients; beat at low speed with an electric mixer just until smooth.
Place a well-greased popover pan (see note following recipe if you don't have a popover pan) in a 425° oven for 3 minutes or until a drop of water sizzles when dropped in it. Remove pan from oven; fill half full with batter.
Bake at 425° for 15 minutes. Reduce heat to 350°, and bake 18 to 20 minutes. Turn oven off. Pierce each popover with the tip of a knife to release steam. Return popovers to oven 5 minutes to crisp. Serve hot. Yield: 6 popovers.

Per popover: Calories 129 (25% from fat); Fat 3.6g (sat 1.4g, mono 1g, poly 0.4g); Protein 5.6g; Carb 17.9g; Fiber 0.6g; Chol 75mg; Iron 1.3mg; Sodium 137mg; Calc 58mg

Note: To bake popovers in muffin pans, preheat regular muffin pans as directed in main recipe. Pour batter into hot muffin pans, filling half full. Bake at 425° for 15 minutes. Reduce heat to 350°; bake 18 to 20 minutes. Turn oven off, and proceed as directed in main recipe. Yield: 1 dozen.

Yorkshire Pudding: Don't grease or preheat muffin pans. Spoon 1 teaspoon beef drippings into each muffin pan; tilt to coat. Add batter; bake as for Popovers.

low calorie
Parmesan Popovers

prep: 15 min.   cook: 45 min.

2	tablespoons grated Parmesan cheese
1	cup all-purpose flour
1	cup milk
2	large eggs
2	egg whites
1	tablespoon butter or margarine, melted
2	teaspoons Worcestershire sauce
½	teaspoon salt
¼	teaspoon garlic powder

Sprinkle bottom and sides of well-greased popover pans or 6-ounce custard cups with Parmesan cheese.
Whisk together flour and remaining ingredients until blended. Spoon batter into pans, filling three-fourths full.
Bake on lowest oven rack at 450° for 15 minutes. Reduce heat to 350°, and bake 30 minutes or until golden. Serve immediately. Yield: 6 popovers.

Per popover: Calories 160 (34% from fat); Fat 6g (sat 2.8g, mono 1.6g, poly 0.5g); Protein 7.5g; Carb 18.6g; Fiber 0.6g; Chol 81mg; Iron 1.4mg; Sodium 310mg; Calc 80 mg

These crusty top hats have a hollow middle just waiting to be filled. Or split and dunk them in soup.

Pecan Popovers

prep: 10 min. cook: 40 min.

½ cup butter or margarine, softened
2 tablespoons honey
4 large eggs
2 cups milk
3 tablespoons butter or margarine, melted
2 cups all-purpose flour
½ teaspoon salt
⅓ cup finely chopped pecans

Stir together ½ cup butter and honey; cover and chill until ready to serve.
Whisk together eggs, milk, and melted butter in a large bowl; add flour and salt, stirring until smooth. Stir in pecans.
Spoon batter into 8 (6-ounce) greased custard cups, filling half full; place cups on a baking sheet.
Bake at 400° for 40 minutes or until firm. Immediately prick popovers with a fork to release steam. Serve immediately with honey butter. Yield: 8 popovers.

Per popover: Calories 380 (58% from fat); Fat 24.4g (sat 12.2g, mono 7.5g, poly 2.3g); Protein 9g; Carb 31.9g; Fiber 1.3g; Chol 153mg; Iron 2.1mg; Sodium 316mg; Calc 95mg

freeze it
Basic Crêpes

prep: 8 min. cook: 1½ min. per crêpe other: 1 hr.

4 large eggs
2 cups all-purpose flour
¼ cup butter or margarine, melted
1 cup cold water
1 cup cold milk
½ teaspoon salt

Process all ingredients in a blender or food processor until smooth, stopping to scrape down sides. Cover and chill 1 hour.
Place a lightly greased 8-inch nonstick skillet over medium heat until skillet is hot.
Pour 3 tablespoons batter into skillet; quickly tilt in all directions so batter covers bottom of skillet.

Cook 1 minute or until crêpe can be shaken loose from skillet. Turn crêpe, and cook about 30 seconds. Repeat procedure with remaining batter. Stack crêpes between sheets of wax paper. Yield: 2 dozen.

Per crêpe: Calories 73 (39% from fat); Fat 3.2g (sat 1.7g, mono 0.9g, poly 0.3g); Protein 2.5g; Carb 8.5g; Fiber 0.3g; Chol 41mg; Iron 0.6mg; Sodium 78mg; Calc 18mg

Make-Ahead Note: Prepare crêpes as directed, and freeze separated by wax paper up to one month in a zip-top freezer bag.

low calorie • low cholesterol • quick
Easy Herb Focaccia

prep: 7 min. cook: 14 min.

For a quick snack, drizzle leftovers with olive oil, and top with chopped tomato and feta or mozzarella cheese.

1 (13.8-ounce) can refrigerated pizza dough
3 tablespoons olive oil
½ teaspoon kosher salt
1 teaspoon freshly ground pepper
1 tablespoon chopped fresh oregano or 1 teaspoon dried oregano
1 tablespoon chopped fresh basil or 1 teaspoon dried basil
1½ teaspoons chopped fresh thyme or ½ teaspoon dried thyme

Shape dough into a ball, and pat or roll into an 11-inch circle onto a lightly greased jelly-roll pan or pizza pan.
Press handle of a wooden spoon into dough to make indentations at 1-inch intervals. Drizzle with oil; sprinkle with salt and remaining ingredients.
Bake at 375° for 14 minutes or until lightly browned. Cut into wedges. Yield: 8 servings.

Per serving: Calories 175 (35% from fat); Fat 6.8g (sat 0.7g, mono 3.7g, poly 0.5g); Protein 4.4g; Carb 23.5g; Fiber 0.8g; Chol 0mg; Iron 1.4mg; Sodium 446mg; Calc 5mg

Mama's Mini-Cinnis

prep: 10 min. cook: 18 min. other: 10 min.

This simple-to-prepare recipe doubles easily for a crowd.

2 (8-ounce) cans refrigerated crescent rolls
6 tablespoons butter or margarine, softened
⅓ cup firmly packed light brown sugar
¼ cup chopped pecans
1 tablespoon granulated sugar
1 teaspoon ground cinnamon
⅔ cup powdered sugar
1 tablespoon milk or half-and-half
¼ teaspoon almond or vanilla extract
⅛ teaspoon salt

Unroll crescent rolls, and separate each dough portion along center perforation to form 4 rectangles; press diagonal perforations to seal.
Stir together butter and next 4 ingredients; spread evenly over 1 side of each rectangle. Roll up, jelly-roll fashion, starting at long end. Gently cut each log into 6 (1-inch-thick) slices, using a serrated knife. Place rolls, ¼ inch apart, into 2 greased (8-inch) cakepans.
Bake at 375° for 15 to 18 minutes or until golden. Cool 5 to 10 minutes.
Stir together powdered sugar and remaining 3 ingredients. Drizzle over warm rolls. Yield: 2 dozen.

Per roll: Calories 136 (52% from fat); Fat 7.9g (sat 2.9g, mono 1.3g, poly 0.4g); Protein 1.5g; Carb 14.5g; Fiber 0.2g; Chol 8mg; Iron 0.6mg; Sodium 182mg; Calc 6mg

Note: To make slicing easier, place unbaked rolls on a baking sheet, and freeze 10 minutes.

Parmesan Cheese Breadsticks

prep: 15 min.   cook: 10 min.

½   cup freshly grated Parmesan cheese
¼   teaspoon paprika
⅛   teaspoon ground cumin
1   (11-ounce) can refrigerated breadsticks
3   tablespoons butter, melted

Combine first 3 ingredients in a shallow dish. **Unroll** breadstick dough, and separate into 12 strips at perforations. Gently pull each strip to a length of 12 inches. Brush both sides of each strip with butter; dredge in cheese mixture. Twist each strip, and place 2 inches apart on greased baking sheets. **Bake** at 400° for 8 to 10 minutes or until browned. Serve warm or at room temperature. Yield: 1 dozen.

Per breadstick: Calories 113 (41% from fat); Fat 5.1g (sat 2.4g, mono 1g, poly 0.2g); Protein 3.3g; Carb 13g; Fiber 0.4g; Chol 11mg; Iron 0.8mg; Sodium 264mg; Calc 38mg

family favorite • for kids • quick

Monkey Bread Bites

prep: 10 min.   cook: 21 min.

This ooey, gooey breakfast treat is baked in individual muffin cups to keep cleanup simple. Find extra-large foil muffin cups on the baking aisle or see option below.

¼   cup granulated sugar
1   tablespoon ground cinnamon
1   (12-ounce) can refrigerated buttermilk biscuits (we tested with Pillsbury Golden Layer Buttermilk Biscuits)
1   (6-ounce) can refrigerated buttermilk biscuits
½   cup butter or margarine
½   cup firmly packed light brown sugar
1   teaspoon vanilla extract
½   cup chopped pecans, toasted
12   extra-large foil muffin cups*

Combine granulated sugar and cinnamon in a large bowl. Cut biscuits into fourths, and add to sugar mixture; toss to coat. Set aside. **Melt** butter in a small saucepan over medium heat. Add brown sugar; cook 3 minutes, stirring until sugar dissolves. Remove from heat; stir in vanilla and pecans.

Monkey Bread Bites

Using extra-large foil muffin cups puts a big serving on everyone's plate.

Arrange 5 coated biscuit pieces in each greased extra-large foil muffin cup; place in a muffin pan. Repeat procedure with remaining biscuit pieces. Sprinkle evenly with remaining cinnamon-sugar mixture. Drizzle evenly with pecan syrup. **Bake** at 400° for 18 minutes or until browned. Yield: 1 dozen.

Per bite: Calories 282 (52% from fat); Fat 16.4g (sat 6.4g, mono 6.7g, poly 1.5g); Protein 3.1g; Carb 31.8g; Fiber 0.8g; Chol 20mg; Iron 1.4mg; Sodium 508mg; Calc 21mg

*You can use standard-size paper muffin liners. Place 4 coated biscuit pieces in each

greased paper liner. Bake at 400° for 15 minutes. Yield: 15 servings.

Monkey Bread Loaf: Prepare biscuits and pecan syrup as directed. Arrange biscuit pieces in a lightly greased 9- x 5-inch loaf-pan. Sprinkle biscuits with remaining cinnamon-sugar mixture, and drizzle with pecan syrup. Bake at 375° for 37 to 40 minutes or until golden and a wooden pick inserted in center of bread loaf comes out clean. Invert bread loaf onto a large plate; invert again onto a serving platter.

versatile dough

Use this basic recipe to make any number of different breads. The dough is quick and easy to work with, requires little kneading, and stores in the refrigerator up to four days. First prepare the dough; then cover and chill it. Next, use part or all of the dough to shape the type of bread you desire.

Basic Yeast Dough

prep: 10 min.   cook: varies with recipe
other: 1 hr. to 4 days

1	(¼-ounce) envelope active dry yeast
1	cup warm water (100° to 110°)
3	tablespoons sugar
2	tablespoons shortening
1	large egg
½	teaspoon salt
3	to 3½ cups all-purpose flour

Combine yeast and warm water in a 1-cup liquid measuring cup; let stand 5 minutes.
Combine yeast mixture, sugar, shortening, egg, salt, and half of flour in a large mixing bowl; beat at low speed with an electric mixer until blended. Gradually stir in enough remaining flour to make a soft dough.

Place dough in a well-greased bowl, turning to grease top. Cover and let rise in a warm place (85°), free from drafts, 1 hour or until doubled in bulk, or cover and store in refrigerator up to 4 days. (If chilled, let dough return to room temperature before proceeding.)

Punch dough down; turn out onto a lightly floured surface, and knead 8 to 10 times. Shape as desired (see options below) and bake at 400° for 10 to 12 minutes or until golden. Yield: 2 dozen.

Per serving: Calories 76 (17% from fat); Fat 1.4g (sat 0.3g, mono 0.6g, poly 0.4g); Protein 2g; Carb 13.6g; Fiber 0.5g; Chol 9mg; Iron 0.8mg; Sodium 52mg; Calc 4mg

shape your own rolls

Try our basic yeast roll recipe or get familiar with store-bought roll dough and use it to create your own butter-rich irresistible dinner rolls. Try one of the shapes below; they adapt easily to most any yeast roll recipe; just make sure the recipe is a fairly stiff dough. If dough is too soft, your rolls won't hold their shape after rising and baking. After rolls have risen, gently brush them with either of the following at right:

Egg wash. This is simply an egg beaten with 1 tablespoon water. It'll make rolls shiny and give them a rich golden top. Or egg white beaten with water can be used to hold toppings like poppy seeds, sesame seeds, or caraway seeds in place during baking.

Melted butter. It's often brushed on rolls before baking, and you can add more butter after baking for extra flavor and shine.

▲ **Fan Tans:** Roll dough into a large rectangle about ¼ inch thick. Spread ¼ cup softened butter over dough. Cut dough lengthwise into 1-inch strips. Stack 5 or 6 strips, buttered side up, on top of one another. Cut each stack into 1-inch sections. Place each stacked section, cut side down, into lightly greased muffin pans. Cover and let rise until doubled in bulk. Bake.

▲ **Parker House Rolls:** Roll dough to ¼-inch thickness; cut with a 2½-inch round cutter. Brush tops lightly with melted butter. Make an off-center crease in each round, using the dull edge of a knife. Fold each round along crease with larger half on top. Place folded rolls on lightly greased baking sheets. Cover and let rise until doubled in bulk. Brush again with melted butter. Bake.

▲ **Crescents:** Roll dough into a 12-inch circle (about ¼ inch thick) on a lightly floured surface. (Reserve excess dough for other uses.) Spread softened butter over dough. Cut into 8 to 12 wedges; roll each wedge tightly, beginning at wide end. Seal points, and place rolls, point side down, on a greased baking sheet, curving into a half-moon shape. Cover and let rise until doubled in bulk. Bake.

▲ **Cloverleaf Rolls (pictured on page 75):** Lightly grease muffin pans. Shape dough into 1-inch balls; place 3 balls in each muffin cup. Cover and let rise in a warm place (85°), free from drafts, 40 minutes or until doubled in bulk. Bake. Brush rolls with ¼ cup melted butter.

sourdough bread

Sourdough bread is centuries old. Ancient Egyptians reportedly combined flour and water, and set the mixture outside where it captured wild yeast spores from the air. The mixture was the ideal environment for the wild yeast to grow. The mixture fermented naturally, leavening the bread and adding the characteristic tang. This was the beginning of what we call sourdough bread.

With commercial yeast so readily available, we no longer depend on a sourdough starter for leavening, but still love it for its distinctive flavor, chewy texture, and the novelty of its fermentation process. As sourdough starter ages, its flavor matures, imparting more sourdough flavor each time it's used.

To make this bread, follow the recipe carefully. Let the starter stand in a warm place for 72 hours, so that it will bubble up and ferment. Stir it two or three times a day; then chill it. The mixture will separate; that's okay. Just stir once a day.

Use the starter at least once every 14 days. Each time that you remove a cup, replenish or "feed" it with Starter Food as directed in the recipe to follow. This maintains the volume and nourishes the yeast. If the starter sits too long without new starter food, it will become overly sour and will lose its leavening quality. If you don't use it within 14 days, pour off one cup of starter, and feed the remaining part as if you had used it. If properly cared for, starter should last indefinitely.

sourdough starter tips

• Mix and store the starter in glass, stoneware, or plastic. Metal can cause a chemical reaction with the starter.
• Place the starter in a bowl large enough to allow it to double in volume as it ferments.
• Never cover the container too tightly. The yeast needs air to live and the gas from the fermentation process needs to escape. Punch a small hole in a plastic wrap cover or leave the lid ajar.
• If a clear liquid forms on top of the mixture, just stir it back in.
• Allow the starter to come to room temperature before using it.

Sourdough bread is prized for its wild tang and chewy texture.

Sourdough Starter

prep: 10 min.   other: 3 days, 1 hr.

Sourdough starter will last indefinitely if you keep "feeding" it with equal amounts of flour and water as well as a tiny bit of sugar.

1   (¼-ounce) envelope active dry yeast
½   cup warm water (100° to 110°)
2   cups all-purpose flour
3   tablespoons sugar
1   teaspoon salt
2   cups warm water (100° to 110°)
Starter Food

Combine yeast and ½ cup warm water in a 1-cup liquid measuring cup; let stand 5 minutes.
Combine flour, sugar, and salt in a medium-size nonmetal bowl, and stir well. Gradually stir in 2 cups warm water. Add yeast mixture, and mix well.
Cover starter loosely with plastic wrap or cheesecloth; let stand in a warm place (85°) 72 hours, stirring 2 or 3 times daily. Place fermented mixture in refrigerator, and stir once a day. Use within 11 days.
To use, remove sourdough starter from refrigerator; let stand at room temperature at least 1 hour.
Stir starter well, and measure amount of starter needed. Replenish remaining starter with Starter Food, and return to refrigerator; use starter within 2 to 14 days, stirring daily. When Sourdough Starter is used again, repeat procedure for using starter and replenishing with Starter Food. Yield: 3 cups.

Starter Food

1   cup all-purpose flour
1   cup water
1   teaspoon sugar

Stir all ingredients into remaining Sourdough Starter.

low calorie • low cholesterol • low fat
Country Crust Sourdough

prep: 25 min.   cook: 35 min.
other: 2 hrs., 30 min.

2   (¼-ounce) envelopes active dry yeast
1¼   cups warm water (100° to 110°)
1   cup Sourdough Starter (at room temperature) (recipe at left)
¼   cup vegetable oil
¼   cup sugar
2   teaspoons salt
2   large eggs, beaten
5½   to 6 cups unbleached all-purpose flour
Vegetable oil
Butter or margarine, melted

Combine yeast and warm water in a 2-cup liquid measuring cup; let stand 5 minutes.
Combine yeast mixture, Sourdough Starter, ¼ cup oil, sugar, salt, eggs, and 3 cups flour in a nonmetal bowl. Gradually stir in enough remaining flour to make a soft dough.
Turn dough out onto a floured surface, and knead until smooth and elastic (8 to 10 minutes). Place in a well-greased bowl, turning to grease top. Cover and let rise in a warm place, (85°), free from drafts, 1 to 1½ hours or until doubled in bulk.
Punch dough down, and divide in half; place on a floured surface. Roll each half into an 18- x 9-inch rectangle. Tightly roll up dough, starting at narrow side; pinch seam and ends together to seal. Place loaves, seam side down, in 2 greased 9- x 5-inch loafpans. Brush tops with oil. Cover and let rise in a warm place, free from drafts, about 1 hour or until doubled in bulk.
Bake at 375° for 30 to 35 minutes or until loaves sound hollow when tapped. Remove loaves from pans; brush with butter. Yield: 2 loaves.

Per ½-inch slice: Calories 117 (23% from fat); Fat 3g (sat 0.6g, mono 1.2g, poly 1g); Protein 3g; Carb 19.1g; Fiber 0.7g; Chol 14mg; Iron 1.3mg; Sodium 177mg; Calc 3mg

rolls

low calorie • low cholesterol

Refrigerator Yeast Rolls

prep: 18 min.   cook: 14 min.
other: 8 hrs., 50 min.

You also know these as Parker House rolls named after the hotel in Boston credited for their creation.

1   (¼-ounce) envelope active dry yeast
2   cups warm water (100° to 110°)
6   cups bread flour
½   cup sugar
2   teaspoons salt
½   cup shortening
2   large eggs, lightly beaten
½   cup butter or margarine, melted

Stir together yeast and warm water in a medium bowl; let stand 5 minutes.
Stir together flour, sugar, and salt in a large bowl. Cut shortening into flour mixture with a pastry blender until crumbly; stir in yeast mixture and eggs just until blended. (Do not overmix.) Cover and chill 8 hours.
Roll dough to ¼-inch thickness on a well-floured surface (dough will be soft); cut with a 2½-inch round cutter.
Brush rounds evenly with butter. Make a crease across each round with the dull edge of a knife; fold in half. Gently press edges to seal. Place rolls on a greased 15- x 10-inch jelly-roll pan with sides touching. Cover and let rise in a warm place (85°), free from drafts, 45 minutes or until doubled in bulk.
Bake at 400° for 14 minutes or until golden. Brush tops with remaining butter. Yield: 4½ dozen.

Per roll: Calories 87 (39% from fat); Fat 3.8g (sat 1.5g, mono 1.4g, poly 0.7g); Protein 2.1g; Carb 11.9g; Fiber 0.4g; Chol 12mg; Iron 0.7mg; Sodium 101mg; Calc 2mg

Refrigerator Yeast Rolls

▲ Cut rolls with a 2½-inch round cutter.

▲ Brush cut rounds with melted butter.

▲ Make a crease across each round with dull edge of a knife.

Few things in the culinary kingdom compare to the aroma and freshness of homemade bread.

freeze it
Sour Cream Yeast Rolls

prep: 45 min.   cook: 12 min.   other: 9 hrs.

The attractive trio of buttery rolls fit neatly into muffin cups for baking. Freeze baked rolls up to one month. To reheat, wrap frozen rolls in aluminum foil, and bake at 400° for 15 minutes.

½   cup sour cream
¼   cup butter or margarine
¼   cup sugar
½   teaspoon salt
1   (¼-ounce) envelope active dry yeast
¼   cup warm water (100° to 110°)
1   large egg, beaten
2   cups all-purpose flour
Melted butter

Cook first 4 ingredients in a saucepan over low heat, stirring occasionally, until butter melts. Cool mixture to 100° to 110°.
Dissolve yeast in ¼ cup warm water in a large bowl; let stand 5 minutes.
Stir in sour cream mixture and egg. Gradually add flour to yeast mixture, mixing well. (Dough will be wet.) Cover and chill 8 hours.
Punch dough down. Shape into 36 (1-inch) balls; place 3 balls in each lightly greased muffin cup. Cover and let rise in a warm place (85°), free from drafts, 1 hour or until doubled in bulk.
Bake at 375° for 10 to 12 minutes or until golden. Brush with melted butter. Yield: 1 dozen.

Per roll: Calories 164 (42% from fat); Fat 7.6g (sat 4.4g, mono 2g, poly 0.4g); Protein 3.3g; Carb 20.8g; Fiber 0.7g; Chol 34mg; Iron 1.2mg; Sodium 142mg; Calc 18mg

freeze it • low calorie • low fat
Butter Rolls

prep: 15 min.   cook: 20 min.
other: 2 hrs., 5 min.

Rolls can also be prepared with a heavy-duty mixer instead of a food processor, if desired.

1   (¼-ounce) envelope active dry yeast
¼   cup warm water (100° to 110°)
2½   to 3 cups all-purpose flour, divided
¼   cup sugar
1¼   teaspoons salt
2   large eggs
¼   cup milk
¼   cup butter or margarine, softened
1   tablespoon water
Sesame or poppy seeds

Stir together yeast and ¼ cup water in a 1-cup liquid measuring cup; let stand 5 minutes.
Pulse 1 cup flour, sugar, and salt in a food processor until blended. Add yeast mixture, 1 egg, and milk; pulse until blended. (Pulsing prevents mixture from overheating, which would kill yeast.)
Add butter, 1 tablespoon at a time, pulsing until combined. Gradually add enough remaining flour until dough is no longer sticky. (Dough should be smooth.)
Place dough in a well-greased bowl, turning to grease top.
Cover and let rise in a warm place (85°), free from drafts, 1 hour or until doubled in bulk. Punch dough down, and divide into fourths; shape each portion into 6 (1-inch) balls. Place in a lightly greased 13- x 9-inch pan. Cover and let rise in a warm place (85°), free from drafts, 1 hour.
Stir together remaining egg and 1 tablespoon water; brush over rolls, and sprinkle with sesame seeds.
Bake at 375° for 15 to 20 minutes or until golden. Freeze up to 3 months, if desired. Yield: 2 dozen.

Per roll: Calories 83 (30% from fat); Fat 2.8g (sat 1.4g, mono 0.8g, poly 0.3g); Protein 2.2g; Carb 12.4g; Fiber 0.5g; Chol 23mg; Iron 0.8mg; Sodium 142mg; Calc 12mg

low calorie • low cholesterol • low fat
Whole Grain Pan Rolls

prep: 30 min.   cook: 20 min.   other: 1 hr.

1   cup water
¼   cup honey
¼   cup butter or margarine
¾   cup whole wheat flour
½   cup uncooked regular oats
2   (¼-ounce) envelopes active dry yeast
1   teaspoon salt
1   large egg
2¼   to 2½ cups all-purpose flour

Combine water, honey, and butter in a small saucepan; heat until butter melts. Remove from heat, and cool to 120°.
Combine wheat flour, oats, yeast, and salt in a mixing bowl; stir well. Gradually add hot liquid mixture; beat at low speed with an electric mixer 1 minute. Add egg; beat 2 minutes at medium speed. Gradually add enough all-purpose flour to make a soft dough.
Turn dough out onto a heavily floured surface; knead until smooth and elastic (about 8 minutes).
Shape into 24 balls; place in a lightly greased 13- x 9-inch pan. Cover and let rise in a warm place (85°), free from drafts, 1 hour or until doubled in bulk.
Bake at 375° for 20 minutes or until lightly browned. Yield: 2 dozen.

Per roll: Calories 97 (23% from fat); Fat 2.5g (sat 1.3g, mono 0.6g, poly 0.2g); Protein 2.6g; Carb 16.4g; Fiber 1.1g; Chol 14mg; Iron 0.9mg; Sodium 114mg; Calc 7mg

low cholesterol • low fat
Bolillos

prep: 25 min.   cook: 10 min.   other: 45 min.

Bolillos are crusty Mexican rolls made in a torpedo shape.

2   (¼-ounce) envelopes active dry yeast
1   cup warm water (100° to 110°)
2   tablespoons sugar
3½   cups bread flour
2   tablespoons shortening
2   teaspoons salt

Stir together first 3 ingredients in a 2-cup liquid measuring cup; let yeast mixture stand 5 minutes.

Stir together flour, shortening, and salt in a mixing bowl of a heavy-duty stand mixer. Add yeast mixture, and beat at medium speed, using dough hook attachment, 6 minutes.

Turn dough out onto a lightly floured surface, and divide into 12 equal portions. Knead each portion 3 times. Shape each portion into a 6-inch log, and place on 2 lightly greased baking sheets (6 loaves per baking sheet).

Cover dough, and let rise in a warm place (85°), free from drafts, 40 minutes (dough will not double in bulk). Cut a shallow slit, lengthwise, in top of each loaf.

Bake at 425° for 10 minutes or until golden. Cool on baking sheets on wire racks. Yield: 1 dozen.

Per roll: Calories 178 (15% from fat); Fat 3g (sat 0.5g, mono 1g, poly 1g); Protein 5.3g; Carb 32.1g; Fiber 1.2g; Chol 0mg; Iron 2mg; Sodium 389mg; Calc 8mg

---

low cholesterol • low fat

Lemon-Orange Rolls

prep: 20 min.   cook: 10 min.   other: 20 min.

If you don't have four miniature muffin pans, you can let these little rolls rise and bake in batches. Just be sure to keep extra dough in the refrigerator until you're ready to fill the pans again.

1   (16-ounce) package hot roll mix (we tested with Pillsbury Hot Roll Mix)
¼   cup butter, softened and divided
⅔   cup granulated sugar
2   tablespoons grated orange rind
1   tablespoon grated lemon rind
2   cups powdered sugar
¼   cup orange juice

Prepare hot roll dough according to package directions.

Divide dough into 2 equal portions. Roll 1 portion of dough into a 12- x 8-inch rectangle on a lightly floured surface. Spread with 2 tablespoons butter.

Stir together granulated sugar and grated rinds; sprinkle half of sugar mixture evenly over butter on rectangle. Roll up rectangle, jelly-roll fashion, starting at a long side. Repeat procedure with remaining half of dough, 2 tablespoons butter, and remaining half of sugar mixture.

Cut each roll into ½-inch-thick slices, and place in lightly greased miniature muffin pans. Cover and let rise in a warm place (85°), free from drafts, 20 minutes.

Bake at 375° for 8 to 10 minutes or until golden. Remove from pans, and place on wire racks.

Stir together powdered sugar and orange juice until smooth; spoon evenly over tops of rolls. Yield: 4 dozen.

Per roll: Calories 76 (17% from fat); Fat 1.4g (sat 0.6g, mono 0.3g, poly 0g); Protein 1g; Carb 14.8g; Fiber 0.3g; Chol 2.5mg; Iron 0.5mg; Sodium 70mg; Calc 1mg.

---

low calorie • test kitchen favorite

Homemade Butter Rolls

prep: 20 min.   cook: 10 min.   other: 10 hrs.

Crescent rolls are fun to shape. Get the kids involved.

2   (¼-ounce) envelopes active dry yeast
1   cup sugar, divided
2   cups warm water (100° to 110°)
1   cup butter or margarine, melted
6   large eggs, lightly beaten
1½ teaspoons salt
8½ to 9½ cups all-purpose flour

Stir together yeast, 2 tablespoons sugar, and 2 cups warm water in a 4-cup glass measuring cup; let stand 5 minutes.

Stir together yeast mixture, butter, and remaining sugar in a large bowl; stir in eggs and salt. Gradually stir in enough flour to make a soft dough. Cover and chill 8 hours.

Divide dough into 4 equal portions. Turn each portion out on a lightly floured surface, and roll into a 12-inch circle. Cut each circle into 12 wedges. Roll up each wedge, starting at wide end; place on greased baking sheets. (Rolls may be frozen at this point.) Cover and let rise in a warm place (85°), free from drafts, 2 hours or until doubled in bulk.

Bake at 400° for 10 minutes or until golden. Yield: 4 dozen.

Per roll: Calories 143 (30% from fat); Fat 4.7g (sat 2.6g, mono 1.3g, poly 0.3g); Protein 3.3g; Carb 21.7g; Fiber 0.7g; Chol 37mg; Iron 1.2mg; Sodium 109mg; Calc 8mg

Note: If unbaked rolls are frozen, place on ungreased baking sheets. Cover and let rise in a warm place, free from drafts, 2 hours or until doubled in bulk. Bake as directed.

Honey Angel Biscuits

prep: 20 min.   cook: 12 min. per batch
other: 5 min.

Honey butter will have you coming back for seconds of these biscuits. Serve them for lunch with chicken salad.

1   (¼-ounce) envelope active dry yeast
2   tablespoons warm water (100° to 110°)
5   cups all-purpose flour
1   tablespoon baking powder
1   teaspoon baking soda
2   teaspoons salt
1   cup shortening
2   cups buttermilk
3   tablespoons honey
Honey Butter

Combine yeast and 2 tablespoons warm water in a 1-cup liquid measuring cup; let stand 5 minutes.

Combine flour, baking powder, baking soda, and salt in a large bowl; cut in shortening with a pastry blender until mixture is crumbly.

Combine yeast mixture, buttermilk, and honey; add to dry ingredients, stirring just until dry ingredients are moistened.

Turn dough out onto a lightly floured surface, and knead 1 minute. Roll dough to ½-inch thickness. Cut with a 2-inch round cutter, and place on ungreased baking sheets.

Bake at 400° for 10 to 12 minutes or until golden. Serve with Honey Butter. Yield: 40 biscuits.

Per biscuit and 1 teaspoon butter: Calories 157 (53% from fat); Fat 9.2g (sat 3.5g, mono 3.3g, poly 1.8g); Protein 2.2g; Carb 17g; Fiber 0.5g; Chol 11mg; Iron 0.8mg; Sodium 200mg; Calc 25mg

---

Honey Butter

prep: 5 min.

½   cup butter or margarine, softened
¼   cup honey

Stir together butter and honey in a small bowl until blended. Yield: ½ cup.

Per tablespoon: Calories 133 (77% from fat); Fat 11.4g (sat 7.2g, mono 2.9g, poly 0.4g); Protein 0.2g; Carb 8.7g; Fiber 0g; Chol 30mg; Iron 0.1mg; Sodium 81mg; Calc 4mg

A dough scraper (above) makes cutting Two-Seed Bread Knots dough into 20 portions easy. Cover dough with plastic wrap or a clean towel to keep it from drying out.

low calorie • low cholesterol • low fat

Two-Seed Bread Knots

prep: 30 min.   cook: 17 min.   other: 35 min.

These rolls are named for their unique shape and sprinkling of sesame and poppy seeds. To create this distinct look, roll each ball of dough into a 7-inch rope; then form into a knot.

1	(¼-ounce) envelope rapid-rise yeast
1	cup warm water (100° to 110°)
3½	cups bread flour
2	tablespoons sugar
1½	teaspoons salt
3	tablespoons olive oil
1	egg yolk
1	tablespoon water
1	tablespoon sesame seeds
1	teaspoon poppy seeds

Preheat oven to 200°. Combine yeast and 1 cup warm water in a 1-cup liquid measuring cup; let stand 5 minutes.

Combine flour, sugar, and salt in a mixing bowl of a heavy-duty stand mixer. Add yeast mixture and oil. Beat at low speed 1 minute; beat at medium speed 5 minutes. Let dough rest, covered, on a lightly floured surface for 10 minutes.

Divide dough into 20 equal portions. Shape each portion into a 7-inch rope, and shape into a knot. Combine egg yolk and 1 tablespoon water; brush over rolls. **Sprinkle** with seeds; place on parchment paper-lined baking sheets. Turn oven off, and cover rolls loosely with plastic wrap; place in oven, and let rise 15 to 20 minutes or until doubled in bulk. Remove from oven, and preheat oven to 400°. Discard plastic wrap.

Bake rolls at 400° for 15 to 17 minutes or until golden. Yield: 20 rolls.

Per roll: Calories 116 (23% from fat); Fat 3g (sat 0.5g, mono 1.7g, poly 0.6g); Protein 3.2g; Carb 18.9g; Fiber 0.7g; Chol 10mg; Iron 1.2mg; Sodium 176mg; Calc 12mg

low calorie • low cholesterol • low fat

Hot Cross Buns

prep: 30 min.   cook: 25 min.
other: 3 hrs., 30 min.

Traditionally served at Easter, these tender sweet rolls have the shape of a cross piped in icing on the roll or snipped into the dough before baking.

2	(¼-ounce) envelopes active dry yeast
½	cup warm water (100° to 110°)
1	cup warm milk (100° to 110°)
½	cup butter, softened
½	cup sugar
½	teaspoon salt
3	large eggs
1½	teaspoons vanilla extract
5	cups all-purpose flour
1½	teaspoons ground cinnamon
1	cup raisins
	Sugar Glaze

Combine yeast and ½ cup warm water in a large mixing bowl; let stand 5 minutes. Add warm milk and next 5 ingredients. Beat at medium speed with an electric mixer until blended.

Combine flour and cinnamon, and gradually add to yeast mixture, beating at medium speed 2 minutes. Stir in raisins. Place dough in a well-greased bowl, turning to grease top.

Cover and let rise in a warm place (85°), free from drafts, 2 hours or until dough is doubled in bulk.

Punch dough down; cover dough, and let rise in a warm place (85°), free from drafts, 30 minutes.

Turn dough out onto a well-floured surface, and roll to ½-inch thickness. Cut with a 2-inch round cutter.

Place on a lightly greased 15- x 10-inch jelly-roll pan. Cover dough, and let rise in a warm place (85°), free from drafts, 45 minutes or until doubled in bulk.

Bake, uncovered, at 350° for 20 to 25 minutes or until lightly browned. Let rolls cool 10 minutes. Pipe Sugar Glaze over rolls in shape of a cross. Yield: 4 dozen.

Per bun: Calories 100 (23% from fat); Fat 2.6g (sat 1.4g, mono 0.7g, poly 0.2g); Protein 2.1g; Carb 17.2g; Fiber 0.8g; Chol 19mg; Iron 0.8mg; Sodium 46mg; Calc 13mg

Sugar Glaze

prep: 5 min.

1	cup powdered sugar
1½	tablespoons milk
½	teaspoon vanilla extract

Whisk together all ingredients until smooth. Yield: ½ cup.

Per tablespoon: Calories: 61 (1% from fat); Fat 0.1g (sat 0.1g, mono 0g, poly 0g); Protein 0.1g; Carb 15.1g; Fiber 0g; Chol 0mg; Iron 0mg; Sodium 1mg; Calc 3mg

low cholesterol

Potato-Caramelized Onion Buns

prep: 35 min.   cook: 18 min.   other: 55 min.

Serve meaty cheeseburgers or grilled fish inside these delicious buns.

2	cups warm water (100° to 110°)
3	(¼-ounce) envelopes active dry yeast
1	cup refrigerated or frozen mashed potatoes, thawed and warmed
2	tablespoons sugar
2	tablespoons butter, melted
7	cups plus 1 tablespoon all-purpose flour
1	tablespoon salt
	Caramelized Onions
1	egg, lightly beaten
1½	teaspoons poppy seeds (optional)

Preheat oven to 200°.

Stir together 2 cups warm water and yeast in a large mixing bowl of a heavy-duty stand mixer until dissolved. Let stand 5 minutes.

Add potatoes, sugar, and butter to yeast mixture; beat at medium speed, using dough hook attachment, until blended. Add 7 cups flour and salt; beat at low speed 2 minutes.

Add Caramelized Onions; beat at medium speed 5 minutes. (Dough will be very sticky.) Sprinkle dough with remaining 1 tablespoon flour, and remove from bowl. **Shape** into a ball, and place in a lightly greased bowl, turning to grease top. Turn off oven. Cover bowl with plastic wrap, and let dough rise in oven 30 minutes or until doubled in bulk.

Remove from oven. Remove and discard plastic wrap. Punch dough down, and turn out onto a lightly floured surface. Divide into 21 portions.

Shape each portion into a ball with floured hands. Place no more than 8 balls on each parchment paper-lined baking sheet. Cover with plastic wrap, and let rise again in a warm place (85°), free from drafts, 15 to 20 minutes or until doubled in bulk. Brush with egg, and sprinkle with poppy seeds, if desired.

Bake at 350° for 15 to 18 minutes or until golden. Remove from pans, and cool on wire racks. Yield: 21 buns.

Per bun: Calories: 205 (18% from fat); Fat 4.1g (sat 2.2g, mono 1g, poly 0.3g); Protein 5.3g; Carb 36.2g; Fiber 1.6g; Chol 19mg; Iron 2.2mg; Sodium 415mg; Calc 14mg

Caramelized Onions

prep: 10 min.   cook: 20 min.

- ¼ cup butter
- 2 large sweet onions, chopped
- ¼ teaspoon salt

Melt butter in a large skillet over medium heat; add onions and salt, and sauté 20 minutes or until caramel-colored. Cool. Yield: 2 cups.

Per tablespoon: Calories: 16 (79% from fat); Fat 1.4g (sat 0.9g, mono 0.4g, poly 0.1g); Protein 0.1g; Carb 0.7g; Fiber 0.1g; Chol 4mg; Iron 0mg; Sodium 29mg; Calc 2mg

yeast bread loaves

family favorite • low cholesterol • low fat
Basic White Bread

prep: 40 min.   cook: 50 min.   other: 2 hrs.

About 7¼ cups all-purpose flour, divided
- 3 tablespoons sugar
- 2½ teaspoons salt
- 2 (¼-ounce) envelopes active dry yeast
- 1½ cups water
- ½ cup milk
- 3 tablespoons butter or margarine

Combine 2 cups flour, sugar, salt, and yeast in a large mixing bowl; stir well. Combine water, milk, and butter; heat until butter melts, stirring often. Cool to 120° to 130°. **Gradually** add liquid mixture to flour mixture, beating well at high speed with an electric mixer. Beat 2 more minutes at medium speed. Gradually add ¾ cup flour, beating 2 minutes at medium speed. Stir in enough remaining flour to make a soft dough. **Turn** dough out onto a floured surface; knead until smooth and elastic (10 minutes). Shape into a ball; place in a well-greased bowl, turning to grease top. Cover and let rise in a warm place (85°), free from drafts, 1 hour or until doubled in bulk. **Punch** dough down; turn out onto a lightly floured surface, and knead lightly 4 or 5 times. Divide dough in half. Roll 1 portion of dough into a 14- x 7-inch rectangle. **Roll up** dough, starting at narrow end, pressing firmly to eliminate air pockets; pinch ends to seal. Place dough, seam side

down, in a well-greased 9- x 5-inch loafpan. Repeat procedure with remaining dough. **Cover** and let rise in a warm place, free from drafts, 1 hour or until doubled in bulk. Bake at 375° for 45 to 50 minutes or until loaves sound hollow when tapped. Remove bread from pans immediately; cool on wire racks. Yield: 2 loaves.

Per 1-inch slice: Calories 216 (11% from fat); Fat 2.7g (sat 1.4g, mono 0.6g, poly 0.3g); Protein 5.6g; Carb 41.3g; Fiber 1.5g; Chol 6mg; Iron 2.4mg; Sodium 341mg; Calc 17mg

Note: You can bake this bread in an 8- x 4-inch loafpan. Bake at 375° for 50 to 55 minutes.

low cholesterol • low fat
Honey-Whole Wheat Bread

prep: 10 min.   cook: 45 min.
other: 1 hr., 45 min.

Equal amounts of whole wheat and all-purpose flour can be used for this bread.

- 4 cups whole wheat flour, divided
- ½ cup instant nonfat dry milk powder
- 1 tablespoon salt
- 2 (¼-ounce) envelopes active dry yeast
- 3 cups water, divided
- ½ cup honey
- 2 tablespoons butter or margarine
- 2 to 3 cups all-purpose flour

Beat 3 cups whole wheat flour, dry milk powder, salt, and yeast at low speed with a

heavy-duty stand mixer until combined. **Bring** 2 cups water to a boil over medium heat; add honey and butter, stirring until butter melts. Remove from heat, and stir in 1 cup cold water. (Thermometer will register about 120°.)

Add honey mixture to flour mixture, beating at low speed 1 minute. Increase speed to medium, and beat 2 more minutes. Gradually add remaining 1 cup wheat flour and enough all-purpose flour to make a soft dough.

Turn dough out onto a well-floured surface, and knead until smooth and elastic (about 5 minutes). Place in a well-greased bowl, turning to grease top. Cover and let rise in a warm place (85°), free from drafts, 1 hour or until doubled in bulk.

Punch dough down, and divide into 2 equal portions. Roll each portion into a 15- x 10-inch rectangle. Roll each up, jelly-roll fashion, beginning with short side. Fold ends under, and place each roll, seam side down, in a 9- x 5-inch loafpan.

Cover and let rise in a warm place, free from drafts, 45 minutes or until dough is doubled in bulk.

Bake at 375° for 40 to 45 minutes, shielding with aluminum foil after 25 minutes to prevent excessive browning. Yield: 2 loaves.

Per 1-inch slice: Calories 193 (9% from fat); Fat 2g (sat 0.9g, mono 0.4g, poly 0.3g); Protein 6.2g; Carb 40g; Fiber 3.8g; Chol 4mg; Iron 1.9mg; Sodium 410mg; Calc 37mg

knead to know

Follow our tips for preparing, kneading, and baking yeast dough.

- Make sure yeast is in date (package is stamped with an expiration date).
- Use 1 envelope of yeast for up to 4½ cups flour unless your recipe specifies otherwise.
- Dissolve yeast in warm water (100° to 110°).
- Measure all ingredients carefully, including salt. Salt plays a significant role in developing the dough's flavor and controlling the rising rate of the dough.
- When kneading dough, flatten and fold it toward you, and use the heels of your hands to push the dough away from you with a rolling motion.
- Rotate dough a quarter turn; repeat the fold, push, and turn steps.
- Use a little more flour if dough becomes too sticky, always working the flour into the dough.
- Don't let dough continue to rise beyond the time called for in recipe.
- Avoid letting the temperature become too high during the dough-rising period; it will kill the yeast. If the temperature is too low, the dough will take longer to rise.

---

low cholesterol

Pumpernickel Bread

prep: 20 min.   cook: 35 min.   other: 35 min.

You'll need a heavy-duty stand mixer to prepare this dough, but after that's done, the rest is simple.

1¾ cups warm water (100° to 110°)
1 (¼-ounce) envelope active dry yeast
2 tablespoons sugar
2 tablespoons instant coffee granules
¼ cup molasses
4½ cups bread flour
1 cup rye flour
2 teaspoons salt
Vegetable cooking spray
2 tablespoons butter or margarine, melted

Preheat oven to 200°. Stir together first 3 ingredients in a large mixing bowl of a heavy-duty stand mixer. Let stand 5 minutes. Add coffee and next 4 ingredients to yeast mixture.

Beat at low speed, using dough hook attachment, 1 minute or until soft dough comes together. Beat at medium speed 4 minutes. (Dough will be slightly sticky.)
Turn dough out onto a lightly floured surface; shape dough into a 9- x 5-inch oval loaf. Place on a parchment paper–lined baking sheet; coat lightly with cooking spray, and cover loosely with plastic wrap. Turn oven off, and place loaf in oven. Let rise 30 minutes or until loaf is doubled in bulk. Remove loaf from oven. Remove and discard plastic wrap. Preheat oven to 375°.
Bake bread for 30 to 35 minutes. Remove from oven, and brush with melted butter. Cool on a wire rack. Yield: 1 loaf.

Per 1-inch slice: Calories 356 (10% from fat); Fat 4g (sat 1.8g, mono 0.8g, poly 0.7g); Protein 9.7g; Carb 69.6g; Fiber 3.5g; Chol 7mg; Iron 3.9mg; Sodium 541mg; Calc 35mg

German-Style Pumpernickel Rolls: Pat dough into a 10-inch square (½ inch thick). Cut into 2-inch squares. Roll into 1½-inch balls, and place on a parchment paper–lined baking sheet. Proceed with recipe as directed. Bake at 375° for 10 to 12 minutes or until lightly browned. Yield: 25 rolls.

---

family favorite • make ahead

Cheddar Casserole Bread

prep: 11 min.   cook: 45 min.   other: 35 min.

This is a dense, cheesy loaf, great for sopping up soup or gravy. Let loaf stand 10 minutes before removing from the dish so it will slice easily.

4½ cups all-purpose flour, divided
2 tablespoons sugar
1½ teaspoons salt
½ teaspoon freshly ground black pepper
2 (¼-ounce) envelopes rapid-rise yeast
1 cup (4 ounces) shredded sharp Cheddar cheese
¼ cup finely chopped onion
2 tablespoons butter, melted
2 cups warm water (120° to 130°)
¼ cup (1 ounce) sharp Cheddar cheese, shredded

Combine 2 cups flour, sugar, salt, pepper, yeast, 1 cup cheese, onion, and butter in a large bowl. Gradually add water, beating at medium speed with an electric mixer

2 minutes or until well blended. Gradually stir in remaining 2½ cups flour. (Dough will be sticky.) Cover; let rest 10 minutes.
Stir batter down; spoon into a lightly greased 2½-quart round baking dish. Cover and let rise in a warm place (85°), free from drafts, 15 minutes or until doubled in bulk. Sprinkle with remaining ¼ cup cheese.
Bake at 350° for 45 minutes or until loaf sounds hollow when tapped. Cool in dish on a wire rack 10 minutes. Remove from dish; cool on a wire rack. Cut into wedges to serve. Yield: 16 servings.

Per serving: Calories 194 (25% from fat); Fat 5.4g (sat 3.2g, mono 1.4g, poly 0.3g); Protein 6.7g; Carb 29.1g; Fiber 1.2g; Chol 15mg; Iron 1.9mg; Sodium 296mg; Calc 84mg

---

low calorie

Cheesy Grits Bread

prep: 15 min.   cook: 50 min.
other: 2 hrs., 15 min.

Grits add a uniquely appealing texture to this loaf.

2 cups milk
¾ cup quick-cooking grits, uncooked
2 teaspoons salt
1 (10-ounce) block white Cheddar cheese, shredded (we tested with Cracker Barrel Vermont Sharp White Cheddar)
1 cup warm water (100° to 110°)
¼ cup sugar
2 (¼-ounce) envelopes rapid-rise yeast
5 to 6 cups bread flour

Bring milk to a boil in a large saucepan over medium heat; stir in grits, and cook, stirring often, 5 minutes (mixture will be very thick). Remove from heat; add salt and cheese, stirring until cheese is melted. Let stand 25 minutes, stirring occasionally.
Combine 1 cup warm water, sugar, and yeast in a mixing bowl of a heavy-duty stand mixer; let stand 5 minutes. Add grits mixture, beating at medium-low speed using the dough hook attachment, until well blended.
Add 4 cups flour, 1 cup at a time, beating until blended after each addition and stopping to scrape down sides as necessary. Gradually add enough flour to make a stiff but slightly sticky dough. Dough will form a ball around mixer attachment.

Shape dough into a ball with well-floured hands, and place in a well-greased bowl, turning to coat top. Cover and let rise in a warm place (85°), free from drafts, 1 hour or until doubled in bulk.

Punch dough down, and divide into thirds; shape each portion into a loaf. Place into lightly greased 9- x 5-inch loafpans; cover and let rise in a warm place, free from drafts, 45 minutes or until doubled in bulk.

Bake at 350° for 35 to 40 minutes or until golden. Let bread cool in pans on wire racks 10 minutes. Remove from pans, and cool completely on wire racks. Yield: 3 loaves.

Per 1-inch slice: Calories 174 (25% from fat); Fat 4.8g (sat 2.8g, mono 1.2g, poly 0.3g); Protein 6.7g; Carb 25.4g; Fiber 0.8g; Chol 12mg; Iron 1.4mg; Sodium 249mg; Calc 86mg

Bacon-Cheddar Grits Bread: Prepare dough as directed. After dividing dough, roll each third into a 14- x 9-inch rectangle on a lightly floured surface. Sprinkle each dough rectangle evenly with ½ cup cooked, crumbled bacon and ¾ cup shredded sharp Cheddar cheese. Roll up, jelly-roll fashion, starting with each short side and ending at middle of dough. You will form 2 rolls per loaf. Place into prepared loafpans; let rise, and bake as directed.

low cholesterol • low fat

Baguettes and Rolls

prep: 24 min.   cook: 20 min. per batch
other: 1 hr., 50 min.

2   (¼-ounce) envelopes rapid-rise yeast
2   tablespoons sugar
2½   cups warm water (100° to 110°)
1   tablespoon salt
1   tablespoon butter, softened
6½   to 7 cups all-purpose flour
2   egg whites
2   tablespoons cold water

Stir together first 3 ingredients in a 4-cup liquid measuring cup; let stand 5 minutes.

Stir together yeast mixture, salt, and butter in a large bowl. Gradually stir in enough flour to make a soft dough. Place in a well-greased bowl, turning to grease top.

Cover and let rise in a warm place (85°), free from drafts, 40 minutes or until doubled in bulk.

Punch dough down; turn out onto a lightly floured surface, and knead lightly 4 or 5 times. Divide dough in half. Shape 1 portion into 12 (3½-inch) ovals; place on a greased baking sheet. Make shallow cuts in tops of rolls; cover and let rise in a warm place, free from drafts, 30 minutes or until doubled in bulk.

Divide remaining portion in half. Turn 1 half onto a floured surface; press with a rolling pin to remove air bubbles. Shape into a 15-inch rope.

Place in a greased baguette pan or large baking sheet. Make deep, 2-inch cuts in top of loaf using a razor blade. Repeat procedure with remaining dough. Let rise in a warm place, free from drafts, 30 minutes or until doubled in bulk.

Bake rolls and baguettes separately at 400° for 15 minutes. Stir together egg whites and water; brush over bread. Bake 5 more minutes or until golden. Cool on a wire rack. Yield: 1 dozen rolls, 2 baguettes.

Per roll: Calories 138 (6% from fat); Fat 0.9g (sat 0.4g, mono 0.2g, poly 0.2g); Protein 4.1g; Carb 27.6g; Fiber 1.1g; Chol 1mg; Iron 1.7mg; Sodium 300mg; Calc 7mg

Per ¼ baguette: Calories 211 (6% from fat); Fat 1.5g (sat 0.6g, mono 0.3g, poly 0.2g); Protein 6.3g; Carb 42.2g; Fiber 1.6g; Chol 2mg; Iron 2.6mg; Sodium 450mg; Calc 10mg

Baguettes and Rolls

bread equipment

Baguette pans: Two long metal half-cylinder pans joined along one side, used for shaping and baking a pair of crusty French baguettes. French bread pans are similar pans, only wider.

Clay stone: A large, thick flat stone made to resemble the floor of a brick oven. When placed on the rack of a very hot oven, it will produce a bread with a superior crisp crust.

Dough hook: A hook attachment for a heavy-duty stand mixer that simulates the kneading process if you'd rather not knead by hand.

Dough scraper: A tool, usually square, made of stainless steel or plastic, convenient for cutting dough or scraping a work surface to lift dough and to prevent it from sticking.

Lame: A sharp, curved razor for scoring the top of a loaf of bread before baking. A single-edged razor blade or a very sharp knife works just as well.

---

low calorie • low cholesterol • low fat

No-Knead French Bread

prep: 45 min.   cook: 25 min.
other: 1 hr., 35 min.

Butter makes this yeast dough rich and luxurious. A series of gentle stirrings allows you to forgo kneading.

½ cup warm water (100° to 110°)
2½ teaspoons sugar
2 (¼-ounce) envelopes active dry yeast
1 cup boiling water
2 tablespoons butter or margarine
2 teaspoons salt
1 cup cold water
6½ to 7 cups all-purpose flour
1 large egg, beaten
2 tablespoons milk

Combine first 3 ingredients in a 1-cup liquid measuring cup; let stand 5 minutes. **Combine** boiling water, butter, and salt in a large mixing bowl. Stir until butter melts. Add cold water; cool mixture to warm (100° to 110°). Stir yeast mixture into liquid mixture. Add 2½ cups flour. Beat at medium speed with an electric mixer until blended. Gradually stir in enough remaining flour to make a soft dough.

Let dough stand in bowl 10 minutes. Stir gently for a few seconds; cover. Repeat gentle stirring every 10 minutes for the next 40 minutes.

Turn dough out onto a floured surface; divide into 3 equal portions. Roll each portion into a 13- x 8-inch rectangle on a floured surface. Roll up, jelly-roll fashion, starting with long side; pinch ends to seal.

Place each loaf, seam side down, on a separate greased baking sheet. Cover and let rise in a warm place (85°), free from drafts, about 40 minutes or until doubled in bulk.

Make diagonal slits about ¼ inch deep down the length of loaves, using a sharp knife or razor blade. Combine egg and milk in a small bowl, beating until blended. Brush gently over loaves after rising.

Bake at 400° for 20 to 25 minutes or until loaves sound hollow when tapped. (Bread freezes well.) Yield: 3 loaves, 12 servings each.

Per serving: Calories 94 (11% from fat); Fat 1.1g (sat 0.5g, mono 0.3g, poly 0.1g); Protein 2.7g; Carb 17.9g; Fiber 0.7g; Chol 8mg; Iron 1.2mg; Sodium 137mg; Calc 6mg

---

Sally Lunn Bread

prep: 10 min.   cook: 45 min.
other: 2 hrs., 5 min.

Here are some bonus ideas for using this slightly sweet yeast bread: as a luscious tomato sandwich, for French toast, or croutons.

2 (¼-ounce) envelopes active dry yeast
½ cup warm water (100° to 110°)
1½ cups milk
¾ cup sugar
½ cup butter or margarine
1 teaspoon salt
2 large eggs
5 cups all-purpose flour
Blackberry Butter (optional)

Combine yeast and ½ cup warm water in a 1-cup measuring cup; let stand 5 minutes. **Heat** milk and next 3 ingredients in a saucepan over medium heat, stirring until butter melts. Cool to 100° to 110°.

Beat yeast mixture, milk mixture, and eggs at medium speed with an electric mixer until blended. Gradually add flour, beating at lowest speed until blended. (Mixture will be a very sticky, soft dough.)

Cover and let rise in a warm place (85°), free from drafts, 1 hour or until dough is doubled in bulk.

Stir dough down; cover and let rise in a warm place, free from drafts, 30 minutes or until dough is doubled in bulk.

Stir dough down, and spoon into a well-greased, 10-inch Bundt pan or tube pan. Cover and let rise in a warm place, free from drafts, 20 to 30 minutes or until dough is doubled in bulk.

Bake at 350° for 35 to 40 minutes or until golden brown and a wooden pick inserted into center of bread comes out clean. Remove from pan immediately. Serve bread with Blackberry Butter, honey, molasses, or jelly, if desired. Yield: 16 servings.

Per 1-inch slice: Calories 255 (26% from fat); Fat 7.5g (sat 4.3g, mono 2g, poly 0.5g); Protein 6g; Carb 40.6g; Fiber 1.2g; Chol 44mg; Iron 2.1mg; Sodium 205mg; Calc 38mg

Blackberry Butter: Stir 2 to 3 tablespoons seedless blackberry jam into ½ cup softened butter.

---

a sweet little bread

Sally Lunn starts with an easy-to-make yeast batter. Eggs offer the yellow color and rich taste. Baking in a Bundt or tube pan gives it the signature shape. And the bread is sturdy enough to serve with supper and sop up gravy.

Where does this versatile food get its name? We don't really know who Sally Lunn was. Some sources contend that she was a woman who sold bread in England. Other historians say the name may have come from the French words "soleil" (which means sun) and "lune" (which means moon). The bread has a top as golden as the sun and a bottom as pale as the moon.

Some food historians believe that the Jamestown colonists made this bread to remind them of their home in England. The recipe shows up in old Southern cookbooks from that time period and beyond.

Whatever its origin, you can make this sweet treat today to enjoy its light, buttery goodness. When you do, smile and raise your cup to Sally Lunn.

doughnuts

family favorite • for kids • freeze it
weekend chef

Raised Doughnuts

prep: 23 min.   cook: 3 min. per batch
other: 1 hr., 10 min.

*For maximum goodness, roll warm dough-
nuts twice in powdered sugar.*

1   cup warm water (100° to 110°)
1   (¼-ounce) envelope active dry yeast
3   tablespoons granulated sugar
3   cups all-purpose flour
1   teaspoon salt
⅓   cup shortening, melted
1   large egg, lightly beaten
Vegetable oil
2   cups powdered sugar

Stir together first 3 ingredients in a large
glass bowl; let stand 5 minutes. Stir in flour
and next 3 ingredients until blended.
Roll dough to ¼-inch thickness; cut with a
2½-inch doughnut cutter. Let stand 1 hour
or until doubled in bulk.
Pour oil to a depth of 2 inches into a Dutch
oven; heat to 375°. Fry doughnuts, in batches, 1 to 1½ minutes on each side or until
golden. Remove with a slotted spoon; drain
on paper towels.
Roll warm doughnuts in powdered sugar.
Cool 5 minutes; repeat procedure using
remaining powdered sugar. Yield: 1½ dozen.

Per doughnut: Calories 379 (69% from fat); Fat 29.2g (sat 3.6g, mono 12.5g, poly 12g); Protein 2.7g; Carb 29.2g; Fiber 0.6g; Chol 12mg; Iron 1.1mg; Sodium 134mg; Calc 5mg

taste of the south beignets

Warm beignets are a sweet invitation to southern Louisiana, and no trip to New Orleans is complete without one. Where else but the South can you get so actively involved and committed to a doughnut? The word "beignet" is French for "fritter," and in the Crescent City, these concoctions come light, yeasty, and without holes.

Of course, you can buy beignet mixes almost any place, but main ingredients are the atmosphere and appreciation of tradition. So if you're craving beignets and New Orleans isn't in your travel plans, make some at home.

Beignets are terrific Saturday morning breakfast treats. No special equipment is necessary—a Dutch oven or deep frying pan is all you need. Let the kids help by dusting the warm beignets with powdered sugar. The easiest method is to pour the sugar in a paper bag, place the hot, drained beignets inside, and shake. Be prepared for lots of giggles, clouds of powdered sugar, and a wonderful taste of a special part of the South.

make ahead

Beignets

prep: 30 min.   cook: 2 min. per batch   other: 1 hr., 30 min.

*Savor these traditional New Orleans doughnuts in your own home.
The dough can even be made ahead.*

1   (¼-ounce) envelope active dry yeast
3   tablespoons warm water (100° to 110°)
¾   cup milk
¼   cup granulated sugar
¼   cup shortening
1   teaspoon salt
1   large egg, lightly beaten
3   cups all-purpose flour
2½   to 3 quarts vegetable oil
Powdered sugar

Combine yeast and 3 tablespoons warm water in a large bowl; let stand 5 minutes.
Heat milk in a small saucepan over medium heat (do not boil). Stir in sugar, shortening, and salt. Cool to lukewarm (100° to 110°).
Add milk mixture, egg, and 2 cups flour to yeast mixture, stirring well. Gradually stir in enough remaining flour to make a soft dough.
Turn dough out onto a floured surface; knead 8 to 10 minutes or until dough is smooth and elastic. Place dough in a well-greased bowl, turning to grease top. Cover and let rise in a warm place (85°), free from drafts, 1 hour or until dough is doubled in bulk.
Punch dough down, and turn out onto a floured surface. Roll dough into a 12- x 10-inch rectangle; cut into 2-inch squares. Place on a floured surface; cover and let rise in a warm place, free from drafts, 30 minutes or until doubled in bulk.
Pour oil to a depth of 2 to 3 inches into a Dutch oven; heat to 375°. Gently lower (don't drop) beignets into oil using a spatula. Fry beignets, in batches, 1 minute on each side or until golden. Drain on paper towels; sprinkle with powdered sugar while still hot. Yield: 2½ dozen.

Per beignet: Calories 141 (62% from fat); Fat 9.7g (sat 1.3g, mono 4.1g, poly 3.8g); Protein 1.9g; Carb 12.2g; Fiber 0.4g; Chol 8mg; Iron 0.7mg; Sodium 83mg; Calc 10mg

Make-Ahead Note: Turn dough out onto a floured surface, and knead 8 to 10 min-utes or until smooth and elastic. Place dough in a well-greased bowl, turning to grease top. Cover and refrigerate over-night. Punch dough down and follow directions above.

specialty yeast breads

The distinct shapes of bagels, brioche, and braided bread define them as special. There's a certain artisanal quality that goes into the preparation of each unique shape. Brush the various breads with melted butter and douse them with fresh herbs, seeds, or coarse salt before baking.

low calorie • low cholesterol

Braided Egg Bread

prep: 25 min. cook: 25 min.
other: 1 hr., 5 min.

This slightly sweet bread is also known as challah (pronounced KHAH-lah).

1½ cups fat-free milk
2   (¼-ounce) envelopes active dry yeast
5½ cups all-purpose flour
1   teaspoon salt
¼   cup shortening
½   cup egg substitute
1   egg yolk
½   cup honey
All-purpose flour
1   large egg, lightly beaten
1   teaspoon sesame seeds (optional)

Preheat oven to 200°.
Microwave 1½ cups milk at HIGH in a microwave-safe glass bowl 2 to 3 minutes or until heated. Stir in yeast, and let stand 5 minutes.
Combine 5½ cups flour and salt in a large bowl; stir in yeast mixture. Add shortening and next 3 ingredients. Beat at low speed with an electric mixer 1 to 2 minutes. Beat at medium speed 5 minutes.
Sprinkle dough with additional flour, and remove from bowl. (Dough will be very sticky.) Place dough in a lightly greased bowl, turning to grease top. Turn off oven. Cover bowl with plastic wrap, and let rise in oven 30 minutes or until doubled in bulk. Remove from oven. Remove and discard plastic wrap.
Punch dough down, and divide in half. Divide each half into 3 equal portions. Roll each portion into a 14-inch-long rope; pinch 3 ropes together at 1 end to seal, and

braid. Repeat with remaining dough portions. Place braids on a parchment paper–lined baking sheet.
Cover braids with plastic wrap; let rise in a warm place (85°), free from drafts, 25 to 30 minutes or until doubled in bulk. Brush evenly with beaten egg; sprinkle with sesame seeds, if desired.
Bake at 350° for 25 minutes or until golden. (A wooden pick should come out clean.) Yield: 2 loaves.

Per 1-inch slice: Calories 153 (19% from fat); Fat 3.2g (sat 0.7g, mono 1.2g, poly 1.1g); Protein 4.3g; Carb 26.9g; Fiber 0.9g; Chol 16mg; Iron 1.5mg; Sodium 109mg; Calc 28mg

family favorite • low cholesterol

Bagels

prep: 1 hr., 15 min. cook: 22 min.
other: 12 to 18 hrs.

1   (¼-ounce) envelope active dry yeast
1¾ cups warm water (100° to 110°)
2   tablespoons honey
5   to 5½ cups bread flour
2   teaspoons salt
3½ quarts water
½   cup sesame seeds or any mix of poppy seeds, caraway seeds, sea salt, or dehydrated onion and garlic flakes

Combine yeast and warm water in a 2-cup liquid measuring cup; let stand 5 minutes. Add honey, stirring well. Combine yeast mixture, 2 cups flour, and salt in a large mixing bowl of a heavy-duty stand mixer; beat at low speed 4 minutes or until smooth.
Gradually stir in enough remaining flour to make a soft dough. Beat at medium-low speed, using a dough hook attachment, 8 minutes or until smooth and elastic. Divide dough into 12 equal pieces. Roll each into a smooth ball. Cover and let rest 5 minutes.
Shape each ball into an 11-inch rope. Bring ends of ropes together, and pinch to seal. Roll bagel around palm of hand to make a ring. Place on greased baking sheets; cover and chill 12 to 18 hours.
Bring water to a boil in a Dutch oven. Boil bagels, 4 at a time, 30 seconds, turning once. Remove with a slotted spoon; place on wire racks. Dip bagels in sesame seeds. Repeat

with remaining bagels and sesame seeds.
Place bagels on lightly greased baking sheets sprinkled with cornmeal, if desired. Bake at 450° for 13 to 14 minutes or until golden. Yield: 1 dozen.

Per bagel: Calories 255 (15% from fat); Fat 4.2g (sat 0.6g, mono 1.2g, poly 1.7g); Protein 8.1g; Carb 46g; Fiber 2.2g; Chol 0mg; Iron 3.5mg; Sodium 391mg; Calc 69mg

English Muffins

prep: 45 min. cook: 14 min. per batch
other: 1 hr., 30 min.

1   (¼-ounce) envelope active dry yeast
½   cup warm water (100° to 110°)
1½ cups milk
3   tablespoons shortening
2   tablespoons sugar
1¼ teaspoons salt
6   to 7 cups all-purpose flour
¼   cup plus 2 tablespoons cornmeal

Combine yeast and warm water in a 1-cup liquid measuring cup; let stand 5 minutes.
Combine milk and next 3 ingredients in a small saucepan; heat until shortening melts, stirring occasionally. Remove from heat, and cool to 100° to 110°.
Combine yeast mixture, liquid mixture, and 3 cups flour in a large mixing bowl; beat at medium speed with an electric mixer until well blended. Gradually stir in enough remaining flour to make a stiff dough.
Turn dough out onto a floured surface, and knead until smooth and elastic (5 to 10 minutes). Place in a well-greased bowl, turning to grease top. Cover and let rise in a warm place (85°), free from drafts, 1 hour or until doubled in bulk.
Punch dough down; turn out onto a lightly floured surface, and knead 4 or 5 times. Divide dough in half. Place half of dough on a smooth surface that has been sprinkled with ¼ cup cornmeal. Pat dough into a circle ¾ inch thick; cut dough into rounds with a 3½-inch round cutter. (Cut carefully, as leftover dough should not be reused.) Repeat procedure with remaining dough.
Sprinkle 2 baking sheets with remaining 2 tablespoons cornmeal. Place dough rounds, cornmeal side down, 2 inches apart on

baking sheets (1 side should remain free of cornmeal). Cover; let rise in a warm place, free from drafts, 30 minutes or until doubled in bulk. Using a wide spatula, transfer rounds to a preheated, lightly greased electric skillet (350°), cornmeal side down. Cook 5 to 7 minutes on each side or until golden. Cool on wire racks. Yield: 8 muffins.

Per muffin: Calories 454 (15% from fat); Fat 7.5g (sat 2g, mono 2.6g, poly 2g); Protein 12.2g; Carb 82.8g; Fiber 3.2g; Chol 5mg; Iron 4.8mg; Sodium 384mg; Calc 67mg

Brioche

prep: 30 min.   cook: 17 min.

other: 15 hrs., 45 min.

1   (¼-ounce) envelope active dry yeast
¼   cup warm water (100° to 110°)
2   tablespoons sugar
1   teaspoon salt
3½   cups all-purpose flour
5   large eggs
1   cup butter, cut into ½-inch pieces and softened
1   tablespoon vegetable oil
1   large egg
1   teaspoon water

Combine yeast and warm water in a 1-cup liquid measuring cup; let stand 5 minutes.
Combine yeast mixture, sugar, salt, and ½ cup flour in a large mixing bowl.
Beat at medium speed with a heavy-duty electric stand mixer, using a paddle attachment, 2 minutes, scraping sides of bowl occasionally.
Add 5 eggs, 1 at a time, beating after each addition. Add butter, a few pieces at a time, beating just until butter is the size of small peas. Gradually add remaining 3 cups flour; beat until blended and creamy. (Dough will be very soft and batterlike.)
Scrape dough into a well-greased bowl. Brush top of dough with oil. Cover and let rise at a cool room temperature 3 hours or until doubled in bulk.
Punch dough down by gently folding edges into center with a rubber spatula; cover and chill 12 hours.
Divide dough into 6 portions; divide each portion into 4 pieces. Working with half of dough at a time (keep remaining dough in refrigerator), roll each piece into a smooth ball. (Do not overhandle the dough.)

Compress 1 side of the dough ball one-third of the way down by gently rocking the edge of your hand back and forth almost all the way through, until dough is shaped like a bowling pin.
Hold dough by the topknot, and gently lower it into a buttered 3½-inch brioche pan. Tuck the topknot down into the dough with a flour-dusted finger, pressing the topknot completely down to the bottom of the pan until firmly tucked in. Repeat with remaining dough pieces.
Combine egg and 1 teaspoon water; brush mixture over brioche. Place brioche pans at least 1 inch apart on a baking sheet. Cover and let rise at a cool room temperature until doubled in bulk (about 45 minutes). Brush again with egg mixture.
Bake at 400° for 15 to 17 minutes or until deep golden. Remove from pans immediately; cool. Yield: 2 dozen.

Per brioche: Calories 165 (54% from fat); Fat 9.9g (sat 5.5g, mono 2.8g, poly 0.8g); Protein 3.7g; Carb 15.2g; Fiber 0.6g; Chol 74mg; Iron 1.1mg; Sodium 171mg; Calc 12mg

bread machine favorite

Graham Cracker Bread

prep: 10 min.   cook: 3 hrs., 25 min.

1¼   cups warm water (100° to 110°)
3   tablespoons butter, cut into pieces
¼   cup honey
2   teaspoons fresh lemon juice
½   teaspoon grated orange rind
2½   cups bread flour
½   cup whole wheat flour
¾   cup cinnamon graham cracker crumbs (about 5 whole crackers)
1   teaspoon salt
1   (¼-ounce) envelope active dry yeast
Bread flour

Combine first 10 ingredients in bread machine according to manufacturer's instructions. Select bake cycle; start machine. (Add more bread flour, 1 tablespoon at a time, to make dough tacky, rather than sticky, if needed.)
Remove bread from pan immediately, and cool on a wire rack. Yield: 1 (2-pound) loaf, 8 servings.

Per serving: Calories 265 (20% from fat); Fat 5.8g (sat 2.9g, mono 1.5g, poly 0.8g); Protein 6.2g; Carb 47.2g; Fiber 1.5g; Chol 11mg; Iron 2.4mg; Sodium 371mg; Calc 12mg

bread machine basics

• Add ingredients in the order recommended by the manufacturer of your machine.
• Make sure liquid ingredients are at room temperature before starting.
• Be precise in measuring ingredients. The slightest over-measuring or under-measuring can affect results.
• When baking sweet or extra-rich breads, use the light setting.
• Don't use the delay cycle for bread recipes that contain eggs or other perishable products like dairy products or meats.

bread machine favorite

Raisin-Walnut Bread

prep: 5 min.   cook: 3 hrs., 25 min.

¾   cup buttermilk
½   cup water
2   tablespoons butter, cut into small pieces
2   cups bread flour
¾   cup whole wheat flour
½   cup uncooked regular oats
¼   cup firmly packed dark brown sugar
1½   teaspoons salt
1   teaspoon ground cinnamon
1   (¼-ounce) envelope active dry yeast
Bread flour
⅓   cup chopped walnuts, toasted
1   cup raisins

Combine first 10 ingredients in bread machine according to manufacturer's instructions. Select bake cycle; start machine. Be sure to check the dough's consistency while machine is in the kneading cycle. (Add more bread flour, 1 tablespoon at a time, to make dough tacky rather than sticky, if needed.) Add walnuts and raisins according to manufacturer's instructions.
Remove bread from pan immediately, and cool on a wire rack. Yield: 1 (2-pound) loaf, 8 servings.

Per serving: Calories 334 (20% from fat); Fat 7.4g (sat 2.3g, mono 1.8g, poly 2.4g); Protein 9.4g; Carb 60.2g; Fiber 4.7g; Chol 8mg; Iron 3.2mg; Sodium 490mg; Calc 58mg

breakfast &
brunch

Scrambled Eggs

prep: 2 min.   cook: 4 min.

4   large eggs
2   tablespoons water or milk
¼   teaspoon salt
Dash of pepper
1   tablespoon butter or margarine

Combine first 4 ingredients; stir briskly with a fork until blended. Melt butter in an 8-inch skillet over medium heat, tilting pan to coat bottom; pour in egg mixture. **Cook,** without stirring, until mixture begins to set on bottom. Draw a spatula across bottom of pan to form large curds. Continue cooking until eggs are thickened and firm throughout, but still moist. (Do not stir constantly.) Yield: 2 servings.

Per serving: Calories 197 (71% from fat); Fat 15.6g (sat 6.7g, mono 5.3g, poly 1.6g); Protein 12.7g; Carb 0.8g; Fiber 0g; Chol 438mg; Iron 1.9mg; Sodium 471mg; Calc 55mg

Cream Cheese Scrambled Eggs

prep: 10 min.   cook: 6 min.

8   large eggs
¼   cup milk
½   teaspoon salt
½   teaspoon pepper
1   tablespoon butter
1   (3-ounce) package cream cheese, cut into cubes
⅓   cup chopped fresh basil (optional)

Whisk together first 4 ingredients. **Melt** butter in a large nonstick skillet over medium heat; add egg mixture, and cook, without stirring, until eggs begin to set on bottom. Sprinkle cream cheese cubes evenly over egg mixture; draw a spatula across bottom of skillet to form large curds. **Cook** until eggs are thickened but still moist. (Do not stir constantly.) Remove from heat. Stir in chopped basil before serving, if desired. Yield: 4 servings.

Per serving: Calories 256 (73% from fat); Fat 20.7g (sat 9.9g, mono 6.8g, poly 1.8g); Protein 14.7g; Carb 2.2g; Fiber 0.1g; Chol 455mg; Iron 2.2mg; Sodium 520mg; Calc 89mg

Shown on previous page: Cream Cheese Scrambled Eggs (above), Brown Sugar Bacon (page 129), Ambrosia (page 127), and Bourbon Sunrise (page 71)

These creamy curds need no adornment other than seasoning. Take care not to stir them too much while they cook. Simply draw a heat-resistant spatula through egg mixture as it begins to set on the bottom, forming large curds. Continue until eggs are thickened but still moist; do not stir constantly or they'll become dry and crumbly.

Hard-Cooked Eggs

prep: 20 min.

Place desired number of eggs in a single layer in a saucepan. Add enough water to measure at least 1 inch above eggs. Cover and quickly bring to a boil. Remove from heat. Let stand, covered, in hot water 15 minutes for large eggs. (Adjust time up or down by about 3 minutes for each size larger or smaller.) Pour off water. Immediately run cold water over eggs, or place them in ice water until completely cooled.

To remove shell, gently tap egg all over, roll between hands to loosen egg shell; then hold egg under cold running water as you peel off shell.

Per egg: Calories 74 (61% from fat); Fat 5g (sat 1.6g, mono 1.9g, poly 0.7g); Protein 6.3g; Carb 0.4g; Fiber 0g; Chol 212mg; Iron 0.9mg; Sodium 70mg; Calc 27mg

Bacon-and-Egg Quesadillas

prep: 20 min.   cook: 23 min.

Instead of using the egg mixture to make quesadillas, you can also spoon it into warmed tortillas to make wraps.

6   large eggs
2   tablespoons minced onion
2   tablespoons finely chopped green bell pepper
6   pickled jalapeño pepper slices, finely chopped
½   teaspoon seasoned salt
½   teaspoon seasoned pepper
½   cup Ranch dressing
½   cup salsa
1   (8-ounce) package shredded Mexican four-cheese blend
4   (10-inch) flour tortillas
4   bacon slices, cooked and crumbled
½   cup diced ham
Vegetable cooking spray

Whisk together first 6 ingredients. Cook in a lightly greased large skillet over medium heat, without stirring, until eggs begin to set on bottom. Draw a spatula across bottom of skillet to form large curds. Continue cooking until eggs are thickened but still moist. (Do not stir constantly.) Remove egg mixture from skillet, and set aside. Wipe skillet clean. **Stir** together Ranch dressing and salsa; set salsa mixture aside. **Sprinkle** ¼ cup cheese evenly onto half of each tortilla; top evenly with one-fourth of egg mixture, bacon, and ham. Top each half with ¼ cup more cheese. Fold tortilla in half over filling, pressing gently to seal. **Heat** skillet coated with cooking spray over medium-high heat. Add quesadillas, in 2 batches, and cook 3 to 4 minutes on each side or until golden brown. Serve with salsa mixture. Yield: 4 servings.

Per serving: Calories 796 (58% from fat); Fat 51.7g (sat 19.8g, mono 16.5g, poly 11.9g); Protein 35.7g; Carb 45.7g; Fiber 3.1g; Chol 395mg; Iron 4.5mg; Sodium 2180mg; Calc 561mg

No covered-dish dinner in the South is complete without those cheery little yellow-and-white ovals known as deviled eggs. Our staff likes them prepared any number of ways, but all agree that a modest amount of mayonnaise (no runny fillings for us), a touch of mustard, and a little sweet pickle are requirements.

Pipe, rather than spoon, the yolk mixture into egg white halves for a fancier look. Fill a small freezer bag with the yolk mixture, cut a hole in one corner, and press the bag to squeeze out the yolk mixture.

low calorie • low carb • make ahead

Basic Deviled Eggs

prep: 20 min.   cook: 5 min.
other: 1 hr., 15 min.

This basic recipe is the foundation for some creative additions, among them bacon, shrimp, chives, crabmeat, and pimiento. Whether or not to dust with paprika before serving is a purely personal decision.

6   large eggs
2   tablespoons mayonnaise
1½   tablespoons sweet pickle relish
1   teaspoon prepared mustard
⅛   teaspoon salt
Dash of pepper
Garnish: paprika

Place eggs in a single layer in a saucepan; add water to a depth of 3 inches. Bring to a boil; cover, remove from heat, and let stand 15 minutes.
Drain immediately, and fill saucepan with cold water and ice. Tap each egg firmly on the counter until cracks form all over the shell. Peel under cold running water.
Slice eggs in half lengthwise, and carefully remove yolks. Mash yolks with mayonnaise. Add sweet pickle relish, mustard, salt, and pepper; stir well.
Spoon yolk mixture into egg whites. Cover and chill at least 1 hour or until ready to serve. Garnish, if desired. Yield: 6 servings.

Per serving: Calories 116 (69% from fat); Fat 8.9g (sat 2.2g, mono 3g, poly 2.7g); Protein 6.4g; Carb 2.1g; Fiber 0.1g; Chol 214mg; Iron 0.7mg; Sodium 178mg; Calc 26mg

entertaining • low carb • make ahead

Deviled Eggs With Capers

prep: 18 min.   other: 1 hr.

6   large eggs, hard-cooked and peeled
2   tablespoons mayonnaise
1   tablespoon butter, softened
2   teaspoons drained capers
1   teaspoon chopped fresh chives or parsley
⅛   teaspoon dry mustard
⅛   teaspoon pepper
Paprika (optional)
Fresh chives or parsley sprigs (optional)

Cut eggs in half lengthwise; carefully remove yolks. Mash yolks; stir in mayonnaise and next 5 ingredients.
Spoon or pipe egg yolk mixture evenly into egg white halves. Cover and chill at least 1 hour or until ready to serve. Sprinkle with paprika and top with chives or parsley sprigs, if desired. Yield: 6 servings.

Per serving: Calories 128 (76% from fat); Fat 10.8g (sat 3.4g, mono 3.4g, poly 2.7g); Protein 6.4g; Carb 0.8g; Fiber 0.1g; Chol 219mg; Iron 0.7mg; Sodium 130mg; Calc 27mg

the deal on peeling

Opinions vary on the easiest way to peel eggs and keep those pesky shells from sticking. Some of our staff swear by this method.

Remove cooked eggs from heat, and pour off the water. Add about 1 inch of cold water and several ice cubes to the saucepan (it's okay if the insides of the eggs are still warm). Cover the pot, and shake vigorously so that the eggs crack all over. Peel under cold running water, starting at the large end—the air pocket will give you something to grip.

low carb

Chive-Tarragon Deviled Eggs

prep: 15 min.   other: 1 hr.

Lemon juice replaces pickle relish for the tang in these herbed jewels.

12   large eggs, hard-cooked and peeled
½   cup mayonnaise
1   tablespoon lemon juice
⅛   teaspoon hot sauce
2   tablespoons finely chopped fresh chives
2   teaspoons finely chopped fresh tarragon
½   teaspoon salt
½   teaspoon dry mustard
Garnishes: chopped fresh chives, fresh
    flat-leaf parsley sprigs

Cut eggs in half lengthwise; carefully remove yolks. Mash egg yolks; stir in mayonnaise, lemon juice, hot sauce, and next 4 ingredients.
Spoon or pipe egg yolk mixture evenly into egg white halves. Cover and chill at least 1 hour or until ready to serve. Garnish, if desired. Yield: 12 servings.

Per serving: Calories 145 (78% from fat); Fat 12.6g (sat 2.7g, mono 3.8g, poly 4.6g); Protein 6.5g; Carb 1.1g; Fiber 0g; Chol 216mg; Iron 0.7mg; Sodium 213mg; Calc 28mg

poached eggs make a simple, yet fancy, offering. For special occasions, serve them on English muffins, and top them with a rich sauce like hollandaise (page 432).

Poaching is tricky so follow the recipe carefully. Keep the water at a gentle simmer, and make sure it's no more than 2 inches deep. You can trim away ragged edges of eggs if the shape is important to you.

To poach eggs in advance, immediately after cooking, place eggs in ice water, and refrigerate until serving time. Drain eggs; place in boiling water 45 seconds, and drain again. Serve immediately.

low calorie • low carb • quick
Poached Eggs

prep: 2 min.   cook: 5 min.

Lightly grease a large saucepan. Add water to a depth of 2 inches in pan. Bring water to a boil; reduce heat, and maintain at a light simmer. Break eggs, 1 at a time, into a measuring cup or saucer; slip eggs, 1 at a time, into water, holding cup as close as possible to surface of water. Simmer 5 minutes or until done. Remove eggs with a slotted spoon. Trim edges, if desired.

Per egg: Calories 74 (61% from fat); Fat 5g (sat 1.6g, mono 1.9g, poly 0.7g); Protein 6.3g; Carb 0.4g; Fiber 0g; Chol 212mg; Iron 0.9mg; Sodium 70mg; Calc 27mg

Note: To cook eggs in poaching cups, grease each cup. Place poacher in a pan of simmering water so water is below the bottom of poacher. Break eggs into cups. Cover and cook 5 minutes or until done.

family favorite
Traditional Eggs Benedict

prep: 25 min.   cook: 10 min.

8   (½-ounce) Canadian bacon slices
Vegetable cooking spray
2   English muffins, split and toasted
4   poached eggs (recipe above)
Hollandaise Sauce (page 432)
Coarsely ground pepper
Paprika

Cook bacon in a skillet coated with cooking spray over medium heat until thoroughly heated, turning once. Drain on paper towels. **Place** 2 bacon slices on each muffin half. Top each with a poached egg, and drizzle evenly with Hollandaise Sauce. Sprinkle with pepper and paprika; serve immediately. Yield: 2 servings.

Per serving (with ⅓ cup Hollandaise Sauce): Calories 792 (68% from fat); Fat 60.1g (sat 31.7g, mono 18.4g, poly 4.5g); Protein 33.5g; Carb 28.9g; Fiber 1.6g; Chol 743mg; Iron 4.2mg; Sodium 1699mg; Calc 189mg

entertaining • family favorite
Eggs Sardou

prep: 9 min.   cook: 35 min.

Meant for a special brunch, this recipe requires a bit of advance preparation to poach eggs (see box above, left) and prepare Hollandaise.

2   green onions, chopped
2   teaspoons butter or margarine, melted
2   (10-ounce) packages frozen chopped spinach, thawed and well drained
1   (8-ounce) container sour cream
¼   cup whipping cream
¼   cup grated Parmesan cheese
¼   teaspoon ground nutmeg
⅛   teaspoon salt
Dash of pepper
3   (14-ounce) cans artichoke bottoms, drained
16   poached eggs (recipe at left)
2   recipes Hollandaise Sauce (page 432)
Paprika

Sauté green onions in butter in a large skillet until tender; stir in spinach and next 6 ingredients. Cook over low heat until thoroughly heated. (Do not boil.) **Place** 16 artichoke bottoms on a 15- x 10-inch jelly-roll pan, reserving any extra for another use. Bake at 350° for 10 minutes or until artichoke bottoms are heated; cover and keep warm. **For each serving,** spoon ¼ cup spinach mixture onto each individual serving plate; top with 2 artichoke bottoms. Arrange a poached egg on each artichoke bottom. Spoon Hollandaise Sauce over each egg. Sprinkle with paprika. Serve immediately. Yield: 8 servings.

Per serving (with ⅓ cup Hollandaise Sauce): Calories 761 (83% from fat); Fat 70.1g (sat 39.7g, mono 20.4g, poly 4.1g); Protein 22g; Carb 12.4g; Fiber 1.5g; Chol 774mg; Iron 5.1mg; Sodium 1159mg; Calc 227mg

baking is a good choice If you need to serve a lot of eggs at one time, baking is a good choice. Eggs require little attention as they bake, and they look attractive served in individual portions. Spooning milk over the eggs before cooking gives them a softer finish than fried or poached eggs. Serve baked eggs immediately.

low calorie • low carb • quick
Baked (Shirred) Eggs

prep: 3 min.   cook: 15 min.

4   large eggs
Salt and pepper to taste
¼   cup half-and-half or milk (optional)

Grease 4 (6-ounce) custard cups. Break and slip 1 egg into each custard cup. Sprinkle each egg with salt and pepper. Spoon 1 tablespoon half-and-half over each serving, if desired. Bake eggs, uncovered, at 325° for 15 minutes or until eggs reach desired doneness. Yield: 4 servings.

Per serving: Calories 74 (63% from fat); Fat 5g (sat 1.6g, mono 1.9g, poly 0.7g); Protein 6.3g; Carb 0.4g; Fiber 0g; Chol 212mg; Iron 0.9mg; Sodium 143mg; Calc 27mg

Quiche Lorraine

prep: 22 min.   cook: 47 min.   other: 10 min.

Filled with crunchy bits of bacon and melted Swiss, this classic quiche tempts the taste buds any time of day.

½   (15-ounce) package refrigerated piecrusts
8   bacon slices, cut into ½-inch pieces
4   green onions, chopped
2   cups (8 ounces) shredded Swiss cheese, divided
6   large eggs
1   cup whipping cream
½   teaspoon salt
⅛   teaspoon ground red pepper
⅛   teaspoon ground white pepper
⅛   teaspoon ground nutmeg

Fit piecrust into a 9-inch pieplate according to package directions; fold edges under, and crimp.

Bake at 400° for 7 minutes; remove from oven. Cool on a wire rack.

Meanwhile, cook bacon pieces in a large skillet until crisp; drain on paper towels, and crumble. Sprinkle bacon, green onions, and 1 cup cheese into prepared crust.

Whisk together eggs and next 4 ingredients; pour into piecrust, and sprinkle with remaining 1 cup cheese and nutmeg.

Bake at 350° for 35 to 40 minutes or until set. Let stand 10 minutes. Yield: 6 servings.

Per serving: Calories 568 (67% from fat); Fat 42.3g (sat 21.6g, mono 14.4g, poly 5.5g); Protein 22g; Carb 23.1g; Fiber 0.3g; Chol 318mg; Iron 1.3mg; Sodium 725mg; Calc 334mg

---

low carb

Crustless Canadian Bacon-and-Brie Quiche

prep: 10 min.   cook: 30 min.   other: 5 min.

Canadian bacon forms a surprise crust in this updated brunch dish.

14 thin Canadian bacon slices (about 10 ounces)
1   (8-ounce) round Brie cheese
8   large eggs, lightly beaten
½   cup mayonnaise
½   teaspoon ground white pepper
¼   cup grated Parmesan cheese
½   teaspoon dried basil

Arrange bacon slices on bottom and up sides of a lightly greased 9-inch pieplate, slightly overlapping slices.

Remove rind from Brie, and cut Brie into cubes. Whisk together eggs and mayonnaise; stir in Brie, pepper, Parmesan cheese, and basil. Pour filling into prepared pieplate.

Bake at 375° for 30 minutes or until a knife inserted in center comes out clean. Let stand 5 minutes before serving. Yield: 6 servings.

Per serving: Calories 446 (72% from fat); Fat 35.8g (sat 12.5g, mono 10.9g, poly 9.4g); Protein 27.5g; Carb 2.5g; Fiber 0.1g; Chol 353mg; Iron 1.9mg; Sodium 1157mg; Calc 149mg

---

Chicken-Olive-Cheddar Quiche

prep: 16 min.   cook: 48 min.
other: 10 min.

This is a tasty use for leftover chicken.

½   (15-ounce) package refrigerated piecrusts
1   (8-ounce) package sliced fresh mushrooms, drained
1   garlic clove, minced
Vegetable cooking spray
1½ cups chopped cooked chicken
3   green onions, chopped
2   tablespoons chopped fresh or 1 teaspoon dried basil
1   (2.25-ounce) can sliced black olives, drained
¼   teaspoon ground red pepper
1   cup (4 ounces) shredded Cheddar cheese
1   cup half-and-half
4   large eggs
¼   teaspoon salt
¼   teaspoon black pepper

Fit piecrust into a 9-inch pieplate according to package directions. Fold edges under, and crimp. Bake on lowest oven rack at 400° for 8 minutes. Cool.

Sauté mushrooms and garlic in a skillet coated with cooking spray over medium-high heat 5 minutes. Combine sautéed mushrooms, garlic, chicken, and next 4 ingredients. Spoon mixture into prepared crust. Sprinkle with cheese.

Whisk together half-and-half and remaining 3 ingredients. Pour over cheese.

Bake at 400° on lowest oven rack for 35 minutes or until set. Let stand 10 minutes before serving. Yield: 6 servings.

Per serving: Calories 401 (59% from fat); Fat 26.1g (sat 12.4g, mono 9.5g, poly 4.8g); Protein 19.7g; Carb 21.9g; Fiber 1g; Chol 203mg; Iron 1.7mg; Sodium 505mg; Calc 216mg

---

entertaining

Crabmeat-Parmesan Quiche

prep: 15 min.   cook: 44 min.   other: 15 min.

A hint of lemon enhances the succulent, sweet goodness of crab.

½   (15-ounce) package refrigerated piecrusts
4   green onions, chopped
2   teaspoons olive oil
1   pound fresh lump crabmeat, drained*
1   teaspoon grated lemon rind
½   teaspoon Old Bay seasoning
⅛   teaspoon ground red pepper
1   cup half-and-half
3   large eggs
¼   teaspoon salt
¼   teaspoon black pepper
1   (5-ounce) package shredded Parmesan cheese

Fit piecrust into a 9-inch pieplate according to package directions; fold edges under, and crimp. Bake on lowest oven rack at 400° for 8 minutes. Cool.

Sauté green onions in hot oil in a large skillet over medium-high heat 2 minutes. Stir in crabmeat and next 3 ingredients; sauté 2 minutes.

Whisk together half-and-half and next 3 ingredients in a large bowl; stir in cheese and crabmeat mixture. Pour filling into prepared crust.

Bake on lowest oven rack at 400° for 32 minutes or until set. Let stand 15 minutes before serving. Yield: 6 servings.

Per serving: Calories 419 (54% from fat); Fat 25g (sat 12g, mono 9.5g, poly 4.6g); Protein 26.7g; Carb 20.7g; Fiber 0.4g; Chol 196mg; Iron 1.4mg; Sodium 929mg; Calc 418mg

*Substitute 2 (6-ounce) cans lump crabmeat, rinsed and drained, for fresh crabmeat.

Plain Omelet

prep: 2 min.   cook: 3 min.

2   large eggs
⅛   teaspoon salt
Dash of ground white pepper
1   tablespoon water
1   tablespoon butter or margarine
Omelet fillings (optional)

Combine first 4 ingredients; whisk just until blended.
Heat a 6- or 8-inch omelet pan or heavy skillet over medium heat until hot enough to sizzle a drop of water. Add butter; rotate pan to coat bottom. Pour egg mixture into pan. As mixture starts to cook, gently lift edges of omelet with a spatula, and tilt pan so uncooked portion flows underneath.
Sprinkle half of omelet with 1 or more of the following fillings, if desired: 2 slices bacon, cooked and crumbled; 2 tablespoons sautéed mushrooms; 2 tablespoons shredded cheese; 2 tablespoons diced cooked ham; 1 tablespoon chopped fresh or 1 teaspoon dried herbs. Fold omelet in half, and transfer to plate. Yield: 1 serving.

Per serving (with no fillings): Calories 248 (77% from fat); Fat 21.3g (sat 10.3g, mono 6.8g, poly 1.8g); Protein 12.7g; Carb 0.9g; Fiber 0g; Chol 453mg; Iron 1.8mg; Sodium 512mg; Calc 57mg

Ham-and-Cheese Omelets

prep: 5 min.   cook: 5 min. per omelet

Havarti, a creamy, buttery-flavored cheese, is a nice update to this traditional omelet.

6   large eggs
2   tablespoons chopped fresh chives
¼   teaspoon salt
¼   teaspoon pepper
Vegetable cooking spray
2   teaspoons butter or margarine, divided
1   cup chopped smoked ham
½   cup (2 ounces) shredded Havarti cheese
1   cup (4 ounces) shredded Swiss cheese

Whisk together first 4 ingredients.
Melt 1 teaspoon butter in a 9- or 10-inch omelet pan or heavy skillet coated with cooking spray over medium heat, rotating pan to coat bottom evenly.

Add half of egg mixture to skillet. As egg mixture starts to cook, gently lift edges of omelet with a spatula, and tilt pan so uncooked portion flows underneath. Cook 1 to 2 minutes or until almost set. Flip omelet over.
Sprinkle 1 side of omelet with half each of ham and cheeses. Fold omelet in half. Cook 2 to 3 minutes or until cheese melts. To make next omelet, repeat with remaining 1 teaspoon butter, egg mixture, ham, and cheeses. Serve immediately. Yield: 4 servings.

Per serving: Calories 344 (65% from fat); Fat 24.8g (sat 12.8g, mono 8.1g, poly 1.9g); Protein 26.1g; Carb 2.3g; Fiber 0.1g; Chol 379mg; Iron 1.5mg; Sodium 821mg; Calc 391mg

Spanish Omelets With Fresh Avocado Salsa

prep: 10 min.   cook: 10 min. per omelet

1   cup chopped chorizo sausage (about 4 ounces)*
1   small sweet onion, chopped
½   small green bell pepper, chopped
1   garlic clove, minced
6   large eggs
¼   teaspoon salt
¼   teaspoon pepper
Vegetable cooking spray
2   teaspoons butter or margarine, divided
1   (3-ounce) package goat cheese, crumbled
Fresh Avocado Salsa
Garnishes: sour cream, freshly ground pepper

Cook first 4 ingredients in a 9- or 10-inch nonstick skillet over medium-high heat 5 minutes or until vegetables are tender. Remove chorizo mixture from skillet, and set aside. Wipe skillet clean.
Whisk together eggs, salt, and ¼ teaspoon pepper.
Melt 1 teaspoon butter in skillet coated with cooking spray over medium-high heat, rotating pan to coat bottom evenly. Add half of egg mixture. As egg mixture starts to cook, gently lift edges of omelet with a spatula, and tilt pan so uncooked portion flows underneath. Cook 3 minutes or until almost set. Flip omelet over.
Sprinkle 1 side of omelet with half each of chorizo mixture and goat cheese. Fold in

half. To make next omelet, repeat with remaining 1 teaspoon butter, egg mixture, chorizo mixture, and cheese.
Top with Fresh Avocado Salsa; garnish, if desired. Yield: 4 servings.

Per serving: Calories 448 (69% from fat); Fat 34.3g (sat 13.1g, mono 15g, poly 3.3g); Protein 23g; Carb 13.6g; Fiber 5g; Chol 364mg; Iron 2.8mg; Sodium 1023mg; Calc 131mg

*Substitute spicy smoked sausage for chorizo, if desired.

Fresh Avocado Salsa

prep: 20 min.

For best results, serve salsa within 4 hours.

4   plum tomatoes, chopped
1   small avocado, chopped
1   small sweet onion, chopped
1   small jalapeño pepper, seeded and minced
¼   cup chopped fresh cilantro
2   tablespoons fresh lime juice
½   teaspoon salt

Combine all ingredients, stirring gently. Cover and chill. Yield: 2 cups.

Per tablespoon: Calories 13 (69% from fat); Fat 1g (sat 0.2g, mono 0.6g, poly 0.1g); Protein 0.2g; Carb 1g; Fiber 0.5g; Chol 0mg; Iron 0.1mg; Sodium 38mg; Calc 2mg

Farmer's Oven-Baked Omelet

prep: 20 min.   cook: 35 min.

12   large eggs
½   cup sour cream
2   tablespoons chopped fresh thyme
1   teaspoon salt
¾   teaspoon freshly ground pepper
¼   teaspoon baking powder
2   tablespoons butter or margarine
6   small plum tomatoes, seeded and chopped
8   ounces farmer cheese, shredded
½   cup chopped fresh basil
Garnish: fresh basil leaves

Beat first 6 ingredients at medium speed with an electric mixer 2 to 3 minutes or until well blended.

Melt butter in a 12-inch ovenproof skillet; add egg mixture.

Bake at 350° for 15 minutes. Remove omelet from oven; sprinkle with tomatoes, cheese, and chopped basil. Return to oven, and bake 15 to 20 more minutes or until set. Garnish, if desired; serve immediately. Yield: 10 servings.

Per serving: Calories 238 (71% from fat); Fat 18.9g (sat 10.5g, mono 5.7g, poly 1.3g); Protein 12.4g; Carb 2.8g; Fiber 0.6g; Chol 285mg; Iron 1.4mg; Sodium 475mg; Calc 224mg

Note: Farmer cheese is a mild, part-skim, semisoft cheese. Substitute Havarti or Monterey Jack cheese, if you'd like.

low calorie • low carb • vegetarian

Creamy Veggie Omelets

prep: 13 min.   cook: 10 min. per omelet

Two cheeses flavor this savory egg dish that's chockful of veggies.

6   large eggs
¼   teaspoon salt
¼   teaspoon pepper
½   small red bell pepper, chopped
½   small green bell pepper, chopped
1   cup sliced fresh mushrooms
1   cup chopped fresh broccoli
¼   teaspoon salt
¼   teaspoon pepper
2   teaspoons butter or margarine, melted
Vegetable cooking spray
2   teaspoons butter or margarine, divided
3   tablespoons soft cream cheese with chives and onion
3   tablespoons crumbled feta cheese

Whisk together first 3 ingredients; set aside.
Sauté red bell pepper and next 5 ingredients in 2 teaspoons melted butter in a 9- or 10-inch omelet pan or nonstick skillet 10 minutes or until bell pepper is tender. Remove vegetables from skillet; set aside. Wipe skillet clean with a paper towel.
Coat skillet with cooking spray; add 1 teaspoon butter to skillet, and melt over medium heat. Add half of egg mixture (about ¾ cup). As egg mixture starts to cook, gently lift edges of omelet with a spatula, and tilt pan so uncooked portion flows underneath. Flip omelet over.

Sprinkle 1 side of omelet with half of vegetables. Dollop with half of cream cheese; sprinkle with half of feta cheese. Fold in half. Cook 2 minutes or until cheese melts. To make next omelet, repeat with remaining butter, egg mixture, vegetable mixture, and cheeses. Serve immediately. Yield: 4 servings.

Per serving: Calories 224 (68% from fat); Fat 16.9g (sat 8.5g, mono 5.2g, poly 1.4g); Protein 12.3g; Carb 5.5g; Fiber 1.4g; Chol 345mg; Iron 1.9mg; Sodium 559mg; Calc 104mg

family favorite • quick

Potato-Bacon Frittata

prep: 6 min.   cook: 17 min.

Serve with fresh fruit for breakfast or a quick supper.

3   tablespoons butter or margarine
2   cups frozen potatoes with onions and peppers (we tested with Ore Ida Potatoes O'Brien)
6   large eggs
2   tablespoons milk
¼   teaspoon salt
¼   teaspoon pepper
1   cup (4 ounces) shredded Cheddar cheese
6   bacon slices, cooked and crumbled
Garnish: diced fresh tomato or picante sauce

Melt butter in a 9- or 10-inch nonstick ovenproof skillet over medium heat; add frozen potatoes, and cook, uncovered, 10 minutes or until browned, stirring occasionally.
Combine eggs and next 3 ingredients, stirring with a wire whisk; pour over potatoes. As mixture starts to cook, gently lift edges of frittata with a spatula, and tilt pan so uncooked portion flows underneath. Sprinkle with cheese. Broil 2 minutes or until set.
Sprinkle with bacon; garnish, if desired. Serve immediately. Yield: 6 servings.

Per serving: Calories 346 (54% from fat); Fat 20.8g (sat 10.8g, mono 6.6g, poly 1.4g); Protein 16.3g; Carb 21.2g; Fiber 2g; Chol 256mg; Iron 2.3mg; Sodium 1145mg; Calc 172mg

Frittatas are more forgiving than omelets—you don't have to flip them in half.

Avocado-and-Black Bean Frittata

prep: 15 min.   cook: 34 min.   other: 5 min.

This hearty brunch dish is an authentic beginning to a border-style meal.

1   medium onion, chopped
1   tablespoon vegetable oil
2   large avocados, chopped
1   (15-ounce) can black beans, rinsed and drained
10   large eggs
½   cup sour cream
½   teaspoon salt
¼   teaspoon pepper
¼   teaspoon ground cumin
1   cup (4 ounces) shredded Cheddar cheese
Toppings: avocado slices, plum tomato slices, sour cream
Chunky salsa (optional)

Sauté onion in hot oil in a 12-inch ovenproof skillet over medium-high heat 3 to 4 minutes or until tender. Remove from heat; sprinkle top evenly with chopped avocados and beans.
Whisk together eggs and next 4 ingredients; pour over avocado mixture in skillet.
Bake at 350° for 25 minutes; sprinkle top evenly with cheese, and bake 5 more minutes. Remove from oven, and let stand 5 minutes before serving. Serve with desired toppings and, if desired, with salsa. Yield: 6 servings.

Per serving: Calories 417 (68% from fat); Fat 31.4g (sat 10.8g, mono 13.7g, poly 4.1g); Protein 20g; Carb 15.9g; Fiber 7.5g; Chol 381mg; Iron 3.2mg; Sodium 596mg; Calc 231mg

Brunch Egg Nests

prep: 20 min.   cook: 40 min.

A classic brunch recipe is revisited with convenience products.

½   tablespoon butter or margarine
1   (8-ounce) package fresh mushrooms, quartered
¾   cup chopped cooked ham
1   (10-ounce) container refrigerated Alfredo sauce
¼   cup sour cream
3   to 4 tablespoons sherry, white wine, or milk
1   to 2 tablespoons chopped fresh chives
1   (10-ounce) package frozen puff pastry shells, baked
4   hard-cooked eggs, coarsely chopped
Garnish: chopped fresh chives

Melt butter in a saucepan over medium-high heat; add mushrooms and ham, and sauté 7 minutes or until tender and golden. Reduce heat to low; whisk in Alfredo sauce, sour cream, sherry and 1 to 2 tablespoons chives, stirring until thoroughly heated. (Don't let mixture come to a boil.)
Fill each baked pastry shell with ½ cup mushroom mixture. Sprinkle evenly with chopped egg. Garnish, if desired. Yield: 6 servings.

Per serving: Calories 493 (65% from fat); Fat 35.7g (sat 11.5g, mono 9.3g, poly 13.2g); Protein 16.3g; Carb 27.6g; Fiber 1.2g; Chol 185mg; Iron 2.1mg; Sodium 770mg; Calc 113mg

Breakfast Ham 'n' Egg Casserole

prep: 15 min.   cook: 55 min.
other: 8 hrs., 5 min.

10   hearty white bread slices, cubed (we tested with Pepperidge Farm Hearty White)
2   cups cubed cooked ham (about 1 pound)
2   cups (8 ounces) shredded sharp Cheddar cheese
6   large eggs
1½   cups milk
1   teaspoon salt
1   teaspoon dry mustard
½   teaspoon Worcestershire sauce

Place bread cubes in a lightly greased 13- x 9-inch baking dish. Top evenly with ham and cheese. Whisk together eggs and remaining 4 ingredients; pour evenly over bread. Cover and chill 8 hours.
Bake, uncovered, at 350° for 50 to 55 minutes or until set. Let stand 5 minutes before serving. Yield: 8 servings.

Per serving: Calories 375 (46% from fat); Fat 19.3g (sat 9.1g, mono 6g, poly 1.4g); Protein 25g; Carb 26.6g; Fiber 2.5g; Chol 214mg; Iron 2.3mg; Sodium 1304mg; Calc 305mg

English Muffin Breakfast Strata

prep: 20 min.   cook: 48 min.
other: 8 hrs., 10 min.

Pepper-Jack cheese is a good substitute for either of the cheeses in this casserole, and it adds a little extra heat.

1   (16-ounce) package ground pork sausage
1   (12-ounce) package English muffins, split, toasted, and buttered
1   (10-ounce) block sharp Cheddar cheese, shredded
1   (8-ounce) block mozzarella cheese, shredded
8   large eggs
1½   cups sour cream
1   (4.5-ounce) can chopped green chiles, drained

Cook sausage in a skillet, stirring until sausage crumbles and is no longer pink; drain on paper towels, and set aside.
Cut muffin halves into quarters, and arrange in an even layer in a lightly greased 13- x 9-inch baking dish.
Sprinkle half each of sausage, Cheddar cheese, and mozzarella cheese evenly over muffins.
Whisk together eggs, sour cream, and chiles in a large bowl; pour evenly over sausage and cheeses. Top with remaining sausage and cheeses. Cover and chill 8 hours.
Bake, uncovered, at 350° for 40 minutes. Let stand 10 minutes before serving. Yield: 8 servings.

Per serving: Calories 717 (67% from fat); Fat 53g (sat 26.9g, mono 17.5g, poly 4.2g); Protein 33.7g; Carb 25.6g; Fiber 1.4g; Chol 330mg; Iron 3mg; Sodium 1086mg; Calc 684mg

Italian Sausage Brunch Casserole

prep: 20 min.   cook: 1 hr., 10 min.
other: 8 hrs.

This recipe sneaks a couple of veggies into a brunch casserole that's equally good for lunch or supper.

1   (8-ounce) package sweet Italian sausage
8   green onions, sliced
2   zucchini, diced (3 cups)
1   teaspoon salt
½   teaspoon pepper
1   (7-ounce) jar roasted red bell peppers, drained and chopped
1   (16-ounce) Italian bread loaf, cut into 1-inch cubes (about 8 cups)
2   cups (8 ounces) shredded sharp Cheddar cheese
6   large eggs
1½   cups milk

Remove and discard casings from sausage. Cook sausage in a large skillet, stirring until sausage crumbles and is no longer pink; drain. Add green onions and next 3 ingredients to skillet.
Sauté 4 minutes or until vegetables are tender. Stir in roasted bell peppers. Remove from heat, and cool.
Spread 4 cups bread cubes in a lightly greased 13- x 9-inch baking dish. Top with half each of the sausage mixture and cheese. Repeat with remaining bread, sausage, and cheese.
Whisk together eggs and milk. Pour egg mixture over bread. Cover and chill 8 hours.
Bake, covered, at 325° for 1 hour or until bubbly and hot. Yield: 8 servings.

Per serving: Calories 414 (42% from fat); Fat 19.3g (sat 9.5g, mono 6g, poly 1.9g); Protein 24g; Carb 35.7g; Fiber 2.6g; Chol 201mg; Iron 3.5mg; Sodium 1118mg; Calc 349mg

Breakfast Enchiladas

prep: 31 min.   cook: 47 min.

Our Test Kitchens staff likes the make-ahead ease of this casserole. Prepare as directed, without baking, and refrigerate overnight. Let stand at room temperature 30 minutes; bake as directed. Tip: Prepare the Cheese Sauce before scrambling the eggs so it will be ready to add at the proper time.

1 (1-pound) package hot ground pork sausage
2 tablespoons butter or margarine
4 green onions, thinly sliced
2 tablespoons chopped fresh cilantro
14 large eggs, beaten
¾ teaspoon salt
½ teaspoon pepper
Cheese Sauce
10 (8-inch) flour tortillas
1 cup (4 ounces) shredded Monterey Jack cheese with jalapeños
Toppings: halved grape tomatoes, sliced green onions, chopped fresh cilantro

Breakfast Enchiladas

Cook sausage in a large nonstick skillet over medium-high heat, stirring until sausage crumbles and is no longer pink. Remove from pan; drain well, pressing between paper towels.

Melt butter in a large nonstick skillet over medium heat. Add green onions and cilantro, and sauté 1 minute. Add eggs, salt, and pepper, and cook, without stirring, until eggs begin to set on bottom. Draw a spatula across bottom of pan to form large curds. Continue to cook until eggs are thickened but still moist. (Do not stir constantly.) Remove from heat, and gently fold in 1½ cups Cheese Sauce and sausage.

Spoon about ½ cup egg mixture down center of each flour tortilla; roll up. Place seam side down in a lightly greased 13- x- 9-inch baking dish. Pour remaining Cheese Sauce evenly over tortillas; sprinkle evenly with Monterey Jack cheese.

Bake, uncovered, at 350° for 30 minutes or until sauce is bubbly. Serve with desired toppings. Yield: 10 servings.

Per serving: Calories 625 (62% from fat); Fat 43.1g (sat 20g, mono 14.8g, poly 3.8g); Protein 29.2g; Carb 29.5g; Fiber 0.7g; Chol 385mg; Iron 3mg; Sodium 1204mg; Calc 501mg

Cheese Sauce

prep: 3 min.   cook: 8 min.

⅓ cup butter
⅓ cup all-purpose flour
3 cups milk
2 cups (8 ounces) shredded Cheddar cheese
1 (4.5-ounce) can chopped green chiles, undrained
¾ teaspoon salt

Melt butter in a saucepan over medium-low heat; whisk in flour until smooth. Cook, whisking constantly, 1 minute. Gradually whisk in milk; cook over medium heat, whisking constantly, 5 minutes or until thickened. Remove from heat, and whisk in cheese and remaining ingredients until smooth. Yield: 4 cups.

Per tablespoon: Calories 32 (70% from fat); Fat 2.5g (sat 1.6g, mono 0.4g, poly 0.1g); Protein 1.3g; Carb 1.2g; Fiber 0g; Chol 8mg; Iron 0.1mg; Sodium 65mg; Calc 40mg

Breakfast Pizza

prep: 8 min.   cook: 20 min.

1 (14-ounce) prebaked Italian pizza crust
1 (8-ounce) package shredded Italian cheese blend, divided
8 bacon slices, cooked and crumbled
4 plum tomatoes, sliced
½ teaspoon freshly ground pepper
2 large eggs
½ cup milk
¼ cup chopped fresh basil

Place pizza crust on a greased jelly-roll pan. Sprinkle half of cheese over pizza crust; top with bacon, tomato, and pepper.

Whisk together eggs, milk, and basil; slowly pour onto center of pizza (it will spread to edges). Sprinkle with remaining cheese.

Bake at 425° for 20 minutes or until egg mixture is set. Yield: 4 servings.

Per serving: Calories 652 (41% from fat); Fat 29.8g (sat 12.7g, mono 9.2g, poly 2.3g); Protein 36.3g; Carb 61g; Fiber 3.2g; Chol 167mg; Iron 4.3mg; Sodium 1452mg; Calc 602mg

taste of the south 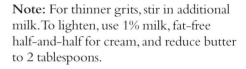 grits

Through the years grits have been the workhorse of the Southern table. Grits act as a foundation for flavorful items such as gravy, hash, or over-easy eggs. However, in the past decade or so, grits have experienced a renaissance, appearing on upscale dinner menus with the likes of shrimp, beef, and a host of herbs and cheeses.

Confusion abounds over what grits actually are. Commercially produced grits are made from ground, degerminated, dried white or yellow corn kernels that have been soaked in a solution of water and lye. The only grits for purists are produced by the old-fashioned method of stone grinding with a water-turned stone. These grits retain a more natural texture and rich flavor. Stone-ground grits are sometimes labeled as "speckled heart" because the remaining germ—or heart of the kernel—looks like a tiny black fleck.

At their most basic appearance, grits are cooked quickly in water and seasoned with salt and pepper. At their best, grits are luxuriously rich when cooked slowly in broth or whipping cream.

Creamy Grits

prep: 5 min.   cook: 45 min.

Serve these grits with either Tomato Gravy (page 441) or Country Ham With Redeye Gravy (page 321) for an authentic and delicious Deep South twist.

2   cups milk
2   cups water
1   to 1½ teaspoons salt
1   cup regular grits, uncooked
1   cup whipping cream
¼   cup butter or margarine
1   to 2 teaspoons freshly ground pepper

Bring first 3 ingredients to a boil in a large saucepan; gradually stir in grits. Reduce heat; simmer, stirring occasionally, 30 to 40 minutes or until thickened.
Stir in whipping cream, butter, and pepper; simmer, stirring occasionally, 5 minutes. Yield: 6 servings.

Per serving: Calories 346 (62% from fat); Fat 23.9g (sat 14.4g, mono 3.2g, poly 1.1g); Protein 5g; Carb 27.3g; Fiber 0.5g; Chol 82mg; Iron 1.2mg; Sodium 476mg; Calc 98mg

Creamy Grits

Note: For thinner grits, stir in additional milk. To lighten, use 1% milk, fat-free half-and-half for cream, and reduce butter to 2 tablespoons.

Jalapeño-Cheese Grits

prep: 20 min.   cook: 1 hr.

1   (32-ounce) container chicken broth
1¾   cups quick-cooking grits, uncooked
½   cup butter or margarine
1   medium onion, chopped
2   jalapeño peppers, seeded and diced
1   large red or green bell pepper, chopped
2   garlic cloves, pressed
2   cups (8 ounces) shredded sharp Cheddar cheese
2   cups (8 ounces) shredded Monterey Jack cheese
5   large eggs, lightly beaten
¼   teaspoon salt

Bring broth to a boil in a large saucepan; stir in grits. Reduce heat, and simmer, stirring occasionally, 5 minutes. Cover and remove from heat.
Melt butter in a large skillet; add chopped onion and next 3 ingredients, and sauté 5 minutes or until tender. Stir in grits, Cheddar cheese, and remaining ingredients. Pour into a lightly greased 13- x 9-inch baking dish.
Bake, covered, at 350° for 45 minutes or until set; serve immediately. Yield: 8 servings.

Per serving: Calories 515 (58% from fat); Fat 33.1g (sat 19.7g, mono 9.4g, poly 1.6g); Protein 22.7g; Carb 31.5g; Fiber 1.7g; Chol 217mg; Iron 2.7mg; Sodium 720mg; Calc 450mg

Grits go beyond breakfast these days. Let them replace rice or pasta. They're great for supper with shrimp or even pork roast.

Garlic Shrimp and Grits

prep: 10 min.   cook: 15 min.

If you want to cook shrimp yourself, start with 1 pound raw shrimp in the shell.

3   cups water
1   cup whipping cream
¼   cup butter or margarine
1   teaspoon salt
1   cup quick-cooking grits, uncooked
½   pound cooked, peeled medium-size, fresh shrimp
1   cup (4 ounces) extra-sharp shredded Cheddar cheese
2   garlic cloves, minced

Bring 3 cups water, whipping cream, butter, and salt to a boil in a large saucepan over medium-high heat. Reduce heat to medium, and whisk in grits. Cook, whisking constantly, 7 to 8 minutes or until mixture is smooth. Stir in shrimp, cheese, and garlic, and cook 1 to 2 minutes or until thoroughly heated. Yield: 6 servings.

Per serving: Calories 455 (57% from fat); Fat 28.8g (sat 17.1g, mono 7.3g, poly 1.7g); Protein 22.5g; Carb 24.6g; Fiber 0.4g; Chol 208mg; Iron 3mg; Sodium 673mg; Calc 183mg

Smoked Gouda Grits

prep: 5 min.   cook: 18 min.

A 7- to 8-ounce wheel of Gouda cheese is enough to yield the amount of shredded cheese needed in this recipe. Pair these grits with grilled pork for dinner.

6   cups chicken broth
2   cups milk
½   teaspoon pepper
2   cups quick-cooking grits, uncooked
1⅔   cups shredded smoked Gouda cheese
3   tablespoons butter or margarine

Bring first 3 ingredients to a boil in a 3- or 4-quart saucepan; gradually whisk in grits. Cover, reduce heat, and simmer, stirring occasionally, 8 minutes or until thickened. Add cheese and butter, stirring until melted. Yield: 12 servings.

Per serving: Calories 241 (38% from fat); Fat 10.1g (sat 5.7g, mono 2.9g, poly 0.7g); Protein 13.1g; Carb 23.9g; Fiber 0.4g; Chol 31mg; Iron 1.6mg; Sodium 950mg; Calc 164mg

Baked Garlic-and-Herb Grits

prep: 30 min.   cook: 55 min.

4   cups water
4   cups milk
1¼   teaspoons salt
2   cups regular grits, uncooked
2   (6.5-ounce) containers garlic-and-herb-flavored spreadable cheese (we tested with Alouette)
1   teaspoon seasoned pepper
1   cup shredded Parmesan cheese
4   large eggs, lightly beaten
¼   cup chopped fresh parsley
8   bacon slices, cooked and crumbled

Bring first 3 ingredients to a boil in a large saucepan or Dutch oven; gradually stir in grits. Cover, reduce heat, and simmer, stirring occasionally, 20 minutes or until thickened. Stir in spreadable cheese, pepper, and Parmesan cheese.

Gradually stir about one-fourth of grits into beaten eggs; add to remaining grits, stirring constantly. Stir in parsley. Pour into a lightly greased 13- x 9-inch baking dish. Sprinkle with crumbled bacon.

Bake, uncovered, at 350° for 50 to 55 minutes or until lightly browned and set. Yield: 12 servings.

Per serving: Calories 333 (52% from fat); Fat 19.3g (sat 10.6g, mono 5.7g, poly 1.2g); Protein 12.9g; Carb 26.6g; Fiber 0.5g; Chol 116mg; Iron 1.6mg; Sodium 675mg; Calc 216mg

Hot Tomato Grits

prep: 10 min.   cook: 30 min.   other: 5 min.

2   bacon slices, chopped
2   (14-ounce) cans chicken broth
½   teaspoon salt
1   cup quick-cooking grits, uncooked
2   large tomatoes, peeled and chopped
2   tablespoons canned chopped green chiles
1   cup (4 ounces) shredded Cheddar cheese
Garnishes: chopped tomato, cooked and crumbled bacon, shredded Cheddar cheese

Cook bacon in a heavy saucepan until crisp, reserving drippings in pan. Gradually add broth and salt; bring to a boil.
Stir in grits, tomato, and chiles; return to a

boil, stirring often. Reduce heat, and simmer, stirring often, 15 to 20 minutes. **Stir** in 1 cup cheese; cover and let stand 5 minutes or until cheese melts. Garnish, if desired. Yield: 6 servings.

Per serving: Calories 231 (40% from fat); Fat 10.3g (sat 5.2g, mono 3.5g, poly 0.8g); Protein 9.9g; Carb 25.5g; Fiber 1.7g; Chol 25mg; Iron 1.8mg; Sodium 625mg; Calc 150mg

Note: To decrease fat and calories, drain bacon on paper towels, discarding drippings; substitute reduced-fat sharp Cheddar cheese for regular.

Chile-Blue Cheese Grits

prep: 20 min.   cook: 1 hr.   other: 1 hr.

Saga blue is a soft, mellow-flavored blue cheese that has a white, edible rind.

3   cups milk
1   garlic clove, minced
1¼   teaspoons salt, divided
1   cup quick-cooking grits, uncooked
½   cup crumbled Saga blue cheese
⅓   cup butter or margarine, cubed
½   cup whipping cream
2   large eggs, lightly beaten
2   egg whites, lightly beaten
1   (4.5-ounce) can chopped green chiles, drained
2   tablespoons freshly grated Parmesan cheese
2   teaspoons chopped fresh basil
1   teaspoon chopped fresh thyme
¼   teaspoon pepper

Bring milk, garlic, and 1 teaspoon salt to a boil in a medium saucepan; gradually stir in grits. Cover, reduce heat, and simmer, stirring occasionally, 10 minutes.
Whisk in blue cheese and butter until melted. Whisk in remaining ¼ teaspoon salt, cream, and remaining ingredients; pour into a lightly greased 1½-quart soufflé dish.
Bake, uncovered, at 325° for 1 hour. (Center may be slightly soft.) Yield: 6 servings.

Per serving: Calories 413 (58% from fat); Fat 26.5g (sat 15.6g, mono 7.3g, poly 1.3g); Protein 13.3g; Carb 30.1g; Fiber 1.1g; Chol 146mg; Iron 1.5mg; Sodium 847mg; Calc 234mg

Croissant French Toast With
Fresh Strawberry Syrup

Caramel-Pecan French Toast

prep: 11 min.   cook: 45 min.

Caramel nut roll meets French toast in this recipe.

1	cup firmly packed light brown sugar
½	cup butter or margarine
2	tablespoons light corn syrup
12	honey white bread slices (we tested with Sara Lee)
1	cup chopped pecans, toasted and divided
¾	cup raisins
6	large eggs
½	cup milk
2	teaspoons grated lemon rind
1	teaspoon vanilla extract
½	teaspoon ground cinnamon
1½	cups whipping cream, divided
¼	cup powdered sugar

Maple syrup

Combine first 3 ingredients in a small saucepan; cook over medium heat 3 to 5 minutes, stirring constantly, until sugar dissolves.

Pour brown sugar mixture into a lightly greased 13- x 9-inch baking dish. Arrange 5 to 6 bread slices over brown sugar mixture, cutting slices as necessary to fit in dish. Sprinkle ¾ cup chopped pecans and raisins over bread. Top with remaining bread slices.

Whisk together eggs, next 4 ingredients, and 1 cup whipping cream. Pour egg mixture evenly over bread slices.

Bake, uncovered, at 350° for 30 to 40 minutes or until a wooden pick inserted in center comes out clean.

Meanwhile, beat remaining ½ cup whipping cream until foamy; gradually add powdered sugar, beating until soft peaks form. Top each serving with maple syrup, a sprinkling of remaining ¼ cup chopped pecans, and sweetened whipped cream. Yield: 8 servings.

Per serving: Calories 692 (56% from fat); Fat 42.7g (sat 18.9g, mono 15.1g, poly 5.3g); Protein 10g; Carb 70g; Fiber 3g; Chol 250mg; Iron 3.3mg; Sodium 413mg; Calc 140mg

Croissant French Toast With Fresh Strawberry Syrup

prep: 15 min.   cook: 4 min. per batch

½	cup whipping cream
1½	tablespoons powdered sugar
4	large day-old croissants
¾	cup milk
2	large eggs
1	teaspoon vanilla extract
2	tablespoons butter
3	tablespoons powdered sugar

Fresh Strawberry Syrup

Beat whipping cream at medium speed with an electric mixer until soft peaks form. Add 1½ tablespoons powdered sugar, beating until stiff peaks form. Chill.

Slice croissants in half lengthwise.

Whisk together milk, eggs, and vanilla. Pour into a shallow dish. Dip croissant halves into egg mixture, coating well.

Melt 1 tablespoon butter in a large nonstick skillet over medium heat. Add 4 croissant halves, and cook about 2 minutes on each side or until golden. Repeat procedure with remaining butter and croissant halves.

Sprinkle with 3 tablespoons powdered sugar; top each serving with whipped cream and 2 tablespoons Fresh Strawberry Syrup. Yield: 4 servings.

Per serving: Calories 576 (55% from fat); Fat 34.9g (sat 19.9g, mono 9.7g, poly 1.9g); Protein 11.1g; Carb 53g; Fiber 2.6g; Chol 211mg; Iron 2mg; Sodium 604mg; Calc 118mg

Fresh Strawberry Syrup

prep: 10 min.   cook: 5 min.   other: 30 min.

1	quart fresh strawberries, sliced
½	cup sugar
¼	cup orange liqueur or orange juice
1	teaspoon grated orange rind

Combine all ingredients in a saucepan; let stand 30 minutes or until sugar dissolves. Cook over low heat, stirring occasionally, 5 minutes or until warm. Yield: about 2 cups.

Per tablespoon: Calories 25 (4% from fat); Fat 0.1g (sat 0g, mono 0g, poly 0g); Protein 0.1g; Carb 5.3g; Fiber 0.4g; Chol 0mg; Iron 0.1mg; Sodium 0mg; Calc 3mg

Cinnamon Bread French Toast

prep: 8 min.   cook: 6 min. per batch

2   cups all-purpose baking mix
1½ cups water
1   teaspoon vanilla extract
¼   teaspoon ground cinnamon
2½ tablespoons butter or margarine, divided
2½ tablespoons vegetable oil, divided
14 cinnamon bread slices (we tested with Pepperidge Farm Cinnamon Swirl Bread)
2   bananas, sliced
¼   cup chopped pecans, toasted
Maple syrup

Whisk together first 4 ingredients.
Melt ½ tablespoon butter and ½ tablespoon oil in a large skillet over medium heat. Dip 3 bread slices in batter; cook 2 to 3 minutes on each side or until golden.
Repeat procedure with remaining butter, oil, bread slices, and batter.
Top with sliced banana and pecans. Serve with maple syrup. Yield: 7 servings.

Per serving (without syrup): Calories 441 (46% from fat); Fat 22.3g (sat 5.8g, mono 10.1g, poly 3.7g); Protein 9.2g; Carb 58.2g; Fiber 6.2g; Chol 11mg; Iron 2.9mg; Sodium 692mg; Calc 58mg

Pain Perdu

prep: 11 min.   cook: 4 min. per batch
other: 30 min.

French toast is called pain perdu, or "lost bread," because it's made from stale bread.

1   (12-ounce) French bread loaf
4   large eggs
2   cups whipping cream
½   cup granulated sugar
1   tablespoon ground cinnamon
1   teaspoon ground nutmeg
4   teaspoons vanilla extract
Powdered sugar
4   cups raspberries and blueberries
Maple syrup

Cut French bread into 12 (1-inch-thick) diagonal slices. Whisk together eggs and next 5 ingredients until blended.

Place bread slices in a lightly greased 13- x 9-inch baking dish; pour egg mixture evenly over bread. Let stand 30 minutes, or overnight (covered in refrigerator), or until most of liquid is absorbed.
Remove bread slices from egg mixture, letting excess drip off. Cook bread slices, in batches, in a greased nonstick skillet or griddle over medium-high heat 2 minutes on each side or until golden.
Arrange bread slices on serving plates; sprinkle with powdered sugar. Top with raspberries and blueberries. Serve with maple syrup. Yield: 6 servings.

Per serving (without syrup): Calories 535 (44% from fat); Fat 26.2g (sat 14g, mono 8g, poly 1.8g) Protein 9.3g; Carb 64.4g; Fiber 6.1g; Chol 198mg; Iron 2.7mg; Sodium 384mg; Calc 82mg

Dried Cherry-Walnut Sweet Rolls

prep: 10 min.   cook: 15 min.   other: 30 min.

1   (25-ounce) package frozen roll dough, thawed according to package directions
½   cup chopped walnuts
¼   cup butter, melted
1   (3-ounce) package dried cherries, chopped
3   tablespoons granulated sugar
¾   teaspoon pumpkin pie spice
2   cups powdered sugar
3   tablespoons hot water

Preheat oven to 200°.
Place dough balls in 2 greased 9-inch round cakepans. Turn off oven. Cover dough balls with plastic wrap; let rise in oven 25 to 30 minutes or until doubled in bulk. Remove from oven. Remove and discard plastic wrap.
Stir together walnuts and next 4 ingredients. Sprinkle nut mixture evenly over dough in pans.
Bake at 350° for 12 to 15 minutes or until golden. Cool.
Stir together powdered sugar and 3 tablespoons hot water. Drizzle evenly over rolls. Yield: 2 dozen.

Per roll: Calories 161 (29% from fat); Fat 5.1g (sat 1.3g, mono 1.4g, poly 1.2g); Protein 3.4g; Carb 26.5g; Fiber 1g; Chol 5mg; Iron 1.1mg; Sodium 129mg; Calc 4mg

Pecan Crescent Twists

prep: 15 min.   cook: 12 min.

Keep crescent roll dough on hand to make this special morning treat. Kids can help roll out the dough.

2   (8-ounce) cans refrigerated crescent rolls
3   tablespoons butter or margarine, melted and divided
½   cup chopped pecans
¼   cup granulated sugar
1   teaspoon ground cinnamon
⅛   teaspoon ground nutmeg
½   cup powdered sugar
2½ teaspoons maple syrup or milk

Unroll crescent rolls, and separate each can into 2 rectangles, pressing perforations to seal. Brush evenly with 2 tablespoons melted butter.
Stir together chopped pecans and next 3 ingredients; sprinkle 3 tablespoons pecan mixture onto each rectangle, pressing in gently.
Roll up, starting at 1 long side, and twist. Cut 6 shallow ½-inch-long diagonal slits in each roll.
Shape rolls into rings, pressing ends together; place on a lightly greased baking sheet. Brush rings with remaining 1 tablespoon butter.
Bake at 375° for 12 minutes or until rings are golden.
Stir together powdered sugar and maple syrup until smooth; drizzle over warm rings. Cut rings in half, and serve. Yield: 8 servings.

Per serving: Calories 367 (54% from fat); Fat 21.9g (sat 6.2g, mono 10.8g, poly 3.4g); Protein 4.8g; Carb 37.4g; Fiber 0.9g; Chol 11mg; Iron 1.8mg; Sodium 476mg; Calc 12mg

Everyday Granola

prep: 12 min.   cook: 50 min.

The key to crisp granola is to bake it in a thin, even layer. We recommend two large rimmed baking sheets. Otherwise, simply bake it in batches on smaller pans.

1	cup orange juice
1	cup firmly packed light brown sugar
½	cup honey
⅓	cup canola oil
4	cups whole-wheat toasted oat cereal
3	cups uncooked regular oats
1	cup toasted wheat germ
1	cup coarsely chopped walnuts
1	cup pecan halves
½	cup nutlike cereal nuggets
½	cup unsalted soy nuts
¼	cup flaxseed
¼	cup unsalted sunflower seed kernels
1	cup dried cranberries (about 6 ounces)
1	cup dried blueberries (about 8 ounces)

Heat first 4 ingredients in a saucepan over medium heat 5 minutes, stirring until sugar dissolves; set aside.

Combine oat cereal and next 8 ingredients in a large bowl. Pour juice mixture over dry ingredients; toss well to coat. Divide mixture in half; spread evenly over 2 lightly greased 17¼- x 12¼-inch rimmed baking sheets.

Bake at 300° for 45 minutes or until dry and crisp, stirring gently every 15 minutes. Remove from oven; stir in dried fruit. Press granola lightly onto pans. Cool completely. Store in an airtight container. Yield: 16 cups.

Per cup: Calories 436 (37% from fat); Fat 18g (sat 1.6g, mono 7.4g, poly 7.3g); Protein 10.1g; Carb 63.8g; Fiber 7.1g; Chol 0mg; Iron 7.6mg; Sodium 81mg; Calc 69mg

Sour Cream Coffee Cake

prep: 21 min.   cook: 1 hr.   other: 1 hr., 10 min.

1	cup coarsely chopped pecans, toasted
1	cup firmly packed light brown sugar
1	tablespoon ground cinnamon
3	cups all-purpose flour
2½	teaspoons baking powder
½	teaspoon baking soda
¾	teaspoon salt
¾	cup butter, softened
1½	cups granulated sugar
3	large eggs
2	teaspoons vanilla extract
1	(16-ounce) container sour cream
1	cup powdered sugar
1½	tablespoons orange juice

Grease a 12-cup nonstick Bundt pan with shortening.

Combine pecans, brown sugar, and cinnamon; set aside.

Combine flour, baking powder, baking soda, and salt.

Beat butter and 1½ cups sugar at medium speed with an electric mixer until light and fluffy. Add eggs, 1 at a time, and beat just until blended. Add vanilla, beating until blended. Add flour mixture to butter mixture alternately with sour cream, beginning and ending with flour mixture.

Pour one-third of batter into prepared pan. Sprinkle batter with half of pecan mixture. Repeat procedure with remaining batter and pecan mixture, ending with batter.

Bake at 350° for 1 hour or until a wooden pick inserted in center comes out clean. Cool in pan on a wire rack 10 minutes. Run a knife around edges to loosen sides. Gently turn cake out onto wire rack to cool completely. Transfer to a serving plate.

Whisk together powdered sugar and orange juice. Drizzle over coffee cake. Yield: 16 servings.

Per serving: Calories 449 (42% from fat); Fat 21.1g (sat 9.9g, mono 7.4g, poly 2.4g); Protein 5.5g; Carb 61.5g; Fiber 1.6g; Chol 75mg; Iron 2mg; Sodium 319mg; Calc 111mg

Cinnamon Breakfast Rolls

prep: 31 min.   cook: 30 min.
other: 9 hrs., 30 min.

These homemade-tasting rolls start with a mix.

1	(18.25-ounce) package French vanilla cake mix (we tested with Betty Crocker)
5¼	cups all-purpose flour
2	(¼-ounce) envelopes active dry yeast
1	teaspoon salt
2½	cups warm water (120° to 130°)
½	cup sugar
2	teaspoons ground cinnamon
½	cup butter, divided and melted
½	cup raisins, divided
¾	cup chopped pecans, divided
1	cup powdered sugar
3	tablespoons milk
½	teaspoon vanilla extract

Stir together first 5 ingredients in a large bowl; cover and let rise in a warm place (85°), free from drafts, 1 hour.

Combine ½ cup sugar and cinnamon.

Turn dough out onto a well-floured surface; divide in half. Roll one portion into an 18- x 12-inch rectangle.

Brush with half of butter; sprinkle with half of sugar mixture, half of raisins, and ¼ cup pecans.

Roll up, jelly-roll fashion, starting at long side; cut crosswise into 16 (1-inch-thick) slices. Place rolls into a lightly greased 13- x 9-inch pan. Repeat procedure with remaining rectangle. Cover and chill 8 hours.

Remove from refrigerator, and let stand 30 minutes.

Bake at 350° for 20 to 25 minutes or until golden; cool slightly.

Stir together powdered sugar, milk, and vanilla; drizzle over rolls. Sprinkle with remaining pecans. Yield: 32 rolls.

Per roll: Calories 165 (35% from fat); Fat 6.5g (sat 2.6g, mono 1.9g, poly 0.7g); Protein 11.8g; Carb 25.5g; Fiber 1.1g; Chol 8mg; Iron 0.8mg; Sodium 196mg; Calc 8mg

Tip: To cut rolls, use a piece of waxed dental floss. It works wonders to get a clean-cut edge without flattening the rolls.

Caramel Sticky Buns

prep: 25 min.   cook: 16 min.   other: 40 min.

1	(16-ounce) package hot roll mix
1½	cups Caramel Sauce (page 442)
1	cup chopped pecans, toasted
3	tablespoons butter, softened
¼	cup sugar
2	teaspoons ground cinnamon

Prepare roll dough according to package directions. Let stand 5 minutes.

Pour Caramel Sauce into a lightly greased 13- x 9-inch pan or 2 lightly greased 8-inch square pans. Sprinkle with pecans.

Roll dough into a 15- x 10-inch rectangle. Spread with butter, and sprinkle with sugar and cinnamon.

Roll up, starting at a long side. Cut into 1-inch-thick slices. Arrange slices, cut side down, over Caramel Sauce and pecans.

Cover and let rise in a warm place (85°), free from drafts, 30 minutes or until doubled in bulk.

Bake at 375° for 16 minutes. Let stand on a wire rack 5 minutes. Invert onto a serving plate. Yield: 15 sticky buns.

Per bun: Calories 437 (47% from fat); Fat 22.8g (sat 10.3g, mono 8.6g, poly 4g); Protein 3.8g; Carb 54.7g; Fiber 1.7g; Chol 57mg; Iron 1.8mg; Sodium 282mg; Calc 11mg

Freezing Note: Buns can be frozen before rising. Remove from freezer, and let thaw at room temperature; continue as directed above.

Overnight Caramel Sticky Buns: Allow dough to rise in refrigerator overnight. Remove from refrigerator, and let stand 30 minutes. Bake as directed above.

Caramel Sticky Buns

◄ Roll up dough, starting at long side.

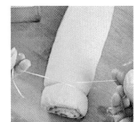

◄ Use dental floss to cut dough into 1-inch slices.

◄ Arrange slices in pan over pecans and Caramel Sauce.

family favorite
Cheese Blintzes

prep: 25 min.   cook: 8 min.   other: 20 min.

These brunch or dessert crêpes are filled with a slightly sweet cheese. They're folded into plump pillows that brown nicely in a hot skillet.

2 (3-ounce) packages cream cheese, softened
1 (12-ounce) container large-curd cottage cheese
¼ cup egg substitute
2 tablespoons sugar
1 teaspoon grated lemon rind
12 (6-inch) Crêpes (recipe at right)
3 tablespoons butter or margarine, divided
¾ cup sour cream
¾ cup strawberry preserves

Combine cream cheese and cottage cheese; beat at medium speed with an electric mixer 2 minutes or until smooth. Add egg substitute, sugar, and lemon rind, stirring well; cover and chill 20 minutes.
Place about 3 tablespoons cheese filling in center of each crêpe. Fold top and bottom of crêpe over filling; then fold left and right sides of crêpe over filling to form a square.
Repeat procedure with remaining crêpes and filling. Melt 1½ tablespoons butter in a large nonstick skillet over medium heat. Place half of blintzes in skillet. Cook on both sides until lightly browned; remove from skillet, and keep warm.
Melt remaining 1½ tablespoons butter in skillet. Repeat procedure with remaining blintzes.
To serve, place cheese blintzes on serving plates. Top each with 1 tablespoon sour cream and 1 tablespoon strawberry preserves. Yield: 12 servings.

Per serving: Calories 272 (50% from fat); Fat 15.1g (sat 8.9g, mono 4.2g, poly 1g); Protein 7.8g; Carb 26.5g; Fiber 0.5g; Chol 74mg; Iron 1mg; Sodium 257mg; Calc 74mg

Crêpes

prep: 5 min.   cook: 1 to 2 min. per crêpe
other: 1 hr.

1 cup all-purpose flour
¼ teaspoon salt
1¼ cups milk
2 large eggs
2 tablespoons butter, melted
Vegetable cooking spray

Combine first 3 ingredients; beat with a wire whisk until smooth. Add eggs; beat well. Stir in butter. Cover and chill at least 1 hour.
Coat bottom of a 6-inch crêpe pan or heavy skillet with cooking spray; place over medium heat until hot.
Pour 2 tablespoons batter into pan; quickly tilt pan in all directions so batter covers bottom. Cook 1 minute or until crêpe can be shaken loose. Turn crêpe over, and cook 30 seconds. Place crêpe on a cloth towel to cool. Repeat with remaining batter.
Stack crêpes between sheets of wax paper (so they won't stick together), and place in an airtight container, if desired. Store in refrigerator up to 2 days, or freeze up to 3 months. Yield 16 (6-inch) crêpes.

Per crêpe: Calories 62 (39% from fat); Fat 2.7g (sat 1.5g, mono 0.8g, poly 0.2g); Protein 2.2g; Carb 6.9g; Fiber 0.2g; Chol 32mg; Iron 0.5mg; Sodium 63mg; Calc 26mg

low cholesterol • low fat • make ahead
Spiced Mixed Fruit

prep: 30 min.   cook: 20 min.

You can make and chill this fruit a couple of days in advance, but don't add the banana until just before serving.

1 cup sugar
1 cup water
1 cup dry white wine
2 whole cloves
1 (2-inch) cinnamon stick
½ teaspoon vanilla extract
6 navel oranges
3 grapefruit
3 bananas

Bring first 5 ingredients to a boil in a saucepan. Reduce heat to low, and simmer, stirring occasionally, 15 minutes. Stir in vanilla. Cool syrup. Discard cloves and cinnamon stick.
Peel and section oranges and grapefruits, and place in a large bowl. Gently stir in syrup. Chill mixture, if desired. Slice bananas, and stir in just before serving. Yield: 8 servings.

Per serving: Calories 237 (1% from fat); Fat 0.2g (sat 0g, mono 0g, poly 0g); Protein 2.1g; Carb 61.5g; Fiber 8.3g; Chol 0mg; Iron 0.4mg; Sodium 4mg; Calc 63mg

Spiced Apples

prep: 12 min.   cook: 20 min.

Cinnamon spices these apples. They make a nice addition to brunch or a veggie plate.

¼ cup butter or margarine
6 medium Granny Smith apples, peeled, cored, and sliced (about 3 pounds)
¾ cup sugar
1 teaspoon ground cinnamon
½ teaspoon ground nutmeg

Melt butter in a large skillet over medium-high heat; add apples and remaining ingredients. Sauté 15 to 20 minutes or until apples are tender. Yield: 6 servings.

Per serving: Calories 227 (31% from fat); Fat 7.8g (sat 4.9g, mono 2g, poly 0.3g); Protein 0.5g; Carb 41.7g; Fiber 1.9g; Chol 20mg; Iron 0.3mg; Sodium 54mg; Calc 14mg

◄ Apples will be piled high in your skillet as you start cooking.

◄ After 15 to 20 minutes, sautéed apples will have cooked down considerably in the pan.

Ambrosia

prep: 30 min.   other: 2 hrs.

12 navel oranges, peeled and sectioned
1   fresh pineapple, peeled, cored, and cut
    into cubes (see photos at right)
2   tablespoons powdered sugar
1   cup freshly grated coconut

Toss together fruit and powdered sugar in a large bowl.
Place one-third of fruit mixture in a serving bowl. Top with one-third coconut. Repeat layers twice. Cover and chill 2 hours. Yield: 10 servings.

Per serving: Calories 138 (20% from fat); Fat 3g (sat 2.4g, mono 0.2g, poly 0.1g); Protein 2.1g; Carb 29.5g; Fiber 5.1g; Chol 0mg; Iron 0.6mg; Sodium 4mg; Calc 80mg

Note: Three red grapefruit, peeled and sectioned, can be added to fruit mixture, if desired.

Grapefruit Compote in Rosemary Syrup

prep: 20 min.   cook: 5 min.

If you have an abundance of grapefruit during the holidays, this recipe is a great use for it.

1   cup sugar
½   cup water
3   tablespoons honey
3   fresh rosemary sprigs
6   large grapefruit
½   cup maraschino cherries with
    stems
Garnish: fresh rosemary sprigs

Combine first 4 ingredients in a saucepan; bring to a boil over medium heat. Boil 5 minutes. Remove from heat, and let cool completely. Remove and discard rosemary.
Section grapefruit over a large bowl, catching juices. Pour rosemary syrup over fruit in bowl. Add cherries. Cover and chill until ready to serve. Garnish, if desired. Yield: 8 servings.

Per serving: Calories 210 (1% from fat); Fat 0.3g (sat 0g, mono 0g, poly 0g); Protein 1.4g; Carb 54.6g; Fiber 3g; Chol 0mg; Iron 0.2mg; Sodium 0mg; Calc 41mg

cutting a pineapple

▲ Using a sharp knife, cut off a thin slice from top and bottom of pineapple.

▲ Position pineapple upright; thinly slice downward around pineapple to remove rough skin, being careful not to waste fruit.

▲ Cut pineapple lengthwise into eighths.

◄ Cut core away from each slice; discard core.

Chop each slice into chunks. Refrigerate in an airtight container up to three days. ▶

Grand Oranges and Strawberries

prep: 30 min.   other: 8 hrs.

Using Grand Marnier makes this fruit dish fit for company; however, you can substitute fresh squeezed orange juice so the kids can enjoy it, too.

½   cup orange marmalade
1½ cups sparkling white grape juice, chilled
¼   cup orange liqueur (we tested with
    Grand Marnier)
10 to 12 large navel oranges, peeled and
    sectioned
2   cups sliced fresh strawberries

Melt marmalade in a small saucepan over low heat, stirring constantly; remove from heat, and cool slightly.
Stir together marmalade, white grape juice, and orange liqueur in a large serving dish or bowl until blended. Add orange sections, and gently stir. Cover and chill 8 hours.
Add strawberries to oranges in bowl, and gently stir. Serve with a slotted spoon. Yield: 12 servings.

Per serving: Calories 128 (2% from fat); Fat 0.3g (sat 0g, mono 0.1g, poly 0.1g); Protein 1.4g; Carb 30.5g; Fiber 3.2g; Chol 0mg; Iron 0.4mg; Sodium 10mg; Calc 62mg

family favorite • make ahead

Hash Brown Potatoes

prep: 25 min.   cook: 38 min.   other: 8 hrs.

Avoid overstirring potatoes while they brown in a cast-iron skillet.

1½ pounds small red potatoes
2   tablespoons canola or vegetable oil
2   tablespoons butter or margarine
1   small onion, chopped
2   garlic cloves, minced
¼   cup chopped flat-leaf parsley
1½ teaspoons kosher salt
¼   teaspoon pepper

Place potatoes in a Dutch oven with water to cover; bring to a boil. Cook, uncovered, 8 minutes; drain and chill overnight. (Be sure not to overcook potatoes here; they will not be tender at this point.)
Cut potatoes into ¾-inch cubes; set aside.
Melt oil and butter in a 9- or 10-inch cast-iron skillet over medium–high heat. Add potato, and cook 10 minutes, stirring occasionally. Add onion; cook 5 minutes. Reduce heat to medium. Add garlic; cook 15 more minutes or until potatoes are browned on all sides, stirring gently. Stir in parsley, salt, and pepper just before serving. Yield: 4 servings.

Per serving: Calories 246 (48% from fat); Fat 13g (sat 4.2g, mono 5.6g, poly 2.4g); Protein 3.7g; Carb 29.6g; Fiber 3.3g; Chol 15mg; Iron 1.6mg; Sodium 773mg; Calc 31mg

Hash Brown Potatoes

The key to crisp hash browns is cooking them in a single layer in a hot skillet.

family favorite • for kids

Smothered-Covered Hash Browns

prep: 3 min.   cook: 33 min.

Pressing down firmly with a spatula on these hash brown patties will help them hold together easily.

1   medium onion, diced
¼   cup vegetable oil, divided
½   (30-ounce) bag frozen shredded hash browns, thawed (about 4 cups)
1   teaspoon salt
½   teaspoon pepper
8   (¾-ounce) American cheese slices

Sauté onion in 1 tablespoon hot oil in a large nonstick skillet over medium heat 4 to 5 minutes or until tender. Stir together onion, hash browns, salt, and pepper in a large bowl.
Heat 1 tablespoon oil in skillet over medium-high heat. Using a ⅓ cup measure, drop hash brown mixture into hot skillet in 4- to 5-inch rounds.
Cook in batches 5 minutes on each side, or until lightly browned, adding remaining oil as necessary. Press down with a spatula to flatten; top each round with a cheese slice. Cook 5 minutes or until cheese melts. Yield: 8 servings.

Per serving: Calories 183 (67% from fat); Fat 13.7g (sat 4.9g, mono 4.9g, poly 3.2g); Protein 5.5g; Carb 10.6g; Fiber 1.5g; Chol 20mg; Iron 0.3mg; Sodium 623mg; Calc 121mg

make ahead

Hash Brown Breakfast Casserole

prep: 4 min.   cook: 1 hr., 8 min.
other: 8 hrs., 5 min.

1   pound ground hot pork sausage
¼   cup chopped onion
2½ cups frozen cubed hash browns
5   large eggs, lightly beaten
2   cups (8 ounces) shredded sharp Cheddar cheese
1¾ cups milk
1   cup all-purpose baking mix
¼   teaspoon salt
¼   teaspoon pepper
Toppings: green salsa or picante sauce, sour cream (optional)

Cook sausage and onion in a large skillet over medium-high heat 5 to 6 minutes or until meat crumbles. Stir in hash browns, and cook 5 to 7 minutes or until sausage is no longer pink and potatoes are lightly browned. Drain well; spoon into a greased 13- x 9-inch baking dish.

Stir together eggs and next 5 ingredients; pour evenly over sausage mixture. Cover and chill 8 hours.

Bake, covered with nonstick aluminum foil, at 350° for 45 minutes. Uncover and bake 10 more minutes or until a wooden pick inserted in center comes out clean. Remove from oven, and let stand 5 minutes. Serve with desired toppings. Yield: 8 servings.

Per serving: Calories 427 (57% from fat); Fat 27.1g (sat 11.4g, mono 9.8g, poly 2.3g); Protein 23.4g; Carb 22.3g; Fiber 1.5g; Chol 209mg; Iron 1.9mg; Sodium 804mg; Calc 311mg

Bacon-Cheese Cups

prep: 20 min.   cook: 22 min.

Fill the two unused muffin cups with water to keep bottoms from burning.

2   (3-ounce) packages cream cheese, softened
1   large egg
2   tablespoons milk
½   cup (2 ounces) shredded Swiss cheese
1   green onion, chopped
1   (10-ounce) package refrigerated flaky biscuits
5   bacon slices, cooked, crumbled, and divided

Beat first 3 ingredients at medium speed with an electric mixer until combined. Stir in shredded Swiss cheese and chopped green onion.

Separate biscuits, and pat into 5-inch circles. Press circles into greased 3½-inch muffin cups, leaving a ¼-inch border at top of each cup. Sprinkle evenly with half of bacon; top with 2 tablespoons cream cheese mixture.

Bake at 375° for 22 minutes or until set. Remove from oven, and sprinkle with remaining bacon, gently pressing into filling. Yield: 10 servings.

Per serving: Calories 202 (60% from fat); Fat 13.5g (sat 6.4g, mono 5.2g, poly 1g); Protein 6.8g; Carb 13.5g; Fiber 0.5g; Chol 50mg; Iron 1.1mg; Sodium 479mg; Calc 71mg

freeze it • make ahead

Blue Cheese-and-Bacon Puffs

prep: 20 min.   cook: 25 min.

Three of these bite-size bacon pastries alongside a bowl of fruit make a nice meal.

1½   cups water
½   cup butter or margarine
1½   cups all-purpose flour
½   teaspoon salt
¼   teaspoon ground black pepper
¼   teaspoon ground red pepper
6   large eggs
8   ounces crumbled blue cheese
8   bacon slices, cooked and crumbled
4   green onions, finely chopped

Bring 1½ cups water and butter to a boil in a heavy saucepan over medium heat. Add flour and next 3 ingredients all at once; cook, beating with a wooden spoon, until mixture leaves sides of pan and forms a smooth ball of dough. Remove from heat, and cool 4 to 5 minutes.

Add eggs, 1 at a time, beating well with spoon after each addition. Beat in cheese, bacon, and chopped green onions.

Drop dough by rounded teaspoonfuls 2 inches apart onto lightly greased baking sheets.

Bake at 400° for 20 to 25 minutes or until golden. (Puffs will be moist in center.) Serve puffs warm or at room temperature. Yield: 6 dozen.

Per puff: Calories 42 (62% from fat); Fat 2.9g (sat 1.6g, mono 0.9g, poly 0.2g); Protein 1.8g; Carb 2.2g; Fiber 0.1g; Chol 24mg; Iron 0.2mg; Sodium 91mg; Calc 20mg

Note: Baked puffs can be frozen up to 3 months. Thaw in refrigerator overnight, and reheat at 350° for 5 minutes or until thoroughly heated.

Brown Sugar Bacon

prep: 5 min.   cook: 40 min.

Dark brown sugar gives this sinfully good bacon a blackened appearance after baking. Try the sweet-salty strips in a BLT, a grilled cheese-apple slice sandwich, or crumbled over a salad.

10   slices thick-cut bacon (14 ounces)
½   cup firmly packed dark brown sugar

Arrange bacon in a single layer on a wire cooling rack in an aluminum foil-lined jelly-roll or broiler pan. Coat bacon with brown sugar.

Bake at 350° for 38 to 40 minutes or until done. Let stand 2 to 3 minutes or until sugar is set. Yield: 10 servings.

Per serving: Calories 259 (60% from fat); Fat 17.2g (sat 5.6g, mono 7.6g, poly 1.9g); Protein 14.2g; Carb 11.2g; Fiber 0g; Chol 42mg; Iron 0.8mg; Sodium 875mg; Calc 13mg

For Brown Sugar Bacon, arrange bacon in a single layer on a wire rack. Heavily coat bacon with brown sugar, and bake.

cakes

There's great pleasure in cake baking. It's an exacting process that requires precise measuring, mixing, baking, and the proper equipment. The ingredients in a cake promise the joy of creation, but critical oven temperature and the right pan ensure baking success.

Of primary importance are the ingredients. Flour, eggs, butter (or other fat), sugar, salt, flavoring, leavening, and liquid make up the formula of a cake. For best results, let butter, milk, and eggs stand at room temperature 20 to 30 minutes before mixing.

The role of each ingredient is as follows:
• **Flour:** forms the framework of the cake.
• **Eggs:** support the structure, help to incorporate air, supply some of the liquid, and tenderize.
• **Butter or shortening:** tenderizes, helps to incorporate air, and adds flavor.
• **Sugar:** adds flavor, helps to incorporate air, tenderizes, and retains moisture.
• **Salt:** boosts flavor.
• **Leavening (such as baking powder):** lightens the cake.
• **Liquid:** supports the cake's structure and adds moistness; milk products are the preferred liquid for rich flavor.

The two basic types of cakes are butter and foam cakes. Rich with a velvety texture, butter cakes contain a high percentage of butter. Pound cakes and layer cakes are typical butter cakes. Foam cakes contain very little, if any, fat. They're made with a higher ratio of eggs and sugar to flour. Angel food, chiffon, and sponge cake make up this category.

The keys to cake making:

Equipment

Have on hand 2 or 3 each of round cakepans in 8- and 9-inch diameters for layer cakes, and a tube pan or Bundt pan for angel food and pound cakes. Springform pans for cheesecakes are commonly found in 9- and 10-inch sizes but smaller springforms are available, too. Always use shortening to grease cakepans unless recipe specifies otherwise. Butter can burn or cause a cake to stick, so it's best for flavoring the cake, rather than greasing pans. Dust greased pans with flour, tilting pans to coat bottom and sides.

Measuring

Be precise with the measure. Measure any dry ingredient by spooning it lightly into a dry measuring cup, letting it mound slightly. Then level it with a spatula or knife. Measure liquids in a glass or clear plastic measuring cup with a spout.

Mixing

Use a stand mixer for large amounts of batter and a handheld mixer for small amounts. Be sure not to overmix the batter. Mix ingredients just until flour is no longer visible or just until eggs are blended. Use the paddle attachment for creaming or beating the butter and the whisk attachment for whisking egg whites or whipping cream. Immediately after batter is mixed, fill each cakepan with an equal amount of batter. Once filled, handle pans gently.

Baking

Always preheat the oven 10 minutes and make sure it's heating properly; use an oven thermometer to check for accuracy. Place pans on the center oven rack, and don't open the oven door during baking. Cake tests done when a wooden pick inserted in center comes out clean with no crumbs on the pick.

Cooling & Storing

Remove cake from oven, and place pans on wire racks to cool for about 10 minutes (15 minutes for tube or Bundt cakes.) Run a

---

cake baking basics

To grease cakepans: Use a paper towel or wax paper to lightly grease sides and bottoms of pans with shortening.

To flour cakepans: Dust greased pans with flour, shaking pans to coat bottoms and sides. Shake out excess flour.

To bake layers: Pour batter evenly into prepared pans.

To cool cakes: Cool cake in pan 10 minutes; then invert cake onto a wire rack to cool completely.

softened butter

Recipes often call for softened butter, but exactly how soft should it be to incorporate the maximum amount of air needed for a light and tender cake? Butter will usually soften at room temperature in about 30 minutes, but the time can vary depending on the warmth of your kitchen. Before beginning your recipe, test the butter by gently pressing the top

of the stick with your index finger. If an indentation remains but the stick of butter still holds its shape (see center stick), it's perfectly softened. The butter on the left is still too firm, while the butter on the right has become too soft. Avoid softening butter in the microwave because it can melt too quickly and unevenly.

knife around sides of pan to loosen cake, if necessary. Then, invert cake onto wire racks. Be sure to allow cake layers to cool completely before frosting. Store cakes with cream filling or other perishables in the filling or frosting in the refrigerator under a cake dome or a large inverted bowl. Other cakes keep well at room temperature for several days. Most cakes with a creamy-type frosting are good candidates for freezing. Do not freeze cakes with meringue-type frostings. As soon as the layers are cool, wrap them in plastic wrap and put them in the freezer. To freeze a frosted cake, place it uncovered in the freezer just until frozen, then loosely, but thoroughly, wrap and return it to the freezer. It should keep up to three months. Before serving, unwrap frozen cakes, and thaw at room temperature for several hours.

Frosting

Brush off excess crumbs from top and sides of cooled cake layers before you begin. Use a pastry brush or your fingers to do this. To keep the cake plate clean while frosting the cake, tuck strips of wax paper under all sides of bottom cake layer before you begin frosting.

When frosting and stacking cake layers, place the first layer (or the first 2 layers of a 3-layer cake) bottom side up on serving plate; then place top layer right side up. This contributes to a straight and tall cake.

Using an offset spatula, spread between one-fourth to one-fifth of frosting between each cake layer. Spread a very thin layer of frosting on sides of assembled cake to set any remaining crumbs—this is called *crumb coating*. Then spread a generous amount of frosting over the crumb coating. Always keep the frosting just ahead of the spatula; don't backstroke until the entire area is frosted or the spatula may drag up crumbs. Always frost the top of a cake last. When done frosting, gently remove wax paper strips from around bottom edges of cake.

Glazing

Applying a thin glaze is a great way to add extra moistness to a cake. To do this, simply prick holes in top of warm or cooled cake using a long wooden pick, and slowly drizzle glaze over cake allowing it to seep down into cake. Thicker glazes are often drizzled over the top of Bundt or tube cakes for a simple finish.

Serving

You'll get the cleanest slices from your cake if you use a serrated knife. If crumbs and frosting cling to the knife, just wipe the blade with a damp towel before cutting the next slice.

Many cakes slice best if they have a few hours to set up or even chill after they've been assembled. We mention which cakes benefit from this throughout this chapter.

mixer matters

The two basic types of electric mixers are the stand mixer and the portable or handheld mixer.

Stationary or stand mixers are good for mixing large amounts of ingredients and heavy batters; heavy-duty stand mixers are usually sold with three different attachments, each with a unique function.

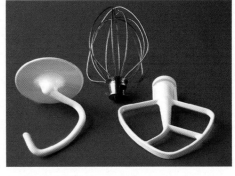

The dough hook (below, left) makes quick work of mixing and kneading bread dough. The wire whisk attachment (center) is meant for whipping egg whites or cream, as well as emulsifying homemade mayonnaise and salad dressing. The flat paddle attachment (far right) is used for creaming butter and sugar, general mixing, in particular cake batter and cookie dough. Brands such as KitchenAid, which is a heavy-duty mixer, mix more quickly and forcefully than regular stand mixers or portable handheld mixers. Most of our cake recipes were tested with a KitchenAid.

Portable or handheld mixers have a smaller motor and don't have as many attachments, but they are usually adequate for mixing most batters. These lightweight mixers offer you great control and are preferred by some home cooks.

We've used all of these mixers successfully in our kitchens. The trick is knowing how long to mix for desired results. Here's one example: When creaming 1 stick butter, the heavy-duty mixer knocked it out in 1 minute on medium speed; a regular stand mixer took 7 to 8 minutes on medium-high speed, stopping several times to scrape down the sides of the bowl; a high-powered handheld mixer creamed butter in 3 minutes on medium speed. With a handheld mixer, you won't have to stop and scrape down the sides of the bowl.

shortening & butter cakes

family favorite
Basic Yellow Cake

prep: 12 min.   cook: 23 min.   other: 10 min.

Almond extract lends a subtle flavor note in addition to vanilla.

1	cup butter or margarine, softened
1½	cups sugar
4	large eggs
3	cups sifted cake flour
2½	teaspoons baking powder
½	teaspoon salt
1	cup milk
2	teaspoons vanilla extract or 1 teaspoon vanilla extract and 1 teaspoon almond extract

Beat butter at medium speed with an electric mixer until creamy; gradually add sugar, beating well. Add eggs, 1 at a time, beating after each addition.
Combine flour, baking powder, and salt; add to butter mixture alternately with milk, beginning and ending with flour mixture. Mix at low speed after each addition until blended. Stir in vanilla.
Pour batter into 3 greased and floured 9-inch round cakepans. Bake at 350° for 23 minutes or until a wooden pick inserted in center comes out clean. Cool in pans on wire racks 10 minutes; remove from pans, and cool completely on wire racks. Frost as desired. Yield: 16 servings.

Per serving: Calories 287 (44% from fat); Fat 14.1g (sat 8.1g, mono 3.9g, poly 1g); Protein 4g; Carb 36.7g; Fiber 0.4g; Chol 85mg; Iron 1.9mg; Sodium 354mg; Calc 73mg

Pair these 3 "workhorse" cakes with just about any flavor of frosting.

family favorite
White Cake Supreme

prep: 20 min.   cook: 30 min.   other: 10 min.

This cake is white because you use egg whites and shortening rather than yolks and butter. The fluffy beaten whites yield a light, airy cake.

¾	cup shortening
1½	cups sugar
2¼	cups sifted cake flour
1	tablespoon baking powder
¾	teaspoon salt
1	cup milk
1½	teaspoons vanilla extract
5	egg whites

Beat shortening at medium speed with an electric mixer until fluffy; gradually add sugar, beating well.
Combine flour, baking powder, and salt; add to shortening mixture alternately with milk, beginning and ending with flour mixture. Mix at low speed after each addition until blended. Stir in vanilla.
Beat egg whites at high speed until stiff peaks form. Gently fold beaten egg whites into batter.
Pour batter into 2 greased and floured 9-inch round cakepans. Bake at 350° for 25 to 30 minutes or until a wooden pick inserted in center comes out clean. Cool in pans on wire racks 10 minutes; remove from pans, and cool completely on wire racks. Frost as desired. Yield: 12 servings.

Per serving: Calories 315 (41% from fat); Fat 14.4g (sat 3.1g, mono 6.2g, poly 4.3g); Protein 3.9g; Carb 43g; Fiber 0.4g; Chol 2mg; Iron 1.7mg; Sodium 299mg; Calc 95mg

White Cupcakes: Spoon batter into paper-lined muffin pans, filling each cup two-thirds full. Bake at 350° for 18 to 20 minutes. Remove from pans, and cool on wire racks. Frost as desired or with Coconut-Cream Cheese Frosting (page 155). Yield: 26 cupcakes.

family favorite
Basic Chocolate Cake

prep: 21 min.   cook: 35 min.   other: 10 min.

Use this chocolate cake to build a grand layer cake, bake cupcakes, or cube the baked layers and make a trifle.

½	cup shortening
2	cups sugar
2	large eggs
4	(1-ounce) unsweetened chocolate squares, melted
2¼	cups sifted cake flour
½	teaspoon baking powder
1	teaspoon baking soda
¾	teaspoon salt
¾	cup buttermilk
¾	cup water
1	tablespoon vanilla extract

Beat shortening at medium speed with an electric mixer until fluffy; gradually add sugar, beating well. Add eggs, 1 at a time, beating after each addition. Add chocolate, mixing well.
Combine flour and next 3 ingredients; add to chocolate mixture alternately with buttermilk, beginning and ending with flour mixture. Mix at low speed after each addition until blended. Add water, mixing well. Stir in vanilla.
Pour batter into 2 greased and floured 9-inch round cakepans. Bake at 350° for 30 to 35 minutes or until a wooden pick inserted in center comes out clean. Cool in pans on wire racks 10 minutes; remove from pans, and cool completely on wire racks. Frost as desired. Yield: 12 servings.

Per serving: Calories 360 (40% from fat); Fat 15.7g (sat 5.5g, mono 6.1g, poly 3.2g); Protein 4.5g; Carb 53.8g; Fiber 1.9g; Chol 37mg; Iron 3.4mg; Sodium 303mg; Calc 45mg

Chocolate Cupcakes: Spoon batter into paper-lined muffin pans, filling each cup half full. Bake at 350° for 15 to 18 minutes. Remove from pans, and cool on wire racks. Frost as desired or with Chocolate-Marshmallow Frosting (page 165). Yield: 3 dozen.

Piña Colada Cake

prep: 20 min.   cook: 25 min.
other: 4 hrs., 10 min.

Piña Colada Filling

½	cup butter, softened
½	cup shortening
2	cups sugar
3	cups sifted cake flour
4	teaspoons baking powder
½	teaspoon salt
⅔	cup milk
⅔	cup water
2	teaspoons vanilla extract
¾	teaspoon almond extract
6	egg whites

Rum Buttercream Frosting
1¾ cups sweetened flaked coconut

Prepare Piña Colada Filling; chill.
Beat butter and shortening at medium speed with an electric mixer until creamy; gradually add sugar, beating well.
Combine flour, baking powder, and salt; add to butter mixture alternately with milk and water, beginning and ending with flour mixture. Beat at low speed until blended after each addition. Stir in flavorings.
Beat egg whites at high speed until soft peaks form; fold about one-third of beaten egg white into batter. Gradually fold in remaining egg white.
Pour batter into 3 greased and floured 8-inch round cakepans.
Bake at 325° for 25 minutes or until a wooden pick inserted in center comes out clean. Cool in pans on wire racks 10 minutes; remove from pans, and cool layers completely on wire racks.
Split layers horizontally. Spread Piña Colada Filling evenly between layers (not on top); cover and chill at least 4 hours.
Spread Rum Buttercream Frosting on top and sides of cake; sprinkle top and sides with flaked coconut, pressing in gently. Store cake in refrigerator. (Cake can be frozen up to 1 month.) Yield: 16 servings.

Per serving: Calories 588 (44% from fat); Fat 29g (sat 15.9g, mono 8.2g, poly 3.1g); Protein 5.2g; Carb 77g; Fiber 0.9g; Chol 97mg; Iron 2mg; Sodium 324mg; Calc 112mg

◄ Beat butter and shortening at medium speed until creamy.

◄ Gradually add sugar, beating well.

◄ Pour batter evenly into greased and floured pans.

Piña Colada Filling

prep: 5 min.   cook: 10 min.   other: 4 hrs.

1	(10-ounce) can frozen piña colada mix concentrate, thawed and undiluted
3	tablespoons cornstarch
4	egg yolks
1½	cups half-and-half
¾	cup sweetened flaked coconut
3	tablespoons butter or margarine, cut up
1	teaspoon vanilla extract

Bring first 4 ingredients to a boil in a 3-quart saucepan over medium heat, whisking constantly. Boil, whisking constantly, 1 minute. Remove from heat; whisk in remaining 3 ingredients. Pour mixture into a bowl. Chill at least 4 hours. Yield: 3½ cups.

Per tablespoon: Calories 29 (65% from fat); Fat 2.1g (sat 1.3g, mono 0.5g, poly 0.1g); Protein 0.4g; Carb 2.3g; Fiber 0.1g; Chol 19mg; Iron 0.1mg; Sodium 10mg; Calc 9mg

Rum Buttercream Frosting

prep: 10 min.

½	cup butter, softened
1	(16-ounce) package powdered sugar, sifted
3	tablespoons rum
3	tablespoons milk
1	teaspoon vanilla extract

cake troubleshooting

Use the following chart to help diagnose and correct any cake-baking problems.

If batter overflows:
- Overmixing
- Too much batter in pan

If cake falls:
- Oven not hot enough
- Undermixing
- Insufficient baking
- Opening oven door during baking
- Too much baking powder, soda, liquid, or sugar

If cake peaks in center:
- Oven too hot at start of baking
- Too much flour
- Not enough liquid

If crust is sticky:
- Insufficient baking
- Oven not hot enough
- Too much sugar

If cake sticks to pan:
- Cake cooling in pan too long
- Pan not properly greased and floured

If cake cracks and falls apart:
- Removing from pan too soon
- Too much shortening, baking powder, soda, or sugar

If texture is heavy:
- Overmixing when adding flour and liquid
- Oven temperature too low
- Too much shortening, sugar, or liquid

If texture is coarse:
- Inadequate mixing
- Oven temperature too low
- Too much baking powder or soda

If texture is dry:
- Overbaking
- Overbeating egg whites
- Too much flour, baking powder, or soda
- Not enough shortening or sugar

Beat butter at medium speed with an electric mixer until creamy; gradually add 1 cup powdered sugar, beating at low speed until blended. Add rum, milk, and vanilla, beating until blended. Gradually add remaining powdered sugar. Yield: 2½ cups.

Per tablespoon: Calories 68 (30% from fat); Fat 2.3g (sat 1.5g, mono 0.6g, poly 0.1g); Protein 0.1g; Carb 11.4g; Fiber 0g; Chol 6mg; Iron 0mg; Sodium 17mg; Calc 2.1mg

Chocolate-Bourbon-Pecan Cake

prep: 28 min.   cook: 23 min.   other: 10 min.

Let cake stand several hours before slicing.

1½ cups semisweet chocolate morsels
½   cup butter, softened
1   (16-ounce) package light brown sugar
3   large eggs
2   cups all-purpose flour
1   teaspoon baking soda
½   teaspoon salt
1   (8-ounce) container sour cream
1   cup hot water
2   teaspoons vanilla extract
Bourbon Buttercream Frosting
2¾ cups chopped pecans, toasted
1   (4-ounce) semisweet chocolate bar, chopped

Melt chocolate morsels in a microwave-safe bowl at HIGH for 30-second intervals until melted (about 1½ minutes total time). Stir until smooth.
Beat butter and sugar at medium speed with an electric mixer, about 5 minutes or until well blended. Add eggs, 1 at a time, beating just until blended after each addition. Add melted chocolate, beating just until blended.
Sift together flour, baking soda, and salt. Gradually add to chocolate mixture alternately with sour cream, beginning and ending with flour mixture. Beat at low speed just until blended after each addition. Gradually add hot water in a slow, steady stream, beating at low speed just until blended. Stir in vanilla. Spoon batter evenly into 3 greased and floured 9-inch square or round cakepans.
Bake at 350° for 23 minutes or until a wooden pick inserted in center comes out clean. Cool in pans on a wire rack 10 minutes. Remove from pans; cool completely on wire rack.
Spread Bourbon Buttercream Frosting between layers; sprinkle with ¼ cup pecans on each layer. Spread remaining frosting on top and sides of cake. Press remaining pecans onto sides of cake. Store in refrigerator. Sprinkle chopped chocolate over top of cake. Yield: 16 servings.

Per serving: Calories 848 (45% from fat); Fat 42.7g (sat 18.3g, mono 15.6g, poly 5.5g); Protein 6.5g; Carb 114.2g; Fiber 3.3g; Chol 91mg; Iron 2.7mg; Sodium 308mg; Calc 75mg

Bourbon Buttercream Frosting

prep: 8 min.

1   cup butter, softened
2   (16-ounce) packages powdered sugar
2   to 3 tablespoons milk
⅓   cup bourbon
1   tablespoon vanilla extract

Beat butter at medium speed with an electric mixer until creamy; gradually add powdered sugar alternately with milk and bourbon, beating at low speed until blended after each addition. Stir in vanilla. Yield: about 5 cups.

Per tablespoon: Calories 67 (31% from fat); Fat 2.3g (sat 1.5g, mono 0.6g, poly 0.1g); Protein 0g; Carb 11.3g; Fiber 0g; Chol 6mg; Iron 0mg; Sodium 16mg; Calc 1mg

Chocolate Truffle Cake

prep: 53 min.   cook: 22 min.   other: 10 min.

Wow your guests with this showy cake wrapped in a fence of rolled wafer cookies. It's a tender cake—for best results, bake layers a day ahead and use a light hand when frosting it.

8   (1-ounce) semisweet chocolate baking squares, chopped
1   cup butter, softened
1¾ cups sugar
3   large eggs
2   teaspoons vanilla extract
2⅔ cups all-purpose flour
1   teaspoon baking soda
½   teaspoon salt
1¾ cups buttermilk
Unsweetened cocoa
Chocolate Truffle Filling
Ganache
2   (14-ounce) containers chocolate hazelnut rolled wafer cookies (we tested with Pirouline®)

Microwave chocolate in a glass bowl at HIGH 1 minute or until melted, stirring once.
Beat butter and sugar at medium speed with an electric mixer until fluffy. Add eggs, 1 at a time, beating just until yellow disappears. Add cooled chocolate and vanilla, beating until blended.
Combine flour, baking soda, and salt; add to butter mixture alternately with buttermilk, beginning and ending with flour mixture. Beat at low speed just until blended after each addition.
Pour batter into 3 greased parchment paper-lined 9-inch round cakepans dusted with cocoa. Bake at 350° for 21 to 22 minutes or until a wooden pick inserted in center comes out clean. Cool in pans 10 minutes. Remove cake layers to wire racks; cool completely.
Spread Chocolate Truffle Filling between layers. Reserving ¼ cup Ganache, spread remaining Ganache on top and sides of cake. Break cookies into long pieces. Line sides of cake with cookies. Spoon reserved Ganache on top center of cake; place broken cookie pieces into mound of Ganache. Yield: 16 servings.

Per serving: Calories 916 (46% from fat); Fat 46.7g (sat 29.4g, mono 12.8g, poly 2.5g); Protein 9.1g; Carb 119g; Fiber 1.3g; Chol 102mg; Iron 2.4mg; Sodium 357mg; Calc 50mg

Chocolate Truffle Filling

prep: 5 min.   cook: 1 min.

4   (1-ounce) semisweet chocolate baking squares, chopped
6   tablespoons butter
6   tablespoons whipping cream
2½ cups powdered sugar, sifted

Microwave chocolate and butter at HIGH 1 minute or until melted, stirring once. Stir in whipping cream. Gradually add powdered sugar, stirring until blended and smooth. Yield: 1¾ cups.

Per tablespoon: Calories 94 (46% from fat); Fat 4.8g (sat 2.9g, mono 1.4g, poly 0.2g); Protein 0.3g; Carb 13.2g; Fiber 0.3g; Chol 11mg; Iron 0.2mg; Sodium 18mg; Calc 3mg

Ganache

prep: 6 min.   cook: 1 min.   other: 20 min.

10 (1-ounce) semisweet chocolate baking squares, chopped
½   cup whipping cream

Microwave chocolate and whipping cream in a medium glass bowl at HIGH 1 minute or until melted and smooth, stirring once. Cool 20 minutes. Yield: 2 cups.

Per tablespoon: Calories 57 (60% from fat); Fat 3.8g (sat 2.3g, mono 1.2g, poly 0.1g); Protein 0.6g; Carb 6g; Fiber 0g; Chol 5mg; Iron 0.2mg; Sodium 1.3mg; Calc 3mg

Chocolate Truffle Cake

Perfect Chocolate Cake

prep: 23 min.   cook: 22 min.   other: 10 min.

Perfect Chocolate Cake is an appropriate name for these towering layers with a whipped cream filling and creamy chocolate frosting.

1   cup unsweetened cocoa
2   cups boiling water
1   cup butter or margarine, softened
2½ cups sugar
4   large eggs
2¾ cups all-purpose flour
2   teaspoons baking soda
½   teaspoon baking powder
½   teaspoon salt
1½ teaspoons vanilla extract
Whipped Cream Filling
Perfect Chocolate Frosting

Combine cocoa and boiling water, stirring until smooth; set aside.
Beat butter at medium speed with an electric mixer about 2 minutes or until creamy. Gradually add sugar, beating 5 to 7 minutes. Add eggs, 1 at a time, beating just until yellow disappears.
Combine flour and next 3 ingredients in a medium bowl; add to butter mixture alternately with cocoa mixture, beginning and ending with flour mixture. Beat at low speed just until blended after each addition. Stir in vanilla. Do not overbeat.
Pour batter into 3 greased and floured 9-inch round cakepans. Bake at 350° for 22 minutes or until a wooden pick inserted in center comes out clean. Cool in pans on wire racks 10 minutes; remove from pans, and cool completely on wire racks.
Spread Whipped Cream Filling between layers; spread Perfect Chocolate Frosting on top and sides of cake. Chill until ready to serve. Store in refrigerator. Yield: 16 servings.

Per serving: Calories 590 (48% from fat); Fat 31.5g (sat 19.3g, mono 7.7g, poly 1.3g); Protein 6.3g; Carb 75.8g; Fiber 2.4g; Chol 129mg; Iron 2.3mg; Sodium 414mg; Calc 49mg

Whipped Cream Filling

prep: 4 min.

1   cup whipping cream
1   teaspoon vanilla extract
¼   cup powdered sugar

Beat whipping cream and vanilla until foamy; gradually add powdered sugar, beating until soft peaks form. Cover and chill. Yield: 2 cups.

Per tablespoon: Calories 28 (80% from fat); Fat 2.5g (sat 1.5g, mono 0.8g, poly 0.1g); Protein 0g; Carb 1.3g; Fiber 0g; Chol 10mg; Iron 0mg; Sodium 3mg; Calc 5mg

Perfect Chocolate Frosting

prep: 17 min.   cook: 5 min.

1   cup semisweet chocolate morsels
½   cup half-and-half
¾   cup butter or margarine
2½ cups sifted powdered sugar

Combine first 3 ingredients in a medium saucepan; cook over medium heat, stirring until chocolate melts. Remove from heat; add powdered sugar, mixing well.
Place saucepan in a large bowl of ice. Beat at low speed with an electric mixer until frosting holds its shape and loses its gloss. Add a few more drops of half-and-half, if needed, for desired spreading consistency. Yield: 2½ cups.

Per tablespoon: Calories 79 (57% from fat); Fat 5g (sat 3.1g, mono 1.4g, poly 0.2g); Protein 0.3g; Carb 9g; Fiber 0.3g; Chol 10mg; Iron 0.1mg; Sodium 26mg; Calc 6mg

freeze it • make ahead • weekend chef
Chocolate-Praline Cake

prep: 50 min.   cook: 22 min.   other: 55 min.

This cake is off-the-charts rich. If you like pralines, you'll love this candylike frosting.

1   cup butter or margarine
¼   cup unsweetened cocoa
1   cup water
½   cup buttermilk
2   large eggs
1   teaspoon baking soda
1   teaspoon vanilla extract
2   cups sugar
2   cups all-purpose flour
½   teaspoon salt
Chocolate Ganache Filling
Praline Frosting

Grease bottoms of 3 (8-inch) round cakepans; line with wax paper. Grease and flour wax paper and sides of pans. Cook first 3 ingredients in a saucepan over low heat, stirring constantly, until butter melts and mixture is smooth; remove from heat. Cool.
Beat buttermilk, eggs, baking soda, and vanilla at medium speed with an electric mixer until smooth. Add butter mixture to buttermilk mixture, beating until blended. Combine sugar, flour, and salt; gradually add to buttermilk mixture, beating until blended. (Batter will be thin.)
Pour batter evenly into prepared pans. Bake at 350° for 20 to 22 minutes or until a wooden pick inserted in center comes out clean. Cool in pans on wire racks 10 minutes. Remove from pans; immediately remove wax paper. Cool completely on wire racks. (Layers will appear thin.)
Spread about ½ cup ganache filling between cake layers; spread remainder on sides of cake. (Do not frost top of cake.) Chill cake 30 minutes. Pour Praline Frosting slowly over center of cake, spreading to edges, allowing some frosting to run over sides of cake. Freeze, if desired; thaw at room temperature 4 to 6 hours. Yield: 12 servings.

Per serving: Calories 785 (51% from fat); Fat 44.3g (sat 23.3g, mono 14.6g, poly 3.6g); Protein 6.2g; Carb 98.6g; Fiber 3.8g; Chol 115mg; Iron 2.9mg; Sodium 403mg; Calc 69mg

Chocolate Ganache Filling

prep: 4 min.   cook: 3 min.   other: 25 min.

1   (12-ounce) package semisweet chocolate morsels
⅓   cup whipping cream
¼   cup butter or margarine, cut into pieces

Microwave chocolate morsels and whipping cream in a glass bowl at MEDIUM (50% power) 2 to 3 minutes or until morsels are melted, stirring after 1½ minutes; whisk until smooth. Gradually add butter, whisking until smooth. Cool, whisking often, about 25 minutes or until spreading consistency. Yield: about 2 cups.

Per tablespoon: Calories 71 (68% from fat); Fat 5.4g (sat 3.3g, mono 1.7g, poly 0.2g); Protein 0.5g; Carb 6.8g; Fiber 0.6g; Chol 7mg; Iron 0.3mg; Sodium 12mg; Calc 6mg

Layer cakes are lofty combinations of textures, flavors, and tradition.

Praline Frosting

cook: 4 min.   other: 5 min.

Don't prepare this frosting ahead because it'll harden very quickly.

- ¼ cup butter or margarine
- 1 cup firmly packed light brown sugar
- ⅓ cup whipping cream
- 1 cup powdered sugar
- 1 teaspoon vanilla extract
- 1 cup chopped pecans, toasted

Bring first 3 ingredients to a boil in a 2-quart saucepan over medium heat, stirring often; boil 1 minute. Remove from heat, and whisk in powdered sugar and vanilla until smooth. Add toasted pecans, stirring gently 3 to 5 minutes or until frosting begins to cool and thicken slightly. Pour frosting immediately over cake. Yield: about 2 cups.

Per tablespoon: Calories 100 (50% from fat); Fat 5.6g (sat 1.9g, mono 2.4g, poly 1g); Protein 0.4g; Carb 12.7g; Fiber 0.4g; Chol 8mg; Iron 0.3mg; Sodium 16mg; Calc 12mg

---

make ahead

Macadamia-Fudge Cake

prep: 13 min.   cook: 25 min.   other: 20 min.

We loved the generous amount of topping that pools around the bottom of this cake. Serve the cake on a rimmed cake plate.

- ½ cup butter or margarine, softened
- ¾ cup sugar
- 1 large egg
- ¾ cup sour cream
- ½ teaspoon vanilla extract
- 1 cup all-purpose flour
- 3 tablespoons unsweetened cocoa
- 1 teaspoon instant coffee granules
- ½ teaspoon baking soda
- ½ teaspoon baking powder
- ¼ teaspoon salt
- Macadamia-Fudge Topping
- Garnish: toasted macadamia nuts

Beat butter at medium speed with an electric mixer until creamy; gradually add sugar, beating until blended. Add egg, sour cream, and vanilla; beat well.
Combine flour and next 5 ingredients; gradually add to butter mixture, beating until blended.

Pour batter into a greased, wax paper-lined 9-inch cakepan. Bake at 350° for 25 minutes or until a wooden pick inserted in center comes out clean. Cool in pan 10 minutes. Remove from pan, and cool on a wire rack 10 minutes. Transfer to a rimmed serving plate. Pour Macadamia-Fudge Topping over cake. Chill until ready to serve. Garnish, if desired. Yield: 9 servings.

Per serving: Calories 664 (64% from fat); Fat 47g (sat 21.1g, mono 20.4g, poly 1.5g); Protein 5.8g; Carb 60.4g; Fiber 2.7g; Chol 101mg; Iron 1.9mg; Sodium 274mg; Calc 82mg

---

Macadamia-Fudge Topping

prep: 3 min.   cook: 7 min.   other: 10 min.

- 4 (1-ounce) semisweet chocolate squares
- 1 (6.85-ounce) jar macadamia nuts, toasted and coarsely chopped
- 1 cup whipping cream
- ¾ cup sugar
- 2 tablespoons butter or margarine
- 1 tablespoon light corn syrup
- 1 teaspoon vanilla extract

Cook first 6 ingredients in a medium saucepan over medium-low heat 7 minutes, stirring constantly, or until sugar dissolves. Remove from heat, and stir in vanilla. Let cool completely. Yield: 2⅓ cups.

Per tablespoon: Calories 97 (71% from fat); Fat 7.6g (sat 2.8g, mono 3.9g, poly 0.2g); Protein 0.6g; Carb 7.5g; Fiber 0g; Chol 10mg; Iron 0.2mg; Sodium 21mg; Calc 8mg

---

Buttermilk Layer Cake With Caramel Frosting

prep: 10 min.   cook: 22 min.   other: 10 min.

- 1 cup shortening
- 2 cups sugar
- 3 large eggs
- 2½ cups all-purpose flour
- ½ teaspoon salt
- ½ teaspoon baking soda
- 1½ cups buttermilk
- 2 teaspoons vanilla extract
- Caramel Frosting

Beat shortening at medium speed with an electric mixer until fluffy. Gradually add sugar, beating well. Add eggs, 1 at a time, beating until blended after each addition.
Combine flour, salt, and soda; add to shortening mixture alternately with buttermilk, beginning and ending with flour mixture.

Beat at low speed until blended after each addition. Beat at medium-high speed 2 minutes. Stir in vanilla.
Pour batter into 3 greased and floured 8-inch round cakepans. Bake at 350° for 22 minutes or until a wooden pick inserted in center comes out clean. Cool in pans on wire racks 10 minutes; remove from pans. Cool completely on wire racks.
Spread Caramel Frosting between layers and on top and sides. Yield: 12 servings.

Per serving: Calories 803 (39% from fat); Fat 34.4g (sat 13.1g, mono 12.8g, poly 6.3g); Protein 5.4g; Carb 120.4g; Fiber 0.7g; Chol 107mg; Iron 1.5mg; Sodium 267mg; Calc 65mg

Chocolate-Buttermilk Cake: Substitute ½ cup cocoa for ½ cup flour. Pour batter into a lightly greased 13- x 9-inch pan. Bake at 350° for 40 minutes or until a wooden pick inserted in center comes out clean.

Caramel Frosting

prep: 18 min.   cook: 20 min.

Beating caramel frosting until spreading consistency is all in the feel. Beat it just until the frosting begins to thicken; test a small portion on the cake to see if it holds its shape. If not, beat a little longer, but be sure not to overbeat or it will be too thick to spread.

- 3¾ cups sugar, divided
- 1½ cups whipping cream
- ¼ cup butter
- ¼ teaspoon baking soda

Bring 3 cups sugar, cream, butter, and baking soda to a boil in a heavy saucepan. Remove from heat, and keep warm.
Sprinkle remaining ¾ cup sugar in a heavy saucepan. Cook over medium heat, stirring constantly, until sugar melts and syrup is light golden brown. (Sugar will clump before melting.) Gradually pour into whipping cream mixture. (Mixture will bubble.) Stir until smooth.
Cook over medium heat, stirring often, 10 to 12 minutes or until a candy thermometer registers 240° (soft ball stage). Remove from heat. Beat at high speed with an electric mixer until spreading consistency (8 to 10 minutes). Yield: 3 cups.

Per tablespoon: Calories 94 (32% from fat); Fat 3.5g (sat 2.1g, mono 1g, poly 0.1g); Protein 0g; Carb 16.1g; Fiber 0g; Chol 13mg; Iron 0mg; Sodium 16mg; Calc 6mg

For easy removal: Line cakepans with precut parchment rounds, or cut wax paper or parchment to fit pans.

family favorite • make ahead

Carrot Cake Supreme

prep: 25 min.   cook: 30 min.
other: 3 hrs., 15 min.

Cover and chill this cake, and serve it the second day; it'll slice neater.

2   cups all-purpose flour
2   teaspoons baking soda
½   teaspoon salt
2   teaspoons ground cinnamon
3   large eggs
2   cups sugar
¾   cup vegetable oil
¾   cup buttermilk
2   teaspoons vanilla extract
2   cups grated carrot
1   (8-ounce) can crushed pineapple, drained
1   (3½-ounce) can flaked coconut
1   cup chopped pecans
Buttermilk Glaze
Deluxe Cream Cheese Frosting

Grease 3 (9-inch) round cakepans; line with wax paper. Lightly grease and flour wax paper. Set aside.
Stir together first 4 ingredients. Beat eggs and next 4 ingredients at medium speed with an electric mixer until smooth. Add flour mixture, beating at low speed until blended. Fold in carrot and next 3 ingredients. Pour batter into prepared pans.

Bake at 350° for 25 to 30 minutes or until a wooden pick inserted in center comes out clean.
Drizzle warm Buttermilk Glaze evenly over warm cake layers; cool in pans on wire racks 15 minutes. Remove from pans, inverting layers. Peel off wax paper; invert again, glaze side up. Cool completely on wire racks.
Spread Deluxe Cream Cheese Frosting between layers and on top and sides of cake. Chill cake several hours before slicing. Store in refrigerator. Yield: 16 servings.

Per serving: Calories 732 (51% from fat); Fat 41.4g (sat 17.5g, mono 14.1g, poly 7.4g); Protein 6.2g; Carb 88.1g; Fiber 2.1g; Chol 101mg; Iron 1.7mg; Sodium 570mg; Calc 63mg

Buttermilk Glaze

prep: 3 min.   cook: 5 min.

1   cup sugar
1½   teaspoons baking soda
½   cup buttermilk
½   cup butter or margarine
1   tablespoon light corn syrup
1   teaspoon vanilla extract

Bring first 5 ingredients to a boil in a Dutch oven over medium heat. Boil 4 minutes, stirring constantly, until glaze is golden.
Remove from heat, and stir in vanilla. Cool slightly. Yield: 1½ cups.

Per tablespoon: Calories 72 (50% from fat); Fat 4g (sat 2.5g, mono 1g, poly 0.2g); Protein 0.2g; Carb 9.3g; Fiber 0g; Chol 11mg; Iron 0mg; Sodium 113mg; Calc 6mg

Deluxe Cream Cheese Frosting

prep: 7 min.

This frosting is slightly softer than the traditional version. Extra cream cheese and butter enrich the frosting and give it a little more volume.

1   (8-ounce) package cream cheese, softened
1   (3-ounce) package cream cheese, softened
¾   cup butter, softened
1   (16-ounce) package powdered sugar, sifted
1½   teaspoons vanilla extract

Beat first 3 ingredients at medium speed with an electric mixer until smooth. Gradually add powdered sugar, beating at low speed until light and fluffy. Stir in vanilla. Yield: 3½ cups.

Per tablespoon: Calories 73 (54% from fat); Fat 4.4g (sat 2.8g, mono 1.2g, poly 0.2g); Protein 0.5g; Carb 8.2g; Fiber 0g; Chol 13mg; Iron 0.1mg; Sodium 34mg; Calc 5mg

family favorite • freeze it • make ahead

Toasted Almond–Butter Cake

prep: 29 min.   cook: 22 min.   other: 10 min.

½   cup butter, softened
½   cup shortening
2   cups sugar
5   large eggs, separated
1¼   cups buttermilk
1   teaspoon almond extract
½   teaspoon vanilla extract
½   teaspoon butter flavoring
2¼   cups all-purpose flour
1¼   teaspoons baking soda
1   cup sweetened flaked coconut
1   cup chopped almonds, toasted
Cream Cheese Frosting
1   cup sliced almonds, toasted

Beat butter and shortening at medium speed with an electric mixer until creamy. Gradually add sugar, beating well. Add egg yolks, 1 at a time, beating just until blended.
Combine buttermilk and flavorings.
Combine flour and baking soda; add to butter mixture alternately with flavored buttermilk. Beat at low speed until blended after each addition.
Stir in coconut and chopped almonds.
Beat egg whites at high speed until stiff peaks form; fold into batter.
Pour into 3 greased and floured 9-inch round cakepans. Bake at 350° for 20 to 22 minutes or until a wooden pick inserted in center comes out clean. Cool cake layers in pans on wire racks 10 minutes; remove from pans, and cool on wire racks.
Spread Cream Cheese Frosting between layers and on top and sides of cake. Sprinkle with sliced almonds. Store in refrigerator. Yield: 12 servings.

Per serving: Calories 933 (45% from fat); Fat 46.6g (sat 19.4g, mono 17.6g, poly 6.7g); Protein 12.1g; Carb 120.8g; Fiber 3g; Chol 153mg; Iron 2.6mg; Sodium 374mg; Calc 110mg

Cream Cheese Frosting

prep: 5 min.

- 1 (8-ounce) package cream cheese, softened
- ½ cup butter, softened
- 1 teaspoon vanilla extract
- 6 cups powdered sugar

Beat first 3 ingredients at medium speed with an electric mixer until creamy; gradually add powdered sugar, beating until blended. Yield: 4¼ cups.

Per tablespoon: Calories 65 (35% from fat); Fat 2.5g (sat 1.6g, mono 0.7g, poly 0.1g); Protein 0.3g; Carb 10.6g; Fiber 0g; Chol 7mg; Iron 0mg; Sodium 19mg; Calc 3mg

family favorite • freeze it • make ahead
Sweet Potato Cake

prep: 30 min.   cook: 28 min.   other: 10 min.

- 6 large eggs, separated
- 1 cup butter, softened
- 3 cups sugar
- 1½ cups mashed cooked sweet potatoes
- 1 (8-ounce) container sour cream
- 3 cups all-purpose flour
- 1 tablespoon baking powder
- ½ teaspoon ground ginger
- ½ teaspoon ground cinnamon
- ¼ teaspoon salt
- 1 cup chopped pecans, toasted
- 1 teaspoon vanilla extract
- Coconut Filling
- Quick Caramel Frosting
- Chopped pecans, toasted (optional)

Beat egg whites at high speed with an electric mixer until stiff peaks form; set aside. **Beat** butter and sugar at medium speed until creamy. Add egg yolks, 1 at a time, beating until blended after each addition. Combine sweet potatoes and sour cream; add to butter mixture, beating until blended. **Combine** flour and next 4 ingredients; add to butter mixture, beating at low speed until blended. Stir in 1 cup pecans and vanilla. Fold in beaten egg whites.
Pour batter into 3 greased and floured 9-inch round cakepans. Bake at 350° for 27 to 28 minutes or until a wooden pick inserted in center comes out clean. Cool in pans 10 minutes. Remove cake layers to wire racks; cool completely.

A general rule in cake baking is to always grease cakepans with shortening unless the recipe states otherwise.

Spread Coconut Filling between layers. **Spread** Quick Caramel Frosting over top and sides of cake. (If frosting becomes too hard to spread, place it over low heat for 1 minute or until spreading consistency, stirring constantly.) Sprinkle with chopped pecans, if desired. Store in refrigerator. Yield: 16 servings.

Per serving: Calories 737 (39% from fat); Fat 32.1g (sat 16.7g, mono 10.1g, poly 2.9g); Protein 7.7g; Carb 108g; Fiber 2.3g; Chol 154mg; Iron 2.5mg; Sodium 357mg; Calc 145mg

Coconut Filling

prep: 4 min.   cook: 5 min.   other: 1 hr.

- ¼ cup sugar
- 2 tablespoons cornstarch
- ⅛ teaspoon salt
- 1 cup milk
- 1 large egg, lightly beaten
- ½ cup sweetened flaked coconut
- 1 teaspoon vanilla extract

Combine first 3 ingredients in a 2-quart saucepan; gradually stir in milk, and cook, stirring constantly, over medium heat 4 minutes or until thickened.
Stir about one-fourth of hot mixture gradually into egg; add egg mixture to remaining hot mixture, stirring constantly. Return to heat, and cook, stirring constantly, 3 minutes. Remove from heat; stir in coconut and vanilla. Place plastic wrap directly on warm filling; chill 1 hour. Yield: 1¼ cups.

Per tablespoon: Calories 33 (35% from fat); Fat 1.3g (sat 0.9g, mono 0.2g, poly 0.1g); Protein 0.8g; Carb 4.6g; Fiber 0.1g; Chol 12mg; Iron 0.1mg; Sodium 23mg; Calc 15mg

Quick Caramel Frosting

prep: 5 min.   cook: 6 min.

Considered a Test Kitchens staff favorite, this frosting has all the anticipated candy-like goodness and requires just minimal stirring with a wooden spoon. It's also great paired with Tennessee Jam Cake on the following page.

- ¾ cup butter
- ¾ cup firmly packed light brown sugar
- ¾ cup firmly packed dark brown sugar
- 6 tablespoons milk or whipping cream
- 3 cups powdered sugar, sifted
- 1½ teaspoons vanilla extract

Bring first 3 ingredients to a boil in a 4-quart saucepan over medium heat, stirring constantly, about 4 minutes. Stir in milk, and bring to a boil; remove from heat. Add powdered sugar and vanilla, stirring with a wooden spoon until smooth (1 to 2 minutes). Use immediately. Yield: 3 cups.

Per tablespoon: Calories 77 (34% from fat); Fat 2.9g (sat 1.8g, mono 0.8g, poly 0.1g); Protein 0.1g; Carb 13g; Fiber 0g; Chol 8mg; Iron 0.1mg; Sodium 24mg; Calc 9mg

Tip: The key to spreading caramel frosting on a cake is to work quickly. If frosting hardens, reheat briefly over low heat, stirring constantly. Or run a metal spatula under hot water and use it to melt and smooth out rough spots on the frosted cake.

Always frost the top of a layer cake last.

test kitchen favorite
Hummingbird Cake

prep: 36 min.   cook: 30 min.   other: 10 min.

3 cups all-purpose flour
1 teaspoon baking soda
½ teaspoon salt
2 cups sugar
1 teaspoon ground cinnamon
3 large eggs, lightly beaten
¾ cup vegetable oil
1½ teaspoons vanilla extract
1 (8-ounce) can crushed pineapple, undrained
1 cup chopped pecans
1¾ cups mashed ripe bananas
Pecan-Cream Cheese Frosting (on facing page)

Combine first 5 ingredients in a large bowl; add eggs and oil, stirring until dry ingredients are moistened. Stir in vanilla, pineapple, pecans, and banana.
Pour batter into 3 greased and floured 9-inch round cakepans. Bake at 350° for 23 minutes or until a wooden pick inserted in center comes out clean. Cool in pans on wire racks 10 minutes; remove from pans, and cool completely on wire racks.
Spread Pecan–Cream Cheese Frosting between layers and on top and sides of cake. Store in refrigerator. Yield: 16 servings.

Per serving: Calories 554 (41% from fat); Fat 25.1g (sat 8.4g, mono 9.3g, poly 6g); Protein 5.4g; Carb 80.1g; Fiber 1.8g; Chol 70mg; Iron 1.7mg; Sodium 248mg; Calc 30mg

family favorite
Caramel Cake

prep: 25 min.   cook: 35 min.   other: 10 min.

1 (8-ounce) container sour cream
¼ cup milk
1 cup butter, softened
2 cups sugar
4 large eggs
2¾ cups all-purpose flour
2 teaspoons baking powder
½ teaspoon salt
1 teaspoon vanilla extract
1 teaspoon rum extract (optional)
Caramel Frosting (page 139)

Combine sour cream and milk in a small bowl; set aside.
Beat butter at medium speed with an electric mixer until creamy; gradually add sugar, beating well. Add eggs, 1 at a time, beating after each addition.
Combine flour, baking powder, and salt; add to butter mixture alternately with sour cream mixture, beginning and ending with flour mixture. Mix at low speed after each addition until blended. Stir in vanilla and, if desired, rum extract.
Pour batter into 2 greased and floured 9-inch round cakepans. (Batter will be very thick.)
Bake at 350° for 30 to 35 minutes or until a wooden pick inserted in center comes out clean. Cool in pans on wire racks 10 minutes; remove from pans, and cool completely on wire racks.
Working quickly, spread Caramel Frosting between layers and on top and sides of cake. Yield: 12 servings.

Per serving: Calories 821 (39% from fat); Fat 35.7g (sat 21.3g, mono 10.1g, poly 1.7g); Protein 6.1g; Carb 122g; Fiber 0.8g; Chol 169mg; Iron 1.8mg; Sodium 385mg; Calc 113mg

family favorite • freeze it • make ahead
Tennessee Jam Cake

prep: 20 min.   cook: 18 min.
other: 1 hr., 10 min.

This cake is best served the second day to allow time for the jam to soak into the layers for a really moist cake.

1 (18.25-ounce) package spice cake mix
1 cup buttermilk
⅓ cup cinnamon applesauce
⅓ cup vegetable oil
3 large eggs
½ teaspoon ground cinnamon
1 cup blackberry jam
Quick Caramel Frosting (page 141)

Beat first 6 ingredients at low speed with an electric mixer for 1 minute. Scrape down sides, and beat at medium speed 2 more minutes until well blended, stopping to scrape down sides, if needed.
Pour batter evenly into 3 greased and floured 9-inch round cakepans. Bake at 350° for 18 minutes or until a wooden pick inserted in center comes out clean. Cool in pans on wire racks for 10 minutes. Remove from pans; cool completely on wire racks.
Spread blackberry jam between layers. Working quickly, spread Quick Caramel Frosting evenly over top and sides of cake. (If frosting becomes too hard to spread, place it over low heat for 1 minute or until spreading consistency, stirring constantly.) Let cake stand at least 1 hour. Yield: 16 servings.

Per serving: Calories 486 (35% from fat); Fat 18.9g (sat 8.1g, mono 6.9g, poly 2.7g); Protein 3.9g; Carb 77.5g; Fiber 0.9g; Chol 65mg; Iron 1.2mg; Sodium 323mg; Calc 50mg

Four-Layer Coconut Cake

prep: 12 min.   cook: 23 min.   other: 10 min.

1   cup shortening
½   cup butter or margarine, softened
2⅔   cups granulated sugar
5   large eggs
3   cups all-purpose flour
1   teaspoon baking powder
½   teaspoon salt
1   cup milk
1   (6-ounce) package frozen flaked coconut, thawed
2   teaspoons coconut extract
1   teaspoon vanilla extract
Coconut Filling
2   cups whipping cream
¼   cup powdered sugar
Garnish: toasted coconut shavings

Beat shortening and butter at medium speed with an electric mixer until creamy; gradually add 2⅔ cups sugar, beating well. Add eggs, 1 at a time, beating after each addition.
Combine flour, baking powder, and salt; add to butter mixture alternately with milk, beginning and ending with flour mixture. Mix at low speed after each addition until blended. Stir in coconut and extracts.
Pour batter into 4 greased and floured 9-inch round cakepans. Bake at 350° for 23 minutes or until a wooden pick inserted in center comes out clean. Cool in pans on wire racks 10 minutes; remove from pans. Cool on wire racks.
Spread Coconut Filling between layers. Beat whipping cream at high speed until foamy. Gradually add powdered sugar, beating until soft peaks form. Spread on top and sides of cake. Store in refrigerator. Garnish, if desired. Yield: 16 servings.

Per serving: Calories 829 (49% from fat); Fat 45.4g (sat 24.1g, mono 12.7g, poly 5.6g); Protein 9.5g; Carb 99g; Fiber 2.1g; Chol 179mg; Iron 2.4mg; Sodium 295mg; Calc 114mg

Coconut Filling

prep: 4 min.   cook: 15 min.

2   cups sugar
¼   cup all-purpose flour
2   cups milk
4   large eggs, lightly beaten
2   (6-ounce) packages frozen flaked coconut, thawed
2   teaspoons vanilla extract

Cook first 4 ingredients in a large saucepan over medium-low heat, whisking constantly, 12 to 15 minutes or until thickened and bubbly. Remove from heat. Stir in coconut and vanilla. Cool completely. Yield: 5½ cups.

Per tablespoon: Calories 44 (35% from fat); Fat 1.7g (sat 1.3g, mono 0.2g, poly 0.1g); Protein 0.6g; Carb 6.9g; Fiber 0.2g; Chol 10mg; Iron 0.1mg; Sodium 15mg; Calc 8mg

make ahead
Fresh Orange Italian Cream Cake

prep: 45 min.   cook: 25 min.
other: 8 hrs., 10 min.

Start this cake a day ahead because the Fresh Orange Curd needs time to chill.

½   cup butter or margarine, softened
½   cup shortening
2   cups sugar
5   large eggs, separated
1   tablespoon vanilla extract
2   cups all-purpose flour
1   teaspoon baking soda
1   cup buttermilk
1   cup sweetened flaked coconut
Fresh Orange Curd
3   cups Pecan-Cream Cheese Frosting
½   cup sweetened flaked coconut, lightly toasted (optional)

Beat butter and shortening at medium speed with an electric mixer until creamy; gradually add sugar, beating well. Add egg yolks, 1 at a time, beating until blended after each addition. Add vanilla; beat until blended.
Combine flour and soda; add to sugar mixture alternately with buttermilk, beginning and ending with flour mixture. Beat at low speed until blended after each addition. Stir in 1 cup flaked coconut.
Beat egg whites until stiff peaks form; fold into batter. Pour batter into 3 greased and floured 9-inch round cakepans.
Bake at 350° for 25 minutes or until a wooden pick inserted in center comes out clean. Cool in pans on wire racks for 10 minutes; remove from pans, and cool completely on wire racks.
Spread ¾ cup chilled Fresh Orange Curd between layers; spread remaining orange curd on top of cake. (The orange curd layer on top of cake will be very thick.) If desired,
loosely cover cake, and chill 8 hours. (Chilling the cake with the curd between the layers helps keep the layers in place and makes it much easier to spread the frosting.)
Spread 3 cups Pecan-Cream Cheese Frosting on sides of cake, reserving remaining frosting for another use. Sprinkle ½ cup toasted coconut over top of cake, if desired. Store in refrigerator. Yield: 16 servings.

Per serving: Calories 635 (46% from fat); Fat 32.4g (sat 14.7g, mono 11g, poly 4.5g); Protein 7.2g; Carb 80.9g; Fiber 1.3g; Chol 153mg; Iron 1.7mg; Sodium 267mg; Calc 53mg

Fresh Orange Curd

prep: 20 min.   cook: 10 min.   other: 8 hrs.

1   cup sugar
¼   cup cornstarch
2   cups fresh orange juice (about 4 pounds navel oranges)
3   large eggs, lightly beaten
¼   cup butter
1   tablespoon grated orange rind

Combine sugar and cornstarch in a 3-quart saucepan; gradually whisk in fresh orange juice. Whisk in eggs. Bring to a boil over medium heat, whisking constantly.
Cook, whisking constantly, 1 to 2 minutes or until mixture reaches a puddinglike thickness. Remove from heat, and whisk in butter and grated orange rind. Cover, placing plastic wrap directly on curd, and chill 8 hours. Yield: 3 cups.

Per tablespoon: Calories 36 (33% from fat); Fat 1.3g (sat 0.7g, mono 0.4g, poly 0.1g); Protein 0.5g; Carb 6g; Fiber 0g; Chol 16mg; Iron 0.1mg; Sodium 11mg; Calc 3mg

Pecan–Cream Cheese Frosting

prep: 10 min.

1   (8-ounce) package cream cheese, softened
½   cup butter, softened
1   tablespoon vanilla extract
1   (16-ounce) package powdered sugar
1   cup chopped pecans, toasted

Beat first 3 ingredients at medium speed with an electric mixer until creamy. Gradually add powdered sugar, beating at low speed until blended. Beat at high speed until smooth; stir in pecans. Yield: 4 cups.

Per tablespoon: Calories 66 (55% from fat); Fat 4g (sat 1.8g, mono 1.5g, poly 0.5g); Protein 0.5g; Carb 7.4g; Fiber 0.2g; Chol 8mg; Iron 0.1mg; Sodium 21mg; Calc 5mg

Chocolate Italian Cream Cake

prep: 24 min.   cook: 24 min.   other: 20 min.

Cocoa in the layers and frosting enlivens this old favorite.

1   cup butter, softened
2   cups sugar
5   large eggs, separated
2½ cups all-purpose flour
¼   cup unsweetened cocoa
1   teaspoon baking soda
1   cup buttermilk
⅔   cup finely chopped pecans
1   (3½-ounce) can flaked coconut
1   teaspoon vanilla extract
½   teaspoon cream of tartar
3   tablespoons light rum
    Chocolate-Cream Cheese Frosting

Grease 3 (9-inch) round cakepans; line with wax paper. Grease and flour wax paper. Set aside.
Beat butter at medium speed with an electric mixer until creamy; gradually add sugar, beating well. Add egg yolks, 1 at a time, beating after each addition.
Combine flour, cocoa, and soda; add to butter mixture alternately with buttermilk, beginning and ending with flour mixture. Mix at low speed after each addition until blended. Stir in pecans, coconut, and vanilla.
Beat egg whites at high speed until foamy. Add cream of tartar; beat until stiff peaks form. Gently fold egg whites into batter.
Pour batter into prepared pans. Bake at 350° for 24 minutes or until a wooden pick inserted in center comes out clean. Cool in pans on wire racks 10 minutes; remove from pans, and peel off wax paper. Cool layers completely on wire racks.
Sprinkle each layer with 1 tablespoon rum. Let stand 10 minutes. Spread Chocolate-Cream Cheese Frosting between layers and on top and sides of cake. Store in refrigerator. Yield: 16 servings.

Per serving: Calories 633 (50% from fat); Fat 34.7g (sat 17.6g, mono 11.2g, poly 3.6g); Protein 7.6g; Carb 76.3g; Fiber 2.7g; Chol 130mg; Iron 2.2mg; Sodium 303mg; Calc 60mg

Chocolate-Cream Cheese Frosting

prep: 10 min.

1   (8-ounce) package cream cheese, softened
½   cup butter, softened
2   teaspoons vanilla extract
¼   teaspoon ground cinnamon
1   (16-ounce) package powdered sugar
¼   cup unsweetened cocoa
¼   cup buttermilk
⅔   cup finely chopped pecans

Beat first 4 ingredients at medium speed with an electric mixer until creamy.
Combine powdered sugar and cocoa; gradually add to butter mixture alternately with buttermilk, beginning and ending with powdered sugar mixture. Beat at low speed until blended after each addition. Stir in pecans. Yield: 4 cups.

Per tablespoon: Calories 63 (51% from fat); Fat 3.6g (sat 1.8g, mono 1.3g, poly 0.4g); Protein 0.5g; Carb 7.6g; Fiber 0.2g; Chol 8mg; Iron 0.1mg; Sodium 22mg; Calc 6mg

Pecan Divinity Cake

prep: 55 min.   cook: 17 min.   other: 2 hrs.

Enjoy this grand Southern cake the day you make it.

1   (18.25-ounce) package white cake mix
2   large eggs
1   (8-ounce) container sour cream
½   cup water
⅓   cup vegetable oil
    Divinity Frosting
    Toasted pecan halves (optional)
    Sugared Cherries and Mint Sprigs (optional)

Beat first 5 ingredients at low speed with an electric mixer 30 seconds or just until moistened; beat at medium speed 2 minutes. Pour batter evenly into 4 greased and floured 8-inch round cakepans.
Bake at 350° for 15 to 17 minutes or until a wooden pick inserted in center comes out clean. Cool in pans on wire racks 10 minutes. Remove from pans, and cool completely on wire racks. Wrap layers in plastic wrap, and freeze 2 hours or up to 1 month, if desired. (It's easier to spread frosting on frozen or partially frozen cake layers.)
Spread about ½ cup Divinity Frosting between each layer, and spread remaining Divinity Frosting on top and sides of cake.
Arrange toasted pecan halves on top of cake, if desired. Arrange Sugared Cherries and Mint Sprigs around bottom edge of cake, if desired. Store at room temperature. Yield: 16 servings.

Per serving: Calories 488 (39% from fat); Fat 21.3g (sat 4.8g, mono 9.5g, poly 5.2g); Protein 4.6g; Carb 73g; Fiber 1.4g; Chol 33mg; Iron 1mg; Sodium 285mg; Calc 45mg

Divinity Frosting

prep: 10 min.

1   (7.2-ounce) package home-style fluffy white frosting mix
½   cup boiling water
⅓   cup light corn syrup
2   teaspoons vanilla extract
1   (16-ounce) package powdered sugar
1½ cups chopped pecans, toasted

Place first 4 ingredients in a 4-quart mixing bowl. Beat at low speed with a heavy-duty electric mixer 1 minute or until mixture is blended. Beat mixture at high speed 3 to 5 minutes or until stiff peaks form. Gradually add powdered sugar, beating at low speed until blended. Stir in toasted pecans. Spread immediately onto cake. Yield: about 4½ cups.

Per tablespoon: Calories 57 (28% from fat); Fat 1.8g (sat 0.2g, mono 1g, poly 0.5g); Protein 0.3g; Carb 10.5g; Fiber 0.2g; Chol 0mg; Iron 0.1mg; Sodium 9mg; Calc 2mg

Sugared Cherries and Mint Sprigs

prep: 45 min.   other: 3 hrs.

20 maraschino cherries with stems, rinsed and well drained
16 fresh mint sprigs, rinsed
1⅓ cups powdered sugar
⅓   cup water
1   tablespoon meringue powder
½   cup granulated sugar

Place cherries and mint on paper towels, and let stand until completely dry.
Beat powdered sugar, ⅓ cup water, and meringue powder at medium speed with an electric mixer 2 to 3 minutes or until smooth and creamy.
Brush cherries and mint sprigs with meringue mixture, using a small paintbrush; sprinkle with granulated sugar, and place on a wire rack. Let stand 2 to 3 hours or until dry. Yield: 20 cherries and 16 mint sprigs.

Pineapple Upside-Down Cake

prep: 29 min.   cook: 50 min.   other: 10 min.

- ½ cup butter or margarine
- 1 cup firmly packed light brown sugar
- 3 (8-ounce) cans pineapple slices, undrained
- 10 pecan halves
- 11 maraschino cherries, halved
- 2 large eggs, separated
- 1 egg yolk
- 1 cup granulated sugar
- 1 cup all-purpose flour
- 1 teaspoon baking powder
- ½ teaspoon ground cinnamon
- ¼ teaspoon salt
- 1 teaspoon vanilla extract
- ¼ teaspoon cream of tartar

Melt butter in a 10-inch cast-iron skillet over low heat. Sprinkle brown sugar in skillet. Remove from heat.

Drain pineapple, reserving ¼ cup juice. Set juice aside. Cut pineapple slices in half, reserving 1 whole slice.

Place whole pineapple slice in center of skillet. Arrange 10 pineapple pieces, spoke fashion, around whole slice in center of skillet. Place a pecan half and a cherry half between each piece of pineapple. Place a cherry half in center of whole pineapple slice.

Arrange remaining pineapple pieces, cut side up, around sides of skillet. Place a cherry half in center of each piece of pineapple around sides of skillet.

Beat 3 egg yolks at high speed with an electric mixer until thick and pale; gradually add 1 cup granulated sugar, beating well.

Combine flour and next 3 ingredients; stir well. Add to egg mixture alternately with reserved ¼ cup pineapple juice. Stir in vanilla.

Beat egg whites and cream of tartar at high speed until stiff peaks form; fold beaten egg whites into batter. Pour batter over pineapple in skillet.

Bake at 350° for 45 to 50 minutes or until cake is set. Let cool 5 to 10 minutes. Invert cake onto a serving plate. Scrape any remaining glaze from skillet onto cake. Cut into wedges to serve. Yield: 8 servings.

Per serving: Calories 450 (29% from fat); Fat 14.7g (sat 7.9g, mono 4.4g, poly 1.2g); Protein 4.1g; Carb 78.6g; Fiber 1.4g; Chol 109mg; Iron 1.9mg; Sodium 245mg; Calc 86mg

Pineapple Upside-Down Cake

This old-fashioned dessert baked in a cast-iron skillet makes great use of canned pineapple.

▲ Sprinkle brown sugar over melted butter in skillet.

▲ Place whole pineapple slice in skillet center; arrange 10 pieces around it.

▲ Place remaining pineapple pieces around sides of skillet.

▲ Pour batter over fruit; bake.

Triple-Decker Strawberry Cake

prep: 25 min. cook: 23 min. other: 10 min.

We doubled the frosting called for in the original recipe to add extra richness to this cake. It keeps best in the refrigerator.

1   (18.25-ounce) package white cake mix (we tested with Duncan Hines Moist Deluxe Classic White Cake Mix without pudding)
1   (3-ounce) package strawberry gelatin
4   large eggs
½   cup sugar
¼   cup all-purpose flour
½   cup finely chopped fresh strawberries
1   cup vegetable oil
½   cup milk
Strawberry Buttercream Frosting
Garnish: whole strawberries

Beat first 8 ingredients at low speed with an electric mixer 1 minute. Scrape down the sides, and beat at medium speed 2 more minutes, stopping to scrape down sides, if needed. (Strawberries should be well blended into batter.) Pour batter into 3 greased and floured 9-inch round cakepans.
Bake at 350° for 23 minutes or until a wooden pick inserted in center comes out clean.
Cool in pans on wire racks 10 minutes. Remove from pans, and cool completely on wire racks.
Spread Strawberry Buttercream Frosting between layers and on top and sides of cake. Garnish, if desired. Serve immediately, or chill up to 1 week (without garnish). Yield: 16 servings.

Per serving: Calories 669 (43% from fat); Fat 31.7g (sat 10.8g, mono 11.3g, poly 7.1g); Protein 4.8g; Carb 95.1g; Fiber 0.7g; Chol 84mg; Iron 1mg; Sodium 344mg; Calc 38mg

Strawberry Buttercream Frosting

prep: 10 min.

1   cup butter, softened
2   (16-ounce) packages powdered sugar, sifted
1   cup finely chopped fresh strawberries

Beat butter at medium speed with an electric mixer 20 seconds or until creamy. Add powdered sugar and strawberries, beating at low speed until creamy. (Add more sugar if frosting is too thin, or add strawberries if too thick.) Yield: 2½ cups.

Per tablespoon: Calories 130 (32% from fat); Fat 4.6g (sat 2.9g, mono 1.2g, poly 0.2g); Protein 0.1g; Carb 22.9g; Fiber 0.1g; Chol 12mg; Iron 0mg; Sodium 33mg; Calc 2mg

To make ahead: Place finished cake in the refrigerator, uncovered, and chill for 20 minutes or until frosting sets. Cover well with wax paper, and store in refrigerator up to 1 week. To freeze, wrap chilled cake with aluminum foil, and freeze up to 6 months. Thaw cake overnight in the refrigerator.

Petits Fours

prep: 1 hr., 20 min. cook: 43 min.
other: 10 min.

These petite cake squares are great for a wedding or baby shower.

1   cup shortening
2   cups granulated sugar
3   cups all-purpose flour
2   teaspoons baking powder
¾   teaspoon salt
1   cup ice water
1½   teaspoons clear imitation butter flavor
1   teaspoon vanilla extract
¾   teaspoon almond extract
4   egg whites
½   teaspoon cream of tartar
10   cups sifted powdered sugar
1   cup water
3   tablespoons light corn syrup
1   teaspoon vanilla or almond extract
Creamy Decorator Frosting

Beat shortening at medium speed with an electric mixer until fluffy; gradually add 2 cups granulated sugar, beating well.

Combine flour, baking powder, and salt; add to shortening mixture alternately with ice water, beginning and ending with flour mixture. Mix at low speed after each addition until blended. Stir in flavorings.
Beat egg whites and cream of tartar at high speed until stiff peaks form. Gently fold one-third of beaten egg white into batter; fold in remaining beaten egg white.
Pour batter into 2 greased and floured 8-inch square pans. Bake at 325° for 40 to 43 minutes. Cool in pans on wire racks 10 minutes; remove from pans, and cool completely on wire racks. Cover; freeze until firm.
Trim crusts from all surfaces, making sure tops of cakes are flat. Cut each cake into 16 (1¾-inch) squares; brush away loose crumbs. Place squares 2 inches apart on wire racks in a jelly-roll pan.
Combine powdered sugar and next 3 ingredients in a large saucepan; cook over low heat, stirring constantly, until smooth. Quickly pour warm icing over cake squares, completely covering top and sides.
Spoon up all excess icing; reheat until smooth. (If necessary, add a small amount of water to maintain icing's original consistency.) Continue pouring and reheating icing until all cakes have been iced twice. Let icing dry completely. Trim any excess icing from bottom of each cake square. Decorate as desired with Creamy Decorator Frosting. Yield: 32 petits fours.

Per petit four: Calories 328 (26% from fat); Fat 9.3g (sat 1.9g, mono 4.1g, poly 2.9g); Protein 1.7g; Carb 60.8g; Fiber 0.3g; Chol 0mg; Iron 0.6mg; Sodium 64mg; Calc 21mg

Creamy Decorator Frosting

prep: 5 min.

2   cups sifted powdered sugar
¼   cup plus 2 tablespoons shortening
2   tablespoons milk
½   teaspoon vanilla or almond extract
Dash of salt
Paste food coloring

Combine first 5 ingredients in a small mixing bowl; beat at low speed with an electric mixer until smooth. Color frosting in small amounts with desired paste food coloring. (Keep frosting covered with a damp cloth or plastic wrap.) Yield: 1¼ cups.

Per tablespoon: Calories 74 (47% from fat); Fat 3.9g (sat 0.8g, mono 1.7g, poly 1.2g); Protein 0.1g; Carb 10g; Fiber 0g; Chol 0.2mg; Iron 0.1mg; Sodium 8mg; Calc 2mg

Party-Perfect Strawberry Shortcakes

prep: 25 min.   cook: 16 min.

This dessert is as impressive as it is easy. Fresh mint makes a surprise appearance in the berry filling.

1   (16-ounce) container fresh strawberries, sliced
½   cup sugar, divided
2   tablespoons chopped fresh mint
2½ cups all-purpose flour
4   teaspoons baking powder
¾   cup butter or margarine, cut into pieces
2   large eggs
1   cup sour cream
1   teaspoon vanilla extract
1   tablespoon sugar
1   cup whipping cream
2   tablespoons sugar
2   tablespoons strawberry jam

Combine sliced strawberries, ¼ cup sugar, and chopped mint. Cover and set aside.
Combine flour, baking powder, and remaining ¼ cup sugar; cut in butter with a pastry blender or fork until mixture is crumbly.
Whisk together eggs, sour cream, and vanilla until blended; add to flour mixture, stirring just until dry ingredients are moistened.
Turn dough out onto a lightly floured surface, and knead 6 times. Pat dough to ½-inch thickness, and cut with a 3-inch round cutter. Place dough on a lightly greased baking sheet; sprinkle evenly with 1 tablespoon sugar.
Bake at 425° for 14 to 16 minutes or until golden.
Beat whipping cream at medium speed with an electric mixer until foamy; gradually add 2 tablespoons sugar, beating at high speed until stiff peaks form.
Remove shortcakes from oven, and split in half horizontally. Spread shortcake bottoms with jam, and top with strawberry mixture. Top with whipped cream and remaining shortcake halves. Serve immediately. Yield: 9 servings.

Per serving: Calories 511 (56% from fat); Fat 31.9g (sat 19.4g, mono 8.8g, poly 1.5g); Protein 6.8g; Carb 50.9g; Fiber 1.9g; Chol 135mg; Iron 2.3mg; Sodium 365mg; Calc 191mg

Party-Perfect Strawberry Shortcake

Ground Pecan Torte

prep: 20 min.   cook: 30 min.   other: 35 min.

1   cup butter or margarine, softened
1   cup sugar
3   large eggs
3   cups pecan meal*
1   tablespoon grated lemon rind
⅓   cup cake flour
1   (8-ounce) package cream cheese, softened
½   cup sugar
1   teaspoon vanilla extract
½   cup seedless raspberry preserves
Garnishes: fresh raspberries, fresh mint sprigs, chopped pecans

Beat butter and 1 cup sugar at medium speed with an electric mixer until creamy. Add eggs, 1 at a time, beating just until blended after each addition; add 3 cups pecan meal and lemon rind, and beat at low speed until blended.
Add flour, and beat at low speed just until blended. Spread into 2 greased and floured 9-inch round cakepans.
Bake at 350° for 25 to 30 minutes or until a wooden pick inserted in center comes out clean. Cool in pans on wire racks 5 minutes; remove from pans, and cool 30 minutes.
Beat cream cheese at medium speed until creamy; gradually add sugar and vanilla, beating well.
Spread half of cream cheese filling on top of 1 cake layer; top evenly with half of raspberry preserves. Top with remaining cake layer; spread with remaining cream cheese filling. Add remaining preserves, spreading to within 1 inch of edge of cake. Chill at least 2 hours. Garnish, if desired. Yield: 12 servings.

Per serving: Calories 525 (66% from fat); Fat 39.9g (sat 15.7g, mono 15.8g, poly 6.1g); Protein 5.6g; Carb 40.5g; Fiber 2.3g; Chol 114mg; Iron 1.3mg; Sodium 181mg; Calc 43mg

*Commercially ground pecans have a very fine texture and are often sold as *pecan meal*. We found this to be more economical than grinding whole or halved pecans. To make your own pecan meal, place 2½ cups pecan halves in a food processor, and pulse about 45 seconds or until pecans are finely ground.

Tip: Stirring the preserves helps make them easier to spread on this torte.

Old-Fashioned Gingerbread

prep: 20 min.   cook: 40 min.

Serve with Vanilla Bean Hard Sauce or Lemon Curd (page 443), or whipped cream.

½   cup butter or margarine, softened
1   cup sugar
1   cup molasses
1   large egg
2½   cups all-purpose flour
1½   teaspoons baking soda
½   teaspoon salt
1   teaspoon ground ginger
1   teaspoon ground cinnamon
1   cup hot water

Beat butter at medium speed with an electric mixer until creamy. Gradually add sugar; beat well. Add molasses and egg; beat well.
Combine flour and next 4 ingredients; add to butter mixture alternately with hot water, beginning and ending with flour mixture. Mix at low speed after each addition until blended. Pour batter into a lightly greased and floured 13- x 9-inch pan.
Bake at 350° for 35 to 40 minutes or until a wooden pick inserted in center comes out clean. Cool slightly in pan on a wire rack. Yield: 12 servings.

Per serving: Calories 313 (24% from fat); Fat 8.3g (sat 5g, mono 2.2g, poly 0.5g); Protein 3.3g; Carb 57.3g; Fiber 0.8g; Chol 38mg; Iron 2.7mg; Sodium 325mg; Calc 67mg

Apple Cider Gingerbread

Apple Cider Gingerbread

prep: 15 min.   cook: 28 min.

½   cup butter or margarine, softened
¾   cup granulated sugar
⅓   cup firmly packed dark brown sugar
1   cup molasses
1   large egg
2   cups all-purpose flour
2   tablespoons crystallized ginger, minced
2   teaspoons ground ginger
1½   teaspoons baking soda
1   teaspoon ground cinnamon
1   teaspoon ground cloves
½   teaspoon salt
1   cup hot apple cider
Powdered sugar (optional)
Ginger-Molasses Whipped Cream
Garnish: fresh berries

Beat butter at medium speed with an electric mixer until creamy; gradually add sugars, beating well. Beat in molasses. Add egg, beating until blended.
Combine flour and next 6 ingredients; add to butter mixture alternately with cider, and beat at medium speed until smooth. Pour batter into a greased and floured 13- x 9-inch pan.
Bake at 350° for 28 minutes or until a wooden pick inserted in center of cake comes out clean. Cool on a wire rack. Cut into 3-inch squares or triangles. Dust with powdered sugar, if desired. Serve with Ginger-Molasses Whipped Cream. Garnish, if desired. Yield: 12 servings.

Per serving: Calories 402 (35% from fat); Fat 15.7g (sat 9.1g, mono 4.5g, poly 0.9g); Protein 2.9g; Carb 63.4g; Fiber 0.8g; Chol 64mg; Iron 2.8mg; Sodium 338mg; Calc 93mg

Ginger-Molasses Whipped Cream

prep: 5 min.

1   cup whipping cream
1   tablespoon powdered sugar
1   tablespoon molasses
¼   teaspoon ground ginger

Beat all ingredients at high speed with an electric mixer until soft peaks form. Yield: 1½ cups.

Per tablespoon: Calories 37 (80% from fat); Fat 3.3g (sat 2g, mono 1g, poly 0.1g); Protein 0g; Carb 1.6g; Fiber 0g; Chol 13mg; Iron 0mg; Sodium 4mg; Calc 9mg

pound cakes

Old-Fashioned Pound Cake

prep: 20 min.   cook: 1 hr., 20 min.

2	cups butter, softened
2¾	cups sugar
6	large eggs
3¾	cups all-purpose flour
¼	teaspoon salt
¼	teaspoon ground nutmeg
½	cup milk
1	teaspoon vanilla extract

Beat butter at medium speed with an electric mixer 2 minutes or until creamy. Gradually add sugar, beating 5 minutes. Add eggs, 1 at a time, beating just until yellow disappears.

Combine flour, salt, and nutmeg in a large bowl; add to butter mixture alternately with milk, beginning and ending with flour mixture. Mix at low speed after each addition just until blended. Stir in vanilla. Spoon batter into a greased and floured 10-inch tube pan.

Bake at 325° for 1 hour and 15 to 20 minutes or until a long wooden pick inserted in center of cake comes out clean. Cool cake in pan on a wire rack 15 minutes; remove from pan, and cool completely on wire rack. Yield: 12 servings.

Per serving: Calories 646 (48% from fat); Fat 34.6g (sat 20.4g, mono 9.4g, poly 2g); Protein 8g; Carb 77.4g; Fiber 1.1g; Chol 187mg; Iron 2.4mg; Sodium 303mg; Calc 40mg

Brown Sugar Pound Cake

prep: 20 min.   cook: 1 hr., 45 min.

Don't preheat the oven for this scrumptious pound cake—it gets its start in a cold oven.

1	cup butter, softened
½	cup shortening
2	cups firmly light packed brown sugar
1	cup granulated sugar
6	large eggs
3	cups cake flour
1	teaspoon baking powder
1	cup evaporated milk
2	teaspoons vanilla extract
2	cups chopped pecans, toasted

▲ Beat butter at medium speed 2 minutes or until creamy.

▲ Gradually add sugar, beating 5 minutes.

▲ Add eggs, 1 at a time, beating just until yellow disappears.

▲ Add milk alternately with flour mixture.

A good old-fashioned pound cake batter should have a velvety, thick texture.

▲ Spoon batter into prepared pan, and bake.

Beat butter and shortening at medium speed with an electric mixer until creamy. Gradually add sugars, beating until light and fluffy. Add eggs, 1 at a time, beating just until yellow disappears.

Sift together flour and baking powder; add to butter mixture alternately with milk, beginning and ending with flour mixture. **Beat** batter at low speed just until blended after each addition. Stir in vanilla and pecans. Pour batter into a greased and floured 10-inch tube pan. Place pan in a cold oven; set oven temperature at 300°. **Bake** for 1 hour and 30 minutes to 1 hour and 45 minutes or until a long wooden pick inserted in center comes out clean. Cool in pan on a wire rack 15 minutes. Remove from pan; cool completely on wire rack. Yield: 12 servings.

Per serving: Calories 729 (53% from fat); Fat 43.3g (sat 14.5g, mono 17.5g, poly 8.3g); Protein 8.9g; Carb 79.9g; Fiber 2.4g; Chol 152mg; Iron 3.8mg; Sodium 220mg; Calc 144mg

Cream Cheese Pound Cake

Cream Cheese Pound Cake

prep: 15 min.   cook: 1 hr., 35 min.
other: 15 min.

1½ cups butter or margarine, softened
1 (8-ounce) package cream cheese, softened
3 cups sugar
6 large eggs
3 cups all-purpose flour
⅛ teaspoon salt
1 tablespoon vanilla extract
Garnishes: powdered sugar, fresh berries, fresh thyme, whipped cream

Beat butter and cream cheese at medium speed with an electric mixer until creamy. Gradually add sugar, beating well. Add eggs, 1 at a time, beating just until yellow disappears.
Combine flour and salt; gradually add to butter mixture, beating at low speed just until blended after each addition. Stir in vanilla. Spoon batter into a greased and floured 10-inch Bundt or tube pan.
Bake at 300° for 1 hour and 35 minutes or until a long wooden pick inserted in center comes out clean. Cool in pan on a wire rack 15 minutes; remove from pan, and cool completely on wire rack. Garnish each serving, if desired. Yield: 12 servings.

Per serving: Calories 628 (48% from fat); Fat 33.2g (sat 19.2g, mono 9.2g, poly 1.9g); Protein 8.2g; Carb 75.7g; Fiber 0.9g; Chol 187mg; Iron 2.2mg; Sodium 277mg; Calc 41mg

Sullivan's Lemon-Almond Pound Cake

prep: 20 min.   cook: 1 hr., 40 min.
other: 15 min.

1 cup butter, softened
3 cups sugar
6 large eggs
2 teaspoons vanilla extract
1 teaspoon lemon extract
1 teaspoon almond extract
3 cups all-purpose flour
1 (8-ounce) container sour cream

Beat butter at medium speed with an electric mixer until creamy. Gradually add sugar, beating at medium speed until light and fluffy. Add eggs, 1 at a time, beating just until yellow disappears. Add flavorings, beating just until blended.
Add flour to butter mixture alternately with sour cream, beginning and ending with flour. Beat at low speed just until blended after each addition. Pour batter into a greased and floured 10-inch tube pan.
Bake at 325° for 1 hour and 40 minutes or until a long wooden pick inserted in center comes out clean. Cool cake in pan on a wire rack 15 minutes. Remove from pan, and cool completely on wire rack. Yield: 12 servings.

Per serving: Calories 537 (39% from fat); Fat 23g (sat 13.1g, mono 6.5g, poly 1.5g); Protein 7.3g; Carb 76g; Fiber 0.9g; Chol 154mg; Iron 2mg; Sodium 153mg; Calc 45mg

Orange-Pecan-Spice Pound Cake

prep: 25 min.   cook: 1 hr., 40 min.
other: 20 min.

Chopped pecans form a crisp coating on this buttery cake with multiple flavorings.

2 cups finely chopped pecans, toasted and divided
2 cups butter, softened
3 cups sugar
6 large eggs
4 cups all-purpose flour
⅛ teaspoon salt
¾ cup milk
2 tablespoons grated orange rind
2 teaspoons ground cinnamon
1 teaspoon ground nutmeg
1 teaspoon vanilla extract
1 teaspoon lemon extract
1 teaspoon orange extract
½ teaspoon ground cloves
Orange Syrup
Pecan halves (optional)

Sprinkle 1¼ cups finely chopped pecans into a generously buttered 10-inch tube pan; shake to evenly coat bottom and sides of pan. (Excess nuts will fall to bottom of pan. Make certain nuts are in an even layer in bottom of pan.) Set aside.
Beat butter at medium speed with an electric mixer until creamy; gradually add sugar, beating well. Add eggs, 1 at a time, beating until blended after each addition.
Combine flour and salt; add to butter mixture alternately with milk, beginning and ending with flour mixture. Beat at low speed until blended after each addition. Stir in remaining ¾ cup pecans, grated orange rind, and next 6 ingredients. Spoon batter evenly into prepared pan.
Bake at 300° for 1 hour and 30 to 40 minutes or until a long wooden pick inserted in center comes out clean. Cool in pan on a wire rack 20 minutes. Remove cake from pan; invert cake, pecan crust-side up, onto a wire rack.
Brush top and sides of cake gently several times with hot Orange Syrup, using a 2-inch-wide pastry brush and allowing the cake to absorb the syrup after each brushing. (Do not pour syrup over cake.) Let cake cool completely on wire rack. Arrange pecan halves around top of cake, if desired. Yield: 12 servings.

Per serving: Calories 891 (50% from fat); Fat 50.3g (sat 23g, mono 17.7g, poly 6.1g); Protein 10.2g; Carb 104g; Fiber 3.4g; Chol 194mg; Iron 3.1mg; Sodium 298mg; Calc 69mg

Orange Syrup

prep: 5 min.   cook: 8 min.

1 large orange
1 cup sugar

Remove rind from orange with a vegetable peeler, avoiding bitter white pith. Squeeze orange to get ½ cup juice.
Combine orange rind, juice, and sugar in a small saucepan. Cook over low heat, stirring until sugar dissolves. Bring to a boil over medium-high heat, and boil 2 minutes. Yield: 1 cup.

Per tablespoon: Calories 52 (0% from fat); Fat 0g (sat 0g, mono 0g, poly 0g); Protein 0.1g; Carb 13.3g; Fiber 0g; Chol 0mg; Iron 0mg; Sodium 0.1mg; Calc 1mg

Chocolate Velvet Pound Cake

prep: 15 min.   cook: 1 hr., 5 min.

other: 15 min.

Ice cream and warm ganache elevate this cake to the ultradessert category.

1½ cups semisweet chocolate morsels

½ cup butter, softened

1 (16-ounce) package light brown sugar

3 large eggs

2 cups all-purpose flour

1 teaspoon baking soda

½ teaspoon salt

1 (8-ounce) container sour cream

1 cup hot water

2 teaspoons vanilla extract

¼ cup powdered sugar

Chocolate Ganache

Vanilla ice cream

Garnishes: fresh strawberries, lavender sprigs

Melt semisweet chocolate morsels in a microwave-safe bowl at HIGH for 30-second intervals until melted (about 1½ minutes total time). Stir until smooth.

Beat butter and brown sugar at medium speed with an electric mixer 5 minutes or until well blended. Add eggs, 1 at a time, beating just until blended after each addition. Add melted chocolate, beating just until blended.

Sift together flour, baking soda, and salt. Gradually add to chocolate mixture alternately with sour cream, beginning and ending with flour mixture. Beat at low speed just until blended after each addition. Gradually add 1 cup hot water in a slow, steady stream, beating at low speed just until blended. Stir in vanilla.

Pour batter into a greased and floured 10-inch tube pan. Bake at 350° for 60 to 65 minutes or until a long wooden pick inserted in center comes out clean. Cool in pan on a wire rack 15 minutes. Remove from pan, and let cool completely on wire rack.

Sift powdered sugar over top of cake. Serve with Chocolate Ganache and ice cream. Garnish, if desired. Yield: 12 servings.

Per serving: Calories 664 (47% from fat); Fat 35g (sat 20.5g, mono 10.7g, poly 1.7g); Protein 6.6g; Carb 89g; Fiber 3.5g; Chol 102mg; Iron 3.5mg; Sodium 328mg; Calc 90mg

Chocolate Velvet Pound Cake

Chocolate Ganache

prep: 10 min.   other: 30 min.

1 (12-ounce) package semisweet chocolate morsels

½ cup whipping cream

3 tablespoons butter

Microwave chocolate morsels and whipping cream in a 2-quart glass bowl at MEDIUM (50% power) 2½ to 3 minutes or until morsels begin to melt. Whisk until smooth. Whisk in butter, and let stand 30 minutes. Beat at medium speed with an electric mixer 3 to 4 minutes. Yield: 1½ cups.

Per tablespoon: Calories 97 (68% from fat); Fat 7.3g (sat 4.4g, mono 2.3g, poly 0.2g); Protein 0.6g; Carb 9.3g; Fiber 0.8g; Chol 10mg; Iron 0.4mg; Sodium 13mg; Calc 8mg

chocolate add-ons:

Dip strawberries in Chocolate Ganache; let berries harden on wax paper. To garnish cake, drip small spoonfuls of warm ganache around edge of cake.

fruit & nut cakes

Caramel-Glazed Pear Cake

prep: 25 min.   cook: 1 hr.   other: 5 min.

Pecans and a brown sugar glaze give this cake a decidedly Southern accent.

4   ripe Bartlett pears, peeled and diced
     (about 3 cups)
1   tablespoon sugar
3   large eggs
2   cups sugar
1¼   cups vegetable oil
3   cups all-purpose flour
1   teaspoon salt
1   teaspoon baking soda
1½   cups pecans, coarsely chopped
2   teaspoons vanilla extract
Caramel Glaze

Toss together pears and 1 tablespoon sugar; let stand 5 minutes.
Beat eggs, 2 cups sugar, and oil at medium speed with an electric mixer until blended.
Combine flour, salt, and baking soda, and add to egg mixture, beating at low speed until blended. Fold in pears, chopped pecans, and vanilla. Pour batter into a greased and floured 10-inch Bundt pan.
Bake at 350° for 1 hour or until a long wooden pick inserted in center comes out clean. Remove from pan, and drizzle Caramel Glaze over warm cake. Yield: 12 servings.

Per serving: Calories 760 (53% from fat); Fat 45g (sat 9.1g, mono 19.1g, poly 14.2g); Protein 7.1g; Carb 88.2g; Fiber 3.6g; Chol 74mg; Iron 2.5mg; Sodium 383mg; Calc 87mg

Caramel Glaze

prep: 5 min.   cook: 8 min.

1   cup firmly packed light brown sugar
½   cup butter, cut into pieces
¼   cup evaporated milk

Stir together brown sugar, butter, and evaporated milk in a small saucepan over medium heat; bring to a boil, and cook, stirring constantly, 2½ minutes or until sugar dissolves. Yield: 1½ cups.

Per tablespoon: Calories 72 (50% from fat); Fat 4g (sat 2.5g, mono 1g, poly 0.2g); Protein 0.2g; Carb 9.2g; Fiber 0g; Chol 11mg; Iron 0.2mg; Sodium 33mg; Calc 16mg

make ahead
Orange Date-Nut Cake

prep: 23 min.   cook: 1 hr., 10 min.

Small slivers of this dense, decadent cake will suffice. Add a dab of whipped cream to dress it up.

1   cup butter or margarine, softened
4   cups sugar, divided
4   large eggs
4   cups all-purpose flour
1   teaspoon baking soda
1½   cups buttermilk
1   (8-ounce) package dried chopped dates
1   cup chopped pecans, toasted
4   teaspoons grated orange rind, divided
1   cup orange juice

Beat butter at medium speed with an electric mixer until creamy. Gradually add 2 cups sugar, beating well. Add eggs, 1 at a time, beating until blended after each addition.
Combine flour and baking soda; add to butter mixture alternately with buttermilk, beginning and ending with flour mixture. Beat at low speed until blended after each addition. Stir in dates, pecans, and 2 teaspoons orange rind. Pour batter into a greased and floured 10-inch tube pan.
Bake at 350° for 1 hour and 10 minutes or until a long wooden pick inserted in center comes out clean.
Bring orange juice, remaining 2 cups sugar, and remaining 2 teaspoons orange rind to a boil in a saucepan; cook, stirring constantly, 1 minute.
Gently run a knife around edge of cake; punch holes in cake with a long wooden skewer. Drizzle glaze over warm cake. Let cake cool in pan on a wire rack. Yield: 16 servings.

Per serving: Calories 550 (33% from fat); Fat 19.9g (sat 8.7g, mono 7g, poly 2.6g); Protein 6.9g; Carb 89.2g; Fiber 2.8g; Chol 86mg; Iron 2.1mg; Sodium 205mg; Calc 52mg

make ahead
Fig Cake

prep: 20 min.   cook: 35 min.

Make and freeze this cake up to two weeks in advance; then thaw and add the glaze the day of serving it.

2   cups all-purpose flour
1½   cups sugar
1   teaspoon salt
1   teaspoon baking soda
1   teaspoon ground cloves
1   teaspoon ground nutmeg
1   teaspoon ground cinnamon
3   large eggs, lightly beaten
1   cup vegetable oil
1   cup buttermilk
1   teaspoon vanilla extract
1   cup chopped fresh figs or fig preserves
1   cup chopped pecans, toasted (optional)
Buttermilk Glaze (page 140)

Stir together first 7 ingredients; stir in eggs, oil, and buttermilk, blending well. Stir in vanilla. Fold in chopped figs and, if desired, pecans. Pour batter into a greased and floured 13- x 9-inch pan.
Bake at 325° for 35 minutes or until a wooden pick inserted in center comes out clean. Pierce top of cake several times with a wooden pick; drizzle Buttermilk Glaze over cake. Yield: 16 servings.

Per serving: Calories 402 (50% from fat); Fat 22.4g (sat 6.1g, mono 8.4g, poly 6.7g); Protein 3.8g; Carb 48.6g; Fiber 0.9g; Chol 58mg; Iron 1mg; Sodium 307mg; Calc 41mg

Chunky Apple Cake With Cream Cheese Frosting

prep: 25 min.   cook: 45 min.

The batter for this moist spice cake will be thick, but resist the temptation to add more liquid.

½   cup butter, melted
2   cups sugar
2   large eggs
1   teaspoon vanilla extract
2   cups all-purpose flour
1   teaspoon baking soda
1   teaspoon salt
2   teaspoons ground cinnamon
4   Granny Smith apples, peeled and sliced
1   cup chopped walnuts, toasted
½   recipe Cream Cheese Frosting (page 141)
Chopped walnuts, toasted (optional)

Stir together first 4 ingredients in a large bowl until blended.

Combine flour and next 3 ingredients; add to butter mixture, stirring until blended. Stir in apple slices and 1 cup walnuts. Spread into a greased 13- x 9-inch pan.

Bake at 350° for 45 minutes or until a wooden pick inserted in center comes out clean. Cool completely in pan on a wire rack. Spread with Cream Cheese Frosting; sprinkle with walnuts, if desired. Store in refrigerator. Yield: 15 servings.

Per serving: Calories 422 (43% from fat); Fat 20g (sat 9.2g, mono 5.4g, poly 3.8g); Protein 5.9g; Carb 57.3g; Fiber 1.6g; Chol 67mg; Iron 1.5mg; Sodium 372mg; Calc 32mg

---

Two fruitcake secrets—Grandma's deep mixing bowl and a strong stirring partner.

make ahead • weekend chef

Sherry-Nut Fruitcake

prep: 35 min.   cook: 3 hrs.
other: 8 hrs., 20 min.

Sherry, instead of bourbon, soaks this classic holiday cake.

2   cups raisins
¾   cup dry sherry
2   cups chopped candied pineapple (about 1 pound)
1½   cups chopped red candied cherries (about ¾ pound)
1½   cups chopped green candied cherries (about ¾ pound)
4   cups chopped pecans
3   cups all-purpose flour, divided
¾   cup butter or margarine, softened
¾   cup granulated sugar
¾   cup firmly packed light brown sugar
6   large eggs
¼   teaspoon salt
1   teaspoon ground allspice
1   teaspoon ground cinnamon
¾   cup whipping cream
1   (10-ounce) jar strawberry preserves
1   teaspoon vanilla extract
¾   teaspoon almond extract
⅔   cup dry sherry (optional)

Soak raisins in ¾ cup sherry 8 hours; drain.

Combine pineapple, candied cherries, pecans, and 1 cup flour, tossing to coat.

Beat butter at medium speed with an electric mixer until creamy; gradually add sugars, beating well. Add eggs, 1 at a time, beating well after each addition.

Combine remaining 2 cups flour, salt, allspice, and cinnamon. Add to butter mixture alternately with cream, beginning and ending with flour mixture. Beat at low speed just until blended after each addition. Add preserves and flavorings, beating well. Stir in raisins and fruit mixture. Spoon into a greased and floured 10-inch tube pan.

Bake at 275° for 3 hours or until a long wooden pick inserted in center comes out clean. Cool fruitcake in pan on a wire rack 20 minutes; remove from pan, and cool completely on wire rack.

If desired, soak cheesecloth in ⅔ cup sherry, wrap around cake, and place in an airtight container. Store in a cool place up to 3 weeks. Yield: 16 servings.

Per serving: Calories 811 (41% from fat); Fat 36.7g (sat 10.3g, mono 16.6g, poly 7.5g); Protein 8.4g; Carb 118g; Fiber 4.8g; Chol 117mg; Iron 3.8mg; Sodium 187mg; Calc 71mg

---

White Fruitcake

prep: 30 min.   cook: 2 hrs.   other: 20 min.

Fruitcakes require time to assemble. Chop fruit and nuts, and combine dry ingredients the night before.

1   cup butter or margarine, softened
1   cup sugar
2   large eggs
1   teaspoon orange extract
1   teaspoon lemon extract
3   cups cake flour, divided
2   teaspoons baking powder
½   teaspoon baking soda
½   teaspoon salt
½   cup peach nectar
1   cup sweetened flaked coconut
1   cup chopped candied pineapple (about ½ pound)
1   cup chopped candied cherries (about ½ pound)
1   cup golden raisins (about ½ pound)
1   cup chopped crystallized ginger
2   cups chopped pecans, toasted
6   egg whites
1   cup peach brandy (optional)

Beat butter and sugar at medium speed with an electric mixer until fluffy. Add eggs, 1 at a time, beating well after each addition. Stir in flavorings.

Combine 2 cups cake flour and next 3 ingredients. Add to butter mixture alternately with nectar, beginning and ending with flour mixture. Beat at low speed just until blended after each addition.

Stir together remaining 1 cup cake flour, coconut, and next 4 ingredients. Stir fruit mixture and pecans into batter.

Beat egg whites at high speed until stiff peaks form. Fold into batter. Pour batter into a greased and floured 10-inch tube pan. **Bake** at 275° for 2 hours or until a long wooden pick inserted in center comes out clean. Cool in pan on wire rack 20 minutes; remove from pan and cool completely on wire rack. If desired, wrap in cheesecloth, and soak with 1 cup peach brandy for 2 weeks. Yield: 16 servings.

Per serving: Calories 554 (41% from fat); Fat 25.2g (sat 9.8g, mono 9.7g, poly 4.1g); Protein 6g; Carb 78.8g; Fiber 3g; Chol 57mg; Iron 3.4mg; Sodium 327mg; Calc 85mg

---

low calorie
Carrot-Raisin Cake

prep: 15 min. cook: 30 min.

This carrot cake boasts all the flavor but less fat than traditional versions lavished with frosting. Cut it into squares, and enjoy with a glass of milk.

1½ cups firmly packed light brown sugar
½ cup butter or margarine, softened
2 large eggs
1 teaspoon vanilla extract
1½ cups all-purpose flour
½ teaspoon baking soda
½ teaspoon salt
½ cup chopped raisins
1½ cups finely grated carrot
½ cup pecans or walnuts, finely chopped

Beat brown sugar and butter at medium speed with an electric mixer until creamy; add eggs and vanilla, beating well.
Stir in flour, baking soda, and salt just until moistened; stir in raisins and carrot. Spread batter into a lightly greased 13- x 9-inch pan. Sprinkle with pecans.
Bake at 350° for 30 minutes or until a wooden pick inserted in center comes out clean. Cool on a wire rack, and cut into squares. Yield: 15 servings.

Per serving: Calories 244 (38% from fat); Fat 10.3g (sat 4.4g, mono 3.7g, poly 1.4g); Protein 2.8g; Carb 36.5g; Fiber 1.2g; Chol 44mg; Iron 1.4mg; Sodium 189mg; Calc 35mg

jelly-roll & sheet cakes

German Chocolate Snack Cake

prep: 15 min. cook: 1 hr.

Pecans and cream cheese make this cake mix recipe taste like a from-scratch dessert.

1 (18.25-ounce) package German chocolate cake mix
4 large eggs
½ cup chopped pecans, toasted
½ cup butter or margarine, melted
1 (16-ounce) package powdered sugar
1 (8-ounce) package cream cheese, softened
Ice cream or whipped topping

Stir together cake mix, 1 egg, pecans, and butter; press mixture into a lightly greased 13- x 9-inch pan.
Beat powdered sugar, cream cheese, and remaining 3 eggs at medium speed with an electric mixer until creamy. Spoon powdered sugar mixture over batter in pan.
Bake at 300° for 1 hour. Cool and cut into bars. Serve with ice cream. Yield: 16 servings.

Per serving: Calories 353 (43% from fat); Fat 16.9g (sat 7.9g, mono 5.8g, poly 1.6g); Protein 4.7g; Carb 47g; Fiber 0.6g; Chol 82mg; Iron 1.3mg; Sodium 293mg; Calc 42mg

---

freeze it
Coconut Sheet Cake

prep: 15 min. cook: 45 min. other: 30 min.

3 large eggs
1 (8-ounce) container sour cream
⅓ cup water
1 (8.5-ounce) can cream of coconut
½ teaspoon vanilla extract
1 (18.25-ounce) package white cake mix
Coconut-Cream Cheese Frosting

Beat eggs at high speed with an electric mixer 2 minutes. Add sour cream, ⅓ cup water, and next 2 ingredients, beating well after each addition. Add cake mix, beating at low speed just until blended. Beat at high speed 2 minutes. Pour batter into a greased and floured 13- x 9-inch pan.
Bake at 325° for 40 to 45 minutes or until a wooden pick inserted in center comes out clean. Cool cake in pan on a wire rack. Cover pan with plastic wrap, and freeze cake 30 minutes. Remove from freezer.
Spread Coconut-Cream Cheese Frosting on chilled cake. Cover and store in refrigerator. Yield: 12 servings.

Per serving: Calories 654 (47% from fat); Fat 34.3g (sat 21.7g, mono 8g, poly 1.5g); Protein 7.6g; Carb 81.4g; Fiber 1.6g; Chol 102mg; Iron 1.6mg; Sodium 498mg; Calc 75mg

---

Note: Cake can be baked in a greased and floured 15- x 10-inch jelly-roll pan for 30 to 32 minutes or until a wooden pick inserted in center comes out clean. Yield: 15 servings.

Coconut-Cream Cheese Frosting

prep: 10 min.

1 (8-ounce) package cream cheese, softened
½ cup butter or margarine, softened
3 tablespoons milk
1 teaspoon vanilla extract
1 (16-ounce) package powdered sugar
1 (7-ounce) package sweetened flaked coconut

Beat cream cheese and butter at medium speed with an electric mixer until creamy; add milk and vanilla, beating well. Gradually add sugar, beating until smooth. Stir in coconut. Yield: 4 cups.

Per tablespoon: Calories 68 (49% from fat); Fat 3.7g (sat 2.6g, mono 0.8g, poly 0.1g); Protein 0.4g; Carb 8.7g; Fiber 0.1g; Chol 8mg; Iron 0.1mg; Sodium 29mg; Calc 5mg

family favorite

Texas Sheet Cake

prep: 10 min. cook: 20 min. other: 15 min.

2 cups sugar
2 cups all-purpose flour
¼ cup unsweetened cocoa
1 teaspoon baking soda
1 cup water
½ cup butter, cut into pieces
½ cup shortening
½ cup buttermilk
2 large eggs
1 teaspoon vanilla extract
Chocolate Icing

Grease and flour a 15- x 10-inch jelly-roll pan. Set aside.
Whisk together first 4 ingredients in a large bowl; set flour mixture aside.
Bring 1 cup water to a boil in a medium saucepan. Remove from heat; add butter and shortening. Let stand 5 minutes or until butter melts, whisking occasionally.
Whisk in buttermilk, eggs, and vanilla. Whisk egg mixture into flour mixture until blended. Pour batter into prepared pan.
Bake at 400° for 18 to 20 minutes or until a wooden pick inserted in center comes out clean. Cool cake in pan 10 minutes. Spread icing over warm cake. Yield: 12 servings.

Per serving: Calories 677 (45% from fat); Fat 34g (sat 13.1g, mono 12.9g, poly 6g); Protein 5.7g; Carb 92.2g; Fiber 2.7g; Chol 78mg; Iron 1.9mg; Sodium 241mg; Calc 43mg

Make this icing 5 minutes before taking the cake out of the oven, and spread it on the hot cake.

Chocolate Icing

prep: 5 min. cook: 10 min.

½ cup butter or margarine
¼ cup unsweetened cocoa
⅓ cup milk
1 (16-ounce) package powdered sugar
1 teaspoon vanilla extract
1 cup chopped pecans

Combine butter, cocoa, and milk in a medium saucepan. Cook over low heat 5 minutes or until butter melts. Bring to a boil over medium heat.
Remove from heat; stir in sugar and vanilla. Beat at medium speed with an electric mixer until mixture is smooth and sugar dissolves. Stir in pecans. Yield: 4 cups.

Per tablespoon: Calories 55 (45% from fat); Fat 2.9g (sat 1.1g, mono 1.2g, poly 0.5g); Protein 0.3g; Carb 7.6g; Fiber 0.3g; Chol 4mg; Iron 0.1mg; Sodium 11mg; Calc 4mg

Cola Cake

prep: 8 min. cook: 35 min. other: 10 min.

1 cup cola-flavored drink
½ cup buttermilk
1 cup butter or margarine, softened
1¾ cups sugar
2 large eggs, lightly beaten
2 teaspoons vanilla extract
2 cups all-purpose flour
¼ cup unsweetened cocoa
1 teaspoon baking soda
1½ cups miniature marshmallows
Cola Frosting (on facing page)
Garnish: ¾ cup chopped pecans, toasted

Combine cola and buttermilk; set aside.
Beat butter at low speed with an electric mixer until creamy. Gradually add sugar; beat until blended. Add eggs and vanilla; beat at low speed until blended.
Combine flour, cocoa, and baking soda. Add to butter mixture alternately with cola mixture, beginning and ending with flour mixture. Beat at low speed just until blended.
Stir in marshmallows. Pour batter into a greased and floured 13- x 9-inch pan. Bake at 350° for 30 to 35 minutes. Remove from oven; cool 10 minutes. Spread Cola Frosting over warm cake. Garnish, if desired. Yield: 12 servings.

Per serving: Calories 599 (37% from fat); Fat 24.6g (sat 15.2g, mono 6.5g, poly 1.1g); Protein 4.5g; Carb 93.3g; Fiber 1.6g; Chol 97mg; Iron 1.6mg; Sodium 298mg; Calc 30mg

Cola Frosting

prep: 5 min.   cook: 5 min.

Plan to make this chocolate-cola frosting while the cake bakes; then spread it over the warm cake.

½   cup butter or margarine
⅓   cup cola-flavored drink
3   tablespoons unsweetened cocoa
1   (16-ounce) package powdered sugar
1   tablespoon vanilla extract

Bring first 3 ingredients to a boil in a large saucepan over medium heat, stirring until butter melts. Remove from heat; whisk in sugar and vanilla. Yield: 2¼ cups.

Per tablespoon: Calories 74 (32% from fat); Fat 2.6g (sat 1.6g, mono 0.7g, poly 0.1g); Protein 0.1g; Carb 13.1g; Fiber 0.2g; Chol 7mg; Iron 0.1mg; Sodium 18mg; Calc 1mg

---

family favorite • freeze it

Mississippi Mud Cake

prep: 20 min.   cook: 30 min.

Sheet cakes like this one are ideal for casual gatherings because they're easy to transport.

1   cup butter, melted
2   cups sugar
½   cup unsweetened cocoa
4   large eggs, lightly beaten
1   teaspoon vanilla extract
⅛   teaspoon salt
1½ cups all-purpose flour
1½ cups coarsely chopped pecans, toasted
1   (10.5-ounce) bag miniature marshmallows
Chocolate Frosting

Whisk together first 6 ingredients in a large bowl. Stir in flour and chopped pecans. Pour batter into a greased and floured 15- x 10-inch jelly-roll pan.

Bake at 350° for 20 to 25 minutes or until a wooden pick inserted in center comes out clean. Remove from oven; top warm cake with marshmallows. Return to oven, and bake 5 more minutes. Drizzle Chocolate Frosting over warm cake. Cool completely. Yield: 15 servings.

Per serving: Calories 593 (41% from fat); Fat 27g (sat 11.5g, mono 10g, poly 3.7g); Protein 5.9g; Carb 88g; Fiber 3.1g; Chol 97mg; Iron 1.9mg; Sodium 166mg; Calc 38mg

---

Note: Substitute 2 (19.5-ounce) packages brownie mix, prepared according to package directions, for first 7 ingredients. Stir in chopped pecans. Bake at 350° for 30 minutes. Proceed with marshmallows and frosting as directed.

Chocolate Frosting

prep: 10 min.

1   (16-ounce) package powdered sugar, sifted
½   cup milk
¼   cup butter, softened
⅓   cup unsweetened cocoa

Beat all ingredients at medium speed with an electric mixer until smooth. Yield: 2 cups.

Per tablespoon: Calories 72 (21% from fat); Fat 1.7g (sat 1g, mono 0.4g, poly 0.1g); Protein 0.3g; Carb 14.8g; Fiber 0.3g; Chol 4mg; Iron 0.1mg; Sodium 12mg; Calc 6mg

---

Cranberry-Apple-Filled Walnut Cake Roll

prep: 18 min.   cook: 22 min.

This cake roll is filled with ingredients of the holiday season—apples, cranberries, and walnuts.

Vegetable cooking spray
2   large cooking apples, peeled, cored, and chopped
1   cup fresh cranberries
¼   cup granulated sugar
¼   cup water
2   tablespoons brandy
1   teaspoon lemon juice
½   teaspoon ground cinnamon
¼   teaspoon ground nutmeg
⅔   cup all-purpose flour
1   teaspoon baking powder
¼   teaspoon salt
3   large eggs
¾   cup granulated sugar
⅓   cup water
1   teaspoon vanilla extract
⅓   cup ground walnuts
2   to 3 tablespoons powdered sugar
1   cup whipping cream
½   teaspoon ground cinnamon
1   teaspoon vanilla extract
Garnish: coarsely chopped walnuts

Coat a 15- x 10- inch jelly-roll pan with cooking spray. Line bottom of pan with wax paper; coat wax paper with cooking spray. Set aside.

Combine chopped apple and next 7 ingredients in a medium saucepan. Cook over medium heat about 10 minutes or until cranberry skins pop and liquid is absorbed, stirring occasionally. Cool completely.

Combine flour, baking powder, and salt. Beat eggs in a large mixing bowl at high speed with an electric mixer 2 minutes. Gradually add ¾ cup sugar, beating 5 minutes or until thick and pale. Stir in ⅓ cup water and 1 teaspoon vanilla. Gradually fold flour mixture and ground walnuts into egg mixture with a wire whisk. Spread batter evenly in prepared pan.

Bake at 375° for 12 minutes or until cake springs back when lightly touched in the center.

Sift powdered sugar in a 15- x 10-inch rectangle on a cloth towel. When cake is done, immediately loosen from sides of pan, and turn out onto towel. Peel off wax paper. Starting at narrow end, roll up cake and towel together; place seam side down on a wire rack to cool.

Unroll cake; spread with cranberry mixture. Reroll cake without towel; place seam side down on a serving plate.

Beat whipping cream, ½ teaspoon ground cinnamon, and 1 teaspoon vanilla at high speed until stiff peaks form. Spread mixture over cake. Loosely cover and chill or partially freeze cake roll before serving. Garnish, if desired. Yield: 6 servings.

Per serving: Calories 442 (41% from fat); Fat 20.2g (sat 9.1g, mono 6g, poly 3.2g); Protein 6.5g; Carb 58.1g; Fiber 2.4g; Chol 159mg; Iron 1.6mg; Sodium 228mg; Calc 102mg

Pumpkin Roll

prep: 25 min.   cook: 15 min.   other: 3 hrs.

Prepare this spice cake a day ahead and keep it chilled; then dust with sugar before serving. Serve slices of the cake with a few pecan halves, if you'd like. Dipping pecan halves in melted chocolate makes them even more special.

Vegetable cooking spray
3   large eggs
1   cup granulated sugar
¾   cup all-purpose flour
2   teaspoons ground cinnamon
1   teaspoon baking soda
1   teaspoon baking powder
1   teaspoon ground ginger
½   teaspoon salt
½   teaspoon ground nutmeg
⅔   cup canned unsweetened pumpkin
½   cup finely chopped pecans, toasted
1   teaspoon lemon juice

1½ cups powdered sugar, divided
2   (3-ounce) packages cream cheese, softened
¼   cup butter or margarine, softened
1   teaspoon vanilla extract
1   teaspoon lemon juice
Garnishes: powdered sugar, pecan halves

Coat bottom and sides of a 15- x 10-inch jelly-roll pan with cooking spray, and line with wax paper. Coat wax paper with cooking spray; set aside.
Beat eggs at medium speed with an electric mixer 5 minutes or until thick and lemon-colored; gradually add granulated sugar, beating until well combined.
Combine flour and next 6 ingredients. Gradually add to egg mixture, beating well. Combine pumpkin, pecans, and 1 teaspoon lemon juice, and gradually add to egg and flour mixture, beating well.
Spread batter evenly into prepared pan. Bake at 375° for 15 minutes or until a wooden pick inserted in center comes out clean.

Sift ½ cup powdered sugar in a 15- x 10-inch rectangle on a clean, dry dish towel. Run a knife around edges of pan to loosen cake, and turn cake out onto prepared towel. Peel off wax paper. Starting at narrow end, roll up cake and towel together; place seam side down on a wire rack to cool completely.
Beat cream cheese and butter at medium speed until creamy; gradually add remaining 1 cup powdered sugar, beating until smooth. Stir in vanilla and 1 teaspoon lemon juice.
Unroll cake; remove towel. Spread cream cheese mixture on cake, leaving a 1-inch border around edges. Reroll cake without towel, and place seam side down on a serving platter. Cover and chill at least 3 hours. Garnish, if desired. Store in refrigerator. Yield: 8 servings.

Per serving: Calories 442 (42% from fat); Fat 20.6g (sat 9.4g, mono 7.3g, poly 2.4g); Protein 6.2g; Carb 60.8g; Fiber 2g; Chol 118mg; Iron 1.9mg; Sodium 543mg; Calc 83mg

cakes from mixes

Triple-Chocolate Snack Cake

prep: 15 min.   cook: 35 min.

This recipe produces 2 moist cakes—serve one as a breakfast coffee cake and give the other as a gift.

1   (18.25-ounce) package devil's food cake mix
1   (3.9-ounce) package chocolate instant pudding mix
2   cups sour cream
1   cup butter or margarine, softened
5   large eggs
1   teaspoon vanilla extract
3   cups semisweet chocolate morsels, divided
1   cup white chocolate morsels
1   cup chopped pecans, toasted

Beat first 6 ingredients at low speed with an electric mixer 30 seconds or just until

moistened; beat at medium speed 2 minutes. Stir in 2 cups semisweet chocolate morsels; pour batter evenly into 2 greased and floured 9-inch square cakepans.
Bake at 350° for 30 to 35 minutes or until a wooden pick inserted in center comes out clean. Cool completely in pans on wire racks.
Microwave white chocolate morsels in a small glass bowl at HIGH 30 to 60 seconds or until morsels melt, stirring at 30-second intervals until smooth. Drizzle evenly over cakes; repeat procedure with remaining 1 cup semisweet morsels. Sprinkle cakes evenly with pecans. Yield: 32 servings.

Per serving: Calories 283 (62% from fat); Fat 19.5g (sat 9.7g, mono 6.7g, poly 1.6g); Protein 3.9g; Carb 26g; Fiber 1.5g; Chol 58mg; Iron 1.4mg; Sodium 230mg; Calc 47mg

Tip: Melt white chocolate and semisweet morsels in separate zip-top freezer bags; then snip off corners of each bag for easy drizzling.

Chocolate Éclair Cake

prep: 24 min.   other: 8 hrs.

Graham crackers simulate cake layers in this indulgent dessert. One box of graham crackers contains three individually wrapped packages of crackers; use one package for each layer. Freeze cake, if desired; thaw a few minutes before serving.

1   (14.4-ounce) box honey graham crackers
2   (3.4-ounce) packages French vanilla instant pudding mix
3   cups milk
1   (12-ounce) container frozen whipped topping, thawed
1   (16-ounce) container ready-to-spread chocolate frosting

Line bottom of an ungreased 13- x 9-inch baking dish with one-third of honey graham crackers.

Whisk together pudding mix and milk; add whipped topping, stirring until mixture thickens slightly. Spread half of pudding mixture over graham crackers. Repeat layers with one-third of graham crackers and remaining pudding mixture. Top with remaining graham crackers. Spread with chocolate frosting. Cover and chill 8 hours. Store in refrigerator. Yield: 12 servings.

Per serving: Calories 467 (32% from fat); Fat 16.8g (sat 8.5g, mono 5.3g, poly 2.2g); Protein 4.7g; Carb 73.9g; Fiber 1.3g; Chol 6mg; Iron 1.8mg; Sodium 524mg; Calc 80mg

Note: To lighten cake, use reduced-fat graham crackers, sugar-free pudding mix, fat-free milk, and fat-free whipped topping.

Root Beer Float Cake

prep: 14 min.   cook: 30 min.   other: 10 min.

Root beer replaces water in this cake mix recipe adding a flavor boost as well as a little extra rise.

1	(18.25-ounce) package German chocolate cake mix
1¼	cups root beer (not diet)
¼	cup vegetable oil
2	large eggs
	Root Beer Frosting

Combine first 4 ingredients in a mixing bowl. Beat at low speed with an electric mixer until dry ingredients are moistened. Pour batter into a greased and floured 13- x 9-inch pan.
Bake at 350° for 30 minutes or until a wooden pick inserted in center comes out clean. Cool in pan 10 minutes. Spread Root Beer Frosting evenly over warm cake. Yield: 12 servings.

Per serving: Calories 479 (36% from fat); Fat 19.2g (sat 7.7g, mono 6.5g, poly 2.9g); Protein 4.5g; Carb 74.3g; Fiber 0.8g; Chol 67mg; Iron 1.7mg; Sodium 377mg; Calc 44mg

Root Beer Frosting

prep: 4 min.   cook: 3 min.

½	cup butter or margarine
7	tablespoons root beer (not diet)
3	tablespoons unsweetened cocoa
1	(16-ounce) package powdered sugar
1	teaspoon vanilla extract

Bring first 3 ingredients to a boil in a large saucepan over medium heat, stirring until butter melts. Remove from heat; whisk in powdered sugar and vanilla until smooth. Yield: 2 cups.

Per tablespoon: Calories 83 (31% from fat); Fat 2.9g (sat 1.8g, mono 0.8g, poly 0.1g); Protein 0.1g; Carb 14.8g; Fiber 0.2g; Chol 8mg; Iron 0.1mg; Sodium 21mg; Calc 2mg

foam cakes

Often grouped together in cookbooks, "foam" cakes include angel food, sponge, and chiffon cakes. These cakes contain an abundance of fluffy egg whites—a common element that's responsible for their similarity and characteristic lightness. But several key differences distinguish the three cakes.

Angel food cake is the purest of the foam cakes. It contains no leavening, egg yolks, or shortening. An angel food cake's structure comes from the high proportion of beaten egg white to flour. And because there's no egg yolk or other fat source, angel food cake is a great dessert for the health conscious.

In contrast, sponge cakes contain both egg whites and yolks and sometimes leavening, but never fat. And chiffon cakes are a blend of shortening cakes and foam cakes. They get their lightness from beaten egg whites, but they also contain yolks, leavening, and shortening or oil.

Foam cakes are commonly baked in an ungreased tube pan. This allows the batter to cling to the sides of the pan and rise

Angel food cake is basically a meringue with added flour for stability and texture.

high. Then, these light cakes are often cooled upside-down in the pan to prevent shrinking and falling.

low calorie • low cholesterol • low fat

Blue Ribbon Angel Food Cake

prep: 20 min.   cook: 35 min.   other: 1 hr.

This feathery light cake is heavenly alone or with fresh berries.

1½	cups sifted cake flour
12	egg whites
1¼	teaspoons cream of tartar
¼	teaspoon salt
1	teaspoon vanilla extract
¼	teaspoon almond extract
1⅓	cups sugar

Sift flour 4 times, and set aside.
Beat egg whites and next 4 ingredients at high speed with an electric mixer until soft peaks form (about 5 minutes). Gradually add sugar, ⅓ cup at a time, beating until blended after each addition. Fold in flour. Pour batter into an ungreased 10-inch tube pan.
Bake at 375° for 35 minutes. Invert pan onto a wire rack, and let stand 1 hour or until cake is completely cool. Run a knife around cake to loosen edges. Yield: 16 servings.

Per serving: Calories 116 (1% from fat); Fat 0.1g (sat 0g, mono 0g, poly 0g); Protein 3.6g; Carb 25g; Fiber 0.2g; Chol 0mg; Iron 0.8mg; Sodium 78mg; Calc 3mg

• Foam cakes should be baked as soon as the batter is ready or egg whites will deflate.
• Slice foam cakes with a serrated knife and a gentle sawing motion.

low calorie • low cholesterol • low fat

Mixed-Berry Angel Cakes With Almond Sugar

prep: 25 min.   cook: 15 min. per batch

Here's an easy way to serve three-berry shortcake to a crowd.

1   (8-ounce) package fresh strawberries (about 1 cup), sliced
1   pint fresh blueberries (about 1 cup)
1   (6-ounce) package fresh raspberries (about 1 cup)
⅔   cup sugar
¾   teaspoon almond extract
1   (1-pound) package angel food cake mix
Frozen whipped topping, thawed

Toss together berries in a large bowl. Stir together sugar and almond extract, and sprinkle over berries, tossing to coat. Cover and chill 1 hour.
Prepare cake mix according to package directions.
Place paper baking cups in muffin pans; spoon batter into cups, filling two-thirds full.
Bake, 1 muffin pan at a time, at 350° for 15 minutes or until lightly browned. Remove cupcakes from pans to wire racks; cool.
Cut cupcakes in half horizontally; spoon 1 tablespoon berry mixture on bottom halves, and cover with tops. Spoon 1 tablespoon berry mixture on top halves, and dollop with whipped topping. Serve immediately. Yield: 32 cupcakes.

Per cupcake: Calories 91 (8% from fat); Fat 0.8g (sat 0.8g, mono 0g, poly 0g); Protein 1.5g; Carb 19.3g; Fiber 0.7g; Chol 0mg; Iron 0.1mg; Sodium 84mg; Calc 83mg

low calorie

Chiffon Cake

prep: 20 min.   cook: 1 hr.   other: 40 min.

This airy cake is distinguished from other foam cakes by the fat it contains. In this case, oil lends tenderness to the cake's delicate texture.

1   cup all-purpose flour
1½   teaspoons baking powder
¼   teaspoon salt
1   cup sugar, divided
¼   cup vegetable oil
4   large eggs, separated
¼   cup water
1   teaspoon vanilla extract
½   teaspoon cream of tartar

Sift together flour, baking powder, salt, and ½ cup sugar in a large mixing bowl. Make a well in center; add oil, egg yolks, water, and vanilla. Beat at high speed with an electric mixer about 5 minutes or until satiny smooth.
Beat egg whites and cream of tartar in a large mixing bowl at high speed until soft peaks form. Add remaining ½ cup sugar, 2 tablespoons at a time, beating until stiff peaks form.
Pour egg yolk mixture in a thin, steady stream over entire surface of egg whites; gently fold whites into yolk mixture.
Pour batter into an ungreased 10-inch tube pan, spreading evenly with a spatula. Bake at 325° for 1 hour or until cake springs back when lightly touched. Invert pan; cool 40 minutes. Loosen cake from sides of pan, using a narrow metal spatula; remove from pan. Yield: 14 servings.

Per serving: Calories 145 (34% from fat); Fat 5.5g (sat 0.9g, mono 2.3g, poly 2g); Protein 2.7g; Carb 21.5g; Fiber 0.2g; Chol 60mg; Iron 0.7mg; Sodium 114mg; Calc 38mg

low calorie • low fat

Vanilla Sponge Cake

prep: 20 min.   cook: 50 min.   other: 40 min.

Enjoy generous slices of sponge cake topped with frozen yogurt or sliced fresh strawberries for an easy and guilt-free dessert.

1   cup sifted cake flour
½   cup sugar
4   egg yolks
1   teaspoon vanilla extract
10   egg whites
1   teaspoon cream of tartar
½   teaspoon salt
¾   cup sugar

Sift flour and ½ cup sugar together 3 times; set aside. Beat egg yolks at high speed with an electric mixer 4 minutes or until thick and pale. Add vanilla; beat at medium speed 5 more minutes or until mixture is thick. Set aside.
Beat egg whites in a large mixing bowl at high speed until foamy. Add cream of tartar and salt; beat until soft peaks form. Add ¾ cup sugar, 2 tablespoons at a time, beating until stiff peaks form.
Sprinkle one-fourth flour mixture over egg whites; gently fold in. Repeat procedure with remaining flour, adding one-fourth of mixture at a time.
Gently fold beaten egg yolks into egg white mixture. Pour batter into an ungreased 10-inch tube pan.
Bake at 350° for 45 to 50 minutes or until cake springs back when lightly touched. Invert pan carefully. Cool in pan 40 minutes. Loosen cake from sides of pan, using a narrow metal spatula; remove from pan. Yield: 14 servings.

Per serving: Calories 126 (10% from fat); Fat 1.4g (sat 0.5g, mono 0.6g, poly 0.2g); Protein 4g; Carb 24.5g; Fiber 0.1g; Chol 59mg; Iron 0.7mg; Sodium 125mg; Calc 9mg

cheesecakes

Deluxe Cheesecake

prep: 12 min.   cook: 1 hr., 25 min.   other: 12 hrs.

You'll need a 9-inch springform pan with 3-inch sides for this recipe.

- 2 cups graham cracker crumbs
- ½ cup butter or margarine, melted
- 2 tablespoons sugar
- 4 (8-ounce) packages cream cheese, softened
- 1¾ cups sugar
- 7 large eggs
- 3 (8-ounce) containers sour cream
- 1 tablespoon vanilla extract

Combine first 3 ingredients; stir well. Press mixture firmly on bottom and up sides of a lightly greased 9-inch springform pan with 3-inch sides. Chill thoroughly.

Beat cream cheese at medium-high speed with a heavy-duty stand mixer until fluffy. Gradually add 1¾ cups sugar, beating well. Add eggs, 1 at a time, beating after each addition. Add sour cream and vanilla; beat at low speed until smooth. Pour batter into prepared pan.

Bake at 300° for 1 hour and 25 minutes. Turn off oven, and leave cheesecake in oven 4 hours. (Do not open oven door.)

Remove from oven; cool completely on a wire rack. Cover and chill 8 hours. Remove sides of springform pan before serving. Store in refrigerator. Yield: 12 servings.

Per serving: Calories 678 (66% from fat); Fat 49.9g (sat 30.5g, mono 12.6g, poly 2.3g); Protein 12.1g; Carb 46.8g; Fiber 0.4g; Chol 251mg; Iron 2mg; Sodium 436mg; Calc 146mg

This tall, dense New York-style cheesecake received our Test Kitchens highest rating—even without any toppings.

Deluxe Cheesecake

freeze it • make ahead

Frozen Peppermint Cheesecake

prep: 24 min.   other: 8 hrs.

For a classic pairing, serve slices with Hot Fudge Sauce (page 441).

- 2½ cups chocolate wafer crumbs
- ½ cup sugar
- ½ cup butter or margarine, melted
- 1 (8-ounce) package cream cheese, softened
- 1 (14-ounce) can sweetened condensed milk
- 1 cup crushed hard peppermint candy,
- 2 cups whipping cream

Combine first 3 ingredients; press mixture on bottom and 2 inches up sides of a 9-inch springform pan. Set aside.

Beat cream cheese at medium speed with an electric mixer until creamy. Gradually add condensed milk, beating until smooth. Stir in ¾ cup crushed candy.

Beat whipping cream until soft peaks form; gently fold whipped cream into cream cheese mixture. Pour into prepared pan; sprinkle remaining ¼ cup crushed candy on top. Cover and freeze 8 hours or until firm. Remove sides of springform pan just before serving. Yield: 12 servings.

Per serving: Calories 561 (54% from fat); Fat 33.7g (sat 19.8g, mono 9.8g, poly 2g); Protein 5.7g; Carb 60.2g; Fiber 0.8g; Chol 106mg; Iron 1.2mg; Sodium 306mg; Calc 146mg

cheesecake tips

- Let cream cheese soften at room temperature before you begin.
- Don't overbeat batter when adding eggs. Beat only until blended.
- To prevent cracks, run a knife or small metal spatula around edge of cheesecake immediately after removing it from the oven. This allows cake to contract freely.
- You can freeze cheesecake up to one month. Remove pan, place cheesecake on a cardboard circle and wrap tightly in heavy-duty aluminum foil. Thaw in the refrigerator the day before serving.

Praline-Crusted Cheesecake

prep: 38 min.   cook: 1 hr., 28 min.
other: 9 hrs.

You'll remember this cheesecake for its shortbread crust and praline center. Use store-bought pralines for a shortcut.

3½ cups crushed shortbread cookies (we tested with 28 Pecan Sandies)
3   tablespoons butter or margarine, melted
4   Pralines (page 188), coarsely crumbled (1 cup)
5   (8-ounce) packages cream cheese, softened
1¾ cups granulated sugar
2   tablespoons all-purpose flour
2   teaspoons vanilla extract
4   large eggs
2   egg yolks
⅓   cup whipping cream
2   (8-ounce) containers sour cream
⅓   cup sifted powdered sugar
Garnish: additional crumbled Pralines

Stir together cookie crumbs and butter. Press on bottom and 1½ inches up sides of a greased 10-inch springform pan.
Bake at 350° for 8 minutes. Cool on a wire rack. Sprinkle coarsely crumbled Pralines over crust.
Beat cream cheese at medium speed with an electric mixer until creamy. Gradually add 1¾ cups sugar, flour, and vanilla, beating until smooth. Add eggs and egg yolks, 1 at a time, beating just until yellow disappears. Stir in whipping cream. Pour into crust (pan will be very full).
Bake at 325° for 1 hour and 20 minutes or until almost set. Cool cheesecake on a wire rack 45 minutes. (Center will settle slightly.)
Stir together sour cream and powdered sugar until smooth; spread over cheesecake to edges of pan. (No additional baking is needed.) Let cool completely. Cover with plastic wrap, and chill 8 hours. Run a sharp knife around sides of pan; remove sides of pan. Garnish, if desired. Store in refrigerator. Yield: 12 servings.

Per serving: Calories 884 (65% from fat); Fat 64g (sat 32.8g, mono 22.4g, poly 4.3g); Protein 13.6g; Carb 66.4g; Fiber 1.1g; Chol 250mg; Iron 2.6mg; Sodium 476mg; Calc 149mg

Key Lime Cheesecake With Strawberry Sauce

prep: 20 min.   cook: 1 hr., 13 min.
other: 8 hrs., 15 min.

2   cups graham cracker crumbs
¼   cup sugar
½   cup butter or margarine, melted
3   (8-ounce) packages cream cheese, softened
1¼ cups sugar
3   large eggs
1   (8-ounce) container sour cream
1½ teaspoons grated lime rind
½   cup Key lime juice
Garnishes: strawberry halves, lime slices
Strawberry Sauce

Stir together first 3 ingredients. Press on bottom and 1 inch up sides of a greased 9-inch springform pan.
Bake at 350° for 8 minutes; cool.
Beat cream cheese at medium speed with an electric mixer until fluffy; gradually add 1¼ cups sugar, beating until blended. Add eggs, 1 at a time, beating after each addition. Stir in sour cream, rind, and juice. Pour batter into crust.
Bake at 325° for 1 hour and 5 minutes; turn oven off. Partially open oven door; let stand in oven 15 minutes. Remove from oven, and immediately run a knife around edge of pan, releasing sides.
Cool completely in pan on a wire rack; cover and chill 8 hours. Remove sides of springform pan before serving. Garnish, if desired. Serve with Strawberry Sauce. Store in refrigerator. Yield: 12 servings.

Per serving: Calories 510 (61% from fat); Fat 34.7g (sat 20.5g, mono 10.1g, poly 2.1g); Protein 7.7g; Carb 44.4g; Fiber 0.8g; Chol 144mg; Iron 1.5mg; Sodium 334mg; Calc 84mg

Strawberry Sauce

prep: 5 min.

1¼ cups fresh strawberries
¼   cup sugar
1½ teaspoons grated lime rind

Process all ingredients in a food processor until smooth, stopping to scrape down sides. Yield: 1 cup.

Per tablespoon: Calories 16 (0% from fat); Fat 0g (sat 0g, mono 0g, poly 0g); Protein 0.1g; Carb 4g; Fiber 0.2g; Chol 0mg; Iron 0.1mg; Sodium 0mg; Calc 2mg

Chocolate-Coconut-Almond Cheesecake

prep: 12 min.   cook: 1 hr., 8 min.   other: 8 hrs.

This cheesecake is dense and decadent and chock-full of ingredients that make it reminiscent of a popular candy bar.

1½ cups chocolate wafer crumbs (about 30 wafers)
3   tablespoons sugar
¼   cup butter or margarine, melted
4   (8-ounce) packages cream cheese, softened
1   cup sugar
3   large eggs
1   (14-ounce) package sweetened flaked coconut
1   (11.5-ounce) package milk chocolate morsels
1   cup slivered almonds, toasted and divided
1   teaspoon vanilla extract
½   cup semisweet chocolate morsels

Stir together first 3 ingredients; press mixture in bottom of a 10-inch springform pan. Bake at 350° for 8 minutes; cool.
Beat cream cheese at high speed with an electric mixer until creamy; gradually add 1 cup sugar, beating well. Add eggs, 1 at a time, beating at medium speed until blended after each addition. Stir in coconut, milk chocolate morsels, ½ cup almonds, and vanilla. Pour batter into prepared pan.
Bake at 350° for 55 to 60 minutes or until cheesecake is almost set. Remove from oven; cool to room temperature in pan on a wire rack. Cover and chill at least 8 hours. Remove sides of springform pan. Place cheesecake on a serving plate.
Place semisweet chocolate morsels in a small zip-top freezer bag, and seal. Submerge bag in hot water until chocolate melts. Snip a tiny hole in 1 corner of bag, and drizzle melted chocolate over cheesecake. Sprinkle with remaining ½ cup slivered almonds. Store in refrigerator. Yield: 16 servings.

Per serving: Calories 632 (63% from fat); Fat 44.1g (sat 26.2g, mono 12.9g, poly 2.5g); Protein 10.2g; Carb 52.7g; Fiber 3.2g; Chol 114mg; Iron 2.7mg; Sodium 342mg; Calc 115mg

specialty cakes & cupcakes

Honey-Apple Cake

prep: 15 min.   cook: 1 hr.   other: 15 min.

1   cup chopped pecans, divided
2   cups sugar
1   cup vegetable oil
¼   cup honey
3   large eggs
3   cups all-purpose flour
1   teaspoon baking soda
1   teaspoon salt
1   teaspoon ground cinnamon
¼   teaspoon ground nutmeg
1   teaspoon vanilla extract
3   cups chopped Golden Delicious apple
Honey Sauce
Vanilla ice cream (optional)

Grease and flour a 12-cup Bundt pan; sprinkle bottom of pan with ¼ cup pecans. Set pan aside.
Beat sugar, oil, and honey at medium speed with an electric mixer until well blended. Add eggs, 1 at a time, beating just until blended.
Combine flour and next 4 ingredients. Gradually add to sugar mixture, beating at low speed just until blended. Stir in vanilla, remaining ¾ cup pecans, and chopped apple. Spoon batter over pecans in pan.
Bake at 350° for 55 to 60 minutes. Cool in pan on a wire rack 15 minutes; remove from pan, and place on a wire rack over wax paper. Pour ½ cup Honey Sauce over warm cake. Cool.
Heat remaining Honey Sauce; serve with cake and, if desired, ice cream. Yield: 12 servings.

Per serving: Calories 690 (46% from fat); Fat 35.2g (sat 8g, mono 14.6g, poly 10.8g); Protein 6.1g; Carb 93g; Fiber 2.7g; Chol 73mg; Iron 2.5mg; Sodium 381mg; Calc 48mg

Honey Sauce

prep: 5 min.   cook: 2 min.

1   cup firmly packed light brown sugar
½   cup butter or margarine
¼   cup honey
¼   cup milk

Bring all ingredients to a boil in a medium saucepan over medium-high heat, stirring constantly; boil, stirring constantly, 2 minutes. Yield: 1½ cups.

Per tablespoon: Calories 80 (44% from fat); Fat 3.9g (sat 2.4g, mono 1g, poly 0.2g); Protein 0.1g; Carb 12g; Fiber 0g; Chol 10mg; Iron 0.2mg; Sodium 32mg; Calc 12mg

Mocha Fudge Cake

prep: 17 min.   cook: 1 hr., 5 min.   other: 15 min.

A ribbon of cream cheese and coconut runs through this dark chocolate Bundt.

2¼   cups sugar, divided
1   cup vegetable oil
3   large eggs
3   cups all-purpose flour
2   teaspoons baking powder
2   teaspoons baking soda
1½   teaspoons salt
¾   cup unsweetened cocoa
1   cup strong brewed coffee, cooled, or water
1   cup buttermilk
2   teaspoons vanilla extract, divided
1   (8-ounce) package cream cheese, softened
½   cup sweetened flaked coconut
1   cup semisweet chocolate morsels
Chocolate Glaze

Combine 2 cups sugar, oil, and 2 eggs in a large mixing bowl; beat at high speed with an electric mixer 1 minute.
Combine flour and next 4 ingredients; combine coffee and buttermilk. Add dry ingredients and coffee mixture to batter. Beat at medium speed 3 minutes. Stir in 1 teaspoon vanilla. Pour two-thirds of batter into a greased 12-cup Bundt pan.
Beat cream cheese in a small bowl at medium speed until fluffy; add remaining ¼ cup sugar and 1 egg. Beat just until blended. Stir in remaining 1 teaspoon vanilla, coconut, and chocolate morsels; spoon over batter in pan, leaving a ½-inch border around center and edge. Top with remaining chocolate batter.
Bake at 350° for 1 hour and 5 minutes or until a long wooden pick inserted in center comes out clean. Cool in pan on a wire rack 15 minutes. Remove from pan; cool on wire rack. Drizzle with warm Chocolate Glaze. Yield: 12 servings.

Per serving: Calories 733 (53% from fat); Fat 43.3g (sat 16.4g, mono 15.4g, poly 9.4g); Protein 9.3g; Carb 85.9g; Fiber 4.4g; Chol 91mg; Iron 3.7mg; Sodium 714mg; Calc 114mg

Chocolate Glaze

prep: 2 min.   cook: 5 min.

1   cup semisweet chocolate morsels
3   tablespoons butter or margarine
¼   cup whipping cream

Melt chocolate morsels, butter, and cream in a small saucepan over low heat, stirring constantly, until smooth. Yield: about 1 cup.

Per tablespoon: Calories 82 (72% from fat); Fat 6.6g (sat 4g, mono 2g, poly 0.2g); Protein 0.5g; Carb 7g; Fiber 0.6g; Chol 11mg; Iron 0.3mg; Sodium 18mg; Calc 7mg

for kids
Chewy Chocolate Cupcakes

prep: 15 min.   cook: 35 min.

To make ahead, prepare cupcakes one or two days ahead; store in an airtight container. These are superb alone or topped with Chocolate-Marshmallow Frosting (page 165).

1   cup butter
4   (1-ounce) semisweet chocolate baking squares
1½   cups chopped pecans
1½   cups sugar
1   cup all-purpose flour
4   large eggs, lightly beaten
1   teaspoon vanilla extract

Melt together butter and chocolate in a heavy saucepan over medium heat; stir in pecans. Remove from heat.
Combine sugar and next 3 ingredients. (Do not beat.) Stir in chocolate mixture. Place baking cups in muffin pans; spoon batter into cups, filling three-fourths full.
Bake at 325° for 35 minutes. (Do not overbake.) Yield: 16 cupcakes.

Per cupcake: Calories 333 (61% from fat); Fat 22.7g (sat 9.6g, mono 8.7g, poly 3.1g); Protein 4g; Carb 31g; Fiber 1.3g; Chol 83mg; Iron 1.1mg; Sodium 98mg; Calc 19mg

White Cupcakes (page 134) with Coconut-Cream Cheese Frosting (page 155); Brown Sugar-Frosted Cupcakes (opposite); Chocolate Cupcakes (page 134) with Chocolate-Marshmallow Frosting (opposite)

Brown Sugar-Frosted Cupcakes

prep: 17 min.   cook: 20 min.

There's enough frosting with this recipe for generously frosting each cupcake.

1	cup shortening
2	cups sugar
4	large eggs
3	cups sifted cake flour
2½	teaspoons baking powder
½	teaspoon salt
1	cup milk
1	teaspoon almond extract
1	teaspoon vanilla extract

Brown Sugar Frosting

Beat shortening at medium speed with an electric mixer until fluffy; gradually add sugar, beating well. Add eggs, 1 at a time, beating well after each addition.
Combine flour, baking powder, and salt; add to shortening mixture alternately with milk, beginning and ending with flour mixture. Beat at low speed until blended after each addition. Stir in flavorings. Spoon batter into paper-lined muffin pans, filling two-thirds full.
Bake at 350° for 20 minutes. Remove and cool on wire racks. Spread with Brown Sugar Frosting. Yield: 29 cupcakes.

Per cupcake: Calories 284 (37% from fat); Fat 11.8g (sat 4.1g, mono 4.5g, poly 2.5g); Protein 2.1g; Carb 43.2g; Fiber 0.2g; Chol 40mg; Iron 1.2mg; Sodium 126mg; Calc 47mg

Brown Sugar Frosting

prep: 5 min.   cook: 5 min.

½	cup butter or margarine
1	cup firmly packed dark brown sugar
¼	cup dark corn syrup
3	cups sifted powdered sugar
3	tablespoons whipping cream
2	teaspoons vanilla extract

Melt butter in a saucepan over medium heat. Stir in brown sugar and corn syrup; bring to a boil. Boil 3 minutes or until a candy thermometer registers 234°. Remove from heat. Stir in powdered sugar, whipping cream, and vanilla. Beat at medium speed

with an electric mixer 2 minutes. Frost cupcakes immediately. Yield: 2 cups.

Per tablespoon: Calories 100 (30% from fat); Fat 3.3g (sat 2.1g, mono 0.9g, poly 0.1g); Protein 0g; Carb 18.1g; Fiber 0g; Chol 9mg; Iron 0.2mg; Sodium 27mg; Calc 8mg

Red Velvet Cupcakes

prep: 45 min.   cook: 30 min.

1	cup shortening
½	cup butter, softened
3	cups sugar
6	large eggs
2	teaspoons vanilla extract
1	(1-ounce) bottle red food coloring
3	cups all-purpose flour
2	tablespoons unsweetened cocoa
1	teaspoon salt
1	cup milk

Chunky Cherry Icing

Beat first 3 ingredients at medium speed with an electric mixer until fluffy. Add eggs, 1 at a time, beating just until yellow disappears. Stir in vanilla and food coloring until blended.
Combine flour, cocoa, and salt. Add to shortening mixture alternately with milk, beginning and ending with flour mixture, beating just until blended. Spoon batter into greased and floured muffin pans, or line with lightly greased cupcake liners, filling two-thirds full.
Bake at 325° for 30 minutes or until a wooden pick inserted in center comes out clean. Remove from pans, and cool completely on a wire rack. Spread evenly with Chunky Cherry Icing. Store in refrigerator. Yield: 3½ dozen.

Per cupcake: Calories 303 (42% from fat); Fat 14.3g (sat 7g, mono 3.4g, poly 2.2g); Protein 2.8g; Carb 41.7g; Fiber 0.8g; Chol 48mg; Iron 0.8mg; Sodium 117mg; Calc 21mg

Chunky Cherry Icing

prep: 15 min.

1	(8-ounce) package cream cheese, softened
½	cup butter, softened
6	cups powdered sugar
1	cup maraschino cherries, drained and chopped
1	cup chopped pecans, toasted
1	cup sweetened flaked coconut

Beat cream cheese and butter at medium speed with an electric mixer until smooth and creamy. Add powdered sugar, beating until blended. Stir in cherries, chopped pecans, and coconut. Yield: 6 cups.

Per tablespoon: Calories 61 (43% from fat); Fat 2.9g (sat 1.5g, mono 0.8g, poly 0.3g); Protein .03g; Carb 8.8g; Fiber 0.2g; Chol 5mg; Iron 0.1mg; Sodium 14mg; Calc 4mg

Chocolate-Marshmallow Frosting

prep: 15 min.   cook: 5 min.

This thick frosting transforms Chocolate Cupcakes (page 134), especially when topped with chopped candy bars. (pictured on facing page)

3	cups miniature marshmallows
¾	cup butter or margarine, cut into pieces
¾	cup evaporated milk
6	ounces unsweetened chocolate, chopped
6	cups powdered sugar
1	tablespoon vanilla extract

Melt first 4 ingredients in a 2-quart saucepan over medium-low heat, stirring 5 minutes or until mixture is smooth.
Transfer chocolate mixture to a large bowl. Place the bowl into a larger bowl filled with ice and water. Gradually add powdered sugar, beating at low speed with an electric mixer. Increase speed to medium-high, and beat 5 minutes or until frosting is cool, thick, and spreadable. Stir in 1 tablespoon vanilla. Yield: 4½ cups.

Per tablespoon: Calories 78 (38% from fat); Fat 3.3g (sat 2.1g, mono 0.9g, poly 0.1g); Protein 0.5g; Carb 12.6g; Fiber 0.4g; Chol 6mg; Iron 0.4mg; Sodium 19mg; Calc 10mg

cookies & candies

cookies

Cookies are classified by the way they're shaped. You'll find drop, bars and squares, refrigerated, rolled, and shaped cookie categories in this chapter. You'll also find hints to help you with creating, cutting, decorating, and serving cookies.

Equipment

Invest in several sturdy, shiny aluminum baking sheets if you plan to bake a lot of cookies. When you're shopping, pick up a baking sheet and notice how heavy it is. Weight is a good indication of quality. If it's very lightweight, it may warp in your oven.

Select baking sheets that are at least 2 inches narrower and shorter than your oven to allow heat to circulate evenly around them. Don't use pans with high sides for baking cookies because they deflect heat and cause cookies to bake unevenly. If you have baking sheets with nonstick coating, watch the cookies carefully as they bake—dark-surfaced pans of this type tend to overbrown cookies quickly.

A sturdy metal spatula, one or two large wire cooling racks, and an airtight container for storage are other cookie baking essentials.

Cookie scoops (shown at right) are handy for measuring dough. They scoop dough in a uniform size and ensure you of the correct yield.

Silicone baking mats (shown at right) are multipurpose, nonstick reusable liners that come in various sizes to fit most baking sheets. Baking mats are easy to clean (just wipe with soapy water or with a damp sponge), and they're also an excellent surface for kneading and rolling dough. They're safe for freezer and microwave. The only warning is to never use a knife on the mat to avoid marring the finish.

Baking Cookies

Always bake cookies in a preheated oven unless a recipe specifies otherwise. Grease the baking sheet only if directed. Many cookie recipes contain enough fat that greasing the baking sheet isn't necessary. If you do grease the sheet, don't worry about washing or regreasing between batches; just wipe away excess crumbs. Place dough on a cool baking sheet; if you spoon dough onto a hot baking sheet, the dough will spread too quickly and cookies will be flat.

Many bakers use parchment paper (shown at right) to line baking sheets before baking. It eliminates the need to grease and promotes easy removal upon baking. Find it on the grocery aisle near aluminum foil.

For best results, bake only one pan of cookies at a time, placing the pan in the center of the oven. If you have to bake two pans at a time, position oven racks so they divide the oven into thirds, and stagger pans on the racks. If cookies begin to brown unevenly, switch the pans halfway through baking time. Don't bake cookies with one pan directly over another pan. One batch will invariably have tops that are too dark, while the other will have the opposite problem.

Cookies are often difficult to test for doneness. Since personal preference varies as to soft or crisp cookies, we give a range in our baking times. If you prefer soft and chewy cookies, take them out of the oven at the lower end of the time. Leave cookies in one or two minutes longer to crisp them.

We often use the phrase "until lightly browned" to help in determining doneness, too. Unless the recipe states otherwise, remove cookies from baking sheets immediately after removal from the oven. With a spatula, transfer them to a wire rack to cool, being careful not to stack cookies or let the sides touch as they cool.

Storing and Freezing Cookies

Let cookies cool completely before storing. Store soft, chewy cookies in an airtight container to help keep them from drying out. Place crisp cookies in a jar with a loose-fitting lid. Store bar cookies directly in their baking pan, and seal the pan tightly with aluminum foil. You can also stack and store unfrosted bar cookies in airtight containers with wax paper placed between the layers.

You can freeze most cookie dough and baked cookies up to six months. Thaw baked cookies at room temperature an hour before serving. Thaw cookie dough in refrigerator or at room temperature until it's the right consistency for shaping into cookies as the recipe directs. You can even slice some refrigerator cookies straight from the freezer without thawing them. The baking time may be 1 to 2 minutes longer in this case.

Shown on previous page: from front left, Ginger-Oatmeal Sorghum Cookies (page 183), Nutty Oatmeal-Chocolate Chunk Cookies (page 170), Double Chocolate Chunk-Peanut Cookies (page 183)

drop cookies

The name literally gives you all the instruction you need—just drop dough from a spoon onto baking sheets with no further shaping necessary. Drop cookies have somewhat rounded tops and are slightly irregular in shape. For drop cookies in this chapter, we used teaspoons (not measuring spoons) for measuring. Simply pick up the desired amount of dough with one spoon, and use the back of another to push the dough onto the baking sheet (see photo below). Take care to scoop equal amounts of dough each time so cookies will be about the same size. Allow 1 to 2 inches between balls of dough on the baking sheet so they won't run together as they bake.

family favorite • for kids
Ultimate Chocolate Chip Cookies

prep: 30 min. cook: 14 min. per batch

Dark brown sugar adds surprising richness to this cookie dough. Bake each batch 8 minutes for soft and gooey cookies or up to 14 minutes for crisp results.

- ¾ cup butter, softened
- ¾ cup granulated sugar
- ¾ cup firmly packed dark brown sugar
- 2 large eggs
- 1½ teaspoons vanilla extract
- 2¼ cups plus 2 tablespoons all-purpose flour
- 1 teaspoon baking soda
- ¾ teaspoon salt
- 1 (12-ounce) package semisweet chocolate morsels

Beat butter and sugars at medium speed with an electric mixer until creamy. Add eggs and vanilla, beating until blended. **Combine** flour, soda, and salt in a small bowl; gradually add to butter mixture, beating well. Stir in morsels. Drop by table-spoonfuls onto ungreased baking sheets. **Bake** at 350° for 8 to 14 minutes or until desired degree of doneness. Remove to wire racks to cool completely. Yield: 5 dozen.

Per cookie: Calories 89 (43% from fat); Fat 4.3g (sat 2.5g, mono 1.2g, poly 0.2g); Protein 1g; Carb 12.6g; Fiber 0.5g; Chol 13mg; Iron 0.5mg; Sodium 70mg; Calc 7mg

Pecan-Chocolate Chip Cookies

Warm or cold, soft or crisp, chocolate chip cookies deliver in flavor, texture, and appearance.

Peanut Butter-Chocolate Chip Cookies: Decrease salt to ½ teaspoon. Add 1 cup creamy peanut butter with butter and sugars. Increase flour to 2½ cups plus 2 tablespoons. Proceed as directed. (Dough will look a little moist.)

Pecan-Chocolate Chip Cookies: Add 1½ cups chopped, toasted pecans with chocolate morsels. Proceed as directed.

Almond-Toffee Chocolate Chip Cookies: Reduce chocolate morsels to 1 cup. Add ½ cup slivered toasted almonds and 1 cup toffee bits. Proceed as directed.

Note: We tested with Hershey's Heath Bits O'Brickle Toffee Bits.

Dropping dough: Use one teaspoon (not a measuring spoon) to pick up the dough and another to push dough onto the baking sheet.

top 10 cookie secrets

Follow these suggestions for making every batch turn out to perfection.

1. Work with half the cookie dough at a time when rolling and cutting cookies. Too much handling of the dough makes cookies tough. Keep the other half refrigerated. Chilled dough is easier to handle.

2. Bake cookies on shiny, heavy aluminum baking sheets. These sheets with no sides are designed for easily sliding cookies onto a cooling rack. Dark sheets can absorb heat, causing cookies to brown too much on the bottom; nonstick baking sheets work well if not too dark. Insulated baking sheets require a slightly longer baking time.

3. Grease baking sheets with cooking spray or solid shortening instead of butter or margarine. Avoid using tub butter or margarine products labeled as spread, reduced calorie, liquid, or soft-style. These contain less fat than regular butter or margarine and don't give satisfactory results.

4. Use parchment paper or a baking mat to eliminate the need for greasing baking sheets. They also promote even browning.

5. Bake one sheet of cookies at a time on the middle oven rack; if you need to bake more than one at a time, rotate the sheets from the top rack to the bottom rack halfway through baking to encourage even browning.

6. Check cookies for doneness at the minimum baking time.

7. Cool baking sheets between batches before reusing; wipe the surface of each with a paper towel.

8. Place a sheet of wax paper on the counter and sprinkle it with sugar if you're short on cooling racks. Cookies will cool without getting soggy.

9. Cool cookies completely before storing them in airtight containers.

10. To make brownies and bar cookies, line a baking pan with heavy-duty aluminum foil; allow several inches to extend over the sides. Lightly grease foil. Spread batter evenly in the pan; bake and cool. Lift uncut brownies from pan, using edges of foil. Press down the foil sides; cut brownies into desired size and shape with a knife or dough scraper (available at kitchen-supply stores).

---

make ahead

Toffee-Oatmeal Cookies

prep: 15 min.   cook: 10 min. per batch

½   cup butter or margarine, softened
½   cup firmly packed light brown sugar
2   large eggs
1   teaspoon vanilla extract
1½   cups uncooked regular oats
1   cup all-purpose flour
½   teaspoon baking soda
¼   teaspoon salt
½   cup chopped pecans
1   (10-ounce) package toffee bits (we tested with Hershey's Heath Bits O' Brickle Toffee Bits)

Beat butter at medium speed with an electric mixer 2 to 3 minutes or until light and fluffy. Add sugar, beating well. Add eggs and vanilla, beating until blended.

Combine oats and next 3 ingredients; add to butter mixture, beating just until blended. Stir in chopped pecans and toffee bits.

Drop dough by heaping tablespoonfuls onto lightly greased baking sheets.

Bake at 375° for 10 minutes. Cool on wire racks. Yield: 4 dozen.

Per cookie: Calories 88 (53% from fat); Fat 5.2g (sat 2g, mono 1.7g, poly 0.6g); Protein 1.2g; Carb 9.7g; Fiber 0.4g; Chol 16mg; Iron 0.4mg; Sodium 74mg; Calc 6mg

---

family favorite

Chocolate Chubbies

prep: 20 min. cook: 15 min. per batch

Chubby here means a cookie loaded with nuts and chocolate chips.

6   (1-ounce) semisweet chocolate baking squares, chopped
2   (1-ounce) unsweetened chocolate baking squares, chopped
⅓   cup butter
3   large eggs
1   cup sugar
¼   cup all-purpose flour
½   teaspoon baking powder
⅛   teaspoon salt
1   (12-ounce) package semisweet chocolate morsels
2   cups coarsely chopped pecans
2   cups coarsely chopped walnuts

Combine first 3 ingredients in a heavy saucepan; cook, stirring often, over low heat until chocolate melts. Remove from heat; cool slightly.

Beat eggs and sugar at medium speed with an electric mixer until smooth; add chocolate mixture, beating well.

Combine flour, baking powder, and salt; add to chocolate mixture, stirring just until dry ingredients are moistened. Fold in chocolate morsels, pecans, and walnuts.

Drop batter by tablespoonfuls 2 inches apart onto lightly greased baking sheets.

Bake at 325° for 12 to 15 minutes. Cool cookies on baking sheets 1 minute. Remove to wire racks; cool. Yield: 3½ dozen.

Per cookie: Calories 181 (69% from fat); Fat 13.8g (sat 4.2g, mono 5.1g, poly 3.6g); Protein 3.2g; Carb 14.8g; Fiber 1.9g; Chol 19mg; Iron 1.1mg; Sodium 30mg; Calc 19mg

---

family favorite

Nutty Oatmeal-Chocolate Chunk Cookies

prep: 10 min.   cook: 10 min. per batch

Warm chocolate chunk cookies like this one, with chopped candy bars, won't last long. Even while baking, the aroma is just too tempting. (pictured on page 167)

2½   cups uncooked regular oats
1   cup butter or margarine, softened
1   cup granulated sugar
1   cup firmly packed light brown sugar
2   large eggs
1   tablespoon vanilla extract
2   cups all-purpose flour
1   teaspoon baking powder
1   teaspoon baking soda
½   teaspoon salt
3   or 4 (1.55-ounce) milk chocolate candy bars, chopped
1½   cups coarsely chopped pecans

Process oats in a blender or food processor until ground.

Beat butter and sugars at medium speed with an electric mixer until fluffy. Add eggs and vanilla; beat until blended.

Combine ground oats, flour, and next 3 ingredients. Add to butter mixture, beating until blended. Stir in chocolate candy bars and pecans.

Brownie Cookies

troubleshooting cookies

Use the following tips to help correct these common cookie baking problems.

Cookies Spread Too Much:
- Butter was too soft.
- Dough should've been chilled to firm it.
- Baking sheets were not allowed to cool between batches.
- Baking sheets were greased unnecessarily.

Cookies Crumble:
- Undermixing.
- Possibly a soft wheat flour was used. May need flour with a higher protein content (such as Pillsbury or Gold Medal) for better structure.
- Too much butter in the dough.

Cookies are Dry:
- Ingredients weren't accurately measured.
- Heavy handed when measuring flour, resulting in too much flour in dough.
- Oven temperature was too hot.
- Overbaked.

Drop dough by tablespoonfuls onto ungreased baking sheets.
Bake at 375° for 8 to 10 minutes or until golden; remove to wire racks to cool. Yield: 6 dozen.

Per cookie: Calories 97 (48% from fat); Fat 5.2g (sat 2.1g, mono 2g, poly 0.7g); Protein 1.3g; Carb 11.8g; Fiber 0.7g; Chol 13mg; Iron 0.5mg; Sodium 63mg; Calc 15mg

family favorite
Brownie Cookies

prep: 15 min.   cook: 10 min. per batch

½   cup butter
4   (1-ounce) unsweetened chocolate squares, chopped
3   cups semisweet chocolate morsels, divided
1½   cups all-purpose flour
½   teaspoon baking powder
½   teaspoon salt
4   large eggs
1½   cups sugar
2   teaspoons vanilla extract
2   cups chopped pecans, toasted

These scrumptious double-chocolate cookies are similar in texture to a fudgy brownie.

Combine butter, unsweetened chocolate, and 1½ cups chocolate morsels in a large heavy saucepan. Cook over low heat, stirring constantly, until butter and chocolate melt; cool.
Combine flour, baking powder, and salt in a small bowl; set aside.
Beat eggs, sugar, and vanilla at medium speed with an electric mixer. Gradually add dry ingredients to egg mixture, beating well. Add chocolate mixture; beat well. Stir in remaining 1½ cups chocolate morsels and pecans.
Drop dough by 2 tablespoonfuls 1 inch apart onto parchment paper-lined baking sheets.
Bake at 350° for 10 minutes. Cool slightly on baking sheets; remove to wire racks to cool completely. Yield: 2½ dozen.

Per cookie: Calories 254 (58% from fat); Fat 16.5g (sat 6.9g, mono 6.6g, poly 2.2g); Protein 3.5g; Carb 28g; Fiber 2.6g; Chol 36mg; Iron 1.8mg; Sodium 81mg; Calc 25mg

cookie ingredient tips

- Quality ingredients yield the best results. We recommend real butter and good quality vanilla extract in these recipes for premium flavor.
- Don't skimp with store-brand chocolate chips. Brand-name chocolate is best.
- Store nuts in the freezer for optimum freshness, and always taste them before adding to cookie dough.

Crispy Praline Cookies

prep: 10 min.   cook: 15 min. per batch

For this recipe, let the butter sit at room temperature for about an hour, or soften it in the microwave at HIGH for 10 to 20 seconds (do not melt).

1   cup all-purpose flour
1   cup firmly packed dark brown sugar
1   large egg
1   cup chopped pecans
½   cup butter, softened
1   teaspoon vanilla extract

Stir together all ingredients in a large bowl, blending well. Drop cookie dough by tablespoonfuls onto ungreased baking sheets.
Bake at 350° for 13 to 15 minutes. Cool on baking sheets 1 minute; remove cookies to wire racks to cool completely. Yield: 2 dozen.

Per cookie: Calories 125 (55% from fat); Fat 7.6g (sat 2.8g, mono 3.1g, poly 1.3g); Protein 1.3g; Carb 14g; Fiber 0.6g; Chol 19mg; Iron 0.6mg; Sodium 33mg; Calc 14mg

Almond Macaroons

prep: 5 min.   cook: 22 min. per batch

Slivered almonds and extract pack a double almond punch into these chewy nuggets.

2⅔ cups shredded coconut
⅔   cup sugar
¼   cup all-purpose flour
¼   teaspoon salt
4   egg whites
1   teaspoon almond extract
1   cup slivered almonds

Combine first 4 ingredients in a medium bowl; stir well. Add egg whites and almond extract; stir well. Stir in almonds.
Drop dough by teaspoonfuls onto greased baking sheets. Bake at 325° for 22 minutes or until golden. Remove immediately to wire racks to cool completely. Yield: 2 dozen.

Per cookie: Calories 108 (50% from fat); Fat 6g (sat 3.4g, mono 1.6g, poly 0.6g); Protein 2g; Carb 12.4g; Fiber 1g; Chol 0mg; Iron 0.5mg; Sodium 61mg; Calc 14mg

---

low cholesterol
English Rocks

prep: 20 min.   cook: 20 min. per batch

English Rocks are old-fashioned cookies loaded with Christmas colors and flavors.

¾   cup firmly packed light brown sugar
½   cup butter or margarine, softened
2   large eggs
1½ cups all-purpose flour
1   teaspoon ground cinnamon
½   teaspoon baking soda
¼   teaspoon salt
¼   teaspoon ground cloves
¼   teaspoon ground allspice
¼   cup brandy*
2   cups chopped pecans
½   pound candied cherries, halved
½   pound candied pineapple, chopped
1   cup pitted dates, chopped
1   cup raisins

Beat brown sugar and butter at medium speed with an electric mixer until smooth. Add eggs, beating until mixture is blended.
Combine flour and next 5 ingredients; gradually add to butter mixture, beating until blended. Add brandy, beating until blended.
Combine pecans and next 4 ingredients in a large bowl. Pour batter over pecan mixture, and stir until blended.
Drop dough by rounded teaspoonfuls, 2 inches apart, onto lightly greased baking sheets.
Bake at 325° for 20 minutes or until lightly browned. Cool on baking sheets 2 to 3 minutes. Remove to wire racks to cool completely. Yield: 4 dozen.

Per cookie: Calories 129 (40% from fat); Fat 5.8g (sat 1.6g, mono 2.6g, poly 1.2g); Protein 1.3g; Carb 19g; Fiber 1.1g; Chol 14mg; Iron 0.6mg; Sodium 51mg; Calc 13mg

*Substitute ¼ cup apple juice for brandy, if desired.

---

nuts i.d.

Recipes throughout this book call for nuts any number of ways, from pieces to coarsely chopped to ground. Refer to the visual guidelines below for help.

◄ pecan and walnut halves

◄chopped
This is a medium-fine chop of nuts.

◄pecan pieces
These are just large pieces of nuts. Pecans are often sold this way in the bag, so no chopping is needed.

◄finely chopped
This is a fine chop of nuts, but texture is still discernable.

◄coarsely chopped
This is a rough chop of nuts.

◄ground nuts or nutmeal
Use a mini chopper for best results. Don't overprocess nuts or too much oil will be released and you'll have nut butter.

bars & squares

Bar cookies have either a cakelike or a chewy fudgelike texture, depending on the proportion of fat to flour and the number of eggs used. A higher number of eggs yields a more cakelike texture.

If you own a 13- x 9-inch pan or a 9-inch pan, you'll use it repeatedly for bar cookies. The simplest of these recipes involves minimal mixing, spreading batter in the pan, and baking; then once cool, just cut into bars or squares. Be sure to bake in the pan size indicated; otherwise, the baking time and texture of the bars may vary.

entertaining • make ahead

Caramel-Coconut-Pecan Cheesecake Bars

prep: 15 min.   cook: 48 min.   other: 8 hrs.

2   cups graham cracker crumbs
½   cup butter, melted
4   (8-ounce) packages cream cheese, softened
¾   cup sugar
¼   cup all-purpose flour
3   large eggs
1   tablespoon vanilla extract
Quick Coconut-Pecan Frosting

Stir together graham cracker crumbs and butter; press into bottom of a lightly greased 13- x 9-inch pan.
Bake at 350° for 8 minutes. Remove from oven, and cool on a wire rack.
Beat cream cheese at medium speed with an electric mixer until smooth. Combine sugar and flour; gradually add to cream cheese, beating just until blended.
Add eggs, 1 at a time, beating until blended after each addition. Stir in vanilla. Pour mixture over prepared crust, spreading evenly to edges of pan.
Bake at 350° for 40 minutes or until set. Remove from oven, and cool on a wire rack.
Pour warm Quick Coconut-Pecan Frosting over cheesecake, spreading evenly to edges of pan. Cover and chill 8 hours. Cut into bars. Yield: 2 dozen.

Per bar: Calories 466 (61% from fat); Fat 31.8g (sat 17g, mono 10.1g, poly 2.9g); Protein 7.8g; Carb 39.5g; Fiber 1.1g; Chol 99mg; Iron 1.3mg; Sodium 272mg; Calc 141mg

Quick Coconut-Pecan Frosting

prep: 5 min.   cook: 10 min.

Fast and foolproof, this frosting is ready to remove from heat when it thickens to a puddinglike consistency.

2   (14-ounce) cans sweetened condensed milk
½   cup firmly packed light brown sugar
½   cup butter
1   teaspoon vanilla extract
1½   cups sweetened flaked coconut
1½   cups chopped pecans, toasted

Place first 4 ingredients in a heavy 3-quart saucepan; bring to a boil, stirring constantly, over medium-low heat. Cook, stirring constantly, 3 to 5 minutes or until mixture reaches a puddinglike thickness. Remove from heat. Stir in coconut and pecans.

Per tablespoon: Calories 87 (53% from fat); Fat 5.1g (sat 2.3g, mono 1.8g, poly 0.7g); Protein 1.3g; Carb 9.6g; Fiber 0.3g; Chol 8mg; Iron 0.2mg; Sodium 31mg; Calc 39mg

entertaining • make ahead

Pecan Pie Bars

prep: 12 min.   cook: 55 min.

Move over pieplate; the beauty of this recipe is that you can cut and stack these rich bars. They're great for gift giving.

2   cups all-purpose flour
½   cup granulated sugar
⅛   teaspoon salt
¾   cup butter or margarine, cut into pieces
1   cup firmly packed brown sugar
1   cup light corn syrup
½   cup butter or margarine
4   large eggs, lightly beaten
2½   cups finely chopped pecans
1   teaspoon vanilla extract

Combine flour, sugar, and salt in a large bowl; cut in ¾ cup butter thoroughly with a pastry blender until mixture resembles very fine crumbs. Press mixture evenly into a greased 13- x 9-inch pan, using a piece of plastic wrap to press crumb mixture firmly

in pan. Bake at 350° for 17 to 20 minutes or until lightly browned.
Combine brown sugar, corn syrup, and ½ cup butter in a saucepan; bring to a boil over medium heat, stirring gently. Remove from heat. Stir one-fourth of hot mixture into beaten eggs; add to remaining hot mixture. Stir in pecans and vanilla. Pour filling over crust.
Bake at 350° for 34 to 35 minutes or until set. Cool completely in pan on a wire rack. Cut into bars. Yield: 16 large bars.

Per bar: Calories 467 (56% from fat); Fat 29g (sat 10.6g, mono 11.8g, poly 4.8g); Protein 5g; Carb 50.6g; Fiber 2.2g; Chol 91mg; Iron 1.7mg; Sodium 167mg; Calc 39mg

family favorite

Blonde Brownies

prep: 11 min.   cook: 32 min.

Brown sugar is what defines these brownies as blonde. Top them with vanilla ice cream and caramel sauce for a bonus.

1   (16-ounce) package brown sugar
¾   cup butter or margarine
3   large eggs
2¾   cups all-purpose flour
2½   teaspoons baking powder
½   teaspoon salt
1   cup chopped pecans
2   teaspoons vanilla extract

Heat sugar and butter in a saucepan over medium heat until butter melts and mixture is smooth. Remove from heat. Cool slightly. Add eggs, 1 at a time, beating after each addition.
Combine flour, baking powder, and salt; add to sugar mixture, stirring well. Stir in pecans and vanilla. Pour into a greased and floured 13- x 9-inch pan. Bake at 350° for 25 to 28 minutes. Cool in pan on a wire rack. Cut into bars. Yield: 2 dozen.

Per bar: Calories 220 (41% from fat); Fat 10g (sat 4.1g, mono 3.5g, poly 1.4g); Protein 2.8g; Carb 30.5g; Fiber 0.9g; Chol 41mg; Iron 1.3mg; Sodium 156mg; Calc 55mg

Lemon Bars

Lemon Bars

prep: 12 min. cook: 43 min.

We cut these bars into large servings for big lemon flavor.

2   cups all-purpose flour
½   cup sifted powdered sugar
1   cup butter or margarine, softened
1   teaspoon vanilla extract
2   cups granulated sugar
2   tablespoons cornstarch
5   large eggs, lightly beaten
1   tablespoon grated lemon rind
¼   cup plus 2 tablespoons lemon juice
2   tablespoons butter or margarine, melted
¼   cup powdered sugar
Garnish: fresh raspberries

Combine first 4 ingredients; beat at medium speed with an electric mixer until blended. Pat mixture into a greased 13- x 9-inch baking dish. Bake at 350° for 18 minutes or until golden.
Combine 2 cups granulated sugar and cornstarch. Add eggs and next 3 ingredients; beat well. Pour mixture over crust.

Bake at 350° for 20 to 25 minutes or until set. Cool completely. Chill well.
Sift ¼ cup powdered sugar over top. Cut into bars. Garnish, if desired. Yield: 1 dozen.

Per bar: Calories 425 (42% from fat); Fat 20g (sat 11.6g, mono 5.6g, poly 1.2g); Protein 5g; Carb 57.6g; Fiber 0.7g; Chol 133mg; Iron 1.4mg; Sodium 151mg; Calc 21mg

Cranberry-Nut Triangles

prep: 15 min. cook: 45 min.

½   cup butter or margarine, softened
½   cup powdered sugar
1   large egg yolk
1½ cups all-purpose flour
1¼ cups chopped pecans
¾   cup dried cranberries
1   cup firmly packed light brown sugar
5   tablespoons butter
3   tablespoons whipping cream
3   tablespoons light corn syrup
2   tablespoons maple syrup

Beat ½ cup softened butter and powdered sugar at medium speed with an electric mixer until creamy. Add egg yolk, beating just until blended. Add flour, and beat at low speed just until mixture is crumbly.
Press flour mixture on bottom and slightly up sides of a lightly greased 13- x 9-inch baking dish.
Bake at 350° for 20 to 25 minutes or until edges and surface are lightly browned. Remove from oven; sprinkle crust evenly with chopped pecans and cranberries, and let cool.
Bring brown sugar and next 4 ingredients to a boil, stirring constantly, in a saucepan over medium-high heat. Pour brown sugar mixture evenly over chopped pecans and cranberries in baking dish.
Bake at 350° for 15 minutes or until golden. Remove from oven, and let cool completely. Cut into 15 squares; cut squares in half diagonally to form triangles. Yield: 2½ dozen.

Per triangle: Calories 162 (52% from fat); Fat 9.3g (sat 3.8g, mono 3.5g, poly 1.3g); Protein 1.2g; Carb 19.7g; Fiber 0.8g; Chol 22mg; Iron 0.6mg; Sodium 41mg; Calc 15mg

Fudgy Candy Bar Brownies

prep: 20 min. cook: 30 min.

These rich gooey brownies are the ultimate candy lover's indulgence. After baking and cooling, try freezing for 10 minutes for easy slicing.

1⅓ cups all-purpose flour
1¼ cups sugar
½   cup unsweetened cocoa
1   teaspoon baking powder
½   teaspoon salt
4   large eggs
¾   cup butter or margarine, melted
1   cup semisweet chocolate morsels
½   cup milk chocolate morsels
½   cup white chocolate morsels
3   (2.07-ounce) chocolate-coated caramel-peanut nougat bars, coarsely chopped (we tested with Snickers)

Stir together first 5 ingredients in a large bowl. Add eggs and butter, stirring well. Stir in morsels. Spoon batter into a lightly greased 13- x 9-inch pan. Sprinkle evenly with candy pieces; gently press candy into batter.
Bake at 350° for 30 minutes or until a wooden pick inserted in center comes out clean. Cool completely before cutting into bars. Yield: 16 servings.

Per brownie: Calories 373 (48% from fat); Fat 20.1g (sat 11g, mono 6.6g, poly 1.3g); Protein 5.6g; Carb 46.1g; Fiber 2.3g; Chol 80mg; Iron 1.7mg; Sodium 220mg; Calc 76mg

Layered Brownies

prep: 25 min. cook: 23 min. other: 3 hrs.

The Vanilla Cream Topping and Brownie Glaze add layers of texture and richness to this recipe.

4   (1-ounce) unsweetened chocolate baking squares
1   cup butter or margarine
2   cups sugar
4   large eggs, lightly beaten
1   cup all-purpose flour
1   cup chopped pecans, toasted
Vanilla Cream Topping
Brownie Glaze

Microwave chocolate and butter in a 2-quart glass bowl at HIGH 1½ minutes or until melted, stirring twice. Add sugar and eggs, stirring until blended. Stir in flour and chopped pecans. Pour into a lightly greased, aluminum foil-lined 13- x 9-inch pan. **Bake** at 350° for 20 to 23 minutes. Cool on a wire rack 1 hour.

Spread cooled brownies with Vanilla Cream Topping; chill 45 minutes. Pour Brownie Glaze over Vanilla Cream Topping, and spread evenly. Chill 1 hour. Let stand at room temperature 15 minutes; cut into 1-inch squares. Yield: 4 dozen.

Per brownie: Calories 202 (57% from fat); Fat 12.9g (sat 7g, mono 4g, poly 1g); Protein 1.6g; Carb 22.4g; Fiber 0.8g; Chol 41mg; Iron 0.8mg; Sodium 68mg; Calc 12mg

Vanilla Cream Topping

prep: 5 min.

1 cup butter, melted
1 (16-ounce) package powdered sugar
¼ cup half-and-half
2 teaspoons vanilla extract

Stir together all ingredients in a bowl until smooth. Yield: 1½ cups.

Per tablespoon: Calories 145 (49% from fat); Fat 7.9g (sat 5g, mono 2.1g, poly 0.3g); Protein 0.2g; Carb 19g; Fiber 0g; Chol 21mg; Iron 0mg; Sodium 55mg; Calc 5mg

Brownie Glaze

prep: 5 min.

4 (1-ounce) semisweet chocolate baking squares
¼ cup butter

Microwave chocolate squares and butter in a 1-quart glass bowl at HIGH 1½ minutes or until melted, stirring twice. Yield: ½ cup.

Per tablespoon: Calories 118 (76% from fat); Fat 9.9g (sat 6.1g, mono 2.9g, poly 0.4g); Protein 0.7g; Carb 9g; Fiber 0.8g; Chol 15mg; Iron 0.5mg; Sodium 42mg; Calc 6mg

test kitchen favorite

Cream Cheese Brownies

prep: 15 min.   cook: 45 min.

4 (1-ounce) unsweetened chocolate baking squares
4 (1-ounce) semisweet chocolate baking squares
⅓ cup butter or margarine
2 (3-ounce) packages cream cheese, softened
¼ cup butter or margarine, softened
2 cups sugar, divided
6 large eggs, divided
1 teaspoon vanilla extract
2 tablespoons all-purpose flour
1½ cups semisweet chocolate morsels, divided
2 teaspoons vanilla extract
1 cup all-purpose flour
1 teaspoon baking powder
1 teaspoon salt

Microwave first 3 ingredients in a 1-quart glass bowl at HIGH 2 minutes or until melted, stirring once. Cool and set aside.

Beat cream cheese and ¼ cup butter at medium speed with an electric mixer until creamy; gradually add ½ cup sugar, beating well. Add 2 eggs, 1 at a time, beating until blended. Stir in 1 teaspoon vanilla. Fold in 2 tablespoons flour and ½ cup chocolate morsels; set aside.

Beat remaining 4 eggs in a large bowl at medium speed. Gradually add remaining 1½ cups sugar, beating well. Add melted chocolate mixture and 2 teaspoons vanilla; beat mixture until well blended.

Combine 1 cup flour, baking powder, and salt; fold into chocolate batter until blended, and stir in remaining 1 cup chocolate morsels.

Reserve 3 cups chocolate batter; spread remaining batter evenly in a greased 13- x 9-inch pan. Pour cream cheese mixture over batter. Top with reserved 3 cups chocolate batter; swirl mixture with a knife. **Bake** at 325° for 40 to 45 minutes. Cool and cut brownies into squares. Yield: 1½ dozen.

Per brownie: Calories 267 (52% from fat); Fat 15.3g (sat 9g, mono 4.6g, poly 0.7g); Protein 4g; Carb 32.7g; Fiber 1.9g; Chol 72mg; Iron 1.9mg; Sodium 190mg; Calc 36mg

Cream Cheese Brownies

▲ Drop spoonfuls of chocolate batter over cream cheese batter.

▲ Swirl batters together with a knife.

Double Chocolate Brownies With Caramel Frosting

prep: 15 min.   cook: 40 min.

Freeze these awesome bars up to a month.

2   (1-ounce) unsweetened chocolate baking squares
2   (1-ounce) semisweet chocolate baking squares
1   cup butter, softened
2   cups sugar
4   large eggs
1   cup all-purpose flour
½   teaspoon salt
1   teaspoon vanilla extract
¾   cup chopped, toasted pecans, divided
¾   cup semisweet chocolate morsels, divided
Caramel Frosting

Microwave chocolate squares in a small microwave-safe bowl at MEDIUM (50% power) 1½ minutes or until melted. Stir chocolate until smooth.

Beat butter and sugar at medium speed with an electric mixer until light and fluffy. Add eggs, 1 at a time, beating just until blended after each addition. Add melted chocolate, beating just until blended.

Add flour and salt, beating at low speed just until blended. Stir in vanilla, ½ cup pecans, and ½ cup chocolate morsels. Spread batter into a greased and floured 13- x 9-inch pan. Sprinkle with remaining ¼ cup pecans and ¼ cup chocolate morsels.

Bake at 350° for 40 minutes or until set. Cool completely on a wire rack. Spread evenly with Caramel Frosting. Yield: 32 brownies.

Per brownie: Calories 280 (50% from fat); Fat 15.6g (sat 8.4g, mono 5g, poly 1.3g); Protein 2.2g; Carb 35.7g; Fiber 1g; Chol 53mg; Iron 0.9mg; Sodium 144mg; Calc 17mg

Caramel Frosting

prep: 10 min.   cook: 30 min.

¾   cup butter
2   cups sugar
½   cup buttermilk
12   large marshmallows
1   tablespoon light corn syrup
½   teaspoon baking soda

Melt butter in a large saucepan over low heat. Stir in sugar and remaining ingredients. Cook over medium heat, stirring occasionally, 25 to 30 minutes or until a candy thermometer registers 234° (soft ball stage).

Remove from heat. Beat at high speed 5 to 7 minutes or until frosting thickens and begins to lose its gloss. Yield: 2 cups.

Per tablespoon: Calories 99 (40% from fat); Fat 4.4g (sat 2.8g, mono 1.1g, poly 0.2g); Protein 0.2g; Carb 15.4g; Fiber 0g; Chol 12mg; Iron 0mg; Sodium 57mg; Calc 5mg

Double Chocolate Brownies With Caramel Frosting

Chocolate-Peanut Squares

prep: 13 min.   other: 1 hr., 10 min.

¾   cup butter or margarine, softened
1   cup crunchy peanut butter
1   (16-ounce) package powdered sugar
1½   cups vanilla wafers, crushed (about 45 cookies)
1   (12-ounce) package semisweet chocolate morsels
2   teaspoons shortening

Beat butter and peanut butter at medium speed with an electric mixer until blended. Add powdered sugar and vanilla wafer crumbs; beat until blended. Press mixture evenly into a lightly greased 13- x 9-inch pan lined with wax paper.

Combine chocolate morsels and shortening in a glass measuring cup. Microwave at HIGH 1 to 2 minutes or until morsels melt, stirring after 1 minute. Stir until smooth. Spread evenly on top of peanut butter mixture. Chill 1 hour or until firm.

Remove pan from refrigerator, and let stand at room temperature 10 minutes or until slightly softened. Cut into 48 squares. Yield: 4 dozen.

Per square: Calories 147 (53% from fat); Fat 8.6g (sat 3.7g, mono 3.1g, poly 1.1g); Protein 1.7g; Carb 17.9g; Fiber 1g; Chol 8mg; Iron 0.5mg; Sodium 59mg; Calc 8mg

Classic Shortbread

prep: 10 min.   cook: 45 min.

Five ingredients are all it takes for cookie perfection.

1 cup butter, softened
½ cup sugar
⅛ teaspoon vanilla extract
2¼ cups all-purpose flour
⅛ teaspoon salt
Sugar

Beat butter at medium speed with an electric mixer until creamy; gradually add ½ cup sugar, beating well. Stir in vanilla. **Combine** flour and salt; gradually add to butter mixture, beating at low speed after each addition.
Roll dough to ½-inch thickness on a lightly floured surface. Cut with a 3-inch heart-shaped cookie cutter, and place 2 inches apart on ungreased baking sheets. Sprinkle with additional sugar.
Bake at 275° for 45 minutes or until edges begin to brown. Remove to wire racks to cool completely. Yield: 1 dozen.

Per cookie: Calories 258 (54% from fat); Fat 15.4g (sat 9.6g, mono 3.9g, poly 0.7g); Protein 2.7g; Carb 27.8g; Fiber 0.7g; Chol 40mg; Iron 1.1mg; Sodium 132mg; Calc 8mg

Mocha-Chocolate Shortbread

prep: 9 min.   cook: 24 min.   other: 30 min.

1¼ cups all-purpose flour
½ cup powdered sugar
2 teaspoons instant coffee granules
⅔ cup butter or margarine, softened
½ teaspoon vanilla extract
1½ cups semisweet chocolate morsels, divided
Coffee ice cream (optional)

Combine first 3 ingredients in a medium bowl; add butter and vanilla, and beat at low speed with an electric mixer until blended. Stir in ½ cup chocolate morsels.
Press dough into an ungreased 9-inch square pan; prick dough with a fork.
Bake at 325° for 22 to 24 minutes or until lightly browned.
Sprinkle remaining 1 cup morsels over top, and spread to cover. Cut shortbread into 25 (about 1¾-inch) squares. Let cool 30 minutes in pan before removing. Serve with coffee ice cream, if desired. Yield: 25 squares.

Per cookie: Calories 124 (57% from fat); Fat 7.9g (sat 4.9g, mono 2.3g, poly 0.3g); Protein 1.1g; Carb 13.6g; Fiber 0.8g; Chol 13mg; Iron 0.6mg; Sodium 36mg; Calc 6mg

Rosemary Shortbread

prep: 8 min.   cook: 30 min.   other: 1 hr.

Fresh rosemary updates basic but timeless shortbread.

1 cup butter, softened
¾ cup sifted powdered sugar
¼ cup cornstarch
1¾ cups all-purpose flour
1 tablespoon chopped fresh rosemary

Beat butter at medium speed with an electric mixer until creamy; gradually add powdered sugar and cornstarch, beating well. Stir in flour and rosemary. (Dough will be stiff.)
Divide dough in half. Shape 1 portion of dough into a 6½-inch circle on an ungreased baking sheet. Crimp edges with a fork. Cut dough into 8 wedges (do not separate). Repeat procedure with remaining dough. Cover and chill 1 hour.
Bake at 300° for 30 minutes or until done. Cool on baking sheet 5 minutes. Remove shortbread wedges to a wire rack, and cool completely. Yield: 16 wedges.

Per wedge: Calories 176 (59% from fat); Fat 11.5g (sat 7.2g, mono 3g, poly 0.5g); Protein 1.5g; Carb 17g; Fiber 0.4g; Chol 30mg; Iron 0.7mg; Sodium 81mg; Calc 6mg

refrigerator cookies

You may know them as icebox cookies or slice 'n' bake, but the most notable thing about refrigerator cookies is their make-ahead quality.

You can roll the dough into a log, chill it up to a week, and when it's baking time, just slice the dough directly from the refrigerator, and bake only the number of cookies you want. They bake crisp and thin, make great dunkers for coffee, and are easy to stack and give as gifts.

If you don't bake all the cookies at once, you can easily return the remaining dough to the refrigerator or freezer to use at another time.

freeze it • low cholesterol

Lemon Icebox Cookies

prep: 20 min.   cook: 14 min. per batch
other: 8 hrs.

1 cup butter, softened
1 cup granulated sugar
1 cup firmly packed light brown sugar
2 large eggs
1 teaspoon grated lemon rind
2 tablespoons fresh lemon juice
3½ cups all-purpose flour
1 teaspoon baking soda
½ teaspoon salt

Beat butter and sugars at medium speed with an electric mixer until fluffy. Add eggs, 1 at a time, beating well after each addition. Add lemon rind and juice, beating until blended.

Combine flour, baking soda, and salt; gradually add to butter mixture, beating just until blended. Divide dough into 3 equal portions; roll each portion on wax paper into a 12-inch log. Cover and chill 8 hours.
Cut each log into ½-inch slices (about 28 slices); place on lightly greased baking sheets.
Bake at 350° for 12 to 14 minutes or until edges are lightly browned. Remove to wire racks to cool. Store cookies in an airtight container, or freeze, if desired. Yield: 7 dozen.

Per cookie: Calories 60 (36% from fat); Fat 2.4g (sat 1.4g, mono 0.6g, poly 0.1g); Protein 0.7g; Carb 9g; Fiber 0.1g; Chol 11mg; Iron 0.3mg; Sodium 47mg; Calc 4mg

Lemon–Poppy Seed Cookies: Add 2 teaspoons poppy seeds; proceed as directed.

Lemon–Pecan Cookies: Add 1 cup finely chopped pecans, toasted; proceed as directed.

Cinnamon Chip Icebox Cookies

prep: 12 min.   cook: 15 min. per batch
other: 8 hrs.

These cookies are a delicious departure from chocolate chip cookies.

1   cup butter or margarine, softened
2   cups sugar
2   large eggs
2   teaspoons vanilla extract
4   cups all-purpose flour
1   (10-ounce) package cinnamon-flavored morsels
1   cup chopped pecans, toasted

Beat butter at medium speed with an electric mixer until creamy. Gradually add sugar, beating well. Add eggs and vanilla, beating until blended. Gradually add flour, beating at low speed just until blended. Stir in cinnamon morsels and pecans.
Divide dough into 3 (2-cup) portions; roll each portion into a 12-inch log. Wrap logs in wax paper. Chill 8 hours, or freeze in an airtight container up to 3 months.
Cut each log into 24 (½-inch-thick) slices, and place slices on ungreased baking sheets.
Bake at 350° for 13 to 15 minutes or until edges are lightly browned. Cool on baking sheets 5 minutes. Remove cookies to wire racks to cool completely. Yield: 6 dozen.

Per cookie: Calories 104 (43% from fat); Fat 5g (sat 2.3g, mono 2.8g, poly 0.5g); Protein 1.3g; Carb 13.5g; Fiber 0.4g; Chol 13mg; Iron 0.4mg; Sodium 29mg; Calc 14mg

Note: Cookie dough can be dropped by rounded tablespoonfuls, 2 inches apart, onto ungreased baking sheets, and then baked.

Candy Wrap Cookies

prep: 15 min.   cook: 14 min. per batch

These are quick, easy, and fun cookies to make with kids.

1   (18-ounce) package refrigerated sugar cookie dough
24   bite-size chocolate-coated caramel-and-creamy nougat bars (we tested with Milky Way Miniatures)
Unsweetened cocoa

Cut dough into ¼-inch slices. Wrap each slice around 1 candy bar, and place on ungreased baking sheets. Bake at 350° for 14 minutes. Cool 1 minute; remove to a wire rack to cool completely. Dust with cocoa. Yield: 2 dozen.

Per cookie: Calories 129 (40% from fat); Fat 5.8g (sat 1.8g, mono 3g, poly 0.6g); Protein 1.3g; Carb 18.7g; Fiber 0.4g; Chol 7mg; Iron 0.5mg; Sodium 110mg; Calc 28mg

rolled cookies

Rolled cookies are prepared from dough that has been rolled to a designated thickness and cut with cookie cutters. Cut and baked plain, sprinkled with decorator candies before baking, or spread with frosting after baking, rolled cookies are particularly popular around the holidays. And they provide a good opportunity to show off your collection of cookie cutters, too.

To be rolled and shaped properly, dough needs to be firmer than dough for most cookies. Many recipes call for chilling dough to firm it before rolling. Large amounts of dough can be divided so you can work with one portion while the rest remains chilled. If your dough still seems too soft to roll after chilling, roll it directly onto baking sheet, cut with cutters, and peel away the scraps. This eliminates transferring cut dough to baking sheets, a task that can be tricky when dough is soft.

Swedish Holiday Cookies

prep: 20 min.   cook: 8 min. per batch
other: 8 hrs., 6 min.

1   cup butter or margarine, softened
¾   cup sugar
1½   tablespoons dark molasses
2   teaspoons ground cinnamon
½   teaspoon ground cardamom
1   tablespoon water
1   teaspoon baking powder
2½   cups all-purpose flour
2   egg whites, lightly beaten
Sugar

Beat butter at medium speed with an electric mixer until creamy. Add ¾ cup sugar, beating until smooth. Add molasses, cinnamon, and cardamom, beating until blended.
Combine 1 tablespoon water and baking powder, stirring until baking powder is dissolved; add to butter mixture. Gradually add flour to butter mixture, beating until blended. Cover and chill 8 hours.

Turn dough out onto a lightly floured surface; roll to ¼-inch thickness. Cut with a 2-inch round or other desired shape cutter. Place 2 inches apart on lightly greased baking sheets. Brush evenly with egg white, and sprinkle with additional sugar.
Bake at 375° for 8 minutes or until lightly browned. Cool on baking sheets 5 to 6 minutes. Remove to wire racks to cool completely. Yield: about 5 dozen.

Per cookie: Calories 62 (46% from fat); Fat 3.2g (sat 1.9g, mono 0.8g, poly 0.1g); Protein 0.7g; Carb 7.9g; Fiber 0.2g; Chol 8mg; Iron 0.4mg; Sodium 32mg; Calc 10mg

cutting out cookies

• For the cleanest cutouts, when you make an impression with a cookie cutter, cut straight down into dough—don't twist. Best results come when you're working with a firm or chilled dough that's just been rolled.
• When you begin to cut out cookies, start at the top edge of dough, and make cutouts as close together as possible to get the most yield with the first rolling of the dough.

Tea Cakes

prep: 20 min.   cook: 12 min. per batch
other: 1 hr., 5 min.

1   cup butter, softened
2   cups sugar
3   large eggs
1   teaspoon vanilla extract
3½   cups all-purpose flour
1   teaspoon baking soda
½   teaspoon salt

Beat butter at medium speed with an electric mixer until creamy; gradually add sugar, beating well. Add eggs, 1 at a time, beating until blended after each addition. Add vanilla, beating until blended.
Combine flour, soda, and salt; gradually add flour mixture to butter mixture, beating at low speed until blended after each addition.
Divide dough in half; wrap each portion in plastic wrap, and chill 1 hour.
Roll half of dough to ¼-inch thickness on a floured surface. Cut out cookies with a 2½-inch round cutter, and place 1 inch apart on parchment paper–lined baking sheets.
Bake at 350° for 10 to 12 minutes or until edges begin to brown; cool on baking sheets 5 minutes. Remove to wire racks to cool completely. Repeat procedure with remaining dough. Yield: 3 dozen.

Per tea cake: Calories 140 (36% from fat); Fat 5.6g (sat 3.3g, mono 1.5g, poly 0.3g); Protein 1.9g; Carb 20.8g; Fiber 0.3g; Chol 31mg; Iron 0.7mg; Sodium 109mg; Calc 6mg

Cranberry-Pecan Rugelach

Cranberry-Pecan Rugelach

prep: 45 min.   cook: 20 min.
other: 8 hrs., 30 min.

1   cup butter, softened
1   (8-ounce) package cream cheese, softened
½   cup sugar
2¾   cups all-purpose flour
½   teaspoon salt
Cranberry-Pecan Filling
1   large egg, lightly beaten
2   teaspoons water
½   cup sugar or sparkling sugar

Beat butter and cream cheese at medium speed with an electric mixer until creamy; gradually add ½ cup sugar, beating until fluffy. Stir in flour and salt until blended. Divide dough into 4 equal portions; flatten each portion into a disk, and wrap each disk separately in plastic wrap. Chill 8 hours.
Roll 1 portion of dough at a time into an 8-inch circle on a lightly floured surface (keep remaining dough chilled until ready to use). Spread with 3 heaping tablespoons Cranberry-Pecan Filling, leaving a ½-inch border around edge. Using a sharp knife, cut circle into 8 wedges; roll up each wedge, starting at wide end, to form a crescent shape. Place crescents, point side down, on a baking sheet lined with parchment paper. Chill cookies on baking sheets 30 minutes.
Combine egg and water in a small bowl; brush cookies gently with egg wash, and sprinkle with ½ cup sugar.
Bake at 350° for 18 to 20 minutes or until golden. Remove to wire racks to cool completely. Yield: 32 cookies.

Per cookie: Calories 176 (54% from fat); Fat 10.5g (sat 6g, mono 3.1g, poly 0.7g); Protein 2.1g; Carb 19.1g; Fiber 0.6g; Chol 32mg; Iron 0.7mg; Sodium 108mg; Calc 13mg

Cranberry-Pecan Filling

prep: 10 min.

⅔   cup sugar
½   cup finely chopped pecans, toasted
½   cup finely chopped sweetened dried cranberries*
¼   cup butter, melted
1½   teaspoons ground cinnamon
¾   teaspoon ground allspice

Stir together all ingredients until blended. Yield: about 1 cup.

Per tablespoon: Calories 96 (53% from fat); Fat 5.6g (sat 2g, mono 2.3g, poly 0.9g); Protein 0.4g; Carb 12.2g; Fiber 0.7g; Chol 8mg; Iron 0.2mg; Sodium 20mg; Calc 7mg

*Substitute ⅔ cup finely chopped dried cherries or apricots, if desired.

Linzer Cookies

prep: 25 min.   cook: 15 min. per batch
other: 1 hr.

A dough scraper, which can be purchased inexpensively at kitchen stores, makes transferring these star cutouts onto baking sheets a breeze.

1¼ cups butter, softened
1   cup powdered sugar, sifted
2½ cups all-purpose flour
½   cup finely chopped pecans, toasted
¼   teaspoon salt
¼   teaspoon ground cloves
¼   teaspoon ground cinnamon
1   teaspoon grated lemon rind
¼   cup seedless raspberry jam
Powdered sugar

Beat butter at medium speed with an electric mixer; gradually add 1 cup powdered sugar, beating until light and fluffy.
Combine flour and next 5 ingredients; gradually add to butter mixture, beating just until blended.
Divide dough into 2 equal portions. Cover and chill 1 hour.
Roll each portion to ⅛-inch thickness on a lightly floured surface; cut with a 3-inch star-shaped cutter. Cut centers out of half of cookies with a 1½-inch star-shaped cutter. Place all stars on lightly greased baking sheets.
Bake at 325° for 15 minutes; cool on wire racks. Spread solid cookies with jam; sprinkle remaining stars with powdered sugar. Top each solid jam-covered cookie with a hollow star. Yield: 3 dozen.

Per cookie: Calories 92 (57% from fat); Fat 5.8g (sat 3.1g, mono 1.7g, poly 0.5g); Protein 0.9g; Carb 9.6g; Fiber 0.3g; Chol 13mg; Iron 0.4mg; Sodium 46mg; Calc 4mg

Date Pinwheel Cookies

prep: 20 min.   cook: 14 min. per batch
other: 2 hrs., 3 min.

Slather this dough with date-nut filling, roll it jelly-roll fashion, and then slice and bake it into pretty swirled cookies.

1   (10-ounce) package chopped dates
¾   cup granulated sugar, divided
½   cup water
¼   teaspoon salt, divided
1   cup chopped walnuts
½   cup butter or margarine, softened
½   cup firmly packed light brown sugar
1   large egg
½   teaspoon vanilla extract
2   cups all-purpose flour
¼   teaspoon baking soda

Stir together dates, ¼ cup granulated sugar, ½ cup water, and ⅛ teaspoon salt in a saucepan; bring mixture to a boil over medium-high heat. Reduce heat; simmer 3 to 5 minutes. Remove from heat; stir in walnuts, and set aside.
Beat remaining ½ cup granulated sugar, softened butter, and brown sugar at medium speed with an electric mixer until light and fluffy.
Add egg and vanilla, beating until blended. Gradually add remaining ⅛ teaspoon salt, flour, and baking soda, beating until blended. Cover and chill 1 hour.
Turn dough out onto floured wax paper, and roll into an 18- x 12-inch rectangle. Spread date mixture evenly over dough, leaving a ½-inch border.
Roll up dough, jelly-roll fashion, beginning at 1 long side. Wrap in wax paper, and chill 1 hour.
Cut roll into ¼-inch-thick slices; place on lightly greased baking sheets.
Bake in batches at 375° for 12 to 14 minutes or until lightly browned. Cool cookies 2 to 3 minutes on baking sheets, and remove to wire racks to cool completely. Yield: 2½ dozen.

Per cookie: Calories 149 (35% from fat); Fat 5.8g (sat 2.1g, mono 1.5g, poly 1.6g); Protein 2.4g; Carb 23.1g; Fiber 1.2g; Chol 15mg; Iron 0.7mg; Sodium 55mg; Calc 14mg

for kids • freeze it • low cholesterol
Gingerbread Boys

prep: 30 min.   cook: 8 min. per batch
other: 8 hrs.

You can freeze these cookies for several months in airtight containers.

1   cup butter, softened
1   cup sugar
½   teaspoon salt
1   cup molasses
2   tablespoons white vinegar
1   large egg
5   cups all-purpose flour
1½ teaspoons baking soda
1   tablespoon ground ginger
1   teaspoon ground cinnamon
1   teaspoon ground cloves
Royal Icing

Beat butter at medium speed with an electric mixer until creamy; gradually add sugar and salt, beating well. Add molasses, vinegar, and egg, beating at low speed just until blended.
Combine flour and next 4 ingredients; add to butter mixture, beating at low speed until blended. Cover and chill 8 hours.
Divide dough into fourths. Roll each portion to ⅛-inch thickness on a floured surface. Cut with a 3-inch gingerbread-boy cookie cutter. Place on lightly greased or parchment paper–lined baking sheets.
Bake at 375° for 8 minutes. Cool on pans 1 minute; place on wire racks to cool. Decorate with Royal Icing. Yield: 6 dozen.

Per cookie: Calories 81 (31% from fat); Fat 2.8g (sat 1.6g, mono 0.7g, poly 0.3g); Protein 1.1g; Carb 13.2g; Fiber 0.3g; Chol 10mg; Iron 0.7mg; Sodium 63mg; Calc 13mg

Royal Icing

prep: 5 min.

1   (16-ounce) package powdered sugar
3   tablespoons meringue powder
6   tablespoons hot water
Liquid food coloring (optional)

Stir together first 3 ingredients until smooth. Stir in food coloring, if desired. Pour into a decorating bag or a large zip-top freezer bag. Snip a tiny hole in 1 corner of bag, and decorate as desired. Yield: about 3 cups.

Per tablespoon: Calories 39 (0% from fat); Fat 0g (sat 0g, mono 0g, poly 0g); Protein 0.2g; Carb 9.7g; Fiber 0g; Chol 0mg; Iron 0mg; Sodium 2mg; Calc 4mg

shaped cookies

For these cookies, roll dough into balls with palms of your hands. Dough for this type of cookie needs to be firm so you can form it in your hands without making a mess. If dough seems too soft to shape, chill it for an hour or so until it's firm enough to shape.

When shaping the cookies, take care to roll all the balls the same size so cookies will be uniform after baking. Many of these cookies may spread as they bake, so allow 1 to 2 inches between them so they won't run together. And grease the baking sheet only if the recipe specifies.

Many of the recipes in this section evolve from balls into other shapes or are coated or frosted.

family favorite • for kids

Old-Fashioned Peanut Butter Cookies

prep: 25 min.   cook: 8 min. per batch
other: 3 hrs.

1   cup butter or margarine, softened
1   cup creamy peanut butter
1   cup granulated sugar
1   cup firmly packed light brown sugar
2   large eggs
2½   cups all-purpose flour
2   teaspoons baking soda
¼   teaspoon salt
1   teaspoon vanilla extract
     Granulated sugar

Beat butter and peanut butter at medium speed with an electric mixer until creamy; gradually add sugars, beating well. Add eggs, beating well.
Combine flour, soda, and salt in a medium bowl; add to butter mixture, beating well. Stir in vanilla. Cover and chill 3 hours.
Shape into 1¼-inch balls; place 3 inches apart on ungreased baking sheets. Dip a fork in additional granulated sugar; flatten cookies in a crisscross design. Bake at 375° for 7 to 8 minutes. Remove to wire racks to cool. Yield: 6 dozen.

Per cookie: Calories 85 (48% from fat); Fat 4.5g (sat 2g, mono 1.6g, poly 0.6g); Protein 1.5g; Carb 10.1g; Fiber 0.3g; Chol 13mg; Iron 0.4mg; Sodium 81mg; Calc 6mg

family favorite • for kids • quick

Peanut Butter–Kiss Cookies

prep: 10 min.   cook: 11 min. per batch

This simple cookie celebrates the union of peanut butter and chocolate.

1   (14-ounce) can sweetened condensed milk
¾   cup creamy peanut butter
2   cups all-purpose baking mix
1   teaspoon vanilla extract
¼   cup sugar
1   (13-ounce) package milk chocolate kisses

Beat condensed milk and peanut butter at medium speed with an electric mixer until creamy. Add baking mix and vanilla, beating at low speed just until blended.
Shape dough into 1-inch balls; roll in sugar. Place on lightly greased baking sheets.
Bake at 350° for 11 minutes. Remove from oven, and immediately place a chocolate kiss in center of each cookie. Remove cookies to wire racks to cool. Yield: 3 dozen.

Per cookie: Calories 153 (46% from fat); Fat 7.9g (sat 3.3g, mono 3g, poly 1g); Protein 3.4g; Carb 18.6g; Fiber 0.8g; Chol 6mg; Iron 0.5mg; Sodium 131mg; Calc 63mg

family favorite

Chocolate-Dipped Orange Cookies

prep: 45 min.   cook: 12 min. per batch
other: 1 hr.

1   cup butter, softened
½   cup powdered sugar
1   teaspoon grated orange rind
1   teaspoon orange extract
2   cups all-purpose flour
1   cup semisweet chocolate morsels, melted
¾   cup finely chopped almonds, toasted (optional)
¾   cup sweetened flaked coconut, toasted (optional)

Beat butter at medium speed with an electric mixer until creamy; gradually add powdered sugar, beating well. Stir in orange rind and extract. Gradually add flour, beating well. Cover and chill 1 hour.
Divide dough in half. Cover and chill 1 portion. Divide remaining portion into 24 pieces; shape each piece of dough into a 2½- x ½-inch log on a lightly floured surface. Repeat procedure with reserved portion. Place cookies 2 inches apart on baking sheets.
Bake at 350° for 12 minutes. Cool on baking sheets 3 minutes; remove to wire racks to cool completely.
Dip tips of cookies in melted chocolate, and, if desired, chopped nuts or coconut. Place on wire racks; let stand until firm. Yield: 4 dozen.

Per cookie: Calories 76 (59% from fat); Fat 5g (sat 3g, mono 1.3g, poly 0.2g); Protein 0.8g; Carb 7.7g; Fiber 0.4g; Chol 10mg; Iron 0.4mg; Sodium 27mg; Calc 3mg

Chocolate Wedding Cookies

prep: 23 min.   cook: 10 min. per batch

Powdered sugar blended with cocoa dusts these cookies and hints at the novel flavor twist to an old favorite.

½   cup powdered sugar
2   tablespoons unsweetened cocoa
½   cup butter or margarine, softened
¾   cup all-purpose flour
⅓   cup granulated sugar
¼   cup unsweetened cocoa
1   teaspoon vanilla extract
1   cup finely chopped pecans, toasted

Sift together powdered sugar and 2 tablespoons cocoa. Set aside.
Beat butter at medium speed with an electric mixer until creamy. Add flour and next 3 ingredients, beating until blended. Stir in pecans. (Dough will be stiff.) Shape into 1-inch balls, and place on ungreased baking sheets.
Bake at 400° for 10 minutes. Remove cookies to wire racks, and cool slightly. Roll warm cookies in powdered sugar mixture, and cool completely on wire racks. Yield: 2 dozen.

Per cookie: Calories 106 (65% from fat); Fat 7.6g (sat 2.8g, mono 3.1g, poly 1.2g); Protein 1.2g; Carb 9.7g; Fiber 1g; Chol 10mg; Iron 0.5mg; Sodium 27mg; Calc 7mg

Pecan Crescents

prep: 52 min.   cook: 14 min. per batch
other: 1 hr.

These nutty cookies are much like traditional wedding cookies. Let your kids help shape and roll the dough.

1   cup pecan pieces, toasted
1   cup butter, softened
¾   cup powdered sugar, sifted
2   teaspoons vanilla extract
2½ cups sifted all-purpose flour
2   cups powdered sugar

Pulse pecans in a food processor 5 or 6 times or until ground.
Beat butter and ¾ cup powdered sugar at medium speed with an electric mixer until creamy. Stir in vanilla and ground pecans. Gradually stir in flour until a soft dough forms. Cover and chill dough 1 hour.
Divide dough into 5 portions; divide each portion into 12 pieces. Shape each piece into a 2-inch crescent. Place on ungreased baking sheets.
Bake at 350° for 12 to 14 minutes or until lightly browned. Cool 5 minutes on wire racks. Roll warm cookies in 2 cups powdered sugar. Roll cookies again in remaining powdered sugar. Yield: 5 dozen.

Per cookie: Calories 77 (51% from fat); Fat 4.4g (sat 2g, mono 1.5g, poly 0.5g); Protein 0.7g; Carb 9.1g; Fiber 0.3g; Chol 8mg; Iron 0.3mg; Sodium 22mg; Calc 3mg

Note: For this recipe, remember to sift flour before measuring and sift the ¾ cup powdered sugar after measuring.

Peppermint Crescents

prep: 30 min.   cook: 18 min. per batch
other: 5 min.

1   cup butter, softened
1⅔ cups powdered sugar, divided
1¼ teaspoons peppermint extract, divided
⅛   teaspoon salt
2   cups all-purpose flour
Sifted powdered sugar
2   tablespoons milk
Hard peppermint candies, crushed

Beat butter at medium speed with an electric mixer until creamy. Gradually add ⅔ cup powdered sugar, 1 teaspoon peppermint extract, and salt, beating well. Gradually add flour, beating until blended.
Divide dough into 3 portions; divide each portion into 12 pieces. Roll each piece into a 2-inch log, curving ends to form a crescent. Place crescents 2 inches apart on lightly greased baking sheets.
Bake at 325° for 15 to 18 minutes or until lightly browned. Cool 5 minutes. Carefully roll warm cookies in sifted powdered sugar. Cool completely on wire racks.
Stir together milk, remaining 1 cup powdered sugar, and remaining ¼ teaspoon extract until smooth. Drizzle cookies with glaze, and sprinkle with crushed candies, gently pressing candies into glaze. Store in airtight containers. Yield: 3 dozen.

Per cookie: Calories 103 (45% from fat); Fat 5.2g (sat 3.2g, mono 1.3g, poly 0.2g); Protein 0.8g; Carb 13.6g; Fiber 0.2g; Chol 13mg; Iron 0.3mg; Sodium 44mg; Calc 4mg

Cupcake Cookies

prep: 23 min.   cook: 14 min. per batch

Spraying the paper candy liners with cooking spray is the key to keeping these tiny treasures from sticking.

1   (14.4-ounce) package graham crackers, finely crushed (about 3¾ cups) (we tested with Honey Maid)
1   cup firmly packed light brown sugar
1   cup whipping cream
½   cup unsalted butter, melted
1   cup semisweet chocolate morsels
1   cup chopped pecans
1   cup chopped walnuts

Stir together first 4 ingredients until blended. Stir in morsels and nuts until blended.
Shape dough into 1-inch balls (about 1 tablespoon of dough). Place into miniature paper candy liners coated with cooking spray; place on 2 baking sheets.
Bake at 375° for 12 to 14 minutes. Let cool 1 minute on baking sheets; remove to wire racks to cool completely. Yield: 5½ dozen.

Per cookie: Calories 99 (58% from fat); Fat 6.4g (sat 2.3g, mono 2.3g, poly 1.4g); Protein 1.2g; Carb 10.3g; Fiber 0.6g; Chol 9mg; Iron 0.5mg; Sodium 41mg; Calc 11mg

Easy Sugar Cookies

prep: 30 min.   cook: 11 min. per batch

1   cup butter, softened
1   cup powdered sugar
1   cup granulated sugar
2   large eggs
1   cup vegetable oil
2   teaspoons vanilla extract
1   tablespoon fresh lemon juice
5¼ cups all-purpose flour
1   teaspoon cream of tartar
1   teaspoon baking soda
¼   teaspoon salt
Decorator sugar crystals

Beat butter at medium speed with an electric mixer until fluffy; add sugars, beating well. Add eggs, oil, vanilla, and lemon juice, beating until blended.
Combine flour and next 3 ingredients; gradually add to sugar mixture, beating until blended.
Shape dough into 1-inch balls; roll in colored sugar, and place about 2 inches apart on lightly greased baking sheets.
Bake in batches at 350° for 9 to 11 minutes or until set. (Do not brown.) Remove to wire racks to cool. Yield: 7 dozen.

Per cookie: Calories 97 (46% from fat); Fat 5g (sat 1.7g, mono 1.8g, poly 1.3g); Protein 1g; Carb 12.2g; Fiber 0.2g; Chol 11mg; Iron 0.4mg; Sodium 39mg; Calc 3mg

Thumbprint Cookies

prep: 35 min.   cook: 15 min. per batch
other: 1 hr.

A dollop of jelly brings vibrant color to these classic cookies. This version is rolled in chopped nuts for added texture.

1   cup butter, softened
¾   cup sugar
2   large eggs, separated
1   teaspoon almond extract
2   cups all-purpose flour
¼   teaspoon salt
1¼ cups finely chopped pecans
½   cup red currant or other flavored jelly, stirred

Beat butter at medium speed with an electric mixer until creamy; gradually add sugar, beating well. Add egg yolks and almond extract, beating until blended.

Combine flour and salt; add to butter mixture, beating at low speed until blended. Cover and chill dough 1 hour.

Shape dough into 1-inch balls. Lightly beat egg whites. Dip each ball in egg white; roll in pecans. Place 2 inches apart on ungreased baking sheets. Press thumb in each cookie to make an indentation.

Bake at 350° for 15 minutes. Cool 1 minute on baking sheets; remove to wire racks to cool completely. Press centers again with thumb while cookies are still warm; fill center of each cookie with jelly. Yield: 3½ dozen.

Per cookie: Calories 130 (58% from fat); Fat 8.4g (sat 3.6g, mono 3.1g, poly 1.2g); Protein 1.5g; Carb 13g; Fiber 0.6g; Chol 25mg; Iron 0.5mg; Sodium 57mg; Calc 7mg

Ginger–Oatmeal Sorghum Cookies

prep: 30 min.   cook: 12 min. per batch

Rolling these cookie dough balls in sugar transforms them during baking into sugar-crusted treasures. (pictured on page 166)

4	cups all-purpose flour
1	tablespoon baking soda
1½	teaspoons salt
4	cups uncooked quick-cooking oats
1½	cups raisins
1¼	cups sugar
1½	teaspoons ground ginger
1	cup butter or margarine, melted
1	cup sorghum
1	cup chopped walnuts
2	tablespoons hot water
2	large eggs, lightly beaten
½	cup sugar

Combine first 7 ingredients in a large bowl; add butter and next 4 ingredients, stirring until blended.

Divide dough into 20 (2-inch) balls. Roll in ½ cup sugar. Place 2 inches apart on lightly greased baking sheets; flatten each ball to ½-inch thickness.

Bake at 375° for 10 to 12 minutes or until lightly browned. Yield: 20 cookies.

Per cookie: Calories 440 (30% from fat); Fat 14.9g (sat 6.4g, mono 3.9g, poly 3.2g); Protein 7.6g; Carb 71.1g; Fiber 3.5g; Chol 45mg; Iron 3.3mg; Sodium 443mg; Calc 62mg

Chocolate Chunk–Peanut Cookies

prep: 20 min.   cook: 15 min. per batch

A hint of cinnamon gives these cookies a delicious, subtly different flavor.

½	cup butter, softened
½	cup shortening
1	cup chunky peanut butter
1	cup granulated sugar
1	cup firmly packed light brown sugar
2	large eggs
2½	cups all-purpose flour
1½	teaspoons baking soda
1	teaspoon baking powder
½	teaspoon salt
1	teaspoon ground cinnamon
1	cup unsalted dry-roasted peanuts
1	(11.5-ounce) package chocolate chunks or 1 (12-ounce) package semisweet chocolate morsels

Beat butter and shortening at medium speed with an electric mixer until creamy; add chunky peanut butter and sugars, beating well. Add eggs, beating until blended.

Combine flour and next 4 ingredients. Add to butter mixture, beating well.

Stir in peanuts and chocolate chunks.

Shape dough into 2-inch balls (about 2 tablespoons for each cookie). Flatten slightly, and place on ungreased baking sheets.

Bake at 375° for 12 to 15 minutes or until lightly browned. Cool on pan 1 to 2 minutes; remove to wire rack to cool completely. Yield: 28 cookies.

Per cookie: Calories 305 (53% from fat); Fat 18g (sat 6.1g, mono 7.3g, poly 3.6g); Protein 5.6g; Carb 33.9g; Fiber 2.2g; Chol 24mg; Iron 1.4mg; Sodium 204mg; Calc 33mg

Double Chocolate Chunk–Peanut Cookies *(pictured on page 167)*: Reduce flour to 2 cups; add ⅓ cup unsweetened cocoa, sifted. Proceed as directed.

Per cookie: Calories 300 (54% from fat); Fat 18.1g (sat 6.1g, mono 7.3g, poly 3.6g); Protein 5.5g; Carb 32.8g; Fiber 2.3g; Chol 24mg; Iron 1.5mg; Sodium 204mg; Calc 32mg

Chocolate-Chip Supreme Cookies

prep: 15 min.   cook: 12 min. per batch

Set out a plate of these fresh-from-the-oven cookies, and watch how fast they disappear. Pudding mix is the secret ingredient that makes these chip cookies tender.

½	cup shortening
½	cup butter or margarine, softened
¾	cup firmly packed dark brown sugar
¾	cup granulated sugar
2	large eggs
1	(3.4-ounce) package vanilla instant pudding mix
1	tablespoon vanilla extract
2¼	cups all-purpose flour
1	tablespoon baking soda
1	teaspoon ground cinnamon
½	teaspoon ground nutmeg
½	teaspoon salt
1	(12-ounce) package semisweet chocolate morsels
1½	cups chopped pecans
1	cup uncooked quick-cooking oats

Beat shortening and butter at medium speed with an electric mixer until creamy; gradually add sugars, beating well. Add eggs, beating until blended. Add pudding mix and vanilla; beat until blended.

Combine flour and next 4 ingredients. Gradually add to butter mixture, beating until blended. Stir in morsels, chopped pecans, and oats.

Shape dough into 1½-inch balls; place on lightly greased baking sheets, and press to 1-inch thickness.

Bake at 375° for 10 to 12 minutes. Remove cookies to wire racks to cool. Yield: 3 dozen.

Per cookie: Calories 213 (52% from fat); Fat 12.4g (sat 4.3g, mono 5.1g, poly 2.3g); Protein 2.3g; Carb 25.4g; Fiber 1.5g; Chol 18mg; Iron 1.1mg; Sodium 201mg; Calc 16mg

Italian biscotti are long-slivered, intensely crunchy cookies made for dunking into a cup of joe or dessert wine such as Vin Santo.

Biscotti With Lavender and Orange

freeze it • make ahead

Biscotti With Lavender and Orange

prep: 13 min.   cook: 55 min.

Lavender's aromatic appeal combined with fresh orange essence makes this crunchy cookie better than bakery fare.

½   cup sugar
¼   cup butter, softened
1½ to 2 tablespoons coarsely chopped fresh lavender
½   teaspoon grated orange rind
2   large eggs
2   cups all-purpose flour
2   teaspoons baking powder
½   teaspoon salt
½   cup sliced almonds, toasted
½   teaspoon vanilla extract

Beat first 4 ingredients at medium speed with an electric mixer until well blended. Add eggs, 1 at a time, beating until blended. **Combine** flour, baking powder, and salt. Gradually add flour mixture to sugar mixture; beat until blended. Stir in almonds and vanilla. **Turn** dough out onto a lightly greased baking sheet. Shape dough into a 10-inch log; flatten to 1-inch thickness. Bake at 350° for 30 minutes. Remove log from baking sheet, and cool completely on a wire rack. Reduce oven temperature to 300°.
Cut log diagonally into ½-inch-thick slices using a serrated knife. Place slices on an ungreased baking sheet. Bake at 300° for 20 to 25 minutes (cookies will be slightly soft in center but will harden as they cool). Remove from baking sheet; cool completely on wire rack. Yield: 15 cookies.

Per cookie: Calories 143 (35% from fat); Fat 5.5g (sat 2.3g, mono 2.1g, poly 0.7g); Protein 3.3g; Carb 20.3g; Fiber 0.8g; Chol 36mg; Iron 1mg; Sodium 174mg; Calc 52mg

Note: Store in an airtight container. Freeze up to 6 months in an airtight container.

◄Shape dough into a log for the first baking.

◄Cool cookie log on a wire rack.

◄Cut log diagonally into ½-inch slices and then bake the logs until crisp.

make ahead

Chocolate Chip Biscotti

prep: 38 min.   cook: 53 min. per batch

½   cup butter or margarine, softened
½   cup firmly packed light brown sugar
½   cup granulated sugar
1   tablespoon instant coffee or espresso granules (we tested with Café Bustelo)
2   large eggs
2   cups all-purpose flour
2   teaspoons baking powder
½   teaspoon salt
½   teaspoon ground cinnamon (optional)
1   cup chopped walnuts or pecans, toasted
1   cup semisweet chocolate mini-morsels

Combine first 4 ingredients in a large mixing bowl; beat at medium speed with an electric mixer until light and fluffy. Add eggs, 1 at a time, beating until blended. **Combine** flour, baking powder, salt, and, if desired, cinnamon; add to butter mixture,

stirring until blended. Fold in nuts and chocolate morsels. Divide dough in half.
Shape each portion of dough into a 13- x 2-inch log on a lightly greased baking sheet; pat dough to 1-inch thickness.
Bake at 350° for 23 minutes or until firm. Let cool on baking sheet 5 minutes. Transfer logs to wire racks to cool completely. Reduce oven temperature to 300°.
Cut each log diagonally into ½-inch-thick slices with a serrated knife, using a gentle sawing motion. Place slices on ungreased baking sheets.
Bake at 300° for 15 minutes; turn cookies over, and bake 15 more minutes. Transfer to wire racks to cool. Yield: 3½ dozen.

Per biscotto: Calories 102 (49% from fat); Fat 5.5g (sat 2.3g, mono 1.5g, poly 1.2g); Protein 1.8g; Carb 12.5g; Fiber 0.6g; Chol 16mg; Iron 0.6mg; Sodium 71mg; Calc 21mg

low calorie • low cholesterol • make ahead
Chocolate-Hazelnut Biscotti

prep: 26 min.   cook: 40 min. per batch
other: 30 min.

2   large eggs
¾   cup sugar
1   tablespoon Frangelico or other hazelnut liqueur (optional)
2   cups all-purpose flour
3   tablespoons unsweetened cocoa
2   teaspoons baking powder
¼   teaspoon salt
1   cup hazelnuts, toasted, skinned, and chopped

Beat eggs at medium speed with an electric mixer until foamy. Gradually add sugar, beating at high speed until thick and pale. Add liqueur, beating until blended.
Combine flour and next 3 ingredients; fold into egg mixture. Fold in nuts. Cover and chill 30 minutes.
Divide dough into 3 portions, and spoon portions 2 inches apart onto a lightly greased baking sheet.
Shape each portion of dough into an 8-inch log.
Bake at 350° for 20 minutes or until lightly browned. Transfer to wire racks to cool. Reduce oven temperature to 300°. Cut logs diagonally into ½-inch-thick slices. Place slices, cut side down, on baking sheets. Bake at 300° for 10 minutes; turn slices over, and

bake 5 to 10 more minutes. Transfer to wire racks to cool. Yield: 3 dozen.

Per cookie: Calories 69 (34% from fat); Fat 2.6g (sat 0.3g, mono 1.7g, poly 0.4g); Protein 1.6g; Carb 10.3g; Fiber 0.7g; Chol 12mg; Iron 0.6mg; Sodium 47mg; Calc 22mg

make ahead
Orange-Pecan Biscotti

prep: 27 min.   cook: 1 hr.   other: 15 min.

3⅓   cups all-purpose flour
1   cup sugar
1½   tablespoons grated orange rind
2   teaspoons baking powder
¼   teaspoon salt
4   large eggs
2   tablespoons vegetable oil
1   teaspoon vanilla extract
1   teaspoon almond extract
1   cup chopped pecans

Combine first 5 ingredients in a heavy-duty stand mixer; stir until blended.
Whisk together eggs, oil, and extracts; add to flour mixture. Beat at medium speed until blended. Stir in pecans.
Divide dough in half; shape each portion into an 8-inch log on a lightly floured surface. Transfer logs to a lightly greased baking sheet. Shape into 2 (8- x 4-inch) rectangles. Bake at 350° for 30 minutes or until firm. Remove from oven, and let cool 15 minutes.
Reduce oven temperature to 300°. Cut each log crosswise into ½-inch slices using a serrated knife. Stand slices upright on same baking sheet. Carefully return baking sheet to oven.
Bake at 300° for 30 minutes or until dry and crisp, but not brown. Remove cookies to wire racks to cool. Yield: 34 cookies.

Per cookie: Calories 111 (35% from fat); Fat 4.3g (sat 0.6g, mono 2.1g, poly 1.3g); Protein 2.4g; Carb 16.1g; Fiber 0.7g; Chol 25mg; Iron 0.8mg; Sodium 54mg; Calc 24mg

Lemon Butter Cookies

prep: 40 min.   cook: 15 min. per batch

These dainty cookies have a delicate flavor with a citrus zing.

2   cups butter, softened
1   cup powdered sugar
3   cups all-purpose flour
1   teaspoon lemon extract
1   teaspoon grated lemon rind (optional)

Beat butter until creamy; gradually add powdered sugar, beating well. Add flour, 1 cup at a time, beating well after each addition. Stir in extract and, if desired, rind.
Form dough into desired shapes using a cookie press, and place onto parchment paper–lined baking sheets.
Bake at 325° for 12 to 15 minutes. Cool on wire racks. Yield: 8 dozen.

Per cookie: Calories 54 (63% from fat); Fat 3.8g (sat 2.4g, mono 1g, poly 0.2g); Protein 0.4g; Carb 4.5g; Fiber 0.1g; Chol 10mg; Iron 0.2mg; Sodium 27mg; Calc 2mg

Madeleines

prep: 26 min.   cook: 10 min. per batch

A madeleine is a small, featherlike sponge cake eaten as a cookie.

2   large eggs
⅛   teaspoon salt
⅓   cup granulated sugar
½   cup all-purpose flour
1   teaspoon grated lemon rind
½   cup butter, melted and cooled
Powdered sugar

Beat eggs and salt at high speed with an electric mixer until foamy. Gradually add granulated sugar; beat at high speed 15 minutes or until thick and pale. Combine flour and lemon rind, and fold into batter 2 tablespoons at a time. Fold in butter, 1 tablespoon at a time. Spoon 1 tablespoon batter into greased and floured madeleine molds.
Bake at 400° for 8 to 10 minutes or until lightly browned. Cool in molds about 3 minutes. Remove from molds, and cool on a wire rack, flat side down. Sprinkle with powdered sugar. Yield: 2 dozen.

Per cookie: Calories 75 (64% from fat); Fat 5.3g (sat 2.8g, mono 1.6g, poly 0.5g); Protein 0.9g; Carb 6.2g; Fiber 0.1g; Chol 28mg; Iron 0.2mg; Sodium 45mg; Calc 4mg

candies

Equipment

You'll need several sizes of heavy saucepans. Candy mixtures usually triple in volume as they cook, so you'll need pans large enough to allow candy mixtures to boil freely without boiling over. For smaller candy recipes, use smaller pans. If the pan is too large for the amount of mixture you're boiling, the mixture won't be deep enough in the pan for you to insert a candy thermometer to get an accurate temperature reading.

Wooden spoons are the preferred utensil because you'll need to stir some candy mixtures while they're cooking, and wooden spoons don't absorb heat like metal spoons.

While you can test for the proper candy temperature by using the cold-water test alone, a candy thermometer is almost a necessity because it allows you to cook candy to precisely the right temperature and candy stage. Always test the accuracy of your thermometer before cooking with it by letting it stand in boiling water 2 minutes. If thermometer doesn't register 212°, allow for the inaccuracy when cooking. Always read a thermometer at eye level.

Cooking Candy

In candy making, it's important to follow a few special rules. Measure ingredients precisely to keep them in proper proportions. Assemble equipment and measure ingredients before starting to cook, because you may not have time once the process begins.

The main goal of candy making is to control the formation of sugar crystals. We recommend buttering the sides of a saucepan as an initial way of preventing sugar crystals from clustering on the pan. Stir candy mixture gently until it comes to a boil and the sugar dissolves, still trying to prevent crystals from clustering on the pan.

The next step is to cover the pan, and cook over medium heat 2 to 3 minutes to wash down sugar crystals. Then remove the lid and continue cooking. After this point, avoid stirring unless recipe specifies. Occasional stirring of candies made with milk or cream is necessary, however, to avoid scorching. Our recipes indicate whether you need to stir. If so, stir gently with a wooden spoon so mixture doesn't splash onto sides of pan.

Avoid doubling a candy recipe. It's safer to make a second batch. During humid or rainy weather, cook candy until thermometer registers 1 to 2 degrees higher than the recipe directions specify.

Testing for Doneness

The most accurate test for doneness is to use a candy thermometer. When using one, make sure the bulb is in the boiling mixture but not touching the bottom of the pan. Watch the thermometer carefully, because the temperature rises quickly as the candy nears doneness.

If you don't have a candy thermometer, use the cold-water test to check all candy stages except the thread stage and caramel stage. Remove the syrup from the heat while testing. Drop a small amount of syrup into a cup of very cold water; then test with your

A good rule of thumb is to do your candy making on a dry, sunny day, and you shouldn't have any problems.

fingers to determine consistency. Use fresh, cold water each time you test a sample. For thread stage, syrup should spin a 2-inch thread when you dip a metal spoon into the syrup and then gently shake the spoon back and forth. For caramel stage, syrup will be medium honey-colored when spooned onto a white plate.

Cooling Candy

Some recipes call for candy mixtures to cool in the pan until lukewarm (110°). Let pan sit undisturbed during this period; don't stir unless instructed to do so or the candy might become grainy.

When the mixture is ready for pouring, do so quickly, and take care not to scrape the sides of the pan since this may add sugar crystals to the candy. Let candy cool completely before cutting or packaging it.

Storing Candy

Store all candies in airtight containers as soon as they're cool; this prevents them from picking up moisture from the atmosphere. Most candies will stay fresh up to a week; fudgelike candies will keep up to a week or two if properly stored.

The recipe will indicate if the candy needs refrigerating. Some chocolate-dipped candies need refrigerating to keep the coating firm. In general, candy is not a good candidate for freezing.

tests for candy stages

Thread Stage — 215° to 232°
- Syrup spins a 2-inch thread when dropped from a metal spoon.

Soft Ball Stage — 234° to 240°
- In cold water, syrup forms a soft ball that flattens when removed from water.

Firm Ball Stage — 242° to 248°
- In cold water, syrup forms a firm ball that doesn't flatten when removed from water.

Hard Ball Stage — 250° to 268°
- Syrup forms a hard, yet pliable, ball when removed from cold water.

Soft Crack Stage — 270° to 290°
- When dropped into cold water, syrup separates into threads that are hard but not brittle.

Hard Crack Stage — 300° to 310°
- When dropped into cold water, syrup separates into threads that are hard and brittle.

Caramel Stage — 320° to 350°
- Syrup will be honey-colored when spooned onto a white plate. The longer it's cooked, the darker it will be.

classic candies

These traditional candies include the crunchy and chewy sweets you remember from childhood—peanut brittle, taffy, toffee, and divinity. All are cooked to a precise temperature. You won't have any trouble making them if you follow the basic guidelines for minimizing sugar crystals and check for the specific end temperature as described on the opposite page. Avoid making these candies on a humid or rainy day because they can pick up moisture from the air and become sticky.

low cholesterol • low fat

Mrs. Floyd's Divinity

prep: 30 min.   cook: 20 min.

Editor in Chief John Floyd's mom was known across the South for her featherlight and tender divinity.

2½   cups sugar
½   cup water
½   cup light corn syrup
¼   teaspoon salt
2   egg whites
1   teaspoon vanilla extract
1   cup chopped pecans, toasted
Garnish: toasted pecan halves

Cook first 4 ingredients in a heavy 2-quart saucepan over low heat until sugar dissolves and a candy thermometer registers 248° (about 15 minutes). Remove from heat.
Beat egg whites at high speed with an electric mixer until stiff peaks form. Pour half of hot syrup in a thin stream over egg whites, beating constantly at high speed, 5 minutes.
Cook remaining half of syrup over medium heat, stirring occasionally, until a candy thermometer registers 272° (about 4 to 5 minutes). Slowly pour hot syrup and vanilla over egg white mixture, beating constantly at high speed until mixture holds its shape (about 6 to 8 minutes). Stir in 1 cup chopped pecans.

Drop mixture quickly by rounded teaspoonfuls onto lightly greased wax paper. Garnish, if desired. Cool. Yield: 4 dozen (1¾ pounds).

Per piece: Calories 69 (25% from fat); Fat 1.9g (sat 0.2g, mono 1g, poly 0.5g); Protein 0.4g; Carb 13.5g; Fiber 0.2g; Chol 0mg; Iron 0.1mg; Sodium 19mg; Calc 2mg

make ahead

Pecan Toffee

prep: 10 min.   cook: 20 min.   other: 1 hr.

1½   cups chopped, toasted pecans, divided
1   cup sugar
1   cup butter
1   tablespoon light corn syrup
¼   cup water
1   cup semisweet chocolate morsels

Spread 1 cup pecans into a 9-inch circle on a lightly greased baking sheet.
Bring sugar and next 3 ingredients to a boil in a heavy saucepan over medium heat, stirring constantly. Cook until mixture is golden brown and a candy thermometer registers 290° to 310° (about 15 minutes). Pour sugar mixture over pecans on baking sheet.
Sprinkle with morsels; let stand 30 seconds. Spread melted morsels evenly over top; sprinkle with remaining ½ cup chopped pecans. Chill 1 hour. Break into bite-size pieces. Store in an airtight container. Yield: 12 servings (1½ pounds).

Per serving: Calories 374 (72% from fat); Fat 30.1g (sat 13g, mono 11.4g, poly 3.9g); Protein 2.1g; Carb 28.9g; Fiber 2.3g; Chol 40mg; Iron 0.8mg; Sodium 111mg; Calc 20mg

Almond Toffee: Substitute 1 cup chopped, toasted slivered almonds for 1 cup of chopped pecans to sprinkle on baking sheet. Substitute ½ cup toasted sliced almonds for ½ cup chopped pecans to sprinkle over chocolate. Proceed as directed.

Bourbon-Pecan Toffee: Substitute ¼ cup bourbon for ¼ cup water. Proceed with recipe as directed.

family favorite • quick

Classic Peanut Brittle

prep: 5 min.   cook: 8 min.   other: 5 min.

Make this old-fashioned favorite in the microwave or on the stove.

1   cup sugar
½   cup light corn syrup
⅛   teaspoon salt
1   cup dry-roasted or shelled raw peanuts
2   tablespoons butter
1   teaspoon baking soda
2   teaspoons vanilla extract

Combine first 3 ingredients in a large glass bowl. Microwave at HIGH 5 minutes; add peanuts, and microwave 2 more minutes with 1,000-watt microwave. Microwave 4 more minutes if using a 700-watt microwave. Stir in butter and remaining ingredients.
Pour into a buttered 15- x 10-inch jelly-roll pan; shake pan to spread thinly. Cool until firm, and break into pieces. Store in an airtight container. Yield: 8 servings (1 pound).

Per serving: Calories 304 (39% from fat); Fat 13.3g (sat 4g, mono 5.6g, poly 3g); Protein 4.4g; Carb 45.4g; Fiber 1.5g; Chol 11mg; Iron 0.4mg; Sodium 250mg; Calc 12mg

Cooktop Brittle: Cook first 3 ingredients in a medium-size heavy saucepan over medium heat, stirring constantly, until mixture starts to boil. Boil without stirring 5 minutes or until a candy thermometer reaches 310°. Add peanuts, and cook 2 to 3 more minutes or to 280°. (Mixture should be golden brown.) Remove from heat, and stir in butter and remaining ingredients. Pour mixture onto a metal surface or into a shallow pan. Allow to stand 5 minutes or until hardened. Break into pieces.

Chocolate-Dipped Peanut Brittle: Prepare peanut brittle as directed. Melt 2 (2-ounce) chocolate bark coating squares; dip peanut brittle pieces into melted chocolate. Place on wax paper, and let harden.

Popcorn Peanut Brittle: Prepare brittle as directed. Stir in 1 cup popped popcorn before pouring into pan.

Once divinity holds its shape upon beating, quickly spoon it by teaspoonfuls onto wax paper.

taste of the south pralines

Few confections are so readily identified with the South as pralines—irresistible nuggets made of caramel and pecans. Whether you pronounce it "PRAY-leen" or "PRAH-leen," you'll love this candy's rich flavor.

Different Southern cooks swear by a variety of recipes—with or without brown sugar or baking soda; with evaporated milk, buttermilk, or half-and-half; and dropped large or small. We tasted them all before determining our favorite recipe, a combination of white and brown sugars with evaporated milk.

Pralines aren't difficult to make, but they can be tricky. The requirements are plenty of stirring, patience, and careful attention. Two big questions usually come up during preparation: when to remove the candy mixture from the heat, and when to stop beating and start spooning it. (You're allowed to enlist an extra set of hands at this stage.)

If the mixture gets too hot, the candy will be dry and crumbly. If it isn't cooked long enough, the mixture will be runny and sticky.

One trick we learned after making several batches in our Test Kitchens: Use a candy thermometer for the best temperature reading—it will take out most of the guesswork. We like to use two thermometers for accuracy.

Beat the mixture with a wooden spoon just until it begins to thicken. You'll feel the mixture become heavier, and its color will become lighter. Often the last few pralines that you spoon will be thicker and less perfectly shaped than the first, but they'll still taste just as good. The candy tastes best if eaten within a day or two; pralines become sugary and gritty with age. Be sure to store them in an airtight container for best results (a metal tin or other container with a tight-fitting lid works well).

family favorite
Pralines

prep: 10 min.   cook: 30 min.

1½ cups granulated sugar
1½ cups firmly packed light brown sugar
1 cup evaporated milk
¼ cup butter or margarine
2 cups pecan halves, toasted
1 teaspoon vanilla extract

Bring sugars and milk to a boil in a 3- or 4-quart saucepan, stirring often. Cook over medium heat, stirring often, 11 minutes or until a candy thermometer registers 228° (thread stage).
Stir in butter and pecans, and cook, stirring constantly, until candy thermometer registers 232°.
Remove from heat; stir in vanilla. Beat with a wooden spoon 1 to 2 minutes or just until mixture begins to thicken and lose its gloss. Quickly drop by heaping tablespoonfuls onto buttered wax paper or parchment paper; let stand until firm. Yield: 2½ dozen.

Per praline: Calories 158 (43% from fat); Fat 7.6g (sat 2g, mono 3.6g, poly 1.6g); Protein 1.2g; Carb 22.5g; Fiber 0.7g; Chol 8mg; Iron 0.4mg; Sodium 26mg; Calc 36mg

▲ Cook candy mixture to 228°.

▲ Stir in butter and pecans, and cook to 232°.

▲ Beat with a wooden spoon until candy begins to thicken.

▲ Quickly drop by heaping tablespoonfuls onto buttered paper.

Coffee-Pecan Fudge

Mama's Fudge

prep: 10 min.   cook: 20 min.   other: 30 min.

2	cups sugar
⅔	cup milk
¼	cup unsweetened cocoa
1	tablespoon light corn syrup
¼	teaspoon salt
3	tablespoons butter
1	teaspoon vanilla extract

Stir together first 5 ingredients in a 2-quart saucepan. Bring mixture to a boil over medium–high heat, and cook until a candy thermometer registers 240° (soft ball stage). Remove mixture from heat; add butter, and let melt. (Do not stir.) Let cool 10 to 15 minutes or until pan is cool to the touch. Stir in vanilla.

Beat mixture at medium–low speed with an electric mixer 2 to 3 minutes or until mixture begins to lose its gloss. Working quickly, pour fudge onto a buttered 11- x 7-inch platter. Let cool 15 minutes. Cut fudge into 1-inch pieces. Yield: 20 (1-inch) pieces.

Per piece: Calories 108 (23% from fat); Fat 2.7g (sat 1.7g, mono 0.7g, poly 0.1g); Protein 0.5g; Carb 21.8g; Fiber 0.4g; Chol 7mg; Iron 0.2mg; Sodium 50mg; Calc 12mg

family favorite • quick

Fast Fudge

prep: 18 min.   cook: 8 min.

2	cups sugar
1	(5-ounce) can evaporated milk (⅔ cup)
½	cup butter
12	large marshmallows
Pinch of salt	
1	cup semisweet chocolate morsels
1	cup chopped pecans, toasted
1	teaspoon vanilla extract

Combine first 5 ingredients in a large heavy saucepan. Cook over medium heat, stirring constantly, until mixture comes to a boil; boil 5 minutes, stirring constantly. Remove from heat.

Add chocolate morsels to marshmallow mixture, stirring until chocolate melts. Add pecans and vanilla, stirring well. Spread evenly in a buttered 8- or 9-inch square pan. Cool and cut into squares. Yield: 3 dozen squares (2 pounds).

Per square: Calories 125 (48% from fat); Fat 6.7g (sat 2.9g, mono 2.6g, poly 0.9g); Protein 0.9g; Carb 16.8g; Fiber 0.6g; Chol 9mg; Iron 0.2mg; Sodium 30mg; Calc 17mg

Coffee-Pecan Fudge: Add 2 tablespoons instant coffee granules with first 5 ingredients. Proceed as directed.

foolproof fudge

Our Test Kitchens turn out countless pounds of candy each year. Here's their best advice:

• If it's a humid day, the candy may have a more sugary texture. Best results generally occur when the weather is dry.
• Have all your ingredients chopped, measured, and ready before you begin cooking.
• Use a heavy saucepan with thick sides and bottom. It will conduct heat evenly.
• Butter the inside of saucepan before you begin. This keeps sugar from clinging to sides of pan and helps prevent fudge from becoming grainy.
• An important early step in making creamy fudge is to be sure sugar dissolves completely before boiling the candy mixture. Otherwise, fudge may be grainy and crumbly. To test this, dip a metal spoon into sugar syrup mixture and press spoon against side of pan. If sugar's dissolved, you shouldn't feel any grains of sugar on back of spoon.
• Use a clip-on candy thermometer. Always read thermometer at eye level. Test it for accuracy by placing thermometer in boiling water 2 minutes; it should register 212°. If not, adjust temperature given in recipe by the amount that your reading deviates from 212°. For example, if your thermometer registers 210° in boiling water, it's 2° low. And you should remove candy from heat when thermometer registers 2° below what the recipe specifies.
• Don't scrape sides of pan when pouring out fudge. It could lead to grainy fudge.

Fudge has good keeping quality, so you can make a lot of it and store it easily in an airtight container.

Coffee Penuche

prep: 10 min. cook: 28 min.
other: 1 hr., 40 min.

These morsels have a fudgelike texture with brown-sugar flavor.

3   cups firmly packed light brown
    sugar
1   cup brewed coffee
2   tablespoons light corn syrup
2   tablespoons butter or margarine
1   teaspoon vanilla extract
⅛   teaspoon salt
1   cup chopped pecans

Cook first 3 ingredients in a large heavy saucepan over low heat, stirring until sugar dissolves. Cover and cook over medium heat 2 to 3 minutes to wash down sugar crystals from sides of pan. Uncover and cook, without stirring, until a candy thermometer registers 238° (soft ball stage).

Remove from heat, and add butter, vanilla, and salt (do not stir). Cool to 175°, about an hour. Stir in pecans, and beat with a wooden spoon until mixture thickens and begins to lose its gloss (about 10 minutes). Spread into a buttered 8-inch square pan. Cool 30 minutes or until firm. Cut into 1-inch squares. Store in an airtight container. Yield: 5⅓ dozen squares (2 pounds).

Per piece: Calories 58 (28% from fat); Fat 1.8g (sat 0.4g, mono 0.9g, poly 0.4g); Protein 0.2g; Carb 10.8g; Fiber 0.2g; Chol 1mg; Iron 0.2mg; Sodium 12mg; Calc 10mg

low cholesterol • low fat
Old-Fashioned Taffy

prep: 45 min. cook: 40 min.

2½ cups sugar
½   cup water
¼   cup white vinegar
1   tablespoon butter or margarine
⅛   teaspoon salt
1   teaspoon vanilla extract

Combine first 5 ingredients in a small Dutch oven; cook over low heat until sugar dissolves, stirring gently. Cover and cook over medium heat 2 to 3 minutes to wash down sugar crystals from sides of pan. Uncover and cook over medium heat, without stirring, to soft crack stage or until a candy thermometer registers 270°. Remove from heat. Stir in vanilla.

Pour candy into a buttered 15- x 10-inch jelly-roll pan or onto a slab of marble. Cool to touch; butter hands, and pull candy until light in color and difficult to pull. Divide candy in half, and pull into a rope, 1 inch in diameter. Cut into 1-inch pieces; wrap each piece in wax paper. Yield: 40 (1-inch) pieces.

Per piece: Calories 61 (13% from fat); Fat 0.9g (sat 0.5g, mono 0.2g, poly 0g); Protein 0g; Carb 13.7g; Fiber 0g; Chol 2mg; Iron 0mg; Sodium 15mg; Calc 1mg

chocolate candies

entertaining • freeze it • make ahead
Chocolate-Hazelnut Truffles

prep: 40 min. cook: 13 min. other: 5 hrs.

¼   cup whipping cream
1   (4-ounce) bittersweet chocolate baking
    bar, chopped
1   (4-ounce) semisweet chocolate baking
    bar, chopped
2   tablespoons hazelnut spread (we tested
    with Nutella)
1   cup hazelnuts

Bring cream to a simmer in a saucepan over medium-high heat; remove from heat. **Whisk** in chocolates and hazelnut spread until blended and smooth. Transfer mixture to a glass bowl; cover and chill 3 hours or until firm.
Place hazelnuts on a baking sheet. Bake at 350° for 10 minutes or until hazelnuts are toasted and skins begin to split. Place warm hazelnuts in a dish towel, and rub vigorously to remove skins.

Process toasted hazelnuts in a food processor until ground. Place in a shallow dish.
Shape chilled chocolate mixture into 1-inch balls; roll in ground hazelnuts. Cover and chill truffles 2 hours or until ready to serve. Yield: 2 dozen.

Per truffle: Calories 92 (74% from fat); Fat 7.6g (sat 2.6g, mono 3.8g, poly 0.6g); Protein 1.3g; Carb 7.2g; Fiber 1.2g; Chol 3mg; Iron 0.6mg; Sodium 2mg; Calc 10mg

◄Shape chilled chocolate mixture into balls. We recommend using a cookie scoop.

◄Roll truffles in ground hazelnuts.

entertaining • make ahead
Raspberry-Fudge Truffles

prep: 30 min. cook: 5 min. other: 3 hrs.

Use a sturdy wooden pick to dip chilled or frozen truffle balls in chocolate.

1   (12-ounce) package semisweet chocolate
     morsels
2   (8-ounce) packages cream cheese,
     softened
1   cup seedless raspberry preserves
2   tablespoons raspberry liqueur
1½   cups vanilla wafer crumbs
10   (2-ounce) chocolate bark coating squares
3   (1-ounce) white chocolate squares
1   tablespoon shortening

Microwave chocolate morsels in a 4-cup glass measuring cup at HIGH 1½ to 2½ minutes or until melted, stirring every 30 seconds.
Beat cream cheese at medium speed with an electric mixer until smooth.

Add melted chocolate, preserves, and liqueur, beating until blended.
Stir in crumbs; cover and chill 2 hours.
Shape mixture into 1-inch balls; cover and freeze 1 hour or until firm.
Microwave chocolate coating in a 4-cup glass measuring cup at HIGH 1½ to 2½ minutes or until melted, stirring every 30 seconds. Dip balls in coating; place on wax paper.
Place white chocolate and shortening in a small zip-top freezer bag; seal. Submerge in hot water until chocolate melts; knead until smooth.
Snip a tiny hole in 1 corner of bag, and drizzle mixture over truffles. Let stand until firm. Store in refrigerator or freezer, if desired. Yield: 6 dozen.

Per truffle: Calories 115 (52% from fat); Fat 6.7g (sat 4.6g, mono 1.4g, poly 0.2g); Protein 0.9g; Carb 13.9g; Fiber 0.3g; Chol 8mg; Iron 0.3mg; Sodium 27mg; Calc 11mg

chocolate coating

- Chocolate-dipped candies can be challenging. It takes a little practice to achieve the same smooth and symmetrical coating as commercially dipped candies.
- There are two mediums you can use for dipping—real chocolate or chocolate-flavored bark coating. Most people prefer real chocolate because of its premium flavor; its biggest disadvantage is that after melting under home conditions, it doesn't harden again completely and can be sticky. Many of our recipes add a little shortening to the chocolate to firm it.
- Chocolate-flavored bark coating isn't actually real chocolate at all, but is flavored and colored to look like chocolate. It melts like real chocolate (only a little faster and easier), and when the coating cools to room temperature, there's usually not a problem with stickiness.
- When dipping candies in either medium, melt the chocolate according to recipe directions. You can use two forks, a wooden pick, or a candy dipping utensil to dip and remove candy from melted chocolate. Let excess chocolate drip back into the pan; then transfer chocolates to wax paper to cool and harden.

Texas Millionaires

prep: 25 min.   other: 1 hr.

1   (14-ounce) package caramels
2   tablespoons butter or margarine
2   tablespoons water
3   cups pecan halves
1   cup semisweet chocolate morsels
8   (2-ounce) vanilla bark coating squares

Cook first 3 ingredients in a heavy saucepan over low heat, stirring constantly, until smooth. Stir in pecan halves. Cool in pan 5 minutes.
Drop by tablespoonfuls onto lightly greased wax paper. Chill 1 hour, or freeze 20 minutes until firm.
Melt morsels and vanilla coating in a heavy saucepan over low heat, stirring until smooth. Dip caramel candies into chocolate mixture, allowing excess to drip; place on lightly greased wax paper. Let stand until firm. Yield: 4 dozen.

Per piece: Calories 150 (59% from fat); Fat 9.8g (sat 4.3g, mono 4.3g, poly 1.6g); Protein 1.2g; Carb 16.3g; Fiber 1g; Chol 2mg; Iron 0.3mg; Sodium 24mg; Calc 19mg

Buckeyes

prep: 25 min.

Buckeyes are a chocolate-covered peanut butter candy ball made to resemble the nut by the same name.

1¼ cups butter, softened
1   (18-ounce) jar creamy peanut butter
7   cups sifted powdered sugar (about 1½ pounds)
3   cups semisweet chocolate morsels
1½ tablespoons shortening

Process butter and peanut butter in a food processor until thoroughly blended. Add 3 cups powdered sugar, and process until smooth. Gradually add remaining powdered sugar in 2 batches, processing after each addition until mixture pulls away from sides and is no longer crumbly. Shape into 1-inch balls. Cover and chill thoroughly.
Combine chocolate morsels and shortening in top of a double boiler; bring water to a boil. Reduce heat to low; cook until chocolate melts, stirring occasionally.

Remove pan from heat, leaving chocolate mixture over hot water.
Use a wooden pick to dip each ball in chocolate, coating three-fourths of ball; place on wax paper. Carefully smooth wooden pick holes. Let candies stand until chocolate hardens. Store in an airtight container in refrigerator. Yield: 8 dozen.

Per buckeye: Calories 108 (58% from fat); Fat 6.9g (sat 3g, mono 2.5g, poly 0.9g); Protein 1.6g; Carb 11.7g; Fiber 0.6g; Chol 6mg; Iron 0.3mg; Sodium 42mg; Calc 5mg

make ahead

Bourbon Balls

prep: 45 min.   other: 17 hrs.

If you'd rather forgo dipping these bourbon bites in chocolate, roll them in powdered sugar instead.

1   (16-ounce) package powdered sugar
⅓   cup bourbon
¼   cup butter, softened
50 pecan halves (about 1¼ cups)
1   (12-ounce) package semisweet chocolate morsels
1   tablespoon shortening

Stir together first 3 ingredients in a bowl until blended. Cover and chill 8 hours.
Shape mixture into 1-inch balls. Gently press pecan halves into 2 sides of each ball. Chill 8 hours.
Melt chocolate and shortening in a saucepan over medium heat. Remove from heat. Dip bourbon balls in chocolate, and place on wax paper. Chill 1 hour or until hardened. Yield: 25 balls.

Per candy: Calories 183 (42% from fat); Fat 8.5g (sat 3.9g, mono 3.2g, poly 1g); Protein 0.9g; Carb 27.1g; Fiber 1.1g; Chol 5mg; Iron 0.5mg; Sodium 15mg; Calc 7mg

Cordial Cherries

prep: 10 min.   cook: 10 min.   other: 8 hrs.

Brandy-soaked cherries can be left in the freezer for up to two days before you dip them into the chocolate.

1   (10-ounce) jar maraschino cherries with stems
½   cup brandy (optional)
1   (8-ounce) package semisweet chocolate baking squares, chopped

Drain maraschino cherries, and return to jar. Pour brandy, if desired, in jar; cover with a lid, and freeze 8 hours. Drain cherries, and pat dry, reserving brandy for another use.
Melt two-thirds of chocolate baking squares in a saucepan over medium heat, stirring until a candy thermometer reaches 115°. Remove from heat; add remaining chocolate, and stir until candy thermometer reaches 89° and chocolate is smooth.
Dip cherries quickly into melted chocolate, coating well. Place cherries on wax paper, stem sides up, and cool. Yield: 2½ dozen.

Per cherry: Calories 46 (45% from fat); Fat 2.3g (sat 1.3g, mono 0.8g, poly 0.1g); Protein 0.3g; Carb 7.8g; Fiber 0.5g; Chol 0mg; Iron 0.2mg; Sodium 1mg; Calc 2mg

---

make ahead • test kitchen favorite

Chocolate-Dipped Caramels

prep: 5 min.   cook: 17 min.   other: 16 hrs.

These creamy confections received our Test Kitchens highest rating.

1   cup sugar
1   cup butter
1   cup dark corn syrup
1   (14-ounce) can sweetened condensed milk
1   teaspoon vanilla extract
2½ cups semisweet chocolate morsels
2   tablespoons shortening

Bring first 3 ingredients to a boil in a saucepan over medium heat; cook 7 minutes, without stirring. Stir in condensed milk, and bring to a boil; cook, stirring constantly, 10 minutes or until a candy thermometer reaches 245°.
Remove from heat, and stir in vanilla. Pour into a lightly greased aluminum foil-lined 8- x 8-inch dish. Let stand 8 hours at room temperature.
Cut caramel into ½-inch squares, and shape into balls.
Melt chocolate and shortening in a saucepan over medium heat. Remove from heat. Dip balls into melted chocolate mixture; place on wax paper. Chill 8 hours. Yield: 10 dozen.

Per piece: Calories 57 (49% from fat); Fat 3.1g (sat 1.8g, mono 0.9g, poly 0.2g); Protein 0.4g; Carb 7.8g; Fiber 0.2g; Chol 5mg; Iron 0.1mg; Sodium 20mg; Calc 11mg

---

make ahead • quick

Chocolate Mint Snowballs

prep: 20 min.

1   (18-ounce) package cream-filled chocolate sandwich cookies
1   (8-ounce) package ⅓-less-fat cream cheese
1   (12.5-ounce) package chocolate-covered creamy mints (we tested with Junior Mints)
2   (12-ounce) packages semisweet chocolate morsels
1   tablespoon shortening

Pulse half of cookies in a food processor 3 or 4 times or until crumb consistency. Add remaining cookies to crumbs in food processor, and pulse until crumb consistency.
Cut cream cheese into 4 pieces; add to food processor, 1 piece at a time, processing well after each addition.
Roll cream cheese mixture into 1-inch balls. Push 1 chocolate-covered mint into the center of each ball; roll each ball smooth.
Microwave chocolate morsels and shortening in a glass bowl at HIGH for 90 seconds or until melted, stirring every 30 seconds. Dip balls into melted chocolate mixture; place on wax paper to harden. Store in refrigerator. Yield: 5 dozen.

Per snowball: Calories 132 (46% from fat); Fat 6.8g (sat 3.4g, mono 2.5g, poly 0.4g); Protein 1.5g; Carb 18.4g; Fiber 1g; Chol 3mg; Iron 0.8mg; Sodium 77mg; Calc 6mg

---

specialty candies

family favorite • for kids

Old-Fashioned Popcorn Balls

prep: 15 min.   cook: 20 min.

2   cups firmly packed dark brown sugar
¾   cup light corn syrup
¾   cup water
½   teaspoon salt
½   cup butter or margarine
1   teaspoon vanilla extract
6   quarts popped corn

Combine first 4 ingredients in a saucepan; cook over low heat until sugar dissolves, stirring gently. Cook over medium heat, without stirring, to hard ball stage or until a candy thermometer registers 254°. Remove from heat, and stir in butter and vanilla.
Place popped corn in a large pan (we used a large roasting pan). Pour hot syrup over top, stirring well with a wooden spoon. Grease hands with butter, and shape mixture into balls. Place on wax paper to dry. Wrap in plastic wrap; store in a cool, dry place. Yield: 2 dozen.

Per ball: Calories 192 (35% from fat); Fat 7.4g (sat 3.2g, mono 2g, poly 1.6g); Protein 1g; Carb 32.3g; Fiber 1.1g; Chol 11mg; Iron 0.7mg; Sodium 196mg; Calc 18mg

popcorn ball pointers

- Air-popped corn and corn popped in a Dutch oven with oil work equally well in this recipe.
- Remove any unpopped kernels of corn before combining the sugar mixture and popped corn.
- We used a large roasting pan to combine the sugar mixture with the popped corn. A very large bowl works, too.
- Make sure your hands are well greased in order to keep the sticky popcorn mixture from clinging to them.

Butter Mints

prep: 20 min. cook: 5 min.   other: 4 hrs.

Freeze extra mints in a zip-top freezer bag for up to three months.

½   (8-ounce) package cream cheese
2   tablespoons butter
1   (16-ounce) package powdered sugar
¼   teaspoon peppermint extract
⅛   teaspoon vanilla extract

Melt cream cheese and butter in a large saucepan over low heat, stirring constantly until smooth. Gradually stir in powdered sugar; add peppermint and vanilla extracts, stirring until well blended.
Divide cream cheese mixture into 10 (¼-cup) portions; roll each into a 12-inch rope. Cut into ½-inch pieces. Let stand, uncovered, 4 hours or until firm. Yield: 20 dozen.

Per mint: Calories 10 (30% from fat); Fat 0.3g (sat 0.2g, mono 0.1g, poly 0g); Protein 0g; Carb 1.9g; Fiber 0g; Chol 1mg; Iron 0mg; Sodium 2mg; Calc 0mg

Lollipops

prep: 10 min. cook: 40 min.

Vegetable oil
1   cup sugar
¼   cup water
¼   cup light corn syrup
1   or 2 drops of desired food coloring
¼   teaspoon oil of cinnamon or peppermint
8   white craft sticks

Brush inside surfaces of metal lollipop molds with vegetable oil; set molds aside.
Combine sugar, water, and corn syrup in a medium saucepan. Cook over low heat, stirring gently, until sugar dissolves. Cover and cook mixture over medium heat 2 to 3 minutes to wash down sugar crystals from sides of pan. Uncover and cook, without stirring, to hard crack stage (300°). Remove mixture from heat, and stir in desired food coloring and oil of cinnamon. Immediately pour hot mixture into prepared molds.
Press sticks in indentations of molds, gently twirling sticks to embed. Cool completely; lift lollipops out of molds. Immediately wrap in plastic wrap. Store in a cool, dry place. Yield: 8 (2-inch) lollipops.

Per lollipop: Calories 138 (8% from fat); Fat 1.3g (sat 0.1g, mono 0.6g, poly 0.6g); Protein 0g; Carb 33.2g; Fiber 0g; Chol 0mg; Iron 0mg; Sodium 13mg; Calc 1mg

easy candies

Cracker Candy

prep: 10 min. cook: 11 min.

2   sleeves round buttery crackers (76 crackers), broken in half
¾   cup butter
¾   cup firmly packed light brown sugar
1   (12-ounce) package milk chocolate morsels
¾   cup chopped pecans, toasted
½   cup chopped white chocolate

Place crackers on a greased aluminum foil-lined 15- x 10-inch jelly-roll pan.
Bring butter and brown sugar to a boil in a saucepan, stirring constantly; cook 3 minutes, stirring often. Pour mixture over crackers.
Bake at 350° for 5 minutes. Turn oven off. Sprinkle crackers with chocolate morsels. Let stand in oven 3 minutes or until chocolate melts. Spread melted chocolate evenly over crackers. Top with pecans and white chocolate. Cool completely, and break candy into pieces. Store in refrigerator. Yield: 8 servings (2 pounds).

Per serving: Calories 834 (58% from fat); Fat 53.9g (sat 25.6g, mono 9g, poly 3.1g); Protein 7.8g; Carb 82.3g; Fiber 1.1g; Chol 69mg; Iron 2mg; Sodium 430mg; Calc 83mg

Cherry-Pistachio Bark

prep: 10 min. cook: 10 min. other: 1 hr.

Lightly grease the cookie cutter with cooking spray to make cutting easier.

1¼ cups dried cherries
2   tablespoons water
2   (12-ounce) packages white chocolate morsels
6   (2-ounce) vanilla bark coating squares
1¼ cups chopped red or green pistachios

Microwave cherries and 2 tablespoons water in a small glass bowl at HIGH 2 minutes; drain.
Melt white chocolate morsels and vanilla coating in a heavy saucepan over low heat. Remove from heat; stir in cherries and pistachios. Spread into a wax paper-lined 15- x 10-inch jelly-roll pan.
Chill 1 hour or until firm. Cut with a 3-inch heart-shaped cookie cutter. Store in an airtight container. Yield: 40 servings (3½ pounds).

Per serving: Calories 181 (51% from fat); Fat 10.3g (sat 6g, mono 4.1g, poly 0.9g); Protein 2.3g; Carb 20.5g; Fiber 0.6g; Chol 4mg; Iron 0.3mg; Sodium 27mg; Calc 54mg

Pecan Clusters

prep: 20 min. cook: 13 min.

Little helpers can lend a hand dropping these easy confections onto wax paper.

1   (7-ounce) jar marshmallow cream
1½ pounds milk chocolate kisses
5   cups sugar
1   (12-ounce) can evaporated milk
½   cup butter or margarine
6   cups pecan halves

Place marshmallow cream and chocolate in a large bowl.
Bring sugar, milk, and butter to a boil in a large heavy saucepan, stirring constantly. Boil, stirring constantly, 8 minutes. Add to marshmallow cream mixture, stirring until chocolate melts. Stir in pecans.
Drop by rounded teaspoonfuls onto wax paper-lined baking sheets; chill 2 hours or until firm. Cover; store in airtight containers in refrigerator. Yield: 12 dozen.

Per cluster: Calories 95 (52% from fat); Fat 5.5g (sat 1.7g, mono 2.5g, poly 1.1g); Protein 0.9g; Carb 11.7g; Fiber 0.6g; Chol 3mg; Iron 0.2mg; Sodium 12mg; Calc 18mg

desserts

Equipment

Simple or spectacular, dessert is often the highlight of a meal. And since desserts take on many shapes, our recipes make use of a variety of pans, molds, and other equipment. Always read through a recipe before you begin preparation to be sure you have the equipment you need or a suitable substitute.

Rich puddings and sauces serve many purposes on these pages; therefore, a few wire whisks, large spoons, and a heavy saucepan will come in handy for creating their thick and velvety-smooth texture.

Ovenproof ramekins or custard cups are ideal for making individual custards, and a large soufflé dish is a simple piece of equipment that produces a showy dessert. You'll need a large roasting pan or baking dish when making some baked custards like crème brûlée. The pan holds custard cups in a gently simmering "water bath," which insulates the custard and prevents overcooking.

And no summer cookout would be complete without the universal favorite, homemade ice cream. An ice-cream freezer, whether electric or hand-crank, is easy to use when you follow the manufacturer's instructions. Be diligent about carefully cleaning and drying your ice-cream freezer after each use to prevent it from rusting.

Storing and Freezing

Store desserts that contain fresh fruit or cream in the refrigerator, both before serving if you make them ahead, and afterward if there are leftovers.

If the dessert recipe doesn't mention freezing as an option, then it's probably not a good candidate for making ahead and freezing. The low temperatures of freezing alter the texture of most fruit dishes, and pudding-based recipes have a tendency to break down. Avoid freezing a dessert that contains gelatin unless instructed to do so; some gelatin desserts freeze well, and some don't, depending on the ingredients.

One dessert component that does freeze well is crêpes. You can make extra crêpes, stack them between wax paper, and freeze up to three months sealed in a freezer bag. They'll thaw quickly and be ready for you to fill with ice cream or fruit.

custards & puddings

In their purest form, custards and puddings are simply sweetened egg and milk mixtures. Their procedure is virtually foolproof if you stir patiently over the proper heat. Served alone or combined with fruit and cake into trifles and parfaits, custards and puddings are classic comfort food.

Many of these recipes are thickened with flour or cornstarch; usually eggs contribute to the thickening also. Most require frequent, if not constant, stirring to ensure a smooth base. Avoid using high heat or overcooking the mixture because this can cause the custard to curdle.

It's important to acclimate eggs slowly to a heated mixture. This procedure is called *tempering*. To temper beaten eggs into a hot mixture, stir a small amount of the heated mixture into beaten eggs, and then slowly add it all back to the original heated mixture, continuing to gently stir constantly to maintain a smooth texture.

If you end up with curdled bits of egg in your custard, strain the custard to remove the egg or place the custard over a bowl of ice water and whisk to remove lumps.

Shown on previous page: Peach-Pecan Ice Cream (page 210).

As thickened puddings cool, they sometimes form a thin "skin" across the top. You can prevent this skin from forming by placing a piece of plastic wrap directly on top of a hot pudding. Once pudding has cooled, remove the covering, and spoon the pudding into dessert dishes.

family favorite • low calorie • low fat
make ahead

Stirred Custard

prep: 10 min.   other: 2 hrs.

3   cups milk
2   large eggs
⅔   cup sugar
1½ tablespoons all-purpose flour
1   teaspoon vanilla extract

Cook milk in a heavy saucepan over medium heat, stirring often, until heated. Beat eggs at medium speed with an electric mixer until frothy. Add sugar and flour, beating until thickened. Gradually stir in about 1 cup hot milk; add to remaining hot milk, stirring constantly. Cook over low heat, stirring occasionally, until custard coats a spoon (about 10 minutes). Remove from heat; stir in vanilla. Chill 2 hours. Yield: 3½ cups.

Per ½ cup: Calories 165 (26% from fat); Fat 4.8g (sat 2.4g, mono 1.4g, poly 0.4g); Protein 5.3g; Carb 25.2g; Fiber 0.1g; Chol 71mg; Iron 0.4mg; Sodium 62mg; Calc 126mg

family favorite • make ahead

Vanilla Pudding

prep: 10 min.   cook: 22 min.   other: 2 hrs.

½   cup sugar
3   tablespoons cornstarch
½   teaspoon salt
4   egg yolks
3   cups milk
2   tablespoons butter or margarine
2   teaspoons vanilla extract

Bring first 5 ingredients to a boil in a heavy saucepan over medium heat (about 20 minutes), whisking constantly; boil, whisking constantly, 1 minute or until thickened. Remove from heat.
Stir in butter and vanilla. Place plastic wrap directly on surface of custard (to keep "skin" from forming); chill 2 hours. Yield: 4 cups.

Per cup: Calories 339 (42% from fat); Fat 16g (sat 8.6g, mono 4.9g, poly 1.3g); Protein 8.6g; Carb 39.6g; Fiber 0.1g; Chol 238mg; Iron 0.6mg; Sodium 413mg; Calc 231mg

Sabayon

prep: 9 min.   cook: 10 min.

Sabayon is a French cooked custard with a splash of Marsala, a sweet fortified wine. The custard makes a beautiful dessert when drizzled over fresh berries.

15   egg yolks
½   cup sugar
3   to 4 tablespoons sweet Marsala
2   cups fresh raspberries
2   cups fresh blueberries
2   cups fresh blackberries
1   cup sweetened whipped cream

Beat egg yolks in top of a double boiler at high speed with a handheld electric mixer 5 minutes; add sugar, 1 tablespoon at a time, beating until yolks are thick and pale. Gradually add Marsala, beating well.
Bring water to a boil in bottom of double boiler. Place egg yolk mixture over water, and cook, stirring constantly with a wire whisk, 10 minutes or until mixture reaches 160°. Remove from heat, and place top of double boiler in a large bowl of ice water, stirring until mixture is cold.
Toss berries in a bowl. Arrange berries in wine glasses or other serving dishes; immediately spoon sauce over fruit. Dollop with whipped cream. Yield: 10 servings.

Per serving: Calories 210 (47% from fat); Fat 11g (sat 4.8g, mono 4.2g, poly 1.4g); Protein 4.9g; Carb 22.8g; Fiber 3.8g; Chol 323mg; Iron 1.1mg; Sodium 17mg; Calc 57mg

cooking custard

When cooking custards and puddings in a saucepan, stir with a gentle figure 8 motion. This helps to ensure a smooth sauce with no lumps. Don't stir too vigorously, though, or you'll break down the thickening.

make ahead

Pots de Crème

prep: 6 min.   cook: 24 min.   other: 4 hrs.

Using premium chocolate helps ensure the velvety texture of this decadent dessert.

2   cups half-and-half
½   cup sugar
2   large eggs, lightly beaten
1   tablespoon instant espresso granules
¼   cup unsweetened cocoa
¼   cup brandy
8   ounces semisweet chocolate, chopped

Whisk together first 6 ingredients in top of a double boiler; add chocolate. Bring water to a boil. Reduce heat to medium-low; cook, whisking constantly, 24 minutes or until mixture reaches 160° (mixture will be moderately thickened).
Remove from heat. Spoon chocolate mixture into ramekins, demitasse cups, or chocolate pots. Cover and chill at least 4 hours. Yield: 8 servings.

Per serving: Calories 296 (52% from fat); Fat 17g (sat 9.9g, mono 5.4g, poly 0.7g); Protein 5.1g; Carb 34.7g; Fiber 2.6g; Chol 75mg; Iron 1.6mg; Sodium 46mg; Calc 83mg

low calorie • low fat • make ahead

Caramel Custard

prep: 30 min.   cook: 1 hr., 10 min.   other: 3 hrs.

This classic custard is one of life's simple indulgences. You can also make it in a 9-inch cakepan. Just caramelize sugar in cakepan instead of saucepan.

1½   cups sugar, divided
3   large eggs
2   egg yolks
2½   cups warm milk
1   tablespoon vanilla extract

Place 1 cup sugar in a heavy saucepan; cook over medium heat 10 minutes or until sugar caramelizes, stirring occasionally. Remove from heat. Pour evenly into 8 (4-ounce) custard cups.
Whisk together eggs, egg yolks, and remaining ½ cup sugar until blended. Gradually add warm milk, whisking constantly; stir in vanilla.
Pour mixture into prepared custard cups.

custard dictionary

Baked Custard: This is the simplest of the custard desserts; it uses the highest ratio of milk to eggs. Unlike many of its rich custard cousins, this one's not unmolded before serving.

Crème Brûlée: Served in ramekins, it's a thick creamy custard beneath a thin sheet of sugar crust. The sugar is caramelized (or burnt) under extremely high heat, like a broiler, just before serving. Compared to crème caramel or flan, crème brûlée is a richer custard because it usually contains heavy cream and numerous egg yolks.

Crème Caramel: This fairly light custard is typically made with milk; egg yolks are added for richness. It's baked in a metal mold lined with caramelized sugar. You unmold it for serving, and the caramel drips out of the mold and becomes a sauce.

Flan: The custard of choice in Spain, flan is similar to crème caramel; it bakes in a caramel-lined mold and is turned out before serving. Flan, though, is richer than crème caramel because the custard is made with more eggs and yolks as well as half-and-half, evaporated milk, or sweetened condensed milk.

Pots de Crème: A French custard whose name means "pot of cream." This very rich, velvety custard laden with egg yolks is often flavored with chocolate and traditionally served in little lidded porcelain cups.

Stirred Custard: Very soft and fluid, stirred custard is almost sauce consistency. It will thicken slightly as it cools, but remains fluid enough to pour.

Cover each with aluminum foil; place in a 13- x 9-inch pan. Add hot water to pan to a depth of ¼ to ½ inch.
Bake at 325° for 1 hour and 10 minutes or until a knife inserted in center comes out clean. Remove custard cups from water; uncover. Cool in cups on a wire rack. Cover and chill 3 hours.
Run a knife around edge of custard to loosen; invert each onto a dessert plate. Yield: 8 servings.

Per serving: Calories 236 (21% from fat); Fat 5.4g (sat 2.4g, mono 1.8g, poly 0.6g); Protein 5.5g; Carb 41.4g; Fiber 0g; Chol 138mg; Iron 0.5mg; Sodium 59mg; Calc 102mg

Black-and-White Crème Brûlée

prep: 10 min.   cook: 1 hr., 10 min.
other: 8 hrs., 5 min.

Crème brûlée sounds fancy, but it's really a simple custard with a crunchy sugar top. In this version, chocolate adds an extra layer of flavor. If you're entertaining friends, get a kitchen torch and let them brûlée their own dessert.

2½ cups whipping cream, divided
1 cup semisweet chocolate morsels
5 egg yolks
½ cup granulated sugar
1 tablespoon vanilla extract
6 tablespoons light brown sugar

Heat ½ cup whipping cream and chocolate morsels in a saucepan over low heat, stirring until chocolate melts. Cool slightly. Pour mixture evenly into 6 (6-ounce) ramekins. Set aside.

Whisk together remaining 2 cups whipping cream, egg yolks, ½ cup granulated sugar, and vanilla until sugar dissolves and mixture is smooth. Pour evenly into prepared baking dishes; place dishes in a 13- x 9-inch pan. Add hot water to pan to a depth of ½ inch.

Bake at 275° for 1 hour and 10 minutes or until almost set. Cool custards in water in

Black-and-White
Crème Brûlée

For a water bath, add hot water to roasting pan to depth specified in recipe.

pan on a wire rack. Remove custards from pan; cover and chill at least 8 hours.

Sprinkle 1 tablespoon brown sugar over each custard; place custards in pan.

Broil 5½ inches from heat until sugar melts. Let stand 5 minutes to allow sugar to harden. Yield: 6 servings.

Per serving: Calories 617 (66% from fat); Fat 45.4g (sat 26.3g, mono 14.4g, poly 1.7g); Protein 3.4g; Carb 50.6g; Fiber 1.7g; Chol 304mg; Iron 1.4mg; Sodium 47mg; Calc104mg

Piña Colada Crème Brûlée

prep: 10 min.   cook: 1 hr., 2 min.
other: 8 hrs., 50 min.

1 (8-ounce) can crushed pineapple
1 cup whipping cream
1 cup coconut milk
8 egg yolks
⅓ cup sugar
¼ cup coconut rum*
1 teaspoon vanilla extract
6 teaspoons sugar
½ cup sweetened flaked coconut, toasted

Drain pineapple, and pat dry with paper towels.

Stir together pineapple, whipping cream, and next 5 ingredients. Pour mixture evenly into 6 (6-ounce or ¾-cup) ramekins; place ramekins in a large roasting pan. Add hot water to pan to a depth of ½ inch.

Bake at 300° for 50 to 55 minutes or until almost set. Cool 30 to 45 minutes in water in pan on a wire rack. Remove ramekins from pan; cover and chill at least 8 hours.

Sprinkle 1 teaspoon sugar evenly over each custard, and place ramekins in pan.

Broil 5½ inches from heat 7 minutes or until sugar melts. Let custard stand 5 minutes to allow sugar to harden. Sprinkle coconut evenly over each custard. Yield: 6 servings.

Per serving: Calories 395 (67% from fat); Fat 29.3g (sat 19g, mono 7g, poly 1.4g); Protein 4.6g; Carb 26.7g; Fiber 1g; Chol 326mg; Iron 2mg; Sodium 45mg; Calc 68mg

Note: Make a second batch (rather than double the recipe) for a larger crowd.

*Substitute 1 teaspoon coconut extract for coconut rum, if desired.

Pineapple Flan

prep: 12 min.   cook: 1 hr.,10 min.   other: 8 hrs.

- ½ cup sugar
- 1 (14-ounce) can sweetened condensed milk
- 1 cup whipping cream
- ½ cup pineapple juice
- 3 large eggs
- 3 egg yolks
- 1 teaspoon vanilla extract
- 1 cup finely chopped fresh pineapple

Sprinkle sugar in an 8-inch round cakepan; place over medium heat, and cook, shaking pan constantly, until sugar melts and turns a light golden brown. Remove from heat.
Process condensed milk and next 5 ingredients in a blender until smooth, stopping to scrape down sides; stir in pineapple. Pour custard over caramelized sugar in pan. Cover with aluminum foil; place in a roasting pan. Add hot water to roasting pan to a depth of 1 inch.
Bake at 350° for 1 hour and 10 minutes or just until barely set. Remove cakepan from water, and uncover; cool flan completely in cakepan on a wire rack. Cover and chill at least 8 hours.
Run a knife around edge of flan to loosen; invert onto a serving plate. Cut into wedges to serve. Yield: 6 servings.

Per serving: Calories 503 (45% from fat); Fat 25.2g (sat 14.3g, mono 7.8g, poly 1.5g); Protein 10.7g; Carb 60.5g; Fiber 0.4g; Chol 285mg; Iron 1mg; Sodium 139mg; Calc 245mg

Coco Loco Custard

prep: 30 min.   cook: 1hr., 10 min.   other: 3 hrs.

- 1½ cups sugar, divided
- ½ cup water
- 3 large eggs
- 2 egg yolks
- 2½ cups warm milk
- ½ cup sweetened flaked coconut, toasted
- 2 tablespoons dark rum
- 1 tablespoon vanilla extract

Combine 1 cup sugar and ½ cup water in a 9-inch cakepan; cook over low heat 10 minutes or until sugar caramelizes, tipping pan to cover bottom evenly.

Whisk together eggs, yolks, and remaining ½ cup sugar until blended. Gradually add milk, whisking constantly; stir in coconut, rum, and vanilla.
Pour mixture into prepared pan. Cover with foil; place on a jelly-roll pan. Add hot water to jelly-roll pan to a depth of ¼ to ½ inch.
Bake at 325° for 1 hour and 10 minutes or until a knife inserted in center comes out clean. Remove from water, and uncover; cool in cakepan on a wire rack. Cover and chill 3 hours.
Run a knife around edge of custard to loosen; invert onto a serving plate. Yield: 8 servings.

Per serving: Calories 262 (24% from fat); Fat 6.9g (sat 3.7g, mono 1.9g, poly 0.6g); Protein 5.6g; Carb 43.6g; Fiber 0.2g; Chol 138mg; Iron 0.6mg; Sodium 71mg; Calc 103mg

Note: Substitute 8 (4-ounce) custard cups for cakepan, if desired. Caramelize sugar in a heavy saucepan instead of cakepan.

Creamy Rice Pudding

prep: 5 min.   cook: 43 min.

There's no need to save this comfort food for dessert—try it for brunch, too.

- 1 quart milk
- 1 cup uncooked medium-grain rice
- ½ teaspoon salt
- 1½ teaspoons vanilla extract
- 4 egg yolks, beaten
- ½ cup sugar
- ½ cup half-and-half
- 1 teaspoon ground cinnamon
- 1 cup raisins

Combine first 4 ingredients in a medium saucepan. Cover and cook over low heat about 40 minutes or until rice is tender, stirring occasionally.
Combine egg yolks and next 3 ingredients in a small bowl. Gradually stir about one-fourth of hot mixture into yolk mixture; add yolk mixture to remaining hot mixture.
Cook over low heat, stirring constantly, until mixture reaches 160° and is thickened and bubbly (about 3 minutes). Stir in raisins. Serve warm or chilled. Yield: 10 servings.

Per serving: Calories 249 (23% from fat); Fat 6.5g (sat 3.4g, mono 2g, poly 0.6g); Protein 6.3g; Carb 42g; Fiber 1g; Chol 96mg; Iron 1.2mg; Sodium 166mg; Calc 153mg

English Rice Pudding

prep: 5 min.   cook: 1 hr.

- 3 cups cooked long-grain rice
- 2 cups hot milk
- 2 cups hot whipping cream
- 4 large eggs, lightly beaten
- 1½ cups sugar
- 1 cup raisins
- 1 teaspoon vanilla extract
- ¼ teaspoon salt
- 2 tablespoons butter or margarine, cut into pieces
- ¼ teaspoon ground nutmeg
- Lemon Sauce

Stir together first 8 ingredients until thoroughly blended. Pour into a greased 13- x 9-inch baking dish; dot with butter, and sprinkle evenly with nutmeg. Place dish in a large pan; add hot water to a depth of 1 inch.
Bake at 350° for 1 hour or until lightly browned and set. Cool slightly, and cut into squares. Serve with Lemon Sauce. Yield: 16 servings.

Per serving and 1½ tablespoons sauce: Calories 324 (40% from fat); Fat 14.5g (sat 8.3g, mono 4.3g, poly 0.6g); Protein 3.7g; Carb 45.5g; Fiber 0.6g; Chol 102mg; Iron 0.8mg; Sodium 112mg; Calc 75mg

Lemon Sauce

prep: 5 min.   cook: 5 min.

- 1 cup water
- ½ cup sugar
- 2 tablespoons cornstarch
- ⅛ teaspoon salt
- 1 tablespoon butter or margarine
- 1 tablespoon grated lemon zest
- ½ cup fresh lemon juice

Stir together first 4 ingredients in a small saucepan until smooth. Cook, stirring constantly, over medium heat 5 minutes or until thickened. Remove from heat, and stir in butter, zest, and lemon juice. Serve warm or cold. Yield: 1½ cups.

Per tablespoon: Calories 24 (19% from fat); Fat 0.5g (sat 0.3g, mono 0.1g, poly 0g); Protein 0g; Carb 5.3g; Fiber 0.1g; Chol 1mg; Iron 0mg; Sodium 16mg; Calc 1mg

Banana Pudding

Chocolate Cookie Pudding

prep: 15 min.   other: 5 min.

1   (5.9-ounce) package chocolate instant
    pudding mix
2   cups milk
1   (3-ounce) package cream cheese,
    softened
1   (8-ounce) container frozen whipped
    topping, thawed
16 double-stuffed cream-filled chocolate
    sandwich cookies, crushed (about 2 cups)
¾   cup chopped pecans, toasted

Whisk together pudding mix and milk for
2 minutes. Cover and chill 5 minutes.
Stir together cream cheese and whipped
topping, blending well.
Place 1 cup crushed cookies in a 2-quart
bowl. Spread half of cream cheese mixture
over crushed cookies; sprinkle with half of
pecans. Spread all of pudding over top;
spread remaining cream cheese mixture
over pudding. Sprinkle with remaining
cookies and pecans. Chill. Yield: 8 servings.

Per serving: Calories 448 (52% from fat); Fat 25.8g (sat 10.5g, mono 10.8g, poly 3.5g);
Protein 5.3g; Carb 49.2g; Fiber 2.8g; Chol 18mg; Iron 1.8mg; Sodium 490mg; Calc 88mg

Blueberry Bread Pudding

prep: 15 min.   cook: 1 hr.
other: 8 hrs., 5 min.

1   (16-ounce) French bread loaf, cubed
1   (8-ounce) package cream cheese, cut up
3   cups fresh blueberries, divided
6   large eggs
4   cups milk
½   cup sugar
¼   cup butter or margarine, melted
¼   cup maple syrup
1   (10-ounce) jar blueberry preserves
Garnishes: fresh mint leaves, edible pansies

Arrange half of bread cubes in a lightly
greased 13- x 9-inch pan. Sprinkle evenly
with cream cheese and 1 cup blueberries;
top with remaining bread cubes.
Whisk together eggs, milk, sugar, butter,
and maple syrup; pour over bread mixture,
pressing bread cubes to absorb egg mixture.
Cover and chill 8 hours.

Banana Pudding

prep: 21 min.   cook: 35 min.

*Banana Pudding just might be the ultimate
comfort food.*

3½ tablespoons all-purpose flour
1⅓ cups sugar
Dash of salt
3   large eggs, separated
3   cups milk
1   teaspoon vanilla extract
1   (12-ounce) package vanilla wafers
6   medium bananas
6   tablespoons sugar
1   teaspoon vanilla extract

Combine first 3 ingredients in a heavy
saucepan. Beat egg yolks; combine egg yolks
and milk, stirring well. Stir into dry ingredients; cook over medium heat, stirring constantly, until smooth and thickened. Remove
from heat; stir in 1 teaspoon vanilla.
Layer one-third of wafers in a 3-quart
baking dish. Slice 2 bananas, and layer over
wafers. Pour one-third of custard over
bananas. Repeat layers twice.
Beat egg whites at high speed with an electric mixer until foamy. Gradually add ¼ cup
plus 2 tablespoons sugar, 1 tablespoon at a
time, beating until stiff peaks form. Add
1 teaspoon vanilla, and beat until blended.
Spread meringue over custard, sealing
to edge of dish. Bake at 325° for 25 to
30 minutes or until golden. Yield: 8 servings.

Per serving: Calories 532 (19% from fat); Fat 11.5g (sat 3.6g, mono 3.5g, poly 0.5g);
Protein 7.7g; Carb 103.3g; Fiber 4.4g; Chol 95mg; Iron 2.2mg; Sodium 214mg; Calc 141mg

Bake, covered, at 350° for 30 minutes. Uncover and bake 30 more minutes or until lightly browned and set. Let stand 5 minutes before serving.

Stir together remaining 2 cups blueberries and blueberry preserves in a saucepan over low heat until warm. Serve blueberry mixture over bread pudding. Garnish, if desired. Yield: 8 servings.

Per serving: Calories 628 (36% from fat); Fat 25.3g (sat 13.6g, mono 7.4g, poly 1.8g); Protein 16.2g; Carb 86.1g; Fiber 3g; Chol 217mg; Iron 2.8mg; Sodium 572mg; Calc 235mg

entertaining • weekend chef

Chocolate Bread Pudding

prep: 30 min.   cook: 1 hr.
other: 1 hr., 5 min.

1   cup heavy whipping cream
1   (8-ounce) package semisweet chocolate, coarsely chopped
⅔   cup sugar
½   cup unsalted butter, melted
5   large eggs
1   tablespoon vanilla extract
2   cups heavy whipping cream
½   cup milk
1   pound ciabatta loaf or French bread, cut into 1-inch chunks
Custard Sauce

Bring 1 cup whipping cream to a simmer in a small saucepan. Remove from heat; cool 5 minutes.

Process chocolate in a food processor 15 to 20 seconds or until finely chopped. With processor running, slowly add warm cream; process until smooth. Add sugar and butter. Add eggs, 1 at a time; process until smooth. Add vanilla, and process until blended; pour mixture into a large bowl. Stir in 2 cups whipping cream and milk.

Combine bread cubes and chocolate mixture, stirring until blended. Spoon into a lightly greased 13- x 9-inch baking dish. Let stand 1 hour, gently pressing bread into custard with the back of a spoon.

Bake at 350° for 55 minutes to 1 hour or until a knife inserted in center comes out clean. Serve warm with Custard Sauce. Yield: 8 servings.

Per serving and ¼ cup sauce: Calories 981 (60% from fat); Fat 65.4g (sat 37.2g, mono 19.8g, poly 4.3g); Protein 16.5g; Carb 86.5g; Fiber 3.2g; Chol 446mg; Iron 3.5mg; Sodium 450mg; Calc 234mg

Custard Sauce

prep: 10 min.   cook: 20 min.

This sauce can be prepared a day ahead and chilled.

6   egg yolks
⅔   cup sugar, divided
2   cups milk
1   tablespoon brandy
1   teaspoon vanilla extract

Whisk together egg yolks and ⅓ cup sugar in a large bowl 1 minute or until blended.

Bring milk and remaining ⅓ cup sugar to a boil in a heavy saucepan, whisking constantly. Stir about one-fourth of hot milk mixture gradually into yolks; add to remaining hot mixture, stirring constantly.

Cook over medium-low heat, stirring constantly, 20 minutes or until custard is thick enough to coat the back of a spoon. Remove from heat. Pour custard through a fine wire-mesh strainer into a bowl. Stir in brandy and vanilla. Chill, if desired. Yield: 2 cups.

Per tablespoon: Calories 36 (33% from fat); Fat 1.3g (sat 0.6g, mono 0.5g, poly 0.2g); Protein 1g; Carb 5g; Fiber 0g; Chol 40mg; Iron 0.1mg; Sodium 8mg; Calc 21mg

Chocolate Bread Pudding

the classic trifle

Trifle is a classic dessert from Victorian England made of layers of sherry-moistened cake cubes or ladyfingers, fresh berries, jam or preserves, and rich custard. The top is crowned with whipped cream. Trifle recipes have evolved using different liqueurs as well as cake and fruit layers.

make ahead

Strawberry-Sugar Biscuit Trifle

prep: 35 min.   other: 4 hrs.

When prepping for this recipe, make the custard first; then bake the biscuits, and prepare the fruit.

Trifle Custard
Sugar Biscuits
6   tablespoons orange liqueur or orange juice, divided
2½ pounds strawberries, halved
1½ cups whipping cream
¼   cup plus 2 tablespoons powdered sugar
Garnishes: fresh strawberries, fresh mint leaves

Prepare Trifle Custard.
Bake Sugar Biscuits.
Cut Sugar Biscuits in half; brush cut sides evenly with 5 tablespoons orange liqueur. **Line** bottom of a 4-quart bowl or trifle bowl with 8 Sugar Biscuit halves. Arrange strawberry halves around lower edge of bowl. Spoon one-third of Trifle Custard evenly over Sugar Biscuit halves; top with one-third of remaining strawberry halves. Repeat layers twice, ending with strawberry layer. Drizzle remaining orange liqueur evenly over top. Cover and chill 3 to 4 hours. **Beat** whipping cream until foamy; gradually add powdered sugar, beating until soft peaks form. Spread over trifle; serve immediately. Garnish, if desired. Yield: 12 servings.

Per serving: Calories 538 (46% from fat); Fat 27.2g (sat 11.8g, mono 9.3g, poly 4.2g); Protein 7.4g; Carb 65.2g; Fiber 2.5g; Chol 163mg; Iron 2.4mg; Sodium 584mg; Calc 156mg

Trifle Custard

prep: 5 min.   cook: 8 min.   other: 2 hrs.

1   cup sugar
⅓   cup cornstarch
6   egg yolks
2   cups milk
1¾   cups half-and-half
1   teaspoon vanilla extract

Whisk together all ingredients in a heavy saucepan. Bring to a boil over medium heat, whisking constantly, 1 minute or until thickened. Remove from heat. Place pan in ice water; whisk occasionally until cool. Chill completely, about 2 hours. Yield: 4 cups.

Per ½ cup: Calories 264 (39% from fat); Fat 11.3g (sat 6.1g, mono 3.7g, poly 0.9g); Protein 5.5g; Carb 35.4g; Fiber 0.1g; Chol 179mg; Iron 0.5mg; Sodium 52mg; Calc 141mg

Sugar Biscuits

prep: 10 min.   cook: 20 min.

1   (12-count) package frozen buttermilk biscuits
2   tablespoons whipping cream
1   tablespoon sugar
¼   teaspoon ground cinnamon

Brush tops of frozen biscuits with whipping cream; sprinkle with sugar and cinnamon. Place on a lightly greased baking sheet. Bake at 350° for 20 minutes. Cool. Yield: 1 dozen.

Per biscuit: Calories 199 (42% from fat); Fat 9.3g (sat 1.8g, mono 3.8g, poly 3.2g); Protein 3.2g; Carb 26g; Fiber 0.7g; Chol 4mg; Iron 1.7mg; Sodium 537mg; Calc 27mg

make ahead

Jumbleberry Trifle

prep: 45 min.   other: 50 min.

1   (10-ounce) package frozen unsweetened raspberries, thawed
1   (18-ounce) jar seedless blackberry jam or preserves, divided
1   (10.75-ounce) frozen pound cake, thawed
2   tablespoons cream sherry
1½   cups whipping cream
1   (10-ounce) jar lemon curd
Garnishes: whipped cream, fresh berries

Stir together 1 package raspberries and 1 cup jam. Press mixture through a wire-mesh strainer into a bowl; discard seeds. Cover sauce, and chill 20 minutes.

Cut pound cake into ¼-inch-thick slices. Spread remaining jam on 1 side of half of slices; top with remaining slices. Cut sandwiches into ½-inch cubes; drizzle with sherry, and set aside.
Beat whipping cream and lemon curd at low speed with an electric mixer until blended. Gradually increase mixer speed, beating until medium peaks form. Cover and chill 30 minutes.
Spoon 1 tablespoon berry sauce into 8 large wine glasses; top with about ¼ cup each of cake cubes and lemon curd mixture. Repeat layers once, ending with berry sauce. Serve immediately, or chill until ready to serve. Garnish, if desired. Yield: 8 servings.

Per serving: Calories 602 (37% from fat); Fat 24.8g (sat 13.9g, mono 9.7g, poly 2.4g); Protein 2.3g; Carb 90.7g; Fiber 0.8g; Chol 142mg; Iron 0.7mg; Sodium 190mg; Calc 43mg

Georgia Peach Trifle

prep: 15 min.   other: 2 hrs., 5 min.

1   (3.4-ounce) package vanilla instant pudding mix
2   cups milk
6   large fresh peaches, peeled and sliced
3   tablespoons granulated sugar
½   (20-ounce) package pound cake
⅓   cup bourbon
1   cup whipping cream
2   tablespoons powdered sugar
½   cup sliced almonds, toasted

Prepare pudding mix according to package directions, using 2 cups milk. Cover and chill 5 minutes.
Toss sliced peaches with granulated sugar.
Cut pound cake into ½-inch slices. Place half of cake slices on bottom of a trifle dish or deep bowl; drizzle evenly with half of bourbon. Spoon half of peach mixture evenly over cake slices. Spread half of pudding over peaches. Repeat with remaining cake slices, bourbon, peach mixture, and pudding. Cover and chill at least 2 hours.
Beat whipping cream in a medium bowl at medium speed with an electric mixer until foamy; gradually add powdered sugar, beating until soft peaks form. Spread whipped cream over trifle; sprinkle with almonds. Yield: 8 servings.

Per serving: Calories 451 (43% from fat); Fat 21.7g (sat 9.1g, mono 9g, poly 2g); Protein 6.1g; Carb 54.2g; Fiber 2.7g; Chol 67mg; Iron 1.2mg; Sodium 355mg; Calc 137mg

Tiramisù

prep: 37 min.   cook: 8 min.   other: 8 hrs.

This popular Italian dessert that means "pick-me-up" has a coffee- and alcohol-soaked cake layer, sweetened cream cheese, and grated chocolate. Look for ladyfingers in the bakery section of the store.

6   egg yolks
1¼   cups sugar
1¼   cups mascarpone cheese*
1¾   cups whipping cream
½   cup water
2   teaspoons instant coffee granules
¼   cup brandy

2   (3-ounce) packages ladyfingers, split
½   cup whipping cream, whipped
1   teaspoon grated unsweetened chocolate

Combine yolks and sugar in top of a double boiler; beat at medium speed with a hand-held mixer until thick and pale. Bring water to a boil in bottom of double boiler; reduce heat to low, and cook, stirring constantly, 8 minutes or until mixture reaches 160°. Remove from heat. Add mascarpone; beat until smooth.
Beat 1¾ cups whipping cream at medium speed until soft peaks form; fold into cheese mixture. Combine ½ cup water, coffee granules, and brandy; brush cut side of ladyfingers with ½ cup coffee mixture.

Line sides and bottom of a 3-quart trifle bowl with 36 ladyfingers, cut sides in; pour in half of filling mixture. Layer remaining ladyfingers on top; drizzle with remaining ¼ cup coffee mixture. Cover with remaining filling. Garnish with whipped cream and grated chocolate. Cover and chill 8 hours. Yield: 12 servings.

Per serving: Calories 415 (62% from fat); Fat 28.7g (sat 15.9g, mono 8.8g, poly 1.2g); Protein 3.8g; Carb 33.8g; Fiber 0.1g; Chol 207mg; Iron 0.8mg; Sodium 68mg; Calc 78mg

*As a substitute for mascarpone cheese, combine 2 (8-ounce) packages cream cheese, softened, ⅓ cup sour cream, and ¼ cup whipping cream; beat well. Use 1¼ cups mixture for recipe, reserving remainder for other uses.

mousses, soufflés & gelatin desserts

Light and lofty desserts such as these get their lift from whipped cream or egg whites folded into them. Make one of these popular "chill-until-set" desserts ahead, and store it in the refrigerator until serving time. The texture of these shapely desserts is similar, but each has distinguishing characteristics.

Mousse is a French term for "froth." Any dessert that has a foamy, frothy texture can actually be called a mousse. Its consistency is light because of the air incorporated into it. Traditionally, uncooked beaten egg whites were the common ingredient that gave a mousse its volume, but in order to keep up with current egg safety standards, we switched to cooked, beaten egg whites or whipped cream.

Soufflés are similar in consistency but usually lighter in texture than mousses. They always have fluffy beaten egg whites and sometimes contain whipped cream, too. Savory dinner soufflés are usually baked, whereas dessert soufflés can be baked or just chilled. When they're not baked, soufflés typically contain sweetened cooked egg whites referred to as Italian meringue and gelatin. Soufflés have a reputation for being hard to make when, in fact, if you follow directions for beating egg whites properly, they can be one of the simplest dessert offerings you can stir together.

Unflavored gelatin enables chilled, molded dessert soufflés to hold their shape. The key to working with gelatin is first to soften it in a liquid before completely dissolving it over heat.

Chocolate Mousse

prep: 10 min.   other: 2 hrs., 5 min.

1   (12-ounce) package semisweet chocolate morsels
2½   cups whipping cream, divided
1   teaspoon vanilla extract
1   tablespoon rum
Garnishes: whipped cream, grated chocolate

Microwave morsels and ½ cup cream in a glass bowl at HIGH 1½ minutes or until melted, stirring twice. Stir in vanilla and rum, blending well. Cool 5 minutes.
Beat remaining 2 cups cream at medium speed with an electric mixer until soft peaks form; fold cream into chocolate mixture. Cover and chill 2 hours.
Pipe or spoon into a serving bowl or dessert dishes. Garnish, if desired. Yield: 6 servings.

Per serving: Calories 612 (74% from fat); Fat 50.3g (sat 30.1g, mono 15.7g, poly 1.4g); Protein 2.4g; Carb 42.5g; Fiber 3.4g; Chol 133mg; Iron 1.8mg; Sodium 40mg; Calc 87mg

White Chocolate Mousse

prep: 3½ min.   other: 15 min.

2   (4-ounce) packages white chocolate bars, chopped
1   cup whipping cream

Microwave white chocolate and whipping cream in a 2-quart microwave-safe bowl at MEDIUM (50% power) 3½ minutes (do not boil). Whisk until mixture is smooth.
Place bowl in a pan of ice water; let stand 10 to 15 minutes or until very cold, stirring often. Remove from ice water, and beat at medium speed with an electric mixer just until soft peaks form. Cover and chill until serving time. Yield: 4 servings.

Per serving: Calories 524 (66% from fat); Fat 38.2g (sat 24.2g, mono 16.2g, poly 1.6g); Protein 4.1g; Carb 36.4g; Fiber 0g; Chol 100mg; Iron 0mg; Sodium 81mg; Calc 122mg

container ideas

If you're looking for creative serving dish options for mousses, soufflés, and gelatins, use wine goblets, vintage sherbet glasses, or champagne flutes for an attractive and easy presentation.

chocolate dictionary

Semisweet and bittersweet chocolates: These *real* chocolates contain at least 35% chocolate liquor (the liquor qualifying them as real), and 27% cocoa butter. Because they are sold under a variety of names including semisweet, bittersweet, bitter, special dark, dark sweet, and German sweet, buying them can be confusing. In fact, it's possible that a bittersweet chocolate may taste sweeter than a semisweet. Tasting them is the best way to become familiar with brands of choice.

Milk chocolate: Made of at least 10% chocolate liquor, this *real* chocolate is recognized by its light color. Its most popular form is the candy bar.

Unsweetened chocolate: Including 45% chocolate liquor, the important thing to remember about this *real* chocolate is that it has no sugar or flavoring added —so don't substitute it for bittersweet or semisweet. These chocolates include baking chocolate and bitter chocolate and are used primarily for baking.

Chocolate-flavored products: These contain oil rather than cocoa butter, and aren't real chocolates. An example is chocolate bark coating.

White chocolate: Not a real chocolate, because it doesn't contain chocolate liquor. It's extremely sweet and has a buttery mouthfeel. Because it's rich in fat, white chocolate's quite perishable, so buy it in small amounts.

Unsweetened cocoa:
Nonalkaline cocoa (made by Hershey's) is the most popular cocoa used in the U.S. It's an acidic cocoa with a strong, full flavor. Dutch-processed cocoa is another type available; it's a darker powder with a richer, yet more delicate flavor.

All About Chocolate

What is Bloom? Bloom happens when chocolate becomes too warm or is exposed to too much moisture. Chocolate changes color during storage and it may take on a gray or grainy appearance. Follow our storage tips below to avoid bloom.

Storage Wrap opened chocolate in aluminum foil and then in plastic wrap. Keep chocolate tightly covered in a cool, dry place with low humidity (65° is ideal). In hot weather, you can refrigerate chocolate, but wrap it in foil and seal in a plastic bag so it won't absorb flavors from other foods. When bringing refrigerated chocolate to room temperature, leave it wrapped so moisture doesn't condense on it and cause it to seize (stiffen and become lumpy) when melted.

Shelf Life The shelf life of chocolate is determined by the amount of cocoa butter it contains. Unsweetened, semisweet, and bittersweet, if stored properly, will keep for several years. Milk chocolate should be used within 1 year and white chocolate within 6 months of purchase.

Melting Chocolate can be melted in a heavy pan over low heat on the cooktop or in a microwave-safe container in the microwave oven. Be sure all utensils are dry, because even a little water will cause the chocolate to seize.

To melt in the microwave oven, place 1 cup chocolate pieces or 6 (1-ounce) squares in a microwave-safe measuring cup or large custard cup. Microwave, uncovered, at MEDIUM (50% power) for 2 to 3 minutes or until soft enough to stir smooth; start checking after 1½ minutes.

Top
(dark chocolates):
extra dark chocolate,
dark chocolate, bittersweet chocolate,
semisweet chocolate
Middle (white chocolates): premium white chocolate,
white chocolate baking squares
Bottom: milk chocolate
Foreground left to right: milk chocolate morsels,
classic white morsels, milk chocolate toffee bits, special dark morsels

Separate eggs while cold (it's easiest). A cupped hand makes a great egg separator.

make ahead

Raspberry Mousse

prep: 15 min.   cook: 20 min.
other: 8 hrs., 30 min.

2	(6-ounce) packages fresh raspberries*
1	tablespoon lemon juice
1	tablespoon cold water
1	envelope unflavored gelatin
¾	cup granulated sugar
2	large eggs
2	egg yolks
1	tablespoon raspberry liqueur
1½	cups whipping cream
¼	cup powdered sugar

Process raspberries in a blender or food processor until smooth. Pour through a wire-mesh strainer into a bowl, discarding seeds; set aside. (Pulp and liquid should equal about 1½ cups.)

Stir together lemon juice and 1 tablespoon cold water; sprinkle gelatin over lemon juice mixture. Stir and let stand 1 minute; set aside.

Whisk together 1 cup raspberry puree, granulated sugar, eggs, and egg yolks in top of a double boiler. Bring water to a slight boil in bottom of double boiler; reduce heat to low, and cook, whisking constantly, 20 minutes or until mixture thickens and reaches 160°. Remove pan from heat.

Whisk gelatin mixture into raspberry puree mixture in pan, whisking constantly, 1½ minutes or until blended. Whisk in remaining ½ cup raspberry puree and raspberry liqueur; cover and chill 30 minutes or until consistency of unbeaten egg white.

Beat cream until foamy; gradually add powdered sugar, beating until soft peaks form. Fold in raspberry mixture. Pour into an oiled 6-cup mold; cover and chill 8 hours or until firm. Unmold onto a serving plate. Yield: 8 servings.

Per serving: Calories 317 (50% from fat); Fat 17.7g (sat 9.8g, mono 5.5g, poly 0.9g); Protein 5.8g; Carb 33.1g; Fiber 2.8g; Chol 164mg; Iron 0.7mg; Sodium 42mg; Calc 56mg

*Substitute 1 (10-ounce) package frozen raspberries, thawed, if desired.

family favorite • make ahead

Baked Lemon Pudding

prep: 23 min.   cook: 50 min.   other: 1 hr.

With beaten egg whites folded into the batter, this delicate lemon dessert has a soufflélike finish.

3	large eggs, separated
2	teaspoons grated lemon rind
1½	cups milk
¼	cup fresh lemon juice
2	teaspoons butter, melted
1½	cups sugar, divided
½	cup all-purpose flour
½	teaspoon baking powder
¼	teaspoon salt
Whipped cream	
Garnishes: grated lemon zest, fresh berries	

Beat egg yolks at medium speed with an electric mixer until thick and pale; add lemon rind and next 3 ingredients, beating well.

Combine 1 cup sugar and next 3 ingredients; add to lemon mixture, beating until smooth.

Beat egg whites until soft peaks form; add remaining ½ cup sugar, and beat until blended. Fold into lemon mixture. Pour into a lightly greased 2-quart baking dish. Place baking dish in a large shallow pan. Add hot water to pan to a depth of 1 inch.

Bake at 350° for 50 minutes or just until center is set. Remove baking dish from pan; cool completely on a wire rack. Cover and chill at least 1 hour. Top with whipped cream, and garnish, if desired. Yield: 8 servings.

Per serving: Calories 295 (30% from fat); Fat 9.9g (sat 5.5g, mono 2.9g, poly 0.6g); Protein 5g; Carb 48.1g; Fiber 0.3g; Chol 107mg; Iron 0.8mg; Sodium 160mg; Calc 91mg

entertaining • test kitchen favorite

Grand Marnier Soufflés

prep: 22 min.   cook: 46 min.

Butter	
1	tablespoon sugar
1	cup milk
¼	cup butter
¼	cup all-purpose flour
4	egg yolks
2	tablespoons Grand Marnier or other orange liqueur
¾	cup sugar
2	tablespoons cornstarch
5	egg whites
1	tablespoon sugar
Custard Sauce (page 201)	

Lightly butter 6 (6-ounce) custard cups; coat bottom and sides of cups with 1 tablespoon sugar. Set aside.

Heat milk in a heavy saucepan. Cover and set aside.

Melt ¼ cup butter in a large saucepan over medium heat; add flour, stirring until smooth. Cook, stirring constantly, 1 minute. Gradually stir in warm milk, and cook, stirring constantly, until mixture thickens and begins to leave sides of pan.

Beat egg yolks until thick and pale. Gradually stir about one-fourth of hot mixture into yolks; add to remaining hot mixture, stirring constantly. Stir in Grand Marnier; set aside.

Combine ¾ cup sugar and cornstarch; set aside. Beat egg whites at high speed with an electric mixer until foamy. Slowly add sugar mixture; beat until stiff peaks form and sugar dissolves (4 to 5 minutes). Gradually stir about one-fourth of sauce mixture into egg whites; gently fold into remaining sauce mixture.

Spoon evenly into prepared custard cups. (Cups will be very full, but will firm up during baking and will not overflow.) Sprinkle custards with 1 tablespoon sugar. Place cups in a large shallow pan. Add hot water to pan to a depth of 1 inch.

Bake at 400° for 10 minutes.

Reduce oven temperature to 350°, and bake 20 to 25 minutes or until golden. Remove custard cups from water. Serve immediately with Custard Sauce. Yield: 6 servings.

Per serving and ¼ cup sauce: Calories 475 (44% from fat); Fat 23.7g (sat 13.4g, mono 7.2g, poly 1.5g); Protein 9g; Carb 54.8g; Fiber 0.2g; Chol 276mg; Iron 0.8mg; Sodium 171mg; Calc 124mg

Gingerbread Soufflés With Lemon Cream

prep: 20 min. cook: 30 min. other: 20 min.

Sugaring the cups helps the soufflé batter cling to the cups and rise high.

Butter or margarine
Granulated sugar
¼ cup butter or margarine
¼ cup all-purpose flour
1¼ cups milk
⅔ cup granulated sugar
¼ cup molasses
2 teaspoons ground ginger
1 teaspoon ground cinnamon
¼ teaspoon salt
1 teaspoon vanilla extract
5 large eggs, separated
Garnish: powdered sugar
Lemon Cream

Grease bottom and sides of 8 (6-ounce) custard cups or ramekins evenly with butter. Lightly coat bottom and sides evenly with granulated sugar, shaking out excess. Place cups in a 13- x 9-inch pan. Set aside.
Melt ¼ cup butter in a large saucepan over medium heat; whisk in flour. Cook, whisking constantly, 1 minute. Gradually whisk in milk, whisking constantly until thickened. Remove from heat. Whisk in ⅔ cup granulated sugar and next 5 ingredients.

steps to great soufflés

• Be sure mixing bowl and beaters are grease free. If any fat is present, egg whites won't whip to their maximum volume.
• Separate eggs while cold (it's easiest), but for best volume, let the whites come to room temperature before beating them.
• Beat egg whites until stiff, but not dry. Overbeaten egg whites can cause a soufflé to collapse.
• Be ready to fold the rest of the ingredients together as soon as you beat the egg whites. Stir a small amount of beaten whites into soufflé mixture to lighten it; then gently and quickly fold in remaining whites, being careful not to deflate mixture.

Whisk egg yolks until thick and pale. Gradually stir about one-fourth of hot mixture into yolks; add to remaining hot mixture, stirring constantly. Cook over medium heat 1 minute. Cool 20 minutes.
Beat egg whites at high speed with an electric mixer until soft peaks form. Gradually fold egg whites into custard. Spoon evenly into custard cups.
Bake at 400° for 18 to 20 minutes or until puffed and set. Garnish, if desired. Serve immediately with Lemon Cream. Yield: 8 servings.

Per serving: Calories 386 (55% from fat); Fat 23.9g (sat 13.7g, mono 7g, poly 1.1g); Protein 5.7g; Carb 37.4g; Fiber 0.4g; Chol 201mg; Iron 1.4mg; Sodium 213mg; Calc 110mg

Lemon Cream

prep: 5 min.

1 cup whipping cream
2 tablespoons sugar
1 tablespoon grated lemon rind
1 tablespoon fresh lemon juice

Beat whipping cream at medium speed until foamy; gradually add sugar, rind, and juice, beating until soft peaks form. Yield: 2 cups.

Per tablespoon: Calories 28 (81% from fat); Fat 2.5g (sat 1.5g, mono 0.8g, poly 0.1g); Protein 0g; Carb 1.4g; Fiber 0g; Chol 10mg; Iron 0mg; Sodium 3mg; Calc 5mg

Gingerbread Soufflés
With Lemon Cream

Coffee-and-Cream Chill

prep: 20 min.   cook: 2 min.   other: 4 hrs.

Coffee-flavored gelatin and whipped cream make a pretty presentation layered in parfait glasses.

2   envelopes unflavored gelatin
½   cup cold water
½   cup sugar
1½ cups water
2   tablespoons instant coffee granules
1   cup whipping cream
2   tablespoons sugar
2   tablespoons coffee liqueur
Garnish: grated chocolate

Sprinkle gelatin over ½ cup cold water in a small saucepan; let stand 1 minute.
Cook over low heat, stirring until gelatin dissolves (about 2 minutes).
Stir in ½ cup sugar, 1½ cups water, and coffee granules until dissolved. Pour into a 1-quart bowl. Chill 4 hours or until mixture is firm.
Beat whipping cream at medium speed with an electric mixer until foamy; gradually add 2 tablespoons sugar and coffee liqueur, beating until soft peaks form.
Pull a fork through gelatin to break into small pieces.
Spoon ½ cup gelatin into each of 4 parfait glasses; top evenly with half of whipped cream. Repeat procedure with remaining gelatin and whipped cream. Garnish, if desired. Yield: 4 servings.

Per serving: Calories 365 (49% from fat); Fat 20g (sat 12g, mono 6g, poly 0.5g); Protein 3.2g; Carb 39.9g; Fiber 0g; Chol 80mg; Iron 0.1mg; Sodium 31mg; Calc 48mg

Molded French Cream

prep: 15 min.   cook: 5 min.   other: 4 hrs.

This silky smooth dessert carries a slight tang from sour cream.

2   (8-ounce) containers sour cream
3   cups whipping cream, divided
1½ cups superfine sugar
2   envelopes unflavored gelatin
½   cup cold water
2   (8-ounce) packages cream cheese, softened
2   teaspoons vanilla extract
1   tablespoon superfine sugar
Garnishes: edible violas, fresh mint leaves

Whisk together sour cream and 2 cups whipping cream in a medium saucepan; gradually add 1½ cups sugar, whisking with each addition. Cook over low heat, whisking often, until warm.
Sprinkle gelatin over ½ cup cold water in a saucepan; let stand 1 minute. Cook over medium heat, stirring until gelatin dissolves. Add to sour cream mixture.
Beat cream cheese at medium speed with an electric mixer fitted with a whisk attachment until light and fluffy. Gradually add sour cream mixture and vanilla, beating until smooth.
Pour into a lightly greased 8-cup mold or 2-quart bowl; chill until firm, or, if desired, up to 2 days. Unmold onto a serving platter.
Beat remaining 1 cup whipping cream until foamy; add 1 tablespoon sugar, beating until soft peaks form. Spoon whipped cream into a pastry bag fitted with a star-shaped tip. Pipe whipped cream around base of mold. Garnish, if desired. Yield: 16 servings.

Per serving: Calories 390 (71% from fat); Fat 30.9g (sat 18.9g, mono 9g, poly 1g); Protein 3.8g; Carb 24.6g; Fiber 0g; Chol 104mg; Iron 0.4mg; Sodium 116mg; Calc 87mg

Mocha Charlottes

prep: 20 min.   cook: 5 min.   other: 8 hrs.

For a quick version of this dessert, line dainty cups with ladyfingers, fill with chocolate ice cream, and top with whipped cream.

1   envelope unflavored gelatin
¼   cup cold water
½   cup granulated sugar
2   large eggs
1   cup milk
⅓   cup semisweet chocolate morsels
1½ teaspoons instant coffee granules
2   teaspoons vanilla extract
1½ cups whipping cream, divided
2   (3-ounce) packages ladyfingers, split
3   tablespoons powdered sugar
Garnish: 8 (3-inch) cinnamon sticks

Sprinkle gelatin over ¼ cup cold water; stir and let stand 1 minute. Set gelatin aside.
Beat granulated sugar and eggs at medium speed with an electric mixer 2 to 3 minutes or until thick and pale.
Heat milk in a large saucepan over low heat. Gradually add about one-fourth of milk to egg mixture; add to remaining hot milk, stirring constantly. Cook over low heat, stirring constantly, 4 to 5 minutes or until mixture coats a spoon. Remove from heat; stir in gelatin mixture until gelatin dissolves.
Whisk in chocolate morsels, coffee granules, and vanilla until coffee granules dissolve and chocolate melts.
Pour mixture into a metal bowl; place bowl over ice, and let stand, stirring often, 6 to 8 minutes or until cold and slightly thickened.
Beat 1 cup whipping cream at high speed until soft peaks form, and gradually fold into coffee mixture.
Line each of 8 teacups with 6 ladyfinger halves, placing rounded sides of ladyfingers against edge of each cup. Spoon custard evenly into cups; cover and chill 8 hours.
Beat remaining ½ cup whipping cream and powdered sugar until soft peaks form. Top custards with whipped cream; garnish, if desired. Yield: 8 servings.

Per serving: Calories 359 (49% from fat); Fat 19.9g (sat 11.4g, mono 6.1g, poly 0.8g); Protein 7.1g; Carb 38.1g; Fiber 0.5g; Chol 138mg; Iron 1.1mg; Sodium 105mg; Calc 92mg

ice creams & frozen desserts

Ice cream is a worldwide favorite. Few desserts compare in flavor and texture. Each ingredient in ice cream plays a pivotal role. Fat from cream gives ice cream its smooth texture and mouthfeel. Sugar sweetens it, and eggs add body and help thicken it.

In keeping with today's egg safety standards, eggs must be cooked (and then chilled) for ice cream custards. And there are many easy ice cream recipes that don't contain eggs or a cooked custard.

Before you begin, get acquainted with your ice-cream freezer. Read the manufacturer's instructions carefully. Freezers are made of different materials, and this makes a difference in the recommended ice-salt ratio. Don't skimp on the ice and salt; they're essential for proper freezing. The ice cream freezes because its heat is absorbed by the ice and salt. Ice alone is not cold enough to freeze ice cream. If you use too little salt, the ice won't be cold enough to freeze ice cream. With too much salt, ice cream will freeze too quickly, causing large ice crystals to form. Rock salt is preferred over table salt because rock salt is slower to dissolve.

Fill the freezer container only as full as recommended by the manufacturer. Most

should be filled no more than two-thirds or three-fourths of their capacity. When adding ice and salt, make four fairly thick layers of ice and four thin layers of salt, beginning with ice and ending with salt. Add more ice and salt as the ice melts during the freezing process as well as after ice cream is frozen.

Most ice cream needs to "ripen" or stand an hour or so after freezing and before serving. This allows the ice cream to harden and the flavors to blend. To ripen ice cream, first remove the dasher. Then cover the ice cream with foil, and replace the lid. Pack the freezer bucket with ice and salt, using a higher ratio of salt to ice than was used for freezing. Wrap the top well with a towel or newspaper; let stand in a cool place for an hour or the amount of time recommended. Drain off the salty water; check ice and salt often, adding more if needed. As you serve the ice cream, take care not to let any salt solution get into the ice cream container. Spoon any leftover ice cream into small freezer containers. Cover tightly, and freeze.

To firm up ice cream after it's frozen, lift ice cream dasher and scrape ice cream back into container. Cover ice cream, and let ripen as explained above, right.

freeze it • make ahead
test kitchen favorite

Peanut Butter Ice Cream

prep: 25 min. cook: 7 min. other: 2 hrs.

1   (12-ounce) jar chunky peanut butter
1½ quarts half-and-half
6   large eggs
1   (14-ounce) can sweetened condensed milk
1   cup milk
1   tablespoon vanilla extract
2   cups sugar
2   tablespoons all-purpose flour

Cook peanut butter, 2 cups half-and-half, and eggs in a Dutch oven over low heat, whisking constantly, 7 minutes or until a thermometer registers 160°. Whisk in remaining 4 cups half-and-half, condensed milk, milk, and vanilla.

Combine sugar and flour; whisk into hot mixture until sugar dissolves. Cook just until

slightly thickened. Remove from heat. Cool completely. Cover and chill at least 1 hour.

Pour into freezer container of a 5-quart hand-turned or electric freezer. Freeze according to manufacturer's instructions.

Pack freezer with additional ice and rock salt, and let stand 1 hour before serving. Yield: 1 gallon.

Per cup: Calories 461 (50% from fat); Fat 25.5g (sat 10.4g, mono 9.7g, poly 3.9g); Protein 12.7g; Carb 48.6g; Fiber 1.7g; Chol 123mg; Iron 0.9mg; Sodium 204mg; Calc202mg

freeze it • make ahead

Banana–Coconut Ice Cream

prep: 30 min. cook: 30 min. other: 4 hrs.

Use very ripe bananas for the sweetest flavor.

2   cups sweetened flaked coconut
1   cup sugar
6   egg yolks
4   cups milk
2   cups half-and-half
1   (15-ounce) can cream of coconut
2   teaspoons vanilla extract
3   ripe bananas, mashed
Garnish: toasted sweetened flaked coconut

Bake 2 cups coconut in a shallow pan at 350°, stirring occasionally, 10 minutes or until toasted.

Whisk together sugar, egg yolks, and milk in a heavy saucepan over medium heat; cook, whisking constantly, 20 minutes or until mixture thickens and coats back of a spoon. (Do not boil.)

Remove from heat; whisk in 2 cups toasted coconut, half-and-half, cream of coconut, and vanilla. Fold in banana. Cover and chill 3 hours.

Pour mixture into freezer container of a 1-gallon hand-turned or electric freezer. Freeze according to manufacturer's instructions.

Pack freezer with additional ice and rock salt, and let stand 1 hour before serving. Garnish, if desired. Yield: 2½ quarts.

Per cup: Calories 416 (51% from fat); Fat 23.8g (sat 17.2g, mono 4.1g, poly 1g); Protein 8.1g; Carb 45.5g; Fiber 2.8g; Chol 150mg; Iron 1mg; Sodium 88mg; Calc 176mg

Vanilla Ice Cream

prep: 10 min.   cook: 24 min.   other: 8 hrs.

Make the cooked custard for this old-fashioned favorite recipe a day ahead.

4   cups milk
2¼   cups sugar
¼   cup all-purpose flour
¼   teaspoon salt
6   large eggs, lightly beaten
4   cups half-and-half
1   tablespoon vanilla extract

Whisk together first 4 ingredients in a Dutch oven over medium heat, stirring constantly, 15 to 20 minutes or until mixture thickens and coats a spoon. Do not boil.

frozen desserts dictionary

Granita: An Italian frozen ice; see next entry.
Ice: An ice is a frozen mixture of water, sugar, and another liquid such as coffee, wine, or fruit juice. It's called *granita* in Italy and *granité* in France. The proportion is usually 4 parts liquid to 1 part sugar. During the freezing process, the mixture is stirred occasionally to produce a slightly granular texture. Before serving, most ices are scraped with the tines of a fork to fluff up the crystals. You won't get a firm scoop when serving an ice; just mound it in glasses and serve it right away.
Ice Cream: A creamy, frozen blend of milk products, a sweetener, various flavorings, and sometimes eggs. Fat from cream imparts richness, smoothness, and flavor. Generally, the higher the fat content, the creamier the ice cream.
Sherbet: Sherbet is made much like ice cream but is not as rich and creamy. It's made of sweetened fruit juice, water, and sometimes added milk, cooked and beaten egg white, or gelatin.
Sorbet: Sorbet differs from sherbet because it doesn't contain milk. Sorbet is typically served as a palate cleanser between courses. A sorbet is not as granular in texture as an ice.

Stir about one-fourth of hot milk mixture gradually into eggs; add egg mixture to remaining hot mixture, stirring constantly. Cook 4 minutes; remove from heat. Stir in half-and-half and vanilla; cool completely. Cover and chill at least 8 hours.
Pour into freezer container of a 4-quart hand-turned or electric freezer. Freeze according to manufacturer's instructions. Serve immediately, or remove container from ice-cream freezer, and place in freezer 15 minutes. Transfer to an airtight container, and freeze 2 hours or until firm. Store leftover ice cream in an airtight container. Yield: ½ gallon.

Per cup: Calories 521 (37% from fat); Fat 21.5g (sat 12g, mono 6.4g, poly 1.3g); Protein 12.6g; Carb 70.4g; Fiber 0.1g; Chol 215mg; Iron 1mg; Sodium 223mg; Calc 285mg

Peach-Pecan Ice Cream

prep: 40 min.   cook: 25 min.
other: 1 hr., 47 min.

For best results, make this recipe midsummer when peaches are at their prime. (pictured on page 195)

6   cups mashed ripe peaches (about 2½ pounds)
1   cup sugar
3   large eggs
1½   cups sugar
2   tablespoons all-purpose flour
½   teaspoon salt
4   cups milk
1   cup whipping cream
1   tablespoon vanilla extract
1   cup chopped pecans

Combine peaches and 1 cup sugar; stir well, and set aside.
Beat eggs at medium speed with an electric mixer until frothy. Combine 1½ cups sugar, flour, and salt; stir well. Gradually add sugar mixture to eggs; beat until thickened. Gradually add milk; beat until blended.
Pour custard mixture into a large heavy saucepan.
Cook over medium-low heat, stirring constantly, until mixture thickens and coats the back of a metal spoon (about 25 minutes). Remove from heat, and set pan over a bowl of ice water; stir gently until custard cools.

Stir in peaches, whipping cream, vanilla, and pecans.
Pour mixture into freezer container of a 1-gallon hand-turned or electric freezer. Freeze according to manufacturer's instructions. Pack freezer with additional ice and rock salt, and let ripen 1 hour before serving. Yield: 11 cups.

Per cup: Calories 440 (40% from fat); Fat 19.5g (sat 7.1g, mono 7.9g, poly 3g); Protein 6.5g; Carb 62.3g; Fiber 2.4g; Chol 96mg; Iron 0.9mg; Sodium 168mg; Calc 136mg

Mocha Ice Cream

prep: 20 min.   cook: 20 min.   other: 3 hrs.

1   (8-ounce) package semisweet chocolate squares, coarsely chopped
¼   cup strong brewed coffee
2   cups whipping cream
1   cup half-and-half
¾   cup sugar, divided
3   tablespoons instant coffee granules
4   egg yolks

Microwave chopped chocolate in a 1-quart microwave-safe bowl at HIGH 1½ minutes or until melted, stirring twice; stir in brewed coffee. Set chocolate mixture aside.
Bring whipping cream, half-and-half, ½ cup sugar, and coffee granules to a boil in a heavy saucepan over medium heat, stirring until sugar and coffee dissolve.
Beat egg yolks and remaining ¼ cup sugar at high speed with an electric mixer until thick and pale. With mixer at low speed, gradually pour hot cream mixture into yolk mixture; return to saucepan.
Cook over medium heat, stirring constantly, 6 to 8 minutes or until mixture thickens and coats a spoon. Remove from heat; stir in chocolate mixture. Cover and chill 2 hours.
Pour mixture into freezer container of a 5-quart hand-turned or electric freezer, and freeze according to manufacturer's instructions.
Pack freezer with additional ice and rock salt, and let stand 1 hour before serving. Yield: 5 cups.

Per cup: Calories 763 (65% from fat); Fat 54.7g (sat 32g, mono 17.3g, poly 2g); Protein 5.6g; Carb 68.2g; Fiber 2.7g; Chol 310mg; Iron 1.9mg; Sodium 64mg; Calc151mg

For Rum-Raisin Ice Cream, scrape tiny seeds from vanilla bean into custard, using the tip of a paring knife.

freeze it • make ahead

Rum-Raisin Ice Cream

prep: 20 min.   cook: 15 min.
other: 9 hrs., 30 min.

The raisins in this lavish treat soak up just enough rum flavor.

1¼ cups raisins
½ cup dark rum
3 cups milk
1 vanilla bean
1 cup sugar
9 egg yolks
2 cups whipping cream

Combine raisins and rum in a small bowl; let stand 8 hours.

Cook milk and vanilla bean in a heavy saucepan over medium heat, stirring often, just until steaming. Remove from heat; cover and let stand 20 to 30 minutes. Remove vanilla bean; split in half lengthwise, scraping to remove seeds. Return seeds and pod to milk mixture.

Whisk together sugar and yolks in a bowl until thick and pale. Gradually whisk in hot milk mixture; return to saucepan.

Cook, whisking constantly, over medium-low heat until custard mixture thickens and coats a spoon. (Do not overcook.)

Pour custard mixture through a wire-mesh strainer into a medium bowl, discarding vanilla bean pod and seeds. Place bowl in a larger bowl filled with ice, and stir custard until cool.

Pour raisin mixture through a wire-mesh strainer, discarding rum. Stir raisins and whipping cream into custard. Pour mixture into freezer container of a 5-quart hand-turned or electric freezer. Freeze according to manufacturer's instructions.

Pack freezer with additional ice and rock salt, and let stand 1 hour before serving. Yield: 2 quarts.

Per cup: Calories 488 (52% from fat); Fat 28g (sat 15.5g, mono 9g, poly 1.5g); Protein 6.6g; Carb 51.7g; Fiber 0.8g; Chol 320mg; Iron 1mg; Sodium 68mg; Calc 180mg

---

family favorite • for kids • freeze it
make ahead

Turtle Ice Cream

prep: 25 min.   other: 5 hrs.

2 cups milk
1 (14-ounce) can sweetened condensed milk
1 (5-ounce) can evaporated milk
2 tablespoons sugar
2 teaspoons vanilla extract
1 cup caramel sauce (we tested with Hershey's Classic Caramel Topping)
1½ cups chopped pecans, toasted
¾ cup chopped chocolate-covered turtle candy (we tested with Russell Stover)

Whisk first 5 ingredients in a 2-quart pitcher or large bowl until blended. Cover and chill 30 minutes. Pour milk mixture into freezer container of a 2-quart electric freezer, and freeze according to manufacturer's instructions.

Remove container with ice cream from ice-cream maker, and place in freezer 15 minutes. Spoon half of ice cream into an 11- x 7-inch dish. Spoon ½ cup caramel sauce over ice cream; sprinkle with ¾ cup pecans. Repeat with remaining ice cream, caramel, and pecans. Cover and freeze at least 4 hours or until firm. Sprinkle with chopped candy before serving. Let stand 10 minutes before serving. Yield: 9 cups.

Per cup: Calories 530 (46% from fat); Fat 27.1g (sat 7.7g, mono 12.4g, poly 5.6g); Protein 9.5g; Carb 65.6g; Fiber 2.7g; Chol 28mg; Iron 1mg; Sodium 242mg; Calc 277mg

---

ice cream ideas

• Chill ice-cream custard 30 minutes before churning to ensure a smoother texture.
• To speed freezing, place the freshly churned ice cream (in the freezing container from your ice-cream maker) directly into the freezer for 15 minutes. Add any stir-ins, and then transfer to an airtight container; refreeze.
• Freeze ice cream 8 hours or longer after churning for the best texture. Allow to stand at room temperature 30 minutes before serving.
• Customize with stir-ins: Add 1 cup chopped toasted nuts, chocolate morsels, crushed cream-filled chocolate sandwich cookies, or toasted coconut to your favorite variation.

freeze it • make ahead

Cherry Ice Cream

prep: 30 min.   cook: 9 min.   other: 1 hr.

2 cups sugar
¼ cup all-purpose flour
Dash of salt
3 cups milk
4 large eggs
3 cups pitted fresh cherries (about 1¼ pounds)
3 cups whipping cream
1 teaspoon almond extract

Stir together first 3 ingredients in a large heavy saucepan; gradually whisk in milk. Cook over medium heat, whisking constantly, 8 minutes or until slightly thickened.

Beat eggs until thick and pale. Whisk about one-fourth of hot mixture into eggs; add to remaining hot mixture, whisking constantly. Cook, stirring constantly, 1 minute. Cool.

Pulse half of cherries in a food processor until finely chopped; remove. Pulse remaining cherries until coarsely chopped. Stir cherries, cream, and extract into custard.

Pour mixture into freezer container of a 1-gallon hand-turned or electric freezer. Freeze according to manufacturer's instructions.

Pack freezer with additional ice and rock salt, and let stand 1 hour before serving. Yield: 9 cups.

Per cup: Calories 565 (50% from fat); Fat 31.7g (sat 18.2g, mono 9.5g, poly 1.2g); Protein 6.3g; Carb 64.1g; Fiber 1.1g; Chol 209mg; Iron 0.8mg; Sodium 107mg; Calc 166mg

Lemon Ice Cream

prep: 8 min.   other: 6 hrs.

2   cups sugar
2   cups milk
2   cups half-and-half
2   teaspoons grated lemon rind
1   cup fresh lemon juice
6   drops of yellow liquid food coloring
Garnish: fresh mint sprigs

Combine first 6 ingredients. Pour into a
13- x 9-inch pan; freeze at least 2 hours.
Process half of mixture in a food processor
until smooth. Remove from processor.
Repeat procedure with remaining mixture.
Return all of mixture to pan. Freeze 4 hours
or until firm. Garnish, if desired. Yield:
1½ quarts.

Per cup: Calories 421 (24% from fat); Fat 11.9g (sat 7.2g, mono 3.3g, poly 0.5g);
Protein 5.2g; Carb 77.4g; Fiber 0.2g; Chol 38mg; Iron 0.1mg; Sodium 66mg; Calc 180mg

No-Cook Vanilla Ice Cream

prep: 5 min.   other: 2½ hrs.

*You'll need an ice-cream maker larger than
1-quart for any of these flavor variations.*

1   (14-ounce) can sweetened condensed
     milk
1   (5-ounce) can evaporated milk
2   tablespoons sugar
2   teaspoons vanilla extract
2   cups milk

Whisk together all ingredients in a 2-quart
pitcher or large bowl until blended. Cover
and chill 30 minutes.
Pour milk mixture into freezer container
of a 1-quart electric freezer, and freeze
according to manufacturer's instructions.
(Instructions and times will vary.)
Remove container with ice cream from
ice-cream maker, and place in freezer
15 minutes. Transfer to an airtight container;
freeze until firm, about 1 to 1½ hours.
Yield: 1 quart.

Per cup: Calories 475 (30% from fat); Fat 15.6g (sat 9.5g, mono 4.3g, poly 0.7g);
Protein 14.5g; Carb 70g; Fiber 0g; Chol 57mg; Iron 0.3mg; Sodium 217mg; Calc 523mg

Note: We tested with a Rival 4-quart
Durable Plastic Bucket Ice Cream Maker
and a Cuisinart Automatic Frozen Yogurt-
Ice Cream & Sorbet Maker.

No-Cook Chocolate Ice Cream: Omit
sugar, vanilla extract, and whole milk.
Add 2 cups whole chocolate milk and
⅔ cup chocolate syrup. Proceed as directed.
Yield: 1 quart.

**No-Cook Chocolate-Almond Ice
Cream:** Prepare No-Cook Chocolate Ice
Cream as directed. Remove container with
ice cream from ice-cream maker, and place
in freezer. Freeze 15 minutes. Stir ¾ cup
toasted sliced almonds into prepared ice
cream. Place in an airtight container; freeze
until firm. Yield: 1¼ quarts.

No-Cook Strawberry Ice Cream: Omit
vanilla, and reduce whole milk to 1½ cups.
Process 1 (16-ounce) container fresh strawberries or 1 (16-ounce) package thawed
frozen strawberries, 2 tablespoons lemon
juice, and ¼ teaspoon salt in a blender or
food processor until smooth. Stir into
milk mixture. Proceed as directed. Yield:
1½ quarts.

No-Cook Fig-Mint Ice Cream: Prepare
No-Cook Vanilla Ice Cream as directed.
Remove container with prepared ice cream
from ice-cream maker, and place in freezer.
Freeze 15 minutes. Stir together 2 cups
chopped peeled fresh figs, ¼ cup fresh
lemon juice, 2 tablespoons sugar, and
2 teaspoons chopped fresh mint. Stir mixture into prepared ice-cream mixture. Place
in an airtight container; freeze until firm.
Yield: 1½ quarts.

Note: We used Black Mission figs; any fresh
figs in season will work in this recipe,
including green figs.

No-Cook Fig-Mint
Ice Cream

Blackberry Sherbet

prep: 15 min.   other: 11 hrs., 30 min.

4 cups fresh blackberries*
2 cups sugar
2 cups buttermilk
Garnishes: fresh blackberries, fresh mint
   sprigs

Stir together 4 cups blackberries and sugar
in a bowl; let mixture stand 30 minutes.
Process blackberry mixture in a food
processor or blender until smooth, stopping
to scrape down sides. Pour blackberry mixture through a fine wire-mesh strainer into
a 9-inch square pan, discarding solids; stir in
buttermilk. Cover and freeze 8 hours.
Break frozen mixture into chunks, and
place in a bowl; beat at medium speed with
an electric mixer until smooth. Return to
pan; cover and freeze 3 hours or until firm.
Garnish, if desired. Yield: 1 quart.

Per cup: Calories 524 (8% from fat); Fat 4.7g (sat 2.5g, mono 1.1g, poly 0.6g);
Protein 6g; Carb 119.9g; Fiber 7.4g; Chol 18mg; Iron 0.9mg; Sodium 146mg; Calc 168mg

*Substitute 2 (14-ounce) packages frozen
blackberries, thawed, for fresh blackberries,
if desired.

Easy Orange Sherbet

prep: 35 min.   other: 1 hr., 30 min.

*Two simple ingredients pack lots of flavor
into this kids favorite.*

2 (14-ounce) cans sweetened condensed
   milk
6 (12-ounce) cans orange carbonated
   beverage

Combine condensed milk and carbonated
beverage in freezer container of a 6-quart
hand-turned or electric freezer, stirring
well. Freeze according to manufacturer's
instructions.
Pack freezer with additional ice and rock
salt, and let stand 1 hour before serving.
Yield: 15 cups.

Per cup: Calories 248 (17% from fat); Fat 4.6g (sat 2.9g, mono 1.3g, poly 0.2g);
Protein 4.2g; Carb 49.8g; Fiber 0g; Chol 18mg; Iron 0.1mg; Sodium 85mg; Calc 150mg

Lime Sherbet

prep: 50 min.

4 teaspoons finely grated lime rind
   (about 1 large lime)
1 cup sugar
3 cups half-and-half
½ cup fresh lime juice (about 4 limes)
½ cup water
⅛ teaspoon salt
Garnishes: fresh mint sprigs, thinly sliced
   lime wedges

Stir together first 6 ingredients in a large
bowl, stirring until well blended.
Pour lime mixture into freezer container of
a 4-quart hand-turned or electric freezer;
freeze according to manufacturer's instructions. Garnish, if desired. Yield: 5 cups.

Per cup: Calories 349 (41% from fat); Fat 16.6g (sat 10.3g, mono 4.8g, poly 0.6g);
Protein 4.4g; Carb 48.5g; Fiber 0.3g; Chol 53mg; Iron 0.1mg; Sodium 118mg; Calc158mg

Raspberry-Buttermilk Sherbet

prep: 50 min.

2 cups fresh raspberries or 1 (14-ounce)
   package frozen raspberries, thawed
1 cup sugar
2 cups buttermilk
1 teaspoon vanilla extract
Garnishes: fresh mint sprigs, fresh
   raspberries

Process 2 cups raspberries in a food processor or blender until smooth, stopping to
scrape down sides. Press raspberry puree
through a fine wire-mesh strainer into a
large bowl, discarding solids. Add sugar,
buttermilk, and vanilla, and stir until well
blended.
Pour raspberry mixture into freezer container of a 4-quart hand-turned or electric
freezer, and freeze according to manufacturer's
instructions. Garnish, if desired. Yield: 4 cups.

Per cup: Calories 304 (13% from fat); Fat 4.4g (sat 2.5g, mono 1g, poly 0.5g);
Protein 4.7g; Carb 63.5g; Fiber 4g; Chol 18mg; Iron 0.4mg; Sodium 146mg; Calc 141mg

refreshing sorbet

Unlike ice cream and sherbet, sorbet is made
without cream or eggs, so it's the perfect
light pick-me-up for the dog days of summer.
Sugar is the key to a good sorbet—too little
and the crystals will be too big, too much
and the sorbet will be slushy. Make sure you
select the ripest, most fragrant fruits to add
even more punch. Cover leftover sorbet with
plastic wrap (directly on the surface), and
store in a plastic container in the freezer up
to two weeks.

Watermelon Sorbet

prep: 15 min.   cook: 5 min.   other: 2 hrs.

*The healthy nature of this dessert belies its
delightful flavor and texture.*

3 cups water
1 cup sugar
4 cups seeded, chopped watermelon
¼ cup lime juice

Bring 3 cups water and sugar just to a boil
in a medium saucepan over high heat, stirring until sugar dissolves. Remove from
heat. Cool.
Process sugar syrup and watermelon, in
batches, in a blender until smooth. Stir in
lime juice. Cover and chill 2 hours.
Pour mixture into freezer container of a
1-gallon hand-turned or electric freezer,
and freeze according to manufacturer's
instructions. Yield: ½ gallon.

Per cup: Calories 118 (0% from fat); Fat 0g (sat 0g, mono 0g, poly 0g); Protein 0.3g;
Carb 32.3g; Fiber 0.5g; Chol 0mg; Iron 0.2mg; Sodium 6mg; Calc 8mg

Cantaloupe Sorbet: Substitute 4 cups
chopped cantaloupe for watermelon and
lime juice. Proceed as directed.

Raspberry Sorbet: Substitute 5 cups fresh
or frozen raspberries for watermelon and
lime juice. Proceed as directed.

Ambrosia Sorbet

prep: 30 min.   cook: 5 min.
other: 2 hrs., 20 min.

11 or 12 navel oranges
2   cups water
1   cup sugar
1   cup cream of coconut

Grate enough orange rind in a small bowl to equal 2 teaspoons. Cut oranges in half, and squeeze halves to equal 3 cups juice; set aside.
Bring 2 cups water and sugar to a boil in a large saucepan over high heat. Cook, stirring constantly, 3 minutes or just until sugar dissolves; remove from heat, and cool.
Stir in cream of coconut, orange juice, and grated rind; cover and chill at least 2 hours.
Pour mixture into freezer container of a 4-quart hand-turned or electric freezer, and freeze according to manufacturer's instructions. Yield: 2 quarts.

Per cup: Calories 210 (29% from fat); Fat 6.7g (sat 5.8g, mono 0.3g, poly 0.1g); Protein 1.7g; Carb 37.9g; Fiber 1.1g; Chol 0mg; Iron 0.4mg; Sodium 21mg; Calc 13mg

Fresh Mango Sorbet

prep: 20 min.

Look for unblemished mangoes with yellow skin and a reddish blush. Ripe mangoes will hold for a couple of days in a plastic bag in the refrigerator.

2   large ripe mangoes, chopped
1   cup mango nectar
¾   cup sugar
1   tablespoon grated lime rind
½   cup fresh lime juice

Process all ingredients in a food processor until smooth. Pour mixture into freezer container of a 2-quart hand-turned or electric freezer. Freeze according to manufacturer's instructions. Yield: 4 cups.

Per cup: Calories 257 (1% from fat); Fat 0.4g (sat 0.1g, mono 0.1g, poly 0.1g); Protein 0.8g; Carb 67.4g; Fiber 2.6g; Chol 0mg; Iron 0.2mg; Sodium 4.3mg; Calc 20mg

Chocolate Sorbet

prep: 45 min.   cook: 36 min.   other: 2 hrs.

5   cups water
2¼ cups sugar
1   cup unsweetened cocoa, sifted
10   (1-ounce) bittersweet chocolate squares, chopped

Bring 5 cups water and sugar to a boil in a medium saucepan. Boil mixture, stirring occasionally, 1 minute or until sugar dissolves. Whisk in cocoa until blended. Reduce heat, and simmer, whisking occasionally, 30 minutes. Remove from heat; gradually add chopped chocolate, whisking until smooth after each addition. Let stand 1 hour.
Pour into freezer container of a 4-quart hand-turned or electric freezer. Freeze according to manufacturer's instructions 45 minutes.
Pack freezer with additional ice and rock salt. Let stand 1 hour before serving. Yield: 5 cups.

Per cup: Calories 671 (31% from fat); Fat 26.7g (sat 13.5g, mono 8.9g, poly 0.9g); Protein 7.4g; Carb 128g; Fiber 9.8g; Chol 0mg; Iron 3.9mg; Sodium 8mg; Calc 28mg

Lemon Ice

prep: 15 min.   other: 8 hrs., 45 min.

You won't need an ice-cream freezer to make this tart refresher; your regular freezer does the trick.

1   (12-ounce) can frozen lemonade concentrate, thawed
3   cups ice cubes
1   cup water
⅓   cup sugar

Process all ingredients in a food processor or blender until smooth. Pour mixture into a 13- x 9-inch pan, and freeze 45 minutes.
Process mixture in a food processor or blender until smooth. Return to pan, and freeze 8 hours. Yield: 4 cups.

Per cup: Calories 218 (1% from fat); Fat 0.2g (sat 0g, mono 0g, poly 0.1g); Protein 0.3g; Carb 56.7g; Fiber 0.2g; Chol 0mg; Iron 0.6mg; Sodium 8mg; Calc 11mg

making sorbets & granitas

To make sorbets and granitas, keep the following in mind:

• To help develop the desired icy consistency, chill the ingredients before freezing.
• Use a metal pan; it helps mixture freeze quickly.
• Cover sorbets and granitas while they freeze; otherwise, they may pick up flavors from other foods.
• To achieve the granular texture of a granita, stir several times while it freezes.
• For the smooth but icy consistency of sorbet, process the mixture in a food processor just until fluffy after it's almost frozen. Freeze again until firm.
• Sorbet left in the freezer more than a few days can become too crystallized. If this happens, partially thaw sorbet, and process it again in food processor. Refreeze and use it within 24 hours.

Margarita Granita

prep: 15 min.   other: 8 hrs.

3   cups water
1   cup sugar
½   cup fresh lime juice
⅓   cup fresh lemon juice
6   tablespoons orange liqueur
6   tablespoons gold tequila
2   teaspoons grated lime rind
Sugar

Bring 3 cups water and 1 cup sugar to a boil in a saucepan, stirring constantly. Pour into a large bowl; add lime juice and next 4 ingredients. Cover and freeze 8 hours.
Process frozen mixture in a blender or food processor until slushy.
Dip margarita glass rims into water; dip rims in sugar. Spoon granita into glasses. Yield: 5 cups.

Per cup: Calories 280 (0% from fat); Fat 0.1g (sat 0g, mono 0g, poly 0g); Protein 0.2g; Carb 55.3g; Fiber 0.3g; Chol 0mg; Iron 0.1mg; Sodium 5mg; Calc 9mg

Note: For a nonalcoholic version, omit liquors, and add ½ cup fresh orange juice.

freeze it • low cholesterol • low fat
make ahead

Grapefruit Freeze

prep: 20 min.   other: 4 hrs., 35 min.

1½ cups sugar
1   cup water
½   cup fresh mint leaves, chopped
1   (64-ounce) bottle Ruby Red grapefruit
    juice
Garnish: fresh mint sprigs

Bring sugar and 1 cup water to a boil in a saucepan. Add chopped mint; cover and let stand 5 minutes. Pour through a fine wire-mesh strainer into an 8-cup container; discard chopped mint. Add grapefruit juice. **Divide** mixture into 2 (1-quart) freezer containers; cover and freeze at least 4 hours. Let stand 30 minutes before serving. Scrape with a spatula, or process, in batches, in a food processor. Garnish, if desired. Yield: 8 cups.

Per cup: Calories 235 (0% from fat); Fat 0g (sat 0g, mono 0g, poly 0g); Protein 1g; Carb 59.5g; Fiber 0g; Chol 0mg; Iron 0mg; Sodium 1mg; Calc 21mg

entertaining • freeze it • make ahead

Toffee-Coffee Ice-Cream Torte

prep: 30 min.   cook: 5 min.   other: 8 hrs.

This torte is made in two loafpans so you can serve one and keep one frozen for later.

6   tablespoons coffee liqueur, divided
1   tablespoon instant coffee granules
1   quart chocolate ice cream, softened
1   (12-ounce) bag chocolate-covered toffee
    candy bars, finely chopped (we tested
    with Hershey's Heath Snack Bars)
½   gallon coffee ice cream, softened
1   (3-ounce) package ladyfingers
1   cup strong brewed coffee or espresso
½   cup sugar
1½ tablespoons cornstarch
Garnishes: whipped topping, additional
    chopped toffee candy bars

Line 2 (9- x 5-inch) loafpans with plastic wrap, allowing excess to hang over sides. **Stir** together 1 tablespoon liqueur and coffee granules until dissolved. Combine coffee mixture, chocolate ice cream, and half of the chopped toffee bars in a large bowl. In a separate bowl, combine ½ gallon coffee ice cream and remaining chopped toffee bars from bag. Spread half of chocolate ice-cream mixture evenly into 1 prepared loafpan; top with half of coffee ice-cream mixture. Repeat layers in remaining loafpan. **Brush** ladyfingers with 3 tablespoons coffee liqueur; place ladyfingers, brushed sides down, evenly over ice cream in loafpans. Fold plastic wrap over to seal; freeze at least 8 hours. **Stir** together brewed coffee, sugar, and cornstarch in a heavy saucepan over medium-high heat; cook, stirring constantly, until mixture starts to boil. Reduce heat to low, and cook 2 to 3 minutes or until thickened and clear. Remove from heat; cool. Stir in remaining 2 tablespoons liqueur; cover and chill coffee sauce until ready to serve. **Invert** tortes onto serving plates; remove and discard plastic wrap. Garnish, if desired. Serve with chilled coffee sauce. Yield: 12 servings.

Per serving: Calories 701 (49% from fat); Fat 37.8g (sat 21.4g, mono 10.8g, poly 1.5g); Protein 9.5g; Carb 75.6g; Fiber 1.3g; Chol 189mg; Iron 0.6mg; Sodium 263mg; Calc 268mg

entertaining • for kids • make ahead

Mint-Chocolate Chip Ice-Cream Cupcakes

prep: 20 min.   cook: 25 min.
other: 8 hrs., 10 min.

Ice cream and candy provide more than just a hint of mint in these cool, chocolaty cupcakes.

1   (19.8-ounce) package fudge brownie mix
½   cup water
½   cup vegetable oil
3   large eggs
½   gallon mint-chocolate chip ice cream,
    softened
1   (8-ounce) container frozen whipped
    topping, thawed
2   to 3 tablespoons green crème de menthe
    (optional)
½   (4.67-ounce) package chocolate mints
    (we tested with Andes)

Stir together first 4 ingredients until blended. Place 12 foil baking cups into muffin pans; spoon batter into cups.

Bake at 350° for 20 to 25 minutes. (A wooden pick inserted in center does not come out clean.) Cool in pans on wire racks 10 minutes; remove from pans, and cool completely on wire racks.
Return baking cups to muffin pans, and spoon ice cream evenly over each brownie. Freeze 8 hours or until firm.
Stir together whipped topping and, if desired, liqueur. Dollop evenly over ice cream. Freeze until ready to serve.
Pull a vegetable peeler down sides of mints, making tiny curls; sprinkle curls over cupcakes just before serving. Yield: 1 dozen.

Per cupcake: Calories 545 (39% from fat); Fat 23.4g (sat 8.8g, mono 8.2g, poly 6.5g); Protein 8.8g; Carb 72g; Fiber 2.9g; Chol 60mg; Iron 1.9mg; Sodium 264mg; Calc 152mg

family favorite

Cream Cheese Brownie Sundaes

prep: 20 min.   cook: 50 min.

1   (18.25-ounce) package chocolate cake
    mix (we tested with Pillsbury Moist
    Supreme Devil's Food Double Pudding)
½   cup butter or margarine, melted
3   large eggs
1   (8-ounce) package cream cheese,
    softened
1   (16-ounce) package powdered sugar
⅓   cup unsweetened cocoa
6   cups mint-chocolate chip ice cream
1½ cups chocolate sauce

Beat cake mix, butter, and 1 egg at medium speed with an electric mixer until combined. Press mixture into bottom of a lightly greased 13- x 9-inch baking dish.
Beat cream cheese at medium speed until creamy. Gradually add powdered sugar, beating until smooth. Add remaining 2 eggs, 1 at a time, beating well after each addition. Gradually add cocoa, beating until blended. Pour mixture evenly over chocolate layer.
Bake at 350° for 45 to 50 minutes or until a wooden pick inserted in center comes out clean. Cool and cut into squares. Top each serving with mint-chocolate chip ice-cream and chocolate sauce. Yield: 12 servings.

Per serving: Calories 734 (30% from fat); Fat 24.4g (sat 13.2g, mono 8.2g, poly 1.8g); Protein 10.3g; Carb 118.5g; Fiber 3.9g; Chol 99mg; Iron 2.8mg; Sodium 640mg; Calc 266mg

Turtle Dessert

◄ Place 8 ½ ice-cream sandwiches in baking dish.

◄ Spread evenly with caramel topping.

◄ Sprinkle with 1 cup pecans.

◄ Spread with remaining whipped topping.

family favorite • freeze it • make ahead

Turtle Dessert

prep: 10 min.   other: 2 hrs., 5 min.

Here's a great recipe for the beach, for a supper club, or a children's party.

17   ice-cream sandwiches (we tested with Mayfield)
1   (12.25-ounce) jar caramel topping
1¼   cups chopped pecans, toasted
1   (12-ounce) container frozen whipped topping, thawed
¾   cup hot fudge topping, heated

Place 8½ ice-cream sandwiches in a 13- x 9-inch baking dish. Spread evenly with caramel topping, and sprinkle with 1 cup pecans. Top with 2 cups whipped topping and remaining ice-cream sandwiches. Spread remaining whipped topping evenly over sandwiches. Sprinkle with remaining ¼ cup pecans. Cover and freeze at least 2 hours. Let stand 5 minutes before serving; cut into squares. Drizzle with fudge topping. Yield: 10 servings.

Per serving: Calories 609 (41% from fat); Fat 28g (sat 13g, mono 9.8g, poly 3.9g); Protein 7.4g; Carb 83.8g; Fiber 3.3g; Chol 34mg; Iron 1.3mg; Sodium 262mg; Calc 154mg

meringue desserts

Baked meringues grace a dessert table with high style. In contrast to soft, puffy meringues that top pies, baked meringues produce a firm and crisp dessert.

The basic meringue mixture is piped or spread on baking sheets into freestanding shapes and baked long and slowly on a low temperature setting. This method gives the shaped meringue its characteristic crisp, melt-in-your-mouth texture without browning the meringue.

Superfine sugar is best for making meringues. It dissolves quicker than regular granulated sugar.

For maximum volume from beaten egg whites, separate the eggs while cold, and then let whites sit at room temperature 20 minutes before whipping them. If you're fortunate enough to own a large copper bowl, it produces beaten whites with great volume due to a stabilizing chemical reaction that takes place between the egg white

and copper. Otherwise, a clean, grease-free glass bowl works, too.

Don't beat egg whites for meringue until you're absolutely ready to pipe or spread and then bake once the mixture is beaten. If beaten egg whites sit too long before being baked, they'll deflate and lose their shape in the oven.

The ideal baking temperature ranges from 200° to 225°. Bake meringues until they're firm and almost dry; then turn the oven off, and leave meringues in the oven to cool several hours or overnight.

Store baked meringues in an airtight container at room temperature up to two days. For longer storage, freeze them up to a month in an airtight freezer container.

If meringues feel soft or sticky after storage, crisp them in a 200° oven for 5 minutes. Then turn off oven and let meringues cool in the oven until dry. Fill meringues just before serving to keep them crisp.

Avoid making meringues on humid or rainy days; the extra moisture outside can make the end product soft and sticky.

low calorie • low carb • low cholesterol
low fat

Meringues

prep: 20 min. cook: 2 hrs. other: 8 hrs.

4   egg whites
1   teaspoon cream of tartar
¼   teaspoon almond extract
¼   cup superfine sugar

Beat egg whites at medium speed with an electric mixer until foamy; add cream of tartar and almond extract, beating until blended. Gradually add sugar, beating until stiff peaks form and sugar dissolves.

Pipe or spread mixture into small 2-inch cookie shapes or other desired shapes onto a parchment paper–lined baking sheet. **Bake** at 200° for 2 hours. Turn off oven; let meringues stand in closed oven with light on for 8 hours. Yield: 2½ dozen.

Per meringue: Calories 9 (1% from fat); Fat 0g (sat 0g, mono 0g, poly 0g); Protein 0.5g; Carb 1.8g; Fiber 0g; Chol 0mg; Iron 0mg; Sodium 7mg; Calc 0mg

make ahead

Strawberry Meringue Parfaits

prep: 10 min. cook: 15 min. other: 6 hrs.

You can substitute store-bought meringue cookies for the homemade Meringues.

1   quart fresh strawberries, sliced
1¾   cups sugar, divided
¼   cup cornstarch
4   egg yolks
3   cups milk or half-and-half
¼   cup butter or margarine
2   teaspoons vanilla extract
Meringues (recipe at left)

Sprinkle strawberries with ¼ cup sugar. **Combine** remaining 1½ cups sugar and cornstarch in a large saucepan over medium heat. Gradually whisk in egg yolks and milk; cook milk mixture, whisking often,

Strawberry Meringue Parfaits

12 minutes or until thickened. Bring milk mixture to a boil, and cook, stirring constantly, 1 minute. Remove mixture from heat; stir in butter and vanilla. Cover and chill 6 hours.

Spoon half of custard into 6 parfait glasses; top with half of sliced strawberries and 3 Meringues. Repeat layers, ending with 1 Meringue on top of each serving. Yield: 6 servings.

Per serving: Calories 493 (27% from fat); Fat 14.8g (sat 8.1g, mono 4.3g, poly 1.1g); Protein 8.4g; Carb 83.7g; Fiber 2g; Chol 169mg; Iron 0.8mg; Sodium 139mg; Calc 172mg

fruit desserts

Desserts made with fresh fruit are often the simplest, most beautiful, and the most healthful dessert options available. Those without a lot of sugar or heavy sauces emphasize the freshness and flavor of the fruit without a lot of extra fat and calories.

For the fullest flavor, buy fruit in season. Evaluate its quality by the ripeness, texture, aroma, and color. Don't buy soft or bruised fruit because it will deteriorate quickly. Whenever possible, buy loose fruit rather than prepackaged so you can best evaluate its quality.

Frozen fruits and some canned fruits offer good alternatives to fresh fruit. Fruits frozen whole without added syrup will have flavor and texture closest to fresh.

low calorie • low fat • make ahead

Spicy Tropical Fruit

prep: 10 min. other: 2 hrs.

1   (8-ounce) container light sour cream
1   (8-ounce) container plain yogurt
¼   cup honey
2   tablespoons chopped crystallized ginger
¼   teaspoon ground allspice
¼   teaspoon salt
⅛   to ¼ teaspoon ground red pepper (optional)
3   ripe mangoes, peeled, seeded, and diced
3   bananas, peeled and diced
1   (15.25-ounce) can pineapple tidbits, drained
Garnish: toasted pistachio nuts

Stir together first 6 ingredients, and, if desired, ground red pepper in a medium bowl. Fold in mangoes, bananas, and pineapple. Cover and chill at least 2 hours. Garnish, if desired. Yield: 7 cups.

Per cup: Calories 199 (19% from fat); Fat 4.2g (sat 2.5g, mono 1.2g, poly 0.2g); Protein 3.9g; Carb 39.8g; Fiber 3.7g; Chol 13.3mg; Iron 0.5mg; Sodium 132mg; Calc 122mg

Berry Sundaes

prep: 10 min.   other: 2 hrs.

We used blueberries, blackberries, and raspberries for mixed fresh berries.

2¼ cups fresh strawberries, halved
2¼ cups mixed fresh berries
3   tablespoons sugar
2   tablespoons orange liqueur
2   teaspoons grated orange rind
½   teaspoon chopped fresh mint
3   cups fruit sorbet
Garnishes: orange zest, fresh mint sprigs

Combine first 6 ingredients, tossing lightly to combine. Cover and chill up to 2 hours. **Scoop** ½ cup sorbet into each of 6 serving dishes. Spoon two-thirds cup of berries over sorbet in each dish. Garnish, if desired. Serve immediately. Yield: 6 servings.

Per serving: Calories 178 (2% from fat); Fat 0.4g (sat 0g, mono 0.1g, poly 0.2g); Protein 1.4g; Carb 42.1g; Fiber 3.6g; Chol 0mg; Iron 1mg; Sodium 9mg; Calc 29mg

Berry Sundae

Bananas Foster

prep: 5 min.   cook: 4 min.

If you don't have banana liqueur, just double the rum.

¼   cup butter or margarine
⅓   cup firmly packed dark brown sugar
½   teaspoon ground cinnamon
4   bananas, quartered
⅓   cup banana liqueur
⅓   cup dark rum
1   pint vanilla ice cream

Melt butter in a large skillet over medium-high heat; add brown sugar and next 3 ingredients. Cook, stirring constantly, 2 minutes or until bananas are tender. Remove from heat. Pour rum into a small long-handled saucepan; heat just until warm. Remove from heat. Ignite with a long match, and pour over bananas. Baste bananas with sauce until flames die down. Serve over ice cream. Yield: 4 servings.

Per serving: Calories 460 (37% from fat); Fat 18.7g (sat 11.7g, mono 4.9g, poly 0.7g); Protein 3.4g; Carb 66g; Fiber 4.6g; Chol 59mg; Iron 0.9mg; Sodium 141mg; Calc 107mg

Poached Pears With White Caramel Sauce

prep: 10 min.   cook: 15 min.   other: 8 hrs.

To core whole fruit, insert an apple corer into the bottom, cutting to, but not through, the stem end, and twist.

8   cups water
¾   cup sugar
6   small firm pears, peeled and cored
White Caramel Sauce

Bring 8 cups water and sugar to a boil in a Dutch oven. Add cored pears; cover, reduce heat, and simmer 12 to 15 minutes or until pears are tender. Remove from heat; uncover and cool.
Cover pears and chill 8 hours, if desired.
Drain pears, and cut into thin slices, keeping stems intact. Serve with White Caramel Sauce. Yield: 6 servings.

Per serving: Calories 578 (64% from fat); Fat 41.1g (sat 25g, mono 11.2g, poly 1.3g); Protein 0.9g; Carb 52g; Fiber 2.7g; Chol 131mg; Iron 0mg; Sodium 180mg; Calc 111mg

White Caramel Sauce

prep: 4 min.   cook: 30 min.

¾   cup sugar
⅓   cup water
1⅓ cups whipping cream
2   tablespoons vanilla extract
¾   cup butter or margarine

Cook sugar and ⅓ cup water in a heavy saucepan over medium heat, stirring often, about 15 minutes or until reduced to 6 tablespoons.
Add whipping cream and vanilla. (Mixture will be lumpy.) Cook over medium heat, stirring often, 15 minutes or until reduced to 1 cup. Remove from heat.
Stir in butter. Cover sauce, and chill up to 3 days, if desired. Serve warm. Yield: 1½ cups.

Per tablespoon: Calories 122 (75% from fat); Fat 10.1g (sat 6.3g, mono 2.8g, poly 0.3g); Protein 0.1g; Carb 7.3g; Fiber 0g; Chol 33mg; Iron 0mg; Sodium 45mg; Calc 11mg

Orange-Ginger Roasted Apples

prep: 12 min.   cook: 35 min.

Trim about ⅛ inch off the bottom of the apples, if necessary, so they will sit level in the dish.

4   medium Braeburn apples*
⅓   cup honey
1   teaspoon grated orange rind
¼   cup fresh orange juice
1   tablespoon lime juice
1½   teaspoons grated fresh ginger
¼   cup sour cream
½   cup granola

Remove cores from apples, leaving a ½-inch core on bottom of each. Place apples in a lightly greased 8-inch square baking dish.
Stir together honey and next 4 ingredients. Drizzle mixture over apples, filling apple centers.
Bake, covered, at 425° for 30 minutes. Uncover; baste with pan juices, and bake 5 more minutes. Serve each apple with 1 tablespoon sour cream and 2 tablespoons granola. Yield: 4 servings.

Per serving: Calories 290 (21% from fat); Fat 6.9g (sat 2.5g, mono 2.2g, poly 1.7g); Protein 2.9g; Carb 58.3g; Fiber 6.2g; Chol 6mg; Iron 1.2mg; Sodium 49mg; Calc 32mg

*Substitute McIntosh, Golden Delicious, or Fuji apples for Braeburn, if desired.

Apple Fritters

prep: 10 min.   cook: 4 min. per batch

Try these fritters with caramel sauce or lemon curd for dipping.

1½   cups all-purpose flour
¼   teaspoon salt
1¼   teaspoons baking powder
½   cup milk
1   large egg, lightly beaten
2   tablespoons butter or margarine, melted
3   Mutsu or McIntosh apples, peeled and coarsely chopped (about 3 cups)
Peanut oil
Powdered sugar

Combine first 6 ingredients in a medium bowl. Add apples, stirring well.
Pour oil to a depth of 3 inches into a Dutch oven; heat to 350°. Drop batter by tablespoonfuls into hot oil, and fry in batches until golden, turning once. Drain on paper towels. Sprinkle fritters with powdered sugar; serve hot. Yield: 30 fritters.

Per fritter: Calories 61 (43% from fat); Fat 2.9g (sat 0.9g, mono 1.1g, poly 0.7g); Protein 1g; Carb 7.9g; Fiber 0.3g; Chol 9.5mg; Iron 0.4mg; Sodium 49mg; Calc 19mg

Caramel Apples

prep: 20 min.   other: 35 min.

6   large Granny Smith apples
6   wooden craft sticks
1   (14-ounce) bag caramels
1   tablespoon vanilla extract
1   tablespoon water
2   cups chopped pecans, toasted
1   (12-ounce) package semisweet chocolate morsels

Wash and dry apples; remove stems. Insert a craft stick into stem end of each apple.
Combine caramels, vanilla, and 1 tablespoon water in a microwave-safe glass bowl. Microwave at HIGH 90 seconds or until melted, stirring twice.
Quickly dip each apple into the caramel mixture, allowing excess caramel to drip off. Roll in chopped pecans; place on lightly greased wax paper. Chill at least 15 minutes.
Microwave chocolate morsels at HIGH 90 seconds or until melted, stirring twice; cool 5 minutes. Pour chocolate where craft stick and apple meet, allowing chocolate to drip down sides of apples. Chill 15 minutes or until set. Yield: 6 apples.

Per apple: Calories 850 (54% from fat); Fat 50.8g (sat 16.6g, mono 22.4g, poly 9.2g); Protein 9.3g; Carb 106g; Fiber 10.5g; Chol 4mg; Iron 3.1mg; Sodium 158mg; Calc 138mg

Black-and-White Caramel Apples: Microwave 6 ounces white chocolate morsels at HIGH 1 minute or until melted, stirring once; drizzle evenly over semisweet chocolate on each apple.

Black-and-White Caramel Apple

fish & shellfish

fish

Fish has much to offer the health-conscious cook. Relatively low in total fat and saturated fat, fish contains predominantly heart-healthy polyunsaturated fat and monounsaturated fat. It boasts beneficial omega-3 fatty acids as well as zinc and other nutrients. Fish comes from saltwater and freshwater and is both wild and farmed.

Fat and Lean Fish

Fish is classified as fat and lean. Fat fish has an oil content of more than 5 percent and tends to be higher in calories and stronger in flavor than lean fish (see the Flavors of Fish, page 225). The color of fat fish is usually darker due to oil distributed throughout the flesh. The oil produces a pronounced flavor as well as more of a meatlike texture than in lean fish. Fat fish requires less basting during cooking than lean fish to keep the flesh moist and tender.

Lean fish has an oil content of less than 5 percent. The oil is concentrated in the liver, which is removed when fish is cleaned. Lean fish is milder in flavor and whiter in appearance than fat fish because the oil is not distributed throughout the body of the fish. Lean fish tends to dry out during cooking because of its low fat content; therefore, moist heat methods like poaching and baking are best. Lean fish can be grilled successfully if basted often.

When substituting one fish for another in a recipe, it's best to choose a substitute from the same classification. Use the chart below as a guide.

fish classification

Fat Fish	Lean Fish	
Amberjack	Cod	Scrod
Freshwater Catfish	Flounder	Sea Bass
Herring	Grouper	Snapper
Lake Trout or	Haddock	Sole
Rainbow Trout	Halibut	Swordfish
Mackerel	Mahi-mahi	Tilapia
Mullet	Orange Roughy	Tilefish
Pompano	Pike	Triggerfish
Salmon	Pollock	Turbot
Sardines	Redfish	Walleye
Tuna	Rockfish	Whiting
Whitefish	Scamp	

Selecting Fish

Fish is highly perishable, so it's important to follow some basic guidelines for buying and storing it properly. When shopping for fish, deal with a reputable seafood market. Buy fish from a store that has quick turnover, regularly replenishes its stock, and uses refrigerated cases to store its fish. Get to know the seafood market manager, and before purchasing, ask where and when the fish was caught.

The eyes of whole fresh fish should be clear, clean, and full, almost bulging. The gills should be pinkish-red and not slippery. Fish flesh should be firm and elastic (that means it should spring back when lightly touched). The skin should have no faded markings; it should be shiny with scales firmly attached. Cut surfaces of fish steaks and fillets should be moist, not dried out. There should be no signs of yellowing or browning edges. Perhaps, though, the best indicator of freshness is odor. Fresh fish should have a clean, mild, "sea-breeze" smell, not an offensive "fishy" odor.

Handling Fish

Fresh fish is best if cooked the day of purchase, but may be stored in the original wrapping in the coldest part of the refrigerator up to two days if the wrapping is moisture- and vapor-resistant. If it's not, wrap the fish carefully before storing. Place a damp cloth over the fish, inside the wrapping, to prevent fish from drying out. Fresh fish should be frozen within two days of purchase. Freeze fish up to three months.

Some fish sold in the unfrozen state has been flash-frozen or blast-frozen to maintain quality. Once flash-frozen fish has thawed, do not refreeze. If you intend to freeze the fish, ask if fish was previously frozen.

If you're not going directly home after buying fish, have the package placed in a plastic bag filled with ice. When you arrive home, remove fish from the wrapper, rinse the fish in cold water, and pat dry with paper towels. Then repackage fish in wax paper and an airtight plastic bag. Place bag directly on ice in a colander set in a larger bowl in the refrigerator.

When buying frozen fish, make sure the package is tightly wrapped and sealed. There should be little or no air within the wrapping. Be sure there's no blood visible inside or out, that the fish is solidly frozen and free of ice crystals, which can jeopardize its texture and freshness.

Thaw frozen fish in the refrigerator. If you need to thaw fish quicker than that, place frozen fish wrapped in plastic wrap under cold running water until thawed. Drain and blot thawed fish with paper towels before cooking.

Frozen breaded fish products should not be thawed before cooking; prepare these according to package directions. Leftover cooked fish will keep two days in the refrigerator.

Always marinate fish in the refrigerator.

Shown on previous page: Cedar-Planked Salmon (page 230)

Cooking Fish

Fish can be successfully baked, broiled, grilled, fried, poached, steamed, or microwaved. Dry heat methods of cooking such as grilling, broiling, and smoking are ideal for fat fish, while lean fish remains moister when cooked by moist heat methods. You can, however, cook lean fish by a dry heat method if basted often.

Overcooking and cooking at too high a temperature are the most common problems in cooking fish. These factors dry and toughen fish and can destroy the flavor.

Be sure to check the fish for doneness occasionally while cooking. To do this, pierce the thickest part of the fish with a fork, and twist fork slightly; most fish will flake easily and come away from the bones readily when done. The flesh becomes opaque, and the juices should be a milky white.

Microwaving Fish

Generally, it's best to microwave fish at HIGH power to quickly seal in juices and flavor. Arrange thicker portions to the outside of the dish so they'll get done without overcooking the thinner areas. When fish turns opaque, it's done.

The microwave oven also works well for defrosting frozen fish. Fillets can be left in their original package for defrosting. Fish defrosts rapidly, so be careful not to toughen it by overdefrosting in the microwave. Remove fish from the packaging while still slightly icy; hold under cold, running water to complete the defrosting.

Grilling Fish

Fish properly grilled is a delicacy. Almost any type of fish is suitable for the grill; just remember that lean fish will need frequent basting during grilling. And you'll want to choose fish fillets or steaks that are at least ¾ inch thick for the grill.

Before you put fish on the grill, be sure to grease the grill grate. Our Test Kitchens staff recommends spraying the grate with vegetable cooking spray before placing it over a hot fire.

A fish basket is a handy piece of equipment for grilling thin pieces of fish. The basket holds the fish securely and keeps it from sticking to the grill. Grease the basket, arrange fish in the basket, and fasten shut. Place basket flat on the grill. To turn the fish during grilling, simply flip the basket.

You can also steam fish on the grill. Place fish (fillets work well) on a large piece of heavy-duty aluminum foil; sprinkle with your favorite seasonings or herbs. Seal foil, and cook on the grill 4 to 5 inches above the heat, approximately 7 to 10 minutes per inch of thickness. (To determine thickness, measure thickest part of fish with a ruler.)

It's easy to overcook fish, so don't leave fish unattended during grilling. Begin checking for doneness halfway through cooking time; the time will vary according to the thickness and size of the fish, the wind, the temperature of the coals, and whether or not the grill is covered.

Poaching Fish

Poaching is an excellent low-fat cooking method for fish. It preserves the delicate texture of the fish and enhances its flavor. It's

fish i.d.

You can buy fresh fish in a variety of market forms, and the listings on the board at the fish market can sometimes have you guessing. Knowing these terms will help you pick the right type and amount for your needs.

Whole fish: marketed just as it comes from the water. It needs to be cleaned completely. When cooked, a whole fish makes a dramatic presentation on the plate. Count on 1 pound per serving.

Drawn fish: a whole fish that has been eviscerated (internal organs removed), but it still needs to be scaled or skinned. Allow 1 pound per serving.

Dressed fish: a fish that has been eviscerated, scaled, and has head and fins removed. The tail may or may not be removed as well. Smaller fish that have been dressed are referred to as *pan-dressed*. Allow ½ pound per serving.

Fish steaks: thick slices cut crosswise through the whole dressed fish (right, top). They're usually cut about 1 inch thick. The only bone is a cross section of the backbone and ribs. Plan on about ⅓ to ½ pound per serving.

Fish steaks

Fillet

Fish fillets: boneless pieces cut lengthwise away from the backbone (at right). They're often skinned and are practically boneless (though small pinbones may be present). For *butterfly fillets,* the fillets are held together by the uncut belly skin. Skinless fillets tend to dry out quickly during cooking, so watch them carefully. Allow ⅓ to ½ pound per serving for fillets.

Cold-smoked: cured and partially dried.
Smoked: cooked over heat.

important to immerse the fish completely in the poaching liquid so that an exchange of flavors between the fish and the cooking liquid will take place.

It's easy to cook large fish in a fish poacher, a long narrow piece of cookware with a lid and removable tray. Or cut fish in half crosswise so that pieces will fit in a smaller container. Use a large skillet or saucepan to poach smaller fish, fish steaks, and fillets. Most firm-fleshed fish is suitable for poaching.

To poach fish, have the poaching liquid simmering when fish is lowered into it; then reheat the liquid to barely simmering for cooking. Poach 7 to 10 minutes per inch of thickness.

timetable for cooking fish & shellfish

cooking method	product	market form	approximate weight or thickness	cooking temperature	approximate total cooking time by minutes
Baking	Fish	Dressed	3 to 4 pounds	350°	40 to 60
		Pan-dressed	½ to 1 pound	350°	25 to 30
		Steaks	½ to 1 inch	350°	25 to 35
		Fillets	1 inch	350°	10 per inch
	Clams	Live		450°	15
	Lobster	Live	¾ to 1 pound	400°	15 to 20
			1 to 1½ pounds	400°	20 to 25
	Oysters	Live		450°	15
		Shucked		400°	10
	Scallops	Shucked		350°	25 to 30
	Shrimp	Headless		350°	20 to 25
	Spiny lobster tails	Headless	4 ounces	450°	20 to 25
			8 ounces	450°	25 to 30
Broiling	Fish	Pan-dressed	½ to 1 pound	Broil	10 to 15
		Steaks	½ to 1 inch	Broil	10 to 15
		Fillets	1 inch	Broil	10 per inch
	Clams	Live		Broil	5 to 8
	Lobster	Live	¾ to 1 pound	Broil	10 to 12
		1 to 1½ pounds		Broil	12 to 15
	Oysters	Live		Broil	5
		Shucked		Broil	5
	Scallops	Shucked		Broil	8 to 10
	Shrimp	Headless		Broil	8 to 10
	Spiny lobster tails	Headless	4 ounces	Broil	8 to 10
			8 ounces	Broil	10 to 12
Poaching	Fish	Pan-dressed	½ to 1 pound	Simmer	10
	Steaks		½ to 1 inch	Simmer	10
	Fillets		1 inch	Simmer	9 per inch
	Crabs	Live		Simmer	15
	Lobster	Live	¾ to 1 pound	Simmer	10 to 15
			1 to 1½ pounds	Simmer	15 to 20
	Scallops	Shucked		Simmer	4 to 5
	Shrimp	Headless		Simmer	3 to 5
	Spiny lobster tails	Headless	4 ounces	Simmer	10
			8 ounces	Simmer	15
Frying	Fish	Pan-dressed	½ to 1 pound	375°	2 to 4
	Steaks		½ to 1 inch	375°	2 to 4
	Fillets		1 inch	375°	1 to 5
	Clams	Shucked		375°	2 to 3
	Crabs	Soft-shell	¼ pound	375°	3 to 4
	Lobster	Live	¾ to 1 pound	375°	3 to 4
		1 to 1½ pounds		375°	4 to 5
	Oysters	Shucked		375°	2
	Scallops	Shucked		350°	3 to 4
	Shrimp	Headless		350°	2 to 3
	Spiny lobster tails	Headless	4 ounces	350°	3 to 4
			8 ounces	350°	4 to 5

Spicy Catfish With Vegetables and Basil Cream

prep: 25 min. cook: 25 min.

Creole seasoning puts the spice in this dish.

- 3 tablespoons butter, divided
- 1 (16-ounce) package frozen whole kernel corn, thawed
- 1 medium onion, chopped
- 1 medium-size green bell pepper, chopped
- 1 medium-size red bell pepper, chopped
- ¾ teaspoon salt
- ¾ teaspoon pepper
- ½ cup all-purpose flour
- ¼ cup yellow cornmeal
- 1 tablespoon Creole seasoning
- 4 (6- to 8-ounce) catfish fillets
- ⅓ cup buttermilk
- 1 tablespoon vegetable oil
- ½ cup whipping cream
- 2 tablespoons chopped fresh basil
- Garnish: fresh basil sprigs

Melt 2 tablespoons butter in a large skillet over medium-high heat. Add corn, onion, and bell peppers; sauté 6 to 8 minutes or until tender. Stir in salt and pepper; spoon vegetables onto serving dish, and keep warm.

Combine flour, cornmeal, and Creole seasoning in a large shallow dish. Dip fillets in buttermilk, and dredge in flour mixture.

Melt remaining 1 tablespoon butter with oil in skillet over medium-high heat. Cook fillets, in batches, 2 to 3 minutes on each side or until golden. Remove and arrange over vegetables.

Add cream to skillet, stirring to loosen particles from bottom of skillet. Add chopped basil, and cook, stirring often, 1 to 2 minutes or until thickened. Serve fillets and vegetables with sauce. Garnish, if desired. Yield: 4 servings.

Per serving: Calories 624 (53% from fat); Fat 36.8g (sat 15.4g, mono 13.3g, poly 5.3g); Protein 32.8g; Carb 43.9g; Fiber 5.3g; Chol 145mg; Iron 2.5mg; Sodium 1318mg; Calc 79mg

When a recipe calls for firm-textured, mild fish fillets, you can always use orange roughy, flounder, or tilapia.

entertaining

Pecan-Crusted Catfish With Lemon-Thyme Butter

prep: 11 min. cook: 30 min.

Catfish takes an upscale turn with a pecan crust and an herb butter sauce.

- 1½ cups pecan halves, toasted and divided
- ¾ cup all-purpose flour
- 2½ teaspoons Creole seasoning, divided
- 1 large egg
- 1 cup milk
- 6 (6-ounce) catfish, flounder, tilapia, or trout fillets
- ¾ cup plus 2 tablespoons butter, divided
- 1 tablespoon Worcestershire sauce
- 6 large fresh thyme sprigs
- ½ teaspoon kosher salt
- ¼ teaspoon pepper
- ¼ cup plus 3 tablespoons fresh lemon juice
- Garnishes: fresh thyme sprigs, lemon slices

Process ¾ cup pecans, flour, and 1½ teaspoons Creole seasoning in a food processor until finely ground; place in a large shallow bowl.

Whisk together egg and milk in a large bowl; set aside.

Sprinkle both sides of fillets evenly with remaining 1 teaspoon Creole seasoning. Dip fillets in egg mixture, draining off excess; dredge in pecan mixture, coating both sides, and shake off excess.

Melt 2 tablespoons butter in a large skillet over medium heat until butter starts to bubble. Place 2 fillets in skillet; cook 4 to 6 minutes on each side or until golden. Drain on a wire rack in a jelly-roll pan; keep warm in a 200° oven. Wipe skillet clean; repeat procedure with remaining fillets.

Wipe skillet clean. Melt remaining ½ cup butter in skillet over high heat; add remaining ¾ cup pecans, and cook, stirring occasionally, 2 to 3 minutes or until toasted. Stir in Worcestershire sauce, 6 thyme sprigs, salt, and pepper; cook 30 seconds or until thyme becomes very aromatic. Stir in lemon juice. Discard thyme sprigs.

Place fish on a serving platter; spoon pecan butter over fish. Garnish, if desired. Yield: 6 servings.

Per serving: Calories 674 (76% from fat); Fat 56.8g (sat 21.5g, mono 22.6g, poly 8.9g); Protein 24.4g; Carb 19.7g; Fiber 3.1g; Chol 163mg; Iron 2.3mg; Sodium 1213mg; Calc 94mg

the flavors of fish

Do you like mild-flavored fish or those with robust flavors? Here's a guide to help you select or substitute fish according to your taste preferences.

- Mild fish such as catfish, cod, flounder, grouper, orange roughy, and tilapia readily accept the flavor of seasonings and sauces.
- Medium-flavored fish like tuna, farm-raised salmon, swordfish, and mahi-mahi have a fishier taste compared to the mild group.
- Wild salmon, mackerel and kingfish are the most full-flavored fish.
- Shellfish such as blue crabs, shrimp, scallops, and lobster are mild in flavor.
- King and Dungeness crabs, oysters, mussels, and clams are medium-flavored shellfish.

taste of the south fried catfish

Members of our Foods staff have a tough time arriving at a consensus when it comes to the Southern delicacy of fried catfish. These words seem to evoke a flood of personal memories.

In searching for the perfect fried catfish recipe, we tried a variety of techniques, from soaking catfish overnight to combining the best ingredients from several different recipes. The more we sampled, the more we realized that it's hard not to go back to what you know or grew up eating.

Now available year-round at grocery seafood counters and in the freezer section, farm-raised catfish delivers a mild flavor and a firm texture that's perfect for anything from pan-frying to grilling. Our Test Kitchens found 4- to 6-ounce, thin-cut fillets easy to manage in the skillet, and they curl up when cooked, giving great eye appeal. And cornmeal offers that sought-after delicate crunchy coating for the fish without a greasy taste. (If you purchase frozen fillets, place them in a colander with a pan underneath, and thaw in the refrigerator overnight; otherwise, keep them in the coldest part of your refrigerator, and use within two days.)

Enhance crispy fish fillets with your favorite side dishes. Our choices include hush puppies, baked beans, and coleslaw. As for condiments, the number one item is hot sauce, but a dab of ketchup and tartar sauce and a squeeze of lemon are also high on the list.

Jack's Fried Catfish

family favorite
Jack's Fried Catfish

prep: 10 min.   cook: 8 min. per batch
other: 1 hr., 10 min.

6   (4- to 6-ounce) catfish fillets
2   cups milk
2   cups yellow cornmeal
1   tablespoon seasoned salt
2   teaspoons pepper
½   teaspoon onion powder
½   teaspoon garlic powder
1   teaspoon salt
Peanut oil

Place catfish in a single layer in a shallow dish; cover with milk. Cover and chill 1 hour.
Combine cornmeal and next 4 ingredients in a shallow dish.
Remove catfish fillets from refrigerator, and let stand at room temperature 10 minutes. Remove from milk, allowing excess to drip off. Sprinkle evenly with 1 teaspoon salt.
Dredge catfish fillets in cornmeal mixture, shaking off excess. Pour oil to a depth of 1½ inches into a large skillet; heat to 350°. Fry fillets, in batches, about 3 to 4 minutes on each side or until golden. Drain on wire racks over paper towels. Yield: 6 servings.

Per serving: Calories 410 (58% from fat); Fat 26.2g (sat 5.6g, mono 12g, poly 6.7g); Protein 28.8g; Carb 13.1g; Fiber 1.2g; Chol 83mg; Iron 1.7mg; Sodium 774mg; Calc 105mg

fish frying tips

• Remove excess moisture from fish before dredging by patting dry with a paper towel.
• Keep one hand clean for dredging and the other hand available for frying.
• Select an oil, such as peanut oil, with a high smoke point.
• Use a large Dutch oven or deep cast-iron skillet to keep the hot oil from popping out.
• Use a deep-fat thermometer to maintain an accurate temperature.
• Don't overcrowd the skillet; fry in batches, two or three fillets at a time. Bring remaining oil back to the proper temperature before frying the next batch.
• Remove fish from skillet with a wide, slotted, curved spoon.
• To keep warm, place fried fish on a wire rack with a foil-lined pan underneath; place in a 250° oven. For a crisp texture, do not cover fillets.

Grilled Snapper With Orange-Almond Sauce

prep: 20 min.   cook: 12 min.

Fresh thyme sprigs smoke and sizzle right on the hot coals, sending an herbal essence up into the fish.

6   (8-ounce) snapper or grouper fillets
2   tablespoons olive oil
1   teaspoon coarse sea salt
1   teaspoon freshly ground pepper
4   fresh thyme sprigs
Vegetable cooking spray
½   cup butter
½   cup sliced almonds
½   to 1 tablespoon grated orange rind
Garnishes: orange wedges, fresh thyme sprigs

Rub fish fillets with oil. Sprinkle evenly with salt and pepper.
Arrange 4 thyme sprigs on hot charcoal or lava rocks on grill. Coat food rack with cooking spray; place on grill over high heat (400° to 500°). Place fish on rack; grill 5 to

fish substitutions

Can't find a particular fish? Use this substitution list, selecting the same form as called for in the recipe—whole, fillets, or steaks.

Catfish: haddock, pollock, flounder
Flounder: ocean perch, orange roughy, sole, turbot
Grouper: halibut, sea bass, snapper
Haddock: cod, ocean catfish, flounder
Halibut: sea bass, snapper, monkfish
Mackerel: bluefish, lake trout
Perch: walleyed pike, orange roughy, flounder, turbot, sole
Pompano: snapper, sea bass, yellowtail, redfish
Salmon: swordfish, halibut, lake trout
Sea Bass: grouper, halibut, snapper
Snapper: sea bass, grouper, redfish, pompano
Sole: flounder, turbot, orange roughy, ocean perch
Swordfish: halibut, shark, marlin, tuna
Tuna: blackfish, bluefish, mackeral, mahi-mahi, salmon

6 minutes on each side or until fish flakes with a fork.
Melt butter in a saucepan over medium-high heat; add almonds, and sauté 5 minutes or until butter is brown. Remove from heat. Stir in orange rind. Pour sauce over fish. Garnish, if desired. Yield: 6 servings.

Per serving: Calories 439 (55% from fat); Fat 26.7g (sat 11.1g, mono 10.4g, poly 3g); Protein 46.6g; Carb 1.8g; Fiber 1g; Chol 120mg; Iron 3.9mg; Sodium 461mg; Calc 94mg

Broiled Grouper

prep: 10 min.   cook: 10 min.

2   pounds grouper fillets
½   cup grated Parmesan cheese
1   tablespoon butter or margarine, softened
3   tablespoons reduced-fat mayonnaise
3   tablespoons chopped green onions
1   garlic clove, pressed
¼   teaspoon salt
Dash of hot sauce

Place fillets in a single layer in a lightly greased 13- x 9-inch pan.
Stir together cheese and next 6 ingredients; spread over fillets.
Broil 5½ inches from heat 10 minutes or until lightly browned and fish flakes with a fork. Yield: 6 servings.

Per serving: Calories 200 (29% from fat); Fat 6.5g (sat 3g, mono 1.6g, poly 1.2g); Protein 32g; Carb 1.7g; Fiber 0.1g; Chol 67mg; Iron 1.5mg; Sodium 358mg; Calc 119mg

Note: Don't broil on the top rack or the topping may burn before the fish is done.

Orange Roughy Dijon

prep: 10 min.   cook: 10 min.

4   (6- to 8-ounce) orange roughy fillets
½   teaspoon salt
¼   teaspoon pepper
¼   cup butter or margarine, softened
2   tablespoons Dijon mustard
1   tablespoon lemon juice
2   teaspoons Worcestershire sauce
1   garlic clove, minced
½   cup fine, dry breadcrumbs

Sprinkle fish with salt and pepper; place in a lightly greased 13- x 9-inch baking dish.

Combine butter and next 4 ingredients; spread on fish. Top with breadcrumbs.
Bake at 450° for 10 minutes or until fish flakes with a fork. Yield: 4 servings.

Per serving: Calories 286 (44% from fat); Fat 14.1g (sat 7.4g, mono 4.1g, poly 0.9g); Protein 27.5g; Carb 11.8g; Fiber 0.8g; Chol 64mg; Iron 1.4mg; Sodium 795mg; Calc 95mg

Moroccan Broiled Fish

prep: 13 min.   cook: 10 min.   other: 30 min.

2   garlic cloves, halved
1   (2-inch) piece fresh ginger, peeled and chopped (about 2 tablespoons chopped)
½   cup chopped fresh cilantro
1   small jalapeño pepper, seeded and quartered
1   teaspoon salt
½   teaspoon ground hot paprika
½   teaspoon ground turmeric
½   teaspoon ground coriander
2   teaspoons vegetable oil
2   pounds catfish, grouper, or flounder fillets (about 6 fillets)
Fresh lime wedges (optional)

Process first 9 ingredients in a food processor until finely chopped.
Spread spice mixture evenly over both sides of each fillet. Cover and chill 30 minutes. Place fillets on a lightly greased rack in a broiler pan. Broil fish 5½ inches from heat 10 minutes or until fish flakes with a fork. Serve with fresh lime wedges, if desired. Yield: 6 servings.

Per serving: Calories 198 (50% from fat); Fat 11.1g (sat 2.3g, mono 5.6g, poly 2.3g); Protein 22.3g; Carb 1.1g; Fiber 0.3g; Chol 75mg; Iron 1.2mg; Sodium 483mg; Calc 15mg

Note: For a different serving idea, prepare recipe as directed, let cooked fish stand 15 minutes, and then flake with a fork. Serve on warm flour tortillas with a squeeze of lime and a dollop of sour cream.

on orange roughy

Orange roughy is a chameleon, of sorts. Its pearl-white color, tender texture, and mild flavor allow it to take on whatever seasoning comes its way. It's ideal for baking, frying, or stuffing. Catfish fillets make a nice substitute.

Broiled Mahi-Mahi
With Parsleyed
Tomatoes

Blackened Fish

prep: 5 min.   cook: 24 min.   other: 20 min.

Blackening fish creates a lot of smoke, so it's best to cook it outside over a burner or on a stove with a strong exhaust fan.

6   (6- to 8-ounce) redfish, grouper, or catfish fillets (about ½ inch thick)
1   cup unsalted butter, melted
2   tablespoons blackened fish seasoning (we tested with Paul Prudhomme's Magic Seasoning Blends Blackened Redfish Magic)
Lemon wedges

Dip fillets in melted butter. Sprinkle 1 teaspoon seasoning evenly over both sides of each fillet. Press seasoning into fish, and place on wax paper.
Heat a large cast-iron skillet over medium-high heat 10 minutes or until smoking. Place 2 fillets in the skillet, and cook 4 minutes on each side or until lightly charred. Transfer fillets to a serving dish; cover and keep warm. Drain butter from skillet, and carefully wipe clean with paper towels.
Heat skillet 5 minutes or until smoking. Place 2 fillets in skillet, and repeat cooking procedure. Repeat with remaining 2 fillets. Serve with lemon wedges. Yield: 6 servings.

Per serving: Calories 292 (52% from fat); Fat 16.9g (sat 10g, mono 4.3g, poly 1.1g); Protein 33.2g; Carb 0.5g; Fiber 0g; Chol 103mg; Iron 1.5mg; Sodium 453mg; Calc 33mg

---

Broiled Mahi-Mahi With Parsleyed Tomatoes

prep: 15 min.   cook: 21 min.

2   medium onions, sliced
2   tablespoons olive oil
2   tomatoes, seeded and chopped
2   tablespoons chopped fresh parsley
¼   cup white wine
1   tablespoon tomato paste
2   garlic cloves, chopped
½   teaspoon salt, divided
½   teaspoon pepper, divided
6   (6- to 8-ounce) mahi-mahi fillets
1   (4-ounce) package crumbled feta cheese
Garnish: lemon slices

Sauté sliced onions in hot olive oil over medium-high heat 8 minutes or until tender. Add chopped tomatoes, next 4 ingredients, and ¼ teaspoon each of salt and pepper. Simmer, stirring occasionally, 5 minutes. Set onion-and-tomato mixture aside.
Place fish in a single layer on a lightly greased rack in an aluminum foil-lined broiler pan; sprinkle with remaining ¼ teaspoon each of salt and pepper.
Broil 5½ inches from heat 8 minutes or until fish flakes with a fork.
Spoon onion-and-tomato mixture evenly onto a platter; top with fish fillets. Sprinkle evenly with crumbled feta cheese, and garnish, if desired. Yield: 6 servings.

Per serving: Calories 265 (34% from fat); Fat 10g (sat 3.8g, mono 4.4g, poly 0.9g); Protein 35.1g; Carb 7.6g; Fiber 1.2g; Chol 142mg; Iron 2.6mg; Sodium 583mg; Calc 135mg

---

Coastal Bend Redfish With Shrimp and Crab

prep: 18 min.   cook: 11 min.

½   pound unpeeled, large fresh shrimp
1   cup Beurre Blanc (page 431)
⅓   cup tomato puree
1   teaspoon sugar
2   shallots, minced
1   garlic clove, minced
1   small jalapeño pepper, seeded and diced
¼   cup olive oil, divided
2   plum tomatoes, peeled, seeded, and diced
½   pound fresh jumbo lump crabmeat
6   (6- to 8-ounce) redfish or red snapper fillets, skinned
1   teaspoon salt
1   teaspoon pepper

Peel and chop shrimp. Whisk together Beurre Blanc and next 2 ingredients.
Sauté shallots, garlic, and jalapeño in 2 tablespoons hot oil in a large skillet over medium heat 1 minute. Add shrimp; cook 1 minute or just until shrimp turn pink. Add diced tomato; sauté 30 seconds. Stir in crabmeat and Beurre Blanc; keep sauce warm.
Brush fillets with remaining 2 tablespoons olive oil; sprinkle with salt and pepper. Place on a lightly greased rack in a broiler pan.
Broil 3 inches from heat 4 minutes on each side or until fish flakes. Top with shrimp and crab sauce. Yield: 6 servings.

Per serving: Calories 440 (73% from fat); Fat 35.6g (sat 17.1g, mono 13.8g, poly 2.3g); Protein 20.5g; Carb 10g; Fiber 0.7g; Chol 164mg; Iron 1.9mg; Sodium 925mg; Calc 94mg

---

Classic Trout Amandine

prep: 20 min.   cook: 25 min.   other: 2 hrs.

2   cups milk
2   teaspoons salt, divided
¼   teaspoon hot sauce
6   (8- to 10-ounce) trout fillets
¾   cup all-purpose flour
½   teaspoon pepper
1¼   cups butter or margarine, divided
1   tablespoon olive oil
¾   cup sliced almonds
2   tablespoons lemon juice
2   teaspoons Worcestershire sauce
¼   cup chopped fresh parsley
Hot cooked couscous with chopped parsley and red bell pepper (optional)

Stir together milk, 1 teaspoon salt, and hot sauce in a 13- x 9-inch baking dish; add fillets, turning to coat. Cover and chill 2 hours. **Combine** flour and ½ teaspoon pepper in a shallow dish.

Melt ¼ cup butter in a large skillet over medium heat; add oil. Remove fillets from marinade, discarding marinade. Dredge fillets in flour mixture. Add to skillet; cook 2 minutes on each side or until golden. Transfer to a serving platter; keep warm. **Combine** remaining 1 cup butter and almonds in a saucepan, and cook over medium heat until lightly browned. **Stir** in lemon juice, Worcestershire sauce, and remaining 1 teaspoon salt; cook 2 minutes. Remove from heat, and stir in chopped parsley; pour over fillets. Serve immediately over couscous. Yield: 6 servings.

Per serving: Calories 786 (68% from fat); Fat 59.5g (sat 28.9g, mono 19g, poly 7.3g); Protein 52.2g; Carb 10.6g; Fiber 1.7g; Chol 237mg; Iron 1.8mg; Sodium 673mg; Calc 235mg

Peppered Tuna With Mushroom Sauce

prep: 15 min.   cook: 20 min.

If you can't find fresh tuna, frozen tuna steaks will work just fine; just be sure to thaw before using.

3	tablespoons butter
1	cup sliced fresh mushrooms
¾	cup plum sauce*
¼	cup lite soy sauce
1	teaspoon ground ginger
2	tablespoons vegetable oil
6	(6-ounce) tuna steaks (about 1½ inches thick)
1	tablespoon freshly ground multicolored peppercorns or 2 teaspoons freshly ground black pepper

Melt butter in a large skillet over medium-high heat until lightly browned. Add mushrooms, and sauté 4 to 7 minutes or until lightly browned and tender. Stir in plum sauce, soy sauce, and ginger. Bring to a boil, reduce heat, and simmer, stirring often, 3 to 4 minutes. Keep warm.
Heat oil in a large nonstick skillet over medium-high heat. Sprinkle tuna evenly with pepper, and cook 4 minutes on each side (rare) or to desired degree of doneness.

Serve with warm mushroom sauce. Yield: 6 servings.

Per serving: Calories 419 (41% from fat); Fat 19.2g (sat 6.3g, mono 6.3g, poly 4.9g); Protein 41.5g; Carb 18.4g; Fiber 0.8g; Chol 80mg; Iron 2.7mg; Sodium 716mg; Calc 25mg

*Look for plum sauce on the ethnic foods aisle of the supermarket.

entertaining • from the grill

Grilled Salmon With Sweet Soy Slaw and Dipping Sauce

prep: 5 min.   cook: 26 min.   other: 10 min.

The dipping sauce will keep in the refrigerator, covered, for several weeks. Warm sauce over medium-low heat before serving. Use as a marinade on steaks or shrimp, too.

2	cups soy sauce
2	tablespoons canola oil
8	pieces crystallized ginger
2	garlic cloves, minced
3	cups sugar
6	(6-ounce) salmon fillets
2	(12-ounce) packages broccoli slaw
¼	cup chopped green onions
1	tablespoon sesame seeds, toasted
Salt and pepper to taste	

Combine first 4 ingredients in a small saucepan. Stir in sugar. Cook over medium heat 10 minutes or until sugar dissolves, stirring occasionally. Remove from heat. (Mixture will thicken.) Set aside 1½ cups soy mixture for slaw and to serve as a dipping sauce.
Brush both sides of salmon generously with remaining soy mixture; cover and let stand 10 minutes.
Grill salmon, covered with grill lid, over medium-high heat (350° to 400°) 6 to 8 minutes on each side.
Toss together broccoli slaw, green onions, sesame seeds, and ½ cup reserved soy mixture; top with grilled salmon. Season with salt and pepper to taste. Serve with reserved 1 cup soy mixture for dipping. Yield: 6 servings.

Per serving: Calories 632 (32% from fat); Fat 22.5g (sat 4.9g, mono 10g, poly 4.9g); Protein 43.5g; Carb 62.5g; Fiber 4g; Chol 123mg; Iron 3.5mg; Sodium 2727mg; Calc 98mg

low carb

Baked Salmon With Caribbean Fruit Salsa

Prep: 5 min.   cook: 25 min.   other: 2 hrs.

A whole salmon fillet makes a dramatic presentation. Ask the butcher at your grocery store to remove salmon skin.

1	(3-pound) whole skinless salmon fillet
1	tablespoon Caribbean jerk seasoning*
1½	tablespoons olive oil
Caribbean Fruit Salsa	
Garnish: lime wedges	

Place salmon fillet in a roasting pan; sprinkle evenly on 1 side with jerk seasoning. Drizzle with oil. Cover and chill 2 hours.
Bake salmon at 350° for 20 to 25 minutes or until fish flakes with a fork. Serve with Caribbean Fruit Salsa. Garnish, if desired. Yield: 8 servings.

Per serving: Calories 346 (43% from fat); Fat 16.4g (sat 2.5g, mono 7g, poly 5.4g); Protein 39.1g; Carb 9.2g; Fiber 1.4g; Chol 108mg; Iron 1.8mg; Sodium 192mg; Calc 35mg

*Substitute Jamaican jerk seasoning, if desired. Caribbean jerk seasoning has a hint of sweetness.

Caribbean Fruit Salsa

prep: 20 min.   other: 2 hrs.

This salsa's also great as an appetizer served with tortilla chips.

1	mango (about ½ pound), peeled and diced*
1	papaya (about ½ pound), peeled and diced*
1	medium-size red bell pepper, diced
1	medium-size green bell pepper, diced
1	cup diced fresh pineapple
1	small red onion, diced
3	tablespoons chopped fresh cilantro
2	tablespoons fresh lime juice
1	tablespoon olive oil

Stir together all ingredients. Cover and chill at least 2 hours. Yield: 5 cups.

Per ¼ cup: Calories 24 (30% from fat); Fat 0.8g (sat 0.1g, mono 0.5g, poly 0.1g); Protein 0.3g; Carb 4.6g; Fiber 0.7g; Chol 0mg; Iron 0.1mg; Sodium 1mg; Calc 6mg

*Substitute 1 cup each diced, refrigerated jarred mango and papaya, if desired.

Cedar-Planked Salmon

all about planking

- Look for 1-inch-thick wood planks. Thinner planks can burn and warp on the grill.
- Look for cedar planks marked "untreated."
- Always soak the plank before grilling with it. A soaked plank produces maximum smoke and is less likely to burn. Submerge it in water at least an hour or up to 24 hours. Weight it down with a small can.
- If the fillet is skinless, lightly coat the plank with cooking spray.
- After placing the plank on the grill, immediately cover the grill so that the smoke quickly surrounds the food.
- Use oven mitts to remove the plank and place it on a heatproof platter or baking sheet. The edges may be charred and smoldering.
- If you're serving fillets, cut them into serving-size portions; then serve directly from the plank, carefully sliding a thin spatula between skin and meat.

Woods that work
- Alder produces a delicate flavor that works well with mild foods. Alder and seafood—especially salmon—are a great match.
- Pair cedar with hearty foods such as salmon or pork. Cedar also stands up nicely to spicy dishes.
- Hickory gives an intense smoky flavor that works well with beef and chicken.
- Maple imparts a mild smoky flavor with subtle sweetness. It works nicely with fish, chicken, and pork.
- Oak offers a medium aroma. Expect a pleasantly acidic note similar to the essence oak barrels give Chardonnay. Pair oak with most any food, especially chicken, fish, and pork.

from the grill • low calorie • low carb
low fat • weekend chef

Cedar-Planked Salmon

prep: 5 min.   cook: 30 min.

Look for cedar planks at your local hardware or home improvement store with the outdoor grilling accessories. The aromatic planks infuse fish with just enough smoky flavor to leave you wanting more.

Cedar plank
2   teaspoons sugar
1   teaspoon mesquite smoked sea salt or table salt
1   teaspoon pepper
1½ tablespoons chopped fresh dill
1   (2-pound) wild salmon fillet, skin on* (such as Coho or Sockeye)

Soak cedar plank in water according to package directions. Drain plank.
Combine sugar and next 3 ingredients in a small bowl. Rub seasoning blend over flesh side of salmon and place skin side down on prepared cedar plank.
Grill, covered with grill lid, over medium-high heat (350° to 400°) 25 to 30 minutes or until salmon flakes with a fork. Yield: 6 servings.

Per serving: Calories 222 (39% from fat); Fat 9.5g (sat 1.4g, mono 1.1g, poly 1.9g); Protein 29.7g; Carb 1.6g; Fiber 0.1g; Chol 68mg; Iron 1.1mg; Sodium 455mg; Calc 2mg

*If wild salmon is not available, you can substitute Atlantic or farm-raised salmon.

from the grill

Shredded Grilled Tilapia Tacos

prep: 10 min.   cook: 6 min.   other: 10 min.

1   tablespoon ground chipotle seasoning
1½ teaspoons ground cumin
½   teaspoon salt
6   (6-ounce) tilapia fillets
2   tablespoons olive oil
1   teaspoon grated lime rind
2   tablespoons fresh lime juice
Vegetable cooking spray
12 corn tortillas
Sweet-and-Spicy Slaw (page 409)
Fruity Black Bean Salsa
Fresh lime wedges

Combine first 3 ingredients. Rub seasoning mixture evenly over fillets.
Stir together oil, grated lime rind, and juice; drizzle over fillets. Let stand 10 to 15 minutes to marinate, if desired.
Arrange fillets in a grill basket coated with cooking spray.
Grill over medium-high heat (350° to 400°) 3 minutes on each side or just until fish flakes with a fork. Cool slightly.
Shred fish. Spoon 2 to 3 tablespoons fish into each tortilla, and top each with ¼ cup Sweet-and-Spicy Slaw and ¼ cup Fruity Black Bean Salsa. Serve with a squeeze of lime. Yield: 6 servings.

Per serving (including slaw and salsa): Calories 411 (32% from fat); Fat 14.4g (sat 4g, mono 5.5g, poly 1.8g); Protein 39.7g; Carb 33.7g; Fiber 6.5g; Chol 121mg; Iron 2.2mg; Sodium 473mg; Calc 81mg

Fruity Black Bean Salsa

prep: 15 min.

1   (15-ounce) can black beans, rinsed and drained
1   small papaya, peeled, seeded, and cut into ½-inch cubes*
½   red or green bell pepper, seeded and chopped
1   large ripe avocado, cut into ½-inch cubes
2   jalapeño peppers, seeded and minced
¼   cup chopped fresh cilantro
1   teaspoon grated lemon rind
2   tablespoons fresh lemon juice
1   tablespoon honey
½   teaspoon salt

Combine first 6 ingredients in a glass bowl. Whisk together lemon rind and next 3 ingredients in a small bowl, and drizzle over bean mixture. Toss gently to coat. Cover and chill salsa until ready to serve. Yield: 3½ cups.

Per tablespoon: Calories 12 (38% from fat); Fat 0.5g (sat 0.1g, mono 0.3g, poly 0.1g); Protein 0.4g; Carb 1.7g; Fiber 0.6g; Chol 0mg; Iron 0.1mg; Sodium 37mg; Calc 3mg

*Substitute ½ (24-ounce) jar papaya available in the produce section of your supermarket for fresh, if desired. If you can't find papaya, substitute 2 ripe mangoes, cubed.

shellfish

Shellfish are divided into two groups: *crustaceans* and *mollusks*. Crustaceans have long bodies with soft, jointed shells and legs. These include shrimp, crabs, crawfish, and lobster. Mollusks have soft bodies with no spinal column and are covered by a shell of one or more pieces. These include clams, mussels, oysters, and scallops as well as squid, snails, and octopus.

Freshness is critical for shellfish because they spoil quickly out of water. Many shellfish are kept alive in water tanks or on beds of ice until time to cook them, but most are also available fresh, frozen, cooked, or frozen cooked.

The majority of shrimp sold has been frozen, often while still at sea. The fast-freezing method preserves freshness.

shrimp

Fresh raw shrimp vary in color from light gray to pink. The color is an indication of the type of water the shrimp came from, not quality. (All shrimp turn pale pink during cooking.) The flesh should feel firm and slippery and have a mild, almost sweet odor. Avoid any with an odor of ammonia, which indicates deterioration.

Shrimp vary in size from small to colossal. Small and medium shrimp are good in salads and casseroles. Large and jumbo shrimp are ideal stuffed, grilled, or in entrées for entertaining.

Store shrimp in the refrigerator for up to two days. Shrimp can be frozen raw in the shell or cooked, peeled, and frozen for longer storage.

Shrimp are usually sold headless, but if they are whole, twist off heads, being sure to remove all parts of the head region. Though the heads are typically removed before cooking, you can save them to flavor sauces, stocks, and soups.

To peel shrimp, run your thumb along the inside curl of the shrimp between the legs and remove shell. The tail can be left on the shrimp for show, if desired. Using a small knife or deveiner, make a slit down the back of the shrimp, and remove the sand vein, if you'd like. (See text at right.)

Shrimp are easy to prepare, and many chefs believe they taste best when cooked simply. Cook just until they turn pink. Small shrimp will cook in just 1 to 3 minutes; larger shrimp will take only moments longer.

You can cook shrimp peeled or unpeeled, deveined or with the vein still intact. They are sold according to the number per pound, which varies from region to region. See the chart on the following page for examples.

---

family favorite • low calorie • low carb
low fat • quick

Boiled Shrimp

prep: 25 min.   cook: 5 min.

6   cups water
2   tablespoons salt
2   bay leaves
1   lemon, halved
1   celery rib with leaves, cut into 3-inch pieces
2   pounds unpeeled fresh shrimp
Cocktail Sauce (optional, page 435)

Combine first 5 ingredients in a Dutch oven; bring to a boil. Add shrimp, and cook 3 to 5 minutes. Drain well; rinse with cold water. Cover and chill. Peel shrimp, and devein, if desired. Serve with Cocktail Sauce, if desired. Yield: 4 servings.

Per serving (without sauce): Calories 171 (10% from fat); Fat 1.9g (sat 0.5g, mono 0.3g, poly 0.8g); Protein 36g; Carb 0g; Fiber 0g; Chol 336mg; Iron 5.3mg; Sodium 2130mg; Calc 68mg

---

low calorie • low carb • low fat

Steamed Shrimp

prep: 15 min.   cook: 15 min.

We used 15- to 19-count shrimp per pound when testing this recipe.

6   cups water
1   (12-ounce) bottle beer
1   large onion, quartered
4   to 6 tablespoons Old Bay seasoning
6   pounds unpeeled, jumbo fresh shrimp
Cocktail Sauce (optional, page 435)
Lemon wedges (optional)

Bring first 4 ingredients to a boil in a large Dutch oven. Add shrimp, and cook, covered, 8 to 10 minutes or just until shrimp turn pink, stirring often. Turn off heat, and let stand 2 minutes; drain. If desired, serve shrimp with cocktail sauce and lemon wedges. Yield: 12 servings.

Per serving (without sauce): Calories 173 (10% from fat); Fat 1.9g (sat 0.5g, mono 0.3g, poly 0.8g); Protein 36.1g; Carb 0.6g; Fiber 0g; Chol 336mg; Iron 5.3mg; Sodium 714mg; Calc 68mg

---

do I need to devein?

That little black line that runs down the back of a shrimp (the sand vein) is its intestinal tract. In small shrimp, the vein is really not noticeable and is generally left in. But for larger shrimp, it's unappealing and adds a gritty, muddy taste. While there's no harm in eating cooked shrimp that haven't been deveined, most people prefer cleaned shrimp.

Marinated Shrimp

prep: 30 min.   cook: 2 min.   other: 1 hr.

A cool and easy dish for a summer cookout.

2	pounds unpeeled, large fresh shrimp
6	cups water
2	teaspoons salt
½	cup sugar
1½	cups white vinegar
1	cup vegetable oil
¼	cup capers, undrained
1	teaspoon salt
1½	teaspoons celery salt
1	medium-size red onion, sliced and separated into rings

Peel shrimp, and devein, if desired. Bring water and 2 teaspoons salt to a boil; add shrimp, and cook 2 minutes or just until shrimp turn pink. Drain; rinse with cold water. Chill.

Whisk together sugar and next 5 ingredients in a large shallow dish; add shrimp alternately with onion. Cover and chill 1 hour to 6 hours, turning often. Drain and discard marinade before serving. Yield: 10 appetizer servings.

Per serving: Calories 80 (16% from fat); Fat 1.4g (sat 0.3g, mono 0.4g, poly 0.6g); Protein 14.5g; Carb 1.4g; Fiber 0.2g; Chol 134mg; Iron 2.2mg; Sodium 198mg; Calc 29mg

Butterflying shrimp: Split and flatten shrimp for a pretty appearance and even cooking.

barbecue shrimp notes

● Offer plenty of napkins, paper towels, or, if you have them, bibs. (If you don't like getting your hands dirty when you eat, this isn't the dish for you.)

● Leftover shrimp keep well in the refrigerator for a day or two. Be careful not to overcook them when reheating. You can also peel them, and serve them over pasta.

New Orleans Barbecue Shrimp

prep: 5 min.   cook: 20 min.   other: 2 hrs.

Spicy, buttery, and decidedly hands-on, this dish is a New Orleans classic. Serve with a green salad and corn on the cob for a complete meal.

4	pounds unpeeled, large fresh shrimp or 6 pounds shrimp with heads on
½	cup butter
½	cup olive oil
¼	cup chili sauce
¼	cup Worcestershire sauce
2	lemons, sliced
4	garlic cloves, chopped
2	tablespoons Creole seasoning
2	tablespoons lemon juice
1	tablespoon chopped fresh parsley
1	teaspoon paprika
1	teaspoon dried oregano
1	teaspoon ground red pepper
½	teaspoon hot sauce

Spread shrimp in a shallow, aluminum foil-lined broiler pan.

Combine butter and remaining ingredients in a medium saucepan over low heat, stirring until butter melts; pour over shrimp. Cover and chill 2 hours, turning shrimp every 30 minutes.

Bake, uncovered, at 400° for 20 minutes, turning shrimp once. Serve with French bread. Yield: 8 servings.

Per serving: Calories 396 (56% from fat); Fat 24.7g (sat 14.9g, mono 6.2g, poly 1.6g); Protein 36.5g; Carb 6.3g; Fiber 0.3g; Chol 396mg; Iron 6mg; Sodium 2254mg; Calc 91mg

Sautéed Shrimp With Country Ham and Capers

prep: 25 min.   cook: 6 min.

Crusty bread is a must for sopping up the buttery goodness.

3	pounds unpeeled, extra-large fresh shrimp
⅓	cup butter
⅓	cup olive oil
1	cup (4 ounces) thinly sliced country ham, prosciutto, or baked ham
¼	cup vermouth or dry white wine
2	to 3 tablespoons fresh lemon juice
2	tablespoons capers
1	teaspoon salt-free Cajun seasoning
2	tablespoons minced fresh parsley

Peel shrimp, and devein, if desired.

Melt butter with olive oil in a large deep skillet over medium-high heat. Increase heat to high, and add shrimp and ham; cook, stirring constantly, 3 to 5 minutes or until shrimp turn pink. Reduce heat to medium high, add vermouth and next 3 ingredients; bring to a boil. Pour into a large deep serving platter or individual bowls. Sprinkle with parsley; serve immediately. Serve with French bread. Yield: 8 servings.

Per serving: Calories 304 (57% from fat); Fat 19.2g (sat 6.8g, mono 9.4g, poly 1.9g); Protein 31.2g; Carb 0.7g; Fiber 0.1g; Chol 282mg; Iron 4.3mg; Sodium 790mg; Calc 57mg

shrimp statistics

1 pound raw, unpeeled shrimp

= 12 ounces raw, peeled, deveined shrimp

= 8 to 9 ounces cooked peeled shrimp

colossal = 11 shrimp per pound

jumbo = 15 to 19 shrimp per pound

large = 26 to 29 shrimp per pound

medium = 37 to 40 shrimp per pound

small = 45+ shrimp per pound

Speedy Scampi

prep: 20 min.   cook: 8 min.

2	pounds unpeeled, large fresh shrimp
⅓	cup butter or margarine
2	green onions, sliced
4	large garlic cloves, minced
1	tablespoon grated lemon rind
½	cup fresh lemon juice
½	teaspoon salt
½	cup chopped fresh parsley
½	teaspoon hot sauce
12	ounces angel hair pasta, cooked

Peel shrimp, and devein, if desired.
Melt butter in a large skillet over medium-high heat. Add green onions, minced garlic, lemon rind, lemon juice, and salt; cook 2 to 3 minutes or until bubbly.
Reduce heat to medium; add shrimp, and cook, stirring constantly, 5 minutes or just until shrimp turn pink. Stir in parsley and hot sauce. Toss with hot pasta. Yield: 4 servings.

Per serving: Calories 627 (27% from fat); Fat 19.1g (sat 10.5g, mono 4.6g, poly 2.6g); Protein 48.2g; Carb 66.8g; Fiber 3.7g; Chol 376mg; Iron 8.4mg; Sodium 799mg; Calc 115mg

Shrimp Cakes With
Watercress Rémoulade

These savory cakes also make great sandwiches.

Shrimp Cakes With Watercress Rémoulade

prep: 25 min.   cook: 30 min.   other: 2 hrs.

Serve these cakes with lemon juice or tartar sauce, if desired.

⅓	cup butter or margarine
¼	cup minced sweet onion
¼	cup all-purpose flour
1	cup milk
1	tablespoon seafood seasoning
½	teaspoon ground red pepper
2	large eggs, lightly beaten
4	cups chopped cooked shrimp*
1	sleeve saltine crackers, crushed (about 1½ cups crumbs)
1½	cups Japanese breadcrumbs (panko)
9	tablespoons vegetable oil, divided

Watercress Rémoulade
Garnishes: whole cooked shrimp, watercress

Melt butter in a large saucepan over medium heat; add onion, and sauté 3 minutes or until onion is tender.

Whisk in flour; cook, whisking constantly, about 1 minute. Gradually whisk in milk; cook, whisking constantly, until thickened. Remove from heat; stir in seafood seasoning and red pepper. Cool.
Whisk in beaten eggs; stir in shrimp and cracker crumbs. Shape into 15 (3-inch) patties; dredge in breadcrumbs. Cover and chill 2 hours.
Heat 3 tablespoons oil in a large nonstick skillet over medium heat. Add 5 shrimp cakes; cook 5 minutes on each side or until golden. Repeat procedure twice with remaining oil and shrimp cakes. Serve with Watercress Rémoulade. Garnish, if desired. Yield: 15 cakes.

Per shrimp cake and 1 tablespoon rémoulade: Calories 411 (72% from fat); Fat 32.8g (sat 6.9g, mono 10.1g, poly 13.8g); Protein 16.3g; Carb 31.1g; Fiber 0.7g; Chol 167mg; Iron 3mg; Sodium 569mg; Calc 75mg

Note: To make consistent-sized patties, try this easy method: Using a 3-inch round cutter, pat ⅓ cup shrimp cake batter into center of cutter on a wax paper-lined baking sheet.

Watercress Rémoulade

prep: 11 min.

1½	cups mayonnaise
½	cup chopped fresh chives
2	tablespoons Dijon mustard
3	green onions, sliced
1	bunch watercress leaves, chopped (about ½ cup)
1	garlic clove, minced
¼	teaspoon ground red pepper

Stir together all ingredients in a medium bowl. Yield: 2 cups.

Per tablespoon: Calories 76 (97% from fat); Fat 8.2g (sat 1.2g, mono 2.1g, poly 4.4g); Protein 0.3g; Carb 0.7g; Fiber 0.1g; Chol 4mg; Iron 0.1mg; Sodium 83mg; Calc 6mg

*We tested this recipe using 1 (32-ounce) package frozen cooked large shrimp, thawed and patted dry with paper towels.

Cracker-Breaded Fried Shrimp

prep: 30 min.   cook: 2 min. per batch

We found that coarsely crushed crackers work best for this recipe. Place crackers in a zip-top plastic bag, and crush with a rolling pin.

2   pounds unpeeled, large fresh shrimp
1½ cups crushed buttery round crackers (about 26 crackers)
½   cup all-purpose flour
¾   teaspoon pepper, divided
½   teaspoon salt
½   cup buttermilk
2   or 3 drops of hot sauce
1   large egg
Vegetable oil

Peel shrimp, leaving tails intact, and devein, if desired.
Combine crushed crackers, flour, ½ teaspoon pepper, and salt in a shallow dish. Stir together buttermilk, hot sauce, egg, and remaining ¼ teaspoon pepper in a bowl until blended. Dip shrimp in buttermilk mixture; dredge in cracker mixture.
Pour oil to a depth of 2½ inches into a large deep cast-iron or heavy-duty skillet; heat to 375°. Fry shrimp, in batches, 1 to 2 minutes or until golden; drain on wire racks over paper towels. Yield: 6 servings.

Per serving: Calories 459 (61% from fat); Fat 30.9g (sat 4.2g, mono 13.8g, poly 11.6g); Protein 27.9g; Carb 18.1g; Fiber 0.6g; Chol 262mg; Iron 4.8mg; Sodium 595mg; Calc 93mg

Curry-Ginger Shrimp

prep: 50 min.   cook: 49 min.

3   pounds unpeeled, large fresh shrimp
2   cups water
¾   cup port wine, divided
6   large garlic cloves, minced
2   tablespoons minced fresh ginger
2   teaspoons red wine vinegar
¼   cup butter or margarine, divided
¼   cup peanut oil, divided
1   teaspoon salt, divided
¼   teaspoon pepper
4   green onions, chopped
1   tablespoon curry powder
½   teaspoon hot sauce
¼   cup dry white wine
½   cup whipping cream
2   (6-ounce) packages fresh baby spinach
6   cups hot cooked basmati rice

Peel shrimp, and devein, if desired, reserving shells; set shrimp aside. Bring shells and 2 cups water to a boil in a large saucepan over medium-high heat. Cover, reduce heat, and simmer 20 minutes. Strain shrimp stock, reserving ½ cup; discard shells and remaining stock.
Bring ⅓ cup port wine and next 3 ingredients to a boil in a skillet over medium-high heat; boil 4 to 5 minutes or until liquid is reduced to 2 tablespoons.
Melt 2 tablespoons butter with 2 tablespoons oil in a large skillet over medium-high heat. Add shrimp, ½ teaspoon salt, and pepper; sauté 6 to 8 minutes or until shrimp turn pink. Remove from skillet; keep warm.
Add onions, curry powder, and hot sauce to skillet; sauté over medium-high heat 1 minute. Stir in shrimp stock, remaining port wine, and white wine; cook 8 minutes or until reduced by half. Stir in cream; cook 4 minutes or until reduced by half. Stir in reserved wine reduction and remaining 2 tablespoons butter. Add shrimp; cook until thoroughly heated.
Sauté spinach in remaining 2 tablespoons hot oil 1 to 2 minutes or until wilted; sprinkle with remaining ½ teaspoon salt. Serve with shrimp and rice. Yield: 6 servings.

Per serving: Calories 652 (36% from fat); Fat 25.9g (sat 11.1g, mono 9g, poly 4.4g); Protein 43.7g; Carb 61.2g; Fiber 6.6g; Chol 383mg; Iron 11.5mg; Sodium 1033mg; Calc 201mg

Shrimp and Grits

prep: 18 min.   cook: 28 min.

There are many variations of this Southern classic; this is one of our staff's favorites.

2   cups water
1   (14-ounce) can chicken broth
¾   cup half-and-half
¾   teaspoon salt
1   cup uncooked regular grits
1   cup (4 ounces) shredded Cheddar cheese
⅓   cup grated Parmesan cheese
2   tablespoons butter
½   teaspoon hot sauce
4   bacon slices
1   pound unpeeled, medium-size fresh shrimp
¼   teaspoon salt
¼   teaspoon pepper
¼   cup all-purpose flour
1   (8-ounce) package sliced fresh mushrooms
½   cup chopped green onions
2   garlic cloves, minced
½   cup chicken broth
2   tablespoons fresh lemon juice
¼   teaspoon hot sauce

Bring first 4 ingredients to a boil in a medium saucepan; gradually whisk in grits. Reduce heat, and simmer, stirring occasionally, 10 minutes or until thickened. Add Cheddar cheese and next 3 ingredients. Keep warm.
Cook bacon in a large skillet until crisp. Remove and drain on paper towels, reserving 1 tablespoon drippings in skillet. Crumble bacon.
Peel shrimp, and devein, if desired. Sprinkle shrimp with ¼ teaspoon salt and pepper; dredge in flour.
Sauté mushrooms in hot drippings in skillet 5 minutes or until tender. Add ½ cup green onions, and sauté 2 minutes. Add shrimp and garlic, and sauté 2 minutes or until shrimp are lightly browned. Stir in ½ cup chicken broth, lemon juice, and ¼ teaspoon hot sauce; cook 2 more minutes, stirring to loosen particles from bottom of skillet.
Serve shrimp mixture over hot cheese grits. Top with crumbled bacon. Yield: 4 servings.

Per serving: Calories 615 (46% from fat); Fat 31.4g (sat 16.6g, mono 9.4g, poly 2.4g); Protein 38.3g; Carb 44.8g; Fiber 1.9g; Chol 209mg; Iron 4.9mg; Sodium 1795mg; Calc 392mg

Frogmore Stew

prep: 10 min. cook: 30 min.

5   quarts water
¼   cup Old Bay seasoning
4   pounds small red potatoes
2   pounds kielbasa or hot smoked link
     sausage, cut into 1½-inch pieces
6   ears fresh corn, halved
4   pounds unpeeled, large fresh
     shrimp
Old Bay seasoning (optional)
Cocktail sauce (optional)

This stew at its most basic contains shrimp, seafood seasoning, smoked sausage, corn on the cob, and potatoes. But onions, crab, and butter are welcome additions.

Bring 5 quarts water and ¼ cup Old Bay seasoning to a rolling boil in a large covered stockpot.

Add potatoes; return to a boil, and cook, uncovered, 10 minutes.

Add sausage and corn, and return to a boil. Cook 10 minutes or until potatoes are tender.

Add shrimp to stockpot; cook 3 to 4 minutes or until shrimp turn pink. Drain. If desired, serve with Old Bay seasoning and cocktail sauce. Yield: 12 servings.

Per serving (without sauce): Calories 496 (41% from fat); Fat 22.5g (sat 8g, mono 10.2g, poly 3.2g); Protein 38.4g; Carb 34.2g; Fiber 3.8g; Chol 275mg; Iron 6mg; Sodium 1727mg; Calc 94mg

scallops

A scallop is a milky white delicacy that's shucked immediately after harvest because it never closes its shells once removed from the water.

There's a vast difference in the two sizes of scallops available. Bay scallops are the small, tender scallops with a delicate flavor. Sea scallops can be as large as 2 to 3 inches in diameter. The two types can be used interchangeably in most recipes, but cooking times will vary.

Fresh scallops should have a moist sheen, sweet smell, and a color range between pinkish and beige. Rinse them well before cooking because sand accumulates in the crevices. Scallops are highly perishable so store them loosely covered in the coldest part of the refrigerator, and use within two days of purchase.

Bay scallops are usually only available fresh. Count on 40 to a pound. You'll find sea scallops fresh or in the frozen foods section of your market. Allow ¼ to ⅓ pound of shucked scallops per person, whether they're the smaller bay scallops or the larger sea scallops.

low carb • quick
Coquilles St. Jacques

prep: 15 min. cook: 8 min.

1   cup dry white wine
1   tablespoon minced fresh parsley
1½   teaspoons chopped fresh thyme or
     ½ teaspoon dried thyme
1   bay leaf
¼   teaspoon coarsely ground pepper
1½   pounds bay scallops
¼   cup butter or margarine
¼   cup all-purpose flour
½   cup half-and-half
1   teaspoon lemon juice
1   tablespoon chopped fresh parsley
¼   teaspoon salt
¼   cup soft breadcrumbs
¼   cup grated Parmesan cheese

Combine first 5 ingredients in a large saucepan; bring to a boil. Add scallops; cook 2 minutes, stirring often. Discard bay leaf. Drain scallops, reserving liquid.

Melt butter in saucepan over low heat; add flour, stirring until smooth. Cook 1 minute, stirring constantly. Gradually add reserved scallop liquid and half-and-half; cook over medium heat, stirring constantly, until mixture is thickened and bubbly. Stir in scallops, lemon juice, 1 tablespoon parsley, and salt.

Spoon into 6 lightly greased individual baking dishes or baking shells. Sprinkle each with 2 teaspoons breadcrumbs and 2 teaspoons Parmesan cheese. Broil 3 inches from heat 1 to 2 minutes or until lightly browned. Yield: 6 servings.

Per serving: Calories 234 (45% from fat); Fat 11.8g (sat 6.9g, mono 3g, poly 0.8g); Protein 21.8g; Carb 9.4g; Fiber 0.3g; Chol 68mg; Iron 1mg; Sodium 409mg; Calc 97mg

low calorie • low carb • low fat • quick
Seared Scallops

prep: 6 min. cook: 9 min.

1½   pounds sea scallops
3   tablespoons all-purpose flour
½   teaspoon salt
½   teaspoon pepper
1½   tablespoons olive oil
½   cup dry white wine
1   tablespoon balsamic vinegar
Garnish: fresh parsley sprigs

Pat scallops dry with a paper towel.

Combine flour, salt, and pepper in a large zip-top plastic bag; add scallops. Seal bag, and shake to coat.

Heat oil in a large nonstick skillet over medium-high heat. Add scallops; cook 3 minutes on each side or until done. Remove from pan; keep warm.

Add wine and vinegar to pan; cook 3 minutes or until slightly thickened, stirring with a whisk. Stir in scallops; remove from heat. Garnish, if desired. Yield: 4 servings.

Per serving: Calories 223 (26% from fat); Fat 6.4g (sat 0.8g, mono 3.8g, poly 1g); Protein 29.2g; Carb 10.4g; Fiber 0.2g; Chol 56mg; Iron 1mg; Sodium 568mg; Calc 46mg

Creamy Scallop-and-Shrimp Casserole

prep: 29 min.   cook: 35 min.   other: 10 min.

Crisp strips of phyllo dough provide an elegant topping on this party casserole.

16   frozen phyllo pastry sheets, thawed and divided
Vegetable cooking spray
2½   pounds unpeeled, medium-size fresh shrimp
2   (10-ounce) packages frozen chopped spinach, thawed
5   tablespoons butter, divided
2   garlic cloves, minced
1   pound fresh bay scallops
1   (8-ounce) package cream cheese, softened

1   (8-ounce) container sour cream
⅓   cup shredded Parmesan cheese
1   teaspoon salt
½   teaspoon ground red pepper
¼   cup all-purpose flour
2   cups half-and-half

Stack 8 phyllo sheets in a lightly greased 13- x 9-inch baking dish, lightly coating each sheet with cooking spray. Bake on lowest oven rack at 400° for 5 minutes or until lightly browned; set aside. Keep remaining phyllo sheets covered with a damp towel to prevent drying out.

Peel shrimp, and devein, if desired. Drain spinach well, pressing between paper towels to remove excess moisture.

Melt 1 tablespoon butter in a large skillet over medium heat; add garlic, and sauté 1 minute. Add shrimp and scallops; cook 5 minutes or just until shrimp turn pink. Stir in cream cheese and next 4 ingredients until blended; remove from heat. Stir in spinach.

Melt remaining ¼ cup butter in a small saucepan over medium heat. Add flour, whisking constantly; cook 1 minute. Gradually add half-and-half; cook, whisking constantly, 6 minutes or until thickened. Stir flour mixture into shrimp mixture. Spoon into prepared baking dish.

Stack reserved phyllo sheets, coating each sheet with cooking spray. Cut into thin strips, using a pizza cutter. Arrange strips, in a lattice pattern, over casserole; coat strips with cooking spray. Bake at 400° for 16 to 18 minutes or until golden. Let stand 10 minutes before serving. Yield: 8 servings.

Per serving: Calories 551 (48% from fat); Fat 29.4g (sat 16g, mono 8.1g, poly 2.1g); Protein 40.8g; Carb 30.3g; Fiber 2.3g; Chol 245mg; Iron 6mg; Sodium 995mg; Calc 250mg

crabs

Known for their succulent white meat, crabs are second only to shrimp in seafood popularity in the United States.

Crabmeat comes from several types of crabs. The most common is the blue crab, which weighs about ½ pound. Dungeness crabs are the pride of the Pacific waters, from Alaska to Mexico. These large crabs range from 2 to 3 pounds each, while the Alaskan king crab weighs 10 pounds plus. Usually just the legs of Alaskan king crabs are sold and eaten. The stone crab comes in abundance from Florida waters. Its name comes from its rocklike oval shell. Only the claw meat of a stone crab is eaten.

Blue crabs (found along the Atlantic and Gulf coasts) are commonly eaten in their soft-shell state. There's a period of a few days between April and September in which blue crabs shed their hard shells to grow new, larger ones. During this brief time before the new shells harden, these softshells are considered a delicacy. Whether grilled or fried to a golden crispness, the entire crab is edible.

Crabs are available live, cooked fresh or frozen in the shell, and cooked fresh or frozen out of the shell. You can get cooked lump crabmeat (whole pieces of the white body meat) or cooked flaked crabmeat (small pieces of meat from the body and claws).

Fresh crabmeat should smell clean and fresh and have no odor of ammonia. When buying fresh crabmeat, avoid any that's gray or yellow—a sign that it's old. Use it within a day of purchase.

how to remove crabmeat

1. To get to cooked meat, first twist off crab legs and claws intact. Crack claws, and remove meat with a small cocktail fork.

2. Invert the crab, and pry off the apron (or tail flap), and discard it. Turn crab right side up again.

3. Insert thumb under top shell by apron hinge; pry off the shell, and discard it.

4. Pull away the inedible gray gills; discard them along with internal organs. Break the body; remove meat from the pockets.

crab cake rules

Start with absolutely fresh crab, preferably jumbo lump. Add an egg or some mayonnaise to moisten the meat; season to taste. Use your hands to gently add in just enough cracker crumbs or breadcrumbs to bind the mixture; form into cakes. Some recipes recommend that you place cakes on a baking sheet and chill at least an hour before sautéing or deep-frying to help the cakes hold together. Cook until slightly crusty and golden.

low carb • quick

Crab Cakes Our Way

prep: 20 min.   cook: 10 min.

You'll love how simple these are to prepare. The spicy rémoulade sauce enhances the delicate crab cakes. The sauce is good on sandwiches, too.

1   pound fresh crabmeat
6   to 8 multigrain saltine crackers, finely crushed
½   cup mayonnaise
1   large egg, lightly beaten
1   tablespoon minced fresh parsley
1½   teaspoons Old Bay seasoning
½   teaspoon dry mustard
½   teaspoon pepper
½   teaspoon Worcestershire sauce
2   tablespoons butter or margarine
Red Pepper Rémoulade Sauce

Drain and flake crabmeat, removing any bits of shell.
Combine crushed crackers and next 7 ingredients; gently fold crabmeat into mixture. Shape into 6 thin patties.
Melt butter in a skillet over medium heat. Add crab cakes; cook 4 to 5 minutes on each side or until golden. Drain on paper towels. Serve with Red Pepper Rémoulade Sauce. Yield: 6 cakes.

Per crab cake and 2 tablespoons sauce: Calories 361 (75% from fat); Fat 30g (sat 6.3g, mono 7.5g, poly 13.8g); Protein 18g; Carb 5.8g; Fiber 0.4g; Chol 110mg; Iron 1.1mg; Sodium 815mg; Calc 72mg

Red Pepper Rémoulade Sauce

prep: 5 min.   other: 30 min.

1   (7.5-ounce) jar roasted red bell peppers, drained
1   cup mayonnaise
¼   cup chopped fresh parsley
¼   cup dill pickle relish
1   green onion, minced
1   tablespoon grated lemon rind
1½   to 2 tablespoons prepared horseradish
1   tablespoon drained capers
¼   teaspoon salt
¼   teaspoon pepper

Process bell peppers and mayonnaise in a blender or food processor until smooth, stopping to scrape down sides. Add parsley and remaining ingredients; process until almost smooth. Cover and chill 30 minutes. Yield: 2¼ cups.

Per tablespoon: Calories 49 (90% from fat); Fat 4.9g (sat 0.7g, mono 1.2g, poly 2.6g); Protein 0.2g; Carb 1.3g; Fiber 0.2g; Chol 2mg; Iron 0.1mg; Sodium 98mg; Calc 3mg

entertaining • low calorie

Deviled Crab

prep: 1 hr.   cook: 20 min.

¾   cup chopped celery
¾   cup chopped onion
¼   cup chopped red bell pepper
⅓   cup butter or margarine, melted
1   pound fresh lump crabmeat, drained
1   cup saltine cracker crumbs, divided
½   cup chopped fresh parsley
¼   cup whipping cream
1   tablespoon Dijon mustard
1   teaspoon dry mustard
½   teaspoon freshly ground black pepper
½   teaspoon hot sauce
¼   teaspoon salt
1   tablespoon butter or margarine, melted
Paprika
Lemon wedges (optional)

Cook first 3 ingredients in ⅓ cup butter in a large skillet over medium-high heat, stirring constantly, until tender. Remove from heat. Gently stir in crabmeat, ¾ cup cracker crumbs, and parsley.

Combine whipping cream and next 5 ingredients; gently stir into crabmeat mixture. Spoon into 6 baking shells or individual baking dishes.
Brown remaining ¼ cup cracker crumbs in 1 tablespoon butter in a small skillet over medium heat, stirring often. Sprinkle each serving with cracker crumbs and paprika.
Bake, uncovered, at 350° for 15 to 20 minutes or until thoroughly heated. Serve with lemon wedges, if desired. Yield: 6 servings.

Per serving: Calories 274 (59% from fat); Fat 18.1g (sat 10g, mono 5.1g, poly 1.2g); Protein 15.2g; Carb 12.4g; Fiber 1.2g; Chol 111mg; Iron 1.8mg; Sodium 546mg; Calc 107mg

quick • test kitchen favorite

Crab-Stuffed Potatoes

prep: 10 min.   cook: 15 min.

This superior spud received our Test Kitchens highest rating.

4   large baking potatoes, baked
½   cup butter or margarine
½   cup whipping cream
2   cups fresh lump crabmeat, drained
1   cup (4 ounces) shredded Cheddar cheese
1   tablespoon grated onion
1½   teaspoons salt
Paprika

Cut a 1-inch-wide strip from the top of each baked potato. Carefully scoop out the pulp, leaving shells intact.
Mash pulp with butter and whipping cream; stir in crabmeat and next 3 ingredients. Spoon evenly into shells, and place on a baking sheet. Sprinkle with paprika.
Bake at 425° for 15 minutes. Yield: 4 servings.

Per serving: Calories 754 (52% from fat); Fat 43.6g (sat 26.6g, mono 11.7g, poly 2g); Protein 26.7g; Carb 65.9g; Fiber 6.6g; Chol 189mg; Iron 4mg; Sodium 1414mg; Calc 339mg

Crab Cake Sandwiches

prep: 20 min. cook: 6 min. per batch
other: 1 hr.

Onion sandwich buns partner perfectly with the crispy, golden cakes.

¾   cup Italian-seasoned breadcrumbs
1   large egg
3   tablespoons mayonnaise
2   tablespoons chopped fresh parsley
1   tablespoon fresh lemon juice
1   teaspoon Dijon mustard
½   teaspoon salt
½   teaspoon ground red pepper
1   pound fresh lump crabmeat, drained
⅓   cup fine, dry breadcrumbs
2   tablespoons butter or margarine
6   onion sandwich buns
Tartar Sauce (page 433)
Store-bought coleslaw

Combine first 8 ingredients; gently fold in crabmeat. Shape crab mixture into 6 patties; dredge in ⅓ cup breadcrumbs. Cover and chill 1 hour.
Melt butter in a large nonstick skillet over medium-high heat; cook crab cakes, in batches, 3 minutes on each side or until golden. Drain on paper towels. Serve on buns with 1 tablespoon Tartar Sauce and 2 tablespoons coleslaw. Yield: 6 servings.

Per serving: Calories 460 (42% from fat); Fat 21.4g (sat 7g, mono 5.2g, poly 7.6g); Protein 23.1g; Carb 44g; Fiber 2.4g; Chol 121mg; Iron 3.5mg; Sodium 1094mg; Calc 195mg

low calorie • low carb
Steamed Blue Crabs

prep: 10 min. cook: 35 min.

¼   cup plus 2 tablespoons Old Bay seasoning
¼   cup plus 2 tablespoons coarse salt
3   tablespoons ground red pepper
3   tablespoons pickling spice
2   tablespoons celery seeds
1   tablespoon dried crushed red pepper (optional)
White vinegar
12   live hard-shell blue crabs
Lemon Butter (page 433)

Combine first 5 ingredients and, if desired, crushed red pepper; set aside.

Combine water and vinegar in equal amounts to a depth of 1 inch in a very large pot with a lid; bring to a boil. Place a rack in pot over boiling liquid; arrange half of crabs on rack. Sprinkle with half of seasoning mixture. Top with remaining crabs, and sprinkle with remaining seasoning mixture.
Cover tightly, and steam 20 to 25 minutes or until crabs turn bright red. Rinse with cold water, and drain well. Serve crabs hot or cold with Lemon Butter. Yield: 1 dozen.

Per serving and 1 tablespoon butter: Calories 88 (81% from fat); Fat 7.9g (sat 4.9g, mono 2g, poly 0.4g); Protein 3.9g; Carb 0.9g; Fiber 0.1g; Chol 36mg; Iron 0mg; Sodium 596mg; Calc 24mg

Fried Soft-Shell Crabs

prep: 40 min. cook: 20 min. other: 15 min.

12   fresh soft-shell crabs
3   large eggs
½   teaspoon ground black pepper
1½   cups yellow cornmeal
1   cup all-purpose flour
2   teaspoons baking powder
1   teaspoon salt
½   teaspoon ground black pepper
½   teaspoon garlic powder
⅛   teaspoon ground red pepper
Vegetable oil

To clean crabs, remove spongy gills that lie under the tapering points on either side of back shell. Place crabs on back, and remove the small piece at lower part of shell that terminates in a point (the apron). Wash crabs thoroughly; drain well.
Combine eggs and ½ teaspoon black pepper in a large shallow dish. Add crabs, turning to coat. Let stand 10 minutes.
Combine cornmeal and next 6 ingredients. Remove crabs from egg mixture, and dredge in cornmeal mixture. Let stand 5 minutes; dredge in cornmeal mixture again.
Pour oil to a depth of ½ inch into a large heavy skillet or an electric skillet; heat oil to 375°. Fry crabs 2 minutes on each side or until browned. Drain; serve immediately. Yield: 1 dozen.

Per serving: Calories 257 (34% from fat); Fat 9.6g (sat 1.4g, mono 3.6g, poly 3.8g); Protein 28.2g; Carb 13.2g; Fiber 1g; Chol 146mg; Iron 2mg; Sodium 593mg; Calc 160mg

When crabs are in their molting state, they shed their hard outer shell, leaving a soft shell, which is entirely edible.

Fried Soft-Shell Crabs

crawfish

Crawfish, also called *crayfish* (and *crawdads* in Louisiana), are tiny crustaceans that resemble lobsters. Louisiana, the self-proclaimed crawfish capital of the world, harvests much of our nation's supply from its nearby waters.

Crawfish are sold either live or cooked. They can be prepared by most of the same methods as lobster, and like lobster, turn bright red when cooked. Crawfish are usually eaten with just fingers. The sweet bites of meat must be picked from the tail and juices and fat sucked from the heads.

Crawfish Étouffée

low carb • low fat
Crawfish Boil

prep: 1 hr.   cook: 55 min.   other: 30 min.

The longer you allow the cooked crawfish to soak, the more flavorful and spicy they become.

1½	gallons water
10	bay leaves
1	cup salt
¾	cup ground red pepper
¼	cup whole allspice
2	tablespoons mustard seeds
1	tablespoon coriander seeds
1	tablespoon dill seeds
1	tablespoon dried crushed red pepper
1	tablespoon black peppercorns
1	teaspoon whole cloves
4	celery ribs, quartered
3	medium onions, halved
3	garlic bulbs, halved crosswise
5	pounds live crawfish

Bring 1½ gallons water to a boil in a 19-quart stockpot over high heat. Add bay leaves and next 12 ingredients to water. Return to a rolling boil.

Reduce heat to medium, and cook, uncovered, 30 minutes. Add crawfish. Bring to a rolling boil over high heat; cook 5 minutes. Remove stockpot from heat; let stand 30 minutes. (For spicier crawfish, let stand 45 minutes.) Drain crawfish. Serve on large platters or newspaper. Yield: 6 servings.

Per serving: Calories 336 (14% from fat); Fat 5.3g (sat 0.9g, mono 1.1g, poly 1.7g); Protein 66.5g; Carb 1.2g; Fiber 0.7g; Chol 518mg; Iron 4.4mg; Sodium 2111mg; Calc 203mg

crawfish count

- **1 pound unpeeled whole crawfish** = 3 to 4 ounces peeled tail meat
- **1 pound unpeeled crawfish tails** = 10 ounces (just over 1 cup) peeled tail meat
- **1 pound peeled crawfish tails** = 1 to 2 cups meat

family favorite • low fat
Crawfish Étouffée

prep: 17 min.   cook: 28 min.

This Creole classic is quick enough to make any night of the week.

¼	cup butter or margarine
1	medium onion, chopped
2	celery ribs, chopped
1	medium-size green bell pepper, chopped
4	garlic cloves, minced
1	large shallot, chopped
¼	cup all-purpose flour
1	teaspoon salt
½	to 1 teaspoon ground red pepper
1	(14-ounce) can chicken broth
2	pounds cooked, peeled crawfish tails
¼	cup chopped fresh parsley
¼	cup chopped fresh chives
6	cups hot cooked rice

Melt butter in a large Dutch oven over medium-high heat. Add onion and next 4 ingredients; sauté 5 to 6 minutes or until tender.

Add flour, salt, and ½ to 1 teaspoon ground red pepper; cook stirring constantly, until caramel-colored (about 12 minutes). Add broth; cook, stirring constantly, 3 to 5 minutes or until thick and bubbly.

Stir in crawfish; cook 5 minutes or until thoroughly heated. Stir in herbs. Serve with hot cooked rice. Yield: 6 servings.

Per serving: Calories 446 (21% from fat); Fat 10.5g (sat 5.3g, mono 2.5g, poly 1.1g); Protein 32.4g; Carb 52.9g; Fiber 2.2g; Chol 227mg; Iron 4.4mg; Sodium 884mg; Calc 136mg

crawfish eatin' 101

- Begin by snapping apart the head and tail.
- If you're not a fan of the head, toss it aside, and then peel the tail by working your thumbs down the sides of the hard shell to release the sweet meat.
- For the true crawfish lover, the renowned sucking of the head gives full access to a fiery concoction of spices and fat.

oysters, mussels & clams

The bivalves—oysters, mussels, and clams—offer a stunning presentation when served from their shapely shells. And there's a simple pleasure that comes from extracting the plump meat. Please a crowd by serving fresh steamed shellfish accompanied with a simple sauce, broth, or pasta.

You can buy oysters, mussels, and hard-shelled clams live in the shell. They're displayed on beds of crushed ice in the market and will keep their shells tightly closed once harvested from the water. If mussel and clam shells are broken or open and don't close when lightly tapped, discard them. If oysters are live, their shells will be tightly closed. Discard any open shells.

Never store mussels or clams in airtight containers. You can cover the containers with clean damp cloths. Refrigerate for no more than two days. They should be cooked, steamed, or sautéed until the shells pop open.

Oysters and clams are available fresh shucked or shucked and canned. If they're fresh shucked and in their liquor, don't discard the liquor; it contains flavor you can add to the recipe. For best flavor, serve fresh oysters within five minutes of shucking.

Fresh shucked oysters should be plump, uniform in size, have good color, smell fresh, and be packed in clear, not cloudy, oyster liquor.

Oysters are graded by size. The smaller the oyster, the younger and more tender it will be. Fresh oysters are available year-round, but are best during the fall and winter months because oysters spawn during the summer and become soft and fatty. Allow six live oysters in the shell per person or ⅓ to ½ pint of shucked oysters per serving. The same serving sizes apply for clams and mussels.

Shucking oysters: Scrape knife between the oyster and the bottom shell to free the meat.

Scalloped Oysters

prep: 15 min.   cook: 30 min.
other: 8 hrs., 30 min.

1   quart fresh oysters, undrained
2½ sleeves rectangle buttery crackers
     (about 66 crackers), crushed (we tested
     with Keebler Club Original crackers)
1   teaspoon salt
1   cup butter, melted
1½ cups half-and-half
1   teaspoon Worcestershire sauce
½   teaspoon freshly ground pepper

Drain oysters, reserving ½ cup oyster liquor (liquid from oyster container).
Place cracker crumbs in a large bowl; sprinkle evenly with salt. Drizzle butter over crumbs, tossing to combine.
Whisk together ½ cup reserved oyster liquor, half-and-half, and Worcestershire sauce.
Place one-third crumb mixture evenly in a lightly greased 2-quart baking dish; top with half of oysters. Sprinkle with ¼ teaspoon pepper. Pour half of cream mixture evenly over oysters. Repeat layers, ending with crumb mixture. Cover and chill at least 8 hours.
Let stand at room temperature 30 minutes before baking. Bake oysters at 350° for 30 minutes or until bubbly. Yield: 8 servings.

Per serving: Calories 457 (70% from fat); Fat 36g (sat 19.3g, mono 12.5g, poly 2.1g); Protein 8.5g; Carb 25.8g; Fiber 0.3g; Chol 100mg; Iron 5.7mg; Sodium 1023mg; Calc 114mg

from the grill • low calorie • low fat • quick
Grilled Oysters With Paul's Cocktail Sauce

prep: 5 min.   cook: 20 min.

2   dozen fresh oysters (in the shell)
Paul's Cocktail Sauce

Grill oysters, covered with grill lid, over medium heat (300° to 350°) 20 minutes or until oysters open. Serve with Paul's Cocktail Sauce. Yield: 6 servings.

Per serving and ¼ cup sauce: Calories 107 (12% from fat); Fat 1.4g (sat 0.4g, mono 0.2g, poly 0.6g); Protein 4g; Carb 20g; Fiber 0.2g; Chol 30mg; Iron 4.2mg; Sodium 1649mg; Calc 32mg

Paul's Cocktail Sauce

prep: 5 min.   other: 30 min.

1   (12-ounce) jar chili sauce
½   cup cider or white vinegar
2   teaspoons pepper
2   teaspoons Worcestershire sauce
1   teaspoon lemon juice

Stir together all ingredients. Cover and chill 30 minutes. Yield: 1½ cups.

Per tablespoon: Calories 17 (0% from fat); Fat 0g (sat 0g, mono 0g, poly 0g); Protein 0g; Carb 4.5g; Fiber 0.1g; Chol 0mg; Iron 0.1mg; Sodium 383mg; Calc 2mg

are oysters safe?

Cooked oysters are generally safe to eat. Raw oysters, though, can harbor a variety of ills, among them Norwalk virus, which causes upset stomach, and hepatitis (though such occurrences are extremely rare).

The seafood industry has come up with ways to treat raw oysters to kill the bacteria, called post-harvest processing or PHP. Oysters can be frozen, treated with hydrostatic pressure, or pasteurized. Oysters treated this way are designated virtually bacteria-free by the FDA. If you're concerned about eating raw ones, ask your seafood market to order post-harvest processed oysters. In a restaurant, ask if the oysters have been post-harvest processed. If not, order cooked oysters instead.

Oysters Rockefeller

There is much ado over the original recipe for Oysters Rockefeller. We do know that it was invented by Jules Alciatore, the second-generation proprietor of Antoine's restaurant in New Orleans. We don't know, however, what exactly went into the original dish—just that there was a wealth of bright green herbs, and it was rich, like John D. Rockefeller himself.

A true Rockefeller is bold and strong with freshly blended ingredients including parsley, celery leaf, and fennel bulb. The addition of anise-flavored liqueur such as Pernod only enhances the green herbaceous flavor. When making these baked bivalves, it's important to choose the freshest oysters and herbs available.

low carb
Oysters Rockefeller

prep: 45 min.   cook: 23 min.

1	cup unsalted butter, divided	2	tablespoons anise liqueur (we tested with Pernod)
½	cup chopped flat-leaf parsley	¼	teaspoon salt
¼	cup chopped green onions	¼	teaspoon pepper
¼	cup chopped fennel bulb	⅛	to ¼ teaspoon hot sauce
1	teaspoon chopped fresh chervil or tarragon	½	(4-pound) box rock salt
2	to 3 celery leaves, chopped	2	dozen fresh oysters on the half shell
2	cups watercress or baby spinach leaves		Rock salt
⅓	cup fine, dry breadcrumbs		Garnish: lemon wedges

Melt 3 tablespoons butter in a skillet over medium-high heat; add parsley and next 4 ingredients. Sauté 2 to 3 minutes. Add watercress, and cook 2 to 3 minutes or until wilted. Cool.

Pulse parsley mixture in a food processor with the remaining 13 tablespoons butter, breadcrumbs, and liqueur until smooth, stopping to scrape down sides.

Add salt, pepper, and hot sauce.

Fill pieplates or a large baking sheet with 2 pounds rock salt. Dampen salt slightly, and arrange oysters on the beds of salt.

Top each oyster with a spoonful of the parsley mixture.

Bake at 450° for 12 to 15 minutes or until lightly browned and bubbly. Serve on a bed of rock salt, and garnish, if desired. Yield: 6 servings.

Per serving: Calories 344 (84% from fat); Fat 32.1g (sat 19.7g, mono 8.1g, poly 1.8g); Protein 5.6g; Carb 8.8g; Fiber 0.7g; Chol 110mg; Iron 4.5mg; Sodium 274mg; Calc 71mg

A true Rockefeller recipe is bold and strong with freshly blended ingredients.

Mussels Steamed in Wine

prep: 35 min.   cook: 24 min.

6	dozen fresh mussels
½	cup butter, divided
1	large onion, chopped
2	shallots, chopped
2	garlic cloves, minced
2½	cups finely chopped fresh parsley
½	teaspoon freshly ground pepper
1½	cups dry white wine
½	cup fresh lemon juice

Scrub mussels with a brush; remove beards. Discard any opened, cracked, or heavy mussels (they're filled with sand).

Melt ¼ cup butter in a large Dutch oven over medium-high heat. Add mussels, onion, and next 5 ingredients. Cover and cook 4 minutes or until mussels open, shaking pan several times.

Transfer mussels to a serving dish with a slotted spoon, discarding any unopened mussels. Cover serving dish, and keep warm.

Pour remaining liquid in pan through a wire-mesh strainer into a large skillet, discarding parsley mixture. Bring to a boil. Cook 20 minutes or until thickened. Remove from heat; whisk in remaining ¼ cup butter. Stir in lemon juice; pour over mussels. Yield: 6 servings.

Per serving: Calories 370 (51% from fat); Fat 21g (sat 10.7g, mono 5.3g, poly 2.1g); Protein 31.2g; Carb 13.5g; Fiber 0.4g; Chol 112mg; Iron 10.8mg; Sodium 851mg; Calc 87mg

shellfish savvy

• Some shellfish benefit from being stored on ice in the refrigerator. Mussels, clams, crabs, and oysters fare well when stored in the crisper covered with wet paper towels or newspaper.

• Only cook live shellfish. If bivalves are open, tap on the shell to see if they close. Still not sure? Leave shellfish at room temperature for about 15 minutes, and then tap the shell again. Crabs often appear dead when they are cool. To check, gently pull on a claw with a pair of tongs; if it pulls back slightly, the crab is still alive. Otherwise, discard it.

low calorie • low fat • quick

Mussels Marinara

prep: 15 min.   cook: 15 min.

Serve this Italian dish in pasta bowls to hold all the juices.

2   pounds fresh mussels
5   large garlic cloves, minced
2   teaspoons olive oil
1   (28-ounce) can whole Italian plum tomatoes, undrained
5   large fresh basil leaves, coarsely chopped
¼   teaspoon salt
¼   teaspoon pepper
1   (6-ounce) package fresh spinach
Garnish: chopped fresh basil

Scrub mussels thoroughly with a scrub brush, removing beards. Discard any opened, cracked, or heavy mussels (they're filled with sand).
Sauté garlic in hot oil in a Dutch oven over medium heat 1 to 2 minutes. Add tomatoes, 5 chopped basil leaves, salt, and pepper; simmer, stirring occasionally, 5 minutes.
Add mussels and spinach; cook, covered, 5 minutes or until all mussels have opened. Remove from heat. Serve with Italian bread. Garnish, if desired. Yield: 4 servings.

Per serving: Calories 265 (26% from fat); Fat 7.8g (sat 1.3g, mono 2.9g, poly 1.8g); Protein 30.1g; Carb 19g; Fiber 2.9g; Chol 64mg; Iron 12.2mg; Sodium 1082mg; Calc 171mg

Cleaning clams: Scrub clams under cold running water with a stiff brush to remove sand and dirt. Shuck clams; release meat from bottom shells.

entertaining • low carb

Littleneck Clams With Cilantro–Walnut Pesto

prep: 35 min.   cook: 10 min.

other: 1 hr., 10 min.

¾   cup olive oil
2   cups fresh cilantro leaves
½   cup walnut halves
8   garlic cloves
½   cup freshly grated Parmesan cheese
½   cup grated Romano cheese
½   teaspoon salt
¼   teaspoon freshly ground pepper
2   cups dry white wine
2   garlic cloves, chopped
1   shallot, chopped
40 littleneck clams, scrubbed
Garnish: chopped pimiento

Process first 8 ingredients in a blender or food processor until smooth; set pesto aside.
Bring white wine, chopped garlic, and shallot to a boil in a Dutch oven. Add clams, and cook 5 minutes or until clams open. Drain and cool.
Remove clams from shells, reserving 40 half shells. Chill clams at least 1 hour.
Stir pesto into clams; spoon pesto and 1 clam into each reserved shell. Garnish, if desired. Yield: 20 appetizer servings.

Per serving: Calories 145 (74% from fat); Fat 11.9g (sat 2.3g, mono 6.5g, poly 2.4g); Protein 7.8g; Carb 1.9g; Fiber 0.3g; Chol 18.7mg; Iron 5.6mg; Sodium 183mg; Calc 104mg

low calorie • low fat

Fried Calamari

prep: 15 min.   cook: 1 min. per batch

other: 30 min.

1   (2.5-pound) package cleaned calamari (tubes and tentacles), rinsed
1   cup all-purpose flour
¾   teaspoon salt
1½ teaspoons dried oregano
1½ teaspoons paprika
½   teaspoon pepper
Vegetable oil

Cut calamari tubes into ¼-inch-thick rings. Soak calamari in cold water 30 minutes; drain. Pat dry with paper towels.
Combine flour and next 4 ingredients in a bowl. Dredge calamari in flour mixture.
Pour oil to a depth of 6 inches into a Dutch oven. Heat to 400°. Fry calamari, in batches, 1 minute, allowing oil to reach 400° before cooking next batch. Drain on paper towels. Serve immediately. Yield: 6 servings.

Per serving: Calories 247 (25% from fat); Fat 6.6g (sat 1.1g, mono 1.2g, poly 3.8g); Protein 21.3g; Carb 24.1g; Fiber 1g; Chol 276mg; Iron 2.3mg; Sodium 295mg; Calc 48mg

lobster

Lobsters are known as the king of shellfish, sporting a confident red when served in prized regional recipes across the globe. There are two types of lobsters found in U.S. waters, the spiny or rock lobster and the clawed lobster. A favorite of Maine residents and tourists, the American clawed lobster is the meatier choice. It contains a good bit of claw meat in addition to the succulent tail meat. Farmed along various coasts ranging from Florida to South Africa, spiny lobsters have a distinguishable spiky body, a reddish-brown shell, and no claws. Often only its tail section is sold.

Both types turn bright red when cooked.

You can purchase lobsters live, fresh or frozen cooked in the shell, or cooked, shelled, and canned.

Whole lobsters should be purchased alive and kept alive until you're ready to cook them. Live lobsters should be moving and should curl their tails when lifted from water. Look for medium-size lobsters that are lively in water. The most tender meat comes from lobsters that weigh 2 pounds or less. A 1½- to 2-pound lobster is considered a single serving.

Boiled Lobster

prep: 15 min.   cook: 10 min.

2	(1¼-pound) live lobsters
3	quarts water
2	tablespoons salt

Clarified Butter (page 433)

Plunge lobsters headfirst into boiling salted water (photo 1); return water to a boil. Cover, reduce heat, and simmer 10 minutes. Drain.
Place each lobster on its back; twist the body and tail shell apart; then cut the body shell open using kitchen shears (photo 2). Remove liver and coral roe (photo 3). Remove meat from tail shell (photo 4). Remove intestinal vein that runs from the stomach to tip of the tail (photo 5). Crack claws (photo 6). Serve with Clarified Butter. Yield: 2 servings.

Per lobster and ¼ cup butter: Calories 545 (76% from fat); Fat 46.3g (sat 28.9g, mono 12g, poly 1.8g); Protein 30.4g; Carb 1.9g; Fiber 0g; Chol 226mg; Iron 0.6mg; Sodium 2040mg; Calc 103mg

Crab-Stuffed Lobster Tails

prep: 20 min.   cook: 22 min.

2	quarts water
2	tablespoons salt
2	(1½- to 1¾-pound) live lobsters
½	pound fresh lump crabmeat
1	garlic clove, minced
1	tablespoon chopped fresh parsley
2	tablespoons freshly grated Parmesan cheese
2	tablespoons fine, dry breadcrumbs
¼	teaspoon salt
¼	teaspoon Old Bay seasoning
¼	teaspoon pepper
2	tablespoons butter, melted
1	teaspoon lemon juice

Garlic-Butter Sauce

Garnish: lemon halves

preparing live lobster

1. Grasp live lobster just behind the eyes with long tongs. Plunge lobster, headfirst, into boiling water.

2. After cooking, remove lobster from water. Place lobster on its back. Using kitchen shears, cut apart the body shell and tail shell.

3. Scoop out the green tomalley (liver) and the coral roe (in female lobster only).

4. Using kitchen shears, cut down center of shell on tail underside to expose meat. Pull meat from shell in one piece.

5. Cut ¼ inch deep along outer curve of tail meat to expose intestinal vein. Discard vein.

6. Crack the claws with a seafood cracker or nut cracker, and extract the claw meat.

Combine water and salt in a large Dutch oven; bring to a boil. Plunge lobsters headfirst into boiling water; return to a boil. Cover, reduce heat, and simmer 10 minutes; drain and cool.
For each lobster, break off large claws and legs. Crack claw and leg shells, using a seafood or nut cracker; remove meat. Break off tail. Cut top side of tail shell lengthwise, using kitchen shears. Cut through center of meat; remove vein. Leave meat in shell; rinse.
Drain crabmeat, removing any bits of shell. Combine crabmeat, garlic, and next 8 ingredients; toss gently. Spoon crab filling into lobster tails. Place on a baking sheet.
Bake at 400° for 12 minutes or just until heated. Serve with Garlic-Butter Sauce and claw and leg meat. Garnish, if desired. Yield: 2 servings.

Per serving and ⅓ cup sauce: Calories 882 (68% from fat); Fat 66.4g (sat 40.8g, mono 17.3g, poly 3.1g); Protein 60.5g; Carb 10.6g; Fiber 0.6g; Chol 390mg; Iron 2.2mg; Sodium 3068mg; Calc 313mg

Garlic-Butter Sauce

prep: 2 min.   cook: 3 min.

½	cup butter
2	tablespoons whipping cream
1	garlic clove, minced
2	tablespoons lemon juice

Melt butter in a saucepan over medium-low heat; add whipping cream and garlic, and cook 1 minute, stirring constantly with a wire whisk. Stir in lemon juice. Remove from heat. Yield: ⅔ cup.

Per tablespoon: Calories 86 (100% from fat); Fat 9.6g (sat 6g, mono 2.5g, poly 0.4g); Protein 0.2g; Carb 0.4g; Fiber 0g; Chol 26mg; Iron 0mg; Sodium 62mg; Calc 5mg

from the grill

There's no substitute for the smoky flavors and aromas that come from cooking over an open flame.

One of the most important things to know about grilling is how and when to cook over direct vs. indirect heat. The biggest difference is that direct heat works best on foods that cook quickly, no more than 20 or 30 minutes. If something needs to cook more than 30 minutes, consider using indirect heat. Most of the recipes in this chapter use direct-heat grilling; those that require indirect heat give specific instructions.

Direct-heat grilling is exactly that: Food cooks directly over the heat source. Quick-cooking foods suitable for direct heat include hamburgers, steaks, chops, boneless chicken pieces, fish fillets, and vegetables. To ensure even cooking, turn foods once. Use direct heat to sear meat and to get grill marks for food that looks as good as it tastes.

Indirect-heat grilling means the fire is off to one side of the grill, opposite the food. The heat rising and reflecting off the lid and inside surfaces of the grill circulates around the food and cooks it slowly and evenly on all sides. Foods that are fit for indirect heat include roasts, ribs, whole chickens, turkeys, and other large cuts of meat or poultry.

When grilling, you need to be able to determine how hot the fire is. Some cooks determine coal temperature by how long they can hold their hands above the coals at cooking level, but a grill thermometer offers a more accurate measurement; the only problem with a thermometer is it gives an accurate reading only when the grill is covered. For a "hands-on" technique, follow this guide: A hot fire allows a 2-second hand count and is between 400° and 500°, with coals that are barely covered with ash. A medium fire allows a 4-second hand count, is between 300° and 350°, and has coals that are glowing through the gray ash. A low fire allows a 5-second hand count and is under 300°; the coals are covered with a thick layer of ash.

Easy Smoked Cheddar

prep: 30 min.   cook: 2 hrs.

Hickory wood chips
2   (16-ounce) blocks Cheddar cheese
Vegetable cooking spray
Cheesecloth

Soak wood chips in water for at least 30 minutes.
Prepare charcoal fire in smoker; let burn 15 to 20 minutes.
Place 1 cheese block on top of the other; coat with cooking spray. Place lengthwise in center of a 24-inch piece of cheesecloth. Tightly wrap cheesecloth around stacked cheese. Place wrapped cheese crosswise in center of another 24-inch piece of cheese-cloth; tightly wrap.
Drain wood chips, and place on coals. Place water pan in smoker; add water to depth of fill line. Place wrapped cheese, seam side down, on upper food rack; cover with smoker lid.
Cook cheese 2 hours. Cool completely. Yield: 2 (16-ounce) blocks.

Per 2 ounces: Calories 229 (74% from fat); Fat 18.8g (sat 12g, mono 5.3g, poly 0.5g); Protein 14.1g; Carb 0.7g; Fiber 0g; Chol 60mg; Iron 0.4mg; Sodium 352mg; Calc 409mg

Grilled Andouille Grits

prep: 5 min.   cook: 23 min.   other: 8 hrs.

Once chilled, the sturdy wedges of grits will hold their shape; just make sure the grill is good and hot to keep them from sticking.

½   large Vidalia onion, chopped
½   cup chopped andouille or spicy smoked sausage
2   tablespoons vegetable oil
1   (14½-ounce) can chicken broth
¾   cup half-and-half
1   cup uncooked quick-cooking grits
½   teaspoon salt
2   tablespoons butter or margarine, melted

Sauté onion and sausage in hot oil in a 3-quart saucepan over medium-high heat until tender. Add chicken broth and half-and-half; bring to a boil. Gradually stir in grits and salt. Cover, reduce heat, and simmer, stirring occasionally, 10 minutes or until thickened.

smoked for flavor

Smoking makes for take-it-easy cooking. Aromatic, smoldering wood chips "wrap" food in a blanket, sealing in the natural juices. It's an easy process, but it isn't quick. You'll get tender meats and vegetables, but don't stop there: Fill your smoker with shrimp, cheese, and pecans (page 39), too. If you don't have a smoker, your grill with a lid and a pan of water underneath the food that's grilling works well. The liquid in the water pan keeps foods moist.

Pour grits onto a lightly greased baking sheet into a 10½-inch circle (should be about ⅓ inch thick); cover and chill 8 hours.
Invert grits circle onto a flat surface; cut into 8 wedges. Brush top and bottom of each wedge with melted butter.
Grill, without grill lid, over medium heat (about 300° to 350°) 3 to 4 minutes on each side. Remove and keep warm. Yield: 6 servings.

Per serving: Calories 261 (56% from fat); Fat 16.4g (sat 6.4g, mono 5.7g, poly 3g); Protein 5.2g; Carb 23.6g; Fiber 0.6g; Chol 29mg; Iron 1.2mg; Sodium 507mg; Calc 39mg

Note: Grits can be broiled, if desired. Prepare as directed, and arrange buttered wedges on a baking sheet. Broil 6 inches from heat 2 minutes on each side or until golden.

entertaining • low carb

Texas Rockets

prep: 30 min.   cook: 35 min.   other: 30 min.

You'll want to make more than one batch of these meaty appetizers. For less heat, look for jalapeño peppers with rounded tips.

½   pound chicken breast strips
¾   cup Italian dressing, divided
½   (8-ounce) package cream cheese, softened
⅛   teaspoon salt
⅛   teaspoon pepper
12   jalapeño peppers (about 3½ to 4 inches long)
12   thin bacon slices

Keep your outdoor grill in tip-top shape. All you need are a few inexpensive tools and a little bit of elbow grease.

Place chicken and ½ cup Italian dressing in a shallow dish or zip-top freezer bag; cover or seal, and chill 30 minutes.

Remove chicken from marinade, discarding marinade. Grill chicken, covered with grill lid, over medium heat (300° to 350°) 4 to 5 minutes on each side or until done, basting with remaining ¼ cup Italian dressing. Let chicken cool slightly, and finely chop.

Stir together chicken, cream cheese, salt, and pepper in a bowl.

Cut jalapeño peppers lengthwise down 1 side, leaving other side intact; remove seeds. Spoon 1½ to 2 tablespoons chicken mixture into cavity of each pepper. Wrap each pepper with 1 bacon slice, securing with 2 wooden picks.

Grill stuffed jalapeños, without grill lid, turning often, over medium heat 20 to 25 minutes or until bacon is crisp. Yield: 1 dozen.

Per stuffed pepper: Calories 193 (79% from fat); Fat 16.9g (sat 6.1g, mono 6.3g, poly 2.6g); Protein 8g; Carb 2.3g; Fiber 0.4g; Chol 38mg; Iron 0.5mg; Sodium 414mg; Calc 13mg

Bistro Grilled Chicken Pizza

prep: 15 min.   cook: 10 min.

Use long-handled grilling tongs and a spatula to turn this dough with ease.

1	(13.8-ounce) can refrigerated pizza crust dough
1	teaspoon olive oil
¾	cup pizza sauce
4	plum tomatoes, sliced
2	cups chopped cooked chicken
1	(4-ounce) package tomato-and-basil feta cheese
1	cup (4 ounces) shredded mozzarella cheese
2	tablespoons chopped fresh basil

Unroll dough, and place on a lightly greased 18- x 12-inch sheet of heavy-duty aluminum foil. Starting at center, press out dough with hands to form a 13- x 9-inch rectangle. Brush dough evenly with olive oil.

Invert dough onto grill cooking grate; peel off foil. Grill, covered with grill lid, over medium heat (300° to 350°) 2 to 3 minutes or until bottom of dough is browned. Turn dough over, and grill, covered, 1 to 2 minutes or until bottom is set. Carefully remove crust from grill to an aluminum foil-lined baking sheet.

Microwave pizza sauce in a small glass bowl at HIGH 30 seconds or until warm, stirring once. Spread sauce evenly over crust; top with tomatoes and chicken. Sprinkle with cheeses and basil. Return pizza to cooking grate (pizza should slide easily).

Grill, covered, 3 to 5 more minutes or until crust is done and cheese is melted. Yield: 6 servings.

Per serving: Calories 392 (33% from fat); Fat 14.4g (sat 6.3g, mono 4.6g, poly 1.5g); Protein 27.8g; Carb 36g; Fiber 1.9g; Chol 69mg; Iron 2.9mg; Sodium 872mg; Calc 244mg

low carb
Lemon Barbecued Chicken

prep: 8 min.   cook: 45 min.   other: 3 hrs.

Cooking for more than just two? This recipe can be doubled or tripled easily.

2	bone-in chicken breasts
¾	teaspoon salt
½	teaspoon grated lemon rind
1	teaspoon Worcestershire sauce
¼	teaspoon dry mustard
¼	teaspoon dried oregano
¼	cup vegetable oil
¼	cup lemon juice
1	tablespoon chopped green onion
	Vegetable cooking spray

Place chicken breasts in a large zip-top freezer bag. Combine salt and next 4 ingredients in a small bowl. Gradually add oil and lemon juice, stirring well. Stir in green onion. Pour over chicken; seal bag. Marinate in refrigerator 3 hours, turning occasionally.

Remove chicken from marinade, reserving marinade. Place marinade in a small saucepan. Bring to a boil; set aside.

grilling 101

Become a grillmaster in no time with these helpful hints.

• To prevent food from sticking, lightly coat the grate with an oil that has a high smoke point before turning on the grill. Peanut oil is a good choice. Cooking spray works, too.

• For charcoal grills, use a chimney-type starter with a few pieces of newspaper and a match; this helps coals heat quickly. Expect about 20 minutes for coals to burn down to gray ash.

• Fire needs oxygen to burn, so be sure grill vents are open enough to keep the fire burning. The wider the vent, the hotter the fire. Cleaning out old ashes will also allow better air flow, which equals more oxygen.

• Basting brushes made of natural bristles are handy for dabbing on marinades and sauces.

• Long-handled tongs and spatulas are great for turning hot foods on the grill. Tongs won't pierce the flesh and will keep juices inside.

• Keep a spray bottle filled with water nearby to control flare-ups. Be careful to tame the fire, not to douse it.

• Test for doneness. Instant-read and digital thermometers with forklike prongs are available at kitchen and home-supply stores. Best used on cuts at least 1 inch thick, they should be inserted into the thickest portion of the food. Cook chicken breasts to 170°, thighs to 180°, beef to 145° (medium rare) or 160° (medium), and pork to 160° (medium). Fish should flake at its thickest part. Chicken should have no pink areas, and juices should run clear.

Light gas grill on 1 side to medium; coat grill rack on opposite side with cooking spray. Place rack over cool lava rocks, and let grill preheat 10 to 15 minutes.

Arrange chicken breasts on rack opposite hot coals; cover and grill 30 to 45 minutes, basting with reserved marinade and turning once. Yield: 2 servings.

Per serving: Calories 581 (64% from fat); Fat 41.5g (sat 6.6g, mono 17g, poly 14.8g); Protein 49.6g; Carb 3g; Fiber 0.4g; Chol 139mg; Iron 2.2mg; Sodium 1024mg; Calc 37mg

Molasses–Glazed Chicken Thighs

prep: 15 min.   cook: 12 min.   other: 8 hrs.

Skinned and boned chicken thighs are available in the fresh poultry section of most supermarkets.

¾ cup molasses
⅓ cup soy sauce
¼ cup fresh lemon juice
¼ cup olive oil
3 garlic cloves, minced
1 teaspoon pepper
12 skinned and boned chicken thighs

Combine first 6 ingredients in a shallow dish or large zip-top freezer bag; add chicken thighs. Cover or seal, and chill 8 hours, turning occasionally.
Remove chicken from marinade, discarding marinade.
Grill chicken thighs, covered with grill lid, over medium heat (300° to 350°) 5 to 6 minutes on each side or until done. Yield: 6 servings.

Per serving: Calories 332 (44% from fat); Fat 16.2g (sat 3.9g, mono 7.8g, poly 3.1g); Protein 28.8g; Carb 16.6g; Fiber 0.2g; Chol 102mg; Iron 2.7mg; Sodium 548mg; Calc 59mg

Stuffed Border Burger

entertaining • family favorite
Beef and Chicken Fajitas

prep: 20 min.   cook: 30 min.   other: 2 hrs.

Chipotle seasoning contributes a smoky essence to the marinade for these fajitas.

2 tablespoons chili powder
2 teaspoons ground cumin
1 teaspoon brown sugar
1 teaspoon pepper
¼ teaspoon salt
¼ teaspoon garlic powder
¼ teaspoon chipotle seasoning (optional)
1 cup Italian dressing
6 skinned and boned chicken breasts
4 pounds flank steak
20 (8-inch) flour tortillas, warmed
Toppings: sour cream, shredded lettuce, chopped tomato, shredded Cheddar cheese

Combine first 6 ingredients and, if desired, chipotle seasoning.

Stir together chili powder mixture and dressing. Pour half of marinade into a shallow dish or large zip-top freezer bag; add chicken. Cover or seal.
Pour remaining marinade into a separate shallow dish or large zip-top freezer bag; add beef. Cover or seal; chill chicken and beef 2 hours.
Remove chicken and beef from marinade, discarding marinade.
Grill, covered with grill lid, over medium heat (300° to 350°) about 15 minutes on each side or until chicken is done and beef is to desired degree of doneness.
Cut chicken and beef into strips. Serve in warmed flour tortillas with desired toppings. Yield: 10 servings.

Per serving (without toppings): Calories 697 (30% from fat); Fat 23.2g (sat 6.5g, mono 8.9g, poly 3.9g); Protein 67.3g; Carb 52.6g; Fiber 0.2g; Chol 118mg; Iron 5.4mg; Sodium 865mg; Calc 238mg

family favorite
Stuffed Border Burgers

prep: 25 min.   cook: 10 min.

Uniform-sized patties are the key to success when making these cheese-stuffed burgers.

1½ pounds lean ground beef
½ cup finely chopped onion
1 (4.25-ounce) can chopped ripe olives, drained
2 tablespoons ketchup
1 teaspoon chili powder
1 teaspoon fajita seasoning
½ teaspoon salt
6 (1-ounce) slices Monterey Jack cheese with peppers
6 onion rolls, split and toasted
Tex-Mex Secret Sauce (page 433)
Toppings: shredded lettuce, sliced tomatoes, guacamole

Combine first 7 ingredients. Shape mixture into 12 (4-inch) patties. Fold cheese slices into quarters; place cheese on each of 6 patties. Top with remaining 6 patties, pressing to seal edges.

Grill, covered with grill lid, over medium-high heat (350° to 400°) 4 to 5 minutes on each side or until done. Serve on rolls with Tex-Mex Secret Sauce and desired toppings. Yield: 6 servings.

Per serving: Calories 597 (52% from fat); Fat 34.3g (sat 16.5g, mono 13.1g, poly 2.1g); Protein 34.7g; Carb 37.6g; Fiber 2.9g; Chol 114mg; Iron 4.3mg; Sodium 1169mg; Calc 333mg

family favorite • make ahead
Sweet-and-Savory Burgers

prep: 20 min.   cook: 14 min.   other: 4 hrs.

¼ cup soy sauce
2 tablespoons corn syrup
1 tablespoon lemon juice
½ teaspoon ground ginger
¼ teaspoon garlic powder
2 green onions, thinly sliced
2 pounds ground chuck
¼ cup chili sauce
¼ cup jalapeño jelly
8 hamburger buns
Toppings: grilled red onions, grilled
    pineapple slices*

Stir together first 6 ingredients; pour into a shallow pan or baking dish.

Shape beef into 8 patties; place in a single layer in marinade, turning to coat both sides. Cover and chill 4 hours. Drain, discarding marinade.

Grill patties over medium-high heat (350° to 400°) 6 to 7 minutes on each side or until beef is no longer pink.

Stir together chili sauce and jelly. Serve patties on buns with chili sauce mixture and grilled toppings. Yield: 8 servings.

Per serving: Calories 451 (34% from fat); Fat 17.2g (sat 6.2g, mono 7.2g, poly 1.3g); Protein 27.3g; Carb 46.7g; Fiber 2.8g; Chol 77mg; Iron 4mg; Sodium 622mg; Calc 101mg

*One cored fresh pineapple easily yields 8 slices. Grill pineapple and red onion slices over medium-high heat 4 to 5 minutes on each side.

ground rules for grilling

Use this chart as a general guide when cooking beef, fish, lamb, pork, or poultry on the grill at medium to medium-high heat.

Meat	Cooking Time	Method	Instructions
Beef			
Ground beef patties	8 to 12 minutes	Direct	Cook, without grill lid, until no longer pink.
Steaks (1 to 1½ inches thick)	8 to 12 minutes	Direct	Cook, without grill lid, to at least 145°.
Steaks (2 inches thick)	18 to 22 minutes	Direct; Indirect	Sear over direct heat; then move to indirect to cook to at least 145°.
Tenderloin (3 pounds)	30 to 45 minutes	Direct; Indirect	Sear over direct heat; then move to indirect to cook to at least 145°.
Brisket (6 pounds)	3 to 4 hours	Indirect	Cook, covered with grill lid, to at least 145°.
Fish			
Whole fish (per inch of thickness)	10 to 12 minutes	Direct	Cook, covered with grill lid.
Fish fillets (per inch of thickness)	7 to 10 minutes	Direct	Cook, without grill lid.
Lamb			
Chops or steaks (1 inch thick)	10 to 12 minutes	Direct	Cook, without grill lid, to at least 145°.
Leg of lamb (boneless or butterflied)	40 to 50 minutes	Indirect	Cook, covered with grill lid, to at least 145°.
Pork			
Chops (½ inch thick)	7 to 11 minutes	Direct	Cook, covered with grill lid, to 160°.
Chops (¾ inch thick)	10 to 12 minutes	Direct	Cook, covered with grill lid, to 160°.
Chops (1½ inches thick)	16 to 22 minutes	Direct	Cook, covered with grill lid, to 160°.
Kabobs (1-inch cubes)	9 to 13 minutes	Direct	Cook, covered with grill lid, to 160°.
Tenderloin (½ to 1½ pounds)	16 to 21 minutes	Indirect	Cook, covered with grill lid, to 160°.
Ribs	1½ to 2 hours	Indirect	Cook, covered with grill lid, to 160°.
Poultry			
Chicken (whole, halves, quarters, and thighs)	50 to 60 minutes	Indirect	Cook, covered with grill lid, to 180°.
Chicken (bone-in breast)	30 minutes	Indirect	Cook, covered with grill lid, to 170°.
Chicken (boneless breast)	10 to 12 minutes	Direct	Cook, without grill lid.
Turkey (bone-in breast, cut lengthwise in half)	45 minutes	Indirect	Cook, covered with grill lid, to 170°.

Steak-and-Vegetable Kabobs

prep: 20 min.   cook: 12 min.
other: 2 hrs., 20 min.

If you use wooden skewers instead of metal, soak wooden skewers in water 30 minutes before grilling.

½   cup dry sherry
½   cup olive oil
2   tablespoons grated orange rind
½   cup fresh orange juice
¼   cup soy sauce
4   garlic cloves, minced
2   tablespoons minced fresh ginger
½   teaspoon dried crushed red pepper (optional)
1½   pounds rib-eye steak, cut into 1-inch pieces
1   small red onion, cut into 1½-inch pieces
1   medium-size yellow bell pepper, cut into ½- to ¾-inch pieces
2   small zucchini, cut into 8 slices
4   cups mixed salad greens

Whisk together first 7 ingredients, and, if desired, crushed red pepper. Remove and reserve ¾ cup marinade. Pour remaining marinade into a shallow dish or large zip-top freezer bag; add steak. Cover or seal, and chill 2 hours. Add onion, bell pepper, and zucchini; toss to coat. Cover or seal, and chill 20 minutes.
Remove steak and vegetables from marinade, discarding marinade. Thread steak and vegetables, separately, onto 6 to 8 (12-inch) metal skewers.
Grill, covered with grill lid, over medium-high heat (350° to 400°) 10 to 12 minutes or until done. Serve over mixed salad greens with reserved ¾ cup marinade. Yield: 4 servings.

Per serving: Calories 565 (64% from fat); Fat 40g (sat 10.6g, mono 22.6g, poly 2.8g); Protein 36g; Carb 12g; Fiber 3g; Chol 153mg; Iron 3.9mg; Sodium 792mg; Calc 84mg

smoke signals

● Soak wood chips in water at least 30 minutes and wood chunks 1 to 24 hours before grilling. If you're after an abundance of smoke flavor, be sure the wood is waterlogged.
● Start your fire and let coals burn down until they're covered with gray ash. Cover coals with soaked chips, and set smoker vents to produce a smooth, even draft. Add herbs, citrus peel, or spices to the fire for more complex flavor.
● Get creative when it comes to filling the smoker's water pan. Add beer, wine, cola, fruit juice, or a marinade instead of water. The liquid imparts even more flavor to the food as it steams and smokes.
● For best results, smoke only one type of food at a time, and use pieces that are the same size and weight.

entertaining • low carb

Smoked Prime Rib

prep: 25 min.   cook: 6 hrs.   other: 1 hr., 35 min.

When it comes to beef, it's hard to beat prime rib. And when cooked on a smoker, the results redefine delicious.

Hickory wood chunks
4   garlic cloves, minced
1   tablespoon salt
2   tablespoons coarsely ground pepper
1   tablespoon fresh or dried rosemary
1   teaspoon dried thyme
1   (6-pound) beef rib roast
1½   cups dry red wine
1½   cups red wine vinegar
½   cup olive oil

Soak wood chunks in water at least 1 hour.
Combine minced garlic and next 4 ingredients; rub garlic mixture on beef roast.
Stir together wine, vinegar, and olive oil; set wine mixture aside.
Prepare charcoal fire in smoker; let burn 15 to 20 minutes.
Drain wood chunks, and place on coals. Place water pan in smoker, and add water to just below fill line. Place beef roast in center on lower food rack. Gradually pour wine mixture over beef roast.

Cook beef roast, covered, 6 hours or until a meat thermometer inserted in thickest portion of beef roast registers 145° (medium rare), adding more water to depth of fill line, if necessary. Remove beef roast from smoker, and let stand 15 minutes before slicing. Yield: 10 servings.

Per serving: Calories 617 (72% from fat); Fat 49.1g (sat 19.3g, mono 22.4g, poly 2g); Protein 39.7g; Carb 1.7g; Fiber 0.6g; Chol 136mg; Iron 4.3mg; Sodium 803mg; Calc 37mg

entertaining

Ribs McCoy

prep: 20 min.   cook: 3 hrs., 30 min.

Whip up this quick spice rub and add a favorite store-bought barbecue sauce to mop on these ribs.

⅓   cup Melvyn's Seasoning Mix
5   pounds spareribs
1   (32-ounce) bottle barbecue sauce

Prepare a hot fire by piling charcoal on 1 side of grill, leaving other side empty. (For gas grills, light only 1 side to high heat [400° to 500°]).
Rub Melvyn's Seasoning Mix on all sides of ribs. Arrange ribs on food rack over unlit side.
Grill, covered with grill lid, 3 to 3½ hours, turning once and basting with barbecue sauce during last 30 minutes. Serve with additional barbecue sauce, if desired. Yield: 10 servings.

Per serving: Calories 530 (55% from fat); Fat 32.3g (sat 11.7g, mono 14.2g, poly 2.9g); Protein 31.4g; Carb 25.1g; Fiber 1.2g; Chol 128mg; Iron 2.8mg; Sodium 1602mg; Calc 68mg

Melvyn's Seasoning Mix

prep: 5 min.

⅓   cup Creole seasoning
⅓   cup garlic powder
⅓   cup pepper
1½   tablespoons Greek seasoning

Stir together all ingredients. Store mix in an airtight container. Yield: 1¼ cups.

Per tablespoon: Calories 12 (1% from fat); Fat 0.1g (sat 0g, mono 0g, poly 0g); Protein 0.6g; Carb 2.7g; Fiber 0.7g; Chol 0mg; Iron 0.6mg; Sodium 698mg; Calc 9mg

Marinated London Broil

Marinated London Broil

prep: 5 min. cook: 30 min. other: 24 hrs.

For the juiciest flavor, pull this hearty cut of beef off the grill before it reaches medium doneness. It will continue to cook as it stands.

1   (12-ounce) can cola soft drink
1   (10-ounce) bottle teriyaki sauce
1   (2½- to 3-pound) London broil

Combine cola and teriyaki sauce in a shallow dish or large zip-top freezer bag; add London broil. Cover or seal, and chill 24 hours, turning occasionally.
Remove London broil from marinade, discarding marinade.
Grill, covered with grill lid, over medium heat (300° to 350°) 12 to 15 minutes on each side or to desired degree of doneness. Let stand 10 minutes; cut diagonally across the grain into thin slices. Yield: 8 servings.

Per serving: Calories 228 (35% from fat); Fat 8.8g (sat 3.6g, mono 3.5g, poly 0.3g); Protein 30.7g; Carb 6.1g; Fiber 0g; Chol 48mg; Iron 2.2mg; Sodium 923mg; Calc 27mg

London Broil is best carved across the grain into thin slices.

low calorie • low carb

Rosemary Grilled Flank Steak

prep: 20 min. cook: 20 min. other: 4 hrs.

Use long rosemary branches to brush flavor onto the meat.

1   cup dry red wine
½   cup olive oil
½   teaspoon Worcestershire sauce
2   tablespoons chopped fresh parsley
2   bay leaves
2   green onions, chopped
3   garlic cloves, minced
1   teaspoon dried oregano
1   teaspoon salt
½   teaspoon pepper
2   pounds flank steak
Rosemary sprigs
½   lemon

Combine first 10 ingredients. Reserve ⅓ cup red wine mixture.
Place flank steak in a large shallow dish or a large zip-top freezer bag. Pour red wine mixture over steak. Cover or seal, and chill 2 to 4 hours, turning occasionally.
Remove flank steak from marinade, discarding marinade.
Grill, covered with grill lid, over medium–high heat (350° to 400°) 8 to 10 minutes on each side or to desired degree of doneness, brushing with reserved wine mixture using rosemary sprigs. Cut steak diagonally across the grain into thin strips. Squeeze lemon over steak before serving. Yield: 8 servings.

Per serving: Calories 215 (51% from fat); Fat 12.3g (sat 3.2g, mono 7.2g, poly 0.9g); Protein 23.9g; Carb 1g; Fiber 0.2g; Chol 37mg; Iron 1.7mg; Sodium 199mg; Calc 23mg

low carb • quick

Grilled Porterhouse Steaks

prep: 6 min. cook: 20 min.

¼   cup olive oil
2   tablespoons minced fresh basil
4   garlic cloves, pressed
2   (2-pound) porterhouse steaks
1   tablespoon seasoned salt
1   tablespoon freshly ground pepper

Combine first 3 ingredients in a small bowl. Rub oil mixture on both sides of steaks; sprinkle with seasoned salt and pepper. Grill, covered with grill lid, over medium–high heat (350° to 400°) 10 minutes on each side or to desired degree of doneness. Yield: 4 servings.

Per serving: Calories 736 (62% from fat); Fat 50.7g (sat 16.4g, mono 25.3g, poly 2.8g); Protein 64.4g; Carb 2.1g; Fiber 0.5g; Chol 209mg; Iron 5.7mg; Sodium 1185mg; Calc 54mg

low carb • quick

Grilled New York Steaks

prep: 5 min. cook: 20 min.

To keep costs down, you can buy thick-cut New York strip steaks and cut them in half to mimic the look of the more expensive filet mignons.

4   (1½-inch-thick) New York strip steaks, cut in half
1   tablespoon kosher salt
2½ teaspoons freshly ground pepper
Garnish: fresh flat-leaf parsley sprigs

Sprinkle steaks evenly on both sides with salt and pepper.
Grill steaks, covered with grill lid, over medium–high heat (350° to 400°) 8 to 10 minutes on each side or to desired degree of doneness. Garnish, if desired. Yield: 8 servings.

Per serving: Calories 451 (57% from fat); Fat 28.6g (sat 11.3g, mono 11.9g, poly 1.1g); Protein 45.1g; Carb 0.4g; Fiber 0.2g; Chol 150mg; Iron 3.1mg; Sodium 812mg; Calc 35mg

annual upkeep

- Give your grill a thorough cleaning once a year. If you cook out year-round, clean your grill in the spring and fall.
- Combine one part distilled white vinegar and one part water in a spray bottle, and then coat the interior of the grill. Close the grill lid and allow to stand for one hour. The solution will break up burnt particles, making them easier to remove with a brush. Wipe clean with a wet cloth.
- Clean the grate with a sponge and mild dish-washing soap, or try an oven or grill cleaner, following manufacturer's instructions carefully. Note: Use oven cleaner only on the grate because it can damage painted surfaces.

---

low carb • quick

Grilled Veal Chops

prep: 10 min.   cook: 12 min.

Pair these herbed chops with garlic mashed potatoes.

¼	cup olive oil
1	tablespoon salt
1	tablespoon chopped fresh or dried rosemary
1	tablespoon chopped fresh thyme
2	tablespoons chopped fresh oregano
1	tablespoon coarsely ground pepper
8	(12-ounce) bone-in veal chops

Garnish: fresh thyme sprigs

Stir together first 6 ingredients. Rub evenly on both sides of veal chops.
Grill, covered with grill lid, over medium-high heat (350° to 400°) 12 minutes or until a meat thermometer inserted in thickest portion registers 160°, turning once. Garnish, if desired. Yield: 8 servings.

Per serving: Calories 324 (49% from fat); Fat 17.2g (sat 4.8g, mono 8.7g, poly 1.5g); Protein 39.1g; Carb 1g; Fiber 0.4g; Chol 157mg; Iron 1.7mg; Sodium 1015mg; Calc 47mg

---

quick

Smoked Pork Chops With Jalapeño-Cherry Sauce

prep: 10 min.   cook: 12 min.

6	(1-inch-thick) boneless smoked pork chops
1	(14-ounce) can dark, sweet pitted cherries
1	cup jalapeño jelly
½	teaspoon ground coriander

Grill pork chops, covered with grill lid, over medium-high heat (350° to 400°) 5 to 6 minutes on each side or until done. Transfer to a serving dish.
Bring cherries, jelly, and coriander to a boil in a saucepan, stirring constantly. Pour over pork chops. Yield: 6 servings.

Per serving: Calories 619 (53% from fat); Fat 36.3g (sat 13.1g, mono 17.3g, poly 4g); Protein 35.4g; Carb 35.8g; Fiber 1g; Chol 99mg; Iron 2mg; Sodium 1892mg; Calc 26mg

---

family favorite • low carb • make ahead
weekend chef

Baby Back Ribs

prep: 20 min.   cook: 3 hrs., 10 min.   other: 8 hrs.

The Sweet Sauce in this recipe makes a large yield—it's so good, though, you won't mind having plenty left over for serving with grilled chicken or burgers.

2	slabs baby loin back ribs (about 4 pounds)
3	tablespoons Dry Spices
½	cup Basting Sauce, divided
½	cup Sweet Sauce

Place ribs in a large shallow roasting pan. Rub Dry Spices evenly on ribs. Cover and chill 8 hours.
Brush ribs with ¼ cup Basting Sauce. Bake, covered, at 300° for 1½ hours. Uncover and brush with remaining ¼ cup Basting Sauce. Bake, covered, 1½ more hours or until ribs are tender. Remove from pan; place on a large tray.
Brush ribs with Sweet Sauce. Grill ribs, covered with grill lid, over medium heat (300° to 350°) 5 minutes on each side. Serve with additional Sweet Sauce. Yield: 4 servings.

Per serving: Calories 806 (70% from fat); Fat 62.8g (sat 23.3g, mono 28.2g, poly 5.1g); Protein 51.3g; Carb 7g; Fiber 1.5g; Chol 247mg; Iron 4.1mg; Sodium 740mg; Calc 113mg

---

Dry Spices

prep: 5 min.

3	tablespoons paprika
2	teaspoons seasoned salt
2	teaspoons garlic powder
2	teaspoons black pepper
1	teaspoon dry mustard
1	teaspoon ground oregano
1	teaspoon ground red pepper
½	teaspoon chili powder

Combine all ingredients in a small bowl. Yield: 6 tablespoons.

Per tablespoon: Calories 15 (36% from fat); Fat 0.6g (sat 0.1g, mono 0.1g, poly 0.3g); Protein 0.8g; Carb 2.8g; Fiber 1.4g; Chol 0mg; Iron 1mg; Sodium 407mg; Calc 13mg

---

Basting Sauce

prep: 3 min.   other: 8 hrs.

1	tablespoon light brown sugar
1½	teaspoons Dry Spices
½	cup red wine vinegar
½	cup water
1	tablespoon Worcestershire sauce
⅛	teaspoon hot sauce
1	bay leaf

Stir together all ingredients; cover and chill 8 hours. Remove and discard bay leaf. Yield: about 1 cup.

Per tablespoon: Calories 3 (5% from fat); Fat 0g (sat 0g, mono 0g, poly 0g); Protein 0g; Carb 0.9g; Fiber 0.1g; Chol 0mg; Iron 0.1mg; Sodium 24mg; Calc 2mg

---

Sweet Sauce

prep: 10 min.   cook: 30 min.

1	cup ketchup
1	cup red wine vinegar
1	(8-ounce) can tomato sauce
½	cup spicy honey mustard
½	cup Worcestershire sauce
¼	cup butter or margarine
2	tablespoons light brown sugar
2	tablespoons hot sauce
1	tablespoon seasoned salt
1	tablespoon paprika
1	tablespoon lemon juice
1½	teaspoons garlic powder
⅛	teaspoon chili powder
⅛	teaspoon ground red pepper
⅛	teaspoon black pepper

Combine all ingredients in a large saucepan; bring to a boil. Reduce heat, and simmer, uncovered, 30 minutes, stirring occasionally. Store in refrigerator or freezer. Yield: 4 cups.

Per tablespoon: Calories 19 (43% from fat); Fat 0.9g (sat 0.5g, mono 0.2g, poly 0.1g); Protein 0.2g; Carb 3g; Fiber 0.2g; Chol 2mg; Iron 0.2mg; Sodium 179mg; Calc 5mg

family favorite • make ahead
Smoked Pork

prep: 40 min.   cook: 7 hrs., 20 min.
other: 1 hr., 20 min.

Most barbecue sauces have either a ketchup or mustard base; this one has both.

Hickory wood chunks
2   cups prepared mustard
1½ cups ketchup
¾   cup cider vinegar
2   tablespoons sugar
2   tablespoons Worcestershire sauce
1   tablespoon hot sauce
2   tablespoons butter or margarine
1   (5- to 6-pound) Boston butt pork roast
5   garlic cloves, chopped
2   tablespoons salt
1   tablespoon pepper

Soak wood chunks in water at least 1 hour. **Cook** mustard and next 6 ingredients in a large saucepan over low heat, stirring often, 20 minutes; remove from heat, and set aside. **Cut** several deep slits in roast using a paring knife. Stir together garlic, salt, and pepper; rub on all sides of roast.
Prepare charcoal fire in smoker; let burn 15 to 20 minutes.
Drain wood chunks; place on coals. Place water pan in smoker; add water to fill line.
Place pork roast in center of lower food rack. Pour 1 cup mustard mixture over roast.
Cook, covered, 6 to 7 hours or until a meat thermometer inserted in thickest portion registers 160°, adding additional wood chunks and charcoal every hour as needed. Remove roast from smoker; cool slightly. Chop and serve with remaining mustard sauce. Yield: 10 servings.

Per serving: Calories 546 (58% from fat); Fat 35.1g (sat 12.9g, mono 15.4g, poly 3.4g); Protein 41.7g; Carb 16g; Fiber 1.8g; Chol 150mg; Iron 3.9mg; Sodium 2399mg; Calc 98mg

low calorie • low fat
Adobo Grilled Pork Tacos With Cucumber-Radish Salsa

prep: 40 min.   cook: 23 min.
other: 2 hrs., 32 min.

Toasted cumin seed contributes an earthy, nutty essence to the grilled pork.

1   (2-ounce) package dried mild New Mexico chiles
3   cups boiling water
2   teaspoons cumin seeds
1   tablespoon dried oregano
3   garlic cloves
2   tablespoons cider vinegar
1   teaspoon sugar
1   teaspoon salt
¼   teaspoon ground red pepper
2   (¾-pound) pork tenderloins
½   teaspoon salt
1   (8-ounce) container sour cream
Cucumber-Radish Salsa
2   (17.5-ounce) packages soft taco-size flour tortillas, warmed
Garnishes: lime wedges, fresh cilantro

Slice chiles in half lengthwise. Remove and discard stems and seeds. Place chiles in a bowl, and cover with boiling water. Let stand 20 minutes or until chiles are softened. Drain chiles, reserving liquid.
Cook cumin seeds in a skillet over medium heat 30 seconds. Add oregano, and cook, stirring constantly, 30 seconds or until cumin is toasted.
Process cumin mixture, soaked chiles, 1 cup reserved liquid, garlic, and next 4 ingredients in a blender or food processor until smooth, adding more reserved liquid if needed.
Place pork in a shallow dish or zip-top freezer bag; sprinkle each tenderloin with ¼ teaspoon salt. Pour chile mixture over meat, reserving ½ cup for basting. Cover or seal, and chill 1 to 2 hours. Remove pork from marinade, discarding marinade.
Stir together sour cream and ½ cup Cucumber-Radish Salsa; cover and chill until ready to serve.

Grill pork, covered with grill lid, over medium-high heat (350° to 400°), turning occasionally and basting with reserved chile mixture, 22 minutes or until a meat thermometer inserted in thickest portion registers 155°. Remove from grill; let stand 10 minutes. Coarsely chop pork. Serve in warm tortillas with remaining Cucumber-Radish Salsa and sour cream mixture. Garnish, if desired. Yield: 20 servings.

Per serving: Calories 239 (31% from fat); Fat 8.3g (sat 3.3g, mono 2.3g, poly 2.3g); Protein 12.1g; Carb 28.1g; Fiber 0.5g; Chol 29mg; Iron 2.3mg; Sodium 517mg; Calc 94mg

Cucumber-Radish Salsa

prep: 10 min.

1   cucumber, peeled, seeded, and chopped
1   (6-ounce) package radishes, grated (about 1½ cups)
1   small onion, minced
2   tablespoons chopped fresh cilantro
¼   cup lime juice
½   teaspoon salt
¼   teaspoon ground red pepper

Stir together all ingredients. Cover and chill, if desired. Yield: 3 cups.

Per tablespoon: Calories 2 (5% from fat); Fat 0g (sat 0g, mono 0g, poly 0g); Protein 0.1g; Carb 0.5g; Fiber 0.1g; Chol 0mg; Iron 0mg; Sodium 26mg; Calc 2mg

grilling safety

• Always keep the grill at least 10 feet away from your house, garage, or any flammable materials. Never use a grill indoors or under a covered patio.
• Never add lighter fluid to a lit fire.
• Never use a grill that wobbles, leans, or is otherwise unstable.
• Never spray or brush oil on a hot cooking grate. Oil the food instead.
• Don't wear loose or highly flammable clothing when grilling. Always use heat-resistant barbecue mitts and long-handled tools to tend the fire and food.
• Keep a fire extinguisher handy in case of a mishap. Never pour water on a grease fire. Instead, cover charcoal grill with lid and close all vents; turn off gas grills at the source.
• Keep children and pets away from hot grills.

Few things rival the aroma of an outdoor barbecue.

Margarita Pork
Tenderloin

Wrap chips in heavy-duty aluminum foil, and poke several holes in foil.

Light gas grill on 1 side to medium; place foil-wrapped chips directly on hot coals. Coat grill rack on opposite side with cooking spray. Place rack over cool lava rocks; let grill preheat 10 to 15 minutes or until chips smoke.

Remove lamb from marinade, discarding marinade. Place lamb on rack opposite hot coals. Grill, covered with grill lid, 40 minutes or until a meat thermometer inserted in thickest portion registers 150° (medium rare) or 160° (medium). Let stand 10 minutes. Slice diagonally across the grain into thin slices. Yield: 8 servings.

Per serving: Calories 430 (53% from fat); Fat 25.5g (sat 9g, mono 11.6g, poly 2.2g); Protein 46g; Carb 2.6g; Fiber 0.3g; Chol 151mg; Iron 4mg; Sodium 875mg; Calc 45mg

Note: If pecan shell chips are hard to find in your area, substitute whole pecans. Just crack them, leaving the nuts in the shell.

---

low calorie • low carb • low fat

Margarita Pork Tenderloin

prep: 15 min.   cook: 8 min.   other: 1 hr.

3   garlic cloves, minced
1   green onion, minced
½   jalapeño pepper, minced
3   tablespoons chopped fresh cilantro
2   tablespoons fresh lime juice
1½   tablespoons tequila
1   tablespoon fresh orange juice
1   teaspoon salt
1   teaspoon ground cumin
½   teaspoon chili powder
2   (1-pound) pork tenderloins

Combine first 10 ingredients in a shallow dish or large zip-top freezer bag. Cut pork diagonally into 1-inch-thick slices, and add to tequila mixture. Cover or seal, and chill 1 hour, turning occasionally.

Remove pork from marinade, discarding marinade.

Grill, covered with grill lid, over high heat (400° to 500°) 3 to 4 minutes on each side or until a meat thermometer inserted in thickest portion registers 160°. Yield: 6 servings.

Per serving: Calories 187 (26% from fat); Fat 5.3g (sat 1.8g, mono 2.1g, poly 0.5g); Protein 30.3g; Carb 1.7g; Fiber 0.3g; Chol 84mg; Iron 1.8mg; Sodium 454mg; Calc 16mg

---

low carb

Grilled Leg of Lamb Dijon

prep: 12 min.   cook: 40 min.

other: 8 hrs., 25 min.

Pecan shells add smoky essence to this lamb.

1   (5- to 6-pound) leg of lamb, boned and butterflied
4   garlic cloves, pressed
2   (8-ounce) jars Dijon mustard
¼   cup plus 1 tablespoon soy sauce
¼   cup plus 1 tablespoon olive oil
2   tablespoons minced fresh ginger
1   tablespoon chopped fresh or dried rosemary
1   tablespoon dried thyme
1   teaspoon salt
1   teaspoon ground red pepper
Pecan shell chips
Vegetable cooking spray

Trim fat from lamb. Combine garlic and next 8 ingredients in a medium bowl; stir well with a wire whisk.

Pour half of marinade into a 13- x 9-inch baking dish. Place lamb in dish. Spread remaining half of marinade on lamb. Cover and marinate in refrigerator 8 hours.

Soak pecan shell chips in water to cover 1 hour. Drain well.

---

low carb

Basil Grilled Lamb Chops

prep: 10 min.   cook: 12 min.   other: 2 hrs.

Honey and soy sauce paint these chops with goodness on the grill.

8   (5-ounce) lean lamb loin chops (1 inch thick)
½   cup minced onion
¼   cup honey
3   tablespoons chopped fresh basil
3   tablespoons vegetable oil
1½   tablespoons soy sauce
1   tablespoon minced fresh garlic
1   teaspoon salt
1   teaspoon freshly ground pepper

Place chops in a large zip-top freezer bag. Combine onion and remaining ingredients. Pour over chops. Seal bag; marinate in refrigerator 2 hours, turning once.

Remove chops from marinade, reserving marinade. Bring marinade to a boil. Remove from heat, and set aside.

Grill chops, uncovered, over medium-high heat (350° to 400°) 5 to 6 minutes on each side or to desired degree of doneness, basting often with marinade. Yield: 8 servings.

Per serving: Calories 345 (63% from fat); Fat 24.2g (sat 8.6g, mono 10.2g, poly 3.6g); Protein 21.2g; Carb 10.5g; Fiber 0.3g; Chol 82mg; Iron 1.8mg; Sodium 543mg; Calc 25mg

Hickory-Smoked Bourbon Turkey

prep: 30 min. cook: 6 hrs.
other: 49 hrs., 15 min.

The sweetness of maple syrup combined with bourbon seals Southern goodness into this bird.

1   (11-pound) fresh or frozen whole turkey, thawed
2   cups maple syrup
1   cup bourbon
1   tablespoon pickling spice
Hickory wood chunks
1   large carrot
1   celery rib
1   medium onion, peeled and halved
1   lemon
1   tablespoon salt
2   teaspoons pepper

Remove giblets and neck from turkey; reserve for other uses, if desired. Rinse turkey thoroughly with cold water, and pat dry with paper towels.
Add water to a stockpot, filling half full; stir in maple syrup, bourbon, and pickling spice. Add turkey and, if needed, additional water to cover. Cover and chill 2 days.
Soak wood chunks in fresh water at least 1 hour. Prepare charcoal fire in smoker; let fire burn 20 to 30 minutes.
Remove turkey from water, discarding water mixture; pat turkey dry. Cut carrot and celery in half crosswise. Stuff cavity with carrot, celery, and onion. Pierce lemon with a fork; place in neck cavity.
Combine salt and pepper; rub mixture on turkey. Fold wings under, and tie legs together with string, if desired.
Drain wood chunks, and place on coals. Place water pan in smoker, and add water to depth of fill line. Place turkey in center of lower food rack; cover with smoker lid.
Cook 6 hours or until a meat thermometer inserted into thickest portion of turkey thigh registers 180°, adding more water, charcoal, and wood chunks as needed. Remove from smoker, and let stand 15 minutes before slicing. Yield: 12 servings.

Per serving: Calories 516 (40% from fat); Fat 23g (sat 6.7g, mono 7.6g, poly 5.9g); Protein 66.5g; Carb 4.9g; Fiber 0.1g; Chol 194mg; Iron 4.4mg; Sodium 743mg; Calc 68mg

Smoked Turkey Breast

prep: 10 min. cook: 5 hrs. other: 1 hr., 30 min.

Hickory wood chunks
1   tablespoon salt
1   tablespoon garlic powder
1   tablespoon chopped fresh or dried rosemary
1   tablespoon pepper
1   (5-pound) bone-in turkey breast

Soak wood chunks in water at least 1 hour.
Combine salt and next 3 ingredients; rub mixture on turkey breast.
Prepare charcoal fire in smoker; let burn 15 to 20 minutes.
Drain wood chunks, and place on coals. Place water pan in smoker; add water to depth of fill line. Place turkey in center of lower food rack; cover with smoker lid.
Cook 4 to 5 hours or until a meat thermometer inserted into thickest portion registers 170°, adding more water to depth of fill line, if necessary. Remove from smoker; let stand 10 minutes before slicing. Yield: 8 servings.

Per serving: Calories 396 (35% from fat); Fat 15.4g (sat 4.4g, mono 5.1g, poly 3.7g); Protein 59.4g; Carb 1.6g; Fiber 0.5g; Chol 152mg; Iron 3.3mg; Sodium 1003mg; Calc 54mg

Fresh Herb-Rubbed Salmon Fillets

prep: 15 min. cook: 10 min. other: 1 hr.

This fish with a light coating of fresh herbs cooks up in minutes.

¼   cup tightly packed fresh parsley leaves
¼   cup tightly packed fresh cilantro leaves
¼   cup chopped onion
2   garlic cloves, pressed
3   tablespoons olive oil
1½   teaspoons chili powder
1   teaspoon dried oregano
½   teaspoon salt
6   (6-ounce) salmon fillets

Process first 8 ingredients in a food processor until smooth.
Place salmon fillets, skin side down, in a 13- x 9-inch baking dish. Spread herb mixture evenly on fillets; cover and chill 1 hour.
Grill, skin side down, covered with grill lid, over high heat (400° to 500°) 6 to 10 minutes or until fish flakes with a fork. Yield: 6 servings.

Per serving: Calories 403 (59% from fat); Fat 26.2g (sat 5.6g, mono 13.3g, poly 4.5g); Protein 37.5g; Carb 1.8g; Fiber 0.4g; Chol 123mg; Iron 1.8mg; Sodium 298mg; Calc 54mg

Grilled Tuna Sandwiches

prep: 10 min. cook: 16 min.

1   (1-inch-thick) tuna steak (about ¾ pound)
2   tablespoons olive oil, divided
½   teaspoon salt
½   teaspoon pepper
8   slices sourdough bread
¼   teaspoon ground red pepper (optional)
¼   cup finely chopped green onions
¼   cup mayonnaise
2   tablespoons fresh lime juice
2   teaspoons prepared horseradish
1   large tomato, thinly sliced
1   ripe avocado, sliced

Rub tuna with 1 tablespoon olive oil, and sprinkle salt and pepper evenly on both sides of tuna.
Grill, covered with grill lid, over medium-high heat (350° to 400°) 6 to 7 minutes on each side or to desired degree of doneness.
Brush bread slices with remaining 1 tablespoon olive oil, and grill 1 minute on each side or until golden.
Flake tuna; combine with ground red pepper, if desired, and next 4 ingredients. Spread tuna mixture evenly on 1 side of each of 4 grilled bread slices; top with tomato and avocado slices. Cover with remaining 4 bread slices. Yield: 4 servings.

Per serving: Calories 623 (42% from fat); Fat 29g (sat 4.5g, mono 14g, poly 8.5g); Protein 29.9g; Carb 61.5g; Fiber 7.3g; Chol 42mg; Iron 4mg; Sodium 1038mg; Calc 109mg

For the juiciest seafood possible, grill it hot and fast. The smaller the seafood is, the hotter the fire should be. Intense heat prevents seafood from sticking to the grill.

Grilled Shrimp With Tropical Fruit Sauce

prep: 20 min.   cook: 58 min.   other: 1 hr.

2 pounds unpeeled, large fresh shrimp
1 (33.8-ounce) jar peach nectar
¼ cup fresh lime juice, divided
2 tablespoons dark sesame oil
1 tablespoon grated fresh ginger
½ teaspoon salt
4 plum tomatoes, seeded and diced
2 papayas or mangoes, peeled and cubed*
3 green onions, sliced
¼ cup minced fresh cilantro
½ to 1 teaspoon chili-garlic paste
3 cups hot cooked rice

Peel shrimp, and devein, if desired; set aside.
Bring nectar to a boil in a medium saucepan; boil 45 minutes or until reduced to 1 cup. Stir in 2 tablespoons lime juice and next 3 ingredients. Remove from heat; cool.
Pour half of nectar mixture into a large zip-top freezer bag; add shrimp. Cover or seal, and chill 1 hour.
Remove shrimp from marinade, discarding marinade.
Grill in 2 batches in a grill basket over medium-high heat (350° to 400°) 3 to 4 minutes or until shrimp turn pink.
Add remaining 2 tablespoons lime juice, tomato, and next 4 ingredients to remaining nectar mixture. Cook over medium heat until thoroughly heated. Stir in shrimp; serve over hot cooked rice. Yield: 6 servings.

Per serving: Calories 375 (12% from fat); Fat 5g (sat 0.9g, mono 1.7g, poly 2.1g); Protein 27g; Carb 55.8g; Fiber 3.2g; Chol 224mg; Iron 5.3mg; Sodium 438mg; Calc 106mg

Note: Select unblemished papayas or mangoes that yield slightly to pressure. If underripe, place in a paper bag at room temperature to speed up the process.

*Substitute 1 pineapple, chopped, for papaya, if desired.

Grilled-Shrimp Gyros With Herbed Yogurt Spread

prep: 25 min.   cook: 10 min.   other: 30 min.

1½ pounds unpeeled, medium-size fresh shrimp
2 tablespoons Greek seasoning
2 tablespoons olive oil
6 (12-inch) wooden skewers
4 (6-inch) pita rounds or gyro rounds
Herbed Yogurt Spread
½ cup crumbled feta cheese
1 large tomato, chopped
1 cucumber, thinly sliced

Peel shrimp, and devein, if desired.
Combine seasoning and olive oil in a zip-top freezer bag; add shrimp. Seal and chill 30 minutes.
Soak skewers in water 30 minutes while shrimp marinates; thread shrimp onto skewers.
Grill, covered with grill lid, over medium-high heat (350° to 400°) about 3 minutes on each side or just until shrimp turn pink.
Wrap each pita round in a damp cloth; microwave at HIGH 10 to 15 seconds or until soft. Spread 1 side of each pita round with Herbed Yogurt Spread. Top evenly with shrimp, cheese, tomato, and cucumber; roll up. Yield: 4 servings.

Per serving: Calories 445 (28% from fat); Fat 13.5g (sat 4.5g, mono 6.3g, poly 1.8g); Protein 38g; Carb 41.4g; Fiber 2.7g; Chol 271mg; Iron 6.3mg; Sodium 2293mg; Calc 275mg

Herbed Yogurt Spread

prep: 5 min.

½ cup low-fat yogurt
1 garlic clove, minced
1 tablespoon chopped fresh or
   ¾ teaspoon dried oregano
1 teaspoon chopped fresh mint
2 teaspoons lemon juice
¼ teaspoon pepper

Whisk together all ingredients; cover and chill until ready to serve or up to 8 hours. Yield: ½ cup.

Per tablespoon: Calories 11 (25% from fat); Fat 0.3g (sat 0.2g, mono 0.1g, poly 0g); Protein 0.9g; Carb 1.4g; Fiber 0g; Chol 1mg; Iron 0mg; Sodium 11mg; Calc 32mg

Grilled Asparagus Salad With Orange Vinaigrette

prep: 35 min.   cook: 10 min.   other: 1 hr.

1½ pounds fresh asparagus
1½ tablespoons grated orange rind
⅓ cup fresh orange juice
½ cup olive oil
⅓ cup balsamic vinegar
2 teaspoons Dijon mustard
¾ teaspoon salt
½ teaspoon pepper
1½ pounds mixed gourmet salad greens
6 bacon slices, cooked and crumbled (optional)

Snap off tough ends of asparagus; place asparagus in a shallow dish.
Whisk together grated orange rind and next 6 ingredients. Pour one-third of vinaigrette over asparagus; cover and chill 1 hour. Set aside remaining vinaigrette.
Drain asparagus. Grill, covered with grill lid, over medium-high heat (350° to 400°) 8 to 10 minutes or until crisp-tender; cool.
Combine greens, remaining vinaigrette, and, if desired, bacon; place evenly on 6 salad plates. Arrange asparagus over salad. Yield: 6 servings.

Per serving: Calories 365 (39% from fat); Fat 15.7g (sat 2.1g, mono 11.1g, poly 1.8g); Protein 4.5g; Carb 48.6g; Fiber 4.2g; Chol 0mg; Iron 3.3mg; Sodium 365mg; Calc 101mg

Three-Pepper Grill

prep: 25 min.   cook: 25 min.   other: 4 hrs.

Toss these veggies on the fire and serve up a sassy side dish for grilled chicken or burgers. Use a grill wok to contain the pieces.

4 large tomatoes
1 medium eggplant
1 large red bell pepper
1 large green bell pepper
1 large yellow bell pepper
¼ cup olive oil
1 tablespoon fresh thyme leaves
3 tablespoons lemon juice
2 garlic cloves, pressed
½ teaspoon salt

Cut tomatoes in half; peel eggplant, and cut into cubes. Cut bell peppers into 2-inch pieces. Combine vegetables, oil, and remaining ingredients in a large zip-top freezer bag; seal and chill 2 to 4 hours. Remove vegetables, reserving marinade.

Grill eggplant and bell pepper, in batches, in a grill wok, covered with grill lid, over high heat (400° to 500°), stirring occasionally, 10 minutes or until tender. Place bell pepper and eggplant in a large bowl.

Grill tomato, cut sides up, covered, over high heat 4 to 5 minutes. Coarsely chop tomato, and toss with bell pepper mixture. Drizzle with reserved marinade, tossing to coat. Yield: 6 servings.

Per serving: Calories 145 (60% from fat); Fat 9.7g (sat 1.3g, mono 6.7g, poly 1.2g); Protein 2.7g; Carb 15.3g; Fiber 5.5g; Chol 0mg; Iron 1.2mg; Sodium 209mg; Calc 24mg

low calorie • low carb

Grilled Red Onions

prep: 20 min.   cook: 10 min.   other: 8 hrs.

If you've tried to grill onions only to have the rings separate and end up in the fire, then we have a solution. Insert skewers through onion slices to hold them together.

12 (8-inch) wooden skewers
3   medium-size red or sweet onions
1½ cups dry white wine
¼   cup butter or margarine
1   teaspoon chopped fresh thyme
⅛   teaspoon pepper
Garnish: fresh thyme

Insert 4 wooden skewers (1 at a time) through each onion about ½ inch apart to create horizontal segments. Cut onions into slices between skewers. (Leave skewers in place to hold onion slices together during marinating and cooking.)

Place onion slices in a shallow container; add wine. Cover and chill 8 hours, turning occasionally. Drain.

Melt butter in a small saucepan; stir in thyme and pepper. Brush onion slices with butter mixture, reserving some for basting.

Grill onions, covered with grill lid, over medium-high heat (350° to 400°) 10 minutes, turning and basting often with reserved butter mixture. Serve on a platter. Garnish, if desired. Yield: 6 servings.

Per serving: Calories 92 (74% from fat); Fat 7.6g (sat 4.8g, mono 2g, poly 0.3g); Protein 0.7g; Carb 6.1g; Fiber 0.8g; Chol 20mg; Iron 0.3mg; Sodium 58mg; Calc 17mg

low calorie • low cholesterol • low fat

Grilled Corn and Squash

prep: 25 min.   cook: 25 min.

Add a bit of Monterey Jack cheese to this grilled mix, and roll it up in tortillas.

4   ears fresh corn
4   medium-size yellow squash
½   medium-size sweet onion
Vegetable cooking spray
3   poblano chile peppers
1   garlic clove, pressed
2   tablespoons chopped fresh basil
1   tablespoon chopped fresh oregano
½   teaspoon salt
½   teaspoon ground cumin

Remove husks from corn; cut squash in half lengthwise, and cut onion into ¼-inch-thick slices. Coat corn, squash, and onion with cooking spray, and set aside.

Grill chile peppers, covered with grill lid, over medium-high heat (350° to 400°) 5 minutes on each side.

Grill corn and onion, covered, over medium-high heat 4 minutes on each side.

Grill squash, cut sides down, covered, over medium-high heat 5 minutes; turn squash, and grill 2 more minutes.

Cut corn kernels from cob. Chop vegetables, discarding chile pepper seeds; place corn kernels and vegetables in a large bowl. Toss with garlic and remaining ingredients. Yield: 6 servings.

Per serving: Calories 100 (21% from fat); Fat 2.4g (sat 0.1g, mono 0g, poly 0.2g); Protein 4.9g; Carb 18.5g; Fiber 3.3g; Chol 0mg; Iron 1.1mg; Sodium 199mg; Calc 33mg

Corn on the Cob With Garlic-Chive Butter

prep: 30 min.   cook: 20 min.   other: 1 hr.

6   ears fresh corn with husks
½   cup butter or margarine, softened
2   garlic cloves, minced
¼   cup finely chopped fresh chives

Pull back corn husks; remove and discard silks. Pull husks over corn. Cover corn with water; let stand 1 hour (this keeps husks from burning). Drain.

Stir together butter, garlic, and chives.

Grill corn, without grill lid, over medium heat (300° to 350°) 20 minutes or until tender, turning often. Remove husks. Spread desired amount of butter mixture over corn. Yield: 6 servings.

Per serving: Calories 226 (70% from fat); Fat 17.7g (sat 9.6g, mono 3.9g, poly 0.6g); Protein 4.3g; Carb 16.4g; Fiber 2.1g; Chol 40mg; Iron 0.4mg; Sodium 108mg; Calc 8mg

Grilled Red Onions

Grilled Balsamic-Glazed
Peaches

Serve this simple peach side with grilled chicken or beef, or even as dessert.

Grill tomatoes, cut sides up, covered with grill lid, over medium-high heat (350° to 400°) about 4 to 5 minutes (do not turn). Sprinkle tomatoes evenly with basil and coarse salt. Yield: 10 servings.

Per serving: Calories 45 (60% from fat); Fat 3g (sat 0.4g, mono 2g, poly 0.4g); Protein 0.9g; Carb 4.6g; Fiber 1.1g; Chol 0mg; Iron 0.5mg; Sodium 241mg; Calc 10mg

low calorie • low cholesterol

Marinated Grilled Vegetables

prep: 20 min.   cook: 24 min.   other: 30 min.

Serve these grilled vegetables as an antipasto at your next cookout.

10	large fresh mushrooms
2	zucchini
2	yellow squash
1	green bell pepper
1	red bell pepper
½	cup balsamic vinegar
2	tablespoons olive oil
3	garlic cloves, minced
1	teaspoon salt
2	teaspoons minced fresh thyme
1	teaspoon freshly ground pepper

Vegetable cooking spray

Remove mushroom stems, and discard. Cut zucchini and yellow squash into ½-inch slices. Cut bell peppers into 1-inch strips.
Combine vegetables, vinegar, and next 5 ingredients in a large zip-top freezer bag; seal and chill 30 minutes.
Remove vegetables with a slotted spoon, reserving marinade.
Coat a grill wok with cooking spray; arrange vegetables in basket. Grill, covered with grill lid, over medium heat (300° to 350°) 12 minutes on each side or until crisp-tender. Place vegetables in a large bowl; drizzle with reserved marinade, tossing to coat. Yield: 6 servings.

Per serving: Calories 96 (44% from fat); Fat 5.1g (sat 0.7g, mono 3.4g, poly 0.7g); Protein 3.3g; Carb 11.2g; Fiber 2.8g; Chol 0mg; Iron 1mg; Sodium 405mg; Calc 30mg

low cholesterol

Grilled Balsamic-Glazed Peaches

prep: 15 min.   cook: 14 min.   other: 10 min.

Freestone peaches are the best choice for this recipe, because the pits can be easily removed.

½	cup balsamic vinegar
3	tablespoons light brown sugar
1	teaspoon cracked pepper
⅛	teaspoon salt
6	firm, ripe peaches, halved
¼	cup vegetable oil

Combine first 4 ingredients in a saucepan. Bring to a boil; reduce heat, and simmer 2 to 3 minutes.
Remove pits from peaches; do not peel. Place peaches in a shallow dish. Pour vinegar mixture over peaches, tossing to coat. Let stand 10 minutes.
Remove peaches from vinegar mixture, reserving 2 tablespoons. Set remaining vinegar mixture aside.
Whisk together reserved 2 tablespoons vinegar mixture with oil, blending well. Set vinaigrette aside.
Place peach halves, cut sides down, on a lightly greased grill rack. Grill, covered with grill lid, over medium heat (300° to 350°) 5 minutes on each side or until firm and golden, basting with remaining vinegar mixture. Serve with vinaigrette. Yield: 6 servings.

Per serving: Calories 165 (53% from fat); Fat 9.7g (sat 1g, mono 4.1g, poly 4.1g); Protein 0.9g; Carb 21.1g; Fiber 1.6g; Chol 0mg; Iron 0.6mg; Sodium 54mg; Calc 14mg

low calorie • low carb • low cholesterol
low fat • quick

Grilled Tomatoes

prep: 10 min.   cook: 5 min.

Here's a quick, healthy side dish you can throw on the grill alongside a steak or burgers. Leftovers make a great addition for pasta salad.

2	garlic cloves, minced
2	tablespoons olive oil
5	large tomatoes, cut in half crosswise
½	teaspoon salt
½	teaspoon pepper
½	cup chopped fresh basil
½	teaspoon coarse salt

Stir together garlic and olive oil. Brush cut sides of tomatoes evenly with garlic mixture, and sprinkle with ½ teaspoon salt and pepper.

Potato-Stuffed Grilled Bell Peppers

prep: 25 min.   cook: 1 hr., 48 min.   other: 15 min.

Think twice-baked potato, except the potato filling is stuffed and served in a bell pepper half. The peppers roast and char on the bottom; the upper edges stay crisp-tender.

4	large baking potatoes (3½ to 4 pounds)
4	large red bell peppers
1	(16-ounce) container sour cream
½	cup (2 ounces) shredded Gouda cheese
¼	cup sliced green onions
3	tablespoons butter
3	tablespoons chopped fresh flat-leaf parsley
¾	teaspoon salt
½	teaspoon ground pepper
¼	teaspoon paprika

Pierce each potato 3 or 4 times with a fork, and place directly on oven rack.
Bake at 450° for 1 hour and 30 minutes. Let cool slightly, about 15 minutes.
Cut bell peppers in half lengthwise, cutting through stems and keeping intact. Remove and discard seeds and membranes; rinse and pat dry. Set aside.
Cut baked potatoes in half. Scoop out pulp into a large bowl, discarding shells. Add sour cream and next 6 ingredients to pulp, blending well with a fork or potato masher.
Spoon potato mixture evenly into bell pepper halves. Sprinkle with paprika.
Grill peppers, covered with grill lid, over medium-high heat (350° to 400°) 18 minutes or until peppers are blistered and potato filling bubbles around edges. Serve immediately. Yield: 8 servings.

Per serving: Calories 350 (48% from fat); Fat 18.5g (sat 11.4g, mono 5.1g, poly 0.9g); Protein 7.5g; Carb 40.9g; Fiber 4.1g; Chol 44mg; Iron 1.1mg; Sodium 347mg; Calc 135mg

Note: We tried microwaving the potatoes, but the texture is mealy; baking is best for this recipe.

Grilled Pineapple Skewers With Rum Sauce

prep: 20 min.   cook: 18 min.   other: 30 min.

16	(6-inch) wooden skewers
1	cup firmly packed light or dark brown sugar
½	cup butter
⅓	cup dark rum
½	teaspoon ground cinnamon
¼	teaspoon ground nutmeg
1	large fresh pineapple
	Vegetable cooking spray

Soak skewers in water 30 minutes.
Stir together brown sugar and next 4 ingredients in a small saucepan over medium heat, stirring constantly, until blended. Cook over low heat, without stirring, 10 minutes or until sauce begins to thicken. Remove from heat; keep warm, if desired.
Peel pineapple; remove frond. Cut pineapple lengthwise into quarters; discard core. Cut pineapple pieces in half lengthwise. Cut each long pineapple wedge into 6 crosswise pieces. Thread 3 pieces of pineapple onto each skewer.
Spray food grate with cooking spray, and place on grill. Place pineapple on grate. Grill, covered with grill lid, over medium-high heat (350° to 400°) 4 minutes on each side or until thoroughly heated.
Arrange skewers on dessert plates, and drizzle with warm rum sauce. Yield: 16 skewers.

Per skewer and 1 tablespoon sauce: Calories 123 (42% from fat); Fat 5.7g (sat 3.6g, mono 1.5g, poly 0.2g); Protein 0.2g; Carb 17.2g; Fiber 0.5g; Chol 15mg; Iron 0.4mg; Sodium 46mg; Calc 18mg

for kids • quick
Grilled "Banana Splits"

prep: 10 min.   cook: 5 min.

The only way to improve upon this dessert is to add ice cream to the plate.

4	firm, ripe bananas, unpeeled
¼	cup miniature marshmallows
¼	cup semisweet chocolate mini-morsels
¼	cup chunky peanut butter

Cut a lengthwise slit to, but not through, bottom of each banana. Stuff banana slit with 1 tablespoon each of marshmallows, chocolate morsels, and peanut butter.
Place each banana, bottom side down, on 4 squares of aluminum foil folded to resemble a boat. Grill bananas, without grill lid, over medium coals (300° to 350°) 5 minutes or until chocolate morsels melt. Yield: 4 servings.

Per serving: Calories 269 (37% from fat); Fat 11.2g (sat 3.2g, mono 5g, poly 2.5g); Protein 5.4g; Carb 42.4g; Fiber 5.9g; Chol 0mg; Iron 1mg; Sodium 83mg; Calc 11mg

Grilled Pineapple Skewers With Rum Sauce

healthy
favorites

You'll find lots of healthy attributes in these recipes you'll want to prepare often for your family.

Dried Cherry-and-Pecan Oatmeal

prep: 10 min.   cook: 20 min.

Whole oats take a little longer to cook than instant, but they're higher in fiber, have a chewier texture, and stick to your ribs longer.

3   cups water
3   cups fat-free milk
2   cups uncooked whole oats
½   cup dried cherries, coarsely chopped
½   teaspoon salt
5   tablespoons brown sugar
1   tablespoon butter
¼   teaspoon ground cinnamon
¼   teaspoon vanilla extract
2   tablespoons chopped pecans, toasted

Bring first 5 ingredients to a boil; reduce heat, and simmer, stirring occasionally, 20 minutes or until thickened. Remove from heat. Stir in 4 tablespoons brown sugar and next 3 ingredients. Spoon 1 cup oat-meal into each of 6 bowls. Sprinkle with pecans and remaining 1 tablespoon brown sugar. Serve immediately. Yield: 6 servings.

Per cup: Calories 394 (18% from fat); Fat 8g (sat 2.3g, mono 2.9g, poly 2.1g); Protein 13.3g; Carb 66g; Fiber 7.7g; Chol 8mg; Iron 3.2mg; Sodium 280mg; Calc 197mg

oatmeal for a healthy heart

One key to maintaining a healthy heart is keeping cholesterol levels in check. While cholesterol levels are due, in part, to genetics, a diet high in saturated fat can cause choles-terol levels to rise, which can damage and clog arteries and lead to an increased risk for heart disease and stroke. But oatmeal can actually help decrease cholesterol levels. It's low in saturated fat, and the soluble fiber in oats binds to cholesterol in the small intes-tine, preventing it from being absorbed.

Shown on previous page: Savory Spinach-Gorgonzola Custards (page 266), Creamy Gorgonzola Dressing (page 273)

Mixed Fruit Granola

prep: 10 min.   cook: 30 min.

Serve with nonfat vanilla yogurt.

6   cups uncooked regular oats
½   cup wheat germ
½   cup sunflower kernels
½   cup chopped pecans
¼   cup sesame seeds
½   cup honey
2   tablespoons vegetable oil
½   tablespoon ground cinnamon
1½   teaspoons vanilla extract
Vegetable cooking spray
1½   cups chopped mixed dried fruit

Combine first 9 ingredients; spread on 2 pans coated with cooking spray.
Bake at 350° for 25 to 30 minutes, stirring 3 times. Cool. Stir in dried fruit. Yield: 7½ cups.

Per ¼ cup: Calories 145 (33% from fat); Fat 5.3g (sat 0.6g, mono 2.1g, poly 2.2g); Protein 4g; Carb 22g; Fiber 3g; Chol 0mg; Iron 1.4mg; Sodium 2mg; Calc 28mg

Note: Store in an airtight container up to 2 weeks.

Creamy Potato-Garlic Spread

prep: 5 min.   cook: 15 min.

Baked pita chips, raw veggies, or low-fat crackers make healthy dippers.

1   pound baking potatoes, peeled and cut into 2-inch cubes
3   tablespoons fresh lemon juice
1   tablespoon olive oil
1   teaspoon bottled minced roasted garlic
½   to 1 teaspoon grated lemon rind
½   teaspoon salt
½   teaspoon freshly ground pepper
1   green onion, chopped (optional)

Cook potato in boiling water to cover in a Dutch oven 15 minutes or until tender. Drain.

Process potato, juice, and next 5 ingredients in a food processor until smooth, stopping to scrape down sides. Transfer mixture to a serving dish, and sprinkle with green onion, if desired. Yield: 6 servings.

Per ¼ cup: Calories 76 (28% from fat); Fat 2.4g (sat 0.3g, mono 1.8g, poly 0.2g); Protein 1.2g; Carb 13g; Fiber 1g; Chol 0mg; Iron 0.2mg; Sodium 197mg; Calc 5mg

Note: To make your own pita chips, cut 2 (6-inch) pita rounds into wedges; split in half at seams. Place on a baking sheet coated with vegetable cooking spray; coat wedges with cooking spray. Bake at 450° for 4 to 5 minutes or until crisp.

Chunky Black-Eyed Pea Salsa

prep: 30 min.   cook: 10 min.

Black-eyed peas contain soluble fiber, which aids in reducing blood cholesterol. They also decrease the risk of some cancers.

1   large poblano chile pepper
1   (15.8-ounce) can black-eyed peas, rinsed and drained
1   ripe mango, peeled and chopped
½   small sweet onion, chopped
½   small red bell pepper, chopped
¼   cup chopped fresh cilantro
½   teaspoon grated lime rind
3   tablespoons fresh lime juice
2   teaspoons olive oil
¼   to ½ teaspoon salt
¼   to ½ teaspoon freshly ground pepper

Broil poblano pepper on an aluminum foil-lined baking sheet 5½ inches from heat about 5 minutes on each side or until pepper looks blistered.
Place pepper in a zip-top freezer bag; seal and let stand 10 minutes to loosen skin. Peel pepper; remove and discard seeds. Chop pepper.
Stir together pepper, peas, and remaining ingredients. Cover and chill. Serve with tortilla chips. Yield: 2 cups.

Per ¼ cup: Calories 70 (18% from fat); Fat 1.4g (sat 0.2g, mono 0.9g, poly 0.2g); Protein 3.5g; Carb 12g; Fiber 2g; Chol 0mg; Iron 1.1mg; Sodium 244mg; Calc 32mg

adobo sauce

This spiced Mexican marinade is generally found canned with chipotle chiles (smoked jalapeños); it has a smoky, slightly sweet flavor with a medium heat index. For those trying to watch their sodium intake, beware—this sauce is high in sodium, and a little goes a long way, too.

low calorie • low carb

Spicy Crab Ball

prep: 17 min.   other: 2 hrs.

½   small sweet onion, chopped
1   teaspoon olive oil
1   (8-ounce) package reduced-fat cream cheese, softened
1   (6-ounce) can jumbo lump crabmeat, rinsed and drained
1   to 2 tablespoons adobo sauce (from canned chipotles)
10   smoked almonds, finely chopped

Sauté onion in hot oil in a nonstick skillet over medium heat until tender.
Stir together onion, cream cheese, crabmeat, and adobo sauce. Cover and chill 2 hours.
Shape crab mixture into a ball; roll top in almonds. Cover; chill until ready to serve. Serve with fresh vegetables or low-fat crackers. Yield: 8 servings.

Per serving: Calories 107 (63% from fat); Fat 7.5g (sat 3g, mono 0.5g, poly 0.3g); Protein 6.8g; Carb 3g; Fiber 0.3g; Chol 29mg; Iron 0.4mg; Sodium 232mg; Calc 58mg

low cholesterol • low fat • quick

Low-Fat Cappuccino Cooler

prep: 5 min.

1½   cups brewed coffee, chilled
1½   cups low-fat chocolate ice cream
¼   cup chocolate syrup
Reduced-fat frozen whipped topping, thawed (optional)

Process first 3 ingredients in a blender until smooth. Serve immediately over crushed ice. Top with whipped topping, if desired. Yield: 3 cups.

Per cup: Calories 168 (11% from fat); Fat 2g (sat 1g, mono 0g, poly 0g); Protein 2.8g; Carb 35g; Fiber 0g; Chol 5mg; Iron 0.6mg; Sodium 74mg; Calc 82mg

low cholesterol • low fat • quick

Banana-Berry Smoothie

prep: 5 min.

Freeze leftover fruit to use in shakes, smoothies, or any blended treat.

1   cup low-fat plain yogurt
3   cups frozen strawberries
2   bananas, sliced
¾   cup fat-free milk
¼   cup crushed ice
¼   cup honey

Process all ingredients in a blender until smooth. Serve immediately. Yield: 5 cups.

Per cup: Calories 168 (5% from fat); Fat 1g (sat 0.6g, mono 0.3g, poly 0.1g); Protein 4.8g; Carb 38g; Fiber 3.1g; Chol 4mg; Iron 0.9mg; Sodium 53mg; Calc 153mg

low calorie • low fat

Berry-and-Spice Whole Wheat Muffins

prep: 15 min.   cook: 21 min.   other: 5 min.

¼   cup firmly packed light brown sugar
1   tablespoon all-purpose flour
3   tablespoons chopped pecans
1   tablespoon butter, melted
1   cup all-purpose flour
1   cup whole wheat flour
¼   cup granulated sugar
¾   teaspoon baking powder
¾   teaspoon baking soda
½   teaspoon ground cinnamon
¼   teaspoon ground allspice
1   large egg
1¼   cups buttermilk
1½   tablespoons vegetable oil
1   cup fresh or frozen blueberries

Combine brown sugar, 1 tablespoon flour, and pecans in a small bowl. Stir in melted butter; set aside.
Combine 1 cup all-purpose flour and next 6 ingredients in a large bowl; make a well in center of mixture.
Stir together egg, buttermilk, and oil; add to dry ingredients, stirring just until moistened. Fold in blueberries.
Spoon about ⅓ cup batter into each of 12 lightly greased muffin cups. Sprinkle batter evenly with reserved pecan mixture.
Bake at 375° for 19 to 21 minutes or until lightly browned. Cool in pans on a wire rack 5 minutes. Remove from pans, and cool slightly on wire rack. Serve warm. Yield: 1 dozen.

Per muffin: Calories 168 (27% from fat); Fat 5g (sat 1.2g, mono 2g, poly 1.4g); Protein 4.2g; Carb 28g; Fiber 2g; Chol 21mg; Iron 1.2mg; Sodium 151mg; Calc 61mg

low calorie • low cholesterol • quick

Parmesan Corn Muffins

prep: 10 min.   cook: 15 min.

2   cups white cornmeal mix
¾   cup all-purpose flour
½   cup grated Parmesan cheese
¼   teaspoon ground red pepper
2½   cups fat-free buttermilk
½   cup egg substitute
2   tablespoons vegetable oil
Vegetable cooking spray

Combine first 4 ingredients in a mixing bowl, and make a well in center of mixture.
Stir together buttermilk, egg substitute, and oil; add to dry ingredients, stirring just until moistened. Spoon into muffin pans coated with cooking spray, filling two-thirds full.
Bake at 425° for 15 minutes or until golden. Remove from pans immediately, and cool on wire racks. Yield: 17 muffins.

Per muffin: Calories 118 (28% from fat); Fat 3.7g (sat 1g, mono 1.5g, poly 0.9g); Protein 5g; Carb 16g; Fiber 1g; Chol 5mg; Iron 1.2mg; Sodium 284mg; Calc 138mg

10 snacks under 50 calories

1 cucumber, sliced
12 baby carrots
16 celery sticks
1 large tomato, cut into wedges
22 fat-free pretzel sticks
1½ cups broccoli florets
½ apple, sliced
12 radishes
4 low-fat crackers
12 medium strawberries

English Muffin French Toast

prep: 5 min.   cook: 6 min. per batch
other: 8 hrs.

1   cup egg substitute
1   cup fat-free milk
1   teaspoon vanilla extract
6   English muffins, split
Vegetable cooking spray
Chopped kiwifruit, blueberries, nectarines,
      strawberries (optional)
Garnish: fresh mint sprigs

Stir together egg substitute, milk, and vanilla. Place in a large zip-top freezer bag; add English muffins. Seal and chill 8 hours, turning occasionally. Remove muffins from bag, discarding remaining liquid.
Cook English muffins, in batches, in a large skillet coated with cooking spray over medium-high heat 2 to 3 minutes on each side or until muffins are golden. Serve with light pancake syrup and, if desired, kiwifruit, blueberries, nectarines, and strawberries. Garnish, if desired. Yield: 6 servings.

Per serving: Calories 326 (8% from fat); Fat 3g (sat 0.7g, mono 0.4g, poly 0.2g); Protein 15.2g; Carb 60g; Fiber 2.3g; Chol 5mg; Iron 3mg; Sodium 468mg; Calc 309mg

make ahead

Light Tiramisù

prep: 15 min.   cook: 30 min.   other: 2 hrs.

This creamy, coffee-inspired concoction has less than half the fat of the traditional version.

½   cup granulated sugar
1   cup whipping cream, divided
2   cups fat-free milk
½   cup egg substitute
2   egg yolks
1   tablespoon all-purpose flour
½   vanilla bean, split
1   (8-ounce) package fat-free cream cheese, softened
1   (8-ounce) package ⅓-less-fat cream cheese, softened
½   cup brewed espresso or dark-roast coffee
3   tablespoons Marsala
3   (3-ounce) packages ladyfingers
3   tablespoons powdered sugar
1   tablespoon unsweetened cocoa

Stir together granulated sugar, ½ cup cream, milk, and next 4 ingredients in a heavy saucepan. Cook over medium heat, stirring constantly, 30 minutes or until thickened. Cool completely. Discard vanilla bean. Whisk in cream cheeses.
Stir together espresso and Marsala. Layer one-fourth of ladyfingers in a trifle bowl; brush with espresso mixture. Top with one-fourth of cream cheese mixture. Repeat 3 times with remaining ladyfingers, coffee mixture, and cream cheese mixture.
Beat remaining ½ cup whipping cream at high speed with an electric mixer until foamy; gradually add powdered sugar, beating until soft peaks form. Spoon over cream cheese mixture, and sprinkle with cocoa. Cover and chill 2 hours. Yield: 10 servings.

Per serving: Calories 345 (43% from fat); Fat 16.6g (sat 9.5g, mono 4.3g, poly 1.1g); Protein 12.3g; Carb 35g; Fiber 0.4g; Chol 182mg; Iron 1.4mg; Sodium 325mg; Calc 166mg

Note: This can also be prepared in a 13- x 9-inch baking dish, layering ladyfingers and cream cheese mixture. Spread with whipped cream mixture.

make ahead

Blueberry Cheesecake

prep: 20 min.   cook: 1 hr., 15 min.   other: 9 hrs.

At less than half the calories and one-third the fat of a classic cheesecake, this version is a keeper.

1   cup graham cracker crumbs
3   tablespoons butter, melted
1   tablespoon sugar
2   (8-ounce) packages ⅓-less-fat cream cheese, softened
1   (8-ounce) package fat-free cream cheese, softened
1   cup sugar
3   tablespoons all-purpose flour
½   teaspoon salt
2   large eggs
2   egg whites
1   (8-ounce) container light sour cream
1   teaspoon vanilla extract
1   tablespoon grated lemon rind
1½   cups fresh or frozen blueberries
1   cup fat-free frozen whipped topping, thawed
¼   cup light sour cream

Combine first 3 ingredients in a small bowl. Press mixture on bottom and 1½ inches up sides of a 9-inch springform pan coated with cooking spray.
Bake at 350° for 5 minutes. Remove from oven; set aside.
Beat cream cheese at medium speed with an electric mixer until smooth.
Combine 1 cup sugar, flour, and salt. Add to cream cheese, beating until blended. Add eggs, 1 at a time, beating well after each addition. Add egg whites, beating until blended.
Add 8-ounce container sour cream, vanilla, and lemon rind, beating just until blended. Gently stir in blueberries. Pour mixture into prepared pan.
Bake at 300° for 1 hour and 10 minutes or until center of cheesecake is firm. Turn off oven, and let cheesecake stand in oven, with oven door partially open, 30 minutes.
Remove cheesecake from oven; cool in pan on a wire rack 30 minutes. Cover cheesecake, and chill 8 hours. Gently run a knife around edges of pan to release sides.
Stir together whipped topping and ¼ cup sour cream. Spread over cheesecake. Yield: 12 servings.

Per serving: Calories 315 (45% from fat); Fat 15.6g (sat 9.5g, mono 1.5g, poly 0.5g); Protein 10.2g; Carb 33.4g; Fiber 0.8g; Chol 83mg; Iron 0.6mg; Sodium 469mg; Calc 110mg

low calorie • low cholesterol • low fat

Black-Eyed Susans

prep: 20 min.   cook: 8 min. per batch

Get out your cookie gun for this recipe. Let the kids help add chocolate morsels.

½   cup butter, softened
½   cup granulated sugar
½   cup firmly packed light brown sugar
1   cup creamy peanut butter
1   large egg
1½   tablespoons warm water
1   teaspoon vanilla extract
1½   cups all-purpose flour
½   teaspoon salt
½   teaspoon baking soda
½   cup semisweet chocolate morsels

Beat butter and sugars at medium speed with an electric mixer until light and fluffy. Add peanut butter and next 3 ingredients, beating well.

Combine flour, salt, and baking soda. Add to butter mixture, beating until blended. Use a cookie gun fitted with a flower-shaped disc to make cookies, following manufacturer's instructions. Place cookies on lightly greased baking sheets. Place a chocolate morsel in center of each cookie. Bake at 350° for 8 minutes or until lightly browned. Remove to wire racks to cool. Freeze up to 1 month, if desired. Yield: 8 dozen.

Per cookie: Calories 45 (52% from fat); Fat 2.6g (sat 1.1g, mono 1g, poly 0.4g); Protein 1g; Carb 4.7g; Fiber 0.3g; Chol 5mg; Iron 0.2mg; Sodium 39mg; Calc 3mg

low calorie • low cholesterol
Cranberry–Walnut Swirls

prep: 15 min.   cook: 15 min. per batch

other: 9 hrs.

½   cup butter, softened
¾   cup sugar
1   large egg
1   teaspoon vanilla extract
1½   cups all-purpose flour
¼   teaspoon baking powder
¼   teaspoon salt
½   cup ground walnuts
⅓   cup finely chopped fresh cranberries
1   tablespoon grated orange rind

Beat butter and sugar at medium speed with an electric mixer until light and fluffy. Add egg and vanilla, beating until blended. Gradually add flour, baking powder, and salt, beating until blended. Cover and chill dough 1 hour.
Combine ground walnuts, cranberries, and orange rind.
Turn dough out onto a lightly floured surface, and roll into a 10-inch square. Sprinkle with cranberry mixture, leaving a ½-inch border on 2 opposite sides.
Roll up dough, jelly-roll fashion, beginning at a bordered side. Cover and freeze 8 hours.
Cut roll into ¼-inch-thick slices. Place slices on lightly greased baking sheets.
Bake on top oven rack at 375° for 14 to 15 minutes or until lightly browned. Freeze up to 1 month, if desired. Yield: 3 dozen.

Per swirl: Calories 68 (45% from fat); Fat 3.4g (sat 1.7g, mono 0.8g, poly 0.7g); Protein 0.9g; Carb 8.5g; Fiber 0.3g; Chol 13mg; Iron 0.3mg; Sodium 40mg; Calc 6mg

storing berries

Store blueberries in airtight containers in the refrigerator up to five days. Remember not to wash the berries until you're ready to eat them or use them in a recipe. If you're lucky enough to have more than you can eat in five days, freeze the rest. Place unwashed berries in a single layer on a baking sheet. Place the baking sheet in the freezer. Transfer the frozen berries into airtight containers, and store them in the freezer up to five months.

low calorie • low cholesterol • low fat
make ahead • quick
Blueberry Sherbet

prep: 15 min.   other: 8 hrs.

All you need to make this easy and flavorful dessert is just 5 ingredients, a pan, your freezer, and a blender.

2   cups fresh or frozen blueberries, thawed
1   cup fat-free buttermilk
½   cup sugar
1   tablespoon fresh lemon juice
½   teaspoon vanilla extract
Garnish: fresh mint sprig

Process first 5 ingredients in a blender until smooth. Pour into a 9-inch square pan; cover and freeze 4 hours or until firm.
Process frozen mixture, in batches, in a blender until smooth. Cover and freeze 4 hours or until frozen. Garnish, if desired. Yield: 3 cups.

Per ½ cup: Calories 110 (4% from fat); Fat 0.5g (sat 0.2g, mono 0.1g, poly 0.1g); Protein 1.7g; Carb 26g; Fiber 1.3g; Chol 1mg; Iron 0.1mg; Sodium 46mg; Calc 51mg

low cholesterol • low fat • make ahead
Blackberry–Lemon Sorbet

prep: 40 min.   cook: 20 min.   other: 13 hrs.

This tart, refreshing dessert is a terrific source of calcium.

10   cups fresh blackberries*
2¼   cups sugar
1   teaspoon grated lemon rind
¼   cup fresh lemon juice
4   cups fat-free buttermilk

Blueberry Sherbet

Bring first 4 ingredients to a boil in a saucepan, stirring constantly; reduce heat, and simmer 15 minutes. Cool.
Process blackberry mixture, in batches, in a blender or food processor until smooth, stopping to scrape down sides.
Pour blackberry puree through a fine wire-mesh strainer into a bowl, pressing pulp with back of a wooden spoon. Discard pulp, and stir in buttermilk. Freeze 8 hours.
Process frozen blackberry mixture, in batches, until smooth. Freeze 5 hours. Yield: 14 cups.

Per cup: Calories 207 (4% from fat); Fat 1g (sat 0.4g, mono 0.2g, poly 0.3g); Protein 3g; Carb 49g; Fiber 5.5g; Chol 2mg; Iron 0.6mg; Sodium 74mg; Calc 115mg

*Substitute 5 (14-ounce) packages frozen blackberries, thawed, if desired.

strike a healthy balance

Confused about what to eat? Mom's nutrition advice still applies.

- **Eat your vegetables.** There are no bad vegetables, but some are less caloric than others. So fill your dish with low-cal, low-starch veggies such as green beans, cabbage, broccoli, yellow squash, zucchini, snap peas, tomatoes, bell peppers, and spinach. Take smaller portions of higher calorie, starchy vegetables such as corn, potatoes, and peas. Choose sweet potatoes—they're a great source of fiber and cancer-fighting antioxidants.
- **Choose your protein.** Protein-rich foods keep us satisfied longer, but many are high in saturated fat. Choose lean meats: pork loin, lean sirloin, any fish/shellfish, and skinless chicken/turkey. Dried beans are also a great source of protein and supply plenty of cholesterol-lowering soluble fiber. Nuts are a terrific choice, too, but at about 170 calories per ounce, you'll want to stick to a single serving.
- **Go for hardworking carbs.** Highly processed starchy foods (snack crackers, bagels, muffins, and some instant cereals) are a breeze for your body to break down, so you may be snacking soon after you eat. Enjoy whole grain breads and cereals to help keep hunger pangs at bay.
- **Fruit is still your friend.** Your best bet for getting the most nutrients from fruit is to grab whole fresh fruit (eating the skin or peel, when possible) instead of juices, which are high in calories (about 120 per cup) and contain virtually no fiber. So don't count on them for staying with you through the morning or afternoon. Oranges, peaches, pears, cantaloupe, and apples are delicious, versatile, and help you feel full.

low carb • vegetarian

Savory Spinach-Gorgonzola Custards

prep: 30 min.   cook: 1 hr., 5 min.
other: 10 min.

Serve these bold, cheesy custards with a big tossed salad dressed in tangy vinaigrette alongside crusty multigrain rolls or bread. (pictured on page 261)

½ cup frozen chopped spinach, thawed
2   large onions, halved and thinly sliced
2   teaspoons olive oil
2   teaspoons brown sugar
Vegetable cooking spray
3   ounces crumbled Gorgonzola cheese*
½ (8-ounce) package fat-free cream cheese, softened
1   large egg
1   cup 2% reduced-fat milk
½ cup egg substitute
¼ teaspoon salt
¼ teaspoon ground nutmeg
¼ teaspoon pepper
Garnish: fresh spinach leaves

Drain spinach well, pressing between layers of paper towels. Set aside.
Sauté onion in hot oil in a large nonstick skillet over medium heat 5 minutes.
Stir in brown sugar; cook, stirring occasionally, 20 minutes or until onion is caramel-colored. Reserve ¼ cup onion. Spoon remaining onion evenly into 6 (6-ounce) custard cups coated with cooking spray; sprinkle evenly with Gorgonzola cheese.
Beat cream cheese with an electric mixer until smooth. Add egg and next 5 ingredients, beating just until blended. Stir in spinach. Spoon evenly over cheese in custard cups.
Place cups in a 13- x 9-inch pan. Add hot water to pan to a depth of 1 inch.
Bake at 350° for 35 to 40 minutes or until almost set. Remove cups from pan. Let stand 10 minutes; unmold, and top each custard with reserved onions. Garnish platter, if desired. Yield: 6 servings.

Per serving: Calories 160 (48% from fat); Fat 8.6g (sat 3.9g, mono 2g, poly 0.6g); Protein 11.6g; Carb 9.4g; Fiber 1.3g; Chol 56mg; Iron 1.1mg; Sodium 422mg; Calc 206mg

*Substitute 1 (4-ounce) package crumbled blue cheese, if desired.

from the grill • low calorie • low fat

Grilled Flank Steak With Molasses Barbecue Glaze

prep: 3 min.   cook: 12 min.   other: 2 hrs.

Flank steak provides an excellent source of iron in this sweet 'n' tangy grilled dinner.

½ cup molasses
¼ cup coarse-grained mustard
1   tablespoon olive oil
1   (1½-pound) flank steak
6   (8-inch) flour tortillas
1   cup shredded lettuce
1   large tomato, chopped
¾ cup (3 ounces) shredded reduced-fat Cheddar cheese
½ cup light sour cream

Whisk together first 3 ingredients.
Place steak in a shallow dish or large zip-top freezer bag. Pour molasses mixture over steak, reserving ¼ cup for basting. Cover or seal, and chill 2 hours, turning occasionally. Remove meat from marinade, discarding marinade.
Grill, covered with grill lid, over medium-high heat (350° to 400°) 6 minutes on each side or to desired degree of doneness, brushing often with reserved marinade. Cut steak diagonally across the grain into very thin strips. Serve steak with tortillas and remaining ingredients. Yield: 6 servings.

Per serving: Calories 283 (30% from fat); Fat 9.4g (sat 3g, mono 3.9g, poly 1.3g); Protein 9.5g; Carb 40.7g; Fiber 1.4g; Chol 14mg; Iron 2.8mg; Sodium 376mg; Calc 181mg

rub lean meats such as flank steak, pork tenderloin, or chicken with spice rubs, or marinate them; freeze in zip-top freezer bags. When thawed, meats will be perfectly seasoned and ready to go on the grill.

Lettuce-Wrapped Picadillo

prep: 10 min.   cook: 30 min.

Pronounced pee-cah-DEE-yo, this warm and zesty ground beef mixture is tasty rolled in crisp iceberg lettuce leaves. Also try it in whole wheat tortillas layered with fat-free refried beans, fat-free sour cream, and salsa.

1   pound extra-lean ground beef*
2   garlic cloves, minced
Vegetable cooking spray
½   (10-ounce) package frozen onion-and-
       pepper medley, thawed
½   cup golden raisins
½   cup tomato sauce
2   to 3 teaspoons hot sauce
½   teaspoon ground cumin
½   teaspoon salt
¼   teaspoon pepper
Iceberg lettuce leaves
Lime wedges (optional)

Cook ground beef and minced garlic in a large nonstick skillet coated with cooking spray over medium-high heat 10 minutes or until beef crumbles and is no longer pink. Drain and pat with paper towels.
Add onion-and-pepper medley to skillet; cook over medium-high heat, stirring often, 10 minutes or until onions are tender.
Stir in beef mixture, raisins, and next 5 ingredients. Bring mixture to a boil. Reduce heat, and simmer 10 minutes or until most of liquid evaporates. Serve beef mixture in lettuce leaves. Serve with lime wedges, if desired. Yield: 6 servings.

Per serving: Calories 175 (29% from fat); Fat 5.6g (sat 2.2g, mono 2.4g, poly 0.3g); Protein 14.5g; Carb 17g; Fiber 2.2g; Chol 22mg; Iron 2.7mg; Sodium 351mg; Calc 39mg

*Substitute lean ground pork for extra-lean ground beef. Use trimmed boneless pork loin chops; cut into chunks, and process in food processor until ground. Proceed according to recipe.

Note: For testing purposes only, we used McKenzie's Seasoning Blend. If you can't find it in your market, substitute 1 onion, chopped; 1 green bell pepper, chopped; and 1 celery rib, chopped.

Gyro Burgers With Tahini Sauce

prep: 20 min.   cook: 12 min.

Extra-lean ground beef and a small amount of feta cheese keep these burgers healthier than their full-fat cousins. Find tahini paste on the imported foods aisle of large supermarkets or in Mediterranean markets.

1   pound extra-lean ground beef
1   teaspoon Greek seasoning
4   (6-inch) pita rounds
4   lettuce leaves
8   large tomato slices
4   thin red onion slices
Tahini Sauce
¼   cup crumbled feta cheese

Combine beef and seasoning. Shape into 4 patties. Grill, covered with grill lid, over medium-high heat (350° to 400°) 5 to 6 minutes on each side or until beef is no longer pink.
Cut off 2 inches of bread from 1 side of each pita round, forming a pocket. Line each with 1 lettuce leaf, 2 tomato slices, and 1 red onion slice. Add burger. Drizzle each with 2 tablespoons Tahini Sauce, and sprinkle with 1 tablespoon feta cheese. Yield: 4 servings.

Per serving: Calories 377 (31% from fat); Fat 13g (sat 2.8g, mono 4.7g, poly 4.3g); Protein 26.4g; Carb 41g; Fiber 3g; Chol 48mg; Iron 4mg; Sodium 551mg; Calc 81mg

Tahini Sauce

prep: 10 min.

¼   cup tahini paste
¼   cup water
2   tablespoons fresh lemon juice
⅛   teaspoon garlic powder
¼   teaspoon salt

Whisk together all ingredients. Yield: ½ cup.

Per tablespoon: Calories 47 (84% from fat); Fat 4.4g (sat 0.6g, mono 1.7g, poly 1.9g); Protein 1.5g; Carb 1.5g; Fiber 0.7g; Chol 0mg; Iron 0.2mg; Sodium 74mg; Calc 9mg

Sweet Pork Tenderloin With Lime and Chipotle

prep: 18 min.   cook: 20 min.
other: 2 hrs., 10 min.

Chipotle peppers, sweet honey mustard, and tangy citrus join for an intensely flavored sauce to accompany this juicy pork tenderloin.

1   (10.4-ounce) bottle honey-Dijon mustard
       (about 1 cup)
⅔   cup chopped fresh cilantro
½   cup fresh lime juice
2   to 3 tablespoons canned chipotle
       peppers in adobo sauce, minced
4   garlic cloves, minced
1   teaspoon ground cumin
¾   teaspoon salt
¾   teaspoon ground cinnamon
2   (¾-pound) pork tenderloins
¼   cup water
¼   cup chopped honey-roasted peanuts
Garnish: chopped fresh cilantro

Stir together first 8 ingredients; reserve 1 cup mustard mixture.
Place pork in a large shallow dish or zip-top freezer bag; pour remaining mustard mixture over pork. Cover or seal, and chill, turning occasionally, 2 hours.
Remove pork from marinade, discarding marinade.
Grill pork, covered with grill lid, over medium-high heat (350° to 400°) 8 to 9 minutes on each side or until a meat thermometer inserted into thickest portion registers 155°. Remove from grill, and let stand 5 to 10 minutes or until thermometer rises to 160°. Cut pork into slices.
Bring reserved 1 cup mustard mixture and ¼ cup water to a boil in a saucepan; reduce heat, and simmer 2 minutes. Sprinkle peanuts over pork, and serve with sauce. Garnish, if desired. Yield: 6 servings.

Per serving: Calories 280 (55% from fat); Fat 17g (sat 2.8g, mono 3.3g, poly 1.3g); Protein 25.3g; Carb 7.3g; Fiber 0.9g; Chol 84mg; Iron 1.7mg; Sodium 363mg; Calc 13mg

Make-Ahead Pork Dumplings

prep: 2 hrs.   cook: 25 min.

This recipe makes a bunch, so ask a friend to help you assemble the dumplings; then freeze some for later.

1½	pounds lean boneless pork loin chops, cut into chunks
1	(12-ounce) package 50%-less-fat ground pork sausage
1½	teaspoons salt
15	water chestnuts, finely chopped
1	to 2 tablespoons minced fresh ginger
½	cup cornstarch
2	teaspoons lite soy sauce
½	cup low-sodium fat-free chicken broth
¼	cup sugar
1	teaspoon teriyaki sauce
1	teaspoon sesame oil
¼	cup chopped fresh parsley
4	green onions, diced
2	(16-ounce) packages won ton wrappers

Oyster sauce (optional)
Thai chili sauce (optional)
Ginger Dipping Sauce (optional)

Process pork loin in a food processor until finely chopped.
Combine pork loin, pork sausage, and next 11 ingredients.
Cut corners from won ton wrappers to form circles. Drop 1 teaspoon mixture onto middle of each skin. Gather up won ton sides, letting dough pleat naturally. Lightly squeeze the middle while tapping the bottom on a flat surface so it will stand upright.
Arrange dumplings in a bamboo steam basket over boiling water. Cover and steam 20 to 25 minutes. Serve with sauces, if desired. Yield: 116 dumplings.

Per dumpling: Calories 40 (18% from fat); Fat 0.8g (sat 0.2g, mono 0.3g, poly 0.2g); Protein 2.5g; Carb 6g; Fiber 0.2g; Chol 6mg; Iron 0.4mg; Sodium 101mg; Calc 7mg

Note: To freeze, arrange dumplings on a baking sheet; freeze 2 hours. Place in zip-top freezer bags; label and freeze for up to 3 months. To cook dumplings from frozen state, steam 22 to 25 minutes.

Ginger Dipping Sauce

prep: 10 min.   cook: 1 min.

1	garlic clove, minced
1	tablespoon minced fresh ginger
1	teaspoon dark sesame oil
2	tablespoons lite soy sauce
1	tablespoon rice wine vinegar
2	teaspoons teriyaki sauce
1	green onion, minced

Sauté garlic and ginger in hot oil 1 minute; remove from heat. Whisk in soy sauce and remaining ingredients. Yield: ⅓ cup.

Per tablespoon: Calories 17 (48% from fat); Fat 0.9g (sat 0.1g, mono 0.4g, poly 0.4g); Protein 0.7g; Carb 1.4g; Fiber 0.1g; Chol 0mg; Iron 0.1mg; Sodium 335mg; Calc 4mg

Creamy Lamb Curry

prep: 20 min.   cook: 1 hr., 15 min.

Serve this aromatic, full-flavored dish over basmati rice, a nutty-tasting long-grain variety. Look for garam masala, a fragrant spice mixture, in Indian markets or in the spice or ethnic sections of supermarkets. It's available in the McCormick Gourmet Collection, or you can find it online at www.ethnicgrocer.com.

2	pounds lean boneless lamb, cut into 2-inch pieces
½	teaspoon salt

Vegetable cooking spray

1	medium onion, chopped (1 cup)
1	(1-inch) piece fresh ginger, peeled and minced
2	garlic cloves, minced
2	teaspoons ground coriander
1	teaspoon ground cumin
⅛	teaspoon ground cloves
2	bay leaves
1	(1-inch) cinnamon stick
2	cups low-sodium fat-free chicken broth
1	(14.5-ounce) can diced tomatoes, undrained
½	cup plain nonfat yogurt
1	tablespoon garam masala
8	fresh mint leaves, chopped

Sprinkle lamb pieces with salt. Cook lamb, in batches, in a Dutch oven coated with cooking spray over medium-high heat, stirring often, 5 minutes or until lamb is lightly browned. Remove and set aside.
Sauté onion and ginger in Dutch oven coated with cooking spray over medium-high heat 1 to 2 minutes. Add garlic; cook 1 minute. Stir in coriander and next 4 ingredients. Add cooked lamb, broth, and tomatoes; bring to a boil. Cover, reduce heat, and simmer 1 hour or until lamb is tender. Remove bay leaves and cinnamon stick. Remove from heat; add yogurt and garam masala, stirring until blended. Sprinkle with mint. Yield: 6 servings.

Per serving: Calories 257 (39% from fat); Fat 11g (sat 4.5g, mono 4g, poly 0.5g); Protein 29.6g; Carb 9.2g; Fiber 1.3g; Chol 101mg; Iron 2.4mg; Sodium 512mg; Calc 109mg

Marinated Chicken Strips and Vegetables

prep: 25 min.   cook: 15 min.   other: 2 hrs.

¾	cup lite soy sauce
⅔	cup honey
⅓	cup dry sherry*
½	teaspoon garlic powder
¼	teaspoon ground ginger
1½	pounds fresh asparagus spears
6	(6-ounce) skinned and boned chicken breasts, cut into ¼-inch strips
¼	cup stone-ground mustard
2	tablespoons sesame seeds, toasted
3	medium tomatoes, cut into wedges
8	cups mixed salad greens

Honey-Mustard Dressing

Stir together first 5 ingredients; set ½ cup mixture aside.
Pour remaining soy sauce mixture evenly into 2 zip-top freezer bags. Snap off tough ends of asparagus, and place asparagus spears in 1 bag. Add chicken to remaining bag. Seal and chill at least 2 hours.
Drain chicken and asparagus, discarding marinade. Place chicken on a lightly greased roasting pan. Place asparagus in a lightly greased 13- x 9-inch pan.
Stir together reserved ½ cup soy sauce mixture, mustard, and sesame seeds. Pour ½ cup mixture over chicken and remaining ¼ cup over asparagus.
Bake chicken at 425° for 5 minutes. Place asparagus in oven, and bake chicken and asparagus 10 minutes or until chicken is

done. Cool, if desired. Place separately in zip-top freezer bags, and chill 8 hours, if desired.

Arrange chicken, asparagus, and tomato over salad greens, and drizzle with Honey-Mustard Dressing. Yield: 6 servings.

Per serving: Calories 324 (17% from fat); Fat 6.2g (sat 1.8g, mono 0.9g, poly 1.1g); Protein 30.6g; Carb 37g; Fiber 3.8g; Chol 72mg; Iron 3.8mg; Sodium 834mg; Calc 109mg

*Substitute ⅓ cup pineapple juice for sherry, if desired.

Honey-Mustard Dressing

prep: 5 min.

1   (8-ounce) container light sour cream
¼   cup light mayonnaise
½   cup honey
2   tablespoons stone-ground mustard
2   tablespoons Dijon mustard
2   tablespoons lemon juice

Stir together all ingredients; cover and chill up to 3 days. Yield: 2 cups.

Per tablespoon: Calories 31 (32% from fat); Fat 1.1g (sat 0.4g, mono 0g, poly 0g); Protein 0.3g; Carb 5.5g; Fiber 0g; Chol 3mg; Iron 0mg; Sodium 46mg; Calc 1mg

low calorie • low fat

Chicken Fingers With Honey-Horseradish Dip

prep: 25 min.   cook: 20 min.

This no-fork recipe won our highest rating. We think little and big kids will love it.

16   saltine crackers, finely crushed
¼   cup pecans, toasted and ground
½   teaspoon salt
½   teaspoon pepper
2   teaspoons paprika
4   (6-ounce) skinned and boned chicken breasts
1   egg white
Vegetable cooking spray
Honey-Horseradish Dip

Stir together first 5 ingredients.
Cut each breast half into 4 strips. Whisk egg white until frothy; dip chicken strips into egg white, and dredge in saltine mixture.
Place a rack coated with cooking spray in a broiler pan. Coat chicken strips on each side with cooking spray; arrange on rack.

Bake at 425° for 18 to 20 minutes or until browned. Serve with Honey-Horseradish Dip. Yield: 8 servings.

Per serving: Calories 176 (25% from fat); Fat 4.9g (sat 1g, mono 2.3g, poly 1.1g); Protein 15.5g; Carb 17g; Fiber 1.7g; Chol 34mg; Iron 1.1mg; Sodium 384mg; Calc 48mg

Honey-Horseradish Dip

prep: 5 min.

½   cup plain nonfat yogurt
¼   cup coarse-grained mustard
¼   cup honey
2   tablespoons prepared horseradish

Stir together all ingredients. Yield: 1 cup.

Per tablespoon: Calories 30 (12% from fat); Fat 0.4g (sat 0.2g, mono 0.1g, poly 0g); Protein 0.6g; Carb 5.9g; Fiber 0.5g; Chol 1mg; Iron 0.1mg; Sodium 65mg; Calc 16mg

low fat

White Spaghetti and Meatballs

prep: 30 min.   cook: 58 min.   other: 20 min.

Using the white meat of chicken (or turkey) gives spaghetti a healthy face-lift.

1½   pounds skinned and boned chicken breasts, cut into chunks*
1   large garlic clove
1   large egg
10   saltine crackers, finely crushed
1   teaspoon dried Italian seasoning
Vegetable cooking spray
1   (8-ounce) package sliced fresh mushrooms
⅛   teaspoon ground nutmeg
1   teaspoon olive oil
1   large garlic clove, minced
2   tablespoons all-purpose flour
½   cup dry white wine
3   cups low-sodium fat-free chicken broth
1   (8-ounce) package ⅓-less-fat cream cheese
¼   teaspoon ground red pepper
¼   cup chopped fresh flat-leaf parsley
1   (8-ounce) package uncooked spaghetti

Process chicken and 1 garlic clove in a food processor until ground.
Stir together chicken mixture, egg, crushed crackers, and Italian seasoning in a large bowl. Cover and chill 20 minutes.
Shape mixture into 1-inch balls. Place a rack coated with cooking spray in an

aluminum foil-lined broiling pan. Arrange meatballs on rack; lightly spray meatballs with cooking spray.
Bake at 375° for 13 minutes or until golden and thoroughly cooked.
Sauté mushrooms and nutmeg in hot oil in a Dutch oven over medium-high heat 8 to 10 minutes or until mushrooms are tender. Add minced garlic; sauté 1 minute. Sprinkle with flour; cook, stirring constantly, 1 minute. Add wine, stirring to loosen browned particles from bottom of pan. Whisk in broth.
Bring to a boil; reduce heat, and simmer, stirring occasionally, 15 minutes. Add cream cheese, whisking until smooth and sauce is thickened.
Add meatballs, red pepper, and parsley to sauce; simmer 10 minutes. Meanwhile, cook pasta according to package directions, omitting salt and oil; drain. Serve sauce with meatballs over pasta. Yield: 6 servings.

Per serving: Calories 431 (24% from fat); Fat 11.2g (sat 5.2g, mono 3.5g, poly 1.1g); Protein 40g; Carb 39g; Fiber 1.7g; Chol 122mg; Iron 3.8mg; Sodium 629mg; Calc 78mg

*You can use ground turkey as an option, if desired.

functional foods

Many times, it's what's missing from our diets that can leave us feeling drained. Replace empty calories, such as fatty potato chips and sugary sodas, with foods that provide health benefits beyond basic nutrition.

• Low-fat milk and juices with added calcium: help prevent osteoporosis
• Fruits and vegetables: help reduce blood pressure and risk of cancer and heart disease
• Whole grains: may reduce risk of certain cancers and heart disease
• Oat bran and whole oat products: help reduce bad cholesterol
• Cultured dairy products (yogurt, buttermilk, etc.): help reduce bad cholesterol and risk of cancer; promote a healthy digestive tract
• Garlic: helps control high blood pressure and reduces risk of cancer and heart disease
• Soy products: reduce bad cholesterol and menopausal symptoms
• Fish with omega-3 fatty acids (salmon, halibut, tuna, etc.): help promote a healthy heart

Sweet-and-Sour Chicken and Rice

prep: 20 min.   cook: 1 hr.

Skinned and boned chicken thighs contain a little more fat than breast meat, but they're very nutritious and hold on to lots of flavor and moisture.

½   teaspoon salt
½   teaspoon pepper
2   pounds skinned and boned chicken thighs
Vegetable cooking spray
1   small onion, diced
1   medium-size red bell pepper, chopped
2   garlic cloves, minced
1   cup uncooked long-grain rice
1   cup sweet-and-sour dressing
1   cup low-sodium fat-free chicken broth
2   green onions, chopped

Sprinkle salt and pepper evenly over chicken thighs.
Brown chicken in a Dutch oven coated with cooking spray over medium-high heat 2 to 3 minutes on each side or until browned. Remove chicken from pan, and set aside.
Add onion, bell pepper, and garlic to Dutch oven coated with cooking spray; sauté 5 minutes.
Add rice; sauté 2 minutes or until rice is opaque. Stir in dressing and broth. Add chicken pieces; bring to a boil.
Cover, reduce heat, and simmer 45 minutes or until liquid is absorbed and chicken is done. Sprinkle with green onions. Yield: 8 servings.

Per serving: Calories 289 (16% from fat); Fat 5g (sat 1.3g, mono 1.4g, poly 1.2g); Protein 25g; Carb 35g; Fiber 1.2g; Chol 95mg; Iron 2.4mg; Sodium 739mg; Calc 31mg

Creamy Chipotle Manicotti

prep: 30 min.   cook: 30 min.   other: 10 min.

This calcium-rich recipe (almost 800mg per serving) makes four very hearty portions. For a lighter meal, enjoy one stuffed shell alongside steamed green beans and a colorful salad drizzled with vinaigrette. To reduce the recipe's total fat, use fat-free ricotta cheese and mozzarella cheese, and use ½ cup Monterey Jack cheese with peppers instead of 1 cup.

8   manicotti shells
1   (15-ounce) container part-skim ricotta cheese
2   green onions, chopped
2   tablespoons chopped fresh cilantro
1   cup (4 ounces) shredded part-skim mozzarella cheese
¼   cup egg substitute
Vegetable cooking spray
2   cups chipotle salsa, divided*
1   cup (4 ounces) shredded Monterey Jack cheese with peppers

Cook pasta according to package directions, omitting salt and oil. Rinse with cold water; drain and set aside.
Stir together ricotta cheese and next 4 ingredients.
Coat an 11- x 7-inch baking dish with cooking spray, and pour ½ cup salsa into dish. Spoon cheese mixture evenly into shells, and arrange in dish. Pour remaining salsa over shells.
Bake at 350° for 20 minutes. Sprinkle with Monterey Jack cheese. Bake 10 more minutes or until thoroughly heated and cheese melts. Let stand 10 minutes before serving. Yield: 4 servings.

Per serving: Calories 507 (41% from fat); Fat 23g (sat 14g, mono 6.7g, poly 1.3g); Protein 35g; Carb 40g; Fiber 4.8g; Chol 74mg; Iron 2.6mg; Sodium 1277mg; Calc 794mg

*Substitute 1 or 2 canned chipotle peppers in adobo stirred into 2 cups regular mild salsa for chipotle salsa. Canned chipotle peppers can be found in the Mexican section of the supermarket. Store remaining peppers in a zip-top freezer bag in refrigerator up to 2 weeks or in freezer up to 2 months.

orzo is ideal

Orzo is a tiny, rice-shaped pasta, slightly smaller than a pine nut. It's ideal for soups and casseroles and works well as a substitute for rice. Slightly more plump than rice, you can find orzo in Middle Eastern or Italian markets or in larger grocery stores.

Chicken, Orzo, and Spinach Casserole

prep: 25 min.   cook: 42 min.

Orzo cooks quickly in our homemade broth and adds tender texture to this weeknight one-dish meal.

4   (6-ounce) skinned and boned chicken breasts
⅔   cup uncooked orzo
1   (8-ounce) package sliced fresh mushrooms
Vegetable cooking spray
1   (10-ounce) package chopped frozen spinach, thawed and well drained
1   (10½-ounce) can low-fat cream of mushroom soup
½   cup reduced-fat mayonnaise
2   teaspoons lemon juice
½   teaspoon seasoned pepper
¾   cup (6 ounces) shredded reduced-fat Monterey Jack cheese
¼   cup Italian-seasoned breadcrumbs

Boil chicken and water to cover in a large Dutch oven 12 minutes or until done. Remove chicken, reserving broth. Chop chicken, and set aside.
Cook pasta in reserved broth according to package directions, omitting salt and fat.
Sauté mushrooms until tender in a large nonstick skillet coated with cooking spray.
Remove from heat. Stir in chicken, pasta, spinach, and next 4 ingredients. Spoon mixture into a 13- x 9-inch baking dish coated with cooking spray. Sprinkle with cheese and breadcrumbs.
Bake at 350° for 30 minutes or until thoroughly heated. Yield: 8 servings.

Per serving: Calories 251 (32% from fat); Fat 8.8g (sat 3.8g, mono 0.3g, poly 0.6g); Protein 22.8g; Carb 21.6g; Fiber 2.4g; Chol 49mg; Iron 1.4mg; Sodium 606mg; Calc 252mg

Spicy "Fried" Catfish With Lemon Cream

prep: 25 min.   cook: 30 min.

6   (6-ounce) catfish fillets
½   teaspoon salt, divided
¼   teaspoon black pepper
1½ cups panko breadcrumbs*
¼   teaspoon garlic powder
¼   teaspoon ground red pepper
4   egg whites
Vegetable cooking spray
Lemon Cream
Garnishes: orange slices, parsley sprigs

Sprinkle catfish evenly with ¼ teaspoon salt and ¼ teaspoon black pepper. Set aside.
Combine breadcrumbs, remaining ¼ teaspoon salt, ¼ teaspoon garlic powder, and ¼ teaspoon red pepper in a shallow bowl.
Whisk egg whites in a shallow bowl until frothy. Dip fillets in egg whites, and dredge in breadcrumb mixture.
Arrange fillets on a wire rack coated with cooking spray in an aluminum foil-lined 15- x 10-inch jelly-roll pan. (Do not overlap fillets.) Lightly coat fillets evenly on both sides with cooking spray.
Bake at 375° for 25 to 30 minutes or until fish is golden and flakes with a fork. Serve with Lemon Cream. Garnish, if desired. Yield: 6 servings.

Per serving: Calories 337 (27% from fat); Fat 10.1g (sat 4.1g, mono 1.4g, poly 1.5g); Protein 35g; Carb 24.6g; Fiber 1g; Chol 118mg; Iron 0.6mg; Sodium 480mg; Calc 93mg

*Substitute 1 cup plain dry breadcrumbs for panko breadcrumbs, if desired.

Lemon Cream

prep: 10 min.

1   (8-ounce) container light sour cream
1   tablespoon chopped fresh parsley
½   teaspoon grated lemon rind
2   tablespoons fresh lemon juice
¼   teaspoon salt

Stir together all ingredients until blended. Cover; chill until ready to serve. Yield: 1 cup.

Per tablespoon: Calories 20 (68% from fat); Fat 1.5g (sat 0.9g, mono 0.4g, poly 0.1g); Protein 0.5g; Carb 1.2g; Fiber 0g; Chol 5mg; Iron 0mg; Sodium 47mg; Calc 21mg

---

Glazed Salmon With Stir-Fried Vegetables

prep: 15 min.   cook: 22 min.

2   carrots
1   parsnip
1   small red bell pepper
8   green onions
4   (6-ounce) skinless salmon fillets
¼   teaspoon salt
Vegetable cooking spray
¼   cup apple jelly
3   tablespoons rice wine vinegar
2   tablespoons water
1   tablespoon lite soy sauce
1   teaspoon cornstarch
½   to 1 teaspoon chopped fresh dill (optional)
2   teaspoons vegetable oil
Garnish: fresh dill sprigs

Cut first 4 ingredients into thin strips, and set aside.
Sprinkle salmon fillets evenly with salt. Place on a rack in a broiler pan coated with cooking spray.
Broil 5½ inches from heat 10 to 13 minutes or until fish flakes with a fork.
Whisk together jelly, next 4 ingredients, and, if desired, chopped dill.
Cook carrot and parsnip in hot oil in a large skillet over medium-high heat, stirring often, 2 to 3 minutes. Add bell pepper and onions; cook 1 to 2 minutes or until crisp-tender. Remove vegetables from skillet, and keep warm.
Add jelly mixture to skillet, and cook, stirring constantly, 3 to 4 minutes or until thickened.
Spoon vegetables evenly onto serving plates. Drizzle with half of sauce. Top with salmon fillets, and drizzle with remaining sauce. Garnish, if desired. Yield: 4 servings.

Per serving: Calories 452 (42% from fat); Fat 21.2g (sat 4g, mono 7.6g, poly 7.7g); Protein 35.9g; Carb 29.1g; Fiber 3g; Chol 100mg; Iron 1.5mg; Sodium 425mg; Calc 70mg

Note: Only 8% of the total calories in this recipe comes from saturated fat. The remaining fat calories are from beneficial mono- or polyunsaturated oils.

---

salmon & good omega fats

Salmon, like other cold-water fish, is an excellent source of omega-3 fatty acids. These are a form of polyunsaturated fats that research has found to have a wide variety of benefits—from improving heart health, rheumatoid arthritis, and depression to helping prevent cancer.

Shrimp Tacos With Spicy Cream Sauce

prep: 20 min.   cook: 10 min.   other: 15 min.

Chili powder, cumin, and red pepper add zing to the cool cream sauce.

1   (16-ounce) container nonfat sour cream
2   teaspoons chili powder, divided
1   teaspoon ground cumin, divided
¾   teaspoon ground red pepper, divided
¾   teaspoon salt, divided
¼   teaspoon ground cinnamon
½   cup water
1   pound unpeeled, medium-size fresh shrimp
3   tablespoons orange juice
2   garlic cloves
2   teaspoons olive oil
1   avocado, chopped
8   (8-inch) corn tortillas, warmed

Whisk together sour cream, 1 teaspoon chili powder, ½ teaspoon cumin, ½ teaspoon red pepper, ¼ teaspoon salt, and cinnamon. Add ½ cup water, stirring until smooth. Cover and chill until ready to serve.
Peel shrimp, and devein, if desired; chop. Combine remaining 1 teaspoon chili powder, ½ teaspoon cumin, ¼ teaspoon red pepper, and ½ teaspoon salt in a shallow dish or zip-top freezer bag; add orange juice and shrimp, turning to coat. Cover or seal, and chill 15 minutes. Remove shrimp from marinade, discarding marinade.
Sauté garlic in hot oil in a large skillet over medium-high heat 2 to 3 minutes. Add shrimp; cook 5 minutes or just until shrimp turn pink. Serve with sour cream sauce and avocado in tortillas. Yield: 8 servings.

Per serving: Calories 212 (26% from fat); Fat 6.2g (sat 1g, mono 3.6g, poly 1.1g); Protein 13g; Carb 26g; Fiber 3g; Chol 72mg; Iron 2mg; Sodium 391mg; Calc 140mg

Fresh Mozzarella and Basil Pizza

prep: 30 min.   cook: 10 min.   other: 20 min.

This recipe makes a pizza for one person, but enough dough for six pizzas. If you don't have time to prepare fresh dough, some pizza parlors sell pizza dough on request. Bake pizza on a pizza stone or heavy baking sheet that withstands high baking temperatures. (High heat makes the crust crisp.)

1   (4-ounce) portion Pizza Dough
½   teaspoon extra-virgin olive oil
1   large plum tomato, thinly sliced
1   tablespoon sliced fresh basil
4   thin slices (2 ounces) fresh mozzarella cheese
1   (1-ounce) slice country ham or pancetta ham, cut into thin strips
¼   teaspoon freshly ground pepper

Preheat oven to 450°. Shape Pizza Dough ball into a 6- to 8-inch circle on a lightly floured surface. (Dough doesn't need to be perfectly round.) Place dough on a piece of parchment paper. Fold up edges of dough, forming a 1-inch border. Brush oil evenly over dough using a pastry brush or your fingers.

Cover pizza dough circle loosely with plastic wrap, and let rise in a warm place (85°), free from drafts, 15 to 20 minutes.

Heat pizza stone or heavy baking sheet 10 to 12 minutes in oven.

Remove and discard plastic wrap from dough. Layer tomato and next 3 ingredients on pizza dough. Sprinkle with pepper. Carefully transfer unbaked pizza on parchment paper to hot pizza stone.

Bake at 450° for 10 minutes or until crust is golden. Yield: 1 pizza.

Per pizza: Calories 508 (38% from fat); Fat 21.4g (sat 10.2g, mono 5.4g, poly 1.2g); Protein 23.4g; Carb 52.8g; Fiber 2.9g; Chol 60mg; Iron 4mg; Sodium 1,063mg; Calc 346mg

Note: If you use all this pizza dough and repeat directions above, you'll have 6 personal pan pizzas. You can otherwise divide dough into only 3 larger portions and make 3 large pizzas that bake at 450° for 16 minutes. P.S. Double the toppings, too.

Fresh Mozzarella and Basil Pizza

freeze it • make ahead

Pizza Dough

prep: 15 min.   other: 1 hr., 37 min.

The dough can be frozen up to one month. To freeze, wrap each portion in plastic wrap, and place in zip-top freezer bags. Thaw in refrigerator overnight, or let stand at room temperature 4 hours.

1   cup warm water (100° to 110°)
⅛   teaspoon sugar
1   (¼-ounce) envelope active dry yeast
3   to 3½ cups all-purpose flour
1½   teaspoons salt
1   tablespoon extra-virgin olive oil
Vegetable cooking spray

Stir together 1 cup warm water and sugar in a 2-cup glass measuring cup. Sprinkle with yeast, and let stand 5 to 7 minutes or until mixture is bubbly; stir until blended.

Place 3 cups flour and salt in a food processor. With motor running, add yeast mixture and olive oil; process mixture until dough forms. (If dough is too sticky, add more flour, 2 tablespoons at a time.) Place dough in a large bowl coated with cooking spray; lightly coat dough with cooking spray. Cover with a clean cloth, and let rise in a warm place (85°), free from drafts, 1 hour or until doubled in bulk.

Punch dough down. Turn dough in bowl, and coat with cooking spray; cover with cloth, and let rise in a warm place, free from drafts, 30 minutes or until doubled in bulk. Cut dough into 6 equal portions, shaping each portion into a 3-inch ball. Yield: 6 individual dough rounds.

Per dough round: Calories 253 (11% from fat); Fat 3g (sat 0.4g, mono 1.9g, poly 0.5g); Protein 6.9g; Carb 48.3g; Fiber 2g; Chol 0mg; Iron 3mg; Sodium 586mg; Calc 11mg

Wild Rice-and-Chicken Bowl

prep: 20 min.   cook: 55 min.

If you're pressed for time, buy quick-cooking wild rice or precooked brown rice in microwaveable pouches to equal 8 cups cooked rice.

2   cups uncooked wild rice (we tested with Gourmet House Quick Cooking Wild Rice)
2   cups shredded cooked chicken breasts
½   cup golden raisins
½   cup chopped red bell pepper
¼   cup chopped red onion
2   tablespoons fresh lemon juice
1   tablespoon extra-virgin olive oil
1   tablespoon Dijon mustard
1   tablespoon honey
1   teaspoon white wine vinegar
¼   teaspoon salt
1   tablespoon chopped fresh mint
2   tablespoons chopped fresh parsley
2   tablespoons sliced almonds, toasted
Garnishes: apple slices, fresh flat-leaf parsley sprigs

Cook rice according to package directions.
Combine cooked rice, chicken, and next 3 ingredients in a large bowl.
Whisk together lemon juice and next 5 ingredients. Drizzle over rice mixture, tossing to coat. Stir in mint and parsley. Sprinkle with almonds. Garnish, if desired. Yield: 8 servings.

Per serving: Calories 298 (18% from fat); Fat 6g (sat 1.2g, mono 3g, poly 1.3g); Protein 18g; Carb 45g; Fiber 3.7g; Chol 29mg; Iron 1.7mg; Sodium 152mg; Calc 25mg

get more grains

• Stir whole grain, ready-to-eat cereal into yogurt, or sprinkle it over fruit.
• Top a salad with granola cereal or a crumbled granola bar.
• Make sandwiches with whole grain breads.
• Substitute whole grain pasta for regular semolina pasta.
• Add ½ cup cooked brown rice to a cup of soup.
• Use stone-ground cornmeal for cornbreads.
• Add 1 cup cooked wild rice or barley to bread stuffing.

Creamy Gorgonzola Dressing

prep: 10 min.

Pair this dressing with mixed greens, sliced pears, and strawberries to create a perfect salty-sweet salad. (pictured on page 260)

½   (15-ounce) container part-skim ricotta cheese*
¾   cup fat-free buttermilk
3   ounces Gorgonzola cheese, crumbled*
3   tablespoons rice wine vinegar
1   teaspoon Worcestershire sauce
1   small garlic clove, minced
½   teaspoon freshly ground pepper

Process all ingredients in a food processor or blender until smooth, stopping to scrape down sides. Cover and chill until ready to serve. Yield: 2 cups.

Per 2 tablespoons: Calories 43 (57% from fat); Fat 2.7g (sat 1.7g, mono 0.3g, poly 0g); Protein 3g; Carb 2g; Fiber 0g; Chol 10mg; Iron 0.1mg; Sodium 85mg; Calc 83mg

*You can substitute low-fat cottage cheese for the part-skim ricotta cheese, and mild blue cheese for the Gorgonzola.

Layered Potato Salad

prep: 15 min.   cook: 30 min.   other: 1 hr.

Prepare and chill this salad up to a day ahead.

4   pounds red potatoes, unpeeled
1   (8-ounce) container nonfat sour cream
¾   cup light mayonnaise
2   tablespoons Creole mustard
¼   teaspoon salt
½   teaspoon pepper
1   bunch green onions, chopped
¾   cup chopped fresh flat-leaf parsley
3   reduced-fat, reduced-sodium bacon slices, cooked and crumbled

Bring potatoes and water to cover to a boil in a large Dutch oven over medium-high heat. Boil 25 minutes or until tender. Drain and let cool.
Cut potatoes into thin slices.

Stir together sour cream and next 4 ingredients in a bowl.
Layer one-third each of potatoes, sour cream mixture, green onions, and parsley in a large glass bowl. Repeat layers twice, ending with parsley. Cover and chill 1 hour. Sprinkle with bacon just before serving. Yield: 12 servings.

Per serving: Calories 192 (27% from fat); Fat 5.8g (sat 1g, mono 0g, poly 0g); Protein 4.8g; Carb 30g; Fiber 3.4g; Chol 8mg; Iron 1.5mg; Sodium 270mg; Calc 51mg

Tangy Spinach Salad

prep: 15 min.   cook: 7 min.

Turkey bacon helps keep this salad on the light side.

6   turkey bacon slices
3   tablespoons lemon juice
2   tablespoons brown sugar
2   tablespoons Dijon mustard
1   (10-ounce) package fresh spinach, torn
1   (8-ounce) package sliced fresh mushrooms

Cook bacon in a large skillet over medium-high heat until crisp; remove bacon, reserving drippings in skillet. Crumble bacon, and set aside.
Add lemon juice, brown sugar, and mustard to skillet; cook over low heat, stirring constantly, 1 minute.
Toss together spinach, mushrooms, and lemon juice mixture. Sprinkle with bacon. Yield: 4 servings.

Per serving: Calories 104 (35% from fat); Fat 4g (sat 0.8g, mono 1.5g, poly 1g); Protein 6.2g; Carb 11.3g; Fiber 3.6g; Chol 15mg; Iron 3.1mg; Sodium 583mg; Calc 87mg

Spinach, high in folic acid, is a smart food choice for pregnant women. Eating lots of spinach also has been shown to lessen the chances of age–related blindness.

Lime-Grilled Portobello Mushrooms

prep: 15 min. cook: 14 min.

6   portobello mushroom caps
1   tablespoon olive oil
1   teaspoon salt
1   teaspoon pepper
1   teaspoon grated lime rind
2   tablespoons fresh lime juice
Vegetable cooking spray

Scrape gills from mushroom caps using a metal spoon; discard gills.
Rub mushrooms evenly with oil; sprinkle evenly with salt, pepper, and lime rind. Drizzle with lime juice, tossing to coat.
Grill, covered with grill lid, on a grill rack coated with cooking spray over medium-high heat (350° to 400°) 5 to 7 minutes on each side or until tender. Cut into strips, if desired. Yield: 6 servings.

Per serving: Calories 56 (42% from fat); Fat 2.6g (sat 0.3g, mono 1.8g, poly 0.2g); Protein 1g; Carb 4g; Fiber 1.1g; Chol 0mg; Iron 0mg; Sodium 393mg; Calc 3mg

---

White Bean-and-Asparagus Salad

prep: 20 min.   cook: 4 min.   other: 1 hr.

Once the asparagus is cooked, this is practically a dump-and-stir recipe.

½   pound fresh asparagus, trimmed
7   dried tomatoes
1   garlic clove, minced
1   tablespoon brown sugar
2   tablespoons extra-virgin olive oil
2   tablespoons white wine vinegar
1   tablespoon water
1   teaspoon spicy brown mustard
¼   teaspoon dried rubbed sage
¼   teaspoon salt
¼   teaspoon pepper
1   (19-ounce) can cannellini beans, rinsed and drained
¼   cup chopped red onion
2   teaspoons drained capers
1   (5-ounce) bag gourmet mixed salad greens
1   tablespoon shredded Parmesan cheese

Snap off tough ends of asparagus; arrange asparagus and dried tomatoes in a steamer basket over boiling water. Cover and steam 2 to 4 minutes or until asparagus is crisp-tender. Set tomatoes aside. Plunge asparagus into ice water to stop the cooking process; drain. Cut asparagus into 1-inch pieces, and chill until ready to use. Chop tomatoes.
Whisk together garlic and next 8 ingredients in a medium bowl; add asparagus, tomatoes, beans, onion, and capers, tossing to coat. Cover and chill 1 hour. Serve asparagus mixture over salad greens; sprinkle with cheese. Yield: 6 servings.

Per serving: Calories 127 (39% from fat); Fat 5.5g (sat 1g, mono 3.6g, poly 0.8g); Protein 4.8g; Carb 15.3g; Fiber 4.4g; Chol 1mg; Iron 2mg; Sodium 351mg; Calc 61mg

---

healthy benefits

• Beans and other legumes are rich in soluble (dissolves in water) fiber. A ½-cup serving of cooked beans provides 4 to 10 grams of fiber (adults need 20 to 35 grams per day). Incorporating soluble fiber into your diet is important because it helps lower bad (LDL) cholesterol, thereby reducing the incidence of heart disease. It also helps regulate blood sugar levels, which makes it an excellent nutrient for people with diabetes. Oats, barley, and citrus fruits also contain soluble fiber.

• Iron plays an essential role in getting oxygen from the bloodstream to every cell in your body. Low iron can lead to anemia, weakness, and infections. Besides liver, the best source of readily absorbed iron is lean beef, such as flank steak. Nonmeat sources of iron include fortified breakfast cereals, spinach, beans, and pumpkin seeds. Iron from these sources isn't absorbed as well, but when enjoyed with vitamin C-rich foods such as bell peppers and citrus fruit, iron absorption increases.

• Eat *at least* five servings of vegetables and fruits daily. Here's one reason why: Produce is rich in selenium and vitamins A, C, and E—powerful antioxidants that protect your body's cells from damage caused by aging, smoke, pollution, and sun. They also keep your immune system healthy, reducing your risk of cancer and other diseases.

White Bean-and-Asparagus Salad

bulgur wheat

Bulgur has a tender, chewy texture and packs a nutritional punch. When compared to fiber-rich brown rice, bulgur comes out ahead. Cup for cup, the two are similar in protein, calcium, and sodium, but bulgur has fewer calories, less fat, and more than twice the fiber of rice.

low calorie • low cholesterol • make ahead

Southwestern Tabbouleh Salad

prep: 40 min.   other: 8 hrs., 30 min.

This nutrient-packed salad has both great texture and flavor. Add some whole wheat pita bread on the side.

1	cup uncooked bulgur wheat
1	cup boiling water
2	tomatoes, chopped
4	green onions, chopped
1	(15½-ounce) can black beans, rinsed and drained
¼	cup chopped fresh cilantro
½	teaspoon grated lime rind
¼	cup fresh lime juice
2	tablespoons olive oil
½	teaspoon ground cumin
½	teaspoon ground red pepper
1	(8¾-ounce) can no-salt-added corn kernels, drained
¼	teaspoon salt

Garnish: fresh parsley

Place bulgur in a large bowl, and add 1 cup boiling water. Cover and let stand 30 minutes. Add chopped tomato and next 10 ingredients to bulgur. Toss gently. Cover and chill up to 8 hours. Garnish, if desired. Yield: 8 cups.

Per cup: Calories 157 (23% from fat); Fat 4g (sat 0.6g, mono 2.8g, poly 0.6g); Protein 4g; Carb 28g; Fiber 6.7g; Chol 0mg; Iron 1.3mg; Sodium 226mg; Calc 24mg

Southwestern Tabbouleh Salad

low cholesterol • low fat • quick

Spicy Oven Fries

prep: 8 min.   cook: 20 min.

At about 100 calories for a 5.3-ounce spud, potatoes are not only modest in calories but also very nutritious. So, go ahead and put these potatoes on your plate.

3	large baking potatoes (about 2 pounds)
2	tablespoons olive oil
2	tablespoons Creole seasoning

Vegetable cooking spray

Cut each baking potato lengthwise into 8 wedges.

Combine olive oil and Creole seasoning in a zip-top plastic bag; add potato wedges. Seal bag, and shake to coat. Arrange potato wedges, skin sides down, in a single layer on a baking sheet coated with cooking spray.

Bake potato wedges at 450° for 20 minutes or until browned. Yield: 6 servings.

Per 4 wedges: Calories 181 (24% from fat); Fat 4.9g (sat 0.7g, mono 3.3g, poly 0.4g); Protein 3g; Carb 32g; Fiber 3.2g; Chol 0mg; Iron 1.7mg; Sodium 484mg; Calc 12mg

Healthy Benefits

Being active helps your health in the following ways:

- lowers blood pressure by reducing overall stress
- improves stamina and muscle strength
- reduces feelings of depression and increases feelings of well-being
- preserves lean muscle mass and decreases body fat
- reduces the risk of bone fractures by building strength

Walk with Friends

When it comes to exercise, most folks could use some extra motivation—gather your friends to walk with you.

- As you choose exercise companions, approach people who are at your same fitness level.
- Consider friends and coworkers whose schedules are similar to yours.
- Alternate your walking route; the change of scenery helps keep you invigorated.
- Drink plenty of water before, during, and after your walk to help replenish the fluids your body loses through sweating.

Walking Benefits

- Your heart will thank you for the exercise. Walking for 30 minutes, five times a week, can help reduce your risk for heart disease by lowering blood pressure and cholesterol.
- Flabby muscles will be a thing of the past. Walking is a wonderful way to burn calories and increase your metabolism as well as tone your body.
- Exercise is a proven stress reducer, and when you also have a couple of people to talk to, life's problems may not seem as overwhelming.

---

low calorie • low cholesterol • quick

Thyme-Scented Green Beans With Smoked Almonds

prep: 15 min.   cook: 10 min.

A little bit of seasoning goes a long way in these sautéed beans.

1   pound fresh green beans, trimmed
1   tablespoon light butter
1   teaspoon dried thyme*
¼   teaspoon salt
¼   teaspoon pepper
1   tablespoon chopped smoked almonds*

Arrange green beans in a steamer basket over boiling water. Cover and steam 6 minutes or until crisp-tender.
Melt butter in a large skillet over medium heat. Stir in green beans, thyme, salt, and pepper; cook until thoroughly heated. Sprinkle beans with almonds. Yield: 4 servings.

Per serving: Calories 76 (44% from fat); Fat 3.7g (sat 2g, mono 0.5g, poly 1g); Protein 3.1g; Carb 10g; Fiber 3g; Chol 5mg; Iron 3.5mg; Sodium 196mg; Calc 80mg

*Substitute 1 to 2 tablespoons chopped fresh thyme for the dried thyme, and 1 tablespoon chopped toasted almonds for the smoked almonds.

Note: Smoked almonds can be found in the snack section of the supermarket.

---

low cholesterol

Smoky Mashed Potato Bake

prep: 30 min.   cook: 1 hr.

Smoked Gouda cheese and chipotle peppers put some smoke and fire in these potatoes.

3   garlic cloves, minced
1   teaspoon olive oil
Vegetable cooking spray
3½   pounds new potatoes, cut into chunks
¾   cup (3 ounces) shredded smoked Gouda cheese, divided
1   cup fat-free half-and-half
2   to 3 chipotle peppers in adobo sauce, minced
½   cup light margarine
½   (8-ounce) package fat-free cream cheese, softened
¼   teaspoon salt

Sauté garlic in hot oil in a skillet coated with cooking spray over medium-high heat 2 to 3 minutes or until tender. Cook potato in a Dutch oven in boiling water to cover 30 minutes or until tender; drain.
Mash potato in a large bowl. Stir in garlic, ¼ cup Gouda cheese, half-and-half, and next 4 ingredients until blended. Spoon mixture into a 13- x 9-inch baking dish coated with cooking spray. Sprinkle with remaining ½ cup Gouda cheese.
Bake at 350° for 30 minutes or until cheese is melted. Yield: 10 servings.

Per ½ cup: Calories 245 (32% from fat); Fat 8.8g (sat 1.6g, mono 1g, poly 0.2g); Protein 7.3g; Carb 32g; Fiber 2.9g; Chol 12mg; Iron 2.1mg; Sodium 369mg; Calc 152mg

---

Gnocchi With Olive Oil, Tomato, and Parmesan

prep: 20 min.   cook: 1 hr., 5 min.

1   garlic bulb
2   tablespoons extra-virgin olive oil
10   to 12 fresh sage leaves
1   (16-ounce) package gnocchi
1   (32-ounce) container low-sodium fat-free chicken broth
4   plum tomatoes, chopped
¼   to ½ teaspoon coarsely ground black pepper
2   tablespoons freshly shaved Parmesan or Romano cheese

Cut off pointed end of garlic; place garlic on a piece of aluminum foil. Fold foil to seal.
Bake at 375° for 1 hour; cool. Squeeze pulp from garlic into a bowl, and mash pulp with a fork; set aside.
Stir together oil and sage in a small skillet, and cook over medium-low heat 2 to 3 minutes or until fragrant and crisp. Remove leaves, and drain on a paper towel, reserving oil.
Prepare gnocchi according to package directions, substituting chicken broth for water. Drain, reserving ¼ cup broth. Add gnocchi and reserved oil to roasted garlic in bowl. Add reserved ¼ cup chicken broth, chopped tomatoes, and pepper, tossing to coat. Sprinkle with cheese and sage leaves; serve immediately. Yield: 4 servings.

Per serving: Calories 420 (34% from fat); Fat 16g (sat 6.3g, mono 7.9g, poly 1.1g); Protein 9.1g; Carb 61.2g; Fiber 1.9g; Chol 23mg; Iron 1.3mg; Sodium 692mg; Calc 75mg

Corn-and-Poblano Chowder

prep: 20 min.   cook: 26 min.   other: 10 min.

Frozen creamed corn and fat-free cream cheese are the base for this spicy-sweet, creamy chowder. Have a cupful for a light lunch, or serve it alongside a sandwich for a more substantial supper.

1   large poblano pepper, cut in half lengthwise
1   (20-ounce) tube frozen creamed corn, thawed
1½   cups 1% low-fat or fat-free milk
¼   teaspoon salt
⅛   to ¼ teaspoon ground red pepper
¼   teaspoon ground cumin
1½   to 2 cups low-sodium fat-free chicken broth
½   (8-ounce) package fat-free cream cheese, softened
Garnishes: thinly sliced jalapeño pepper strips, ground black pepper

Broil poblano pepper halves, skin side up, on an aluminum foil-lined baking sheet 5½ inches from heat 5 to 6 minutes or until pepper looks blistered. Fold aluminum foil over pepper to seal, and let stand 10 minutes. Peel pepper; remove and discard seeds. Coarsely chop pepper; set aside.

Bring corn and next 4 ingredients to a boil in a 3-quart saucepan over medium-high heat, stirring constantly. Reduce heat to low, and simmer, stirring often, 10 minutes.

Stir 1½ cups chicken broth into mixture. Whisk in softened cream cheese and chopped poblano pepper; cook, whisking often, 5 minutes or until cream cheese melts and mixture is thoroughly heated. Whisk in additional chicken broth, if necessary, to desired consistency; garnish, if desired. Serve hot. Yield: 4 servings.

Per serving: Calories 222 (37% from fat); Fat 9.2g (sat 0.9g, mono 0.1g, poly 0.2g); Protein 12.5g; Carb 37.5g; Fiber 4.3g; Chol 8mg; Iron 1.2mg; Sodium 803mg; Calc 244mg

Full-of-Veggies Chili

prep: 20 min.   cook: 30 min.

Chili seasoning flavors the ground beef substitute nicely in this soup. You won't miss the meat.

1   large sweet onion, diced
1   large green bell pepper, diced
2   garlic cloves, minced
2   tablespoons vegetable oil
1   (12-ounce) package ground beef substitute
1   large zucchini, diced
1   (11-ounce) can whole kernel corn, undrained
2   (15-ounce) cans no-salt-added tomato sauce
2   (10-ounce) cans diced tomato and green chiles, undrained
1   (15-ounce) can black beans, rinsed and drained
1   (15-ounce) can pinto beans, rinsed and drained
1   teaspoon sugar
1   (1¾-ounce) envelope Texas-style chili seasoning mix

Sauté first 3 ingredients in hot oil in a large stockpot over medium-high heat 5 minutes or until tender. Stir in ground beef substitute and remaining ingredients. Bring to a boil; reduce heat, and simmer, uncovered, stirring often, 20 minutes. Yield: 4 quarts.

Per cup: Calories 128 (14% from fat); Fat 2g (sat 0.4g, mono 0.6g, poly 1g); Protein 16g; Carb 19g; Fiber 3g; Chol 0mg; Iron 1.6mg; Sodium 547mg; Calc 44mg

Note: Freeze chili up to 3 months, if desired.

Cream of Cilantro Soup

prep: 5 min.   cook: 20 min.

1   bunch fresh cilantro
1   (32-ounce) container low-sodium fat-free chicken broth, divided
2   tablespoons butter
2   tablespoons all-purpose flour
1   (8-ounce) package fat-free cream cheese
1   (8-ounce) container light sour cream
1   garlic clove, minced
¼   teaspoon salt
¼   teaspoon ground red pepper
¼   teaspoon ground cumin
Garnishes: fresh cilantro sprigs, light sour cream

Remove stems from cilantro, and coarsely chop leaves.

Process cilantro and 1 cup chicken broth in a blender or food processor until blended, stopping to scrape down sides.

Melt butter in a Dutch oven over medium heat; whisk in flour. Gradually add remaining 3 cups broth, whisking constantly until mixture is smooth. Boil 1 minute. Stir in cilantro mixture, cream cheese, and next 5 ingredients; simmer soup 15 minutes. Garnish, if desired. Yield: 6 cups.

Per cup: Calories 156 (50% from fat); Fat 8.6g (sat 5.2g, mono 2.5g, poly 0.4g); Protein 7.9g; Carb 9.3g; Fiber 1g; Chol 31mg; Iron 1.6mg; Sodium 393mg; Calc 177mg

meatless
main dishes

Meatless meals can help you eat a little lighter, focus on healthy sources of protein, and increase your intake of fruits and vegetables. Recipes in this chapter that are classified as vegetarian are identified that way preceding the recipe title.

If you make the right food choices, a vegetarian diet can supply you with all the nutrients your body needs, especially if you eat dairy products and eggs. If you are a vegan and don't eat dairy products or eggs, be sure to include foods high in protein (legumes, nuts, seeds), vitamins B12 and D (fortified breakfast cereals and soy products), iron (legumes, iron-fortified cereals, and breads), calcium (legumes, broccoli, calcium-fortified tofu, and calcium-fortified juices), and zinc (whole wheat bread and legumes) in your daily diet. All of the recipes in this chapter have at least 10 grams of protein per serving. See page 28 for vegetarian guidelines.

Chickpea-Chipotle Tostadas

prep: 45 min.   cook: 38 min.

(pictured on previous page)

1	tablespoon olive oil
1	medium onion, chopped
½	red bell pepper, chopped
2	garlic cloves, chopped
1½	(16-ounce) cans chickpeas, rinsed and drained
1	cup chicken broth
2	tablespoons chopped fresh cilantro
2	chipotle chiles in adobo sauce, minced
½	teaspoon salt
2	tablespoons fresh lime juice
1	(8-ounce) container sour cream
½	cup salsa verde or green chile sauce
	Vegetable oil
12	corn tortillas
½	head iceberg lettuce, shredded
6	plum tomatoes, chopped
2	cups (8 ounces) shredded Cheddar cheese or 5 ounces feta cheese, crumbled

Heat oil in a large skillet over medium-high heat. Add onion, bell pepper, and garlic; sauté 5 minutes or until tender. Add chickpeas and next 4 ingredients; bring to a boil. Reduce heat, and simmer 5 minutes. Remove from heat; cool slightly.

Process chickpea mixture in a food processor or with a handheld blender until smooth. Return mixture to skillet. Simmer 2 to 3 minutes, stirring occasionally, until very thick. Stir in lime juice, and cook 2 minutes.

Stir together sour cream and salsa; if desired, cover and chill until ready to serve.

Pour oil to a depth of 1 inch in a large skillet. Heat oil to 375°. Fry tortillas, 1 at a time, over medium-high heat 30 seconds on each side or until crisp and lightly browned. Drain on paper towels.

Spread chickpea mixture evenly over tortillas. Top evenly with lettuce and tomato. Drizzle with sour cream mixture, and sprinkle with cheese. Serve immediately. Yield: 6 servings.

Per serving: Calories 500 (62% from fat); Fat 34.5g (sat 14.2g, mono 11.9g, poly 6.1g); Protein 15.9g; Carb 36.5g; Fiber 5.6g; Chol 56mg; Iron 1.5mg; Sodium 768mg; Calc 370mg

---

low calorie • low fat • make ahead

Toasted Barley-Vegetable Salad

prep: 25 min.   cook: 20 min.

other: 3 hrs., 5 min.

Make this salad up to three days ahead. Toss in the cheese and herbs just before serving.

1	cup uncooked quick-cooking barley
2	teaspoons olive oil
2	cups low-sodium fat-free chicken broth
1	(16-ounce) can chickpeas, rinsed and drained
2	medium tomatoes, seeded and chopped
1	medium cucumber, peeled, seeded, and chopped
1	large garlic clove, minced
¾	cup chopped fresh parsley
½	cup chopped fresh mint
½	cup diced celery
⅓	cup finely chopped red onion
1	teaspoon grated lemon rind
3	tablespoons fresh lemon juice
½	teaspoon salt
½	teaspoon freshly ground pepper
1	(4-ounce) package crumbled feta cheese with basil and tomatoes

Sauté barley in hot oil in a medium saucepan over medium-high heat 4 minutes or until lightly browned; stir in broth. Bring to a boil; cover, reduce heat, and simmer 10 to 12 minutes or until barley is just tender. Remove from heat, and let stand 5 minutes. Cover and chill 1 hour.

Stir together chilled barley, chickpeas, and next 11 ingredients in a large bowl. Cover and chill at least 2 hours. Add cheese just before serving, and toss gently. Yield: 6 servings.

Per serving: Calories 250 (28% from fat); Fat 7.7g (sat 3.5g, mono 1.4g, poly 0.8g); Protein 11g; Carb 37g; Fiber 6.6g; Chol 14mg; Iron 2.2mg; Sodium 735mg; Calc 110mg

---

vegetarian

Mac and Texas Cheeses With Roasted Chiles

prep: 20 min.   cook: 1 hr., 18 min.

other: 10 min.

Roasted poblano peppers and goat cheese elevate mac and cheese to gourmet fare.

4	poblano chile peppers
1	pound uncooked elbow macaroni
½	cup butter or margarine
½	cup all-purpose flour
2	cups whipping cream
1	cup milk
3½	cups (14 ounces) shredded Monterey Jack cheese, divided
1	(4-ounce) package goat cheese, crumbled
1	teaspoon salt
¼	cup Italian-seasoned breadcrumbs
½	cup shredded Parmesan cheese

Broil peppers on an aluminum foil-lined baking sheet 5½ inches from heat about 10 minutes on each side or until peppers look blistered. Place peppers in a zip-top freezer bag; seal and let stand 10 minutes to loosen skins. Peel peppers; remove and discard seeds. Cut peppers into strips.

Prepare macaroni according to package directions; drain and set aside.

Melt butter in a Dutch oven over low heat; gradually whisk in flour until smooth. Cook 1 minute, whisking constantly. Gradually add cream and milk; cook over medium heat, whisking constantly, 5 minutes or until mixture is thickened and bubbly.

Add 3 cups Monterey Jack cheese, crumbled goat cheese, and salt; stir until blended. Stir in roasted peppers and macaroni. Pour mixture into a lightly greased 13- x 9-inch baking dish. Top with breadcrumbs and Parmesan cheese.

Bake, uncovered, at 375° for 40 minutes. Remove from oven, and sprinkle with remaining ½ cup Monterey Jack cheese. Broil 5½ inches from heat 3 minutes or until cheese is golden and bubbly. Yield: 8 servings.

Per serving: Calories 835 (60% from fat); Fat 56g (sat 34.2g, mono 15.3g, poly 3.1g); Protein 28.7g; Carb 57.7g; Fiber 4.1g; Chol 169mg; Iron 3.8mg; Sodium 905mg; Calc 554mg

family favorite • make ahead • vegetarian
Three-Cheese Pasta Bake

prep: 20 min.   cook: 30 min.

Ziti pasta is shaped in long, thin tubes; penne or rigatoni pasta can be substituted.

1   (16-ounce) package ziti
2   (10-ounce) containers refrigerated Alfredo sauce
1   (8-ounce) container sour cream
1   (15-ounce) container ricotta cheese
2   large eggs, lightly beaten
¼   cup grated Parmesan cheese
¼   cup chopped fresh parsley
1½ cups (6 ounces) mozzarella cheese

Prepare ziti according to package directions; drain and return to pot.

Stir together Alfredo sauce and sour cream; toss with ziti until well coated. Spoon half of mixture into a lightly greased 13- x 9-inch baking dish.

Stir together ricotta cheese and next 3 ingredients; spread evenly over pasta in baking dish. Spoon remaining pasta mixture evenly over ricotta cheese layer; sprinkle with mozzarella cheese.

Bake at 350° for 30 minutes or until bubbly. Yield: 8 servings.

Per serving: Calories 615 (48% from fat); Fat 32.9g (sat 19.9g, mono 3.8g, poly 0.6g); Protein 26.4g; Carb 52.6g; Fiber 1.9g; Chol 146mg; Iron 2.3mg; Sodium 782mg; Calc 513mg

The demand for great entrées without meat continues to soar.

make ahead • vegetarian
Smoked Mozzarella Pasta Salad

prep: 20 min.   cook: 12 min.   other: 1 hr.

1   (6-ounce) jar marinated artichoke hearts
1   (8-ounce) package rotini pasta, cooked
1   (7-ounce) jar roasted red bell peppers, drained and cut into strips
½   pound smoked mozzarella cheese, cut into ½-inch cubes*
½   (5-ounce) bag baby spinach leaves (about 1½ cups)
½   (4.5-ounce) can chopped green chiles, drained
½   cup mayonnaise
½   cup grated Parmesan cheese
¼   cup pine nuts, toasted
1   garlic clove, minced
½   teaspoon pepper
Garnishes: tomato wedges, baby spinach leaves

Drain artichokes, reserving marinade. Cut artichokes into strips, and place in a large bowl. Add pasta and next 4 ingredients; toss gently.

Stir together reserved artichoke marinade, mayonnaise, and next 4 ingredients until blended. Add to pasta mixture, stirring to combine. Cover and chill. Garnish, if desired. Yield: 6 servings.

Per serving: Calories 481 (57% from fat); Fat 30.5g (sat 8.3g, mono 1.6g, poly 2g); Protein 19.2g; Carb 36.2g; Fiber 3.2g; Chol 33mg; Iron 2.2mg; Sodium 702mg; Calc 122mg

*Substitute ½ pound smoked Gouda or Cheddar cheese for smoked mozzarella, if desired.

low cholesterol • low fat • vegetarian
Vegetables Bolognese

prep: 15 min.   cook: 18 min.   other: 30 min.

Bolognese is classically a robust Italian pasta sauce rich with meat and vegetables. Our version is loaded with vegetables and has a spicy sauce and tangy tomatoes. You won't miss the meat.

½   cup dried tomatoes
½   cup boiling water
2   medium-size sweet onions, chopped
2   small zucchini, chopped
1   medium-size green bell pepper, chopped
1   medium-size red bell pepper, chopped
1   cup sliced fresh mushrooms
2   garlic cloves, minced
2   tablespoons olive oil
1   (26-ounce) jar spicy pasta sauce (we tested with Newman's Own Diavolo Sauce)
½   cup chopped fresh basil
12 ounces penne pasta, cooked

Stir together dried tomatoes and ½ cup boiling water in a bowl; let stand 30 minutes. Drain, chop tomatoes, and set aside.

Sauté onion and next 5 ingredients in hot oil in a large skillet over medium-high heat 6 to 8 minutes or until vegetables are tender. Stir in chopped tomato.

Stir in pasta sauce, and bring to a boil. Reduce heat; stir in basil, and simmer, stirring occasionally, 5 minutes. Serve over hot cooked pasta. Yield: 6 servings.

Per serving: Calories 419 (18% from fat); Fat 8.3g (sat 1.3g, mono 4.1g, poly 1.7g); Protein 14g; Carb 74.2g; Fiber 6.2g; Chol 0mg; Iron 3.6mg; Sodium 477mg; Calc 95mg

Eggplant Parmesan

Thai Noodles With Peanut Sauce

prep: 20 min.   cook: 15 min.

Sugar snap peas, bean sprouts, and basil add fresh flavor and texture to this Asian favorite.

1   cup fresh sugar snap peas
½   pound uncooked wide rice stick noodles
¾   cup coconut milk
½   cup crunchy peanut butter
½   cup vegetable broth
3   tablespoons soy sauce
2   tablespoons lime juice
1   garlic clove, minced
2   teaspoons sugar
1   teaspoon dried crushed red pepper
1   cup bean sprouts, divided
¾   cup firmly packed basil leaves, shredded
     and divided
¼   cup chopped dry-roasted peanuts
Condiments: chopped dry-roasted peanuts,
     lime wedges

Trim peas, and cut in half diagonally.
Bring water to a boil in a large heavy saucepan; add peas, and cook 45 seconds. Drain. Plunge into ice water to stop the cooking process; drain and set aside.
Prepare noodles according to package directions; drain.
Whisk together coconut milk and next 7 ingredients in a large saucepan. Cook over medium-low heat, whisking occasionally, 5 minutes or until thoroughly heated. Add peas, noodles, ¾ cup bean sprouts, and ¾ cup basil; toss and place on a serving platter.
Sprinkle with remaining ¼ cup bean sprouts and ¼ cup chopped peanuts. Serve with condiments. Yield: 4 servings.

Per serving: Calories 583 (47% from fat); Fat 30.3g (sat 11.2g, mono 2.7g, poly 1.6g); Protein 18.1g; Carb 64.7g; Fiber 6.2g; Chol 0mg; Iron 5.6mg; Sodium 1112mg; Calc 95mg

low calorie • vegetarian

Eggplant Parmesan

prep: 35 min.   cook: 1 hr., 9 min.

Try this classic over spaghetti.

3   large eggs
3   tablespoons water
1½   cups Italian-seasoned breadcrumbs or
     panko (Japanese breadcrumbs)
¼   cup freshly grated Parmesan cheese
2   large eggplants, cut into 18
     (½-inch-thick) slices
3   tablespoons olive oil
½   cup freshly grated Parmesan cheese,
     divided
1   (8-ounce) package mozzarella cheese,
     shredded and divided
3   cups Pasta Sauce (page 434)

Whisk together eggs and 3 tablespoons water until blended.

Combine breadcrumbs and ¼ cup Parmesan cheese.
Dip eggplant slices into egg mixture; dredge in breadcrumb mixture.
Cook eggplant, in 3 batches, in 1 tablespoon hot oil (per batch) in a large skillet over medium heat 4 minutes on each side or until tender.
Arrange one-third of eggplant in a single layer in a lightly greased 11- x 7-inch baking dish. Sprinkle with 2 tablespoons Parmesan cheese and ½ cup mozzarella cheese. Repeat layers twice. Spoon 3 cups Pasta Sauce over top.
Bake, covered, at 375° for 35 minutes. Uncover and sprinkle with remaining ½ cup mozzarella cheese and remaining 2 tablespoons Parmesan cheese. Bake 10 more minutes or until cheese melts. Yield: 8 servings.

Per serving: Calories 351 (46% from fat); Fat 18.1g (sat 6.4g, mono 7.7g, poly 2.2g); Protein 17.7g; Carb 32.3g; Fiber 7.4g; Chol 101mg; Iron 2.7mg; Sodium 1284mg; Calc 382mg

Yukon Gold Mash With Morel Sauce

prep: 15 min.   cook: 25 min.

Morel Sauce
6	medium Yukon gold potatoes, peeled and coarsely chopped (2½ pounds)

Roasted Portobello Caps
2	garlic cloves, sliced
¼	cup butter or margarine, melted
1¼	cups milk
1	teaspoon salt
½	teaspoon freshly ground pepper

Garnish: fresh thyme sprigs

Prepare Morel Sauce.

Cook potatoes in boiling salted water to cover 20 minutes or until tender. Drain potatoes, and set aside.

Meanwhile, prepare Roasted Portobello Caps.

Sauté garlic in butter in a large saucepan over medium heat until butter and garlic are golden. Add milk, salt, and pepper. Bring to a simmer; remove from heat, and add potatoes. Mash with a potato masher until almost smooth.

To serve, spoon Yukon Gold Mash into Roasted Portobello Caps; top with Morel Sauce. Garnish, if desired. Yield: 6 servings.

Per serving: Calories 480 (50% from fat); Fat 26.9g (sat 11.1g, mono 12.3g, poly 1.8g); Protein 11.6g; Carb 47.4g; Fiber 4g; Chol 43mg; Iron 3.9mg; Sodium 1292mg; Calc 107mg

Morel Sauce

prep: 15 min.   cook: 22 min.   other: 5 min.

3	(½-ounce) packages dried morel mushrooms, rinsed and drained
2	cups boiling water
2	tablespoons butter or margarine
2	tablespoons olive oil
2	cups coarsely chopped fresh mushrooms (8 ounces)
¾	cup finely chopped onion
¾	cup port wine
2	tablespoons balsamic vinegar
¼	cup all-purpose flour
½	cup water
½	cup half-and-half
1½	tablespoons chopped fresh sage
1	teaspoon salt
½	teaspoon freshly ground pepper

Place morels in 2 cups boiling water; let stand 5 minutes. Remove morels with a slotted spoon, reserving broth. Strain broth, discarding any sandy residue in pan. Chop morels. Set morels and broth aside.

Heat butter and oil in a large deep skillet over medium-high heat until butter melts. Add fresh mushrooms and onion. Cook, stirring constantly, 5 minutes or until onion is browned; add morels, wine, and vinegar. Reduce heat, and simmer, uncovered, 2 minutes. Add reserved broth; bring to a boil, reduce heat, and simmer, uncovered, 3 minutes.

Combine flour and water, stirring until smooth. Add to mushroom mixture. Cook, stirring constantly, 2 minutes or until thickened and smooth. Stir in half-and-half and remaining ingredients. Cook 5 minutes. Serve over Yukon Gold Mash. Yield: 4 cups.

Per tablespoon: Calories 15 (60% from fat); Fat 1g (sat 0.4g, mono 0.5g, poly 0.1g); Protein 0.4g; Carb 1.2g; Fiber 0.1g; Chol 2mg; Iron 0.2mg; Sodium 40mg; Calc 3mg

Roasted Portobello Caps

prep: 3 min.   cook: 15 min.

6	portobello mushroom caps
3	to 4 tablespoons olive oil
1	teaspoon salt
1	teaspoon freshly ground pepper

Place mushroom caps in a large bowl. Drizzle with oil, and sprinkle with seasonings. Toss gently, being careful not to tear mushrooms. Arrange mushrooms, cavity side down, in a single layer in a jelly-roll pan or shallow roasting pan.

Roast at 450° for 15 minutes, turning once. Yield: 6 servings.

Per serving: Calories 88 (71% from fat); Fat 6.9g (sat 0.9g, mono 5g, poly 0.7g); Protein 2.1g; Carb 4.6g; Fiber 1.4g; Chol 0mg; Iron 0.6mg; Sodium 393mg; Calc 8mg

This alluring entrée has three parts: a roasted mushroom cap base, a buttery mashed potato middle, and a hearty mushroom sauce that mimics meat.

Yukon Gold Mash With Morel Sauce

Stuffed Red Peppers With Cheesy Polenta

prep: 25 min.   cook: 45 min.

Bright red bell peppers make a colorful container for this tasty polenta filling.

3   medium-size red bell peppers
¾   cup polenta or yellow cornmeal
3   garlic cloves, minced
2   cups water
1   teaspoon salt
½   teaspoon garlic salt
¼   teaspoon freshly ground pepper
½   cup whipping cream
1   (7-ounce) can whole green chiles, drained and chopped
⅔   cup chopped fresh cilantro
2   cups (8 ounces) shredded Monterey Jack cheese
½   cup freshly grated Parmesan cheese
Garnish: fresh cilantro sprigs

Cut bell peppers in half lengthwise; remove and discard seeds and membranes. Place bell pepper cups in a lightly greased 13- x 9-inch baking dish.

Whisk together polenta and next 5 ingredients in a large saucepan over medium heat; bring to a boil. Cook, whisking constantly, 5 to 7 minutes or until polenta thickens. Stir in whipping cream and next 4 ingredients, blending well.

Spoon mixture into pepper cups.

Bake at 400° for 25 to 30 minutes or until peppers are tender. Garnish, if desired. Yield: 6 servings.

Per serving: Calories 347 (59% from fat); Fat 22.6g (sat 13.4g, mono 6g, poly 0.8g); Protein 15.7g; Carb 21.6g; Fiber 2.9g; Chol 68mg; Iron 2.8mg; Sodium 1009mg; Calc 424mg

Roasted Vegetable Quesadillas

prep: 15 min.   cook: 28 min.

For an extra kick of flavor, add a few drops of hot sauce to the vegetables before cooking.

1   (8-ounce) container sour cream
1   chipotle chile in adobo sauce, minced
1   tablespoon fresh lime juice
½   teaspoon ground cumin
1   pound asparagus, trimmed and cut into ½-inch pieces
½   red onion, vertically sliced
4   garlic cloves, sliced
1   tablespoon olive oil
½   cup roasted red bell peppers from a jar, drained and cut into strips
5   (8-inch) flour tortillas
1½   cups (6 ounces) shredded Monterey Jack cheese

Combine first 4 ingredients, stirring well with a whisk. Cover and chill.

Combine asparagus, onion, and garlic in a greased jelly-roll pan. Drizzle with oil. Roast at 475° for 10 minutes.

Spoon roasted vegetables and roasted peppers over tortillas; sprinkle evenly with cheese. Fold tortillas in half. Place a large nonstick skillet over medium heat. Add quesadillas to pan, 2 at a time, and cook 2 to 3 minutes on each side or until toasted, pressing with a spatula. Cut each quesadilla into wedges, if desired. Serve hot with sour cream mixture. Yield: 5 servings.

Per serving: Calories 400 (58% from fat); Fat 25.9g (sat 13.8g, mono 7.7g, poly 1g); Protein 16.7g; Carb 26.2g; Fiber 3.3g; Chol 50mg; Iron 1.7mg; Sodium 456mg; Calc 337mg

Chiles Rellenos Quiche

prep: 10 min.   cook: 45 min.   other: 10 min.

2   (4.5-ounce) cans diced green chiles, drained
2   cups (8 ounces) shredded sharp Cheddar cheese
1   cup (4 ounces) shredded Monterey Jack cheese with peppers
2   cups milk
1   cup all-purpose baking mix
4   large eggs, lightly beaten
1   cup ricotta cheese

Preheat oven to 350°. Sprinkle green chiles, Cheddar cheese, and Monterey Jack cheese evenly into a lightly greased 11- x 7-inch baking dish.

Beat milk, baking mix, and eggs at low speed with an electric mixer until smooth. Stir in ricotta cheese; spoon mixture over chiles and cheeses in baking dish.

Bake, uncovered, at 350° for 45 minutes or until a knife inserted in center comes out clean. Let stand 10 minutes before cutting. Yield: 6 servings.

Per serving: Calories 472 (62% from fat); Fat 32.3g (sat 18g, mono 3.2g, poly 0.9g); Protein 24.9g; Carb 21.4g; Fiber 1.5g; Chol 216mg; Iron 1.6mg; Sodium 879mg; Calc 751mg

Huevos Con Queso

prep: 30 min.   cook: 12 min.

Here's a Mexican brunch dish for casual entertaining.

1   (12-ounce) package 6-inch corn tortillas
¾   cup vegetable oil
3   tablespoons butter or margarine
1   small onion, finely chopped
½   medium-size red bell pepper, chopped
½   teaspoon ground cumin
2   tablespoons all-purpose flour
1   (8-ounce) container sour cream
1   (8-ounce) loaf Mexican pasteurized prepared cheese product, cubed (we tested with Mexican Velveeta)
1   cup (4 ounces) shredded Monterey Jack cheese with peppers
6   large eggs, lightly beaten
1   (4-ounce) can tomatillo salsa

Cut tortillas into ¼-inch strips.

Pour oil into a Dutch oven; heat to 375°. Fry tortilla strips, in batches, until crisp and golden. Set aside.

Melt butter in a large skillet over medium heat; add onion, bell pepper, and cumin, and sauté until vegetables are tender. Add flour, and cook, stirring constantly, 1 minute; reduce heat to low. Stir in sour cream and cheeses. Cook, stirring constantly, until cheese melts; keep mixture warm.

Cook eggs in a large lightly greased skillet over medium heat, stirring occasionally, until set.

Divide tortilla strips onto 6 serving plates.

Top evenly with cheese mixture and eggs. Drizzle with salsa, and serve immediately. Yield: 6 servings.

Per serving: Calories 650 (65% from fat); Fat 46.6g (sat 20.4g, mono 11.4g, poly 7.2g); Protein 22g; Carb 38.3g; Fiber 3.4g; Chol 294mg; Iron 2.2mg; Sodium 978mg; Calc 445mg

---

vegetarian

Southwestern Tart

prep: 15 min.   cook: 35 min.   other: 25 min.

This irresistible pie with a homemade herb pastry crust tastes as good as it looks.

1   cup all-purpose flour
½   cup grated Parmesan cheese
2   tablespoons chopped fresh cilantro, divided
½   teaspoon salt, divided
⅓   cup shortening
¼   cup ice water
1   (8-ounce) package cream cheese, softened
2   large eggs
2   green onions, chopped
½   teaspoon ground cumin
1   large ripe avocado, chopped
1   to 2 tablespoons fresh lime juice
½   cup sour cream
½   cup (2 ounces) shredded Cheddar cheese
1   tomato, chopped
Salsa (optional)

Combine flour, Parmesan cheese, 1 tablespoon cilantro, and ¼ teaspoon salt; cut in shortening with a pastry blender or fork until crumbly. Add ¼ cup ice water, 1 tablespoon at a time, and stir with a fork until dry ingredients are moistened.
Shape dough into a ball, and press into a 4-inch circle over heavy-duty plastic wrap. Cover with more plastic wrap, and chill 15 minutes.
Roll dough, covered with plastic wrap, into an 11-inch circle. Remove plastic wrap, and fit dough into a 9-inch tart pan with a removable bottom. Line pastry with aluminum foil, and fill with pie weights or dried beans.
Bake at 450° for 10 minutes. Remove weights and foil; bake 4 to 5 more minutes or until lightly browned. Cool on a wire rack.
Beat cream cheese at medium speed with an electric mixer until smooth. Add eggs,

green onions, cumin, and remaining 1 tablespoon cilantro and ¼ teaspoon salt, beating until blended. Spread evenly over crust.
Bake at 400° for 20 minutes. Cool on wire rack 10 minutes.
Toss together avocado and lime juice. Spread pie with ½ cup sour cream, and sprinkle with Cheddar cheese, avocado, and tomato. Serve with salsa, if desired. Yield: 6 servings.

Per serving: Calories 501 (73% from fat); Fat 40.7g (sat 17.6g, mono 15.3g, poly 5.3g); Protein 13.6g; Carb 22.2g; Fiber 2.7g; Chol 136mg; Iron 2.4mg; Sodium 506mg; Calc 218mg

---

vegetarian

Black Bean 'n' Spinach Enchiladas

prep: 21 min.   cook: 30 min.

Frozen spinach soufflé makes quick work of this traditionally time-consuming type recipe.

2   (12-ounce) packages frozen spinach soufflé (we tested with Stouffer's)
2   (15-ounce) cans black beans, rinsed and drained
2   tablespoons fresh lime juice
1   teaspoon Creole seasoning
1   teaspoon chili powder
½   teaspoon ground cumin
½   teaspoon garlic powder
½   teaspoon onion powder
1   (8-ounce) container sour cream
8   (8-inch) flour tortillas
1   (16-ounce) block Monterey Jack cheese, shredded and divided

Cook spinach soufflé according to microwave package directions. Cool slightly.
Combine black beans and next 6 ingredients in a bowl: set aside.
Stir together spinach soufflé and sour cream until blended.
Spoon about ½ cup black bean filling down center of each tortilla. Top each with a heaping ⅓ cup spinach filling, and sprinkle with 3 tablespoons cheese. Roll up each tortilla, and place seam side down in a lightly greased 13- x 9-inch baking dish. Sprinkle with remaining cheese.
Bake, covered, at 350° for 30 minutes or until bubbly. Yield: 8 servings.

Per serving: Calories 529 (58% from fat); Fat 34g (sat 17g, mono 6.7g, poly 0.7g); Protein 27g; Carb 35.8g; Fiber 6g; Chol 149mg; Iron 1.8mg; Sodium 986mg; Calc 553mg

---

low calorie

Spicy Bean Burgers

prep: 20 min.   cook: 14 min.   other: 30 min.

Use a pastry blender to mash two types of beans with ease. The chilling step makes the patties easier to handle and gives the smoky flavors a chance to blend. We recommend topping these burgers with spicy mayo and shredded lettuce.

2   (15.5-ounce) cans pinto beans with jalapeño peppers, rinsed and drained (we tested with Trappey's Jalapinto pinto beans)
1   (15-ounce) can black beans, rinsed and drained
1   cup uncooked regular oats
1   teaspoon garlic salt
4   green onions, chopped
1   large egg, lightly beaten
⅓   cup ketchup
1   teaspoon hot sauce
1   teaspoon Worcestershire sauce
½   teaspoon liquid smoke
¼   cup vegetable oil
8   ounces mozzarella cheese, thinly sliced

Mash beans in a large bowl; stir in oats and next 7 ingredients. Shape bean mixture into 8 (3½-inch) patties. Cover and chill patties 30 minutes.
Heat 2 tablespoons oil in a large skillet over medium-high heat. Cook 4 patties in hot oil 3 minutes on each side or until lightly browned. Repeat with remaining oil and patties. Top each serving with cheese. Yield: 8 servings.

Per serving: Calories 290 (48% from fat); Fat 15.6g (sat 4.8g, mono 5.3g, poly 3.5g); Protein 13.4g; Carb 28.4g; Fiber 7.6g; Chol 49mg; Iron 2.1mg; Sodium 712mg; Calc 203mg

Greek Garbanzo Stew

Stir together first 6 ingredients in a bowl.
Place 1 tablespoon cheese mixture in center
of each won ton wrapper. Moisten won ton
edges with water; fold in 2 opposite sides
over filling. Fold over remaining sides, overlapping edges and pressing to seal.
Pour oil to a depth of 3 inches into a heavy
saucepan; heat to 350°.
Fry dumplings, in batches, 2 to 3 minutes or
until golden (do not overcook); drain on
paper towels. Serve immediately with
Roasted Bell Pepper Vinaigrette. Yield:
5 servings.

Per serving: Calories 594 (81% from fat); Fat 53.4g (sat 10g, mono 21.4g, poly 19.8g);
Protein 10.1g; Carb 24.2g; Fiber 2.4g; Chol 18mg; Iron 2.3mg; Sodium 523mg; Calc 79mg

Note: You can also serve these dumplings
on a mixed green salad. Top with grilled
chicken, and drizzle with Roasted Bell
Pepper Vinaigrette.

Roasted Vegetable-and-Goat Cheese Pizza

prep: 30 min. cook: 1 hr., 15 min.

*You can use more or less cheese depending
on what's available; substituting 2 (4-ounce)
logs of goat cheese or most of an 11-ounce
log works fine.*

1	medium-size sweet onion, cut into ¾-inch pieces
1	teaspoon olive oil
1	medium eggplant, peeled and cut into ¾-inch cubes
1	red bell pepper, cut into ¾-inch pieces
1	small zucchini, cut into ¾-inch cubes
1	teaspoon salt
½	teaspoon pepper
2	teaspoons chopped fresh thyme
1	tablespoon olive oil
1	(24-ounce) package prebaked pizza crusts
1	(7-ounce) container refrigerated prepared pesto sauce
1	(9-ounce) package goat cheese, crumbled
¼	cup pine nuts

Toss onion with 1 teaspoon olive oil;
arrange on an aluminum foil-lined jelly-roll
or broiler pan.
Bake at 425° for 20 minutes or until tender,
stirring after 10 minutes.

Greek Garbanzo Stew

prep: 10 min. cook: 30 min.

*Serve this zesty dish over couscous for a
hearty vegetarian entrée.*

1	medium onion, diced
1	tablespoon olive oil
2	garlic cloves, minced
1	(28-ounce) can diced tomatoes
1	(16-ounce) can garbanzo beans, rinsed and drained
1	(14-ounce) can vegetable broth
2	tablespoons tomato paste
½	teaspoon fresh or dried rosemary
2	teaspoons dried oregano
1	teaspoon Greek seasoning
¼	teaspoon salt
½	teaspoon pepper
1	(6-ounce) package fresh baby spinach
2	tablespoons chopped fresh parsley
4	ounces crumbled feta cheese
Garnish: fresh rosemary

Sauté onion in hot oil in a Dutch oven over
medium-high heat 4 to 5 minutes or until
tender. Add garlic, and cook 1 minute. Stir
in tomatoes and next 8 ingredients. Bring to
a boil; reduce heat to low, and simmer, stirring occasionally, 15 minutes. Stir in spinach
and chopped parsley; cook 5 minutes. Top
with crumbled feta cheese. Garnish, if
desired. Yield: 4 servings.

Per serving: Calories 249 (38% from fat); Fat 10.4g (sat 4.7g, mono 3.8g, poly 0.6g);
Protein 10.8g; Carb 31.1g; Fiber 8.6g; Chol 25mg; Iron 4.1mg; Sodium 1689mg; Calc 252mg

Goat Cheese Dumplings

prep: 30 min. cook: 3 min. per batch

¼	cup diced dried tomatoes in oil, drained
6	ounces goat cheese (¾ cup)
2	garlic cloves, minced
2	tablespoons chopped fresh parsley
3	tablespoons chopped fresh basil
½	teaspoon freshly ground pepper
16	won ton wrappers
Vegetable oil	
Roasted Bell Pepper Vinaigrette (page 417)	

Toss together eggplant and next 6 ingredients; add to onion on jelly-roll pan. Bake 30 more minutes, stirring every 10 minutes. **Place** pizza crusts on 2 lightly greased baking sheets; spread pesto evenly over crusts, and arrange vegetables evenly over pesto. Sprinkle crumbled goat cheese and pine nuts over vegetables.
Bake pizzas at 425° for 25 minutes or until cheese is lightly browned. Yield: 8 servings.

Per serving: Calories 561 (53% from fat); Fat 32.9g (sat 9.9g, mono 13.5g, poly 7.9g); Protein 19.7g; Carb 49.8g; Fiber 4.9g; Chol 23mg; Iron 5mg; Sodium 894mg; Calc 325mg

low calorie • low cholesterol • low fat

Vegetable–Quinoa Pilaf

prep: 15 min.   cook: 22 min.

A delicate-flavored, ricelike grain, quinoa is a rich source of vital nutrients such as protein.

1   cup uncooked quinoa
1¾ cups chicken broth
1   tablespoon olive oil
2   medium leeks, finely chopped
½   cup chopped red bell pepper
½   cup chopped yellow bell pepper
¾   cup finely chopped carrot
½   cup finely chopped celery
2   teaspoons minced garlic
⅓   cup freshly grated Parmesan cheese
½   teaspoon salt
¼   teaspoon freshly ground pepper
¼   cup chopped fresh flat-leaf parsley

Rinse quinoa with cold water according to package directions; drain.
Combine quinoa and broth in a medium saucepan; bring to a boil. Cover, reduce heat, and simmer 15 minutes or until quinoa is tender and liquid is absorbed.
Heat oil in a medium skillet over medium-high heat. Add leeks and next 4 ingredients. Cook 6 minutes or until vegetables are tender, stirring occasionally. Stir in garlic; cook 1 minute. Combine vegetable mixture and quinoa. Stir in cheese, salt, and pepper. Sprinkle with parsley. Yield: 4 servings.

Per serving: Calories 282 (28% from fat); Fat 8.8g (sat 1.9g, mono 3.7g, poly 1.6g); Protein 10.1g; Carb 41.7g; Fiber 4.9g; Chol 6mg; Iron 5.5mg; Sodium 849mg; Calc 149mg

low calorie • low cholesterol • low fat
vegetarian

Bean Chili With Tofu

prep: 10 min.   cook: 38 min.

This recipe uses canned beans for a quick meal. Sautéing ground cumin develops a rich flavor base for the chili.

7   ounces firm tofu, drained and crumbled (about 1 cup)
1½ teaspoons ground cumin, divided
1½ tablespoons soy sauce
2   teaspoons vegetable oil
1½ cups chopped onion
½   teaspoon ground coriander
½   teaspoon dried oregano
1½ tablespoons tomato paste
1½ tablespoons hot chili powder or regular chili powder
1   teaspoon minced drained canned chipotle chile in adobo sauce
½   teaspoon pepper
¼   teaspoon salt
2   garlic cloves, minced
1½ cups water
1   (15-ounce) can pinto beans
1   (15-ounce) can red kidney beans
1   (14.5-ounce) can diced tomatoes, undrained
½   teaspoon cider vinegar
¼   cup chopped fresh cilantro
¼   cup sour cream

Heat a large Dutch oven over medium-high heat. Add tofu and ¾ teaspoon cumin; sauté 3 minutes. Stir in soy sauce; cook 1 minute or until liquid evaporates. Remove tofu mixture from pan.
Heat oil in pan; add remaining ¾ teaspoon cumin, chopped onion, coriander, and oregano; sauté 4 minutes. Add tofu mixture, tomato paste, and next 5 ingredients; stir well. Add water, beans, and tomatoes; bring to a boil. Cover, reduce heat, and simmer 30 minutes. Stir in vinegar. Spoon chili into bowls; top each serving with cilantro and sour cream. Yield: 4 servings.

Per serving: Calories 256 (19% from fat); Fat 5.4g (sat 1.7g, mono 1.5g, poly 1.7g); Protein 12.2g; Carb 42.8g; Fiber 9.6g; Chol 6mg; Iron 4.7mg; Sodium 807mg; Calc 145mg

tofu tidbits

• Regular tofu (soybean curd) is low in calories—3 ounces of tofu carries only 45 to 90 calories. It's a storehouse of vitamins and minerals, including folic acid and iron. Half of tofu's calories or more can come from fat—about 5 grams in 3 ounces—but light versions have only 1 gram per 3 ounces. None of the fat is saturated (the type of fat that increases the risk of heart disease).

• Tofu varies in texture from creamy and smooth to firm enough to slice. It's also sold marinated and smoked, or flavored with seasonings such as teriyaki or garlic and herbs. At some supermarkets and Asian-food specialty stores, you can find it spiced, fermented, freeze-dried, or deep-fried.

• To drain tofu, place it between several layers of paper towels, and press gently to wick away moisture.

• Since tofu is perishable, keep it in the refrigerator for no longer than a week. Tofu can be frozen for up to five months but will shrink during freezing; when defrosted, it will have a chewier texture and caramel appearance that some find appealing, especially when grilled.

meats

The search for a prime-time meat course ends here. These pages serve up beef, veal, lamb, and pork the way they are meant to be—juicy, tender, full-flavored, and cooked to perfection.

Equipment

Stock your kitchen for cooking meat by selecting small and large roasting pans that are thick enough to heat evenly without scorching. Though the pans don't necessarily need lids, they should be equipped with racks to be used for roasting. Add a few heavy skillets with lids, a large sauté pan for pan-frying, and a Dutch oven or other braising pan, and you'll have a set of useful pans for cooking meat. Remember size matters—if the pan is too small and the meat is crowded, browning will be inhibited; if too large, overcooking can result.

Meat can be pounded to the perfect tenderness if you have a meat mallet, though a rolling pin will work in a pinch. There's no need to guess about doneness if you have a meat thermometer or instant-read thermometer. You'll be able to turn meat without piercing it, if you have a pair of spring-loaded metal tongs. And last, invest in a set of sharp knives and a carving set—they'll guarantee a more enjoyable cooking and eating experience.

Shopping

Be aware of the difference between meat inspection and meat grading. The wholesomeness or safety of meat is determined by meat inspection. All meat that is sold must, by law, pass inspection. On the other hand, meat grading has to do with palatability—the tenderness, juiciness, and flavor. Grading is performed by the U.S. Department of Agriculture (USDA), and is determined by the amount of marbling (flecks of fat within the lean), the age of the animal, texture, color, and overall appearance. There are eight grades for beef (in descending order of quality): Prime, Choice, Select, Standard, Commercial, Utility, Cutter, and Canner.

Of the eight quality grades, usually only the top three—Prime, Choice, and Select—are sold at retail. Prime has the most marbling, is produced in limited quantities, and is usually sold only to fine restaurants and specialty meat markets. Choice is what you typically see in the marketplace. In comparison, Select has less marbling, which means it's less tender, less juicy, and not as flavorful. Grades below Standard are used by packers of processed meats and aren't available at retail markets.

USDA grades for pork reflect only two levels of quality: Acceptable and Utility. Acceptable quality is the only fresh pork sold in the marketplace and has a high proportion of lean meat to fat and bone. All pork found in retail stores is either USDA inspected or state inspected for wholesomeness and safety. Much pork is sold cured as bacon or ham, but if buying fresh, look for a relatively small amount of outside fat, a firm texture, and a grayish-pink color.

You might occasionally notice packages of ground beef or other red meat that's bright red on the outside, but dull gray-brown on the inside. Don't be concerned; this condition is largely due to the presence of a natural protein pigment called myoglobin. When the surface of ground beef and other red meat is exposed to air, the myoglobin creates oxymyoglobin, which makes the meat bright red. A darker, purplish-red color is typically found in vacuum-packaged meat due to the lack of oxygen. Once open and exposed to air, these meats also will turn bright red. Sometimes meat appears to have an iridescent sheen; this harmless condition is simply the effect of light on the cut surface of muscle and often occurs on sliced cured ham, dried beef, and corned beef as well as sliced cold roast beef or lamb.

When shopping, make meat selections just before checking out to ensure meats stay as cold as long as possible. Examine each package to determine if it's tightly wrapped and free of tears or punctures. Avoid packages containing excessive liquid, and if purchased frozen, make sure the meat is rock-solid. Meat will remain high quality if purchased by the "sell by" date on the package label.

Shop smarter by considering the cost per serving rather than the cost per pound. A large amount of fat and bone in less expensive cuts will reduce the amount of edible meat, making some more-expensive cuts a better buy. Note that boneless cuts, such as stew meat, ground beef, boneless roasts, and boneless steaks usually serve three or four people per pound. Steaks and roasts with a moderate amount of bone will serve two to three people per pound. Bone-in cuts like ribs will yield 1 to 1½ servings per pound.

Handling and Storing

Refrigerate or freeze meat within 30 minutes after purchasing. If refrigerating, place it in the meat compartment or coldest part of the refrigerator (35° to 40°). If wrapped in transparent film, meat can be refrigerated without rewrapping. Use ground meat within one to two days, and roasts and steaks within three to four days.

If freezing meat (at or below 0°), rewrap the original package with heavy-duty aluminum foil, freezer paper, zip-top freezer bags, or press and seal plastic freezer wrap, removing as much air as possible. Always label frozen meat, identifying the cut, number of servings or weight, and the date frozen. Roasts and steaks stay fresh in the freezer for six to 12 months; ground meat and stew meat up to three months. Leftover cooked meat maintains good quality up to three months in the freezer. Never refreeze meat that has already been frozen and thawed. And most important, thaw frozen meat only in the refrigerator or microwave oven; never defrost at room temperature. Also, when meat is defrosted in a microwave, finish cooking it immediately.

Cooking Methods

The secret to preparing tender meat lies in knowing if the piece you're preparing is a naturally "tender" or "less-tender" cut. This is determined by the location of the cut on the carcass. Tender cuts come from the rib, loin, and short loin sections (along the backbone), and include more costly rib-eye steaks, rib roasts, and sirloin steaks. Dry-heat cooking methods such as grilling, panbroiling, broiling, roasting, pan-frying, and stir-frying work for tender cuts.

Less-tender cuts typically come from the shoulder, legs, breast,

Shown on previous page: Beef Tenderloin With Pan-Roasted Pears (page 296)

and flank sections (heavy muscle development), and include the less expensive chuck, foreshank, brisket, short plate, tip, and round. Moist-heat methods such as braising and stewing are better choices for less-tender cuts.

Grilling: Whether you use charcoal or gas, dry-heat grilling (direct or indirect) gives meat a wonderful smoky flavor. For a 1-inch-thick small to medium-size steak, start by searing one side of the meat over the hottest part of the grill for about a minute. Then, turn it over and sear three to five more minutes. Finish by turning again for another minute or two. Use caution when cooking steak less than an inch thick; unless you use lower heat, it will be well-done on the inside by the time it has seared on both sides. Larger, thicker steaks require longer cooking, so start them out over the hottest part just until seared; then move to the side over lower heat to complete cooking, turning when necessary. Bear in mind that charring is not recommended, and the longer meat is grilled, the more moisture and juices evaporate, leaving you with less flavor. It's recommended that grillers use an instant-read thermometer to determine doneness. This cooking method is best for burgers, steak, ribs, tenderloin, brisket, chops, or kabobs.

Pan-broiling: A dry-heat method accomplished by cooking in an open, heavy, nonstick skillet, pan, or griddle. If the cut of meat is very lean, a small amount of fat may be needed to prevent sticking. The meat is typically seasoned and placed in a preheated skillet where it cooks slowly over medium-low heat and is turned occasionally for even browning. Remove excess drippings from the pan as you cook, or you'll be frying instead of panbroiling. Use this method with most any steak, tenderloin, or burgers.

Broiling: A dry-heat technique where meat is cooked in the oven with the heat element located directly above the meat. Preheat the broiler before you start. Place the seasoned meat on a rack in a broiler pan, and position it on the oven shelf so it's three to five inches from the broiling element. The goal is to broil the top of the meat until brown, then turn it over and broil the other side. This low-fat cooking method is best used with tender steaks (rib-eye, porterhouse, sirloin, and tenderloin) and burgers. If you choose to broil less-tender cuts such as flank steak or top round steak, be sure to marinate them in advance.

Roasting: A dry-heat process where meat is cooked, uncovered, in a hot oven without the addition of liquid. The meat is placed, fat side up, on a rack in a shallow roasting pan. Check doneness by inserting a meat thermometer into the thickest part of the meat, avoiding fat or bone. Use this method for large tender cuts of meat such as rib roast, rolled rump roast, and tenderloin.

Pan-frying: A dry-heat procedure where meat is cooked in a small amount of fat in a sauté pan or skillet over medium heat. Use this method for thin, tender cuts like cubed steak and veal cutlets. A similar method, deep-frying, requires oil to be deep enough to completely cover the meat in a deep heavy skillet or Dutch oven.

Stir-frying: An Asian technique of rapidly frying small pieces of meat in a small amount of oil over high heat in a wok or large heavy nonstick skillet. Use this method for cooking thinly sliced strips of tender sirloin and flat iron steak or, if marinated first, strips of less-tender cubed steak, flank steak, and round steak.

Braising: A moist-heat method that begins with browning or searing meat in hot oil. A small amount of liquid is added before covering and simmering over low heat on the cooktop or in the oven. Cover with a tight-fitting lid or aluminum foil to prevent liquid from evaporating. This long, slow cooking method is ideal for tenderizing tough cuts of meat such as top and bottom round steak, flank steak, eye of round, arm pot roast, and blade roast.

Stewing: A moist-heat method where meat is browned or seared, and then liquid is added to completely cover the meat. Cover with a tight-fitting lid and simmer gently (do not boil) on the cooktop until tender. Any vegetables should be added near the end of cooking so they won't overcook. Use this method for corned beef brisket, stew meat, eye of round roast, and short ribs.

Tenderness and Flavor

Meat is a muscle, and how the animal used that muscle determines the tenderness and taste of the cut. There are several tips for making less-tender cuts of meat more tender and flavorful. This allows for cooking by either dry-heat or moist-heat methods.

For example, marinating in a seasoned acidic mixture such as wine, lemon or lime juice, Italian dressing, salsa, or yogurt adds flavor and tenderizes meat. Acid penetrates the meat and breaks down tough connective tissue. Less-tender meat can marinate in the refrigerator for at least 6 hours, but no longer than 24 hours. In fact, a tender steak should not marinate longer than 2 hours, because marinating too long will result in a mushy texture. Allow about ¼ to ½ cup of marinade for each pound of meat.

Marinating meat: A great no-fuss way to marinate a big piece of meat is in a zip-top freezer bag.

Pounding tough meat with a meat mallet (or rolling pin) is another way to tenderize it. Place meat between sheets of heavy-duty plastic wrap or in a large zip-top freezer bag for easier cleanup. It's also possible to have the butcher run thin cuts of meat, such as round steak, through a cubing machine to tenderize them.

Commercial meat tenderizers also are available. These powders, sometimes flavored with seasoning, are made from tropical fruits that contain *papain,* a natural tenderizer. Be sure to follow directions because meat can quickly become too soft if too much is used.

Rubbing meat with a mixture of seasonings before cooking has become a popular way to add flavor, especially when grilling. Dry rubs usually consist of herbs, spices, and other dry seasonings. Paste rubs are made from dry seasonings held together with a small amount of oil, mustard, soy sauce, or other moist ingredient. Rubs add flavor, help seal in juices, and sometimes form a delicious crust.

Determining Doneness

The most accurate way to determine doneness is by checking the internal temperature with a thermometer. End-point temperatures vary with different meats. The temperature guidelines are:

Beef: at least 145° (medium rare)
Veal: at least 145° (medium rare)
Lamb: at least 145° (medium rare)
Pork: 160° (medium)

Our recipes sometimes suggest removing meats from the oven 5° to 10° before the desired doneness. That's because the internal temperature of roasts will continue to climb several degrees after removing meat from the oven. Always make sure beef, veal, or lamb reaches at least 145° or pork reaches 160° before serving. All ground meats need to cook to 160°.

Two types of thermometers can be used to check the internal temperature of meat. One is an oven-safe meat thermometer that is inserted prior to cooking and left in during the cooking process. The other is an instant-read thermometer, which is not oven-safe. Insert an instant-read thermometer toward the end of cooking time, leave for 10 to 15 seconds, check temperature, and remove. A thermometer is useful when cooking oven roasts, meat loaf, burgers, and steak.

It's also important to visually check for doneness. Medium-rare meat (145° to 150°) will be very pink in the center and only slightly brown toward the exterior. Medium meat (160°) is light pink in the center and brown toward the exterior. Well-done meat (170°) is uniformly brown throughout.

beef

When it comes to meat, beef is king. No other meat offers as much variety in cuts and cooking methods. And thanks to modern breeding and feeding practices, today's beef is leaner and healthier.

There are over 60 different cuts of beef available, so there is enough variety to satisfy all tastes and budgets. Deciding which cut to select, however, can be confusing. So it's a good idea to become familiar with the most common cuts of beef and how they're best prepared. Start by reading the "Cooking Methods" section on the previous page and learn the difference between tender and less-tender cuts and moist- and dry-heat cooking methods. Then glance at the identification chart (opposite) to help you locate various cuts of beef in the supermarket.

Look for beef that's bright red with a relatively thin layer of external white fat. Beef that has been vacuum-packaged and the interior of ground beef will look darker because the meat has not been in direct contact with air. Once opened and exposed to air, meat should turn bright red.

Selections should be fine-textured, firm to the touch, and slightly moist. Tender cuts of meat will have marbling throughout. *Marbling* is flecks or thin streaks of fat that run throughout meat and enhance flavor, tenderness, and juiciness. More marbling means more fat and calories. Therefore, leaner cuts with less marbling are a healthier

choice, but they can be easily overcooked. Always consider tenderizing a lean cut or use a moist-heat cooking method.

Cuts from the center of the steer are the loin and rib sections. They're muscles that are used very little, so they're naturally more tender and are best cooked by dry-heat methods. Tenderloin, rib roast, rib-eye roast, and steak are common cuts. Cuts from the front and rear of the steer are the chuck and round sections; these are heavily used muscles so they're less tender and are best cooked by moist-heat methods. Round steak, top round roast, rump roast, and chuck eye roast are common cuts.

Ground beef can come from any part of the steer, but labels must identify it as coming from the round or the chuck. Meat labeled ground beef must be at least 70% lean according to federal regulations. Ground chuck must be at least 80% lean, while ground round must be 85% lean. One cattle company is currently marketing highly palatable 92% lean ground beef and 96% lean ground round. Upon examination, you can see the differences in the grinds. When ground beef contains more fat, it will look paler and cost less. So remember, just because ground beef is cheaper doesn't make it a better buy. Most of the fat cooks out of the meat anyway and will be discarded. For that reason, expect more shrinkage in recipes made from ground beef. For ground beef recipes

in this chapter, we call for the specific type of grind that we used in testing.

Note that ground beef is more perishable than roasts or steaks, which means it has a shorter shelf life. Immediately freeze ground beef if you don't plan to use within one to two days, and refrigerate leftover cooked meat within two hours of cooking.

Beef can be frozen up to two weeks in its original transparent package. For longer storage (up to three months), rewrap the package in a moisture-proof airtight material like heavy-duty aluminum foil, freezer paper, zip-top freezer bags, or press and seal plastic freezer wrap.

refrigerator/freezer storage for beef

type of beef	refrigerator	freezer
Fresh steaks, roasts	3 to 4 days	6 to 12 months
Fresh ground beef	1 to 2 days	3 months
Leftover cooked beef (all types)	1 to 2 days	2 to 3 months

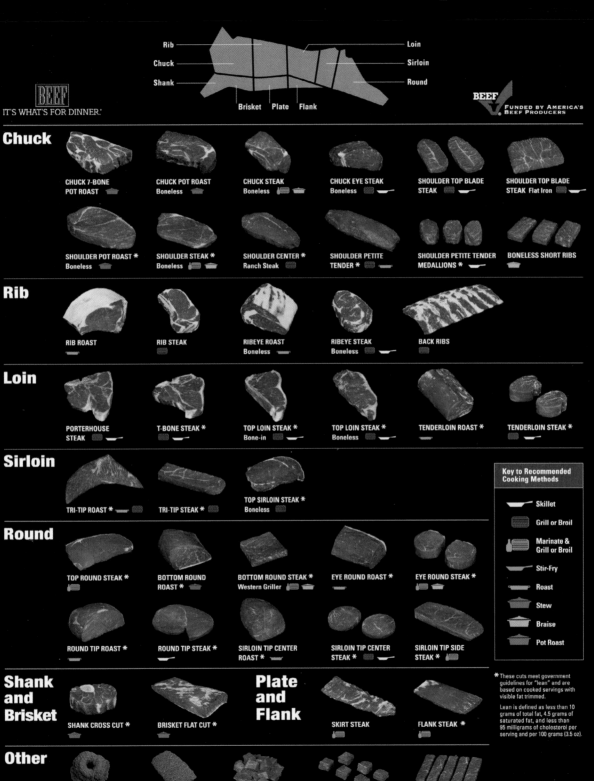

Beef Made Easy®

Rib — Chuck — Shank — Loin — Sirloin — Round — Brisket — Plate — Flank

BEEF IT'S WHAT'S FOR DINNER.®

BEEF FUNDED BY AMERICA'S BEEF PRODUCERS

Chuck

CHUCK 7-BONE POT ROAST

CHUCK POT ROAST Boneless

CHUCK STEAK Boneless

CHUCK EYE STEAK Boneless

SHOULDER TOP BLADE STEAK

SHOULDER TOP BLADE STEAK Flat Iron

SHOULDER POT ROAST * Boneless

SHOULDER STEAK * Boneless

SHOULDER CENTER * Ranch Steak

SHOULDER PETITE TENDER *

SHOULDER PETITE TENDER MEDALLIONS *

BONELESS SHORT RIBS

Rib

RIB ROAST

RIB STEAK

RIBEYE ROAST Boneless

RIBEYE STEAK Boneless

BACK RIBS

Loin

PORTERHOUSE STEAK

T-BONE STEAK *

TOP LOIN STEAK * Bone-in

TOP LOIN STEAK * Boneless

TENDERLOIN ROAST *

TENDERLOIN STEAK *

Sirloin

TRI-TIP ROAST *

TRI-TIP STEAK *

TOP SIRLOIN STEAK * Boneless

Round

TOP ROUND STEAK *

BOTTOM ROUND ROAST *

BOTTOM ROUND STEAK * Western Griller

EYE ROUND ROAST *

EYE ROUND STEAK *

ROUND TIP ROAST *

ROUND TIP STEAK *

SIRLOIN TIP CENTER ROAST *

SIRLOIN TIP CENTER STEAK *

SIRLOIN TIP SIDE STEAK *

Shank and Brisket

SHANK CROSS CUT *

BRISKET FLAT CUT *

Plate and Flank

SKIRT STEAK

FLANK STEAK *

Other

GROUND BEEF

CUBED STEAK

BEEF FOR STEW

BEEF FOR KABOBS

BEEF FOR STIR-FRY OR FAJITAS

Key to Recommended Cooking Methods

- Skillet
- Grill or Broil
- Marinate & Grill or Broil
- Stir-Fry
- Roast
- Stew
- Braise
- Pot Roast

* These cuts meet government guidelines for "lean" and are based on cooked servings with visible fat trimmed.

Lean is defined as less than 10 grams of total fat, 4.5 grams of saturated fat, and less than 95 milligrams of cholesterol per serving and per 100 grams (3.5 oz).

© Cattlemen's Beef Board and National Cattlemen's Beef Association

Standing Rib Roast

prep: 5 min.   cook: 2 hrs., 40 min.   other: 20 min.

This grand holiday roast is encrusted with coarsely ground salt and pepper. For best results, cook a large cut of meat such as this with a combination of high and low heat—first in a very hot oven to sear the outside, and then slowly roasted to keep it juicy.

1   (6-pound) fully trimmed 3-rib roast*
1½ to 2 tablespoons coarse sea salt
1½ teaspoons coarsely ground pepper or
      cracked pepper
Garnish: fresh herbs

Place roast, rib side down, in a lightly greased shallow roasting pan. Rub salt and pepper into fat across entire top of roast, covering completely. Insert a meat thermometer into roast, making sure it does not touch bone or fat.
Roast, uncovered, at 450° for 10 minutes; reduce oven temperature to 325°, and roast 2½ hours or until thermometer registers

---

readying a rib roast

There's a bit of preparation involved in readying a standing rib roast (also called prime rib) for cooking. Most butchers will do the work for you; just be sure to call and give a few days' notice.

A full rib roast contains 7 rib bones that act as a natural roasting rack and make quite an impression upon serving. If you buy less than a full roast, request that it be cut from the loin end; it's where you'll find the largest portion of the rib "eye" meat, the most tender meat.

In trimming the roast, your butcher will "french" (trim fat and gristle) and shorten the rib bones as well as remove the chine bone (back bone). He should also trim the cap fat to just a thin layer covering the outside of the roast. (The cap fat is a thick layer of fat that covers the top of a rib roast.)

Sources vary in serving recommendations from 2 to 4 people per rib. The English method of carving produces fairly thick servings. Other methods call for slicing the roast as thin as ¼ inch.

145° (medium rare). Remove from oven; cover roast with aluminum foil, and let stand 20 minutes. (This allows juices to retreat into the meat; the temperature of roast will rise slightly.) Garnish, if desired. Serve with new potatoes, carrots, and Yorkshire Pudding (page 92). Yield: 10 servings.

Per serving: Calories 611 (73% from fat); Fat 49.7g (sat 20g, mono 21.5g, poly 1.8g); Protein 37.9g; Carb 0.2g; Fiber 0.1g; Chol 141mg; Iron 4.2mg; Sodium 1154mg; Calc 24mg

*Ask your butcher to cut the roast from the loin end and to "french" the bones for you. See Readying a Rib Roast in box at left for more details.

Peppered Rib-Eye Roast

prep: 8 min.   cook: 2 hrs., 20 min.   other: 8 hrs.

This is the boneless version of a standing rib roast. Let the rich gravy dribble onto each slice or over mashed potatoes.

½   cup cracked pepper or coarsely ground
      pepper
1   (5- to 6-pound) boneless rib-eye roast,
      trimmed
1   cup soy sauce
¾   cup red wine vinegar
2   tablespoons tomato paste
1   teaspoon paprika
2   garlic cloves, minced
1   tablespoon cornstarch
1   tablespoon cold water
⅛   teaspoon salt

Lightly press pepper on top and sides of roast. Place roast in a large zip-top freezer bag or large shallow dish. Combine soy sauce and next 4 ingredients; pour over roast. Seal or cover, and marinate in refrigerator 8 hours, turning occasionally.
Remove roast from marinade, discarding marinade. Place roast, fat side up, on a rack in a shallow roasting pan; insert a meat thermometer into thickest part of roast, making sure it does not touch fat.
Bake, uncovered, at 425° for 10 minutes. Reduce temperature to 325°; bake 2 hours and 10 minutes or until thermometer registers 145° (medium rare) or 160° (medium).
Remove roast to a serving platter; cover with aluminum foil, and keep warm. Add

---

carving a rib roast

Place roast on a cutting board with large end down. Insert carving fork just below top rib. Slice horizontally from fat side of the meat through to the rib bone. Slice vertically along rib bone to release each slice. Slide knife under each slice; lift and remove slice to plate.

---

enough water (about ¾ cup) to pan drippings to make 1½ cups; return to pan. **Combine** cornstarch and 1 tablespoon cold water, stirring until smooth. Stir cornstarch mixture and salt into pan drippings. Cook over medium heat, stirring constantly, until mixture is smooth and slightly thickened. Serve roast with gravy. Yield: 12 servings.

Per serving: Calories 530 (71% from fat); Fat 41.8g (sat 17g, mono 18.1g, poly 1.5g); Protein 34.2g; Carb 2.2g; Fiber 0.5g; Chol 129mg; Iron 4.2mg; Sodium 585mg; Calc 27mg

Prime Rib With Spicy Horseradish Sauce

prep: 15 min.   cook: 1 hr., 12 min.   other: 30 min.

During cooking, rock salt's protective covering produces a juicy and perfectly seasoned beef dish. The salt is brushed off after baking.

1   (6-pound) boneless beef rib roast
3   garlic cloves, minced
2   tablespoons coarsely ground pepper
1   tablespoon Worcestershire sauce
2   (4-pound) packages rock salt
½   cup water
Spicy Horseradish Sauce

Rub roast on all sides with garlic, pepper, and Worcestershire sauce.
Pour salt to a depth of ½ inch into a disposable aluminum roasting pan; place roast in center of pan. Pat remaining salt onto roast; sprinkle with ½ cup water.
Bake at 500° for 12 minutes per pound or until a meat thermometer inserted into thickest portion registers 145° (medium rare) or to desired degree of doneness. (Be sure to use a meat thermometer for best results.) Let stand 10 minutes. Crack salt with a hammer; remove roast, and brush

away salt. Let stand 20 minutes. Serve roast with Spicy Horseradish Sauce. Yield: 12 servings.

Per serving: Calories 749 (78% from fat); Fat 64.5g (sat 26.7g, mono 29.5g, poly 7.8g); Protein 37.5g; Carb 1.9g; Fiber 0.3g; Chol 167mg; Iron 4.1mg; Sodium 598mg; Calc 39mg

Spicy Horseradish Sauce

prep: 5 min.   other: 1 hr.

⅔ cup reduced-fat sour cream
3 tablespoons prepared horseradish
2 tablespoons light mayonnaise
1 tablespoon white wine vinegar
1 teaspoon dry mustard
¼ teaspoon salt
¼ teaspoon ground red pepper

Stir together all ingredients. Cover and chill 1 hour. Serve with beef, pork, steamed shrimp, as a sandwich spread, on baked potatoes, or as a dip. Yield: 1 cup.

Per tablespoon: Calories 22 (78% from fat); Fat 1.9g (sat 0.8g, mono 0.5g, poly 0.4g); Protein 0.4g; Carb 1g; Fiber 0.1g; Chol 5mg; Iron 0mg; Sodium 64mg; Calc 13mg

entertaining • low carb • make ahead

Holiday Beef Tenderloin

prep: 10 min.   cook: 35 min.   other: 8 hrs.

1 tablespoon salt
1½ teaspoons onion powder
1½ teaspoons garlic powder
1½ teaspoons black pepper
1 teaspoon ground red pepper
½ teaspoon ground cumin
½ teaspoon ground nutmeg
1 (5-pound) beef tenderloin, trimmed
¼ cup olive oil
Garnish: fresh herbs

Combine first 7 ingredients.
Rub tenderloin with oil; coat with spice mixture. Place in a roasting pan; cover and chill 8 hours.
Bake at 500° for 15 minutes or until lightly browned. Lower temperature to 375°; bake 20 more minutes or to desired degree of doneness. Let stand 10 minutes. Slice and serve with Spicy Horseradish Sauce (above), if desired. Garnish, if desired. Yield: 8 servings.

Per serving: Calories 526 (52% from fat); Fat 30.4g (sat 10.1g, mono 14.6g, poly 1.6g); Protein 58.5g; Carb 1.2g; Fiber 0.3g; Chol 177mg; Iron 4mg; Sodium 991mg; Calc 48mg

timetable for roasting beef

cut	approximate weight in pounds	internal temperature	approximate total cooking times in hours at 325°
Rib roast, bone-in	4	145° (medium rare)	1½
		160° (medium)	1¾
		170° (well-done)	2
	6	145° (medium rare)	2
		160° (medium)	2½
		170° (well-done)	3
Rib roast, boneless rolled	4	145° (medium rare)	1¾
		160° (medium)	2
		170° (well-done)	2½
	6	145° (medium rare)	2¾
		160° (medium)	3
		170° (well-done)	3½
Tenderloin, whole*	4 to 6	145° (medium rare)	¾ to 1
half*	2 to 3	145° (medium rare)	½ to ¾
Rolled rump	5	145° (medium rare)	2¼
		160° (medium)	3
		170° (well-done)	3¼
Sirloin tip	3	145° (medium rare)	1½
		160° (medium)	2
		170° (well-done)	2¼

*Roast at 425°

entertaining • low carb

Garlic-and-Rosemary Beef Tenderloin

prep: 10 min.   cook: 35 min.
other: 8 hrs., 40 min.

½ cup soy sauce
½ cup olive oil
¼ cup balsamic or red wine vinegar
8 garlic cloves, minced
4 teaspoons chopped fresh or dried rosemary
1 (5-pound) beef tenderloin, trimmed
1 tablespoon pepper

Combine first 5 ingredients in a large shallow dish or zip-top freezer bag; add beef. Cover or seal, and chill at least 8 hours, turning occasionally.
Remove beef from marinade, discarding marinade. Place in a roasting pan; sprinkle evenly with pepper; let stand 30 minutes.
Bake at 500° for 15 minutes or until lightly browned. Lower temperature to 375°; bake 20 more minutes or to desired degree of doneness. Let tenderloin stand 10 minutes before slicing. Yield: 8 servings.

Per serving: Calories 457 (42% from fat); Fat 21.2g (sat 7g, mono 10g, poly 1.1g); Protein 61g; Carb 1.5g; Fiber 0.3g; Chol 167mg; Iron 4.2mg; Sodium 465mg; Calc 45mg

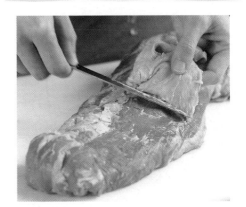

Trimming beef tenderloin: Use a sharp knife and gentle tension to cut away fat.

Beef Tenderloin With Pan-Roasted Pears

prep: 15 min.   cook: 33 min.

(pictured on page 289)

4	(6-ounce) beef tenderloin fillets
½	teaspoon salt
½	teaspoon pepper
2	tablespoons butter or margarine
2	tablespoons olive oil
4	Bartlett pears, halved
1	cup Madeira wine
1	garlic clove, pressed
1	teaspoon fresh thyme leaves or ¼ teaspoon dried thyme
4	ounces blue cheese

Sprinkle fillets with salt and pepper.
Melt butter with oil in a large skillet over medium-high heat; add fillets, and cook 5 minutes on each side or to desired degree of doneness. Remove fillets, and keep warm.
Add pear halves to skillet; cook over medium heat 5 minutes on each side or until browned. Add wine, garlic, and thyme; cook 5 minutes or until pear halves are tender. Remove pear halves from skillet, reserving wine mixture in skillet.
Cook wine mixture in skillet over high heat 6 minutes or until mixture reduces by half. **Stuff** each pear half with cheese. Serve with fillets; drizzle with sauce. Yield: 4 servings.

Per serving: Calories 732 (64% from fat); Fat 51.7g (sat 22.3g, mono 21.9g, poly 2.4g); Protein 40.3g; Carb 27.7g; Fiber 5.3g; Chol 149mg; Iron 3.2mg; Sodium 818mg; Calc 213mg

beef's most popular steaks

A fan of steak? According to the National Cattlemen's Beef Association, the most popular steaks for grilling are (in order):

1. Porterhouse/T-bone steak
2. Rib-eye steak
3. Sirloin steak
4. Tenderloin/Filet mignon
5. New York strip steak
6. Top round steak
7. Flank steak
8. Chuck steak
9. London broil

There are many reasons to appreciate tenderloin. Carved from an area where there's little fat surrounding or running through the meat, this succulent selection is leaner than many other choices. It's pricey, but the nutritional bonus and great flavor make it worth the cost. Remember to keep an eye on cooking time—you don't want to dry out this delicacy.

Beef Tenderloin in Wine Sauce

prep: 20 min.   cook: 50 min.   other: 10 min.

1	(3-pound) beef tenderloin, trimmed
½	teaspoon salt
½	teaspoon pepper
½	cup butter or margarine
1	onion, thinly sliced
1	garlic clove, minced
1	(8-ounce) package sliced fresh mushrooms
½	cup dry red wine
1½	teaspoons Worcestershire sauce
1	teaspoon Italian seasoning
1	teaspoon hot sauce
1	cup beef broth
1	teaspoon all-purpose flour

Sprinkle beef with salt and pepper. Place in an aluminum foil-lined roasting pan.
Bake at 450° for 15 minutes.
Melt butter in a medium saucepan over medium heat. Add onion, garlic, and mushrooms; sauté 7 minutes. Stir in wine and next 3 ingredients. Whisk together beef broth and flour, and stir into wine mixture. Reduce heat, and simmer, stirring occasionally, 10 minutes or until onion is tender.
Remove beef from oven, and top with sauce. Bake beef 18 more minutes or to desired degree of doneness, basting once. Transfer beef to a serving platter, reserving sauce in pan. Let beef stand 10 minutes before slicing. Serve with sauce. Yield: 6 servings.

Per serving: Calories 505 (54% from fat); Fat 30.1g (sat 15.1g, mono 9.9g, poly 1.2g); Protein 52.7g; Carb 4.5g; Fiber 0.9g; Chol 192mg; Iron 4.8mg; Sodium 615mg; Calc 75mg

Mini Beef Wellingtons

prep: 35 min.   cook: 1 hr., 6 min.

6½	tablespoons butter or margarine, divided
8	(3-ounce) beef tenderloin fillets, 1 inch thick
¼	teaspoon salt
¼	teaspoon pepper
3	large fresh mushrooms, chopped
1	(8-ounce) package fresh mushrooms, chopped
2	tablespoons dry sherry or beef broth
1	(17¼-ounce) package frozen puff pastry sheets, thawed
1	egg white, lightly beaten
1½	tablespoons all-purpose flour
1	tablespoon tomato paste
2	(14-ounce) cans beef broth
1	bay leaf, crushed

Melt 3 tablespoons butter in a large skillet over medium heat; add beef, and cook 3 minutes on each side or until browned.
Remove from skillet; sprinkle with salt and pepper, and let cool.
Melt 2 tablespoons butter in skillet; add mushrooms, and sauté 5 minutes. Stir in sherry.
Unfold pastry sheets on a lightly floured surface; roll to ⅛-inch thickness, and cut into fourths. Place 1 fillet in center of each square; top with mushroom mixture. Bring opposite corners of squares together over beef, pressing gently to seal. Place on a baking sheet; brush with egg white.
Bake at 425° on lowest oven rack for 25 to 30 minutes or until golden.
Melt remaining 1½ tablespoons butter in skillet; whisk in flour. Cook, whisking constantly, 2 to 3 minutes or until lightly

browned. Add tomato paste; cook, stirring constantly, 1 to 2 minutes. Gradually whisk in broth. Add bay leaf; simmer 20 minutes. Pour through a wire-mesh strainer into a bowl. Serve sauce with Beef Wellingtons. Yield: 8 servings.

Per serving: Calories 580 (64% from fat); Fat 41.1g (sat 16.6g, mono 12.8g, poly 10.7g); Protein 26.1g; Carb 25.4g; Fiber 1.7g; Chol 81mg; Iron 3.2mg; Sodium 1282mg; Calc 25mg

---

from the grill • low carb • quick

Peppered Rib-Eye Steaks

prep: 5 min.   cook: 16 min.   other: 1 hr.

A mix of black, red, and lemon peppers gives this steak its lively flavor.

3   teaspoons garlic powder
3   teaspoons dried thyme
2   teaspoons ground black pepper
1½ teaspoons salt
1½ teaspoons lemon pepper
1½ teaspoons ground red pepper
1½ teaspoons dried parsley flakes
6   (1½-inch-thick) rib-eye steaks or hanger steaks
3   tablespoons olive oil

Combine first 7 ingredients. Brush steaks with oil; rub with seasoning mixture. Cover and chill 1 hour.
Grill steaks, covered with grill lid, over medium-high heat (350° to 400°) 6 to 8 minutes on each side or to desired degree of doneness. Yield: 6 servings.

Per serving: Calories 608 (60% from fat); Fat 40.8g (sat 14.1g, mono 18.9g, poly 2g); Protein 54.3g; Carb 2.4g; Fiber 0.9g; Chol 255mg; Iron 4.5mg; Sodium 805mg; Calc 52mg

---

family favorite • from the grill

Molasses-Grilled Rib-Eye Steaks

prep: 10 min.   cook: 14 min.   other: 2 hrs.

Serve this flavorful entrée with mashed potatoes and a salad.

½   cup molasses
¼   cup coarse-grain Dijon mustard
1   tablespoon olive oil
4   (10-ounce) boneless rib-eye steaks
¾   teaspoon salt
¾   teaspoon pepper

Combine ½ cup molasses, ¼ cup mustard, and 1 tablespoon olive oil in a shallow dish or large zip-top freezer bag. Add steaks; cover or seal, and chill at least 2 hours, turning occasionally. Remove steaks from marinade, discarding marinade. Sprinkle steaks with salt and pepper.
Grill, covered with grill lid, over medium-high heat (350° to 400°) 5 to 7 minutes on each side or to desired degree of doneness. Yield: 4 servings.

Per serving: Calories 622 (53% from fat); Fat 36.2g (sat 13.4g, mono 15.2g, poly 1.5g); Protein 54.3g; Carb 16.8g; Fiber 0.4g; Chol 255mg; Iron 4.9mg; Sodium 705mg; Calc 86mg

---

entertaining • freeze it • make ahead

Beach Barbecue

prep: 20 min.   cook: 3 hrs.   other: 10 min.

You can prepare and freeze both this meat and sauce. To reheat, place in a 13- x 9-inch baking dish. Cover and bake at 350° for 30 minutes or until bubbly.

1   (4-pound) eye of round roast
1   teaspoon salt
3   (8-ounce) cans tomato sauce
1   (12-ounce) bottle chili sauce
1   medium onion, chopped
½   cup white vinegar
¼   cup firmly packed light brown sugar
¼   cup butter or margarine
¼   cup lemon juice
2   tablespoons Worcestershire sauce
½   teaspoon dry mustard
½   teaspoon chili powder
½   teaspoon paprika
10 hamburger buns

Place roast in a large Dutch oven, and sprinkle with salt; add water to cover, and bring to a boil. Cover, reduce heat to medium, and cook 2 hours or until tender, adding more water as needed after 1 hour.
Stir together tomato sauce and next 10 ingredients in a large saucepan; bring to a boil. Reduce heat to low, and simmer 1 hour, stirring occasionally.
Remove roast from Dutch oven, and let stand 10 minutes before serving. Shred or slice meat, and serve on hamburger buns with sauce. Yield: 10 servings.

Per serving: Calories 480 (25% from fat); Fat 13.3g (sat 5.7g, mono 4.5g, poly 1.4g); Protein 45.1g; Carb 43.4g; Fiber 2g; Chol 86mg; Iron 5.7mg; Sodium 1710mg; Calc 92mg

---

low calorie • low carb • low fat

Roasted Lime-Cilantro Eye of Round Roast

prep: 15 min.   cook: 3 hrs., 15 min.
other: 8 hrs., 10 min.

We enjoyed this spice- and-herb-seasoned shredded roast with warm tortillas, fat-free sour cream, Pico de Gallo (page 301), and an extra squeeze of fresh lime juice.

8   garlic cloves
1   jalapeño pepper, seeded
¼   cup chopped fresh cilantro
¼   cup lime juice
1   tablespoon coriander seeds
1   tablespoon cumin seeds
1   tablespoon coarse salt
1   tablespoon olive oil
1   (4.5-pound) eye of round roast
Garnishes: fresh cilantro sprigs, lime wedges
Corn tortillas (optional)
Sour cream (optional)
Pico de Gallo (optional) (page 301)

Process first 8 ingredients in a food processor until a thick paste forms, stopping to scrape down sides.
Make 3 to 4 (1-inch) cuts in each side of roast with a sharp knife. Fill each cut with about 1 teaspoon of paste. Spread remaining paste over beef. Wrap tightly with plastic wrap; chill at least 8 hours or up to 24 hours. Unwrap roast; place in a 13- x 9-inch pan.
Bake, covered, at 325° for 3 hours and 15 minutes or until meat shreds and a meat thermometer inserted into thickest portion registers 180°. (Meat will not shred below this temperature.) Let stand 10 minutes before shredding or chopping. Garnish, if desired. If desired, serve with corn tortillas, sour cream, and Pico de Gallo. Yield: 12 servings.

Per serving (meat only): Calories 234 (29% from fat); Fat 7.5g (sat 2.4g, mono 3.6g, poly 0.4g); Protein 37.7g; Carb 1.8g; Fiber 0.4g; Chol 69mg; Iron 3.5mg; Sodium 530mg; Calc 22mg

beef made simple

Many cheaper cuts come from the chuck (front) or round (hind) area, both of which tend to be tough. Chuck roasts include shoulder, seven-bone, and chuck eye, while round roasts include eye of round, boneless rump, and top or bottom round. Slow, moist-heat cooking tenderizes them.

Pot Roast With Mushroom Gravy

prep: 25 min.   cook: 3 hrs., 45 min.

Substitute less-expensive chuck roast for rump roast, if desired.

1   (3½-pound) boneless beef rump roast, trimmed
2   large garlic cloves, thinly sliced
1   teaspoon salt
1   teaspoon garlic salt
1   teaspoon pepper
¼   cup all-purpose flour
3   tablespoons vegetable oil
2   cups brewed coffee
1   (10¾-ounce) can cream of mushroom soup
1   tablespoon Worcestershire sauce
1   large onion, sliced
3   tablespoons cornstarch
3   tablespoons water

Cut slits in roast, using a sharp knife; push a garlic slice into each slit. Sprinkle roast with salts and pepper; lightly dredge in flour, patting off excess flour.

Brown roast on all sides in hot oil over medium-high heat in a large Dutch oven. Stir together coffee, soup, and Worcestershire sauce; pour over roast.

Top with onion. Reduce heat, cover, and simmer 3 hours and 40 minutes or until tender. Transfer roast to a serving platter, reserving drippings in Dutch oven; keep roast warm.

Combine cornstarch and 3 tablespoons water; stir into drippings. Bring mixture to a boil, and cook, stirring constantly, 1 minute or until thickened. Pour gravy over roast. Yield: 8 servings.

Per serving: Calories 501 (56% from fat); Fat 31.2g (sat 10.4g, mono 11.7g, poly 4.8g); Protein 41.8g; Carb 11.5g; Fiber 0.8g; Chol 125mg; Iron 4.4mg; Sodium 814mg; Calc 20mg

---

family favorite • make ahead • slow cooker

Italian Pot Roast

prep: 15 min.   cook: 6 hrs., 40 min.

Chuck roast is one of the most economical cuts of beef for pot roast, but it's a high-fat choice. Substitute eye of round or English shoulder roast for a lower fat choice.

8   ounces sliced fresh mushrooms
1   large onion, cut in half and sliced
1   (2½- to 3-pound) boneless beef chuck roast, trimmed
1   teaspoon pepper
2   tablespoons olive oil
1   (1-ounce) envelope dry onion soup mix
1   (14-ounce) can beef broth
1   (8-ounce) can tomato sauce
1   teaspoon dried Italian seasoning
3   tablespoons tomato paste
2   tablespoons cornstarch
2   tablespoons water
3   cups hot cooked egg noodles

Place mushrooms and onion in a 5½-quart slow cooker. Sprinkle roast evenly with pepper. Brown roast on all sides in hot oil in a Dutch oven over medium-high heat. Place roast on mushrooms and onion in slow cooker.

Sprinkle onion soup mix evenly over roast. Pour beef broth and tomato sauce over roast. Cover and cook on HIGH 5 to 6 hours or until meat shreds easily with a fork.

Remove roast from slow cooker, and cut into large chunks; keep warm.

Skim fat from juices in slow cooker; stir in Italian seasoning and tomato paste. Stir together cornstarch and 2 tablespoons water until smooth; add to juices in slow cooker, stirring until blended. Cover and cook on HIGH 20 to 30 more minutes or until thickened. Add roast pieces back to slow cooker. Cover and cook until thoroughly heated. Serve over egg noodles. Yield: 6 servings.

Per serving: Calories 593 (46% from fat); Fat 30.4g (sat 10.5g, mono 14.2g, poly 1.9g); Protein 45.2g; Carb 33.9g; Fiber 2.8g; Chol 120mg; Iron 4.6mg; Sodium 1257mg; Calc 46mg

---

family favorite

Beef Bourguignon

prep: 25 min.   cook: 2 hrs., 48 min.
other: 3 hrs.

1   (4-pound) boneless beef chuck roast, cut into 2-inch cubes
2½   cups dry red wine
8   bacon slices
Bouquet garni*
2   carrots, finely chopped
3   tablespoons butter or margarine, melted
3   tablespoons all-purpose flour
1   (14-ounce) can beef broth
1   teaspoon salt
¼   teaspoon freshly ground pepper
1   garlic clove, minced
1   (16-ounce) package frozen pearl onions, thawed
3   tablespoons butter or margarine, melted
1   pound small fresh mushrooms
2   tablespoons finely chopped fresh parsley
6   cups hot cooked rice or egg noodles

Combine beef cubes and wine in a large zip-top freezer bag; seal bag. Marinate in refrigerator 2 to 3 hours.

Cook bacon in a large skillet over medium heat until crisp. Drain and coarsely crumble bacon, reserving drippings in skillet.

Strain beef, reserving wine. Pat beef dry with paper towels. Brown beef, in batches, in drippings in skillet over medium heat. Transfer beef to a greased 5-quart baking dish. Add bouquet garni; set aside.

Sauté carrot in 3 tablespoons butter in skillet until tender. Add flour; cook 1 minute, stirring constantly. Gradually stir in beef broth and reserved wine. Bring to a boil; cook, stirring constantly, until thickened. Stir in salt, pepper, and garlic. Pour over beef mixture. Cover and bake at 325° for 2½ hours or until meat is tender.

Meanwhile, brown onions in 3 tablespoons butter in skillet over medium heat, stirring often. Remove onions with a slotted spoon, reserving drippings in skillet. Set onions aside. Cook mushrooms in drippings in skillet 2 to 3 minutes, stirring often. Remove from heat, and set aside.

After beef has baked until tender, stir reserved bacon, onions, mushrooms with drippings, and parsley into beef mixture.

Bake, uncovered, 15 more minutes. Remove bouquet garni. Serve beef mixture over hot cooked rice. Yield: 8 servings.

Per serving: Calories 947 (58% from fat); Fat 60.4g (sat 25.4g, mono 24.3g, poly 3.2g); Protein 53.6g; Carb 44.9g; Fiber 2.3g; Chol 188mg; Iron 7mg; Sodium 1376mg; Calc 74mg

*A bouquet garni is a small bundle of fresh herb sprigs such as parsley, thyme, and bay leaves tied together with kitchen twine.

family favorite
Beef Stroganoff

prep: 20 min.   cook: 1 hr., 10 min.

Serve steamed broccoli tossed with melted butter and lemon pepper with this hearty main dish.

1½ pounds sirloin beef tips
½ teaspoon salt
½ teaspoon pepper
3 tablespoons vegetable oil
2 medium-size sweet onions, diced
2 (8-ounce) packages sliced fresh mushrooms
2 cups beef broth
2 tablespoons tomato paste
1 teaspoon Dijon mustard
1 (16-ounce) package egg noodles
½ cup sherry
2 tablespoons all-purpose flour
1 (8-ounce) container sour cream
2 tablespoons chopped fresh parsley (optional)

Sprinkle beef tips with salt and pepper.
Cook beef in hot oil in a large skillet over medium-high heat; add onions and mushrooms, and sauté 3 to 5 minutes or until tender.
Stir broth, tomato paste, and mustard into beef mixture. Cover, reduce heat to low, and cook 1 hour or until beef is tender.
Cook noodles according to package directions; drain.
Combine sherry and flour; stir into beef mixture, and cook, stirring constantly, until thickened. Stir in sour cream. Serve over hot cooked egg noodles; sprinkle with parsley, if desired. Yield: 4 servings.

Per serving: Calories 920 (38% from fat); Fat 38.8g (sat 13.1g, mono 11.6g, poly 9.4g); Protein 57.4g; Carb 86.6g; Fiber 5.8g; Chol 178mg; Iron 9.9mg; Sodium 1425mg; Calc 172mg

Cajun Pepper Steak

prep: 20 min.   cook: 1 hr., 20 min.

You can prep this recipe in 20 minutes, then walk away for an hour or so while slow simmering tenderizes the beef.

1½ pounds sirloin beef tips
1 teaspoon salt-free Cajun seasoning
1 tablespoon vegetable oil
1 medium-size green bell pepper, chopped
1 onion, chopped
3 garlic cloves, minced
1 (14-ounce) can beef broth
1 (14½-ounce) can diced tomatoes, undrained
2 teaspoons Worcestershire sauce
1 teaspoon white wine vinegar
½ teaspoon dried basil
¼ teaspoon salt
⅛ teaspoon pepper
1 (22-ounce) package frozen mashed potatoes
2 tablespoons cornstarch
2 tablespoons cold water

Sprinkle beef tips with Cajun seasoning.
Cook beef in hot oil in a large skillet over medium-high heat 10 minutes or until browned. Add bell pepper, onion, and garlic; sauté 3 minutes. Stir in broth and next 6 ingredients. Bring to a boil; reduce heat, cover, and simmer 1 hour or until meat is tender.
Cook potatoes according to directions.
Stir together cornstarch and water until smooth; stir into meat mixture. Bring to a boil; cook, stirring constantly, 2 minutes or until thickened. Serve over mashed potatoes. Yield: 4 servings.

Per serving: Calories 641 (35% from fat); Fat 24.7g (sat 8.3g, mono 8g, poly 3.2g); Protein 48.3g; Carb 59g; Fiber 6.9g; Chol 93mg; Iron 5mg; Sodium 1247mg; Calc 245mg

from the grill • low carb
Steak-and-Shrimp Kabobs

prep: 16 min.   cook: 12 min.
other: 2 hrs., 20 min.

½ cup dry sherry
½ cup olive oil
¼ cup grated orange rind
½ cup fresh orange juice
¼ cup soy sauce
4 garlic cloves, minced
2 tablespoons minced fresh ginger
½ teaspoon dried crushed red pepper (optional)
1½ pounds rib-eye steak, cut into 1-inch cubes
16 unpeeled jumbo fresh shrimp
4 cups mixed salad greens

Whisk together sherry, next 6 ingredients, and, if desired, crushed red pepper. Reserve 1 cup sherry mixture. Pour remaining mixture into a shallow dish or large zip-top freezer bag; add steak. Cover or seal, and chill 2 hours.
Peel shrimp, and devein, if desired. Add to steak mixture; cover or seal, and chill 20 minutes.
Remove beef and shrimp from marinade, discarding marinade. Thread beef and shrimp alternately onto 4 (12-inch) skewers.
Grill, covered with grill lid, over medium-high heat (350° to 400°) 10 to 12 minutes or until done. Serve kabobs over salad greens with reserved 1 cup sherry mixture. Yield: 4 servings.

Per serving: Calories 593 (63% from fat); Fat 41.5g (sat 10.9g, mono 23.2g, poly 3.2g); Protein 46.2g; Carb 7.5g; Fiber 2g; Chol 257mg; Iron 5.2mg; Sodium 955mg; Calc 92mg

Teriyaki Beef Broil

prep: 20 min.   cook: 6 min.   other: 1 hr.

1¾ pounds top round steak (1 inch thick)
¼ cup soy sauce
¼ cup vegetable oil
2 tablespoons molasses
2 teaspoons ground ginger
2 teaspoons dry mustard
6 garlic cloves, minced
Fresh chives (optional)

Partially freeze steak; slice diagonally across the grain into ¼-inch-thick slices. Place steak in a zip-top freezer bag or shallow dish. Combine soy sauce and next 5 ingredients; pour over steak. Seal or cover, and marinate in refrigerator 1 hour.
Remove steak from marinade, discarding marinade. Thread steak onto 8 (10-inch) bamboo skewers. Place skewers on a lightly greased rack of a broiler pan.
Broil 5½ inches from heat 5 to 6 minutes, turning once. Sprinkle with chives, if desired. Yield: 4 servings.

Per serving: Calories 401 (47% from fat); Fat 20.7g (sat 6g, mono 7.1g, poly 5g); Protein 46.2g; Carb 5.6g; Fiber 0.2g; Chol 85mg; Iron 4.3mg; Sodium 565mg; Calc 29mg

Thai Lemon Beef

prep: 12 min.   cook: 8 min.   other: 30 min.

1½ pounds top round steak (1 inch thick)
⅓ cup soy sauce
¼ cup lemon juice
¼ cup water
2 to 3 teaspoons dried crushed red pepper
4 garlic cloves, minced
1 tablespoon vegetable oil
4 green onions, cut into 2-inch pieces
2 carrots, thinly sliced
2 teaspoons cornstarch
4 cups hot cooked ramen noodles or rice

Cut steak diagonally across the grain into ⅛-inch-thick strips, and place in a bowl.
Combine soy sauce and next 4 ingredients. Reserve half of marinade. Pour remaining marinade over steak. Marinate in refrigerator 30 minutes. Drain steak; discard marinade.
Stir-fry half of steak in ½ tablespoon hot oil in a large nonstick skillet or wok over medium-high heat 1 minute or until outside of

beef is no longer pink. Remove from skillet; repeat procedure with remaining steak and oil. Remove from skillet; set aside.
Add green onions and carrot slices to skillet; stir-fry 3 minutes or until crisp-tender.
Whisk cornstarch into reserved soy sauce mixture; stir into vegetables, and stir-fry until thickened. Add steak; stir-fry until thoroughly heated. Serve over hot cooked noodles or rice. Yield: 4 servings.

Per serving: Calories 465 (35% from fat); Fat 18g (sat 6g, mono 6.9g, poly 3.1g); Protein 42.9g; Carb 31.4g; Fiber 3.5g; Chol 68mg; Iron 4.3mg; Sodium 1113mg; Calc 76mg

Chicken-Fried Steak

prep: 15 min.   cook: 18 min.

¼ teaspoon salt
¼ teaspoon pepper
4 (4-ounce) cubed steaks
38 saltine crackers, crushed (about 1 sleeve)
1¼ cups all-purpose flour, divided
2 teaspoons salt, divided
1½ teaspoons ground black pepper, divided
½ teaspoon ground red pepper
½ teaspoon baking powder
4¾ cups milk, divided
2 large eggs
1 cup peanut oil

Sprinkle ¼ teaspoon salt and ¼ teaspoon pepper evenly over steaks.
Combine crackers, 1 cup flour, 1 teaspoon salt, ½ teaspoon black pepper, red pepper, and baking powder. Whisk together ¾ cup milk and eggs. Dredge steaks in cracker mixture; dip in milk mixture, and dredge again in cracker mixture.
Pour oil into a 12-inch skillet; heat to 360°. (Do not use a nonstick skillet.) Fry steaks 2 to 3 minutes or until golden. Turn and fry steaks 2 to 3 minutes or until golden. Remove steaks to a wire rack in a jelly-roll pan. Keep steaks warm in a 225° oven. Carefully drain hot oil, reserving cooked bits and 1 tablespoon drippings in skillet.
Whisk remaining 4 cups milk, ¼ cup flour, 1 teaspoon salt, and 1 teaspoon black pepper. Add to reserved drippings in skillet; cook, whisking constantly, over medium-high heat, 10 to 12 minutes or until thickened. Serve over steaks. Yield: 4 servings.

Per serving: Calories 765 (52% from fat); Fat 44.3g (sat 14.6g, mono 18.1g, poly 7.2g); Protein 40.7g; Carb 49.2g; Fiber 1.6g; Chol 201mg; Iron 5.2mg; Sodium 1360mg; Calc 406mg

new steaks sizzle

Two new steaks are gaining popularity.

1. Flat iron steak comes from the shoulder blade and is tender enough to grill, broil, or pan-fry, but marinate it first. It's great for fajitas.
2. The Hanger steak comes from near the center of the diaphragm between the last rib and the loin. It has a grainy texture and intense flavor that makes it a first-rate steak, but it also needs to be marinated before cooking.

Beef Fajitas With Pico de Gallo

prep: 5 min.   cook: 10 min.   other: 8 hrs.

1 (8-ounce) bottle zesty Italian dressing
3 tablespoons fajita seasoning (we tested with McCormick Fajita Seasoning)
2 (1-pound) flank steaks or flat iron steaks
12 (6-inch) flour tortillas, warmed
Shredded Cheddar cheese
Pico de Gallo (opposite page)
Garnishes: lime wedges, fresh cilantro sprigs

Combine Italian dressing and fajita seasoning in a shallow dish or large zip-top freezer bag; add steak. Cover or seal, and chill 8 hours, turning occasionally. Remove steak from marinade, discarding marinade.
Grill steaks, covered with grill lid, over medium-high heat (350° to 400°) for 8 minutes. Turn and grill 5 more minutes or to desired degree of doneness. Remove steaks, and let stand 5 minutes.
Cut steaks diagonally across the grain into very thin slices, and serve with tortillas, cheese, and Pico de Gallo. Garnish, if desired. Yield: 6 servings.

Per serving: Calories 665 (47% from fat); Fat 34.5g (sat 12.8g, mono 13.4g, poly 3.4g); Protein 45.1g; Carb 43g; Fiber 5.9g; Chol 87mg; Iron 5mg; Sodium 1318mg; Calc 326mg

Pico de Gallo

prep: 25 min.　other: 1 hr.

1　pint grape tomatoes, chopped
1　green bell pepper, chopped
1　red bell pepper, chopped
1　avocado, peeled and chopped
½　medium-size red onion, chopped
½　cup chopped fresh cilantro
1　garlic clove, pressed
¾　teaspoon salt
½　teaspoon ground cumin
½　teaspoon grated lime rind
¼　cup fresh lime juice

Stir together all ingredients; cover and chill 1 hour. Yield: 3 cups.

Per tablespoon: Calories 10 (63% from fat); Fat 0.7g (sat 0.1g, mono 0.4g, poly 0.1g); Protein 0.2g; Carb 1.1g; Fiber 0.5g; Chol 0mg; Iron 0.1mg; Sodium 37mg; Calc 2mg

---

low calorie • low carb
Flank Steak With Tomato-Olive Relish

prep: 10 min.　cook: 27 min.

1½　pounds flank steak
¾　teaspoon salt
¾　teaspoon coarsely ground pepper
3　tablespoons olive oil
2　garlic cloves, thinly sliced
½　cup red wine or chicken broth
1　(14½-ounce) can Italian-style diced tomatoes
½　cup pitted oil-cured black olives, sliced
1　tablespoon balsamic vinegar
3　tablespoons minced fresh parsley

Sprinkle flank steak with salt and pepper.
Cook steak in hot oil in a large skillet over medium-high heat 6 to 8 minutes on each side or to desired degree of doneness.

---

against the grain

Use an electric knife or sharp chef's knife and place it at an angle against the grain of the meat. Slice into very thin slices. The angle of the knife cutting thin slices across the meat fibers produces tender results. This slicing technique applies whether it's a partially frozen, raw piece of meat or a grilled flank steak.

Drain, reserving 1 tablespoon drippings in skillet; add garlic, and sauté 1 minute. Add wine, tomatoes, olives, and vinegar; cook 10 minutes or until reduced by half. Stir in parsley. Cut steak diagonally across the grain into thin slices, and serve with tomato mixture. Yield: 6 servings.

Per serving: Calories 280 (50% from fat); Fat 15.7g (sat 4.4g, mono 8.9g, poly 1.1g); Protein 25g; Carb 8.5g; Fiber 0.7g; Chol 40mg; Iron 2.6mg; Sodium 804mg; Calc 74mg

---

family favorite • from the grill • low carb
Italian Sirloin Steaks

prep: 15 min.　cook: 9 min.　other: 2 hrs.

4　garlic cloves, pressed
¼　cup olive oil
2　teaspoons dried basil
2　teaspoons dried oregano
2　teaspoons dried parsley
1　teaspoon fresh or dried rosemary
2　(¾-inch-thick) top sirloin steaks (about 2 pounds)
1¼　teaspoons salt, divided
1　teaspoon pepper

Stir together first 6 ingredients. Sprinkle steaks evenly with 1 teaspoon salt and pepper; rub with garlic mixture. Cover and chill steaks at least 2 hours. Sprinkle steaks evenly with remaining ¼ teaspoon salt.
Grill steaks, covered with grill lid, over medium-high heat (350° to 400°) 7 minutes on each side or to desired degree of doneness. Cut steaks in half. Yield: 4 servings.

Per serving: Calories 400 (52% from fat); Fat 22.5g (sat 5.3g, mono 13.4g, poly 1.8g); Protein 45.1g; Carb 2.1g; Fiber 0.8g; Chol 83mg; Iron 3.9mg; Sodium 822mg; Calc 62mg

---

from the grill • low carb (without bun)
Smoked Brisket

prep: 15 min.　cook: 3 hrs., 30 min.　other: 1 hr.

Hickory wood chunks
2　tablespoons fresh or dried rosemary
2　tablespoons paprika
2　tablespoons pepper
2　tablespoons dried garlic flakes
1　teaspoon salt
1　(7-pound) untrimmed beef brisket

Soak wood chunks in water for at least 1 hour. Prepare charcoal fire in smoker; let burn 15 to 20 minutes.

Combine rosemary and next 4 ingredients; rub on brisket.
Drain wood chunks, and place on coals. Place water pan in smoker; add water to depth of fill line. Place brisket on lower food rack; cover with smoker lid.
Cook 3 hours and 30 minutes or until meat thermometer inserted into thickest portion registers 155°. Yield: 12 servings.

Per serving: Calories 620 (71% from fat); Fat 48.7g (sat 19.2g, mono 21.6g, poly 1.7g); Protein 40.6g; Carb 2.3g; Fiber 0.9g; Chol 157mg; Iron 4.5mg; Sodium 312mg; Calc 23mg

---

All-American Meat Loaf

prep: 7 min.　cook: 55 min.

2　pounds ground chuck
¾　cup uncooked quick-cooking oats
1　medium onion, finely chopped
½　cup ketchup
¼　cup milk
2　large eggs, lightly beaten
1　teaspoon salt
½　teaspoon pepper
½　cup ketchup
3　tablespoons brown sugar
2　teaspoons prepared mustard

Combine first 8 ingredients in a large bowl; shape into 2 (7½- x 4-inch) loaves. Place on a lightly greased rack in a broiler pan; bake at 350° for 40 minutes.
Combine ½ cup ketchup, sugar, and mustard. Spoon over meat loaf; bake 15 minutes or until a thermometer inserted into thickest portion registers 160°. Yield: 8 servings.

Per serving: Calories 390 (58% from fat); Fat 25g (sat 9.4g, mono 10.7g, poly 1.1g); Protein 23g; Carb 18.2g; Fiber 1.2g; Chol 134mg; Iron 3.1mg; Sodium 725mg; Calc 51mg

---

Horseradish Meat Loaf: Add 1 tablespoon prepared horseradish to beef mixture and 1 tablespoon horseradish to ketchup topping.

Serve Smoked Brisket with barbecue sauce, hamburger buns, pickles, and bowls of potato salad, baked beans, and slaw.

meat loaf tips

- Mince (very finely chop) the bell pepper and onion. Large pieces cause the loaf to crumble.
- Don't take a shortcut and substitute dry breadcrumbs for soft, or the loaf will be dry. To make soft breadcrumbs, pulse about 8 slices of sandwich bread in a food processor until finely crumbled (yields 4 cups).

---

freeze it • make ahead

Spicy Three-Meat Meat Loaf

prep: 35 min.   cook: 1 hr., 15 min.
other: 10 min.

Make free-form loaves and bake on a broiler pan, or to get more uniform loaves, ideal for sandwiches, bake in two loafpans.

2	pounds ground round
1	pound ground pork
¾	cup finely chopped smoked ham
1	large green bell pepper, minced
1	small onion, minced (about 1 cup)
2	large eggs, lightly beaten
4	cups soft breadcrumbs
⅓	cup ketchup
¼	cup firmly packed light brown sugar
¼	cup maple syrup
3	tablespoons Worcestershire sauce
2	tablespoons hot sauce
1	(15-ounce) can tomato sauce
4	bacon slices

Combine first 12 ingredients in a large bowl; shape into 2 (9- x 4-inch) loaves. Place on a lightly greased rack in a broiler pan. Pour tomato sauce evenly over each loaf, and arrange 2 bacon slices over each.
Bake at 350° for 1 hour and 15 minutes or until a meat thermometer inserted into thickest portion registers 160°. Let meat loaf stand 10 minutes before serving. Yield: 10 servings (2 loaves).

Per serving: Calories 467 (48% from fat); Fat 25g (sat 9.2g, mono 10.7g, poly 2.1g); Protein 31.9g; Carb 28.1g; Fiber 1.5g; Chol 145mg; Iron 4.4mg; Sodium 810mg; Calc 76mg

Note: To make ahead, omit tomato sauce and bacon. Wrap unbaked meat loaf in plastic wrap and foil. Freeze up to 1 month. Thaw in refrigerator overnight, unwrap, and proceed as directed.

Salisbury Steak

prep: 10 min.   cook: 35 min.

Serve this home-style recipe with mashed potatoes or Texas toast.

1	(10¾-ounce) can golden mushroom soup, divided
1½	pounds ground beef
½	cup finely chopped onion
¼	cup Italian-seasoned breadcrumbs
1	large egg, beaten
1	(8-ounce) package sliced fresh mushrooms
⅓	cup beef broth
¼	cup Worcestershire sauce
¼	teaspoon pepper

Combine ¼ cup soup, beef, and next 3 ingredients; stir well. Shape mixture into 6 (½-inch-thick) patties.
Brown patties in a large skillet over medium-high heat. Remove patties, discarding half of pan drippings. Cook mushrooms in remaining drippings in skillet over medium-high heat, stirring constantly, until tender.
Combine remaining soup, beef broth, Worcestershire sauce, and pepper; add to mushroom mixture.
Return patties to skillet; bring to a boil. Cover, reduce heat, and simmer 20 minutes. Yield: 6 servings.

Per serving: Calories 374 (61% from fat); Fat 25.4g (sat 9.4g, mono 10.3g, poly 0.8g); Protein 23.5g; Carb 12.3g; Fiber 1.3g; Chol 118mg; Iron 3.4mg; Sodium 787mg; Calc 51mg

---

family favorite • quick

Sweet Sloppy Joes

prep: 5 min.   cook: 23 min.

1½	pounds ground beef
1	small onion, chopped
1	small green bell pepper, chopped
1	(10¾-ounce) can tomato soup
1	(8-ounce) can tomato sauce
1	cup ketchup
2	tablespoons brown sugar
1	tablespoon Worcestershire sauce
1	tablespoon white vinegar or cider vinegar
1	teaspoon prepared mustard
⅛	teaspoon garlic powder
4	sesame seed hamburger buns, toasted

Cook first 3 ingredients in a large skillet, stirring until beef crumbles and is no longer

pink; drain. Stir in soup and next 7 ingredients; simmer 10 to 15 minutes, stirring often. Serve on toasted buns. Yield: 4 servings.

Per serving: Calories 716 (47% from fat); Fat 37.7g (sat 13.8g, mono 15.8g, poly 2.6g); Protein 36.7g; Carb 59.2g; Fiber 3.2g; Chol 121mg; Iron 7.1mg; Sodium 1752mg; Calc 131mg

---

family favorite • for kids • from the grill • quick

Basic Burgers

prep: 7 min.   cook: 15 min.

1	pound ground chuck
1	large egg, beaten
¼	cup soft breadcrumbs
1	tablespoon grated onion
½	teaspoon all-purpose Greek seasoning
¼	teaspoon salt
¼	teaspoon pepper
2	teaspoons Worcestershire sauce
4	hamburger buns

Combine first 8 ingredients, blending well. Shape into 4 patties. Grill, without grill lid, over medium heat (300° to 350°) 12 to 15 minutes or until done, turning once. Serve on buns. Yield: 4 servings.

Per serving: Calories 437 (53% from fat); Fat 25.9g (sat 9.6g, mono 10.9g, poly 1.7g); Protein 25.4g; Carb 23.7g; Fiber 1g; Chol 134mg; Iron 4.2mg; Sodium 502mg; Calc 95mg

For broiling: Place patties on broiler pan; broil 3 inches from heat 8 to 10 minutes or until done, turning once.

For pan-frying: Heat a heavy skillet until hot. Add patties, and cook over medium heat about 8 minutes or until done, turning once.

---

about ground beef

Ground beef contains varying amounts of fat depending on the type of cut used. For recipes in this book that call for ground beef, we tested with and analyzed for ground chuck, which gets about 20 percent of its calories from fat. Ground round is a leaner cut, with about 10 percent of its calories from fat, while some packages labeled as "ground beef" can contain 30 to 35 percent fat.

Smothered Enchiladas

prep: 10 min.   cook: 30 min.

2   pounds ground beef
1   (1¼-ounce) package mild taco seasoning
    mix
1   (4.5-ounce) can chopped green chiles,
    divided
2   (10¾-ounce) cans cream of chicken soup
1   (16-ounce) container sour cream
8   (8-inch) flour tortillas
2   cups (8 ounces) shredded Cheddar cheese
Garnishes: salsa, sour cream, green onion
    curls, chopped fresh cilantro

Cook ground beef in a large skillet, stirring
until it crumbles and is no longer pink;
drain. Stir in taco seasoning mix and half of
chopped green chiles; set aside.
Stir together remaining green chiles, soup,
and sour cream. Pour half of sour cream
mixture into a lightly greased 13- x 9-inch
baking dish. Spoon beef mixture evenly
down center of each tortilla; roll up. Place
tortillas, seam sides down, over sour cream
mixture in baking dish; top with remaining
sour cream mixture and cheese.
Bake, uncovered, at 350° for 25 minutes or
until thoroughly heated. Garnish, if desired.
Yield: 8 servings.

Per serving: Calories 712 (65% from fat); Fat 51.3g (sat 24.3g, mono 17.6g, poly 2.1g);
Protein 35.1g; Carb 27.7g; Fiber 2.5g; Chol 141mg; Iron 3.2mg; Sodium 1138mg; Calc 322mg

Smothered Enchiladas

Meatball Lasagna

prep: 15 min.   cook: 1 hr.   other: 15 min.

1   (15-ounce) container ricotta cheese
1   (8-ounce) container chive-and-onion
    flavored cream cheese, softened
¼   cup chopped fresh basil
½   teaspoon garlic salt
½   teaspoon seasoned pepper
1   large egg, lightly beaten
2   cups (8 ounces) shredded mozzarella
    cheese, divided
1   (3-ounce) package shredded Parmesan
    cheese, divided
2   (26-ounce) jars tomato-basil pasta sauce
    (we tested with Classico)
1   (16-ounce) package egg roll wrappers
60 to 64 frozen cooked Italian-style meatballs

Stir together first 6 ingredients until blended.
Stir in ½ cup mozzarella cheese and ½ cup
Parmesan cheese; set aside.
Spread 1 cup pasta sauce in a lightly greased
13- x 9-inch baking dish.
Cut egg roll wrappers in half lengthwise;
arrange 10 halves over pasta sauce. (Wrappers will overlap.) Top with meatballs.
Spoon 3 cups pasta sauce over meatballs;
sprinkle with ¾ cup mozzarella cheese.
Arrange 10 egg roll wrappers evenly over
mozzarella. Spread ricotta cheese mixture
over wrappers; top with remaining wrappers
and pasta sauce.
Bake at 350° for 50 minutes. Top with
remaining ¾ cup mozzarella cheese and
remaining ¼ cup Parmesan cheese. Bake
10 more minutes. Let stand 15 minutes.
Yield: 8 servings.

Per serving: Calories 1007 (49% from fat); Fat 54.4g (sat 25.8g, mono 12.9g, poly 1.5g);
Protein 63.9g; Carb 66.6g; Fiber 5.1g; Chol 272mg; Iron 7mg; Sodium 1759mg; Calc 789mg

Liver and Caramelized Onions

prep: 6 min.   cook: 6 min. per batch

2   onions, thinly sliced
3   tablespoons butter or margarine, melted
3   tablespoons olive oil
1   teaspoon salt
½   teaspoon pepper
1   pound thinly sliced calves liver
¼   cup all-purpose flour

Sauté onion in butter in a large skillet over
medium heat 20 minutes or until tender
and golden, stirring occasionally. Remove
onion; add olive oil to skillet.
Sprinkle salt and pepper on both sides of
liver; dredge in flour. Shake off excess flour.
Add liver to skillet, and cook over medium–
high heat 3 minutes on each side or until
browned.
Transfer liver and onion slices to a warm
serving platter; serve immediately. Yield:
4 servings.

Per serving: Calories 376 (58% from fat); Fat 24.3g (sat 8.6g, mono 10.8g, poly 2.3g);
Protein 24g; Carb 15g; Fiber 1.1g; Chol 401mg; Iron 7.9mg; Sodium 731mg; Calc 23mg

veal

Veal comes from a very young beef animal. It has a mild flavor that makes it interesting to prepare. Since veal readily absorbs seasonings, you'll want to try recipes that include various herbs, spices, oils, wines, vinegars, rubs, and bread coatings. Marinades, sauces, and glazes not only enhance veal's flavor, they also tenderize the meat.

Naturally tender and with very little marbling, veal contains less fat than other meats. Though it is classified as "red" meat, fresh veal typically has a pale pink color. Bones should be porous and red, and any visible fat should be firm and very white.

Veal requires careful cooking because it can toughen quickly. Tender cuts, including the leg, veal chops, and rack of veal, are best prepared by dry-heat methods such as grilling, roasting, and pan-frying. Veal cutlets and scallops are best when quickly pan-fried. Moist-heat methods such as braising or simmering in liquid also can be used with these cuts. The less-tender shank, round steak, and roast generally require slow, covered, moist-heat cooking. Prepackaged veal stew meat almost always will be tender enough to make a great stew. We've found it's best to avoid broiling veal because it has a high proportion of connective tissue that could make it tough. Cook veal to 145° for medium rare or 160° for medium.

Pat veal dry with paper towels. This is the key to preventing meat from spattering in the skillet while pan-frying.

what's a piccata?

Veal Piccata is a classic main dish hailing from Italy. Thin cutlets of veal are seasoned and dredged in flour and then quickly pan-fried until golden. Wine and lemon juice are added to deglaze the pan, and the tangy sauce is drizzled over the veal just before serving.

Piccata is so simple and the results so outstanding that it's often applied to boneless chicken breasts that have been pounded to resemble thin cutlets of veal.

---

family favorite • quick

Veal Piccata

prep: 10 min.   cook: 10 min.

1   pound veal cutlets
1   teaspoon salt
½   teaspoon pepper
½   cup all-purpose flour
3   tablespoons butter
2   tablespoons olive oil
3   tablespoons lemon juice
2   garlic cloves, minced
3   tablespoons dry white wine
2   tablespoons chopped fresh flat-leaf parsley

Place veal between 2 sheets of plastic wrap or wax paper, and flatten to ¼-inch thickness, using a meat mallet or rolling pin. Cut veal into 4 serving-size pieces. Pat veal dry. Rub salt and pepper on veal; dredge in flour. **Heat** butter and oil in a large skillet over medium-high heat. Add veal in 2 batches, and cook 1 to 2 minutes on each side. **Remove** veal to a warm platter; cover and keep warm. Drain drippings. **Add** lemon juice, garlic, and white wine to skillet, stirring to loosen brown bits; cook over medium heat 1 to 2 minutes. To serve, spoon pan juices over veal; sprinkle with parsley. Yield: 4 servings.

Per serving: Calories 376 (63% from fat); Fat 26.2g (sat 10.5g, mono 11.4g, poly 1.8g); Protein 20.8g; Carb 13.9g; Fiber 0.6g; Chol 96mg; Iron 1.7mg; Sodium 695mg; Calc 31mg

---

low calorie • low carb • quick

Veal Marsala

prep: 6 min.   cook: 13 min.

Scaloppine is the thinnest piece of veal you can buy. It's so tender that it saves you the time and effort of pounding meat.

1   teaspoon chopped fresh or dried rosemary
½   teaspoon salt
½   teaspoon freshly ground pepper
1   pound (¼-inch-thick) veal scaloppine
2   tablespoons olive oil
1   (8-ounce) package sliced fresh mushrooms
2   garlic cloves, minced
2   teaspoons cornstarch
1   teaspoon chicken bouillon granules
⅔   cup water
⅓   cup dry Marsala

Rub first 3 ingredients over veal. Heat oil in a large nonstick skillet over medium heat. Add half of veal; cook 2 minutes on each side or until lightly browned. Remove veal from skillet; keep warm. Repeat with remaining veal.
Add mushrooms and garlic to skillet; cook over medium-high heat, stirring constantly, 3 minutes or until tender.
Combine cornstarch and remaining 3 ingredients; add to skillet. Cook, stirring constantly, 1 minute or until thick and bubbly. Serve sauce over veal. Yield: 4 servings.

Per serving: Calories 261 (61% from fat); Fat 17.8g (sat 5.2g, mono 9.2g, poly 1.5g); Protein 20.8g; Carb 4.3g; Fiber 0.8g; Chol 74mg; Iron 1.2mg; Sodium 577mg; Calc 26mg

Veal

· RETAIL CUTS ·
WHERE THEY COME FROM
HOW TO COOK THEM

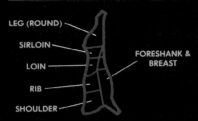

LEG (ROUND)
SIRLOIN
LOIN
RIB
SHOULDER
FORESHANK & BREAST

RIB

Rib Roast
Roast

Boneless Rib Roast
Roast

Crown Roast
Roast

Boneless Rib Chop
Braise, Panfry, Broil

Rib Chop
Braise, Panfry, Broil

Short Ribs
Braise, Cook in Liquid

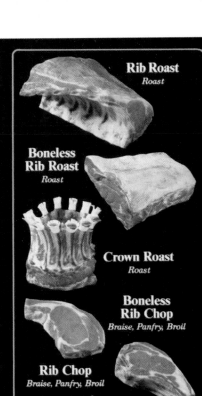

SHOULDER

Blade Roast
Braise, Roast

Arm Roast
Braise, Roast

Blade Steak
Braise, Panfry

Arm Steak
Braise, Panfry

Boneless Shoulder Arm Roast
Braise, Roast

Boneless Shoulder Eye Roast
Braise, Roast

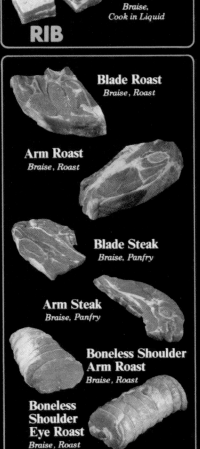

LEG (ROUND)

Boneless Rump Roast
Braise, Roast

Round Steak
Braise, Panfry

Top Round Steak
Braise, Panfry

Leg Cutlet
Braise, Panfry, Broil

FORESHANK & BREAST

Breast
Braise, Roast

Boneless Breast Roast
Braise, Roast

Cross Cut Shank
Braise, Cook in Liquid

Riblet
Braise, Cook in Liquid

Shank
Braise, Cook in Liquid

THIS CHART APPROVED BY

BEEF
USA

National Cattlemen's Beef Association

LOIN

Loin Roast
Roast

Boneless Loin Roast
Roast

Loin Chop
Braise, Panfry, Broil

Kidney Chop
Braise, Panfry

Top Loin Chop
Braise, Panfry, Broil

Butterfly Chop
Braise, Panfry, Broil

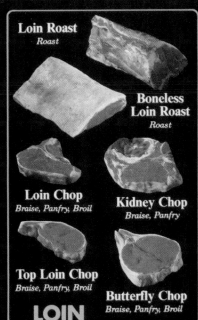

SIRLOIN

Sirloin Roast
Roast

Boneless Sirloin Roast
Roast

Sirloin Steak
Braise, Panfry, Broil

Top Sirloin Steak
Braise, Panfry, Broil

OTHER CUTS

Veal for Stew
Braise, Cook in Liquid

Ground Veal
Panfry, Broil

Cubes for Kabobs
Braise

Cubed Steak
Braise, Panfry

Veal Parmigiana

prep: 20 min. cook: 56 min.

Tender browned veal cutlets star in this Parmigiana. You can also prepare this recipe using chicken.

- 2   (15-ounce) cans tomato sauce
- 1   tablespoon butter or margarine, melted
- 1   tablespoon Worcestershire sauce
- 1   teaspoon dried oregano
- 1   teaspoon dried basil
- 2   garlic cloves, minced
- ¼   teaspoon pepper
- 2   large eggs
- ¼   teaspoon pepper
- 2   pounds veal cutlets, cut into serving-size pieces
- About 4 cups soft breadcrumbs
- ½   cup olive oil
- ¼   cup freshly grated Parmesan cheese
- 1   (8-ounce) package sliced mozzarella cheese

Combine first 7 ingredients in a saucepan; cook over medium heat 5 minutes, stirring occasionally. Set aside.
Combine eggs and ¼ teaspoon pepper; beat well. Place cutlets between 2 sheets of plastic wrap; flatten to ⅛-inch thickness, using a meat mallet or rolling pin.
Dip cutlets into egg mixture, and dredge in breadcrumbs. Brown cutlets in hot oil 4 minutes on each side over medium heat.

Place in a lightly greased 13-x 9-inch baking dish. Pour tomato sauce mixture over veal, and sprinkle with Parmesan cheese. **Bake,** covered, at 350° for 30 minutes. Uncover and top with mozzarella cheese; bake 5 more minutes or until cheese melts. Yield: 6 servings.

Per serving: Calories 615 (55% from fat); Fat 37.6g (sat 14.3g, mono 16.4g, poly 3g); Protein 41.2g; Carb 28g; Fiber 3.1g; Chol 206mg; Iron 4.5mg; Sodium 1367mg; Calc 337mg

Osso Buco

prep: 27 min. cook: 2 hrs., 25 min.

This Milanese specialty of braised veal is a long-simmering dish with layers of flavor. Finish it with a sprinkling of gremolata, a blend of parsley, lemon rind, and garlic.

- 1   large onion, chopped
- 1   cup finely chopped carrot
- ½   cup finely chopped celery
- 2   garlic cloves, minced
- ¼   cup butter or margarine, melted
- 6   (2-inch-thick) crosscut veal shanks (about 6 pounds)
- 1   teaspoon salt
- 1   teaspoon pepper
- ½   cup all-purpose flour
- ½   cup olive oil
- 1   cup dry white wine
- 3   cups coarsely chopped tomato or 1 (28-ounce) can plum tomatoes, undrained and chopped
- 2   cups chicken broth
- ⅓   cup chopped fresh parsley
- 2   bay leaves
- 1½   teaspoons chopped fresh or ½ teaspoon dried basil
- 1½   teaspoons chopped fresh or ½ teaspoon dried thyme
- 3   tablespoons chopped fresh parsley
- 1   teaspoon grated lemon rind
- 1   garlic clove, minced

Sauté first 4 ingredients in butter in a Dutch oven until vegetables are tender. Set aside.
Sprinkle veal with salt and pepper; dredge in flour. Heat oil in a large skillet; add veal, and cook until browned on both sides. Place in Dutch oven with vegetables. Discard oil.
Add wine to skillet; cook over medium-high heat until reduced to ½ cup (about 8 minutes). Stir in tomato and next 5 ingredients. Bring to a boil; pour over veal in Dutch oven. Bake, covered, at 350° for 2 hours or until veal is tender. Discard bay leaves.
Combine 3 tablespoons parsley, lemon rind, and 1 garlic clove; sprinkle over veal. Serve in wide-rimmed pasta bowls. Yield: 6 servings.

Per serving: Calories 683 (38% from fat); Fat 28.5g (sat 8.9g, mono 12.6g, poly 2.5g); Protein 83.9g; Carb 18.4g; Fiber 2.8g; Chol 338mg; Iron 4.7mg; Sodium 1224mg; Calc 130mg

Note: Dip the marrow out of veal bones, using a tiny marrow scoop. It's a delicacy.

lamb

Lamb is versatile, relatively mild-flavored, and comes from sheep less than a year old. The meat of older sheep is called *mutton* and has a much stronger flavor and tougher texture, making it less popular in the United States.

Purchase lamb that has a bright pink color, pink bones, and white fat. Large cuts of lamb are typically covered with a thin, silvery, papery skin called *fell*. Some cooks like to remove the fell, claiming it adds a strong flavor. However, it does help hold the shape of the leg together during roasting, and it also helps retain natural juices.

On small cuts, remove the fell before cooking; if left on, the meat may curl.

Most lamb is tender enough to be cooked by dry-heat methods. This includes basic roasted leg of lamb, chops, and roast. Lamb is best cooked to a rosy-pink, either 145° for medium rare or 160° for medium.

American Lamb
Cuts & How To Cook Them

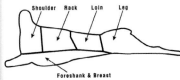

Shoulder   Rack   Loin   Leg

Foreshank & Breast

Leg

Whole Leg
(Roast)

Short Cut Leg, Sirloin Off
(Roast)

Shank Portion Roast
(Roast)

Center Leg Roast
(Roast)

Center Slice
(Broil, Grill, Panbroil, Panfry)

American-Style Roast
(Roast)

Frenched-Style Leg Roast
(Roast)

Boneless Leg Roast (BRT)
(Roast)

Frenched Hindshank
(Braise)

Sirloin Chop
(Braise, Broil, Grill, Panbroil, Panfry)

Boneless Sirloin Roast
(Roast)

Top Round
(Roast)

Rack

Crown Roast
(Roast)

Rib Roast
(Broil, Grill, Roast)

Rib Chop
(Broil, Grill, Panbroil, Panfry, Roast)

Frenched Rib Chop
(Broil, Grill, Panbroil, Pantry, Roast)

Loin

Loin Roast
(Roast)

Boneless Loin Strip (BRT)
(Roast)

Loin Chop
(Broil, Grill, Panbroil, Panfry)

Double Loin Chop
(Broil, Grill, Panbroil, Panfry)

Tenderloin
(Roast)

Shoulder

Square Cut Shoulder Whole
(Braise, Roast)

Saratoga Roast
(Braise, Roast)

Boneless Shoulder Roast (BRT)
(Braise, Roast)

Blade Chop
(Braise, Broil, Grill, Panbroil, Panfry)

Arm Chop
(Braise, Broil, Grill, Panbroil, Panfry)

Foreshank & Breast

Foreshank
(Braise)

Spareribs (Denver Ribs)
(Braise, Broil, Grill, Roast)

Riblets
(Braise, Broil, Grill)

Other Cuts

Lamb for Stew
(Braise)

Ground Lamb
(Broil, Grill, Panbroil)

Cubes for Kabobs
(Braise, Broil, Grill)

AMERICAN LAMB BOARD

www.americanlamb.com

Shish Kabobs

prep: 42 min.   cook: 20 min.   other: 8 hrs.

Cut uniform-sized pieces of vegetables for this traditional skewered meal so they'll cook evenly on the grill. Serve with saffron rice or couscous.

1   cup olive oil
2   tablespoons fresh lemon juice
2   tablespoons chopped fresh mint or parsley
½   tablespoon salt
2   teaspoons dried oregano
1   teaspoon pepper
4   garlic cloves, minced
1   (3-pound) boneless leg of lamb, cut into 2-inch cubes
3   small red onions, cut into fourths
2   green or red bell peppers, cut into fourths
2   tomatoes, cut into fourths, or 8 whole cherry tomatoes
8   whole fresh mushrooms
3   tablespoons fresh lemon juice
3   tablespoons olive oil

Combine first 7 ingredients; stir well. Place lamb in a large zip-top freezer bag or shallow dish. Pour marinade over lamb; seal or cover. Marinate in refrigerator 8 hours, turning occasionally.
Remove lamb from marinade, discarding marinade.
Alternate lamb cubes, onion, and next 3 ingredients onto 8 (12-inch) skewers.
Combine 3 tablespoons lemon juice and 3 tablespoons olive oil; brush on kabobs.
Grill, covered with grill lid, over medium-high heat (350° to 400°) 20 minutes or to desired degree of doneness, turning once. Yield: 8 servings.

Per serving: Calories 519 (68% from fat); Fat 39.5g (sat 11.2g, mono 22.5g, poly 3.4g); Protein 33.6g; Carb 7g; Fiber 1.6g; Chol 117mg; Iron 3.1mg; Sodium 306mg; Calc 32mg

Rosemary-Crusted Lamb With Tzatziki Sauce

prep: 10 min.   cook: 45 min.   other: 10 min.

Grate the lemon rind for the Tzatziki Sauce before squeezing the juice for the lamb.

¼   cup chopped fresh rosemary
3   garlic cloves
3   tablespoons fresh lemon juice
3   tablespoons olive oil
1   teaspoon salt
1   teaspoon pepper
1   (6-pound) boneless leg of lamb, trimmed
Tzatziki Sauce
Garnish: fresh rosemary sprigs

Process first 6 ingredients in a food processor until smooth. Spread rosemary mixture evenly on lamb. Place lamb on a lightly greased rack in a roasting pan.
Bake at 450° for 45 minutes or until a meat thermometer inserted into thickest portion registers 160° (medium).
Let stand 10 minutes before slicing. Serve with Tzatziki Sauce. Garnish, if desired. Yield: 10 servings.

Per serving: Calories 477 (59% from fat); Fat 31.5g (sat 12.4g, mono 14.3g, poly 2.3g); Protein 42g; Carb 3.9g; Fiber 0.5g; Chol 152mg; Iron 3.4mg; Sodium 591mg; Calc 83mg

Tzatziki Sauce

prep: 20 min.

This Greek sauce also can be served as a dip, a spread for sandwiches, or thinned out with good olive oil for a salad dressing.

1   (16-ounce) container plain yogurt
1   large cucumber, peeled, seeded, and diced
1   tablespoon chopped fresh dill
1   tablespoon chopped fresh mint
1   teaspoon salt
1   teaspoon grated lemon rind
1   garlic clove, pressed

Stir together all ingredients in a large bowl. Cover and chill until ready to serve. Yield: 2½ cups.

Per tablespoon: Calories 8 (45% from fat); Fat 0.4g (sat 0.2g, mono 0.1g, poly 0g); Protein 0.4g; Carb 0.7g; Fiber 0.1g; Chol 2mg; Iron 0mg; Sodium 64mg; Calc 15mg

Greek Leg of Lamb

prep: 10 min.   cook: 40 min.
other: 8 hrs., 10 min.

Butterflying a large piece of meat helps it cook quickly and evenly, especially on the grill.

1   (4-pound) boneless leg of lamb, butterflied
½   cup olive oil
½   cup lemon juice
1   tablespoon onion powder
1   tablespoon chopped fresh or 1 teaspoon dried oregano
2   tablespoons fresh or dried rosemary
6   garlic cloves, pressed

Trim fat from lamb. Place lamb in a large zip-top freezer bag or shallow dish.
Combine oil and remaining 5 ingredients; pour over lamb. Seal or cover; marinate in refrigerator 8 hours, turning occasionally.
Remove lamb from marinade, discarding marinade. Grill, without grill lid, over medium coals (300° to 350°) 20 minutes; turn and grill 20 more minutes or until a meat thermometer inserted into thickest portion registers 150° (medium rare) or 160° (medium). Let stand 10 minutes. Slice diagonally across the grain. Yield: 8 servings.

Per serving: Calories 480 (61% from fat); Fat 32.5g (sat 13g, mono 15.4g, poly 1.7g); Protein 43g; Carb 1.4g; Fiber 0.1g; Chol 150mg; Iron 3.6mg; Sodium 120mg; Calc 25mg

Dijon Rack of Lamb

prep: 10 min.   cook: 31 min.   other: 10 min.

This impressive entrée requires only six ingredients. Focaccia breadcrumbs make a special crusty presentation.

2   (8-rib) lamb rib roasts (2 to 2½ pounds each), trimmed
1   teaspoon salt
1   tablespoon pepper
3   tablespoons olive oil
3   tablespoons Dijon mustard
1   cup fresh herb focaccia breadcrumbs*

Rub lamb evenly with salt and pepper.
Cook lamb in hot oil in a large skillet over

Dijon Rack of Lamb

high heat 3 minutes on each side or until browned. Place lamb, fat side up, on a rack in a broiler pan.

Bake at 425° for 20 minutes or until a meat thermometer inserted into thickest portion registers 145° (medium rare).

Remove lamb from oven, leaving oven on. Cover lamb loosely with aluminum foil, and let stand 10 minutes or until meat thermometer registers 150°.

Brush lamb with mustard; cover with breadcrumbs. Return lamb to oven, and bake 4 to 5 minutes or until breadcrumbs are browned. Cut into chops, and serve. Yield: 8 servings.

Per serving: Calories 496 (75% from fat); Fat 41.3g (sat 16.2g, mono 18.9g, poly 3.2g); Protein 26g; Carb 3.4g; Fiber 0.3g; Chol 117mg; Iron 2.4mg; Sodium 491mg; Calc 39mg

*Substitute 1 cup fresh French breadcrumbs for focaccia. Focaccia is an Italian flatbread that can be found in the bakery section of grocery stores.

low carb
Broiled Lamb Chops With Southwestern Butter

prep: 25 min.   cook: 11 min.   other: 2 hrs.

¼   cup olive oil or vegetable oil
2   garlic cloves, chopped
1   tablespoon dried or 2 teaspoons chopped fresh thyme
1½ to 2 tablespoons paprika
18   (2- to 3-ounce) lamb rib chops*
1   teaspoon salt
1   teaspoon pepper
Southwestern Butter (page 434)
Garnish: fresh thyme sprigs

Combine first 4 ingredients in a large shallow dish or large zip-top freezer bag; add lamb chops, turning to coat. Cover or seal, and chill 2 hours.

Remove lamb chops from marinade, discarding marinade. Sprinkle with salt and pepper. Place on a lightly greased aluminum foil-lined rack in a broiler pan.

Broil 3 inches from heat 5 minutes on each side or to desired degree of doneness. Top each lamb chop with a slice of Southwestern Butter; broil 30 more seconds. Serve immediately. Garnish, if desired. Yield: 6 servings.

Per serving: Calories 492 (82% from fat); Fat 44.7g (sat 24g, mono 14.9g, poly 2g); Protein 21.1g; Carb 1.9g; Fiber 0.8g; Chol 147mg; Iron 2.2mg; Sodium 485mg; Calc 35mg

*Substitute 12 loin chops for rib chops. Broil 3 more minutes on each side or to desired degree of doneness.

Fried Lamb Chops

prep: 15 min.   cook: 14 min. per batch

1   cup Italian-seasoned breadcrumbs
¼   cup grated Parmesan cheese
1   teaspoon salt
1   teaspoon garlic powder
1   teaspoon onion powder
1   teaspoon pepper
2   teaspoons paprika
18   (2- to 3-ounce) lamb rib chops*
1   cup all-purpose flour
2   large eggs, lightly beaten
Vegetable oil
Garnishes: lemon wedges, fresh rosemary sprigs

Stir together first 7 ingredients.
Dredge chops in flour; dip into egg, and dredge in breadcrumb mixture.
Pour vegetable oil to a depth of ¼ inch into a skillet; fry chops, in batches, over medium-high heat 5 to 7 minutes on each side. Garnish, if desired. Yield: 6 servings.

Per serving: Calories 592 (61% from fat); Fat 40.3g (sat 13.7g, mono 16.3g, poly 6.4g); Protein 26.9g; Carb 30.1g; Fiber 1.7g; Chol 161mg; Iron 3.8mg; Sodium 1009mg; Calc 114mg

*Substitute 12 loin chops for rib chops. Cook 3 more minutes on each side.

Creamy Dijon Lamb Chops

prep: 15 min.   cook: 28 min.   other: 5 min.

8   (2-inch-thick) lamb chops, trimmed
½   teaspoon salt
¼   teaspoon freshly ground pepper
1   tablespoon olive oil
2   garlic cloves, pressed
½   cup whipping cream
⅓   cup Dijon mustard
2   tablespoons chopped fresh thyme
1   to 2 tablespoons chopped fresh rosemary

Sprinkle lamb chops with salt and pepper.
Brown chops in hot oil in a heavy skillet over medium-high heat 2 minutes on each side; place chops in a 13- x 9-inch baking dish, reserving drippings in skillet.
Bake at 400° for 15 minutes or until a meat thermometer inserted into thickest portion registers 150° (medium rare). Let lamb chops stand 5 minutes before serving.
Sauté garlic in reserved drippings over medium heat 3 minutes or until lightly browned.
Stir together cream and remaining 3 ingredients in a small bowl. Add mixture to skillet, and bring to a boil over medium heat, stirring occasionally. Reduce heat, and simmer 5 minutes. Serve with chops. Yield: 4 servings.

Per serving: Calories 555 (54% from fat); Fat 33.3g (sat 14.1g, mono 13.9g, poly 2g); Protein 58.8g; Carb 1.8g; Fiber 0.3g; Chol 225mg; Iron 4.2mg; Sodium 725mg; Calc 66mg

Easy Baked Lamb Chops

prep: 20 min.   cook: 45 min.

1   tablespoon all-purpose flour
½   teaspoon salt
¼   teaspoon pepper
18   (2- to 3-ounce) lamb rib chops*
1   (1-ounce) envelope onion soup mix
1   red bell pepper, thinly sliced
1   (8-ounce) package sliced fresh mushrooms
½   (14-ounce) can diced tomatoes, undrained
1   tablespoon steak sauce

Combine first 3 ingredients; set aside.
Tear off 1 (28- x 18-inch) heavy-duty aluminum foil sheet. Place in a 13- x 9-inch pan. Place chops in pan; sprinkle evenly with flour mixture. Top with soup mix and remaining ingredients.
Bring up 2 long sides of foil sheet, and double-fold with about 1-inch-wide folds. Double-fold each end to form a packet, leaving room for heat to circulate inside packet. Bake at 375° for 45 minutes. Yield: 6 servings.

Per serving: Calories 365 (67% from fat); Fat 27.3g (sat 11.6g, mono 11.4g, poly 2.1g); Protein 21.2g; Carb 8.5g; Fiber 1.7g; Chol 88mg; Iron 2mg; Sodium 762mg; Calc 38mg

*Substitute 12 loin chops for rib chops. Bake 10 more minutes or to desired degree of doneness.

Maple-Glazed Lamb Chops With Zesty Horseradish Sauce

prep: 10 min.   cook: 14 min.   other: 8 hrs.

⅓   cup maple syrup
¼   cup Dijon mustard
2   tablespoons balsamic vinegar
2   tablespoons olive oil
1   shallot, minced
¼   teaspoon dried crushed red pepper
8   (½-inch-thick) lamb loin chops
½   teaspoon salt
½   teaspoon ground black pepper
      Zesty Horseradish Sauce

Combine first 6 ingredients in a shallow dish or large zip-top freezer bag; add lamb chops. Cover or seal, and chill up to 8 hours, turning occasionally.
Remove lamb chops from marinade, discarding marinade. Sprinkle chops evenly with salt and pepper; place chops on a lightly greased rack in a broiler pan.
Broil chops 3 inches from heat 5 to 7 minutes on each side or to desired degree of doneness. Cover with aluminum foil, and let stand 5 minutes. Serve with Zesty Horseradish Sauce. Yield: 4 servings.

Per serving: Calories 275 (55% from fat); Fat 16.7g (sat 7.2g, mono 7.2g, poly 1g); Protein 19.1g; Carb 11.7g; Fiber 0.2g; Chol 72mg; Iron 1.5mg; Sodium 461mg; Calc 67mg

Zesty Horseradish Sauce

prep: 5 min.

This creamy sauce is great on roast beef sandwiches, too.

½   cup sour cream
2   tablespoons prepared horseradish
2   tablespoons chopped fresh mint

Stir together all ingredients. Cover and chill until ready to serve. Yield: ½ cup.

Per tablespoon: Calories 38 (88% from fat); Fat 3.7g (sat 2.3g, mono 1.1g, poly 0.1g); Protein 0.6g; Carb 0.8g; Fiber 0g; Chol 8mg; Iron 0mg; Sodium 10.2mg; Calc 22mg

Grilled Lamb Chops With Gorgonzola Butter

prep: 28   cook: 20 min.   other: 8 hrs.

16   lamb loin chops (1½ inches thick)
1   cup olive oil
8   shallots, minced
¼   cup minced garlic
1   tablespoon plus 1 teaspoon chopped fresh or dried rosemary
      Gorgonzola Butter (page 434)

Trim excess fat from lamb chops; place in a zip-top freezer bag or shallow dish.
Combine oil and next 3 ingredients; stir well. Pour over chops. Seal or cover, and marinate in refrigerator 8 hours.
Remove chops from marinade, discarding marinade. Drain excess marinade from chops to prevent flare-ups.
Grill chops, covered with grill lid, over medium heat (300° to 350°) 8 to 10 minutes on each side or to desired degree of doneness. Top each chop with Gorgonzola Butter. Yield: 8 servings.

Per serving: Calories 765 (72% from fat); Fat 61.1g (sat 26.2g, mono 24.6g, poly 3.5g); Protein 48.8g; Carb 3.9g; Fiber 0.3g; Chol 218mg; Iron 3.2mg; Sodium 696mg; Calc 153mg

pork

Pork is generally produced from young hogs or domestic swine. Much of a hog is cured and made into ham, bacon, and sausage, but the uncured meat is call "fresh pork." In recent years, fresh pork has become leaner and healthier due to improved breeding and feeding of the hogs, and closer trimming of fat at the processors. This leaves the pork lower in fat, calories, and cholesterol. In fact, there are a wide variety of fresh pork cuts to choose from, many of which are equivalent in fat content and calories to lean poultry. Refer to the identification chart on the next page to help you locate certain cuts of pork when shopping.

When buying fresh pork, look for meat that's firm, with only a small amount of outside white fat. For best results, the meat should have a pink color; it tends to take on a grayish tint when it's been in the meat case too long. For optimum flavor and tenderness, look for cuts with a small amount of marbling.

Store unopened fresh pork in the refrigerator, and use within three days; store ground pork in the refrigerator no longer than two days. If you plan on keeping fresh pork longer, then wrap, seal, and place in the freezer. Generally, fresh cuts of pork like roasts, chops, and tenderloin can be kept in the freezer up to six months; ground pork will keep for about three months.

Today's pork is virtually free of any trichinae (parasites), but it's still recommended that all types of pork be cooked to a medium internal temperature of 160°. Note that even when fresh pork has been cooked to the recommended temperature, it can be slightly pink in the center, but is still safe to eat.

Most pork is naturally tender and can be cooked by dry-heat methods. But keep in mind that today's lean pork cooks fairly quickly, and overcooking can leave it tough and dry. If desired, fresh pork can be marinated in the refrigerator for added flavor and tenderness. We recommend testing pork for perfect doneness with a meat thermometer, especially when grilling.

timetable for roasting fresh pork

cut	approximate weight in pounds	internal temperature	approximate total cooking times in minutes at 325° per pound
Loin			
Center	3 to 5	160°	25 to 30
Half	5 to 7	160°	30 to 35
End	3 to 4	160°	35 to 40
Roll	3 to 5	160°	30 to 35
Boneless top	2 to 4	160°	25 to 30
Crown	4 to 6	160°	25 to 30
Picnic shoulder			
Bone in	5 to 8	170°	25 to 30
Rolled	3 to 5	170°	30 to 35
Boston shoulder	4 to 6	170°	35 to 40
Leg (fresh ham)			
Whole (bone-in)	12 to 16	160°	22 to 26
Whole (boneless)	10 to 14	160°	20 to 25
Half (bone-in)	5 to 8	160°	25 to 30
Tenderloin			
Roast at 375°	½ to 1	160°	20 to 30 minutes
Back ribs		well-done	1½ to 2½ hours
Country-style ribs		well-done	1½ to 2½ hours
Spareribs		well-done	1½ to 2½ hours
Pork loaf	1½ to 2	well-done	1 to 1½ hours

low calorie • low carb • quick

Pan-Fried Pork Chops

prep: 10 min.   cook: 6 min.

These tasty chops go from pan to plate in under 20 minutes.

- ½ cup all-purpose flour
- 1   teaspoon salt
- 1   teaspoon seasoned pepper
- 1½ pounds wafer-thin boneless pork chops (about 12)
- ¼   cup vegetable oil

Combine first 3 ingredients in a shallow dish; dredge pork chops in flour mixture. **Fry** pork chops, in 3 batches, in hot oil in a skillet over medium-high heat 1 minute on each side or until browned. Drain on paper towels. Yield: 6 servings.

Per serving: Calories 308 (56% from fat); Fat 19.1g (sat 5.3g, mono 8.3g, poly 4.1g); Protein 24.8g; Carb 8.6g; Fiber 0.3g; Chol 73mg; Iron 1.4mg; Sodium 438mg; Calc 24mg

Purchasing Pork
A Consumer Guide To Identifying Retail Pork Cuts.

Upper row (l-r): bone-in blade roast, boneless blade roast.
Lower row (l-r): ground pork (The Other Burger®), sausage, blade steak.

Shoulder Butt

Upper row (l-r): smoked picnic, arm picnic roast.
Lower row: smoked hocks.

Picnic Shoulder

Top: spareribs.
Bottom: slab bacon, sliced bacon.

Side

Upper row (l-r): bone-in fresh ham, smoked ham.
Lower row (l-r): leg cutlets, fresh boneless ham roast.

Leg

Upper row (l-r): sirloin chop, rib chop, loin chop.
Lower row (l-r): boneless rib end chop (Chef's Prime Filet™), boneless center loin chop (America's Cut™), butterfly chop.

Upper row (l-r): center rib roast (Rack of Pork), bone-in sirloin roast.
Middle: boneless center loin roast.
Lower row (l-r): boneless rib end roast (Chef's Prime™), boneless sirloin roast.

Chops

Roasts

Loin

Tenderloin & Canadian Style Bacon

Left: tenderloin
Right: Canadian-style bacon

Ribs

Left: country-style ribs.
Right: back ribs.

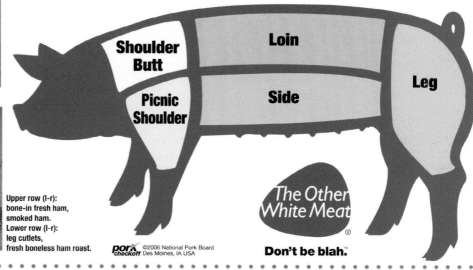

Shoulder Butt

Loin

Picnic Shoulder

Side

Leg

The Other White Meat®

pork checkoff ©2006 National Pork Board Des Moines, IA USA

Don't be blah.™

Roasts
No-fuss family dinner or holiday favorite.

THE MANY SHAPES OF PORK
Cut Loose!

When shopping for pork, consider cutting traditional roasts into a variety of different shapes.

Chops
Dinner, backyard barbecue or gourmet entree.

Cubes
Great for kabobs, stew and chili.

Strips
Super stir fry, fajitas and salads.

Cutlets
Delicious breakfast chops and quick sandwiches.

#03342 01/2006

Balsamic Pork Chops

prep: 5 min.   cook: 15 min.

2½   tablespoons all-purpose flour
1¼   teaspoons lemon pepper-herb seasoning
5   (½-inch-thick) boneless pork loin chops
1½   tablespoons olive oil
⅔   cup balsamic vinegar
½   cup chicken broth

Combine flour and seasoning in a shallow dish; dredge pork chops in flour mixture.
Cook pork in hot oil in a large skillet over medium-high heat 5 minutes on each side or until lightly browned. Remove from skillet, and keep warm.
Add vinegar and broth to skillet, stirring to loosen particles from bottom. Cook, stirring often, over medium-high heat 5 minutes or until slightly thickened. Spoon sauce over pork, and serve immediately. Yield: 5 servings.

Per serving: Calories 204 (52% from fat); Fat 11.8g (sat 3.4g, mono 6.3g, poly 1.1g); Protein 15.5g; Carb 7.9g; Fiber 0.1g; Chol 46mg; Iron 1mg; Sodium 163mg; Calc 24mg

◄ Cook pork chops in hot oil in a large skillet or sauté pan until lightly browned on both sides.

◄ Deglaze skillet with balsamic vinegar and chicken broth.

◄ Cook until sauce is slightly thickened.

Stuffed Pork Chops

prep: 30 min.   cook: 50 min.

Stuffed with fontina cheese, chopped Granny Smith apples, and herbs, these pork chops become something spectacular without losing their homey appeal.

6   bacon slices
2   Granny Smith apples, peeled and diced
2   shallots, finely chopped
1   tablespoon chopped fresh ginger
1   tablespoon chopped fresh sage
1   cup cubed fontina cheese
6   (1½-inch-thick) center-cut pork loin chops
1⅛   teaspoons salt
1¼   teaspoons pepper
2   tablespoons olive oil

Cook bacon in a large skillet until crisp; remove bacon, and drain on paper towels, reserving 2 tablespoons drippings in skillet. Crumble bacon; set aside.
Sauté apple, shallot, and ginger in hot drippings 5 minutes or until tender. Remove from heat; stir in sage.
Stir together apple mixture, bacon, and cheese. Cut a horizontal slit through thickest portion of each pork chop, cutting to, but not through, other side to form a pocket. Sprinkle both sides and pocket of each pork chop with salt and pepper. Spoon apple mixture evenly into pockets; secure with wooden picks.
Cook chops, in 2 batches, in hot olive oil in a large skillet over medium-high heat 1 to 2 minutes on each side or until golden. Place in a lightly greased roasting pan or large shallow baking dish.
Bake at 425° for 25 to 30 minutes or until done. Yield: 6 servings.

Per serving: Calories 447 (57% from fat); Fat 28.1g (sat 11g, mono 12.6g, poly 2.4g); Protein 36.2g; Carb 11.5g; Fiber 1.1g; Chol 118mg; Iron 1.5mg; Sodium 817mg; Calc 155mg

Southwest Pork in Black Bean Sauce

prep: 15 min.   cook: 16 min.

For less spice, substitute a can of regular diced tomatoes for the mild diced tomatoes with green chiles.

1½   pounds boneless pork loin chops
1   tablespoon ground cumin
1   teaspoon ground chipotle chile pepper (we tested with McCormick Gourmet Collection Chipotle Chile Pepper)
1   teaspoon garlic salt
1   teaspoon paprika
2   (10-ounce) cans mild diced tomatoes with green chiles
1   (15-ounce) can black beans, rinsed and drained
1   (8-ounce) can whole kernel corn, drained
1   tablespoon vegetable oil
1   small red onion, diced
1   cup uncooked instant rice
1   cup (4 ounces) grated Cheddar cheese
2   tablespoons chopped fresh cilantro
Flour tortillas
Lime wedges

Cut pork into ½-inch cubes.
Combine cumin, chipotle chile pepper, garlic salt, and paprika in a large zip-top freezer bag. Remove 2 teaspoons cumin mixture, and reserve. Add pork to zip-top bag. Seal and shake to coat. Set aside.
Stir together reserved 2 teaspoons cumin mixture, diced tomatoes with green chiles, black beans, and corn in a large bowl.
Heat vegetable oil in a large skillet over medium-high heat. Add pork and red onion, and sauté 6 to 8 minutes or until pork is browned. Stir in tomato mixture; bring mixture to a boil, and stir in rice. Cover and remove from heat. Let stand 5 minutes.
Sprinkle evenly with Cheddar cheese and chopped fresh cilantro. Serve with flour tortillas and lime wedges. Yield: 6 servings.

Per serving: Calories 424 (45% from fat); Fat 21.6g (sat 8.8g, mono 8.1g, poly 2.3g); Protein 32.7g; Carb 26.6g; Fiber 4.8g; Chol 93mg; Iron 2.7mg; Sodium 913mg; Calc 208mg

Tuscan Pork Chops

prep: 10 min.   cook: 10 min.

¼   cup all-purpose flour
1   teaspoon salt
¾   teaspoon seasoned pepper
4   (1-inch-thick) boneless pork chops
1   tablespoon olive oil
3   to 4 garlic cloves, minced
⅓   cup balsamic vinegar
⅓   cup chicken broth
3   plum tomatoes, seeded and diced
2   tablespoons capers

Combine first 3 ingredients in a shallow dish; dredge pork chops in flour mixture.
Cook pork chops in hot oil in a large non-stick skillet over medium–high heat 1 to 2 minutes on each side or until golden brown. Remove chops from skillet.
Add garlic to skillet, and sauté 1 minute. Add vinegar and broth, stirring to loosen particles from bottom of skillet; stir in tomatoes and capers. Return pork chops to skillet; bring sauce to a boil. Cover, reduce heat, and simmer 4 to 5 minutes or until pork is done. Serve pork chops with tomato mixture. Yield: 4 servings.

Per serving: Calories 321 (48% from fat); Fat 17.2g (sat 5.6g, mono 8.5g, poly 1.6g); Protein 28.6g; Carb 12.5g; Fiber 0.8g; Chol 82mg; Iron 1.8mg; Sodium 882mg; Calc 44mg

Greek-Style Baked Pork Chops

prep: 20 min.   cook: 14 min.

½   cup bottled diced roasted red bell peppers
1   tablespoon chopped fresh parsley
2   tablespoons olive oil
2   teaspoons grated lemon rind
1   tablespoon fresh lemon juice
2   teaspoons minced garlic
½   teaspoon dried oregano
¼   cup all-purpose flour
1   teaspoon coarsely ground pepper
4   (¾-inch-thick) center-cut pork chops
½   cup crumbled feta cheese
⅓   cup kalamata olives, chopped

Stir together first 7 ingredients.
Stir together flour and pepper. Coat both sides of pork chops evenly with flour mixture. Cook pork chops in a lightly greased ovenproof skillet over medium heat 2 minutes on each side. Spoon red bell pepper mixture over pork chops.
Bake, covered, at 400° for 5 minutes. Combine feta cheese and olives in a small bowl. Spoon mixture evenly over pork chops, and bake, covered, 5 more minutes. Yield: 4 servings.

Per serving: Calories 323 (61% from fat); Fat 22g (sat 7.1g, mono 11.6g, poly 1.9g); Protein 19.6g; Carb 9.9g; Fiber 0.7g; Chol 65mg; Iron 1.4mg; Sodium 473mg; Calc 120mg

Pork-Stuffed Poblanos With Walnut Cream Sauce

prep: 25 min.   cook: 55 min.   other: 10 min.

8   large poblano chile peppers*
1   pound ground pork
1   tablespoon olive oil
1   medium onion, chopped
1   large garlic clove, minced
1   teaspoon ground cumin
¾   teaspoon ground cinnamon
¼   teaspoon ground red pepper
2   large tomatoes, chopped
1   small apple, chopped
⅓   cup raisins
⅓   cup diced almonds, toasted
1   tablespoon cider vinegar
1   teaspoon salt
1   cup tomato sauce
1   teaspoon sugar
¼   teaspoon salt
¼   teaspoon dried crushed red pepper
Walnut Cream Sauce
Garnish: cinnamon sticks

Broil chile peppers on an aluminum foil-lined baking sheet 5 inches from heat about 5 minutes on each side or until peppers look blistered.
Place chile peppers in a zip-top freezer bag; seal and let stand 10 minutes to loosen skins. Peel peppers. Gently split chile peppers open lengthwise, keeping stems intact; remove and discard seeds. Set peppers aside.
Cook pork in hot oil in a large skillet over medium–high heat, stirring until it crumbles and is no longer pink; drain. Add chopped onion and next 4 ingredients; cook, stirring often, 7 minutes or until onion is tender.
Stir in tomato and next 4 ingredients. Cover, reduce heat, and simmer 5 minutes. Stir in 1 teaspoon salt.
Stir together tomato sauce and next 3 ingredients in a small saucepan over low heat 5 minutes. Spoon about ½ cup pork mixture into each pepper, and place in a lightly greased 13- x 9-inch baking dish. Pour tomato sauce mixture over peppers.
Bake, covered, at 350° for 30 minutes. Top with Walnut Cream Sauce. Garnish, if desired. Yield: 8 servings.

Per serving: Calories 357 (60% from fat); Fat 23.9g (sat 8.2g, mono 9g, poly 4.6g); Protein 17.4g; Carb 21.7g; Fiber 3.9g; Chol 59mg; Iron 2.7mg; Sodium 679mg; Calc 90mg

Tuscan Pork Chops

*Substitute small green bell peppers for poblanos. (Do not roast.) Proceed as directed. Bake 45 minutes or until peppers are tender.

Walnut Cream Sauce

prep: 10 min.

1 (3-ounce) package cream cheese, softened
½ cup walnuts, toasted
½ cup sour cream
¼ cup milk
1 teaspoon ground cinnamon
½ teaspoon ground red pepper
½ teaspoon sugar
¼ teaspoon salt

Process all ingredients in a food processor or blender until smooth, stopping to scrape down sides. Yield: 1½ cups.

Per tablespoon: Calories 41 (86% from fat); Fat 3.9g (sat 1.5g, mono 1.1g, poly 1g); Protein 1.1g; Carb 0.9g; Fiber 0.2g; Chol 6mg; Iron 0.2mg; Sodium 38mg; Calc 14mg

---

family favorite
Pork Scaloppine

prep: 25 min. cook: 10 min.

1½ pounds pork loin
4 large eggs
¼ cup milk
½ cup freshly grated Romano cheese
1½ teaspoons garlic powder
½ teaspoon salt
½ cup all-purpose flour
¼ cup butter or margarine
¼ cup olive oil
2 lemons, quartered

Cut pork loin into ½-inch-thick slices. Place pork between 2 sheets of heavy-duty plastic wrap; flatten to ¼-inch thickness, using a meat mallet or rolling pin.
Whisk together eggs and next 4 ingredients. Dredge pork in flour, shake to remove excess, and dip in egg mixture.
Melt butter with olive oil in a large skillet over medium-high heat. Cook pork, in batches, 1 minute on each side or until browned. Serve with lemon quarters. Yield: 4 servings.

Per serving: Calories 629 (59% from fat); Fat 41.3g (sat 15.6g, mono 19g, poly 3.3g); Protein 46.8g; Carb 16.3g; Fiber 0.6g; Chol 353mg; Iron 3.7mg; Sodium 666mg; Calc 193mg

---

entertaining
Festive Pork Roast

prep: 30 min. cook: 2 hrs., 30 min.
other: 8 hrs., 10 min.

A robust marinade infuses this roast with intense flavor.

1½ cups dry red wine
⅔ cup firmly packed light brown sugar
½ cup ketchup
½ cup water
¼ cup vegetable oil
4 garlic cloves, minced
3 tablespoons soy sauce
2 teaspoons curry powder
1 teaspoon ground ginger
½ teaspoon pepper
1 (5-pound) boneless rolled pork roast
4 teaspoons cornstarch

Combine first 10 ingredients in a large zip-top freezer bag; add pork. Seal and chill 8 hours, turning occasionally.
Remove pork from marinade, reserving 2½ cups marinade. Bring reserved marinade to a boil in a saucepan; whisk in cornstarch, and cook, stirring constantly, 2 to 3 minutes or until thickened. Cool.
Pat pork dry; place on a rack in a shallow roasting pan.
Bake at 325° for 2½ hours or until a meat thermometer inserted into thickest portion registers 160°, basting with ¼ cup reserved sauce the last 15 minutes. Allow roast to stand 10 minutes before slicing. Serve with reserved sauce. Yield: 10 servings.

Per serving: Calories 485 (50% from fat); Fat 26.7g (sat 9.2g, mono 10.8g, poly 4.4g); Protein 45.4g; Carb 13.6g; Fiber 0.2g; Chol 136mg; Iron 2.2mg; Sodium 403mg; Calc 62mg

---

entertaining
Roast Pork Loin

prep: 20 min. cook: 1 hr. other: 10 min.

You can easily halve this recipe if you're not serving a large group. Sweet potatoes and dried fruit make it a healthy one-dish meal.

2 (4-pound) center-cut boneless pork loins
1 teaspoon salt
1 teaspoon pepper
⅓ cup all-purpose flour
2 tablespoons olive oil
4 large sweet potatoes, peeled and cut into ½-inch slices
1 (12-ounce) package medium-size pitted prunes
2 (6-ounce) packages dried apricots
2 cups chicken broth
1 cup Madeira wine

Rub pork loins evenly with salt and pepper; dredge in flour.
Brown pork loins on all sides, 1 at a time, in hot oil in a large skillet over medium heat. Place browned pork in a large lightly greased roasting pan. Arrange sweet potatoes and prunes around pork.
Combine apricots, broth, and wine in a large saucepan; bring to a boil, and cook 5 minutes. Pour apricot mixture over pork, sweet potato slices, and prunes.
Bake at 375° for 1 hour or until a meat thermometer inserted into thickest portion of pork registers 160°, basting every 15 minutes. Let stand 10 minutes before serving. Yield: 16 servings.

Per serving: Calories 639 (43% from fat); Fat 30.7g (sat 10.2g, mono 14.1g, poly 3.3g); Protein 47.9g; Carb 38.9g; Fiber 3.7g; Chol 153mg; Iron 3.7mg; Sodium 426mg; Calc 82mg

Crown Pork Roast With Cranberry Stuffing

prep: 10 min.   cook: 3 hrs., 30 min.
other: 15 min.

3   teaspoons coarse salt, divided
1   tablespoon pepper
1   (16-rib) crown pork roast, trimmed and tied (about 10¼ pounds)
2   cups reserved unbaked Cranberry Stuffing
2   tablespoons all-purpose flour
¾   cup water
Garnishes: fresh cranberries, fresh rosemary and thyme sprigs, fresh sage leaves

Rub 2 teaspoons salt and 1 tablespoon pepper evenly over all sides of pork roast. Place roast, rib ends down, in a 1-quart round soufflé or casserole dish. Place soufflé dish in an aluminum foil-lined roasting pan.
Bake at 325° for 2½ hours. Remove from oven. Remove dish from pan; remove roast from dish, and invert. Place rib ends up on aluminum foil in roasting pan. Pour drippings from dish into roasting pan. Spoon 2 cups reserved unbaked Cranberry Stuffing into center of roast; cover with a 12-inch square of heavy-duty aluminum foil, and fold foil over tips of roast.
Bake roast 45 minutes to 1 hour more or until a meat thermometer registers 155°. Remove foil, and let stand 15 minutes or until thermometer registers 160° before slicing.
Pour pan drippings into a skillet, and cook over medium-high heat until mixture comes to a boil.
Stir together 2 tablespoons flour, remaining 1 teaspoon salt, and ¾ cup water. Whisk into pan drippings; cook, whisking constantly, 5 minutes or until thickened. Serve with roast. Garnish, if desired. Yield: 12 servings.

Per serving: Calories 527 (53% from fat); Fat 31.3g (sat 11.8g, mono 14.3g, poly 3.1g); Protein 51.7g; Carb 6.4g; Fiber 0.8g; Chol 138mg; Iron 2.1mg; Sodium 630mg; Calc 60mg

Cranberry Stuffing

prep: 15 min.   cook: 40 min.

¼   cup butter or margarine
1   cup chopped celery
1   cup chopped onion
1   (16-ounce) package herb-seasoned cornbread stuffing mix (we tested with Pepperidge Farm Corn Bread Stuffing)
2   cups chicken broth
1   (16-ounce) can whole-berry cranberry sauce
1   cup chopped pecans

Melt ¼ cup butter in a large Dutch oven over medium heat; add celery and onion, and sauté 5 minutes or until tender.
Stir in stuffing mix and remaining ingredients, stirring just until moistened. Remove 2 cups unbaked stuffing; reserve to stuff in pork roast. Spoon remainder into a lightly greased 11- x 7-inch baking dish.
Bake, covered, at 325° for 30 to 35 minutes or until thoroughly heated. Serve stuffing with pork roast. Yield: 10 servings.

Per serving: Calories 224 (56% from fat); Fat 13.9g (sat 3.5g, mono 6.2g, poly 3.2g); Protein 2.3g; Carb 24.3g; Fiber 2.8g; Chol 10mg; Iron 0.6mg; Sodium 356mg; Calc 24mg

Peppered Pork Tenderloin With Roasted Fennel

prep: 7 min.   cook: 34 min.

2   fennel bulbs
3   large portobello mushroom caps
1   (2-pound) package pork tenderloins, trimmed
¼   cup olive oil, divided
2   tablespoons coarsely ground black peppercorns, divided
½   teaspoon salt
½   cup dry sherry
1   cup whipping cream

Trim base from fennel bulbs; cut bulbs into sixths, discarding fronds. Cut mushroom caps into fourths. Set aside.
Brown tenderloins in 2 tablespoons hot oil in a large skillet over medium-high heat 4 minutes on each side. Place pork in a shallow roasting pan; sprinkle with 1 tablespoon pepper and salt. Arrange fennel and mushrooms around tenderloins; drizzle with remaining 2 tablespoons oil.

Removing silver skin: Use a sharp boning knife to trim tough silver skin from pork tenderloin.

Bake at 425° for 20 minutes or until a meat thermometer inserted in thickest portion registers 155°. Transfer tenderloins to a serving platter; let stand, covered, 5 minutes or until thermometer registers 160°.
Place roasting pan over 2 burners of cooktop; add sherry, stirring with a whisk to loosen any browned bits from bottom of pan. Whisk in whipping cream and remaining 1 tablespoon pepper; bring to a boil. Cook, whisking constantly, 3 to 4 minutes or until sauce is slightly thickened. Serve over sliced tenderloin and vegetables. Yield: 4 servings.

Per serving: Calories 660 (57% from fat); Fat 41.6g (sat 16.5g, mono 19.5g, poly 2.7g); Protein 50.9g; Carb 18.6g; Fiber 5.6g; Chol 227mg; Iron 4.5mg; Sodium 497mg; Calc 134mg

Grilled Pork Tenderloins With Rosemary Pesto

prep: 30 min.   cook: 50 min.
other: 8 hrs., 10 min.

½   cup walnut halves, toasted
¼   cup chopped fresh rosemary (about 4 long sprigs)
3   tablespoons Creole mustard
3   garlic cloves, chopped
½   cup olive oil, divided
4   (½- to ¾-pound) pork tenderloins
1½   teaspoons salt
½   teaspoon black pepper

Process first 4 ingredients in a food processor until smooth, stopping to scrape down sides. With processor running, pour ¼ cup oil through food chute in a slow stream; process until smooth.

Place tenderloins between 2 sheets of heavy-duty plastic wrap, and flatten to ½-inch thickness, using a meat mallet or rolling pin. Spread rosemary pesto evenly over top of 2 tenderloins; top with remaining tenderloins, and tie together with kitchen string.

Rub remaining ¼ cup oil over pork; sprinkle with salt and pepper. Cover and chill 8 hours.

Grill, covered with grill lid, over medium heat (300° to 350°) 10 minutes, turning once. Move pork to indirect heat for 40 minutes or until a meat thermometer inserted into thickest portion registers 155°. Let stand, covered, 10 minutes or until meat thermometer registers 160°. Yield: 10 servings.

Per serving: Calories 271 (61% from fat); Fat 18.4g (sat 3g, mono 10.5g, poly 3.6g); Protein 24.3g; Carb 1.8g; Fiber 0.6g; Chol 63mg; Iron 1.6mg; Sodium 490mg; Calc 14mg

Note: To prepare grill for cooking process, pile charcoal on 1 side of grill, leaving other side empty. (For gas grills, light only 1 side.) Use heated side during first stage of cooking, and move to unlit side for indirect cooking.

Sweet-and-Sour Pork Stir-fry

prep: 30 min.   cook: 16 min.

1½   pounds pork tenderloin, cubed
¼   cup cornstarch
3   tablespoons dark sesame oil, divided
1   (20-ounce) can pineapple tidbits
2   tablespoons lite soy sauce
1   red bell pepper, chopped
1   green bell pepper, chopped
4   green onions, diagonally sliced
½   cup hoisin sauce
1   tablespoon Asian chili garlic sauce (we tested with A Taste of Thai Garlic Chili Pepper Sauce)
3   cups hot cooked brown rice
1   tablespoon sesame seeds, toasted

Dredge pork in cornstarch.

Heat 2 tablespoons oil in a wok or large

Sweet-and-Sour Pork Stir-fry

skillet over medium-high heat; stir-fry pork, in batches, 3 minutes or until browned. Remove pork from skillet; set aside.

Drain pineapple, reserving ¼ cup juice. Add reserved juice and soy sauce to skillet, stirring to loosen browned particles.

Add remaining 1 tablespoon sesame oil to skillet; stir-fry pineapple, bell pepper, and green onions 5 minutes or until bell pepper is tender.

Stir together hoisin sauce and chili garlic sauce; add to skillet. Add pork, and stir-fry 5 minutes. Serve over hot cooked brown rice. Sprinkle with sesame seeds. Yield: 6 servings.

Per serving: Calories 426 (29% from fat); Fat 13.2g (sat 2.7g, mono 5.3g, poly 4.3g); Protein 28.7g; Carb 47.9g; Fiber 4.1g; Chol 74mg; Iron 2.9mg; Sodium 659mg; Calc 59mg

hot tips for stir-fry

● Heat a wok or large skillet until a few beads of water dropped in the pan sizzle and evaporate immediately.

● "Ring" the wok with oil drizzled near the top edge of the wok or skillet, allowing it to run down the sides. This gives the pan a smooth surface with minimal oil.

Boston Butt Roast With Gravy

prep: 20 min.   cook: 3 hrs., 45 min.
other: 10 min.

For the ultimate in comfort food, serve with roasted potatoes, carrots, and onions.

1	(5- to 6-pound) Boston butt pork roast, trimmed
1½	tablespoons salt
½	tablespoon dried Italian seasoning
1	teaspoon garlic powder
1	teaspoon pepper
6	tablespoons all-purpose flour, divided
2	cups water
¼	cup white vinegar
1	onion, chopped
4	garlic cloves
¼	cup hot sauce
2	tablespoons butter or margarine
1	cup low-sodium beef broth
¼	cup red wine
½	teaspoon dried Italian seasoning

Salt and pepper to taste

Place roast in an aluminum foil-lined roasting pan. Sprinkle pork evenly with 1½ tablespoons salt and next 3 ingredients. Sprinkle evenly with 4 tablespoons flour. Pour 2 cups water and vinegar into roasting pan. Add onion and garlic cloves. Drizzle pork evenly with hot sauce.

Bake at 375° for 3½ hours or until tender. Remove pork from roasting pan, and wrap in aluminum foil. Pour about 1 cup pan drippings into a 2-cup glass measuring cup. Let stand 10 minutes, and skim fat from drippings.

Melt butter in a large skillet over medium-high heat; whisk in remaining 2 tablespoons flour, pan drippings, broth, wine, and ½ teaspoon Italian seasoning. Bring to a boil, whisking constantly; reduce heat to medium, and simmer 10 minutes. Season with salt and pepper to taste. Serve gravy over sliced pork. Yield: 10 servings.

Per serving: Calories 505 (62% from fat); Fat 34.7g (sat 13.4g, mono 14.7g, poly 3.2g); Protein 40.5g; Carb 4.8g; Fiber 0.3g; Chol 152mg; Iron 2.9mg; Sodium 1463mg; Calc 56mg

Chalupa Dinner Bowl

slow cooker
Chalupa Dinner Bowl

prep: 30 min.   cook: 11 hrs.

Serve this pork-and-bean mixture spooned over cornbread or rolled up, burrito-style, in flour tortillas. Make hearty nachos, quesadillas, or tacos with it, too.

1	pound dried pinto beans
1	(3½-pound) bone-in pork loin roast
2	(4.5-ounce) cans chopped green chiles
2	garlic cloves, chopped
1	tablespoon chili powder
2	teaspoons salt
1	teaspoon dried oregano
1	teaspoon ground cumin
1	(32-ounce) container chicken broth
1	(10-ounce) can diced tomatoes and green chiles with lime juice and cilantro
8	taco salad shells
1	small head iceberg lettuce, shredded

Toppings: shredded Monterey Jack cheese, pickled jalapeño slices, halved grape tomatoes, sour cream, avocado slices

Rinse and sort beans according to package directions.

Place pinto beans in a 6-quart slow cooker; add roast and next 6 ingredients. Pour chicken broth over roast.

Cover and cook on HIGH 1 hour; reduce heat to LOW, and cook 9 hours. Or, cover and cook on HIGH 6 hours. Remove bones and fat from roast; pull roast into large pieces with 2 forks. Stir in diced tomatoes and green chiles. Cook roast, uncovered, on HIGH 1 more hour or until liquid is slightly thickened.

Heat taco salad shells according to package directions; place shredded lettuce evenly into shells. Spoon about 1 cup pork-and-bean mixture into each shell using a slotted spoon. Serve with desired toppings. Yield: 8 servings.

Per serving: Calories 545 (28% from fat); Fat 17.2g (sat 4.5g, mono 4.2g, poly 1g); Protein 42.7g; Carb 54.5g; Fiber 15.2g; Chol 85mg; Iron 5.2mg; Sodium 1673mg; Calc 154mg

Garlic-Orange Roast Pork

prep: 30 min.   cook: 3 hrs., 56 min.
other: 20 min.

2   cups chopped fresh parsley
¼   cup herbes de Provence
2   tablespoons grated lemon rind
¼   cup fresh lemon juice
1   (5- to 6-pound) Boston butt pork roast
1   tablespoon salt, divided
1   tablespoon pepper, divided
10   garlic cloves, divided
2   large oranges, sliced
2   tablespoons olive oil
2¼   cups orange juice, divided
4   pints cherry tomatoes
1   tablespoon cornstarch
Garnishes: cilantro sprigs, fresh orange
    slices

Combine first 4 ingredients. Set aside.
Butterfly roast by making a lengthwise cut
down center of 1 flat side, cutting to within
1 inch of bottom. Open roast; sprinkle
evenly with 1 teaspoon each of salt and
pepper. Chop 2 garlic cloves, and sprinkle
evenly over pork. Rub half of parsley mixture evenly over pork, and fold pork over
to close; tie pork at 1-inch intervals with
string. Sprinkle evenly with remaining
2 teaspoons each of salt and pepper on
outside of pork.
Place orange slices in a roasting pan with
remaining 8 garlic cloves; drizzle with oil.
Place pork on top of orange slices; pour
2 cups orange juice over pork.
Bake at 450° for 15 minutes; reduce heat to
325°, and bake, basting every 20 minutes, for
1 hour and 30 minutes. Add tomatoes to
pan, and bake 2 more hours or until a meat
thermometer inserted into thickest portion
registers 150°, basting occasionally with pan
drippings. Remove pork from oven, and
coat evenly with remaining parsley mixture.
Bake 10 more minutes or until meat thermometer registers 155°. Remove pork,
orange slices, and tomatoes from pan; cover
with aluminum foil, and let stand 20 minutes or until temperature rises to 160° and
juices settle. Reserve drippings in pan.
Combine cornstarch and remaining ¼ cup
orange juice; stir into drippings. Bring mixture to a boil, and cook, stirring constantly,
1 minute or until thickened. Pour sauce

through a wire-mesh strainer, if desired.
Serve pork with tomatoes, orange slices, and
sauce. Garnish, if desired. Yield: 10 servings.

Per serving: Calories 598 (59% from fat); Fat 39.2g (sat 12.9g, mono 18.1g, poly 4.4g);
Protein 42.6g; Carb 18.2g; Fiber 3.5g; Chol 161mg; Iron 4.7mg; Sodium 856mg; Calc 133mg

Fig-Balsamic Roasted Pork Loin

prep: 45 min.   cook: 1 hr., 48 min.
other: 15 min.

*Purchase a pork loin roast, not a rolled
pork loin roast (which has two loins tied
together). Don't trim away the entire fat
cap on top of the loin; this layer prevents
the meat from drying out. See photos below.*

½   pound ground pork sausage
1¾   cups herb-seasoned stuffing mix
1   large ripe Bartlett pear, peeled and
    chopped
½   red bell pepper, finely chopped
⅓   cup chopped dried figs
½   cup hot chicken broth
1   tablespoon minced fresh thyme
1   (4-pound) boneless pork loin roast
1   teaspoon salt
1   to 2 tablespoons cracked black pepper
1   (11.5-ounce) jar fig preserves
1   cup Madeira wine
2   tablespoons balsamic vinegar
¼   cup butter or margarine
¼   cup all-purpose flour
Garnishes: dried figs, Bartlett pear slices,
    fresh parsley sprigs

Cook sausage in a skillet over medium-high
heat, stirring often, 4 to 5 minutes, stirring
until it crumbles and is no longer pink.
Drain well. Stir together sausage, stuffing
mix, and next 5 ingredients.
Butterfly pork loin roast by making a
lengthwise cut down center of 1 flat side,
cutting to within ½ inch of the bottom.
(Do not cut all the way through roast.)
Open roast, forming a rectangle, and place
between 2 sheets of heavy-duty plastic
wrap. Flatten to ½-inch thickness, using a
meat mallet or rolling pin. Sprinkle roast
with salt and pepper. Spoon sausage mixture
evenly over roast, leaving a ½-inch border.
Roll up roast, and tie with string at 1½-inch
intervals. Place roast, seam side down, in a
greased shallow roasting pan.
Bake at 375° for 55 to 60 minutes or until a
meat thermometer inserted into thickest
portion registers 145°. Remove roast from
pan; reserve drippings. Return roast to pan.
Stir together fig preserves, Madeira, and balsamic vinegar. Spoon half of preserves mixture evenly over roast.
Bake at 375° for 20 to 30 more minutes or
until meat thermometer registers 160°. Let
stand 15 minutes before slicing.
Melt butter in a medium saucepan; whisk in
flour until smooth. Cook, whisking constantly, 3 minutes. Whisk in reserved pan
drippings and remaining fig preserves mixture, and cook over medium-high heat
5 minutes. Serve sauce with roast; garnish, if
desired. Yield: 8 servings.

Per serving: Calories 786 (46% from fat); Fat 40.4g (sat 14.8g, mono 16.7g, poly 4.1g);
Protein 52.4g; Carb 50.6g; Fiber 3g; Chol 188mg; Iron 3.7mg; Sodium 851mg; Calc 99mg

▲ Pounding the pork loin with
the flat, smooth side of a meat
mallet to ½-inch thickness
produces an even surface and
allows for easier rolling of the
stuffed meat.

▲ Leave a ½-inch border on the
edge of the meat to prevent
stuffing from spilling out.

▲ Using butcher's twine, tie the
roast at 1½-inch intervals.

Chinese-Style Spareribs

prep: 20 min.   cook: 2 hrs., 10 min.

- 2 pounds pork spareribs, cut into small pieces
- 2 garlic cloves, minced
- 1 teaspoon grated fresh ginger
- 1 tablespoon vegetable oil
- 1 (8-ounce) jar black bean sauce
- ¼ cup teriyaki sauce
- 2 tablespoons chili garlic sauce

Rub ribs with garlic and ginger.
Brown ribs in hot oil in a Dutch oven over medium-high heat 4 to 5 minutes on each side. Stir together sauces. Pour over ribs; reduce heat, and simmer, stirring occasionally, 1 hour. Arrange ribs in a 13- x 9-inch pan. Pour sauce mixture over ribs.
Bake at 350° for 1 hour. Yield: 3 servings.

Per serving: Calories 684 (69% from fat); Fat 52.4g (sat 18g, mono 21.6g, poly 8.2g); Protein 35.4g; Carb 15.8g; Fiber 1.2g; Chol 146mg; Iron 2.8mg; Sodium 1856mg; Calc 86mg

glossary of ribs

Spareribs yield the least amount of meat per bone, and because they're less tender than other ribs, may take a bit longer to cook. However, they are considered the most flavorful.

Baby back ribs have lots of meat between their short bones. These may cost a bit more per pound than spareribs.

Country-style ribs are the meatiest ribs of all, and can be eaten with a knife and fork. They're usually sold in packages of six to eight pieces already cut apart for easy grilling.

Buy ribs with as much meat and as little fat as possible.

Spicy-Sweet Ribs and Beans

prep: 15 min.   cook: 6 hrs. (HIGH) or 10 hrs. (LOW), 22 min.

Bottled hickory-flavored barbecue sauce and hot jalapeño jelly make preparation a breeze, and the long, slow cooking makes these ribs extra tender.

- 2 (16-ounce) cans pinto beans, drained
- 4 pounds country-style pork ribs, trimmed
- 1 teaspoon garlic powder
- ½ teaspoon salt
- ½ teaspoon pepper
- 1 medium onion, chopped
- 1 (18-ounce) bottle hickory-flavored barbecue sauce (we tested with Kraft Thick 'n' Spicy Hickory Smoke Barbecue Sauce)
- 1 (10.5-ounce) jar red jalapeño jelly
- 1 teaspoon green hot sauce (we tested with Tabasco Green Pepper Sauce)

Place beans in a 5-quart slow cooker; set aside.
Cut ribs into serving-size portions.
Combine garlic powder, salt, and pepper. Sprinkle both sides of ribs with seasoning mixture. Place ribs on a lightly greased rack in a broiler pan.
Broil 5½ inches from heat 10 to 11 minutes on each side or until browned. Add ribs to slow cooker, and sprinkle with onion.
While ribs broil, combine barbecue sauce, jelly, and hot sauce in a large saucepan. Cook over medium heat 4 minutes or until smooth, stirring constantly. Pour over rib mixture; stir gently.
Cover and cook on HIGH 6 hours or on LOW 9 to 10 hours. Remove ribs. Drain bean mixture, reserving sauce. Skim fat from sauce. Arrange ribs over bean mixture; serve with sauce. Yield: 8 servings.

Per serving: Calories 610 (39% from fat); Fat 26.2g (sat 9.7g, mono 11.2g, poly 2.5g); Protein 32.2g; Carb 57g; Fiber 3.7g; Chol 104mg; Iron 2.6mg; Sodium 1204mg; Calc 70mg

---

Maple Spareribs

Maple Spareribs

prep: 15 min.   cook: 2 hrs.

- 3 to 4 pounds pork spareribs
- 1 cup maple syrup
- ⅓ cup soy sauce
- 1 tablespoon garlic powder
- 3 tablespoons sweet rice wine (we tested with Kikkoman Aji-Mirin Sweet Cooking Rice Wine)
- 2 teaspoons salt
- ½ teaspoon sugar

Bring ribs and water to cover to a boil in a large Dutch oven; reduce heat, and simmer 30 minutes. Drain. Place ribs in a lightly greased 13- x 9-inch baking dish.
Stir together maple syrup and remaining ingredients; pour over ribs in dish.
Prepare a hot fire by piling charcoal on 1 side of grill, leaving other side empty. (For gas grills, light only 1 side.) Arrange ribs over unlit side, reserving sauce in dish.
Grill spareribs, covered with grill lid, 1 hour and 30 minutes, basting occasionally with reserved sauce. Yield: 4 servings.

Per serving: Calories 803 (54% from fat); Fat 48.1g (sat 17.6g, mono 21.4g, poly 4.4g); Protein 48.1g; Carb 42.9g; Fiber 0.3g; Chol 191mg; Iron 4.2mg; Sodium 2024mg; Calc 121mg

Oven-Baked Maple Spareribs: Prepare as directed. Wrap ribs in foil, and bake at 350° for 2 hours. Remove foil, and bake 30 more minutes, basting occasionally.

ham & sausage

If a leg of pork has been cured and rubbed with salt and spices, soaked in a brine solution, and/or smoked, it becomes known as ham. Look for the label on the ham to identify the type of processing and whether it has been cooked. Several varieties are available: ham with natural juices, ham with water added, and a ham and water product commonly known as deli ham. Country ham is extremely dry and salty and is usually served in small, thinly sliced portions.

Most hams are fully cooked and do not require further heating. Though they can be eaten cold, heating to an internal temperature of 140° will make them more flavorful. Uncooked hams must be cooked to 160° before serving.

Bone-in hams are sold whole, as halves, in butt or shank portions, or as center cut slices. The butt half generally has a higher proportion of meat to bone and is more expensive than the shank. Boneless hams are easier to slice, and are sold as halves, quarter, or steaks. Canned hams are boneless and fully cooked.

Cured ham will keep in the refrigerator up to a week, cooked or uncooked. Unopened, canned hams will keep up to a year; once opened, refrigerate them. We do not recommend freezing ham because its texture and flavor will decline, but if you do so, it will keep up to two months.

Bacon, from the side section of the pig, is sold in slices of varying thickness or in slab form. Other variations include lower salt bacon, ready-to-microwave bacon, and precooked bacon. Flavored bacon, such as peppered or applewood-smoked, is also available. Canadian-style bacon comes from smoked pork tenderloin, and is a lean alternative to regular bacon.

Sausage is seasoned fresh, smoked, or cured ground pork that sometimes, but not always, is enclosed in a casing. Many different varieties are available. Sausage might be mild, seasoned, or hot, and different ingredient combinations yield a host of ethnic favorites, including sweet Italian links, spicy French or Cajun andouille, German bratwurst links, and Spanish chorizo.

low calorie • low fat

Country Ham

prep: 1 hr.   cook: 4 hrs.   other: 24 hrs.

1   (12- to 14-pound) uncooked country ham
2   quarts cider vinegar
1   tablespoon whole cloves
Hot biscuits (optional)

Place ham in a large container. Add water to cover, and soak 24 hours. Drain. Scrub ham 3 or 4 times in cold water with a stiff brush, and rinse well.
Place ham, fat side up, in a large roasting pan. Pour vinegar over ham; sprinkle with cloves. Cover with lid or aluminum foil.
Bake at 325° for 4 hours or until a meat thermometer registers 140°. Remove from oven; cool slightly. Slice ham, and serve with hot biscuits, if desired. Yield: 40 servings.

Per serving: Calories 228 (38% from fat); Fat 9.6g (sat 3.2g, mono 4.4g, poly 1.1g); Protein 32.2g; Carb 0.4g; Fiber 0g; Chol 81mg; Iron 1.3mg; Sodium 3118mg; Calc 12mg

low calorie • low carb • low fat • quick

Country Ham With Redeye Gravy

prep: 5 min.   cook: 25 min.

2   cups hot strong brewed coffee
¼   cup firmly packed brown sugar
1   pound center-cut country ham slices

Stir together coffee and sugar.
Cook ham in a large cast-iron skillet over medium heat 5 minutes on each side or until browned. Remove ham; reserve drippings in skillet.
Add coffee mixture to skillet, stirring to loosen particles from bottom; bring coffee to a boil.
Boil, stirring occasionally, until reduced by half (about 15 minutes). Serve with ham. Yield: 6 servings.

Per serving: Calories 184 (31% from fat); Fat 6.3g (sat 2.1g, mono 2.9g, poly 0.7g); Protein 21.1g; Carb 9.5g; Fiber 0g; Chol 53mg; Iron 1.1mg; Sodium 2043mg; Calc 19mg

timetable for roasting smoked pork

cut	approximate weight in pounds	internal temperature	approximate total cooking times in minutes at 325° per pound
Ham (cook before eating)			
Whole	10 to 14	160°	18 to 20
Half	5 to 7	160°	22 to 25
Shank portion	3 to 4	160°	35 to 40
Butt portion	3 to 4	160°	35 to 40
Ham (fully cooked)			
Whole	10 to 12	140°	15 to 18
Half	5 to 7	140°	18 to 24
Loin	3 to 5	160°	25 to 30
Picnic shoulder (cook before eating)	5 to 8	170°	30 to 35
Picnic shoulder (fully cooked)	5 to 8	140°	25 to 30
Shoulder roll (butt)	2 to 4	170°	35 to 40
Canadian-style bacon	2 to 4	160°	35 to 40

ham know how

Simple Mathematics

Wondering how much to buy? Say you want to serve eight people: Allotting two to three servings per pound for a bone-in ham, you'll need to buy a 7- to 9-pound ham.

Which to Buy

Overall, we find the taste and texture of a bone-in ham to be the best. Besides, you've got prime real estate—the ham bone—underneath all that goodness. Save this prize for your next pot of beans, greens, or soup.

You'll find half hams cut into shank and butt portions. Though pricier, the butt portion offers more meat because there's not as much bone as in the shank. Also available are spiral-sliced hams, which are easier to serve, but you'll pay for this added convenience. You can substitute a reduced-sodium ham in our recipes if you're watching your sodium count.

To Cook or Not?

The label on a ham tells you whether it's ready to eat or should be cooked. We recommend that you bake a fully cooked ham at 325° for 15 to 20 minutes per pound or until it reaches an internal temperature of 140°. Even though it technically doesn't require additional cooking, reheating it thoroughly maximizes its goodness. Fresh hams should be baked at 325° for 18 to 22 minutes per pound or until a meat thermometer registers 160°.

How to Store It

If you don't plan on using all the meat within four to five days, slice or cube it; then wrap tightly in heavy-duty plastic wrap. Freeze it in an airtight container up to two months. Or package it in small, manageable portions so there's no waste.

Carving Clues

Carving a ham is easy. A sharp carving knife, a meat fork, and these simple instructions are all you need. Hold the knife perpendicular to the bone. Cut full slices just until you feel the knife touching the bone. Then, place your knife at a 90-degree angle to the slices, parallel to the bone, and cut to release the slices. Once all the meat has been cut from this side, turn the ham over, and repeat the procedure.

Molasses–Coffee Glazed Ham

prep: 20 min.   cook: 2 hrs.   other: 30 min.

You wouldn't expect coffee and vanilla to be key components in this yummy basting sauce. It's also great on turkey.

1	cup molasses
1	(12-ounce) jar apricot jam
2	tablespoons cider vinegar
1	tablespoon Dijon mustard
1	teaspoon salt
1	teaspoon vanilla extract
¾	cup strong brewed coffee
1	(8- to 9-pound) bone-in, fully cooked smoked ham half

Stir together first 7 ingredients until blended. Reserve 1 cup molasses–coffee sauce in a small bowl; set reserved sauce aside.

Trim ham, and, if desired, score top of ham in a diamond pattern. Place ham in a lightly greased 13- x 9-inch pan. Pour remaining molasses–coffee sauce evenly over ham.

Bake on lower oven rack at 350° for 2 hours or until a meat thermometer inserted into thickest portion of ham registers 140°, basting with sauce in pan every 15 minutes. Cover ham loosely with lightly greased aluminum foil the last 30 minutes to prevent excessive browning, if necessary.

Remove ham from pan; let stand 30 minutes. Heat reserved molasses–coffee sauce, and serve with ham. Yield: 12 servings.

Per serving: Calories 661 (48% from fat); Fat 35.6g (sat 13g, mono 16g, poly 3.4g); Protein 45g; Carb 38.9g; Fiber 0.1g; Chol 163mg; Iron 3.2mg; Sodium 336mg; Calc 89mg

Baked Ham With Bourbon Glaze

prep: 10 min.   cook: 2 hrs., 30 min.

1	cup honey
½	cup molasses
½	cup bourbon or orange juice
¼	cup orange juice
2	tablespoons Dijon mustard
1	(6- to 8-pound) smoked ham half

Microwave honey and molasses in a 1-quart glass dish at HIGH 1 minute. Whisk to blend. Whisk in bourbon, orange juice, and mustard.

---

ham dictionary

Bone-in ham: This ham has the entire bone intact. It's available whole, butt end, or shank end only.

Boneless ham: This ham has the entire bone removed, and the ham is rolled or packed in a casing.

Country ham: Ham prepared with a dry-rub cure. Most country hams are very dry and salty and require soaking before cooking.

Dry-cured ham: The ham's surface is rubbed with a mixture of salt, sugar, nitrites, and seasonings, and then air-dried.

Fresh ham: Uncured pork leg.

Pancetta: Italian bacon cured with salt and aromatic herbs and spices. It's often eaten cold in thin slices.

Prosciutto ham: Prosciutto is a broadly used term to describe ham that has been seasoned, salt-cured, and air-dried. Italy's Parma ham is a true prosciutto. It's usually sold very thinly sliced and eaten as an appetizer.

Smoked ham: Ham that's been hung in a smokehouse after the curing process in order to take on the smoky flavor of the wood used.

Remove skin and fat from ham; place ham in a lightly greased 13- x 9-inch pan. Make ¼-inch-deep cuts in ham in a diamond pattern. Pour glaze over ham.

Bake on lower oven rack at 350° for 2 to 2½ hours or until a meat thermometer inserted into thickest portion registers 140°, basting every 15 minutes with glaze.

Remove from pan, reserving drippings. Cover ham, and chill, if desired. Chill reserved drippings.

Remove and discard fat from drippings. Bring drippings to a boil in a small saucepan. Serve warm with ham. Yield: 12 servings.

Per serving: Calories 534 (45% from fat); Fat 26.6g (sat 9.8g, mono 12g, poly 2.5g); Protein 33.7g; Carb 34g; Fiber 0.1g; Chol 122mg; Iron 2.1mg; Sodium 117mg; Calc 50mg

Baked Burgundy Ham

Tackling an uncooked ham can be overwhelming. Ask your butcher to cut a little bit off the top of the hock; doing so will give you extra room in the roasting pan. Don't discard this moist piece of meat. It provides a seasoning base for soups and beans, and the aroma is an excellent indicator of the ham's quality.

family favorite

Ham-Broccoli Pot Pie

prep: 20 min.   cook: 35 min.

Convenience items make this one-dish meal very appealing.

1   (10-ounce) package frozen chopped broccoli, thawed
1   (11-ounce) can sweet whole kernel corn, drained
1   (10¾-ounce) can cream of mushroom soup
2   cups diced cooked ham
2   cups (8 ounces) shredded colby-Jack cheese blend
1   (8-ounce) container sour cream
½   teaspoon pepper
½   teaspoon dry mustard
½   (15-ounce) package refrigerated piecrusts

Arrange chopped broccoli in a lightly greased 11- x 7-inch baking dish.
Stir together corn and next 6 ingredients. Spoon over broccoli.
Unroll piecrust; pat or roll into an 11- x 7-inch rectangle, and place over ham mixture. Crimp edges, and cut 4 slits for steam to escape.
Bake at 400° for 30 to 35 minutes or until golden. Yield: 6 servings.

Per serving: Calories 585 (62% from fat); Fat 40.5g (sat 19.9g, mono 6.4g, poly 1.8g); Protein 24.6g; Carb 29.7g; Fiber 2g; Chol 96mg; Iron 1.5mg; Sodium 849mg; Calc 339mg

Baked Burgundy Ham

prep: 20 min.   cook: 3 hrs.   other: 8 hrs.

Red wine and fragrant spices in the marinade richly flavor this ham that deserves center-piece status on the holiday table.

1   (6- to 8-pound) smoked fully cooked ham half, well trimmed
6   cups water
2   cups cran-apple juice drink, divided
2   cups dry red wine, divided
2   cups firmly packed dark brown sugar, divided
2   (3-inch) cinnamon sticks
1   tablespoon whole cloves
Garnish: fresh rosemary

Score top of ham in a diamond pattern.
Place ham in a large Dutch oven. Add water, 1 cup juice drink, 1 cup wine, 1 cup brown sugar, cinnamon sticks, and cloves.
Bring to a boil; cover, reduce heat, and simmer 20 minutes. Remove from heat; let stand until cool. Remove ham and marinade from Dutch oven, and place in a large nonmetallic bowl. Cover and marinate in refrigerator 8 hours.
Remove ham from marinade; reserve 2 cups marinade. Discard remaining marinade. Place ham in a lightly greased shallow roasting pan; cover.
Bake, covered, at 325° for 1½ hours, basting ham occasionally with reserved marinade. Uncover and bake 20 minutes or until a meat thermometer inserted into thickest portion registers 140°, basting ham occasionally with pan juices. Remove ham, reserving pan juices.
Combine pan juices, remaining 1 cup juice, 1 cup wine, and 1 cup brown sugar in a saucepan. Bring to a boil; reduce heat, and simmer, uncovered, 40 minutes or until sauce coats the back of a metal spoon. Serve sauce with ham. Garnish, if desired. Yield: 12 servings.

Per serving: Calories 531 (45% from fat); Fat 26.6g (sat 9.8g, mono 12g, poly 2.5g); Protein 33.7g; Carb 37.9g; Fiber 0g; Chol 122mg; Iron 2.1mg; Sodium 94mg; Calc 52mg

Note: Buy ham halves in either butt or shank portions. The butt half has a rounded end, more meat, and usually costs a little more. The shank half has a tapered end, and is easier to slice because of its bone configuration.

quick

Sausage and Peppers With Parmesan Cheese Grits

prep: 15 min.   cook: 15 min.

1 (19-ounce) package sweet Italian sausage
3 red, yellow, or green bell peppers, cut into strips
1 large sweet onion, cut in half and thinly sliced
2 garlic cloves, minced
1 to 2 teaspoons dried Italian seasoning
½ teaspoon garlic powder
1 teaspoon salt
½ teaspoon pepper
Parmesan Cheese Grits

Remove and discard sausage casings. Cook sausage and next 7 ingredients in a large skillet over medium-high heat, stirring until sausage crumbles and is no longer pink and vegetables are tender. Serve over Parmesan Cheese Grits. Yield: 4 servings.

Per serving: Calories 579 (41% from fat); Fat 26.1g (sat 11.9g, mono 8.6g, poly 4.5g); Protein 42.4g; Carb 43.5g; Fiber 3g; Chol 146mg; Iron 3.8mg; Sodium 2621mg; Calc 471mg

Parmesan Cheese Grits

prep: 5 min.   cook: 5 min.

1 cup uncooked quick-cooking grits
4 cups water
¾ teaspoon salt
1 tablespoon butter or margarine
1 (5-ounce) package shredded Parmesan cheese

Cook grits according to package directions, using 4 cups water. Stir in salt, butter, and Parmesan cheese. Yield: 4 servings.

Per serving: Calories 323 (36% from fat); Fat 13g (sat 8g, mono 4g, poly 0.6g); Protein 17.1g; Carb 34.2g; Fiber 0.8g; Chol 33mg; Iron 1.9mg; Sodium 1062mg; Calc 453mg

quick

Sausage-and-Bean Supper

prep: 10 min.   cook: 20 min.

1 pound smoked sausage, cut into ¼-inch slices
3 bacon slices, diced
1 small sweet onion, diced
½ (10-ounce) bag shredded carrot
2 celery ribs, chopped
1 (19-ounce) can cannelloni beans or navy beans, rinsed and drained
1 (14-ounce) can chicken broth
1 teaspoon dried rosemary
½ teaspoon dried thyme
½ teaspoon pepper
2 tablespoons butter or margarine
1 cup fresh breadcrumbs
½ cup grated Parmesan cheese

Cook sausage, bacon, onion, carrot, and celery in a large skillet over medium-high heat 10 minutes or until sausage is browned and vegetables are tender.
Stir in beans, broth, rosemary, thyme, and pepper; cook over medium heat 10 minutes or until mixture is hot and bubbly.
Melt butter in a small skillet over medium heat; add breadcrumbs, and sauté until lightly browned. Remove from heat, and stir in Parmesan cheese. Sprinkle breadcrumb topping over sausage and beans. Serve hot. Yield: 4 servings.

Per serving: Calories 747 (62% from fat); Fat 50.6g (sat 19g, mono 19.8g, poly 5.2g); Protein 36g; Carb 34.8g; Fiber 5.7g; Chol 107mg; Iron 3.3mg; Sodium 2599mg; Calc 215mg

from the grill • low carb (without buns) • quick

Grilled Brats

prep: 2 min.   cook: 20 min.

A quick simmer infuses these brats with beer before they hit the grill. Serve them with or without a bun, but a mug of beer shouldn't be optional.

2 pounds bratwurst
3 (12-ounce) cans beer or 4½ cups water

Prick sausage with a fork. Bring beer to a boil in a large saucepan; add sausage, and return to a boil.
Cover, reduce heat, and simmer 5 minutes. Remove sausage, and pat dry. Grill, without grill lid, over medium coals (300° to 350°) 9 to 10 minutes, turning often. Serve with coarse-grained mustard. Yield: 4 servings.

Per serving: Calories 364 (77% from fat); Fat 31.1g (sat 10.8g, mono 15.7g, poly 2.8g); Protein 14.8g; Carb 5.2g; Fiber 0g; Chol 79mg; Iron 0.6mg; Sodium 934mg; Calc 33mg

game meats

Venison and other game meats have an undeserved reputation as being tough and dry. Since game is generally lean and lacks the marbling of other meat, it can be tough and dry if not cooked properly.

The key is putting the right marinade and cooking method to work to ensure tender, juicy results. Try a marinade with an acidic component such as wine, vinegar, or citrus juice to break down tough muscle fiber. And then cook by a moist-heat method such as braising or stewing.

low calorie • low fat • quick

Venison Burgers

prep: 10 min.   cook: 10 min.

1 pound ground venison
1 pound ground chuck
3 tablespoons lemon pepper
2 tablespoons Worcestershire sauce
½ teaspoon garlic powder
2 teaspoons coarse-grained mustard
Hamburger buns, toasted

Combine first 6 ingredients in a bowl. Shape into 8 (¾-inch-thick) patties.
Place patties on a lightly greased rack of a broiler pan. Broil patties 5½ inches from heat 5 minutes on each side, turning once. Serve burgers on toasted buns with your choice of condiments. Yield: 8 servings.

Per serving: Calories 304 (31% from fat); Fat 10.5g (sat 3.7g, mono 4.1g, poly 1.3g); Protein 27.5g; Carb 22.9g; Fiber 1.1g; Chol 83mg; Iron 4.7mg; Sodium 844mg; Calc 83mg

Grilled Venison Steaks

prep: 5 min.   cook: 10 min.   other: 8 hrs.

4   (4-ounce) lean, boneless venison loin
    steaks (1 inch thick)
1   cup cranberry-orange crushed fruit,
    divided
½   cup dry red wine
2   tablespoons Dijon mustard
2   teaspoons minced garlic
2   teaspoons fresh or dried rosemary
½   teaspoon pepper
Vegetable cooking spray

Trim fat from steaks. Place steaks in a large zip-top freezer bag. Combine ½ cup crushed fruit, wine, and next 4 ingredients; pour over steaks. Seal bag; turn to coat steaks. Marinate in refrigerator 4 to 8 hours, turning bag occasionally. Remove steaks from marinade, discarding marinade.
Lightly spray grill rack with cooking spray. Grill steaks over medium-high heat (350° to 400°), 8 to 10 minutes, or to desired degree of doneness, turning once. Serve with remaining ½ cup crushed fruit. Yield: 4 servings.

Per serving: Calories 224 (15% from fat); Fat 3.7g (sat 1.1g, mono 0.9g, poly 0.7g); Protein 26.2g; Carb 21g; Fiber 0.2g; Chol 95mg; Iron 4.2mg; Sodium 156mg; Calc 23mg

Pepper-Crusted Venison Tenderloin

prep: 5 min.   cook: 55 min.
other: 2 hrs., 10 min.

Cola as a marinade mellows the sometimes gamey taste of venison. Horseradish, cracked pepper, and coarse-grained mustard deliver robust flavor.

2   venison tenderloins (2 to 2½ pounds
    total)
1   (12-ounce) can cola-flavored beverage
¼   cup coarse-grained mustard
2   tablespoons coarsely ground or cracked
    pepper
½   cup red currant jelly
2   tablespoons prepared horseradish
1   tablespoon coarse-grained mustard

Place venison and cola in a large zip-top freezer bag; seal and marinate in refrigerator 2 hours. Remove venison from bag, discarding marinade.
Spread 2 tablespoons mustard over top and sides of each tenderloin; pat pepper over mustard. Place tenderloins on a greased rack in broiler pan. Bake, uncovered, at 450° for 15 minutes; reduce heat to 350°, and bake 40 minutes or until a meat thermometer inserted into thickest portion registers 160° (medium).
Combine jelly, horseradish, and 1 tablespoon mustard; stir well. Let venison stand 10 minutes before slicing; serve with sauce. Yield: 8 servings.

Per serving: Calories 208 (16% from fat); Fat 3.6g (sat 1.1g, mono 0.9g, poly 0.6g); Protein 26.4g; Carb 17.1g; Fiber 0.7g; Chol 95mg; Iron 4.3mg; Sodium 250mg; Calc 19mg

Venison Pot Roast

prep: 30 min.   cook: 5 hrs.   other: 8 hrs.

Five hours of slow simmering in the oven tenderizes this roast and leaves you time for other things.

1   (5-pound) venison chuck roast, trimmed
2   cups water
1   cup white vinegar
3   garlic cloves, finely chopped
2   celery ribs with leaves, finely chopped
1   large onion, finely chopped
1   medium-size green bell pepper, finely
    chopped
2   tablespoons vegetable oil
¾   cup dry red wine, divided
1   tablespoon salt
1   tablespoon black pepper
½   teaspoon garlic powder
¼   teaspoon ground red pepper
2   lemons, sliced
8   bacon slices
½   cup butter or margarine
½   cup orange juice
½   cup honey
1   teaspoon chopped fresh or dried
    rosemary
2   tablespoons cornstarch
2   tablespoons water
2   tablespoons chopped fresh parsley
4   green onions, thinly sliced

Place roast in a large zip-top freezer bag. Add 2 cups water and vinegar to roast. Seal bag; marinate in refrigerator 8 hours, turning occasionally. Remove roast from marinade, discarding marinade.
Sauté chopped garlic and next 3 ingredients in hot oil in a large roasting pan 5 minutes or until tender. Add roast to pan and pour ½ cup wine over roast.
Combine salt and next 3 ingredients; sprinkle over roast. Arrange lemon slices over roast; top with bacon.
Combine remaining ¼ cup wine, butter, and next 3 ingredients in a small saucepan; cook over medium heat until butter melts, stirring occasionally. Baste roast once with half of butter mixture.
Insert a meat thermometer into thickest portion of roast, making sure it does not touch bone or fat. Bake, covered, at 275° for 4 hours, basting often with remaining butter mixture. Uncover and bake 1 more hour or until meat thermometer registers 170°. Remove roast to a serving platter, reserving drippings in pan.
Combine cornstarch and 2 tablespoons water; gradually add to pan drippings. Bring to a boil over medium-high heat, stirring constantly; cook, stirring constantly, until thickened and bubbly. Stir in parsley and green onions. Serve sauce with roast. Yield: 8 servings.

Per serving: Calories 607 (36% from fat); Fat 24.5g (sat 11.2g, mono 7.6g, poly 3.6g); Protein 68.6g; Carb 26.6g; Fiber 1.3g; Chol 278mg; Iron 10.5mg; Sodium 1258mg; Calc 46mg

pasta, rice &
grains

pasta

The passion for pasta is alive and well in today's kitchen. While simple to cook and versatile, it's also protein- and carbohydrate-packed, high in fiber, and easily affordable. And many of the basic recipes boil down to a few easy steps that don't require a chef's skill. The main thing to remember is that pasta is best eaten hot without delay.

Equipment

Cooking pasta doesn't require any special cookware. In fact, a sturdy set of saucepans and a large pot and colander will get you through this section with ease. A stainless steel pasta insert makes a convenient replacement for a colander. When the pasta's ready, simply lift out the insert for perfectly drained pasta.

Pasta Basics

Most pasta is made from semolina flour, a flour high in gluten-forming protein, ground from durum wheat.

Pasta comes in about as many shapes and flavors as there are ways to prepare it. And it's available in two forms—dried or refrigerated fresh.

Dried pasta is popular because it's easy on the budget and has a long shelf life. Look for a package that has unbroken pieces.

Fresh pasta is sold in the refrigerated section at the supermarket. It's a bit more pricey, but it cooks up superfast. Fresh pasta varies in weight from dried pasta; ounce for ounce, you'll need to buy about 50 percent more fresh pasta to end up with the same amount of cooked dried pasta.

Storing Pasta

Store uncooked pasta in a cool, dry place free from dust and moisture up to one year; store uncooked egg noodles up to six months. Store plain cooked pasta in the refrigerator up to four days or in the freezer up to one month. You can refrigerate prepared pasta dishes one to two days (depending on any meat or seafood it contains), or freeze them as long as six months. To store fresh homemade pasta, wrap in plastic and refrigerate up to three days, or freeze up to one month.

Measuring Pasta

Uncooked dried pasta of similar sizes and shapes can be interchanged in recipes if it's measured by weight, not volume. Cooked pasta, however, can be substituted cup for cup. When cooked, noodles swell slightly; spaghetti and macaroni double in size. In general, allow 2 ounces of uncooked dried pasta, 3 ounces of uncooked refrigerated pasta, or 1 to 1½ cups cooked pasta per person.

Cooking Pasta

Pasta needs plenty of room to roam in rapidly boiling salted water. Whether you start with hot or cold tap water matters not. Using hot tap water will simply get the water boiling faster. Using plenty of water and stirring two or three times during cooking keeps pasta from sticking or clumping. Resist the urge to add oil to pasta water. Most reliable sources discourage this, claiming the oil merely coats the pasta and prevents sauce from sticking to it.

Use a pot with a 6- to 8-quart capacity to cook one pound of pasta. Fill the pot three-fourths full with water. Cover pot, and bring water to a rolling boil over high heat; then add salt. (We recommend 1 tablespoon salt per pound of pasta.) Uncover and add pasta to boiling salted water, and stir with a wooden spoon. Bring water back to a rolling boil, and maintain boil for remainder of cook time.

When cooking long pasta shapes (spaghetti, linguine, and fettuccine), it's not necessary to break the pasta into pieces. Simply hold one end of pasta by the handful, and dip the other end into boiling water, pushing pasta gently until it softens enough to submerge.

Cooking times will vary with a pasta's size, shape, and moisture content. Fresh pasta cooks in one to three minutes, while dried pasta requires five to 15 minutes. Follow the package directions.

Taste-test a piece of pasta for doneness near the end of cooking. Pasta's ready when it's *al dente* ("to the tooth" in Italian)—firm but tender, chewy not soggy. Slightly undercook pasta such as lasagna that will be used as part of a recipe requiring further cooking.

It's often a good idea to save a small ladleful of pasta water before you drain the pasta. You may want to add it to the sauce before serving. The small amount of starch in pasta water encourages a light sauce to cling to pasta.

Drain pasta in a colander, and shake gently to remove excess liquid. Rinse pasta only if you are making a pasta salad. The starch that clings to cooked pasta will help the sauce cling. If serving is delayed, return cooked and drained pasta to its warm cooking pot. Cover and let stand up to 10 minutes.

When cooked *al dente,* pasta can be reheated. Simply drop cooked pasta into boiling water that has been removed from heat, and let stand one to two minutes; then drain.

Serving Pasta

Serving long, thin pastas such as linguine or fettuccine can be tricky. Use kitchen tongs or a pasta fork to transfer the pasta. This long-handled fork has pegs protruding from the flat surface that allow you to grab the pasta and easily lift it to plates.

The variety of pastas available today creates endless options for pairing pastas and sauces. Keep in mind this general rule of thumb—thin strands for light sauces; small shapes for soups; bolder shaped pastas deserve chunky, robust sauces; and ribbons or tube shapes for layered dishes. Filled pastas are great partners with smooth, light sauces or a simple drizzle of olive oil. And, remember that pasta need only be lightly coated with sauce, not smothered in it; you want to taste the pasta, too.

> Pasta needs plenty of room to roam in rapidly boiling salted water.

pasta dictionary

Long shapes: Team thick strands with hearty sauces and thin strands with light, delicate sauces.▼

Shells and wide noodles: These are great for stuffing and layering with hearty ingredients. ▼

Small shapes: Use these petite pastas for soups and salads. ▼

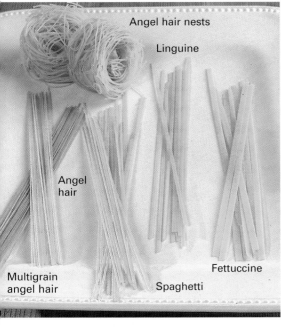

Angel hair nests
Linguine
Angel hair
Multigrain angel hair
Spaghetti
Fettuccine

Lasagna
Manicotti
Jumbo shells

Ditalini
Orzo
Alphabet pasta

Medium shapes: These pastas have holes and ridges and pair well with chunky, hearty sauces and are popular in salads, casseroles, and stews.

▼   ▼

Tricolor rotini
Fusilli
Corkscrews
Ziti
Multigrain rotini
Cavatelli
Radiatore
Vegetable corkscrews

Rigatoni
Mostaccioli
Multigrain penne
Seashells
Gemelli
Multigrain elbow macaroni
Farfalle

When our recipes call for freshly grated Parmesan cheese, we recommend you grate from a wedge of cheese.

Pasta With Spring Vegetables

family favorite
Easy Spaghetti

prep: 8 min.   cook: 30 min.

Scores of popular entrées begin with a skillet full of ground beef and onion. Here the duo stars in a foolproof spaghetti.

1   pound ground beef
1   small onion, chopped
1   (28-ounce) can tomatoes, undrained and chopped
2   (6-ounce) cans tomato paste
1   teaspoon dried oregano
1   teaspoon dried basil
1   large garlic clove, minced, or
     ½ teaspoon garlic powder
½   (16-ounce) package uncooked spaghetti
1   cup freshly grated Parmesan cheese

Cook ground beef and onion in a large skillet, stirring until meat crumbles and is no longer pink; drain. Stir in tomatoes, tomato paste, and seasonings. Cook over medium heat about 20 minutes, stirring occasionally. **Cook** spaghetti according to package directions; drain. Serve sauce over spaghetti; sprinkle with cheese. Yield: 4 main-dish servings.

Per serving: Calories 691 (39% from fat); Fat 29.6g (sat 12.3g, mono 11.8g, poly 1.3g); Protein 38.2g; Carb 68.2g; Fiber 9.8g; Chol 98mg; Iron 7.5mg; Sodium 993mg; Calc 330mg

Sicilian Spaghetti Sauce

prep: 20 min.   cook: 2 hrs., 40 min.

½   pound mild Italian sausage
½   pound lean ground beef
1   large onion, chopped
2   garlic cloves, minced
4   (8-ounce) cans tomato sauce
1   (6-ounce) can Italian-style tomato paste
3   cups water
¼   cup sugar
1   teaspoon salt
1   teaspoon dried parsley
1   teaspoon dried basil
¼   to ½ teaspoon ground red pepper
1   cup sliced fresh mushrooms
12   ounces uncooked spaghetti
1   cup freshly grated Parmesan cheese

Remove and discard casings from sausage. Cook sausage and ground beef in a large skillet or Dutch oven over medium heat 6 minutes, stirring until meat crumbles and is no longer pink. Add onion and garlic, and sauté 4 minutes. Drain and set aside. Wipe skillet clean.
Combine tomato sauce and next 7 ingredients in skillet or Dutch oven; cook, stirring occasionally, 1 hour. Add sausage mixture and mushrooms. Cook, stirring occasionally, 1 hour and 30 minutes or until thickened.
Cook spaghetti according to package directions; drain. Serve sauce over spaghetti; sprinkle with cheese. Yield: 6 main-dish servings.

Per serving: Calories 527 (25% from fat); Fat 14.7g (sat 5.9g, mono 5.4g, poly 1.4g); Protein 27.2g; Carb 71.8g; Fiber 5.6g; Chol 46mg; Iron 5.6mg; Sodium 2116mg; Calc 238mg

vegetarian
Pasta With Spring Vegetables

prep: 25 min.   cook: 20 min.

Great as a vegetarian dish, or add some chopped grilled chicken.

12   ounces uncooked whole grain spaghetti or fettuccine (we tested with Barilla Plus)
1   pound fresh asparagus
1   pound broccoli florets
½   cup rice vinegar
¼   cup peanut oil
3   tablespoons sesame oil
1   medium cucumber
3   large carrots, thinly sliced
1   (8-ounce) can sliced water chestnuts, drained
5   large radishes, thinly sliced (optional)
¾   teaspoon salt
¼   teaspoon pepper

Cook pasta according to package directions; remove pasta with tongs, reserving boiling water. Drain pasta, and set aside.
Snap off tough ends of asparagus; cut asparagus into ½-inch pieces. Add asparagus and broccoli to boiling water, and cook 3 minutes; drain. Plunge asparagus and broccoli into ice water to stop the cooking process; drain and set aside.

Whisk together vinegar and oils. Pour over pasta, and toss.
Cut cucumber in half lengthwise; remove seeds, and thinly slice cucumber. Add cucumber, asparagus, broccoli, carrot, chestnuts, radishes, if desired, and salt, and pepper to pasta mixture; toss well. Yield: 6 main-dish servings.

Per serving: Calories 404 (38% from fat); Fat 17.2g (sat 2.8g, mono 7.3g, poly 6.4g); Protein 12.5g; Carb 56.4g; Fiber 13.1g; Chol 0mg; Iron 3.3mg; Sodium 638mg; Calc 93mg

low calorie • low fat
Asian Shrimp With Pasta

prep: 25 min.   cook: 8 min.

1   pound unpeeled, medium-size fresh shrimp
1   (9-ounce) package refrigerated angel hair pasta
¼   cup lite soy sauce
¼   cup seasoned rice wine vinegar
2   teaspoons sesame oil
6   green onions, chopped
1   cup frozen sweet peas, thawed
¾   cup shredded carrot
1   (8-ounce) can sliced water chestnuts, drained
¼   cup chopped fresh cilantro
2   tablespoons minced fresh ginger
2   garlic cloves, minced
1   teaspoon vegetable oil
2   tablespoons fresh lime juice
½   teaspoon freshly ground pepper
⅓   cup chopped unsalted dry-roasted peanuts

Peel shrimp, and devein, if desired. Set shrimp aside.

Cook pasta according to package directions, omitting salt and fat. Drain and place in a large bowl or on a platter.

Stir together soy sauce, vinegar, and sesame oil. Drizzle over pasta. Add green onions and next 4 ingredients to pasta; toss.

Sauté ginger and garlic in hot vegetable oil 1 to 2 minutes. (Do not brown.) Add shrimp, lime juice, and pepper; cook 3 to 5 minutes or just until shrimp turn pink. Add shrimp mixture to pasta mixture, and toss. Sprinkle with peanuts. Serve immediately. Yield: 6 main-dish servings.

Per serving: Calories 305 (25% from fat); Fat 8.4g (sat 1.1g, mono 3.1g, poly 3.3g); Protein 21.8g; Carb 37.2g; Fiber 5.8g; Chol 112mg; Iron 4mg; Sodium 804mg; Calc 56mg

---

low calorie • low fat
Chicken Vermicelli

prep: 25 min.   cook: 10 min.

1   (8-ounce) package vermicelli rice noodles
1   onion, diced
2   tablespoons sesame oil
4   carrots, shredded
3   medium celery ribs, diced
2   cups shredded cooked chicken
2   garlic cloves, minced
1   small napa cabbage, finely chopped
1   cup low-sodium chicken broth
1   tablespoon cornstarch
¼   cup soy sauce
1   tablespoon oyster sauce
Garnish: chopped green onions

Soak noodles in hot water 10 minutes; drain and set aside.

Sauté diced onion in hot oil in a large skillet over medium-high heat 5 minutes or until tender. Add carrot and next 4 ingredients; cook, stirring occasionally, 2 minutes.

Stir together broth and cornstarch until smooth; add to chicken mixture. Add soy sauce and oyster sauce; bring to a boil, and cook 1 minute. Serve over noodles. Garnish, if desired. Yield: 6 main-dish servings.

Per serving: Calories 322 (22% from fat); Fat 8g (sat 1.6g, mono 3g, poly 2.7g); Protein 18.4g; Carb 43.2g; Fiber 3.4g; Chol 42mg; Iron 1.5mg; Sodium 950mg; Calc 94mg

---

low calorie • low cholesterol • low fat • quick
Fresh Tomato Sauce With Linguine

prep: 19 min.   cook: 6 min.

1   (12-ounce) package uncooked linguine
3   garlic cloves, thinly sliced
½   teaspoon dried crushed red pepper
3   tablespoons olive oil
4   cups cherry or grape tomatoes, halved
½   cup fresh basil leaves, coarsely chopped
2   tablespoons chopped fresh parsley
2   tablespoons red wine vinegar
1   teaspoon salt

Cook pasta according to package directions. **Meanwhile,** sauté garlic and red pepper in hot oil in a large skillet over medium-low heat. Add tomato and next 4 ingredients; cook 3 to 5 minutes.

Toss together hot cooked pasta and tomato mixture. Yield: 6 side-dish servings.

Per serving: Calories 288 (24% from fat); Fat 7.8g (sat 1.2g, mono 5.1g, poly 1.2g); Protein 8.8g; Carb 46.9g; Fiber 3.2g; Chol 0mg; Iron 2.4mg; Sodium 687mg; Calc 31mg

---

Creamy Crawfish Pasta

prep: 20 min.   cook: 20 min.

To speed up the chopping, use a food processor.

1   (8-ounce) package uncooked linguine
½   cup butter
⅓   cup all-purpose flour
1   bunch green onions, finely chopped
1   small onion, minced
4   garlic cloves, minced
½   green bell pepper, minced
2   celery ribs, minced
1   chicken bouillon cube
1   pint whipping cream
1   (2-pound) package frozen crawfish tails, thawed
1   (10-ounce) can diced tomatoes and green chiles, drained
1   tablespoon Creole seasoning
1   tablespoon chopped fresh parsley
¼   teaspoon pepper
⅛   teaspoon salt
Hot sauce (optional)
1   cup freshly grated Parmesan cheese

Cook linguine according to package directions; drain. Keep warm.

Melt butter in a Dutch oven over medium heat. Add flour, and cook, stirring constantly, 2 minutes or until blended.

Add green onions and next 4 ingredients; sauté 5 minutes or until tender. Add bouillon cube and next 7 ingredients; cook 10 minutes or until thickened. Stir in hot sauce, if desired.

Serve over linguine; sprinkle with Parmesan cheese. Yield: 8 main-dish servings.

Per serving: Calories 566 (57% from fat); Fat 35.8g (sat 21.3g, mono 10.1g, poly 1.6g); Protein 25.9g; Carb 33.7g; Fiber 2g; Chol 239mg; Iron 2.3mg; Sodium 991mg; Calc 234mg

---

family favorite • make ahead
Smoked Turkey Tetrazzini

prep: 21 min.   cook: 41 min.

1   (12-ounce) package uncooked linguine
¼   cup butter or margarine
1   medium onion, coarsely chopped (1 cup)
3   tablespoons all-purpose flour
1   teaspoon salt
1   teaspoon freshly ground pepper
¼   teaspoon hot sauce
3   cups milk
½   cup white wine
3   cups chopped smoked turkey (1 pound)
1   (14-ounce) jar quartered artichoke hearts, drained and coarsely chopped
1   (6-ounce) jar sliced mushrooms, drained
1   cup freshly grated Parmesan cheese
1   cup sliced almonds
3   tablespoons chopped fresh flat-leaf parsley

Cook pasta according to package directions; drain.

Melt butter in a large skillet over medium-high heat; add onion, and sauté 6 minutes. Gradually stir in flour and next 3 ingredients until smooth; add milk, and cook, stirring constantly, 10 minutes or until thickened. Remove from heat; very gradually add wine. Stir in turkey, artichokes, and mushrooms.

Layer a lightly greased 13- x 9-inch baking dish with half each of pasta, turkey mixture, and cheese. Repeat layers with remaining pasta, turkey mixture, and cheese. Sprinkle with almonds and parsley.

Bake, uncovered, at 400° for 20 to 25 minutes or until bubbly and golden. Yield: 8 main-dish servings.

Per serving: Calories 516 (38% from fat); Fat 21.8g (sat 8.9g, mono 7.8g, poly 3.1g); Protein 34.3g; Carb 47g; Fiber 5.3g; Chol 77mg; Iron 3.3mg; Sodium 1625mg; Calc 333mg

Herbed Seafood Pasta

quick
Herbed Seafood Pasta

prep: 15 min.   cook: 7 min.

1   (16-ounce) package uncooked fettuccine
½   pound unpeeled, medium-size fresh shrimp
2   tablespoons olive oil
5½ tablespoons Herb-Pesto Butter, divided
½   pound large sea scallops
6   green onions, cut into 2-inch strips
1   cup freshly grated Parmesan cheese, divided

Cook pasta according to package directions; drain and set aside. Keep warm.
Peel shrimp, and devein, if desired.
Heat oil and 2 tablespoons Herb-Pesto Butter in a large skillet over medium-high heat. Add shrimp, scallops, and green onions; cook, stirring often, 3 to 5 minutes or just until shrimp turn pink. Stir in 2 more table-spoons Herb-Pesto Butter. Remove mixture from skillet, and keep warm.
Melt remaining 1½ tablespoons Herb-Pesto Butter in skillet; remove from heat. Add warm pasta and ½ cup cheese, tossing to coat. Divide pasta mixture evenly among 4 pasta bowls; top evenly with seafood mix-ture and remaining ½ cup cheese. Serve immediately. Yield: 4 main-dish servings.

Per serving: Calories 779 (31% from fat); Fat 26.7g (sat 10.7g, mono 10.2g, poly 2.5g); Protein 46.8g; Carb 88.3g; Fiber 4.4g; Chol 144mg; Iron 5.8mg; Sodium 1335mg; Calc 480mg

Herb-Pesto Butter

prep: 10 min.

1½ cups fresh basil leaves
½   cup chopped fresh parsley
¼   cup pine nuts
3   tablespoons Marsala or white wine
2   tablespoons chopped fresh oregano
8   garlic cloves, chopped
1   cup butter, softened
1   to 2 tablespoons olive oil

Process first 6 ingredients in a food proces-sor until smooth, stopping to scrape down sides. Add butter and 1 tablespoon olive oil, and process until combined; add remaining 1 tablespoon oil, if necessary, to achieve desired consistency. Yield: 2 cups.

Per tablespoon: Calories 63 (99% from fat); Fat 6.9g (sat 3.7g, mono 2g, poly 0.6g); Protein 0.3g; Carb 0.6g; Fiber 0.2g; Chol 15mg; Iron 0.2mg; Sodium 41mg; Calc 9mg

family favorite
Chicken-Artichoke Pasta With Rosemary

prep: 13 min.   cook: 26 min.

4   skinned and boned chicken breasts, cut into 1-inch pieces
½   teaspoon salt
1   teaspoon pepper
½   cup butter or margarine, divided
1   small sweet onion, halved and sliced
2   garlic cloves, pressed
6   plum tomatoes, seeded and chopped
1   (8-ounce) package sliced fresh mushrooms
1   (12-ounce) jar marinated artichoke heart quarters, drained
2   tablespoons chopped fresh rosemary
⅓   cup dry white wine
2   cups whipping cream
1   (9-ounce) package refrigerated fettuccine, cooked
¾   cup freshly grated Parmesan cheese

Sprinkle chicken pieces evenly with salt and pepper.
Melt ¼ cup butter in a large skillet over medium-high heat; add chicken, and cook 5 minutes or until lightly browned, tossing frequently. Remove chicken with a slotted spoon, and set aside.
Add onion and next 5 ingredients to skillet; sauté 7 to 8 minutes or until vegetables are tender. Add wine, and cook 2 to 3 minutes or until wine evaporates. Remove vegetables from skillet.
Add remaining ¼ cup butter and whipping cream to skillet. Cook over medium-high heat 10 minutes or until thickened, stirring often. Add chicken, vegetables, cooked fettuccine, and Parmesan cheese. Toss gently. Serve immediately. Yield: 6 main-dish servings.

Per serving: Calories 724 (62% from fat); Fat 49.7g (sat 27.9g, mono 14.7g, poly 2.5g); Protein 32.3g; Carb 37.4g; Fiber 3.9g; Chol 202mg; Iron 2.3mg; Sodium 1036mg; Calc 285mg

Fettuccine Alfredo

prep: 7 min.   cook: 11 min.

8	ounces uncooked fettuccine
½	cup butter
½	cup whipping cream
¾	cup freshly grated Parmesan cheese
¼	teaspoon salt
¼	teaspoon pepper
2	tablespoons chopped fresh parsley
⅛	teaspoon ground nutmeg (optional)

Cook fettuccine according to package directions; drain. Place in a serving bowl. **Meanwhile,** combine butter and whipping cream in a saucepan; cook over low heat until butter melts. Stir in cheese and next 3 ingredients; add nutmeg, if desired. Pour sauce over hot fettuccine; toss well. Serve immediately. Yield: 6 side-dish servings.

Per serving: Calories 399 (60% from fat); Fat 26.4g (sat 15.8g, mono 7.3g, poly 1.1g); Protein 11.4g; Carb 29.6g; Fiber 1.3g; Chol 77mg; Iron 1.3mg; Sodium 658mg; Calc 227mg

Pasta Primavera

prep: 30 min.   cook: 15 min.

Primavera means spring style, referring to these crisp-tender, bright vegetables.

8	ounces uncooked fettuccine or linguine
⅓	cup pine nuts
2	cups fresh broccoli florets
1½	cups fresh or frozen snow peas, trimmed
2	large carrots, diagonally sliced
¼	cup butter or margarine
10	large fresh mushrooms, sliced
2	garlic cloves, minced
1½	cups freshly grated Parmesan cheese
1	cup whipping cream
6	green onions, sliced
12	cherry tomatoes, cut in half
¼	cup chopped fresh flat-leaf parsley
⅓	cup chopped fresh basil
½	teaspoon salt
½	teaspoon pepper
	Freshly grated Parmesan cheese (optional)

Cook fettuccine according to package directions; drain and set aside.
Toast pine nuts at 350° in a shallow roasting pan or skillet over medium heat 3 to 5 minutes, stirring once; set aside.

Cook broccoli, snow peas, and carrot in a Dutch oven in boiling water to cover 1 to 2 minutes or until crisp-tender. Drain and plunge vegetables into ice water to stop the cooking process. Drain.
Melt butter in Dutch oven. Add mushrooms and garlic; sauté over medium heat just until tender. Add 1½ cups cheese and whipping cream, stirring until cheese melts. Add broccoli mixture, green onions, and next 5 ingredients, stirring well. Add fettuccine, and toss to coat. Spoon onto a serving platter. Sprinkle with pine nuts, and, if desired, additional cheese. Yield: 4 main-dish servings.

Per serving: Calories 831 (57% from fat); Fat 52.6g (sat 26.1g, mono 15g, poly 5.7g); Protein 32.4g; Carb 61.4g; Fiber 7g; Chol 140mg; Iron 4.6mg; Sodium 1482mg; Calc 733mg

Baked Rotini

prep: 10 min.   cook: 1 hr.

Although the ingredient list looks long, you probably already have most of these items on hand. Elbow macaroni makes a fine substitute for rotini.

1	pound ground beef
1	small onion, chopped
1	small green bell pepper, chopped
1	(28-ounce) can crushed tomatoes
1	(6-ounce) can tomato paste
1	(4.5-ounce) jar sliced mushrooms, undrained
1	teaspoon salt
½	teaspoon dried basil
¼	teaspoon garlic powder
¼	teaspoon dried oregano
¼	teaspoon dried crushed red pepper
8	ounces rotini, cooked
3	cups (12 ounces) shredded mozzarella cheese

Cook first 3 ingredients in a large skillet, stirring until beef crumbles and is no longer pink; drain and return to skillet.
Stir in crushed tomatoes and next 7 ingredients; bring to a boil. Reduce heat, and simmer, stirring occasionally, 20 minutes. Stir in rotini and cheese. Spoon into a lightly greased 13- x 9-inch baking dish.
Bake, uncovered, at 350° for 35 minutes. Yield: 8 main-dish servings.

Per serving: Calories 400 (37% from fat); Fat 16.4g (sat 8.2g, mono 5.6g, poly 0.8g); Protein 28.7g; Carb 36.3g; Fiber 4.5g; Chol 61mg; Iron 4.3mg; Sodium 1056mg; Calc 374mg

Grilled Chicken With Spicy Soba Noodles

prep: 30 min.   cook: 12 min.   other: 4 hrs.

These Japanese noodles made from buckwheat flour are thin, flat, and have a grayish-brown color.

3	tablespoons soy sauce
2	teaspoons grated fresh ginger
2	garlic cloves, minced
4	skinned and boned chicken breasts
2	(6-ounce) packages uncooked soba noodles
1	red bell pepper, cut into thin strips
1	cup snow peas, cut into thin strips
5	green onions, sliced
	Asian Dressing
2	tablespoons sesame seeds, toasted

Combine first 3 ingredients in a shallow dish or large zip-top freezer bag; add chicken. Cover or seal, and chill 4 hours, turning occasionally.
Remove chicken from marinade, discarding marinade.
Grill, covered with grill lid, over medium-high heat (350° to 400°) 6 minutes on each side or until chicken is done. Cool; slice thinly, and set aside.
Cook noodles in boiling water 6 to 8 minutes; drain. Rinse and drain.
Combine chicken, noodles, bell pepper, snow peas, and green onions. Drizzle with Asian Dressing, tossing to coat. Sprinkle with sesame seeds. Yield: 4 main-dish servings.

Per serving: Calories 631 (28% from fat); Fat 19.9g (sat 3.3g, mono 6.3g, poly 9.3g); Protein 43.2g; Carb 76.1g; Fiber 2.4g; Chol 73mg; Iron 5.3mg; Sodium 1755mg; Calc 118mg

Asian Dressing

prep: 5 min.

2	tablespoons light brown sugar
2	tablespoons chili-garlic sauce
2½	tablespoons rice vinegar
2½	tablespoons soy sauce
2	tablespoons vegetable oil
2	tablespoons sesame oil

Whisk together all ingredients in a bowl. Yield: ¾ cup.

Per tablespoon: Calories 50 (83% from fat); Fat 4.6g (sat 0.7g, mono 1.4g, poly 2.5g); Protein 0.6g; Carb 2.2g; Fiber 0.1g; Chol 0mg; Iron 5.3mg; Sodium 212mg; Calc 2mg

Spinach and Noodle Casserole

prep: 22 min.   cook: 30 min.

1½ pounds ground beef
3   garlic cloves, minced
¾   teaspoon salt
½   teaspoon pepper
1   (26-ounce) jar spaghetti sauce
1   teaspoon dried Italian seasoning
1   (10-ounce) package frozen chopped spinach, thawed and drained
2   cups (8 ounces) shredded Monterey Jack cheese
1½ cups sour cream
1   large egg, lightly beaten
1   teaspoon garlic salt
8   ounces wide egg noodles, cooked
1   (5-ounce) package shredded Parmesan cheese

Cook first 4 ingredients in a large nonstick skillet over medium-high heat, stirring until beef crumbles and is no longer pink. Drain and return to skillet. Stir in spaghetti sauce and Italian seasoning.
Combine spinach and next 4 ingredients. Fold in noodles, and spoon mixture into a lightly greased 13- x 9-inch baking dish. Sprinkle with half of Parmesan cheese; top with beef mixture and remaining cheese.
Bake, uncovered, at 350° for 30 minutes or until golden and bubbly. Yield: 8 main-dish servings.

Per serving: Calories 632 (53% from fat); Fat 37.5g (sat 18.6g, mono 12.8g, poly 2.3g); Protein 38g; Carb 35.1g; Fiber 3.4g; Chol 161mg; Iron 4.6mg; Sodium 1381mg; Calc 596mg

Lemon Orzo

prep: 5 min.   cook: 18 min.

Greek pasta is tossed with a warm, buttery blend of lemon and Parmesan.

6   cups chicken broth
16 ounces uncooked orzo (rice-shaped pasta)
¼   cup butter or margarine
2   tablespoons grated fresh lemon rind
2   tablespoons fresh lemon juice
1½ cups freshly grated Parmesan cheese
½   teaspoon freshly ground pepper
Garnish: freshly grated Parmesan cheese

Bring broth to a boil in a Dutch oven. Stir in orzo; cook, uncovered, 11 minutes or until tender, stirring occasionally to prevent sticking. Drain.
Melt butter in same pan over medium heat. Add orzo, lemon rind, and next 3 ingredients. Stir gently just until cheese melts. Garnish, if desired. Serve hot. Yield: 8 side-dish servings.

Per serving: Calories 359 (32% from fat); Fat 12.8g (sat 6.8g, mono 3.5g, poly .7g); Protein 17.5g; Carb 43.6g; Fiber 2g; Chol 33mg; Iron 1.9mg; Sodium 1092mg; Calc 315mg

Couscous With Raisins, Almonds, and Lemon

prep: 15 min.   cook: 35 min.

A staple in North African cuisine, couscous is a tiny pasta made from coarsely ground semolina wheat.

1   (14-ounce) can vegetable broth
¼   cup water
3   tablespoons olive oil, divided
1   (4.8-ounce) package Israeli couscous (we tested with Marrakesh Express Couscous)
½   cup raisins
⅓   cup chopped fresh flat-leaf parsley
1   (2.25-ounce) package slivered almonds
1   tablespoon lemon juice
2   small celery ribs, diced
3   garlic cloves, pressed
4   skinned and boned chicken breasts, cut into strips

Bring broth, ¼ cup water, and 1 tablespoon oil to a boil in a saucepan over medium heat. Stir in couscous and seasoning packet. Cover, reduce heat, and simmer 15 minutes or until liquid is absorbed and couscous is tender. Fluff with a fork. Stir in raisins and next 4 ingredients.
Heat remaining 2 tablespoons oil in a large skillet over medium heat. Add garlic; sauté 2 to 3 minutes or until tender. Add chicken; sauté 8 minutes or until browned. Spoon couscous onto a serving platter; top with chicken. Yield: 4 main-dish servings.

Per serving: Calories 507 (36% from fat); Fat 20g (sat 2.5g, mono 12.9g, poly 3.5g); Protein 35.9g; Carb 46.8g; Fiber 4.6g; Chol 68mg; Iron 2.8mg; Sodium 504mg; Calc 85mg

Macaroni and Cheese

prep: 10 min.   cook: 35 min.

Comfort food finds its definition in this traditional cheesy macaroni. For a little extra zip, add a shake of hot sauce.

1   (8-ounce) package uncooked elbow macaroni
¼   cup butter or margarine
¼   cup all-purpose flour
1½ cups milk
1   teaspoon salt
2   cups (8 ounces) shredded sharp Cheddar cheese or American cheese
Paprika (optional)

Cook macaroni according to package directions, omitting salt. Drain and set aside.
Melt butter in a heavy saucepan over low heat; add flour, stirring until smooth. Cook 1 minute, stirring constantly. Gradually add milk; cook over medium heat, stirring constantly, until thickened and bubbly. Add salt and cheese, stirring until cheese melts.
Stir macaroni into cheese sauce. Cook over medium-low heat 5 minutes; let stand 5 minutes before serving. Sprinkle with paprika, if desired. Yield: 6 side-dish servings.

Per serving: Calories 415 (49% from fat); Fat 22.7g (sat 14g, mono 6.1g, poly 1g); Protein 16.9g; Carb 35.5g; Fiber 1.4g; Chol 66mg; Iron 1.9mg; Sodium 896mg; Calc 352mg

Golden Macaroni and Cheese

prep: 10 min.   cook: 1 hr.

For a divine main dish, stir in chopped cooked ham before baking; then sprinkle the top with chopped cooked bacon before serving.

1   (8-ounce) package uncooked elbow macaroni
2   cups milk
¼   cup all-purpose flour
1   teaspoon onion salt
2   (10-ounce) blocks sharp Cheddar cheese, shredded (about 4½ cups) and divided
1   cup soft breadcrumbs
¼   cup butter or margarine, melted

Cook macaroni according to package directions; drain well. Set aside.

Place milk, flour, and onion salt in a quart jar; cover tightly, and shake vigorously 1 minute.

Stir together flour mixture, 3½ cups cheese, and macaroni.

Pour macaroni mixture into a lightly greased 13- x 9-inch baking dish or 2 (11-inch) oval baking dishes. Sprinkle evenly with breadcrumbs and remaining 1 cup cheese; drizzle evenly with melted butter.

Bake at 350° for 45 minutes or until golden. Yield: 8 side-dish servings.

Per serving: Calories 508 (57% from fat); Fat 31.9g (sat 19.8g, mono 8.7g, poly 1.3g); Protein 24.2g; Carb 30.7g; Fiber 1.2g; Chol 96mg; Iron 1.9mg; Sodium 915mg; Calc 596mg

entertaining • test kitchen favorite

Caramelized Onion Macaroni and Cheese

prep: 30 min.   cook: 1 hr., 20 min.
other: 10 min.

Our favorite thing about this dish is tasting the crunchy pecan topping in the same bite with the sharp white Cheddar and mellow, sweet onions.

1   (8-ounce) package uncooked elbow macaroni
2   tablespoons butter or margarine
2   large onions, halved and thinly sliced
1   teaspoon sugar
1   (16-ounce) block white Cheddar cheese, shredded
1   cup shredded Parmesan cheese
32 whole grain saltine crackers, finely crushed and divided
6   large eggs
4   cups milk
1   teaspoon salt
½   teaspoon pepper
2   tablespoons butter, melted
½   cup chopped pecans

Cook macaroni according to package directions; drain and set aside.

Melt 2 tablespoons butter in a large skillet over medium-high heat. Add sliced onions and sugar. Cook, stirring often, 15 to 20 minutes or until onions are caramel-colored.

Layer half each of cooked macaroni, onions, cheeses, and cracker crumbs in a lightly greased 13- x 9-inch baking dish. Layer with remaining macaroni, onions, and cheeses.

Whisk together eggs and next 3 ingredients; pour over macaroni.

Stir together remaining cracker crumbs, 2 tablespoons melted butter, and pecans. Sprinkle evenly over macaroni.

Bake at 350° for 1 hour or until browned and set. Let stand 10 minutes before serving. Yield: 10 side-dish servings.

Per serving: Calories 561 (57% from fat); Fat 35.7g (sat 19.3g, mono 11.1g, poly 3.3g); Protein 25.4g; Carb 32.7g; Fiber 1.8g; Chol 205mg; Iron 2.1mg; Sodium 1061mg; Calc 606mg

quick

Penne Pasta With Bacon and Cream

prep: 5 min.   cook: 25 min.

This rich penne dish is much like mac and cheese—hearty enough to be an entrée.

15 bacon slices
1   (8-ounce) package sliced fresh mushrooms
2   garlic cloves, minced
16 ounces penne pasta, cooked
1   cup freshly grated Parmesan cheese
2   cups whipping cream
½   teaspoon pepper
4   green onions, sliced

Cook bacon in a large skillet over medium heat until crisp; remove bacon, reserving 2 tablespoons drippings in skillet. Coarsely crumble bacon.

Sauté sliced mushrooms and garlic in reserved drippings 3 minutes or until tender. Stir in pasta, Parmesan cheese, whipping cream, and pepper; simmer over medium-low heat, stirring often, until sauce thickens (about 5 minutes). Stir in bacon and green onions. Serve hot. Yield: 6 main-dish servings.

Per serving: Calories 779 (53% from fat); Fat 45.5g (sat 23.3g, mono 15.1g, poly 2.7g); Protein 27.3g; Carb 64.4g; Fiber 3.1g; Chol 147mg; Iron 3.1mg; Sodium 1241mg; Calc 349mg

Spicy Vegetables With Penne

low cholesterol • low fat • vegetarian

Spicy Vegetables With Penne

prep: 30 min.   cook: 15 min.   other: 30 min.

½   cup dried tomatoes
½   cup boiling water
12 ounces uncooked penne pasta
2   medium-size sweet onions, chopped
2   small zucchini, chopped
1   medium-size green bell pepper, chopped
1   medium-size red bell pepper, chopped
1   cup sliced fresh mushrooms
2   garlic cloves, minced
2   tablespoons olive oil
1   (24-ounce) jar hot-and-spicy pasta sauce (we tested with Newman's Own Fra Diavolo Sauce)
½   cup chopped fresh basil
½   teaspoon salt

Stir together dried tomatoes and ½ cup boiling water in a bowl; let stand 30 minutes. Drain, chop, and set aside.

Cook pasta according to package directions.

Sauté onions and next 5 ingredients in hot oil in a large skillet over medium-high heat 6 to 8 minutes or until vegetables are tender. Stir in chopped tomatoes.

Stir in pasta sauce; bring to a boil. Reduce heat to medium; stir in basil and salt, and simmer, stirring occasionally, 5 minutes. Serve over pasta. Yield: 6 main-dish servings.

Per serving: Calories 404 (21% from fat); Fat 9.6g (sat 1.5g, mono 5.2g, poly 1.9g); Protein 11.9g; Carb 70.1g; Fiber 7.1g; Chol 0mg; Iron 3.7mg; Sodium 1082mg; Calc 58mg

Two-Step Lasagna

Meat Lover's Chunky Sauce

prep: 15 min.   cook: 35 min.

- 1   pound ground chuck
- 1   pound Italian sausage, casings removed
- 1   green bell pepper, chopped
- 1   medium onion, diced
- 1   (8-ounce) package sliced fresh mushrooms
- 2   teaspoons olive oil
- 2   (25-ounce) jars roasted garlic spaghetti sauce
- 3   tablespoons chopped fresh parsley
- 2   tablespoons chopped fresh basil

Salt and pepper to taste

Cook ground chuck and sausage in a large Dutch oven, stirring until mixture crumbles and is no longer pink. Drain well on paper towels. Wipe Dutch oven clean.
Sauté bell pepper, onion, and mushrooms in hot oil in Dutch oven over medium-high heat 11 to 12 minutes or until pepper is tender and liquid is slightly reduced. Stir in beef mixture, spaghetti sauce, parsley, and basil. Bring to a boil, stirring occasionally; add salt and pepper to taste. Reduce heat, and simmer, uncovered, 15 minutes. Yield: 9 cups.

Per ¼ cup: Calories 76 (53% from fat); Fat 4.5g (sat 1.2g, mono 2g, poly 0.6g); Protein 4.5g; Carb 4.4g; Fiber 0.8g; Chol 12mg; Iron 0.4mg; Sodium 288mg; Calc 18mg

Two-Step Lasagna

prep: 15 min.   cook: 1 hr., 10 min.

- 1   (10-ounce) package frozen chopped spinach, thawed
- 1   (15-ounce) container ricotta cheese

Meat Lover's Chunky Sauce
- 12   no-cook lasagna noodles
- 1   (16-ounce) package shredded mozzarella cheese (4 cups), divided

Drain spinach well, pressing between paper towels.
Stir together spinach and ricotta cheese.
Spread 3 cups Meat Lover's Chunky Sauce in a lightly greased 13- x 9-inch baking dish. Arrange 4 noodles over sauce. Spread spinach mixture evenly over noodles. Sprinkle one-third mozzarella cheese evenly over spinach mixture; arrange 4 noodles over mozzarella. Top with 3 cups sauce and one-third mozzarella cheese. Top with remaining noodles and sauce. Cover tightly with aluminum foil.
Bake at 350° for 1 hour. Uncover and sprinkle evenly with remaining one-third mozzarella cheese. Bake 10 more minutes. Let stand 5 minutes before serving. Yield: 8 main-dish servings.

Per serving: Calories 724 (49% from fat); Fat 39.3g (sat 17.3g, mono 14.2g, poly 2.7g); Protein 45.8g; Carb 45.9g; Fiber 5.7g; Chol 112mg; Iron 3.9mg; Sodium 1665mg; Calc 659mg

Ravioli in Basil-Cream Sauce

prep: 10 min.   cook: 15 min.

- 1   (24-ounce) package frozen beef ravioli (we tested with Rosina Celentano Beef Ravioli)
- 2   tablespoons butter
- 1   (8-ounce) package sliced fresh mushrooms
- 3   green onions, chopped
- 2   garlic cloves, minced
- 1   teaspoon dried Italian seasoning
- 1   (10-ounce) can diced mild tomatoes and green chiles, drained
- 2   tablespoons chopped fresh basil
- 1   cup whipping cream
- ½   cup grated Parmesan cheese
- ½   teaspoon salt

Prepare ravioli according to package directions; drain and keep warm. Melt butter in a Dutch oven over medium-high heat. Add mushrooms and next 3 ingredients; sauté

6 minutes or until mushrooms are tender. Stir in tomatoes and green chiles, basil, and cream; bring to a boil. Reduce heat, and simmer, stirring occasionally, 5 minutes. Stir in Parmesan cheese; add salt. Stir in hot cooked ravioli, tossing to coat. Yield: 4 main-dish servings.

Per serving: Calories 668 (52% from fat); Fat 38.8g (sat 21.8g, mono 12g, poly 1.4g); Protein 22.8g; Carb 56g; Fiber 2.6g; Chol 193mg; Iron 3.1mg; Sodium 1736mg; Calc 318mg

vegetarian

Wild Mushroom Ragoût With Tortellini

prep: 10 min.   cook: 35 min.

- 1   pound refrigerated cheese-filled tortellini
- 2   cups whipping cream
- 1   teaspoon salt, divided
- 1   pinch fresh ground nutmeg
- 4   tablespoons unsalted butter
- ¼   cup minced shallots
- 2   large garlic cloves, minced
- ½   pound crimini mushroom caps, sliced, or sliced fresh button mushrooms
- ½   pound shiitake mushrooms, sliced
- ½   pound oyster mushrooms, sliced
- 1   large portobello mushroom cap, minced
- 1   cup freshly grated Parmigiano-Reggiano cheese, divided
- ½   teaspoon freshly ground pepper

Cook tortellini according to package directions. Drain and set aside.
Stir together cream, ½ teaspoon salt, and nutmeg in a saucepan over medium heat; bring to a boil, reduce heat, and cook 15 minutes or until cream thickens and coats the back of a spoon. Remove from heat.
Melt butter in a large skillet over medium heat. Add shallots and garlic; cook, covered, 2 to 3 minutes, stirring occasionally. Increase heat to medium-high; add mushrooms and remaining ½ teaspoon salt. Cover and cook 8 minutes. Uncover and cook until liquid evaporates.
Add cream mixture, ⅓ cup grated cheese, and pepper to skillet; stir until blended.
Toss pasta with mushroom sauce.
Sprinkle with remaining ⅔ cup grated cheese. Serve pasta in warmed bowls. Yield: 4 main-dish servings.

Per serving: Calories 949 (63% from fat); Fat 66.9g (sat 39.8g, mono 19.3g, poly 2.2g); Protein 28.7g; Carb 60.9g; Fiber 5.1g; Chol 237mg; Iron 3.1mg; Sodium 2007mg; Calc 641mg

Cheesy Sausage Manicotti

prep: 25 min.   cook: 29 min.   other: 10 min.

- 1   (8-ounce) package uncooked manicotti
- 1   (15-ounce) can tomato sauce
- 1   (10-ounce) can diced tomatoes and green chiles with garlic, oregano, and basil
- 1   pound Italian sausage
- 1   (8-ounce) package cream cheese
- 1   cup ricotta cheese
- 4   cups (16 ounces) shredded mozzarella cheese, divided
- ½   cup chopped fresh parsley

Cook pasta according to package directions; rinse with cold water. Drain.

Process tomato sauce and tomatoes in a blender 20 seconds or until smooth. Set aside.

Remove and discard casings from sausage. Cook sausage in a large skillet over medium-high heat, stirring until meat crumbles and is no longer pink. Stir in cream cheese, ricotta cheese, and 2 cups mozzarella cheese. Spoon into manicotti shells; arrange stuffed shells in a lightly greased 13- x 9-inch baking dish.

Pour tomato mixture over shells; sprinkle with remaining 2 cups mozzarella cheese.

Bake at 350° for 20 minutes or until cheese is melted and bubbly. Let stand 10 minutes before serving. Sprinkle with chopped fresh parsley. Yield: 6 main-dish servings.

Per serving: Calories 865 (61% from fat); Fat 58.3g (sat 30g, mono 20.5g, poly 4.3g); Protein 44.1g; Carb 41g; Fiber 2.4g; Chol 161mg; Iron 3.9mg; Sodium 1913mg; Calc 721mg

Note: Assemble casserole and freeze up to 1 month. Thaw in the refrigerator overnight; bake, covered, at 350° for 30 minutes. Uncover and bake 15 more minutes or until cheese is melted and bubbly. If you prefer, use 2 (11- x 7-inch) baking dishes. Proceed as directed.

rice

Rice teams readily with all types of food and can easily become any course of the meal. It's divided into three categories based on the size of the seed—long grain, medium grain, and short grain. The length of the grain determines the texture and consistency.

Long-grain rice has long, slender kernels that cook up separate, light, and fluffy. Short-grain rice, with its fat, almost round grains and high starch content, tends to stick together. As a rule, the shorter the grain, the more tender and clingy the cooked rice. This makes short-grain rice ideal for risotto and sushi. Medium-grain rice is shorter and plumper than long grain, tends to cling like short grain, and produces a fluffy product that can be molded.

You can store regular-milled white, parboiled, and precooked rice indefinitely in airtight containers. Brown and wild rice are subject to rancidity due to the presence of bran, which limits shelf life to six months in an airtight container.

Each type of rice requires a different cooking time and amount of water and yields a different amount of cooked grain. Cook rice, tightly covered, until all liquid is absorbed. Resist the urge to peek or stir while cooking—this causes rice to be gummy.

Cooked rice freezes well by itself or in dishes that are suitable for freezing. It may be frozen in an airtight container up to four months. Store cooked rice in the refrigerator up to one week.

Basic Rice

prep: 2 min.   cook: 22 min.

Omit the salt and substitute chicken broth for water for a simple chicken-flavored rice.

- 2½   cups water
- ½   teaspoon salt
- 1   cup uncooked long-grain rice

Bring water and salt to a boil in a medium saucepan; add rice. Cover, reduce heat, and simmer 20 minutes or until water is absorbed and rice is tender. Yield: 4 side-dish servings.

Per serving: Calories 173 (3% from fat); Fat 0.5g (sat 0.1g, mono 0.1g, poly 0.2g); Protein 3.8g; Carb 37.2g; Fiber 1g; Chol 0mg; Iron 2.4mg; Sodium 295mg; Calc 29mg

Saffron Rice Pilaf

prep: 5 min.   cook: 20 min.

This brilliant yellow rice with flecks of red makes a colorful statement on your plate.

- 1   (5-ounce) package saffron yellow rice mix
- ½   red bell pepper, diced
- ½   cup currants
- 1   tablespoon chopped fresh thyme

Prepare rice according to package directions. Stir in bell pepper, currants, and thyme. Yield: 4 side-dish servings.

Per serving: Calories 214 (12% from fat); Fat 2.9g (sat 1.8g, mono 0.8g, poly 0.2g); Protein 4.1g; Carb 45.1g; Fiber 1.6g; Chol 8mg; Iron 1.6mg; Sodium 329mg; Calc 20mg

Lemon Rice Pilaf

prep: 15 min.   cook: 30 min.

- ¼   cup butter or margarine
- 4   celery ribs, sliced
- 6   green onions, sliced
- 2   cups uncooked long-grain rice
- 1   (32-ounce) container chicken broth
- 2   tablespoons grated lemon rind
- ½   teaspoon salt
- ¼   teaspoon pepper

Melt butter in a large skillet over medium-high heat; sauté celery and green onions until tender. Stir in rice; sauté 2 minutes or until golden. Add broth; bring to a boil. Cover, reduce heat, and simmer 20 minutes or until rice is tender. Stir in rind, salt, and pepper. Yield: 6 side-dish servings.

Per serving: Calories 313 (24% from fat); Fat 8.4g (sat 5g, mono 2.1g, poly 0.5g); Protein 6.2g; Carb 53.9g; Fiber 2.7g; Chol 20mg; Iron 3.7mg; Sodium 612mg; Calc 67mg

rice & grains dictionary

Arborio rice: This Italian short-grain rice with a high-starch kernel contributes the characteristic creamy texture to risotto.

Aromatic rices: These rices have a perfumy aroma and taste like toasted nuts or popped corn. Popular varieties are *basmati, jasmine, Texmati,* and *wild pecan rice.*

Barley: Pearl barley has the bran removed and has been steamed and polished. It's available in coarse, medium, and fine grinds and is often used in soups. Whole grain (or hulled) barley has only the outer husk removed and is the most nutritious form of the grain.

Brown rice: Brown rice has the outer hull removed, but retains the bran layers that give it a tan color, chewy texture, and nutlike flavor. Brown rice has more minerals, vitamins, and fiber than white rice.

Bulgur: Similar to cracked wheat, bulgur consists of wheat kernels that have been steamed, dried, and crushed. Bulgur has a tender, chewy texture and comes in coarse, medium, and fine grinds. It's used in the Middle Eastern salad tabbouleh.

Couscous: It's a tiny pasta that cooks instantly.

Instant rice: This precooked rice has been milled, cooked, and dried. This creates a porous, open grain that rehydrates quickly. The processing destroys much of the flavor and texture.

Parboiled rice: Parboiled rice is soaked, steamed, and dried to remove the outer hull. Grains are firmer and more separate and retain more nutrients than regular rice.

Regular-milled white rice: Also known as polished rice, this is the least expensive and most common rice form. The husk, bran, and germ are milled away until the grain is white. It's available in long, medium, and short grain.

Wild rice: Not really rice at all, wild rice is the long-grain seed of a marsh grass native to the Great Lakes area. The unpolished, dark brown, long and slender grains are high in fiber and have a nutty taste. It's often sold as a blend with other rice.

Orphan's Rice

family favorite
Orphan's Rice

prep: 10 min.   cook: 30 min.   other: 10 min.

The name of this dish comes from the Spanish name, arroz huerfano, *which loosely translated means "feast for orphans." The original recipe used white rice and saffron; we used packaged yellow rice to streamline.*

1	tablespoon butter
¾	cup pecan halves
½	cup slivered almonds
⅓	cup pine nuts
½	small onion, minced
1	garlic clove, minced
2	tablespoons vegetable oil
1	(10-ounce) package yellow rice
3	cups low-sodium chicken broth
2	bacon slices, cooked and crumbled
¼	cup finely chopped cooked ham
1	tablespoon chopped fresh flat-leaf parsley

Melt butter in a skillet over medium heat. Add pecan halves, slivered almonds, and pine nuts; cook, stirring often, 3 minutes or until almonds are light golden. Set aside.
Sauté minced onion and garlic in hot oil in a saucepan over medium-high heat 5 minutes or until onion is tender. Add rice, and sauté, stirring constantly, 1 minute. Add chicken broth; cover and cook 18 minutes. Remove saucepan from heat.
Stir in nuts, bacon, ham, and fresh parsley. Cover and let stand 10 minutes. Serve immediately. Yield: 6 side-dish servings.

Per serving: Calories 482 (53% from fat); Fat 28.6g (sat 4.3g, mono 12.5g, poly 10g); Protein 13.5g; Carb 47.9g; Fiber 2.8g; Chol 13mg; Iron 2.7mg; Sodium 527mg; Calc 42mg

Persian Rice Pilaf

prep: 10 min.   cook: 35 min.

Basmati rice has a distinctive nutty flavor and fragrant aroma. If you can't find it, try American-grown Texmati, which is a cross between long-grain and basmati rices, or substitute regular long-grain rice.

2	tablespoons butter or margarine
1	small onion, chopped
½	cup slivered almonds
1½	cups uncooked basmati rice
½	cup golden raisins
1½	teaspoons ground turmeric
¼	teaspoon ground cinnamon
½	teaspoon salt
3	cups chicken broth

Melt butter in a skillet over medium-high heat; add onion and almonds, and sauté 7 minutes or until onion is tender and almonds are golden. Stir in rice and next 4 ingredients; sauté 2 minutes. Add broth, and bring to a boil; cover, reduce heat, and simmer 20 to 25 minutes or until rice is tender. Yield: 6 side-dish servings.

Per serving: Calories 218 (35% from fat); Fat 8.5g (sat 2.8g, mono 3.9g, poly 1.3g); Protein 4.3g; Carb 31.8g; Fiber 2.3g; Chol 10mg; Iron 1.3mg; Sodium 470mg; Calc 37mg

Toasted Herb Rice

prep: 10 min.   cook: 55 min.

1	cup uncooked long-grain rice
2	tablespoons butter or margarine
1	(10½-ounce) can condensed chicken broth, heated
¾	cup boiling water
4	green onions, chopped
1	teaspoon dried basil
¼	cup pine nuts, toasted

Place rice in an ovenproof Dutch oven; cover with lid.
Bake at 325° for 20 to 25 minutes or until rice is golden. Add butter, and stir until melted. Carefully stir in broth and ¾ cup boiling water; cover. Bake 30 more minutes or until water is absorbed and rice is tender.
Stir in green onions, basil, and pine nuts; serve hot. Yield: 4 side-dish servings.

Per serving: Calories 310 (37% from fat); Fat 12.8g (sat 4.4g, mono 3.6g, poly 3.4g); Protein 8.8g; Carb 40.1g; Fiber 1.8g; Chol 16mg; Iron 3.6mg; Sodium 536mg; Calc 50mg

Quick Hoppin' John

prep: 7 min.   cook: 20 min.

This good-luck peas-and-rice dish is the ideal accompaniment with pork or ham, and not just on New Year's Day, but year-round, too.

3   bacon slices, chopped
½   cup chopped celery
⅓   cup chopped onion
1   cup water
1   (15-ounce) can black-eyed peas, undrained
1   cup uncooked quick long-grain rice
2   tablespoons chopped fresh parsley
½   teaspoon dried thyme
Garnish: celery leaves

Cook bacon in a large saucepan until crisp, stirring often. Add celery and onion; sauté until vegetables are tender.
Stir in water and peas; bring to a boil. Cover, reduce heat, and simmer 5 minutes. Stir in rice, parsley, and thyme. Remove from heat; cover and let stand 5 minutes or until liquid is absorbed and rice is tender. Garnish, if desired. Yield: 4 side-dish servings.

Per serving: Calories 198 (10% from fat); Fat 2.2g (sat 0.7g, mono 0.9g, poly 0.3g); Protein 7.9g; Carb 35.3g; Fiber 4.4g; Chol 5mg; Iron 2.1mg; Sodium 461mg; Calc 37mg

Caribbean Rice and Peas

prep: 10 min.   cook: 30 min.

Pigeon peas, nicknamed no-eyed peas, are of African origin. They're yellow-gray and about the size of green peas.

1   small onion, finely chopped
2   garlic cloves, pressed
1   tablespoon olive oil
2   cups uncooked basmati rice
2½ cups water
1   (10½-ounce) can condensed chicken broth
½   cup unsweetened coconut milk
1   (15-ounce) can pigeon peas, rinsed and drained*
1   tablespoon chopped fresh parsley
2   teaspoons grated lemon rind
1   teaspoon salt
Garnish: fresh parsley sprigs

Sauté onion and garlic in hot oil in a Dutch oven over medium-high heat 1 to 2 minutes or until translucent.
Add rice and next 3 ingredients; bring to a boil. Cover, reduce heat, and simmer 25 minutes or until liquid is absorbed and rice is tender. Stir in peas, chopped parsley, lemon rind, and salt. Garnish, if desired. Yield: 8 side-dish servings.

Per serving: Calories 171 (28% from fat); Fat 5.3g (sat 3g, mono 1.4g, poly 0.6g); Protein 4.3g; Carb 27g; Fiber 2.9g; Chol 1mg; Iron 1.3mg; Sodium 536mg; Calc 24mg

*Substitute 1 (15-ounce) can field peas, if desired.

Black Beans and Rice

prep: 25 min.   cook: 40 min.

The trick to this recipe is substituting canned black beans for dried beans and using pantry ingredients for big flavor.

2   cups uncooked long-grain rice
5   (15-ounce) cans black beans, divided
1   cup chopped onion
½   cup chopped green bell pepper
½   cup chopped red bell pepper
5   garlic cloves, minced
2   tablespoons seeded, minced jalapeño pepper
2   teaspoons olive oil
1   (14-ounce) can chicken broth
1   (6-ounce) can tomato paste
1   tablespoon red wine vinegar
1   teaspoon ground cumin
1   teaspoon dried crushed red pepper
¼   teaspoon black pepper
Salt to taste
Toppings: shredded Cheddar cheese, sour cream, chopped tomatoes, chopped fresh cilantro, chopped green onions, sliced jalapeño peppers (optional)

Cook rice according to package directions; set aside and keep warm.
Rinse and drain 3 cans black beans. (Do not drain other 2 cans.)
Sauté onion and next 4 ingredients in hot oil in a Dutch oven over medium-high heat 5 minutes or until tender. Stir in drained and undrained beans, chicken broth, and next 5 ingredients. Bring to a boil; reduce heat, and simmer, uncovered, 30 minutes, stirring occasionally. Add salt to taste. Serve with hot cooked rice and desired toppings. Yield: 6 main-dish servings.

Per serving: Calories 501 (8% from fat); Fat 4.8g (sat 0.4g, mono 1.3g, poly 2.7g); Protein 20.4g; Carb 103g; Fiber 20g; Chol 1mg; Iron 8.6mg; Sodium 1660mg; Calc 140mg

Spicy Red Beans and Rice

prep: 30 min.   cook: 3 hrs., 30 min.
other: 8 hrs.

2   pounds dried red kidney beans
5   bacon slices, chopped
1   pound smoked sausage, cut into ¼-inch-thick slices
½   pound salt pork, quartered
6   garlic cloves, minced
5   celery ribs, sliced
2   green bell peppers, chopped
1   large onion, chopped
2   (32-ounce) containers chicken broth
2   cups water
1   teaspoon salt
1   teaspoon ground red pepper
1   teaspoon black pepper
4   cups hot cooked rice

Place kidney beans in a Dutch oven. Cover with water 2 inches above beans, and let soak 8 hours. Drain beans; rinse thoroughly, and drain again.
Sauté bacon in Dutch oven over medium-high heat 5 minutes. Add smoked sausage and salt pork; sauté 5 minutes or until sausage is browned. Add garlic and next 3 ingredients; sauté 5 minutes or until vegetables are tender.
Stir in beans, broth, 2 cups water, and next 3 ingredients; bring to a boil. Boil 15 minutes; reduce heat, and simmer, stirring occasionally, 3 hours or until beans are tender. Remove salt pork before serving. Serve over rice. Yield: 8 main-dish servings.

Per serving: Calories 791 (35% from fat); Fat 31.3g (sat 10.5g, mono 13.8g, poly 4.2g); Protein 38.1g; Carb 90.1g; Fiber 27g; Chol 51mg; Iron 9.9mg; Sodium 2406mg; Calc 221mg

Note: For quick soaking, place kidney beans in a Dutch oven; cover with water 2 inches above beans, and bring to a boil. Boil 1 minute; cover, remove from heat, and let stand 1 hour. Drain and proceed with recipe.

Fried Rice

prep: 15 min. cook: 15 min.

Cook and chill rice a day ahead. Chilled rice has a firm texture that's easy to stir-fry.

- ¼ cup vegetable oil, divided
- 2 large eggs, lightly beaten
- 1 cup diced cooked ham
- ½ large red bell pepper, diced
- ½ large sweet onion, diced
- ½ cup frozen petite peas, thawed
- 3 cups cooked rice
- ¼ cup soy sauce
- 1 teaspoon chili-garlic sauce
- 4 green onions, sliced

Heat 1 tablespoon oil in a skillet or wok at medium-high heat 2 minutes. Add eggs, and cook 1 minute on each side or until done. Remove from skillet; chop and set aside.
Heat remaining 3 tablespoons oil in skillet or wok; add ham, and stir-fry 1 to 2 minutes or until browned. Add bell pepper and onion; stir-fry 5 minutes. Add peas and next 3 ingredients; stir-fry 3 to 4 minutes or until thoroughly heated.
Stir in reserved egg, and sprinkle with green onions. Yield: 4 main-dish servings.

Per serving: Calories 440 (45% from fat); Fat 21.8g (sat 4.7g, mono 6.2g, poly 10g); Protein 19.6g; Carb 41.6g; Fiber 2.4g; Chol 138mg; Iron 3.3mg; Sodium 1553mg; Calc 53mg

Dirty Rice

prep: 37 min. cook: 1 hr., 30 min.

Chopped giblets give this rice a "dirty" look and great flavor.

- 2 cups uncooked long-grain rice
- 1 quart water
- 5 chicken wings (about ¾ pound)
- 5 chicken gizzards (about ¼ pound)
- 5 chicken hearts (about 1 ounce)
- 5 chicken livers (about ¼ pound)
- 1 pound ground hot pork sausage
- ¼ cup butter, margarine, or bacon drippings
- 1 large onion, chopped
- 1 cup chopped green bell pepper
- 3 celery ribs, chopped
- 1 tablespoon dried parsley flakes

Cook rice according to package directions; set aside.
Combine water and next 3 ingredients in a Dutch oven; bring to a boil. Cover, reduce heat, and simmer 20 minutes; add chicken livers, and cook 10 to 12 minutes or until tender. Drain, reserving ¾ cup liquid.
Remove meat from wings; coarsely chop wing meat, gizzards, hearts, and livers. Set meat aside.
Cook sausage in Dutch oven, stirring until it crumbles and is no longer pink; drain and set aside.
Melt butter in Dutch oven; add onion, bell pepper, and celery. Cook over medium heat 5 minutes or until tender, stirring often. Add sausage, chopped meat, and reserved liquid. Bring to a boil; cover, reduce heat, and simmer 15 minutes. Stir in cooked rice and parsley. Serve warm. Yield: 8 main-dish servings.

Per serving: Calories 294 (47% from fat); Fat 15.3g (sat 6.9g, mono 5.4g, poly 1.5g); Protein 16.1g; Carb 22g; Fiber 1.3g; Chol 121mg; Iron 3mg; Sodium 432mg; Calc 32mg

Mushroom Brown Rice

prep: 15 min. cook: 45 min.

- 1½ cups uncooked brown rice
- ¼ pound sliced fresh mushrooms
- 2 small green bell peppers, chopped
- 1 large onion, chopped
- 1 garlic clove, minced
- 2 tablespoons butter or margarine, melted
- 2 cups peeled, chopped tomato
- 2 tablespoons soy sauce
- 1 tablespoon minced fresh cilantro or parsley
- ⅛ teaspoon pepper

Cook brown rice according to package directions; set aside.
Sauté mushrooms, bell pepper, onion, and garlic in butter in a large skillet 5 to 7 minutes or until vegetables are tender. Stir in cooked rice, tomato, and remaining ingredients; cook until thoroughly heated. Yield: 8 side-dish servings.

Per serving: Calories 184 (21% from fat); Fat 4.2g (sat 2.1g, mono 1.2g, poly 0.6g); Protein 4.8g; Carb 32.9g; Fiber 3.6g; Chol 8mg; Iron 1mg; Sodium 284mg; Calc 24mg

Creole Jambalaya

prep: 25 min. cook: 1 hr.

- 2 tablespoons butter or margarine
- 1 large onion, chopped
- 1 green bell pepper, chopped
- 8 green onions, chopped
- 2 celery ribs, chopped
- 3 cups cubed cooked ham (1 pound)
- 1 pound Cajun-flavored or smoked sausage, sliced
- 1 (8-ounce) can tomato sauce
- ½ teaspoon salt
- ½ teaspoon ground black pepper
- ¼ teaspoon ground red pepper
- 5 cups hot cooked rice

Melt butter in a large skillet over medium heat. Add onion and next 3 ingredients; sauté until tender. Add ham, sausage, and next 4 ingredients. Cook, stirring occasionally, 20 minutes.
Stir in rice; cover and cook over low heat 30 minutes, stirring occasionally. Yield: 8 main-dish servings.

Per serving: Calories 472 (42% from fat); Fat 22.2g (sat 9.2g, mono 4.8g, poly 1.1g); Protein 26.7g; Carb 39.9g; Fiber 1.6g; Chol 96mg; Iron 3.9mg; Sodium 821mg; Calc 32mg

Rice Jardin

prep: 8 min. cook: 20 min.

- 3 tablespoons butter or margarine
- 3 medium zucchini, sliced
- 1 medium onion, chopped
- 1 (8¾-ounce) can whole kernel corn, drained
- 1 (10-ounce) can diced tomato and green chiles
- 3 cups cooked rice
- 1½ teaspoons salt
- ¼ teaspoon dried oregano
- ¼ teaspoon pepper
- ¼ teaspoon ground coriander (optional)

Melt butter in a Dutch oven over medium-high heat. Add zucchini and onion; sauté 5 minutes or until tender. Stir in corn, next 5 ingredients, and, if desired, coriander. Cover and cook over low heat 15 minutes. Yield: 6 side-dish servings.

Per serving: Calories 211 (27% from fat); Fat 6.4g (sat 3.7g, mono 1.6g, poly 0.4g); Protein 4.1g; Carb 33.2g; Fiber 2.3g; Chol 15mg; Iron 1.5mg; Sodium 1277mg; Calc 46mg

Lemon-Lime Risotto

prep: 12 min. cook: 49 min.

6	cups chicken broth
1	teaspoon grated lemon rind
1	teaspoon grated lime rind
3	tablespoons fresh lemon juice
3	tablespoons fresh lime juice
1	large onion, chopped
2	tablespoons olive oil
2	cups uncooked Arborio rice
2	tablespoons butter or margarine
½	cup freshly grated Parmesan cheese

Bring first 5 ingredients to a boil in a large saucepan. Set aside on low heat.

Sauté onion in hot oil in a large sauté pan over medium-high heat 4 minutes or until tender. Add rice, and cook, stirring constantly, 5 minutes.

Reduce heat to medium; add ½ cup hot broth. Cook, stirring constantly, until broth is absorbed. Repeat procedure with remaining hot broth, ½ cup at a time. (Cooking time is 20 to 30 minutes.)

Remove from heat; stir in butter and cheese. Serve immediately. Yield: 8 side-dish servings.

Per serving: Calories 277 (31% from fat); Fat 9.5g (sat 3.3g, mono 4.3g, poly 0.8g); Protein 8g; Carb 41g; Fiber 2.4g; Chol 13mg; Iron 0.3mg; Sodium 843mg; Calc 107mg

Lemon-Lime Risotto

▲ Sauté rice with onion until browned.

▲ Add ½ cup hot broth; cook until liquid is absorbed. Repeat, adding ½ cup broth at a time.

▲ Stir in butter and cheese before serving.

Serve risotto immediately to capture its pearly look on your plate.

Risotto

prep: 8 min.   cook: 1 hr.

Using Arborio rice makes the best risotto; find it in large supermarkets, specialty food stores, or online.

½   cup butter or margarine
1   medium onion, chopped
2¼   cups uncooked Arborio rice
2   garlic cloves, chopped
2   cups dry white wine*
2   bay leaves
5½   cups hot chicken broth
¼   teaspoon salt
¼   teaspoon pepper
⅛   teaspoon hot sauce

Melt butter in a Dutch oven over medium-high heat; add onion, and sauté 5 to 7 minutes or until tender.
Stir in rice and garlic; sauté 2 minutes. Reduce heat to medium; add wine and bay leaves. Cook 5 minutes or until liquid is reduced by half.
Add 1 cup hot chicken broth, salt, pepper, and hot sauce; cook, stirring often, until liquid is absorbed.
Repeat procedure with remaining broth, ½ cup at a time. (Cooking time is about 45 minutes.) Remove and discard bay leaves. Yield: 6 side-dish servings.

Per side-dish serving: Calories 354 (46% from fat); Fat 18g (sat 10g, mono 4.7g, poly 1.3g); Protein 7g; Carb 41.2g; Fiber 0.9g; Chol 49mg; Iron 0.6mg; Sodium 1626mg; Calc 20mg

*Substitute 1 cup chicken broth for white wine, if desired.

Green Bean Risotto

prep: 19 min.   cook: 54 min.

1   pound fresh green beans
1   (32-ounce) container chicken broth, divided
¼   cup butter or margarine
1   red onion, coarsely chopped
2   garlic cloves, pressed
1   cup uncooked Arborio rice
1   cup dry white wine or chicken broth
1   teaspoon chopped fresh thyme
½   teaspoon freshly ground pepper
1   cup freshly shredded Parmesan cheese

Trim beans, and cut into bite-size pieces. Bring beans and ½ cup broth to a boil in a Dutch oven over medium-high heat; cook 10 minutes or until crisp-tender. Remove beans with a slotted spoon, and set aside.
Bring remaining broth to a simmer in a saucepan, keeping warm over low heat.
Add butter, onion, and garlic to broth in Dutch oven; cook 3 minutes. Add rice and wine; cook, stirring constantly, 5 minutes or until liquid is absorbed. Reduce heat.
Add 1 cup simmering broth to rice in Dutch oven, and cook, stirring often, until liquid is absorbed. Repeat procedure with remaining broth, 1 cup at a time. (Cooking time is about 20 minutes.)
Stir in beans, thyme, pepper, and cheese; serve immediately. Yield: 6 side-dish servings.

Per side-dish serving: Calories 224 (52% from fat); Fat 13g (sat 7.5g, mono 3.4g, poly 0.5g); Protein 9g; Carb 19.1g; Fiber 2.5g; Chol 33mg; Iron 0.9mg; Sodium 967mg; Calc 230mg

grains

Grains are the edible seeds from the grass family. Some of the most common grains are barley, bulgur, corn, oats, quinoa, rice, and wild rice. They provide an affordable source of fiber, protein, and carbohydrate. In addition, some grains are ground into flours.

Grains have uses that go beyond the basic side dish. They blend well into casseroles, salads, and stuffings. Grits, the small flakes of hulled, dried corn, are eaten more in the South than in other regions of the country. Hominy, whole kernels of the same corn, are a heartier option. Hominy often replaces meat in vegetarian entrées.

You'll find oatmeal and muesli on breakfast tables throughout the winter months. Serve bulgur and barley as side dishes like rice. They add nutrients and fiber to the diet.

When cooking grains and cereals, add them to boiling water in a slow, steady stream. This prevents lumping as the boiling water instantly surrounds and plumps the individual granules.

Whole grains contain more nutrients than processed ones; as a result, they have a short storage life because they contain an oil-rich germ that can become rancid. So, for this reason, buy whole grains in small quantities and keep them in airtight containers.

grits dictionary

Grits can be very different, depending on whether they're ground at a gristmill or purchased at the supermarket. This guide will help you with the different choices.

Hominy: Dried white or yellow corn kernels from which the hull and germ have been removed. It's sold dried or ready-to-eat in cans. When dried hominy is ground, it's called hominy grits. Grits are available in three grinds—fine, medium, and coarse.

Instant grits: These fine-textured grits have been precooked and dehydrated. To prepare them, simply add boiling water.

Quick and regular grits: The difference between these types is in granulation. Quick grits are ground fine and cook in 5 minutes; regular grits are medium grind and cook in 10 minutes.

Whole-ground or stone-ground grits: These grits are a coarse grind. You'll find stone-ground grits at gristmill gift shops and specialty food stores.

Southwestern Grits Wedges

prep: 10 min.   cook: 20 min.   other: 2 hrs.

2⅔ cups chicken broth
2 tablespoons butter or margarine
⅔ cup uncooked quick-cooking grits
½ (8-ounce) loaf pasteurized cheese product, cubed
1 (10-ounce) can diced tomatoes and green chiles, drained
1 tablespoon butter or margarine, melted
¼ cup plus 2 tablespoons sour cream
Chopped fresh cilantro

Bring broth and 2 tablespoons butter to a boil in a large saucepan over medium heat; add grits, and cook, stirring often, 5 minutes or until thickened. Remove from heat, and add cheese, stirring until melted and combined. Stir in tomatoes and green chiles. Pour mixture into a lightly greased 9-inch pieplate. Cover and chill 2 hours.
Unmold grits, and cut into 6 wedges; lightly brush each side with melted butter.
Cook wedges on a hot, lightly greased griddle 4 minutes on each side or until golden. Dollop wedges with sour cream. Sprinkle with cilantro. Yield: 6 side-dish servings.

Per serving: Calories 235 (59% from fat); Fat 15.3g (sat 8.8g, mono 4.4g, poly 0.8g); Protein 6.9g; Carb 16.7g; Fiber 0.3g; Chol 43mg; Iron 0.7mg; Sodium 1100mg; Calc 160mg

low calorie • low cholesterol • low fat • quick
Basic Polenta

prep: 2 min.   cook: 10 min.

Polenta is a coarse grind of cornmeal that's famous for taking on trendy shapes and flavors. It's available in most grocery stores; regular yellow cornmeal works, too.

3½ cups water or milk
¾ teaspoon salt
1 cup yellow cornmeal

Bring water and salt to a boil over high heat in a heavy saucepan. Whisk in cornmeal. Reduce heat; simmer 10 minutes or until thick and creamy, whisking often. Yield: 7 side-dish servings.

Per serving: Calories 72 (4% from fat); Fat 0.3g (sat 0g, mono 0.1g, poly 0.1g); Protein 1.7g; Carb 15.3g; Fiber 1.5g; Chol 0mg; Iron 0.8mg; Sodium 252mg; Calc 4mg

quick
Serrano Chile Polenta

prep: 8 min.   cook: 10 min.

Serve this polenta as you would mashed potatoes. Our recommendation: meatloaf.

3 cups water
1 cup white cornmeal
½ cup butter or margarine, cut into pieces
1 cup shredded Parmesan cheese
2 serrano chiles, seeded and chopped, or jalapeño peppers, seeded and chopped
1 tablespoon chopped fresh cilantro
¼ teaspoon salt
¼ teaspoon pepper

Bring 3 cups water to a boil in a large heavy saucepan; gradually add cornmeal, whisking until smooth. Cook 3 to 5 minutes or until thickened. Remove from heat.
Whisk in butter and remaining ingredients. Serve warm or spread into a lightly greased 9-inch square pan. Cool slightly. Cut into desired shapes. Yield: 4 side-dish servings.

Per serving: Calories 413 (63% from fat); Fat 29g (sat 17.9g, mono 7.8g, poly 1.2g); Protein 10.8g; Carb 27.8g; Fiber 2.7g; Chol 75mg; Iron 1.7mg; Sodium 651mg; Calc 264mg

low cholesterol • low fat • quick
Cranberry-Almond Wild Rice

prep: 5 min.   cook: 20 min.

1 (6-ounce) package long-grain and wild rice
1 (3.5-ounce) bag quick-cooking brown rice
¾ cup sweetened dried cranberries
⅓ cup slivered almonds, toasted

Cook long-grain and wild rice according to package directions. Prepare brown rice according to package directions. Stir together rice, cranberries, and almonds. Yield: 4 side-dish servings.

Per serving: Calories 354 (15% from fat); Fat 5.8g (sat 0.4g, mono 3.2g, poly 1.6g); Protein 7.3g; Carb 71.7g; Fiber 4.7g; Chol 0mg; Iron 1.7mg; Sodium 585mg; Calc 57mg

Wild Rice With Grapes

prep: 5 min.   cook: 1 hr., 4 min.

This healthy side dish sports beautiful colors with the addition of red and green grapes. Stir in some chopped cooked chicken, and serve it as an entrée.

2 tablespoons butter or margarine, divided
2 tablespoons sliced almonds
¼ cup chopped green onions
1 (14-ounce) can chicken broth
3 tablespoons water
½ teaspoon salt
¼ teaspoon pepper
⅔ cup uncooked wild rice
½ cup seedless green grapes, halved
½ cup seedless red grapes, halved

Melt 1 tablespoon butter in a large saucepan over medium heat; add almonds, and cook 2 minutes, stirring constantly, until golden. Remove almonds from pan; set aside.
Melt remaining 1 tablespoon butter in pan. Add green onions; cook, stirring constantly, until tender. Add broth and next 3 ingredients; bring to a boil. Stir in rice; return to a boil. Cover, reduce heat, and simmer 1 hour or until rice is tender. Drain any liquid. Stir in grapes. Sprinkle with almonds. Yield: 4 side-dish servings.

Per serving: Calories 213 (35% from fat); Fat 8.4g (sat 3.8g, mono 2.9g, poly 1g); Protein 5.7g; Carb 29.7g; Fiber 2.5g; Chol 20mg; Iron 0.8mg; Sodium 1037mg; Calc 27mg

pies & pastries

Equipment

You can bake tender, flaky pies with just a few pieces of equipment—basically all you need is a pieplate and rolling pin. A pastry blender is a useful tool to help cut fat into flour on its way to becoming dough. And a pastry wheel will cut straight strips of dough for a lattice-topped crust. A metal dough scraper is another tool for cutting dough and releasing it from a work surface with ease. And a wire rack is the best place to cool your pie so the bottom crust doesn't get soggy.

Nonshiny pieplates such as ovenproof glass or dull metal perform the best. Avoid shiny metal pans; they reflect heat and keep pastry crusts from browning evenly. Always use the size pieplate specified in a recipe. Standard sizes range from 9 to 10 inches in diameter and typically measure 1¼ inches deep. Always measure pieplates across the top.

Commercial Crusts

There is a variety of store-bought piecrusts available to help speed up your pie making. Frozen pastry shells and crumb crusts already in pans offer good quality but hold less filling than most homemade pastries and commercial refrigerated piecrusts. Even though their packages state they are 9-inch crusts, most are not an equivalent substitute. Piecrusts labeled "extra serving size" and "deep dish" are closer substitutes for homemade 9-inch crusts. Our favorite shortcut is refrigerated piecrust that you unroll and simply place in your pieplate, and flute.

Freezing Pies

You can freeze balls or flattened discs of pastry dough up to six months if wrapped tightly in wax paper or plastic wrap and then in an airtight container. When ready to use, allow time to thaw the dough overnight in the refrigerator. (When thawed, pastry will be slightly more fragile than if it had not been frozen.)

You can also freeze baked or unbaked pastry directly in a pieplate. Unbaked frozen pastry can be baked without thawing; just bake frozen pastry as the recipe directs, and add two or three more minutes to the baking time.

Some baked pies, particularly fruit pies, freeze well. The texture of the pastry, however, may lose crispness when baked due to the freezing and defrosting. The texture of the fruit may soften slightly, too.

To freeze baked pies, freeze them unwrapped first; then wrap them so that they're airtight, label, and return them to the freezer. Use frozen pies within two months. Thaw baked pies at room temperature 30 minutes; then reheat at 350° until warm.

It's not a good idea to freeze custard, cream, or chiffon pies that contain meringue toppings. The meringue will deteriorate in the freezing and thawing stages.

pastry

The key to making flaky pastry begins with measuring ingredients accurately and mixing them properly. If proportions of fat to flour to liquid are off even slightly, or if you overwork the dough, your pastry can turn out tough or crumbly.

Making Basic Pastry

Cut cold fat (typically butter or shortening) into flour, using a pastry blender or two knives until the mixture is crumbly and resembles the size of peas. During baking, the fat particles that coat the flour will melt and leave behind pockets of air that separate layers of pastry and create a flaky crust.

Sprinkle ice water, one tablespoon at a time, over the flour mixture; stir with a fork just enough to moisten the dry ingredients. Don't overwork the dough. The more you stir and handle it, the more gluten (structure) will develop and toughen the pastry. Add the minimum amount of water to moisten the dough; too much can make pastry soggy.

Gather dough into a flattened disc or ball, cover tightly with plastic wrap or wax paper, and chill thoroughly. Chilling the dough makes it easier to handle and helps to achieve a flaky crust.

When ready to roll dough, let it stand briefly until it's pliable but still firm—almost like clay. Lightly dust the work surface with flour, and place chilled dough in the center; flatten dough with the heel of your hand. Carefully and quickly roll dough from the center outward in all directions rather than back and forth across the dough; this stretches the dough and will cause it to shrink during baking.

Lift dough circle periodically as you roll it to make sure it's not sticking to the work surface. If it does stick, loosen underneath the dough with a dough scraper or spatula and sprinkle a little more flour under the dough onto the work surface.

Roll pastry to desired thickness and about two inches larger than the pieplate. To transfer pastry to the pieplate without tearing it, carefully and quickly fold dough in half, and then in half again. Place the point of the fold in the center of the pieplate, and unfold. Be careful not to stretch the dough as you're fitting it into the pieplate.

Trim edges of pastry dough, leaving about ½ inch overhang over rim of pieplate. Kitchen shears or a knife make easy work of trimming. Fold the overhang dough under itself, creating a thick rim around edge of pieplate; then crimp as desired. Chill pastry until you're ready to bake it.

Shown on previous page: Fresh Peach Pie (page 352)

Single or Double Crusts

Pies that aren't topped with a top crust are known as single-crust pies. For this type of pie, crimp the pastry edge before adding filling. If the filling is unbaked, bake the crust before adding filling.

Some of our pastry recipes offer directions for blind baking (baking a crust without filling). When you do this, prick the bottom and sides of the pastry dough in the pieplate to keep pastry from puffing during baking. Do not, however, prick the dough if a filling will be baked in it from the dough state. If you do, the filling is likely to seep through the crust to the pieplate during baking.

Double-crust pies have both a top and bottom crust, and the filling is baked between the crusts. To make a double-crust pie, use a pastry recipe specifically for this type of pie. You can also double a recipe for a single-crust pie. Divide the dough in half; keep one portion covered and chilled while working with the other. Line a pieplate with one portion of pastry, following directions for a single-crust pie and omitting the crimping step; then add filling. Roll remaining pastry about an inch larger than the pieplate. Moisten the edge of bottom pastry with water or beaten egg; fit the top pastry over the filling. Trim edge of pastry so ½ inch of overhang remains. Fold the overhang under the edge of the bottom pastry, pressing firmly to seal. Then crimp the thick edge. Cut a few slits in top pastry to allow steam to escape during baking.

A lattice topping gives a decorative finish to a double-crust fruit pie. It allows plump berries or other fruit to peek through its woven design. A lattice-topped pie requires the same amount of pastry as a double-crust pie. Just roll and fit the bottom pastry as a single- or double-crust pie, leaving a 1-inch overhang around the edge. Then roll out remaining pastry to the same thickness and cut into ½-inch strips (10 to 14 strips is plenty for a typical lattice). Use a fluted pastry wheel for more decorative strips, if desired. If you choose to make a lattice with wider strips, you might need only eight to 10 strips.

To weave the lattice, first moisten the edge of pastry in the pieplate. Then place five or seven strips evenly across the pie going in the same direction, leaving ½ to ¾ inch between strips; fold every other strip back a little over halfway. Place one of the remaining strips across the center of the pie, perpendicular to first row of strips. Carefully fold back the flat strips and unfold the folded ones. Place another strip parallel to the center strip, leaving ½ to ¾ inch between strips. Repeat the folding and unfolding step and adding more cross strips until the lattice is completely woven. Trim edges, and press the ends of strips to seal the pastry. Then crimp the edges, if desired.

quick
Basic Pastry for a 9-inch Pie

prep: 8 min.   cook: 12 min.

Use this pastry with recipes throughout the chapter. It's a blend of basic ingredients that forms a flaky base for a multitude of sweet fillings. We give you three pieplate sizes from which to choose. See following page for 8-inch and 10-inch pastry.

1¼ cups all-purpose flour
½   teaspoon salt
⅓   cup plus 1 tablespoon chilled shortening
3   to 4 tablespoons ice water

Combine flour and salt; cut in shortening with a pastry blender until mixture is crumbly (photo 1). Sprinkle ice water, 1 tablespoon at a time, evenly over surface (photo 2); stir with a fork until dry ingredients are moistened. Shape into a ball (photo 3); cover and chill until ready to use.
Roll pastry to ⅛-inch thickness on a lightly floured surface. Place in pieplate (photos 4 and 5); trim off excess pastry along edges. Fold edges under, and crimp. Chill.
For baked pastry shell, prick bottom and sides of pastry shell with a fork (photo 6). Chill pastry until ready to bake. Bake at 450° for 10 to 12 minutes or until golden. Yield: 8 servings.

basic pastry steps

1. Cut fat into flour mixture, using a pastry blender, until mixture is crumbly.

2. Sprinkle ice water evenly over surface. Stir just until dry ingredients are moistened.

3. Gather dough into a ball or flat disc. Cover and chill at least 30 minutes.

4. Roll dough with a rolling pin to ⅛-inch thickness; carefully roll dough onto pin, and then unroll into pieplate.

5. Another way to transfer dough is to fold it in half and then in half again; place point in center of pieplate. Unfold.

6. When baking pastry without a filling, prick bottom and sides with a fork. Do not prick pastry if it's to be filled before baking.

Basic Pastry for an 8-inch Pie

prep: 8 min.   cook: 12 min.

1   cup all-purpose flour
½   teaspoon salt
⅓   cup chilled shortening
2   to 3 tablespoons ice water

Follow directions on previous page. Yield:
6 servings.

Per serving: Calories 174 (56% from fat); Fat 10.9g (sat 2.7g, mono 3.6g, poly 2.8g);
Protein 2.2g; Carb 16g; Fiber 0.6g; Chol 0mg; Iron 1mg; Sodium 194mg; Calc 3mg

Basic Pastry for a 10-inch Pie

prep: 8 min.   cook: 12 min.

1½   cups all-purpose flour
¾   teaspoon salt
½   cup chilled shortening
4   to 5 tablespoons ice water

Follow directions on previous page. Yield:
10 servings.

Per serving: Calories 156 (57% from fat); Fat 9.8g (sat 2.4g, mono 3.2g, poly 2.5g);
Protein 1.9g; Carb 14.3g; Fiber 0.5g; Chol 0mg; Iron 0.9mg; Sodium 175mg; Calc 3mg

pick your piecrust

We offer a variety of homemade piecrusts on
these pages; however, if you're in a pinch for
time, a 15-ounce package of refrigerated
piecrusts works fine in all our recipes calling for
pastry for a 9-inch pie. Two piecrusts come in a
package.

Piecrust Pointers

Our Test Kitchens staff shares these tips for a
"perfect crust every time" when using a refrigerated piecrust to ensure top quality.
• Use crust by the expiration date on the box.
• Pinch the same amount of dough each time
you crimp the edges to promote even browning.
• To keep the crust from sliding down the
pieplate during baking, anchor the crust in
four spots by attaching small dough scraps
from the crust to a spot underneath the lip of
the pieplate. Remove after crust is baked.
• Shield the outer edges of the crust with aluminum foil to prevent excessive browning.

pretty pastry edges

For all designs: Fold over-
hanging pastry under, creating
a thick edge even with
pieplate rim. Be careful not to
stretch the pastry.

Fork Edge: Press firmly around
pastry edge with tines of a fork.
To prevent sticking, dip fork in
flour.

Pinch Edge: Place index finger
on outside of pastry rim and
thumb and other index finger
on inside. Pinch pastry into a
V shape along the edge.

Rope Edge: Place side of
thumb on pastry rim at an
angle. Pinch pastry by pressing
knuckle of index finger into
pastry toward thumb.

Scalloped Edge: Press indentions into pastry edge using
the rim of a small spoon, creating a scalloped appearance.

Eyelet Edge: Create the pinch
edge (shown above). With the
end of a wooden spoon, make
small indentions into the V
shape openings.

Double-Crust Pastry

prep: 5 min.

2   cups all-purpose flour
1   teaspoon salt
⅔   cup plus 2 tablespoons chilled shortening
4   to 5 tablespoons ice water

Combine flour and salt; cut in shortening
with a pastry blender until mixture is crumbly. Sprinkle ice water, 1 tablespoon at a
time, evenly over surface; stir with a fork
until dry ingredients are moistened. Shape
into a ball; cover and chill until ready to use.
Roll and fit pastry into pieplate as pie recipe
directs. Yield: 8 servings.

Per serving: Calories 288 (60% from fat); Fat 19.3g (sat 4.8g, mono 6.4g, poly 4.9g);
Protein 3.2g; Carb 23.9g; Fiber 0.8g; Chol 0mg; Iron 1.5mg; Sodium 291mg; Calc 4.9mg

Oil Pastry

prep: 6 min.

1¼   cups all-purpose flour
½   teaspoon salt
¼   cup plus 2 tablespoons vegetable oil
3   to 4 tablespoons ice water

Combine flour and salt; add oil, stirring
until mixture is crumbly. Sprinkle with ice
water, 1 tablespoon at a time, stirring quickly.
Gather dough into a ball.
Roll pastry to ⅛-inch thickness on a lightly
floured surface. Place in a 9-inch pieplate;
trim off excess pastry along edges. Fold
edges under, and crimp. Yield: 8 servings.

Per serving: Calories 154 (54% from fat); Fat 9.2g (sat 2.3g, mono 3g, poly 2.3g);
Protein 2g; Carb 15g; Fiber 0.5g; Chol 0mg; Iron 0.9mg; Sodium 146mg; Calc 3mg

Sweet Flaky Pastry (Pâte Sucrée)

prep: 20 min.   cook: 15 min.   other: 8 hrs.

Pâte sucrée is a sweet crust used for fruit tarts, pies, and other desserts.

3   cups all-purpose flour
½   cup sugar
1   cup cold butter, cut into pieces
½   cup ice water

Combine flour and sugar in a large bowl; cut in butter with a pastry blender until mixture is crumbly. Sprinkle ice water, 1 tablespoon at a time, evenly over surface; stir with a fork just until dry ingredients are moistened.

Divide dough into 4 equal portions; wrap each portion of dough in plastic wrap, and chill 8 hours.

Roll each portion to ⅛-inch thickness on a lightly floured surface, and cut into 12 equal portions. Fit dough into 1- or 2-inch tartlet pans; trim excess pastry from edges. Fill and bake as filling recipe directs.

For baked tart shells, prick bottoms of pastry with a fork. Place pans on a baking sheet. Bake at 400° for 12 to 15 minutes. Yield: enough pastry for 4 dozen tartlet shells.

Per shell: Calories 70 (50% from fat); Fat 3.9g (sat 2.4g, mono 1g, poly 0.2g); Protein 0.9g; Carb 8.1g; Fiber 0.2g; Chol 10mg; Iron 0.4mg; Sodium 27mg; Calc 2mg

crumb crusts

Crumb crusts provide shortcuts to pie making. They're popular, easy to make, and pair well with many chilled and frozen pies. When teamed with chilled fillings, crumb crusts are usually baked briefly to set the crumbs. When used with frozen fillings like ice cream, no baking is needed. Freezing firms the crumbs sufficiently to make the crust sliceable.

Cookies and graham crackers are the best choices for a crumb crust. A food processor is the best tool for making fine, uniform crumbs. You also can use a blender to make crumbs, or place cookies or crackers in a plastic bag and tap with a heavy rolling pin to make crumbs.

The goal of a crumb crust is to make sure it's an even thickness in the pieplate. To achieve this, use the bottom of a drinking glass to press the crumbs into the pieplate or use a slightly smaller pieplate, place it on top of the crumbs, and press down firmly and evenly.

family favorite • quick
Chocolate Wafer Crust

prep: 4 min.   cook: 8 min.

1¼   cups chocolate wafer crumbs (about 24 wafers)
⅓   cup butter or margarine, melted

Combine chocolate wafer crumbs and butter. Firmly press crumb mixture evenly in bottom and up sides of a 9-inch pieplate.

For frozen pies, crust can be used without baking. For other pies, bake crust at 350° for 6 to 8 minutes. Cool on a wire rack. Yield: 8 servings.

Per serving: Calories 143 (64% from fat); Fat 10.1g (sat 5.5g, mono 2.8g, poly 1g); Protein 1.2g; Carb 12.7g; Fiber 0.6g; Chol 20mg; Iron 0.7mg; Sodium 155mg; Calc 8mg

family favorite • quick
Gingersnap Crumb Crust

prep: 4 min.   cook: 10 min.

1½   cups gingersnap crumbs (26 cookies)
¼   cup sugar
⅓   cup butter or margarine, melted

Combine all ingredients. Firmly press crumb mixture in bottom and up sides of a 9-inch pieplate.

For frozen pies, crust can be used without baking. For other pies, bake at 350° for 8 to 10 minutes. Cool on a wire rack. Yield: 8 servings.

Per serving: Calories 186 (47% from fat); Fat 9.8g (sat 5.4g, mono 3.2g, poly 0.6g); Protein 1.4g; Carb 23.8g; Fiber 0.5g; Chol 20mg; Iron 1.5mg; Sodium 203mg; Calc 20mg

family favorite • quick
Graham Cracker Crust

prep: 5 min.   cook: 9 min.

Slightly sweetened and crisp-baked, this crumb crust is a universal favorite for popular pies such as Key lime.

1   (5⅓-ounce) packet graham crackers, crushed (about 1⅔ cups)
¼   cup sugar
6   tablespoons butter or margarine, melted

Combine all ingredients. Firmly press crumb mixture evenly in bottom and up sides of a 9-inch pieplate.

For frozen pies, crust can be used without baking. For other pies, bake crust at 350° for 7 to 9 minutes. Cool on a wire rack. Yield: 8 servings.

Per serving: Calories 179 (52% from fat); Fat 10.4g (sat 5.7g, mono 3g, poly 1g); Protein 1.4g; Carb 20.8g; Fiber 0.5g; Chol 23mg; Iron 0.7mg; Sodium 175mg; Calc 7mg

fruit pies & tarts

Among desserts, fruit pies and tarts are Southern favorites. For best results buy and use fresh fruit in season. Some frozen sliced fruit is acceptable in pie making, providing a year-round option. Just be sure to follow recipe directions when using frozen fruit. For some recipes you'll need to thaw the fruit. Some recipes tell you to toss fruit with a little flour to absorb excess liquid.

You can store most fruit pies and tarts at room temperature for short periods of time, but refrigerate those that contain eggs or dairy products as soon as they cool.

Applesauce Pie

make ahead
Applesauce Pie

prep: 40 min.   cook: 1 hr., 10 min.

10	large Granny Smith apples (about 4½ pounds), peeled and chopped
1	large lemon, sliced and seeded
2½	cups sugar
3	tablespoons butter or margarine
1	teaspoon vanilla extract
1	(15-ounce) package refrigerated piecrusts

Cook first 3 ingredients in a Dutch oven over medium heat, stirring often, 30 to 35 minutes or until thickened. Remove from heat. Discard lemon slices. Add butter and vanilla. Cool.

Fit 1 piecrust into a 9-inch pieplate according to package directions. Pour applesauce filling into crust.

Unroll remaining piecrust; cut into ½-inch strips. Arrange strips in a lattice design over filling; fold edges under, and crimp.

Bake on lowest oven rack at 425° for 30 to 35 minutes or until golden, shielding with aluminum foil to prevent excessive browning, if necessary. Cool completely on a wire rack. Yield: 8 servings.

Per serving: Calories 596 (28% from fat); Fat 18.3g (sat 8.6g, mono 7.1g, poly 3.8g); Protein 2.5g; Carb 109g; Fiber 2.1g; Chol 21mg; Iron 0.1mg; Sodium 227mg; Calc 10mg

family favorite
Apple Pie

prep: 40 min.   cook: 1 hr., 5 min.

Double-Crust Pastry (page 348)

6	cups peeled, sliced cooking apple
1	tablespoon lemon juice
½	cup granulated sugar
½	cup firmly packed light brown sugar
2	tablespoons all-purpose flour
½	teaspoon ground cinnamon
¼	teaspoon ground nutmeg
2	tablespoons butter or margarine
1	egg yolk, lightly beaten
2	teaspoons granulated sugar (optional)
⅛	teaspoon ground cinnamon (optional)

Roll half of pastry to ⅛-inch thickness on a lightly floured surface. Place in a 9-inch pieplate; set aside.

Combine apple and lemon juice in a large bowl. Combine ½ granulated cup sugar and next 4 ingredients. Spoon over apple mixture, tossing gently. Spoon filling evenly into pastry shell, and dot with butter.

Roll remaining pastry to ⅛-inch thickness; transfer to top of pie. Trim off excess pastry along edges. Fold edges under, and crimp.

Cut slits in top crust for steam to escape. Brush pastry lightly with beaten egg yolk. If desired, combine 2 teaspoons granulated sugar and ⅛ teaspoon cinnamon to sprinkle on pie.

Cover edges of pastry with aluminum foil to prevent excessive browning. Bake at 450° for 15 minutes; reduce heat to 350°, and bake 50 more minutes. Yield: 8 servings.

Per serving: Calories 468 (44% from fat); Fat 22.8g (sat 6.8g, mono 7.4g, poly 5.1g); Protein 4g; Carb 62.2g; Fiber 2.1g; Chol 33mg; Iron 2mg; Sodium 318mg; Calc 27mg

Cheddar-Pear Pie

prep: 25 min.   cook: 53 min.

5	medium-size ripe pears, peeled and chopped
⅓	cup sugar
2	tablespoons butter
¼	teaspoon vanilla extract
1	(9-inch) frozen unbaked pastry shell
½	cup (2 ounces) shredded sharp Cheddar cheese
½	cup all-purpose flour
¼	cup sugar
¼	teaspoon salt
¼	cup butter, melted

Combine pears and ⅓ cup sugar in a 3½-quart saucepan. Cook, stirring often, over medium-low heat 12 to 14 minutes or until pears are tender. Remove from heat. (Drain excess liquid, if necessary.)
Process pears in a blender until smooth; stir in 2 tablespoons butter and vanilla. Set aside.
Line pastry shell with aluminum foil; fill with pie weights or dried beans.
Bake on lowest oven rack at 425° for 10 minutes. Remove weights and foil; bake 4 more minutes.
Combine cheese and next 3 ingredients. Stir in ¼ cup melted butter.
Spoon pear mixture into prepared piecrust; sprinkle with cheese mixture. Cover edges with aluminum foil.
Bake at 425° for 25 minutes. Yield: 6 servings.

Per serving: Calories 405 (44% from fat); Fat 21.6g (sat 10.3g, mono 6g, poly 3.2g); Protein 4.7g; Carb 59.7g; Fiber 2.7g; Chol 38.4mg; Iron 1.2mg; Sodium 377mg; Calc 89mg

Cranberry Streusel Pie

prep: 10 min.   cook: 50 min.

½	(15-ounce) package refrigerated piecrusts
2	cups fresh or frozen cranberries
¼	cup granulated sugar
¼	cup firmly packed light brown sugar
½	cup chopped walnuts
½	teaspoon ground cinnamon
1	large egg
⅓	cup granulated sugar
¼	cup butter or margarine, melted
3	tablespoons all-purpose flour

Fit piecrust into a 9-inch pieplate according to package directions; fold edges under, and

apple dictionary

• Apples will keep longer if they're not touching other apples.
• Generally speaking, when peaches and melons are in season, stay away from apples. For juiciest results, buy apples just a month or two later when there's a snap in the air.

Mildly tart **Cameos** are great for use in salads, making applesauce or pies.
Mutsu apples (also called *Crispin*) are juicy, crisp, all-purpose fruit. They make great applesauce.
Honey Crisp apples are fairly new on the scene. Hailed for their crisp, juicy texture, they're great in salads or for baking, and they keep up to two months in the refrigerator.
Fuji is a Japanese apple with great appeal—it's super sweet, super juicy, and very crisp. It's a great snacking apple out of hand.
Gala and **Braeburn** apples are popular New Zealand varieties. Galas are aromatic juicy apples with a firm, crisp texture and a very sweet flavor. They're tops for eating out of hand, and are also excellent in salads, pies, and other baked goods. Braeburns are firm with sweet yet slightly tart flavor; they're nice in salads and desserts or as a snack.
Jonagold is a cross between Golden Delicious and Jonathon apples. They're crisp, sweet, firm apples, great for eating out of hand or in salads. They hold their shape fairly well in baking.
Rome apples are superb baking apples that retain their shape as well as their mildly tart flavor.

Granny Smith is a hard, crunchy, green-skinned apple with a tart flavor. It's a juicy apple that keeps well. Peeling is often recommended because the green skin tends to be tough. The Granny Smith is a great pie apple.
Golden Delicious apples have a fairly long season—they're a good all-purpose apple year-round, though they tend to lose flavor when cooked.
Red Delicious are large, elongated, brilliant red apples. They're juicy and sweet, good for snacking and in salads but not for cooking.

crimp. Stir together cranberries and next 4 ingredients, and spoon into piecrust.
Whisk together egg and remaining ingredients, and pour over cranberry mixture.
Bake at 400° for 20 minutes. Reduce oven temperature to 350°, and bake 30 more minutes or until streusel is golden. Yield: 6 servings.

Per serving: Calories 445 (48% from fat); Fat 23.5g (sat 8.7g, mono 3.6g, poly 4.3g); Protein 4.7g; Carb 54.6g; Fiber 2.1g; Chol 59mg; Iron 0.9mg; Sodium 214mg; Calc 24mg

Fresh Peach Pie

prep: 38 min.   cook: 55 min.

A golden lattice artfully adorns summer's favorite pie. (pictured on page 344)

5½ cups peeled, sliced fresh peaches
    (3½ pounds)*
1   cup sugar
¼   cup all-purpose flour
½   teaspoon ground cinnamon
3   tablespoons butter or margarine
1   teaspoon vanilla extract
Pastry for double-crust 9-inch pie (page 348)

Combine first 4 ingredients in a saucepan; set aside until syrup forms. Bring mixture to a boil; reduce heat to low, and cook 10 minutes or until peaches are tender, stirring often. Remove from heat; add butter and vanilla, blending well.
Roll half of pastry to ⅛-inch thickness on a lightly floured surface. Place pastry in a 9-inch pieplate; trim off excess pastry along edges of pieplate. Spoon filling into pastry shell. Roll remaining pastry to ⅛-inch thickness; cut into ½-inch or 1-inch strips.
Arrange strips in lattice design over peaches. Trim strips even with pieplate edges; fold edges under, and crimp.
Bake at 425° for 15 minutes; reduce oven temperature to 350°, and bake 25 to 30 more minutes or until crust is browned. Serve warm with ice cream, if desired. Yield: 8 servings.

Per serving: Calories 484 (44% from fat); Fat 23.9g (sat 7.5g, mono 7.6g, poly 5.2g); Protein 4.8g; Carb 63.2g; Fiber 2.8g; Chol 11mg; Iron 2mg; Sodium 322mg; Calc 16mg

*Substitute 1½ (16-ounce) packages frozen unsweetened sliced peaches, if fresh peaches are out of season.

A good pie or pastry simply wraps a superb filling in a tender, flaky crust.

Pineapple Buttermilk Pie

prep: 16 min.   cook: 50 min.

You can serve this pie warm, at room temperature, or chilled; our Test Kitchens staff preferred it chilled.

½   (15-ounce) package refrigerated
    piecrusts
2   cups sugar
2   tablespoons cornmeal
5   large eggs, lightly beaten
⅔   cup buttermilk
½   cup drained crushed pineapple
½   cup sweetened flaked coconut
¼   cup butter, melted
2   teaspoons grated lemon rind
2   teaspoons fresh lemon juice
1   teaspoon vanilla extract

Unroll piecrust; fit into a 9-inch pieplate. Fold edges under, and crimp.
Combine sugar and cornmeal in a large bowl. Stir in eggs and buttermilk until blended. Stir in pineapple and remaining ingredients. Pour filling into piecrust.
Bake at 350° for 45 to 50 minutes or until filling is set and top is lightly browned. Yield: 8 servings.

Per serving: Calories 459 (35% from fat); Fat 17.7g (sat 9.3g, mono 5.9g, poly 2.5g); Protein 6.1g; Carb 69.8g; Fiber 0.6g; Chol 155mg; Iron 0.8mg; Sodium 208mg; Calc 43mg

---

Ginger-Peach Fried Pies

prep: 30 min.   cook: 50 min.   other: 1 hr., 30 min.

1½ cups water
1   (6-ounce) package dried peaches, chopped
½   cup sugar
2   tablespoons minced crystallized ginger
¾   teaspoon vanilla extract
1   (15-ounce) package refrigerated piecrusts
Vegetable oil

Combine 1½ cups water and peaches in a saucepan; let stand 1 hour. Stir in sugar, ginger, and vanilla; bring to a boil over medium heat. Reduce heat, and simmer, stirring often, 30 minutes or until peaches are tender and liquid has evaporated. Process peach mixture in a food processor until smooth, stopping to scrape down sides. Chill mixture 30 minutes.
Roll piecrusts into 12-inch circles; cut each crust into 9 (4-inch) circles.
Spoon 2 rounded teaspoonfuls peach mixture onto half of each pastry circle. Moisten edges with water; fold dough over fruit mixture, pressing edges with a fork to seal. Crimp edges with a fork dipped in flour. Chill pies until ready to fry.
Pour oil to a depth of ½ inch into a large heavy skillet; heat to 350°. Fry pies, in batches, 2 minutes on each side. Yield: 1½ dozen.

Per pie: Calories 270 (66% from fat); Fat 19.8g (sat 3.6g, mono 6g, poly 6g); Protein 0.9g; Carb 22.8g; Fiber 0.7g; Chol 2mg; Iron 0.3mg; Sodium 92mg; Calc 0.9mg

Note: To bake, place pies on lightly greased baking sheets; bake at 425° for 12 minutes.

Oven-Fried Strawberry Pies

prep: 25 min.   cook: 20 min.   other: 1 hr.

Baking certainly doesn't sacrifice flavor here—these pies are delicious and healthier than traditional fried pies.

2   cups fresh strawberries, mashed
¾   cup sugar
¼   cup cornstarch
1   (15-ounce) package refrigerated piecrusts
1   large egg, lightly beaten
2   tablespoons water
Vegetable cooking spray

Combine first 3 ingredients in a saucepan. Bring strawberry mixture to a boil over medium heat. Cook 1 minute or until thickened, stirring constantly; cool completely.
Unroll 1 piecrust; cut into 6 circles with a 4½-inch round cutter. Spoon 1 tablespoon strawberry mixture in the center of each circle; moisten edges with water, fold over, pressing edges with a fork to seal. Repeat

with remaining piecrust and strawberry mixture.

Place pies in a single layer on a baking sheet, and freeze at least 1 hour.

Transfer pies to a baking sheet coated with cooking spray. Combine egg and water; brush pies with egg wash. Bake at 425° for 20 minutes or until golden. Yield: 1 dozen.

Per pie: Calories 230 (38% from fat); Fat 9.7g (sat 4.1g, mono 4.4g, poly 2.5g); Protein 2g; Carb 33.9g; Fiber 0.5g; Chol 24mg; Iron 0.2mg; Sodium 138mg; Calc 6mg

Pear Frangipane Tart

prep: 28 min.　cook: 55 min.　other: 2 hrs.

This showy French tart is superb served with vanilla bean ice cream. Frangipane refers to the buttery ground almond filling.

½	cup cold butter, cut into pieces
1½	cups all-purpose flour
¼	teaspoon salt
3	tablespoons ice water
1¼	cups slivered almonds
½	cup granulated sugar
2	tablespoons all-purpose flour
½	cup butter, softened
2	large eggs
2	tablespoons powdered sugar
¼	teaspoon salt
1	cup dry white wine
2	cups water
1	cup granulated sugar
2	teaspoons vanilla extract
3	large Bosc pears, peeled
1	tablespoon butter or margarine, melted
1	tablespoon cornstarch

Pear Frangipane Tart

Pulse first 3 ingredients in a food processor until mixture is crumbly. Slowly add ice water through food chute, pulsing until mixture forms a ball. Flatten dough to a 6-inch disc; wrap in plastic wrap and chill 1 hour.

Process almonds in food processor until finely ground. Combine almonds, ½ cup granulated sugar, and 2 tablespoons flour in a small bowl; set aside.

Beat softened butter, eggs, powdered sugar, and ¼ teaspoon salt at medium speed with an electric mixer until creamy. Combine almond and butter mixtures. Cover and chill 1 hour.

Roll pastry to ⅛-inch thickness on a floured surface. Fit pastry into a 10-inch tart pan; place on a baking sheet. Bake at 425° for 12 minutes. Cool. Reduce heat to 400°.

Combine wine, 2 cups water, 1 cup sugar, and vanilla in a large saucepan; bring just to a boil. Add pears, and simmer 8 minutes. Remove from heat. Cool pears completely in liquid. Remove pears; pat dry. Reserve 1 cup poaching liquid.

Cut pears in half vertically, remove cores, and cut pears into ¼-inch-thick lengthwise slices, keeping stem ends intact.

Spread almond mixture into baked tart shell. Arrange sliced pear halves over almond mixture, stem ends toward center. Fan pears slightly. Brush pears with melted butter. Bake at 400° for 30 minutes or until golden.

Combine reserved 1 cup poaching liquid and cornstarch in a small saucepan, stirring until smooth. Cook over medium heat, stirring constantly, until mixture thickens. Boil 1 minute, stirring constantly. Remove from heat. Brush tart with glaze mixture. Remove sides of tart pan before serving. Yield: 8 servings.

Per serving: Calories 536 (56% from fat); Fat 34.3g (sat 16.4g, mono 12.2g, poly 3.3g); Protein 8.3g; Carb 57.2g; Fiber 3.9g; Chol 117mg; Iron 2.3mg; Sodium 336mg; Calc 67mg

Grapefruit Tart

prep: 40 min.   cook: 24 min.
other: 2 hrs., 30 min.

1   (5.3-ounce) package pure butter shortbread (we tested with Walkers)
3   tablespoons sugar
2   tablespoons butter, melted
½   cup sugar
6   tablespoons cornstarch
⅛   teaspoon salt
2   cups fresh red grapefruit juice
4   egg yolks
3   tablespoons butter
2   teaspoons grated red grapefruit rind
3   red grapefruit, peeled and sectioned
2   tablespoons sugar

Process shortbread in a blender or food processor until graham cracker crumb consistency (about 1⅓ cups of crumbs).
Stir together shortbread crumbs, 3 tablespoons sugar, and 2 tablespoons melted butter in a small bowl. Press mixture lightly into a greased 9-inch tart pan.
Bake at 350° for 10 to 12 minutes or until lightly browned. Set aside.
Combine ½ cup sugar, cornstarch, and salt in a medium-size heavy saucepan. Whisk in juice and egg yolks. Cook over medium-high heat, whisking constantly, 10 to 12 minutes or until mixture thickens and boils. Remove from heat; stir in 3 tablespoons butter and rind.
Pour filling into prepared tart shell. Cover surface of filling directly with plastic wrap. Chill 2½ hours.
Place red grapefruit sections in an 8-inch square baking dish. Sprinkle with 2 tablespoons sugar; chill until ready to assemble. Drain grapefruit.
Arrange grapefruit segments, with outer part of segments facing the edge, around border of tart. Arrange remaining segments around tart, slightly overlapping to cover filling completely. Serve immediately. Chill leftovers. Yield: 8 servings.

Per serving: Calories 339 (37% from fat); Fat 14g (sat 6.5g, mono 5.4g, poly 1.2g); Protein 3.4g; Carb 51.5g; Fiber 1.5g; Chol 125mg; Iron 0.9mg; Sodium 177mg; Calc 37mg

To make ahead: Prepare the crust and filling up to 2 days ahead, but do not top with fruit. Top with grapefruit just before serving.

---

entertaining
Almond-Apple Tart

prep: 42 min.   cook: 45 min.   other: 15 min.

1   (15-ounce) package refrigerated piecrusts
6½ tablespoons butter or margarine, softened and divided
4   ounces almond paste, crumbled
5   tablespoons sugar, divided
¼   cup brandy, divided
⅓   cup plus 2 tablespoons all-purpose flour, divided
1   large egg
1   teaspoon vanilla extract
¼   teaspoon almond extract
2   medium Granny Smith apples, peeled and thinly sliced
½   cup apricot preserves
1   tablespoon whipping cream
Garnishes: sweetened whipped cream, sliced almonds, ground cinnamon

Unroll piecrusts; stack on a lightly floured surface. Roll into a 12-inch circle. Fit into a 10-inch tart pan with removable bottom; trim excess pastry.
Beat 4 tablespoons butter, almond paste, 1 tablespoon sugar, 2 tablespoons brandy, ⅓ cup flour, and next 3 ingredients at medium speed with an electric mixer until blended; spread in crust.
Toss together 2 tablespoons sugar and apple slices; arrange in circles, overlapping slices, on filling.
Cook preserves in a saucepan over low heat until melted. Pour through a fine wire-mesh strainer, discarding solids. Stir in 1 tablespoon butter, remaining 2 tablespoons brandy, and cream; drizzle over apples.
Combine remaining 2 tablespoons sugar and remaining 2 tablespoons flour; cut in remaining 1½ tablespoons butter with a fork until crumbly. Sprinkle evenly over apples.
Bake at 425° on lowest oven rack 45 minutes. Cool in pan on a wire rack 15 minutes. Garnish, if desired. Yield: 10 servings.

Per serving: Calories 421 (49% from fat); Fat 23.4g (sat 10.2g, mono 9.2g, poly 4g); Protein 4.1g; Carb 49.6g; Fiber 1.1g; Chol 51mg; Iron 0.8mg; Sodium 224mg; Calc 31mg

---

Tangy Lemon Tart

prep: 25 min.   cook: 37 min.
other: 4 hrs., 20 min.

1   (15-ounce) package refrigerated piecrusts
1   tablespoon coarse sparkling sugar
2   cups granulated sugar
6   tablespoons cornstarch
1   cup fresh lemon juice (8 large lemons)
8   large eggs, lightly beaten
½   cup butter, melted
4   drops yellow liquid food coloring

Unroll 1 piecrust, and place on a lightly floured surface; lightly brush top of crust with water. Unroll remaining crust, and place over bottom crust; gently roll or press crusts together into a 12-inch circle. Fit piecrust into a 9-inch deep-dish tart or quiche pan (about 1½ to 1¾ inches deep). Prick bottom of crust with a fork. Freeze 10 minutes.
Line piecrust with parchment paper; fill with pie weights or dried beans.
Bake at 425° for 10 minutes. Remove weights and parchment paper; sprinkle crust with sparkling sugar, and bake 12 to 15 more minutes or until lightly browned.
Whisk together granulated sugar and cornstarch in a heavy nonaluminum medium saucepan; gradually whisk in lemon juice, eggs, and butter. Cook, whisking constantly, over medium-low heat 12 minutes or until thick and bubbly. Remove from heat; add food coloring, and let stand 10 minutes.
Pour filling into crust; cover and chill 4 hours or until set. Yield: 8 servings.

Per serving: Calories 641 (42% from fat); Fat 30.1g (sat 13.7g, mono 4.9g, poly 1.1g); Protein 7.5g; Carb 85.9g; Fiber 0.2g; Chol 248mg; Iron 1mg; Sodium 368mg; Calc 33mg

---

Key Lime Curd Tartlets

prep: 39 min.   cook: 30 min.   other: 6 hrs.

4   large eggs
⅔   cup Key lime juice
¾   cup sugar
6   tablespoons unsalted butter
2   teaspoons grated Key lime rind
2   cups all-purpose flour
¼   cup sugar
¾   teaspoon salt
¼   teaspoon baking powder
¾   cup cold butter, cut into pieces
6   tablespoons ice water

Whisk together first 4 ingredients in a saucepan; cook over medium-low heat, whisking constantly, 10 to 12 minutes or until mixture is thickened. Pour carefully through a wire-mesh strainer into a bowl. Stir in lime rind. Cover lime curd, and refrigerate 4 to 6 hours.

Pulse flour, ¼ cup sugar, salt, and baking powder in a food processor until combined.

Add ¾ cup butter, and pulse until mixture is crumbly. Add ice water, 1 tablespoon at a time, pulsing after each addition. Remove dough, and wrap in plastic wrap; chill at least 2 hours.

Shape dough into 36 (1-inch) balls, and press balls into lightly greased miniature tart pans or miniature (1¾ inch) muffin pans. Prick with a fork.

Bake at 375° for 17 to 18 minutes or until golden. Remove from pans, and let cool on wire racks.

Spoon 1 heaping teaspoon lime curd into each tart shell. Yield: 3 dozen.

Per tartlet: Calories 109 (54% from fat); Fat 6.6g (sat 3.8g, mono 1.7g, poly 0.3g); Protein 1.5g; Carb 11.3g; Fiber 0.2g; Chol 39mg; Iron 0.4mg; Sodium 87mg; Calc 8mg

custard & cream pies

Custard pies are basically sugar, milk or cream, and flavorings thickened with eggs. Custard pies must always be kept chilled.

When baking custard pies, avoid spills by placing the pastry-lined pieplate on the oven rack before pouring in the filling. To check for doneness, use the jiggle test and/or the knife test: When a knife inserted near the center of the pie comes out clean, the pie is done. The center should still be a little jiggly when you remove the pie from the oven; the pie will firm when cooled.

Cream pies are custard pies thickened with cornstarch or flour and topped with whipped cream. If the pie is thickened with flour or cornstarch, never add it directly to a hot mixture—this would cause the mixture to lump. Typically the thickening agent is blended with a cold liquid before the cooking process begins.

Whether thickened with cornstarch or flour, cook the filling until it comes to a full boil; then boil 1 minute, stirring gently. If the filling also contains eggs, you'll need to boil it 3 minutes. This additional boiling kills an enzyme present in eggs that could otherwise break down their thickening ability. The filling should hold its shape when sliced but shouldn't be too firm.

If a recipe states to chill the filling before adding a topping, press plastic wrap directly on the surface of the filling to prevent a "skin" from forming as the filling cools.

Allow custard and cream pies to cool completely before slicing and serving them. Otherwise, you run the risk of serving a runny pie. Always refrigerate leftover custard and cream pies.

Lemon-Blueberry Cream Pie

prep: 18 min.   cook: 9 min.   other: 2 hrs.

1⅔ cups graham cracker crumbs
¼ cup granulated sugar
6 tablespoons butter or margarine, melted
1 (8-ounce) package cream cheese, softened
1 (14-ounce) can sweetened condensed milk
¼ cup powdered sugar
1 (3.4-ounce) package lemon instant pudding mix
2 teaspoons grated lemon rind
½ cup fresh lemon juice
1 pint fresh blueberries
2 tablespoons blueberry preserves
1 cup whipping cream

Stir together first 3 ingredients; press evenly in bottom and up sides of a 9-inch pieplate.
Bake crust at 350° for 8 to 9 minutes; remove crust to a wire rack, and let cool.
Beat cream cheese, milk, and powdered sugar at medium speed with an electric mixer until creamy. Add pudding mix, lemon rind and juice; beat until blended. Spread half of lemon mixture evenly into prepared crust.
Stir together blueberries and preserves; spread evenly over lemon mixture. Spread remaining lemon mixture over blueberry mixture; cover and chill 2 hours or until set.
Beat whipping cream at high speed with an electric mixer until soft peaks form; spread whipped cream around outer edge of pie, forming a 3-inch border. Yield: 8 servings.

Per serving: Calories 632 (49% from fat); Fat 34.7g (sat 20.6g, mono 10g, poly 1.9g); Protein 7.7g; Carb 75.4g; Fiber 1.5g; Chol 111mg; Iron 1.2mg; Sodium 484mg; Calc 195mg

Coconut Cream Pie

prep: 10 min.   cook: 10 min.   other: 1 hr.

½ (15-ounce) package refrigerated piecrusts
½ cup sugar
¼ cup cornstarch
2 cups half-and-half
4 egg yolks
3 tablespoons butter
1 cup sweetened flaked coconut
2½ teaspoons vanilla extract, divided
2 cups whipping cream
⅓ cup sugar
Garnish: toasted coconut

Fit piecrust into a 9-inch pieplate; fold edges under, and crimp. Prick bottom and sides of piecrust with a fork. Bake according to package directions.
Combine ½ cup sugar and cornstarch in a large heavy saucepan. Whisk together half-and-half and egg yolks. Gradually whisk egg mixture into sugar mixture; bring to a boil over medium heat, whisking constantly. Boil 1 minute; remove from heat.
Stir in butter, 1 cup coconut, and 1 teaspoon vanilla. Cover with plastic wrap, placing wrap directly on filling; let stand 30 minutes. Spoon custard filling into prepared crust; cover and chill 30 minutes or until set.
Beat whipping cream at high speed with an electric mixer until foamy; gradually add ⅓ cup sugar and remaining 1½ teaspoons vanilla, beating until soft peaks form. Spread or pipe whipped cream over pie filling. Garnish, if desired. Yield: 8 servings.

Per serving: Calories 609 (67% from fat); Fat 45.2g (sat 26.6g, mono 10.6g, poly 1.6g); Protein 5.2g; Carb 46.4g; Fiber 0.4g; Chol 220mg; Iron 0.5mg; Sodium 214mg; Calc 115mg

Black-Bottom Chocolate Cream Pie

prep: 17 min.   cook: 8 min.

other: 6 hrs., 30 min.

Thick and rich is the most fitting description for this pie. Find dark chocolate bars on the grocer's candy aisle.

1½ (3-ounce) dark chocolate bars, melted (we tested with Ghirardelli)
1   baked 9-inch pastry shell
⅔   cup granulated sugar
⅓   cup cornstarch
3   tablespoons unsweetened cocoa
⅛   teaspoon salt
4   egg yolks, lightly beaten
2   cups milk
1   cup half-and-half
2   tablespoons butter or margarine
1   (3-ounce) dark chocolate bar, finely chopped
1   teaspoon vanilla extract
1   tablespoon bourbon (optional)
1   cup whipping cream
¼   cup sifted powdered sugar
Garnish: chocolate shavings

Pour melted chocolate into baked pastry shell, spreading evenly. Chill until chocolate hardens.

Meanwhile, combine ⅔ cup granulated sugar, cornstarch, cocoa, and salt in a heavy saucepan; stir well. Stir together egg yolks, milk, and half-and-half; gradually stir into sugar mixture. Cook over medium heat, stirring constantly, until mixture thickens and boils. Boil 3 minutes, stirring constantly. Remove from heat; stir in butter, 3 ounces chocolate, vanilla, and, if desired, bourbon.

Pour filling into a bowl; cover with plastic wrap, placing directly on filling, and cool 30 minutes. Pour filling into pastry shell; cover tightly with plastic wrap, and chill at least 6 hours.

Beat whipping cream at medium speed with an electric mixer until foamy; gradually add powdered sugar, beating until soft peaks form. Spread whipped cream over pie. Garnish, if desired. Store in refrigerator. Yield: 8 servings.

Per serving: Calories 506 (57% from fat); Fat 31.9g (sat 18.8g, mono 6.5g, poly 1.1g); Protein 6.8g; Carb 50.6g; Fiber 3.2g; Chol 170mg; Iron 1.4mg; Sodium 128mg; Calc 135mg

Egg Custard Pie

prep: 5 min.   cook: 1 hr., 10 min.

An old-fashioned recipe, this egg custard bakes with a sprinkling of nutmeg on top.

Pastry for 9-inch pie (page 347)
4   large eggs, lightly beaten
⅔   cup sugar
1½ teaspoons vanilla extract
¼   teaspoon salt
¼   teaspoon ground nutmeg
2   cups milk
¼   cup whipping cream
Ground nutmeg

Bake pastry shell at 450° for 8 to 10 minutes or until golden.

Meanwhile, combine eggs and next 4 ingredients; beat at medium speed with an electric mixer until blended. Gradually stir in milk and whipping cream; mix well.

Without removing baked pastry shell from oven, pour filling into hot pastry shell; sprinkle with additional nutmeg.

Reduce heat to 325°; bake 1 hour or until 2 inches from center is set when jiggled. Cool completely; store in refrigerator. Yield: 8 servings.

Per serving: Calories 324 (47% from fat); Fat 16.9g (sat 6g, mono 5.4g, poly 3g); Protein 7.3g; Carb 34.9g; Fiber 0.5g; Chol 122mg; Iron 1.4mg; Sodium 281mg; Calc 90mg

Pumpkin Cream Pie

prep: 14 min.   cook: 8 min.   other: 8 hrs.

This make-ahead holiday dessert's good chilled or frozen.

25 (2-inch) gingersnap cookies, finely crushed (we tested with Murray's)
¼   cup butter or margarine, melted
1   (8-ounce) package cream cheese, softened
1   (15-ounce) can pumpkin
1   teaspoon ground cinnamon
½   teaspoon ground allspice
½   teaspoon ground ginger
¼   teaspoon ground nutmeg
½   cup heavy whipping cream
1½ cups powdered sugar
Garnishes: whipped cream, gingersnaps

Stir together crushed gingersnaps and butter; press into a greased 9-inch pieplate. Bake at 350° for 8 minutes. Cool completely on a wire rack.

Beat cream cheese in a large bowl at medium speed with an electric mixer until creamy. Add pumpkin and next 4 ingredients; beat until blended.

Beat whipping cream until foamy; gradually add powdered sugar, beating until stiff peaks form. (Mixture will be very thick.) Fold whipped cream into pumpkin filling until blended. Spoon into crust. Cover and chill pie at least 8 hours. Garnish, if desired. Yield: 8 servings.

Per serving: Calories 399 (53% from fat); Fat 23.4g (sat 13.9g, mono 7.1g, poly 1.1g); Protein 4.4g; Carb 45.1g; Fiber 2.3g; Chol 67mg; Iron 2.6mg; Sodium 276mg; Calc 70mg

Classic Chess Pie

prep: 23 min.   cook: 1 hr.

Remarkable in its simplicity, timeless in appeal, this is the ultimate pantry pie.

½   (15-ounce) package refrigerated piecrusts
2   cups sugar
2   tablespoons cornmeal
1   tablespoon all-purpose flour
¼   teaspoon salt
½   cup butter or margarine, melted
¼   cup milk
1   tablespoon white vinegar
½   teaspoon vanilla extract
4   large eggs, lightly beaten

Fit piecrust into a 9-inch pieplate according to package directions; fold edges under, and crimp.

Line pastry with aluminum foil, and fill with pie weights or dried beans.

Bake at 425° for 4 to 5 minutes. Remove weights and foil; bake 2 more minutes or until golden. Cool completely.

Stir together sugar and next 7 ingredients until blended. Add eggs, stirring well. Pour filling into piecrust.

Bake at 350° for 50 to 55 minutes, shielding edges with aluminum foil after 10 minutes to prevent excessive browning. Cool completely on a wire rack. Yield: 8 servings.

Per serving: Calories 465 (41% from fat); Fat 21g (sat 10.6g, mono 4g, poly 0.8g); Protein 4.3g; Carb 65.7g; Fiber 0.2g; Chol 140mg; Iron 0.6mg; Sodium 329mg; Calc 33mg

meringue pies

Meringue is made of egg whites and sugar whipped into a fluffy mass for topping pies. The key to successful meringue is to work with a clean, grease-free bowl and beaters.

When properly beaten, meringue should look glossy and have firm peaks. Spread it quickly onto a hot filling and anchor it to the edges of the pie. The residual heat carried by the hot filling helps cook the meringue from the bottom, making it less prone to shrinking. To prevent a meringue from weeping (tiny beads of moisture that form on the surface), don't overbake it. Food-safety issues mandate chilling meringue pies, and, unfortunately, chilling increases the likelihood of weeping, too.

make ahead • quick
Key Lime Pie

prep: 5 min. cook: 15 min.

- 3   large egg yolks
- ½   cup Key lime juice
- 1   (14-ounce) can sweetened condensed milk
- ¼   teaspoon vanilla extract
- Pinch of salt
- 1   (6-ounce) ready-made graham cracker crust
- Garnishes: whipped cream, lime slices

Whisk egg yolks until blended; whisk in Key lime juice. Add condensed milk, vanilla, and salt, whisking until blended. Pour filling into crust. Bake at 350° for 15 minutes. **Remove** from oven; cool completely on a wire rack. Chill until ready to serve. Garnish, if desired. Yield: 8 servings.

Per serving: Calories 329 (36% from fat); Fat 13.3g (sat 4.9g, mono 5.3g, poly 2.5g); Protein 6.2g; Carb 48.7g; Fiber 0.5g; Chol 94mg; Iron 0.9mg; Sodium 252mg; Calc 157mg

Meringue-Topped Key Lime Pie: Prepare filling (above); pour into crust. Beat 3 egg whites and ¼ teaspoon cream of tartar at high speed with an electric mixer until foamy. Add 2 tablespoons sugar, 1 tablespoon at a time, beating until soft peak forms and sugar dissolves (2 to 4 minutes). Spread meringue over filling. Bake at 325° for 25 to 28 minutes. Chill 8 hours, if desired.

family favorite
Lemon Meringue Pie

prep: 25 min. cook: 50 min. other: 10 min.

- 1   (15-ounce) package refrigerated piecrusts
- 1   cup sugar
- ¼   cup cornstarch
- ⅛   teaspoon salt
- 4   large egg yolks
- 2   cups milk
- ⅓   cup fresh lemon juice
- 3   tablespoons butter or margarine
- 1   teaspoon grated lemon rind
- ½   teaspoon vanilla extract
- 6   egg whites
- ½   teaspoon vanilla extract
- 6   tablespoons sugar

Unroll 1 piecrust, and place on a lightly floured surface; lightly brush top of crust with water. Unroll remaining crust, and place over bottom crust; gently roll or press crusts together. Fit into a 9-inch pieplate; fold edges under, and crimp. Prick bottom and sides of piecrust with a fork. Freeze piecrust 10 minutes.
Line piecrust with parchment paper; fill with pie weights or dried beans.
Bake at 425° for 10 minutes. Remove weights and parchment paper; bake 12 to 15 more minutes or until crust is lightly browned. (Shield edges of pie with aluminum foil to prevent excessive browning, if necessary.)
Whisk together 1 cup sugar, cornstarch, and salt in a heavy nonaluminum medium saucepan. Whisk together egg yolks, milk, and lemon juice in a bowl; whisk into sugar mixture in pan over medium heat. Bring to a boil, and boil, whisking constantly, 1 minute. Remove pan from heat; stir in butter, lemon rind, and ½ teaspoon vanilla until smooth. Pour into piecrust. Cover with plastic wrap, placing directly on filling. (Proceed immediately with next step to ensure that the meringue is spread over the pie filling while it's still warm.)
Beat egg whites and ½ teaspoon vanilla at high speed with an electric mixer until foamy. Add 6 tablespoons sugar, 1 tablespoon at a time, and beat 2 to 4 minutes or until stiff peaks form and sugar dissolves.
Remove plastic wrap from pie, and spread meringue evenly over warm filling, sealing edges.
Bake at 325° for 25 minutes or until golden. Cool pie completely on a wire rack. Store leftovers in the refrigerator. Yield: 8 servings.

Per serving: Calories 385 (36% from fat); Fat 15.4g (sat 7.1g, mono 2.6g, poly 0.6g); Protein 6.6g; Carb 55.1g; Fiber 0.1g; Chol 123mg; Iron 0.3mg; Sodium 245mg; Calc 84mg

beating egg whites

1. Foamy stage: When lightly beaten to this stage, egg whites will look bubbly and foamy.

2. Soft peak stage: When beaten to soft peak stage, egg whites will mound, but no sharp tips will form.

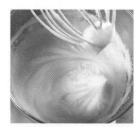

3. Stiff peak stage: When beaten to stiff peaks, sharp tips will form when beaters are lifted.

4. Overbeaten egg whites: When whites are overbeaten, they look curdled and dry. There's no restoring them.

Brown Sugar Meringue Pie

prep: 34 min.   cook: 35 min.

Here's a mile-high showstopper meringue dessert. Pies like this are meant to be served the day they're made. For best results, time the beating of the egg whites as close as possible to the readiness of the syrup. Since this meringue is baked for only 9 minutes, it's essential that the syrup be at 250° when added to the egg whites to bring them to a safe temperature.

1	cup firmly packed light brown sugar
⅓	cup cornstarch
⅛	teaspoon salt
2	cups half-and-half
4	egg yolks
2	teaspoons vanilla extract
¼	cup butter, cut into pieces
¾	cup firmly packed light brown sugar
⅔	cup granulated sugar
6	tablespoons water
5	egg whites
½	teaspoon cream of tartar
1	baked 9-inch pastry shell

Combine first 3 ingredients in a 4-quart heavy saucepan. Stir in half-and-half. Cook, stirring constantly, over medium heat 9 minutes or until mixture comes to a boil and thickens. Boil 2 minutes, stirring constantly. Remove from heat.

Lightly beat egg yolks with a wire whisk. Gradually stir about one-fourth of hot mixture into yolks; add to remaining hot mixture, stirring constantly. Cook, stirring constantly, 3 minutes over medium heat. Remove from heat, and stir in vanilla and butter. Cover and set aside while preparing meringue.

Stir together ¾ cup brown sugar, ⅔ cup granulated sugar, and 6 tablespoons water in a 1-quart heavy saucepan. Bring to a boil over medium heat, stirring constantly, until sugar dissolves. Wash down crystals with a small pastry brush dipped in hot water. Bring to a boil over medium heat, and cook, stirring often, until a candy thermometer registers 250° (firm ball stage).

While syrup cooks, beat egg whites and cream of tartar in a large mixing bowl at high speed with a heavy-duty stand mixer until soft peaks form. Pour hot syrup mixture in a heavy stream over beaten egg whites, beating constantly at high speed until stiff peaks form (about 2 to 3 minutes). (Do not overbeat.)

Pour hot filling into pastry shell. Spoon one-third of meringue over hot filling in about 5 large dollops. Using back of a large spoon, spread meringue, sealing to edge of pastry and forming decorative swirls. Spread another third of meringue over pie, using same procedure. Spread remaining third of meringue over pie, and spread to edge.

Bake at 375° for 9 minutes or until meringue is lightly browned. Let cool completely on a wire rack. Yield: 8 servings.

Per serving: Calories 465 (31% from fat); Fat 16.2g (sat 9g, mono 4.4g, poly 0.8g); Protein 5.7g; Carb 75.8g; Fiber 0.1g; Chol 140mg; Iron 1.4mg; Sodium 178mg; Calc 119mg

Note: Be sure to use a heavy-duty stand mixer with at least a 4-quart bowl to accommodate the large volume of meringue. Don't be tempted to spread on all the meringue at once. It's necessary to apply it in three batches in order to fit it all on the pie and ensure maximum volume.

chilled & frozen pies

Pies that require chilling or freezing make excellent desserts for entertaining because you can prepare them in advance and then forget about them until serving time.

The two most common types of chilled pies are cream-based and ice cream- or yogurt-based. The secret to frozen pies is not to freeze pies as hard as a rock, but long enough so they're firm for slicing and soft enough to spoon into.

You can make a chilled pie using a baked pastry or a baked crumb crust, and a frozen pie with a baked pastry or an unbaked crumb crust.

entertaining • freeze it • make ahead
weekend chef

Tiramisù Toffee Trifle Pie

prep: 24 min.   other: 8 hrs., 10 min.

This frozen version of the beloved coffee-soaked cake grabbed our undivided attention.

1½	tablespoons instant coffee granules
¾	cup warm water
1	(16-ounce) frozen pound cake (we tested with Sara Lee)
1	(8-ounce) package cream cheese, softened
1	cup plus 2 tablespoons powdered sugar, divided
½	cup chocolate syrup
4	cups whipping cream
2	(1.4-ounce) chocolate-covered toffee candy bars, coarsely chopped

Stir together coffee granules and warm water in a small bowl until granules dissolve. Cool.

Cut frozen pound cake into 16 slices; arrange slices evenly on bottom and up sides of a 9-inch springform pan. Brush coffee evenly over cake.

Beat cream cheese, ½ cup powdered sugar, and chocolate syrup at medium speed with an electric mixer until smooth.

Beat whipping cream in a large bowl at high speed until foamy; gradually add ½ cup plus 2 tablespoons powdered sugar, beating until stiff peaks form. Gradually fold 5 cups whipped cream into cream cheese mixture, reserving remaining whipped cream. Pour filling over cake slices in pan. Sprinkle chopped candy bar over pie. Pipe remaining whipped cream around edge of pie. Freeze 8 hours or until firm. Let stand 5 to 10 minutes before serving. Yield: 12 servings.

Per serving: Calories 590 (66% from fat); Fat 43.3g (sat 24.9g, mono 12.8g, poly 1.4g); Protein 4g; Carb 44.8g; Fiber 0.4g; Chol 184mg; Iron 0.9mg; Sodium 239mg; Calc 84mg

Fudgy Peanut
Butter Cup Pie

Process first 3 ingredients in a food processor until finely crushed. Firmly press mixture onto bottom of a lightly greased 10-inch springform pan.

Bake at 350° for 10 minutes. Cool completely in pan on a wire rack.

Let vanilla ice cream stand at room temperature 20 minutes or until slightly softened.

Meanwhile, process strawberries and 2 tablespoons powdered sugar in a food processor until pureed, stopping to scrape down sides; remove strawberry mixture, and set aside.

Process blueberries and 1 tablespoon powdered sugar in food processor until pureed, stopping to scrape down sides; set aside.

Mash bananas with a fork in a large bowl; stir in remaining 1 tablespoon powdered sugar. Set aside.

Place 1 quart of ice cream in a large bowl; cut into large (3-inch) pieces. Fold strawberry mixture into ice cream until blended. Place in freezer until slightly firm.

Divide remaining quart of ice cream in half, placing halves in separate bowls. Stir blueberry mixture into half and mashed banana mixture into remaining half. Place bowls in freezer.

Spread half of strawberry mixture evenly into prepared crust in springform pan. Place pan and remaining strawberry mixture in freezer. Freeze 30 minutes or until strawberry layer in pan is slightly firm. Spread banana mixture evenly over strawberry layer in pan; return pan to freezer, and freeze 30 minutes or until banana layer is slightly firm. Repeat procedure with blueberry mixture. Spread remaining strawberry mixture over blueberry layer in pan, and freeze 3 hours or until all layers are firm. Let pie stand at room temperature 15 minutes before serving. Garnish, if desired. Yield: 12 servings.

Per serving: Calories 415 (51% from fat); Fat 23.4g (sat 13.7g, mono 6.1g, poly 0.9g); Protein 5.3g; Carb 49.8g; Fiber 2g; Chol 76mg; Iron 0.6mg; Sodium 119mg; Calc 130mg

---

family favorite • freeze it
make ahead

Fudgy Peanut Butter Cup Pie

prep: 15 min.   other: 2 hrs., 40 min.

For an impressive presentation, carefully transfer frozen pie from aluminum pieplate to a serving plate.

1   (1.75-quart) container vanilla ice cream with peanut butter cups swirled with fudge (we tested with Mayfield's Moose Tracks Ice Cream)
⅓   cup creamy or chunky peanut butter
1   (6-ounce) ready-made chocolate crumb piecrust
6   (0.55-ounce) peanut butter cup candies, halved
½   cup chocolate-peanut butter shell coating

Allow container of ice cream to stand at room temperature 20 to 30 minutes to soften.

Spread peanut butter over crust; freeze 10 minutes.

Spread softened ice cream evenly over peanut butter in crust. Arrange peanut butter cup candy halves, cut sides down, around edges of crust. Drizzle chocolate-peanut

butter shell coating over ice cream. Freeze at least 2 hours.

Cut frozen pie with a warm knife to serve. Yield: 8 servings.

Per serving: Calories 657 (56% from fat); Fat 41.2g (sat 17.4g, mono 4.2g, poly 2.2g); Protein 10.3g; Carb 66.2g; Fiber 4.5g; Chol 44mg; Iron 1.9mg; Sodium 316mg; Calc 154mg

---

freeze it • make ahead • test kitchen favorite

Strawberry Smoothie Ice Cream Pie

prep: 50 min.   cook: 10 min.

other: 4 hrs., 45 min.

This tall pie has four stripes of fruity flavor layered on top of a waffle-cone crust.

1   (7-ounce) package waffle cones, broken into pieces
6   tablespoons butter, melted
1   tablespoon granulated sugar
2   (1-quart) containers premium vanilla ice cream, divided
1   (16-ounce) container fresh strawberries (1 quart), stemmed
¼   cup powdered sugar, divided
1   pint fresh blueberries
2   ripe bananas

Garnishes: waffle cone pieces, fresh berries

make ahead
Orange Dream Pie

prep: 25 min.   cook: 8 min.   other: 2 hrs.

Orange curd can be found in the jams-and-jellies area of the supermarket. Specialty butter cookies as the crust earn this pie top billing.

1   (7.25-ounce) package butter cookies, crushed (we tested with Pepperidge Farm Chessman Cookies)
¼   cup butter or margarine, melted
1   (8-ounce) package cream cheese, softened
⅓   cup powdered sugar
1   teaspoon vanilla extract
    Orange liquid food coloring (optional)
1   (12-ounce) container frozen whipped topping, thawed and divided
1   (10-ounce) jar orange curd
2   teaspoons grated orange rind
2   tablespoons fresh orange juice
    Garnishes: whipped topping, orange zest

Stir together cookie crumbs and butter; press evenly in bottom and up sides of a 9-inch pieplate.

Bake at 350° for 8 minutes; remove to a wire rack, and cool completely.

Beat cream cheese and powdered sugar at medium speed with an electric mixer until smooth. Stir in vanilla and, if desired, food coloring until blended; fold in 2 cups whipped topping. Spread cream cheese filling evenly into prepared crust.

Stir together curd, orange rind, juice, and 2 tablespoons whipped topping. Spread evenly over cheese filling; cover and chill 2 hours or until set. Garnish, if desired. Yield: 8 servings.

Per serving: Calories 520 (54% from fat); Fat 31.3g (sat 18.7g, mono 5.7g, poly 0.8g); Protein 3.8g; Carb 51.4g; Fiber 0.3g; Chol 103mg; Iron 0.9mg; Sodium 232mg; Calc 33mg

nut pies

entertaining • freeze it • make ahead
Coconut-Pecan Cookie Tarts

prep: 30 min.   cook: 24 min.
other: 1 hr., 10 min.

A thicker, cookie-type crust sets the bar pretty high for these pecan tassies.

1   cup butter, softened
2   (3-ounce) packages cream cheese, softened
½   cup sweetened flaked coconut
2   cups all-purpose flour
1   cup firmly packed light brown sugar
¾   cup chopped pecans, toasted
2   large eggs, lightly beaten
1½   tablespoons butter, melted
¾   teaspoon vanilla extract
¼   teaspoon salt

Beat 1 cup butter and cream cheese at medium speed with an electric mixer until creamy; stir in coconut. Gradually add flour to butter mixture, beating at low speed after each addition. Shape dough into 36 balls; cover and chill 1 hour. Place dough balls in lightly greased miniature muffin pans, shaping each into a thick shell.

Whisk brown sugar and remaining ingredients. Spoon into tart shells. Bake at 350° for 24 minutes or until set. Cool in pan on a wire rack 10 minutes. Remove from pan; cool on wire rack. Yield: 3 dozen.

Per tart: Calories 142 (63% from fat); Fat 9.9g (sat 5.1g, mono 3g, poly 0.9g); Protein 1.7g; Carb 12.2g; Fiber 0.5g; Chol 32mg; Iron 0.6mg; Sodium 76mg; Calc 15mg

entertaining
Chocolate-Bourbon Pecan Pie

prep: 10 min.   cook: 1 hr.

½   (15-ounce) package refrigerated piecrusts
1½   cups chopped pecans
1   cup semisweet chocolate morsels
1   cup dark corn syrup
½   cup granulated sugar
½   cup firmly packed light brown sugar
¼   cup bourbon
4   large eggs
¼   cup butter or margarine, melted
2   teaspoons cornmeal
2   teaspoons vanilla extract
½   teaspoon salt

Fit piecrust into a 9-inch deep-dish pieplate according to package directions; fold edges under, and crimp. Sprinkle pecans and chocolate morsels into piecrust; set aside.

Combine corn syrup and next 3 ingredients in a large saucepan, and bring to a boil over medium heat. Cook, stirring constantly, 3 minutes. Remove from heat.

Whisk together eggs and remaining ingredients. Gradually whisk about one-fourth of hot mixture into egg mixture; add to remaining hot mixture, whisking constantly. Pour filling into prepared piecrust.

Bake at 325° for 55 minutes or until set; cool on a wire rack. Yield: 8 servings.

Per serving: Calories 692 (49% from fat); Fat 37.4g (sat 11.9g, mono 13.6g, poly 5.6g); Protein 6.7g; Carb 87.8g; Fiber 3.4g; Chol 124mg; Iron 2.1mg; Sodium 400mg; Calc 57mg

Chocolate-Bourbon Pecan Pie

Macadamia Pie

prep: 15 min.   cook: 50 min.

This is a rich pie meant for the holiday table.

2   (3½-ounce) jars macadamia nuts
⅓   cup flaked coconut
1   unbaked 9-inch pastry shell
4   large eggs, lightly beaten
1   cup light corn syrup
½   cup sugar
1½   teaspoons vanilla extract
¼   teaspoon salt
1½   tablespoons cream of coconut
½   cup whipping cream, whipped

Rinse nuts with hot water; drain and pat dry with paper towels. Coarsely chop nuts; set aside. Press coconut into bottom and up sides of pastry shell; set aside.

Combine eggs and next 4 ingredients; stir in nuts. Pour filling into prepared pastry shell. Bake at 350° for 15 minutes. Reduce oven temperature to 325°, and bake 35 more minutes or until set.

Fold cream of coconut into whipped cream; serve whipped cream with pie. Yield: 8 servings.

Per serving: Calories 582 (55% from fat); Fat 35.5g (sat 10.8g, mono 17.6g, poly 0.9g); Protein 5.9g; Carb 65.1g; Fiber 2.4g; Chol 129mg; Iron 1mg; Sodium 284mg; Calc 36mg

Mom's Pecan Pie

prep: 10 min.   cook: 55 min.

To prevent filling from seeping under the crust, some of our recipes call for using two crusts stacked and rolled together.

1   (15-ounce) package refrigerated piecrusts
3   large eggs
1   cup sugar
¾   cup light corn syrup
2   tablespoons butter or margarine, melted
2   teaspoons vanilla extract
¼   teaspoon salt
1½   cups pecan halves*

Unroll 1 piecrust, and place on a lightly floured surface; lightly brush top of crust with water. Unroll remaining crust, and place over bottom crust; gently roll or press crusts together. Fit into a 9-inch pieplate; fold edges under, and crimp.

Stir together eggs and next 5 ingredients; stir in pecans.

Pour filling into piecrust. Bake at 350° for 55 minutes or until set. Serve warm or cold. Yield: 8 servings.

Per serving: Calories 619 (48% from fat); Fat 33.1g (sat 8.6g, mono 9.7g, poly 4.7g); Protein 5.2g; Carb 78.2g; Fiber 1.9g; Chol 93mg; Iron 0.9mg; Sodium 373mg; Calc 26mg

*Substitute chopped pecans, a less expensive choice, for pecan halves, if desired.

Mystery Pecan Pie

prep: 10 min.   cook: 55 min.

Taste pecan pie and cheesecake together in this decadent dessert.

1   (15-ounce) package refrigerated piecrusts
1   (8-ounce) package cream cheese, softened
4   large eggs
¾   cup sugar, divided
2   teaspoons vanilla extract, divided
¼   teaspoon salt
1   cup chopped pecans
1   cup light corn syrup
2   tablespoons butter, melted

Unroll 1 piecrust, and place on a lightly floured surface; lightly brush top of crust with water. Unroll remaining crust, and place over bottom crust; gently roll or press crusts together. Fit into a 9-inch pieplate; fold edges under, and crimp.

Beat cream cheese, 1 egg, ½ cup sugar, 1 teaspoon vanilla, and salt at medium speed with an electric mixer until smooth. Pour into piecrust. Sprinkle with pecans.

Stir together corn syrup, melted butter, remaining 3 eggs, remaining ¼ cup sugar, and remaining 1 teaspoon vanilla; pour filling over pecans.

Bake at 350° for 50 to 55 minutes or until set. Cool completely. Yield: 8 servings.

Per serving: Calories 696 (51% from fat); Fat 39.7g (sat 14.6g, mono 10.5g, poly 4g); Protein 7.7g; Carb 80.1g; Fiber 1.4g; Chol 150mg; Iron 1.2mg; Sodium 478mg; Calc 49mg

Triple Nut Tart

pre: 15 min.   cook: 1 hr., 5 min.

Three types of nuts crown this tart.

½   (15-ounce) package refrigerated piecrusts
1   cup sugar
½   cup light corn syrup
¼   cup butter or margarine
4   large eggs, lightly beaten
1   teaspoon vanilla extract
¼   teaspoon salt
½   cup pecan or walnut halves
½   cup macadamia nuts
⅓   cup blanched whole almonds, toasted

Unroll piecrust, and fit piecrust into a greased and floured 9½-inch round tart pan with a removable bottom. Prick bottom of piecrust with a fork.

Bake at 400° for 10 minutes or until golden. Cool on a wire rack. Reduce oven temperature to 325°.

Stir together sugar, corn syrup, and butter in a saucepan; cook over medium heat until butter melts and sugar dissolves, stirring often. Remove from heat; cool slightly. Add eggs, vanilla, and salt; stir well. Stir in nuts. Spoon filling into crust.

Bake at 325° for 55 minutes or until set. Cool on a wire rack. Serve with unsweetened whipped cream or ice cream. Yield: 8 servings.

Per serving: Calories 505 (52% from fat); Fat 29.4g (sat 8.5g, mono 12.2g, poly 2.9g); Protein 6.3g; Carb 57.6g; Fiber 2.1g; Chol 124mg; Iron 1mg; Sodium 283mg; Calc 37mg

Honey-Pecan Tart

prep: 35 min.   cook: 40 min.
other: 2 hrs., 30 min.

1   cup sugar
¼   cup water
1   cup whipping cream
¼   cup unsalted butter, cut into pieces
¼   cup honey
½   teaspoon salt
2½ cups coarsely chopped pecans
1   (15-ounce) package refrigerated piecrusts
2   teaspoons sugar, divided
½   (4-ounce) bittersweet chocolate bar,
    chopped (we tested with Ghirardelli)

Honey-Pecan Tart

Bring 1 cup sugar and ¼ cup water to a boil in a 2-quart saucepan, stirring until sugar dissolves. Boil over medium-high heat, without stirring, 8 minutes or until golden, swirling pan occasionally. (Wash down sides of pan with a pastry brush dipped in water, if sugar crystals form on sides.)
Remove from heat, and gradually stir in whipping cream (mixture will bubble). Add butter, honey, and salt, stirring until smooth (caramel will form a hard ball that will dissolve when stirred). Stir in pecans; simmer over medium heat, stirring occasionally, 5 minutes. Remove from heat, and cool completely.

Fit 1 piecrust into a 9-inch tart pan with removable bottom or 9-inch pieplate allowing crust to overhang slightly. Spread pecan mixture into crust. Unroll remaining crust. Place crust over mixture, pressing firmly into bottom crust to seal; trim edges. Sprinkle with 1 teaspoon sugar. Freeze 30 minutes.
Bake at 400° for 40 minutes, shielding crust with aluminum foil after 30 minutes, if necessary. Cool completely on a wire rack.

Place chocolate in a small zip-top plastic bag; seal. Submerge in hot water until chocolate melts. Snip a tiny hole in 1 corner of bag; drizzle chocolate over tart. Sprinkle with remaining 1 teaspoon sugar. Let stand 2 hours or until chocolate sets. Yield: 8 servings.

Per serving: Calories 819 (65% from fat); Fat 59.6g (sat 19.1g, mono 20g, poly 8.7g); Protein 5.6g; Carb 70.4g; Fiber 4.1g; Chol 62mg; Iron 1mg; Sodium 375mg; Calc 48mg

cobblers & other comfort foods

Fruit cobblers, crisps, and apple dumplings all fall into the comfort food category. With bumpy or flaky tops and juicy centers, these deep-dish baked desserts with a fruit filling topped with strips or dollops of biscuitlike dough are a bit more rustic than other desserts.

Quick Apple Dumplings

prep: 25 min.   cook: 54 min.

½   cup sugar
½   cup water
½   teaspoon ground cinnamon, divided
½   teaspoon ground nutmeg, divided
1   tablespoon butter or margarine
⅔   cup sugar
1½ (15-ounce) packages refrigerated
    piecrusts
6   medium Granny Smith apples, peeled
    and cored
2   tablespoons cold butter, cut into 6 pieces
Vanilla ice cream (optional)

Bring ½ cup sugar, ½ cup water, ¼ teaspoon cinnamon, and ¼ teaspoon nutmeg to a boil in a small saucepan over medium-high heat, stirring constantly; reduce heat, and simmer, stirring occasionally, 5 minutes. Remove from heat, and stir in 1 tablespoon butter. Set syrup aside.
Combine ⅔ cup sugar, remaining ¼ teaspoon ground cinnamon, and remaining ¼ teaspoon ground nutmeg.
Cut piecrusts in half, and roll each portion into an 8-inch circle. Place 1 apple in center of each circle. Sprinkle each evenly with sugar mixture; dot evenly with butter.
Fold dough over apples, pinching to seal. Place in a lightly greased 13- x 9-inch

baking dish. Drizzle each apple with 1 tablespoon syrup, reserving remaining syrup.

Bake at 375° for 45 to 48 minutes or until golden. Serve with reserved syrup and, if desired, ice cream. Yield: 6 servings.

Per serving: Calories 737 (41% from fat); Fat 33.6g (sat 15.4g, mono 1.5g, poly 0.3g); Protein 4.4g; Carb 106.7g; Fiber 1.8g; Chol 35mg; Iron 0.2mg; Sodium 435mg; Calc 11mg

Plum Galette

prep: 20 min. cook: 40 min. other: 40 min.

1	cup all-purpose flour
3½	tablespoons cold butter, cut into pieces
¼	teaspoon salt
3	tablespoons ice water
1	tablespoon cornmeal
4	medium plums, each cut into 8 wedges
1	tablespoon cornstarch
¼	cup Plum Jam
1	tablespoon Plum Jam
1	tablespoon sugar

Combine flour, butter, and salt in a food processor; process until mixture resembles coarse meal. With processor on, slowly add ice water through food chute, processing just until combined (do not form a ball). Press mixture gently into a 4-inch circle on plastic wrap. Cover and chill 30 minutes.
Line a baking sheet with parchment paper; sprinkle paper with cornmeal. Unwrap dough; roll dough into a 9-inch circle on a lightly floured surface. Place dough on baking sheet.
Combine plums and cornstarch in a large bowl, tossing to coat. Add ¼ cup Plum Jam; toss well to coat. Spread plum mixture on dough, leaving a 1½-inch border. Fold edges of dough over plum mixture.
Bake at 425° for 20 minutes. Remove galette from oven (do not turn oven off). Brush crust with 1 tablespoon Plum Jam; sprinkle galette with sugar.
Bake at 425° for 20 minutes or until crust is golden. Cool in pan on a wire rack 10 minutes before serving. Yield: 6 servings.

Per serving: Calories 210 (30% from fat); Fat 7g (sat 4.2g, mono 1.8g, poly 0.4g); Protein 2.8g; Carb 35g; Fiber 1.6g; Chol 18mg; Iron 1.1mg; Sodium 145mg; Calc 6mg

Plum Jam

prep: 10 min. cook: 1 hr., 5 min.

4½	cups chopped ripe red plums (about 8 medium)
1	cup sugar
1	cup water

Combine plums, sugar, and water in a large saucepan; bring to a boil. Cover, reduce heat, and simmer 10 minutes. Uncover and simmer 50 minutes or until mixture begins to thicken, skimming foam from surface of mixture occasionally. Cool; pour into an airtight container. (Mixture will thicken as it cools.) Cover and chill. Yield: 2 cups.

Per tablespoon: Calories 37 (2% from fat); Fat 0.1g (sat 0g, mono 0.1g, poly 0g); Protein 0.2g; Carb 9.3g; Fiber 0.4g; Chol 0mg; Iron 0mg; Sodium 0mg; Calc 1mg

make ahead • test kitchen favorite
Tropical Pineapple Crisp

prep: 15 min. cook: 30 min.

1	fresh pineapple, peeled, cored, and cubed (about 4 cups)*
2	tablespoons dark rum
⅓	cup all-purpose flour
⅓	cup firmly packed dark brown sugar
⅓	cup cold butter or margarine, cut into pieces
1	cup crumbled white chocolate-and-macadamia nut cookies (we tested with Pepperidge Farm Tahoe White Chocolate Macadamia Cookies)
½	cup sweetened flaked coconut
	Simple Coconut Ice Cream (above right)

Combine pineapple and rum; spoon into an ungreased 8- x 8-inch baking dish.
Combine flour and sugar; cut in butter with a pastry blender or fork until mixture is crumbly. Stir in cookie crumbs and coconut; sprinkle over pineapple.
Bake at 400° for 30 minutes or until golden. Serve with Simple Coconut Ice Cream. Yield: 6 servings.

Per serving: Calories 735 (53% from fat); Fat 43.2g (sat 30.2g, mono 8.4g, poly 1.1g); Protein 8.4g; Carb 82.5g; Fiber 4.8g; Chol 80mg; Iron 2.3mg; Sodium 276mg; Calc 180mg

*Substitute 2 (20-ounce) cans pineapple chunks in juice, drained, if desired.

Simple Coconut Ice Cream

prep: 7 min. other: 8 hrs.

½	gallon vanilla ice cream, softened
1	(15-ounce) can cream of coconut
¾	cup sweetened flaked coconut

Stir together all ingredients in a large bowl until blended. Cover and freeze 8 hours or until firm. Yield: 9 cups.

Per 1 cup: Calories 383 (61% from fat); Fat 25.9g (sat 19.5g, mono 4g, poly 0.7g); Protein 6g; Carb 35.5g; Fiber 2.5g; Chol 52mg; Iron 0.5mg; Sodium 126mg; Calc 152mg

test kitchen favorite
Blueberry Crisp

prep: 5 min. cook: 40 min.

9	cups fresh blueberries
⅓	cup granulated sugar
⅓	cup firmly packed light brown sugar
⅓	cup all-purpose flour
½	teaspoon ground cinnamon
¼	teaspoon ground nutmeg
	Streusel Topping

Stir together first 6 ingredients in a large bowl; toss until berries are coated.
Spoon berry mixture into a lightly greased 13- x 9-inch baking dish. Spoon Streusel Topping over berry mixture.
Bake at 375° for 40 minutes or until golden. Yield: 12 servings.

Per serving: Calories 350 (23% from fat); Fat 8.9g (sat 5g, mono 2.2g, poly 0.7g); Protein 4.2g; Carb 67g; Fiber 4.1g; Chol 20mg; Iron 2.2mg; Sodium 65mg; Calc 39mg

Streusel Topping

prep: 5 min.

1½	cups all-purpose flour
1½	cups uncooked regular oats
1	cup firmly packed light brown sugar
½	cup butter, melted

Combine flour, oats, and brown sugar; stir in butter with a fork until mixture is crumbly. Yield: 4 cups.

Per tablespoon: Calories 19 (47% from fat); Fat 1g (sat 0.5g, mono 0.3g, poly 0.1g); Protein 0.2g; Carb 2.5g; Fiber 0.1g; Chol 2mg; Iron 0.1mg; Sodium 8mg; Calc 2mg

family favorite

Apple-Vinegar Biscuit Cobbler

prep: 25 min.   cook: 55 min.   other: 10 min.

Vanilla ice cream contrasts nicely with the cider vinegar tang in this sweet-tart dessert. As a bonus, you'll have three or four extra biscuits to serve anytime.

8	medium Granny Smith apples, peeled and sliced
2	cups sugar
1	(3-ounce) package cream cheese
⅓	cup cold butter or margarine, cut into pieces
2½	cups self-rising flour
1	cup milk
¼	cup butter or margarine
⅓	cup cider vinegar or apple cider
1	teaspoon grated lemon rind
1	teaspoon ground cinnamon
1	teaspoon ground allspice
¼	teaspoon ground cloves
Vanilla ice cream (optional)	

Combine apple and sugar, tossing gently; set aside. Cut cream cheese and ⅓ cup butter into flour with a pastry blender until crumbly; stir in milk.

Turn dough out onto a lightly floured surface; knead 3 or 4 times. Roll dough to ½-inch thickness. Cut with a 2½-inch round cutter; set aside.

Melt ¼ cup butter in a large skillet over medium-high heat; add apple mixture. Cook, stirring often, 20 minutes or until apple is tender and syrup thickens slightly. Stir in vinegar and next 4 ingredients. Pour mixture into a lightly greased 11- x 7-inch baking dish; place dish on an aluminum foil-lined baking sheet. Arrange 12 biscuits over hot apple mixture. Place remaining biscuits on a baking sheet.

Bake cobbler at 425° for 20 minutes or until biscuits are golden. Bake remaining biscuits at 425° for 12 to 15 minutes.

Let cobbler stand 10 minutes before serving. Press biscuits down into juices before serving; serve cobbler with ice cream, if desired. Yield: 6 servings.

Per serving: Calories 678 (27% from fat); Fat 20.6g (sat 12.6g, mono 5.3g, poly 1g); Protein 6.5g; Carb 121.5g; Fiber 3.8g; Chol 55mg; Iron 2.4mg; Sodium 648mg; Calc 198mg

Sweet Potato Cobbler

prep: 25 min.   cook: 55 min.

Enjoy sweet potatoes in this rustic biscuit-topped cobbler. For an added Southern tradition, drizzle some heavy cream over each serving, or top with a scoop of vanilla ice cream.

½	cup butter or margarine
2	tablespoons whipping cream
1	cup granulated sugar
¼	cup firmly packed light brown sugar
1	teaspoon ground cinnamon
¼	teaspoon ground nutmeg
¼	teaspoon salt
3	large sweet potatoes, peeled and cubed (about 2 pounds)
⅓	cup butter or margarine
1⅔	cups self-rising flour
½	cup buttermilk
Streusel Topping	

Melt ½ cup butter in a 10½-inch cast-iron skillet over medium heat. Whisk in whipping cream and next 5 ingredients. Remove from heat.

Add sweet potatoes, and spread evenly in skillet. Cover with aluminum foil, and place on a baking sheet. Bake at 350° for 25 to 30 minutes or until sweet potatoes are tender. Uncover.

Cut ⅓ cup butter into flour with a pastry blender until crumbly; add buttermilk, stirring just until dry ingredients are moistened. Turn dough out onto a lightly floured surface; gently knead 3 or 4 times. Pat or roll dough into a 10½-inch circle; place over cobbler. Sprinkle with Streusel Topping.

Bake, uncovered, at 350° for 25 minutes or until golden. Yield: 8 servings.

Per serving: Calories 624 (44% from fat); Fat 30.6g (sat 17.1g, mono 9g, poly 2.3g); Protein 6.1g; Carb 83.9g; Fiber 4g; Chol 72mg; Iron 2.8mg; Sodium 626mg; Calc 160mg

Streusel Topping

prep: 5 min.

⅓	cup uncooked regular oats
⅓	cup all-purpose flour
⅓	cup firmly packed light brown sugar
¼	cup cold butter or margarine, cut into pieces
⅓	cup chopped pecans

Combine oats, flour, and sugar; cut in butter with a pastry blender or fork until crumbly. Stir in chopped pecans. Yield: 1⅔ cups.

Per tablespoon: Calories 129 (57% from fat); Fat 8.2g (sat 3.4g, mono 3.1g, poly 1.2g); Protein 1.4g; Carb 13.5g; Fiber 0.8g; Chol 13mg; Iron .6mg; Sodium 38mg; Calc 13mg

family favorite

Double-Crust Peach Cobbler

prep: 12 min.   cook: 42 min.

A double crust and perfectly sweetened and spiced peach filling make this an ultimate Southern dessert.

8	cups sliced fresh peaches (about 5 pounds)
2	cups sugar
3	tablespoons all-purpose flour
½	teaspoon ground nutmeg
1	teaspoon almond or vanilla extract
⅓	cup butter or margarine
Pastry for double-crust 9-inch pie (page 348)	

Stir together first 4 ingredients in a Dutch oven; set aside until syrup forms. Bring peach mixture to a boil; reduce heat to low, and cook 10 minutes or until tender. Remove from heat; add almond extract and butter, stirring until butter melts.

Roll half of pastry to ⅛-inch thickness on a lightly floured surface; cut into a 9-inch square. Spoon half of peaches into a lightly buttered 9-inch square pan; top with pastry square. Bake at 475° for 12 minutes or until lightly browned. Spoon remaining peaches over baked pastry square.

Roll remaining pastry to ⅛-inch thickness, and cut into 1-inch strips; arrange in a lattice design over peaches. Bake 15 to 18 more minutes or until browned. Yield: 8 servings.

Per serving: Calories 629 (39% from fat); Fat 27.4g (sat 9.6g, mono 8.4g, poly 5.3g); Protein 5.2g; Carb 92.4g; Fiber 3.5g; Chol 20mg; Iron 2mg; Sodium 345mg; Calc 18mg

Blackberry Cobbler

Blackberry Cobbler

prep: 10 min.   cook: 45 min.

1⅓ cups sugar
½   cup all-purpose flour
½   cup butter or margarine, melted
2   teaspoons vanilla extract
2   (14-ounce) bags frozen blackberries,
     unthawed*
½   (15-ounce) package refrigerated piecrusts
1   tablespoon sugar
Vanilla ice cream (optional)

Stir together first 4 ingredients in a large bowl. Gently stir in blackberries until sugar mixture is crumbly. Spoon fruit mixture into a lightly greased 11- x 7-inch baking dish. **Cut** piecrust into 1-inch-wide strips, and arrange strips in a lattice design over blackberry mixture. Sprinkle top with 1 tablespoon sugar.

Bake at 425° for 45 minutes or until crust is golden and center is bubbly. Serve with ice cream, if desired. Yield: 8 servings.

Per serving: Calories 448 (38% from fat); Fat 18.8g (sat 9.7g, mono 3g, poly 0.7g); Protein 2.6g; Carb 69.3g; Fiber 5.2g; Chol 33mg; Iron 1.2mg; Sodium 190mg; Calc 34mg

*Substitute 5 (6-ounce) packages fresh blackberries, if desired.

cream puff pastries

Cream puff paste, also called pâte à choux or choux pastry, is simply a dough of butter, flour, and eggs stirred vigorously on the cooktop and baked into delicate pastries. The high proportion of eggs in the rich dough causes the pastries to "puff" to great heights. The center dough is then removed, creating a tiny pastry bowl to hold a luscious filling.

Cream puffs and éclairs start from this same pastry, but they're different in shape. Both pastries are prettiest when piped from a pastry bag fitted with a large fluted tip, but you can also just spoon the dough onto a baking sheet if you'd rather. The piped pastry will be more shapely and the other more smooth.

When piping or spooning the dough onto the baking sheet, work quickly and take care to make all the puffs the same size so they'll bake evenly. Space the puffs several inches apart on the baking sheet so they'll have room to expand during baking.

After making the dough, spoon it out, and bake immediately. The longer you wait to bake cream puffs, the less they'll rise in the oven.

You can bake cream puffs a day ahead and store them in airtight containers. Just don't fill them more than a few hours before serving or they'll become soggy.

quick • low calorie (without filling)
Cream Puff Paste

prep: 10 min. cook: 40 min.

Also called pâte à choux, this pastry is the basis for many fabulous desserts, such as éclairs. Fill these puffs with your favorite pudding.

1   cup water
½   cup butter or margarine
1   cup all-purpose flour
⅛   teaspoon salt
4   large eggs

Combine water and butter in a medium saucepan; bring to a boil. Add flour and salt, all at once (photo 1), stirring vigorously over medium-high heat until mixture leaves sides of pan and forms a smooth ball (photo 2). Remove from heat; cool 4 to 5 minutes. **Add** eggs, 1 at a time, beating thoroughly with a wooden spoon after each addition (photo 3); beat until dough is smooth. **Drop** Cream Puff Paste into 10 equal mounds 3 inches apart on an ungreased baking sheet. Bake at 400° for 30 to 35 minutes or until golden and puffed. Cool away from drafts. Cut off top of each cream puff; pull out soft dough inside, and discard. Yield: 10 (2-inch) cream puffs.

Per cream puff: Calories 124 (65% from fat); Fat 9g (sat 5.1g, mono 2.5g, poly 0.5g); Protein 3.1g; Carb 7.8g; Fiber 0.3g; Chol 87mg; Iron 0.8mg; Sodium 97mg; Calc 12mg

making cream puff paste

1. When making cream puff paste, add flour and salt to butter mixture all at once, stirring vigorously.

2. Continue to stir vigorously until mixture leaves sides of pan and forms a smooth ball.

3. Add eggs, 1 at a time, beating with a wooden spoon until dough is smooth after each addition.

entertaining • freeze it • make ahead
weekend chef
Vanilla Custard–Filled Éclairs

prep: 28 min. cook: 29 min. other: 2 hrs.

Each puff is filled with creamy vanilla custard and topped with a velvety glazing of chocolate ganache. Using piecrust mix simplifies a classic pastry. Prepare the custard a day ahead and chill it overnight.

1⅓ cups water
1   (11-ounce) package piecrust mix (we tested with Betty Crocker)
3   large eggs
2   egg whites
Vanilla Custard
Chocolate Glaze

Bring 1⅓ cups water to a boil in a 3-quart saucepan over medium-high heat.
Stir in piecrust mix, beating vigorously with a wooden spoon 1 minute or until mixture leaves sides of pan.
Place dough in bowl of a heavy-duty stand mixer; cool 5 minutes. Beat dough at medium speed with electric mixer using paddle attachment.
Add eggs and egg whites, 1 at a time, beating until blended after each addition. (If desired, eggs and egg whites can be added 1 at a time and beaten vigorously with a wooden spoon.)
Spoon dough into a large zip-top freezer bag. (A large pastry bag can also be used.) Cut a 1½-inch opening across 1 bottom corner of the bag. Pipe 3-inch-long strips of dough 2 inches apart onto ungreased baking sheets.
Bake at 425° for 20 to 25 minutes or until puffed and golden. (Do not underbake.) Remove from oven, and cut a small slit in side of each éclair to allow steam to escape. Cool on wire racks.
Split éclairs lengthwise using a serrated

knife, starting at 1 long side, cutting to, but not through, opposite side. Pull out soft dough inside, and discard.

Carefully spoon about 3 tablespoons Vanilla Custard into each éclair; close top of each éclair over custard.

Spoon Chocolate Glaze evenly over each éclair. Chill éclairs 2 hours, or freeze up to 1 month. (Thaw éclairs in the refrigerator overnight or at room temperature 30 minutes.) Store leftovers in refrigerator. Yield: 20 éclairs.

Per éclair: Calories 237 (48% from fat); Fat 12.7g (sat 5.6g, mono 5.2g, poly 1.1g); Protein 4.5g; Carb 27.5g; Fiber 0.8g; Chol 75mg; Iron 0.9mg; Sodium 222mg; Calc 64mg

Vanilla Custard

prep: 5 min.   cook: 28 min.   other: 8 hrs.

1   cup sugar
3   tablespoons all-purpose flour
3   tablespoons cornstarch
½   teaspoon salt
3   cups milk
3   egg yolks
1   tablespoon butter
1   teaspoon vanilla extract

Combine first 4 ingredients in top of a double boiler; gradually stir in milk.

Cook over medium heat over simmering water, stirring constantly, until thickened and bubbly. Beat egg yolks until thick and pale. Gradually stir about one-fourth of hot mixture into yolks; add to remaining hot mixture, stirring constantly.

Cook over medium heat, stirring constantly, 2 minutes or until mixture is thickened. Stir in butter and vanilla.

Remove from heat, and cool completely. Cover with plastic wrap, placing directly on custard, and chill 8 hours. Yield: 3½ cups.

Per tablespoon: Calories 30 (27% from fat); Fat 0.9g (sat 0.5g, mono 0.3g, poly 0.1g); Protein 0.6g; Carb 4.9g; Fiber 0g; Chol 13mg; Iron 0.1mg; Sodium 28mg; Calc 16mg

Chocolate Glaze

prep: 5 min.

1   cup semisweet chocolate morsels
¼   cup whipping cream
2   tablespoons butter, softened

Microwave morsels and whipping cream at HIGH 30 seconds to 1 minute or until melted, stirring twice. Whisk in butter until blended, and spoon immediately over éclairs. Yield: 1 cup.

Per tablespoon: Calories 75 (70% from fat); Fat 5.8g (sat 3.5g, mono 1.8g, poly 0.2g); Protein 0.5g; Carb 6.9g; Fiber 0.6g; Chol 9mg; Iron 0.3mg; Sodium 13mg; Calc 6mg

entertaining • low calorie • make ahead

Cheesecake Cream Puffs

prep: 15 min.   cook: 20 min.

Here's an over-the-top, bite-size dessert for serving company or gift giving.

Cheesecake Pastry Cream
1⅓ cups water
1   (11-ounce) package piecrust mix (we tested with Betty Crocker)
4   large eggs
Chocolate Ganache

Prepare Cheesecake Pastry Cream. Cover and chill.

Bring 1⅓ cups water to a boil in a medium saucepan. Add piecrust mix, stirring vigorously over medium-high heat until mixture leaves sides of pan and forms a smooth ball. Remove from heat, and cool 5 minutes.

Add eggs, 1 at a time, beating thoroughly with a wooden spoon after each addition; beat until dough is smooth. Drop dough by heaping teaspoonfuls onto ungreased baking sheets.

Bake at 425° for 20 minutes or until golden and puffed; cool completely on a wire rack.

Pipe Cheesecake Pastry Cream into cream puffs through side of each cream puff, using a pastry bag fitted with a round pastry tip. Dip half of each cream puff in warm Chocolate Ganache. Store cream puffs in refrigerator. Yield: 30 cream puffs.

Per cream puff: Calories 169 (60% from fat); Fat 11.3g (sat 5.5g, mono 4.4g, poly 0.8g); Protein 2.9g; Carb 15.5g; Fiber 0.9g; Chol 54mg; Iron 0.8mg; Sodium 110mg; Calc 29mg

Cheesecake Pastry Cream

prep: 8 min.   cook: 10 min.   other: 4 hrs.

1   large egg
1   egg yolk
¼   cup sugar
3   tablespoons cornstarch
1   cup half-and-half
½   (8-ounce) package cream cheese, softened
1   tablespoon butter, softened
1   teaspoon vanilla extract
1   teaspoon grated orange rind

Whisk first 4 ingredients in a heavy saucepan. Gradually add half-and-half. Bring to a boil over medium heat, whisking constantly. Cook 1 to 2 minutes or until thickened and bubbly. Remove from heat; whisk in cream cheese and remaining ingredients until smooth. Transfer to a small bowl; cover and chill at least 4 hours. (Cheesecake Pastry Cream will be thick.) Yield: 2 cups.

Per tablespoon: Calories 39 (65% from fat); Fat 2.8g (sat 1.6g, mono 0.8g, poly 0.1g); Protein 0.8g; Carb 2.7g; Fiber 0g; Chol 21mg; Iron 0.1mg; Sodium 19mg; Calc 12mg

Chocolate Ganache

prep: 5 min.   cook: 2 min.

6   tablespoons whipping cream
1   (12-ounce) package semisweet chocolate morsels

Microwave whipping cream in a small glass bowl at HIGH 1 minute. Add morsels, and microwave 1 more minute; stir until smooth. Yield: 2 cups.

Per tablespoon: Calories 60 (63% from fat); Fat 4.2g (sat 2.5g, mono 1.3g, poly 0.1g); Protein 0.5g; Carb 6.7g; Fiber 0.6g; Chol 3.8mg; Iron 0.3mg; Sodium 2.2mg; Calc 5mg

phyllo

Phyllo is tissue-thin sheets of pastry dough that's used to make sweet and savory pastries.

Frozen phyllo is readily available in supermarkets in the frozen foods aisle. It keeps up to a year.

Thaw phyllo in its package as the label directs, typically overnight. If used before completely thawed, the thin sheets may tear. Once opened, use phyllo within three days. Work with only one sheet at a time; keep the remaining sheets covered with a damp towel. If phyllo is left uncovered, it becomes brittle. Brush each sheet generously with melted butter; this makes the layers crisp when baked.

family favorite • low calorie • make ahead

Baklava

prep: 45 min.   cook: 50 min.   other: 24 hrs.

- 1   (16-ounce) package frozen phyllo pastry, thawed
- 1   cup butter, melted
- 3   cups finely chopped or ground pecans, walnuts, pistachios, or almonds
- ¼   cup sugar
- 1½   teaspoons ground cinnamon
- ½   teaspoon ground nutmeg
- Syrup

Assembling Baklava: Layer 10 sheets of phyllo in pan, brushing each sheet with butter. Top with nuts; repeat layers.

Butter a 13- x 9-inch pan. Set aside.

Cut phyllo in half crosswise, and cut each half to fit prepared pan; discard trimmings. Cover phyllo with a slightly damp towel.

Layer 10 sheets of phyllo in pan, brushing each sheet with melted butter. Set aside.

Combine nuts and next 3 ingredients; stir well. Sprinkle one-third of mixture over phyllo in pan; drizzle with melted butter.

Top nut mixture with 11 sheets of phyllo, brushing each sheet with butter. Repeat twice with remaining nut mixture, phyllo, and butter, ending with buttered phyllo.

Cut stack into diamond shapes, using a sharp knife. Bake at 350° for 45 minutes or until golden. Cool completely. Drizzle Syrup over Baklava. Cover and let stand at room temperature 24 hours. Yield: 3 dozen.

Per piece: Calories 185 (63% from fat); Fat 13g (sat 4g, mono 5.8g, poly 2.5g); Protein 1.9g; Carb 17g; Fiber 1.3g; Chol 13mg; Iron 0.7mg; Sodium 97mg; Calc 11mg

Syrup

prep: 5 min.   cook: 5 min.

- 1   cup sugar
- ½   cup water
- ¼   cup honey

Combine all ingredients in a saucepan, and bring to a boil. Reduce heat, and simmer, uncovered, 4 minutes. Yield: 1¼ cups.

Per tablespoon: Calories 52 (0% from fat); Fat 0g (sat 0g, mono 0g, poly 0g); Protein 0g; Carb 13.5g; Fiber 0g; Chol 0mg; Iron 0mg; Sodium 0.2mg; Calc 0.4mg

entertaining • low calorie

Creamy Lemon Tartlets

prep: 12 min.   cook: 5 min.   other: 1 hr.

- 2   (2.1-ounce) packages frozen mini phyllo pastry shells
- 1   cup whipping cream
- ⅔   cup lemon curd
- ½   teaspoon almond extract

Bake pastry shells according to package directions; cool completely.

Beat cream, lemon curd, and almond extract at medium speed with an electric mixer just until thickened and cream mounds slightly. Spoon mixture into pastry

shells. Chill tartlets 1 hour. Yield: 30 tartlets.

Per tartlet: Calories 70 (51% from fat); Fat 4g (sat 1.8g, mono 0.8g, poly 0.1g); Protein 0.5g; Carb 7.9g; Fiber 0.7g; Chol 16mg; Iron 0.2mg; Sodium 15mg; Calc 6mg

Dried Fruit Strudels

prep: 45 min.   cook: 33 min.

- ¾   cup pitted prunes, coarsely chopped
- ¾   cup dried apricots, coarsely chopped
- ½   cup sugar, divided
- ½   cup orange juice
- ¼   cup apricot brandy or orange juice
- 2   teaspoons ground cinnamon
- 1   teaspoon vanilla extract
- 1   (6-ounce) package sweetened dried cranberries
- ½   cup pistachios, coarsely chopped
- ½   cup toasted walnuts, coarsely chopped
- 1   cup apricot preserves
- 12   frozen phyllo pastry sheets, thawed
- ½   cup butter, melted

Stir together prunes, apricots, ¼ cup sugar, and next 3 ingredients in a saucepan; bring to a boil over medium-high heat. Reduce heat to low; cook 3 minutes.

Process fruit mixture and vanilla in a food processor until smooth, stopping to scrape down sides. Stir in dried cranberries and next 3 ingredients; set aside.

Unfold phyllo, and cover with a damp towel to prevent pastry from drying out.

Stack 6 phyllo sheets on a flat surface covered with wax paper, brushing each sheet with melted butter.

Spoon half of fruit mixture down short edge of 1 end of phyllo stack, leaving a 1-inch border around edge. Repeat procedure with remaining phyllo and fruit mixture. Fold in long edges 1 inch.

Roll up, starting at short edge nearest filling. Place each, seam side down, in a lightly greased jelly-roll pan. Cut ¼-inch-deep diagonal slits, 1 inch apart, across top. Brush strudels with melted butter; sprinkle with remaining ¼ cup sugar.

Bake at 375° for 30 minutes. Cool on a wire rack. Yield: 12 servings.

Per serving: Calories 392 (33% from fat); Fat 14.4g (sat 5.6g, mono 4.6g, poly 3.3g); Protein 4.6g; Carb 64.2g; Fiber 3.2g; Chol 20mg; Iron 1.8mg; Sodium 148mg; Calc 26mg

puff pastry

Rich, delicate puff pastry is made with a sheet of butter incorporated into layers of pastry dough in a roll, fold, and chill method. The process involves a formula of rolling the butter-filled dough, folding it into thirds, turning and rolling out, and chilling it. This process gives the dough its characteristic lightness and crispness when baked. The method creates the hundreds of layers of dough and butter. In turn, when the dough is baked, the moisture in the butter creates steam causing the dough to rise or "puff" into hundreds of flaky layers.

Puff pastry is used for croissants, tarts, and napoleons. Fortunately for today's busy cooks puff pastry is available frozen.

Apricot-Cheese Rum Tarts

prep: 20 min.   cook: 15 min.

1   (8-ounce) package cream cheese, softened
1¼   cups sifted powdered sugar, divided
1   teaspoon rum flavoring
1   (17.3-ounce) package frozen puff pastry sheets, thawed
½   cup apricot preserves
1   egg yolk, beaten
1   tablespoon milk
Vegetable cooking spray

Beat cream cheese at medium speed with an electric mixer until creamy. Add 1 cup sugar and rum flavoring; beat until smooth.
Cut each sheet of puff pastry into 4 squares. Spoon cream cheese mixture evenly into center of each square of pastry; top each with 1 tablespoon apricot preserves.
Combine egg yolk and milk in a small bowl; stir well. Brush edges of pastry squares lightly with egg mixture. Fold each square of pastry into a triangle; press edges together with a fork to seal. Place tarts on a baking sheet lightly coated with cooking spray. Brush tarts with remaining egg mixture.
Bake at 400° for 10 to 15 minutes or until puffed and golden. Remove tarts to wire racks to cool; sprinkle with remaining ¼ cup powdered sugar. Yield: 8 tarts.

Per tart: Calories 575 (54% from fat); Fat 33.9g (sat 12.4g, mono 16.3g, poly 3.5g); Protein 7g; Carb 61.1g; Fiber 0.9g; Chol 57mg; Iron 2mg; Sodium 248mg; Calc 34mg

Pistachio Pastry Twists

prep: 28 min.   cook: 19 min. per batch

2   egg yolks
1   tablespoon water
⅓   cup sugar
½   teaspoon ground cinnamon
½   teaspoon ground cardamom
1   (17.3-ounce) package frozen puff pastry sheets, thawed
½   cup finely chopped roasted pistachios
2   tablespoons butter or margarine, melted

Whisk together egg yolks and water in a small bowl.
Combine sugar, cinnamon, and cardamom.
Carefully roll each sheet of puff pastry into a 9½-inch square on a lightly floured work surface. Brush each sheet with egg wash, and sprinkle with 2 tablespoons sugar mixture. Sprinkle chopped pistachios evenly over 1 sheet, leaving a ¼-inch border; top with remaining sheet, sugar side down. Firmly press edges to seal. Brush pastry with melted butter; sprinkle with remaining sugar mixture. Cut pastry into ¾-inch-thick strips, using a pizza cutter. Twist each strip 3 times, and place 2 inches apart on lightly greased baking sheets.
Bake at 400° for 19 minutes or until golden. Remove from pans immediately, and cool on wire racks. Yield: 10 twists.

Per twist: Calories 364 (61% from fat); Fat 24.8g (sat 6.8g, mono 13.1g, poly 3.5g); Protein 5.5g; Carb 30.8g; Fiber 1.5g; Chol 47mg; Iron 1.7mg; Sodium 141mg; Calc 19mg

---

entertaining • freeze it • low cholesterol
make ahead • weekend chef

Palmiers

prep: 8 min.   cook: 23 min. per batch
other: 1 hr.

Thaw dough at room temperature for about 1 hour or overnight in the refrigerator. Store palmiers in an airtight container at room temperature up to three days; freeze to store longer.

1   cup plus 2 tablespoons sugar, divided
1   (17.3-ounce) package frozen puff pastry sheets, thawed

Palmiers

Sprinkle work surface with ¼ cup sugar. Lay 1 sheet of puff pastry flat on surface, and sprinkle evenly with ¼ cup sugar. Beginning at 1 side, tightly roll up dough to the center of square. Repeat to roll up the other side so the 2 rolls are touching and rolled tightly to meet in middle; wrap tightly in plastic wrap or wax paper, and freeze 1 hour. Repeat rolling and freezing procedure with remaining sugar and puff pastry.
With a sharp knife, cut rolls crosswise into ½-inch-thick slices. Lay pastries flat, 1 inch apart, on parchment-lined baking sheets. Sprinkle pastries evenly with remaining 2 tablespoons sugar.
Bake at 400° for 21 to 23 minutes or until golden. Transfer to wire racks to cool completely. Yield: 2½ dozen.

Per palmier: Calories 120 (47% from fat); Fat 6.3g (sat 0.9g, mono 1.4g, poly 3.6g); Protein 1.2g; Carb 15g; Fiber 0.3g; Chol 0mg; Iron 0.4mg; Sodium 41mg; Calc 2mg

poultry

Today's poultry is rich in nutrients, low in fat, reasonably priced, and abundant.

Equipment

A good sharp boning knife, poultry shears, and a large cutting board will serve you well if you plan to cut up whole chickens. A roasting pan and meat thermometer are essential when roasting a bird. Vertical roasting racks are popular as a naturally low-fat cooking rack.

Poultry Primer

Chicken is prized for its tender white meat and moist dark meat. White meat of poultry has less fat than dark meat; dark meat has less fat than many cuts of red meat. Small whole chickens such as broiler-fryers are leaner than roasters, and roasters are leaner than hens and capons. Most of the fat in poultry comes from the skin and pockets of fat under the skin. You can remove the skin and cut away excess fat before or after cooking. With fat, however, comes flavor. Some fat will naturally be rendered during cooking if you leave the skin intact.

The neck and giblets (liver, heart, and gizzard) are usually packaged separately and placed in the bird's body and neck cavities. They're also sold individually. When cooking a whole bird, remove the packages from cavities before cooking.

Determine the type of poultry you buy by how you want to cook it. If your recipe calls for cut-up chicken or assorted pieces, you can cut up a broiler-fryer yourself, buy it precut, or take advantage of packaged chicken "parts," buying all legs or thighs if dark meat is your preference, or all breasts if white meat is your choice.

Domesticated birds commonly found at the meat counter of most supermarkets are as follows:

Cornish hens are one of the smallest members of the poultry family, weighing from 1 to 2 pounds. They're often split when cooked on the grill. One bird typically serves one, but larger or stuffed hens can be split to serve two.

Petit Poussin is French for a very young, small chicken weighing no more than 1½ pounds. It's best grilled or broiled.

The **broiler-fryer** is the all-purpose whole bird, ranging from 2 to 4 pounds. This young, tender economical bird can be baked, grilled, fried, and roasted. A 3-pound broiler-fryer yields four to six servings or about 3 cups chopped cooked chicken.

Roasters are slightly larger and a little older than broiler-fryers; they weigh from 4 to 6 pounds. They are higher in fat than fryers, too, which makes them ideal for ovenroasting and rotisserie cooking. The cooked chicken is tasty in salads, soups, and casseroles.

Hens or stewing chickens range from 3 to 8 pounds. They're flavorful mature birds, but less tender. Moist-heat cooking such as stewing or braising suits these tougher birds.

A **capon** is a castrated rooster. It weighs from 4 to 10 pounds and is full-breasted with tender, succulent meat that's particularly suited to roasting.

Free-range or **free-roaming** chickens are not necessarily organic chickens, but they are chickens that have been allowed access to the outside. They're fed a special vegetarian diet, and they have more freedom of movement than chickens that are mass produced. These added amenities can cause free-range birds to cost more. They weigh 4 to 5 pounds typically.

Ducklings have a lower proportion of meat to bone than most poultry. They weigh from 3 to 6 pounds. Plan on 1 pound per serving. Ducklings are available in the frozen meat section.

Geese range from 6 to 15 pounds, and they, too, have a lower proportion of meat to bone. One pound per person is a good average per serving. Look for them in the frozen meat section.

Turkeys can range from 5 to 30 pounds. Count on one serving per pound of turkey. So if you buy a 12-pound turkey, it will serve 12 people. Turkeys are available year-round in the frozen meat section and fresh during the holiday season.

Buying and Storing Poultry

Fresh poultry is highly perishable. When shopping, check the "sell by" date and choose the freshest product available. It should look and smell fresh. Never purchase poultry with an off odor or skin that looks dry. Poultry skin should be smooth and soft. Chicken with yellow skin is no more or less nutritious than chicken with cream-colored skin. Skin color is due to the type of feed the chicken is given.

Pick up poultry items last, and make sure they're bagged separately from other food at the checkout counter. Juices from raw poultry should not touch other foods. As soon as possible, store poultry well-wrapped in plastic wrap in the coldest part of your refrigerator for a day or two. Don't store raw chicken next to food you plan on eating raw such as lettuce. Most cooked chicken or turkey can be refrigerated up to four days after preparation; however, cooked ground chicken and chicken in gravy should be used within two days.

Freezing Poultry

You can freeze properly packaged uncooked poultry parts up to six months and a whole bird up to a year. Freeze giblets and ground chicken up to four months. For best results, remove poultry from its packaging, rinse, and pat dry. Wrap poultry tightly in heavy-duty plastic wrap or freezer paper. Label and date the package before freezing.

Freeze cooked poultry dishes four to six months. First cool the dish in the refrigerator and then wrap securely and freeze. Avoid freezing poultry dishes that contain mayonnaise or hard-cooked egg; these items will suffer a loss of quality in the freezing process. And never refreeze chicken that has been thawed. Use it within a day or two.

Safe Poultry Pointers

Always rinse chicken before cooking, and use a clean knife and cutting board. Wash your hands, knife, and cutting board with hot, soapy water immediately after use to prevent cross-contamination with other foods.

The safest place to thaw poultry is in the refrigerator. To safely thaw frozen poultry more quickly, place the wrapped package in a large bowl of cold water and allow it to stand at room temperature 30 minutes. Change the water and repeat the process until the poultry is thawed. Never leave a package of poultry sitting on the counter to thaw—bacteria thrive at room temperature. Cook thawed chicken or turkey immediately or refrigerate it until cooking time.

Never place cooked chicken or other poultry on the same platter that held the uncooked meat. And don't leave cooked poultry at room temperature more than one hour. Chicken salad is safe to take on a picnic as long as it's packed on ice in a cooler. Never refrigerate a raw or cooked whole bird with stuffing inside the body or neck cavities because of the risk of increased bacterial growth. Instead, store the bird and stuffing separately. Read more on stuffing versus dressing on page 386.

In 2006 the USDA determined a new minimum doneness temperature of 165° for both white and dark meat poultry; however, this minimum internal temperature for food safety may not achieve the desired doneness for personal preferences and best quality. The recipes in this chapter reflect slightly higher temperatures preferred by our Foods staff when testing these recipes. We consider cooked poultry to be at an ideal doneness when the juices run clear.

chicken

A *broiler-fryer* is a young, tender bird, and perhaps the most economical form of chicken you can buy. When buying these whole chickens, always choose a meaty, full breasted bird with plump short legs.

For many chicken recipes you can substitute one cut for another. Just remember that bone-in chicken pieces require longer cooking times than boneless pieces. See our detailed definitions below for help in the supermarket.

A *cut-up chicken* is conveniently cut into eight pieces: two breasts, two thighs, two drumsticks, and two wings. Some producers offer a popular combination package of three breasts, three thighs, and three drumsticks.

A package of *chicken halves* or *splits* contains two halves of a broiler-fryer. These are ideal for outdoor grilling.

Chicken *breast quarters* and *leg quarters* are often packaged separately. A breast quarter is all white meat and includes the wing, breast, and back portion. The leg quarter is all dark meat and includes a drumstick, thigh, and back portion. Each chicken quarter usually yields one serving.

The chicken breast or *split breast* is the leanest cut of chicken. Purchase four chicken breasts with bone and skin or four skinned, boned chicken breasts for four servings. Two chicken breasts will yield about 1 cup chopped cooked chicken.

The *chicken leg* is all dark meat and includes the whole leg with unseparated drumstick and thigh. One chicken leg is considered a serving. It's sometimes called a *chicken leg quarter.*

The *drumstick* is the lower portion of the chicken leg. Two drumsticks make a serving.

The *thigh* is that portion of the leg above the knee joint. It's usually packaged with skin and bone intact. Skinned, boned thighs are also available and can typically be substituted for skinned, boned chicken breasts. You may have to cook thighs a little longer, though. Plan on one or two thighs for each serving.

The *wing* contains three sections and is all white meat. A *drummette* is the meaty first section of the wing and is often used as an hors d'oeuvre.

Ground chicken is typically made from skinned, boned chicken thighs. It's a great alternative to ground beef in meat loaf, soups, or sandwiches. You can also ask your butcher to grind skinned, boned chicken breasts for a leaner white meat grind. One pound of ground chicken yields four servings.

In addition to these choices, you can also purchase *chicken tenders, nuggets, patties* and other semi-prepared (marinated) and frozen chicken products. Canned chicken is another option for busy cooks. Just keep in mind that it tends to be high in sodium.

low carb
Glazed Roasted Chicken

prep: 20 min.   cook: 50 min.   other: 8 hrs.

¼   cup teriyaki sauce
2   tablespoons frozen orange juice
      concentrate, thawed and undiluted
1½ tablespoons dark sesame oil
2   garlic cloves, minced
1   (3-pound) whole chicken
¼   teaspoon freshly ground pepper
Garnish: green onion strips

Stir together first 4 ingredients.
Sprinkle chicken with pepper. Place in a large zip-top freezer bag, and pour half of teriyaki mixture over chicken. Chill remaining teriyaki mixture. Seal bag, and chill 8 hours, turning chicken, if desired.
Remove chicken from marinade, discarding marinade. Place chicken, breast side up, in a lightly greased aluminum foil-lined 13- x 9-inch pan.
Bake at 450° for 40 to 50 minutes or until a meat thermometer inserted into thigh registers 180°, shielding with foil after 30 minutes. Brush with reserved teriyaki mixture during last 5 minutes of baking. Garnish, if desired. Yield: 4 servings.

Per serving: Calories 452 (55% from fat); Fat 27.6g (sat 7.1g, mono 11g, poly 6.7g); Protein 43.3g; Carb 5.2g; Fiber 0.1g; Chol 134mg; Iron 2.5mg; Sodium 647mg; Calc 29mg

The key to an evenly browned bird is turning the pan a few times in the oven.

family favorite

Lemon–Thyme Roasted Chicken

prep: 20 min.   cook: 1 hr., 35 min.
other: 10 min.

We start off at a higher temperature to first brown the skin and lock in juices and flavor. Reducing the heat ensures that the bird cooks evenly. (pictured on cover and page 371)

1	lemon, cut in half
½	medium onion
1	(5-pound) whole roasting chicken
¼	cup butter or margarine, softened
3	garlic cloves, minced
2	teaspoons chopped fresh thyme
1	teaspoon coarse salt
1	teaspoon coarsely ground pepper
1	cup chicken broth
½	cup dry white wine
2	tablespoons all-purpose flour

Garnishes: fresh thyme, roasted garlic
Roasted New Potatoes (page 472)

Place 1 lemon half and onion half into chicken cavity.

Stir together butter, garlic, and 2 teaspoons thyme. Starting at neck cavity, loosen skin from breast and drumsticks by inserting fingers and gently pushing between skin and meat. (Do not totally detach skin.) Rub half of butter mixture evenly under skin.

Tie ends of legs together with string; tuck wing tips under. Rub remaining half of butter mixture over chicken. Squeeze remaining lemon half over chicken. Place chicken, breast side up, on a lightly greased rack in a lightly greased shallow roasting pan. Sprinkle with salt and pepper.

Bake at 450° for 30 minutes.

Reduce heat to 400°, and bake for 55 to 60 minutes or until a meat thermometer inserted into thigh registers 180°, basting occasionally with drippings and turning pan for even browning. Cover loosely with aluminum foil to prevent excessive browning, if necessary. Remove to a serving platter, reserving drippings in pan. Cover chicken with foil; let stand 10 minutes before slicing.

Add broth to reserved drippings in pan, stirring to loosen browned bits from bottom.

Whisk together pan drippings, wine, and flour in a small saucepan. Cook, stirring often, over medium heat 5 minutes or until thickened. Serve with chicken. Garnish, if desired. Yield: 5 servings.

Per serving: Calories 754 (66% from fat); Fat 55g (sat 18.7g, mono 21.2g, poly 10.1g); Protein 56.8g; Carb 4.9g; Fiber 0.3g; Chol 251mg; Iron 3.2mg; Sodium 969mg; Calc 45mg

Note: To roast and serve garlic with chicken, toss 8 unpeeled large garlic cloves with 1 tablespoon olive oil. Scatter garlic around chicken in pan and roast. Remove garlic from pan if it gets browned before chicken is done.

▲ Place lemon half and onion half into chicken cavity.

▲ Rub half of butter mixture under skin.

Lemon-Thyme Roasted Chicken

▲ Rub remaining butter mixture over chicken.

▲ Squeeze remaining lemon half over chicken.

▲ Sprinkle with salt and freshly ground pepper.

Jan's Roasted Chicken

prep: 15 min.   cook: 1 hr., 30 min.

Jan Karon, best-selling author of the Mitford series, shares her favorite roasted chicken recipe with us. We were charmed by her roasted potatoes, too.

1   (3- to 4-pound) whole chicken
3   tablespoons olive oil, divided
3   garlic cloves, halved
1   teaspoon salt
1   tablespoon coarsely ground pepper
3   fresh rosemary sprigs
1   lemon, quartered
Jan's Roasted Potatoes (optional)

Rub chicken and cavities with 2 table-spoons olive oil, garlic cloves, salt, and pepper.
Tuck chicken wings under; tie legs together with string, if desired. Pour remaining 1 tablespoon oil into a large cast-iron skillet; place chicken, breast side up, in skillet.
Place 1 rosemary sprig and 2 lemon quarters into neck cavity of chicken; repeat in lower cavity. Place remaining rosemary sprig underneath skin.
Bake at 450° for 30 minutes; reduce heat to 350°, and bake 1 more hour or until meat thermometer inserted in thigh registers 180°. Serve with Jan's Roasted Potatoes, if desired. Yield: 4 servings.

Per serving: Calories 493 (62% from fat); Fat 33.8g (sat 8g, mono 16.9g, poly 6.2g); Protein 42.6g; Carb 2.9g; Fiber 0.6g; Chol 134mg; Iron 2.8mg; Sodium 712mg; Calc 35mg

Jan's Roasted Potatoes

prep: 5 min.   cook: 1 hr.

8   medium-size new potatoes, halved
3   tablespoons butter or margarine, melted
1   teaspoon salt
1   teaspoon pepper

Place potatoes on a baking sheet. Drizzle with butter; sprinkle with salt and pepper.
Bake potatoes at 350° for 1 hour, turning every 20 minutes. Yield: 4 servings.

Per serving: Calories 322 (25% from fat); Fat 9g (sat 5.5g, mono 2.2g, poly 0.4g); Protein 6.5g; Carb 54.4g; Fiber 5.1g; Chol 23mg; Iron 2.1mg; Sodium 664mg; Calc 30mg

Chicken With White Barbecue Sauce

prep: 30 min.   cook: 2 hrs.
other: 8 hrs., 20 min.

1   cup mayonnaise
½   cup white vinegar
1   tablespoon lemon juice
1   teaspoon salt
1   teaspoon pepper
Hickory wood chips
2   (2½-pound) whole chickens
1   teaspoon salt
1   teaspoon pepper
2   lemons, cut in half

Stir together first 5 ingredients; cover and chill sauce 8 hours.
Soak wood chips in water at least 30 minutes.
Prepare charcoal fire in smoker; let burn 15 to 20 minutes.
Rinse chickens, and pat dry. Sprinkle each chicken with ½ teaspoon salt and ½ teaspoon pepper. Place 2 lemon halves into the cavity of each chicken.
Drain wood chips, and place on hot coals. Place water pan in smoker; add water to depth of fill line. Place chickens on lower food rack; cover with smoker lid.
Cook 1 hour and 30 minutes to 2 hours or until a meat thermometer inserted into thigh registers 180°. Serve prepared White Barbecue Sauce with chicken. Yield: 8 servings.

Per serving: Calories 530 (70% from fat); Fat 41.3g (sat 8.8g, mono 13.3g, poly 16.1g); Protein 35.6g; Carb 2.6g; Fiber 0.2g; Chol 122mg; Iron 2.2mg; Sodium 846mg; Calc 26mg

Cajun Fried Chicken

prep: 40 min.   cook: 36 min.

See box on page 390 for frying safety tips.

3   (3-pound) whole chickens
3   tablespoons Cajun seasoning
1½   gallons peanut oil

Remove giblets and necks, and rinse chickens with cold water. Drain cavities well; pat dry. Rub inside and outside of chickens with seasoning; set aside.
Pour oil into a deep propane turkey fryer;

heat to 350° according to manufacturer's instructions over medium-low flame. Place 1 chicken on fryer rod; carefully lower into hot oil. Fry 12 minutes or until a meat thermometer inserted into thigh registers 180°. (Keep oil temperature at 350°.)
Remove from oil, and drain. Repeat procedure for 2 remaining chickens. Cool slightly before serving. Yield: 12 servings.

Per serving: Calories 562 (70% from fat); Fat 42.8g (sat 11.2g, mono 18.2g, poly 10.1g); Protein 41.8g; Carb 0g; Fiber 0g; Chol 168mg; Iron 2mg; Sodium 607mg; Calc 25mg

Make-ahead Note: Fry chickens; wrap in foil and then newspaper. Refrigerate up to 2 days.

Beer-Can Chicken

prep: 20 min.   cook: 1 hr., 20 min.
other: 8 hrs.

The benefit of a beer-can chicken recipe is that the meat cooks up juicy and tender and is infused with a hint of beer.

3   (2- to 3-pound) whole chickens
4   (12-ounce) cans beer
1   (8-ounce) bottle Italian dressing
¼   to ⅓ cup fajita seasoning

Place each chicken in a large zip-top freezer bag.
Combine 1 can beer, Italian dressing, and fajita seasoning; pour evenly over chickens. Seal bags, and chill 8 hours, turning occasionally.
Remove chicken from marinade, discarding marinade.
Open remaining 3 cans beer. Place each chicken upright onto a beer can, fitting can into cavity. Pull legs forward to form a tripod, allowing chickens to stand upright.
Prepare a hot fire by piling charcoal on 1 side of grill, leaving other side empty. (For gas grills, light only 1 side.) Place food grate on grill. Place chickens upright on unlit side of grill. Grill, covered with grill lid, 1 hour and 20 minutes or until golden and a meat thermometer inserted in thigh registers 180°. Carefully remove beer cans, and cut chickens into quarters. Yield: 12 servings.

Per serving: Calories 303 (58% from fat); Fat 19.4g (sat 5g, mono 7.2g, poly 5.1g); Protein 28.3g; Carb 2.1g; Fiber 0g; Chol 89mg; Iron 1.6mg; Sodium 657mg; Calc 16mg

Chicken Pot Pie

prep: 35 min.   cook: 2 hrs., 5 min.

1   (3½-pound) whole chicken
5   cups water
2   celery ribs with leaves
1¼   teaspoons salt
¼   teaspoon pepper
3   to 4 bacon slices
3   green onions, sliced
2   large celery ribs, chopped
½   cup all-purpose flour
3   hard-cooked eggs, sliced
3   carrots, cooked and diced
1   cup frozen petit peas or 1 (8.5-ounce) can
     sweet green peas, drained
1   teaspoon salt
¼   teaspoon pepper
½   teaspoon chopped fresh or ⅛ teaspoon
     dried thyme
½   (15-ounce) package refrigerated piecrusts

Bring first 5 ingredients to a boil in a large Dutch oven; reduce heat, and simmer 1½ hours or until chicken is done.
Remove chicken, reserving 3½ cups broth in Dutch oven; discard celery tops. Let chicken cool; skin, bone, and cut chicken into bite-size pieces.
Meanwhile, cook bacon in a large skillet until crisp; remove bacon, and drain on paper towels, reserving 3 tablespoons drippings in skillet. Crumble bacon, and set aside.
Sauté green onions and chopped celery in hot drippings in skillet over medium heat 5 minutes or until tender. Gradually whisk in flour until blended. Gradually add reserved broth; cook, whisking constantly, 3 to 5 minutes or until thickened and bubbly. Stir in chicken, bacon, eggs, and next 5 ingredients.
Spoon mixture into a greased 3-quart baking dish, and top with refrigerated piecrust, sealing crust to edge of dish. Cut slits in crust for steam to escape.
Bake at 450° for 25 minutes or until golden and bubbly. Yield: 6 servings.

Per serving: Calories 471 (47% from fat); Fat 24.8g (sat 9g, mono 9.4g, poly 4.6g); Protein 26.1g; Carb 34g; Fiber 3g; Chol 173mg; Iron 2.2mg; Sodium 1187mg; Calc 54mg

Note: Speed things up by substituting 3 cups chopped cooked chicken and 3½ cups canned chicken broth. Omit salt.

Chicken Pudding

prep: 38 min.   cook: 1 hr., 30 min.
other: 10 min.

The soft texture of this dish might remind you of your grandmother's Thanksgiving dressing.

1   (5-pound) whole roasting chicken
4   carrots, cut in half
4   celery ribs, cut in half
1   large onion, quartered
1½   teaspoons salt
1   teaspoon pepper
6   tablespoons butter or margarine
1   tablespoon chicken bouillon granules
1½   teaspoons poultry seasoning
¼   cup shortening
2   cups self-rising flour
¾   cup milk
3   large eggs, lightly beaten
1   cup coarsely crushed saltine crackers
     (about 22 crackers)
1   tablespoon butter or margarine, melted

Combine first 6 ingredients and water to cover (we used 12 cups) in a large Dutch oven. Bring to a boil over medium-high heat; reduce heat, and simmer 1 hour or until tender. Remove chicken, and cool.
Pour 6 cups broth through a wire-mesh strainer into a large bowl, discarding solids. Reserve remaining broth for another use. Whisk 6 tablespoons butter, bouillon granules, and poultry seasoning into strained broth until smooth. Set aside to cool.
While chicken cooks, cut shortening into flour with a pastry blender or fork until crumbly. Add milk, stirring just until dry ingredients are moistened. Spread dough to ½-inch thickness on a lightly greased baking sheet, forming 1 (8-inch) biscuit, pressing with floured hands. Bake at 400° for 23 to 25 minutes or until golden. Cool on a wire rack; break into pieces.
Skin, bone, and coarsely chop chicken. Layer half each of chicken and biscuit pieces in a lightly greased 13- x 9-inch baking dish. Whisk together chicken broth mixture and eggs; pour evenly over chicken and biscuit pieces.
Stir together cracker crumbs and 1 tablespoon melted butter; sprinkle evenly over chicken mixture.

Bake at 375° for 30 minutes or until golden and set. Let stand 10 minutes before serving. Yield: 10 servings.

Per serving: Calories 414 (47% from fat); Fat 21.7g (sat 8.5g, mono 7.6g, poly 3.5g); Protein 27.8g; Carb 25.9g; Fiber 1g; Chol 144mg; Iron 3.1mg; Sodium 806mg; Calc 139mg

Note: Speed things up by substituting 4 cups chopped cooked chicken; 6 cups canned broth; and 6 frozen, baked biscuits. (The texture won't be the same if you use canned biscuits.) Our version baked for 50 minutes.

Chicken-and-Smoked Sausage Pilau

prep: 15 min.   cook: 1 hr., 25 min.
other: 15 min.

This winning one-pot rice dish from South Carolina's Lowcountry is a Test Kitchens favorite for entertaining.

1   (5-pound) whole roasting chicken
3   celery ribs, cut in half
2   carrots, cut in half
2   large sweet onions, chopped
8   cups water
1   bay leaf
1½   tablespoons seasoned salt
1½   tablespoons seasoned pepper
1   pound hot or mild smoked pork sausage
     links, cut into ¼-inch slices
4   cups uncooked long-grain rice

Bring first 8 ingredients to a boil in a large Dutch oven or stockpot over medium-high heat. Reduce heat to low, cover, and simmer 1 hour or until chicken is tender. Remove from heat, and let stand 15 minutes.
Remove and discard celery, carrots, and bay leaf, reserving broth in Dutch oven. Remove chicken, and cool slightly; remove skin and bones, and coarsely chop chicken.
Sauté sausage slices in a large skillet over medium-high heat 5 minutes or until browned; drain.
Add chicken and sausage to reserved broth in Dutch oven, and bring to a boil over medium-high heat; stir in rice, and return to boil. Cover, reduce heat to low, and cook 20 minutes or until broth is absorbed and rice is tender. Yield: 8 servings.

Per serving: Calories 921 (41% from fat); Fat 42.3g (sat 13.1g, mono 18.1g, poly 7.8g); Protein 51.2g; Carb 80.9g; Fiber 1.7g; Chol 169mg; Iron 6.2mg; Sodium 1567mg; Calc 72mg

Our Best Southern Fried Chicken

prep: 25 min.   cook: 30 min.   other: 8 hrs.

This fried chicken is one of our all-time favorites. Our friend, Southern historian John Egerton, created it for his book, Southern Food, *published by University of North Carolina Press (1993).*

3 quarts water
1 tablespoon salt
1 (2½- to 3-pound) whole chicken, cut up
1 teaspoon salt
1 teaspoon pepper
1 cup all-purpose flour
2 cups vegetable oil
¼ cup bacon drippings

Combine water and 1 tablespoon salt; add chicken. Cover and chill 8 hours. Drain chicken; rinse with cold water, and pat dry.
Combine 1 teaspoon salt and pepper; sprinkle half of pepper mixture over chicken. Combine remaining pepper mixture and flour in a large zip-top freezer bag. Place 2 pieces of chicken in bag; seal. Shake to coat evenly. Remove chicken, and repeat procedure with remaining chicken, 2 pieces at a time.
Combine oil and bacon drippings in a 12-inch cast-iron skillet or chicken fryer; heat to 360°. Add chicken, a few pieces at a time, skin side down. Cover and cook 6 minutes; uncover and cook 9 minutes. Turn chicken pieces; cover and cook 6 minutes. Uncover and cook 5 to 9 minutes, turning pieces during the last 3 minutes for even browning, if necessary. Drain on paper towels. Yield: 4 servings.

Per serving: Calories 607 (62% from fat); Fat 42g (sat 10.8g, mono 17.6g, poly 10.6g); Protein 37.3g; Carb 18.2g; Fiber 0.8g; Chol 144mg; Iron 2.9mg; Sodium 937mg; Calc 27mg

Island Chicken and Rice

prep: 15 min.   cook: 1 hr., 5 min.

4½ pounds chicken pieces
1½ teaspoons salt, divided
¾ teaspoon black pepper, divided
1 tablespoon vegetable oil
1 tablespoon butter or margarine
1 small onion, chopped
1 cup uncooked long-grain rice
2 garlic cloves, pressed
1 (14-ounce) can chicken broth
1 (13.5-ounce) can coconut milk
¾ cup unsweetened pineapple juice
¼ teaspoon dried crushed red pepper
4 green onions, chopped
1 (3.5-ounce) jar macadamia nuts, toasted and chopped
Garnishes: fresh pineapple, green onions

Sprinkle chicken pieces evenly with 1 teaspoon salt and ½ teaspoon pepper.
Brown chicken in hot oil in a large skillet over medium-high heat 8 to 10 minutes on each side. Remove chicken from skillet, and drain, reserving 1 tablespoon drippings in skillet.
Add butter to skillet, and melt, stirring to loosen particles from bottom of skillet; add 1 chopped onion, and sauté 4 minutes. Add rice, and sauté 4 minutes; add garlic, and sauté 1 minute. Stir in chicken broth and next 3 ingredients; return chicken to skillet. Sprinkle with remaining ½ teaspoon salt and ¼ teaspoon pepper; bring to a boil. Cover, reduce heat to low, and simmer 35 minutes or until rice is tender.
Uncover, fluff rice with a fork, and let stand 5 minutes before serving. Sprinkle with chopped green onions and nuts. Garnish, if desired. Yield: 6 servings.

Per serving: Calories 842 (55% from fat); Fat 51.8g (sat 21.3g, mono 19.8g, poly 6.7g); Protein 58.8g; Carb 35.6g; Fiber 3g; Chol 174mg; Iron 6.5mg; Sodium 1246mg; Calc 74mg

cutting up a chicken

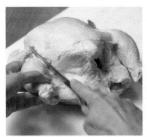

1. With a boning knife or chef's knife, cut through the skin around the leg where it attaches to the breast.

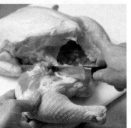

2. Pop the leg out of its socket. Cut through the flesh and skin to detach the leg from body. Repeat with the other leg.

3. Separate drumstick and thigh by cutting through meat at knee joint; break joint, and cut two pieces apart.

4. Bend the wing out from the breast, and cut to remove wing. Repeat with other wing.

5. Using kitchen or poultry shears, cut through ribcage along backbone.

6. Split breast by cutting along breastbone.

Cutting up a chicken gives you these 8 pieces—2 breasts, 2 thighs, 2 drumsticks, and 2 wings.

family favorite
Chicken and Dumplings

prep: 30 min.   cook: 1 hr., 30 min.

This ultimate Southern staple charms as much today as in yesteryear.

1   (3-pound) whole chicken, cut up, if desired
2½   quarts water
2   celery ribs with leaves
2½   tablespoons chicken bouillon granules
1   teaspoon pepper
2   cups all-purpose flour
2   teaspoons baking powder
½   teaspoon salt
¼   cup shortening
⅔   to ¾ cup milk
4   hard-cooked eggs, chopped
Chopped fresh parsley

Bring first 3 ingredients to a boil in a large Dutch oven; partially cover, reduce heat, and simmer 1 hour or until chicken is tender. Remove chicken; cool.
Pour broth through a wire-mesh strainer into a large bowl, discarding solids. Skim off fat. Return 8½ cups broth to Dutch oven; stir in bouillon granules and pepper. Reserve any remaining broth for other uses.
Skin, bone, and chop or shred chicken; cover and keep warm.

Combine flour, baking powder, and salt in a bowl. Cut shortening into flour mixture with a pastry blender until crumbly. Add milk, stirring until dry ingredients are moistened.
Turn dough out onto a lightly floured surface; gather dough into a ball. Press dough with heels of hands, pushing it away from you. Fold top half of dough down and push away from you with heels of hands. Turn dough one-quarter turn, fold top down and push dough away. Continue folding, pushing, and turning 10 to 12 times or until dough is smooth.
Roll dough to ⅛-inch thickness; cut into 1½- x 2-inch strips.
Bring broth mixture to a simmer (do not boil). Drop about 14 dumplings, 1 at a time, into simmering broth. (Dumplings should float in a single layer.) Cover and simmer gently 4 to 5 minutes or until done. (Do not overcook.) Remove to a platter with a large slotted spoon; cover and keep warm. Repeat procedure to cook remaining dumplings.
Stir chicken into broth; simmer 1 minute or until thoroughly heated. Add dumplings and egg to pan. Serve immediately; sprinkle each serving with parsley. Yield: 6 servings.

Per serving: Calories 503 (41% from fat); Fat 22.8g (sat 5.9g, mono 8.9g, poly 5.6g); Protein 34.7g; Carb 39.6g; Fiber 1.3g; Chol 193mg; Iron 4.3mg; Sodium 971mg; Calc 171mg

Chicken and Dumplings

dumpling dos and don'ts

Don't cook more dumplings at once than will lie in a single layer on top of broth. If over-crowded, they'll get soggy and break apart. Keep broth at a gentle simmer. Boiling will tear dumplings apart.

family favorite • make ahead
Chicken Marbella

prep: 10 min.   cook: 1 hr.   other: 8 hrs.

This marinated chicken baked with olives, capers, oregano, and dried plums is the perfect choice for a hearty yet stylish meal.

1   (12-ounce) package pitted, bite-size dried plums
1   (3.5-ounce) jar capers, drained
1   (0.5-ounce) bottle dried oregano
6   bay leaves
1   garlic bulb, minced
1   cup pimiento-stuffed olives
½   cup red wine vinegar
½   cup olive oil
1   tablespoon coarse sea salt
2   teaspoons pepper
8   pounds chicken pieces
1   cup firmly packed light brown sugar
1   cup dry white wine
¼   cup chopped fresh parsley

Combine first 10 ingredients in a large zip-top freezer bag or a large bowl. Add chicken pieces, turning to coat well; seal or cover and chill for at least 8 hours (overnight is best), turning chicken occasionally.
Arrange chicken in a single layer in 2 (13- x 9-inch) baking pans. Pour marinade evenly over chicken, and sprinkle evenly with brown sugar; pour wine around chicken pieces.
Bake, uncovered, at 350° for 50 minutes to 1 hour, basting often.
Remove chicken, dried plums, capers, and olives to a serving platter. Drizzle with ¾ cup pan juices; sprinkle with parsley. Discard bay leaves. Serve chicken with remaining pan juices. Yield: 10 servings.

Per serving: Calories 823 (50% from fat); Fat 45.8g (sat 11.2g, mono 23g, poly 8.5g); Protein 56.4g; Carb 46.2g; Fiber 3.8g; Chol 209mg; Iron 11.4mg; Sodium 1250mg; Calc 107mg

Tandoori Chicken

prep: 20 min.   cook: 35 min.   other: 8 hrs.

This spicy chicken dish calls for quite a few ingredients, but it's well worth it. High-heat roasting makes for a short cooking time.

6   tablespoons fresh lime juice (about 3 limes)
3   tablespoons plain yogurt
1   to 2 small jalapeño or serrano chile peppers, seeded and minced
1½   teaspoons salt
1   teaspoon ground turmeric
1   teaspoon ground coriander
1   teaspoon ground cumin
½   teaspoon ground ginger
½   teaspoon garlic powder
½   teaspoon ground red pepper
¼   teaspoon ground cinnamon
¼   teaspoon ground cloves
2   tablespoons vegetable oil, divided
3   pounds chicken pieces
Garnishes: lime wedges, jalapeño or serrano chile peppers

Stir together first 12 ingredients and 1 tablespoon vegetable oil in a large bowl until blended.
Skin chicken breasts. Remove breast bones by inserting a sharp knife tip between bone and meat, cutting gently to remove as much meat as possible. Cut breast halves into thirds. Cut deep slits, 1-inch apart, into remaining chicken pieces. (Do not skin pieces.) Place chicken in large bowl with spice mixture. Thoroughly rub spice mixture into slits. Cover and chill 8 hours.
Drizzle remaining 1 tablespoon oil in a large aluminum foil-lined roasting pan. Arrange chicken in a single layer in pan. Bake, uncovered, at 450° for 35 minutes or until done.
Arrange chicken on a serving platter. Garnish, if desired. Yield: 8 servings.

Per serving: Calories 220 (51% from fat); Fat 12.4g (sat 2.9g, mono 4.9g, poly 3.4g); Protein 24.1g; Carb 2g; Fiber 0.4g; Chol 80mg; Iron 1.3mg; Sodium 511mg; Calc 25mg

Oven-Baked Barbecue Chicken

prep: 10 min.   cook: 2 hrs., 10 min.

Use any delicious leftovers in tacos or wraps with Cheddar cheese and bacon.

3   cups spicy tomato juice
½   cup cider vinegar
3   tablespoons vegetable oil
2   to 3 garlic cloves, minced
1   bay leaf
2   teaspoons salt
1   teaspoon sugar
½   teaspoon black pepper
¼   teaspoon ground red pepper (optional)
4½   teaspoons Worcestershire sauce
2   cups all-purpose flour
10   chicken thighs, skinned
10   chicken legs, skinned

Stir together first 10 ingredients in a saucepan over medium-high heat; bring to a boil. Reduce heat, and simmer 10 minutes.
Place flour in a shallow dish; dredge chicken pieces on both sides. Arrange thighs, bone side up, and legs in a lightly greased roasting pan. Pour tomato juice mixture evenly over chicken.
Bake, uncovered, at 350° for 1½ to 2 hours, basting occasionally. Discard bay leaf. Yield: 10 servings.

Per serving: Calories 341 (29% from fat); Fat 11.1g (sat 2.5g, mono 3.1g, poly 4g); Protein 41.9g; Carb 16g; Fiber 0.7g; Chol 161mg; Iron 3.2mg; Sodium 687mg; Calc 33mg

Maple-Balsamic Chicken

prep: 10 min.   cook: 25 min.

8   skinned and boned chicken thighs
¾   teaspoon salt
¾   teaspoon paprika
¾   teaspoon dried thyme
1   tablespoon olive oil
1   (14-ounce) can chicken broth
⅓   cup maple syrup
⅓   cup balsamic vinegar
½   teaspoon freshly ground black pepper
¼   teaspoon ground red pepper
3   tablespoons chunky peanut butter

Sprinkle chicken evenly with salt, paprika, and thyme.
Cook chicken in hot oil in a large nonstick skillet over medium-high heat 2 minutes on each side or until golden. Stir in chicken broth and next 4 ingredients, and bring to a boil. Cover, reduce heat to low, and simmer 15 minutes. Remove chicken to a serving platter, and keep warm. Reserve liquid in skillet.
Whisk peanut butter into reserved liquid, and boil over medium-high heat, uncovered, 5 minutes or until sauce is thickened; spoon sauce evenly over chicken. Yield: 4 servings.

Per serving: Calories 369 (41% from fat); Fat 15.8g (sat 2.8g, mono 7.5g, poly 3.7g); Protein 31g; Carb 24.7g; Fiber 1.4g; Chol 119mg; Iron 2.4mg; Sodium 1296mg; Calc 43mg

Breaded Chicken Drumsticks

prep: 10 min.   cook: 1 hr.

A colorful blend of spices coats these drumsticks that bake in the oven to crispy perfection. Dark meats, such as drumsticks, are juicier due to their higher fat content. But don't dismay—most of the fat's in the skin, which you remove before baking.

½   cup fine, dry breadcrumbs
2   teaspoons onion powder
2   teaspoons curry powder
½   teaspoon dry mustard
¼   teaspoon salt
¼   teaspoon garlic powder
¼   teaspoon paprika
¼   to ½ teaspoon ground red pepper
12   chicken drumsticks, skinned (3 pounds)
¼   cup milk
Vegetable cooking spray

Combine first 8 ingredients in a shallow dish. Dip chicken in milk; coat with crumb mixture, and place in a lightly greased 13- x 9-inch baking dish. Coat chicken with cooking spray. Bake, uncovered, at 375° for 1 hour or until done. Yield: 6 servings.

Per serving: Calories 208 (28% from fat); Fat 6.4g (sat 1.6g, mono 1.7g, poly 1.5g); Protein 27.8g; Carb 8.2g; Fiber 0.8g; Chol 104mg; Iron 2mg; Sodium 279mg; Calc 49mg

Honey Barbecue Chicken

prep: 5 min.   cook: 1 hr., 10 min.

Honey Barbecue Sauce can be made up to a week in advance and refrigerated.

Vegetable cooking spray
6   bone-in chicken breasts
8   chicken drumsticks
Honey Barbecue Sauce

Coat food grate with cooking spray; place on grill over medium-high heat (350° to 400°). Place chicken on grate, and grill, covered with grill lid, 5 to 10 minutes on each side. Reduce heat to low (under 300°); grill, covered, 40 to 50 minutes for breasts and 30 to 40 minutes or until done for drumsticks. Brush with 1 cup Honey Barbecue Sauce during the last 10 minutes of grilling. Serve chicken with remaining 1 cup sauce. Yield: 8 servings.

Per serving and ¼ cup sauce: Calories 424 (46% from fat); Fat 21.6g (sat 7.6g, mono 7.8g, poly 3.9g); Protein 41.8g; Carb 14.7g; Fiber 0.3g; Chol 145mg; Iron 2.1mg; Sodium 439mg; Calc 30mg

Honey Barbecue Sauce

prep: 15 min.   cook: 12 min.

¼   cup butter or margarine
1   medium onion, diced (about 1 cup)
1   cup ketchup
⅓   cup water
¼   cup honey
2   tablespoons lemon juice
1   tablespoon Worcestershire sauce
¼   teaspoon pepper

Melt butter in a small saucepan over medium heat; add onion, and sauté 4 to 5 minutes or until tender. Stir in ketchup and remaining ingredients; bring to a boil. Reduce heat, and simmer, uncovered, 5 minutes. Store leftover sauce in refrigerator up to 1 week. Yield: about 2 cups.

Per tablespoon: Calories 30 (45% from fat); Fat 1.5g (sat 0.9g, mono 0.4g, poly 0.1g); Protein 0.2g; Carb 4.6g; Fiber 0.1g; Chol 4mg; Iron 0.1mg; Sodium 99mg; Calc 3mg

Chicken Beer Bake

prep: 15 min.   cook: 1 hr.

Toasted almonds and beer contribute flavor to this easy weeknight dish.

⅓   cup all-purpose flour
½   teaspoon salt
½   teaspoon pepper
6   bone-in chicken breasts
Vegetable oil
2   (10¾-ounce) cans cream of chicken soup
1   tablespoon soy sauce
¼   cup toasted slivered almonds, divided
1   cup beer
1   cup sliced fresh mushrooms

Combine flour, salt, and pepper; dredge chicken in flour mixture. Brown chicken in hot oil in a large skillet over medium-high heat. Remove chicken, and place in a lightly greased 13- x 9-inch baking dish.
Combine soup, soy sauce, 2 tablespoons almonds, beer, and mushrooms; pour over chicken.
Bake, uncovered, at 350° for 1 hour, basting occasionally. Sprinkle with remaining almonds before serving. Yield: 6 servings.

Per serving: Calories 443 (54% from fat); Fat 26.4g (sat 6.2g, mono 11.1g, poly 6.5g); Protein 35.3g; Carb 15.8g; Fiber 1g; Chol 101mg; Iron 2.9mg; Sodium 1141mg; Calc 46mg

Greek Chicken Breasts

prep: 17 min.   cook: 45 min.

Tuck garlic under the skin of these chicken breasts for a flavor surprise in each bite. A sprinkling of olives and feta cheese adds to the Greek accent.

4   bone-in chicken breasts
8   garlic cloves, pressed
2   tablespoons olive oil
1   teaspoon salt
1   teaspoon freshly ground pepper
2   teaspoons dried oregano
4   lemons, thinly sliced
16   to 20 kalamata olives, pitted
1   (4-ounce) container crumbled feta cheese
Garnishes: lemon slices, fresh oregano sprigs

Lift skin gently from each chicken breast without detaching it; place 2 garlic cloves under skin of each chicken breast. Replace skin. Rub chicken breasts evenly with oil; sprinkle with salt, pepper, and oregano.
Place lemon slices in a lightly greased 13- x 9-inch baking dish, and arrange chicken breasts over lemon. Sprinkle olives around chicken.
Bake at 350° for 45 minutes or until done. Remove from oven, and sprinkle with feta cheese. Garnish, if desired. Yield: 4 servings.

Per serving: Calories 396 (56% from fat); Fat 24.7g (sat 7.8g, mono 12.2g, poly 3g); Protein 34.2g; Carb 9.4g; Fiber 0.9g; Chol 108mg; Iron 2mg; Sodium 1214mg; Calc 187mg

Chicken Breasts Saltimbocca

prep: 20 min.   cook: 26 min.

Slivers of salty prosciutto and fresh sage flavor this Italian dish of buttery, sautéed chicken (or veal, traditionally) that's braised in white wine.

4   bone-in chicken breasts
4   fresh sage leaves or 1 teaspoon dried sage leaves
8   thin slices prosciutto
2   teaspoons olive oil
½   teaspoon salt
½   teaspoon freshly ground pepper
3   tablespoons butter or margarine
½   cup dry white wine
1   cup chicken broth
½   cup (2 ounces) shredded mozzarella cheese
2   tablespoons minced fresh flat-leaf parsley

Lift skin gently from each chicken breast without detaching it; place 1 sage leaf (or ¼ teaspoon dried sage), 2 prosciutto slices, and ½ teaspoon oil under skin of each chicken breast. Replace skin. Sprinkle chicken with salt and pepper.
Melt butter in a heavy skillet over medium-high heat; add chicken, and cook 2 to 3 minutes on each side or until golden.
Add wine and broth; cover, reduce heat, and simmer 20 minutes or until chicken is done. Sprinkle with cheese and parsley. Yield: 4 servings.

Per serving: Calories 461 (60% from fat); Fat 30.6g (sat 12.4g, mono 11.8g, poly 4g); Protein 43.7g; Carb 2.8g; Fiber 0.1g; Chol 148mg; Iron 1.8mg; Sodium 1656mg; Calc 131mg

Chicken Divan

prep: 12 min.   cook: 1 hr.

Chicken Divan nestles broccoli spears next to chicken in a subtle curried cream sauce.

4	bone-in chicken breasts, skinned
½	teaspoon salt
¼	teaspoon pepper
2	tablespoons butter or margarine
¼	cup all-purpose flour
1	cup milk
1	egg yolk, beaten
1	(8-ounce) container sour cream
½	cup mayonnaise
½	teaspoon grated lemon rind
2	tablespoons lemon juice
½	teaspoon salt
¼	to ½ teaspoon curry powder
2	(10-ounce) packages frozen broccoli spears, thawed and drained
⅓	cup grated Parmesan cheese
	Paprika

Place first 3 ingredients in a large saucepan; add water to cover. Bring to a boil. Cover, reduce heat, and simmer 20 minutes or until chicken is tender. Drain, reserving ½ cup broth. Let chicken cool slightly. Bone and chop chicken; set aside.

Melt butter in a small heavy saucepan over low heat; add flour, stirring until smooth. Cook 1 minute, stirring constantly. Gradually add milk and reserved broth; cook over medium heat, stirring constantly, until thickened and bubbly.

Stir one-fourth of hot mixture into egg yolk; add to remaining hot mixture and cook 1 minute, stirring constantly. Remove from heat; stir in sour cream and next 5 ingredients.

Layer half each of broccoli, chicken, and sauce in a lightly greased 2-quart casserole. Repeat layers. Sprinkle with Parmesan cheese.

Bake, uncovered, at 350° for 30 to 35 minutes. Sprinkle with paprika. Yield: 4 servings.

Per serving: Calories 661 (65% from fat); Fat 47.5g (sat 17.8g, mono 12.9g, poly 13.5g); Protein 39.9g; Carb 20.1g; Fiber 4g; Chol 187mg; Iron 2.5mg; Sodium 805mg; Calc 301mg

---

Oven-Fried Chicken

prep: 13 min.   cook: 1 hr.

Oven-frying and removing the skin from the chicken significantly reduces the fat content of fried chicken—a healthy and tasty alternative for Southerners who try to watch their fat intake but don't want to part with an old favorite entrée.

12	bone-in chicken breasts, skinned
1	cup Italian-seasoned breadcrumbs
1	cup all-purpose flour
1	tablespoon Old Bay seasoning
½	teaspoon Creole seasoning
½	teaspoon garlic powder
½	teaspoon dried thyme
½	teaspoon dried basil
½	teaspoon dried oregano
⅛	teaspoon freshly ground black pepper
⅛	teaspoon ground red pepper
1	(8-ounce) container plain nonfat yogurt
	Vegetable cooking spray

Line a very large baking sheet with aluminum foil; lightly grease foil, and set aside.

Place chicken in a large bowl of ice water; set aside.

Combine breadcrumbs and next 9 ingredients in a large zip-top freezer bag; seal and shake well.

Remove chicken from water, and pat dry. Brush 2 chicken breasts with yogurt, and place in bag. Seal and shake to coat chicken completely. Place chicken on prepared baking sheet. Repeat procedure with remaining chicken breasts and yogurt.

Coat chicken with cooking spray. Bake, uncovered, on bottom rack of oven at 400° for 1 hour or until done. Yield: 12 servings.

Per serving: Calories 333 (40% from fat); Fat 14.4g (sat 3.9g, mono 5.6g, poly 3.1g); Protein 33.2g; Carb 16.1g; Fiber 0.7g; Chol 93mg; Iron 2mg; Sodium 528mg; Calc 65mg

---

Chicken-Rice Casserole

prep: 9 min.   cook: 1 hr., 7 min.

A casserole like this is a family cook's best friend—easy to prepare and universally popular.

½	cup chopped celery
¼	cup chopped onion
2	garlic cloves, minced
1	tablespoon vegetable oil
1	(8-ounce) package sliced fresh mushrooms
1	cup uncooked regular rice
1	(10¾-ounce) can cream of mushroom soup
1	cup water
1	(8-ounce) can sliced water chestnuts, drained
3	tablespoons chopped fresh parsley
¼	cup dry sherry (optional)
6	bone-in chicken breasts, skinned
½	teaspoon salt
½	teaspoon pepper

Sauté first 3 ingredients in a large nonstick skillet in hot oil over medium heat 5 minutes or until tender. Add mushrooms, and sauté 2 minutes. Stir in rice, next 4 ingredients, and, if desired, sherry; spoon into a lightly greased 13- x 9-inch baking dish. Top with chicken. Sprinkle chicken with salt and pepper.

Bake, covered, at 350° for 1 hour or until chicken is done. Yield: 6 servings.

Per serving: Calories 335 (20% from fat); Fat 7.5g (sat 1.5g, mono 2g, poly 2.2g); Protein 32.2g; Carb 33.6g; Fiber 2.5g; Chol 68mg; Iron 3.5mg; Sodium 614mg; Calc 49mg

Chicken Parmesan

◄ Flatten chicken using a meat mallet.

◄ Dip chicken in egg white.

◄ Dredge chicken in breadcrumb mixture.

◄ Brown chicken in an ovenproof skillet.

family favorite

Chicken Parmesan

prep: 10 min.   cook: 26 min.

1   cup Italian-seasoned breadcrumbs
2   tablespoons all-purpose flour
¼   teaspoon ground red pepper
2   skinned and boned chicken breasts
2   egg whites, lightly beaten
1   tablespoon olive oil
Tomato Sauce
1   cup (4 ounces) shredded mozzarella cheese
½   cup freshly grated Parmesan cheese

Combine first 3 ingredients in a small bowl, and set aside.

Place chicken between 2 sheets of heavy-duty plastic wrap, and flatten to ¼-inch thickness, using a meat mallet or rolling pin.

Dip 1 chicken breast in egg white; coat with breadcrumb mixture. Dip again in egg white; coat again in breadcrumb mixture. Repeat procedure with remaining chicken.

Cook chicken in hot oil in an ovenproof skillet over medium heat 2 to 3 minutes on each side or until done.

Top evenly with Tomato Sauce and cheeses. Bake at 350° for 20 minutes. Yield: 2 servings.

Per serving: Calories 850 (40% from fat); Fat 37.5g (sat 14.1g, mono 15.8g, poly 3.3g); Protein 67.6g; Carb 59.4g; Fiber 4.8g; Chol 120mg; Iron 7mg; Sodium 3355mg; Calc 1063mg

Tomato Sauce

prep: 5 min.   cook: 27 min.

½   small onion, chopped
2   garlic cloves, minced
1   tablespoon olive oil
1   (14½-ounce) can diced tomatoes with basil, garlic, and oregano
¼   cup red wine
¼   teaspoon ground red pepper
½   teaspoon salt
¼   cup chopped fresh basil

Sauté onion and garlic in hot oil over medium heat 5 to 7 minutes or until tender. Add tomatoes, wine, and red pepper; simmer, uncovered, 20 minutes or until thoroughly heated. Add salt and basil. Yield: 1½ cups.

Per tablespoon: Calories 13 (38% from fat); Fat 0.6g (sat 0.1g, mono 0.4g, poly 0.1g); Protein 0.3g; Carb 1.8g; Fiber 0.2g; Chol 0mg; Iron 0.3mg; Sodium 137mg; Calc 13mg

low calorie • low carb • low fat • quick

Chicken Dijon

prep: 5 min.   cook: 25 min.

3   tablespoons butter
6   skinned and boned chicken breasts
1   (14-ounce) can chicken broth
1   medium-size sweet onion, diced
3   tablespoons all-purpose flour
3   tablespoons Dijon mustard

Melt butter in a large skillet over medium-high heat; add chicken, and cook 2 minutes on each side or until golden. Whisk together broth and remaining ingredients; pour over chicken. Cover, reduce heat to low, and simmer 20 minutes. Yield: 6 servings.

Per serving: Calories 214 (33% from fat); Fat 7.8g (sat 4g, mono 2.1g, poly 0.7g); Protein 28.5g; Carb 5.4g; Fiber 0.4g; Chol 97mg; Iron 1.3mg; Sodium 664mg; Calc 19mg

Chicken Pastry Bundles

prep: 1 hr., 15 min.   cook: 1 hr.

Flaky puff pastry encases a savory chicken filling; the combo is wrapped to look like little packages that are perfect for the holidays or any special occasion.

1   pound skinned and boned chicken breasts
¾   teaspoon garlic salt
2   tablespoons butter or margarine
2   shallots, chopped
½   small onion, minced
2   cups sliced fresh mushrooms
½   (8-ounce) package cream cheese, softened
2   tablespoons milk
2   tablespoons dry sherry
1   teaspoon grated Parmesan cheese
⅛   teaspoon salt
⅛   teaspoon pepper
2   (17.3-ounce) packages frozen puff pastry sheets, thawed
12 (1-ounce) Swiss cheese slices
12 (1-ounce) country ham slices
1   egg white, lightly beaten
½   cup butter or margarine, melted
¼   cup Dijon mustard
1   teaspoon poppy seeds
1   teaspoon lemon juice

Sprinkle chicken with garlic salt.
Cook chicken in a lightly greased nonstick skillet over medium-high heat 7 to 8 minutes on each side or until browned. Remove from skillet; chop chicken, and set aside.
Melt 2 tablespoons butter in skillet over medium heat; add shallots and onion, and sauté 3 minutes. Add mushrooms; sauté 5 minutes. Reduce heat to low; add cream cheese and milk, stirring until blended. Remove from heat, and add chopped chicken. Stir in sherry and next 3 ingredients.
Unfold 3 pastry sheets on a lightly floured surface; cut into fourths. Roll each into 10-inch squares. Place 1 cheese slice and 1 ham slice in center of each puff pastry square; top evenly with chicken mixture (about ¼ cup). Bring corners together over filling, gently pressing to seal.
Cut remaining pastry sheet into thin strips; tie each bundle with pastry ribbon. Place on a baking sheet; brush with egg white.
Bake at 400° for 35 minutes or until golden. Whisk together melted butter and remaining ingredients. Serve over pastry bundles. Yield: 12 servings.

Per serving: Calories 804 (63% from fat); Fat 56.2g (sat 18.8g, mono 14.3g, poly 19.6g); Protein 32.7g; Carb 42.1g; Fiber 1.6g; Chol 106mg; Iron 3.3mg; Sodium 1361mg; Calc 268mg

Cheese-Stuffed Chicken in Phyllo

prep: 25 min.   cook: 44 min.

8   skinned and boned chicken breasts
1   teaspoon salt
½   teaspoon pepper
4   cups coarsely chopped fresh spinach
1   medium onion, chopped
2   tablespoons olive or vegetable oil
½   (8-ounce) package cream cheese, softened and cut into pieces
1   cup (4 ounces) shredded mozzarella cheese
½   cup crumbled feta cheese
½   cup (2 ounces) shredded Cheddar cheese
1   egg yolk, lightly beaten
1   tablespoon all-purpose flour
½   teaspoon ground nutmeg
½   teaspoon ground cumin
16 frozen phyllo pastry sheets, thawed
Melted butter or margarine

Place chicken between 2 sheets of heavy-duty plastic wrap, and flatten to ⅛-inch thickness, using a meat mallet or rolling pin. Sprinkle with salt and pepper; set aside.
Sauté spinach and onion in hot oil in a large skillet over medium-high heat 3 to 4 minutes or until onion is tender. Remove from heat, and stir in cream cheese. Stir in mozzarella and next 6 ingredients. Spoon spinach mixture evenly (about ¼ cup) on each chicken breast; roll up, jelly-roll fashion.
Unfold phyllo sheets on a lightly floured surface. Stack 2 sheets, brushing with butter between sheets. (Keep remaining sheets covered with plastic wrap.) Place 1 chicken roll on short side of phyllo stack; gently roll up, folding in long side. Repeat procedure with remaining pastry, butter, and chicken. Place rolls in a shallow pan; brush with butter.
Bake at 350° for 35 to 40 minutes or until chicken is done and pastry is golden. Yield: 8 servings.

Per serving: Calories 536 (52% from fat); Fat 30.8g (sat 16.3g, mono 10.4g, poly 1.9g); Protein 38.5g; Carb 25g; Fiber 1.6g; Chol 161mg; Iron 3mg; Sodium 893mg; Calc 238mg

family favorite
Stuffed Alfredo Chicken

**prep: 25 min.   cook: 1 hr., 10 min.
other: 10 min.**

Pair this entrée with egg noodles and crisp-tender green beans or asparagus.

4   skinned and boned chicken breasts
8   ounces mild ground Italian pork sausage
1   (1.25-ounce) envelope Alfredo sauce mix (we tested with McCormick Creamy Garlic Alfredo Pasta Sauce Blend)
1   cup (4 ounces) shredded mozzarella cheese
1   cup shredded Parmesan cheese
1   (10-ounce) package frozen chopped spinach, thawed and drained
½   cup ricotta cheese
2   plum tomatoes, diced

Place chicken between 2 sheets of heavy-duty plastic wrap, and flatten to ¼-inch thickness using a meat mallet or rolling pin. Set aside.
Cook sausage in a large skillet over medium-high heat 10 minutes, stirring until it crumbles and is no longer pink; drain and set aside.
Prepare Alfredo sauce according to package directions; set aside.
Combine shredded mozzarella and Parmesan cheeses.
Stir together sausage, spinach, ricotta cheese, and ½ cup mozzarella cheese mixture. Spoon mixture evenly down center of each chicken breast, and roll up, jelly-roll fashion. Arrange chicken rolls, seam sides down, in a lightly greased 2-quart baking dish. Pour Alfredo sauce over chicken, and sprinkle evenly with remaining mozzarella cheese mixture.
Bake at 350° for 50 minutes to 1 hour or until chicken is done. Let stand 10 minutes. Cut chicken rolls into slices. Serve with sauce; sprinkle evenly with diced tomatoes just before serving. Yield: 4 servings.

Per serving: Calories 641 (55% from fat); Fat 39g (sat 20.6g, mono 12.1g, poly 4.1g); Protein 57.9g; Carb 13.1g; Fiber 2.8g; Chol 172mg; Iron 3.3mg; Sodium 1469mg; Calc 738mg

Fruity Baked Chicken

prep: 20 min.   cook: 40 min.

2   (6.2-ounce) packages long-grain and wild rice mix
2   teaspoons salt, divided
⅓   cup all-purpose flour
½   teaspoon pepper
½   teaspoon paprika
6   skinned and boned chicken breasts
¼   cup vegetable oil
1   large sweet onion, diced
1   (6-ounce) package chopped mixed dried fruit
2   cups chicken broth
½   cup frozen orange juice concentrate, thawed
2   tablespoons grated fresh ginger
1   teaspoon chile paste with garlic
2   teaspoons cornstarch
¼   cup water

Prepare rice mix according to package directions, omitting seasoning packets; add 1 teaspoon salt. Set aside.
Combine flour, pepper, paprika, and remaining 1 teaspoon salt in a bowl. Dredge chicken in flour mixture.
Cook chicken in hot oil in a large skillet over medium heat about 2 minutes on each side. Remove from skillet; set aside. Add onion to skillet; sauté over medium-high heat, stirring often, 5 minutes. Stir in fruit and next 4 ingredients; bring to a boil.
Combine cornstarch and ¼ cup water. Stir into fruit mixture; cook 1 minute.
Spoon rice into a lightly greased 13- x 9-inch baking dish. Place chicken over rice. Spoon fruit mixture over chicken.
Bake, covered, at 350° for 30 minutes. Yield: 6 servings.

Per serving: Calories 611 (23% from fat); Fat 15.9g (sat 3.9g, mono 5.7g, poly 4.8g); Protein 35.6g; Carb 82.5g; Fiber 4.9g; Chol 78mg; Iron 4.3mg; Sodium 1200mg; Calc 57mg

---

from the grill • low fat • make ahead
Chicken With Polenta

prep: 30 min.   cook: 1 hr., 10 min.

To prepare this recipe ahead, grill the chicken, cut into strips, and chill. Make the polenta just before serving, and reheat the chicken in the microwave.

5   cups chicken broth, divided
1⅓   cups yellow cornmeal*
¾   cup half-and-half
1   cup grated Parmesan cheese
10   skinned and boned chicken breasts
1   teaspoon salt, divided
¼   teaspoon ground black pepper
2   red bell peppers, diced
1   large Vidalia onion, diced
1   tablespoon olive oil
3   cups fresh corn kernels (about 4 ears)
¾   cup dry white wine
½   cup orange juice
⅛   to ¼ teaspoon ground red pepper
Garnish: chopped fresh chives

Bring 4½ cups broth to a boil in a 3-quart saucepan over medium heat. Gradually whisk in cornmeal. Reduce heat to low, and simmer, stirring often, 30 minutes. Remove from heat; stir in half-and-half and cheese.
Sprinkle chicken with ½ teaspoon salt and black pepper.
Grill chicken, without grill lid, over medium-high heat (350° to 400°) 7 minutes on each side or until done. Cool to touch, and cut into thin strips; set aside.
Sauté bell pepper and onion in hot oil in a large nonstick skillet over medium heat 7 minutes or until tender. Add corn; sauté 4 minutes. Stir in wine; simmer 5 minutes. Stir in juice, remaining ½ cup broth, remaining ½ teaspoon salt, and ground red pepper; simmer 10 minutes or until slightly thickened. Serve over polenta and chicken strips. Garnish, if desired. Yield: 10 servings.

Per serving: Calories 337 (27% from fat); Fat 9.9g (sat 3.9g, mono 3.6g, poly 1.4g); Protein 34g; Carb 27.2g; Fiber 3.1g; Chol 89mg; Iron 2.2mg; Sodium 924mg; Calc 130mg

*Substitute 1 cup uncooked regular grits, if desired. Bring 4 cups chicken broth to a boil, and stir in grits. Cover, reduce heat, and simmer 5 minutes. Remove from heat; stir in half-and-half and cheese.

Jalapeño Chicken Casserole

prep: 20 min.   cook: 30 min.

1   (10-ounce) package frozen chopped spinach, thawed
2   tablespoons butter or margarine
1   large onion, chopped
2   green onions, chopped
2   jalapeño peppers, seeded and chopped
1   (10¾-ounce) can cream of chicken soup
1   (8-ounce) container sour cream
1   teaspoon ground cumin
1   (12-ounce) package nacho cheese-flavored tortilla chips
6   cups chopped cooked chicken
1   (8-ounce) package shredded Mexican four-cheese blend
Garnish: green onions

Drain spinach, pressing between paper towels.
Melt butter in a large skillet over medium heat. Add chopped onion, green onions, and jalapeño; sauté until tender. Remove skillet from heat; stir in spinach, soup, sour cream, and ground cumin.
Layer half each of tortilla chips, chicken, spinach mixture, and cheese in a lightly greased 13- x 9-inch baking dish. Repeat layers, ending with spinach mixture and reserving cheese to add later.
Bake at 350° for 10 minutes; sprinkle evenly with remaining cheese, and bake 10 more minutes or until cheese is melted. Garnish, if desired. Yield: 8 servings.

Per serving: Calories 669 (53% from fat); Fat 39.1g (sat 16.1g, mono 11.7g, poly 8.6g); Protein 43.7g; Carb 34.8g; Fiber 3.6g; Chol 143mg; Iron 3.1mg; Sodium 866mg; Calc 384mg

---

chopped chicken choices

Lots of speedy recipes call for chopped cooked chicken. Here are several ways to achieve that.

• Cooking 1 pound of boneless chicken breasts yields about 2 cups chopped chicken.
• Cooking 1 (3½-pound) whole chicken yields about 3 cups chopped chicken.
• Pulling the meat from a deli-roasted chicken yields about 3 cups chopped chicken.
• Freeze leftover chopped cooked chicken or turkey in 1- or 2-cup amounts for up to 1 month to use as needed.

Quick Chicken and Dumplings

prep: 10 min.   cook: 25 min.

4   cups water
3   cups chopped cooked chicken
2   (10¾-ounce) cans cream of chicken soup
2   teaspoons chicken bouillon granules
1   teaspoon seasoned pepper
1   (7.5-ounce) can refrigerated buttermilk
    biscuits

Bring first 5 ingredients to a boil in a Dutch oven over medium-high heat, stirring often. **Separate** biscuits in half, forming 2 rounds; cut each round in half. Drop biscuit pieces, 1 at a time, into boiling mixture; stir gently. Cover, reduce heat to low, and simmer, stirring occasionally, 15 to 20 minutes. Yield: 6 servings.

Per serving: Calories 338 (44% from fat); Fat 16.6g (sat 4.7g, mono 7.1g, poly 3g); Protein 25.1g; Carb 21.8g; Fiber 0g; Chol 71mg; Iron 2.7mg; Sodium 1247mg; Calc 28mg

family favorite
Chicken Enchiladas

prep: 15 min.   cook: 30 min.

3   cups chopped cooked chicken
2   cups (8 ounces) shredded Monterey Jack
    cheese with peppers
½   cup sour cream
1   (4.5-ounce) can chopped green chiles,
    drained
⅓   cup chopped fresh cilantro
8   (8-inch) flour tortillas
Vegetable cooking spray
1   (8-ounce) container sour cream
1   (8-ounce) jar tomatillo salsa
Toppings: diced tomatoes, chopped avocado,
    chopped green onions, sliced ripe olives

Stir together first 5 ingredients. Spoon chicken mixture evenly down center of each tortilla, and roll up. Arrange seam sides down in a lightly greased 13- x 9-inch baking dish. Coat tortillas with cooking spray. **Bake** at 350° for 30 minutes or until golden. **Stir** together 8-ounce container sour cream and salsa. Spoon over hot enchiladas; sprinkle with desired toppings. Yield: 4 servings.

Per serving: Calories 943 (49% from fat); Fat 51.5g (sat 27.1g, mono 16.9g, poly 4.6g); Protein 55g; Carb 62.6g; Fiber 4g; Chol 191mg; Iron 4.9mg; Sodium 1155mg; Calc 651mg

Chicken Lasagna Florentine

prep: 25 min.   cook: 1 hr.   other: 15 min.

2   cups chopped cooked chicken
1   (10¾-ounce) can cream of mushroom
    soup
1   (10-ounce) package frozen chopped
    spinach, thawed and well drained
2   cups (8 ounces) shredded Cheddar cheese
1   (6-ounce) jar sliced mushrooms, drained
¼   teaspoon pepper
1   (8-ounce) container sour cream
6   lasagna noodles, cooked and drained
1   cup grated Parmesan cheese
¾   cup chopped pecans

Stir together first 7 ingredients. **Arrange** 3 noodles in a lightly greased 11- x 7-inch baking dish; top with half of chicken mixture. Repeat layers with remaining noodles and chicken mixture. Sprinkle with Parmesan cheese and pecans. **Bake,** covered, at 350° for 45 minutes; uncover, and bake 15 more minutes or until bubbly. Let lasagna stand 15 minutes before serving. Yield: 6 servings.

Per serving: Calories 630 (60% from fat); Fat 42.2g (sat 18g, mono 14.8g, poly 5.7g); Protein 36.9g; Carb 28.4g; Fiber 4.2g; Chol 110mg; Iron 3.8mg; Sodium 967mg; Calc 568mg

Chicken Livers in Wine

prep: 10 min.   cook: 23 min.

12   bacon slices
4   green onions, finely chopped
½   cup chopped green bell pepper
1   pound chicken livers
⅓   cup all-purpose flour
1   cup dry white wine
1   teaspoon chopped fresh thyme
¼   teaspoon salt
⅛   teaspoon freshly ground pepper
4   cups hot cooked rice

Cook bacon in a large skillet over medium heat until crisp; remove bacon, reserving 3 tablespoons drippings in skillet. Crumble bacon, and set aside.
Cook green onions and bell pepper in reserved bacon drippings over medium heat until tender.
Dredge livers in flour; add to vegetables in skillet, and cook 5 minutes. Add wine and seasonings; cover, reduce heat, and simmer

5 minutes or until livers are done. Serve over hot cooked rice. Sprinkle with crumbled bacon. Yield: 4 servings.

Per serving: Calories 600 (38% from fat); Fat 25.3g (sat 8.9g, mono 10.2g, poly 3.3g); Protein 34.2g; Carb 55.7g; Fiber 1.7g; Chol 427mg; Iron 13.5mg; Sodium 1427mg; Calc 48mg

quick
Sautéed Chicken Livers

prep: 12 min.   cook: 17 min.

¼   cup all-purpose flour
½   teaspoon salt
½   teaspoon pepper
1   pound chicken livers
2   tablespoons olive oil
6   tablespoons butter or margarine, melted
2   medium onions, chopped
2   cups sliced fresh mushrooms
¼   cup dry sherry
¼   cup chopped fresh parsley

Combine flour, salt, and pepper; dredge livers in flour mixture. Heat oil and butter in a large skillet; brown chicken livers over medium-high heat 3 minutes. Remove livers, reserving drippings in skillet. Set livers aside; keep warm.
Add onion to drippings in skillet; sauté 5 minutes or until tender. Add mushrooms, and cook 3 minutes or until tender. Return livers to pan; add sherry, and simmer 6 minutes. Sprinkle with parsley before serving. Yield: 4 servings.

Per serving: Calories 407 (65% from fat); Fat 29.6g (sat 13.6g, mono 10.8g, poly 2.4g); Protein 22.4g; Carb 13.8g; Fiber 1.7g; Chol 436mg; Iron 11.3mg; Sodium 500mg; Calc 37mg

chicken liver is the mildest flavored, most tender liver compared to beef and other livers used in cooking. Whole chicken livers are sold fresh as well as frozen. Purchase liver that has a bright color and slightly moist surface. A quick cooking method like sautéing is recommended because liver can easily be overcooked to disappointingly tough results.

turkey & other birds

Turkey isn't just for Thanksgiving. But it is a standout in the South around the holiday season along with its welcomed companions, cornbread dressing and giblet gravy. A typical-sized roast turkey offers a plentiful amount of both white and dark meat as well as the coveted crispy skin.

Whole ready-to-cook turkeys range in size from 5 to 20 pounds. And the larger 15- to 20-pound birds have a higher ratio of meat per pound.

If it's just the white meat you desire, you can find bone-in and boneless turkey breasts readily available these days. They cook quicker than the whole bird, but stuffing them is not an option. And dark meat fans will find turkey drumsticks and wings sold separately, too.

You'll find turkey in other forms in most supermarkets around the South. When shopping, look for these labels: tenderloins, cutlets, ground turkey, and sausages.

Tenderloins are fillets of turkey cut from the breast; they're especially good for baking, broiling, or grilling.

Cutlets are ⅛- to ¾-inch-thick slices of turkey also cut from the breast. They take only about 3 minutes to cook on each side because they're so thin. Some supermarkets mistakenly label turkey cutlets as steaks, although the term "steak" refers to slices of turkey that are ½ to 1 inch thick.

Ground turkey, either all white meat or a blend of white and dark turkey meat, substitutes well for ground beef in many recipes. The fat content of ground turkey can vary, depending on how much dark meat (higher in fat) is used.

Turkey sausage is available in links and patties in many markets. And just like other types of sausage, turkey sausage can be pan-fried or broiled.

The goose and duckling are other fine offerings for a holiday meal or casual dinner. Both contain a higher fat percentage than other birds, so be sure to prick the skin all over before cooking to render much of the fat during cooking. And don't baste these birds with added fat (butter or oil) during roasting as you might a turkey.

Thawing the Turkey

If you purchase a frozen turkey, it's important from a safety standpoint to thaw it properly before cooking. The best way is to thaw the turkey in the refrigerator. Do not thaw a turkey at room temperature.

Leave the turkey in its original wrapper, place it in a pan to catch any juices, and refrigerate until it's thawed. Allow two to four days for thawing. A 4- to 12-pound bird will take one to two days to thaw; a 12- to 20-pound bird will take two to three days; and a 20- to 24-pound turkey will take up to four days to thaw. Once thawed, a turkey should be cooked immediately.

Stuffing the Turkey

Remove the giblets and neck from a whole turkey, and then rinse and cook them within 12 hours. Use them to make gravy.

Rinse turkey thoroughly, and pat dry. Don't salt the body cavity if you plan to stuff the bird. Stuff turkey just before roasting; never stuff it the night before for food safety reasons. And likewise, never refrigerate a cooked stuffed turkey with stuffing intact. Thoroughly remove the stuffing and refrigerate it in a separate container.

Lightly spoon stuffing into body and neck cavities of turkey, if desired. Don't pack stuffing too tightly, because it needs room to expand during roasting.

If you choose not to stuff turkey, another option is to place a few pieces of onion, celery, fruit, or fresh herb sprigs in the body cavity before roasting. This infuses subtle flavor into the bird as it cooks. Then discard the ingredients before serving.

Stuffing versus Dressing

The main difference in stuffing and dressing is in the moistness as well as where it's cooked—inside the bird or baked separately in a pan. We call it stuffing if it's inside the bird and dressing if it's baked separately in a pan. Many recipes offer a range in the amount of broth or other liquid, so if you like yours moist, add all the liquid recommended, and less if you prefer it drier.

When you make stuffing, spoon it lightly into the bird's cavities just before roasting. When you test the turkey for doneness, check the stuffing, too. The stuffing needs to register 165° on an instant-read thermometer. Promptly remove the stuffing from the turkey before serving.

Cooking the Turkey

Turkeys can be roasted, grilled, or even deep-fried. To roast a turkey, first place it, breast side up, on a rack in a shallow roasting pan or simply in a greased roasting pan. Brush turkey with vegetable oil or melted butter. Roast, uncovered, at 325° without adding any liquid to the pan. Then baste the turkey with pan drippings or melted butter occasionally during roasting. Differing recipes will instruct you to tent or cover the turkey with aluminum foil at different times during roasting to prevent overbrowning.

Deep-frying a turkey involves cooking it in hot peanut oil in an outdoor setting. When it's cooked, you'll have tender, juicy meat under an ultracrispy skin. For safety information on frying turkey, see page 390.

Regardless of how you cook the turkey, the most accurate way to determine doneness of the turkey is to use a meat thermometer. Insert thermometer into the meaty part of thigh, making sure thermometer doesn't touch the bone. When it registers 180°, the turkey is done. At this point, juices should run clear, and drumsticks should move up and down easily.

Storing Leftovers

Always chill leftover turkey meat, stuffing or dressing, and gravy separately. (Remember the two-hour rule: Don't leave food out after serving for longer than two hours after the feast.) You can keep cooked turkey in the refrigerator up to two days.

Extend the storage life of your turkey leftovers by freezing them up to one month. Slice, chop, or shred the meat, and then package it in meal-size portions.

Old-Fashioned Roasted Turkey With Gravy

prep: 30 min.   cook: 5 hrs., 12 min.

other: 15 min.

Start cooking the giblets, neck, and vegetables the last 45 minutes the turkey is baking.

1   (15-pound) whole turkey
1½ teaspoons mixed-up salt, divided
1½ teaspoons garlic powder, divided
1½ teaspoons poultry seasoning, divided
1   teaspoon ground sage
1   teaspoon pepper
5   (14-ounce) cans chicken broth, divided
½   cup butter, melted
2   carrots, sliced
3   celery ribs, sliced
1   medium-size yellow onion, sliced
½   cup chopped fresh parsley
½   cup all-purpose flour
½   cup water
Garnishes: fresh parsley sprigs, orange slices, fresh cranberries

Remove giblets and neck from turkey, and chill for gravy. Rinse turkey with cold water; pat dry with paper towels.

Combine 1 teaspoon each of mixed-up salt, garlic powder, poultry seasoning, sage, and pepper; sprinkle cavity and outside of turkey evenly with mixture.

Place turkey, breast side up, in a large roasting pan, tucking wing tips under. Pour 2 cans chicken broth into roasting pan; drizzle melted butter over turkey.

Bake, uncovered, at 450° for 1 hour. Reduce heat to 425°, and shield with aluminum foil to prevent excessive browning. Bake 3½ to 4 hours or until a meat thermometer inserted into thigh registers 180°, basting every 45 minutes with pan drippings.

Bring remaining 3 cans broth, neck, giblets, carrot, and next 3 ingredients to a boil in a saucepan. Cover, reduce heat, and simmer 45 minutes or until vegetables are tender.

Remove turkey to a serving platter, reserving drippings in roasting pan. Skim excess fat from drippings in pan, if desired. Let turkey stand 15 minutes before carving.

Pour giblet mixture through a wire-mesh strainer into drippings in roasting pan, discarding solids. Bring to a boil in roasting pan

over medium-high heat, stirring to loosen browned bits on bottom of pan.

Stir together flour and ½ cup water until smooth; add to giblet mixture, and cook over medium-high heat, stirring constantly, 10 minutes or until thickened. Stir in remaining ½ teaspoon each of mixed-up salt, garlic powder, and poultry seasoning. Serve gravy with turkey. Garnish, if desired. Yield: 15 servings.

Per serving: Calories 694 (50% from fat); Fat 37.2g (sat 12.6g, mono 12.8g, poly 7.8g); Protein 79.4g; Carb 4.4g; Fiber 0.3g; Chol 308mg; Iron 6.6mg; Sodium 1002mg; Calc 64.8mg

Apple Brandy Turkey

prep: 40 min.   cook: 3 hrs., 35 min.

other: 8 hrs., 15 min.

Soaking this bird in cheesecloth drenched with apple juice keeps it extra juicy.

1   (12-pound) whole turkey
5   cups apple juice
½   cup firmly packed light brown sugar
¼   cup cider vinegar
Cheesecloth
½   cup chicken broth
¼   cup apple brandy
3   tablespoons honey
¼   cup all-purpose flour
Salt and pepper to taste

Remove giblets and neck from turkey; reserve for another use. Rinse turkey with cold water; pat dry with paper towels.

Stir together ½ cup apple juice and brown

sugar in a large saucepan over low heat until sugar dissolves. Remove from heat, and add cider vinegar and remaining 4½ cups apple juice.

Place turkey in a large roasting pan, tucking wing tips under. Cover turkey with cheesecloth. Pour juice mixture over cheesecloth, coating it completely. Cover and chill at least 8 hours, spooning marinade over turkey occasionally.

Remove turkey from pan, discarding cheesecloth and reserving 3¼ cups marinade. Place turkey, breast side up, on a rack in a large roasting pan. Pour 2½ cups reserved apple cider marinade over turkey.

Bake at 325° for 3 hours and 15 minutes or until a meat thermometer inserted into thigh registers 180°, basting every 30 minutes with pan juices. Shield with aluminum foil to prevent excessive browning, if necessary.

Remove turkey to a serving platter, reserving 2 cups pan drippings. Let turkey stand 15 minutes before carving. Pour reserved drippings through a wire-mesh strainer into a saucepan, discarding solids. Add ¼ cup reserved marinade, chicken broth, brandy, and honey to saucepan, whisking until smooth.

Stir together flour and remaining ½ cup reserved marinade; stir into broth mixture. Bring to a boil, stirring constantly. Reduce heat to low; cook, stirring often, 15 minutes or until thickened. Add salt and pepper to taste. Serve with turkey. Yield: 12 servings.

Per serving: Calories 680 (38% from fat); Fat 28.9g (sat 8.1g, mono 10.4g, poly 7.1g); Protein 73.6g; Carb 25.1g; Fiber 0.2g; Chol 244mg; Iron 5.8mg; Sodium 474mg; Calc 69mg

readying a turkey for roasting

1. Remove giblets and neck from turkey.

2. Lift wing tips up and over back, and tuck under bird.

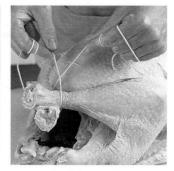

3. Tie legs together with kitchen twine, if desired.

This turkey roasts hands-off. No basting needed.

low carb • test kitchen favorite

Sugar-and-Spice Cured Turkey

prep: 10 min.   cook: 3 hrs., 5 min.
other: 8 hrs., 15 min.

1   (12-pound) whole turkey
¼   cup firmly packed light brown sugar
2   tablespoons coarse sea salt or kosher salt
1   teaspoon onion powder
½   teaspoon garlic powder
½   teaspoon ground allspice
½   teaspoon ground cloves
½   teaspoon ground mace
1   large onion, quartered
2   (14-ounce) cans low-sodium chicken broth
Additional chicken broth
2   tablespoons all-purpose flour
Freshly ground pepper to taste
Garnishes: fresh rosemary sprigs, apples, nuts

Discard giblets and neck from turkey. Rinse turkey with cold water; pat dry with paper towels. Tuck wing tips under. Tie legs together with string.

Combine brown sugar and next 6 ingredients. Rub over turkey. Cover and chill 8 hours.

Place turkey, breast side up, on a rack in a roasting pan. Arrange onion quarters around turkey. Pour 2 cans broth in pan.

Bake, loosely covered with foil, at 325° for 1½ hours. Uncover and bake 1½ more hours or until a meat thermometer inserted into thigh registers 180°. Cover with foil to prevent excessive browning, if necessary. Remove onion, and discard; reserve pan drippings. Let turkey stand 15 minutes before carving.

Combine pan drippings and enough chicken broth to equal 2 cups in roasting pan over medium heat. Whisk in flour, and cook, whisking constantly, 5 minutes or until thickened. Season to taste. Serve gravy with turkey. Garnish, if desired. Yield: 12 servings.

Per serving: Calories 610 (45% from fat); Fat 29.3g (sat 8.3g, mono 10.6g, poly 7.2g); Protein 75g; Carb 6.8g; Fiber 0.2g; Chol 244mg; Iron 5.5mg; Sodium 1219mg; Calc 63mg

Sugar-and-Spice Cured Turkey

1. Rub sugar and spice mixture over turkey.

2. To make gravy, whisk flour into pan drippings and broth.

3. Once gravy has thickened, season to taste before serving.

Roast Turkey With Sage and Thyme

prep: 30 min.   cook: 3 hrs., 30 min.
other: 15 min.

1   (14-pound) whole turkey
¼   cup butter or margarine, softened and divided
½   teaspoon salt
½   teaspoon pepper
¼   cup fresh sage leaves
4   fresh thyme sprigs
1   pear or apple, halved
2   celery ribs, cut in half
1   large onion, cut in half
2   garlic cloves
Garnishes: fresh sage leaves, fresh thyme sprigs

Discard giblets and neck from turkey. Rinse turkey with cold water; pat dry with paper towels.

Loosen skin from turkey breast without totally detaching skin. Stir together 2 tablespoons butter, salt, and pepper. Rub butter mixture evenly over turkey breast under skin. Carefully place sage leaves and thyme sprigs evenly on each side of breast under skin. Replace skin.

Place pear halves, celery ribs, onion halves, and garlic inside cavity. Place turkey, breast side up, on a lightly greased wire rack in an aluminum foil–lined shallow roasting pan. Rub entire turkey evenly with remaining 2 tablespoons butter.

Bake at 325° for 2 hours and 45 minutes to 3 hours and 30 minutes or until a meat thermometer inserted into thigh registers 180°, basting turkey every 30 minutes with pan drippings. Remove turkey from roasting pan, and let stand 15 minutes before carving. Garnish, if desired. Yield: 14 servings.

Per serving: Calories 569 (45% from fat); Fat 28.5g (sat 9.4g, mono 9.1g, poly 6.5g); Protein 72.6g; Carb 0.6g; Fiber 0.1g; Chol 220mg; Iron 4.7mg; Sodium 283mg; Calc 73mg

carving a turkey

To slice turkey easily, allow it to rest at room temperature after it's cooked, covered with aluminum foil, 15 minutes or more before carving. After the meal, remove leftover meat and stuffing from carcass before storing in the refrigerator.

1. Carve the bird, breast side up, on a carving board in the kitchen or on a serving platter at the table.
2. Cut away string first. Remove any stuffing to a serving bowl.
3. Grasp the end of a drumstick, and pull it away from the body. Cut through the skin and meat between the thigh and body; bend the leg away from the bird to expose the leg joint. Slice through the joint, and remove the leg. Cut through the joint that separates the thigh and drumstick. Slice the dark meat from the bones of the leg and thigh rather than placing them whole on the serving platter.
4. Cut the wings off at their second joint, leaving the upper part of the wing intact to steady the bird.
5. To carve the breast meat, steady the bird with a carving fork and make a deep horizontal cut into the breast just above the wing. (Use this cut to mark the end of each slice of breast meat.) Beginning at the outer top edge of breast, cut thin slices from the top down to the horizontal cut. Carve from one side of the turkey at a time, carving only as much meat as needed for serving.
6. Another way to carve breast meat is to remove the whole breast and slice across the meat into thicker, smaller servings.

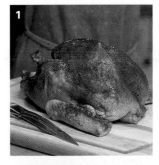
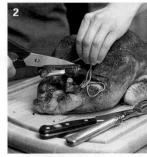

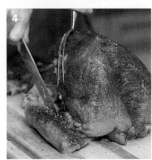

Save the turkey carcass to make broth for homemade soup.

fried turkey tips

- Always fry a turkey outdoors on flat concrete—never indoors, in a garage, on a wooden deck, or on an unstable surface.
- Fry turkey away from buildings and anything flammable.
- Oil will expand in the cooker once you add the turkey; never fill cooker with oil past the oil fill line.
- Use the thermometer provided with the fryer. Don't heat oil above temperature recommended by the manufacturer. Use peanut oil for frying because it cooks at higher temperatures than other oils without smoking.
- Drain all juices from turkey, and thoroughly pat turkey dry before frying. Interior juices can cause hot oil to bubble over.
- If turkey's been frozen, be sure it's totally thawed, drained, and patted dry before lowering it into the hot oil.

Spicy Fried Turkey Breast

prep: 12 min.   cook: 40 min.
other: 8 hrs., 20 min.

1   (6-pound) frozen bone-in turkey breast, thawed
4   cups water
2   tablespoons salt
2   teaspoons garlic salt
2   teaspoons ground red pepper
1   teaspoon ground black pepper
1   cup all-purpose flour
1   teaspoon salt
1   teaspoon ground black pepper
½   teaspoon garlic salt
½   teaspoon ground red pepper
1   to 1½ gallons peanut oil

Rinse turkey with cold water; pat dry. Combine 4 cups water and next 4 ingredients in a large bowl. Place turkey breast, breast side down, in marinade. Cover and marinate in refrigerator at least 8 hours or up to 24 hours.
Thoroughly drain, but don't rinse turkey; discard marinade.
Combine flour and next 4 ingredients. Dredge turkey in seasoned flour, pressing gently to coat; let stand 10 minutes. (This helps the coating adhere during frying.)

Pour peanut oil to fill line into a deep propane turkey fryer, and heat to 325°.
Place turkey on fryer rod. Wearing heavy-duty work gloves or an oven mitt, carefully lower turkey into hot oil using rod attachment. Slowly increase heat so oil temperature returns to 325° to 350° (this may take some time). Fry turkey 40 minutes or until a meat thermometer inserted into thickest part of breast registers 170°. Remove from oil; drain and let stand 10 minutes before serving. Yield: 6 servings.

Per serving: Calories 825 (45% from fat); Fat 40.9g (sat 9.9g, mono 16.4g, poly 10.7g); Protein 91.6g; Carb 16.4g; Fiber 0.8g; Chol 265mg; Iron 6mg; Sodium 1151mg; Calc 59mg

low carb

Citrus-Rosemary Turkey Breast

prep: 20 min.   cook: 2 hrs., 30 min.
other: 10 min.

3   tablespoons butter, softened and divided
3   garlic cloves, minced
1   (6-pound) bone-in turkey breast
1   teaspoon salt
1   teaspoon pepper
1   large orange, sliced
1   large lemon, sliced
4   fresh rosemary sprigs
4   fresh sage leaves
1   teaspoon seasoned pepper
1   onion, quartered
2   cups chicken broth

Stir together 2 tablespoons butter and garlic. Loosen skin from turkey without detaching it; sprinkle salt and pepper under skin. Rub 2 tablespoons garlic mixture over meat. Place fruit slices, rosemary, and sage under skin; replace skin.
Rub remaining 1 tablespoon butter over skin; sprinkle with 1 teaspoon seasoned pepper. Place turkey breast on a lightly greased rack in a broiler pan. Add onion and chicken broth.
Bake at 350° for 1 hour and 30 minutes, basting every 30 minutes. Shield with foil, and bake 1 more hour or until a meat thermometer inserted into breast registers 170°. Let stand 10 minutes before slicing. Serve with pan juices. Yield: 6 servings.

Per serving: Calories 717 (44% from fat); Fat 34.8g (sat 11.4g, mono 12.4g, poly 7.1g); Protein 90.3g; Carb 5.9g; Fiber 1g; Chol 282mg; Iron 5.2mg; Sodium 996mg; Calc 75mg

low carb

Spicy-Sweet Smoked Turkey Breast

prep: 10 min.   cook: 6 hrs.   other: 1 hr., 10 min.

Hickory wood chunks
2   tablespoons coarsely ground pepper
2   (6-pound) bone-in turkey breasts
2   (5-ounce) bottles sweet pepper sauce (we tested with Pickapeppa Sauce)

Soak wood chunks in water 1 hour. Prepare charcoal fire in smoker; let burn 20 to 25 minutes.
Rub pepper evenly over turkey breasts. Pour sauce evenly over breasts.
Drain wood chunks, and place on coals. Place water pan in smoker; add water to depth of fill line. Place turkey breasts side by side on upper food grate, and cover with smoker lid.
Smoke 5 to 6 hours or until a meat thermometer inserted into thickest portion registers 170°, adding more water to depth of fill line, if necessary. Remove from smoker; let stand 10 minutes before slicing. Yield: 6 servings.

Per serving: Calories 647 (34% from fat); Fat 24.5g (sat 6.9g, mono 8.1g, poly 6g); Protein 94.8g; Carb 4.9g; Fiber 0.3g; Chol 244mg; Iron 5mg; Sodium 398mg; Calc 74mg

slow cooker

Slow-Cooker Turkey and Dressing

prep: 12 min.   cook: 7 hrs.

Turkey and dressing has never been so simple. You may never go back to roasting the bird after you try this easy version.

Vegetable cooking spray
1   (8-ounce) package herb-seasoned stuffing mix
1   onion, chopped
2   celery ribs, chopped
1   cup dried cranberries
¾   cup chicken broth
3   tablespoons butter or margarine, melted
1   (3-pound) frozen boneless turkey breast, thawed
¼   teaspoon salt
½   teaspoon pepper
¼   teaspoon dried thyme
1   (0.88-ounce) package turkey gravy mix

Coat inside of a 4-quart slow cooker with cooking spray. Add stuffing mix, onion, celery, and cranberries. Combine broth and melted butter. Pour over stuffing; stir gently. **Remove** string from turkey breast. Rinse turkey breast; pat dry with paper towels. Place turkey in slow cooker on top of stuffing. Combine salt, pepper, and thyme; sprinkle over turkey. Cover and cook at HIGH 1 hour. Reduce to LOW, and cook 5 to 6 hours or until a meat thermometer inserted in turkey registers 170°. **Remove** turkey to a serving platter. Stir stuffing gently in slow cooker; cover and let stand 3 to 4 minutes. Prepare gravy. Spoon stuffing around turkey on platter. Serve with gravy. Yield: 6 servings.

Per serving: Calories 648 (33% from fat); Fat 23.7g (sat 8g, mono 8.2g, poly 4.5g); Protein 55g; Carb 51.3g; Fiber 4.5g; Chol 164mg; Iron 4.7mg; Sodium 1122mg; Calc 87mg

quick

Parmesan Turkey Cutlets

prep: 25 min.   cook: 4 min.

A golden Parmesan crust encases these tender cutlets.

⅔ cup Italian-seasoned breadcrumbs
⅔ cup grated Parmesan cheese
1 teaspoon paprika
½ teaspoon pepper
2 turkey tenderloins (about 1½ pounds)
Vegetable cooking spray
¼ cup olive oil
Lemon wedges

Combine first 4 ingredients; set aside.
Cut tenderloins into 1-inch-thick slices. Place between 2 sheets of heavy-duty plastic wrap, and flatten to ¼-inch thickness, using a meat mallet or rolling pin.
Coat both sides of turkey with cooking spray; dredge in breadcrumb mixture.
Cook half of turkey slices in 2 tablespoons hot olive oil in a large nonstick skillet over medium-high heat 1 minute on each side or until done. Repeat procedure with remaining turkey and hot oil. Serve with lemon wedges. Yield: 4 servings.

Per serving: Calories 411 (44% from fat); Fat 20.3g (sat 4.9g, mono 11.3g, poly 2.5g); Protein 48.1g; Carb 11.8g; Fiber 1g; Chol 76mg; Iron 3.2mg; Sodium 515mg; Calc 141mg

Orange-Ginger Hens With Cranberry Salsa

prep: 12 min.   cook: 1 hr., 6 min.

4 (1½-pound) Cornish hens
1 teaspoon salt
½ teaspoon pepper
¼ cup butter or margarine
¼ cup lemon juice
1 tablespoon grated orange rind
¾ cup fresh orange juice
4 garlic cloves, minced
1 tablespoon grated fresh ginger
1 tablespoon Dijon mustard
1 teaspoon prepared horseradish
Cranberry Salsa

Rub hens evenly with salt and pepper; tie legs together, if desired, and place on a rack in a roasting pan.
Bring butter and next 7 ingredients to a boil in a saucepan; pour over hens.
Bake, uncovered, at 375° for 1 hour or until hens are done, basting often with butter mixture. Serve with Cranberry Salsa. Yield: 4 servings.

Per serving and ¾ cup salsa: Calories 1054 (59% from fat); Fat 67g (sat 31.7g, mono 27.9g, poly 12.2g); Protein 73.1g; Carb 38.3g; Fiber 2.6g; Chol 441mg; Iron 3.7mg; Sodium 1201mg; Calc 80mg

Cranberry Salsa

prep: 14 min.   other: 1 hr., 30 min.

1 cup dried cranberries
½ cup orange juice
½ cup peeled, seeded, and diced cucumber
½ cup diced red onion
¼ cup chopped fresh cilantro
1 garlic clove, minced
1 jalapeño pepper, seeded and diced
¼ cup fresh lime juice
½ teaspoon ground cumin
½ teaspoon salt

Soak cranberries in orange juice in a large bowl 30 minutes. Stir in cucumber and remaining ingredients. Cover and chill 1 hour. Yield: 3 cups.

Per tablespoon: Calories 10 (9% from fat); Fat 0.1g (sat 0g, mono 0g, poly 0g); Protein 0.1g; Carb 2.7g; Fiber 0.2g; Chol 0mg; Iron 0mg; Sodium 25mg; Calc 2mg

Roast Goose With Currant Sauce

prep: 15 min.   cook: 3 hrs., 27 min.
other: 48 hrs., 15 min.

The procedure here for prepping and roasting produces ultracrisp skin and moist meat.

1 (10-pound) dressed goose
1 tablespoon salt
1 tablespoon pepper
1 orange, quartered
1 medium onion, cut into wedges
1 carrot, cut into 4 pieces
1 bay leaf
Currant Sauce (page 435)

Remove loose fat from goose cavity. Remove giblets and neck; reserve for other uses. Chop off wings just below the elbow, if desired. Rinse goose thoroughly with cold water; pat dry with paper towels. Using a trussing needle or sharp skewer, prick skin all over, especially around lower breast and thighs, holding the needle almost parallel to the goose to avoid piercing the meat.
Add water to a tall stockpot, filling two-thirds full; bring to a rolling boil. Gently lower goose into boiling water, neck end down; boil 1 to 2 minutes or until "goose bumps" appear. Remove goose, and repeat procedure, submerging goose, tail end down. Drain; pat goose dry with paper towels. Place goose, breast side up, on a rack in a broiler pan. Refrigerate, uncovered, 24 to 48 hours. (The longer you air-dry the goose, the crispier the skin will be after roasting).
Combine salt and pepper. Rub all over goose and inside cavity. Place orange and next 3 ingredients inside cavity. Place goose, breast side down, on a lightly greased rack in a roasting pan. Roast at 325° for 1½ hours. Remove goose from oven. Drain and discard grease from pan. Return goose, breast side up, to rack in pan; roast 1½ hours. Increase oven temperature to 400°, and roast 15 more minutes or until skin is very crisp and a meat thermometer inserted into thigh registers 180°. Remove goose from oven. Let stand 15 minutes before carving. Serve with Currant Sauce. Yield: 8 servings.

Per serving and ¼ cup sauce: Calories 945 (62% from fat); Fat 64.9g (sat 22.1g, mono 29.1g, poly 7g); Protein 68.3g; Carb 18.7g; Fiber 0.5g; Chol 260mg; Iron 8.3mg; Sodium 1234mg; Calc 51mg

game birds: wild & domestic

The term "game" includes feathered creatures once caught in the wild that are now raised domestically. Quail is a popular example. Game birds tend to be leaner than common domestic birds, which means they can easily become tough when slightly overcooked. So fat is often added, and moist-heat cooking methods are often recommended for this reason. And when roasting game birds, remember to baste them frequently. Some recipes will wrap birds with bacon or other fat to keep them tender and juicy as they cook. This technique is called *barding*.

With younger wild birds, serve only the breasts as an entrée. Small birds can be prepared the same way as quail.

Pheasant is available both domestic and wild. The domestic bird tastes mild and has a texture much like chicken. The wild version has a pronounced gamy flavor.

Quail are lean game birds. They're the smallest game birds commonly eaten in this country. The domestic birds are mild flavored, and the wild ones have a subtle gamy taste. When serving quail as an entrée, allow two birds per person. Look for quail in the frozen meats section at the supermarket.

Be thorough about cleaning and cooking wild game birds. Rinse them in cold water, inside and out, dry them well, and be careful not to overcook them.

entertaining
Roast Duck With Cherry Sauce

prep: 15 min.   cook: 1 hr., 20 min.   other: 10 min.

1	(5-pound) dressed duckling
1	small orange, quartered
2	fresh parsley sprigs
1	small onion, quartered
1	carrot, quartered
1	celery ribs, cut in half
½	teaspoon salt
¼	teaspoon freshly ground pepper

Garnishes: fresh cherries, fresh flat-leaf parsley sprigs, orange slices

Cherry Sauce

Discard giblets and neck from duckling. Rinse duckling thoroughly with cold water; pat dry with paper towels.

Rub 1 orange quarter over skin and inside cavity of duckling. Place remaining orange quarters, 2 parsley sprigs, and next 3 ingredients in cavity of duckling; close cavity with skewers. Tie ends of legs together with string. Lift wing tips up and over back, and tuck under duckling.

Sprinkle duckling with salt and pepper. Place duckling, breast side up, on a rack in a shallow roasting pan. Insert a meat thermometer into thigh, making sure it does not touch bone.

Bake, uncovered, at 425° for 45 minutes. Reduce oven temperature to 400°; bake 35 minutes or until meat thermometer inserted in thigh registers 180°. Turn duckling often during baking for more even browning and crisping of skin, if desired. Transfer duckling to a serving platter; let stand 10 minutes before carving. Garnish, if desired. Serve with Cherry Sauce. Yield: 4 servings.

Per serving and ½ cup sauce: Calories 989 (59% from fat); Fat 65.1g (sat 22.2g, mono 29.6g, poly 8.4g); Protein 44.5g; Carb 55.7g; Fiber 3.2g; Chol 192mg; Iron 6.7mg; Sodium 579mg; Calc 43mg

Cherry Sauce

prep: 8 min.   cook: 6 min.

1	(16½-ounce) can Bing cherries in heavy syrup, undrained
½	cup sugar
1½	tablespoons cornstarch
¼	teaspoon salt
2	tablespoons red wine vinegar
2	tablespoons lemon juice

Drain cherries, reserving ⅔ cup syrup. Combine sugar, cornstarch, and salt in a small saucepan; gradually stir in reserved syrup. Cook over medium-high heat, stirring constantly, until thick and bubbly. Stir in cherries, vinegar, and lemon juice; cook until heated. Yield: 2 cups.

Per tablespoon: Calories 26 (0% from fat); Fat 0g (sat 0g, mono 0g, poly 0g); Protein 0.1g; Carb 6.6g; Fiber 0.4g; Chol 0mg; Iron 0.1mg; Sodium 19mg; Calc 2mg

Duck With Blackberry Sauce

prep: 20 min.   cook: 57 min.

The smooth and spirited blackberry sauce gets a sweet note from pure maple syrup.

2	tablespoons butter or margarine
3	tablespoons sugar
⅓	cup dry white wine
⅓	cup orange juice
2	tablespoons raspberry vinegar
1¼	cups fresh blackberries or 1 (14-ounce) package frozen blackberries, thawed and drained
1	cup beef broth
¾	cup chicken broth
2	tablespoons Cognac
1	tablespoon pure maple syrup
4	boned duck breasts
½	teaspoon salt
¼	teaspoon pepper
1	tablespoon butter or margarine

Melt 2 tablespoons butter in a nonstick skillet over medium heat; add sugar, and cook, stirring constantly, 5 minutes or until sugar melts and turns a light golden brown. Add wine, orange juice, and vinegar. Bring to a boil, stirring constantly, until caramelized sugar dissolves. Add blackberries and broths. Bring to a boil; reduce heat, and simmer, uncovered, 15 minutes or until reduced to 1 cup. Pour mixture through a wire-mesh strainer into a 3-quart saucepan, discarding seeds. Stir in Cognac and syrup; set aside.

Sprinkle duck breasts with salt and pepper; cook skin side down in a hot ovenproof skillet over high heat 7 to 8 minutes or until lightly browned, turning once.

Bake, uncovered, at 400° for 18 to 20 minutes or until a meat thermometer inserted into thickest part of breast registers 170°. Remove from skillet; discard drippings.

Add reserved blackberry mixture to skillet, and cook over high heat 2 minutes, stirring constantly to loosen particles from bottom of skillet. Add 1 tablespoon butter, stirring until butter melts. Slice duck, and serve with sauce. Yield: 4 servings.

Per serving: Calories 428 (48% from fat); Fat 23g (sat 9.1g, mono 9.2g, poly 2.6g); Protein 33.4g; Carb 19.8g; Fiber 2.4g; Chol 197mg; Iron 5.6mg; Sodium 870mg; Calc 39mg

Pan-Braised Dove

prep: 9 min.   cook: 25 min.

¼ cup all-purpose flour
1 teaspoon salt
2 teaspoons freshly ground pepper
16 skinless whole bone-in dove breasts
2 tablespoons butter or margarine, melted
2 tablespoons olive oil
1 cup dry red wine, divided
1 (10½-ounce) can chicken broth, divided
¼ cup red currant jelly
2 tablespoons all-purpose flour

Combine first 3 ingredients; dredge dove breasts in flour mixture. Brown dove all over in butter and olive oil in a large skillet over medium-high heat. Gradually add ½ cup wine, ½ cup broth, and jelly; cover and cook over low heat 20 minutes.
Remove dove from skillet; cover and keep warm. Combine 2 tablespoons flour, remaining ½ cup red wine, and remaining broth, stirring until smooth. Gradually add flour mixture to mixture in skillet; cook over medium heat, stirring constantly, until mixture thickens.
Return dove to skillet to reheat. Serve dove and gravy over hot cooked rice or egg noodles, if desired. Yield: 4 servings.

Per serving: Calories 461 (35% from fat); Fat 15.8g (sat 5.6g, mono 7.5g, poly 1.5g); Protein 40.8g; Carb 24.1g; Fiber 0.8g; Chol 177mg; Iron 8.5mg; Sodium 1063mg; Calc 23mg

low carb
Gin-Marinated Pheasant

prep: 20 min.   cook: 1 hr.   other: 30 min.

¾ cup gin
¾ cup vermouth
1 bay leaf
1 teaspoon ground pepper
1 teaspoon minced garlic
4 pheasants, dressed*
½ teaspoon salt
2 tablespoons olive oil
1 cup red wine
½ cup orange-flavored dried plums, chopped
1 (10-ounce) can chicken broth
2 tablespoons butter

Combine first 5 ingredients in a large zip-top freezer bag, reserving ½ cup of the mixture. Place pheasants in the remaining mixture in freezer bag. Seal and chill at least 30 minutes.
Remove pheasants from marinade, discarding marinade in bag. Sprinkle with salt; brown pheasants on all sides in hot oil in a large roasting pan over medium-high heat. Bake at 400° for 40 to 50 minutes. Remove pheasants from roasting pan; keep warm.
Bring reserved marinade in roasting pan to a boil over high heat, stirring to loosen browned particles. Stir in red wine, and cook 4 to 5 minutes or until liquid is reduced by half. Pour mixture through a fine wire-mesh strainer into a medium saucepan, discarding solids. Add dried plums and broth, and simmer 5 minutes; remove from heat, and stir in butter until melted.
Cut pheasants into quarters; place on a serving platter. Drizzle with sauce; serve. Yield: 8 servings.

Per serving: Calories 839 (46% from fat); Fat 42.7g (sat 12.9g, mono 20.7g, poly 5.1g); Protein 98.1g; Carb 6.7g; Fiber 0.7g; Chol 276mg; Iron 4.6mg; Sodium 452mg; Calc 57mg

*Eight (1- to 1½-pound) Cornish hens make a delicious substitution for the pheasants.

Bacon-Wrapped Quail

prep: 15 min.   cook: 55 min.   other: 10 min.

Make this quail and gravy part of a fall weekend brunch menu.

8 quail, dressed
1 teaspoon salt
½ teaspoon pepper
8 bacon slices
2 tablespoons butter or margarine, melted
Shallot Gravy (page 441)

Sprinkle quail with salt and pepper, and wrap with bacon slices. Place breast side down in a roasting pan. Brush with melted butter.
Bake at 425° for 10 minutes; reduce heat to 325°, and bake, covered, 40 to 45 minutes or until done. Let stand 5 to 10 minutes before serving. Serve with Shallot Gravy. Yield: 4 servings.

Per serving and ¾ cup gravy: Calories 997 (73% from fat); Fat 80.8g (sat 35g, mono 27.1g, poly 10g); Protein 53g; Carb 13.5g; Fiber 1.2g; Chol 294mg; Iron 9.9mg; Sodium 2415mg; Calc 80mg

Chipotle-Marinated Quail

prep: 25 min.   cook: 55 min.   other: 3 hrs.

2 teaspoons black peppercorns
1 teaspoon coriander seeds
2 teaspoons coarse sea salt
10 whole allspice
1 (7-ounce) can chipotle chile peppers in adobo sauce, undrained
½ cup white wine
½ cup frozen orange juice concentrate, thawed and undiluted
⅓ cup white wine vinegar
¼ cup minced onion
4 garlic cloves, minced
12 (3.5-ounce) semiboneless quail
½ teaspoon salt
2 to 4 tablespoons olive oil

Cook first 4 ingredients in a large skillet over medium heat, stirring occasionally, 4 to 5 minutes or until toasted; cool. Process toasted spices in a blender until finely ground.
Process chipotle peppers in a blender until smooth. Measure 2 tablespoons puree, reserving remainder for another use. Stir together 2 tablespoons chipotle puree, spice mixture, wine, and next 4 ingredients.
Pour chipotle puree mixture into a large zip-top freezer bag; add quail. Seal and chill 3 hours, turning every 30 minutes.
Remove quail from marinade, reserving marinade. Sprinkle quail with ½ teaspoon salt. Brown quail, in batches, in hot oil in a large heavy skillet over medium-high heat about 6 minutes on each side, adding more oil, if necessary. Drain on paper towels.
Bring quail and reserved marinade to a boil in skillet. Reduce heat; cover and simmer 25 minutes or until done. Yield: 6 servings.

Per serving: Calories 425 (52% from fat); Fat 24.7g (sat 6.3g, mono 10.3g, poly 5.5g); Protein 36.5g; Carb 12.6g; Fiber 1.6g; Chol 122mg; Iron 6.9mg; Sodium 598mg; Calc 48mg

salads

Some of the simplest, yet best-dressed, food comes from the salad bowl. A well-made salad is a work of art. Often loaded with vegetables and/or fruit, salads are colorful, healthy additions to meals.

Equipment

Not much equipment is needed to produce a pretty salad. In fact, the essentials amount to a wooden salad bowl, salad tongs, and a cruet for serving your favorite dressing. A chef's knife and a cutting board are other basics for chopping fresh vegetables for salad. Of course, a food processor does this job, and swiftly, too. A salad spinner is handy for drying lettuce once you've washed it, and a Microplane® grater will put cheese atop fresh-dressed greens. An egg slicer comes in handy for neatly slicing ingredients such as mushrooms and strawberries that commonly top salads. And keep a pepper mill nearby for adding that last-minute crank of peppery seasoning.

Chill, Don't Freeze

Most salads enhanced with chopped fruits and vegetables don't make good candidates for the freezer. The texture of these ingredients will deteriorate upon freezing. And mayonnaise, a common binding ingredient for creamy-type salads, tends to break down during freezing. Never freeze a gelatin salad that contains fruits or vegetables. The fruits and vegetables may leach liquid during freezing and cause the salad to become watery.

So when you're in the market for a make-ahead type of salad, stick with chilled options. Consider one of our gelatin salads that can be refrigerated overnight. And you can make potato salads, bean salads, and coleslaws, and chill them a day in advance as well.

Chop raw vegetables for salads and package them separately in zip-top bags. You can chill them for a day or two, and then toss with greens and add dressing just before serving.

You can also make salad dressings in advance and chill them several days. Just whisk before serving. Remember to give oil and vinegar dressings time to return to room temperature before serving.

salad greens dictionary

Arugula: This peppery green's assertive flavor is widely used in Italian cuisine. It's slightly bitter and has a hint of mustard. Spinach makes a mild substitute.

Belgian endive: Belgian endive grows in a compact cylindrical shape with a tapered end. Its pale leaves are slightly bitter and can be used as an appetizer, in a salad, or braised and served as a side dish. Store endive in a plastic bag in the refrigerator.

Butter lettuce: Also called *Boston* and *Bibb,* these greens are named for their buttery-textured leaves and slightly sweet flavor. Their delicate texture requires gentle handling because they bruise easily. While Bibb is slightly smaller than Boston, both lettuces impart a similar taste and are delicate additions to salad. The leaves make nice cups for chicken salad.

Curly endive: Often mistakenly referred to as chicory, curly endive has lacy leaves that are slightly bitter. While chicory is a relative of the endive, it's more closely related to the Italian radicchio, which is simply a red chicory. Curly endive is a frilly addition to any salad.

Arugula   Watercress   Baby romaine

Belgian endive

Bibb

Curly endive

Escarole

Dandelion greens: These jagged-edged leaves are bright green with a bitter, tangy taste. They're available year-round, but the best time to find them at their most tender state is early spring. Refrigerate up to five days, and wash thoroughly before using.

Endive: Endive is a relative of chicory and has three main varieties: curly endive, Belgian endive, and escarole.

Escarole: The mildest of the endive varieties, escarole has broad, slightly curved, pale green leaves and only a hint of the bitterness characteristic of the endive varieties. Store escarole tightly wrapped in the refrigerator up to three days.

Green, Red, and Oak leaf lettuces: Leaf lettuce is a variety of lettuce with leaves that splay outward from a central root, rather than forming a compact head like other lettuces. The most common are green leaf, the frilly red leaf with its distinctive burgundy tinge, and oak leaf, named for its shape similar to an oak leaf. Leaf lettuce is generally crisper than head lettuce, but is also more perishable. Choose bunches with no signs of wilting or blemishes; store refrigerated in a plastic bag up to three days.

Kale and Ornamental kale: This member of the cabbage family is highly nutritious with its hearty, richly colored leaves. Choose relatively small bunches of kale devoid of any signs of wilting or discoloration, and use within a few days of purchase. Ornamental kale is used often as a garnish.

Mesclun: Mesclun is simply a mixture of tender, young salad greens. It can include arugula, dandelion, sorrel, and oak leaf lettuce.

Napa cabbage: Also called _Chinese cabbage,_ napa cabbage has crinkly, yellowish-white leaves that have a fairly mild taste compared to other cabbages. Napa cabbage is available year-round and can be stored in the refrigerator up to three days.

Radicchio: The most common radicchio is the Verona variety, which has burgundy-colored leaves and white ribbing. All varieties of radicchio have firm leaves with a slightly bitter flavor. Radicchio adds a splash of color to salad.

Romaine: Romaine leaves grow in heads, ranging from dark green outer leaves to a yellowish-green heart in the center. The lettuce of choice for Caesar salads, romaine adds crisp texture to any lettuce mix.

Sorrel: A spring green sorrel tastes like a lemon-tinged spinach leaf. Young, tender sorrel can be used in salads, while uses of larger sorrel leaves vary from being pureed in soup to being sautéed as an accompaniment with hearty meat dishes. Trim tough stems.

Baby spinach: The mild, tender baby leaves are prime for enjoying raw in salads. There's no need to trim the stems.

Watercress: This green grows in the wild in cool, running streams or brooks. A peppery, slightly bitter green, it's sold in small bunches and is available year-round. To store, place watercress, stems down, in a glass with water, and cover with a plastic bag; refrigerate.

Red leaf lettuce

Kale

Mesclun

Romaine

green salads

When buying bunches of greens, choose those with fresh-looking, brightly colored, healthy leaves with no sign of wilting. Avoid any that are spotted, limp, or yellowing.

A brown core doesn't necessarily indicate poor quality. After lettuce is cut at harvest, the core naturally browns as the cut surface seals to keep the head fresh and to hold in nutrients.

To store salad greens, gently rinse the leaves, and shake off excess moisture. Store in your refrigerator crisper drawer in zip-top bags with a paper towel to absorb moisture, squeezing out as much air as possible before sealing. Use within a day or two. Crisp lettuces such as iceberg hold up longer (sometimes up to a week) than more fragile greens.

In most markets, you can find an abundance of packaged trimmed, torn greens that are ready to use. These packages indicate that the greens are cleaned, but you might want to rinse them lightly to freshen the greens.

The taste, shape, and texture of greens vary, particularly between bunches and heads. Refer to our salad greens photographs and dictionary of greens on the previous pages to familiarize yourself with salad options.

tips of the iceberg

- Thump the core of the lettuce on the counter; you can then twist it out easily.
- Run cold water into the cavity, flushing thoroughly. Invert lettuce head to drain.
- Dry lettuce leaves in a salad spinner, or blot thoroughly with paper towels.
- Wrap lettuce in a damp paper towel, seal in a zip-top plastic bag, squeeze out all the air, and refrigerate up to one week.
- A 1-pound head of iceberg lettuce yields about 6 cups loosely packed, torn leaves.

---

low calorie • low carb • low cholesterol • quick

Caesar Salad

prep: 15 min.

1 head romaine lettuce, torn
½ head iceberg lettuce, torn
¼ cup egg substitute
3 tablespoons olive oil
1 garlic clove, minced
1 tablespoon lemon juice
½ to 1 teaspoon salt
½ teaspoon coarsely ground pepper
½ teaspoon Dijon mustard
1 (2-ounce) can anchovy fillets, drained (optional)
1 cup croutons
¼ cup shredded Parmesan cheese

Place lettuces in a large bowl.
Process egg substitute, next 6 ingredients, and, if desired, anchovies in a blender.
Drizzle dressing over lettuce, tossing well. Sprinkle with croutons and Parmesan cheese. Yield: 8 servings.

Per serving: Calories 100 (66% from fat); Fat 7.3g (sat 1.4g, mono 4.3g, poly 1.2g); Protein 3.4g; Carb 6.3g; Fiber 1.8g; Chol 3mg; Iron 1mg; Sodium 256mg; Calc 71mg

---

quick

Iceberg Lettuce Wedges With Blue Cheese Dressing

prep: 20 min.

A retro salad returns to popularity in this easy recipe. Keep the lettuce wedges well chilled for serving.

Blue Cheese Dressing
1 medium head iceberg lettuce, cut into 4 wedges
8 bacon slices, cooked and crumbled
½ cup shredded Parmesan cheese
¼ cup chopped fresh chives

Pour Blue Cheese Dressing over lettuce wedges placed on individual salad plates. Combine bacon, cheese, and chives; sprinkle over dressing. Yield: 4 servings.

Per serving: Calories 766 (85% from fat); Fat 72.5g (sat 23.1g, mono 20.2g, poly 25.1g); Protein 19.6g; Carb 10.9g; Fiber 1.7g; Chol 92mg; Iron 1.5mg; Sodium 1493mg; Calc 384mg

---

Blue Cheese Dressing

prep: 5 min.

1 cup mayonnaise
1 (8-ounce) container sour cream
1 (4-ounce) package crumbled blue cheese
¼ teaspoon salt
1 tablespoon Worcestershire sauce
1 teaspoon lemon juice

Stir together all ingredients. Cover and chill until ready to serve. Yield: 2½ cups.

Per tablespoon: Calories 62 (93% from fat); Fat 6.4g (sat 1.9g, mono 0.6g, poly 0.1g); Protein 0.8g; Carb 0.4g; Fiber 0g; Chol 7mg; Iron 0mg; Sodium 97mg; Calc 22mg

---

quick

Apple-Spinach Salad

prep: 10 min.

You can chill dressing up to one day.

1 (6-ounce) package fresh baby spinach
2 small Granny Smith apples, chopped
½ cup cashews
¼ cup golden raisins
¼ cup sugar
¼ cup apple cider vinegar
¼ cup vegetable oil
¼ teaspoon garlic salt
¼ teaspoon celery salt

Combine first 4 ingredients in a bowl.
Whisk together sugar and remaining ingredients until blended. Serve dressing with salad. Yield: 4 servings.

Per serving: Calories 346 (57% from fat); Fat 21.8g (sat 2.9g, mono 10.2g, poly 7.4g); Protein 4.2g; Carb 39.1g; Fiber 4.4g; Chol 0mg; Iron 2.9mg; Sodium 275mg; Calc 47mg

---

low carb • quick

Easy Spinach Salad

prep: 20 min.

1 (10-ounce) package fresh spinach*
1 medium-size red onion, thinly sliced
2 hard-cooked eggs, chopped
1 cup garlic-seasoned croutons
2 tablespoons grated Parmesan cheese
Dressing

Toss first 5 ingredients in a large bowl; serve with Dressing. Yield: 6 servings.

Per serving: Calories 210 (63% from fat); Fat 14.7g (sat 3.1g, mono 9g, poly 1.7g); Protein 10.9g; Carb 9.3g; Fiber 1.7g; Chol 87mg; Iron 2mg; Sodium 781mg; Calc 89mg

*Substitute 1 (10-ounce) package salad greens for spinach, if desired.

Dressing

prep: 10 min.

¼   cup olive oil
3   tablespoons fresh lemon juice
1   tablespoon red wine vinegar
1   teaspoon Dijon mustard
½   teaspoon salt
¼   teaspoon freshly ground pepper
6   ounces Canadian bacon, cut into thin strips

Whisk together first 6 ingredients. Add bacon just before serving. Yield: ½ cup.

Per tablespoon: Calories 95 (79% from fat); Fat 8.3g (sat 1.4g, mono 5.6g, poly 0.9g); Protein 4.5g; Carb 1g; Fiber 0.1g; Chol 11mg; Iron 0.2mg; Sodium 461mg; Calc 3mg

quick

Citrus-Almond Salad

prep: 30 min.

⅔   cup vegetable or canola oil
2   teaspoons grated grapefruit rind
½   cup fresh grapefruit juice
1   (0.7-ounce) envelope Italian dressing mix
3   grapefruits, peeled and sectioned*
4   oranges, peeled and sectioned
1   (6-ounce) package baby spinach
3   (5-ounce) packages mixed salad greens
2   celery ribs, sliced
1   green bell pepper, chopped
2   avocados, peeled and sliced
1   cup Sweet-and-Spicy Almonds

Whisk together first 4 ingredients; cover and chill, if desired.
Combine grapefruit and next 6 ingredients in a large bowl. Add citrus dressing, tossing to coat. Sprinkle with Sweet-and-Spicy Almonds. Yield: 10 servings.

Per serving: Calories 358 (72% from fat); Fat 28.6g (sat 4.9g, mono 10.5g, poly 11.6g); Protein 5.9g; Carb 25.6g; Fiber 8g; Chol 7mg; Iron 1.7mg; Sodium 315mg; Calc 116mg

*For year-round appeal, substitute 1 (1-pound, 8-ounce) jar red grapefruit sections.

Citrus-Almond Salad

Sweet-and-Spicy Almonds

prep: 5 min.   cook: 15 min.

1   cup sliced almonds or pecan pieces
1   tablespoon butter or margarine, melted
1½   teaspoons sugar
¼   teaspoon ground cumin
¼   teaspoon chili powder
⅛   teaspoon dried crushed red pepper
Dash of salt

Stir together almonds and butter in a small bowl. Combine sugar and remaining ingredients; sprinkle over almonds, tossing to coat. Spread almonds on a lightly greased baking sheet.
Bake at 325°, stirring occasionally, for 15 minutes. Cool. Yield: 1 cup.

Per tablespoon: Calories 42 (79% from fat); Fat 3.7g (sat 0.7g, mono 2.1g, poly 0.8g); Protein 1.3g; Carb 1.6g; Fiber 0.7g; Chol 2mg; Iron 0.3mg; Sodium 16mg; Calc 15mg

family favorite • quick

Greek Salad

prep: 15 min.

Feta cheese, tangy olives, and pepperoncini are common components of a Greek salad. Try using one of the flavored fetas for variety.

1   medium head iceberg lettuce, torn or chopped
1   small red onion, thinly sliced
1   cucumber, peeled, seeded, and chopped
½   cup pepperoncini salad peppers
½   cup pitted kalamata olives
4   ounces crumbled feta cheese
½   cup red wine vinaigrette
Garnish: tomato wedges

Combine first 7 ingredients in a salad bowl; toss gently, and garnish, if desired. Yield: 4 servings.

Per serving: Calories 261 (72% from fat); Fat 21g (sat 5.5g, mono 7.6g, poly 5.1g); Protein 6.2g; Carb 12.7g; Fiber 2.6g; Chol 25mg; Iron 1.1mg; Sodium 1342mg; Calc 188mg

entertaining
Warm Goat Cheese Salad

prep: 20 min.   cook: 4 min. per batch
other: 2 hrs.

Crumb-coated, fried goat cheese rounds elevate this salad's status to superb.

½   cup olive oil
⅓   cup lemon juice
1   tablespoon thinly sliced green onions
1½   teaspoons Dijon mustard
½   cup Italian-seasoned breadcrumbs
1½   tablespoons grated Parmesan cheese
1½   tablespoons sesame seeds
3   (4-ounce) goat cheese logs
1   large egg, lightly beaten
3   tablespoons butter or margarine
6   cups torn mixed salad greens
12   pitted ripe olives, sliced

Combine first 4 ingredients; set aside.
Combine breadcrumbs, Parmesan cheese, and sesame seeds.
Cut each goat cheese log into 4 slices. Dip in egg, and dredge in breadcrumb mixture. Cover and chill 2 hours.
Melt butter in a large skillet over medium-high heat. Add goat cheese, and fry 1 to 2 minutes on each side or until browned; drain on paper towels.
Toss mixed greens with dressing; add olives, and top with warm goat cheese rounds. Yield: 6 servings.

Per serving: Calories 495 (80% from fat); Fat 44.1g (sat 18.6g, mono 20g, poly 3.3g); Protein 16.2g; Carb 10.6g; Fiber 2.1g; Chol 96mg; Iron 2.9mg; Sodium 613mg; Calc 257mg

test kitchen favorite
Strawberry Salad With Cinnamon Vinaigrette

prep: 20 min.

1   (11-ounce) can mandarin oranges, drained
1   pint fresh strawberries, stemmed and halved
1   small red onion, thinly sliced
½   cup coarsely chopped pecans, toasted
1   avocado, cut into chunks
1   (10-ounce) package romaine lettuce
Cinnamon Vinaigrette

Combine first 6 ingredients in a large bowl. Drizzle with half of Cinnamon Vinaigrette,

tossing to coat. Serve remaining vinaigrette with salad. Yield: 6 servings.

Per serving: Calories 294 (75% from fat); Fat 24.4g (sat 3g, mono 16.1g, poly 4.2g); Protein 2.8g; Carb 19.8g; Fiber 5.9g; Chol 0mg; Iron 1.5mg; Sodium 214mg; Calc 45mg

Cinnamon Vinaigrette

prep: 5 min.   other: 2 hrs.

⅓   cup olive oil
⅓   cup raspberry vinegar
1   tablespoon sugar
½   teaspoon salt
½   teaspoon ground cinnamon
¼   teaspoon pepper
½   teaspoon hot sauce

Combine all ingredients in a jar; cover tightly, and shake vigorously. Cover and chill at least 2 hours. Shake well before serving. Yield: ⅔ cup.

Per tablespoon: Calories 66 (93% from fat); Fat 6.8g (sat 0.9g, mono 5g, poly 0.7g); Protein 0g; Carb 1.7g; Fiber 0.1g; Chol 0mg; Iron 0.2mg; Sodium 115mg; Calc 2mg

family favorite
Chinese Cabbage Salad

prep: 20 min.   cook: 5 min.   other: 1 hr.

2   (3-ounce) packages ramen noodle soup mix
1   Chinese cabbage, shredded
1   bunch green onions, sliced
¼   cup sesame seeds, toasted
½   cup vegetable oil
6   tablespoons rice wine vinegar
2   tablespoons sesame oil
2   (2.5-ounce) packages sliced almonds
2   tablespoons butter or margarine

Remove flavor packets from soup mix, and reserve. Break up ramen noodles; set aside.
Toss together cabbage, green onions, and sesame seeds in a bowl.
Whisk together reserved flavor packets, vegetable oil, vinegar, and sesame oil; toss with cabbage mixture. Cover and chill 1 hour.

Strawberry Salad With Cinnamon Vinaigrette

Sauté ramen noodles and almonds in butter in a large skillet over medium heat until lightly browned; stir into cabbage salad. Yield: 8 servings.

Per serving: Calories 362 (72% from fat); Fat 29.1g (sat 3.5g, mono 11g, poly 13.8g); Protein 7.8g; Carb 22.8g; Fiber 6.4g; Chol 0mg; Iron 2.5mg; Sodium 9mg; Calc 130mg

Cranberry-Strawberry-Jícama Salad

prep: 30 min.

The raw jícama in this salad adds flavor and crunch. Sometimes referred to as the Mexican potato, jícama has a sweet, nutty taste and can be eaten raw or cooked.

- ½ cup olive oil
- ½ cup orange juice
- ¼ cup cranberry-orange relish (we tested with Ocean Spray Cran-Fruit Crushed Fruit)
- 1 small shallot, peeled and chopped
- 2 tablespoons balsamic vinegar
- ¼ teaspoon ground red pepper
- ¼ teaspoon salt
- ¼ teaspoon freshly ground black pepper
- 1 large jícama
- 2 (5-ounce) packages gourmet mixed salad greens
- 2 cups sliced fresh strawberries
- ½ cup sweetened dried cranberries, finely chopped
- 2 large navel oranges, peeled and sectioned (optional)

Garnish: shaved Pecorino Romano or Parmesan cheese

Process first 8 ingredients in a blender until smooth, stopping to scrape down sides.
Cut jícama into cubes, or, if desired, cut into ¼-inch slices, then cut with a 1½-inch star-shaped cutter.
Place jícama, salad greens, strawberries, cranberries, and, if desired, orange sections in a large bowl. Drizzle with vinaigrette, and toss gently to coat. Garnish, if desired. Yield: 10 servings.

Per serving: Calories 211 (48% from fat); Fat 11.3g (sat 1.5g, mono 8g, poly 1.3g); Protein 2g; Carb 27.9g; Fiber 8.2g; Chol 0mg; Iron 1.5mg; Sodium 75mg; Calc 52mg

Salad Greens With Herbed Earl Grey Vinaigrette

prep: 45 min.

This recipe makes 1½ cups vinaigrette; cover and store any remaining vinaigrette in the refrigerator for several days for another use.

- ⅓ cup white wine vinegar
- 2 regular-size Earl Grey tea bags
- 1 teaspoon Dijon mustard
- ½ teaspoon salt
- ½ teaspoon freshly ground pepper
- 1 cup canola oil
- ¼ cup minced fresh basil
- 9 cups mixed salad greens
  Prosciutto Croutons

Bring vinegar to a boil. Pour over tea bags; cover and steep 30 minutes. Discard tea bags.
Process vinegar mixture, mustard, salt, and pepper in a blender until smooth. Turn blender on high; add oil in a slow, steady stream. Stir in basil.
Toss greens with about ¾ cup vinaigrette. Spoon evenly onto 6 salad plates, and top evenly with Prosciutto Croutons. Serve immediately. Yield: 6 servings.

Per serving: Calories 543 (88% from fat); Fat 52.9g (sat 12g, mono 26.3g, poly 11.9g); Protein 15.7g; Carb 4.5g; Fiber 1.9g; Chol 55mg; Iron 2mg; Sodium 1689mg; Calc 136mg

Prosciutto Croutons

prep: 15 min.   cook: 3 min.

- 2 (3-ounce) goat cheese logs
- 18 paper-thin prosciutto or other ham slices, cut into strips (about 6 ounces)
- 2 tablespoons butter or margarine

Shape cheese into 18 balls. Wrap each cheese ball with a prosciutto strip, covering cheese completely.
Melt butter in a large skillet over medium-high heat; add cheese balls, and sauté 1 to 2 minutes, turning often, or until cheese is warm. Serve croutons immediately. Yield: 18 croutons.

Per crouton: Calories 66 (70% from fat); Fat 5.1g (sat 3.1g, mono 1.4g, poly 0.2g); Protein 4.8g; Carb 0.6g; Fiber 0g; Chol 18mg; Iron 0.3mg; Sodium 311mg; Calc 29mg

Bluegrass Salad

prep: 15 min.   cook: 5 min.   other: 1 hr.

Sweet cranberries mingle with creamy blue cheese and toasted walnuts in this inventive salad.

- ½ cup vegetable oil
- ¼ cup rice vinegar
- 1 tablespoon balsamic vinegar
- 2 tablespoons sugar
- 1 teaspoon butter or margarine
- ¾ cup walnuts
- 2 heads romaine lettuce, torn
- 2 pears, chopped
- 1 cup asparagus tips*
- ½ cup crumbled blue cheese
- ½ cup dried cranberries

Whisk together first 4 ingredients. Cover and chill at least 1 hour.
Melt butter in a skillet over medium heat; add walnuts, and sauté 5 minutes or until lightly browned. Remove walnuts with a slotted spoon.
Toss together lettuce, pear, asparagus, and toasted walnuts. Sprinkle with cheese and cranberries; drizzle with dressing. Yield: 8 servings.

Per serving: Calories 308 (72% from fat); Fat 24.5g (sat 4.3g, mono 5.6g, poly 13.4g); Protein 6.4g; Carb 21.1g; Fiber 4.7g; Chol 8mg; Iron 1.7mg; Sodium 131mg; Calc 95mg

*Substitute 1 cup broccoli florets or 1 cup snow peas, if desired.

salad savvy

- Chilling your salad plates or serving bowl will keep salad greens crisp longer.
- The best salads have a balance of textures, colors, and flavors. Contrast crunchy ingredients with smooth dressings, vibrant colors with muted hues, and mellow flavors with spicy bold ones.
- Dress for success: Resist heavy dressings that weigh down ingredients; a lighter dressing lets the freshness shine through.

Italian Bread Salad

prep: 30 min.   cook: 15 min.   other: 15 min.

For ultimate Italian flair, use 1 cup thinly sliced salami, such as Genoa, for 2 cups ham.

4   cups cubed French bread or other rustic bread
6   tablespoons olive oil
3   tablespoons red wine vinegar
2   garlic cloves, minced
1   teaspoon dried oregano
1   teaspoon salt
¾   teaspoon freshly ground black pepper
⅛   to ¼ teaspoon dried crushed red pepper
1   large head romaine lettuce, chopped
4   large plum tomatoes, chopped
2   cups chopped smoked ham
1   (8-ounce) package fresh mozzarella cheese, cubed
3   green onions, chopped

Place bread cubes on a baking sheet. Bake at 325° for 15 minutes or until lightly browned. **Whisk** together oil and next 6 ingredients. **Reserve** 1 cup bread cubes. Scatter remaining cubes on a serving platter. Top with lettuce and next 3 ingredients. Drizzle with dressing; toss. Let stand 15 minutes before serving. Sprinkle with reserved bread cubes and green onions. Yield: 4 servings.

Per serving: Calories 662 (60% from fat); Fat 44.2g (sat 14.1g, mono 23.3g, poly 4g); Protein 37.7g; Carb 29g; Fiber 4.7g; Chol 110mg; Iron 3.8mg; Sodium 1227mg; Calc 383mg

---

low calorie • low cholesterol • make ahead

Tabbouleh

prep: 20 min.   other: 2 hrs.

Tabbouleh is a Middle Eastern salad of bulgur wheat tossed with lots of fresh parsley, mint, and lemon juice. It makes a great sandwich filling, too. Just spoon it into pita pockets with mayonnaise and tomato slices.

½   cup bulgur
1   cup water
3   cups finely shredded lettuce
2   cups tightly packed, chopped fresh parsley (about 1½ large bunches)
2   large tomatoes, seeded and finely chopped
1   small onion, minced
¼   cup chopped fresh mint
1   garlic clove, minced
¼   cup lemon juice
2   tablespoons olive oil
1   teaspoon salt
½   teaspoon pepper

Combine bulgur and water in a bowl; cover and let stand 1 hour or until water is absorbed. Drain well in a strainer or small colander. Press excess water from bulgur, using a fork. (This will prevent the salad from being soggy.)
Press lettuce and parsley between paper towels to remove excess moisture; toss together in a large salad bowl. Add bulgur, tomato, and next 3 ingredients; toss gently.
Combine lemon juice and remaining ingredients in a small bowl. Stir with a wire whisk, and pour dressing over salad; toss gently. Cover and chill 1 hour. Toss again just before serving. Yield: 6 servings.

Per serving: Calories 112 (40% from fat); Fat 5g (sat 0.7g, mono 3.4g, poly 0.7g); Protein 3.1g; Carb 16.3g; Fiber 4.5g; Chol 0mg; Iron 1.9mg; Sodium 416mg; Calc 60mg

---

fruit salads

It's hard to find a salad more refreshing than one made of succulent fresh fruit. Many fruit salads are sweet enough to double as a dessert course.

When preparing fruit salads, don't slice and blend the fruit too far in advance unless the recipe recommends it. Some fruit salads will discolor or become soggy and limp if made ahead.

---

make ahead • quick

Apple Salad

prep: 15 min.

5   to 6 apples, chopped (8 cups)
4   celery ribs, chopped (2 cups)
1   cup coarsely chopped pecans
1   cup chopped pitted dates
1   cup mayonnaise
2   tablespoons sugar
2   tablespoons milk

Combine first 4 ingredients in a large bowl; toss well.
Combine mayonnaise, sugar, and milk, stirring until blended. Add mayonnaise mixture to apple mixture, tossing to coat. Cover and chill. Yield: 12 servings.

Per serving: Calories 296 (66% from fat); Fat 21.8g (sat 2.9g, mono 7.7g, poly 10.1g); Protein 1.9g; Carb 27.1g; Fiber 4.3g; Chol 7mg; Iron 0.6mg; Sodium 122mg; Calc 33mg

---

entertaining • quick

Fruit Salad With Honey-Pecan Dressing

prep: 20 min.

2½   cups fresh orange sections
2½   cups fresh grapefruit sections
1   avocado, sliced
3⅓   cups sliced strawberries
10   cups Bibb lettuce leaves
Honey-Pecan Dressing (page 416)

Arrange fresh orange and grapefruit sections, sliced avocado, and sliced strawberries over Bibb lettuce leaves; drizzle with Honey-Pecan Dressing. Yield: 12 servings.

Per serving: Calories 365 (71% from fat); Fat 28.6g (sat 3.7g, mono 9.7g, poly 14.6g); Protein 2.9g; Carb 30.5g; Fiber 5g; Chol 0mg; Iron 1.3mg; Sodium 53mg; Calc 54mg

Pear Salad With Raspberry Cream

prep: 20 min.

- ¾ cup sour cream
- ¼ cup raspberry preserves
- 3 tablespoons red wine vinegar
- ⅛ teaspoon Dijon mustard
- 4 firm, ripe pears
- 2 tablespoons lemon juice
- 1 head Bibb lettuce, torn
- 1 head romaine lettuce, torn
- ½ cup freshly shredded Parmesan cheese
- 6 bacon slices, cooked and crumbled
- ½ cup fresh raspberries

Whisk together first 4 ingredients. Set dressing aside.
Peel pears, if desired; quarter pears. Brush with lemon juice.
Arrange lettuce on 4 plates. Arrange pear quarters over lettuce. Drizzle with dressing; sprinkle with cheese, bacon, and raspberries. Yield: 4 servings.

Per serving: Calories 389 (45% from fat); Fat 19.3g (sat 9.5g, mono 6g, poly 1.2g); Protein 13.2g; Carb 46.4g; Fiber 7.2g; Chol 45mg; Iron 1.6mg; Sodium 525mg; Calc 267mg

Tropical Fruit Salad

prep: 30 min.   other: 8 hrs.

- 2 (20-ounce) cans sliced pineapple, undrained
- 3 tablespoons honey
- ½ cup fresh lime juice
- 1 teaspoon grated orange rind
- 1 teaspoon grated lime rind
- 6 medium oranges, peeled and sliced
- 4 kiwifruit, peeled, halved, and sliced
- 2 papayas, peeled and cubed
- Garnishes: ½ cup sweetened flaked coconut, fresh mint leaves

Drain pineapple, reserving ½ cup juice. Cut pineapple into cubes.
Stir together reserved juice, honey, and next 3 ingredients in a large bowl; add pineapple and remaining fruit, tossing gently to coat. Cover and chill 8 hours. Garnish, if desired. Yield: 8 servings.

Per serving: Calories 206 (2% from fat); Fat 0.5g (sat 0g, mono 0.1g, poly 0.2g); Protein 2.1g; Carb 53.6g; Fiber 5.9g; Chol 0mg; Iron 0.8mg; Sodium 9mg; Calc 99mg

Summer Fruit Salad With Blueberry Vinaigrette

prep: 26 min.   other: 1 hr.

If you don't have nectarines, use peaches or chopped cantaloupe.

- 8 cups mixed salad greens
- 1 pint fresh or frozen blueberries, thawed
- 1 pint fresh strawberries, halved
- 2 nectarines, sliced
- Blueberry Vinaigrette
- ½ cup sliced almonds, toasted

Combine first 4 ingredients in a large bowl. Cover and chill 1 hour. Drizzle with ⅓ cup Blueberry Vinaigrette, tossing to coat. Sprinkle with almonds. Yield: 6 servings.

Per serving: Calories 179 (50% from fat); Fat 10g (sat 1.1g, mono 3.8g, poly 4.8g); Protein 4g; Carb 21.9g; Fiber 5.2g; Chol 0mg; Iron 1.8mg; Sodium 106mg; Calc 72mg

Blueberry Vinaigrette

prep: 4 min.

- ¼ cup Blueberry Chutney or store-bought blueberry fruit spread
- ¼ cup minced onion
- ⅓ cup balsamic vinegar
- 1 teaspoon salt
- ½ teaspoon pepper
- ⅔ cup vegetable oil

Whisk together first 5 ingredients. Gradually whisk in oil until blended. Cover and store leftover vinaigrette in the refrigerator up to 2 weeks. Yield: 1½ cups.

Per tablespoon: Calories 59 (95% from fat); Fat 6.2g (sat 0.9g, mono 1.3g, poly 4g); Protein 0g; Carb 1.4g; Fiber 0.1g; Chol 0mg; Iron 0mg; Sodium 98mg; Calc 1mg

Blueberry Chutney

prep: 6 min.   cook: 1 hr., 15 min.

- 1 large Granny Smith apple, peeled and diced
- ½ cup sugar
- 1 tablespoon grated orange rind
- ½ cup orange juice
- 1 teaspoon ground ginger
- ¼ to ½ teaspoon dried crushed red pepper
- ¼ teaspoon pepper
- 4 cups fresh or frozen blueberries
- 3 tablespoons balsamic vinegar

Summer Fruit Salad With Blueberry Vinaigrette

Bring first 7 ingredients to a boil in a medium saucepan. Reduce heat to low, and simmer, stirring occasionally, 15 minutes or until apple is tender. Stir in blueberries and vinegar; bring to a boil. Reduce heat to medium; cook, stirring occasionally, 1 hour or until thickened. Yield: 3 cups.

Per tablespoon: Calories 18 (5% from fat); Fat 0.1g (sat 0g, mono 0g, poly 0g); Protein 0.1g; Carb 4.7g; Fiber 0.4g; Chol 0mg; Iron 0.1mg; Sodium 0mg; Calc 2mg

Watermelon–Prosciutto Salad

prep: 30 min.   cook: 5 min.

- ¼ pound prosciutto, cut into thin strips
- 1 tablespoon chopped fresh basil
- 3 tablespoons white balsamic vinegar
- 2 teaspoons honey
- ⅛ teaspoon paprika
- ⅓ cup olive oil
- 3 cups seeded and cubed watermelon
- 2 bunches watercress
- ½ teaspoon freshly ground pepper

Cook prosciutto in a small nonstick skillet over medium heat 5 minutes. Set aside.
Whisk together basil and next 3 ingredients; gradually whisk in oil until blended.
Arrange watermelon cubes over watercress. Sprinkle with prosciutto and pepper, and drizzle with vinaigrette. Serve immediately. Yield: 4 servings.

Per serving: Calories 279 (69% from fat); Fat 21.3g (sat 3.5g, mono 16.4g, poly 2.3g); Protein 10.1g; Carb 14.9g; Fiber 0.8g; Chol 22mg; Iron 1mg; Sodium 786mg; Calc 73mg

fruit dictionary

1. Red bananas resemble the common yellow banana but with a deep red to purple peel and pinkish-white flesh. Their flavor is similar to that of the yellow banana as well, but with a hint of raspberry. Red bananas are available year-round in specialty and large supermarkets.

2. Kiwano, also called a *horned melon,* is an oblong, yellow fruit studded with characteristic "horns." Look for kiwanos in specialty markets. Store in the refrigerator up to a month.

3. Avocado is a green, buttery-textured and slightly nutty fruit recognizable as the main component of guacamole. For immediate use, choose avocados whose flesh yields slightly when pressed. If firm, store at room temperature until ripe; then refrigerate five to seven days.

4. Mango is a tropical fruit recognizable by its blended green, yellow, and red skin, and fragrant smell. The oblong fruit has a flat seed that can be avoided by cutting the flesh away from either side with a sharp knife. Look for fresh mangoes from May to September. Sweeten your unripe mango by storing it in a paper bag on your kitchen counter for about a week. Once ripened, store in the refrigerator up to two weeks.

5. Prickly Pear is the fruit of a variety of cactus named for its resemblance to the pear's shape. It has a melon fragrance and slightly aromatic flesh. Generally served in chilled, peeled wedges, prickly pear is popular in Mexico and Latin American countries. Look for prickly pear at Mexican and specialty markets from fall through spring. Store in the refrigerator up to one week.

6. Persimmons, when ripe, are soft with red-orange skin and flesh. Store in the refrigerator up to three days. Use in baked goods.

7. Kumquat is a miniature member of the citrus family that can be eaten in its entirety, but the tart flesh and sweet peel are usually candied or cooked for marmalade. In season from November through March, kumquats can be refrigerated in a plastic bag up to one month.

8. Passion Fruit is a tropical fruit available from March through September. Passion fruit is deep purple with soft, golden flesh. Use it raw as a garnish for salad, or cook it as a sauce to accompany a dessert. Store in the refrigerator up to one week.

9. Papaya is a pear-shaped tropical fruit. Ripe papayas have golden-yellow skin and smooth, fragrant flesh, and a center of black seeds. Choose papayas with rich color and flesh that yields slightly to pressure; store in the refrigerator only a day or two once ripe.

10. Rainier Cherry is a sweet cherry in season in June and July. Rainier cherries are a fickle crop that requires an immense amount of attention to achieve their characteristic sweetness and blushing golden and red skin. Rainier cherries are a cross between a Bing and Van cherry, two sweet red varieties. Store in the refrigerator, and use within three to five days.

11, 12. Peaches are available from May to October and can range from a whitish-pink to a blushed yellow in both their fuzzy skin and flesh. Choose fragrant peaches that yield to pressure. Ripen firm peaches in a perforated paper bag at room temperature; then store them in the refrigerator up to five days. White peaches, some say, are the most flavorful, fragrant, and best-tasting peaches available.

13. Apricots are summer fruit that are plump, golden relatives of the peach. This popular fruit is enjoyed in a variety of ways, from eating out of hand to filling a pie. Store apricots in the refrigerator in a plastic bag up to five days.

14. Plums have deeply colored, smooth skin and a center pit. Japanese plums, varying from yellow with sweet flesh to large with dark red skin and sweet flesh, are generally larger than the European varieties. European varieties include a range of plums from the D'Agen plum that's used to make prunes, to the Robe de Sergeant, with its dark bluish purple skin

and sweet flesh. Store ripe plums in the refrigerator up to four days.

15. Bing Cherries are garnet-colored cherries available in grocery stores from May through August. Enjoy Bing cherries as a snack or a pie filling. Store in the refrigerator, and use within three to five days.

16. Honeydew, with its light green flesh, is a relative of the American cantaloupe. Honeydews are available year-round. Choose heavy melons with a slightly wrinkled texture for peak ripeness. Store melon wrapped in plastic wrap up to two weeks.

17. Cantaloupe, when ripe, has textured, grayish-beige skin and sweet, juicy flesh. To detect a ripe melon, choose one that's heavy for its size, yields slightly to pressure on its blossom end, and has a sweet, but not overpowering fragrance. Cantaloupe can absorb refrigerator odors over a period of a few days, so store it wrapped in plastic wrap up to a week.

18. Pepino has a violet-streaked, smooth golden skin and fragrant golden flesh that tastes slightly milder than a cantaloupe. Ranging in size from an apricot to a papaya, pepinos are available from late fall to early spring. Pepinos, if unripe, can be left at room temperature to mature. Ripe pepino fruits should be stored in the refrigerator up to two weeks.

19. Asian Pear is a crunchy, yellow- or brown-skinned pear that's subtly sweet and firm to the touch. Asian pears are champions of the pear family for storage—keep them refrigerated up to three months.

20, 21. Bartlett Pears are bell-shaped pears with a light yellowish-green or red skin and sweet, juicy flesh. Refrigerate up to three weeks.

22. Bosc pears are recognizable by their rough yellow and brown skin and slender necks. Bosc pears are available from October through April, and are often used in cooking because they hold their shape well. To prolong the life of Bosc pears, store them in the refrigerator up to a month. Bosc pears are the best choice for poaching.

23. Anjou is a winter pear that can be red or green. The green variety is a large and yellowish-green pear flushed with red, while the red variety is the same size but maroon in color. Both varieties have the same juicy sweetness that can be appreciated either cooked or raw. Store in the refrigerator for three to five days. For the best flavor, be sure to bring them back to room temperature before eating.

24. Kiwifruit (not shown) has vibrant green, sweet, and slightly tart flesh and a fuzzy brown skin. Try kiwis halved, scooping out the flesh like you would a melon, or peeled and sliced as a garnish for salad. Store ripe kiwis in the refrigerator up to three weeks.

25. Nectarines (not shown) are a blushing golden yellow relative of the peach, slightly firmer with a characteristic sweet fragrance. Look for brightly colored, firm nectarines from mid-spring to September. Prepare, store, and eat nectarines as you would a peach or apricot. To ripen nectarines, place in a paper bag, and store at room temperature up to one week. If you aren't ready for them once they're ripe, store in the refrigerator up to three days.

26. Oranges (not shown) are divided into three categories: sweet, loose-skinned, and bitter. Sweet oranges, such as the navel orange or the blood orange, are prized for their juice and flavor and are generally larger than other varieties. Oranges with skins that can be easily peeled and eaten out of hand like the mandarin orange are appropriately called loose-skinned oranges. Bitter oranges, like the Seville that's usually prepared in marmalades or liqueurs due to its sour flavor, are mainly valued for their peels. Store oranges in your refrigerator two weeks or more.

27. Rhubarb (not shown), though eaten as a fruit, is a tart vegetable with a peak season from April to June. It's characterized by its red, celerylike stalks. Due to its tartness, rhubarb is generally prepared with a considerable amount of sugar and is used in desserts. Rhubarb is highly perishable and should be refrigerated and eaten shortly after purchase.

Fresh Fruit Salad With Orange–Ginger Syrup

prep: 25 min.

1   large cantaloupe, cut into 2-inch cubes
2   pints fresh strawberries, halved
1   pint fresh blueberries
1   pineapple, peeled, cored, and cubed
Orange-Ginger Syrup

Combine first 4 ingredients in a large bowl. Serve with chilled Orange-Ginger Syrup. Yield: 10 servings.

Per serving: Calories 167 (3% from fat); Fat 0.5g (sat 0.1g, mono 0.1g, poly 0.2g); Protein 1.6g; Carb 42.2g; Fiber 3.5g; Chol 0mg; Iron 0.7mg; Sodium 15mg; Calc 27mg

Orange–Ginger Syrup

prep: 10 min.   cook: 5 min.
other: 1 hr., 15 min.

Make this citrusy-sweet syrup up to three days ahead. It's also tasty in unsweetened iced tea.

1   cup sugar
½   cup water
2   tablespoons chopped fresh ginger
2   teaspoons orange rind
¼   teaspoon lemon juice

Cook all ingredients in a small saucepan over low heat until sugar dissolves. Bring to a boil; reduce heat, and simmer 1 minute. **Remove** from heat; let stand 15 minutes. Remove and discard ginger and orange rind. Cool syrup; cover and chill 1 hour or up to 3 days. Yield: ¾ cup.

Per tablespoon: Calories 66 (0% from fat); Fat 0g (sat 0g, mono 0g, poly 0g); Protein 0g; Carb 16.9g; Fiber 0.1g; Chol 0mg; Iron 0mg; Sodium 0mg; Calc 1mg

gelatin salads

Gelatin makes a molded salad keep its shape, and it's important to know the basics of using the little packet of powder. Two types of gelatin are available, and they're not interchangeable. With both types, it's crucial that you properly soften and dissolve the granules before adding other ingredients; otherwise, the end product will not gel enough to hold its shape.

Types of Gelatin

Flavored gelatin comes in an assortment of fruit flavors and colors and has sugar or sugar substitute added. All recipes that specify flavored gelatin make sweet salads. For flavored gelatin, stir boiling water into gelatin until granules dissolve; then stir in cold liquid and other ingredients. Follow the label for the exact cup amounts of solids that flavored gelatin will suspend.

Unflavored gelatin is colorless, flavorless, and has no added sugar. It's packaged in envelopes that contain enough gelatin to gel 2 cups of liquid. When working with unflavored gelatin, first soften it in cold water 1 to 5 minutes to allow the granules to swell. Then dissolve it by adding hot water and cooking and stirring over low heat until it's clear and no granules remain.

Salad Additions

You can add fruits and vegetables to a salad in amounts specified on the gelatin package. Just don't add more than directions recommend or the salad won't gel. In general, finely chop the ingredients you add; large pieces may cause the salad to fall apart upon serving.

Selecting a Mold

Always use the size mold recommended in the recipe. If the mold is too small, you'll have mixture left over. If the mold is too large, the ingredients won't completely fill the mold, and you'll lose the effect of the shape. For ease in unmolding, lightly oil the mold with vegetable oil or vegetable cooking spray before adding the mixture.

Chill to the Proper Consistency

Chilling a gelatin mixture to the consistency of unbeaten egg white means to refrigerate the gelatin mixture until it's slightly thick—and looks like an egg white from a just-broken egg. This chilling takes from 30 minutes to several hours, depending on the amount of mixture. Check the mixture periodically. Don't let the mixture congeal too much or it will be difficult to fold in remaining ingredients. If the gelatin gets too firm, set the container of gelatin in a bowl of warm water, and stir until the mixture softens enough to add other ingredients to it.

tips for unmolding

- Lightly spray mold with vegetable cooking spray before filling.
- Be sure salad is firm before unmolding it.
- Loosen edges of mold using a small knife.
- Dip bottom of mold in warm water for 15 seconds before unmolding.
- Moisten platter with a little water before inverting mold to help gelatin adhere to surface. Invert and gently shake to loosen mold.
- If mold sticks, return to warm water for five more seconds, and try again.

Raspberry–Tomato Aspic

prep: 15 min.   cook: 5 min.   other: 8 hrs.

Here's a classic aspic with a raspberry flavor twist and a fun serving suggestion—punch cups in lieu of molds.

1⅔ cups tomato juice
2   tablespoons sugar
2   tablespoons finely chopped fresh mint
2   tablespoons red wine vinegar
2   tablespoons fresh lemon juice
½   bay leaf
⅛   teaspoon crushed dried rosemary
1   envelope unflavored gelatin
½   cup cold water
1   (3-ounce) package raspberry-flavored gelatin
Garnishes: fresh mint sprigs, lemon slices
Shrimp Salad (optional)

Bring first 7 ingredients to a boil in a large saucepan; reduce heat, and simmer 5 minutes. Pour tomato juice mixture through a wire-mesh strainer into a large bowl, discarding solids.
Sprinkle unflavored gelatin over ½ cup cold water; let stand 1 minute. Stir softened gelatin mixture into tomato juice mixture, stirring until gelatin dissolves.
Prepare raspberry-flavored gelatin according to package directions; do not chill. Add to tomato juice mixture, stirring until combined. Pour mixture into 10 (6-ounce) punch cups; cover and chill 8 hours or until firm. Garnish, if desired. Serve with Shrimp Salad (below) or Chicken Salad (page 412), if desired. Yield: 10 servings.

Per serving (aspic only): Calories 51 (0% from fat); Fat 0g (sat 0g, mono 0g, poly 0g); Protein 1.7g; Carb 11.8g; Fiber 0.2g; Chol 0mg; Iron 0.2mg; Sodium 141mg; Calc 5mg

Shrimp Salad

prep: 15 min.

6   cups chopped cooked shrimp
1¼   cups mayonnaise
6   green onions, thinly sliced
3   celery ribs, finely chopped
1   tablespoon grated lemon rind
½   teaspoon ground red pepper
Salt and black pepper to taste

Stir together all ingredients. Cover and chill, if desired. Yield: 10 servings.

Per serving: Calories 298 (70% from fat); Fat 23.1g (sat 3.3g, mono 0.2g, poly 0.4g); Protein 19.8g; Carb 1.2g; Fiber 0.5g; Chol 192mg; Iron 3.1mg; Sodium 401mg; Calc 49mg

Lime Congealed Salad

prep: 15 min.   cook: 5 min.   other: 6 hrs.

1   cup milk
16   large marshmallows
1   (3-ounce) package lime-flavored gelatin*
1   (3-ounce) package cream cheese, softened
1   (15½-ounce) can crushed pineapple, drained
½   cup chopped toasted pecans
1   cup whipping cream

Heat milk and marshmallows in a medium saucepan over low heat, stirring until marshmallows melt. Add gelatin, stirring until dissolved.
Combine cream cheese, pineapple, and pecans. Stir into gelatin mixture until blended. Let cool completely.
Beat whipping cream at medium speed with an electric mixer until stiff peaks form. Fold whipped cream into cream cheese mixture, and spoon into a lightly greased 8-cup mold or an 11- x 7-inch baking dish. Chill 6 hours or until firm. Yield: 8 servings.

Per serving: Calories 308 (58% from fat); Fat 19.7g (sat 9.3g, mono 7.1g, poly 1.9g); Protein 3.8g; Carb 30.9g; Fiber 1.1g; Chol 55mg; Iron 0.4mg; Sodium 114mg; Calc 74mg

*Substitute any flavor gelatin, if desired.

Apricot Congealed Salad

prep: 15 min.   cook: 5 min.   other: 6 hrs.

2   (11.5-ounce) cans apricot nectar
2   (3-ounce) packages apricot-flavored gelatin
1   (15¼-ounce) can apricots, drained and chopped
1½   cups buttermilk
½   cup apricot preserves
1   (8-ounce) container frozen whipped topping, thawed

Bring apricot nectar to a boil in a medium saucepan. Remove from heat; add gelatin, stirring until gelatin dissolves. Cool and chill until the consistency of unbeaten egg white. **Stir** in apricots, buttermilk, and preserves. Fold in whipped topping, and spoon into a lightly greased 9-cup mold. Cover and chill 6 hours or until firm. Yield: 12 servings.

Per serving: Calories 209 (19% from fat); Fat 4.3g (sat 3.8g, mono 0.3g, poly 0.1g); Protein 2.8g; Carb 40.2g; Fiber 1g; Chol 4mg; Iron 0.4mg; Sodium 96mg; Calc 40mg

Bing Cherry-and-Cranberry Salad

prep: 15 min.   cook: 5 min.   other: 8 hrs.

This updated congealed salad adds rich color and sweet-tart flavor to a meal.

2½   cups water
3   (3-ounce) packages black cherry-flavored gelatin
2   cups cola soft drink
1   (16-ounce) can whole-berry cranberry sauce
1   (15-ounce) can pitted Bing cherries, drained and quartered
2   cups chopped pecans, toasted

Bring 2½ cups water to a boil in a large saucepan over high heat; remove from heat. Add gelatin, stirring 2 minutes or until gelatin dissolves.
Stir cola and next 3 ingredients into gelatin mixture; pour into a lightly greased 12-cup ring mold. Cover and chill 8 hours or until firm. Unmold onto a serving platter. Yield: 12 servings.

Per serving: Calories 303 (43% from fat); Fat 14.4g (sat 1.2g, mono 8.1g, poly 4.3g); Protein 3.9g; Carb 44.1g; Fiber 3g; Chol 0mg; Iron 0.6mg; Sodium 89mg; Calc 17mg

vegetable salads

Salads made with vegetables are an important part of a healthy diet. Vegetables boost the nutritional impact of a simple green salad and add texture and a depth of flavor.

Crisp vegetable salads add a splash of color to menus, and many of them are quick to make. Some are as simple as opening cans of beans and vegetables and adding a briefly boiled marinade. You can keep most marinated salads in the refrigerator for several days.

Fresh vegetable salads can take a few extra minutes to prepare since you'll need to clean and trim the vegetables, but their unmatched fresh flavor makes up for the time spent. Put the food processor to work for you when you can.

BLT Potato Salad

test kitchen favorite
BLT Potato Salad

prep: 48 min.   cook: 14 min.

This recipe puts a spin on traditional potato salad with cream cheese, Ranch dressing, and Romano cheese. This salad is best served at room temperature right after it's tossed.

3½ pounds Yukon gold potatoes, cut into ¾-inch chunks
1 (8-ounce) package cream cheese, softened
½ cup sour cream
⅓ cup milk
1 cup mayonnaise
1 (1-ounce) package dry Ranch dressing mix
½ cup chopped fresh flat-leaf parsley
¼ cup chopped fresh basil
½ teaspoon onion salt
½ teaspoon ground white pepper
1 cup finely shredded Romano cheese, divided
2 (2.1-ounce) packages fully cooked bacon
1 pint grape tomatoes, halved
3 cups coarsely chopped romaine lettuce
1 tablespoon chopped fresh flat-leaf parsley

Cook potatoes in boiling water to cover 10 to 12 minutes or until tender. Drain well, and set aside to cool completely.
Meanwhile, beat cream cheese and next 3 ingredients at medium speed with an electric mixer until smooth. Add Ranch dressing mix and next 4 ingredients; stir well. Stir in ½ cup Romano cheese.
Heat bacon according to package directions to desired crispness; cool and coarsely chop.
Combine potatoes, cream cheese mixture, 1 cup bacon, and tomatoes in a large bowl; stir gently to blend.
Place lettuce on a serving platter. Mound potato salad on top of lettuce; sprinkle with remaining ½ cup Romano cheese, remaining ½ cup bacon, and 1 tablespoon parsley. Yield: 12 servings.

Per serving: Calories 459 (55% from fat); Fat 28.3g (sat 9.7g, mono 8.2g, poly 8.7g); Protein 10.9g; Carb 28.3g; Fiber 2.3g; Chol 47mg; Iron 2mg; Sodium 802mg; Calc 125mg

family favorite • make ahead
Creamy Potato Salad

prep: 15 min.   cook: 30 min.

4 pounds small red potatoes
1½ cups light mayonnaise
1½ cups light sour cream
1½ teaspoons prepared horseradish
1 teaspoon salt
½ teaspoon celery seeds
1 cup chopped fresh parsley
1 bunch green onions, finely chopped

Cook potatoes in boiling water to cover in a Dutch oven 30 minutes. Drain and cool. Thinly slice potatoes.
Stir together mayonnaise and next 5 ingredients. Gently stir into potato.
Cover and chill. Top with green onions. Yield: 10 servings.

Per serving: Calories 306 (45% from fat); Fat 15.2g (sat 3.7g, mono 3.9g, poly 6.7g); Protein 6.5g; Carb 35.7g; Fiber 3.7g; Chol 25mg; Iron 2mg; Sodium 562mg; Calc 112mg

Sweet Potato Salad

prep: 20 min.   cook: 25 min.

2   pounds sweet potatoes, peeled and cut into 1-inch cubes
Vegetable cooking spray
¾   teaspoon salt, divided
2   celery ribs, diced
1   jalapeño pepper, seeded and finely chopped
½   cup diced onion
⅓   cup diced green bell pepper
3   tablespoons brown sugar
2   tablespoons chopped fresh or 1 tablespoon dried parsley flakes
5   tablespoons white vinegar
1   tablespoon vegetable oil
1   teaspoon hot sauce
1   teaspoon prepared mustard
3   slices peppered or regular bacon, cooked and crumbled (optional)
Garnish: fresh flat-leaf parsley sprigs

Arrange potatoes in an even layer in a 15- x 10-inch jelly-roll pan. Coat with cooking spray; sprinkle with ½ teaspoon salt. **Bake** at 400° for 25 minutes or just until tender. Let cool slightly.
Stir together remaining ¼ teaspoon salt, celery, and next 9 ingredients in a large bowl until blended. Add potatoes, and toss gently to coat. Sprinkle with crumbled bacon, if desired; garnish, if desired. Serve warm or chilled. Yield: 4 servings.

Per serving: Calories 246 (24% from fat); Fat 6.5g (sat 1.4g, mono 1.9g, poly 2.7g); Protein 5.4g; Carb 42.4g; Fiber 5.6g; Chol 7mg; Iron 1.8mg; Sodium 703mg; Calc 75mg

Sweet-and-Spicy Slaw

prep: 8 min.

Serve this slaw with Shredded Grilled Tilapia Tacos (page 230).

1   cup sour cream
2   tablespoons rice wine vinegar
2   tablespoons pineapple or orange marmalade
½   teaspoon salt
¼   to ½ teaspoon dried chipotle seasoning
1   (16-ounce) package cabbage slaw mix

Whisk together first 5 ingredients in a medium glass bowl until blended. Add slaw mix, tossing to coat. Cover and chill until ready to serve. Yield: 12 servings.

Per serving: Calories 58 (64% from fat); Fat 4.1g (sat 2.5g, mono 1.2g, poly 0.2g); Protein 1.2g; Carb 5.2g; Fiber 0.9g; Chol 8mg; Iron 0.2mg; Sodium 116mg; Calc 41mg

Best Barbecue Coleslaw

prep: 10 min.   other: 2 hrs.

½   cup sugar
½   cup mayonnaise
¼   cup milk
¼   cup buttermilk
2½   tablespoons lemon juice
1½   tablespoons white vinegar
½   teaspoon salt
⅛   teaspoon pepper
2   (10-ounce) packages finely shredded cabbage
1   carrot, shredded

Whisk together first 8 ingredients in a large bowl; add vegetables, tossing to coat. Cover and chill at least 2 hours. Yield: 10 servings.

Per serving: Calories 143 (56% from fat); Fat 9.1g (sat 1.6g, mono 2.3g, poly 4.8g); Protein 1.4g; Carb 15.1g; Fiber 1.5g; Chol 6mg; Iron 0.4mg; Sodium 203mg; Calc 45mg

Sweet-and-Tart Red Cabbage Coleslaw

prep: 20 min.   other: 1 hr.

⅓   cup pineapple juice
¼   cup sugar
¼   cup olive oil
¼   cup lemon or lime juice
¼   cup rice wine vinegar
½   teaspoon salt
½   teaspoon pepper
⅛   teaspoon hot sauce
1   large red cabbage, finely shredded
1   small Granny Smith apple, chopped
1   large carrot, shredded
1   small sweet onion, minced
5   to 6 bacon slices, cooked and crumbled

Whisk together first 8 ingredients in a large bowl until sugar dissolves. Add cabbage and next 3 ingredients, tossing to coat.

Cover and chill at least 1 hour. Sprinkle with bacon before serving. Yield: 10 servings.

Per serving: Calories 141 (46% from fat); Fat 7.2g (sat 1.3g, mono 4.7g, poly 0.9g); Protein 3.4g; Carb 18.1g; Fiber 3g; Chol 4mg; Iron 1.1mg; Sodium 252mg; Calc 59mg

Broccoli Slaw

prep: 6 min.   cook: 4 min.   other: 3 hrs.

This attractive picnic slaw is a bit on the sweet side. If you'd like, reduce the sugar to ½ cup.

½   cup cider vinegar
¾   cup sugar
½   teaspoon salt
½   teaspoon mustard seeds
3   tablespoons vegetable oil
1   (16-ounce) package broccoli slaw
2   small Gala apples, chopped
½   cup raisins

Combine first 4 ingredients in a small saucepan. Bring to a boil. Boil until sugar dissolves. Remove from heat. Cool. Gradually whisk in oil.
Combine broccoli slaw, apple, and raisins in a large bowl; add vinaigrette, and toss well. Cover and chill 3 hours. Yield: 8 servings.

Per serving: Calories 184 (26% from fat); Fat 5.4g (sat 0.8g, mono 1.2g, poly 3.4g); Protein 2g; Carb 33g; Fiber 2.7g; Chol 0mg; Iron 0.7mg; Sodium 167mg; Calc 22mg

Broccoli Slaw

Grilled Marinated Vegetable Salad

prep: 35 min.   cook: 14 min.

4   tablespoons olive oil, divided
3   tablespoons honey
2   tablespoons balsamic vinegar
1   teaspoon salt
½   teaspoon pepper
3   large yellow squash
3   large zucchini
2   medium-size green bell peppers
2   medium-size red bell peppers
2   medium-size orange bell peppers
2   medium-size yellow bell peppers
1   pound fresh green beans

Stir together 1 tablespoon oil, honey, and next 3 ingredients until blended. Set aside.
Slice squash and zucchini; cut bell peppers into 1-inch pieces. Trim green beans. Toss squash, zucchini, and bell pepper with 2 tablespoons oil. Toss beans with remaining 1 tablespoon oil.
Grill squash, zucchini, and bell pepper in a grill wok, covered with grill lid, over medium-high heat (350° to 400°), stirring occasionally, 5 to 7 minutes or until vegetables are tender. Remove from wok.
Grill green beans in grill wok, covered, over medium-high heat, stirring occasionally, 5 to 7 minutes or until tender.
Toss vegetables with honey mixture; cover and chill. Yield: 10 servings.

Per serving: Calories 136 (40% from fat); Fat 6.1g (sat 0.9g, mono 4g, poly 0.9g); Protein 4g; Carb 20.5g; Fiber 5.4g; Chol 0mg; Iron 1.6mg; Sodium 250mg; Calc 52mg

Cool Cucumber Salad

prep: 10 min.   other: 2 hrs.

2   cups plain yogurt
1   cucumber, peeled, seeded, and diced
1   medium-size sweet onion, chopped
½   to 1 small jalapeño pepper, seeded and minced
¼   cup chopped fresh cilantro
1   teaspoon cumin seeds or ½ teaspoon ground cumin
1   teaspoon lemon pepper
½   teaspoon salt

Despite their distinct colors, bell peppers can be substituted for one another in many recipes.

Stir together all ingredients in a bowl. Cover and chill at least 2 hours. Yield: 4 servings.

Per serving: Calories 98 (39% from fat); Fat 4.3g (sat 2.6g, mono 1.2g, poly 0.2g); Protein 5.1g; Carb 10.5g; Fiber 1g; Chol 16mg; Iron 0.7mg; Sodium 466mg; Calc 171mg

Layered Southwestern Salad

prep: 15 min.

⅓   cup chopped fresh cilantro
½   cup lime juice
½   cup olive oil
½   cup sour cream
1   teaspoon sugar
½   teaspoon salt
½   teaspoon pepper
1   (16-ounce) package romaine lettuce, shredded or chopped
5   plum tomatoes, chopped
1   (15-ounce) can black beans, rinsed and drained
1   small red onion, chopped
1   (8-ounce) package shredded Mexican four-cheese blend
1   (15-ounce) can whole kernel corn with red and green bell peppers, drained
1   (6-ounce) can sliced ripe olives, drained
2   cups crushed tortilla chips
Garnish: fresh cilantro

Process first 7 ingredients in a blender or food processor until smooth, stopping to

scrape down sides. Layer lettuce and next 7 ingredients in a 3-quart glass bowl. Pour vinaigrette over salad just before serving; gently toss. Garnish, if desired; serve immediately. Yield: 8 servings.

Per serving: Calories 447 (65% from fat); Fat 32.5g (sat 10.7g, mono 16g, poly 3.5g); Protein 11.1g; Carb 32.9g; Fiber 6.2g; Chol 32mg; Iron 2mg; Sodium 1000mg; Calc 300mg

Green Bean Salad With Feta

prep: 5 min.   cook: 8 min.   other: 2 hrs.

1½   pounds green beans, trimmed
1   small red onion, chopped (about ½ cup)
½   cup Lemon Vinaigrette (page 417)
2   ounces crumbled feta cheese
¾   cup walnuts, toasted and coarsely chopped

Cook green beans in boiling salted water to cover 8 minutes or until crisp-tender. Drain and plunge into ice water to stop the cooking process; drain and pat dry. Place in a serving bowl; cover and chill at least 2 hours.
Add chopped onion and Lemon Vinaigrette to beans, tossing to coat. Sprinkle with feta and walnuts. Yield: 6 servings.

Per serving: Calories 241 (78% from fat); Fat 20.8g (sat 3.3g, mono 4.8g, poly 11.6g); Protein 7.1g; Carb 10.9g; Fiber 4.7g; Chol 8mg; Iron 1.7mg; Sodium 192mg; Calc 98mg

Tomato Salad

prep: 25 min.

This salad begs for your best summer tomatoes—any variety, shape, and color. The more variety you add, the more beautiful and delicious the results will be. (pictured on page 2)

2   (8-ounce) packages mozzarella cheese, cut into cubes
3   large tomatoes, chopped
1   cucumber, chopped
1   cup chopped red onion
½   cup chopped fresh basil leaves
1   cup whole kalamata olives, pitted
½   cup extra-virgin olive oil
¼   cup balsamic vinegar
3   garlic cloves, minced
½   to 1 teaspoon freshly ground pepper
¾   teaspoon salt

Most of the heat in chile peppers
is in the membranes and seeds. Remove them
to lessen the intensity.

Combine first 6 ingredients in a salad bowl; toss gently.

Combine oil and remaining ingredients; whisk until blended. Pour desired amount of vinaigrette over salad; toss well. Serve at room temperature. Yield: 6 servings.

Per serving: Calories 474 (71% from fat); Fat 37.2g (sat 12.6g, mono 20.4g, poly 3g); Protein 21.5g; Carb 14.4g; Fiber 2.1g; Chol 41mg; Iron 1.2mg; Sodium 934mg; Calc 585mg

low calorie • low carb • low cholesterol
make ahead • quick

Grape Tomatoes With Capers

prep: 15 min. other: 15 min.

3   tablespoons drained small capers
3   tablespoons balsamic vinegar
2   tablespoons olive oil
½   teaspoon salt
½   teaspoon pepper
2   pints grape tomatoes
6   large fresh basil leaves, shredded
3   tablespoons shredded Parmesan cheese
Bibb lettuce leaves (optional)

Plum (Roma) tomatoes

Cherry tomatoes

Grape tomatoes

● Grape and cherry tomatoes make a sweet snack picked right off the vine.
● Plum tomatoes are an all-purpose, year-round pick that aren't overly juicy.

Stir together first 5 ingredients. Drizzle over tomatoes; toss to coat. Let stand at least 15 minutes or up to 1 hour. Sprinkle with basil and cheese. Serve over lettuce leaves, if desired. Yield: 6 servings.

Per serving: Calories 75 (65% from fat); Fat 5.4g (sat 1.1g, mono 3.6g, poly 0.6g); Protein 2g; Carb 5.3g; Fiber 1.4g; Chol 2mg; Iron 0.5mg; Sodium 371mg; Calc 45mg

low carb • make ahead

Hot Tomato Salad

prep: 15 min. other: 4 hrs.

4   yellow banana peppers
2   green banana peppers
2   jalapeño peppers
4   to 5 large tomatoes
2   garlic cloves, minced
1   tablespoon chopped fresh basil
1   tablespoon chopped fresh parsley
1   teaspoon chopped fresh rosemary
1   teaspoon chopped fresh oregano
2   ounces smoked Cheddar cheese, cubed
½   cup olive oil
1   tablespoon lemon juice
1   teaspoon salt
½   teaspoon pepper
2   teaspoons sugar
Garnish: fresh basil sprig

Remove and discard seeds from peppers and tomatoes. Dice peppers and tomatoes; place in a large bowl. Add garlic, herbs, and cheese.

Stir together oil and next 4 ingredients; add to tomato mixture, tossing to coat. Cover and chill 2 to 4 hours. Serve with a slotted spoon. Garnish, if desired. Yield: 6 servings.

Per serving: Calories 244 (80% from fat); Fat 21.7g (sat 4.2g, mono 14.1g, poly 2.3g); Protein 4.3g; Carb 10.8g; Fiber 3.2g; Chol 10mg; Iron 1mg; Sodium 466mg; Calc 86mg

peppers dictionary

1. Poblano: These summer peppers have rich, zesty flavor. Their dried state is called *ancho*.

2. Anaheim: A slightly sweet chile with mild heat, the Anaheim pepper is often stuffed.

3. Jalapeño: These popular peppers are known for their fiery hot seeds and veins. *Chipotles* are the smoked, dried form.

4. Cubanelle: Enjoy these sweet peppers raw on a salad, or in any way you'd use bell pepper.

5. Hot cherry: Also called the *Hungarian cherry pepper,* cherry peppers are small, slightly rounded, bright red peppers that pack a medium punch.

6. Serrano: Serranos are small, spicy chiles.

7. Sweet mini: Miniature versions of bell peppers. Use interchangeably.

8. Yellow caribe: A hot yellow pepper, caribe chiles carry a sweetly spicy, intense flavor.

9.Hungarian wax: A pale yellow chile with a medium-hot flavor.

10. Red Fresno: Comparably spicy to the jalapeño, red Fresno chiles are short, cone-shaped chiles. Use them sparingly because their assertive flavor will surprise you.

11. Thai chiles: Also known as *bird chiles,* these intensely hot chiles are grades hotter than jalapeños.

12. Shishito: Only about two inches in length, the Japanese shishito chile is sweet and mild.

entrée salads

Meat and seafood salads are hearty enough to be a meal's main attraction. They include adequate amounts of protein to meet main-dish requirements, and the serving size is typically larger than other salads. Don't forget to give these salads time to chill for the flavors to mingle and blend.

low calorie • make ahead

Chicken Salad

prep: 9 min.   other: 1 hr.

Chicken salad is definitive comfort food. This version is colored with red and green grapes for a sweet touch.

3   cups chopped cooked chicken
1   cup thinly sliced celery
2   tablespoons lemon juice
1   tablespoon minced onion
½   cup mayonnaise
½   teaspoon salt
½   teaspoon pepper
½   cup seedless green grapes, halved lengthwise
½   cup seedless red grapes, halved lengthwise
1   (2.25-ounce) package sliced almonds, toasted
Bibb lettuce

Combine first 4 ingredients; cover and chill at least 1 hour.
Combine mayonnaise, salt, and pepper. Add mayonnaise mixture, grapes, and almonds to chilled chicken mixture; toss gently. Serve chicken salad in lettuce cups. Yield: 6 servings.

Per serving: Calories 329 (60% from fat); Fat 22.1g (sat 3.1g, mono 3.9g, poly 1.7g); Protein 24.3g; Carb 8.3g; Fiber 1.9g; Chol 66mg; Iron 1.5mg; Sodium 383mg; Calc 51mg

quick • test kitchen favorite

Honey Chicken Salad

prep: 20 min.

The mayonnaise-and-honey mixture that dresses this salad is reminiscent of poppy seed dressing. Reduce the amount of honey for a less sweet taste.

4   cups chopped cooked chicken
3   celery ribs, finely chopped (about 1½ cups)
1   cup sweetened dried cranberries
½   cup chopped pecans, toasted
1½   cups mayonnaise
⅓   cup orange-blossom honey
¼   teaspoon salt
¼   teaspoon pepper
Garnish: chopped toasted pecans

Stir together first 4 ingredients.
Whisk together mayonnaise and next 3 ingredients. Add to chicken mixture, stirring gently until combined. Garnish, if desired. Yield: 4 servings.

Per serving: Calories 1120 (66% from fat); Fat 82.2g (sat 11.4g, mono 7.9g, poly 4.5g); Protein 45.2g; Carb 51.7g; Fiber 3.9g; Chol 149mg; Iron 2.2mg; Sodium 827mg; Calc 55mg

quick

Sweet Peanut-Chicken Salad

prep: 30 min.

1   (8-ounce) can crushed pineapple, drained
¾   cup mayonnaise
1   teaspoon grated lime rind
1   tablespoon fresh lime juice
1½   teaspoons lite soy sauce
½   teaspoon pepper
2   cups coarsely chopped cooked chicken
1   small Granny Smith apple, chopped
½   cup chopped salted peanuts
1   head green leaf lettuce
1   fresh pineapple, peeled, cored, and cut into 1-inch pieces
2   oranges, cut into wedges
2   kiwifruit, peeled and sliced
2   cups red or green seedless grapes
2   tablespoons chopped salted peanuts

Stir together first 6 ingredients in a large bowl. Stir in chicken, apple, and ½ cup peanuts.
Arrange lettuce leaves on a large platter. Spoon chicken mixture in center of platter, and arrange pineapple and remaining fruit around platter. Sprinkle with 2 tablespoons chopped peanuts. Yield: 6 servings.

Per serving: Calories 531 (56% from fat); Fat 33.1g (sat 5.8g, mono 0.6g, poly 0.6g); Protein 20.9g; Carb 39.2g; Fiber 6.3g; Chol 50mg; Iron 1.8mg; Sodium 377mg; Calc 74mg

low fat

Chicken-and-Fruit Salad

prep: 40 min.   cook: 12 min.   other: 8 hrs.

¾   cup orange marmalade
3   tablespoons soy sauce
3   tablespoons lemon juice
1½   tablespoons chopped fresh ginger
6   skinned and boned chicken breasts
1   cored fresh pineapple
1   large jícama, peeled (optional)
Vegetable cooking spray
2   cups fresh strawberry halves
1   cup fresh raspberries
Orange-Raspberry Vinaigrette
Lettuce leaves

Combine first 4 ingredients; remove ¼ cup marmalade mixture, and chill.
Place chicken in a shallow dish or large zip-top freezer bag; pour remaining marmalade mixture over chicken. Cover or seal, and chill 8 hours, turning occasionally.
Cut pineapple into spears; cut jícama into ½-inch slices.
Place pineapple and jícama in a shallow dish or large zip-top freezer bag; pour ¼ cup reserved marmalade mixture over pineapple mixture. Cover or seal, and chill 8 hours.
Remove chicken from marinade, discarding marinade; drain pineapple mixture. Coat chicken and pineapple mixture with cooking spray.
Grill chicken, covered with grill lid, over medium-high heat (350° to 400°) 5 to 6 minutes on each side or until done. Grill pineapple and jícama 2 to 3 minutes on each side.

Cut chicken and jícama into thin strips; cut pineapple into bite-size pieces.

Combine chicken, jícama, pineapple, strawberry halves, and raspberries; toss gently with Orange-Raspberry Vinaigrette. Serve over lettuce leaves. Yield: 6 servings.

Per serving: Calories 355 (16% from fat); Fat 6.4g (sat 1g, mono 3.7g, poly 1g); Protein 27.6g; Carb 50.2g; Fiber 4.6g; Chol 64mg; Iron 1.8mg; Sodium 435mg; Calc 66mg

Orange-Raspberry Vinaigrette

prep: 10 min.

½ cup orange marmalade
¼ cup raspberry vinegar
1 medium jalapeño pepper, seeded and minced
2 tablespoons finely chopped fresh cilantro
2 tablespoons olive oil

Whisk together all ingredients in a small bowl. Yield: 1 cup.

Per tablespoon: Calories 40 (38% from fat); Fat 1.7g (sat 0.2g, mono 1.3g, poly 0.2g); Protein 0.1g; Carb 6.7g; Fiber 0.1g; Chol 0mg; Iron 0.1mg; Sodium 6mg; Calc 4mg

make ahead

Wild Rice–Chicken Salad

prep: 40 min.   other: 8 hrs.

2 (6.2-ounce) packages long-grain and wild rice mix
2 (6-ounce) jars marinated artichoke quarters, undrained
4 cups chopped cooked chicken
1 medium-size red bell pepper, chopped
2 celery ribs, thinly sliced
5 green onions, chopped
1 (2.25-ounce) can sliced ripe olives, drained
1 cup mayonnaise
1½ teaspoons curry powder
Leaf lettuce

Cook rice mix according to package directions.

Drain artichoke quarters, reserving ½ cup liquid. Stir together rice, artichoke, chicken, and next 4 ingredients.

Stir together artichoke liquid, mayonnaise, and curry powder; toss with rice mixture. Cover and chill 8 hours. Serve on leaf lettuce. Yield: 8 servings.

Per serving: Calories 548 (52% from fat); Fat 31.9g (sat 5.1g, mono 1.3g, poly 0.7g); Protein 27.3g; Carb 38.3g; Fiber 2.4g; Chol 70mg; Iron 2.7mg; Sodium 1017mg; Calc 61mg

Spicy Beef Salad

from the grill • low calorie • low fat

Spicy Beef Salad

prep: 15 min.   cook: 12 min.   other: 1 hr.

1 pint grape tomatoes, halved
1 large red onion, cut in half and thinly sliced
1 cucumber, seeded and diced
2 green onions, chopped
1 pound flank steak
1½ teaspoons salt, divided
2 teaspoons ground coriander, divided
2 small fresh Thai chile peppers or serrano peppers
1 stalk lemon grass, coarsely chopped*
2 garlic cloves
1 tablespoon chopped fresh ginger
2 tablespoons fresh lemon juice
1 tablespoon rice wine vinegar
¼ cup fish sauce
1 tablespoon vegetable oil
1 teaspoon sugar
Mixed salad greens
Garnish: sliced green onions

Combine first 4 ingredients; set aside.

Rub steak with ½ teaspoon salt and 1 teaspoon coriander.

Process remaining 1 teaspoon salt, remaining 1 teaspoon coriander, and next 9 ingredients in a food processor or blender until smooth. Cover and chill dressing 1 hour.

Grill steak, covered with grill lid, over medium-high heat (350° to 400°) 6 minutes on each side or to desired degree of doneness. Let stand 5 minutes. Thinly slice steak across the grain.

Place steak and vegetable mixture in a large bowl, and drizzle with dressing, tossing to coat. Serve over salad greens. Garnish, if desired. Yield: 6 servings.

Per serving: Calories 185 (39% from fat); Fat 8.1g (sat 2.6g, mono 3.3g, poly 1.4g); Protein 18.8g; Carb 10.2g; Fiber 2.9g; Chol 26mg; Iron 2.4mg; Sodium 1568mg; Calc 79mg

*Substitute 2 teaspoons grated lemon rind, if desired.

Taco Salad

prep: 15 min. cook: 10 min.

1   pound ground beef
2   garlic cloves, minced
1¾   cups taco sauce, divided
1   (1¼-ounce) envelope taco seasoning mix
1   (15¼-ounce) can Mexican-style whole kernel corn, drained
1   (15-ounce) can red kidney beans, drained
½   (9-ounce) package tortilla chips, coarsely crushed
1   medium head iceberg lettuce, shredded
2   cups (8 ounces) shredded Colby-Jack or Cheddar cheese
2   tomatoes, chopped
¾   cup sour cream

Cook ground beef and garlic in a large skillet, stirring until beef crumbles and is no longer pink; drain. Stir in 1 cup taco sauce and next 3 ingredients. Remove from heat, and cool slightly.

Layer half each of tortilla chips, meat mixture, lettuce, cheese, and tomato in a large serving bowl; repeat layers. Serve immediately with remaining ¾ cup taco sauce and sour cream. Yield: 6 servings.

Per serving: Calories 660 (55% from fat); Fat 40g (sat 18.7g, mono 11.7g, poly 1.6g); Protein 28.2g; Carb 43.6g; Fiber 9.3g; Chol 100mg; Iron 3mg; Sodium 1587mg; Calc 378mg

Old-Fashioned Layered Salad

prep: 15 min. other: 8 hrs.

1   cup mayonnaise
1   cup salad dressing (we tested with Miracle Whip)
1   tablespoon milk
1   teaspoon dry mustard
½   teaspoon salt
½   teaspoon pepper
1   head romaine or iceberg lettuce, coarsely chopped
2   cups (8 ounces) shredded Swiss cheese
1   (10-ounce) package frozen sweet peas, thawed
1   medium-size red onion, diced
6   hard-cooked eggs, chopped
1½   cups chopped smoked turkey or crumbled cooked bacon
1   large cucumber, seeded and chopped (optional)

Stir together first 6 ingredients.
Layer half each of lettuce, next 5 ingredients, and, if desired, cucumber in a bowl. Spread half of dressing over top; repeat layers. Cover and chill 8 hours. Yield: 8 servings.

Per serving: Calories 594 (75% from fat); Fat 49.2g (sat 11.1g, mono 1.7g, poly 0.9g); Protein 23.2g; Carb 13.8g; Fiber 2.9g; Chol 222mg; Iron 1.7mg; Sodium 670mg; Calc 350mg

Curried Shrimp Salad

prep: 30 min. cook: 5 min.

6   cups water
2   pounds unpeeled, medium-size fresh shrimp*
1   head iceberg lettuce, shredded
4   celery ribs, diced
4   green onions, diced
1¾   cups Curried Dressing
Toppings: toasted slivered almonds, toasted coconut, golden raisins, sliced green onions

Bring 6 cups water to a boil; add shrimp, and cook 3 to 5 minutes or just until shrimp turn pink. Drain shrimp and rinse with cold water.

Peel shrimp, and devein, if desired.
Combine lettuce, celery, and diced green onions, and place on a large platter. Arrange shrimp over lettuce. Chill, if desired.
Serve with Curried Dressing and desired toppings. Yield: 6 servings.

Per serving: Calories 502 (64% from fat); Fat 35.5g (sat 4.9g, mono 2.3g, poly 2.6g); Protein 25.3g; Carb 19.3g; Fiber 2g; Chol 237mg; Iron 4.6mg; Sodium 866mg; Calc 82mg

*Substitute 4 cups chopped cooked chicken for boiled shrimp, if desired.

Curried Dressing

prep: 5 min.

1   cup mayonnaise
½   cup hot mango chutney
2   teaspoons curry powder
2   tablespoons tarragon vinegar
2   tablespoons vegetable oil

Process all ingredients in a blender or food processor until smooth. Yield: about 1¾ cups.

Per tablespoon: Calories 79 (83% from fat); Fat 7.3g (sat 1g, mono 0.4g, poly 0.4g); Protein 0g; Carb 3.2g; Fiber 0.1g; Chol 3mg; Iron 0.1mg; Sodium 124mg; Calc 0.7mg

Salad Niçoise

prep: 20 min. cook: 18 min. other: 30 min.

2   pounds unpeeled small red potatoes
1½   pounds fresh green beans
Herb Dressing
2   heads romaine lettuce
6   (3-ounce) packages albacore tuna, flaked
1   (2-ounce) can anchovy fillets, drained (optional)
5   hard-cooked eggs, quartered
5   plum tomatoes, cut into wedges, or 1 (8-ounce) container grape tomatoes
1   cup sliced ripe olives

Cook potatoes in boiling water to cover 15 minutes or until tender; drain. Cool slightly; cut into slices. Set aside.
Cook green beans in boiling water to cover 3 minutes; drain. Plunge into ice water to stop the cooking process.
Toss together potato slices, green beans, and ½ cup Herb Dressing in a large bowl. Chill at least 30 minutes.
Tear 1 head romaine lettuce into bite-size pieces. Line a platter with leaves of remaining head of romaine. Arrange potato mixture over lettuce. Top with torn lettuce pieces.
Mound tuna in center of greens. Arrange anchovies around tuna, if desired. Place egg and tomato wedges on salad. Sprinkle with sliced olives. Serve with remaining Herb Dressing. Yield: 8 servings.

Per serving: Calories 534 (59% from fat); Fat 34.9g (sat 5.5g, mono 23.1g, poly 4.4g); Protein 25.3g; Carb 32.8g; Fiber 9.3g; Chol 159mg; Iron 5.7mg; Sodium 728mg; Calc 156mg

Herb Dressing

prep: 10 min.

1   cup olive oil
½   cup red wine vinegar
¼   cup drained capers
2   green onions, chopped
2   teaspoons dried basil
2   teaspoons dried marjoram
2   teaspoons dried oregano
2   teaspoons dried thyme
½   teaspoon dry mustard
½   teaspoon salt
½   teaspoon freshly ground pepper

Whisk all ingredients. Yield: 1½ cups.

Per tablespoon: Calories 82 (99% from fat); Fat 9.1g (sat 1.2g, mono 6.7g, poly 0.9g); Protein 0.1g; Carb 0.5g; Fiber 0.3g; Chol 0mg; Iron 0.4mg; Sodium 92mg; Calc 8mg

Sewee Preserve's Seafood Salad

prep: 20 min.   cook: 13 min.   other: 1 hr.

1   pound unpeeled, cooked medium-large fresh shrimp (about 24-30)
1   (1-pound) skinless flounder or grouper fillet
2   teaspoons olive oil
¼   teaspoon salt
¼   teaspoon pepper
1   pound fresh lump crabmeat, drained and picked
½   cup chopped red onion
¼   cup finely chopped dill pickle
2   tablespoons drained capers
Dill Vinaigrette
Watercress

Peel shrimp and devein, if desired; set aside. **Place** fillet on a lightly greased rack in a broiler pan. Brush fillet with olive oil, and sprinkle with salt and pepper. Broil 5½ inches from heat 10 to 13 minutes or until fish flakes with a fork. Remove from pan, and cool. **Break** cooled fish into large pieces, and place in a large bowl. Add shrimp, crabmeat, and next 3 ingredients; toss gently to combine. Drizzle with Dill Vinaigrette; toss gently to coat. Cover and chill at least 1 hour. Arrange seafood on watercress. Yield: 8 servings.

Per serving: Calories 221 (39% from fat); Fat 9.6g (sat 1.5g, mono 6.1g, poly 1.5g); Protein 29.8g; Carb 2.9g; Fiber 0.5g; Chol 155mg; Iron 2.2mg; Sodium 788mg; Calc 122mg

Dill Vinaigrette

prep: 10 min.

¼   cup red wine vinegar
¼   cup olive oil
2   tablespoons fresh lemon juice
2   tablespoons finely chopped sweet onion
2   tablespoons minced fresh dill
2   tablespoons minced dill pickle
2   teaspoons liquid from jarred capers
¾   teaspoon salt
¾   teaspoon coarsely ground black pepper
½   teaspoon sugar

Whisk together all ingredients. Cover and chill. Yield: ¾ cup.

Per tablespoon: Calories 43 (94% from fat); Fat 4.5g (sat 0.6g, mono 3.3g, poly 0.5g); Protein 0.1g; Carb 0.7g; Fiber 0.1g; Chol 0mg; Iron 0.1mg; Sodium 193mg; Calc 2mg

Chicken-and-Bow Tie Pasta Salad

prep: 15 min.

This recipe makes more dressing than you'll need for the pasta salad. Serve remaining dressing over salad greens or toss with left-over pasta salad; it'll continue to soak up flavors the longer it sits.

8   ounces bow tie pasta, cooked
2   cups shredded or chopped cooked chicken
1   medium-size green bell pepper, finely chopped
1   medium-size red bell pepper, finely chopped
½   cup crumbled feta cheese
1   celery rib, thinly sliced
30 kalamata olives, pitted
½   teaspoon salt
¼   teaspoon pepper
½   cup Pasta Salad Dressing
Garnish: fresh basil sprigs

Toss together first 10 ingredients; add more dressing as desired. Serve salad at room temperature or chilled. Garnish, if desired. Yield: 6 servings.

Per serving: Calories 395 (44% from fat); Fat 19.1g (sat 4.2g, mono 10.3g, poly 3.5g); Protein 22.2g; Carb 33.9g; Fiber 2.3g; Chol 51mg; Iron 2.3mg; Sodium 780mg; Calc 94mg

Pasta Salad Dressing

prep: 5 min.

¼   cup balsamic vinegar
¼   cup vegetable oil
¼   cup olive oil
1   tablespoon chopped fresh parsley
1   green onion, thinly sliced
1   garlic clove, minced
1   teaspoon lemon juice
½   teaspoon dried basil
½   teaspoon dried tarragon
½   teaspoon salt

Whisk together all ingredients in a small bowl until blended. Yield: 1 cup.

Per tablespoon: Calories 63 (99% from fat); Fat 6.9g (sat 0.8g, mono 4g, poly 1.8g); Protein 0.1g; Carb 0.8g; Fiber 0.1g; Chol 0mg; Iron 0.1mg; Sodium 74mg; Calc 4mg

Chicken-and-Bow Tie Pasta Salad

salad dressings

The dressing is a salad's key flavoring. It can tie together a blend of tender greens and fresh vegetables. Or, if the dressing is too salty, too oily, or too spicy, it can ruin a good salad. The amount of dressing is critical, too. Too much wilts the greens, and they'll be swimming in the salad bowl. When adding dressing, remember the drier the leaves, the better the dressing will cling.

Dressings can be broken down into four types: vinaigrettes, mayonnaise-based dressings, cooked dressings, and creamy dressings. A true vinaigrette is three parts oil to one part vinegar with added seasonings. Many vinaigrette recipes stray from these basic proportions and still provide great flavor. Creamy dressings often have yogurt, buttermilk, or sour cream as a base.

The best way to dress a salad is to drizzle a small amount of dressing over greens just before serving. Then toss lightly (ideally with your hands) to coat the greens and other ingredients, and serve the remaining dressing at the table. This way, each person can add the desired amount of dressing.

Store dressings in the refrigerator up to five days.

low carb • make ahead • quick

Green Goddess Dressing

prep: 10 min.

1⅓ cups mayonnaise
½   cup chopped fresh parsley
2   tablespoons chopped fresh chives
2   teaspoons Champagne vinegar or white wine vinegar
1   teaspoon anchovy paste
1   teaspoon grated lemon rind
2   tablespoons fresh lemon juice
¼   teaspoon pepper

Process all ingredients in a food processor until smooth, stopping to scrape down sides. Cover and chill. Yield: 1⅓ cups.

Per tablespoon: Calories 102 (97% from fat); Fat 11g (sat 1.5g, mono 0g, poly 0g); Protein 0.1g; Carb 0.3g; Fiber 0.1g; Chol 5mg; Iron 0.2mg; Sodium 123mg; Calc 4mg

family favorite • low carb • make ahead
quick

Thousand Island Dressing

prep: 15 min.

Thousand Island Dressing comes from ingredients that you probably have on hand. Try it on sandwiches and some vegetables.

1   cup mayonnaise
½   cup chili sauce
3   tablespoons chopped pimiento-stuffed olives
1   tablespoon chopped fresh parsley
1   tablespoon diced pimiento
1   tablespoon honey
½   teaspoon lemon juice
¼   teaspoon onion powder
12   capers

Combine mayonnaise and chili sauce; stir in olives and remaining ingredients. Cover and chill. Serve over salad greens. Yield: 1¾ cups.

Per tablespoon: Calories 66 (87% from fat); Fat 6.4g (sat 0.9g, mono 0.1g, poly 0g); Protein 0g; Carb 2.1g; Fiber 0g; Chol 3mg; Iron 0mg; Sodium 218mg; Calc 1mg

Russian Dressing: Omit olives and capers; add 1 teaspoon each prepared horseradish, paprika, and 1 tablespoon sugar.

quick

Tart Poppy Seed Dressing

prep: 5 min.

⅓   cup sugar
¼   cup white vinegar
1½   teaspoons chopped onion
¼   teaspoon paprika
¼   teaspoon Worcestershire sauce
½   cup vegetable oil
1   tablespoon poppy seeds

Process first 5 ingredients in a blender for 30 seconds. With blender running, pour oil through food chute in a slow, steady stream, and process until smooth. Stir in poppy seeds. Serve over fruit or greens. Yield: 1 cup.

Per tablespoon: Calories 79 (82% from fat); Fat 7.2g (sat 0.8g, mono 3g, poly 3.2g); Protein 0.1g; Carb 4.4g; Fiber 0.1g; Chol 0mg; Iron 0.1mg; Sodium 1mg; Calc 8mg

quick

Honey-Pecan Dressing

prep: 5 min.

3   tablespoons sugar
1   tablespoon chopped sweet onion
½   teaspoon dry mustard
¼   teaspoon salt
½   cup honey
¼   cup red wine vinegar
1   cup vegetable oil
1   cup chopped pecans, toasted

Pulse first 6 ingredients in a blender 2 or 3 times until blended. With blender running, pour oil through food chute in a slow, steady stream; process until smooth. Stir in pecans. Serve over fruit or salad greens. Yield: 2½ cups.

Per tablespoon: Calories 85 (83% from fat); Fat 7.8g (sat 0.8g, mono 3.6g, poly 3g); Protein 0.3g; Carb 4.9g; Fiber 0.3g; Chol 0mg; Iron 0.1mg; Sodium 15mg; Calc 3mg

low calorie • low carb • low cholesterol

Fresh Tomato Dressing

prep: 20 min.   other: 9 hrs.

Mix-and-match a variety of heirloom tomatoes, such as the sweet and fruity Sun Gold or Snow White with a more tart variety such as Green Zebra. Store dressing in refrigerator up to two weeks.

1   cup olive oil
½   cup balsamic vinegar
3   garlic cloves, sliced
1   tablespoon sugar
1   tablespoon salt
1   teaspoon pepper
4   large tomatoes, peeled and chopped
2   tablespoons fresh thyme leaves or 4 thyme sprigs

Whisk together first 6 ingredients in a large glass bowl. Stir in tomato and fresh thyme. Cover and let stand at room temperature 1 hour, stirring occasionally. Cover and chill 8 hours. Serve over salad greens. Yield: 4 cups.

Per tablespoon: Calories 34 (90% from fat); Fat 3.4g (sat 0.5g, mono 2.5g, poly 0.4g); Protein 0.1g; Carb 1g; Fiber 0.2g; Chol 0mg; Iron 0.1mg; Sodium 110mg; Calc 3mg

Lime-Peanut Dressing

prep: 10 min.

½ cup lime juice
4 garlic cloves, minced
3 tablespoons sugar
2 tablespoons finely chopped unsalted dry-roasted peanuts
1 tablespoon minced fresh ginger
1 tablespoon chopped fresh cilantro
2 tablespoons fish sauce

Stir together all ingredients until blended. Serve over vegetables. Yield: 1 cup.

Per tablespoon: Calories 20 (27% from fat); Fat 0.6g (sat 0.1g, mono 0.3g, poly 0.2g); Protein 0.5g; Carb 3.6g; Fiber 0.2g; Chol 0mg; Iron 0.1mg; Sodium 174mg; Calc 4mg

quick

Sweet-and-Sour Dressing

prep: 5 min.

⅓ cup sugar
2½ tablespoons white vinegar
1 tablespoon diced onion
¼ teaspoon salt
¼ teaspoon garlic salt
⅛ teaspoon pepper
½ cup vegetable oil

Pulse first 6 ingredients in a blender until smooth. With blender running, pour oil through food chute in a slow, steady stream; process until smooth. Yield: 1 cup.

Per tablespoon: Calories 76 (83% from fat); Fat 7g (sat 0.8g, mono 3g, poly 3g); Protein 0g; Carb 4.2g; Fiber 0g; Chol 0mg; Iron 0mg; Sodium 51mg; Calc 0mg

low carb • quick

Sesame Dressing

prep: 10 min.

¾ cup canola oil
½ cup rice vinegar
¼ cup sesame oil
1 tablespoon salt
1 tablespoon sugar
2 tablespoons grated orange rind
1 teaspoon pepper
1 teaspoon minced fresh ginger
1 teaspoon soy sauce
½ teaspoon minced garlic
¼ teaspoon dried crushed red pepper

Process all ingredients in a blender or food processor until smooth, stopping to scrape down sides. Serve over vegetables or salad greens. Yield: 1⅔ cups.

Per tablespoon: Calories 77 (98% from fat); Fat 8.4g (sat 0.7g, mono 4.5g, poly 2.7g); Protein 0g; Carb 0.7g; Fiber 0.1g; Chol 0mg; Iron 0mg; Sodium 278mg; Calc 1mg

low calorie • low carb • low cholesterol

Roasted Bell Pepper Vinaigrette

prep: 20 min.   cook: 10 min.   other: 10 min.

2 large red bell peppers
¼ cup red wine vinegar
¼ cup chopped fresh cilantro
2 garlic cloves
1 tablespoon sugar
½ teaspoon salt
½ teaspoon pepper
½ cup vegetable oil

Place bell peppers on an aluminum foil-lined baking sheet. Broil 5½ inches from heat 5 minutes on each side or until blistered.
Place bell peppers in a large zip-top freezer bag; seal and let stand 10 minutes to loosen skins. Peel bell peppers; discard seeds.
Process bell pepper, vinegar, and next 5 ingredients in a blender until smooth, stopping to scrape down sides. Turn on high; add oil in a slow, steady stream, and process until smooth. Serve over salad greens. Yield: about 1⅔ cups.

Per tablespoon: Calories 42 (92% from fat); Fat 4.3g (sat 0.5g, mono 1.8g, poly 1.8g); Protein 0.2g; Carb 1.3g; Fiber 0.3g; Chol 0mg; Iron 0.1mg; Sodium 44mg; Calc 2mg

low carb • quick

Dijon Vinaigrette

prep: 5 min.

Serve over salad greens, or use as a marinade for vegetables, chicken, or pork.

1 cup olive oil
½ cup cider vinegar
1 tablespoon Dijon mustard
1 teaspoon dried dill
½ teaspoon salt
¼ teaspoon sugar
¼ teaspoon pepper

Whisk together all ingredients. Cover and chill until ready to serve. Yield: 1½ cups.

Per tablespoon: Calories 81 (100% from fat); Fat 9g (sat 1.2g, mono 6.7g, poly 0.9g); Protein 0g; Carb 0.4g; Fiber 0g; Chol 0mg; Iron 0.1mg; Sodium 57mg; Calc 1mg

low carb • quick

Lemon Vinaigrette

prep: 5 min.

3 tablespoons fresh lemon juice
3 tablespoons white wine vinegar
1 tablespoon Dijon mustard
½ teaspoon sugar
¼ teaspoon salt
⅛ teaspoon freshly ground pepper
½ cup vegetable or olive oil

Whisk together first 6 ingredients in a small bowl; gradually whisk in oil until blended. Serve over salad greens, or use to marinate artichoke hearts or chicken. Yield: 1 cup.

Per tablespoon: Calories 62 (100% from fat); Fat 7.1g (sat 1g, mono 1.5g, poly 4.2g); Protein 0.1g; Carb 0.5g; Fiber 0g; Chol 0mg; Iron 0mg; Sodium 60mg; Calc 2mg

quick • test kitchen favorite

Balsamic Vinaigrette

prep: 5 min.

½ cup balsamic vinegar
3 tablespoons Dijon mustard
3 tablespoons honey
2 large garlic cloves, minced
2 small shallots, minced
¼ teaspoon salt
¼ teaspoon pepper
1 cup olive oil

Whisk together first 7 ingredients until blended. Gradually whisk in olive oil until blended. Serve over fruit or salad greens. Yield: 2 cups.

Per tablespoon: Calories 69 (89% from fat); Fat 6.8g (sat 0.9g, mono 5g, poly 0.7g); Protein 0.1g; Carb 2.5g; Fiber 0g; Chol 0mg; Iron 0.1mg; Sodium 38mg; Calc 2mg

sandwiches

Grilled Apple and Cheese Sandwiches

prep: 15 min.   cook: 3 min.

Try this yummy combination of sharp Cheddar, crisp-sweet apple, and olives.

1   cup (4 ounces) shredded sharp Cheddar cheese
1   cup finely chopped apple
⅓   cup minced pimiento-stuffed olives
¼   cup mayonnaise
8   slices white or whole wheat bread
2   tablespoons softened butter or margarine

Combine cheese, apple, olives, and mayonnaise in a bowl; stir well.
Spread cheese mixture evenly on 1 side of 4 slices of bread to within ¼ inch of edges. Top with remaining bread slices; brush top slices of bread with softened butter, and invert onto a hot griddle. Immediately brush other sides of sandwiches with softened butter; cook over medium heat until golden. Turn sandwiches, and brown other sides. Yield: 4 servings.

Per serving: Calories 508 (53% from fat); Fat 30g (sat 11.3g, mono 2.4g, poly 0.3g); Protein 16.3g; Carb 45.5g; Fiber 0.9g; Chol 45mg; Iron 1.7mg; Sodium 1062mg; Calc 290mg

Checkerboard Cheese Sandwiches

prep: 30 min.

You can also serve this cheesy filling as a dip with fresh veggies and crackers.

1   (10-ounce) block extra-sharp Cheddar cheese, shredded
1   (10-ounce) block Swiss cheese, shredded
1¼ cups light or regular mayonnaise
1   (4-ounce) jar diced pimiento, drained
1   teaspoon dried onion flakes
¼   teaspoon freshly ground pepper
20   thin white bread slices (we tested with Pepperidge Farm Very Thin White Bread)
20   thin wheat bread slices (we tested with Pepperidge Farm Very Thin Wheat Bread)
Garnishes: grape tomatoes and black olives, secured with wooden picks

Shown on previous page: Smoked Chicken and Fontina Panini (page 427)

Stir together first 6 ingredients. Spread half of mixture evenly on half of white bread slices; top with remaining half of white bread slices. Spread remaining half of mixture evenly on half of wheat bread slices; top with remaining half of wheat bread slices.
Remove crusts with a serrated knife; cut each sandwich into 4 squares. Arrange, stacked in pairs, on a serving plate in a checkerboard pattern, alternating white and wheat. Garnish, if desired. Yield: 80 mini sandwiches.

Per sandwich: Calories 67 (51% from fat); Fat 3.8g (sat 1.7g, mono 0.1g, poly 0.1g); Protein 2.6g; Carb 5.6g; Fiber 0.4g; Chol 8mg; Iron 0.4mg; Sodium 121mg; Calc 66mg

Egg Salad Club Sandwiches

prep: 25 min.

Substitute fresh arugula for the spinach if you prefer its spicy bite. If you want to serve only the salad, just omit the bread, spinach, and ⅓ cup mayonnaise.

⅔   cup mayonnaise, divided
4   large hard-cooked eggs, chopped
1   celery rib, diced
4   bacon slices, cooked and crumbled
¼   cup chopped fresh chives
1   tablespoon minced sweet onion
¼   teaspoon seasoned salt
½   teaspoon freshly ground pepper
12   thin white or wheat sandwich bread slices, lightly toasted (we tested with Pepperidge Farm Very Thin Bread)
1   cup firmly packed fresh spinach
Garnish: whole fresh chives

Stir together ⅓ cup mayonnaise and next 7 ingredients.
Spread remaining ⅓ cup mayonnaise evenly over 1 side of each bread slice. Spread 4 bread slices, mayonnaise side up, evenly with half of egg salad. Top evenly with half of spinach and 4 bread slices.
Repeat procedure with remaining egg salad, spinach, and bread slices. Cut each sandwich into quarters; garnish, if desired. Yield: 4 servings.

Per serving: Calories 498 (70% from fat); Fat 38.9g (sat 6.7g, mono 3.5g, poly 1.8g); Protein 12.6g; Carb 22.9g; Fiber 1.5g; Chol 233mg; Iron 2.3mg; Sodium 781mg; Calc 88mg

Floyd's Favorite Tomato Sandwich

prep: 10 min.   other: 8 hrs.

Large heirloom beefsteak varieties such as Red Brandywine and Aunt Ginny's Purple slice well for sandwiches and have a classic rich and juicy tomato flavor.

1   large ripe tomato, peeled
1   large onion
3   tablespoons mayonnaise
1   tablespoon prepared mustard
16   sandwich bread slices
⅛   teaspoon salt
⅛   teaspoon pepper

Cut tomato and onion into 8 (¼-inch-thick) slices each. Layer slices in a shallow dish; cover and chill 8 hours. Discard onion.
Stir together mayonnaise and mustard; spread on 1 side of each bread slice. Place 1 tomato slice on each of 8 bread slices; sprinkle lightly with salt and pepper. Top with remaining bread slices. Cover and chill up to 2 days. Yield: 8 sandwiches.

Per sandwich: Calories 265 (25% from fat); Fat 7.5g (sat 0.6g, mono 0.1g, poly 0.2g); Protein 10.2g; Carb 41.1g; Fiber 0.2g; Chol 2mg; Iron 1.6mg; Sodium 596mg; Calc 81mg

Open–Faced Summer Sandwiches

prep: 17 min.   cook: 24 min.

2   large tomatoes, cut into ½-inch-thick slices
1   teaspoon salt
½   teaspoon pepper
4   (¾-inch-thick) rustic bread slices
¼   cup olive oil, divided
2   large sweet onions, cut into ½-inch-thick slices
½   cup mayonnaise
3   tablespoons pesto
1   cup sliced kalamata or ripe olives
3   tablespoons thinly sliced fresh basil

Sprinkle tomato slices evenly with salt and pepper; set aside.
Brush both sides of bread slices with 3 tablespoons olive oil. Brush onion slices with remaining 1 tablespoon olive oil.

Grill bread, covered with grill lid, over medium-high heat (350° to 400°) 2 minutes on each side or until lightly browned. Grill onion, covered with grill lid, over medium-high heat (350° to 400°) 8 to 10 minutes on each side or until tender and browned.

Stir together mayonnaise and pesto; spread evenly on 1 side of each bread slice. Top evenly with tomato and onion slices; sprinkle with olives and basil. Yield: 4 servings.

Per serving: Calories 623 (74% from fat); Fat 51.4g (sat 7.4g, mono 20.1g, poly 2.9g); Protein 7.1g; Carb 33.4g; Fiber 3.5g; Chol 14mg; Iron 2.4mg; Sodium 1649mg; Calc 143mg

low calorie
The Grinder

prep: 8 min.   cook: 38 min.

The Grinder is a huge sandwich that's a cousin to the hoagie and hero. You may want to cut it in half to fit it in the oven easily.

1   green bell pepper, cut into rings
1   garlic clove, minced
3   tablespoons olive oil
½   teaspoon onion salt
½   pound thinly sliced ham
2   small tomatoes, thinly sliced
1   (14-ounce) loaf French bread, split horizontally
1½ teaspoons chopped fresh or ½ teaspoon dried oregano
Freshly ground pepper
8   ounces sliced mozzarella cheese

Sauté bell pepper and garlic in hot oil in a skillet until pepper is crisp-tender. Sprinkle with onion salt. Remove bell pepper, reserving olive oil mixture.
Layer ham, tomato, and bell pepper on bottom half of French bread. Drizzle olive oil mixture over bell pepper. Sprinkle with oregano and freshly ground pepper; top with cheese. Cover with top of bread.
Cut sandwich in half, if necessary; wrap in aluminum foil, and place on a baking sheet. Bake at 350° for 35 minutes or until cheese melts. Slice before serving. Yield: 6 servings.

Per serving: Calories 391 (40% from fat); Fat 17.5g (sat 5.9g, mono 7.5g, poly 1g); Protein 20.8g; Carb 37.1g; Fiber 2.5g; Chol 47mg; Iron 2.6mg; Sodium 1320mg; Calc 233mg

Italian Club Sandwich

Italian Club Sandwich

prep: 25 min.   cook: 6 min.

½   (16-ounce) Italian bread loaf
¼   cup Italian dressing
⅓   cup shredded Parmesan cheese
½   cup mayonnaise
½   cup mustard
½   pound thinly sliced Genoa salami
½   pound thinly sliced mortadella or bologna
4   (1-ounce) provolone cheese slices
Romaine lettuce leaves
3   plum tomatoes, sliced
8   bacon slices, cooked and cut in half

Cut bread diagonally into 12 (¼-inch-thick) slices; arrange on a baking sheet. Brush slices evenly with Italian dressing, and sprinkle with Parmesan cheese.
Bake at 375° for 5 to 6 minutes or until lightly toasted. Spread mayonnaise and mustard on untoasted sides of bread slices.
Layer 4 bread slices, mayonnaise side up, with salami, mortadella, and provolone.
Top with 4 bread slices, mayonnaise side up; layer with lettuce, tomato, and bacon.
Top with remaining 4 bread slices, mayonnaise side down. Cut sandwiches in half; secure with wooden picks, if desired. Yield: 4 servings.

Per serving: Calories 1039 (70% from fat); Fat 80.7g (sat 23.6g, mono 23.7g, poly 10.9g); Protein 40.8g; Carb 36.6g; Fiber 2.4g; Chol 140mg; Iron 3.9mg; Sodium 3050mg; Calc 375mg

make ahead • slow cooker
French Dip Sandwiches

prep: 5 min.   cook: 7 hrs.

Reserve the meat juices that gather from the long simmer to use for dipping the sandwiches.

1   (3½- to 4-pound) boneless chuck roast, trimmed
½   cup soy sauce
1   beef bouillon cube
1   bay leaf
3   to 4 peppercorns, crushed
1   teaspoon fresh or dried rosemary
1   teaspoon dried thyme
1   teaspoon garlic powder
12   French rolls, split

Place roast in a 5-quart slow cooker.
Combine soy sauce and next 6 ingredients; pour over roast. Add hot water to slow cooker until roast is almost covered.
Cover and cook on LOW 7 hours or until very tender. Remove and discard bay leaf; remove roast, reserving broth; shred roast with 2 forks. Place shredded meat evenly in rolls, and serve with reserved broth for dipping. Yield: 12 servings.

Per serving: Calories 459 (45% from fat); Fat 23.1g (sat 9.2g, mono 9.6g, poly 0.9g); Protein 30.7g; Carb 28.5g; Fiber 1.1g; Chol 90mg; Iron 4.8mg; Sodium 1243mg; Calc 13mg

Caramelized Onion BLT

prep: 8 min.   cook: 7 min.

Using premium bacon here, in tandem with caramelized onion, makes this sandwich a gourmet treat.

12	bacon slices
2	medium tomatoes
	Olive oil
8	sourdough bread slices
½	cup mayonnaise
1	tablespoon chopped fresh basil
4	curly leaf lettuce leaves
	Caramelized Onions
4	(½-ounce) Swiss cheese slices
	Salt and pepper to taste

Cook bacon in a large skillet until crisp; remove bacon, and drain on paper towels, reserving 1 tablespoon drippings for Caramelized Onions. Cut each tomato into 4 slices.

Brush 1 side of each bread slice lightly with olive oil. Grill bread 45 seconds or until toasted.

Stir together mayonnaise and basil; spread on 1 side of each bread slice. Top 4 bread slices with lettuce, 2 tomato slices, Caramelized Onions, cheese, and 3 bacon slices; sprinkle with salt and pepper to taste. Top with remaining bread slices. Yield: 4 servings.

Per serving: Calories 824 (52% from fat); Fat 47.7g (sat 14g, mono 8g, poly 2.4g); Protein 23.8g; Carb 75.2g; Fiber 5.5g; Chol 63mg; Iron 4mg; Sodium 1768mg; Calc 260mg

Caramelized Onion BLT

Caramelized Onions

prep: 5 min.   cook: 30 min.

2	tablespoons butter
1	tablespoon bacon drippings
2	sweet onions, sliced
½	teaspoon salt
¼	teaspoon freshly ground black pepper

Melt butter with bacon drippings in a skillet over medium heat. Add onion, salt, and pepper; cook 20 to 30 minutes or until caramelized, stirring often. Yield: about 1½ cups.

Per ¼ cup: Calories 69 (78% from fat); Fat 6g (sat 3.2g, mono 2g, poly 0.4g); Protein 0.5g; Carb 3.8g; Fiber 0.5g; Chol 12mg; Iron 0.1mg; Sodium 228mg; Calc 12mg

Grilled Chicken-and-Pesto Clubs

prep: 40 min.   cook: 20 min.   other: 10 min.

4	skinned and boned chicken breasts
½	teaspoon salt
½	teaspoon pepper
	Homemade Pesto* (page 435)
12	large whole wheat bread slices, toasted
1	(3-ounce) package goat cheese, crumbled
1	(5.2-ounce) jar roasted red bell peppers, drained and thinly sliced
4	plum tomatoes, sliced
8	bacon slices, cooked and cut in half
2	cups mixed salad greens

Sprinkle chicken with salt and pepper. Grill, covered with grill lid, over medium-high heat (350° to 400°) 10 minutes on each side or until chicken is done. Let stand 10 minutes; cut into ¼-inch-thick slices.

Spread Homemade Pesto evenly on 1 side of each bread slice.

Layer 4 bread slices, pesto side up, with chicken, goat cheese, and roasted bell pepper slices.

Top with 4 bread slices, pesto side up; layer with tomato, bacon, and salad greens. Top with remaining 4 bread slices, pesto side down.

Cut sandwiches into quarters, and secure with wooden picks. Yield: 4 servings.

Per serving: Calories 1007 (55% from fat); Fat 61.8g (sat 15.5g, mono 30.7g, poly 10.9g); Protein 68g; Carb 48.7g; Fiber 8g; Chol 144mg; Iron 6.9mg; Sodium 1702mg; Calc 438mg

*Substitute ¾ cup prepared pesto for homemade, if desired.

Spicy Coleslaw Reubens

prep: 15 min.   cook: 13 min.

1   (10-ounce) package finely shredded cabbage
4   green onions, sliced
1   teaspoon olive oil
½   cup Thousand Island dressing
3   tablespoons spicy brown mustard
12 sourdough sandwich bread slices
6   (1-ounce) Monterey Jack cheese with peppers slices
16 ounces thinly sliced corned beef

Sauté cabbage and green onions in hot oil in a large nonstick skillet over medium-high heat 3 to 5 minutes or until cabbage wilts. Remove from heat, and stir in dressing.
Spread mustard evenly on 1 side of 6 bread slices. Layer evenly with cheese slices, corned beef, and cabbage mixture. Top with remaining bread slices.
Cook sandwiches on a lightly greased nonstick griddle or skillet 3 to 4 minutes on each side or until golden. Yield: 6 servings.

Per serving: Calories 648 (34% from fat); Fat 24.4g (sat 9.7g, mono 3.8g, poly 4.8g); Protein 30.6g; Carb 75.6g; Fiber 6.3g; Chol 77mg; Iron 5.9mg; Sodium 2102mg; Calc 338mg

Kentucky Hot Browns

prep: 20 min. cook: 4 min.

8   thick white bread slices
1   pound roasted turkey slices
    Cheese Sauce
1   cup shredded Parmesan cheese
8   bacon slices, cooked
2   large tomatoes, sliced and halved

Trim crusts from bread slices; discard. Place bread on a baking sheet; broil 3 inches from heat until toasted, turning once.
Arrange 2 bread slices in each of 4 lightly greased individual baking dishes. Top bread with turkey. Pour hot Cheese Sauce over turkey, and sprinkle with Parmesan cheese.
Broil 5½ inches from heat 4 minutes or until bubbly and lightly browned; remove from oven. Top evenly with bacon and tomato. Serve immediately. Yield: 4 servings.

Per serving: Calories 828 (51% from fat); Fat 47.1g (sat 25.7g, mono 13g, poly 2.9g); Protein 50.8g; Carb 49.6g; Fiber 2.6g; Chol 157mg; Iron 3.9mg; Sodium 2556mg; Calc 712mg

Cheese Sauce

prep: 5 min.   cook: 8 min.

½   cup butter or margarine
⅓   cup all-purpose flour
3½ cups milk
½   cup shredded Parmesan cheese
¼   teaspoon salt
¼   teaspoon pepper

Melt butter in a 3-quart saucepan over medium-high heat. Whisk in flour, and cook, whisking constantly, 1 minute. Gradually whisk in milk.
Bring to a boil, and cook, whisking constantly, 1 to 2 minutes or until thickened. Whisk in cheese, salt, and pepper. Remove from heat. Yield: 4 cups.

Per tablespoon: Calories 26 (69% from fat); Fat 2g (sat 1.3g, mono 0.5g, poly 0.1g); Protein 0.8g; Carb 1.1g; Fiber 0g; Chol 6mg; Iron 0mg; Sodium 35mg; Calc 23mg

Barbecue Meat Loaf Sandwiches

prep: 10 min.   cook: 20 min.

In order to simplify this recipe, we baked our onion rings at 425° for 15 minutes, added the Texas toast to the baking sheet, and baked 5 more minutes.

1   (9.5-ounce) box frozen five-cheese Texas toast (we tested with Pepperidge Farm Five Cheese Texas Toast)
1   (8-ounce) box frozen onion rings (we tested with Ore-Ida Vidalia O's)
6   (1-inch-thick) cold meat loaf slices
½   cup barbecue sauce
1   cup prepared coleslaw

Cook Texas toast and onion rings according to package directions.
Spray a large nonstick skillet with cooking spray, and heat over medium-high heat.
Add meat loaf slices; cook 5 minutes. Turn, brush evenly with barbecue sauce, and cook 5 more minutes or until thoroughly heated.
Top each slice of toast evenly with meat loaf slices, coleslaw, and onion rings. Serve sandwiches immediately. Yield: 6 servings.

Per serving: Calories 510 (53% from fat); Fat 29.9g (sat 10.6g, mono 6.8g, poly 1.1g); Protein 22.3g; Carb 40g; Fiber 3.1g; Chol 104mg; Iron 4.1mg; Sodium 962mg; Calc 98mg

Meat Loaf Sandwich

prep: 23 min.   cook: 1 hr., 23 min.

Here's a weeknight sandwich the whole family will enjoy. Just add a tossed salad.

1   (16-ounce) Italian or sourdough bread loaf
2½   tablespoons butter or margarine, divided
1   small onion, chopped
½   (8-ounce) package sliced fresh mushrooms
1   large egg
6   to 7 tablespoons ketchup, divided
1½   cups (6 ounces) shredded Cheddar cheese, divided
1   pound lean ground beef
½   cup dry red wine or beef broth
1   teaspoon garlic salt
¼   teaspoon dried thyme
2   to 3 tablespoons mayonnaise

Cut bread loaf in half lengthwise. Scoop out bread, leaving ¼-inch-thick shells. Tear reserved bread into small pieces, and measure 1½ cups crumbs, reserving remaining bread pieces for another use. Set bread shells and 1½ cups breadcrumbs aside.
Melt 1½ tablespoons butter in a large skillet over medium heat; add chopped onion and mushrooms, and sauté 8 minutes or until tender.
Stir together egg and 2 tablespoons ketchup in a large bowl. Add onion mixture, 1½ cups breadcrumbs, ½ cup cheese, ground beef, and next 3 ingredients, blending well. Shape mixture into a loaf slightly smaller than reserved bread shell (about 10 inches long). Place loaf on a lightly greased rack in a roasting pan.
Bake at 350° for 1 hour or until done.
Spread bottom bread shell with mayonnaise; top with meat loaf. Top with remaining ketchup; sprinkle with remaining 1 cup cheese. Top with remaining bread half. Melt remaining 1 tablespoon butter; brush over bread top. Wrap in aluminum foil.
Bake at 350° for 10 to 15 minutes or until heated. Yield: 6 servings.

Per serving: Calories 575 (51% from fat); Fat 32.5g (sat 14.8g, mono 9.7g, poly 1.9g); Protein 29.2g; Carb 40.7g; Fiber 2.4g; Chol 131mg; Iron 4.3mg; Sodium 1031mg; Calc 282mg

Portobello
Mushroom
Burger

from the grill
Portobello Mushroom Burgers

prep: 20 min.   cook: 10 min.   other: 30 min.

1½   cups mesquite wood chips
⅓   cup olive oil
1   tablespoon minced garlic
1   medium-size red onion, cut into 6 slices
6   large portobello mushroom caps
6   hamburger buns, split
1   cup light mayonnaise
⅓   cup chopped fresh basil
2   tablespoons Dijon mustard
1   teaspoon lemon juice
½   teaspoon salt
½   teaspoon pepper
6   romaine lettuce leaves
2   tomatoes, cut into 6 slices each

Soak wood chips in water at least 30 minutes; drain.
Prepare a charcoal fire on grill; scatter wood chips over hot coals.
Whisk together oil and garlic; brush on both sides of onion and mushrooms.
Grill onion slices and mushroom caps, covered with grill lid, over medium-high heat

(350° to 400°) 4 minutes on each side or until tender. Grill bun halves, cut sides down, 2 minutes or until lightly toasted.
Stir together mayonnaise and next 5 ingredients. Layer 6 bottom bun halves with lettuce, onion, mushrooms, mayonnaise mixture, and 2 tomato slices; top with remaining bun halves. Yield: 6 servings.

Per serving: Calories 412 (61% from fat); Fat 27.7g (sat 4.8g, mono 9.4g, poly 2.1g); Protein 6.9g; Carb 32.8g; Fiber 3.3g; Chol 13mg; Iron 2.4mg; Sodium 794mg; Calc 82mg

family favorite • from the grill
Big Juicy Burgers

prep: 20 min.   cook: 18 min.

2   (6-ounce) cans vegetable juice
3   white sandwich bread slices, torn into pieces
3   pounds ground chuck
1   large egg
1½   teaspoons salt
1   teaspoon pepper
10   hamburger buns

Microwave vegetable juice in a glass bowl at HIGH 1 minute; add sandwich bread

pieces, and let cool. Combine with hands.
Combine vegetable juice mixture, ground chuck, and next 3 ingredients. Shape into 10 patties.
Grill patties, covered with grill lid, over medium-high heat (350° to 400°) 6 to 8 minutes on each side or until beef is no longer pink.
Spray cut sides of buns with cooking spray; place buns, cut sides down, on grill rack, and grill 1 to 2 minutes or until lightly browned. Serve hamburgers on buns. Yield: 10 servings.

Per serving: Calories 500 (54% from fat); Fat 29.8g (sat 11.1g, mono 12.6g, poly 1.7g); Protein 29g; Carb 26.6g; Fiber 1.4g; Chol 118mg; Iron 4.6mg; Sodium 791mg; Calc 105mg

for kids
Corn Dogs and Taters

prep: 10 min.   cook: 5 min. per batch

16   (8-inch) wooden sticks
8   hot dogs
2   baking potatoes, cut into ½-inch cubes (about ¾ pound)
¾   cup all-purpose flour
½   teaspoon baking powder
½   teaspoon salt
1   large egg
½   cup milk
1   tablespoon vegetable oil
Peanut oil

Insert a stick into each hot dog, leaving about a 3-inch handle; set aside.
Thread potatoes onto remaining sticks. Whisk together flour and next 5 ingredients; pour into a tall glass.
Pour peanut oil to a depth of 1½ inches into a large skillet; heat to 350°.
Dip hot dogs into batter, covering well.
Fry hot dogs and potatoes, in batches, 4 to 5 minutes or until golden. Serve with mustard or ketchup, if desired. Yield: 8 servings.

Per serving: Calories 395 (69% from fat); Fat 30.2g (sat 9g, mono 13.9g, poly 5.7g); Protein 13.1g; Carb 17.6g; Fiber 1.1g; Chol 78mg; Iron 3.8mg; Sodium 814mg; Calc 245mg

Note: Substitute 1 (8-ounce) package hush puppy mix and ¾ cup milk or 1 (8½-ounce) package corn muffin mix, 1 large egg, and ⅓ cup milk for homemade batter, if desired.

White Bean–and–Tuna Salad Sandwiches

prep: 11 min.   other: 1 hr.

1   (15.5-ounce) can cannellini beans or navy beans, rinsed and drained
1   (12-ounce) can solid white tuna in spring water, drained and flaked
6   bacon slices, cooked and crumbled
2   plum tomatoes, seeded and chopped
¼   cup chopped red onion
¼   cup mayonnaise
3   tablespoons fresh lemon juice
2   tablespoons chopped fresh chives
2   teaspoons Dijon mustard
1   teaspoon minced fresh dill
¼   teaspoon freshly ground black pepper
16 sourdough bread slices, toasted
Curly leaf lettuce

Combine first 11 ingredients in a large bowl; cover and chill 1 hour. Line 8 bread slices with lettuce, and top each with ½ cup tuna salad. Cover with remaining bread slices. Yield: 8 servings.

Per serving: Calories 502 (22% from fat); Fat 12.5g (sat 2.5g, mono 2.7g, poly 1.6g); Protein 21.8g; Carb 73.7g; Fiber 5.8g; Chol 20mg; Iron 4.3mg; Sodium 1109mg; Calc 119mg

make ahead • test kitchen favorite

Shrimp Burgers

prep: 16 min.   cook: 14 min.   other: 2 hrs.

If you like crab cakes, you'll enjoy shrimp prepared in similar fashion for a sandwich. Finely chopping the shrimp and chilling the patties for at least two hours will help them stay together when cooking.

1   pound unpeeled, medium-size fresh shrimp, cooked
¼   cup chopped green onions
¼   cup chopped fresh flat-leaf parsley
1½ teaspoons grated lemon rind
1¼ cups cornbread crumbs
3   tablespoons mayonnaise
1   large egg, beaten
½   teaspoon salt
½   teaspoon pepper
3   tablespoons canola oil
6   hamburger buns, toasted
Toppings: shredded lettuce, tomato slices, tartar sauce (optional)

Peel shrimp, and devein, if desired; finely chop. Combine shrimp and next 3 ingredients in a large bowl. Add cornbread crumbs and next 4 ingredients, stirring until blended.
Shape shrimp mixture into 6 patties. Place patties on a wax paper–lined baking sheet; cover and chill at least 2 hours.
Heat oil in a large nonstick skillet over medium heat. Cook shrimp patties 6 to 7 minutes on each side or until golden. Drain on paper towels. Serve shrimp burgers on hamburger buns with desired toppings. Yield: 6 servings.

Per serving: Calories 435 (41% from fat); Fat 20g (sat 3.3g, mono 7.2g, poly 3.8g); Protein 20.3g; Carb 42.1g; Fiber 2.3g; Chol 175mg; Iron 4.4mg; Sodium 912mg; Calc 125mg

family favorite

Dressed Mini Oyster Po'boys

prep: 19 min.   cook: 16 min.

Serve two of these mini sandwiches for a meal or make them part of an appetizer buffet.

1¼ cups self-rising cornmeal mix
2   tablespoons Creole seasoning
1   (16-ounce) container fresh Select oysters, drained
Peanut or vegetable oil
1   cup mayonnaise, divided
2   tablespoons white vinegar
2   tablespoons Dijon mustard
1   (10-ounce) package finely shredded cabbage
2   tablespoons ketchup
1   tablespoon prepared horseradish
1   teaspoon Creole seasoning
¾   teaspoon paprika
12 (1.4-ounce) French rolls, split and toasted
Garnish: lemon wedges

Combine cornmeal mix and 2 tablespoons Creole seasoning. Dredge oysters in cornmeal mixture.
Pour oil to a depth of 1 inch into a Dutch oven; heat to 375°. Fry oysters, in 4 batches, 3 to 4 minutes or until golden. Drain oysters on paper towels.
Stir together ½ cup mayonnaise, vinegar, and mustard. Stir in shredded cabbage, and set slaw aside.
Stir together remaining ½ cup mayonnaise, ketchup, and next 3 ingredients in a bowl.

Spread cut sides of French bread rolls with ketchup mixture. Place oysters and slaw evenly on bottom halves of each roll. Cover with tops. Serve po'boys immediately. Garnish, if desired. Yield: 6 servings.

Per serving: Calories 830 (58% from fat); Fat 53.6g (sat 8.3g, mono 10.3g, poly 7.3g); Protein 14.9g; Carb 74.9g; Fiber 5.4g; Chol 30mg; Iron 7.6mg; Sodium 2031mg; Calc 239mg

family favorite • make ahead

Shrimp Rolls

prep: 27 min.   cook: 15 min.   other: 2 hrs.

These are a delicious Southern twist on New England's lobster rolls.

3   quarts water
1   (3-ounce) package crab and shrimp boil seasoning
2   pounds unpeeled, large fresh shrimp
⅓   cup mayonnaise
1   small onion, finely chopped
2   celery ribs, finely chopped
2   tablespoons lemon juice
½   teaspoon salt
¼   teaspoon seasoned pepper
3   tablespoons butter, softened
1   garlic clove, minced
8   French rolls, split
8   green leaf lettuce leaves
2   avocados, thinly sliced

Bring 3 quarts water and crab seasoning to a boil in a Dutch oven; add shrimp, and cook, stirring occasionally, 3 to 5 minutes or just until shrimp turn pink. Drain and cool.
Peel cooked shrimp, and devein, if desired; coarsely chop shrimp.
Stir together mayonnaise and next 5 ingredients in a large bowl; stir in shrimp. Chill 2 hours.
Stir together butter and garlic; spread evenly on cut side of bread halves. Bake at 375° for 10 minutes or until toasted.
Line each roll with a lettuce leaf; spoon shrimp mixture evenly on each roll. Top with avocado slices; cover with tops. Yield: 8 servings.

Per serving: Calories 516 (37% from fat); Fat 21.2g (sat 5.2g, mono 6.1g, poly 1.5g); Protein 27.8g; Carb 51.4g; Fiber 4.7g; Chol 183mg; Iron 6.3mg; Sodium 812mg; Calc 51mg

taste of the south muffulettas

Take a bite of a well-prepared muffuletta, and you'll know why these large, round sandwiches remain enduring standards of the New Orleans food scene. Filled with layers of salami, ham, cheese, and olive salad, muffulettas are cold-cut competitors of the po'boy. The flavors are bold, and the servings are generous.

Who created the muffuletta is a matter still debated, but historian and food critic Gene Bourg uncovered a likely scenario. He interviewed elderly Sicilians who lived in the French Quarter for many years. "They told me vendors used to sell them on the streets, as did Italian groceries," he says. "The name refers to the shape of the bread. 'Muffuletta' means 'little muffin.' Italian bakers made muffuletta loaves and sold them to Italian delis. The delis then wrapped the sandwiches in the same paper the bread came in, so the sandwich took on the name."

make ahead · quick
Muffuletta

prep: 10 min.

1 (10-inch) round Italian bread loaf
2 cups Olive Salad
½ pound sliced hard salami
½ pound sliced cooked ham
6 Swiss cheese slices
6 thin provolone cheese slices

Cut bread loaf in half horizontally.
Spoon 1 cup Olive Salad onto bottom bread shell; top with salami, ham, cheeses, and remaining 1 cup Olive Salad. Cover with bread top, press gently, and cut crosswise into wedges or quarters. Yield: 4 servings.

Per serving: Calories 1228 (43% from fat); Fat 58.4g (sat 23.1g, mono 25.7g, poly 6.4g); Protein 64.3g; Carb 110.7g; Fiber 7.8g; Chol 143mg; Iron 8.5mg; Sodium 4114mg; Calc 868mg

Olive Salad

prep: 15 min. other: 8 hrs.

1 (1-quart) jar mixed pickled vegetables
1 red onion, quartered
1 (16-ounce) jar pitted green olives, drained
1 (6-ounce) can medium-size pitted ripe olives, drained
¼ cup sliced pepperoncini salad peppers
2 tablespoons capers
1 tablespoon minced garlic
½ cup olive oil
1½ teaspoons dried parsley flakes
1 teaspoon dried oregano
1 teaspoon dried basil
½ teaspoon ground black pepper
1 (7.25-ounce) jar roasted red bell peppers, drained and coarsely chopped (optional)

Drain pickled vegetables, reserving ¼ cup liquid.
Pulse pickled vegetables 4 times in a food processor or until coarsely chopped; pour into a large bowl. Pulse onion 4 times in food processor or until coarsely chopped; add to pickled vegetables in bowl. Pulse olives and salad peppers in food processor 4 times or until coarsely chopped; add to vegetable mixture. Stir in capers, next 6 ingredients, reserved ¼ cup pickled vegetable liquid, and, if desired, chopped bell peppers. Cover and chill 8 hours. Cover and chill leftover salad up to 2 weeks. Yield: 6 cups.

Per tablespoon: Calories 18 (85% from fat); Fat 1.7g (sat 0.2g, mono 1.3g, poly 0.2g); Protein 0.1g; Carb 0.8g; Fiber 0.3g; Chol 0mg; Iron 0.1mg; Sodium 81mg; Calc 5mg

Note: We used mixed pickled vegetables that contained cauliflower, onions, carrots, peppers, and celery.

Turkey, Bacon, and Havarti Sandwich

make ahead
Turkey, Bacon, and Havarti Sandwich

prep: 20 min. other: 1 hr.

1 (7-inch) round sourdough bread loaf
¼ cup balsamic vinaigrette
½ pound thinly sliced smoked deli turkey
1 (12-ounce) jar roasted red bell peppers, drained and sliced
6 (1-ounce) slices Havarti cheese
4 fully cooked bacon slices
Garnish: dill pickle spears

Cut off top 2 inches of sourdough loaf, reserving top; hollow out loaf, leaving a 1-inch-thick shell. (Reserve soft center of bread loaf for other uses, if desired.)
Drizzle 2 tablespoons vinaigrette in bread shell; layer with half each of turkey, peppers, and cheese. Repeat layers, and top with bacon. Drizzle with remaining 2 tablespoons vinaigrette, and cover with reserved bread top; press down firmly. Wrap in plastic wrap, and chill at least 1 hour or up to 8 hours before serving. Cut into 4 wedges. Garnish, if desired. Yield: 4 servings.

Per serving: Calories 547 (44% from fat); Fat 26.7g (sat 12.5g, mono 2.1g, poly 0.8g); Protein 31.4g; Carb 44.3g; Fiber 2.3g; Chol 85mg; Iron 2.4mg; Sodium 1732mg; Calc 286mg

hot off the press

Quick and easy to make, grilled sandwiches are big on flavor. The popular Italian-style sandwiches known as panini are prepared in a special grill press that eliminates the need for turning. The top and bottom heating units cook sandwiches quickly and evenly, compressing and searing the bread to create distinctive ridges. Floating hinges on the press accommodate thick-sliced breads.

quick
Smoked Chicken and Fontina Panini

prep: 7 min.   cook: 4 min.

Pick up a smoked chicken from the deli or your local barbecue joint, or use rotisserie chicken for this sandwich. (pictured on page 419)

1   (8-ounce) loaf ciabatta bread, cut in half lengthwise
3   tablespoons jarred pesto
2   plum tomatoes, sliced
1   cup shredded smoked chicken
2   ounces fontina cheese, sliced

Preheat panini press according to manufacturer's instructions.
Spread bottom half of bread with pesto. Top with tomatoes, chicken, and cheese. Top with bread.
Place sandwich in panini press; cook 3 to 4 minutes or until cheese melts and bread is toasted. Cut in half, and serve hot. Yield: 2 servings.

Per serving: Calories 702 (41% from fat); Fat 32.2g (sat 11.1g, mono 15.7g, poly 3.5g); Protein 40.1g; Carb 66.1g; Fiber 3.4g; Chol 107mg; Iron 5.5mg; Sodium 1246mg; Calc 336mg

quick
Tangy Roast Beef Wraps

prep: 15 min.

¼   cup Dijon mustard
¼   cup pineapple preserves
2   tablespoons prepared horseradish
4   (9-inch) wheat wraps (we tested with Toufayan Bakeries Wheat Wraps)
½   pound thinly sliced deli roast beef
4   green leaf lettuce leaves
1   (8-ounce) package Cheddar cheese slices
¼   cup chopped walnuts, toasted
2   tablespoons sliced green onions

Stir together first 3 ingredients. Spread mixture on wraps. Layer each wrap with roast beef, lettuce, and cheese slices; sprinkle each with nuts and green onions. Roll up tightly. Cut in half diagonally. Yield: 4 servings.

Per serving: Calories 588 (47% from fat); Fat 30.7g (sat 14.6g, mono 6.7g, poly 3.5g); Protein 32.4g; Carb 47.7g; Fiber 2.7g; Chol 83mg; Iron 3.4mg; Sodium 1510mg; Calc 477mg

quick • vegetarian
Mediterranean Wrap

prep: 25 min.

¼   cup garlic-and-herb spreadable cheese or softened cream cheese (we tested with Alouette)
4   (9-inch) tomato-basil or spinach wraps or tortillas (we tested with Toufayan Bakeries Wraps)
3   cups chopped fresh baby spinach
2   small ripe avocados, sliced
4   ounces crumbled feta cheese
1   cup chopped plum tomato
½   cup sliced black olives
¼   cup red wine vinaigrette (we tested with Brianna's Blush Wine Vinaigrette)
12   fresh basil leaves

Spread 1 tablespoon cheese over 1 side of each tortilla. Divide baby spinach and remaining ingredients among tortillas; roll up each tortilla. Cut each wrap in half diagonally. Yield: 4 servings.

Per serving: Calories 499 (55% from fat); Fat 30.3g (sat 9.8g, mono 8.8g, poly 1.7g); Protein 13.5g; Carb 47.6g; Fiber 6.8g; Chol 38mg; Iron 4.2mg; Sodium 1331mg; Calc 251mg

quick
Club Wraps

prep: 25 min.

½   cup creamy mustard-mayonnaise blend
4   (10-inch) flour tortillas
½   pound thinly sliced smoked turkey
½   pound thinly sliced honey ham
1   cup (4 ounces) shredded smoked provolone or mozzarella cheese
2   cups shredded leaf lettuce
2   medium tomatoes, seeded and chopped
½   small red onion, diced
8   bacon slices, cooked and crumbled
½   teaspoon salt
½   teaspoon pepper

Spread mustard–mayonnaise blend evenly over 1 side of each tortilla, leaving a ½-inch border.
Layer turkey and next 6 ingredients evenly over tortillas; sprinkle with salt and pepper.
Roll up tortillas; cut in half diagonally, and secure with wooden picks. Yield: 4 servings.

Per serving: Calories 624 (44% from fat); Fat 30.5g (sat 8.1g, mono 3.1g, poly 1.8g); Protein 43g; Carb 39.4g; Fiber 7.7g; Chol 84mg; Iron 2.2mg; Sodium 2154mg; Calc 227mg

Club Wraps

grilling tips and tidbits

• If you don't have a panini press, place sandwiches in a hot skillet, and press gently with a smaller heavy pan or clean brick wrapped in aluminum foil. Grill sandwiches over medium to low heat rather than high heat so the bread doesn't burn before the cheese melts.
• For a super-crisp crust, lightly coat bread with vegetable cooking spray or brush with a mixture of melted butter and olive oil before grilling.
• Pantry items such as roasted red bell peppers, green chiles, artichoke hearts, and olives are all delicious additions to grilled sandwiches.

sauces & condiments

sauces

Equipment

Sauce recipes often have short ingredient lists, but they require a few key tools to produce the proper results. A top-quality 1½- to 3-quart heavy saucepan is a worthwhile investment. For many basic sauces you'll need a straight-sided or sloping-sided saucepan. Consider investing in one made of heavy copper or copper-bottomed stainless steel with iron handles, not brass; brass handles get too hot too fast. Saucepans with sloping sides are excellent for reducing or cooking down sauces to concentrate their flavor; they allow sauces to boil down quickly, and the slanted sides facilitate whisking and stirring. Avoid aluminum saucepans, which may react with some ingredients and cause an off flavor or color.

Many sauces such as Hollandaise Sauce (page 432) are egg-based and require a double boiler to prevent curdling.

One utensil that you'll use repeatedly in sauce making is an elongated wire whisk. A whisk is essential for making emulsified sauces like hollandaise. There are several sizes of whisks to choose from in kitchen shops. A medium-size stainless steel whisk is a good all-purpose choice. Serious cooks will collect small, medium, and large whisks as well as a balloon whisk, which is used mainly for beating egg whites.

You'll need spatulas and wooden spoons, and occasionally a ladle, strainer, or sieve. A fat separator will come in handy for gravy making. It's a glass or plastic pitcher with a spout attached to the base. Fat floats to the top of the pitcher and liquid is then poured off from the bottom.

You'll find that a food processor is your best tool for chopping ingredients for condiments like Chowchow (page 446), a blend of several vegetables.

Sauce Basics

The base of many sauces is a fat and flour mixture called a roux. A roux has several color stages that are each used for different types of sauces and soups. A white roux cooks about 1 minute and is the beginning of the versatile White Sauce (facing page). This brief cooking time is just long enough to release the starch from the flour and eliminate a raw flour taste. This type of sauce takes approximately 2 tablespoons flour to thicken 1 cup liquid. (See page 490 for more discussion on the rich brown roux that cooks in 20 to 30 minutes and develops a nutty flavor that's the trademark of a good gumbo.) Sauces made with a roux need constant stirring as they cook to prevent lumping.

Cornstarch is a thickening agent commonly used for sauces. It has twice the thickening power of flour; 1 tablespoon cornstarch will thicken 1 cup liquid. Sauces thickened with cornstarch have a transparent look; that's why it's often used for fruit dessert sauces.

Never add cornstarch (or flour) directly to a hot mixture because it will lump. Instead, combine it with a cold liquid, and

Shown on previous page: Homemade Pesto (page 435)

stir until smooth. Then gradually stir the cold mixture into the hot mixture. Cook, stirring gently, until it comes to a full boil. Boil for 1 minute. It takes only a short time for the starch granules to swell, absorb some of the liquid, and thicken the sauce.

Don't think that the longer you cook a cornstarch mixture, the thicker it will become. Overcooking can cause the sauce to break down and be runny. Remember that some sauces may look thin while they're cooking but will thicken as they cool.

If you're making a sauce with an acidic ingredient like lemon juice, first cook the cornstarch mixture until thickened. Then remove it from heat and gently stir in the acid component. If you cook an acid in a sauce, it negates the thickening power and results in a runny sauce.

Eggs are another thickening agent for sauces. They lend luscious consistency to classic French sauces like hollandaise and béarnaise. Keep in mind that thickening with eggs can be touchy. Handle eggs carefully over heat to prevent curdling. Don't overcook eggs or use heat that's too high. The gentle heat of a double boiler keeps this from happening. Always heat egg mixtures slowly and stir constantly.

When a recipe requires adding eggs to a hot mixture, use a technique called tempering to prevent curdling or lumping. First, beat eggs slightly; then warm them by gradually stirring in one-fourth of the hot mixture. Next, stir the tempered egg mixture into the remaining hot mixture. Cook, stirring constantly, until sauce is thickened.

A reduction is a technique of simmering a sauce to concentrate its flavor and reduce its yield. And, in so doing, the sauce naturally becomes thicker and syrupy. This happens quickest when you use a large skillet rather than a saucepan because a skillet has more surface area.

Freezing Sauces

Many sauces have such small yields that they're eaten entirely at one meal. When you do have a little left over, remember that most flour-based and tomato-based sauces freeze best. Pack them in rigid plastic containers, leaving ½ inch headspace. Thaw sauces in refrigerator or over low heat in a heavy saucepan, stirring often.

What Went Wrong

You can often rectify a lumpy sauce by vigorously whisking or by pouring the sauce through a fine wire-mesh sieve. Thin the consistency of an overly thick sauce by gradually adding milk, 1 tablespoon at a time, as the sauce cooks. If too thin, blend additional flour and milk or water together and add to the sauce, cooking and stirring until thickened.

To rescue a curdled hollandaise or béarnaise sauce, combine a teaspoon of lemon juice and a tablespoon of curdled sauce. Beat with a wire whisk until mixture is thick and creamy. Gradually beat in remaining sauce, 1 tablespoon at a time, making sure each addition has thickened before adding the next.

savory sauces

White Sauce, Basic Brown Sauce, and Hollandaise Sauce are three of the classic "mother sauces." White Sauce on its own is mild in flavor, but offers endless possibilities for variation and is the basis for many creamy casseroles and soups as well.

Rich emulsions of hollandaise and béarnaise are close cousins of mayonnaise, except they're served hot. These egg-enriched sauces pair well with brunch egg dishes and beef entrées. Use a double boiler for gentle simmering and never let water in the bottom of the boiler touch the insert. With the addition of herbs and wine, Basic Brown Sauce becomes bordelaise, which dresses up a good steak. Conquer these basic sauces, and you'll gain confidence for pesto, marinara, and a host of other options.

low calorie • low carb • quick

White Sauce

prep: 2 min.   cook: 4 min.

2   tablespoons butter or margarine
2   tablespoons all-purpose flour
1   cup milk
¼   teaspoon salt
Dash of ground white pepper

Melt butter in a heavy saucepan over low heat; add flour, stirring until smooth. Cook 1 minute, stirring constantly.
Gradually add milk; cook over medium heat, stirring constantly, until thickened. Stir in salt and pepper.
Serve over poached eggs, poultry, seafood, or vegetables. Yield: 1 cup.

Per tablespoon: Calories 25 (68% from fat); Fat 1.9g (sat 1.2g, mono 0.5g, poly 0.1g); Protein0.6g; Carb 1.4g; Fiber 0g; Chol 5mg; Iron 0.1mg; Sodium 53mg; Calc 18mg

Note: For thin White Sauce, decrease butter and flour each to 1 tablespoon. For thick White Sauce, increase butter and flour each to 3 tablespoons.

Microwave Directions: Place butter in a 4-cup liquid measuring cup. Microwave at HIGH 45 seconds or until melted. Add flour, stirring until smooth. Gradually add milk, and stir well. Microwave at HIGH 3 to 4 minutes or until thickened and bubbly, stirring after 2 minutes, and then at 1-minute intervals. Stir in salt and pepper.

Velouté Sauce: Substitute 1 cup chicken, beef, or fish broth for milk.

Cheddar Cheese Sauce: Stir in 1 cup (4 ounces) shredded Cheddar cheese and ¼ teaspoon dry mustard with salt and pepper.

low calorie • low carb • low fat • quick

Basic Brown Sauce

prep: 4 min.   cook: 5 min.

4   thin slices onion
1½   tablespoons butter or margarine, melted
1½   tablespoons all-purpose flour
1   teaspoon beef bouillon granules
1   cup water
⅛   teaspoon pepper

making a white sauce

1. Melt butter in a heavy saucepan over low heat; add flour, and stir until smooth.

2. Gradually add milk to "white roux," stirring constantly.

3. Cook, stirring constantly, until thickened and bubbly. Add salt and pepper.

Sauté onion in butter in a heavy skillet until onion is tender; discard onion. Cook butter over low heat until it begins to brown. Add flour, stirring until smooth. Cook 1 minute, stirring constantly. Add bouillon granules, and gradually stir in water. Cook over medium heat, stirring constantly, until thickened and bubbly. Stir in pepper. Serve sauce with beef or pork. Yield: 1 cup.

Per tablespoon: Calories 12 (83% from fat); Fat 1.1g (sat 0.7g, mono 0.3g, poly 0g); Protein 0g; Carb 0.6g; Fiber 0g; Chol 3mg; Iron 0mg; Sodium 36mg; Calc 1mg

Bordelaise Sauce: Substitute ⅓ cup dry red wine for ⅓ cup of the water, and stir in ¾ teaspoon dried parsley flakes and ¼ teaspoon dried thyme; increase pepper to ¼ teaspoon. Serve with beef or pork.

Beurre Blanc

prep: 15 min.   cook: 30 min.

This pearly white sauce enhances poultry, fish, and vegetables. Use it for the Coastal Bend Redfish recipe (page 228).

¾   cup dry white vermouth
2   shallots, minced
2   tablespoons white wine vinegar
¾   cup whipping cream
½   cup butter or margarine, cut into pieces
1   tablespoon fresh lemon juice
½   teaspoon salt
⅛   teaspoon ground white pepper

Bring first 3 ingredients to a boil in a small saucepan; cook 15 minutes or until liquid is reduced to ¼ cup. Stir in whipping cream, and cook 10 minutes or until liquid is reduced to ⅓ cup.
Reduce heat, and whisk in butter, 1 tablespoon at a time; cook, whisking constantly, 5 minutes or until sauce thickens. Stir in lemon juice, salt, and pepper. Yield: 1 cup.

Per tablespoon: Calories 92 (92% from fat); Fat 9.4g (sat 5.9g, mono 2.6g, poly 0.3g); Protein 0.2g; Carb 1.8g; Fiber 0g; Chol 30mg; Iron 0.1mg; Sodium 118mg; Calc 10mg

Hollandaise Sauce

prep: 5 min.   cook: 10 min.

Add just a hint of cayenne pepper to this classic sauce, if desired.

4	large egg yolks
2	tablespoons fresh lemon juice
1	cup butter, cut into pieces
¼	teaspoon salt

Whisk yolks in top of a double boiler; gradually whisk in lemon juice. Place over hot water (do not boil). Add butter, ⅓ cup at a time, whisking until smooth; whisk in salt. Cook, whisking constantly, 10 minutes or until thickened and a thermometer registers 160°. Serve immediately. Yield: 1½ cups.

Per tablespoon: Calories 76 (98% from fat); Fat 8.3g (sat 5.1g, mono 2.3g, poly 0.4g); Protein 0.5g; Carb 0.2g; Fiber 0g; Chol 54mg; Iron 0.1mg; Sodium 79mg; Calc 6mg

1. Whisk egg yolks in top of a double boiler. Gradually add lemon juice.

2. Add about one-third of butter to egg mixture, whisking until butter melts.

3. As sauce begins to thicken, keep adding pieces of butter, whisking constantly until smooth. Whisk in salt.

4. Cook until sauce temperature reaches 160°; remove from heat, and serve immediately.

Béarnaise Sauce

prep: 8 min.   cook: 2 min.

Swirl this tarragon-vinegar reduction into Hollandaise Sauce, and serve it over fish or beef, particularly the well-known London Broil (page 251).

3	tablespoons white wine vinegar
1	teaspoon minced green onion
¼	teaspoon coarsely ground pepper
½	teaspoon dried tarragon
	Hollandaise Sauce

Combine first 3 ingredients in a small saucepan; bring to a boil over medium heat. **Reduce** heat to low, and simmer until half the liquid evaporates. Pour mixture through a strainer, reserving liquid; discard solids. Cool vinegar mixture slightly; stir in tarragon.
Add to thickened Hollandaise Sauce just before removing from heat. Serve sauce with vegetables, fish, or beef. Yield: 1½ cups.

Per tablespoon: Calories 76 (98% from fat); Fat 8.3g (sat 5.1g, mono 2.3g, poly 0.4g); Protein 0.5g; Carb 0.3g; Fiber 0g; Chol 54mg; Iron 0.1mg; Sodium 80mg; Calc 7mg

Cream Sauce

prep: 8 min.   cook: 8 min.

Use this wine-enhanced sauce for Potato-Butternut Squash-and-Gruyère Gratin (page 474).

¼	cup butter or margarine
⅓	cup all-purpose flour
2½	cups milk
1	cup dry white wine
¼	teaspoon salt

Melt butter in a heavy saucepan over low heat; whisk in flour until smooth. Cook, whisking constantly, 1 minute. Gradually whisk in milk and wine; cook over medium heat, whisking constantly, until sauce is thickened and bubbly. Stir in salt. Yield: 3½ cups.

Per tablespoon: Calories 17 (64% from fat); Fat 1.2g (sat 0.7g, mono 0.3g, poly 0.1g); Protein 0.4g; Carb 1.1g; Fiber 0g; Chol 3mg; Iron 0.1mg; Sodium 21mg; Calc 13mg

Mornay Sauce

prep: 10 min.   cook: 6 min.

Mornay Sauce is a basic white sauce enriched with egg and cheese. It's particularly delicious when spooned over fancy brunch egg dishes.

1	tablespoon butter or margarine
1	tablespoon all-purpose flour
1	cup milk
½	teaspoon salt
⅛	teaspoon ground white pepper
1	egg yolk, beaten
2	tablespoons whipping cream
2	tablespoons (½ ounce) shredded Swiss cheese
2	tablespoons freshly grated Parmesan cheese

Melt butter in a heavy saucepan over low heat; add flour, stirring until smooth. Cook 1 minute, stirring constantly.
Gradually add milk; cook over medium heat, stirring constantly, until mixture is thickened and bubbly. Stir in salt and pepper.
Combine egg yolk and whipping cream. Gradually stir about one-fourth of hot mixture into yolk mixture; add to remaining hot mixture, and cook, stirring constantly, until thickened (2 to 3 minutes). Add cheeses, stirring until melted. Remove from heat. Yield: 1¼ cups.

Per tablespoon: Calories 26 (73% from fat); Fat 2.1g (sat 1.2g, mono 0.6g, poly 0.1g); Protein 1g; Carb 1g; Fiber 0g; Chol 16mg; Iron 0.1mg; Sodium 77mg; Calc 28mg

Mushroom–Wine Sauce

prep: 15 min.   cook: 13 min.

½	cup butter or margarine
12	shallots, chopped
4	green onions, chopped
1	garlic clove, minced
1	(8-ounce) package sliced fresh mushrooms
¼	cup all-purpose flour
2	(10¾-ounce) cans beef consommé
½	cup dry red wine

Melt butter in a large skillet over medium-high heat. Add shallots, green onions, and garlic; sauté 2 minutes. Add mushrooms;

sauté 5 minutes. Add flour, and cook, stirring constantly, 1 minute. Gradually stir in consommé and wine. Cook, stirring constantly, 5 minutes until slightly thickened. Yield: 4 cups.

Per tablespoon: Calories 21 (60% from fat); Fat 1.4g (sat 0.9g, mono 0.4g, poly 0.1g); Protein 0.6g; Carb 1.5g; Fiber 0.1g; Chol 4mg; Iron 0.1mg; Sodium 76mg; Calc 3mg

low carb • make ahead • quick
Clarified Butter

prep: 4 min.

Also called drawn butter, Clarified Butter and its lemon variation are great for dipping succulent bites of seafood like lobster and crabmeat.

1   cup butter

Melt butter over low heat; fat will rise to the top, and milk solids will sink to the bottom. Skim off white froth that appears on top. Then strain off the clear, yellow butter, keeping back the sediment of milk solids. Chill clarified butter until ready to serve; then reheat. Yield: about ¾ cup.

Per tablespoon: Calories 80 (100% from fat); Fat 9.1g (sat 5.8g, mono 2.4g, poly 0.3g); Protein 0.1g; Carb 0g; Fiber 0g; Chol 24mg; Iron 0mg; Sodium 65mg; Calc 3mg

Lemon Butter: Add ½ cup lemon juice to Clarified Butter, stirring well. Yield: 1¼ cups.

Melt butter in a skillet or saucepan over low heat. Skim white foam off top; then strain clear yellow butter, leaving behind the milk solids. ▶

To *clarify* is to clear a cloudy liquid by removing sediment. Clarified butter has a higher smoke point than regular butter, can be cooked at a higher temperature, and will keep longer. ▶

Marinara Sauce (page 435)

Hollandaise Sauce

Rémoulade Sauce

Cheddar Cheese Sauce (page 431)

low carb • make ahead
Rémoulade Sauce

prep: 5 min.   other: 30 min.

Rémoulade is a classic French sauce that's easy to stir together and has a tangy flavor that complements fish particularly well.

1   cup mayonnaise
1   to 2 tablespoons lemon juice
1½   tablespoons Dijon mustard
1   tablespoon chopped gherkin pickle
1   tablespoon capers
1   teaspoon dried tarragon
1   teaspoon dried chervil
½   teaspoon anchovy paste

Combine all ingredients, stirring well. Cover and chill at least 30 minutes. Serve with hot or cold meat, fish, or shellfish. Yield: 1 cup.

Per tablespoon: Calories 102 (97% from fat); Fat 11g (sat 1.5g, mono 0g, poly 0g); Protein 0.1g; Carb 0.4g; Fiber 0g; Chol 5mg; Iron 0.1mg; Sodium 151mg; Calc 3mg

Tartar Sauce

prep: 5 min.

¼   cup sour cream
3   tablespoons mayonnaise
2   teaspoons grated lemon rind
1   tablespoon chopped fresh parsley
1   tablespoon minced green onions
1   teaspoon fresh lemon juice
¼   teaspoon hot sauce

Stir together all ingredients. Yield: ½ cup.

Per tablespoon: Calories 53 (95% from fat); Fat 5.6g (sat 1.6g, mono 1.5g, poly 2.3g); Protein 0.3g; Carb 0.7g; Fiber 0.1g; Chol 5mg; Iron 0.1mg; Sodium 35mg; Calc 11mg

low calorie • low carb • low fat
make ahead • quick
Tex-Mex Secret Sauce

prep: 5 min.

½   cup sour cream
⅓   cup ketchup
1   (4.5-ounce) can chopped green chiles
1   tablespoon minced fresh cilantro

Stir together all ingredients. Cover and chill until ready to serve. Yield: 1 cup.

Per tablespoon: Calories 22 (65% from fat); Fat 1.6g (sat 1g, mono 0.4g, poly 0.1g); Protein 0.4g; Carb 2g; Fiber 0.2g; Chol 3mg; Iron 0.1mg; Sodium 91mg; Calc 12mg

Lemon-Rosemary Mayonnaise

prep: 8 min.

2 cups mayonnaise
2 tablespoons chopped fresh rosemary*
1½ tablespoons grated lemon rind
1 garlic clove, pressed

Stir together all ingredients. Use in place of tartar sauce when serving fresh seafood. Toss with canned tuna, or spread on a smoked turkey sandwich. Yield: 2 cups.

Per tablespoon: Calories 100 (99% from fat); Fat 11g (sat 1.5g, mono 0g, poly 0g); Protein 0g; Carb 0.1g; Fiber 0.1g; Chol 5mg; Iron 0mg; Sodium 90mg; Calc 1mg

*If you prefer a milder flavor, substitute fresh parsley for rosemary.

Spicy Thai Mayonnaise

prep: 15 min. other: 1 hr.

Use as a dressing or sandwich spread. It enlivens potato salad, chicken, or roast-beef sandwiches.

1 cup mayonnaise
3 green onions, chopped
2 tablespoons chili-garlic paste
1 tablespoon chopped fresh cilantro
1 jalapeño pepper, seeded and chopped
1 teaspoon red wine vinegar
¼ teaspoon curry powder

Process all ingredients in a blender or food processor until smooth, stopping to scrape down sides. Cover and chill at least 1 hour. Yield: 1⅓ cups.

Per tablespoon: Calories 76 (98% from fat); Fat 8.3g (sat 1.1g, mono 0g, poly 0g); Protein 0.1g; Carb 0.5g; Fiber 0.1g; Chol 4mg; Iron 0.1mg; Sodium 104mg; Calc 2mg

Chinese Hot Mustard

prep: 2 min. other: 8 hrs.

¼ cup dry mustard
1 teaspoon sugar
¼ cup boiling water
2 teaspoons vegetable oil

Combine mustard and sugar; stir in water and oil. Cover and let stand 8 hours before serving. Store in refrigerator. Yield: ⅓ cup.

Per tablespoon: Calories 50 (70% from fat); Fat 3.9g (sat 0.6g, mono 0.8g, poly 0.8g); Protein 1.9g; Carb 2g; Fiber 0.5g; Chol 0mg; Iron 0.5mg; Sodium 0mg; Calc 16mg

Southwestern Butter

prep: 5 min. other: 6 hrs.

1 cup unsalted butter, softened
1½ teaspoons chili powder
¼ teaspoon ground cumin
1 teaspoon ground red pepper
1 teaspoon dried oregano
1 teaspoon Worcestershire sauce
⅛ teaspoon garlic powder
⅛ teaspoon onion powder

Stir together all ingredients. Shape mixture into a log, using parchment paper or wax paper. Chill 4 to 6 hours. Yield: 1 cup.

Per tablespoon: Calories 103 (100% from fat); Fat 11.4g (sat 7.2g, mono 3g, poly 0.4g); Protein 0.2g; Carb 0.4g; Fiber 0.1g; Chol 30mg; Iron 0.1mg; Sodium 10.7mg; Calc 7mg

Gorgonzola Butter

prep: 8 min. other: 3 hrs.

1 cup butter, softened
6 ounces Gorgonzola cheese, softened
2 tablespoons olive oil
2 tablespoons fresh lemon juice
1 tablespoon plus 1 teaspoon minced shallot
2 teaspoons minced garlic
½ teaspoon kosher salt
½ teaspoon freshly ground pepper

Combine all ingredients in a large mixing bowl; beat at medium speed with an electric mixer until smooth. Shape mixture into 16 (1-inch) patties. Cover and freeze 3 hours or until firm. Yield: 1¾ cups.

Per tablespoon: Calories 89 (95% from fat); Fat 9.4g (sat 5.5g, mono 2.4g, poly 0.3g); Protein 1.4g; Carb 0.5g; Fiber 0g; Chol 23mg; Iron 0mg; Sodium 163mg; Calc 34mg

Jalapeño-Pecan-Mustard Butter

prep: 10 min. cook: 5 min.

Enjoy this flavor-packed butter with cornbread or grilled pork chops.

½ cup chopped pecans
2 cups butter or margarine, softened
⅓ cup Creole mustard
¼ cup minced red onion
2 garlic cloves
2 jalapeño peppers, seeded and minced

Bake pecans in a shallow pan at 350°, stirring occasionally, 5 minutes or until toasted; cool. **Stir** together pecans, butter, and remaining ingredients in a large bowl until well blended. Yield: 2½ cups.

Per tablespoon: Calories 91 (100% from fat); Fat 10.2g (sat 5.9g, mono 3g, poly 0.7g); Protein 0.3g; Carb 0.4g; Fiber 0.2g; Chol 24mg; Iron 0.1mg; Sodium 87mg; Calc 4mg

Pasta Sauce

prep: 15 min. cook: 2 hrs., 10 min.

This big-yield sauce freezes beautifully.

2 small onions, chopped
4 garlic cloves, chopped
¼ cup vegetable oil
2 (28-ounce) cans diced tomatoes, undrained
2 (12-ounce) cans tomato paste
8 cups water
¼ cup sugar
2 tablespoons dried Italian seasoning
1 tablespoon salt
1 tablespoon dried basil
2 teaspoons black pepper
1 teaspoon dried crushed red pepper

Sauté onion and garlic in hot oil in a Dutch oven over medium heat 10 minutes or until onion is tender. Stir in diced tomatoes and remaining ingredients. Bring to a boil; reduce heat, and simmer, stirring often, 2 hours. **Divide** into 1 cup portions; set aside 3 cups for Eggplant Parmesan (page 282), and freeze remaining portions. Yield: 12 cups.

Per tablespoon: Calories 9 (30% from fat); Fat 0.3g (sat 0g, mono 0.1g, poly 0.1g); Protein 0.2g; Carb 1.5g; Fiber 0.3g; Chol 0mg; Iron 0.2mg; Sodium 77mg; Calc 4mg

family favorite • low calorie • low carb
low cholesterol • low fat

Marinara Sauce

prep: 10 min.   cook: 35 min.

1 small onion, chopped
5 garlic cloves, minced
¼ cup olive oil
2 (28-ounce) cans diced tomatoes,
   undrained, or 2 (28-ounce) cans whole
   tomatoes, undrained and chopped
½ cup chopped fresh flat-leaf parsley or
   basil or ¼ cup each
2 tablespoons lemon juice
½ teaspoon sugar

Sauté onion and garlic in hot oil in a large
saucepan or Dutch oven, stirring constantly,
over medium heat until tender. Add tomatoes and remaining ingredients; bring mixture to a boil. Reduce heat to medium, and
cook, uncovered, 30 minutes or until mixture thickens and liquid evaporates, stirring
often. Yield: 6 cups.

Per tablespoon: Calories 9 (60% from fat); Fat 0.6g (sat 0.1g, mono 0.4g, poly 0.1g);
Protein 0.2g; Carb 1g; Fiber 0.3g; Chol 0mg; Iron 0.1mg; Sodium 21mg; Calc 4mg

low calorie • low cholesterol • low fat
make ahead • quick • test kitchen favorite

Grandpa Jim's Shrimp Sauce

prep: 5 min.

½ cup chili sauce
⅓ cup prepared horseradish
⅓ cup ketchup
2 tablespoons lemon juice
1½ teaspoons Worcestershire sauce
½ to 1 teaspoon hot sauce
¼ teaspoon salt
¼ teaspoon pepper

Stir together all ingredients until blended.
Cover and chill until ready to serve. Yield:
1⅓ cups.

Per tablespoon: Calories 19 (33% from fat); Fat 0.7g (sat 0.5g, mono 0.2g, poly 0g);
Protein 0.2g; Carb 3.2g; Fiber 0.1g; Chol 2mg; Iron 0.1mg; Sodium 256mg; Calc 5mg

low calorie • low cholesterol • quick

Cocktail Sauce

prep: 5 min.

½ cup mayonnaise
½ cup ketchup
½ cup chili sauce
2⅓ tablespoons lemon juice
1 tablespoon lime juice
2 teaspoons prepared horseradish
½ to 1 teaspoon hot sauce

Stir together all ingredients. Cover and chill
until ready to serve. Yield: 1¾ cups.

Per tablespoon: Calories 40 (72% from fat); Fat 3..2g (sat 0.5g, mono 0g, poly 0g);
Protein 0.1g; Carb 2.7g; Fiber 0.1g; Chol 2mg; Iron 0mg; Sodium 211mg; Calc 1.3mg

low calorie • low cholesterol • low fat

Sweet-Hot Ketchup

prep: 5 min.   other: 2 hrs.

1 cup ketchup
2 tablespoons to ¼ cup honey
1 tablespoon lime juice
1 teaspoon chipotle chile pepper seasoning

Stir together all ingredients until blended.
Cover and chill 2 hours. Yield: 1⅓ cups.

Per tablespoon: Calories 17 (5% from fat); Fat 0.1g (sat 0g, mono 0g, poly 0g);
Protein 0.2g; Carb 4.6g; Fiber 0.1g; Chol 0mg; Iron 0.1mg; Sodium 134mg; Calc 2mg

low calorie • low carb • low cholesterol
low fat

Tomatillo Sauce

prep: 20 min.   cook: 6 min.   other: 20 min.

10 fresh tomatillos, husks removed
1   small onion
½   cup water
⅓   cup packed fresh cilantro
1   small jalapeño pepper, halved
½   teaspoon salt

Combine tomatillos, onion, and water to
cover in a saucepan. Bring to a boil; cook
5 minutes. Turn off heat; let stand 20 minutes or until tomatillos are tender. Drain.
Process tomatillo mixture, ½ cup water, and
remaining ingredients in a blender until
smooth. Cover and chill. Yield: 1¼ cups.

Per tablespoon: Calories 7 (26% from fat); Fat 0.2g (sat 0g, mono 0g, poly 0.1g)
Protein 0.2g; Carb 1.4g; Fiber 0.4g; Chol 0mg; Iron 0.1mg; Sodium 58mg; Calc 2mg

low carb • quick

Homemade Pesto

prep: 10 min.

(pictured on page 428)

1 cup firmly packed fresh basil leaves
1 cup shredded Parmesan cheese
½ cup pine nuts, toasted
½ cup olive oil
3 garlic cloves

Process all ingredients in a blender or food
processor until smooth, stopping occasionally
to scrape down sides. Yield: ¾ cup.

Per tablespoon: Calories 147 (90% from fat); Fat 14.7g (sat 2.7g, mono 8.3g, poly 2.9g);
Protein 3.4g; Carb 1.4g; Fiber 0.4g; Chol 5mg; Iron 0.6mg; Sodium 114mg; Calc 91mg

quick

Currant Sauce

prep: 5 min.   cook: 1 min.

½ cup red currant jelly
½ cup dry red wine (we tested with Burgundy)
¼ cup ketchup
¼ cup butter
2 tablespoons Worcestershire sauce
2 teaspoons cornstarch
¼ teaspoon dry mustard

Combine all ingredients in a small saucepan.
Bring to a boil over medium heat, stirring
constantly; cook 1 minute. Yield: 2 cups.

Per tablespoon: Calories 29 (43% from fat); Fat 1.4g (sat 0.9g, mono 0.4g, poly 0.1g);
Protein 0.1g; Carb 4.2g; Fiber 0g; Chol 4mg; Iron 0.1mg; Sodium 42mg; Calc 2mg

Tomatillos are an apple-green fruit with
tangy flavor and a papery husk that splits
open as the fruit matures.

Fresh Cranberry Sauce

prep: 20 min.   cook: 10 min.   other: 1 hr.

1 cup sugar
1 cup water
1 (12-ounce) package fresh cranberries
1 tablespoon grated orange rind
1 tablespoon orange liqueur or fresh orange juice
¼ cup chopped pecans or sliced almonds, toasted

Bring sugar and 1 cup water to a boil in a saucepan, stirring until sugar dissolves. Add cranberries, rind, and liqueur; return to a boil, reduce heat, and simmer 10 minutes. Stir in toasted pecans. Cover and chill 1 hour or until firm. Yield: 2 cups.

Per tablespoon: Calories 37 (17% from fat); Fat 0.7g (sat 0.1g, mono 0.4g, poly 0.2g); Protein 0.1g; Carb 7.9g; Fiber 0.6g; Chol 0mg; Iron 0.1mg; Sodium 0mg; Calc 2mg

Cranberry Jezebel Sauce

prep: 5 min.   cook: 15 min.

1 cup water
½ cup granulated sugar
½ cup firmly packed light brown sugar
1 (12-ounce) package fresh cranberries
½ cup pineapple preserves
3 tablespoons prepared horseradish
1 tablespoon Dijon mustard

Bring first 3 ingredients to a boil, stirring often, in a saucepan over medium-high heat; add cranberries.
Return mixture to a boil. Reduce heat, and simmer, stirring often, 10 minutes or until cranberry skins begin to pop and mixture begins to thicken. Remove from heat.
Stir in preserves, horseradish, and mustard; remove pan from heat, and let sauce cool. Cover and chill until ready to serve. Yield: about 3 cups.

Per tablespoon: Calories 31 (6% from fat); Fat 0.2g (sat 0.1g, mono 0.1g, poly 0g); Protein 0g; Carb 7.4g; Fiber 0.3g; Chol 0mg; Iron 0mg; Sodium 6mg; Calc 3mg

Note: Store sauce in an airtight container in the refrigerator up to 2 weeks.

barbecue sauces, marinades & rubs

Sampling barbecue sauce is like taking a mini tour of the South. North Carolina is famous for its vinegar-based varieties, while South Carolina is mustard-tart and sugar-sweet. Texas serves up a thick, sweet sauce with brisket, while in North Alabama, a mayonnaise-based sauce is synonymous with barbecued chicken.

Generally speaking, barbecue sauce should be applied to food during the last 15 to 45 minutes of cooking, depending on how sweet the sauce is. If the sauce has much sugar in it, wait until the last 15 minutes to apply it; this keeps the meat or poultry from burning on the grill. A non-sweet sauce, however, can be brushed on at any point during cooking. Always be sure to save a little sauce for passing at the table. The sauces on these pages can all be made ahead and refrigerated up to one week.

A marinade is added to uncooked food for flavor and sometimes tenderizing. Marinades can be cooked or uncooked; many contain an acid such as wine, citrus juice, or vinegar that helps tenderize meat.

Marinate food in nonmetal containers like glass dishes, plastic bowls, or zip-top freezer bags that won't react with acidic components in the marinade. Allow ½ cup marinade for every pound of meat, poultry, or seafood. Always marinate food, covered, in the refrigerator, turning occasionally.

To simply add flavor, marinate most foods 30 minutes to 2 hours. To tenderize meat, marinating 8 hours is ideal, but you can marinate large cuts of meat up to 24 hours with good results. Meat that marinates longer than that can become mushy.

Never reuse a marinade in which raw meat, fish, or poultry has soaked until you first bring it to a boil. This will kill any bacteria that may have been transferred from the raw food to the marinade.

A rub is a blend of dry seasonings, usually spices and dried herbs, applied to meat, seafood, or poultry before cooking. The dry rub forms something of a crust that seals in the juices during cooking. You can team a sauce with a rub, which many cooks do.

When a small amount of liquid like olive oil or crushed garlic with its juice is added to a rub, it becomes a paste. A paste is easy to apply to meat, because it clings to the food well. You can apply a rub or paste to food and then chill it up to 24 hours before cooking for maximum flavor.

North Carolina Eastern-Style Barbecue Sauce

prep: 5 min.

This is widely used for North Carolina-style pig pickin's, where the cavity of the pig is sloshed with sauce so the sauce seeps into the meat during hours of smoking. The mixture is later chopped into the cooked pork. Some purists might fuss at us for adding ginger ale, but we were partial to this recipe passed on from a prizewinning North Carolina barbecue smoker.

7 cups white vinegar
1 cup ginger ale
3 tablespoons plus 1 teaspoon dried crushed red pepper
1 to 2 tablespoons ground red pepper

Stir together all ingredients until blended. Serve sauce over pork barbecue. Yield: 8 cups.

Per tablespoon: Calories 3 (0% from fat); Fat 0g (sat 0g, mono 0g, poly 0g); Protein 0g; Carb 1g; Fiber 0.1g; Chol 0mg; Iron 0mg; Sodium 0mg; Calc 0mg

Thick-and-Robust Barbecue Sauce

prep: 10 min.   cook: 40 min.

The first nationally branded barbecue sauces were likely based on a Kansas City-style sauce like this one—thick, tomatoey, and sweet, with just a hint of hot.

- ¾ cup cider vinegar
- ½ cup ketchup
- ¼ cup Worcestershire sauce
- 1 garlic clove, minced
- ¼ cup chili sauce
- 2 tablespoons chopped onion
- 1 tablespoon brown sugar
- 1 tablespoon lemon juice
- ½ teaspoon dry mustard
- Dash of ground red pepper

Stir together all ingredients in a medium saucepan over medium heat; bring to a boil. Reduce heat; simmer, stirring occasionally, 40 minutes.

Divide sauce into separate containers for basting and serving at the table. (Basting brushes used on raw food should not be dipped into table sauce.) Use as a basting sauce during the last 10 minutes of cooking for steak, pork, burgers, or chicken. Discard any remaining basting sauce, and refrigerate leftover table sauce. Yield: 1¼ cups.

Per tablespoon: Calories 16 (6% from fat); Fat 0.1g (sat 0g, mono 0g, poly 0g); Protein 0.2g; Carb 4.4g; Fiber 0.1g; Chol 0mg; Iron 0.3mg; Sodium 196mg; Calc 6mg

White Barbecue Sauce

prep: 10 min.

White sauce is a trademark of North Alabama barbecued chicken, but it's just as good spooned over shredded pork.

- 1½ cups mayonnaise
- ⅓ cup cider vinegar
- ¼ cup lemon juice
- 2 tablespoons sugar
- 2 tablespoons freshly ground pepper
- 2 tablespoons white wine Worcestershire sauce
- 1 teaspoon salt

Whisk together all ingredients in a small bowl until blended. Store in refrigerator. Yield: 2 cups.

Per tablespoon: Calories 81 (92% from fat); Fat 8.3g (sat 1.1g, mono 0g, poly 0g); Protein 0.1g; Carb 1.6g; Fiber 0.1g; Chol 4mg; Iron 0.1mg; Sodium 151mg; Calc 3mg

Brisket Red Sauce

prep: 10 min.   cook: 7 min.

Southern Living staff member Troy Black perfected this red sauce for brisket. It's thinner than a Texas sauce, but it blends perfectly with the smoky beef flavor.

- 1½ cups cider vinegar
- 1 cup ketchup
- ½ cup firmly packed light brown sugar
- ¼ cup Worcestershire sauce
- 2 tablespoons butter
- 1½ teaspoons onion powder
- 1½ teaspoons garlic powder
- 1½ teaspoons ground cumin
- 1 teaspoon salt
- ½ teaspoon freshly ground black pepper
- ½ teaspoon ground red pepper

Stir together all ingredients in a medium saucepan. Bring to a boil, reduce heat, and simmer, stirring occasionally, 5 to 7 minutes or until sugar dissolves. Yield: 3 cups.

Per tablespoon: Calories 21 (21% from fat); Fat 0.5g (sat 0.3g, mono 0.1g, poly 0g); Protein 0.1g; Carb 4.4g; Fiber 0.1g; Chol 1mg; Iron 0.2mg; Sodium 122mg; Calc 6mg

Sweet Mustard Barbecue Sauce

prep: 5 min.   cook: 10 min.

This is a sweeter, slightly thicker version of a traditional South Carolina sauce.

1   cup cider vinegar
⅔   cup prepared mustard
½   cup sugar
2   tablespoons chili powder
1   teaspoon ground white pepper
1   teaspoon ground black pepper
¼   teaspoon ground red pepper
½   teaspoon hot sauce
2   tablespoons butter or margarine
½   teaspoon soy sauce

Stir together first 8 ingredients in a saucepan over medium heat; bring to a boil, reduce heat, and simmer 10 minutes. Remove from heat, and stir in butter and soy sauce. Yield: 2 cups.

Per tablespoon: Calories 28 (48% from fat); Fat 1.5g (sat 0.5g, mono 0.4g, poly 0.4g); Protein 0.1g; Carb 4.1g; Fiber 0.1g; Chol 2mg; Iron 0.1mg; Sodium 35mg; Calc 2mg

Cider Vinegar Barbecue Sauce

prep: 10 min.   cook: 7 min.

This sauce is often referred to as Lexington-Style Dip, but there are many variations. Most folks can't resist adding their own touch.

1½ cups cider vinegar
⅓   cup firmly packed brown sugar
¼   cup ketchup
1   tablespoon hot sauce (we tested with Texas Pete Hot Sauce)
1   teaspoon browning and seasoning sauce (we tested with Kitchen Bouquet Browning & Seasoning Sauce)
½   teaspoon salt
½   teaspoon onion powder
½   teaspoon pepper
½   teaspoon Worcestershire sauce

Stir together all ingredients in a medium saucepan; cook over medium heat, stirring constantly, 7 minutes or until sugar dissolves.

Cover and chill sauce until ready to serve. Serve with smoked pork shoulder. Yield: 2 cups.

Per tablespoon: Calories 13 (0% from fat); Fat 0g (sat 0g, mono 0g, poly 0g); Protein 0g; Carb 3.6g; Fiber 0g; Chol 0mg; Iron 0.1mg; Sodium 61mg; Calc 3mg

Drunken Sauce

prep: 10 min.   cook: 12 min.   other: 5 min.

This Mexican barbecue sauce is often served with slow-roasted, shredded beef or lamb.

6   medium-size fresh tomatillos, husks removed
3   pasilla chiles, stemmed, seeded, and chopped*
1   garlic clove, minced
¼   cup flat beer
1   tablespoon vegetable oil
½   tablespoon red or rice wine vinegar
½   teaspoon dried oregano
½   teaspoon salt
1   tablespoon (1 ounce) finely crumbled feta cheese*

Combine tomatillos, chiles, and water to cover in a saucepan. Bring mixture to a boil. Reduce heat, and cook, covered, 5 to 7 minutes or until tender. Drain. Allow to cool for 5 minutes.
Pulse tomatillo mixture, garlic, and next 5 ingredients 3 or 4 times in a blender until chopped. Stir in cheese. Yield: 1½ cups.

Per tablespoon: Calories 12 (60% from fat); Fat 0.8g (sat 0.1g, mono 0.3g, poly 0.3g); Protein 0.3g; Carb 1.2g; Fiber 0.3g; Chol 0mg; Iron 0.1mg; Sodium 53mg; Calc 4mg

*Substitute 1 large dried ancho chile for pasilla chiles, if desired. Substitute cotija cheese for feta, if desired. Look for cotija cheese in Latin markets.

Green Barbecue Sauce

prep: 15 min.   cook: 2 hrs.

Serve this over grilled chicken, fish, or shrimp.

2½ pounds green tomatoes, coarsely chopped
1½ pounds tomatillos, husked and coarsely chopped
2   garlic cloves, pressed
½   to 1 cup sugar
1   cup white vinegar
1   large sweet onion, coarsely chopped
1   tablespoon dry mustard
½   teaspoon dried crushed red pepper
1   teaspoon salt

Cook all ingredients in a stockpot over medium-low heat 2 hours or until tomatoes and tomatillos are tender. Cool.
Process green tomato mixture, in batches, in a food processor or blender until smooth. Yield: 3 cups.

Per tablespoon: Calories 20 (14% from fat); Fat 0.3g (sat 0g, mono 0g, poly 0.1g); Protein 0.5g; Carb 4g; Fiber 0.6g; Chol 0mg; Iron 0.3mg; Sodium 52mg; Calc 5mg

Note: Store sauce in refrigerator up to 1 week.

Citrus–Honey Mustard Marinade

prep: 5 min.

Serve grilled chicken made with this marinade with picnic-style side dishes, baked potatoes, and grilled vegetables, or your best lettuce or spinach salad.

⅓   cup honey
¼   cup orange juice
¼   cup olive oil
3   tablespoons coarse-grained Dijon mustard
2   tablespoons red wine vinegar
¼   teaspoon salt
¼   teaspoon freshly ground pepper

Whisk together all ingredients. Cover and chill up to 4 days. Yield: 1 cup.

Per tablespoon: Calories 57 (57% from fat); Fat 3.6g (sat 0.5g, mono 2.5g, poly 0.3g); Protein 0.2g; Carb 6.5g; Fiber 0.2g; Chol 0mg; Iron 0.1mg; Sodium 101mg; Calc 4mg

Lemon Marinade

prep: 10 min.

Splash this lively marinade over chicken before grilling or over hot cooked vegetables.

1   cup vegetable oil
1   cup red wine vinegar
2   tablespoons grated lemon rind
¼   cup fresh lemon juice
3   tablespoons sugar
2   tablespoons hot sauce
2   tablespoons Dijon mustard
2   garlic cloves, pressed
½   teaspoon salt

Whisk together all ingredients in a bowl. Yield: 2½ cups.

Per tablespoon: Calories 53 (95% from fat); Fat 5.6g (sat 0.6g, mono 2.4g, poly 2.4g); Protein 0g; Carb 1.2g; Fiber 0g; Chol 0mg; Iron 0.1mg; Sodium 42mg; Calc 1mg

Note: To prepare ahead, store in an airtight container in the refrigerator up to 1 week. Bring to room temperature, and whisk before using.

Asian Marinade

prep: 12 min.

1   cup thinly sliced green onions
1   cup chopped fresh cilantro
2   tablespoons sesame seeds, toasted
2   garlic cloves, pressed
½   cup soy sauce
¼   cup dark sesame oil
¼   cup honey
1   teaspoon hot sauce

Combine first 4 ingredients in a small bowl. Combine soy sauce and remaining ingredients; stir well. Add onion mixture to soy sauce mixture; stir well. Use to marinate fish or chicken. Yield: 2 cups.

Per tablespoon: Calories 30 (60% from fat); Fat 2g (sat 0.3g, mono 0.8g, poly 0.8g); Protein 0.6g; Carb 2.7g; Fiber 0.2g; Chol 0mg; Iron 0.1mg; Sodium 232mg; Calc 9mg

Southwestern Rub

prep: 5 min.

We recommend this rub for pork ribs, chicken, and catfish.

¼   cup chili powder
1   tablespoon onion powder
1   tablespoon ground cumin
2   teaspoons salt
1½   teaspoons dried oregano
1   teaspoon garlic powder
1   teaspoon ground red pepper

Combine all ingredients; store in an airtight container. Rub on meat of choice before smoking or grilling. Yield: ⅓ cup.

Per tablespoon: Calories 13 (28% from fat); Fat 0.4g (sat 0g, mono 0g, poly 0g); Protein 0.5g; Carb 2.2g; Fiber 0.8g; Chol 0mg; Iron 0.7mg; Sodium 1056mg; Calc 22mg

Jamaican Jerk Rub

prep: 5 min.

⅓   cup freeze-dried chives
1   tablespoon fine-grain sea salt
1   tablespoon onion powder
1   tablespoon dried onion flakes
1   tablespoon garlic powder
1   tablespoon ground ginger
1   tablespoon dried thyme
1   tablespoon light brown sugar
1   tablespoon ground red pepper
2   teaspoons ground allspice
2   teaspoons coarsely ground black pepper
2   teaspoons ground coriander
1   teaspoon ground cinnamon
½   teaspoon ground nutmeg
½   teaspoon ground cloves

Process all ingredients in a blender until ground and well blended. Rub on meat of choice before smoking or grilling. Yield: ¾ cup.

Per tablespoon: Calories 16 (11% from fat); Fat 0.2g (sat 0g, mono 0g, poly 0.1g); Protein 0.4g; Carb 3.5g; Fiber 1g; Chol 0mg; Iron 0.5mg; Sodium 577mg; Calc 17mg

Chipotle Rub

prep: 5 min.

2   to 3 canned chipotle chile peppers
¼   cup firmly packed brown sugar
1   tablespoon chili powder
1   teaspoon salt

Chop chipotle chile peppers; stir together peppers, brown sugar, chili powder, and salt to form a paste. Rub on meat of choice before smoking or grilling. Yield: ⅓ cup.

Per tablespoon: Calories 48 (6% from fat); Fat 0.3g (sat 0g, mono 0g, poly 0g); Protein 0.3g; Carb 11.4g; Fiber 0.5g; Chol 0mg; Iron 0.6mg; Sodium 611mg; Calc 17mg

All-Purpose Barbecue Rub

prep: 5 min.

¼   cup coarse salt
¼   cup firmly packed dark brown sugar
¼   cup sweet paprika
2   tablespoons pepper

Combine all ingredients. Store mixture in an airtight jar, away from heat, up to 6 months. Rub on meat of choice before smoking or grilling. Yield: 1 cup.

Per tablespoon: Calories 11 (0% from fat); Fat 0g (sat 0g, mono 0g, poly 0g); Protein 0.1g; Carb 2.7g; Fiber 0.2g; Chol 0mg; Iron 0.3mg; Sodium 1412mg; Calc 5mg

Caribbean Spice Rub

prep: 5 min.

2   tablespoons ground allspice
1   tablespoon ground ginger
1   tablespoon dried thyme, crushed
1   tablespoon garlic powder
1   tablespoon onion powder
2   teaspoons salt
½   teaspoon freshly ground black pepper
⅛   teaspoon ground red pepper

Combine all ingredients. Store in an airtight container. Rub on meat of choice before smoking or grilling. Yield: ⅓ cup.

Per tablespoon: Calories 25 (7% from fat); Fat 0.2g (sat 0g, mono 0g, poly 0g); Protein 0.7g; Carb 5.2g; Fiber 2.2g; Chol 0mg; Iron 0.9mg; Sodium 875mg; Calc 34mg

Store dry spice rubs in an airtight jar up to six months.

gravies

A gravy is a "jus," the natural juice from a cooked roast, that has been thickened with flour. Gravies made from meat pan drippings are some of the richest flavored and easiest sauces to make. It's really just a matter of properly adding the flour to get a thickened smooth sauce. These recipes add an equal amount of flour to fat already in the pan; another method is to make a slurry of water and flour and add it to the gravy. Try one of these six easy gravies for starters.

family favorite • low calorie • low carb • quick

Cream Gravy

prep: 5 min.   cook: 5 min.

If you have drippings from fried chicken or other meat, you can substitute those for the butter.

1 cup milk
1 (¼-inch-thick) onion slice
1 fresh parsley sprig
2 tablespoons butter or margarine
2 tablespoons all-purpose flour
2 tablespoons whipping cream
⅛ teaspoon salt
⅛ teaspoon ground white pepper
Dash of ground nutmeg

Bring first 3 ingredients to a boil, and remove from heat. Pour milk mixture through a wire-mesh strainer into a small bowl, discarding solids.
Melt butter in a skillet over low heat; whisk in flour until smooth. Cook, whisking constantly, 1 minute. Gradually whisk in reserved hot milk, and cook, whisking constantly, over medium heat, until thickened and bubbly. Whisk in whipping cream and remaining ingredients. Yield: ¾ cup.

Per tablespoon: Calories 42 (75% from fat); Fat 3.5g (sat 2.2g, mono 0.9g, poly 0.2g); Protein 0.9g; Carb 2g; Fiber 0g; Chol 10mg; Iron 0.1mg; Sodium 47mg; Calc 25mg

family favorite • low calorie • low carb
low cholesterol • low fat • quick

Pan Gravy

prep: 2 min.   cook: 4 min.

Make Pan Gravy from the natural drippings left in the roasting pan from roasts, steaks, chops, and other meats.

2 tablespoons pan drippings (fat and juice)
2 tablespoons all-purpose flour
1 cup meat juices, broth, or water
¼ teaspoon salt
⅛ teaspoon pepper

Pour off all except 2 tablespoons drippings from pan in which meat was cooked. Add flour, stirring until smooth. Cook 1 minute, stirring constantly. Gradually stir in meat juices; cook over medium heat, stirring constantly, until mixture is thickened and bubbly. Stir in salt and pepper. Serve hot with roast and mashed potatoes. Yield: 1 cup.

Per tablespoon: Calories 10 (9% from fat); Fat 0.1g (sat 0.1g, mono 0.1g, poly 0g); Protein 1.4g; Carb 0.9g; Fiber 0g; Chol 3mg; Iron 0.1mg; Sodium 145mg; Calc 0.7mg

family favorite • low calorie • low carb

Giblet Gravy

prep: 10 min.   cook: 1 hr., 5 min.

We used egg yolks and flour as thickeners in this luscious recipe.

Giblets and neck from 1 turkey
4 cups water
½ cup butter or margarine
1 small onion, chopped
1 celery rib, chopped
1 carrot, chopped
¼ cup all-purpose flour
2 egg yolks
½ cup half-and-half
½ teaspoon salt
½ teaspoon pepper
½ teaspoon poultry seasoning

Bring giblets, neck, and 4 cups water to a boil in a medium saucepan over medium heat. Cover, reduce heat, and simmer

45 minutes or until tender. Drain, reserving broth. Chop giblets and neck meat, and set aside.
Melt butter in a large skillet over medium heat; add chopped vegetables, and sauté 5 minutes. Add flour, stirring until smooth. Add reserved broth; cook, stirring constantly, 10 minutes or until thickened. Reduce heat to low. Remove vegetables using a hand-held, wire-mesh strainer, and discard, leaving gravy in skillet.
Whisk together egg yolks and half-and-half. Gradually stir about one-fourth of hot gravy into yolk mixture; add to remaining hot gravy. Add giblets and neck meat; cook, stirring constantly, 4 to 5 minutes or until a thermometer registers 160°. Stir in salt, pepper, and seasoning. Serve immediately. Yield: 4 cups.

Per tablespoon: Calories 43 (55% from fat); Fat 2.6g (sat 1.3g, mono 0.7g, poly 0.3g); Protein 3.9g; Carb 0.9g; Fiber 0g; Chol 64mg; Iron 1.3mg; Sodium 46mg; Calc 5mg

low calorie • low carb • quick

Sawmill Gravy

prep: 5 min.   cook: 20 min.

½ pound ground pork sausage
¼ cup butter
⅓ cup all-purpose flour
3¼ cups milk
½ teaspoon salt
¾ teaspoon pepper
⅛ teaspoon dried Italian seasoning (optional)

Cook sausage in a large skillet over medium heat, stirring until it crumbles and is no longer pink. Remove sausage, and drain on paper towels. Wipe skillet clean.
Melt butter in skillet over low heat. Whisk in flour until smooth. Cook, whisking constantly, 1 minute. Gradually whisk in milk, and cook, whisking constantly, over medium heat about 10 to 12 minutes or until thickened and bubbly. Stir in sausage, salt, pepper, and, if desired, Italian seasoning. Yield: 3¾ cups.

Per tablespoon: Calories 29 (68% from fat); Fat 2.2g (sat 1.1g, mono 0.8g, poly 0.2g); Protein 1.1g; Carb 1.1g; Fiber 0g; Chol 6mg; Iron 0.1mg; Sodium 54mg; Calc 16mg

Tomato Gravy

prep: 2 min.   cook: 6 min.

2   tablespoons butter
2   tablespoons all-purpose flour
½   cup chicken broth
1   (14½-ounce) can diced tomatoes with
    basil, oregano, and garlic
1   teaspoon sugar
½   teaspoon seasoned pepper

Melt butter in a large saucepan over medium heat; add flour, stirring until smooth. Cook, stirring constantly, 1 minute. Add broth, stirring until smooth. Add diced tomatoes, sugar, and pepper; cook, stirring often, 3 to 5 minutes or until thickened. Yield: 2 cups.

Per tablespoon: Calories 14 (45% from fat); Fat 0.7g (sat 0.5g, mono 0.2g, poly 0g); Protein 0.3g; Carb 1.7g; Fiber 0.1g; Chol 2mg; Iron 0.2mg; Sodium 86mg; Calc 8mg

low calorie • low carb • quick

Shallot Gravy

prep: 15 min.   cook: 10 min.

Spoon this creamy gravy over Bacon-Wrapped Quail (page 393).

6   tablespoons butter or margarine,
    divided
½   pound fresh whole mushrooms,
    quartered
3   shallots, finely chopped
¼   cup all-purpose flour
1½   cups chicken broth
⅓   cup whipping cream
¼   cup sour cream
1   teaspoon salt
½   teaspoon pepper
Garnish: chopped parsley

Melt 2 tablespoons butter in a large saucepan over medium-high heat; add mushrooms and shallots, and sauté 3 to 5 minutes or until tender. Remove from pan. **Melt** remaining 4 tablespoons butter in saucepan over medium-high heat; whisk in flour. Cook, whisking constantly, 1 minute. Whisk in chicken broth until smooth, and cook, whisking constantly, until slightly thickened. Stir in whipping cream and sour cream. Add mushrooms, shallots, salt, and pepper. Cook, stirring constantly, until thoroughly heated. Garnish, if desired. Yield: 3 cups.

Per tablespoon: Calories 27 (80% from fat); Fat 2.4g (sat 1.4g, mono 0.6g, poly 0.1g); Protein 0.4g; Carb 1.1g; Fiber 0.1g; Chol 7mg; Iron 0.1mg; Sodium 108mg; Calc 4mg

dessert sauces

Whether it's fudge sauce, caramel, or crème anglaise, a dessert sauce is an easy and impressive way to dress up store-bought cake, pie, or ice cream. Typically quick to make, most dessert sauces keep for several days in the refrigerator.

There's a variety of flavors from which to choose—from fudge and chocolate sauces to please the chocoholics to tangy lemon curd for filling tarts.

for kids • quick

Chocolate Sauce

prep: 5 min.   cook: 3 min.

1   cup semisweet chocolate morsels
¼   cup whipping cream
2   tablespoons butter

Stir together all ingredients in a small saucepan over low heat, and cook, stirring constantly, until chocolate and butter melt and sauce is warm. Yield: 1 cup.

Per tablespoon: Calories 76 (71% from fat); Fat 6g (sat 3.6g, mono 1.8g, poly 0.2g); Protein 0.5g; Carb 6.7g; Fiber 0.6g; Chol 9mg; Iron 0.3mg; Sodium 13mg; Calc 6mg

entertaining • quick

Champagne-Chocolate Sauce

prep: 10 min.

A little bubbly brings special appeal to chocolate sauce.

2   (6-ounce) dark chocolate candy bars,
    finely chopped (we tested with Hershey's
    Special Dark Chocolate candy bars)
1   tablespoon butter
½   cup Champagne or sparkling wine

Microwave chocolate and butter in a small microwave-safe bowl at HIGH 1 minute or just until chocolate begins to melt, stirring after 30 seconds. Whisk in Champagne, whisking until chocolate melts and mixture is smooth. (Mixture may appear broken, but continue to whisk until smooth.) Yield: 1¾ cups.

Per tablespoon: Calories 72 (55% from fat); Fat 4.4g (sat 2.8g, mono 0.1g, poly 0g); Protein 0.6g; Carb 7.2g; Fiber 1.1g; Chol 2mg; Iron 0.3mg; Sodium 3mg; Calc 0mg

for kids • make ahead • quick

Hot Fudge Sauce

prep: 1 min.   cook: 6 min.

This heavenly sauce dresses up Frozen Peppermint Cheesecake (page 161).

1   (12-ounce) package semisweet chocolate
    morsels
1   cup half-and-half
1   tablespoon butter or margarine
1   teaspoon vanilla extract

Combine all ingredients in a saucepan. Cook over medium-low heat until chocolate melts and sauce is smooth, stirring often. Serve warm. Yield: 2 cups.

Per tablespoon: Calories 64 (62% from fat); Fat 4.4g (sat 2.7g, mono 1.4g, poly 0.2g); Protein 0.7g; Carb 7.1g; Fiber 0.6g; Chol 4mg; Iron 0.3mg; Sodium 7mg; Calc 11mg

German Chocolate Sauce

prep: 5 min.   cook: 7 min.

½   cup butter
1   (4-ounce) package sweet baking
    chocolate
1½ cups sugar
1   teaspoon vanilla extract
⅛   teaspoon salt
1   (5-ounce) can evaporated milk

Melt butter and chocolate in a small saucepan over low heat, stirring until melted. Stir in sugar, vanilla, salt, and milk; bring to a boil over medium heat. Cook 7 minutes, stirring constantly. Serve warm over ice cream or pound cake. Yield: 2 cups.

Per tablespoon: Calories 84 (44% from fat); Fat 4.1g (sat 2.6g, mono 0.8g, poly 0.1g); Protein 0.6g; Carb 12g; Fiber 0.3g; Chol 9mg; Iron 0.1mg; Sodium 34mg; Calc 13mg

Coffee Syrup

prep: 6 min.

Serve this versatile syrup over cheesecake or crème brûlée, or stir it into a milk shake, cup of coffee, or hot chocolate.

½   cup water
1   cup sugar
¼   cup instant coffee granules
¼   cup chocolate syrup

Bring ½ cup water to a boil; add sugar and coffee granules, stirring until dissolved. Stir in chocolate syrup. Store in refrigerator. Yield: 1¼ cups.

Per tablespoon: Calories 50 (0% from fat); Fat 0g (sat 0g, mono 0g, poly 0g); Protein 0.2g; Carb 12.6g; Fiber 0g; Chol 0mg; Iron 0.1mg; Sodium 3mg; Calc 1mg

Grand Marnier Cream

prep: 6 min.

Grand Marnier laces this fluffy topping with a hint of orange. Dollop it over fresh strawberries for the ultimate indulgence.

⅔   cup whipping cream
1½ teaspoons Grand Marnier
1   teaspoon brandy
1   teaspoon vanilla extract
¼   cup sugar
2   tablespoons sour cream

Combine first 4 ingredients in a small mixing bowl; beat at medium speed with an electric mixer 1 minute. Add sugar and sour cream; beat until stiff peaks form. Serve with fresh strawberries. Yield: 1½ cups.

Per tablespoon: Calories 36 (68% from fat); Fat 2.7g (sat 1.7g, mono 0.8g, poly 0.1g); Protein 0.2g; Carb 2.4g; Fiber 0g; Chol 10mg; Iron 0mg; Sodium 3mg; Calc 6mg

Crème Anglaise

prep: 4 min.   cook: 14 min.

Crème Anglaise is a thin, pourable custard sauce. You'll need to stir it constantly and gently as it cooks. Dribble sauce around a poached pear, dessert soufflé, cream puff, or slice of pie.

2   cups milk or 1 cup milk and 1 cup
    half-and-half
½   cup sugar
5   egg yolks
1   teaspoon vanilla extract

Bring milk to a simmer over medium heat.
Beat sugar and egg yolks at high speed with an electric mixer until pale and mixture forms a ribbon.
Gradually add hot milk to egg yolk mixture, whisking until blended; return to saucepan. Cook over low heat, stirring constantly, until custard thickens and coats a spoon. Remove from heat; pour through a wire-mesh strainer into a bowl, and cool 10 minutes. Stir in vanilla. Cover and chill. Yield: 2 cups.

Per tablespoon: Calories 30 (36% from fat); Fat 1.2g (sat 0.5g, mono 0.4g, poly 0.1g); Protein 0.9g; Carb 3.9g; Fiber 0g; Chol 34mg; Iron 0.1mg; Sodium 7mg; Calc 21mg

Easy Caramel Sauce

prep: 5 min.   cook: 10 min.

1   cup butter
2   cups sugar
2   teaspoons fresh lemon juice
1½ cups whipping cream

Melt butter in a heavy saucepan over medium heat.
Add sugar and lemon juice, and cook, stirring constantly, 6 to 8 minutes or until mixture turns a deep caramel color. Gradually add cream; cook, stirring constantly, 1 to 2 minutes or until smooth. Remove from heat, and cool.
Pour into hot, sterilized jars, and seal. Store sauce in refrigerator up to 1 month. Yield: 3 cups.

Per tablespoon: Calories 91 (64% from fat); Fat 6.5g (sat 4.1g, mono 1.8g, poly 0.2g); Protein 0.2g; Carb 8.6g; Fiber 0g; Chol 20mg; Iron 0mg; Sodium 30mg; Calc 6mg

Caramel Sauce

prep: 10 min.   cook: 30 min.

2   cups whipping cream
¼   cup butter
½   teaspoon baking soda
2   cups sugar
½   cup water
2   teaspoons lemon juice

Cook first 3 ingredients in a Dutch oven over medium heat, stirring occasionally, until butter melts; remove mixture from heat.
Bring sugar, water, and lemon juice to a boil in a Dutch oven over high heat, stirring occasionally.
Reduce heat to medium-high; boil, stirring occasionally, 8 minutes or until mixture begins to brown. Reduce heat to medium, and cook, stirring occasionally, 5 minutes or until caramel-colored.
Pour sugar mixture gradually into whipping cream mixture. Remove from heat; let stand 1 minute. Whisk until smooth.
Cook over medium-low heat, stirring occasionally, until a candy thermometer registers 230° (thread stage); cool. Yield: 2½ cups.

Per tablespoon: Calories 150 (52% from fat); Fat 8.6g (sat 5.2g, mono 2.4g, poly 1g); Protein 0g; Carb 18g; Fiber 0g; Chol 32mg; Iron 8mg; Sodium 40mg; Calc 1mg

Sour Cream Sauce

prep: 10 min.

- ⅓ cup butter or margarine, softened
- 1 cup powdered sugar
- ½ cup sour cream
- ½ teaspoon lemon juice
- ¼ teaspoon vanilla extract

Beat butter and powdered sugar at medium speed with an electric mixer until smooth. Add sour cream, lemon juice, and vanilla, beating until sauce is creamy. Cover and chill until ready to serve or up to 8 hours. Yield: about 1¾ cups.

Per tablespoon: Calories 45 (60% from fat); Fat 3g (sat 1.9g, mono 0.8g, poly 0.1g); Protein 0.2g; Carb 4.5g; Fiber 0g; Chol 8mg; Iron 0mg; Sodium 18mg; Calc 5mg

make ahead

Lemon Curd

prep: 10 min. cook: 20 min. other: 8 hrs.

Lemon Curd adds a nice citrus flavor when served alongside shortbread or banana-nut bread. Or pour into a decorative jar for holiday gift giving.

- 2 cups sugar
- ½ cup butter, cut into pieces
- ¼ cup grated lemon rind
- 1 cup fresh lemon juice (about 6 lemons)
- 4 large eggs, lightly beaten

Stir together sugar, butter, lemon rind, and juice in a large heavy, nonaluminum saucepan over medium heat. Cook, stirring constantly, until sugar dissolves and butter melts. **Whisk** about one-fourth hot sugar mixture gradually into eggs; add egg mixture to remaining hot sugar mixture, whisking constantly.
Cook over medium-low heat, stirring constantly, 15 minutes or until mixture thickens and coats a spoon. Remove from heat; cool. Cover and chill at least 8 hours or up to 2 weeks. Yield: 2 cups.

Per tablespoon: Calories 85 (37% from fat); Fat 3.5g (sat 2g, mono 1g, poly 0.2g); Protein 0.9g; Carb 13.3g; Fiber 0.1g; Chol 34mg; Iron 0.1mg; Sodium 29mg; Calc 6mg

Italian Cottage Cheese

prep: 15 min.   other: 8 hrs., 30 min.

- 8 cups milk
- ½ cup whipping cream
- 2 cups buttermilk
- ½ teaspoon salt

Heat milk and whipping cream in a saucepan over medium heat to 190°. (Do not boil.) Add buttermilk, stirring until large curds form.
Line a colander with several layers of cheesecloth or a coffee filter; pour mixture into colander. Let stand 20 to 30 minutes to drain. Press cheese mixture slightly to remove remaining liquid.
Invert cottage cheese onto a serving dish; sprinkle with salt. Cover and chill 8 hours. Serve with fresh fruit, if desired. Yield: 1½ cups.

Per tablespoon: Calories 78 (59% from fat); Fat 5.1g (sat 3.1g, mono 1.2g, poly 0.2g); Protein 3.4g; Carb 4.8g; Fiber 0g; Chol 18mg; Iron 0mg; Sodium 107mg; Calc 95mg

Vanilla Bean Hard Sauce

prep: 8 min.

Hard sauce melts like ice cream over cobbler or any piping hot fruit dessert.

- 1 vanilla bean, split lengthwise
- 1 cup butter, softened
- 2 cups sifted powdered sugar

Scrape seeds from vanilla bean into a mixing bowl with butter. Beat butter at medium speed with an electric mixer until creamy. Gradually add sugar, beating well. Cover and chill until ready to serve. Soften slightly before serving. Yield: 1½ cups.

Per tablespoon: Calories 100 (68% from fat); Fat 7.6g (sat 4.8g, mono 2g, poly 0.3g); Protein 0.1g; Carb 8.3g; Fiber 0g; Chol 20mg; Iron 0mg; Sodium 54mg; Calc 2mg

Note: One 6-inch vanilla bean equals about 1 tablespoon vanilla extract if you want to substitute extract.

Lemon Curd

condiments

Canning Basics

Canning is a way of preserving food by heating jars of food hot enough and long enough to keep food from spoiling. Use the freshest ingredients picked at the peak of their season—then you'll know they'll be prime for canning.

There are two basic methods of home canning. The boiling-water method (for recipes in this chapter) is used for high-acid foods such as fruits, fruit spreads, tomatoes, pickles, and relishes, and it processes the food in a water-bath canner (at 212°). The steam pressure method is used for low-acid foods like most vegetables, meats, poultry, and seafood. It processes food in a pressure canner at a higher temperature (240°).

Equipment

Before you begin canning, be sure you have the proper equipment. You'll need a water-bath canner with a round kick rack that fits inside or you can use a large kettle. Just make sure it has a tight-fitting lid and that the jars fit easily inside. You'll need a jar lifter, a funnel or filler, a narrow nonmetal spatula, and a kitchen timer.

Use only standard canning jars and lids; old-style or antique canning jars and recycled commercial jelly jars are not safe for home canning. Check jars for cracks, scratches, and chips before you begin. Today's jars are reusable, as are the metal bands as long as they aren't dented or rusty. Lids are not reusable because the sealing compounds on them work only once. Always buy new jar lids with each use. Most canning supplies are available at grocery stores.

The Preparation

As with any recipe, prepare your work area and collect all the equipment you'll need before you get started. And read the recipe through more than once.

Select produce that's in season, firm, ripe, and has no bruises or bad spots. Wash produce well, and prepare as recipe directs.

The USDA recommends using hot, sterilized jars for high-acid and low-acid foods and jellies regardless of the processing time in a water-bath canning recipe. Wash jars in the dishwasher or in hot, soapy water; rinse well. To sterilize jars, place jars, right side up, on the rack in a boiling-water canner, pressure canner, or large stockpot. Cover jars with water, one inch above the jar tops, and bring water to a simmer over high heat (180°); reduce heat, and keep jars in hot water until ready to use. Carefully remove the hot jars with a jar lifter, and drain, saving the hot water for processing the filled jars. Follow manufacturer's instructions to sterilize lids. Don't use the dishwasher for sterilizing jars or lids.

Place food in hot jars using a funnel. It's important to be accurate in filling jars to the recommended headspace. Headspace is the space between the inside of the lid and the top of the food in the jar. Headspace is critical for expansion of food as it's processed and for forming a vacuum seal in the cooled jars. Too much headspace occurs when air bubbles trapped inside the jar rise to the top during processing; this can prevent proper sealing.

Once jars are filled, remove air bubbles by running a nonmetal spatula around the edge of the jar, gently shifting the food so that any trapped air escapes. Don't use anything metallic to remove air bubbles because metal might scratch the glass and cause it to break during processing. After removing air bubbles you may need to adjust headspace.

Wipe each jar rim with a clean, damp cloth to help ensure a tight seal. Then place the lid on the jar rim and screw on the metal band with your fingertips just until you feel resistance. If the band is too loose, liquid can escape during processing, and the seal can fail. If the band is too tight during processing, air can't vent, and this can cause food to discolor during storage.

When processing in a water-bath canner, use a jar lifter and position filled jars on rack in the canner, leaving space for water to flow evenly around them. If necessary, add more hot water so that the water level is 2 to 3 inches above capped jars. Bring water to a boil; cover and reduce heat to maintain a gentle boil throughout the specified processing time. Set your timer for processing when water returns to a boil.

Once jars have been processed, carefully remove each jar with a jar lifter and place right side up on a cloth towel or wire rack to cool. Let jars cool naturally 12 to 24 hours. When removing jars from the boiling water, don't be tempted to retighten the bands; you could interfere with the seal that's forming. As the jars cool you might hear loud pops indicating the vacuum seal has occurred.

When jars are completely cooled, check each jar for a proper seal. The center of the lid should dip downward. Press down on the center of the lid; it should not spring back when released.

Wipe off processed jars; label and date each jar. If a lid fails to seal, the food should be repacked and reprocessed in hot jars within 24 hours with new, properly prepared lids. Or, if you don't have time to reprocess, store food in the refrigerator. Length of storage will vary, depending on the type of food.

Storage

Foods properly processed in a water-bath canner or a pressure canner need no refrigeration until you open them. Store unopened canned foods in a cool, dark, dry place up to one year.

pickles

Summer is prime time for pickling fresh garden produce. It's the best and safest way to reap fruit and vegetable rewards all year long. With your efforts, the pantry becomes a canvas painted with jar after jar of pickles and vibrant-colored vegetables.

The Pickling Process

Always start with just-ripe produce that's free from deformities, bruises, or bad spots. It's best to begin pickling within 24 hours after picking fruits or vegetables. If it's not possible for you to start pickling right away, refrigerate the produce, unwashed, or spread it in a cool, ventilated area. Remember that cucumbers deteriorate quickly at room temperature.

Vinegar and salt are essential for making pickles, and amounts should never be reduced or diluted. Vinegar provides the acidity necessary for preservation of fresh-pack pickles. Always use vinegar of at least 5% acidity.

Be sure to use granulated uniodized pickling or canning salt. Table salt may leave white sediment on the pickles or cloud the brine.

Most pickling recipes call for some sugar because it helps crisp and plump the pickles. Unless the recipe specifies brown sugar, use white granulated sugar.

Spices give pickles their distinctive flavor. Dill, garlic, cinnamon, mustard seeds, and cloves are just a few typically used. It's best to start with fresh, whole spices; powdered spices can darken and cloud the pickled product.

---

low calorie • low cholesterol • low fat
make ahead • quick • test kitchen favorite

No-Cook Sweet-and-Spicy Pickles

prep: 5 min.

1   (46-ounce) jar hamburger dill chips
½   cup sugar
2   large garlic cloves, thinly sliced
2   tablespoons hot sauce (we tested with Tabasco Pepper Sauce)

Drain liquid from jar; remove pickles from jar. Rinse pickles with water, and drain.
Layer half each of pickles, sugar, garlic, and hot sauce in jar. Press down gently. Repeat layers. Twist on lid to seal; invert jar, and shake 2 or 3 times to combine ingredients. Store pickles in refrigerator up to 4 weeks. Yield: 4 cups.

Per ¼ cup: Calories 34 (3% from fat); Fat 0.1g (sat 0g, mono 0g, poly 0.1g); Protein 0.4g; Carb 8.5g; Fiber 0g; Chol 0mg; Iron 0.3mg; Sodium 670mg; Calc 6mg

---

family favorite • low cholesterol • low fat
make ahead

Watermelon Rind Pickles

prep: 20 min.   cook: 1 hr., 15 min.
other: 16 hrs., 10 min.

1   large watermelon, quartered
¾   cup salt
12 cups water
8   cups ice cubes
1   tablespoon whole cloves
1   tablespoon whole allspice
9   cups sugar
3   cups white vinegar (5% acidity)
3   cups water
1   lemon, thinly sliced
5   (3-inch) cinnamon sticks

Peel watermelon; remove pulp, and reserve for another use. Cut rind into 1-inch cubes; reserve 12 cups rind cubes in a container.
Stir together salt and 12 cups water; pour over rind. Add ice; cover and let stand 8 hours. Rinse well, and drain.
Cook rind and water to cover in a Dutch oven over high heat 10 minutes or until tender. Drain.
Place cloves and allspice on a 3-inch square of cheesecloth; tie with a string.
Stir together sugar, vinegar, and 3 cups water; add spice bag, and bring to a boil. Boil 5 minutes, and pour over rind. Stir in lemon slices. Cover and let stand 8 hours.
Bring rind and syrup mixture to a boil; reduce heat, and simmer 1 hour, stirring occasionally. Discard spice bag.
Pack rind mixture into hot, sterilized jars, filling to ½ inch from top. Add 1 cinnamon stick to each jar. Remove air bubbles; wipe jar rims.
Cover at once with metal lids, and screw on bands. Process in boiling water bath 10 minutes. Yield: 5 (12-ounce) jars (30 servings).

Per ¼ cup: Calories 162 (1% from fat); Fat 0.2g (sat 0g, mono 0.1g, poly 0.1g); Protein 0.9g; Carb 41.5g; Fiber 0.6g; Chol 0mg; Iron 0.4mg; Sodium 1397mg; Calc 12mg

---

family favorite • low calorie • low cholesterol
low fat • make ahead

Bread and Butter Pickles

prep: 1 hr., 45 min.   other: 3 hrs., 10 min.

6   pounds pickling cucumbers (about 25 cucumbers)
6   medium onions, sliced
2   medium-size green bell peppers, chopped
3   garlic cloves
⅓   cup pickling salt
Crushed ice
5   cups sugar
3   cups cider vinegar (5% acidity)
2   tablespoons mustard seeds
1½ teaspoons ground turmeric
1½ teaspoons celery seeds

Wash cucumbers, and thinly slice. Combine cucumber, onion, and next 3 ingredients in a large Dutch oven. Cover with ice; mix thoroughly, and refrigerate 3 hours. Drain.
Combine sugar and next 4 ingredients; pour over cucumber mixture. Heat just until boiling.
Pack hot mixture into hot, sterilized jars, filling to ½ inch from top. Remove air bubbles; wipe jar rims. Cover at once with metal lids, and screw on bands. Process jars in boiling water bath 10 minutes. Yield: 9 pints (72 servings).

Per ¼ cup: Calories 38 (2% from fat); Fat 0.1g (sat 0g, mono 0g, poly 0g); Protein 0.4g; Carb 9.2g; Fiber 0.5g; Chol 0mg; Iron 0.2mg; Sodium 260mg; Calc 9mg

low calorie • low cholesterol • low fat
make ahead

Pickled Asparagus

prep: 15 min.   cook: 6 min.   other: 8 hrs.

4   cups white vinegar (5% acidity)
3   cups water
½   cup sugar
¼   cup pickling salt
1   tablespoon dried crushed red pepper
1   tablespoon pickling spices

3   pounds fresh asparagus spears (about
    3 bunches)
6   fresh dill sprigs
3   garlic cloves

Cook first 6 ingredients in a medium saucepan over medium-high heat 4 to 6 minutes or until sugar is dissolved. Remove saucepan from heat, and cool mixture completely.
Snap off tough ends of asparagus.
Pack 1 bunch asparagus, 2 dill sprigs, and 1 garlic clove into 1 (1-quart) canning jar; repeat process with 2 remaining jars, asparagus, dill sprigs, and garlic.
Pour vinegar mixture evenly into jars; seal jars. Chill at least 8 hours; store in refrigerator up to 1 week. Yield: 3 quarts (18 servings).

Per ⅔ cup: Calories 21 (4% from fat); Fat 0.1g (sat 0g, mono 0g, poly 0.1g); Protein 1g; Carb 4.7g; Fiber 0.9g; Chol 0mg; Iron 0.9mg; Sodium 776mg; Calc 13mg

relishes

Pickle relishes are the fruition of chopped, seasoned, and pickled fruits and vegetables. The pickling process for relishes is similar to that of most pickles, but more time is required in preparation because the ingredients must be chopped. If you have a food processor, use it here. Just be careful not to overprocess ingredients because they can quickly go from chopped to mushy with a few pulses in the food processor.

family favorite • low calorie • low cholesterol
low fat • make ahead

Sweet Pickle Relish

prep: 30 min.   cook: 15 min.
other: 2 hrs., 10 min.

4   cups chopped cucumber
2   cups chopped onion
1   green bell pepper, chopped
1   red bell pepper, chopped
¼   cup pickling salt
1¾   cups sugar
1   cup cider vinegar or white vinegar
     (5% acidity)
1½   teaspoons celery seeds
1½   teaspoons mustard seeds

Combine first 4 ingredients in a large bowl; sprinkle evenly with pickling salt, and cover vegetables with cold water. Let stand 2 hours. Drain.
Combine sugar, vinegar, and spices in a Dutch oven; bring to a boil, and add vegetables. Return to a boil; reduce heat, and simmer 10 minutes.

Pack hot mixture into hot, sterilized jars, filling to ½ inch from top. Remove air bubbles; wipe jar rims.
Cover at once with metal lids, and screw on bands. Process in boiling water bath 10 minutes. Yield: 4 half-pints.

Per tablespoon: Calories 15 (0% from fat); Fat 0g (sat 0g, mono 0g, poly 0g); Protein 0.1g; Carb 3.8g; Fiber 0.2g; Chol 0mg; Iron 0.1mg; Sodium 218mg; Calc 3mg

low calorie • low cholesterol • low fat

Hot Relish

prep: 1 hr.   cook: 45 min.

6   large red tomatoes
6   large green tomatoes
3   large onions
1   large red bell pepper
2   cups sugar
3   cups white vinegar (5% acidity)
⅓   cup black peppercorns, cracked
2   to 3 jalapeño peppers, finely chopped
2   tablespoons salt
1   tablespoon ground pepper

Chop first 4 ingredients coarsely. Pulse in a food processor 2 or 3 times or until chopped; drain.
Combine tomato mixture, sugar, and remaining ingredients in a Dutch oven; bring to a boil over medium-low heat, stirring constantly. Reduce heat, and simmer, stirring often, 45 minutes.
Pack mixture into hot, sterilized jars, filling to ½ inch from top. Remove air bubbles; wipe jar rims. Cover at once with metal lids, and screw on bands.

Process in boiling water bath 10 minutes. Yield: 10 (12-ounce) jars (60 servings).

Per 2 tablespoons: Calories 39 (2% from fat); Fat 0.1g (sat 0g, mono 0g, poly 0.1g); Protein 0.5g; Carb 9.5g; Fiber 0.7g; Chol 0mg; Iron 0.2mg; Sodium 254mg; Calc 8mg

low cholesterol • low fat

Chowchow

prep: 20 min.   cook: 5 min.
other: 8 hrs., 15 min.

5   green bell peppers
5   red bell peppers
2   large green tomatoes
2   large onions
½   small cabbage
¼   cup pickling salt
3   cups sugar
2   cups white vinegar (5% acidity)
1   cup water
1   tablespoon mustard seeds
1½   teaspoons celery seeds
¾   teaspoon turmeric

Chop first 5 ingredients. Stir together chopped vegetables and salt in a large Dutch oven. Cover and chill 8 hours. Rinse and drain; return mixture to Dutch oven. Stir in sugar and remaining ingredients. Bring to a boil; reduce heat, and simmer 3 minutes.
Pack hot mixture into hot, sterilized jars, filling to ½ inch from top. Remove air bubbles; wipe jar rims. Cover at once with metal lids, and screw on bands. Process in boiling water bath 15 minutes. Yield: 5½ pints.

Per ¼ cup: Calories 67 (3% from fat); Fat 0.2g (sat 0g, mono 0.1g, poly 0.1g); Protein 0.6g; Carb 16.8g; Fiber 0.9g; Chol 0mg; Iron 0.3mg; Sodium 260mg; Calc 11mg

jellies, jams & preserves

Jelly Making

The proper amount of sugar is important for achieving a good gel, so never reduce the recommended amount. Sugar contributes to taste and acts as a preservative, preventing the growth of microorganisms.

In jelly making, jars need to be sterilized and hot before filling. Sealed jellied products should keep well up to one year if stored in a cool, dark, dry place. However, they should be used as soon as possible since flavor and quality begin to decrease within a few months.

low calorie • low cholesterol • low fat
make ahead

Easiest Pepper Jelly

prep: 5 min.   cook: 5 min.   other: 8 hrs.

- ½   cup apple jelly
- ½   cup orange marmalade
- 1   teaspoon apple cider vinegar
- 1   tablespoon seeded and chopped jalapeño pepper
- 1   tablespoon chopped green onion

Stir together all ingredients in a large saucepan over low heat until jelly and marmalade melt and mixture is blended. Cool. Cover and chill 8 hours. Store in refrigerator up to 2 weeks. Yield: 1 cup.

Per tablespoon: Calories 50 (0% from fat); Fat 0g (sat 0g, mono 0g, poly 0g); Protein 0g; Carb 13.2g; Fiber 0.1g; Chol 0mg; Iron 0mg; Sodium 6mg; Calc 4mg

family favorite • low calorie • low cholesterol
low fat • make ahead • quick

Quick Grape Jelly

prep: 10 min.   cook: 5 min.

- 2   cups bottled unsweetened grape juice
- 3½   cups sugar
- 1   (3-ounce) package liquid pectin

Combine grape juice and sugar in a Dutch oven; bring to a boil, stirring constantly. Stir in pectin; boil 1 minute, stirring constantly. Remove from heat; skim off foam with a metal spoon. Pour hot jelly quickly into hot, sterilized jars, filling to ¼ inch from top;

wipe jar rims. Cover at once with metal lids, and screw on bands. Process in boiling water bath 10 minutes. Yield: 4 half-pints.

Per tablespoon: Calories 47 (0% from fat); Fat 0g (sat 0g, mono 0g, poly 0g); Protein 0g; Carb 12.2g; Fiber 0g; Chol 0mg; Iron 0mg; Sodium 0mg; Calc 1mg

low calorie • low cholesterol • low fat • quick

Tart Basil Jelly

prep: 5 min.   cook: 10 min.

- 6¼   cups sugar
- 2   cups water
- 1   cup white vinegar (5% acidity)
- 1   cup loosely packed fresh basil leaves
- 6   drops of green liquid food coloring
- 2   (3-ounce) packages liquid pectin

Bring first 5 ingredients to a boil in a large saucepan. Add pectin, and bring to a full rolling boil. Boil 1 minute. Remove from heat. Remove and discard basil leaves; skim off foam with a metal spoon.
Pour hot mixture immediately into hot, sterilized jars, filling to ¼ inch from top. Remove air bubbles; wipe jar rims. Cover at once with metal lids, and screw on bands.
Process in boiling water bath 10 minutes. Yield: 7 half-pints.

Per tablespoon: Calories 43 (0% from fat); Fat 0g (sat 0g, mono 0g, poly 0g); Protein 0g; Carb 11.2g; Fiber 0g; Chol 0mg; Iron 0mg; Sodium 0mg; Calc 0mg

Mint Jelly: Substitute 1 cup mint leaves for 1 cup basil leaves.

low calorie • low cholesterol • low fat

Blueberry Jam

prep: 5 min.   cook: 10 min.

- 6   cups stemmed blueberries, crushed
- 1   teaspoon grated lemon rind
- 2   tablespoons fresh lemon juice
- 7   cups sugar
- 2   (3-ounce) packages liquid pectin

Combine first 4 ingredients in a Dutch oven. Bring to a boil; cook until sugar dissolves, stirring occasionally. Boil 2 minutes, stirring often; remove from heat. Add pectin to mixture, and stir 5 minutes. Skim

off foam with a metal spoon. Pour hot jam quickly into hot, sterilized jars, leaving ¼-inch headspace; wipe jar rims. Cover at once with metal lids, and screw on bands. Process in boiling water bath 10 minutes. Yield: 8 half-pints.

Per tablespoon: Calories 46 (0% from fat); Fat 0g (sat 0g, mono 0g, poly 0g); Protein 0.1g; Carb 12g; Fiber 0.2g; Chol 0mg; Iron 0mg; Sodium 0mg; Calc 1mg

low calorie • low cholesterol • low fat

Strawberry-Port Jam

prep: 15 min.   cook: 10 min.   other: 10 min.

- 2   (10-ounce) packages frozen unsweetened strawberries, thawed
- 1½   cups ruby port
- 1   teaspoon grated lemon rind
- ½   teaspoon ground nutmeg
- 1   (1¾-ounce) package powdered fruit pectin
- 4   cups sugar

Chop or crush thawed strawberries in a 4-cup measuring cup. Add water to strawberries to measure 2½ cups.
Stir together strawberry mixture, port, lemon rind, and nutmeg in a large saucepan. Stir in pectin.
Bring mixture to a full rolling boil, and boil, stirring constantly, 1 minute. Add sugar, stirring constantly, and bring to a full rolling boil. Boil 1 minute. Remove from heat, and skim off foam with a metal spoon.
Pour hot jam immediately into hot, sterilized jars, filling to ¼ inch from top. Remove air bubbles; wipe jar rims. Cover at once with metal lids, and screw on bands.
Process in boiling water bath 10 minutes. Yield: 7 half-pints.

Per tablespoon: Calories 32 (0% from fat); Fat 0g (sat 0g, mono 0g, poly 0g); Protein 0g; Carb 7.8g; Fiber 0.1g; Chol 0mg; Iron 0mg; Sodium 0mg; Calc 1mg

Note: Ruby port is a deep red–colored sweet wine typically enjoyed as an after-dinner drink. It's usually sold in liquor stores because of its high alcohol content.

Peach-Rosemary Jam, Carrot-Orange Marmalade, Strawberry-Port Jam (page 447)

Decorative jars make pretty serving containers, but don't use them for processing canned items.

test kitchen favorite
Peach-Rosemary Jam

prep: 25 min.   cook: 10 min.   other: 10 min.

4   cups peeled and chopped fresh peaches
1   teaspoon grated lime rind
¼   cup fresh lime juice
2   rosemary sprigs
1   (1¾-ounce) package powdered fruit pectin
5   cups sugar

Bring first 5 ingredients to a full rolling boil in a Dutch oven. Boil 1 minute, stirring constantly. Add sugar to peach mixture, and bring to a full rolling boil; boil 1 minute, stirring constantly. Remove from heat. Remove and discard rosemary sprigs; skim off foam with a metal spoon.
Pour hot mixture immediately into hot, sterilized jars, filling to ¼ inch from top. Remove air bubbles; wipe jar rims. Cover at once with metal lids, and screw on bands. Process in boiling water bath 10 minutes. Yield: 7 half-pints.

Per tablespoon: Calories 37 (0% from fat); Fat 0g (sat 0g, mono 0g, poly 0g); Protein 0.1g; Carb 9.6g; Fiber 0.1g; Chol 0mg; Iron 0mg; Sodium 0mg; Calc 1mg

low calorie • low cholesterol • low fat
Carrot-Orange Marmalade

prep: 15 min.   cook: 25 min.   other: 10 min.

4   cups sugar
3   large oranges, thinly sliced
1   (10-ounce) bag matchstick carrots
2   teaspoons lemon rind (rind from 1 lemon)
2   tablespoons fresh lemon juice

Bring all ingredients to a full rolling boil over medium heat in a Dutch oven, stirring occasionally, until sugar is dissolved and syrup thickens. Reduce heat, and simmer, stirring occasionally, 15 to 20 minutes. Remove from heat; skim off foam with a metal spoon.
Pour hot marmalade immediately into hot, sterilized jars, filling to ¼ inch from top. Remove air bubbles; wipe jar rims. Cover at once with metal lids, and screw on bands. Process in boiling water bath 10 minutes. Yield: 7 half-pints.

Per tablespoon: Calories 31 (0% from fat); Fat 0g (sat 0g, mono 0g, poly 0g); Protein 0.1g; Carb 8g; Fiber 0.2g; Chol 0mg; Iron 0mg; Sodium 2mg; Calc 3mg

family favorite • low calorie • low cholesterol low fat
Fig Preserves

prep: 10 min.   cook: 2 hrs.
other: 8 hrs., 15 min.

Shop for figs from late June through October. Handle fresh ones gently, and store them in the refrigerator up to two or three days.

2   quarts fresh figs (about 4 pounds)
8   cups sugar

Layer figs and sugar in a Dutch oven. Cover and let stand 8 hours.
Cook over medium heat 2 hours, stirring occasionally, until syrup thickens and figs are clear.
Pack figs into hot, sterilized jars, filling to ½ inch from top. Cover fruit with boiling syrup, filling to ½ inch from top. Remove

air bubbles; wipe jar rims. Cover at once with metal lids, and screw on bands. **Process** in boiling water bath 15 minutes. Yield: 4 quarts.

Per tablespoon: Calories 29 (0% from fat); Fat 0g (sat 0g, mono 0g, poly 0g); Protein 0.1g; Carb 7.6g; Fiber 0.2g; Chol 0mg; Iron 0mg; Sodium 0mg; Calc 3mg

low calorie • low cholesterol • low fat
make ahead
Mango Chutney

prep: 30 min.   cook: 35 min.

1½   cups orange juice
1   cup golden raisins
3   cups chopped mango (2 medium)
2   to 3 jalapeño peppers, seeded and chopped
1   medium-size red onion, chopped
2   tablespoons brown sugar
2   to 3 tablespoons lime juice
2   teaspoons ground coriander
1   teaspoon ground cumin
1   teaspoon ground ginger
¼   teaspoon ground cloves
¼   teaspoon ground nutmeg
⅛   teaspoon ground red pepper

Combine all ingredients in a medium saucepan. Cover; bring to a boil over medium heat, stirring occasionally. Reduce heat; simmer, uncovered, 30 minutes or until mixture thickens, stirring occasionally. Cool slightly. Chill up to one week. Yield: 2 cups.

Per tablespoon: Calories 34 (3% from fat); Fat 0.1g (sat 0g, mono 0g, poly 0g); Protein 0.4g; Carb 8.6g; Fiber 0.6g; Chol 0mg; Iron 0.2mg; Sodium 2mg; Calc 8mg

Count yourself lucky if neighbors or friends offer you some of their fig harvest.

Cranberry Conserve

prep: 10 min.   cook: 30 min.   other: 3 hrs.

4   cups fresh cranberries
1   cup water
1   orange
1   cup raisins
2½   cups sugar
½   cup finely chopped pecans

Combine cranberries and 1 cup water in a large saucepan; bring to a boil. Cover, reduce heat, and simmer 6 to 8 minutes or until cranberry skins pop.
Grate rind of orange; peel, seed, and dice orange. Stir together cranberries, orange, grated rind, raisins, sugar, and pecans.
Cook over low heat, stirring often, 20 minutes or until mixture thickens. Remove from heat; cool. Cover and chill at least 3 hours. Yield: 4 cups.

Per tablespoon: Calories 47 (13% from fat); Fat 0.7g (sat 0.1g, mono 0.4g, poly 0.2g); Protein 0.2g; Carb 10.7g; Fiber 0.5g; Chol 0mg; Iron 0.1mg; Sodium 0mg; Calc 3mg

taste of the south apple butter

You don't have to go to the county fair to stir up childhood memories of sugar and spice. Instead, you can make jars of apple butter for year-round enjoyment. As the fall season approaches, take a road trip through the Appalachian Mountains and stop at community festivals and quaint crossroads stores. Buy a jar of the sweet preserve or buy some Granny Smith apples and prepare this easy oven recipe. Then you can enjoy the tastes of fall all year long.

Some folks have a fondness for spreading apple butter between layers of graham crackers, a dessert similar to an apple stack cake. But truth be told, nothing can beat tender flaky biscuits hot from the oven slathered with freshly made apple butter.

low calorie • low cholesterol • low fat

Oven Apple Butter

prep: 25 min.   cook: 5 hrs.

8   Granny Smith apples, peeled and diced
1   cup apple juice
1   cup sugar
1   teaspoon ground cinnamon

Cook diced apple and juice in a Dutch oven over medium heat 30 minutes or until apple is tender. Stir until apple is mashed.
Stir in sugar and cinnamon. Pour apple mixture into a lightly greased 11- x 7-inch baking dish. Bake at 275° for 4½ hours, stirring every hour, or until spreading consistency. Cover and chill. Yield: 3 cups.

Per tablespoon: Calories 24 (0% from fat); Fat 0g (sat 0g, mono 0g, poly 0g); Protein 0.1g; Carb 7.7g; Fiber 0.3g; Chol 0mg; Iron 0.1mg; Sodium 0mg; Calc 2mg

vinegars

Making your own vinegar isn't hard. For flavor and color variations, just pour cider vinegar, red or white wine vinegar, or Champagne vinegar over fresh berries, herbs, and spices. Bring vinegar almost to a boil (190°) before pouring over herbs.

Use flavored vinegars in homemade vinaigrettes for salads, add a spoonful to black bean soup or beef stew, or splash some over steaming hot roasted vegetables.

low calorie • low carb • low cholesterol
low fat • make ahead

Raspberry Vinegar

prep: 5 min.   cook: 5 min.   other: 2 weeks

1   pint fresh raspberries
4   cups white wine vinegar
⅓   cup sugar

Place raspberries in a widemouthed glass jar or bowl; crush berries with the back of a spoon. Pour vinegar over berries; cover and let stand at room temperature 2 weeks.
Pour raspberry mixture through a wire-mesh strainer lined with 2 layers of cheesecloth into a saucepan, discarding raspberries; stir in sugar.
Bring mixture to a boil over medium-high heat, stirring constantly. Pour into hot, sterilized bottles; cool. Seal or cork bottles, and store in refrigerator. Yield: 4 cups.

Per tablespoon: Calories 5 (0% from fat); Fat 0g (sat 0g, mono 0g, poly 00g); Protein 0g; Carb 1.2g; Fiber 0.1g; Chol 0mg; Iron 0.1mg; Sodium 2mg; Calc 1mg

low calorie • low carb • low cholesterol
low fat • make ahead

Tomato–Herb Vinegar

prep: 10 min.   cook: 5 min.   other: 2 weeks

10   large sprigs fresh rosemary
6   large sprigs fresh basil
4   large sprigs fresh oregano
12   small garlic cloves, peeled and halved
10   dried tomato halves
1   teaspoon black peppercorns
3   (32-ounce) bottles red wine vinegar
Fresh rosemary sprigs (optional)

Clean and rinse herbs. Twist stems of herbs gently to bruise leaves, and press garlic with back of a spoon to crush it. Place herbs and garlic in a large glass container. Add tomato and peppercorns. Set aside.
Bring vinegar just to a boil, and pour over herb mixture. Cover and let stand at room temperature 2 weeks.
Pour vinegar mixture through a large wire-mesh strainer into hot, sterilized decorative bottles, discarding solids. Add additional cleaned and rinsed rosemary sprigs, if desired. Seal bottles, and store in refrigerator. Yield: 11 cups.

Per tablespoon: Calories 1 (0% from fat); Fat 0g (sat 0g, mono 0g, poly 0g); Protein 0g; Carb 0.1g; Fiber 0g; Chol 0mg; Iron 0.1mg; Sodium 2mg; Calc 1mg

side dishes

The way Southerners prepare vegetables has evolved over the years. The legacy of long-cooked vegetables still lingers, however, and we pay tribute to it with a few recipes in this chapter. Today's cooking procedures leave you with fuller flavor, better texture, and more nutrients.

Equipment

If you like steamed vegetables, you'll benefit from a selection of saucepans with snug-fitting lids as well as a collapsible metal steamer basket. A large skillet or an electric wok will serve you well for sautéing and stir-frying vegetables.

Both fresh and frozen vegetables will put your microwave oven to its best use. A sharp paring knife, chef's knife, and sturdy vegetable peeler are must-have tools for trimming, peeling, and slicing vegetables. A couple of cutting boards will supply the stable surface to complete the task.

Always Buy in Season

Buying vegetables in season not only yields the highest quality and flavor, but they'll be reasonably priced. When selecting fresh produce, look for bright color and crisp appearance. Small vegetables tend to be sweeter and more tender than larger ones in the same family. Generally speaking, buy firm vegetables rather than soft. Avoid buying any vegetables that are bruised or limp.

Storing Vegetables

For maximum flavor and nutritive value, use fresh vegetables within one to two days of purchase. Store most vegetables dry and unwashed. Wash vegetables just before using. Too much moisture causes vegetables to deteriorate rapidly. Leafy greens are the exception. Rinse leafy green vegetables under cool water, and drain using a colander or a salad spinner. Wrap in paper towels, place in zip-top plastic bags, squeeze out air, and refrigerate.

Store potatoes and onions away from each other in a cool, dry, well-ventilated place such as a pantry out of direct sunlight. Store tomatoes at room temperature in a basket or on a windowsill out of direct sunlight.

Corn, beans, and peas lose sweetness as their natural sugar turns to starch during storage. Store these vegetables dry and unwashed in plastic bags in the refrigerator, and use as soon as possible.

It's a good idea to check vegetables daily for spoilage no matter where they're stored (pantry, refrigerator, or simply at room temperature). If one piece shows signs of spoilage, it can quickly ruin the whole lot. So if you detect spoilage, promptly discard those vegetable pieces. Once cut, all vegetables should be stored in the refrigerator in plastic bags.

Freezing Vegetables

Most vegetables require blanching before freezing in order to maintain good quality. Blanching is a brief boiling that arrests maturation of food. See photo on page 27 for more detail.

Leftover cooked vegetables and vegetable casseroles freeze fairly well, although when reheated, their texture won't be as crisp.

Preparing Vegetables

Brush off loose dirt before washing vegetables. Use a stiff vegetable brush to remove dirt from some root vegetables. A sinkful of luke-warm water is recommended for removing sand and grit from vegetables such as artichokes, zucchini, leafy greens, and leeks.

Peel vegetables when a recipe specifies. Many vegetables such as small eggplant, summer squash, and potatoes don't have to be peeled; just wash them well. Leaving the skin on helps retain nutrients.

Some vegetables discolor quickly once they're peeled or sliced. To prevent discoloration, briefly dip vegetables in acidulated water, a solution of 1 tablespoon lemon juice to 1 cup water.

Cooking Vegetables

Cook most vegetables as briefly as possible in as little liquid as possible to retain nutrients, color, and texture. The microwave oven is ideal for cooking fresh vegetables because you need only a scant amount of water. In turn, vegetables cook quickly, retaining good color and nutrients.

Steaming fresh vegetables in a steamer basket over boiling water preserves more vitamins than cooking in boiling water. Be sure the boiling water level does not touch the basket.

Cook vegetables such as artichokes, large green beans, cabbage, and some greens uncovered in a large pot of boiling water. The boiling activity softens tough vegetable fibers.

Sautéing and stir-frying are quick and easy cooking methods ideal for many vegetables. Sautéing them in a small amount of hot fat over medium to medium-high heat preserves color, texture, and nutrients. When stir-frying, it's often recommended that you cut vegetables on the diagonal to expose the most surface area for quick cooking. See photo on page 25 for details.

Braising (cooking slowly, covered, in a flavorful liquid) is a recommended cooking method for many root vegetables, as well as cabbage and brussels sprouts. These vegetables will absorb the flavor of the braising liquid during long, slow cooking.

Roasting enhances the natural sweetness of many vegetables. This dry-heat cooking method with no added liquid preserves nutrients and concentrates flavor. You can roast any number of vegetables by this simple method: Cut similarly textured vegetables into same-size pieces. Prepare to roast only enough vegetables to create a single layer in a roasting pan. Drizzle vegetables with 1 to 2 tablespoons of olive oil, and sprinkle with salt and pepper. Roast at 450° or 500° for 6 to 8 minutes, stirring once. Some vegetables such as potatoes will take much longer to cook. See individual recipes for recommended times. Roasted vegetables are simple to prepare and are quite versatile. You can match them with many entrées.

Shown on previous page: Field Peas, Okra, and Corn (page 466)

vegetable side dishes

Whole Cooked Artichokes

prep: 15 min.   cook: 35 min.

To eat an artichoke, pluck the leaves from the cooked veggie, one at a time, beginning at the base; dip the meaty end of each leaf into desired sauce (see suggestions below). Draw each leaf between your teeth, scraping off the meat. Discard leaves. Under the inedible fuzzy choke that remains in the center of the artichoke lies the prized heart. Quarter and dip it as well.

4   large artichokes
Lemon wedge
3   tablespoons lemon juice

Wash artichokes by plunging up and down in cold water. Cut off stem ends, and trim about ½ inch from top of each artichoke. Remove any loose bottom leaves. With scissors, trim one-fourth off top of each outer leaf, and rub cut edges with lemon wedge to prevent discoloration.
Place artichokes in a stainless steel Dutch oven; cover with water, and add lemon juice.
Bring to a boil; cover, reduce heat, and simmer 35 minutes or until lower leaves pull out easily. Drain artichokes. Serve with Clarified Butter (page 433), Beurre Blanc (page 431), or Hollandaise Sauce (page 432). Yield: 4 servings.

Per serving: Calories 79 (2% from fat); Fat 0.2g (sat 0.1g, mono 0g, poly 0.1g); Protein 5.4g; Carb 18.1g; Fiber 8.8g; Chol 0mg; Iron 2.1mg; Sodium 152mg; Calc 72mg

Microwave Directions: Stand artichokes in an 11- x 7-inch baking dish, and add 1 cup water to dish. Cover dish with heavy-duty plastic wrap. Microwave at HIGH 15 to 20 minutes, giving dish a quarter-turn halfway through cooking time. Let stand 5 minutes. (When done, the petal near the center will pull out easily.) Yield: 4 servings.

Asparagus Amandine

prep: 5 min.   cook: 15 min.

2   pounds fresh asparagus
2   tablespoons butter or margarine
¼   cup sliced almonds
¼   cup diced red bell pepper
1   tablespoon fresh lemon juice
½   teaspoon salt
½   teaspoon pepper

Snap off tough ends of asparagus.
Cook asparagus in boiling salted water to cover in a large skillet 3 minutes or until crisp-tender; drain. Plunge asparagus into ice water to stop the cooking process; drain.
Melt butter in a large skillet over medium heat; add almonds, and sauté 2 to 3 minutes or until browned.
Add asparagus and diced red bell pepper; cook 3 to 5 minutes. Toss with lemon juice, salt, and pepper, and serve hot. Yield: 8 servings.

Per serving: Calories 56 (71% from fat); Fat 4.4g (sat 1.9g, mono 1.7g, poly 0.5g); Protein 2.1g; Carb 3.5g; Fiber 1.7g; Chol 8mg; Iron 1.5mg; Sodium 167mg; Calc 24mg

Roasted Asparagus With Balsamic Browned Butter

prep: 5 min.   cook: 15 min.

2   pounds fresh asparagus
Vegetable cooking spray
½   teaspoon kosher salt
¼   teaspoon pepper
2   tablespoons butter
2   teaspoons soy sauce
1   teaspoon balsamic vinegar

Snap off tough ends of asparagus.
Arrange asparagus in a single layer on a baking sheet; coat with cooking spray. Sprinkle with salt and pepper.
Bake at 400° for 12 minutes or until tender.
Melt butter in a small skillet over medium heat; cook 3 minutes or until lightly browned, shaking pan occasionally. Remove from heat; stir in soy sauce and vinegar.

Drizzle over asparagus, tossing well to coat. Serve hot. Yield: 8 servings.

Per serving: Calories 39 (67% from fat); Fat 2.9g (sat 1.8g, mono 0.7g, poly 0.2g); Protein 1.5g; Carb 2.6g; Fiber 1.3g; Chol 8mg; Iron 1.3mg; Sodium 249mg; Calc 16mg

Lemon-Marinated Asparagus

prep: 20 min.   cook: 3 min.   other: 10 hrs.

Fresh lemon juice makes an impressive difference in this make-ahead side dish. Add the asparagus near the final stage to preserve its green color.

½   cup fresh lemon juice
3   tablespoons olive oil
2   tablespoons sugar
¼   teaspoon salt
¼   teaspoon pepper
1   garlic clove, minced
1   (14-ounce) can quartered artichoke hearts, drained
1   (4-ounce) jar diced pimiento, drained
2   pounds fresh asparagus

Whisk together first 6 ingredients in a large bowl; add artichoke heart quarters and diced pimiento, and gently toss. Cover and chill 8 hours or overnight.
Snap off tough ends of asparagus; cook in boiling salted water to cover 3 minutes or until crisp-tender.
Drain asparagus, and plunge into ice water to stop the cooking process. Place cooked asparagus in a large zip-top freezer bag, and store overnight in refrigerator, if desired.
Add asparagus to artichoke mixture, and gently toss. Cover and chill 2 hours. Yield: 8 servings.

Per serving: Calories 87 (54% from fat); Fat 5.2g (sat 0.7g, mono 3.8g, poly 0.6g); Protein 2.3g; Carb 9.3g; Fiber 1.5g; Chol 0mg; Iron 1.9mg; Sodium 151mg; Calc 17mg

Barbecue Beans

prep: 9 min.   cook: 1 hr., 6 min.

Use your favorite barbecue sauce here.

½   pound ground chuck
¾   cup chopped onion
10   bacon slices, cooked and crumbled
⅔   cup firmly packed light brown sugar
¾   cup barbecue sauce (we tested with KC
     Masterpiece Original Barbecue Sauce)
1   (15-ounce) can pork and beans, undrained
1   (15-ounce) can dark red kidney beans,
     rinsed and drained
1   (15-ounce) can butter beans, rinsed and
     drained
2   tablespoons molasses
2   teaspoons Dijon mustard
½   teaspoon salt
½   teaspoon pepper
½   teaspoon chili powder

Cook ground chuck and onion in a Dutch oven, stirring until meat crumbles and is no longer pink. Drain and return to pan. Stir in bacon and remaining 10 ingredients. Spoon bean mixture into a lightly greased 2½–quart baking dish. Chill 8 hours, if desired.
Bake, covered, at 350° for 1 hour, stirring once. Yield: 10 servings.

Per serving: Calories 242 (16% from fat); Fat 4.4g (sat 1.6g, mono 1.6g, poly 0.4g); Protein 12.2g; Carb 41.2g; Fiber 4.3g; Chol 19mg; Iron 2.5mg; Sodium 732mg; Calc 59mg

Note: If you desire thicker beans, bake this dish uncovered.

Best Pinto Beans

prep: 14 min.   cook: 1 hr., 45 min.

This pinto bean recipe packs the perfect balance of smokiness from the ham hock and spiciness from the diced tomatoes with chiles and hot sauce. Serve these beans with or without the juices; eat them with cornbread for a simple supper.

1   pound dried pinto beans
1   smoked ham hock
1   (10-ounce) can diced tomatoes and green
     chiles
1   (32-ounce) container chicken broth
1   green bell pepper, chopped
1   celery rib, chopped
½   onion, chopped
1   teaspoon salt
1   teaspoon garlic powder
1   teaspoon dried oregano
½   teaspoon dried thyme
½   teaspoon black pepper
1   teaspoon Worcestershire sauce
½   teaspoon hot sauce
Hot cooked rice (optional)

Sort and rinse beans; place in a Dutch oven. Cover with water 2 inches above beans. Bring to a boil; let boil 1 minute. Cover and remove from heat. Let stand 1 hour. Drain.
Return beans to Dutch oven, and add water to cover. Bring to a boil, and cook, uncovered, 30 minutes. Drain.
Add ham hock, tomatoes, and next 11 ingredients to Dutch oven with beans; bring to a boil. Reduce heat; simmer, covered, over low heat 1 hour or until beans are tender. Serve over hot cooked rice, if desired. Yield: 8 servings.

Per serving: Calories 220 (8% from fat); Fat 1.9g (sat 0.3g, mono 0.4g, poly 0.3g); Protein 13.7g; Carb 38.6g; Fiber 13g; Chol 2mg; Iron 3.2mg; Sodium 923mg; Calc 80mg

vegetable dictionary

Artichoke: While the hearty artichoke is available year-round, its peak season is March through May. Artichokes vary greatly in size so it's a good rule to remember the smaller the artichoke, the more tender it will be. When you're purchasing artichokes, look for deep green, intact leaves without cracks or discoloration.

Beets: Traditionally, beets bring to mind a garnet red color and earthy flavor, but this isn't true of all varieties. In fact, beets can vary from the common garnet red to white to a golden color. A versatile vegetable, beets are equally as good served hot or chilled. One thing to remember—always cook them separately from other ingredients since their color stains. Peel beets after they're cooked to ensure minimal nutrient and color loss, and store them, sealed in a plastic bag, in the refrigerator up to five days.

Bok choy: Bok choy has an appearance and texture similar to celery, but it's much broader and whiter in color. Choose bok choy for its firm, white stalks and crisp green leaves. While cooked bok choy is a staple for stir-fry dishes, its raw crunchiness can add fresh flavor to salads. Store bok choy in the refrigerator in an airtight bag for three or four days.

Broccoli rabe: Broccoli rabe has 6- to 9-inch stalks, large green leaves, and little broccoli-like buds. Available mainly during the fall through spring, broccoli rabe is a favorite in Italian cooking. Steaming, braising, or frying it offsets the vegetable's bitterness. The leaves, stems, and flower heads are cooked and eaten just like regular broccoli. To maintain crispness, refrigerate, unwashed, loosely wrapped in a plastic bag for up to three days.

Brussels sprouts: This member of the cabbage family grows in rows of buds on thick stalks and resembles small green cabbage heads. Brussels sprouts are a vitamin-rich food and are in season during late August through March. Look for brussels sprouts that are small, bright green, and have tightly compacted leaves.

Chayote squash: Recognizable by its pale green skin and gourdlike shape, chayote squash is available mainly during winter months. It can be cooked similarly to summer squash, eaten raw or stuffed, and it can take on assertive seasoning due to its mild flavor.

Corn: Corn's best season is May through September. It should be eaten just-picked, if possible, because the sugar in corn kernels quickly converts to starch and depletes flavor.

Eggplant: Peak season is August and September. Choose eggplants with a smooth, firm skin and substantial weight. Use eggplants shortly after purchase, and avoid cutting them until ready to use. Also look for Japanese or Asian eggplant, Italian or baby eggplant, and white eggplant.

Fennel: The common form of fennel is called *Florence fennel* and is available from fall through spring. With its white bulbs, celery-like stalks, and feathery green leaves, fennel's mainly used for its sweet, delicately anise-flavored bulb. Enjoy it braised, sautéed, or raw as well as incorporated into stocks. Florence fennel's relative, referred to as common fennel, produces fennel seeds.

Haricots verts: French green beans, haricots verts, are small, thin beans that can be used in the same manner as their American counterpart. They need only brief cooking.

Jerusalem artichoke: Also labeled as *sunchokes,* Jerusalem artichokes are available from October to March. Their nutty, crunchy flesh is encased in a lumpy brown skin that resembles gingerroot. An iron-rich vegetable, the Jerusalem artichoke can be cooked peeled, or simply washed and cooked.

Jícama: A root vegetable available year-round in many Latin American markets, jícama is hailed for its sweet, nutty flavor and crisp texture. Store it in the refrigerator in a sealed plastic bag.

Kohlrabi: Also called a *cabbage turnip,* kohlrabi looks and tastes similar to a turnip with its stem's slightly purple hue and edible greens. Choose a firm, unblemished kohlrabi with deep green leaves, and try it steamed or in your favorite stir-fry.

Okra: A popular vegetable in Southern cuisine, okra is recognizable by its long, ridged, tapered body and green skin. Okra can be fried, baked, or braised as well as paired with other vegetables. It exudes a viscous substance when cooked that provides thickening to gumbos or stews.

Opo: Also referred to as the *Calabash Gourd,* the Asian Opo gourds are the edible products of a prolific tropical climbing vine. While prepared similarly to squash, Opo gourds are not a member of the squash family. Opo gourds grow in a variety of forms, ranging from long and

green, like zucchini, to the short, plump, and white variety popular in Japan.

Parsnip: This white root vegetable is available year-round, though its peak season is during the colder months. When choosing parsnips, look for ones that are firm and unblemished. Store in the refrigerator in a plastic bag up to two weeks.

Pattypan squash: A summer squash with a dainty, scalloped edge, pattypan squash have pale green, bumpy skin and are 3 to 4 inches in diameter. Use pattypan squash in recipes interchangeably with any summer squash.

Rutabaga: These pale yellow vegetables are thought to be a cross between a cabbage and turnip, which proves likely considering the slightly sweet taste and firm texture of this root vegetable. Try rutabagas as a substitute for turnips in your favorite root vegetable recipe.

Swiss chard: Chard is part of the beet family. It's really like two vegetables in one—use the stems like celery; cook the large ruffly leaves like spinach.

Turnip: Turnips have white skins and pale purple tops. Choose turnips that have crisp, firm roots and greens. Ideally, turnips should be stored in a cool, dark place, but the vegetable drawer of your refrigerator will work fine for its shelf life of about two weeks.

Winter Squash

Acorn: Most commonly halved, baked, and eaten directly from its shell, acorn squash is an oblong, dark green vegetable with ribbed skin.

Butternut: This winter squash is long and cylindrical. Prepare it as you would use any winter squash; you'll enjoy its sweet orange flesh in savory or sweet recipes.

Spaghetti: Even when judged by its watermelon-shaped and pale yellow exterior, the reason for spaghetti squash's name is evident. Once cooked, its mild-flavored flesh separates into spaghetti-like strands, striking such a resemblance to the pasta that it can be used as a substitute.

Baked Beans

prep: 10 min.   cook: 49 min.

4	bacon slices
1	(28-ounce) can pork and beans, drained
1	small onion, diced
¼	cup firmly packed light or dark brown sugar
¼	cup sorghum
¼	cup ketchup
1	teaspoon Worcestershire sauce
½	teaspoon dry mustard

Cook bacon in a large skillet over medium-high heat 3 to 4 minutes; drain.
Stir together pork and beans and next 6 ingredients in a lightly greased 1-quart baking dish. Top with bacon slices. Bake at 350° for 45 minutes. Yield: 4 servings.

Per serving: Calories 335 (16% from fat); Fat 5.8g (sat 1.9g, mono 2.3g, poly 0.7g); Protein 12.6g; Carb 62.5g; Fiber 9.8g; Chol 19mg; Iron 3.9mg; Sodium 1037mg; Calc 114mg

Smoky Speckled Butterbeans

prep: 10 min.   cook: 3 hrs., 30 min.

You'll know when this dish is ready—the pork shreds easily, and the beans are creamy on the inside.

3	quarts water
1	pound smoked pork shoulder
2	pounds fresh or frozen speckled butterbeans
2	teaspoons salt
1	teaspoon pepper
1	jalapeño pepper, sliced
	Hot cooked rice (optional)
	Toppings: chopped sweet onion, hot sauce, chowchow (optional)

Bring first 6 ingredients to a boil in a Dutch oven. Reduce heat to medium. Cover and simmer 3 hours or until beans are tender, stirring occasionally. Remove pork, and shred. Return to Dutch oven. If desired, serve with hot cooked rice and toppings. Yield: 8 servings.

Per serving: Calories 544 (16% from fat); Fat 9.4g (sat 3g, mono 3.5g, poly 0.8g); Protein 35.1g; Carb 80.9g; Fiber 25.3g; Chol 37mg; Iron 7.5mg; Sodium 623mg; Calc 114mg

Five-Bean Bake

prep: 20 min.   cook: 1 hr., 40 min.

This dish resembles traditional baked beans but it's five times better—it boasts a quintuplet of beans.

8	bacon slices, chopped
1	large onion, diced
1	(28-ounce) can pork and beans
1	(19.75-ounce) can black beans, rinsed and drained
1	(16-ounce) can chickpeas, rinsed and drained
1	(15.5-ounce) can kidney beans, rinsed and drained
1	(15.25-ounce) can lima beans, rinsed and drained
1	cup ketchup
½	cup firmly packed light or dark brown sugar
½	cup water
¼	cup cider vinegar

Cook bacon in a large skillet over medium-high heat until crisp; remove bacon, and drain on paper towels, reserving 2 tablespoons drippings in skillet. Add onion; sauté in hot drippings 5 minutes or until tender.
Combine bacon, onion, pork and beans, and remaining ingredients in a lightly greased 13- x 9-inch baking dish.
Bake, covered, at 350° for 1 hour; uncover and bake 30 more minutes. Yield: 8 servings.

Per serving: Calories 338 (15% from fat); Fat 5.6g (sat 1.5g, mono 2.2g, poly 1.1g); Protein 14.1g; Carb 65.3g; Fiber 13g; Chol 14mg; Iron 4.1mg; Sodium 1208mg; Calc 114mg

Sautéed Green Beans

prep: 10 min.   cook: 20 min.

2	pounds fresh green beans, trimmed
1	red bell pepper, thinly sliced lengthwise
2	tablespoons olive oil
2	garlic cloves, minced
1	teaspoon Creole seasoning (we tested with Tony Chachere's Creole Seasoning)

Cook green beans in boiling salted water to cover 5 to 8 minutes or until crisp-tender. Drain and plunge into ice water to stop the cooking process; drain.
Sauté sliced red bell pepper in 2 tablespoons hot oil in a large skillet over medium heat 5 minutes or until crisp-tender; add minced garlic, and sauté 2 minutes. Add green beans; sprinkle with 1 teaspoon Creole seasoning, and cook, just until thoroughly heated. Yield: 6 servings.

Per serving: Calories 88 (48% from fat); Fat 4.7g (sat 0.7g, mono 3.3g, poly 0.6g); Protein 2.7g; Carb 11g; Fiber 4.9g; Chol 0mg; Iron 1.5mg; Sodium 109mg; Calc 52mg

Green Beans in Tomato Sauce

prep: 10 min.   cook: 28 min.

If you're tired of plain old green beans, try this tangy combination with tomato sauce. Although you can substitute frozen green beans for fresh, we recommend using fresh for the best flavor.

1	pound fresh green beans, trimmed*
1	small sweet onion, chopped
1	garlic clove, minced
2	tablespoons olive oil
1	(8-ounce) can tomato sauce
1	tablespoon sugar
½	teaspoon salt
½	teaspoon freshly ground pepper
1	tablespoon red wine vinegar
1	tablespoon chopped fresh flat-leaf parsley

If desired, snap beans into 1-inch pieces. Cook beans in boiling water to cover 8 to 12 minutes or until crisp-tender; drain and set aside.
Sauté onion and garlic in hot oil in a large skillet over medium-high heat 5 minutes or until onion is tender.
Add tomato sauce and next 4 ingredients; cook 5 minutes, stirring often. Add green beans, and cook 3 minutes or until beans are heated. Sprinkle with parsley, and serve hot. Yield: 4 servings.

Per serving: Calories 132 (48% from fat); Fat 7g (sat 1g, mono 5g, poly 0.8g); Protein 2.8g; Carb 17.2g; Fiber 4.6g; Chol 0mg; Iron 1.8mg; Sodium 592mg; Calc 52mg

*Substitute 1 pound frozen whole green beans for fresh green beans, if desired. Cook according to package directions; drain well.

green grows the bean

- There are two general types of green beans (also known as snap beans). Bush beans come in round and flat varieties, are basically stringless, and very tender. They grow on bushes, making them easy to harvest commercially. Pole beans grow on running vines trained on trellises or fences. Pole beans also come in round and flat varieties. Most have strings, but a couple of types are stringless. Because pole beans are labor-intensive to grow and must be picked by hand, they often cost more and are not as widely available.
- Choose bush beans for their tender, quick-cooking qualities, and pole beans for long, slow-cooking dishes.
- We tested with stringless beans in this chapter; if you purchase beans with strings, remove them before cooking for best results.

low calorie

Green Beans With Caramelized Onion

prep: 20 min.   cook: 50 min.

Texas Sweet, Vidalia, or Walla Walla are three sweet onion options here.

2 pounds fresh green beans
2 large sweet onions
3 tablespoons butter or margarine, divided
3 tablespoons light brown sugar
1½ tablespoons balsamic vinegar

Trim beans. Cook beans in boiling water to cover 12 to 15 minutes or until tender. Drain and set aside, or cover and chill overnight, if desired.

Meanwhile, cut onions into thin slices, and cut each slice in half.

Melt 1 tablespoon butter in a large nonstick skillet over medium-high heat, and add onion; cook 8 to 10 minutes (do not stir). Continue cooking onion, stirring often, 15 to 20 minutes or until golden. Reduce heat to medium; stir in remaining 2 tablespoons butter and brown sugar.

Add green beans, and cook 5 minutes or until thoroughly heated. Add vinegar; toss to coat. Yield: 8 servings.

Per serving: Calories 95 (42% from fat); Fat 4.4g (sat 2.7g, mono 1.1g, poly 0.2g); Protein 2.2g; Carb 13.6g; Fiber 3.7g; Chol 11mg; Iron 1.2mg; Sodium 41mg; Calc 49mg

low calorie • low cholesterol • low fat
make ahead

Winter Beets

prep: 5 min.   cook: 8 min.   other: 8 hrs.

Spoon these chilled beets over a bed of gourmet mixed greens.

½ cup sugar
2 tablespoons all-purpose flour
½ cup white vinegar
¼ cup water
⅛ teaspoon salt
2 tablespoons butter or margarine
2 (15-ounce) cans sliced beets, drained

Combine sugar and flour in a heavy saucepan; whisk in vinegar and ¼ cup water. Bring to a boil over medium heat, and boil, whisking constantly, 1 minute or until thickened. Remove from heat; stir in salt and butter.

Stir beets into sugar mixture; cook over low heat 5 minutes or until thoroughly heated, stirring often. Serve immediately, or let cool, and spoon beet mixture into an airtight container; chill 8 hours. Yield: 8 servings.

Per serving: Calories 100 (26% from fat); Fat 2.9g (sat 1.8g, mono 0.8g, poly 0.1g); Protein 0.7g; Carb 19g; Fiber 0.8g; Chol 8mg; Iron 0.5mg; Sodium 70mg; Calc 10mg

Green Beans With Caramelized Onion

Broccoli and Parsnips With Horseradish

prep: 15 min. cook: 16 min.

If you can't find parsnips, carrots make a fine substitute.

1 pound fresh parsnips, peeled and diagonally sliced
1 pound fresh broccoli crowns, cut into florets
3 tablespoons butter or margarine
2 tablespoons prepared horseradish
2 tablespoons fresh lemon juice
¾ teaspoon salt
½ cup coarsely chopped walnuts, toasted

Arrange parsnips in a steamer basket over boiling water. Cover and steam 8 minutes. Add broccoli; cover and steam 4 to 5 minutes or until crisp-tender. Place parsnips and broccoli in a large bowl.

Melt butter in a small saucepan over medium-low heat. Cook 3 minutes or until lightly browned. Remove from heat. Stir in horseradish, lemon juice, and salt. Pour sauce over vegetables, tossing to coat. Sprinkle with walnuts. Serve hot. Yield: 6 servings.

Per serving: Calories 196 (57% from fat); Fat 12.4g (sat 4g, mono 3.2g, poly 4.1g); Protein 5.9g; Carb 19.5g; Fiber 5.9g; Chol 15mg; Iron 1.5mg; Sodium 375mg; Calc 77mg

Stir-fried Broccoli

prep: 10 min. cook: 7 min.

2 slices peeled fresh ginger
3 tablespoons vegetable oil
1 (16-ounce) package fresh broccoli florets*
½ teaspoon salt
¼ teaspoon sugar
½ cup hot water
½ teaspoon chicken bouillon granules
1 tablespoon sesame oil
1 tablespoon sesame seeds, toasted

Sauté ginger in hot vegetable oil in a large skillet or wok over medium-high heat 1 minute. Add broccoli; stir-fry 2 minutes. Sprinkle with salt and sugar.
Stir together ½ cup water and bouillon granules until dissolved. Pour over broccoli mixture. Cover, reduce heat to medium, and cook 2 to 3 minutes. Drizzle with sesame oil; sprinkle with sesame seeds. Yield: 6 servings.

Per serving: Calories 113 (81% from fat); Fat 10.2g (sat 1.1g, mono 3.9g, poly 4.1g); Protein 2.5g; Carb 4.6g; Fiber 2.2g; Chol 0mg; Iron 2.8mg; Sodium 225mg; Calc 37mg

*You can use 1 pound broccoli crowns. Chop florets and about 2 inches of stalks.

Brussels Sprouts With Apples

prep: 25 min. cook: 42 min.

2¼ pounds fresh brussels sprouts, halved
3 tablespoons fresh lemon juice
2 teaspoons salt, divided
¼ cup butter or margarine, divided
1 medium onion, diced
¼ cup apple juice
1 large Red Delicious apple, diced
1 garlic clove, minced
1 teaspoon sugar
1 (8-ounce) can sliced water chestnuts, drained
½ cup golden raisins
2 teaspoons grated lemon rind
½ teaspoon freshly ground pepper
⅛ teaspoon grated nutmeg

Bring brussels sprouts, lemon juice, 1½ teaspoons salt, and water to cover to a boil in a saucepan. Cover, reduce heat, and simmer

5 to 10 minutes or until tender. Drain and keep warm.
Melt 2 tablespoons butter in a large skillet over medium-high heat; add onion, and sauté 15 to 20 minutes or until caramel-colored. Add apple juice, and cook 2 minutes, stirring to loosen browned particles.
Add apple, garlic, and sugar; cook, stirring constantly, 5 to 6 minutes or until apple is tender. Add water chestnuts, next 4 ingredients, remaining ½ teaspoon salt, and remaining 2 tablespoons butter; cook, stirring constantly, 3 to 4 minutes. Gently toss in brussels sprouts. Yield: 8 servings.

Per serving: Calories 168 (33% from fat); Fat 6.2g (sat 3.7g, mono 1.5g, poly 0.4g); Protein 4.7g; Carb 28g; Fiber 6.1g; Chol 15mg; Iron 1.9mg; Sodium 654mg; Calc 64mg

Shredded Brussels Sprouts

prep: 20 min. cook: 11 min.

This recipe will make anyone a fan of brussels sprouts. Clean and slice them ahead, and store in a zip-top plastic bag. Then heat your skillet for a fast stir-fry with tangy-sweet flavor.

2 pounds brussels sprouts
2 tablespoons butter or margarine
2 tablespoons olive oil
2 garlic cloves, minced
½ small red onion, cut into slivers (½ cup)
½ teaspoon salt
½ teaspoon pepper
¼ cup plus 2 tablespoons red wine vinegar
1½ tablespoons light brown sugar

Rinse brussels sprouts; remove discolored leaves. Cut off stem ends, and thinly slice brussels sprouts. (They should look shredded.)
Heat butter and oil in a large deep skillet over medium-high heat until hot. Add shredded brussels sprouts, garlic, and onion.
Sauté 8 to 10 minutes or until brussels sprouts are tender and onion is lightly caramelized. Season with salt and pepper; transfer to a serving bowl. Add vinegar and brown sugar to skillet. Simmer over medium heat 30 seconds; pour over brussels sprouts, and toss gently. Yield: 8 servings.

Per serving: Calories 109 (54% from fat); Fat 6.5g (sat 2.3g, mono 3.3g, poly 0.6g); Protein 3.6g; Carb 11.6g; Fiber 4g; Chol 8mg; Iron 1.6mg; Sodium 193mg; Calc 49mg

Spicy Cabbage Stir-fry

prep: 14 min.   cook: 10 min.

The beautiful color and fresh flavor of this dish will entice even picky eaters.

2   tablespoons vegetable oil
½   medium head red cabbage, thinly sliced (about 4 cups)
1   green bell pepper, thinly sliced
1   small onion, thinly sliced
3   tablespoons jalapeño jelly
¾   cup chopped fresh cilantro
1   tablespoon lime juice
1   teaspoon salt
½   teaspoon pepper

Heat oil in large skillet or wok at high heat 3 to 4 minutes. Add cabbage, bell pepper, onion, and jalapeño jelly, and stir-fry 7 to 10 minutes or until crisp-tender or to desired degree of doneness. Stir in cilantro and remaining ingredients. Yield: 6 servings.

Per serving: Calories 87 (50% from fat); Fat 4.8g (sat 0.5g, mono 2g, poly 2.1g); Protein 1g; Carb 11.8g; Fiber 1.8g; Chol 0mg; Iron 0.5mg; Sodium 401mg; Calc 30mg

Scalloped Cabbage

prep: 11 min.   cook: 1 hr., 5 min.

This cabbage recipe is not your typical casserole. It's cheesy and crunchy in the same bite. This casserole is full to the brim before baking. Don't worry—the cabbage cooks down.

2   cups crushed cornflakes cereal
¼   cup butter or margarine, melted
1   (10-ounce) package shredded angel hair cabbage
1   large sweet onion, halved and thinly sliced
½   cup milk
½   cup mayonnaise
1   (10¾-ounce) can cream of celery soup, undiluted
1   cup (4 ounces) shredded sharp Cheddar cheese

Stir together cereal and butter; spoon half of mixture into a lightly greased 11- x 7-inch baking dish. Top with cabbage and onion.
Stir together milk, mayonnaise, and soup.

Pour over cabbage. Sprinkle with cheese and remaining cereal mixture.
Bake, covered, at 350° for 45 minutes; uncover and bake 20 more minutes or until top is golden and crispy. Yield: 6 servings.

Per serving: Calories 379 (74% from fat); Fat 31.3g (sat 11.9g, mono 8.1g, poly 9.4g); Protein 7.8g; Carb 18.8g; Fiber 2g; Chol 55mg; Iron 3.5mg; Sodium 745mg; Calc 209mg

Balsamic Baby Carrots

prep: 8 min.   cook: 15 min.

Crisp-tender little carrots are bathed in a tangy glaze.

3   cups water
1   (1-pound) package baby carrots
2   large shallots, thinly sliced
1   medium-size red bell pepper, diced into ½-inch pieces
1   tablespoon olive oil
3   tablespoons balsamic vinegar
1½ tablespoons sugar
½   teaspoon salt
¼   teaspoon freshly ground pepper
2   tablespoons chopped fresh flat-leaf parsley

Bring 3 cups water to a boil in a 3-quart saucepan; add carrots, return to a boil, and cook 4 minutes. Remove from heat; drain.
Sauté shallots and bell pepper in hot oil in a large skillet over medium-high heat 3 minutes or until crisp-tender. Add carrots, balsamic vinegar, and next 3 ingredients, and cook 4 minutes or until liquid is reduced and vegetables begin to glaze. Remove from heat, and stir in chopped parsley. Yield: 6 servings.

Per serving: Calories 83 (26% from fat); Fat 2.4g (sat 0.3g, mono 1.7g, poly 0.3g); Protein 1g; Carb 15.3g; Fiber 1.9g; Chol 0mg; Iron 1.1mg; Sodium 257mg; Calc 33mg

Carrot Soufflé

prep: 10 min.   cook: 1 hr., 30 min.

1   pound carrots, peeled and chopped
3   large eggs, lightly beaten
½   cup sugar
½   cup butter or margarine, melted
3   tablespoons all-purpose flour
1   teaspoon baking powder
1   teaspoon vanilla extract

Bring carrots and water to cover to a boil in a medium saucepan; cook 45 minutes or until very tender. Drain.
Process carrots in a food processor until smooth.
Stir together carrot puree, eggs, and remaining ingredients. Spoon into a lightly greased 1-quart baking dish.
Bake at 350° for 45 minutes or until set. Yield: 8 servings.

Per serving: Calories 210 (57% from fat); Fat 13.4g (sat 7.8g, mono 3.7g, poly 0.8g); Protein 3.3g; Carb 20g; Fiber 1.5g; Chol 109mg; Iron 0.7mg; Sodium 203mg; Calc 64mg

Lemon-Baked Cauliflower

prep: 10 min.   cook: 1 hr.

For a splash of color, stir diced pimiento into the buttery topping for this cauliflower.

⅓   cup finely chopped shallots
¼   cup butter or margarine, softened
¼   cup finely chopped fresh parsley
2   garlic cloves, minced
1   tablespoon grated lemon rind
1   teaspoon salt
¼   teaspoon pepper
⅛   teaspoon ground nutmeg
1   large cauliflower, cored

Stir together first 8 ingredients.
Place cauliflower on a large sheet of heavy-duty aluminum foil; spread butter mixture over cauliflower. Bring sides of foil to top; seal edges. Place on a baking sheet. Bake at 375° for 1 hour or until tender. Yield: 6 servings.

Per serving: Calories 112 (63% from fat); Fat 7.8g (sat 4.8g, mono 2g, poly 0.4g); Protein 3.2g; Carb 9.7g; Fiber 3.8g; Chol 20mg; Iron 0.9mg; Sodium 486mg; Calc 44mg

Fresh Basil Corn on the Cob

prep: 15 min.   cook: 7 min.

4	ears fresh corn with husks
¼	cup butter or margarine, softened
½	teaspoon grated orange rind
2	tablespoons chopped fresh basil

Remove heavy outer husks from corn; pull back inner husks. Remove and discard silks. Pull husks back over corn, and arrange, spoke fashion, on a glass plate.
Microwave at HIGH 7 minutes, turning corn after 3½ minutes.
Stir together butter, orange rind, and basil. Pull back husks, and brush the butter mixture evenly over corn. Yield: 4 servings.

Per serving: Calories 178 (63% from fat); Fat 12.4g (sat 7.4g, mono 3.3g, poly 0.9g); Protein 3.1g; Carb 17.3g; Fiber 2.5g; Chol 30mg; Iron 0.5mg; Sodium 94mg; Calc 8mg

Buttermilk Fried Corn

prep: 15 min.   cook: 15 min.   other: 30 min.

A quick soak in buttermilk and a toss in a peppery cornmeal coating produce a crispy corn for a vegetable plate or appetizers.

3	cups fresh corn kernels
2¼	cups buttermilk
1	cup all-purpose flour
1	cup cornmeal
1	teaspoon salt
1½	teaspoons pepper
Corn oil	

Stir together corn and buttermilk; let stand 30 minutes. Drain.
Combine flour and next 3 ingredients in a large zip-top freezer bag. Add corn to flour mixture, a small amount at a time, and shake bag to coat.
Pour oil to a depth of 1 inch in a Dutch oven; heat to 375°. Fry corn, in small batches, 2 minutes or until golden. Drain on paper towels. Serve immediately. Yield: 6 servings.

Per serving: Calories 289 (35% from fat); Fat 11.2g (sat 1.8g, mono 2.7g, poly 6.2g); Protein 6.5g; Carb 43g; Fiber 4g; Chol 3mg; Iron 2.1mg; Sodium 347mg; Calc 7mg

Skillet Creamed Corn

Skillet Creamed Corn

prep: 20 min.   cook: 27 min.

Smoky bacon enhances this simple side dish.

6	bacon slices
½	Vidalia onion, finely chopped
1	garlic clove, finely chopped
3	cups fresh corn kernels (about 6 ears)
¼	cup all-purpose flour
1½	cups half-and-half
½	teaspoon salt
¼	teaspoon pepper
1	tablespoon butter or margarine
1	tablespoon chopped fresh basil

Cook bacon in a large skillet until crisp; remove bacon, and drain on paper towels, reserving 2 tablespoons drippings in skillet. Crumble bacon, and set aside.
Sauté onion and garlic in hot drippings 5 minutes or until tender. Stir in corn; cook 5 to 7 minutes or until golden. Remove from heat.
Cook flour in a large clean skillet over medium heat, stirring occasionally, about 5 minutes or until golden. Gradually whisk in half-and-half until smooth. Add corn mixture, salt, and pepper; cook 5 minutes or until thickened. Remove from heat; stir in butter and basil. Sprinkle with bacon. Yield: 6 servings.

Per serving: Calories 283 (58% from fat); Fat 18.3g (sat 8.1g, mono 5.6g, poly 1.1g); Protein 8.9g; Carb 24.2g; Fiber 2.4g; Chol 38mg; Iron 0.8mg; Sodium 385mg; Calc 70mg

Corn Pudding

prep: 18 min.   cook: 47 min.

9   ears fresh corn
4   large eggs, beaten
½   cup half-and-half
1½   teaspoons baking powder
⅓   cup butter or margarine
2   tablespoons sugar
2   tablespoons all-purpose flour
1   tablespoon butter or margarine, melted
⅛   teaspoon freshly ground pepper

Remove and discard husks and silks from corn. Cut off tips of corn kernels into a bowl; scrape milk and remaining pulp from cob with a paring knife to measure 3 cups. Set corn aside.

Combine eggs, half-and-half, and baking powder, stirring well with a wire whisk.

Melt ⅓ cup butter in a large saucepan over low heat; add sugar and flour, stirring until smooth. Remove from heat; gradually add egg mixture, stirring constantly with a wire whisk until smooth. Stir in corn.

Pour corn mixture into a greased 1½-quart baking dish. Bake, uncovered, at 350° for 40 to 45 minutes or until pudding is set. Drizzle with 1 tablespoon butter; sprinkle with pepper. Broil 5½ inches from heat 2 minutes or until golden. Let stand 5 minutes before serving. Yield: 6 servings.

Per serving: Calories 323 (53% from fat); Fat 19.2g (sat 10.3g, mono 5.5g, poly 1.8g); Protein 9.5g; Carb 33.3g; Fiber 3.7g; Chol 180mg; Iron 1.6mg; Sodium 282mg; Calc 113mg

To prepare corn for Corn Pudding, cut tips of corn kernels, using a paring knife. Scrape milk and pulp from cob into a bowl.

Cornbread Dressing

prep: 45 min.   cook: 1 hr.

Serve this holiday favorite with pork roast or turkey.

2   cups cornmeal
½   cup all-purpose flour
2   teaspoons baking powder
1   teaspoon baking soda
1   teaspoon salt
1   teaspoon sugar (optional)
6   large eggs, divided
2   cups buttermilk
2   tablespoons bacon drippings or melted butter
½   cup butter or margarine
3   bunches green onions, chopped
4   celery ribs, chopped
1   (16-ounce) package herb-seasoned stuffing mix
5   (14-ounce) cans chicken broth

Combine first 5 ingredients and, if desired, sugar in a large bowl. Stir together 2 eggs and buttermilk; add to dry ingredients, stirring just until moistened.

Heat bacon drippings in a 10-inch cast-iron skillet or 9-inch round cakepan in oven at 425° for 5 minutes. Stir hot drippings into batter. Pour batter into hot skillet.

Bake at 425° for 25 minutes or until cornbread is golden; cool and crumble. Freeze in a large zip-top freezer bag up to 1 month, if desired. Thaw in refrigerator.

Melt ½ cup butter in a large skillet over medium heat; add green onions and celery, and sauté until tender.

Stir together remaining 4 eggs in a large bowl; stir in cornbread, onion mixture, stuffing mix, and chicken broth until blended.

Spoon dressing into 1 lightly greased 13- x 9-inch baking dish and 1 lightly greased 9-inch square baking dish. Cover and freeze dressing up to 3 months, if desired; thaw in refrigerator 8 hours.

Place 13- x 9-inch dish (uncovered) and 9-inch square dish (uncovered) in oven at 350°. Bake 13- x 9-inch dish for 1 hour and 9-inch square dish for 50 minutes or until each is lightly browned. Yield: 16 servings.

Per serving: Calories 323 (35% from fat); Fat 12.4g (sat 5.8g, mono 3.3g, poly 0.7g); Protein 9.8g; Carb 41.5g; Fiber 3.6g; Chol 108mg; Iron 2.6mg; Sodium 1632mg; Calc 80mg

---

Rustic Corn Dressing

prep: 25 min.   cook: 1 hr., 10 min.

Smoked bacon and roasted corn make this dressing unique.

1   (29-ounce) can whole kernel corn, drained (2¾ cups)
1   pound smoked bacon (we tested with Nueske's)
2   cups chopped onion
1½   cups chopped celery
4   garlic cloves, chopped
½   cup butter or margarine, melted
6   cups (12 ounces) stuffing (we tested with Pepperidge Farm cubed country-style stuffing)
1½   cups coarsely chopped pecans, toasted
1   large egg, lightly beaten
2   to 2¾ cups chicken or turkey broth
½   teaspoon salt
1   teaspoon freshly ground pepper

Press corn between several layers of paper towels to remove excess moisture. Set aside.

Cook bacon in a large skillet over medium heat until crisp; remove bacon, reserving 2 tablespoons drippings in skillet. Crumble bacon; set aside. Add corn to skillet; toss to coat. Cook over high heat, stirring constantly, until corn is roasted in appearance. Transfer to a large bowl.

Sauté onion, celery, and garlic in butter in large skillet over medium-high heat, until tender. Transfer to a large bowl. Add stuffing, crumbled bacon, and pecans, stirring well. Add egg, desired amount of broth, salt, and pepper to stuffing mixture; stir gently.

Spoon dressing into a lightly greased 13- x 9-inch pan. Bake, uncovered, at 325° for 1 hour or until well browned. Yield: 10 servings.

Per serving: Calories 397 (69% from fat); Fat 30.3g (sat 9.1g, mono 12.7g, poly 5.2g); Protein 14.2g; Carb 40.1g; Fiber 5.3g; Chol 64mg; Iron 2.3mg; Sodium 1170mg; Calc 40mg

Fruited Wild Rice Dressing

prep: 20 min.   cook: 1 hr., 20 min.

Dried fruits add sweetness and color to this dressing that's equally at home with turkey, chicken, or pork.

1   (6-ounce) package long-grain and wild rice mix
6   cups (½-inch cubes) country-style bread (we tested with ciabatta)
1   pound ground pork sausage
2   small onions, chopped
4   celery ribs, chopped
¼   cup butter, melted
1   cup dried apricots, coarsely chopped
¾   cup dried cherries
½   cup chopped fresh flat-leaf parsley
½   teaspoon salt
½   teaspoon pepper
1   cup chicken broth

Prepare rice mix according to package directions. Transfer to a large bowl, and fluff with a fork. Set aside.
Place bread cubes on a large-rimmed pan, and toast at 325° for 20 minutes or until dry.
Cook sausage in a large skillet over medium heat, stirring until it crumbles and is well browned; drain.
Sauté onion and celery in butter in a large skillet over medium heat until tender.
Combine rice, bread, sausage, sautéed vegetables, dried fruit, parsley, salt, and pepper in a large bowl; toss well. Drizzle broth evenly over dressing. Toss well. Transfer dressing to a lightly greased 3-quart baking dish.
Bake, covered, at 375° for 20 minutes. Uncover and bake 25 to 30 more minutes or until browned. Yield: 10 servings.

Per serving: Calories 409 (40% from fat); Fat 18.2g (sat 7g, mono 7.5g, poly 2g); Protein 12.5g; Carb 48.7g; Fiber 3.4g; Chol 46mg; Iron 3mg; Sodium 1021mg; Calc 48mg

Garden Succotash

prep: 25 min.   cook: 40 min.

¾   cup fresh lima or butter beans
1¼   cups fresh corn kernels (2 small ears)
1   cup chopped shiitake mushrooms
1   red bell pepper, seeded and diced
1   green bell pepper, seeded and diced
¾   teaspoon salt
¼   teaspoon pepper
2   tablespoons olive oil
½   teaspoon chopped garlic
¼   cup dry white wine
¾   cup whipping cream
2   tablespoons butter
1   medium tomato, peeled, seeded, and chopped
1   tablespoon chopped fresh parsley
1   tablespoon chopped fresh chives

Place beans in boiling water to cover in a small saucepan; simmer 3 minutes or until crisp-tender. Drain; rinse with cold water, and drain.
Sauté corn kernels, chopped mushrooms, bell pepper, salt, and pepper in hot oil in a medium skillet over medium-high heat for 5 minutes or until corn is crisp-tender. Add chopped garlic; sauté 30 seconds. Stir in wine, and cook 1 minute. Add whipping cream and beans; reduce heat to medium-low, and simmer, covered, 25 to 30 minutes or until beans are tender. Remove from heat, and stir in butter. Add chopped tomato, parsley, and chives, and stir just until combined. Yield: 6 servings.

Per serving: Calories 309 (59% from fat); Fat 20.1g (sat 10g, mono 7.6g, poly 1.2g); Protein 7.4g; Carb 28.2g; Fiber 7.2g; Chol 51mg; Iron 2mg; Sodium 339mg; Calc 50mg

low cholesterol
Fried Eggplant

prep: 15 min.   cook: 3 min. per batch
other: 1 hr.

2   eggplants, peeled and cut into ¼-inch-thick slices
1   teaspoon salt
1   cup buttermilk
¾   cup self-rising flour
½   cup self-rising cornmeal
½   teaspoon pepper
½   teaspoon salt
Vegetable oil

Sprinkle both sides of eggplant slices with salt; place on paper towels. Let stand 30 minutes. Rinse and pat dry. Soak slices in buttermilk 30 minutes.
Combine flour and next 3 ingredients. Drain eggplant; dredge in flour mixture.
Pour oil to a depth of 1½ inches in a large cast-iron skillet; heat to 375°. Fry eggplant slices, in batches, 3 minutes or until golden. Yield: 8 servings.

Per serving: Calories 170 (53% from fat); Fat 10.1g (sat 1.2g, mono 4.1g, poly 4.2g); Protein 3g; Carb 19g; Fiber 4.6g; Chol 1mg; Iron 1.2mg; Sodium 656mg; Calc 68mg

Creamy Pan-Braised Fennel

prep: 20 min.   cook: 40 min.

4   large fennel bulbs (2 pounds without fronds)
1½   cups whipping cream
½   teaspoon salt
½   teaspoon pepper
¼   teaspoon ground nutmeg
¼   cup Italian-seasoned breadcrumbs
½   cup shredded Parmesan cheese
3   tablespoons butter or margarine, cut up

Trim bases from fennel bulbs; cut into eighths, reserving fronds for another use.
Arrange fennel in a greased 11- x 7-inch baking dish.
Whisk together whipping cream and next 3 ingredients, and pour over fennel slices. Sprinkle fennel slices with breadcrumbs and Parmesan cheese, and dot with butter.
Bake at 425° for 40 minutes or until fennel is tender. Serve hot. Yield: 4 servings.

Per serving: Calories 499 (76% from fat); Fat 42.2g (sat 25.2g, mono 12.2g, poly 1.3g); Protein 7g; Carb 23.6g; Fiber 5.5g; Chol 150mg; Iron 1.7mg; Sodium 768mg; Calc 285mg

Southern Turnip Greens and Ham Hocks

These luscious greens have all the makings of a simple Southern dish—classic ingredients and lots of love.

Southern Turnip Greens and Ham Hocks

prep: 30 min.   cook: 3 hrs.

We simmered the ham hocks for about 2 hours until the meat easily pulled away from the bones. If you want to save time, just simmer 30 to 45 minutes to release the flavor.

1¾	pounds ham hocks, rinsed
2	quarts water
2	bunches fresh turnip greens with roots (about 10 pounds)
1	tablespoon sugar

Bring ham hocks and 2 quarts water to a boil in an 8-quart Dutch oven. Reduce heat, and simmer 1½ to 2 hours or until meat is tender.
Remove and discard stems and discolored spots from greens. Chop greens, and rinse thoroughly; drain. Peel turnip roots, and cut in half.
Add greens, roots, and sugar to Dutch oven; bring to a boil. Reduce heat; cover and simmer 45 to 60 minutes or until greens and roots are tender. Yield: 10 servings.

Per serving: Calories 278 (47% from fat); Fat 14.6g (sat 5g, mono 6.1g, poly 1.8g); Protein 15.9g; Carb 23.9g; Fiber 10.2g; Chol 44mg; Iron 4mg; Sodium 148mg; Calc 607mg

---

low calorie

Sweet Skillet Turnips

prep: 20 min.   cook: 25 min.

1	tablespoon butter or margarine
1	small onion, finely chopped
1	pound turnips, peeled and shredded
½	cup chicken broth
1	tablespoon sugar
½	teaspoon salt
¼	teaspoon pepper

Melt butter in a large skillet over medium heat; add onion, and sauté 3 to 5 minutes or until tender.
Stir in turnips and remaining ingredients. Cook, stirring often, 20 minutes or until turnips are tender. (Turnips will turn a light brown–caramel color as they cook.) Yield: 3 servings.

Per serving: Calories 101 (38% from fat); Fat 4.3g (sat 2.4g, mono 1g, poly 0.2g); Protein 1.7g; Carb 14.9g; Fiber 2.6g; Chol 12mg; Iron 0.5mg; Sodium 754mg; Calc 44mg

---

cleaning greens

Cleaning greens is a time-consuming task, but it's well worth the effort. If you don't clean them well, they'll be gritty. To ease the removal of dirt and grit from the leaves, our Test Kitchens staff recommends coarsely chopping the greens first, and then soaking them. It's best to soak and rinse the leaves four or five times. The result is perfectly clean greens.

Choosing the proper seasoning can be a touchy subject in the South. Some argue that it's better to add salt pork to the pot, while others insist on ham hocks. Some cooks opt to embellish their greens with other ingredients such as chicken broth, bacon, garlic, onions, and even wine.

---

leafy greens 101

• Choose crisp greens with even color. Avoid those that are wilted, yellowing, or have dark green, slimy patches.
• Store fresh greens in a tightly sealed, large plastic bag in the refrigerator up to three days.
• Leafy greens are an excellent source of vitamins A and C, antioxidants known to help prevent heart disease and certain types of cancer. Greens also contain significant amounts of fiber, calcium, and folic acid.

---

low calorie • low cholesterol

Nana's Collard Greens

prep: 20 min.   cook: 1 hr., 15 min.

The carrot is used in this recipe to sweeten the pot. Try serving these greens over grits.

4	bacon slices
1	large carrot, chopped
1	large onion, chopped
2	garlic cloves, minced
2	to 3 tablespoons balsamic vinegar
4	(1-pound) packages fresh collard greens, cleaned, trimmed, and chopped
1½	cups low-sodium fat-free chicken broth
½	teaspoon dried crushed red pepper
½	teaspoon salt
¼	teaspoon pepper

Cook bacon in a Dutch oven until crisp. Drain bacon on paper towels, reserving 2 tablespoons drippings. Crumble bacon.
Cook carrot in hot bacon drippings in Dutch oven over medium–high heat, stirring occasionally, 5 minutes. Add onion, and cook, stirring occasionally, 5 minutes or until carrot and onion begin to caramelize.
Add garlic; cook, stirring constantly, 30 seconds. Add balsamic vinegar, and cook 30 seconds. Add collards, crumbled bacon, broth, and remaining ingredients.
Bring to a boil; cover, reduce heat, and simmer 1 hour or until tender. Yield: 8 servings.

Per serving: Calories 103 (45% from fat); Fat 5.2g (sat 1.8g, mono 2.1g, poly 0.8g); Protein 5.3g; Carb 10.9g; Fiber 5.2g; Chol 7mg; Iron 0.4mg; Sodium 364mg; Calc 196mg

Creamed Swiss Chard

prep: 4 min.   cook: 16 min.

Swiss chard has broad green leaves and big ribs. Cook it as you would spinach.

3   pounds fresh Swiss chard
2   tablespoons butter or margarine
1½ tablespoons all-purpose flour
1   cup half-and-half or milk
½   teaspoon salt
¼   teaspoon pepper
¼   teaspoon ground nutmeg

Rinse chard leaves thoroughly; remove and discard ribs from larger leaves. Coarsely chop chard leaves.

Place chard in a large Dutch oven. (Do not add water.) Cover and cook over medium heat 10 minutes or until tender. Drain chard well; squeeze between paper towels until barely moist. Return chard to Dutch oven.

Melt butter in a heavy saucepan over low heat; add flour, stirring until smooth. Cook 1 minute, stirring constantly. Gradually add half-and-half; cook over medium heat, stirring constantly, until thickened and bubbly.

Stir in salt, pepper, and nutmeg. Stir creamed mixture into chard. Yield: 6 servings.

Per serving: Calories 133 (60% from fat); Fat 8.9g (sat 5.3g, mono 2.4g, poly 0.5g); Protein 5.2g; Carb 11.1g; Fiber 3.4g; Chol 25mg; Iron 3.9mg; Sodium 682mg; Calc 150mg

Leeks With Brussels Sprouts and Almonds

prep: 15 min.   cook: 14 min.

3   large leeks
½   pound small fresh brussels sprouts
2   to 3 tablespoons butter or margarine
1   large Granny Smith apple, diced
¼   cup water
¼   teaspoon salt
¼   teaspoon pepper
½   cup sliced almonds, toasted
2   bacon slices, cooked and crumbled

Remove root, tough outer leaves, and tops from leeks, leaving 2 inches of dark leaves. Thinly slice leeks; rinse well, and drain.

Remove discolored leaves from brussels sprouts. Cut off stem ends, and cut a shallow X in the bottom of each sprout. Cook in boiling water to cover 3 to 4 minutes; drain.

Melt butter in a large skillet over medium-high heat; add leeks, and sauté 5 minutes. Add brussels sprouts, apple, and next 3 ingredients; sauté 5 minutes or until apple and brussels sprouts are crisp-tender. Stir in almonds and bacon. Serve hot. Yield: 4 servings.

Per serving: Calories 214 (56% from fat); Fat 13.4g (sat 4.6g, mono 5.9g, poly 2g); Protein 6.6g; Carb 20.8g; Fiber 5.2g; Chol 19mg; Iron 2.8mg; Sodium 285mg; Calc 95mg

Marinated Mirlitons, Artichokes, and Peppers

prep: 30 min.   cook: 50 min.   other: 2 hrs.

2   (12-ounce) jars marinated artichoke hearts
6   large mirlitons*
½   cup chopped fresh basil
¼   cup chopped fresh parsley
½   cup white balsamic vinegar
2   garlic cloves, minced
1   teaspoon salt
¼   teaspoon Creole seasoning
1   (7-ounce) jar roasted red bell peppers
Mixed salad greens

Drain artichoke hearts, reserving liquid in a large bowl.

Bring mirlitons and water to cover to a boil in a Dutch oven, and boil 45 to 50 minutes or until tender. Drain and cool. Peel mirlitons. Cut in half lengthwise; remove seeds, if desired. Cut mirliton halves into ¼-inch-thick slices.

Whisk together reserved liquid, basil, and next 5 ingredients. Add mirlitons, artichoke hearts, and bell pepper; toss well. Cover and chill 2 hours, stirring occasionally. Serve over salad greens. Yield: 6 servings.

Per serving: Calories 175 (34% from fat); Fat 6.7g (sat 0.1g, mono 0.1g, poly 0.3g); Protein 8.3g; Carb 27.8g; Fiber 7.8g; Chol 0mg; Iron 1.6mg; Sodium 971mg; Calc 66mg

*Substitute 6 large yellow squash or zucchini for mirlitons, if desired. Cut in half lengthwise; cut halves crosswise into ¼-inch-thick slices. Cook in boiling water to cover 5 minutes or until tender; drain, and cool.

Mushrooms in Sour Cream

prep: 15 min.   cook: 14 min.

This simple mushroom side dish can be used in a variety of ways to liven up an ordinary meal. Try using it to top a steak or burger, or serve over egg noodles.

1   (8-ounce) container sour cream
¼   cup butter or margarine
1   (8-ounce) package fresh button mushrooms, quartered
1   (8-ounce) package fresh crimini mushrooms, quartered (we tested with baby bellas)
2   garlic cloves, minced
½   cup dry white wine or Marsala wine
½   teaspoon salt
¼   teaspoon pepper
1½ teaspoons all-purpose flour
¼   cup chopped fresh flat-leaf parsley

Set out sour cream to come to room temperature.

Melt butter in a large skillet over medium-high heat; add mushrooms and garlic, and cook 8 minutes, stirring occasionally. Add wine, salt, and pepper. Cook, stirring often, 5 minutes or until liquid is reduced by half. Stir in flour, and cook 1 minute. Add sour cream and parsley, stirring just until thoroughly heated. Yield: 4 servings.

Per serving: Calories 256 (82% from fat); Fat 23.4g (sat 14.6g, mono 6.4g, poly 0.9g); Protein 4.7g; Carb 8.7g; Fiber 0.6g; Chol 55mg; Iron 0.9mg; Sodium 413mg; Calc 93mg

mushroom dictionary

Enoki

Oyster

Crimini

Chanterelle

Wood ear

Shiitake

Bluefoot

Honshimeji

Morels

Enoki: These mild white mushrooms almost grow in a bouquet and are sold in clusters. Because of their unique appearance and slightly crunchy texture, these mushrooms are best eaten raw in salads or used as a garnish. Enokis keep up to a week refrigerated in a paper bag; before using, trim roots at their cluster base.

Oyster: Oyster mushrooms are distinguishable by the fluted shape of their cap as well as their velvety texture. They're perhaps best sautéed in butter with onions and served alongside a meat or seafood dish to bring out their full flavor.

Crimini: Also sold as *Baby Bellas,* crimini mushrooms are harvested about a week earlier than their mature counterparts, portobellos. Criminis can be substituted for white mushrooms in recipes because they have a similar texture but impart a deeper, earthier flavor. Store refrigerated in a paper bag for five to seven days.

Chanterelle: Golden trumpet-shaped mushrooms, chanterelles are mainly imported from Europe and can be found dried or canned, if not fresh during the summer and winter months. Their chewy texture and nutty flavor allow them to act as a solo side dish as well as an ingredient in recipes. Choose spongy, intact chanterelles and avoid ones with broken or shriveled caps. Chanterelles tend to toughen when overcooked, so incorporate them into a recipe near the end of cooking.

Wood ear: Also called *cloud ear* or *tree ear,* wood ear mushrooms are slightly crunchy, delicate mushrooms often associated with Asian stir-fry dishes. They have a subtle flavor and tend to absorb the prominent flavors of a dish. Look for them in Asian markets, either fresh, distinguishable by their dark brown, floppy caps, or dried, resembling small black chips.

Shiitake: Meaty mushrooms with umbrella-shaped caps, shiitakes enhance savory recipes. Before using, discard their woody stems. Store shiitakes refrigerated in a paper bag up to a week.

Bluefoot: Also commonly referred to as *blewit* mushrooms, the bluefoot is a medium-sized mushroom with a violet-blue color, which it retains even after cooking. Keep young, firm bluefoot mushrooms in the refrigerator in a paper bag for up to a week.

Honshimeji: Small in size, this Asian mushroom grows in bunches of delicate, compact white stems topped with light brown or off-white caps. Their texture is crisp, providing a crunchy and juicy meat that tastes slightly nutty when cooked. Not a mushroom to eat raw, a quick sauté in olive oil or a quick grilling shows these off best. They stand up well in soups, stews, and stir-fries. Use within a week. To prepare them, cut off base of cluster so that each individual mushroom is cut at the stem.

Morels: These distinct, tan, yellow, or black mushrooms have pointed caps with grooves similar to sea coral. Their shape traps sauce like a dream.

Porcini: Also called *cèpes,* porcinis are pale brown and have a smooth, meaty texture and

Baby bellas

Portobellos

woodsy flavor. While the elusive porcinis are sold dried in many supermarkets, look for fresh porcinis in the late spring or autumn in specialty food stores.

Portobello: These meaty mushrooms are a culinary favorite, due to their broad size that facilitates a range of uses including being stuffed. The broad cap is often grilled whole to maintain its dramatic shape, which mimics a burger on a bun.

All about Mushrooms

Mushrooms add earthy goodness to recipes or can stand alone as a side dish. White button, brown crimini, and portobello are popular cultivated types. Shiitake, morel, oyster, porcino, enoki, and chanterelle are favored wild varieties.

Remove any plastic wrap immediately, and store mushrooms, unwashed, in a paper bag in the refrigerator. Use within five to seven days. Don't peel or wash. Clean with a mushroom brush or damp paper towels just before cooking. Discard tough or shriveled stems.

For maximum flavor, sauté mushrooms before adding to a recipe. Use a hot skillet and a small amount of butter or oil. Don't crowd the skillet or mushrooms will steam and become watery.

Dried mushrooms are ready to add to a dish after they've had a 30-minute to 1-hour soak in warm water; use the soaking liquid in place of water in the recipe for added flavor.

Smoked Gouda- and Apple-Stuffed Mushrooms

prep: 18 min. cook: 25 min.

The flavor blend of apple, pecans, and Gouda cheese is wonderful in these mushroom caps. Serve them as an appetizer or a side dish.

2 pounds very large fresh mushrooms (about 30)
2 tablespoons butter or margarine
¼ cup finely chopped onion
1 garlic clove, minced
2 cups (8 ounces) shredded smoked Gouda cheese
¼ cup soft breadcrumbs
1 Granny Smith apple, chopped
¼ teaspoon salt
¼ teaspoon freshly ground pepper
3 tablespoons ground pecans
1 tablespoon butter or margarine, melted

Remove and chop mushroom stems; set mushroom caps aside.

Melt 2 tablespoons butter in a large skillet over medium heat. Add mushroom stems, onion, and garlic; sauté 3 to 5 minutes or until tender. Remove from heat. Stir in cheese and next 4 ingredients. Spoon evenly into mushroom caps; place caps on a rack in a broiler pan.

Combine pecans and 1 tablespoon melted butter. Sprinkle evenly over each filled mushroom cap.

Bake at 350° for 15 to 17 minutes or until thoroughly heated. Change oven setting to broil, and broil mushrooms 1 to 2 minutes or just until browned on top. Yield: 30 appetizers.

Per mushroom: Calories 51 (67% from fat); Fat 3.8g (sat 2.1g, mono 1.1g, poly 0.3g); Protein 2.9g; Carb 2.1g; Fiber 0.5g; Chol 12mg; Iron 0.2mg; Sodium 93mg; Calc 56mg

Okra Creole

prep: 15 min. cook: 25 min.

3 bacon slices
1 (16-ounce) package frozen sliced okra
1 (14.5-ounce) can chopped tomatoes
1 cup frozen onion seasoning blend
1 cup frozen whole kernel corn
½ cup water
1 teaspoon Creole seasoning
¼ teaspoon pepper
Hot cooked rice (optional)

Cook bacon in a Dutch oven until crisp; drain bacon on paper towels, reserving drippings. Crumble bacon, and set aside.

Cook okra and next 6 ingredients in hot drippings in Dutch oven over medium-high heat, stirring occasionally, 5 minutes. Reduce heat to low, cover, and simmer 15 minutes or until vegetables are tender. Top with crumbled bacon. Serve over hot cooked rice, if desired. Yield: 4 servings.

Per serving: Calories 154 (34% from fat); Fat 5.8g (sat 2g, mono 2.5g, poly 0.8g); Protein 5.9g; Carb 22.6g; Fiber 4.5g; Chol 8mg; Iron 0.9mg; Sodium 439mg; Calc 94mg

Fried Okra and Green Tomatoes

prep: 18 min. cook: 6 min. per batch

1 cup buttermilk
1 large egg
1¾ cups cornmeal
¾ teaspoon salt, divided
¼ teaspoon pepper
1 pound fresh okra, sliced
2 green tomatoes, cut into ½-inch pieces
Vegetable oil

Whisk together buttermilk and egg.

Combine cornmeal, ¼ teaspoon salt, and pepper. Dip okra and tomato, in batches, into buttermilk mixture; coat in cornmeal mixture.

Pour oil to a depth of 2 inches into a Dutch oven. Heat oil to 375°.

Fry okra and tomato, in batches, 6 minutes turning once, or until golden. (Turning too soon will cause breading to fall off.) Drain on paper towels; sprinkle with remaining ½ teaspoon salt. Yield: 8 servings.

Per serving: Calories 216 (38% from fat); Fat 9g (sat 1.5g, mono 3.5g, poly 3.4g); Protein 5.4g; Carb 29.8g; Fiber 4.2g; Chol 24mg; Iron 1.9mg; Sodium 265mg; Calc 75mg

Field Peas, Okra, and Corn

prep: 10 min. cook: 1 hr.

Enjoy this colorful combo as a side dish or as a one-dish meal. (pictured on page 450)

2 celery ribs, sliced
1 large onion, halved and sliced
½ large red bell pepper, diced ½-inch
1 garlic clove, minced
1 tablespoon olive oil
1 tablespoon Worcestershire sauce
2 teaspoons Creole seasoning
1 teaspoon freshly ground pepper
1 teaspoon hot sauce
½ teaspoon salt
1 (14-ounce) can chicken broth plus ½ cup chicken broth
1 (16-ounce) package frozen field peas with snaps, unthawed
1 (16-ounce) package frozen sliced okra, unthawed
1 (16-ounce) package frozen whole kernel corn, unthawed
Hot cooked rice
Garnishes: chopped tomato, diagonally sliced green onions

Sauté first 4 ingredients in hot oil in a Dutch oven over medium heat 8 minutes or until onion is browned. Add Worcestershire sauce and next 4 ingredients, and cook, stirring constantly, 3 minutes.

Stir in broth, and bring to a boil. Stir in field peas, and return to a boil. Cover, reduce heat, and simmer 25 minutes.

Stir in okra, corn, and, if needed, up to ½ cup water; bring to a boil. Cover, reduce heat, and simmer 10 minutes or until vegetables are tender. Serve over hot cooked rice. Garnish, if desired. Yield: 8 servings.

Per serving: Calories 198 (15% from fat); Fat 3.4g (sat 0.7g, mono 1.8g, poly 0.8g); Protein 11.2g; Carb 34.3g; Fiber 6.5g; Chol 1mg; Iron 2.5mg; Sodium 743mg; Calc 81mg

Note: You can use 1 pound fresh okra, sliced, and 1 pound fresh lady peas or pinkeye peas instead of frozen items.

Florentine Stuffed Onions

prep: 19 min.   cook: 1 hr., 6 min.

Look for baby spinach in the organic section of the grocery store or in the produce section. It's pricier than other spinach, but you save time because you don't have to trim the stems.

4	medium-size sweet onions (about 2 pounds)
1	(6-ounce) package fresh baby spinach
1	garlic clove, minced
1	tablespoon olive oil
1	tablespoon butter or margarine
1	tablespoon all-purpose flour
½	teaspoon salt
¼	teaspoon pepper
⅛	teaspoon dry mustard
⅓	cup milk
½	(8-ounce) package cream cheese
½	cup freshly shredded Parmesan cheese

Peel onions, and cut in half crosswise. Cut a thin slice from bottom of each half, forming a base for onions to stand. Place onions in a lightly greased 13- x 9-inch baking dish.

Remove onion centers, leaving 1–inch-thick shells. Chop centers, reserving 1 cup chopped onion for the stuffing. Reserve remaining onion for another use, if desired.

Sauté spinach, garlic, and 1 cup chopped onion in hot oil in a large skillet over medium–high heat about 3 minutes or until spinach is wilted. Remove mixture from skillet.

Melt butter in same skillet over medium heat. Stir in flour and next 3 ingredients until smooth. Stir in milk, and cook, stirring constantly, 2 to 3 minutes or until thick-ened. Reduce heat to low; stir in cream cheese, stirring until melted. Stir in spinach mixture. Spoon hot mixture evenly into onion halves.

Bake at 350° for 45 minutes. Sprinkle evenly with Parmesan cheese, and bake 15 more minutes or until golden and bubbly. Yield: 8 servings.

Per serving: Calories 164 (57% from fat); Fat 10.3g (sat 5.5g, mono 3.7g, poly 0.5g); Protein 5.2g; Carb 14.3g; Fiber 2.6g; Chol 25mg; Iron 1.1mg; Sodium 346mg; Calc 136mg

onion dictionary

Boiler onions: Boiler onions are very small white or yellow onions that have been harvested early for their mild flavor. They can be found in yellow, red, and white varieties and are usually served in stew or as a pickled or boiled side dish.

Cipollini: Though hard to find in the U.S., this variety can be found in farmers markets in the fall or at your specialty grocer. Cipollini are small Italian onions with a flat oval shape. They add a bittersweet accent to pot roast, soups, stews, and vegetable dishes. If kept whole, these onions will last up to two months.

Green onions: Often confused with their relative, the scallion, green onions are immature white onions that had not yet formed a bulb before they were harvested. While green onions are available year-round, their prime season is spring and summer. Store green onions in a plastic bag in the vegetable crisper section of your refrigerator for up to five days.

Pearl onions: The smallest of the onion family, pearl onions are marble-sized summer onions that have a mild flavor. They're often cooked or creamed as a side dish. Blanch them for easy peeling.

Red onions: Also referred to as Italian or purple onions, red onions have a milder, sweeter flavor than the stronger yellow onion. The flesh of red onions is white, stained a reddish-purple only on the outer edge of each layer.

Shallots: Shallots, unlike other onions, grow in heads similar to garlic. With the papery skin characteristic of other onions, shallots have a sweetly acidic flavor and are a favorite in French cooking.

Spanish onions: Seasonal from August to May, Spanish onions are a bit sweeter than, but can also be substituted for, the yellow onion.

Sweet onions: The most succulent of onions are the sweet onions, notably the Texas Sweet, Maui, Vidalia, and Walla Walla varieties. Georgia's Vidalia and Washington's Walla Walla are both large, golden, spring-to-summer onions with a sweet, juicy flavor. Maui onions have a white to pale yellow color, and a mild flavor. You can use sweet onions interchangeably in recipes.

Buttermilk Batter-Fried Onion Rings

prep: 20 min.   cook: 10 min.

These are best served right out of the fryer.

2   large onions
1   cup all-purpose flour
2   cups buttermilk
1   tablespoon sugar
1   teaspoon baking powder
½   teaspoon salt
Peanut oil

Cut onions into ½-inch slices, and separate into rings. Set aside.
Whisk together flour and next 4 ingredients until smooth.
Pour oil to a depth of 2 inches into a Dutch oven; heat to 375°.
Dip onion rings in batter, coating well. Fry a few rings at a time until golden. Drain on paper towels. Serve immediately. Yield: 4 servings.

Per serving: Calories 345 (47% from fat); Fat 17.9g (sat 4.9g, mono 6.8g, poly 4.7g); Protein 7.6g; Carb 39.4g; Fiber 1.9g; Chol 17mg; Iron 1.7mg; Sodium 553mg; Calc 89mg

Slow-Cooker Caramelized Onions

prep: 5 min.   cook: 6 hrs.

Use a slotted spoon for serving, and save the broth to make soup.

2   extra-large sweet onions (about 2 pounds)
¼   cup butter or margarine, melted
½   teaspoon salt
⅛   teaspoon pepper

Cut onions in half; cut each half into ½-inch-thick slices.
Combine all ingredients in a 3-quart slow cooker. Cook, covered, on HIGH 6 hours or until golden and very soft. Store in an airtight container; chill up to 2 weeks, or if desired, freeze up to 2 months. Yield: 2½ cups.

Per ¼ cup: Calories 53 (78% from fat); Fat 4.6g (sat 2.9g, mono 1.2g, poly 0.2g); Protein 0.3g; Carb 3.1g; Fiber 0.4g; Chol 12mg; Iron 0.1mg; Sodium 149mg; Calc 8mg

Vidalia Onion Soufflé

prep: 30 min.   cook: 40 min.

2   tablespoons butter or margarine
5   medium Vidalia or other sweet onions, chopped (about 4 cups)
2   cups fresh bread cubes (about 10 slices, crusts removed)
1   (15-ounce) can fat-free evaporated milk
3   large eggs, lightly beaten
1¼   cups shredded Parmesan cheese
1   teaspoon salt

Melt butter in a large skillet over medium heat; add chopped onion, and sauté 10 to 15 minutes or until tender.
Place onion and bread cubes in a large bowl. Stir in milk, egg, 1 cup cheese, and salt. Pour into a lightly greased 1½-quart soufflé or baking dish. Sprinkle with remaining ¼ cup cheese.
Bake at 350° for 25 minutes or until set. Yield: 8 servings.

Per serving: Calories 203 (38% from fat); Fat 8.6g (sat 4.7g, mono 2.7g, poly 0.6g); Protein 12.5g; Carb 19.1g; Fiber 1.3g; Chol 98mg; Iron 1.1mg; Sodium 672mg; Calc 353mg

Sweet Onion Pudding

prep: 5 min.   cook: 1 hr., 32 min.

½   cup butter or margarine
6   medium-size sweet onions (3¼ pounds), thinly sliced and separated into rings
2   cups whipping cream
1   (3-ounce) package shredded Parmesan cheese
6   large eggs, lightly beaten
3   tablespoons all-purpose flour
2   tablespoons sugar
2   teaspoons baking powder
1   teaspoon salt

Melt butter in a large skillet over medium heat; add onion. Cook, stirring often, about 1 hour or until caramel-colored. Remove from heat.
Meanwhile, stir together whipping cream, cheese, and eggs in a large bowl. Combine flour and next 3 ingredients; gradually stir in egg mixture.

Stir onion into egg mixture; spoon into a lightly greased 13- x 9-inch baking dish. Bake, uncovered, at 350° for 30 to 32 minutes or until slightly firm, puffed, and golden. Yield: 8 servings.

Per serving: Calories 487 (74% from fat); Fat 40.2g (sat 23.9g, mono 11.7g, poly 1.8g); Protein 11.9g; Carb 21.9g; Fiber 1.7g; Chol 278mg; Iron 1.5mg; Sodium 763mg; Calc 300mg

Slow-Roasted Winter Vegetables

prep: 25 min.   cook: 1 hr.

¼   cup butter or margarine, melted
¼   cup firmly packed light brown sugar
½   teaspoon ground cinnamon
½   teaspoon pepper
¼   teaspoon ground nutmeg
4   medium parsnips, peeled and cut into 1-inch cubes (about 1 pound)
4   medium carrots, peeled and cut into 1-inch cubes (about 1 pound)
2   medium-size sweet potatoes, peeled and cut into 1-inch cubes (about 1½ pounds)
½   medium rutabaga, peeled and cut into 1-inch cubes (about 1 pound)

Heat a roasting pan or broiler pan in a 400° oven for 5 minutes.
Stir together first 5 ingredients in a large bowl; add vegetables, tossing to coat. Arrange vegetables in a single layer in hot pan. Bake at 400° for 55 to 60 minutes or until tender, stirring after 30 minutes. Yield: 6 servings.

Per serving: Calories 269 (27% from fat); Fat 8.2g (sat 4.9g, mono 2.1g, poly 0.5g); Protein 3.5g; Carb 48.1g; Fiber 9g; Chol 20mg; Iron 1.9mg; Sodium 147mg; Calc 113mg

A Mess of Peas

prep: 5 min.   cook: 1 hr.

1   quart water
1   (8- to 10-ounce) smoked ham hock
8   cups fresh field peas
4   to 6 hot peppers in vinegar, drained
1   teaspoon sugar
1   teaspoon salt
1   teaspoon pepper

Bring 1 quart water and smoked ham hock to a boil in a large Dutch oven over medium-high heat. Reduce heat to low, and simmer 30 minutes. Stir in peas and remaining ingredients; cover and simmer 25 to 30 minutes or until peas are done. Yield: 12 servings.

Per serving: Calories 156 (28% from fat); Fat 4.8g (sat 1.7g, mono 2g, poly 0.6g); Protein 8.4g; Carb 20g; Fiber 4.9g; Chol 21mg; Iron 1.5mg; Sodium 500mg; Calc 121mg

low calorie • low cholesterol • low fat

Green Peas With Bacon

prep: 20 min.   cook: 18 min.

Mint and orange brighten this often under-rated legume, while the bacon lends a smoky flavor. When in season, use fresh sweet peas.

2   smoked bacon slices
1   shallot, sliced
½   teaspoon grated orange rind
½   cup fresh orange juice
½   teaspoon pepper
¼   teaspoon salt
1   (16-ounce) bag frozen sweet peas, thawed*
1   teaspoon butter or margarine
1   tablespoon chopped fresh mint
Garnish: fresh mint

Cook bacon in a medium skillet until crisp; remove bacon, and drain on paper towels, reserving 1 teaspoon drippings in skillet. Crumble bacon, and set aside.
Sauté shallot in hot bacon drippings over medium-high heat 2 minutes or until tender. Stir in orange rind, orange juice, pepper, and salt. Cook, stirring occasionally, 5 minutes or until reduced by half. Add peas, and cook 5 more minutes; stir in butter and mint.
Transfer peas to a serving dish, and sprinkle with crumbled bacon. Garnish, if desired. Yield: 6 servings.

Per serving: Calories 92 (24% from fat); Fat 2.5g (sat 1g, mono 0.9g, poly 0.3g); Protein 4.7g; Carb 13.2g; Fiber 4g; Chol 5mg; Iron 1.3mg; Sodium 203mg; Calc 23mg

*Substitute 3 cups shelled fresh sweet peas for frozen. Cook peas in boiling water 5 minutes, and proceed with recipe.

quick

Sugar Snap Peas and Goat Cheese

prep: 8 min.   cook: 11 min.

For added convenience, look for packaged ready-to-use stringless sugar snap peas in your grocery produce department.

1   pound fresh sugar snap peas, trimmed
2   shallots, minced
1   tablespoon olive oil
1   pint grape tomatoes, halved
2   tablespoons chopped fresh basil
1   (3-ounce) log goat cheese, crumbled
1   teaspoon salt
½   teaspoon freshly ground pepper

Cook peas in boiling water to cover 1 minute; drain. Plunge into ice water to stop the cooking process; drain.
Sauté shallots in hot oil in a large skillet over medium heat until tender. Add peas, and cook just until heated.
Transfer peas to a large bowl. Add tomatoes and remaining ingredients; toss gently. Serve hot. Yield: 4 servings.

Per serving: Calories 178 (51% from fat); Fat 10.1g (sat 4.9g, mono 4g, poly 0.7g); Protein 8.7g; Carb 14.4g; Fiber 3.9g; Chol 17mg; Iron 3.1mg; Sodium 701mg; Calc 126mg

low calorie • low cholesterol • low fat • quick

Orange-Ginger Peas

prep: 5 min.   cook: 7 min.

1   (16-ounce) package frozen sweet peas
1   cup water
1   tablespoon grated orange rind
2   tablespoons honey
¼   to ½ teaspoon salt
¼   teaspoon ground red pepper
1   (1-inch) piece fresh ginger, peeled (optional)

Combine first 6 ingredients and, if desired, ginger, in a large saucepan over medium-high heat. Bring to a boil; reduce heat, and simmer 3 minutes. Remove and discard ginger. Serve with a slotted spoon. Yield: 8 servings.

Per serving: Calories 58 (3% from fat); Fat 0.2g (sat 0g, mono 0g, poly 0.1g); Protein 2.8g; Carb 12.1g; Fiber 3g; Chol 0mg; Iron 0.8mg; Sodium 111mg; Calc 14mg

low carb

Stuffed Banana Peppers

prep: 23 min.   cook: 11 min.

Banana peppers, also known as Hungarian hot wax peppers, are excellent for stuffing. They vary in color from light green to red, with the light green color being mildest in flavor and most available in grocery stores.

7   large banana peppers
¾   cup diced onion
½   small green bell pepper, diced
1   to 2 jalapeño peppers, minced
2   teaspoons olive oil
2   cups (8 ounces) shredded Mexican-blend or Cheddar cheese (we tested with Sargento four-cheese Mexican blend)
1   small tomato, finely chopped
⅛   teaspoon salt
⅛   teaspoon pepper
14   fully cooked bacon slices (we tested with Oscar Mayer)

Cut a slit lengthwise in each banana pepper, cutting to, but not through, other side. Remove seeds.
Sauté onion, bell pepper, and jalapeño in hot oil in a large skillet over medium-high heat 4 minutes or until tender. Stir in cheese and next 3 ingredients.
Spoon vegetable filling evenly into each pepper, and wrap each pepper with 2 bacon slices; secure with wooden picks. Place peppers on a rack in a broiler pan.
Broil 5½ inches from heat 7 minutes or until bacon is crisp and browned. Yield: 7 servings.

Per serving: Calories 215 (64% from fat); Fat 15.3g (sat 8.4g, mono 1g, poly 0.3g); Protein 11.8g; Carb 7.8g; Fiber 3.1g; Chol 39mg; Iron 0.5mg; Sodium 428mg; Calc 245mg

whipped vs. mashed

Some folks like the convenience and light texture that results from whipping potatoes with an electric mixer. Just be careful not to overmix them, or you'll have gummy, gluey spuds. Mashing potatoes with a potato masher provides texture options for creamy or chunky spuds, depending on your preference. Be sure to use a durable masher with a stainless steel or wooden handle.

family favorite

Loaded Garlic Smashed Potatoes

prep: 35 min.   cook: 1 hr., 15 min.

Take it the extra step by roasting your own garlic. While you're at it, roast a few extra bulbs to have on hand.

2	garlic bulbs
1	tablespoon olive oil
6	bacon slices
1	bunch green onions, chopped
4	pounds red potatoes
1	(16-ounce) container sour cream
1½	cups (6 ounces) shredded Cheddar cheese, divided
⅓	cup butter or margarine, softened
¼	cup milk
1	teaspoon salt
¼	teaspoon pepper

Garnish: chopped green onion

Cut off pointed end of garlic; place garlic on a piece of aluminum foil, and drizzle with oil. Fold foil to seal. Bake at 425° for 40 minutes; cool. Squeeze pulp from garlic; set aside.

Cook bacon in a large skillet until crisp; remove bacon, and drain on paper towels, reserving 2 tablespoons drippings in skillet. Crumble bacon, and return to skillet; add 1 bunch chopped green onions. Cook 1 minute or until green onions are tender. Set aside.

Peel potatoes; cut into ¼-inch pieces. Cook potatoes, covered, in a Dutch oven in boiling salted water to cover 15 to 20 minutes or until tender; drain and return to Dutch oven. **Add** roasted garlic pulp, bacon mixture, sour cream, 1 cup cheese, and next 4 ingredients; mash with a potato masher until blended. Spoon into a lightly greased 13- x 9-inch baking dish; top with remaining ½ cup cheese. Bake at 350° for 10 minutes or until cheese melts. Garnish, if desired. Yield: 12 servings.

Per serving: Calories 316 (63% from fat); Fat 22.2g (sat 12.6g, mono 6.9g, poly 1.1g); Protein 9.7g; Carb 19.7g; Fiber 2.3g; Chol 52mg; Iron 1.1mg; Sodium 445mg; Calc 179mg

family favorite

Chile Mashers

prep: 25 min.   cook: 30 min.

4	pounds medium Yukon gold potatoes, peeled and quartered (about 14)
½	cup butter
½	onion, chopped
2	garlic cloves, chopped
2	tablespoons olive oil
2	chipotle chiles in adobo sauce
1	medium tomato, chopped (about ½ cup)
1	teaspoon sugar
1	cup whipping cream or half-and-half
¾	teaspoon salt
⅛	teaspoon pepper

Bring potatoes and salted water to cover to a boil in a Dutch oven. Cook 20 to 30 minutes or until potatoes are tender. Drain and return potatoes to hot, dry pan. Add butter; stir until melted.

Meanwhile, sauté onion and garlic in hot oil in a large skillet over medium-high heat 2 minutes or until tender. Add chiles, tomato, and sugar; cook 3 minutes.

Transfer mixture to a blender, and process until smooth, stopping to scrape down sides.

Mash potatoes and whipping cream with a potato masher. Stir in chile puree, salt, and pepper until blended. Yield: 8 servings.

Per serving: Calories 381 (59% from fat); Fat 24.8g (sat 13.7g, mono 8.5g, poly 1.1g); Protein 4.4g; Carb 34.6g; Fiber 2.5g; Chol 70mg; Iron 1.6mg; Sodium 788mg; Calc 28mg

Whipped Celery Potatoes

prep: 19 min.   cook: 37 min.

2	pounds Yukon gold or red potatoes, peeled and cubed (about 7 medium)
3½	cups water
1½	teaspoons salt
½	cup butter or margarine, divided
3	celery ribs, chopped
½	small onion, diced
⅓	cup milk
¾	teaspoon salt
½	teaspoon pepper

Bring first 3 ingredients to a boil in a large saucepan. Cover, reduce heat, and simmer 30 minutes or until potato is tender. Drain and transfer to a mixing bowl.

Melt 2 tablespoons butter in saucepan; add celery and onion, and sauté until celery is very tender.

Add celery mixture to potatoes; beat at low speed with an electric mixer until potatoes are mashed. Add remaining 6 tablespoons butter, milk, salt, and pepper; beat at high speed until whipped (do not overbeat). Serve hot. Yield: 5 servings.

Per serving: Calories 450 (74% from fat); Fat 36.8g (sat 23.3g, mono 9.5g, poly 1.4g); Protein 4.3g; Carb 26.8g; Fiber 2.2g; Chol 98mg; Iron 1.3mg; Sodium 988mg; Calc 38mg

quick

Mashed Potatoes With Tomato Gravy

prep: 5 min.   cook: 11 min.

1	(22-ounce) package frozen mashed potatoes
2⅓	cups milk
½	(8-ounce) package cream cheese, softened
1	teaspoon salt
1	teaspoon seasoned pepper

Tomato Gravy (page 441)

Stir together potatoes and milk in a large glass bowl. Microwave at HIGH 6 minutes; stir and microwave 5 more minutes. Let stand 2 minutes.

Stir in cream cheese, salt, and seasoned pepper, stirring just until cheese melts and mixture is blended. Serve with Tomato Gravy. Yield: 6 servings.

Per serving: Calories 339 (47% from fat); Fat 17.8g (sat 9.7g, mono 5.4g, poly 1.8g); Protein 8.8g; Carb 40.1g; Fiber 3.5g; Chol 44mg; Iron 1.4mg; Sodium 1196mg; Calc 167mg

potato dictionary

The starch and moisture content of each potato variety determines the best way to prepare it. Waxy, high-moisture potatoes are best for boiling, roasting, and in potato salads. Mealy, drier potatoes are best for baking, mashing, and frying.

Baking Potato: Long, slightly rounded potato, which can weigh more than a pound, is the most widely used variety in the U.S. With its reddish-brown skin and its high-starch white flesh, this potato is meant for baking, mashing, frying, and roasting. As this potato cooks, the large starch granules absorb the internal moisture, expand, and then burst, creating the dry, mealy texture that results in fluffy mashed potatoes. They're also preferred for French fries because the starch on the potato's cut surface expands with heat and dries the surface as it absorbs water from the potato, leaving a fluffy interior and crisp exterior.

White Potato: Waxy variety has smooth white skin and flesh. With more moisture and a lower starch content than a baking potato, this potato works well in recipes in which the potato pieces need to maintain their shape while cooking. It's preferred for boiling, steaming, braising, roasting, and in soups, stews, salads, and casseroles (scalloped and au gratin).

Red-Skinned Potato: Round, waxy potato has smooth red skin and white flesh. It's a low-starch, high-moisture potato that absorbs little water when cooked, so it remains firm, smooth, and creamy. It's best when boiled, roasted,

steamed, or tossed in soup and salad. This variety also has the thinnest skin and is often prepared unpeeled.

Yellow-Flesh Potato: *Yukon Gold* is the most familiar with its dense, creamy texture and buttery flavor, and balance of starch and moisture. It's a versatile variety that can be boiled, steamed, fried, or mashed. With a higher sugar content than some other spuds, this potato tends to brown fairly quickly during cooking.

Purple Potato: This small potato (*Purple Peruvian* is a popular variety) has purple-black skin and a dense interior that can range from deep purple to bright blue. Its starch content also can vary from medium starch to waxy. This potato is a good choice for roasting or mashing and can be used in salads. These purple spuds may stain your hands, so wear gloves while peeling them.

Fingerling: Small, narrow potato is generally 2 to 4 inches in length; a very young tuber with a firm texture that can be moist or dry with a range

of flavors from mildly sweet to rich and nutty. It can be baked, boiled, fried, grilled, roasted, steamed, or sautéed. The French fingerling is a popular variety.

New Potato: Also called *baby red* and *creamer potato*, this potato is harvested very early in its growth and can be sold as small as a marble. It has a high moisture content and high sugar content since the young flesh has not developed the amount of starch common in larger potatoes. The skin is thin and tender and doesn't need to be peeled. New potatoes cook quickly and have a sweet flavor. They're suitable for boiling, baking, frying, or roasting, and can be used in potato salads, soups, stews and casseroles. *Red Bliss* is a common variety.

Choose low-moisture, high-starch potatoes such as russet or Idaho. For crisp fries, wash the cut, uncooked strips in several batches of cold water until the water is clear. However, for the crispiest fries, we found the double-fry method hard to beat. Frying strips twice in the same oil at different temperatures (first at 325° and then 375°) gives you fries like no others.

family favorite

French Fries

prep: 30 min.   cook: 7 min. per batch

4   pounds russet or Idaho potatoes, peeled
Vegetable oil
Salt to taste (optional)

Cut potatoes into ¼-inch-wide strips.
Pour vegetable oil to a depth of 4 inches in a Dutch oven, and heat to 325°.
Fry potato strips, in batches, until lightly golden, but not brown, 4 to 5 minutes per batch. Drain strips on paper towels.
Heat oil to 375°. Fry strips, in small batches, until golden brown and crisp, 1 to 2 minutes per batch. Drain on clean paper towels. Sprinkle with salt, if desired, and serve immediately. Yield: 6 servings.

Per serving: Calories 545 (62% from fat); Fat 37.6g (sat 4.1g, mono 16g, poly 16.1g); Protein 4.8g; Carb 52.1g; Fiber 4.7g; Chol 0mg; Iron 0.8mg; Sodium 10mg; Calc 13mg

family favorite • low cholesterol

Roasted New Potatoes

prep: 12 min.   cook: 37 min.

2   tablespoons olive oil or butter
2   pounds new potatoes, unpeeled and halved
1   tablespoon minced garlic
2   teaspoons chopped fresh thyme
2   teaspoons chopped fresh rosemary
1   teaspoon salt
½   teaspoon pepper

Heat oil in a large cast-iron skillet over medium-high heat. Add potatoes and next 3 ingredients. Toss. Remove skillet from heat; place in oven.
Roast potatoes, uncovered, at 450° for

30 minutes or until potatoes are tender, stirring occasionally. Sprinkle with salt and pepper. Roast, uncovered, 6 more minutes. Serve hot. Yield: 5 servings.

Per serving: Calories 254 (21% from fat); Fat 5.9g (sat 0.8g, mono 4g, poly 0.6g); Protein 3g; Carb 32.5g; Fiber 4.2g; Chol 0mg; Iron 0.7mg; Sodium 473mg; Calc 11mg

Tangy Olive Potatoes

prep: 10 min.   cook: 35 min.

1   (1-pound, 4-ounce) package refrigerated diced potatoes with onion (we tested with Simply Potatoes Diced Potatoes) or 1¼ pounds potatoes, peeled and diced
2   tablespoons butter or margarine
4   ounces Canadian bacon, finely chopped
1   medium onion, chopped
1½   teaspoons chopped fresh or ½ teaspoon dried thyme
1   cup whipping cream
1   teaspoon salt
½   teaspoon pepper
¼   cup sliced pimiento-stuffed olives

Arrange potatoes in a steamer basket over boiling water. Cover and steam 20 minutes or until tender.
Melt butter in a large skillet over medium-high heat; add bacon, onion, and thyme, and cook 10 minutes. Stir in potatoes, whipping cream, salt, and pepper. Cook 5 minutes or until slightly thickened and thoroughly heated; stir in olives. Serve hot. Yield: 4 servings.

Per serving: Calories 415 (62% from fat); Fat 28.8g (sat 16.4g, mono 9.2g, poly 1g); Protein 8g; Carb 28.9g; Fiber 2.2g; Chol 109mg; Iron 1mg; Sodium 1606mg; Calc 59mg

• Scrub a large baking potato with a vegetable brush; pat dry.
• Pierce potato 3 or 4 times with a fork, and rub with butter or olive oil for crispier skin.
• Rub with salt or sea salt, if desired. (Do not wrap in foil. Wrapping holds in moisture, causing a texture similar to a boiled potato. If you like soft skin, wrap potato in foil after baking, and let stand 10 minutes.)
• Bake potato directly on the oven rack at 450° for 1 hour and 10 minutes. If baking more than 4 potatoes, add 5 minutes to the bake time for every additional potato.

Bell's Sweet Potato Casserole

family favorite

Bell's Sweet Potato Casserole

prep: 20 min.   cook: 1 hr., 15 min.

8   medium-size sweet potatoes (6 pounds)
1   cup milk
¼   cup butter
3   tablespoons sugar
1   teaspoon vanilla extract
1   tablespoon orange juice
¼   teaspoon salt
¼   teaspoon ground cinnamon
¼   teaspoon ground nutmeg
1   (10.5-ounce) package miniature marshmallows

Bring sweet potatoes and water to cover to a boil, and cook 30 to 35 minutes or until tender; drain. Peel potatoes, and place in a mixing bowl.
Heat milk and next 3 ingredients in a saucepan over medium heat, stirring until butter melts and sugar dissolves. (Do not boil.) Stir in orange juice, salt, and spices.
Beat potatoes at medium speed with an electric mixer until mashed. Add milk mixture, beating until smooth. Spoon half of mashed sweet potatoes into a lightly greased 13- x 9-inch baking dish; top with half of marshmallows. Spread remaining mashed potatoes over marshmallows.
Bake at 350° for 25 minutes. Top with remaining half of marshmallows, and bake 8 to 10 more minutes or until marshmallows are golden. Yield: 10 servings.

Per serving: Calories 248 (20% from fat); Fat 5.6g (sat 3.4g, mono 1.4g, poly 0.3g); Protein 3.2g; Carb 48.2g; Fiber 3.1g; Chol 14mg; Iron 0.7mg; Sodium 157mg; Calc 66mg

Simple Steamed Rutabagas

prep: 20 min.   cook: 35 min.

Rutabagas resemble large turnips and have a slightly sweet, firm flesh. Here, they're steamed and tossed with a hint of honey.

4   cups peeled, cubed rutabaga
3   tablespoons butter or margarine, melted
1   tablespoon lemon juice
1   tablespoon honey
⅛   teaspoon hot sauce
1   tablespoon chopped fresh parsley
½   teaspoon salt
Dash of pepper

Arrange rutabaga in a steamer basket over boiling water. Cover and steam 30 to 35 minutes or until tender. Drain.
Place rutabaga in a bowl. Add butter and next 3 ingredients; toss. Sprinkle with parsley, salt, and pepper; toss gently. Yield: 6 servings.

Per serving: Calories 95 (56% from fat); Fat 5.9g (sat 3.6g, mono 1.5g, poly 0.3g); Protein 1.2g; Carb 10.8g; Fiber 2.4g; Chol 15mg; Iron 0.6mg; Sodium 254mg; Calc 47mg

Fresh Spinach Sauté

prep: 3 min.   cook: 7 min.

While spinach cooks down considerably, its healthy benefits do not. Each serving is packed full of a peppery lemon and garlic flavor as well as cancer-fighting antioxidants, folate, vitamin A, and potassium.

2   garlic cloves, minced
2   teaspoons olive oil
3   (10-ounce) packages fresh spinach, torn
½   teaspoon salt
½   teaspoon dried crushed red pepper
1   tablespoon fresh lemon juice
¼   cup freshly shredded Parmesan cheese

Sauté garlic in hot oil in a large Dutch oven over medium-high heat 1 minute. Reduce heat to medium; add spinach, salt, and red pepper. Cook 5 minutes or until spinach wilts, stirring occasionally. Add lemon juice. Sprinkle with Parmesan cheese. Serve immediately. Yield: 6 servings.

Per serving: Calories 65 (46% from fat); Fat 3.3g (sat 1g, mono 1.4g, poly 0.4g); Protein 5.7g; Carb 6g; Fiber 3.3g; Chol 3mg; Iron 3.9mg; Sodium 378mg; Calc 193mg

Spinach Pie

prep: 10 min.   cook: 30 min.   other: 10 min.

This is a creamy quichelike pie without the crust.

2   (6-ounce) packages fresh baby spinach
¼   cup butter
3   tablespoons all-purpose flour
¼   teaspoon salt
¼   teaspoon pepper
¼   teaspoon garlic powder
4   large eggs, lightly beaten
¾   cup whipping cream
½   cup shredded Parmesan cheese

Rinse spinach well; drain.
Melt butter in a large skillet over medium heat. Add spinach, and cook just until wilted.
Combine flour, salt, pepper, and garlic powder in a large bowl. Add spinach, eggs, whipping cream, and Parmesan cheese, stirring well. Pour mixture into a lightly greased 9-inch pieplate.
Bake at 350° for 25 minutes or until pie is set. Let stand 10 minutes. Cut pie into wedges. Yield: 8 servings.

Per serving: Calories 213 (75% from fat); Fat 17.8g (sat 10.4g, mono 5.3g, poly 0.9g); Protein 6.9g; Carb 7.8g; Fiber 2.1g; Chol 155mg; Iron 2mg; Sodium 309mg; Calc 123mg

Spinach Soufflé

prep: 15 min.   cook: 40 min.   other: 5 min.

1   (10-ounce) package frozen chopped spinach, thawed
2   tablespoons butter
1   medium onion, chopped (about ¾ cup)
2   garlic cloves, minced
3   large eggs
2   tablespoons all-purpose flour
½   teaspoon salt
¼   teaspoon ground nutmeg
¼   teaspoon pepper
1   cup milk
1   cup freshly grated Parmesan or Romano cheese

Drain spinach well, pressing between paper towels to remove excess liquid.
Melt butter in a large skillet over medium heat; add onion and garlic, and sauté 5 minutes or until garlic is lightly browned

and onion is tender. Remove from heat, and stir in spinach until blended; cool.
Whisk together eggs and next 4 ingredients in a large bowl. Whisk in milk and Parmesan cheese; stir in spinach mixture, and pour into a lightly greased 8-inch square baking dish.
Bake at 350° for 33 to 35 minutes or until set. Let stand 5 minutes before serving. Yield: 4 servings.

Per serving: Calories 279 (57% from fat); Fat 17.8g (sat 9.6g, mono 5.1g, poly 1.2g); Protein 18g; Carb 13.3g; Fiber 2.8g; Chol 197mg; Iron 2.6mg; Sodium 767mg; Calc 432mg

Easy Squash and Corn Casserole

prep: 13 min.   cook: 56 min.   other: 5 min.

This combination of two summertime favorites uses frozen corn soufflé to shortcut preparation.

2   tablespoons butter or margarine
½   small sweet onion, chopped
1   pound yellow squash, sliced
1   (12-ounce) package frozen corn soufflé, thawed (we tested with Stouffer's)
1   cup (4 ounces) shredded sharp Cheddar cheese
¾   cup soft breadcrumbs
2   tablespoons chopped fresh parsley
1   large egg, lightly beaten
½   teaspoon garlic salt
¼   teaspoon pepper

Melt butter in a skillet over medium-high heat; add onion, and sauté 5 minutes or until tender. Add squash, and sauté 5 minutes.
Stir together squash mixture, corn soufflé, and remaining ingredients. Spoon mixture into a lightly greased 8-inch square baking dish. Bake at 350° for 45 minutes or until set. Let stand 5 minutes before serving. Yield: 6 servings.

Per serving: Calories 223 (57% from fat); Fat 14.2g (sat 7.5g, mono 4.2g, poly 1.1g); Protein 9.3g; Carb 15g; Fiber 1.5g; Chol 92mg; Iron 1mg; Sodium 481mg; Calc 181mg

Two-Cheese Squash Casserole

family favorite

Two-Cheese Squash Casserole

prep: 30 min.　cook: 1 hr.

The addition of Parmesan and Cheddar cheeses gives this popular casserole a delicious flavor.

4　pounds yellow squash, sliced
4　tablespoons butter or margarine, divided
1　large sweet onion, finely chopped
2　garlic cloves, minced
2½　cups soft breadcrumbs, divided
1¼　cups shredded Parmesan cheese, divided
1　cup (4 ounces) shredded Cheddar cheese
¼　cup chopped fresh chives
½　cup minced fresh parsley
1　(8-ounce) container sour cream
1　teaspoon salt
1　teaspoon freshly ground pepper
2　large eggs, lightly beaten
¼　teaspoon garlic salt

Cook squash in boiling water to cover in a Dutch oven 8 to 10 minutes or just until tender. Drain well; gently press between paper towels.
Melt 2 tablespoons butter in Dutch oven over medium-high heat; add onion and garlic, and sauté 5 to 6 minutes or until tender. Remove skillet from heat; stir in squash, 1 cup breadcrumbs, ¾ cup Parmesan cheese, and next 7 ingredients. Spoon into a lightly greased 13- x 9-inch baking dish.

Melt remaining 2 tablespoons butter. Stir together melted butter, remaining 1½ cups soft breadcrumbs, ½ cup Parmesan cheese, and garlic salt. Sprinkle mixture evenly over casserole.
Bake at 350° for 35 to 40 minutes or until set. Yield: 10 servings.

Per serving: Calories 256 (61% from fat); Fat 17.5g (sat 10.4g, mono 5g, poly 1g); Protein 11.9g; Carb 14.7g; Fiber 2.5g; Chol 83mg; Iron 1.7mg; Sodium 638mg; Calc 293mg

low calorie • low carb • low cholesterol • quick

Zucchini With Fresh Mint

prep: 10 min.　cook: 10 min.

Combine the fruits of your vegetable and herb garden to make this simple and refreshing side dish.

1½　pounds small zucchini
2　garlic cloves, minced
2　tablespoons olive oil
1　tablespoon chopped fresh mint
1　tablespoon chopped fresh flat-leaf parsley
¾　teaspoon salt
½　teaspoon pepper

Cut zucchini in half lengthwise; then cut crosswise into ¼-inch-thick slices.
Sauté minced garlic in hot oil in a skillet over medium-high heat until lightly browned. Add zucchini, and cook, stirring occasionally, 5 to 6 minutes or until tender.
Remove from heat; add herbs, salt, and pepper. Serve hot. Yield: 4 servings.

Per serving: Calories 70 (89% from fat); Fat 6.9g (sat 0.9g, mono 5g, poly 0.7g); Protein 0.7g; Carb 2.3g; Fiber 0.7g; Chol 0mg; Iron 0.4mg; Sodium 442mg; Calc 13mg

Acorn Squash With Pear Stuffing

prep: 10 min.　cook: 1 hr., 40 min.

2　acorn squash
2　tablespoons butter or margarine
1　small onion, chopped
2　pears, peeled and chopped
2　tablespoons light brown sugar
2　tablespoons bourbon
1　teaspoon salt
½　teaspoon ground ginger
½　teaspoon ground nutmeg
1½　cups orange juice
¾　cup granulated sugar

Cut each squash in half lengthwise; discard seeds and membranes. Place squash halves, cut sides down, in a 13- x 9-inch baking dish. Add water to a depth of 1 inch.
Bake, covered, at 400° for 45 minutes. Drain. Return squash halves to dish, cut sides up. Set aside.
Melt butter in a large skillet over medium heat; add onion, and cook, stirring occasionally, 20 minutes. Add pear and next 5 ingredients; cook, stirring occasionally, 5 minutes. Spoon pear filling into squash halves.
Bake, uncovered, at 350° for 15 to 20 minutes.
Bring orange juice to a boil in a small saucepan. Stir in granulated sugar, and boil 10 minutes. Drizzle orange syrup over squash. Yield: 4 servings.

Per serving: Calories 407 (14% from fat); Fat 6.3g (sat 3.7g, mono 1.6g, poly 0.4g); Protein 3g; Carb 88.9g; Fiber 6.3g; Chol 15mg; Iron 2mg; Sodium 632mg; Calc 100mg

Potato-Butternut Squash-and-Gruyère Gratin

prep: 15 min.　cook: 1 hr., 20 min.

5　medium Yukon Gold potatoes (about 2½ pounds)
1　large butternut squash (about 2 pounds)
2　tablespoons butter or margarine
1　large sweet onion, chopped
1　teaspoon salt
½　teaspoon pepper
2　cups (8 ounces) shredded Gruyère cheese
Cream Sauce (page 432)

Peel and thinly slice potatoes. Peel, seed, and thinly slice squash.
Cook potato in boiling water to cover in a Dutch oven 5 minutes. Add squash; cover and cook 3 minutes. Remove from heat, and drain.
Melt butter in a large skillet; add onion, and sauté 10 to 12 minutes or until golden brown.
Layer half of potato slices and squash in a lightly greased 13- x 9-inch baking dish; sprinkle with half each of salt and pepper. Top with half each of onion, cheese, and Cream Sauce. Repeat layers, ending with Cream Sauce.
Bake at 350° for 1 hour or until browned. Yield: 12 servings.

Per serving: Calories 272 (44% from fat); Fat 13.3g (sat 8g, mono 3.7g, poly 0.7g); Protein 10.2g; Carb 28.7g; Fiber 3.1g; Chol 40mg; Iron 1.5mg; Sodium 374mg; Calc 273mg

Spaghetti Squash

prep: 20 min.   cook: 1 hr., 10 min.

1   (3-pound) spaghetti squash
1   medium onion, chopped
1   garlic clove, minced
2   tablespoons olive oil
1   cup chopped fresh Swiss chard
3   large eggs, lightly beaten
1   cup plus 2 tablespoons fine, dry
    breadcrumbs, divided
½   cup freshly grated Parmesan cheese
1½ teaspoons salt
1   teaspoon dried basil
1   teaspoon dried Italian seasoning
¼   teaspoon pepper
Vegetable cooking spray

Prick squash, and microwave at HIGH 1 minute; cut squash in half lengthwise; discard seeds.
Place squash, cut side up, in a Dutch oven; cover with water. Bring to a boil; cover, reduce heat, and simmer 20 minutes or until tender. Using a fork, remove spaghetti-like strands, leaving 2 (¼-inch-thick) shells; set shells aside. Place strands in a large bowl.
Sauté onion and garlic in hot oil in a large skillet over medium-high heat 3 minutes or until onion is tender.
Combine squash and Swiss chard. Add to onion mixture; cook, uncovered, 3 to 5 minutes or until Swiss chard is wilted and tender. Add eggs, 1 cup breadcrumbs, and next 5 ingredients.
Place reserved squash shells into an ungreased 13- x 9-inch baking dish. Spoon squash mixture evenly into shells. Sprinkle with remaining 2 tablespoons breadcrumbs. Coat breadcrumbs with cooking spray. Bake, uncovered, at 350° for 45 minutes. Yield: 6 servings.

Per serving: Calories 247 (40% from fat); Fat 11g (sat 3g, mono 5.1g, poly 1.7g); Protein 9.8g; Carb 28.7g; Fiber 1.4g; Chol 112mg; Iron 2.3mg; Sodium 918mg; Calc 174mg

---

vegetarian

Herbed Tomato Tart

prep: 30 min.   cook: 25 min.   other: 20 min.

Serve larger portions as a vegetarian entrée.

1   (17.3-ounce) package frozen puff pastry
    sheets, thawed
5   plum tomatoes, thinly sliced
¾   teaspoon salt
1   (8-ounce) package shredded mozzarella
    cheese
1   (4-ounce) package crumbled feta
    cheese
¼   cup chopped onion
1   garlic clove, minced
¼   cup finely chopped mixed fresh herbs*
Freshly ground pepper
1   tablespoon olive oil

Roll each pastry sheet into a 14-inch square on a lightly floured surface; place 1 pastry sheet on an ungreased baking sheet. Cut 2 (14- x 1-inch) strips and 2 (13- x 1-inch) strips from a second pastry sheet. Wet strips with water, and place along edges on top of pastry square, forming a border.
Bake pastry shell at 400° for 10 minutes or until golden. Transfer to a wire rack to cool.
Place tomato slices on paper towels; sprinkle evenly with salt. Let stand 20 minutes.
Place baked pastry shell on baking sheet; sprinkle with mozzarella cheese and next 3 ingredients. Arrange tomato slices in a single layer on top. Sprinkle with herbs and freshly ground pepper; drizzle with oil.
Bake at 400° for 15 minutes or until cheese melts; serve hot. Yield: 8 servings.

Per serving: Calories 484 (64% from fat); Fat 34.3g (sat 11.9g, mono 15.2g, poly 3.3g); Protein 15g; Carb 32g; Fiber 1.5g; Chol 28mg; Iron 2mg; Sodium 705mg; Calc 286mg

*For mixed fresh herbs, we combined 1 tablespoon each of basil, rosemary, chives, and parsley.

---

low carb • make ahead

Charred Tomatoes

prep: 20 min.   cook: 6 min. per batch
other: 1 hr.

8   large tomatoes
⅓   cup plus 2 tablespoons olive oil, divided
⅓   cup sliced fresh basil
3   tablespoons red wine vinegar
1   teaspoon kosher salt
½   teaspoon freshly ground pepper
Garnish: fresh basil leaves

Cut tomatoes into quarters; remove and discard seeds. Pat tomatoes dry, and drizzle with 2 tablespoons olive oil.
Heat a large cast-iron skillet over high heat until very hot. Cook tomatoes, in batches, over high heat 3 minutes on each side or until slightly blackened. Remove tomatoes and juices from skillet to a large bowl; cool.
Toss tomatoes and tomato essence with ⅓ cup olive oil, sliced basil, and next 3 ingredients. Cover and let stand 1 hour; stirring once or twice. Garnish, if desired. Yield: 6 servings.

Per serving: Calories 191 (80% from fat); Fat 17g (sat 2.3g, mono 12.3g, poly 1.9g); Protein 2.2g; Carb 9.8g; Fiber 3.1g; Chol 0mg; Iron 0.9mg; Sodium 327mg; Calc 29mg

Herbed
Tomato
Tart

low calorie • low cholesterol
Honey–Baked Tomatoes

prep: 10 min.   cook: 19 min.

8   medium-size ripe tomatoes, cut into
    1-inch slices
4   teaspoons honey
3   white bread slices (we tested with
    Pepperidge Farm Hearty White bread)
1   tablespoon dried tarragon
1½ teaspoons salt
1½ teaspoons freshly ground pepper
1½ tablespoons butter, melted

Place tomato slices in a single layer in a
lightly greased aluminum foil-lined
15- x 10-inch jelly-roll pan. Drizzle with
honey, spreading honey into hollows.
Process bread in a food processor or
blender until coarse crumbs form.
Stir together breadcrumbs and next 4 ingredients; sprinkle evenly over tomato slices.
Bake at 350° for 15 to 18 minutes or until
tomato skins begin to wrinkle.
Broil 3 inches from heat 1 minute or
until tops are golden. Serve warm. Yield:
8 servings.

Per serving: Calories 93 (30% from fat); Fat 3.1g (sat 1.4g, mono 0.6g, poly 0.3g);
Protein 2.4g; Carb 16.2g; Fiber 2.2g; Chol 6mg; Iron 1.1mg; Sodium 534mg; Calc 24mg

quick tomato peel

◄ To peel a tomato,
first blanch it in
boiling water
30 seconds.

◄ Remove tomato
from water, and
pull skin away,
using a sharp
paring knife.

taste of the south fried green tomatoes

Fried Green Tomatoes

prep: 20 min.   cook: 4 min. per batch

*Golden and crisp, with a pleasingly
rugged exterior, fried green tomatoes are
the quintessential Southern side dish.*

1   large egg, lightly beaten
½   cup buttermilk
½   cup all-purpose flour, divided
½   cup cornmeal
1   teaspoon salt
½   teaspoon pepper
3   medium-size green tomatoes, cut into
    ⅓-inch slices
Vegetable oil
Salt to taste

Combine egg and buttermilk; set aside.
Combine ¼ cup flour, cornmeal, 1 teaspoon salt, and pepper in a shallow bowl
or pan.
Dredge tomato slices in remaining ¼ cup
flour; dip into egg mixture, and dredge in
cornmeal mixture.

Pour oil to a depth of ¼ to ½ inch in a
large cast-iron skillet; heat to 375°. Drop
tomatoes, in batches, into hot oil, and cook
2 minutes on each side or until golden.
Drain on paper towels or a rack. Sprinkle
hot tomatoes with salt to taste. Yield:
4 servings.

Per serving: Calories 299 (51% from fat); Fat 16.9g (sat 2.6g, mono 6.6g, poly 6.4g);
Protein 6.8g; Carb 31.8g; Fiber 2.8g; Chol 57mg; Iron 2.2mg; Sodium 648mg; Calc 23mg

fried tomato tips

• Use a cast-iron skillet or any good heavy
skillet. An electric skillet is great—it keeps an
even heat, so tomatoes cook nicely.
• Use firm tomatoes, and fry them in fairly
shallow oil, about ¼- to ½-inch deep. You don't
want to cover the tomatoes with grease.
• Keep the temperature at 360° to 375°.
• Add about 3 tablespoons bacon drippings for
more flavor.
• Salt the fried tomatoes as they drain, and
serve them hot. They retain their heat for a
while, so let them cool just a little before you
eat them.

Fried Green Tomatoes

Roasted Root Vegetables

prep: 15 min.   cook: 45 min.

1	(1-pound) bag parsnips
6	large turnips
2	large sweet potatoes
1	large rutabaga
6	large beets
	Vegetable cooking spray
1	teaspoon salt, divided
1	teaspoon pepper, divided
2	tablespoons butter or margarine, melted

Peel first 5 ingredients, and cut into large pieces. Coat 2 aluminum foil-lined baking sheets with cooking spray. Arrange parsnip, turnip, sweet potato, and rutabaga on a baking sheet. Lightly coat vegetables with cooking spray, and sprinkle with ¾ teaspoon salt and ¾ teaspoon pepper.

Arrange beets on remaining baking sheet; lightly coat with cooking spray, and sprinkle with remaining ¼ teaspoon salt and ¼ teaspoon pepper.

Roast vegetables at 425° for 35 to 45 minutes or until tender, stirring once or twice after 20 minutes. (Pans may need to be rearranged after 15 to 20 minutes to ensure even cooking.)

Toss vegetables with melted butter in a serving bowl. Yield: 8 servings.

Per serving: Calories 202 (16% from fat); Fat 3.5g (sat 1.9g, mono 0.9g, poly 0.4g); Protein 4.9g; Carb 40.7g; Fiber 10.5g; Chol 8mg; Iron 2.1mg; Sodium 491mg; Calc 133mg

Note: We cooked the beets separately to keep them from bleeding onto the other vegetables.

fruit side dishes

Spiced Applesauce

prep: 20 min.   cook: 20 min.

12	large apples, peeled and coarsely chopped
½	cup granulated sugar
½	cup firmly packed light brown sugar
1	teaspoon ground cinnamon
¼	teaspoon ground cloves

Cook all ingredients in a Dutch oven over medium heat, stirring often, 20 minutes or until apples are tender and juices are thickened. Serve applesauce warm, or let cool, and store in an airtight container in the refrigerator for up to 2 weeks. Yield: 6 cups.

Per ½ cup: Calories 154 (2% from fat); Fat 0.3g (sat 0g, mono 0g, poly 0.1g); Protein 0.5g; Carb 40.5g; Fiber 2.5g; Chol 0mg; Iron 0.4mg; Sodium 4mg; Calc 20mg

Roasted Pears With Gorgonzola Cream

prep: 12 min.   cook: 17 min.

3	large ripe Bosc pears, peeled and halved
2	tablespoons butter or margarine, melted
1	(3-ounce) package cream cheese, softened
3	ounces Gorgonzola cheese, softened
2	tablespoons whipping cream
¼	cup walnuts, finely chopped

Scoop out core from each pear half with a melon baller, leaving at least a 1-inch-thick shell. Slice about ¼ inch from rounded sides to make pear halves sit flat, if necessary.

Brush cut side of each pear half with melted butter, and place cored side up on a greased baking sheet.

Bake, uncovered, at 450° for 15 minutes.

Process cheeses and cream in a food processor until creamy. Spoon mixture into center of each warm pear half.

Broil pears 3 inches from heat 1 to 2 minutes or until lightly browned. Place on serving plates. Sprinkle with walnuts. Serve warm. Yield: 6 servings.

Per serving: Calories 228 (71% from fat); Fat 18.1g (sat 9.9g, mono 3.6g, poly 2.4g); Protein 5.8g; Carb 14.1g; Fiber 2.8g; Chol 45mg; Iron 0.5mg; Sodium 267mg; Calc 101mg

Mixed Fruit With Sour Cream Sauce

prep: 15 min.   cook: 5 min.   other: 1 hr.

⅓	cup sugar
1	cup water
6	fresh mint leaves
1	(8-ounce) can pineapple chunks in juice, drained
1	Granny Smith apple, chopped
1	cup seedless green grapes
1	cup sliced strawberries
1	banana, sliced
	Sour Cream Sauce (page 443)

Bring first 3 ingredients to a boil in a saucepan, and cook, stirring constantly, 4 to 5 minutes or until sugar mixture reaches a syrup consistency. Discard mint leaves, and cool sugar syrup completely.

Combine pineapple, apple, grapes, and strawberries in a large bowl. Pour syrup over fruit mixture; toss gently. Cover and chill at least 1 hour. Add banana just before serving. Serve with Sour Cream Sauce. Yield: 4 servings.

Per serving: Calories 482 (40% from fat); Fat 21.5g (sat 13.4g, mono 5.7g, poly 0.9g); Protein 2.2g; Carb 75.1g; Fiber 2.9g; Chol 52.8mg; Iron 0.6mg; Sodium 125mg; Calc 58mg

Pineapple Casserole

prep: 12 min.   cook: 20 min.

1	(20-ounce) can pineapple chunks in juice, undrained
½	cup sugar
3	tablespoons all-purpose flour
1	cup (4 ounces) shredded Cheddar cheese
1	cup buttery cracker crumbs
3	tablespoons butter or margarine, melted

Drain pineapple, reserving 3 tablespoons juice. Combine sugar and flour; stir in reserved pineapple juice. Stir in cheese and pineapple chunks. Spoon mixture into a greased 1-quart baking dish.

Combine cracker crumbs and butter, stirring well; sprinkle over pineapple mixture. Bake, uncovered, at 350° for 20 minutes or until browned. Serve hot. Yield: 4 servings.

Per serving: Calories 459 (44% from fat); Fat 22.5g (sat 12.5g, mono 4.9g, poly 0.6g); Protein 9.3g; Carb 57.3g; Fiber 0.9g; Chol 52mg; Iron 1.6mg; Sodium 387mg; Calc 245mg

soups & stews

Equipment

Most soups need only a Dutch oven or stockpot to simmer. To begin you'll need the basics—an 8- or 10-quart stockpot for making stock and large-yield soups and a 3- or 4-quart heavy-bottomed pot for other soups. For making a rich brown stock, you'll need a roasting pan for one of its essential steps.

A blender or food processor comes in handy for pureeing soup ingredients to a smooth texture. A large strainer and sieve are needed for broth and stock. A fat separator is also recommended. A wooden spoon and a ladle are essential for stirring and serving soup.

Soup Servings

Our soup yields are given in cup amounts rather than numbers of servings so you can decide how much soup makes a serving. This will depend on which course of the meal the soup will be. For appetizer and dessert soup, allow ¾- to 1-cup servings. Allow 1½ to 2 cups for an entrée soup.

Soups served as the main course tend to be chunkier, meatier recipes like chilis, gumbos, and stews. On the contrary, choose lighter, more delicate soups to serve as an appetizer. An appetizer soup should offer just enough to stimulate the appetite.

Broth Options

Many recipes in this chapter call for broth. We leave it to you to choose between canned broth, our homemade recipe on the next page, or bouillon cubes or granules. Dilute and dissolve granules and cubes according to directions. Be sure to use the exact size can that a recipe specifies. Keep in mind that store-bought broth is saltier than homemade; always taste soup before adding seasoning.

Storing and Freezing Soup

Many soups take on a richer taste if refrigerated overnight to give the flavors time to blend. This makes them a natural make-ahead suggestion for entertaining friends or simply feeding your family.

Most soups freeze well, particularly gumbos, chilis, and stews, which tend to have large yields and the need for storing leftovers. Package soups and stews in pint or quart plastic freezer containers or zip-top freezer bags. Be sure to label them with the recipe name, date, and amount. You can freeze soup up to three months. Thaw in refrigerator and then slowly reheat in a saucepan over low heat, stirring often. Dense soups tend to get thicker during storage. Add a little broth, milk, or water when reheating until soup reaches desired consistency.

broth & stock

Broth is one of the simplest soups to make, has universal appeal, and forms the flavor base for a variety of sauces and gravies. Broth is a thin, clear liquid resulting from simmering meat, poultry, vegetables, or herbs in water. A big difference between broth and stock is that broth counts on flavor from meat, while stock is made using more bones than meat. The bones contribute gelatin, which adds richness and body to stock. So when you're choosing meat or bones for making soup, keep in mind that meat adds flavor and bones contribute body.

Broth simmers less than stock and has a fresher, lighter flavor. Broth preparation is simple. Just wash and cut vegetables; there's no need to peel or trim them since they'll be removed after cooking. Vegetables and herbs add depth of flavor; carrots and onions deepen the color and add sweetness. If you want to be healthy, trim fat from meat before adding meat to the pot.

Shown on previous page: Tortilla Soup (page 487)

After bringing ingredients to a boil, reduce the heat, and let the mixture simmer gently. If the liquid is allowed to boil, the broth will be cloudy. As the broth simmers, remove any scum that collects on the surface.

After broth has cooked, strain it through several thicknesses of cheesecloth to remove meat, vegetables, and herbs. Allow broth to cool completely so the fat can rise to the surface and solidify. Chilling the broth is a quick way to solidify the fat. Then just spoon hardened fat off the top of the broth with a large spoon. The same principal applies to stock.

You can refrigerate fresh broth up to three days or freeze it up to three months in containers of various sizes—anything from pint or quart containers to freezer bags to ice cube trays. Once cubes are frozen, you can easily transfer them to a freezer bag and refreeze. Fish stock is the exception; it needs to be used within two months of being frozen. Degrease broth and stock before freezing because frozen fat can turn rancid.

The characteristics of a good stock are flavor, body, and clarity. The best stock is made from mature vegetables cooked slowly to extract maximum flavor. Stock provides richer taste and more body than broth.

A classic stock begins with bones, simmers for hours, and is then strained and reduced for rich results. If a stock tastes weak after you've strained it, just discard the fat, and simmer stock briskly again to concentrate the flavor.

stock basics

- Use a narrow and high stockpot to prevent excessive evaporation during cooking.
- Start with cold water to cover ingredients. Bring stock slowly just to a boil; cook at a gentle simmer.
- Never rush a stock by boiling it.
- Simmer stock partially covered.
- Never add salt to stock as it's simmering. The long simmering time would concentrate the salt and ruin the resulting stock.

Chicken Broth

prep: 10 min.   cook: 1 hr., 30 min.

This recipe makes a large quantity. Freeze it up to three months and thaw as needed.

6   pounds chicken pieces
2½   quarts water
3   celery ribs with leaves, cut in half
2   onions, quartered
2   fresh thyme sprigs or ½ teaspoon dried thyme
1   bay leaf
1½   teaspoons salt
¾   teaspoon pepper

Combine all ingredients in a large Dutch oven. Bring to a boil; cover, reduce heat, and simmer 1½ hours.

Line a large wire-mesh strainer with a double layer of cheesecloth; place in a large bowl. Pour broth through strainer, discarding chicken pieces, vegetables, and herbs. Cover broth, and chill thoroughly. Skim and discard solidified fat from top of broth.

Store broth in a tightly covered container in the refrigerator up to 3 days, or freeze up to 3 months. Thaw and use as directed in recipes that call for chicken broth. Yield: 10 cups.

Per cup: Calories 19 (19% from fat); Fat 0.4g (sat 0.1g, mono 0.1g, poly 0.1g); Protein 3.5g; Carb 0.2g; Fiber 0.1g; Chol 10mg; Iron 0.2mg; Sodium 357mg; Calc 3mg

Beef Stock

prep: 19 min.   cook: 7 hrs.

Some things in life can't be rushed. Homemade stock is one of them. A good, rich stock begins by roasting bones and vegetables to draw out a natural caramelized flavor. The roasted essence then simmers in the dark stock for several hours to develop its characteristic flavor.

5   pounds beef bones
2   large carrots, quartered
3   large onions, quartered
2   celery ribs, quartered
4   quarts cold water, divided
¼   cup tomato paste
8   fresh parsley sprigs
4   fresh thyme sprigs
½   teaspoon black peppercorns
2   bay leaves
3   garlic cloves, pressed

Place first 4 ingredients in a large roasting pan; roast, uncovered, at 500° for 45 minutes to 1 hour or until well browned, turning occasionally.

Transfer bones and vegetables to a stockpot. Add 2 cups water to roasting pan; bring to a boil over medium-high heat, stirring to loosen bits that cling to bottom of pan; pour into stockpot. Add remaining 3½ quarts water and tomato paste to stockpot. Tie parsley, thyme, and remaining ingredients in a bundle. Add to stockpot.

Bring to a simmer; simmer, partially covered, 6 hours. Skim fat and foam off top of stock after first 10 minutes of simmering.

Line a large wire-mesh strainer with a double layer of cheesecloth; place over a large bowl. Use a ladle to strain stock. Discard solids. (Using a ladle and avoiding sediment in bottom of pot prevents cloudiness.) Cool stock slightly.

Cover and chill stock; discard solidified fat from top of stock. Store stock in a tightly covered container in refrigerator up to 3 days, or freeze up to 3 months. Yield: 8 cups.

Per cup: Calories 78 (7% from fat); Fat 0.6g (sat 0g, mono 0g, poly 0g); Protein 0.2g; Carb 0.6g; Fiber 0.1g; Chol 0mg; Iron 0.1mg; Sodium 14mg; Calc 9mg

cream & puree soups

A cream or pureed soup is ideal to serve as an appetizer or as a light supper along with a green salad. You'll need a food processor or blender to obtain that luxuriously smooth texture known to this family of rich soups. Be careful not to overload the equipment though, because the hot liquid can overflow and leak out. It's always safer to puree soups in batches, filling the blender or processor about half full each time.

The smooth texture of these soups suggests that they can be "sipping soups," rather than being served from a soup bowl. Depending on the formality of the meal, options range from hefty mugs to sleek wine glasses.

Cream soups and purees benefit from a garnish, whether it's a dollop of sour cream, a sprinkling of cheese, or a sprig of fresh herb. Simple is best so that the garnish doesn't overpower the soup.

Some of these soups are served hot; some are best served cold. And some can be served at either temperature, depending on your menu and the time of year. A loose rule of thumb says to serve cold soups in the summer, warm soups during winter.

Tomato-Basil Bisque

prep: 5 min.   cook: 8 min.

2   (10¾-ounce) cans tomato soup
1   (14½-ounce) can diced tomatoes
2½   cups buttermilk
2   tablespoons chopped fresh basil
¼   teaspoon freshly ground pepper
Garnish: shredded fresh basil

Cook first 5 ingredients in a 3-quart saucepan over medium heat, stirring often, 6 to 8 minutes or until thoroughly heated. Garnish, if desired; serve immediately, or serve chilled. Yield: 7 cups.

Per cup: Calories 125 (30% from fat); Fat 4.2g (sat 2g, mono 0.3g, poly 0.7g); Protein 4.8g; Carb 18.7g; Fiber 1.3g; Chol 13mg; Iron 1.4mg; Sodium 661mg; Calc 20mg

soup dictionary

Bouillabaisse: Seafood stew that contains fresh fish and shellfish as well as onions, tomato, white wine, garlic, and herbs. It's typically ladled over French bread in bowls.

Broth: An all-purpose flavorful liquid that results from simmering vegetables, herbs, meat, or poultry in water.

Cassoulet: A rustic French country dish of white beans and a variety of meats stewed very slowly to develop a complex flavor. Cassoulet bakes in the oven with a bread-crumb topping.

Chowder: A general term used to describe any thick, rich soup containing chunky food. Also a specific chunky seafood soup.

Cioppino: A robust tomato-based stew brimming with fish and shellfish.

Consommé: The consummate clear broth, enriched with meat and vegetables and clarified with egg white.

Gumbo: A thick soup that can contain chicken, sausage, ham, shrimp, or oysters. Gumbo gets its flavor base from a rich brown roux that cooks slowly to develop a nutty taste. Gumbo's often thickened with okra or gumbo filé powder, which is added after cooking.

Ragoût: A thick, well-seasoned stew of meat, poultry, or fish, and sometimes vegetables.

Stew: Simmered slowly for several hours in a tightly covered pot, stew is known for yielding melt-in-your-mouth tender meat.

Stock: The strained liquid from vegetables, meat, or fish simmered with seasonings. When making stock, bones are added to contribute flavor and gelatin for body. For a rich brown stock, first roast bones and vegetables to develop a rich flavor base before adding water.

---

low calorie • make ahead

Cream of Pimiento Soup

prep: 10 min.   cook: 20 min.   other: 8 hrs.

2   (4-ounce) jars diced pimiento, undrained
¼   cup butter or margarine
⅓   cup all-purpose flour
2   (14-ounce) cans chicken broth
3   cups half-and-half
1   tablespoon grated onion
1   teaspoon salt
½   teaspoon hot sauce
Garnish: chopped fresh chives

Process pimiento in a blender or food processor until smooth, stopping to scrape down sides; set aside.

Melt butter in a heavy saucepan over low heat; add flour, and stir until mixture is smooth. Cook, stirring constantly, 1 minute.

Add broth and half-and-half gradually to flour mixture; cook over medium heat, stirring constantly, until thickened and bubbly.

Stir in reserved pimiento puree, onion, salt, and hot sauce; cook over low heat, stirring constantly, until thoroughly heated. Cover and chill 8 hours.

Cook soup over medium heat 8 to 10 minutes or until thoroughly heated. Garnish, if desired. Yield: 8 cups.

Per cup: Calories 210 (73% from fat); Fat 17g (sat 10.1g, mono 4.5g, poly 0.7g); Protein 4.4g; Carb 10.3g; Fiber 0.7g; Chol 53mg; Iron 0.8mg; Sodium 1014mg; Calc 99mg

---

low calorie • weekend chef

Roasted Red Pepper Soup

prep: 15 min.   cook: 1 hr., 40 min.
other: 35 min.

4   pounds red bell peppers (about 8 large), halved
3   tablespoons olive oil, divided
2   medium onions, chopped (about 2 cups)
5   garlic cloves, chopped
3½   cups vegetable broth
¼   cup fresh basil leaves, finely chopped
2½   teaspoons salt
1   teaspoon freshly ground pepper
¾   cup whipping cream
1   tablespoon lemon juice
7   tablespoons sour cream

Brush skin side of peppers with 1 tablespoon oil. Roast peppers, skin side up, on

---

lightly greased aluminum foil-lined baking sheets at 400° for 45 minutes or until peppers look blistered.

Place peppers in a large zip-top freezer bag; seal and let stand 20 minutes. Peel peppers; remove and discard seeds.

Sauté onion in remaining 2 tablespoons hot oil in a Dutch oven over medium-high heat 10 minutes or until tender; add garlic, and cook 1 minute. Add vegetable broth and peppers, and bring to a boil; reduce heat to medium, cover, and simmer, stirring occasionally, 30 minutes.

Remove from heat; let stand 15 minutes. Process red pepper mixture, in batches, in a food processor or blender until smooth.

Return pureed mixture to Dutch oven; cook over medium heat 5 minutes. Stir in basil and next 3 ingredients; cook 5 minutes or until thoroughly heated. Stir in lemon juice. Serve with sour cream. Yield: 7 cups.

Per cup: Calories 263 (65% from fat); Fat 19.1g (sat 8.7g, mono 7.9g, poly 1.5g); Protein 4.1g; Carb 22.8g; Fiber 5.8g; Chol 41mg; Iron 1.5mg; Sodium 1325mg; Calc 66mg

---

low calorie • low fat

Saffron Butternut Squash Soup

prep: 25 min.   cook: 45 min.

Just a small amount of saffron adds a distinctive robust flavor and vibrant orange-red color to soups and sauces. If it isn't available, you'll still get great results.

1   (3-pound) butternut squash, halved and seeded
1   large leek
¼   cup butter
Pinch of saffron threads
1   cup dry white wine
2   carrots, diced
1   (32-ounce) container chicken broth
⅛   teaspoon ground cinnamon
⅛   teaspoon ground nutmeg
⅛   teaspoon ground red pepper
¼   cup whipping cream
½   teaspoon salt
¼   teaspoon ground black pepper
Garnish: crushed almond biscotti

Microwave squash in an 11- x 7-inch baking dish 15 minutes. Cool; scoop out pulp into chunks. Set aside.

Cut and discard green top from leek; cut white portion into slices.

Melt butter in a Dutch oven over medium heat; add leek slices and saffron, and sauté 5 minutes or until leek slices are tender. Add wine, and cook 1 to 2 minutes. Add squash, carrot, and and next 4 ingredients, and bring to a boil. Reduce heat, and simmer, uncovered, 20 minutes or until squash and carrot are tender. Remove from heat, and cool slightly.

Process squash mixture, in batches, in a blender or food processor until smooth, stopping to scrape down sides. (A handheld immersion blender can also be used.)

Return squash mixture to Dutch oven. Add cream, salt, and pepper; simmer 10 to 15 minutes or until thickened. Garnish, if desired. Yield: 8 cups.

Per cup: Calories 175 (49% from fat); Fat 9.6g (sat 5.4g, mono 2.3g, poly 0.4g); Protein 3g; Carb 21.4g; Fiber 3.5g; Chol 30mg; Iron 1.4mg; Sodium 942mg; Calc 90mg

freeze it • low calorie • make ahead
test kitchen favorite

Curried Acorn Squash-and-Apple Soup

prep: 40 min.   cook: 1 hr., 35 min.
other: 10 min.

This creamy fall soup takes advantage of slightly sweet winter squash. A trio of spices and a touch of honey make it a favorite.

2   medium acorn squash (about 3 pounds), halved
¼   cup butter or margarine
4¾   cups chicken broth, divided
4   Granny Smith apples, peeled and coarsely chopped
2   baking potatoes, peeled and coarsely chopped
1½   tablespoons curry powder
¾   teaspoon ground red pepper
½   teaspoon ground cinnamon
1   teaspoon salt
2   cups whipping cream
2   tablespoons honey

Place squash halves, cut side down, on an aluminum foil-lined baking sheet.

Bake at 350° for 45 minutes or until squash is tender. Scoop out pulp, discarding shells; set pulp aside.

Melt butter in a Dutch oven over medium heat; add 4 cups chicken broth, apples, and next 5 ingredients. Cook, stirring often, 25 to 30 minutes or until apples and potatoes are tender. Remove from heat, and cool slightly (about 5 to 10 minutes).

Process squash pulp, apple mixture, and remaining ¾ cup chicken broth, in batches, in a food processor or blender until smooth, stopping to scrape down sides.

Return puree to Dutch oven. Stir in whipping cream and honey, and simmer, stirring occasionally, 15 to 20 minutes or until thoroughly heated. Yield: 12 cups.

Per cup: Calories 265 (66% from fat); Fat 19.5g (sat 11.6g, mono 5.3g, poly 0.8g); Protein 3g; Carb 24.6g; Fiber 2.5g; Chol 68mg; Iron 1.1mg; Sodium 850mg; Calc 64mg

freeze it • low calorie • low fat • make ahead

Creamy Southwestern Pumpkin Soup

prep: 15 min.   cook: 55 min.   other: 10 min.

2   tablespoons butter or margarine
1   large onion, chopped (about 2 cups)
1   jalapeño pepper, seeded and chopped
2   garlic cloves, minced
5   cups chicken broth
1   large baking potato, peeled and chopped
1¼   teaspoons salt
½   teaspoon chili powder
½   teaspoon ground cumin
1   (15-ounce) can pumpkin
¼   cup chopped fresh cilantro
2   cups milk
3   tablespoons fresh lime juice
Garnishes: sour cream, fresh cilantro sprigs

Melt butter in a Dutch oven over medium heat. Add onion, jalapeño pepper, and garlic; sauté 15 minutes. Add chicken broth and next 4 ingredients; cook, stirring often, 30 minutes or until potato is tender. Remove from heat, and cool slightly (5 to 10 minutes).

Process potato mixture, pumpkin, and ¼ cup cilantro, in batches, in a food processor or blender until smooth, stopping to scrape down sides.

Return to Dutch oven; stir in milk, and simmer 10 minutes or until thoroughly heated. Stir in lime juice; garnish, if desired. Yield: 10 cups.

Per cup: Calories 112 (41% from fat); Fat 5.1g (sat 2.4g, mono 1g, poly 0.2g); Protein 3.7g; Carb 13.3g; Fiber 2g; Chol 16mg; Iron 0.8mg; Sodium 1105mg; Calc 78mg

Cream of Curried Peanut Soup

prep: 15 min.   cook: 35 min.

Swap the chicken broth for vegetable broth and this surprisingly good soup becomes vegetarian.

2   tablespoons butter or margarine
1   small onion, minced
3   celery ribs, minced
1   garlic clove, minced
2   tablespoons all-purpose flour
2   tablespoons curry powder
⅛   to ¼ teaspoon ground red pepper
3½   cups chicken broth
1   cup creamy peanut butter
2   cups half-and-half
Garnish: chopped peanuts

Melt butter in a saucepan over medium heat; add onion and celery, and sauté 5 minutes. Add garlic; sauté 2 minutes. Stir in flour, curry powder, and red pepper until smooth; cook, stirring constantly, 1 minute. Add broth; bring to a boil. Reduce heat to low, and simmer 20 minutes.

Stir in peanut butter and half-and-half; cook, stirring constantly, 3 to 4 minutes. Remove from heat; cool slightly. Process mixture, in batches, in a food processor or blender until smooth. Garnish, if desired. Serve immediately. Yield: 6 cups.

Per cup: Calories 438 (75% from fat); Fat 36.3g (sat 12.6g, mono 14.1g, poly 6.5g); Protein 15.1g; Carb 18g; Fiber 3.7g; Chol 45mg; Iron 1.6mg; Sodium 1175mg; Calc 123mg

Wildest Rice Soup

prep: 25 min.   cook: 20 min.

This creamy, sophisticated soup gets a convenient boost from canned soup.

1   (6.2-ounce) package long-grain and wild rice mix
1   pound bacon, finely chopped
2   cups chopped fresh mushrooms
1   large onion, diced
3¾ cups half-and-half
2½ cups chicken broth
2   (10¾-ounce) cans cream of potato soup
1   (8-ounce) loaf pasteurized prepared cheese product, cubed

Cook wild rice mix according to package directions, omitting seasoning packet.
Cook bacon, in batches, in a Dutch oven until crisp. Remove bacon, and drain on paper towels, reserving 2 tablespoons drippings in Dutch oven.
Sauté mushrooms and onion in drippings until tender; stir in rice, bacon, half-and-half, and remaining ingredients.

Cook soup over medium-low heat, stirring constantly, until soup is thoroughly heated and cheese melts. Yield: 10 cups.

Per cup: Calories 393 (55% from fat); Fat 24.1g (sat 12.9g, mono 6g, poly 1.3g); Protein 17g; Carb 26.6g; Fiber 0.9g; Chol 74mg; Iron 1.1mg; Sodium 1607mg; Calc 244mg

low calorie • low fat • quick

Chilled Blueberry Soup

prep: 10 min.   cook: 5 min.

4   cups fresh blueberries
1   cup orange juice
½   cup sugar
¼   teaspoon ground cinnamon
⅛   teaspoon salt
1   tablespoon fresh lemon juice
2   cups half-and-half
Garnishes: yogurt, fresh mint sprigs

Bring first 5 ingredients to a boil in a large saucepan over medium-high heat, stirring often. Remove from heat, and cool slightly.
Process blueberry mixture and lemon juice in a blender or food processor until smooth, stopping to scrape down sides. Cover and chill until ready to serve.

Stir in half-and-half just before serving. Serve in stemmed glasses. Garnish, if desired. Yield: 6 cups.

Per cup: Calories 243 (36% from fat); Fat 9.6g (sat 5.8g, mono 2.7g, poly 0.5g); Protein 3.4g; Carb 38.7g; Fiber 2.5g; Chol 30mg; Iron 0.5mg; Sodium 83mg; Calc 96mg

quick

Raspberry Soup

prep: 5 min.

Serve this fruit soup as a first course or an icy dessert.

1   cup fresh or frozen raspberries, thawed
½   cup rosé or dry white wine
½   cup firmly packed light brown sugar
½   cup sour cream
Garnishes: lime slices, fresh raspberries

Process first 4 ingredients in a blender until smooth, stopping to scrape down sides. Pour mixture through a wire-mesh strainer into serving bowls. Cover and chill, if desired. Garnish, if desired. Yield: 2⅓ cups.

Per cup: Calories 348 (28% from fat); Fat 10.7g (sat 6.5g, mono 3g, poly 0.6g); Protein 2.3g; Carb 55.2g; Fiber 3.4g; Chol 22mg; Iron 1.5mg; Sodium 48mg; Calc 115mg

vegetable & bean soups

These hearty soups have many benefits. They can be cooked ahead and easily reheated. They're made from pantry ingredients, dried peas and beans, and often leftovers. And they provide plenty of protein and other nutrients depending on the vegetables included.

When you add vegetables to soup, remember that they don't all cook in the same amount of time. First, add the thickest vegetables that take the longest to cook. Then add remaining vegetables as the recipe directs. Be careful to cut like vegetables the same size so they'll cook evenly. Add frozen vegetables after fresh (no need to thaw them). Add canned vegetables last, and cook just until heated.

low calorie • low cholesterol • low fat • quick

Quick Vegetable Soup

prep: 4 min.   cook: 20 min.

Keep just five ingredients on hand for this fast, great-tasting soup.

1   (14½-ounce) can stewed tomatoes, undrained
1   (8-ounce) can tomato sauce
1   (10-ounce) package frozen mixed vegetables
2   cups water
1½ teaspoons beef bouillon granules
⅛   teaspoon freshly ground pepper

Combine all ingredients in a Dutch oven. Bring to a boil; cover, reduce heat, and simmer 20 minutes, stirring occasionally. Yield: 7 cups.

Per cup: Calories 53 (7% from fat); Fat 0.4g (sat 0.1g, mono 0g, poly 0.1g); Protein 2.5g; Carb 11.3g; Fiber 2.5g; Chol 0mg; Iron 1.4mg; Sodium 426mg; Calc 30mg

Quick Vegetable-Beef Soup: Brown 1 pound ground chuck in a large skillet, stirring until it crumbles and is no longer pink. Drain. Add to soup, and bring to a simmer.

Gazpacho

prep: 40 min.   other: 8 hrs.

8   large tomatoes
2   cucumbers, peeled and seeded
1   large green bell pepper, seeded
1   large yellow bell pepper, seeded
1   small red onion
1   jalapeño pepper, seeded
1   large garlic clove
1   (32-ounce) bottle vegetable juice
⅓   cup red wine vinegar
1   tablespoon grated lemon rind
¼   cup fresh lemon juice
2   teaspoons salt
1   teaspoon paprika
2   to 3 teaspoons hot sauce

Toppings: sour cream, chopped avocado, croutons, boiled shrimp, fresh cilantro sprigs (optional)

Peel tomatoes. Cut tomatoes, cucumbers, bell peppers, and onion into quarters. **Process** vegetables, jalapeño pepper, and garlic in a food processor, in batches, until chunky, stopping to scrape down sides.

Transfer mixture to a large bowl, and stir in vegetable juice and next 6 ingredients. Cover and chill soup, stirring often, 8 hours. Serve with toppings, if desired. Yield: 12½ cups.

Per cup: Calories 52 (7% from fat); Fat 0.4g (sat 0.1g, mono 0.1g, poly 0.2g); Protein 2.2g; Carb 11.2g; Fiber 2.8g; Chol 0mg; Iron 0.8mg; Sodium 568mg; Calc 35mg

Start off a summer's night of entertaining with bowls of this fresh tomato soup.

Gazpacho

test kitchen favorite

Pot Liquor Soup

prep: 1 hr.   cook: 55 min.

Skillet cornbread is in order here.

2   pounds fresh collard greens
¾   pound smoked ham hocks
1   (1½-pound) ham steak, chopped
2   tablespoons hot sauce
3   tablespoons olive oil
3   medium onions, chopped
1   garlic clove, minced
6   red potatoes, diced
3   (14-ounce) cans chicken broth
2   (15.8-ounce) cans field peas with snaps, rinsed and drained
2   (15.8-ounce) cans crowder peas, rinsed and drained
2   cups water
½   cup vermouth
1   tablespoon white vinegar
1   teaspoon salt

Remove and discard stems and discolored spots from collards; rinse with cold water. Drain; tear collards into 1-inch pieces. **Bring** collards, ham hocks, and water to cover to a boil in a large Dutch oven. Remove from heat; drain. Repeat procedure.
Toss together chopped ham and hot sauce; cook in hot oil in Dutch oven over medium-high heat 6 to 8 minutes or until browned. **Add** onion and garlic; sauté until tender. Stir in collards, ham hocks, diced potato, and remaining ingredients. Bring to a boil; reduce heat, and simmer, stirring occasionally, 45 minutes.
Remove meat from ham hocks; discard hocks. Return meat to soup. Yield: 10 cups.

Per cup: Calories 478 (36% from fat); Fat 19.3g (sat 5.5g, mono 9.2g, poly 2.2g); Protein 29.2g; Carb 43g; Fiber 7.9g; Chol 63mg; Iron 2.8mg; Sodium 2163mg; Calc 123mg

French Onion Soup

family favorite • low calorie

French Onion Soup

prep: 20 min.   cook: 1 hr.

¼	cup butter
5	medium-size white onions, thinly sliced (about 3 pounds)
1	(32-ounce) container chicken broth
2	(10½-ounce) cans beef consommé
¼	cup dry white wine
3	fresh thyme sprigs
2	fresh parsley sprigs

Salt and freshly ground pepper to taste

6	(¾-inch-thick) French baguette slices
6	(1-ounce) Swiss cheese slices

Garnish: fresh thyme sprigs

Melt butter in a Dutch oven over medium-high heat; add onion, and cook, stirring often, 40 minutes or until golden.

Add chicken broth and next 4 ingredients; bring to a boil. Reduce heat, and simmer, stirring occasionally, 20 minutes. Remove and discard herbs. Add salt and pepper to taste.

Ladle into 6 ovenproof bowls; top with bread and cheese slices. Broil 5½ inches from heat 4 minutes or until cheese is browned and bubbly. Garnish, if desired. Yield: 6 servings.

Per serving: Calories 297 (51% from fat); Fat 16.7g (sat 9.9g, mono 4g, poly 0.6g); Protein 15g; Carb 22g; Fiber 1.6g; Chol 52mg; Iron 0.8mg; Sodium 1885mg; Calc 296mg

family favorite • low calorie

Baked Potato Soup

prep: 30 min.   cook: 30 min.

5	large baking potatoes, baked
¼	cup butter or margarine
1	medium onion, chopped
⅓	cup all-purpose flour
4	cups half-and-half
3	cups milk
1	teaspoon salt
⅛	teaspoon pepper
2	cups (8 ounces) shredded Cheddar cheese
8	bacon slices, cooked and crumbled

Peel potatoes; coarsely mash with a fork. **Melt** butter in a Dutch oven over medium heat; add onion, and sauté until tender. Add flour, stirring until smooth. **Stir** in potatoes, half-and-half, and next 3 ingredients; cook over low heat until thoroughly heated. Top each serving with cheese and bacon. Yield: 12 cups.

Per cup: Calories 339 (61% from fat); Fat 23.1g (sat 13.8g, mono 6.7g, poly 1g); Protein 12.1g; Carb 21.5g; Fiber 1.3g; Chol 70mg; Iron 0.6mg; Sodium 495mg; Calc 296mg

low calorie • low fat

Okra Soup

prep: 25 min.   cook: 4 hrs.   other: 15 min.

This soup is Lowcountry home cooking at its best.

1	(2½- to 3-pound) boneless chuck roast, trimmed
1	teaspoon salt
1	teaspoon pepper
2	tablespoons vegetable oil
12	cups water
2	medium onions, chopped
2	celery ribs, chopped
2	(16-ounce) bags frozen okra
2	(14½-ounce) cans diced tomatoes
¼	cup sugar
2½	teaspoons salt
1	teaspoon pepper
2½	teaspoons hot sauce
½	teaspoon Worcestershire sauce
3	beef bouillon cubes

Sprinkle roast with 1 teaspoon salt and 1 teaspoon pepper.
Brown roast on all sides in hot oil in a Dutch oven over medium–high heat. Add 12 cups water, and bring to a boil; cover, reduce heat to low, and simmer 2 hours.
Remove roast from broth, reserving broth; cool roast 15 minutes. Shred roast, and return to broth.
Add onion and remaining ingredients to broth; cook, covered, over low heat, stirring occasionally, 2 hours. Yield: 18 cups.

Per cup: Calories 158 (42% from fat); Fat 7.4g (sat 2.2g, mono 3.1g, poly 1g); Protein 13.4g; Carb 10g; Fiber 2.1g; Chol 38mg; Iron 2mg; Sodium 720mg; Calc 58mg

Tortilla Soup

entertaining • family favorite • low calorie

Tortilla Soup

prep: 25 min.   cook: 1 hr., 15 min.

Grilled chicken gives this soup smoky flavor, but chopped rotisserie chicken makes a fine shortcut. (also pictured on page 479)

5	skinned and boned chicken breasts
2	tablespoons olive oil
1	teaspoon salt
½	teaspoon pepper
4	corn tortillas, cut into 1-inch pieces
1	large onion, chopped
5	garlic cloves, minced
3	tablespoons vegetable oil
8	cups chicken broth
1	(14½-ounce) can stewed tomatoes, undrained and chopped
1	(10-ounce) can diced tomatoes and green chiles
2	tablespoons chopped fresh cilantro or parsley
1	tablespoon ground cumin
½	teaspoon pepper
1	bay leaf
6	corn tortillas, cut into ¼-inch strips
½	cup vegetable oil
2	cups (8 ounces) shredded Monterey Jack cheese with peppers, or mozzarella cheese
	Avocado slices (optional)

Drizzle chicken with olive oil; sprinkle with salt and ½ teaspoon pepper. Grill chicken, covered with grill lid, over medium–high heat (350° to 400°) 6 to 8 minutes on

each side or until done. Cool and coarsely chop chicken.
Sauté tortilla pieces, onion, and garlic in 3 tablespoons hot oil in a Dutch oven over medium–high heat 5 minutes or until onion is tender. Add chicken, broth, and next 6 ingredients. Bring to a boil; reduce heat, and simmer 30 minutes. Discard bay leaf.
Fry tortilla strips in ½ cup hot oil in a large skillet until crisp. Drain on paper towels. Sprinkle fried tortilla strips and cheese over each serving. Top with avocado, if desired. Yield: 14 cups.

Per cup: Calories 252 (52% from fat); Fat 14.6g (sat 4.4g, mono 5.6g, poly 3.1g); Protein 17.7g; Carb 13.1g; Fiber 2.4g; Chol 45mg; Iron 1.5mg; Sodium 967mg; Calc 170mg

low calorie • low fat

Hearty Lentil Soup

prep: 28 min.   cook: 3 hrs., 10 min.

The smoky flavor of ham hocks permeates this broth, giving a richness to the lentils.

1	pound dried lentils
1½	pounds smoked ham hocks
4	cups beef broth
4	cups water
1	(28-ounce) can crushed tomatoes
1	(8-ounce) can tomato sauce
½	small cabbage, chopped
4	celery ribs, sliced
2	large onions, chopped
2	carrots, sliced
½	cup chopped fresh parsley
2	bay leaves
2	teaspoons salt
1	teaspoon dried basil
½	teaspoon pepper

Combine all ingredients in a Dutch oven; stir well. Bring to a boil; cover, reduce heat, and simmer 3 hours, stirring occasionally. Remove ham hocks; cool. Remove meat from bones; discard fat and bones. Cut meat into bite-size pieces; stir into soup. Cook over medium–high heat until soup is thoroughly heated. Discard bay leaves. Yield: 15 cups.

Per cup: Calories 241 (26% from fat); Fat 6.9g (sat 2.4g, mono 2.9g, poly 0.9g); Protein 19g; Carb 27.6g; Fiber 9.3g; Chol 30mg; Iron 4.5mg; Sodium 969mg; Calc 67mg

These are hearty soups packed with chunks of meat and seafood. Serve these soups hot with crusty bread.

Seafood soups are stunning when served in shallow, broad-rimmed bowls. Use fresh crab and shrimp for optimum flavor in the seafood soups.

Let our photos on page 491 walk you through the steps of making a rich brown roux, the necessary beginning for a great gumbo.

low calorie

Creamy Chicken Noodle Soup

prep: 20 min.   cook: 55 min.   other: 10 min.

Homemade chicken soup guarantees comfort for the weary.

1   tablespoon butter or margarine
1   large onion, chopped
3   cups chopped cooked chicken
3   (14-ounce) cans chicken broth
1   (10¾-ounce) can cream of mushroom soup
1   (10¾-ounce) can cream of chicken soup
1   (8-ounce) package spaghetti, broken into 2-inch pieces
7   celery ribs, finely chopped
6   carrots, finely chopped
1   teaspoon poultry seasoning
1   teaspoon pepper
1   teaspoon grated lemon rind
2   cups milk
2   cups (8 ounces) shredded sharp Cheddar cheese

Melt butter in a Dutch oven over medium heat; add onion, and sauté until tender. Stir in chicken and next 9 ingredients; bring to a boil. Reduce heat, and simmer 45 minutes. **Stir** in milk; return to a simmer. Remove from heat; let stand 10 minutes. Sprinkle each serving with cheese. Yield: 12 cups.

Per cup: Calories 313 (39% from fat); Fat 13.7g (sat 6.5g, mono 1.1g, poly 0.6g); Protein 20.6g; Carb 25.7g; Fiber 2.7g; Chol 60mg; Iron 1.3mg; Sodium 1213mg; Calc 212mg

low calorie · low fat

Turkey Soup With Green Chile Biscuits

prep: 15 min.   cook: 30 min.

No one will ever recognize the holiday turkey leftovers in this updated turkey soup.

1   medium onion, diced
1   teaspoon vegetable oil
1   garlic clove, minced
3   cups chopped cooked turkey or chicken
1   (16-ounce) can chili beans
3½   cups turkey or chicken broth
1   (11-ounce) can whole kernel corn with red and green bell peppers, drained
1   (10-ounce) can diced tomatoes and green chiles
½   teaspoon chili powder
½   teaspoon ground cumin
⅛   teaspoon salt
⅛   teaspoon pepper
Toppings: sour cream, shredded Mexican four-cheese blend (optional)
Green Chile Biscuits

Sauté onion in hot oil in a large Dutch oven over medium heat 7 minutes or until tender. Add garlic, and sauté 1 minute. Stir in turkey and next 8 ingredients. Bring to a boil, stirring occasionally; reduce heat, and simmer, uncovered, 15 minutes. Serve with desired toppings and Green Chile Biscuits. Yield: 9 cups.

Per cup (without biscuit): Calories 178 (22% from fat); Fat 4.3g (sat 0.9g, mono 0.9g, poly 0.7g); Protein 18.5g; Carb 16.5g; Fiber 3.3g; Chol 45mg; Iron 1.4mg; Sodium 1080mg; Calc 41mg

Green Chile Biscuits

prep: 5 min.   cook: 12 min.

2   cups all-purpose baking mix
1   cup (4 ounces) shredded Mexican four-cheese blend
1   (4.5-ounce) can chopped green chiles, drained
⅔   cup milk

Stir together all ingredients until a soft dough forms. Turn out onto a lightly floured surface; knead 3 or 4 times. Pat or roll dough to ½-inch thickness; cut with a 2½-inch round cutter, and place on an ungreased baking sheet.
Bake at 450° for 10 to 12 minutes or until biscuits are golden. Yield: 1 dozen.

Per biscuit: Calories 103 (32% from fat); Fat 3.7g (sat 2.1g, mono 0.1g, poly 0g); Protein 4.6g; Carb 14.3g; Fiber 1.1g; Chol 10mg; Iron 0.8mg; Sodium 281mg; Calc 171mg

freeze it · low calorie · make ahead

Peasant Soup

prep: 35 min.   cook: 1 hr., 30 min.

Use low-sodium broth if you'd rather reduce the sodium in this soup.

9   baby carrots, sliced
1   large onion, coarsely chopped
2   celery ribs, finely chopped
¼   cup chopped fresh parsley
1   (16-ounce) package kielbasa sausage, cut into ¼-inch-thick slices
1   bay leaf
5   (14-ounce) cans chicken broth
½   (10-ounce) package shredded angel hair coleslaw
2   russet potatoes, peeled and cut into ½-inch cubes
½   cup frozen, cut green beans
1   (15-ounce) can kidney beans, rinsed and drained
¼   teaspoon dried thyme
½   teaspoon pepper

Bring first 6 ingredients and 4 cans chicken broth to a boil in a stockpot; reduce heat, and simmer 45 minutes.
Add remaining can of broth, slaw, and remaining ingredients; simmer 30 minutes or until vegetables are tender. Discard bay leaf. (Freeze leftover soup up to 1 month.) Yield: 10 cups.

Per cup: Calories 231 (55% from fat); Fat 14.2g (sat 4.5g, mono 5.9g, poly 1.5g); Protein 10.5g; Carb 17.9g; Fiber 3.1g; Chol 39mg; Iron 1.8mg; Sodium 1840mg; Calc 54mg

Note: You can cook first 6 ingredients and 4 cans chicken broth in a 5-quart slow cooker on LOW for 4 hours. Add remaining can of broth, slaw, and remaining ingredients; cook on HIGH 1 hour.

taste of the south she-crab soup

A culinary icon of Charleston, South Carolina, she-crab soup was traditionally a rich combination of cream, crabmeat, roe (eggs), and a splash of sherry. The meat from a female crab is said to be sweeter, but it was the addition of her red-orange roe that created the dish's depth of flavor and beautiful pale color, and resulted in the name "she-crab" soup.

These days, roe is not harvested in an ecological effort to preserve the supply of crabs. Is it still she-crab soup if there's no roe? Yes and no. The heart of the recipe remains the same.

You'll find some variations, but purists know the basic recipe is the true Southern tradition. Fresh crabmeat is essential. If you go crabbing for your own, you'll need about a dozen. If you remove the shell of the female crab and discover what looks like a mass of tiny red-orange beads inside, you've struck gold—or roe, that is. Remove it carefully; stir it into the soup with the crabmeat. (Note: Female crabs with roe on the outside must be returned to the water.)

Whether your crabmeat is from crabs you caught yourself or from the supermarket, enjoy a taste of the region with a bowl of this creamy soup.

entertaining
She-Crab Soup

prep: 10 min.   cook: 1 hr., 5 min.

4   cups whipping cream
⅛   teaspoon salt
⅛   teaspoon pepper
2   fish bouillon cubes (we tested with Knorr Fish Bouillon)
2   cups boiling water
¼   cup unsalted butter
⅓   cup all-purpose flour
2   tablespoons lemon juice
¼   teaspoon ground nutmeg
1   pound fresh crabmeat, drained
Garnish: chopped fresh parsley
⅓   cup sherry (optional)*

Combine whipping cream, salt, and pepper in a heavy saucepan; bring to a boil over medium heat. Reduce heat, and simmer 1 hour.

After the cream has simmered 40 minutes, stir together fish bouillon cubes and 2 cups boiling water until bouillon cubes dissolve.
Melt butter in a large heavy saucepan over low heat; add flour, stirring until smooth. Cook 1 minute, stirring constantly. Gradually add hot fish broth; cook over medium heat until thickened. Stir in cream mixture, and cook 5 minutes.
Add lemon juice, nutmeg, and crabmeat. Ladle into individual serving bowls. Garnish, if desired. Add a spoonful of sherry to each serving, if desired. Yield: 6 cups.

Per cup: Calories 714 (86% from fat); Fat 67.9g (sat 41.5g, mono 19.1g, poly 2.8g); Protein 18.1g; Carb 10.3g; Fiber 0.2g; Chol 296mg; Iron 1mg; Sodium 985mg; Calc 175mg

*It's important to use good-quality sherry, not cooking sherry, for this soup.

low calorie • low carb • low fat
Shrimp-Cheese Soup

prep: 15 min.   cook: 30 min.

Feta cheese adds a tangy flavor note to this seafood soup.

1   pound unpeeled, jumbo fresh shrimp
1   tablespoon butter or margarine
2   tablespoons olive oil
1   medium onion, minced
1   to 2 garlic cloves, minced
1   cup dry white wine
1   (8-ounce) bottle clam juice
4   tomatoes, peeled and chopped
1   teaspoon salt
¾   teaspoon dried oregano
½   teaspoon freshly ground pepper
1   (4-ounce) package feta cheese, crumbled
¼   cup chopped fresh parsley

Peel shrimp, and devein, if desired; set aside.
Melt butter with oil in a Dutch oven over medium heat. Add onion and garlic; sauté 5 minutes.
Add wine and next 5 ingredients; bring to a boil. Reduce heat, and simmer 10 minutes or until thickened. Stir in cheese, and simmer 10 minutes. Add shrimp, and cook 3 to 5 minutes or just until shrimp turn pink. Stir in parsley. Yield: 6 cups.

Per cup: Calories 192 (53% from fat); Fat 11.3g (sat 4.8g, mono 4.9g, poly 1g); Protein 16g; Carb 7g; Fiber 1.5g; Chol 135mg; Iron 2.7mg; Sodium 831mg; Calc 144mg

taste of the south gumbo

Gumbo is one of the crowning glories of Louisiana cuisine. This flavorful stew is named for the West African word for okra, *gombo*. It can feature any number of main ingredients, most commonly shrimp, crab, chicken, duck, and sausage. A well-made gumbo offers a savory combination of tastes and textures that's unlike any other dish.

All gumbos start with a roux, but after the initial browning of fat and flour, other decisions are left to the cook's discretion and what ingredients are on hand. Most gumbos are seasoned with garlic and what Louisianans call the "holy trinity"—bell pepper, onion, and celery. Some cooks add okra, but an equal number don't. Other possible ingredients include tomatoes, bay leaves, and filé powder (crushed sassafras leaves).

There are two things to remember before you tackle gumbo: Allow plenty of time; neither a roux or gumbo can be rushed. And keep a wooden spoon handy for stirring the roux and the gumbo occasionally to prevent it from sticking.

White rice is the most traditional accompaniment, but for a truly authentic Cajun touch, serve potato salad on the side.

the secret to gumbo

• Two ingredients—flour and oil—make a roux. The slow-cooked blend contributes a rich depth of flavor to Creole and Cajun dishes and is the heart of every real gumbo.

• Plan to spend from 30 to 40 minutes whisking the precious thickener, depending on the size of your pot and the temperature. You can't rush that nutty flavor. If the heat is too high, the roux will burn, and then you'll need to start over.

• Store roux in an airtight container in the refrigerator up to two weeks. Any time you want gumbo, you'll be ahead of the game.

Most gumbos are seasoned with garlic and what Louisianans call the "holy trinity"—bell pepper, onion, and celery.

entertaining
Shrimp-Crab Gumbo

prep: 35 min.   cook: 4 hrs.

Here's a gumbo recipe for a crowd. You'll need a deep pot for cooking.

1½	cups vegetable oil
2	cups all-purpose flour
9	(14-ounce) cans chicken broth
2½	cups chopped onion
1	cup chopped green onions
½	cup chopped celery
2	garlic cloves, chopped
1	(10-ounce) can diced tomatoes with green chiles
1	(8-ounce) can tomato sauce
1	(16-ounce) package frozen sliced okra
3	pounds unpeeled, medium-size fresh shrimp
1	(16-ounce) container lump crabmeat
½	cup chopped fresh parsley
1	tablespoon filé powder (optional)
10	cups hot cooked rice

Heat oil in a stockpot over medium heat; gradually whisk in flour, and cook, whisking constantly, until roux is a dark mahogany color (about 30 minutes).
Stir in chicken broth and next 7 ingredients; bring to a boil. Reduce heat, and simmer, stirring occasionally, 3 hours.
Peel shrimp, and devein, if desired. Add shrimp to gumbo; cook, stirring often, 15 minutes or just until shrimp turn pink. Stir in crabmeat and parsley. Remove from heat; stir in filé powder, if desired. Serve over hot cooked rice. Yield: 20 cups.

Per cup: Calories 436 (40% from fat); Fat 19.5g (sat 2.1g, mono 7.4g, poly 7.7g); Protein 20.9g; Carb 43.1g; Fiber 1.9g; Chol 126mg; Iron 4.1mg; Sodium 1463mg; Calc 78mg

family favorite • make ahead
Chicken-Andouille Gumbo

prep: 1 hr., 30 min.   cook: 3 hrs., 40 min.

Andouille sausage gives this hearty stew a fiery boost. Make gumbo a day or two ahead because it only improves with time.

16	cups water
1	(4-pound) whole chicken, cut up, if desired
5	bay leaves
5	fresh parsley sprigs
3	garlic cloves, halved
1	cup vegetable oil
1	cup all-purpose flour
2	medium onions, chopped
2	large celery ribs, chopped
1	large green bell pepper, chopped
3	tablespoons minced garlic
1	pound andouille or smoked sausage, sliced
4	chicken bouillon cubes
1	teaspoon ground red pepper
1	teaspoon ground black pepper
1	bunch green onions, chopped
½	cup chopped fresh parsley
1	teaspoon salt
½	teaspoon filé powder (optional)
7	cups hot cooked rice
	Hot sauce (optional)

Bring first 5 ingredients to a boil in a large stockpot; reduce heat, and simmer, partially covered, 1 hour.
While chicken simmers, heat oil in a large heavy skillet or Dutch oven over medium heat; gradually whisk in flour, and cook, whisking constantly, until roux is a chocolate color, (20 to 30 minutes). Remove from heat, and add chopped onion, celery, green bell pepper, and minced garlic. Cook over medium heat, stirring constantly, 8 to 10 minutes or until vegetables are tender. Remove from heat.

Chicken-Andouille Gumbo

Oyster Soup

prep: 25 min.   cook: 55 min.

4 cups water
1 large onion, chopped
2 celery ribs, sliced
2 garlic cloves, minced
2 pints fresh oysters, rinsed and drained
2 cups water
1 cup butter or margarine
½ cup all-purpose flour
2 cups milk
2 tablespoons chicken bouillon granules
2 tablespoons chopped fresh or
   1 tablespoon dried parsley flakes
¾ teaspoon ground white pepper
¾ teaspoon ground black pepper

Bring first 4 ingredients to a boil in a large Dutch oven. Reduce heat, and simmer, stirring occasionally, 35 minutes or just until vegetables are tender.

Bring oysters and 2 cups water to a boil in a 3-quart saucepan, and cook, stirring often, 3 minutes or until edges of oysters begin to curl. Remove oysters, and coarsely chop half of them; set chopped and whole oysters aside. Pour oyster stock into Dutch oven with vegetables.

Melt butter in a saucepan over medium heat; gradually whisk in flour, and cook, whisking constantly, 2 minutes or until smooth and bubbly. Stir flour mixture into vegetable mixture in Dutch oven, and simmer, stirring occasionally, over medium heat 5 minutes.

Stir in chopped oysters, milk, bouillon granules, and remaining ingredients; cook, stirring occasionally, over medium heat 8 minutes or until thickened and bubbly. Stir in remaining whole oysters. Yield: 11 cups.

Per cup: Calories 257 (68% from fat); Fat 19.5g (sat 11.7g, mono 4.8g, poly 1.3g); Protein 7.2g; Carb 13.6g; Fiber 0.5g; Chol 71mg; Iron 5.6mg; Sodium 555mg; Calc 105mg

▲ Add flour to oil in pan, and cook, stirring constantly.

▲ The blonde roux is beginning to brown. Keep cooking and stirring it.

▲ A rich brown roux will give off a nutty aroma. Keep stirring or it will burn.

▲ Add chopped onion, celery, green pepper, and garlic. They'll sizzle and smell great.

When chicken finishes simmering, remove chicken from broth to cool, reserving broth. Pour broth through a wire-mesh strainer into a large bowl, discarding solids. Skim fat from top of broth. Return broth to stockpot (you should have about 13 cups).

Add roux with vegetables to stockpot. Stir in sausage, bouillon cubes, and ground peppers.

Simmer, uncovered, 1 hour and 45 minutes, skimming fat as needed.

Meanwhile, skin, bone, and coarsely chop chicken. Add chicken to soup; simmer 45 more minutes.

Stir green onions, parsley, and salt into gumbo; simmer 10 minutes.

Remove gumbo from heat, and stir in filé powder, if desired. Serve over hot cooked rice. Serve with hot sauce, if desired. Yield: 14 cups.

Per cup: Calories 552 (47% from fat); Fat 28.9g (sat 5.9g, mono 9.3g, poly 8.4g); Protein 32.9g; Carb 38.3g; Fiber 1.4g; Chol 95mg; Iron 4mg; Sodium 772mg; Calc 34mg

chowders, stews & chilis

They all have chunky in common, these chowders, stews, and chilis that are especially appropriate for the winter months. Each is thick with vegetables, meat, or seafood, yet each has a different flavor base. Chowder has milk or cream added for richness as well as crackers crumbled on top. And starchy potato often enhances the thickness, too.

Stews and chilis typically have a tomato base and lots of meat. The pieces of meat and vegetables in a stew are generally larger than in a soup, and the mixture is considerably thicker. There's one important guideline to remember about stews: Don't cheat on the simmering time—the long, slow simmer helps extract maximum flavor and ensure fork-tender results.

Cheesy Vegetable Chowder

prep: 30 min.   cook: 35 min.

A rich cream sauce laden with a pound of cheese forms the base of this hearty chowder.

1   medium onion, chopped
5   celery ribs, sliced
3   carrots, sliced
1   large potato, cut into ¼-inch cubes
1   garlic clove, minced
3½ cups chicken broth
1   (14½-ounce) can whole kernel corn, rinsed and drained
¼   cup butter or margarine
¼   cup all-purpose flour
2   cups milk
1   (16-ounce) loaf pasteurized prepared cheese product, cubed
1   (2-ounce) jar diced pimiento, undrained
1   tablespoon prepared mustard
¼   teaspoon pepper
⅛   teaspoon paprika
Garnish: celery leaves

Bring first 6 ingredients to a boil in a Dutch oven. Cover, reduce heat, and simmer 20 minutes or until potato is tender. Stir in corn; remove from heat.
Melt butter in a heavy saucepan over low heat. Add flour, and stir until mixture is

smooth. Cook, stirring constantly, 1 minute.
Stir in milk and next 5 ingredients.
Cook, stirring constantly, until cheese melts. Gradually stir cheese mixture into vegetable mixture.
Cook over medium heat, stirring constantly, until soup is thoroughly heated. Garnish, if desired, and serve chowder immediately. Yield: 8 cups.

Per cup: Calories 413 (51% from fat); Fat 23.5g (sat 14.3g, mono 2.2g, poly 0.7g); Protein 18.4g; Carb 31.6g; Fiber 3g; Chol 73mg; Iron 1mg; Sodium 1575mg; Calc 414mg

---

low calorie • test kitchen favorite

Potato Chowder With Green Chiles

prep: 30 min.   cook: 45 min.   other: 10 min.

A trio of peppers adds color, texture, and Southwestern flavor to this chunky chowder.

1   large red bell pepper
4   large poblano chile peppers
5   cups chicken broth
1   large potato, peeled and cubed
1   large onion, chopped
1   jalapeño pepper, seeded and chopped
1   teaspoon salt
¼   to ½ teaspoon freshly ground pepper
¼   cup butter or margarine
⅓   cup all-purpose flour
1   teaspoon salt
1   teaspoon dry mustard
¼   to ½ teaspoon freshly ground pepper
2   cups half-and-half
1   cup milk
1   cup (4 ounces) shredded Cheddar cheese
6   bacon slices, cooked and crumbled
1   bunch green onions, chopped

Broil bell pepper and chile peppers on an aluminum foil–lined baking sheet 5½ inches from heat about 5 minutes on each side or until peppers look blistered.
Place peppers in a zip-top freezer bag; seal. Let stand 10 minutes to loosen skins. Peel peppers; remove and discard seeds. Coarsely chop peppers.
Bring chopped roasted peppers, chicken broth, and next 5 ingredients to a boil in a

Dutch oven over medium heat. Reduce heat, and simmer 15 minutes or until potato is tender.
Melt butter in a heavy saucepan over low heat; whisk in flour and next 3 ingredients until smooth. Cook 1 minute, whisking constantly. Gradually whisk in half-and-half.
Stir white sauce and milk into chicken broth mixture; cook over medium heat 8 to 10 minutes or until thickened and bubbly.
Sprinkle each serving with cheese, bacon, and green onions. Yield: 9 cups.

Per cup: Calories 300 (60% from fat); Fat 20g (sat 10.9g, mono 5.3g, poly 1.2g); Protein 10.8g; Carb 20.3g; Fiber 3.1g; Chol 59mg; Iron 1.7mg; Sodium 1366mg; Calc 201mg

---

family favorite • low calorie • low carb
low fat

Quick Shrimp Chowder

prep: 15 min.   cook: 20 min.

We've streamlined this favorite dish by using canned soup as the base.

2   tablespoons butter or margarine
1   medium onion, chopped
2   (10¾-ounce) cans cream of potato soup
3½ cups milk
¼   teaspoon ground red pepper
1½ pounds medium-size fresh shrimp, peeled
1   cup (4 ounces) shredded Monterey Jack cheese
Garnish: chopped fresh parsley
Oyster crackers (optional)

Melt butter in a Dutch oven over medium heat; add onion, and sauté 8 minutes or until tender.
Stir in soup, milk, and pepper; bring to a boil. Add shrimp; reduce heat, and simmer, stirring often, 5 minutes or just until shrimp turn pink.
Stir in cheese until melted. Garnish, if desired. Serve immediately. Serve with oyster crackers, if desired. Yield: 12 cups.

Per cup: Calories 171 (45% from fat); Fat 8.5g (sat 4.9g, mono 2.2g, poly 0.7g); Protein 14.4g; Carb 8.9g; Fiber 0.3g; Chol 107mg; Iron 1.6mg; Sodium 594mg; Calc 178mg

low calorie • low fat
Gulf Coast Cioppino

prep: 40 min.   cook: 1 hr.

When Italian immigrants settled in San Francisco, they brought with them the recipe for cioppino, a tomato-based fish and shellfish stew.

20	fresh mussels
20	fresh clams
2	cups chopped celery
2	cups chopped green bell pepper
1	cup chopped green onions
2	garlic cloves, pressed
¼	cup butter or margarine, melted
1	tablespoon olive oil
1	(16-ounce) can crushed tomatoes
1	(15-ounce) can tomato sauce
1½	tablespoons dried Italian seasoning
1½	teaspoons paprika
1	teaspoon sugar
1	teaspoon salt
1	teaspoon ground red pepper
½	teaspoon black pepper
2	(14-ounce) cans chicken broth
1	pound grouper, amberjack, or sea bass fillets, cut into bite-size pieces

Scrub mussels with a brush, removing beards. Wash clams. Discard any opened or cracked mussels and clams. Set aside.

Sauté celery and next 3 ingredients in butter and hot oil in a Dutch oven over medium-high heat until vegetables are tender. Stir in crushed tomatoes and next 7 ingredients; cook 3 minutes, stirring occasionally. Add chicken broth. Bring to a boil; reduce heat, and simmer, uncovered, 45 minutes, stirring occasionally.

Stir in mussels, clams, and fish; cook 4 minutes, stirring occasionally. (Mussels and clams should open during cooking.) Discard any unopened mussels and clams. Serve immediately. Yield: 12 cups.

Per cup: Calories 172 (37% from fat); Fat 7.1g (sat 2.8g, mono 2.1g, poly 0.7g); Protein 15.8g; Carb 10.4g; Fiber 2.1g; Chol 42mg; Iron 5.7mg; Sodium 1058mg; Calc 61mg

low fat
Brunswick Stew

prep: 2 hrs.   cook: 9 hrs.   other: 30 min.

To make this stew thicker, cook it longer, being sure to stir it often.

Hickory wood chips

2	(2½-pound) whole chickens
1	(3-pound) Boston butt pork roast
3	(14½-ounce) cans diced tomatoes
2	(16-ounce) packages frozen whole kernel yellow corn, thawed
2	(16-ounce) packages frozen butterbeans, thawed
2	medium onions, chopped
1	(32-ounce) container chicken broth
1	(24-ounce) bottle ketchup
½	cup white vinegar
½	cup Worcestershire sauce
¼	cup firmly packed brown sugar
1	tablespoon salt
1	tablespoon pepper
2	tablespoons hot sauce

Soak wood chips in water for at least 30 minutes. Prepare charcoal fire in smoker; let burn 15 to 20 minutes.

Drain wood chips, and place on coals. Place water pan in smoker; add water to depth of fill line.

Remove and discard giblets from chicken. Tuck wing tips under; tie with string, if desired. Place chicken and pork on lower food rack; cover with smoker lid.

Cook chicken 2½ hours; cook pork 6 hours or until a meat thermometer inserted into thickest portion registers 160°. Let meats cool. Remove chicken from bone. Chop chicken and pork.

Stir together chicken, pork, diced tomatoes, corn, and remaining ingredients in a 6-quart Dutch oven. Cover and simmer over low heat, stirring occasionally, 2½ to 3 hours. Yield: 28 cups.

Per cup: Calories 368 (27% from fat); Fat 11.1g (sat 3.7g, mono 4.3g, poly 1.2g); Protein 26.4g; Carb 42.3g; Fiber 9.1g; Chol 62mg; Iron 3.5mg; Sodium 883mg; Calc 68mg

freeze it • low calorie • low fat • make ahead
Kentucky Burgoo

prep: 45 min.   cook: 4 hrs.   other: 8 hrs.

Kentucky Burgoo is a stew of Southern origin. It usually includes at least two types of meat and a garden's worth of fresh vegetables. This recipe serves a crowd, or you can easily freeze it.

1	(4- to 5-pound) hen
2	pounds beef or veal stew meat
1½	to 2 pounds beef or veal bones
1	celery rib with leaves, cut into 1-inch pieces
1	carrot, cut into 1-inch pieces
1	small onion, quartered
1	(6-ounce) can tomato paste
12	cups water
1	red chile pepper pod
1	to 1½ tablespoons salt
1½	to 2 teaspoons ground black pepper
½	teaspoon ground red pepper
2	tablespoons lemon juice
1	tablespoon Worcestershire sauce
6	onions, finely chopped
8	tomatoes, peeled and chopped
1	turnip, peeled and finely chopped
2	green bell peppers, finely chopped
2	cups fresh or frozen butterbeans
2	cups thinly sliced celery
2	cups finely chopped cabbage
2	cups sliced fresh okra
2	cups fresh cut corn

Combine first 14 ingredients in a large Dutch oven. Bring to a boil; cover, reduce heat, and simmer 1 hour. Cool. Strain meat mixture, reserving meat and liquid; discard vegetables. Remove skin, gristle, and meat from bone; finely chop meat. Return meat to liquid; cover and chill 8 hours.

Discard fat layer on mixture; add onion and remaining ingredients. Bring mixture to a boil; reduce heat, and simmer, uncovered, 3 hours or to desired consistency, stirring often to prevent sticking. Yield: 30 cups.

Per cup: Calories 169 (27% from fat); Fat 5.1g (sat 1.8g, mono 2g, poly 0.5g); Protein 14.4g; Carb 17.2g; Fiber 4.7g; Chol 42mg; Iron 1.9mg; Sodium 288mg; Calc 39mg

Hungarian Beef Stew

prep: 25 min.   cook: 2 hrs., 20 min.

5   small onions
2   pounds beef stew meat
⅓   cup all-purpose flour
2   tablespoons vegetable oil
2   garlic cloves, minced
1   (10¾-ounce) can tomato soup
1¾ cups water, divided
2   bay leaves
1   tablespoon dried parsley flakes
1½ teaspoons dried thyme
2   teaspoons salt
½   teaspoon pepper
3   large baking potatoes, peeled and cut
    into 1-inch pieces
1   pound carrots, sliced
4   celery ribs, sliced
1   (16-ounce) package egg noodles, cooked

Peel onions, and set 4 aside. Chop remaining onion.

Dredge beef in flour. Brown in hot vegetable oil in a Dutch oven over medium-high heat. Add chopped onion and garlic; sauté until onion is tender. Stir in soup, 1 cup water, and next 5 ingredients. Cover, reduce heat to low, and simmer 1 hour.

Add whole onions, potato, carrot, celery, and remaining ¾ cup water. Bring to a boil; reduce heat, and simmer 1 hour or until beef is tender. Discard bay leaves. Serve stew over hot cooked egg noodles. Yield: 8 cups.

Per cup: Calories 576 (32% from fat); Fat 20.2g (sat 6.5g, mono 8.4g, poly 2.7g); Protein 29.4g; Carb 68.6g; Fiber 5.5g; Chol 115mg; Iron 5.7mg; Sodium 913mg; Calc 69mg

---

The key to great chili is to slowly build flavor by letting the seasonings simmer awhile.

freeze it
Chunky Beef Chili

prep: 25 min.   cook: 1 hr., 45 min.

Texans take their chili seriously. Opinions vary on what makes a perfect bowl of "red," but chunks of beef and a handful of seasonings guarantee this version is good.

4   pounds boneless chuck roast, cut into
    ½-inch pieces
2   tablespoons chili powder
2   (6-ounce) cans tomato paste
1   (32-ounce) container beef broth
2   (8-ounce) cans tomato sauce
2   teaspoons garlic powder
1   teaspoon salt
1   teaspoon ground oregano
1   teaspoon ground cumin
1   teaspoon paprika
1   teaspoon onion powder
½   teaspoon ground black pepper
¼   teaspoon ground red pepper
Cornbread sticks (optional)
Toppings: crushed tortilla chips, sour cream,
    shredded cheese, chopped onion
    (optional)

Brown meat, in batches, in a Dutch oven over medium-high heat. Remove meat, reserving drippings in Dutch oven. Add chili powder to Dutch oven; cook, stirring constantly, 2 minutes. Stir in tomato paste; cook 5 minutes.

Return beef to Dutch oven. Stir in beef broth and next 9 ingredients; bring to a boil. Reduce heat to low, and simmer, uncovered, stirring occasionally, 1½ hours or until beef is tender. Serve chili with cornbread sticks, if desired, and desired toppings. Yield: 9 cups.

Per cup: Calories 394 (42% from fat); Fat 18.2g (sat 6g, mono 7.6g, poly 0.9g); Protein 42.7g; Carb 13.2g; Fiber 3.1g; Chol 125mg; Iron 5.7mg; Sodium 1478mg; Calc 19mg

---

freeze it • low calorie • low fat
Ground Beef 'n' Tomato Chili

prep: 20 min.   cook: 1 hr., 25 min.

1   pound ground round
1   (14½-ounce) can diced tomatoes with
    green peppers and onions
1   (14½-ounce) can diced tomatoes with
    zesty mild green chiles
1   (10-ounce) can condensed beef broth
2   garlic cloves, pressed
3   tablespoons tomato paste
1   tablespoon chili powder
1   teaspoon ground cumin
½   teaspoon ground black pepper
½   teaspoon ground red pepper
1   (15-ounce) can light kidney beans, rinsed
    and drained
1   (15-ounce) can dark kidney beans, rinsed
    and drained
Toppings: chipotle hot sauce, shredded
    Cheddar cheese, chopped green onions
    (optional)

Cook beef in a Dutch oven over medium heat, stirring occasionally into large chunks, 10 minutes or until no longer pink. (Do not stir beef into crumbles.) Drain and return beef to Dutch oven.

Stir both cans of diced tomatoes and next 7 ingredients into browned beef; reduce heat to medium-low, and simmer, uncovered, stirring occasionally, 1 hour. Stir in beans, and simmer 15 minutes. Serve with desired toppings. Yield: 10 cups.

Per cup: Calories 147 (30% from fat); Fat 4.9g (sat 1.9g, mono 2g, poly 0.2g); Protein 13.4g; Carb 12.3g; Fiber 4.1g; Chol 29mg; Iron 2mg; Sodium 671mg; Calc 46mg

Black Bean Chili

prep: 25 min.   cook: 1 hr., 30 min.

This hearty chili freezes well.

1   pound boneless top sirloin steak, cut into
    1-inch cubes
2   onions, chopped
1   medium-size green bell pepper, seeded
    and chopped
1   jalapeño pepper, seeded and chopped
3   to 4 garlic cloves, minced
1½ teaspoons salt, divided
3   tablespoons olive oil
1   (28-ounce) can crushed tomatoes
1   (12-ounce) bottle dark beer
2   tablespoons chili powder
1   tablespoon ground cumin
2   teaspoons dried oregano
1½ teaspoons ground black pepper
1   teaspoon sugar
¼   teaspoon ground red pepper
2   cups beef broth
3   (15-ounce) cans black beans, rinsed and
    drained
Garnish: shredded Cheddar cheese

Cook first 5 ingredients and ½ teaspoon salt
in hot olive oil in a large Dutch oven over
medium-high heat, stirring constantly,
8 minutes or until beef browns and vegetables are tender.
Stir in remaining 1 teaspoon salt, crushed
tomatoes, ½ cup beer, and next 6 ingredients,
and simmer, stirring occasionally, 30 minutes.
Stir in remaining 1 cup beer, broth, and
beans, and simmer, stirring occasionally,
45 minutes or until thoroughly heated.
Garnish, if desired. Yield: 12 cups.

Per cup: Calories 202 (34% from fat); Fat 7.7g (sat 2g, mono 4.2g, poly 0.5g); Protein 13.8g; Carb 19.1g; Fiber 5.4g; Chol 25mg; Iron 3mg; Sodium 878mg; Calc 60mg

White Bean Chili

prep: 25 min.   cook: 1 hr.

Chicken stars in this popular bean chili.

1   medium onion, chopped
1   tablespoon olive oil
2   garlic cloves, minced
8   skinned and boned chicken breasts,
    cut into bite-size pieces
3   cups water
1   teaspoon salt
2   teaspoons ground cumin
1   teaspoon chili powder
1   teaspoon pepper
1   teaspoon dried oregano
4   (15-ounce) cans cannellini or great
    Northern beans, rinsed, drained, and
    divided
1   (14-ounce) can chicken broth
1   (16-ounce) package frozen shoepeg
    white corn
2   (4.5-ounce) cans chopped green chiles
3   tablespoons lime juice
Garnishes: chopped fresh cilantro, sour
    cream

Sauté chopped onion in hot oil in a large
Dutch oven over medium-high heat 7 minutes; add garlic, and sauté 2 to 3 minutes.
Stir in chicken pieces, and cook, stirring
constantly, until chicken is lightly browned.
Stir in 3 cups water and next 5 ingredients;
reduce heat, and simmer, stirring often,
10 minutes or until chicken is done.
Place 2 cans of beans in a blender; add
broth, and process until smooth, stopping to
scrape down sides.
Stir bean puree, remaining 2 cans of beans,
corn, and chiles into chicken mixture in

Dutch oven; bring to a boil over medium-
high heat. Reduce heat, and simmer, stirring
often, 30 minutes or until thoroughly heated.
Stir in lime juice just before serving. Garnish,
if desired. Yield: 16 cups.

Per cup: Calories 156 (13% from fat); Fat 2.3g (sat 0.3g, mono 0.9g, poly 0.6g); Protein 16.6g; Carb 17g; Fiber 3.7g; Chol 33mg; Iron 1.8mg; Sodium 491mg; Calc 39mg

Note: Use a handheld immersion blender
to puree the beans and broth, if desired.

Quick-and-Easy Chili

prep: 3 min.   cook: 25 min.

*If the beef you buy is lean enough, there's no
need to drain it after browning. Serve this
chili with corn chips piled on each serving.*

1   pound lean ground beef
1   small onion, chopped
1   (16-ounce) can pinto beans, drained
1   (6-ounce) can tomato paste
1½ cups water
2   teaspoons chili powder
½   teaspoon garlic salt

Cook ground beef and onion in a Dutch
oven over medium heat, stirring until meat
crumbles and is no longer pink. Add pinto
beans and remaining ingredients; cover,
reduce heat, and simmer 15 minutes, stirring occasionally. Yield: 5 cups.

Per cup: Calories 317 (52% from fat); Fat 18.2g (sat 7g, mono 8g, poly 0.5g); Protein 19.5g; Carb 17.3g; Fiber 5g; Chol 64mg; Iron 3mg; Sodium 393mg; Calc 38mg

appendices

handy substitutions

ingredient	substitution

baking products

Baking powder, 1 teaspoon
- ½ teaspoon cream of tartar plus ¼ teaspoon baking soda

Chocolate
semisweet, 1 ounce
- 1 ounce unsweetened chocolate plus 1 tablespoon sugar

unsweetened, 1 ounce or square
- 3 tablespoons cocoa plus 1 tablespoon fat

chips, semisweet, 6-ounce package, melted
- 2 ounces unsweetened chocolate, 2 tablespoons shortening plus ½ cup sugar

Cocoa, ¼ cup
- 1 ounce unsweetened chocolate (decrease fat in recipe by ½ tablespoon)

Corn syrup, light, 1 cup
- 1 cup sugar plus ¼ cup water
- 1 cup honey

Cornstarch, 1 tablespoon
- 2 tablespoons all-purpose flour or granular tapioca

Flour
all-purpose, 1 tablespoon
- 1½ teaspoons cornstarch, potato starch, or rice starch
- 1 tablespoon rice flour or corn flour
- 1½ tablespoons whole wheat flour

all-purpose, 1 cup sifted
- 1 cup plus 2 tablespoons sifted cake flour

cake, 1 cup sifted
- 1 cup minus 2 tablespoons all-purpose flour

self-rising, 1 cup
- 1 cup all-purpose flour, 1 teaspoon baking powder plus ½ teaspoon salt

Shortening
melted, 1 cup
- 1 cup cooking oil (don't use cooking oil unless recipe calls for melted shortening)

solid, 1 cup (used in baking)
- 1⅛ cups butter or margarine (decrease salt called for in recipe by ½ teaspoon)

Sugar
brown, 1 cup firmly packed
- 1 cup granulated white sugar

powdered, 1 cup
- 1 cup sugar plus 1 tablespoon cornstarch (processed in food processor)

granulated white, 1 teaspoon
- ⅛ teaspoon noncaloric sweetener solution or follow manufacturer's directions

granulated white, 1 cup
- 1 cup corn syrup (decrease liquid called for in recipe by ¼ cup)
- 1 cup honey (decrease liquid called for in recipe by ¼ cup)

Tapioca, granular, 1 tablespoon
- 1½ teaspoons cornstarch or 1 tablespoon all-purpose flour

dairy products

Butter, 1 cup
- ⅞ to 1 cup shortening or lard plus ½ teaspoon salt
- 1 cup margarine (2 sticks; do not substitute whipped or low-fat margarine)

Cream
heavy (30% to 40% fat), 1 cup
- ¾ cup milk plus ⅓ cup butter or margarine (for cooking and baking; will not whip)

light (15% to 20% fat), 1 cup
- ¾ cup milk plus 3 tablespoons butter or margarine (for cooking and baking)
- 1 cup evaporated milk, undiluted

half-and-half, 1 cup
- ⅞ cup milk plus ½ tablespoon butter or margarine (for cooking and baking)
- 1 cup evaporated milk, undiluted

whipped, 1 cup
- 1 cup frozen whipped topping, thawed

Egg
1 large
- ¼ cup egg substitute

2 large
- 3 small eggs or ½ cup egg substitute
- 1 large egg plus 2 egg whites

1 egg white (2 tablespoons)
- 2 tablespoons egg substitute

Milk
buttermilk, 1 cup
- 1 tablespoon vinegar or lemon juice plus whole milk to make 1 cup (let stand 10 minutes)
- 1 cup plain yogurt
- 1 cup whole milk plus 1¾ teaspoons cream of tartar

fat free, 1 cup
- 4 to 5 tablespoons nonfat dry milk powder plus enough water to make 1 cup
- ½ cup evaporated skim milk plus ½ cup water

whole, 1 cup
- 4 to 5 tablespoons nonfat dry milk powder plus enough water to make 1 cup
- ½ cup evaporated milk plus ½ cup water

handy substitutions, continued

ingredient	substitution
Milk (continued) sweetened condensed, 1 (14-ounce) can (about 1¼ cups)	• Heat the following ingredients until sugar and butter dissolve: ⅓ cup plus 2 tablespoons evaporated milk, 1 cup sugar, 3 tablespoons butter or margarine • Add 1 cup plus 2 tablespoons nonfat dry milk powder to ½ cup warm water. Mix well. Add ¾ cup sugar, and stir until smooth.
Sour cream, 1 cup	• 1 cup plain yogurt plus 3 tablespoons melted butter or 1 tablespoon cornstarch • 1 tablespoon lemon juice plus evaporated milk to equal 1 cup
Yogurt, 1 cup (plain)	• 1 cup buttermilk

miscellaneous

Broth, beef or chicken canned broth, 1 cup	• 1 bouillon cube or 1 teaspoon bouillon granules dissolved in 1 cup boiling water
Garlic 1 small clove garlic salt, 1 teaspoon	• ⅛ teaspoon garlic powder or minced dried garlic • ⅛ teaspoon garlic powder plus ⅞ teaspoon salt
Gelatin, flavored, 3-ounce package	• 1 tablespoon unflavored gelatin plus 2 cups fruit juice
Herbs, fresh, chopped, 1 tablespoon	• 1 teaspoon dried herbs or ¼ teaspoon ground herbs
Honey, 1 cup	• 1¼ cups sugar plus ¼ cup water
Mustard, dried, 1 teaspoon	• 1 tablespoon prepared mustard
Tomatoes, fresh, chopped, 2 cups	• 1 (16-ounce) can (may need to drain)
Tomato sauce, 2 cups	• ¾ cup tomato paste plus 1 cup water

alcohol substitutions

alcohol	substitution
Amaretto, 2 tablespoons	• ¼ to ½ teaspoon almond extract*
Bourbon or Sherry, 2 tablespoons	• 1 to 2 teaspoons vanilla extract*
Brandy, fruit-flavored liqueur, port wine, rum, or sweet sherry: ¼ cup or more	• Equal amount of unsweetened orange or apple juice plus 1 teaspoon vanilla extract or corresponding flavor
Brandy or rum, 2 tablespoons	• ½ to 1 teaspoon brandy or rum extract*
Grand Marnier or other orange liqueur, 2 tablespoons	• 2 tablespoons unsweetened orange juice concentrate or 2 tablespoons orange juice and ½ teaspoon orange extract
Kahlúa or other coffee or chocolate liqueur, 2 tablespoons	• ½ to 1 teaspoon chocolate extract plus ½ to 1 teaspoon instant coffee dissolved in 2 tablespoons water
Marsala, ¼ cup	• ¼ cup white grape juice or ¼ cup dry white wine plus 1 teaspoon brandy
Wine red, ¼ cup or more white, ¼ cup or more	• Equal measure of red grape juice or cranberry juice • Equal measure of white grape juice or nonalcoholic white wine

Add water, white grape juice, or apple juice to get the specified amount of liquid (when the liquid amount is crucial).

equivalent measures

3 teaspoons	= 1 tablespoon	2 tablespoons (liquid)	= 1 ounce	⅛ cup	= 2 tablespoons
4 tablespoons	= ¼ cup	1 cup	= 8 fluid ounces	⅓ cup	= 5 tablespoons plus 1 teaspoon
5⅓ tablespoons	= ⅓ cup	2 cups	= 1 pint (16 fluid ounces)		
8 tablespoons	= ½ cup			⅔ cup	= 10 tablespoons plus 2 teaspoons
16 tablespoons	= 1 cup	4 cups	= 1 quart		
		4 quarts	= 1 gallon	¾ cup	= 12 tablespoons

menu index

Hunter's Feast
Serves 8
Blue Cheese-Bacon Dip (p. 43)   Pear slices
Pepper-Crusted Venison Tenderloin (p. 325)
Loaded Garlic Smashed Potatoes (p. 470)
Roasted Asparagus With Balsamic
Browned Butter (p. 453)
Bakery rolls
Applesauce Pie (p. 350)

Ragin' Cajuns
Serves 8
Parmesan-Artichoke Crostini (p. 54)
Bourbon Sunrise (p. 71)
Chicken-Andouille Gumbo (p. 490)
Soufflé Cornbread (p. 87)
*Bananas Foster (p. 218)

Seaside Supper
Serves 6
Fried Bacon-Wrapped Oysters (p. 59)
Mojitos (p. 73) (prepare by the glass)
Broiled Mahi-Mahi With Parsleyed Tomatoes (p. 228)
Lemon Orzo (p. 334)
French bread
Apricot-Cheese Rum Tarts (p. 369)

Healthy Entertaining
Serves 6
Multi-grain baguette   Herbed olive oil for dipping
White Spaghetti and Meatballs (p. 269)
Salad greens with fat-free raspberry vinaigrette
Chocolate-Hazelnut Biscotti (p. 185)
*Low-Fat Cappuccino Cooler (p. 263)

Asian Pasta Fest
Serves 6
Fiery Cheese-and-Chutney Appetizer (p. 51)
Crackers
Asian Shrimp With Pasta (p. 330)
Stir-Fried Broccoli (p. 458)
Plum Galette (p. 363)

Vegetarian Delight
Serves 6
White Bean Hummus   Pita chips
Yukon Gold Mash With Morel Sauce (p. 283)
Green Bean Salad With Feta (p. 410)
Multi-grain rolls
Spicy Tropical Fruit (p. 217)

Brunch for a Bunch
Serves 10
Breakfast Enchiladas (p. 119)
*Hot Tomato Grits (p. 121)
Fresh melon chunks
Cinnamon Breakfast Rolls (p. 124)
*Spicy Bloody Marys and Virgin Marys (p. 70)

Pork on the Grill
Serves 10
Vidalia Onion-Cheese Dip (p. 43)   Crackers
Salad greens with Sweet-and-Sour Dressing (p. 417)
Grilled Pork Tenderloins With Rosemary Pesto (p. 316)
Smoked Gouda Grits (p. 121)
*Balsamic Baby Carrots (p. 459)
Tiramisù Toffee Trifle Pie (p. 358)

A Cooking Party Menu
Serves 8
Pesto Coins (p. 40)
Whiskey Sour Slushies (p. 73)
Caesar Salad (p. 398)
Grilled New York Steaks (p. 251)
Potato-Stuffed Grilled Bell Peppers (p. 259)
Sweet Onion Pudding (p. 468)
*Bananas Foster (p. 218)

Holidays & Special Occasions

New Year's Gathering
Serves 8
Chunky Black-Eyed Pea Salsa (p. 262)
Pot Liquor Soup (p. 485)
Quick Hoppin' John (p. 339)
Super-Moist Cornbread (p. 86)
Classic Shortbread (p. 177)
Champagne
Maple Coffee (p. 61)

Valentine Dinner
Serves 2
Crab-Stuffed Lobster Tails (p. 243)
Fresh Basil Corn on the Cob (p. 460) (halve recipe)
Iceberg Lettuce Wedges With Blue Cheese
Dressing (p. 398)
Fresh strawberries   Hot Fudge Sauce (p. 441)

Mardi Gras Celebration
Serves 6
Goat Cheese Torta (p. 50)   Baguette slices
Crawfish Étouffée (p. 239)
Salad greens with Balsamic Vinaigrette (p. 417)
Pralines (p. 188)
Maple Coffee (p. 61)

Kids' Sleepover Breakfast
Serves 4
Breakfast Pizza (p. 119)
Tropical Smoothie (p. 68)

Easter Lunch
Serves 8
Chive-Tarragon Deviled Eggs (p. 113)
Molasses-Coffee Glazed Ham (p. 322)
Creamy Potato Salad (p. 408)
Orange-Ginger Peas (p. 469)
Hot Cross Buns (p. 102)
or Party-Perfect Strawberry Shortcakes (p. 147)

July 4th Menu
Serves 6
Big Juicy Burgers (p. 424)
Grilled red onions (p. 249)
Barbecue Beans (p. 454)
Summer Fruit Salad With Blueberry
Vinaigrette (p. 403)
Southern Breeze (p. 66)
Cherry Ice Cream (p. 211)

Rehearsal Dinner
Serves 16
Hot Crabmeat Dip (p. 43)   Crackers
**Fruity Baked Chicken (p. 384)
*Lemon-Marinated Asparagus (p. 453)
Bakery rolls
Fresh Orange Italian Cream Cake (p. 143)
Chocolate Wedding Cookies (p. 181)

Old Southern Breakfast
Serves 6
Country Ham With Redeye Gravy (p. 321)
Creamy Grits (p. 120)
Favorite Buttermilk Biscuits (p. 78)
Fig Preserves (p. 448)

Halloween Happening
Serves 6
Creamy Southwestern Pumpkin Soup (p. 483)
Broccoli Slaw (p. 409)
Ham-and-Cheddar Muffins (p. 83)
Quick Apple Dumplings (p. 362)

Thanksgiving Feast
Serves 10 to 12
*Bluegrass Salad (p. 401)
Sugar-and-Spice Cured Turkey (p. 388)
Cornbread Dressing (p. 461)
Giblet Gravy (p. 440)
Fresh Cranberry Sauce (p. 436)
*Green Peas With Bacon (p. 469)
Bell's Sweet Potato Casserole (p. 472)
Sour Cream Yeast Rolls (p. 100)
Pumpkin Roll (p. 158)
Chocolate-Bourbon Pecan Pie (p. 360)

Make-Ahead Menu to Take a Friend
Serves 6
Cheesy Sausage Manicotti (p. 337)
Bagged Caesar salad kit
French bread
Key Lime Pie (p. 357)

Holiday Appetizer Buffet
Serves 15 to 18
Blue Cheese Biscuits With Beef Tenderloin and
Horseradish Cream (p. 56)
*Garlic-and-Rosemary Shrimp (p. 58)
Spinach-Artichoke Dip (p. 54)   Carrot sticks
*Pepper-Cheese Terrine (p. 50)   Baguette slices
Spicy Pistachios (p. 39)
Cranberry Ambrosia-Cream Cheese Spread (p. 46)
with gingersnaps
Pecan Pie Bars (p. 173)
Brownie Cookies (p. 171)
**Hot Cider Nog (p. 62)
*Almond After-Dinner Coffee (p. 61)

Lazy Christmas Morning
Serves 8
English Muffin Breakfast Strata (p. 118)
Ruby red grapefruit halves
Mama's Mini-Cinnis (p. 93)
*Hot Cocoa (p. 61)

Christmas Dinner
Serves 8
Marinated Cheese Stack (p. 49)   Crackers
Fruit Salad With Honey-Pecan Dressing (p. 402)
Holiday Beef Tenderloin (p. 295)
Loaded Garlic Smashed Potatoes (p. 470)
Green Beans With Caramelized Onion (p. 457)
Bing Cherry-and-Cranberry Salad (p. 407)
Homemade Butter Rolls (p. 101)
Four-Layer Coconut Cake (p. 143)
Chocolate-Hazelnut Truffles (p. 190)
Gingerbread Boys (p. 180)

Recipe Key: *Double recipe   **Triple recipe*

● **for kids**   ● **freeze it**   ● **healthy attribute**   ● **make ahead**   ● **quick**   ● **test kitchen favorite**

● for kids   ● freeze it   ● healthy attribute   ● make ahead   ● quick   ● test kitchen favorite

504   recipe index

● **for kids**　　　● **freeze it**　　　● **healthy attribute**　　　● **make ahead**　　　● **quick**　　　● **test kitchen favorite**

● **for kids**   ● **freeze it**   ● **healthy attribute**   ● **make ahead**   ● **quick**   ● **test kitchen favorite**

● **for kids**   ● **freeze it**   ● **healthy attribute**   ● **make ahead**   ● **quick**   ● **test kitchen favorite**

subject index

credits

Alabama Cattlemen's Association

American Lamb Board

Bromberg's, Birmingham, AL

California Vegetable Specialties,
  Rio Vista, CA

Christine's, Mountain Brook, AL

5-H Farm, Gadsden, AL

Lamb's Ears Ltd., Birmingham, AL

Libeco Home, New York, NY

Mulberry Heights, Birmingham, AL

National Cattlemen's Beef Association

National Pork Producers Council

Potluck, Accord, NY

Pottery Barn, San Francisco, CA

Smith & Hawken, Novato, CA

Star Provisions, Atlanta, GA

Table Matters, Mountain Brook, AL

Tricia's Treasures, Homewood, AL

Williams-Sonoma, San Francisco, CA

Wüsthof-Trident of America, Inc.,
  Briarcliff Manor, NY